W.H. McLEOD

Sikhs and Sikhism

Gurū Nānak and the Sikh Religion
Early Sikh Tradition
The Evolution of the Sikh Community
Who is a Sikh?

OXFORD
UNIVERSITY PRESS

OXFORD
UNIVERSITY PRESS

YMCA Library Building, Jai Singh Road, New Delhi 110 001

Oxford University Press is a department of the University of Oxford. It furthers the University's objective of excellence in research, scholarship, and education by publishing worldwide in

Oxford New York

Auckland Bangkok Buenos Aires Cape Town Chennai Dar es Salaam Delhi Hong Kong Istanbul Karachi Kolkata Kuala Lumpur Madrid Melbourne Mexico City Mumbai Nairobi São Paulo Shanghai Taipei Tokyo Toronto

Oxford is a registered trade mark of Oxford University Press in the UK and in certain other countries

Published in India
By Oxford University Press, New Delhi

First published 1999
Fourth impression 2003

ISBN 0 19 564745 9

Printed by Saurabh Print-O-Pack, Noida
Published by Manzar Khan, Oxford University Press
YMCA Library Building, Jai Singh Road, New Delhi 110 001

To

Jerry Barrier

teacher, scholar, bookseller, friend

Introduction

This collection represents two of the major areas in Sikh history and religion which have absorbed me during the last forty years. The first two books concern the life and teachings of Gurū Nānak. The second two involve my interest in the nature of the Sikh Panth (the Sikh community).

Gurū Nānak and the Sikh Religion is a revised version of the doctoral thesis which I submitted to the University of London in 1965. Although the thesis was originally entitled 'The life and doctrine of Guru Nanak', I was advised that a reference to the religion of the Sikhs in the title would greatly clarify the nature of the book to potential purchasers. This was indeed the case and ever since I have usually managed to work some mention of the Sikhs or Sikhism into the title of any book which I have written.

The book is little changed from the thesis apart from a substitute for the first chapter and the addition of a short chapter at the close. This closing chapter was added at the suggestion of Canon Slater who had also advised me to change the title, and it has produced widely differing reactions from readers. Whereas Sikh readers have strongly approved, many of my western academic readers have regarded it with much more scepticism.

The reverse has been the response to the section dealing with the life of Gurū Nānak. Western readers are generally satisfied; most Sikh readers are emphatically not satisfied. The conclusion to this section of the book amounts to less than one page and the ructions and reverberations concerning it can still be plainly heard. I remain convinced, however, that it stands unchallengeably firm. In contrast to the biographical section my treatment of the teachings of Gurū Nānak has not suffered the same fate. This chapter of the book has actually been translated into Punjabi by Guru Nanak Dev University, thereby signifying Sikh approval of this part of the book.[1]

One criticism of *Gurū Nānak and the Sikh Religion* was that it did not allow for the true value of the *janam-sakhis*, the hagiographic accounts of the Gurū's life which have formed the basis and substance of the traditional 'biographies'. Analysing the janam-sakhis as historical sources was a necessary procedure for a study of Gurū Nānak's life, but I recognized that there was a real value to the janam-sakhis which my first book had not covered. This explains *Early Sikh Tradition*. In it, I attempt to show how the janam-sakhis evolved and to treat them from points of view other than the narrowly historical. The work was completed in 1971 and it is, to my mind, the best book I have ever written.

Early Sikh Tradition, however, was not published until 1980. Meanwhile I had moved on to the second area which absorbed my attention for several more years. This was the nature of the Sikh Panth. In the course of the year 1969–70, which I spent at the University of Cambridge working on *Early Sikh Tradition*, I delivered a series of four lectures in the Faculty of Oriental Studies dealing with the Sikh community. Subsequently I added a contribution on caste in the Sikh Panth, and in 1974 and 1975 these were published as five essays entitled *The Evolution of the Sikh Community*.[2]

In three respects the information contained in *The Evolution of the Sikh Community* has been overtaken by later research. The first is the material relating to the Adi Granth contained in chapter 4, 'The Sikh Scriptures'. This has been greatly expanded by the recent work of Pashaura Singh and Gurinder Singh Mann. Secondly, references to the Singh Sabha are inadequate in the light of Harjot Oberoi's excellent work, *The Construction of Religious Boundaries*.[3] And thirdly, the fresh work being done by Lou Fenech on martyrdom in the Sikh tradition would lead me to enlarge some portions of the book were I to be writing it now. In all other respects, however, the substance of the book still holds firm in my opinion. This includes the theory which explains the growth of militancy in the Panth, a development which I attribute to Jat cultural patterns and to the economic circumstances confronting the early Panth.[4] It is quite false to suggest that this theory has been proven beyond all doubt, and I am aware that it has been challenged by Jagjit Singh in *The Sikh Revolution*.[5] Until a more convincing theory is produced, however, I would maintain that this one should prevail.

This leaves only *Who is a Sikh?* The manuscript for the book was prepared as the Radhakrishnan Lectures which were to be given in the University of Oxford in 1987, but unfortunately a stroke rendered me incapable of delivering them. Although they were never presented in Oxford, the Clarendon Press published them as *Who is a Sikh?* in 1989. No comment seems necessary as far as this book is concerned. In almost all respects it represents views which I still hold.

The one exception in the case of *Who is a Sikh?* applies to all four books in this omnibus. Readers will find that God (or *Akāl Purakh* or *Vāhigurū*) is invariably designated by the masculine pronoun. This usage I now regret. Akāl Purakh is without gender, neither male nor female. Ways of expressing this conviction can be found in passages from the Sikh scripture and if I were providing translations now, I would certainly have avoided the gender trap.

The two areas covered by the four books in this omnibus have not been the only ones which have attracted me in Sikh Studies. One comprises sources of Sikh history and religion. A second is Sikh historiography, particularly the difference between history and tradition generated by the work on the janam-sakhis. A third has been the popular art of the Sikhs, a topic prompted by the discovery in the Victoria and Albert Museum of the Kipling collection of ephemera gathered from the Lahore bazaar in 1870. A fourth has been migration and issues arising from the Sikh diaspora. And a fifth, still continuing and certain to persist for many more years, is the vitally important development of the Khalsa Rahit or code of belief and conduct.

University of Otago
Dunedin, New Zealand

HEW MCLEOD

Notes

1. *Gurū Nānak de udeś.* Part V of *Gurū Nānak and the Sikh Religion.* Amritsar: Guru Nanak Dev University, 1974.
2. *The Evolution of the Sikh Community* was published by the Oxford University Press in Delhi in 1974 and then by the Clarendon Press in Oxford in 1975.
3. Harjot Oberoi, *The Construction of Religious Boundaries: Culture, Identity and Diversity in the Sikh Tradition.* Delhi: Oxford University Press, 1994; Chicago: University of Chicago Press, 1994.
4. *The Evolution of the Sikh Community,* pp. 12–13.
5. Jagjit Singh, *The Sikh Revolution: A Perspective View.* New Delhi: Bahri, 1981.

Gurū Nānak and the Sikh Religion

PREFACE

FOR no one is the injunction to tread softly more relevant than for the historian whose study carries him into regions beyond his own society. Should his study extend to what other men hold sacred the injunction becomes a compelling necessity. For this reason the westerner who ventures upon a study of Sikh history must do so with caution and almost inevitably with a measure of trepidation. In such a field the risk of giving offence is only too obvious.

This risk may perhaps be minimized if we state at the outset the meaning which the title of the book is intended to communicate and the methodology upon which this study is based. It should not be assumed that this book is intended to be, in any direct sense, a study of the faith of modern Sikhs. The book is a study of the man Gurū Nānak. A reference to the Sikh religion has been included in the title because the adherents of that religion quite rightly regard Gurū Nānak as a determinative formulator of the beliefs which have ever since constituted the primary basis of the Sikh religion. For this reason a study of Gurū Nānak must inevitably involve a study of the Sikh religion in its primitive form. The emphasis has, however, been laid upon the man Gurū Nānak. This study is intended to discharge a three-fold task. In the first place it seeks to apply rigorous historical methodology to the traditions concerning the life of Gurū Nānak; secondly, it attempts to provide a systematic statement of his teachings; and thirdly, it endeavours to fuse the glimpses provided by the traditional biographies with the personality emerging from the teachings.

The sources which have been used for the first of these tasks are the hagiographic accounts called 'janam-sākhīs'. A cursory reading at once reveals the unreliable nature of these works as records of the actual life of the Gurū, but they constitute our only source of any importance and we are accordingly compelled to use them as best we can. In order to do so a number of criteria have been posited. These criteria are applied to individual *sākhīs*, or 'incidents', and in this manner a decision is reached concerning the extent to which any such *sākhī* can be accepted. It should be noted that the rejection of much contained in the janam-sākhīs should not imply that these works lack significance and that having rejected many of their traditions in the context of a study of Gurū Nānak we can afford to ignore them altogether. For an understanding of later Sikh history they retain a vital importance which has been obscured by the failure to detach them from the person of the historical Nānak. If, however, our subject is

Gurū Nānak, and if our method is historical, much that they contain must inevitably be rejected.

For the section dealing with the teachings of Gurū Nānak the methodology adopted is much simpler. The works attributed to Gurū Nānak in the *Ādi Granth* have been accepted as authentic and an effort has been made to gather into a systematic form the various beliefs which we find dispersed through his works. This can be done with relative ease, for it is clear that such a pattern was present in the mind of their author.

If we are to indicate a more general purpose beyond the three-fold task pursued in this study it could perhaps be expressed in terms of a quest for creative understanding. We are now beyond the stage where an understanding of one's own society can be accepted as sufficient. This study accordingly represents an initial attempt to know a people of unusual interest and ability. It is no more than a beginning, but it is a necessary beginning. An understanding of later Sikh history or of contemporary Sikh society requires a prior understanding of the man whom Sikhs own as their first Gurū.

As this study is largely based upon Pañjābī sources, words which are common to Pañjābī and other north Indian languages have almost all been transliterated in their Pañjābī forms (*śabad* instead of *śabda*, *gurū* instead of *guru*, etc.). The only exceptions to this rule are a few instances in which a Sanskrit or Hindī form has secured an established place in English usage (e.g. bhakti, *karma*). Transliterated forms have presented the usual problem of when to retain diacritics and when to dispense with them. In almost all cases the diacritics have been retained, the only exceptions being the names of modern authors and a few words which have acquired a standardized form in English usage. Except in quotations from other works the forms *ch* and *chh* have been used in preference to *c* and *ch* (*chitta*, not *citta*).

Almost all passages quoted from the *Ādi Granth* have been given in English translation only, and this pattern has also been followed in the case of quotations from other works in Pañjābī or Hindī. Many of the extracts from the *Ādi Granth* have been translated with some freedom in an effort to bring out their meanings with greater clarity. Bracketed portions indicate words which do not occur in the original but which have been inserted in order to give continuity to a translation. The translations are my own, but in the case of passages from the *Ādi Granth* extensive use has been made of the modern Pañjābī paraphrases provided in a number of vernacular commentaries. One of my great regrets will ever be that when dealing with the compositions of Gurū Nānak I can in no measure reproduce in English translation the beauty of the original utterance. My primary concern in such cases has been to produce an accurate translation and in numerous instances I have felt compelled to sacrifice felicity of style in the interests of exactness.

PREFACE

Except where otherwise indicated dates are all A.D. For all quotations from the *Ādi Granth* I have used the text printed in *Śabadārath Srī Gurū Granth Sāhib Jī*, a work which follows the standard *Ādi Granth* pagination. Attention is drawn to the three indexes. In addition to the General Index a Biographical Index and a Doctrinal Index have been provided.

This book represents a revised version of my thesis *The Life and Doctrine of Gurū Nānak* submitted for the degree of Doctor of Philosophy in the University of London, 1965. To my supervisor, Professor A. L. Basham, I owe a particular debt of gratitude and I take this opportunity of acknowledging it with warmest thanks. For assistance and encouragement I should also like to thank Dr. F. R. Allchin, Dr. John Carman, Dr. Ganda Singh, Dr. J. S. Grewal, Dr. Norvin Hein, Dr. Jodh Singh, Dr. R. S. McGregor, Dr. Maqbul Ahmad, Dr. V. L. Ménage, Dr. Niharranjan Ray, Professor Parkash Singh, Dr. Geoffrey Parrinder, Professor Pritam Singh, Dr. R. H. L. Slater, Dr. Wilfred Cantwell Smith, Dr. Charlotte Vaudeville, and Mr. John C. B. Webster. In fairness to them I must add that for opinions expressed in this book I alone am to be held responsible. I also acknowledge with thanks help received from the Principal and staff of Baring College, Batala; from various people associated with Punjabi University, Patiala; from the office staff of the Shiromani Gurdwara Prabandhak Committee, Amritsar; and from Messrs. Singh Brothers of Bazar Mai Sewan, Amritsar. Finally I should like to thank my wife for her sympathetic endurance.

W. H. McLEOD

Batala, 1967

CONTENTS

ABBREVIATIONS

AG	The *Ādi Granth*.
Aṣṭ	*aṣṭapadī*
Bālā JS	The *Bālā* janam-sākhī lithographed by Hāfaz Qutub Dīn of Lahore in A.D. 1871.
BG	The *Vārs* of Bhāī Gurdās.
BM	British Museum.
GR	The edition of the *Gyān-ratanāvalī* lithographed by Charāg Dīn and Sarāj Dīn, Lahore, A.D. 1891.
IOL	India Office Library
KG	*Kabīr-granthāvalī* (Pāras-nāth Tivārī edition).
Mih JS	*Miharbān Janam-sākhī* (*Pothī Sach-khaṇḍ*), edited by Kirpāl Siṅgh and Shamsher Siṅgh Ashok and published under the title *Janam-sākhī Srī Gurū Nānak Dev Jī*, Amritsar, 1962.
MK	Kāhn Siṅgh Nābhā, *Guruśabad Ratanākar Mahān Koś* (commonly referred to as the *Mahān Koś*), 2nd edition revised with Addendum, Patiala, 1960.
Pur JS	Vīr Siṅgh (ed.), *Purātan Janam-sākhī*, 5th edition, Amritsar, 1959.
S	Samvat, dating according to the Vikrama era.
SOAS	Library of the School of Oriental and African Studies, London.

With references from the *Ādi Granth* a number in brackets indicates the number of a stanza (*aṅk* or *pauṛī*). The designation (1R) indicates a reference from the *rahāu*, or refrain, of a hymn.

1

THE SETTING

1969 was a particularly important year for Sikhs. Gurū Nānak, acknowledged by Sikhs as the founder of their faith, was born in 1469 and it was entirely appropriate that the quincentenary of his birth should have been celebrated with such notable fervour. Although the five centuries which link the birth of Nānak with the present day constitute a comparatively brief span in the history of religions, it has been an eventful period and the product is a significant one. The result is a community with a high degree of ethnic homogeneity, a strong sense of loyalty to the Pañjāb, and above all a common allegiance to a religion of refined and noble quality.

In a strict sense there can be no such thing as a perceptible beginning to Sikh history, for like all religious systems Sikhism has antecedents which defy ultimate scrutiny. This should not, however, suggest that the Sikh people are necessarily mistaken in tracing their beginnings as a religious community to Gurū Nānak. In another sense it is entirely permissible to claim that Sikh history begins with Gurū Nānak. He did indeed receive an inheritance and its influence is abundantly evident in all his works, but it would be altogether mistaken to regard him as a mere mediator of other men's ideas. In his hands the inheritance was transformed. Moreover the pattern which was produced by this transformation has endured. There have been subsequent developments of considerable significance, but this same pattern has remained the core and essence of the continuing Sikh faith.

In this latter sense Sikh history begins with Gurū Nānak and continues for two centuries through a line of nine successors. This initial period, terminating with the death of Gurū Gobind Singh in 1708, is of fundamental importance, for it was during these first two centuries that most of the distinctive features of Sikhism as a religion took shape. Three key events took place during this period, each of them representing a decision made by a Gurū. The first was the formal appointment by Gurū Nānak of a successor to the leadership of the community which had gathered around him. The second was the compilation of a canonical scripture by Gurū Arjan, the fifth Gurū, in 1603–4. The third was the founding of the Khālsā by Gurū Gobind Singh in 1699. The first of these events established a regular, recognized succession within the new community and so provided an effective apostolic continuity in its leadership. The second enshrined in permanent form the teachings of the first five Gurūs soon after the original delivery of those teachings.[1] The third event provided a visible insignia and an explicit discipline which members of the community could renounce only at the cost of virtual excommunication.

The measure of cohesion and stability conferred upon the Sikh community by these three key events was further strengthened by a development which took place during the eighteenth century. Tradition records that Gurū Gobind Singh, immediately before his death, declared that with his departure the line of personal Gurūs would end and that thenceforth the function and authority of the Gurū would vest in the scripture (the *Ādi Granth*) and in the corporate community (the *Panth*, or K͟hālsā). The tradition that this came as a dying declaration from the tenth Gurū himself must be regarded with some doubt,[2] but the distinctive doctrine of the Gurū which it expresses certainly evolved in some manner and has been a concept of fundamental importance in subsequent Sikh history. It is clear that before the eighteenth century had run its course the Sikh community had come to accept the *Ādi Granth* as 'the manifest body of the Gurū', and to accord, at least in theory, a religious sanction to the corporate decisions of the K͟hālsā. It is the first aspect of this doctrine which has been of particular significance. A unique authority was thereby conferred upon the scripture compiled by Gurū Arjan and as a result the inner strength of the community was further consolidated.

The period of almost one hundred years which intervenes between the death of Gurū Gobind Singh and the emergence of Rañjīt Singh is an obscure one. The broad outline of Sikh military and political activity is known and has been recorded many times, but surprisingly little is known about the religious development of the period, and much remains to be done in terms of analysis of the military and political activity. After the death of Gurū Gobind Singh and the succeeding seven years of turmoil associated with the enigmatic figure of Bandā there followed a period of persecution during which the Mughal authorities in the Pañjāb sought to suppress the Sikhs and their religion. It was, however, Mughal authority which met destruction. Out of the confusion of this period, much of it wrought by the successive invasions of Ahmad Shāh Abdālī, there emerged the Sikh *misls*, groups of irregular troops owing primary allegiance to the chieftain of the group but united in a loose confederacy. Eventually one such chieftain, Rañjīt Singh of the Śukerchakīā *misl*, secured an indisputable ascendancy and with his success came the Sikhs' period of political and military triumph. The triumph was qualified by the activities of the British

[1] A number of compositions by the ninth Gurū, Tegh Bahādur, were subsequently added.

[2] J. S. Grewal and S. S. Bal, *Guru Gobind Singh*, Chandigarh, 1967, pp. 188–9. J. S. Grewal, 'The *Prem Sumarg*: a Theory of Sikh Social Order', in the *Proceedings of the First Session of the Punjab History Conference*, Patiala, 1966, p. 110.

on Rañjīt Singh's eastern frontier, but it was a considerable triumph nonetheless and one which still evokes an evident nostalgia.

The political and military successes were, however, accompanied by developments which a later revived Sikhism was to regard as serious deviations from the teachings of the Gurūs.[1] Rañjīt Singh himself provided an illustration in the deference which he showed towards brāhmaṇs, and at his death the rite of *satī* was performed by four queens and seven maidservants. It was this kind of custom which the Gurūs had sought to destroy.[2] During the years which followed the annexation of the Pañjāb by the British in 1849 these developments became even more pronounced.

> The Sikh religion was losing its characteristic vigour and its votaries were relapsing into beliefs and dogmas from which their new faith had extricated them. Absorption into ceremonial Hinduism seemed the course inevitably set for them.[3]

Sikhism was saved from this absorption by two of its distinctive features. The immutable scripture and the recognizable insignia, particularly the uncut hair, preserved it from irrevocable dissolution. When the reformers of the Singh Sabhā Movement began their activities towards the end of the century they had an objective standard to which they could appeal and they knew precisely to whom they should address the appeal. A religious revival followed and although much of the original religious impulse has run out into political sands the effects of the revival were nevertheless considerable and are in appreciable measure still evident today.

The present study takes us back to the very beginning of this period in the history of the Pañjāb and the history of religions. It concerns Gurū Nānak, the acknowledged founder of the Sikh religion and incomparably the greatest of the Gurūs in the shaping of that religion. The sixth Gurū, Hargobind, gave the community a new direction when he assumed military and quasi-political functions, and the conferring of the function of Gurū jointly upon the scripture and the community introduced a highly significant supplement, but the religious content of Sikhism remained, and still remains, the content given it by Gurū Nānak. For this reason the primary and by far the most important part of a study of the Sikh religion must be a study of the life and teachings of its first Gurū.

Gurū Nānak was born on the threshold of a momentous period in Indian history. In the course of his lifetime he witnessed the dominance and the decline of the Lodī Sultanate, and its final extinction by Bābur in 1526. It was not as a casual witness that he observed the events which brought the downfall of the Lodīs and its replacement by Mughal rule. In four of his compositions he comments on the Mughal invasions, interpreting the fall

[1] Teja Singh, *Sikhism: Its Ideals and Institutions*, pp. 86–87.

[2] Cf. Gurū Arjan, *Gauṛī Guārerī* 99, *AG*, p. 185. Gurū Gobind Singh, *Akāl Ustati*, 84.

[3] Harbans Singh, *The Heritage of the Sikhs*, p. 129.

of the Sultanate as the due reward of Lodī unrighteousness.[1] The last eight years of his life were spent in a Pañjāb ruled by Kāmrān, the rebellious brother of Humāyūn. Little is known of this interlude in Pañjāb history and Gurū Nānak himself makes no apparent reference to it.

The birth of Gurū Nānak took place during the reign of Sultan Bahlūl Lodī (1451–89) and the formative years of his life accordingly coincided with the period of Lodī ascendancy under Bahlūl and his son Sikandar. This is a point of some significance in the context of a study of Gurū Nānak's life, for it means that he grew to maturity in a period of comparative peace and prosperity. It is true that the half-century preceding the accession of Sultan Bahlūl had been, for the Pañjāb, a time of political instability accompanied by widespread violence and suffering. The invasion of Tīmūr in 1398–9 brought much damage to the Pañjāb, and the years between 1421 and 1434 brought considerably more. These were the years of Jasrat Khokhar of Siālkoṭ, Faulād Turkbachchā of Bhaṭiṇḍā, and Sheikh 'Alī of Kābul, three agents of havoc and destruction who brought extensive disorder and suffering to the Pañjāb. The effect of their operations would have been even more serious had it not been for the energy and ability of Mubārak Shāh, the second of the Sayyid sultans of Delhi. The activities of these three adventurers have attracted much less attention than the spectacular career of Tīmūr, but in the Pañjāb they were responsible for far more suffering than their celebrated predecessor, for their depredations were spread over a much wider area and over a lengthier period of time.[2]

All this, however, would have been but an unpleasant memory during the years following the birth of Gurū Nānak. By 1469, the year of Gurū Nānak's birth, Bahlūl Lodī had established his authority, and the relative stability which he introduced was further strengthened by his son Sikandar. The praises heaped upon Sikandar Lodī by the Persian chroniclers of the period must be treated with considerable caution, but there is no apparent reason to doubt that his reign provided a period of comparative peace and prosperity. In the circumstances of the time a measure of prosperity would have been a natural development and Bābur seems to imply that it had in fact taken place.[3] A fertile soil, a favourable climate, a relatively limited population, and an appreciable measure of security would all have combined to produce this favourable economic condition. The district around Lahore was, and still is, particularly fertile.[4] Food and other necessities appear to have been readily available, manufactures were developing,

[1] See *infra*, pp. 135–8.

[2] Yāḥyā bin Aḥmad, *Tārikh-i-Mubārak Shāhi* (trans. K. K. Basu), pp. 200–40. Nizāmuddīn Aḥmad, *Tabaqāt-i-Akbari* (trans. B. De), vol. i, pp. 300–21. See also K. S. Lal, *Twilight of the Sultanate*, pp. 84–113, 121.

[3] A. S. Beveridge, *The Bābur-nāma in English*, vol. ii, p. 480.

[4] *Āin-i-Akbari* (trans. H. S. Jarrett), vol. ii, p. 312.

and there was a satisfactory trade balance.[1] Even during the period of Lodī decline under Sultan Ibrāhīm (1517–26) the stability of the Pañjāb appears to have been maintained by the governor, Daulat Khān Lodī, until the last three years of the Sultanate's existence.[2] It seems clear that Gurū Nānak was born into a favoured period, at least as far as security and economic conditions were concerned.

Our sources for the life of Gurū Nānak are, as we shall see, generally unreliable, but it is possible to set out with some assurance a brief outline of his life. He was born in 1469 and grew up in his father's village of Talvaṇḍī.[3] At some point in early manhood he moved to the town of Sultānpur[4] where he probably secured employment in the service of Daulat Khān Lodī. From Sultānpur he began a period of travels within and perhaps beyond India. At the conclusion of this period he settled in the village of Kartārpur on the right bank of the Rāvī river,[5] and it was there that he died, probably in the year 1539.

By the time he died Gurū Nānak had obviously gathered many disciples and within this following his numerous compositions were preserved. The point at which these compositions were committed to writing is not positively known, but it cannot have been long after his death and may well have been during his lifetime. A collection which included the works of Gurū Nānak was prepared at the instance of the third Gurū, Amar Dās, who occupied the office from 1552 until 1574, and this collection was subsequently used by Gurū Arjan when compiling the *Ādi Granth*.[6] The compositions attributed to Gurū Nānak which have been incorporated in the *Ādi Granth* are in an entirely different category from the material offered by the works which purport to record the events of his life. The *Ādi Granth* collection may be unhesitatingly accepted as authentic and consequently we have, in contrast with the paucity of reliable biographical material, ample access to his teachings.

The teachings of Gurū Nānak are dispersed throughout his numerous works, but from these dispersed elements it is possible to reconstruct a coherent theology. The basis of the theology is a belief in a personal God, the omnipotent Creator of the universe, a Being beyond time and human

[1] I. H. Qureshi, *The Administration of the Delhi Sultanate*, pp. 225–6.

[2] Daulat Khān Lodī was appointed governor of Lahore by Sultan Sikandar Lodī sometime between 1500 and 1504. The stability of the Pañjāb during his lengthy term as governor may be safely assumed from the almost total neglect of the Pañjāb by the Persian chroniclers. Serious disorders would have drawn action from the sultan and comment from the chroniclers. Daulat Khān remained governor of Lahore until Bābur's 1524 invasion.

[3] Rāi Bhoi dī Talvaṇḍī, approximately forty miles south-west of Lahore.

[4] Kapūrthalā District.

[5] Opposite the town of Dehrā Bābā Nānak.

[6] The collection commissioned by Gurū Amar Dās was prepared by his grandson Sahansrām. It consisted of two volumes and included the works of the first three Gurūs and of the *bhagats* (*MK*, p. 320 and Addendum, p. 44).

comprehending yet seeking by His grace the salvation of man and for this purpose revealing Himself in His own creation. To the offer of salvation man is called to respond by a life of meditation on the divine self-revelation and of conformity to it. If man responds he progressively grows into the likeness of God and ultimately into an ineffable union with the Timeless One. If he refuses he follows the path of spiritual death and remains firmly bound to the wheel of transmigration.

It is the author of this theology whom we seek, the greatest of the sons of the Pañjāb and the founder of the religion which continues to dominate the attitudes and beliefs of contemporary Pañjāb. We are here engaged in a quest for the historical Nānak, for there is a Nānak of both legend and faith as well as a Nānak of history. It is a quest which must take us to the traditional biographies and to the collection of his works preserved in the *Ādi Granth*. In many places, and indeed in practically all that we find in the traditional biographies, the search must yield disappointing results, but it is a search which should nevertheless be made. Gurū Nānak is too important to be ignored. Without some understanding of him and of his teachings one can understand neither the Sikh religion nor the Pañjāb of today.

2

THE SOURCES

The Ādi Granth

THE obvious place to seek information concerning the life of Gurū Nānak is the *Ādi Granth*, or *Gurū Granth Sāhib*, the scripture compiled by Gurū Arjan in 1603–4. It is the obvious place as it contains numerous works by Gurū Nānak which can safely be accepted as authentic. In this respect, however, the *Ādi Granth* offers an initial disappointment, for it provides us with surprisingly little information concerning the actual events of his life. It contains more than nine hundred of his compositions and yet the biographical details which may be extracted from them are negligible. Indeed, there is no explicit reference at all to any incident in his life, no *śabad* or *ślok*[1] which points unmistakably to an event in which he was directly involved. Even the famous references to Bābur, the so-called *Bābar-vāṇī*, are not exceptions to this rule. They do indicate that Gurū Nānak witnessed something of Bābur's depredations, but if read apart from the traditional biographies (the janam-sākhīs) they do not necessarily point to his presence at the sack of Saidpur.

As far as biographical detail is concerned the most we can do is draw some limited conclusions from the more obvious hints which Gurū Nānak's writings contain. In the case of the *Bābar-vāṇī* we may confidently assume that he witnessed something of the devastation caused by Bābur's army and that accordingly he was in the Pañjāb during at least one of Bābur's incursions into North India. In the same manner we may deduce with confidence that he had frequent contact with Nāth yogīs. The extensive use of their terminology and the frequent instances in which a yogī appears to be addressed makes this aspect of his life perfectly plain. None of these conclusions can, however, take us far in our effort to reconstruct the actual events of Gurū Nānak's life. They are certainly of value, but their scope is obviously very limited.

[1] *śabad* or *śabda*: literally 'word'. In Sikh usage it designates both the divine 'Word' received from God, and the expression of that Word in a hymn or song of praise. In the latter sense it corresponds to the Hindi word *pad*.

ślok: couplet or stanza. Most of Gurū Nānak's *śloks* are incorporated in the composite *vārs* of the *Ādi Granth*. These *vārs* consist of a series of stanzas (*pauṛīs*) each of which is preceded by two or more *śloks*. Some of Gurū Nānak's *śloks* are couplets, but most are stanzas in their own right.

Gurū Nānak himself tells us very little and his four successors, whose works are also recorded in the *Ādi Granth*, add nothing of any importance. Gurū Aṅgad and Gurū Arjan both refer to him,[1] but their references are eulogistic comments, entirely appropriate in their contexts but telling us nothing about Gurū Nānak himself. The same applies to the *savayyās* of the *bhaṭṭs*.[2] Gurū Nānak is mentioned several times,[3] but as one would expect from the nature of the *savayyās* the references are of the same kind as those provided by Gurū Aṅgad and Gurū Arjan. The only work which offers any detail at all is the *Vār* in Rāg Rāmakalī by the *bhaṭṭs* Rāi Balvaṇḍ and Sattā the Ḍūm. In the first four stanzas the authors repeat a single fact, namely that Gurū Nānak appointed Aṅgad as his successor.[4]

As we shall see, the *Ādi Granth* does offer much that is relevant to our biographical concern, but its contribution to our knowledge of the actual events of Gurū Nānak's life is slight. For these we are compelled to resort to our only other available source, the traditional biographies called 'janam-sākhīs'.

The janam-sākhīs

The janam-sākhīs[5] are hagiographic accounts of the life of Gurū Nānak, each consisting of a series of separate incidents, or chapters, entitled *sākhīs* or *goṣṭs*. Although these incidents are normally linked in a chronological sequence the order is frequently erratic and in a few cases it is totally absent. The script used for all the important janam-sākhīs is Gurmukhī, but the language may be either Pañjābī or the composite dialect called *Sādhukkaṛī* or *Sant Bhāṣā*.[6]

These janam-sākhīs are also highly unsatisfactory sources, but for an entirely different reason. Here there is no question of material being in short supply, for the janam-sākhīs provide it in abundance. The problem as far as the janam-sākhīs are concerned is to determine how much of their material can be accepted as historical. A very substantial proportion of it is obviously legend and much of what cannot be summarily dismissed in this way is open to grave suspicion on other grounds. In a number of cases,

[1] Gurū Aṅgad: *Vār Mājh, ślok* 1 of *pauṛī* 27, *AG*, p. 150.
Gurū Arjan: *Soraṭhi* 13 and 14, *AG*, p. 612; *Mārū* 10, *AG*, p. 1001; *Basant Dutukiā* 1, *AG*, p. 1192. *Mājh, Soraṭhi, Mārū*, and *Basant* are four of the *rāgs*, or metres, to which the hymns of the *Ādi Granth* are set.

[2] Panegyrics of the bards. The *bhaṭṭs*, or bards, whose *savayyās* have been included in the *Ādi Granth* were contemporaries of Gurū Arjan.

[3] Rāi Balvaṇḍ and Sattā the Ḍūm: *Vār Rāmakalī* (1–2), *AG*, p. 966. Kal the Poet: *Savayye Mahale Pahile ke* (7), *AG*, p. 1390; *Savayye Mahale Tije ke* (1) *AG*, p. 1392; *Savayye Mahale Chauthe ke* (12), *AG*, p. 1398. Nal the Poet: *Savayye Mahale Chauthe ke* (4), *AG*, p. 1399. There is also a mention of his name in the *Sadu* of Sundar, *AG*, p. 923.

[4] loc. cit., *AG*, pp. 966–7.

[5] Literally 'birth-evidences', or 'evidences of his life'.

[6] See *infra*, p. 153.

however, there is an evident possibility that some historical fact may lie beneath a superstructure of legend. Not all of these possibilities can be satisfactorily tested, but our task must be to examine them all and whereever possible to affirm or reject them.

This must be our method for there is no other way in which a reconstruction of the events of Gurū Nānak's life can be attempted. In spite of their manifest shortcomings we are bound to rely on the janam-sākhīs for almost all of our information concerning these events, for there is nothing to replace them and little to supplement them. There is no piece of external evidence which can be accorded complete trust and, as we have already noted, such indications as his own works contain are at best only hints.

References to Gurū Nānak may be found in other works, but none of these carry us beyond the janam-sākhīs. The *Dabistān*, which of all non-Sikh works containing references to Gurū Nānak lies nearest to his time, is no nearer than the older janam-sākhīs and it is clear that Mohsin Fānī relied largely upon Sikh informants.[1] Much of the chapter in the *Dabistān* entitled 'Nānak-panthīs' deals with the life of Gurū Nānak, but the account which it gives of him amounts to little more than a series of legends. At one point it does offer significant support to a janam-sākhī tradition,[2] but as far as Gurū Nānak is concerned it is more important as a description of the seventeenth-century Sikh understanding of him than as a contribution to authentic biography.

Independent traditions concerning the life of Gurū Nānak did, of course, emerge, but there is no indication that any of them possessed more than the remotest of connexions with historical fact. Beyond the Pañjāb Gurū Nānak's name became a part of the hagiography of the later bhakti movement. Mahīpati's *Bhaktalīlāmrit*, written in A.D. 1774, testifies to both the extent and the nature of his reputation.

> Whoever shows some wonderful event, be he a *bhakta* of God or the chief of the yogīs, his reputation spreads widely and others continue the history of his sect. Hence in that country [the Pañjāb] there are many *bairāgīs* belonging to the sect of Nānak who give the *mantra* to the people and make the dull and ignorant remember God.
>
> If one listens to the lives of the saints, his greatest sins are burnt away; the giver of salvation is pleased with him, and keeps him in the world of Vaikunth.[3]

[1] The Persian *Dabistān-i-Mazāhib* was written in the mid-seventeenth century and is generally attributed to Mohsin Fānī. It appears that the author was personally acquainted with Gurū Hargobind, the sixth Gurū, and he explicitly claims a close acquaintance with Gurū Hari Rāi, the seventh Gurū. (Ganda Singh, English translation of the chapter 'Nānak-panthīs' published under the title *Nanak Panthis or the Sikhs and Sikhism of the 17th Century*, pp. 13, 21.)

[2] The tradition that Gurū Nānak was for a period employed as a steward by Daulat Khān Lodī. Ganda Singh, op. cit., p. 4. See *infra*, p. 108.

[3] Mahīpati, *Bhaktalīlāmrit*, 'The Story of Nānak', 177–9, translated from the Marathi by J. E. Abbot, N. R. Godbole, and J. F. Edwards, p. 195.

For Mahīpati Gurū Nānak was one of the great *bhagats* and his chapter 'The Story of Nānak' is a collection of appropriate legends. Muslim writers also referred to him, but apart from the *Dabistān* their interest appears to have developed later and to have been, for the most part, a polemical one. Colonel Malcolm, who collected the material for his *Sketch of the Sikhs* in 1805, refers to the existence of Muslim accounts of Gurū Nānak, but dismisses them as efforts to misrepresent and denigrate.[1] In other cases the concern of Muslim writers was evidently to claim Gurū Nānak as a believer in the doctrines of Islam.[2]

These independent traditions are almost totally valueless as sources of authentic information and accordingly we are bound to depend on the intensely interesting but largely unreliable janam-sākhīs for practically all of our information concerning the events of the Gurū's life. The best we can hope to do is to discern the historically possible in the midst of accumulated legend, and to test such possibilities against whatever criteria may be available. The outcome must inevitably be that there is little we can categorically affirm concerning the details of his life. There can, however, be no question concerning the basic facts that he was born in the Pañjāb almost five hundred years ago, spent a period in travel, composed the works which are attributed to him in the *Ādi Granth*, and ensured the perpetuation of his teachings by appointing a successor. These are beyond all doubt.

The precise manner in which the janam-sākhīs developed is not known for certain, but it is possible to reconstruct a likely pattern. The beginnings would be the remembered facts about the Gurū which would have circulated orally among the first generation of his followers. With the passage of time these facts would inevitably be embellished by reverent imaginations and practically all of them would undergo gradual change.

It would be remembered, for example, that the Gurū had spent many years travelling outside the Pañjāb. Some of the places he had visited might well be known, but it is unlikely that there would be any reliable knowledge of his complete itinerary. There would doubtless be many gaps in the account and these would soon be filled with the names of places which such a traveller might be expected to visit. These would include the important centres of pilgrimage, both Hindu and Muslim, and names which figured prominently in the current folklore of the Pañjāb. This is not to say that Gurū Nānak did not visit any of these places. On the contrary it is safe to assume that he must surely have visited at least some of them. The point here is that in many cases the name of a certain town or locality will have been added to the collection of *sākhīs*, not because there existed any reliable

[1] J. Malcolm, loc. cit., pp. 4–5.

[2] An example of this interpretation appears in G͟hulām Husain K͟hān's *Siyar-ul-Mutakhirin*, trans. J. Briggs, vol. i, pp. 110–11. The *Siyar-ul-Mutakhirin* was written about the year A.D. 1785.

information in this respect but because the popular imagination believed that he must surely have visited such a place on his travels. In most cases it is impossible to say with anything approaching certainty that he did or did not visit a particular place. Even when the incident which is located in a certain setting is manifestly unhistorical it does not necessarily follow that Gurū Nānak did not pass that way. On the other hand, the fact that an incident bears the marks of probability does not necessarily mean that the location given in the janam-sākhīs is the correct one.

In addition to these remembered facts and their embellishments, stories would have gathered around certain references in his works. It seems clear that this must have happened in the case of *Vār Rāmakalī*, *śloks* 2–7 of *pauṛī* 12.[1] In these six *śloks*, as they appear in the *Ādi Granth*, Gurū Nānak speaks successively as Īśar, Gorakh, Gopīchand, Charapaṭ, Bharatharī, and finally himself. The *śloks* were evidently intended for yogīs of the Nāth sect and this would explain the names used.[2] Subsequently these names must have suggested that Gurū Nānak had actually met these renowned figures and as a result there would have developed the story of his discourse with the Siddhs on Mount Sumeru which we find in stanzas 28–31 of Bhāī Gurdās's *Vār* 1,[3] *sākhī* 50 of the *Purātan Janam-sākhī*,[4] and *goṣṭ* 117 of the *Miharbān Janam-sākhī*.[5] Other similar verses would have assisted the process, notably *Rāmakalī* 4,[6] which refers to Gorakhnāth, and *Rāmakalī* 5,[7] which mentions Machhendranāth. In the *Purātan* janam-sākhīs these two compositions are responsible for a separate *sākhī* involving the two Nāths,[8] but in the *Miharbān Janam-sākhī* they are a part of the lengthy discourse on Mount Sumeru which extends from *goṣṭ* 117 to *goṣṭ* 124.[9]

Obviously there can be no question of historical truth in the story for Gurū Nānak and Gorakhnāth certainly were not contemporaries and Mount Sumeru exists only in legend. The only evident explanation is that a general acceptance of the popular belief in the immortal existence of the nine Nāths and of the eighty-four Siddhs in the fastnesses of the Himālayas[10]

1 *AG*, pp. 952–3.

2 Gorakhnāth, Gopīnāth, and Charapaṭnāth appear in the first of the lists of the nine Nāths given by G. W. Briggs, *Gorakhnāth and the Kānphaṭa Yogis*, p. 136. Īśa is a name of Śiva, the *Ādināth* or 'Primal Master' of the Nāth sect. Bharatharī, or Bhartṛharī, is said to have been a disciple of Gorakhnāth and to have founded the Bairāg sub-sect of the Kānphaṭ order. According to tradition he was a king of Ujjain who abdicated his throne to become a yogī. Ibid., p. 65.

3 See *infra*, pp. 34–35.

4 *Pur JS*, pp. 94–97.

5 *Mih JS*, pp. 384–91. The tradition concerning a discourse on Mount Sumeru is discussed below, pp. 119–22.

6 *AG*, p. 877. *Rāmakali* is one of the *Ādi Granth* metres.

7 *AG*, p. 877.

8 *Pur JS*, *sākhi* 46, pp. 84–86.

9 *Mih JS*, pp. 384–413. The discourse as recorded in this janam-sākhī also includes *Āsā* 37 and 38 (*AG*, pp. 359–60), both of which refer to Bharatharī (ibid., pp. 405–9).

10 The immortal existence of the nine Nāths and the immortal existence of the eighty-four Siddhs constitute two separate traditions, but in the janam-sākhīs the two are confused. See Glossary, p. 243, *Nāth*.

combined with these references in Gurū Nānak's works to produce a story of his having visited them there. The differences in the *Purātan* and *Miharbān* accounts indicate that there must have been an evolution over a period of time, but there seems to be no doubt that the real genesis of the story lay in these compositions which were originally addressed to Nāth yogīs.[1]

The influence of popular belief in this particular case illustrates a fundamental axiom which applies to such works as the janam-sākhīs. All such works will reflect, to some extent, the context in which they evolved, a context which will include not only current beliefs and attitudes but also current needs. In the case of the janam-sākhīs the relevant context is the situation of the Sikh community during the closing years of the sixteenth century and the early decades of the seventeenth century. It can be safely assumed that the janam-sākhīs will express in some measure the beliefs of the community during this period, its more insistent needs, and the answers which it was giving to questions which confronted it. An example of this feature is the recurrent reference to relationships between Hindus and Muslims, and specifically the insistence upon the identity of the Hindu and Muslim ways of salvation. The janam-sākhī attitude towards this issue is most strikingly expressed in the famous pronouncement attributed to Gurū Nānak at the time of his emergence from the waters of the Veīn.

> *nā ko hindū hai nā ko musalamān hai.*
> There is neither Hindu nor Mussulman.[2]

It is quite possible that this aphorism derives from an authentic utterance by Gurū Nānak, but the general unreliability of the janam-sākhīs forbids a positive affirmation on this point. There can, however, be no doubt that it represents a particular doctrinal conviction held by the Sikh community during the early seventeenth century and that this conviction has contributed to the content of the janam-sākhīs. Another example of a theme which evidently reflects both a particular situation and an interpretation of it is the fate of those who place their trust in caste status and the fulfilment of prescribed caste custom.[3]

[1] The story of Kauḍā the Savage (*Pur JS*, *sākhi* 44) appears to be another illustration, the link in this case being the word *karāhā* (cauldron), and likewise the story of Kaliyug (*Pur JS*, *sākhī* 24) where the origin appears to be the exposition of the futility of earthly rewards given in Gurū Nānak's *Sirī Rāgu* 1 (*AG*, p. 14). See also *infra*, p. 83 and Rattan Singh Jaggi, *Vichār-dhārā*, p. 15. The popular story of Sajjaṇ the *Ṭhag* may also owe its origin to this particular process. In a few cases a particular reference or verse has given rise to two different stories. *Basant* 3 (*AG*, p. 1169), which concerns the futility of purified cooking-squares, has produced two entirely different stories in the *Purātan* and *Miharbān* accounts. (*Pur JS*, *sākhī* 38, p. 72; *Mih JS*, *goṣṭ* 41, pp. 120–3.)

[2] *Pur JS*, p. 16. See *infra*, pp. 38, 107. Cf. also *BG* 1. 33; *Mih JS*, p. 489.

[3] Cf. *infra*, pp. 45, 52.

This observation should not suggest that at such points the janam-sākhīs are necessarily in conflict with the teachings of Gurū Nānak. In some instances it seems clear that this is the case, as for example in the measure of deference which the janam-sākhīs pay to sādhūs and faqīrs. Gurū Nānak commended a certain kind of sādhū or faqīr, but not the conventional variety which finds favour in some of the janam-sākhī stories.[1] In other cases, of which the denunciation of caste pretensions serves as an example, there is obvious consonance. The relevant issue at this point is not so much the question of conflict or consonance as the circumstances which prompted certain emphases and the extent to which such emphases have moulded the janam-sākhī traditions.

The contemporary needs of the community can also be regarded as the source of the most prominent of all janam-sākhī characteristics, namely the wonder story. The most cursory reading of any of the janam-sākhīs will soon reveal the dominance of this feature and of the impulse which it represents. Such stories are a compelling need in the popular piety of all religions and the janam-sākhīs provide a natural response. Substantial portions of all the janam-sākhīs can be explained by reference to this necessity.

In this way remembered facts, devout imaginations, suggestive references in Gurū Nānak's works, contemporary beliefs and needs, and the mutations which inevitably result from oral repetition must have combined to create a stock of *sākhīs* or isolated incidents concerning the life of Gurū Nānak. The next step would be to group a number of these *sākhīs* into some sort of chronological pattern and to give the pattern a measure of stability by committing the selected *sākhīs* to writing. Such a selection would still be open to alteration, but to a lesser extent than was inevitably the case while the *sākhīs* were still circulating orally. A selection once recorded would be copied, the copy would be copied, and so a tradition would be established, though still subject to modification by drawing on the oral stock, or perhaps on a different written tradition.

The manuscripts which we now possess are the products of the latter stage in the evolution, being copies of earlier collections rather than original compilations. They fall into four recognizable, though overlapping, traditions:

1. *Purātan.*
2. *Miharbān.*
3. *Bālā*, or *Bhāī Bālā.*
4. The *Gyān-ratanāvalī*, or *Manī Siṅgh Janam-sākhī.*

Of the four the least reliable is the *Bālā* tradition, but its influence has been immense. Ever since the days of Macauliffe, author of the six-volume

[1] Cf. *infra*, pp. 62, 83, 133–4.

work entitled *The Sikh Religion*, it has been the *Purātan* tradition which has been accorded the greatest measure of reliability and which has been used as the basis of all the better biographies. There is now reason to believe that this opinion should be revised and that the *Miharbān Janam-sākhī*, hitherto dismissed as sectarian polemic, should be regarded as at least equal in reliability to the *Purātan* tradition. This description is, however, a relative one. It should not be taken to imply anything resembling consistent reliability.

One important work which does not fit easily into this classification is the first *Vār* of Bhāī Gurdās. It is not a janam-sākhī in the normally accepted sense as apart from four incidents it offers very little information about Gurū Nānak's life. In so far as it does present a pattern it accords with the *Miharbān Janam-sākhī*, but the two could not be said to belong to a common tradition. The primary purpose of this *vār* is to extol the greatness of the first six Gurūs and to serve this purpose in the case of Gurū Nānak, Bhāī Gurdās has made a very limited selection from the available material. In this qualified sense it may be referred to as a janam-sākhī, but it would be unduly optimistic to expect from the relevant stanzas more than the barest sketch of the Gurū's life. Nevertheless, it certainly warrants our closest attention because of its relative nearness to the time of Gurū Nānak, and no treatment of the janam-sākhīs would be complete without it.

Bhāī Gurdās's Vār 1

Bhāī Gurdās Bhallā is a figure of considerable importance in early Sikh history. The date of his birth is not known, but he is said to have been a nephew of the third Gurū, Amar Dās. The year S. 1636 (A.D. 1579) is given as the date of his admission by Gurū Rām Dās to the Sikh community and for a number of years he worked as a missionary in Agra. Gurū Arjan subsequently summoned him back to the Pañjāb and retained him as his amanuensis during the compilation of the *Ādi Granth*. None of his own works were included in the scripture which he transcribed, but his *vārs* are traditionally regarded as 'the key to the *Gurū Granth Sāhib*'[1] and his compositions are specifically approved for recitation in Sikh gurdwārās.[2] After Gurū Arjan's death he became a trusted follower of Gurū Hargobind. His death is said to have taken place in S. 1694 (A.D. 1637).[3]

Bhāī Gurdās's thirty-nine *vārs*[4] and, to a lesser extent, his 556

[1] *Vārān Bhāī Gurdās*, ed. Hazara Singh and Vir Singh, Foreword.

[2] *Sikh Rahit Marayādā*, Śromaṇī Gurduārā Prabandhak Committee (6th ed., 1961), p. 21.

[3] *MK*, p. 311. For a brief account of Bhāī Gurdās's life see Khushwant Singh, *A History of the Sikhs*, vol. i, pp. 310–12.

[4] The published editions of the *vārs* include forty, but the last of these is by a later writer of the same name. Khushwant Singh, op. cit., p. 312. The *vārs* of Bhāī Gurdās differ in form from those of the *Ādi Granth*. Bhāī Gurdās's *vārs* accord more with the customary form, an heroic ode of several stanzas (*pauṛīs*), but no *śloks*.

compositions in the *kabitt* poetic form are of considerable interest as an exposition of contemporary Sikh belief, but they contain relatively little biographical material. In the case of Gurū Nānak such material is confined to *Vār* 1, stanzas 23–45, and *Vār* 11, stanzas 13–14.[1] The second of these extracts is of comparatively slight importance and consequently Bhāī Gurdās's contribution to the biography of Gurū Nānak is almost entirely limited to the twenty-three stanzas of *Vār* 1.

It is clear that these stanzas must have been composed during the first half of the seventeenth century, but impossible to give them an exact date. According to the *Gyān-ratanāvalī* Bhāī Gurdās wrote his account of the life of Gurū Nānak in response to a request made by some Sikhs 'at the time when the fifth Master established the canon of *Srī Granth Sāhib*'.[2] This would mean in, or soon after, A.D. 1604. The *Gyān-ratanāvalī* was, however, written more than a century later than the compilation of the *Ādi Granth*, and the prologue which contains this statement appears to have been written even later than the main work. It has been argued that *Vār* 1 must have been written after A.D. 1628 as stanza 48 contains, with reference to Gurū Hargobind, the line:

> This heroic Gurū was a conqueror of armies, a mighty warrior and one supremely generous.

Gurū Hargobind's first battle, a skirmish with some troops of the Emperor Shāhjahān, took place in 1628 and it is accordingly held that the *vār* must have been written after this date.[3] Such an argument can, however, apply only to the stanza in which the line occurs, for there is no indication that the *vārs* were composed as complete units.

The only safe conclusion is that the twenty-three stanzas would have been composed before A.D. 1637. They may well have been written appreciably earlier, but there is no trustworthy evidence which establishes this beyond doubt and the legendary details which they contain suggest a later rather than an earlier date. The most which can be said with assurance is that this brief account of Gurū Nānak's life was written at some time during a period extending from the close of the sixteenth century to the year 1637, a period which began sixty years after the Gurū's death and ended one hundred years after that date.

The Purātan Janam-sākhīs

The term *Purātan Janam-sākhī*, or 'Ancient Janam-sākhī', is open to some misunderstanding as it has been used in two different senses. Strictly

[1] Other direct references to him are to be found in *Vār* 24. 1–4, and *Vār* 26. 16, 30–31, but with the exception of a line from *Vār*. 24. 1 which refers to his residence in Kartārpur, and another from *Vār*. 24. 4 which describes the levelling of caste within the community established by the Gurū, their content is exclusively eulogistic.

[2] *GR*, p. 3. See *infra*, p. 25.

[3] *Mih JS*, Introductory Essays, p. 62.

speaking it designates no single known work, but rather a small group of janam-sākhīs which are clearly from a common source which has never been found. It is, however, generally used with reference to the composite work which was compiled by Bhāī Vir Singh and first published in 1926. The usage in this present study corresponds to the second of these meanings. The first of them is covered by the plural form *Purātan* janam-sākhīs, or by the term 'the *Purātan* tradition'.

Of the extant *Purātan* janam-sākhīs the two most important are the *Colebrooke* and *Hāfizābād* versions. The first of these was discovered in 1872 by Dr. Trumpp while examining the Gurmukhī manuscripts in the possession of the India Office Library, London.[1] The manuscript had been donated to the Library of East India House by H. T. Colebrooke, probably in 1815 or 1816, and is accordingly known either by his name or as the *Valāitvālī Janam-sākhī*, 'the janam-sākhī from overseas'.

Trumpp's work was published in 1877 and his information aroused the interest of Sikh scholars in the Pañjāb. In 1883 some Amritsar Sikhs petitioned the Lieutenant-Governor of the Pañjāb, Sir Charles Aitcheson, to have the manuscript brought to India for inspection. The petition was granted and in the autumn of the same year the manuscript was sent to the Pañjāb and made available for scrutiny in Lahore and Amritsar. Learning of the Sikhs' desire to have it photographed, Sir Charles made arrangements to have this done at government expense. The manuscript was photographed and printed by means of a zincographic process in 1885 and copies were given to selected institutions as gifts.[2] In the meantime the Lahore Singh Sabhā, a distinguished reform society of Sikhs, had made a copy from the manuscript and this had been lithographed in Lahore in 1884.

In the same year that the photozincograph facsimiles of the *Colebrooke Janam-sākhī* were produced, Macauliffe published another version of the same janam-sākhī. This second version had been acquired the previous year in the town of Hāfizābād by Bhāī Gurmukh Singh of Oriental College, Lahore. Gurmukh Singh passed the manuscript on to Macauliffe who divided off the individual words and had it lithographed at his own expense.[3] The version was designated the *Hāfizābād Janam-sākhī* by Gurmukh Singh and this is its usual title, but it is also referred to as the *Macauliffe-vālī Janam-sākhī*. Gurmukh Singh reported in his introduction to the lithographed edition that there were pages missing from the end of the manuscript and that Macauliffe had used the *Colebrooke Janam-sākhī* to complete the edition.[4]

[1] E. Trumpp, *The Ādi Granth*, p. ii. The manuscript is IOL, MS. Panj. B6.

[2] *Photozincograph Facsimile*, prefatory note, p. iii. Gurmukh Singh, Introduction to Macauliffe's edition of the *Hāfizābād Janam-sākhi*, pp. 3–4. *Pur JS*, Introduction, pp. u–a.

[3] Gurmukh Singh, op. cit., pp. 4–5. The town of Hāfizābād is in Gujranwālā District, West Pakistan. The manuscript is no longer traceable.

[4] Ibid., p. 9.

These were the two manuscripts which Vir Singh used for practically the whole of his composite *Purātan Janam-sākhī*. For the most part the two versions are very close, with only occasional words or phrases differing, but there are a few significant differences. Of the two, the *Hāfizābād* manuscript appears to be closer to the common source, although it is clear that it is not itself the original of the *Purātan* group. This original *Purātan* janam-sākhī has never been found. Macauliffe and Kahn Singh have attributed it to a certain Sevā Dās,[1] but there is no reference to such a person in the janam-sākhī which Macauliffe published and it is clear from a comment which he makes that the information was not based upon anything he had himself seen.[2]

Neither the *Colebrooke* nor the *Hāfizābād Janam-sākhī* bears an explicit date, but a reference in the *Colebrooke* manuscript clearly points to A.D. 1635 as the date of the original composition.[3] The fact that the reference is missing from the *Hāfizābād* manuscript seriously weakens its claims to authenticity, but there are other factors which suggest the same period. One such is the inclusion of works by Gurū Arjan which are erroneously attributed to Gurū Nānak, and another is the evident fact that the author had not seen Bhāī Gurdās's *Vār* 1. It is inconceivable that had he done so he would have omitted reference to the Baghdad incident which Bhāī Gurdās records. This does not prove that the janam-sākhī predated the *Vār*, but it does point to a period which preceded the general dissemination of Bhāī Gurdās's works. Thirdly, there is the obvious age of the language and of the script, both of which resemble those of the Kartārpur version of the *Ādi Granth*.[4] None of these factors could be regarded as determinative, but the second and third are of some significance, particularly the third. It seems safe to conclude that the *Purātan* janam-sākhī must have been committed to writing during the first half of the seventeenth century.

Since the discovery of the *Colebrooke* and *Hāfizābād* janam-sākhīs several other *Purātan* manuscripts have been found. Of these one deserves special mention as it diverges significantly from other janam-sākhīs of this group. It is a manuscript which was acquired by the India Office Library in 1907 and is listed in its catalogue as MSS. Pañjābī B40.[5] This B40 manuscript follows the *Hāfizābād Janam-sākhī* in the early *sākhīs*, but after the *sākhī* which describes Gurū Nānak's departure from Sultānpur it diverges and only a limited amount of the remaining material corresponds even remotely

[1] Macauliffe, *The Sikh Religion*, vol. i, p. lxxxvi. Kahn Singh, *MK*, p. 172 Kahn Singh worked in collaboration with Macauliffe. His reference to Sevā Dās is brief and cryptic.

[2] Macauliffe's comment is as follows: 'The late Sir Atar Singh, Chief of Bhadaur, gave the author this information.' Op. cit., vol. i, p. lxxxvi, n. 1.

[3] *Pur JS*, pp. 116–17.

[4] E. Trumpp, *The Ādi Granth*, p. ii. *Pur JS*, pp. a, e.

[5] It should not be confused with MSS. Pañjābī B41 which belongs to the *Bālā* group of janam-sākhīs.

to the two main *Purātan* manuscripts.[1] Some of the *sākhīs* suggest a connexion with the *Bālā* tradition, but only a very indirect one, the versions recorded in this manuscript having been withdrawn from the oral stock appreciably earlier than the corresponding *Bālā* tradition *sākhīs*. Bhāī Bālā, the person who figures so prominently in the *Bālā* tradition as a companion of Gurū Nānak and from whom the tradition takes its name, is nowhere mentioned. At a few points the text represents an earlier version of what is recorded in the extant version of the *Miharbān Janam-sākhī*. Several of the *sākhīs* are simply discourses rather than incidents and bear appropriately vague titles. Unlike the principal *Purātan* manuscripts it includes the famous story of how Gurū Nānak pretended to water his Lahore fields from Hardwār,[2] and it also refers to a Baghdad visit.[3] The collection follows no logical order after the departure from Sultānpur, simply recording *sākhīs* as isolated incidents.

This manuscript is important, for it represents a more primitive collection than either the *Colebrooke* or *Hāfizābād* janam-sākhīs. Although there is little to distinguish the three as far as language is concerned, the *sākhīs* of this version are, for the most part, more rudimentary than those of the *Colebrooke* and *Hāfizābād* manuscripts. Several of them consist of little more than a verse by Gurū Nānak, with a very brief introduction added to give it a setting. Whether it may be regarded as a version of the *Purātan* tradition is perhaps open to some doubt. If it is to be assigned to any of the recognizable traditions then it must certainly be included within the *Purātan* group, but it would be more accurate to speak of an affiliation with the *Purātan* tradition rather than of inclusion within it.

The Miharbān Janam-sākhī

Of the four traditions the most neglected has been that of the *Miharbān Janam-sākhī*. Until relatively recent years this was inevitably the case as no copy of any substantial portion of the janam-sākhī was known to exist. The absence of such a copy was not, however, regarded as a serious misfortune, for the janam-sākhī had long since acquired a disagreeable reputation. Soḍhī Miharbān, to whom the janam-sākhī is attributed, was closely associated with the Mīṇā sect, and from this association the janam-sākhī derived its unfortunate reputation.[4] The Mīṇās were inimical to the

[1] Examples of correspondence are provided by the following *sākhīs*: Kaliyug, folio 44; Saidpur, folio 66; the wealthy man's flags, folio 189; the first half of the *sākhī* concerning Rājā Śivanābh, corresponding to the *Pur JS sākhī* 41, folio 138.

[2] Loc. cit., folio 76. See *infra*, p. 55.

[3] Loc. cit., folio 200. The *sākhī* does not, however, correspond to Bhāī Gurdās's account of the Gurū's visit to Baghdad (see *infra*, p. 35). According to this manuscript the discourse in Baghdad is said to have been with Sheikh Sharaf.

[4] The Mīṇās were the followers of Prithī Chand (A.D. 1558–1619) the eldest son of the fourth Gurū, Rām Dās. Prithī Chand's behaviour was evidently unsatisfactory as he was passed over in favour of his youngest brother, Arjan, when his father chose a successor.

Gurūs from the period of Gurū Arjan onwards and it has been assumed that this hostility must have informed Miharbān's account of the life of Gurū Nānak. According to the prologue of the *Gyān-ratanāvalī* it was the Mīnā practice of interpolating the traditions concerning Gurū Nānak which prompted Gurū Arjan to commission Bhāī Gurdās's account and which subsequently persuaded Bhāī Manī Siṅgh to write the *Gyān-ratanāvalī* itself.[1] The reference in the prologue of the *Gyān-ratanāvalī* seemed to point directly to the *Miharbān Janam-sākhī* and in the absence of an extant copy of the work there was no evident reason for modifying the hostility which had traditionally been accorded to it.

In 1940, however, a manuscript copy of half of the janam-sākhī was discovered at Damdamā Sāhib.[2] This manuscript comprises the first three *pothīs*, or volumes, of the six which constituted the complete janam-sākhī.[3] The first three are entitled *Pothī Sach-khaṇḍ*, *Pothī Harijī*, and *Pothī Chatarbhuj* respectively, and according to the colophon of *Pothī Sach-khaṇḍ* these three were followed by *Keso Rāi Pothī*, *Abhai Pad Pothī*, and finally *Prem Pad Pothī*.[4] The script is Gurmukhī, but the language is basically Braj with an admixture of words drawn from Eastern and Western Pañjābī, Persian, and Multānī.[5]

Pothī Sach-khaṇḍ, the first volume of the janam-sākhī, is obviously the most important part of the complete work. It is the only *pothī* which is directly attributed to Miharbān himself[6] and it is the only one which contains any appreciable amount of biographical material. The second and

He disputed the succession and following Gurū Arjan's execution in 1606 made further attempts to secure the title. At some point he and his followers were branded 'Mīṇās' and the name stuck. The Mīṇās were a robber tribe of the Gurgāon area, and in Pañjābī the word had come to mean a dissembling rogue, one who took care to conceal his evil intentions. Following the death of Prithī Chand the leadership of the sect passed to his son Miharbān (1581–1640). The Mīṇās were subsequently execrated by Gurū Gobind Singh and declared by him to be one of the five groups with whom orthodox Sikhs were to have no dealings. The sect is now extinct.

[1] *GR*, pp. 3–4. See *infra*, p. 25.

[2] Damdamā Sāhib, originally called Sābo kī Talvaṇḍī, is eighteen miles south of Bhaṭiṇḍā. It acquired importance in Sikh history as a result of a visit by Gurū Gobind Singh following the Battle of Muktsar in 1705. The manuscript is now in the possession of Khalsa College, Amritsar (MS. no. SHR: 427 of the College's Sikh History Research Department). In 1961 Khalsa College acquired a second manuscript (no. SHR: 2190) which covers a much smaller portion of the total janam-sākhī, but which supplies some material which is missing in the first manuscript.

[3] The first *pothī* was published by the Sikh History Research Department of Khalsa College, Amritsar, in 1962 under the title *Janam Sākhī Srī Gurū Nānak Dev Jī* (edited by Kirpal Singh and Shamsher Singh Ashok). The two remaining *pothīs* are forthcoming. The published edition of the first *pothī* incorporates the material which is missing from the Damdamā Sāhib manuscript but supplied by the second Khalsa College manuscript.

[4] *Mih JS*, p. 519.

[5] It is an example of *Sādhukkaṛī*, or *Sant Bhāṣā*. See *infra*, p. 153.

[6] The compiling of the other two sections of the manuscript is attributed, as the titles of the two *pothīs* indicate, to Harijī and Chatarbhuj. Harijī was Miharbān's second son and his successor as *gurū* of the Mīṇās. Chatarbhuj was his third son.

third volumes contain little other than discourse and interpretation of scripture, and it is evident that the same must apply to almost all that was contained in the remaining three volumes which have never been found. Practically all that is of any biographical importance will almost certainly have been incorporated in the first volume. The two which follow it add only an occasional point of interest and it may be safely assumed that the same would have applied to the remaining three volumes.

Even in the case of *Pothī Sach-khaṇḍ* it is at once evident that Miharbān's primary purpose was the exposition of Gurū Nānak's works, and that biographical incidents were included more as settings for discourses than for their own sake. Most of the *goṣṭs*, or 'discourses', into which the *pothī* is divided offer only a few such details and then proceed to discourse, quotations from Gurū Nānak's works, and lengthy interpretations of such quotations. In a few cases an event is described at some length, but in many more no biographical details are given at all. This means that only a small proportion of the janam-sākhī is directly relevant to our biographical concern. There is, however, nothing surprising in this, for all of the janam-sākhīs use most biographical incidents as settings for utterances by Gurū Nānak. In this respect Miharbān's janam-sākhī differs only in that it offers much more extensive interpretations of the scriptures which it quotes.

Pothī Sach-khaṇḍ is accordingly the important portion of the complete *Miharbān Janam-sākhī*, and it provides a valuable addition to the janam-sākhī literature. With such a manuscript available it is possible to determine whether or not Miharbān's account of the life of Gurū Nānak deserves the condemnation which it has traditionally received. An examination of it indicates that Miharbān has been largely misjudged. It is true that certain features of the janam-sākhī could give offence,[1] but such features are by no means as conspicuous as the janam-sākhī's reputation would suggest. The tone, far from being one of denigration, is manifestly one of enthusiastic homage and places this janam-sākhī firmly within the same hagiographic category as the other janam-sākhīs. This is indeed what might have been anticipated. The Mīṇās were schismatics, not heretics, and although they certainly bore enmity towards Gurū Arjan and his successors there was no evident reason why they should have sought to malign Gurū Nānak.

[1] Examples from *Pothi Sach-khaṇḍ* are the claim that Gurū Nānak was a reincarnation of the first Rājā Janak (*Mih JS*, p. 8) and the statement that Gurū Nānak originally began his travels with the intention of finding a *gurū* (ibid., pp. 111, 361). An example from *Pothī Hariji* is its claim that Gurū Nānak remarried following the conclusion of his travels. (Khalsa College MS. no. SHR: 427, folio 387b.) The belief that Gurū Nānak was a reincarnation of Rājā Janak is not confined to the *Miharbān* tradition. There is a *Purātan* janam-sākhī in Hoshiarpur which makes the same claim. (Shamsher Singh Ashok, *Pañjābī hath-likhatān di sūchi*, vol. ii, no. 92, p. 230.) It is possible that the *Colebrooke Janam-sākhi* may have originally included this story as folios 2–6 are missing from the manuscript (*Photozincograph Facsimile*, prefatory note, p. iii).

According to the colophons at the end of all three *pothīs* the copying of the manuscript obtained from Damdamā Sāhib was completed in S. 1885 (A.D. 1828).[1] The colophon of *Pathī Harijī* implies that it is a copy made from the original, a claim which must be treated with some caution. The text is not pure in that it contains references which would not have been possible in the early or mid-seventeenth century,[2] and there are also indications of subsequent alterations by sādhūs of the Udāsī sect.[3]

The date of the original version of *Pothī Sach-khaṇḍ* cannot be determined with certainty, but it seems likely that it would have been finally compiled between A.D. 1640, the year of Miharbān's death, and 1650, the date ascribed to *Pothī Harijī*.[4] The introduction to *Pothī Sach-khaṇḍ*[5] appears to have been written after his death, and the production of *Pothī Harijī* and *Pothī Chatarbhuj* in successive years[6] suggests that the whole collection may have been compiled in a single operation extending over a number of years.

This, of course, applied only to the compilation. The actual composition must have extended over many years of Miharbān's lifetime and been recorded during that time as individual discourses.[7] This means that the composition of Miharbān's janam-sākhī must have taken place during the same period as Bhāī Gurdās's *Vār* 1 and the original *Purātan* janam-sākhī, and that accordingly there can be little to distinguish the three as far as age is concerned. All of them, it appears, had their beginnings in oral traditions which developed during the second half of the sixteenth century, and all three evidently emerged in their present form, or something resembling it, during the first half of the seventeenth century.

The Bālā *janam-sākhīs*

The janam-sākhīs of the *Bālā*, or *Bhāī Bālā*, tradition deserve notice, not because they possess any intrinsic reliability, but because of the immense influence they have exercised in determining what has generally been accepted as the authoritative account of Gurū Nānak's life. Throughout the nineteenth century, until the discovery of the *Purātan* manuscripts, the authority of the *Bālā* version was unchallenged, and even after the *Purātan* tradition had won general acceptance the *Bālā* janam-sākhīs continued to supply many of the incidents required to fill out the relatively

[1] *Mih JS*, p. ix. [2] Ibid., p. ix.

[3] Ibid., Introductory Essays, p. 83. The Udāsīs are an order of celibate ascetics which originally gathered around Sirī Chand, one of Gurū Nānak's two sons. The order still claims numerous followers. There is an important Udāsī temple adjacent to the Golden Temple in Amritsar and many Udāsī sādhūs are to be found in Hardwār. See J. C. Archer, *The Sikhs in relation to Hindus, Moslems, Christians, and Ahmadiyyas*, pp. 226–8.

[4] *Mih JS*, p. ix. [5] Ibid., p. 1. [6] Ibid., p. ix.

[7] This assumption is supported by a work entitled *Goṣṭān Miharvān jī diān*, evidently written during the seventeenth century and attributed to Harijī (Kirpal Singh, *Mih JS*, Introduction, p. vii).

brief accounts given by the *Purātan* manuscripts. Even Macauliffe used them, in spite of his slighting remarks concerning the claims of the *Bālā* version to be the earliest of all janam-sākhīs.[1]

The *Bālā* version is, however, the least trustworthy of all the janam-sākhī traditions. Errors of fact occur with considerable frequency[2] and the fabulous material which it incorporates far exceeds that of the other janam-sākhīs, both in quantity and in degree. The legendary accretions are particularly prominent in its description of Gurū Nānak's mountain-climbing expeditions and of his visits to various Puranic regions (*khands*) and continents (*dīps*).[3] A determined assault was made on the *Bālā* tradition by Karam Singh in 1913,[4] but later authors have generally continued to follow the Macauliffe pattern of using *Bālā* material to augment the *Purātan* account.

If one asks for a janam-sākhī in a Pañjāb bazar bookshop today the book which will be offered will almost invariably be a modern edition of the *Bālā* version. Ever since the janam-sākhīs began to be printed the *Bālā* tradition has monopolized the Pañjābī market, and with the passing years these printed editions have grown progressively bulkier. An edition lithographed in 1871 is, for the most part, a copy of a version which is found in several extant *Bālā* manuscripts,[5] but another edition lithographed in the same year by Dīvān Būṭā Singh of Lahore is substantially longer,[6] and yet another produced in 1890 is longer still.[7] Finally we have the letterpress version which still sells well in Pañjāb bookshops.[8] It is to the earliest of the lithographed editions, the one which was published by Hāfaz Qutub Dīn of Lahore in 1871, that reference will normally be made in the section

[1] Macauliffe, i. lxxvii–ix.

[2] Karam Singh provides a lengthy list in his *Kattak ki Visākh*, pp. 36–138.

[3] *Bālā JS*, pp. 200 ff. See especially pp. 265–8. An illustration of the *Bālā* variety of fantasy is its account of Gurū Nānak's ride on a fish measuring thirty-five *kos* in length and five *kos* in breadth. The fish turns out to be a former Sikh who had been reincarnated in this form as a result of Gurū Nānak having once commented that he writhed like a fish whenever he was instructed to do anything (ibid., pp. 137–40).

[4] Karam Singh, *Kattak ki Visākh*, Amritsar, 1913. The book was primarily intended to prove that Gurū Nānak was born in the month of Vaisākh, and not in Kārtik as popularly believed, but practically the whole of the book consists of a vigorous attack upon the *Bālā* janam-sākhīs, the source of the Kārtik tradition.

[5] Published in Lahore by Hāfaz Qutub Dīn in S. 1928 (A.D. 1871). There is a copy of this edition in the IOL (Panj. 1522). Also in the IOL are two reprints, one dated A.D. 1874 (IOL, Panj. 30. E. 3) and the other A.D. 1886 (IOL, Panj. 1523). Although this edition generally follows the IOL manuscript Panj. B41 it is not, as Trumpp claimed, 'nearly identical' (E. Trumpp, *The Ādi Granth*, p. lii, n. 1). It contains four substantial interpolations from a *Purātan* source, it omits some portions which appear derogatory to Gurū Nānak, and it adds an account of the Gurū's death.

[6] *Bālā Janam-sākhī*, Mālik Dīvān Būṭā Singh, Lahore, S. 1928 (A.D. 1871). There is a copy in the IOL (Panj. 31.1.9) and another in the BM (14162. d. 3). A reprint was published in A.D. 1890 (IOL, Panj. 31.1.7).

[7] *Bālā Janam-sākhi*, Maulvī Maibūb Ahmad, Lahore, A.D. 1890 (IOL, Panj. 31.1.10).

[8] Copies available in London are IOL, Panj. H. 18, and BM, 14162 d. 26.

dealing with the life of Gurū Nānak.[1] Occasional reference will also be made to two other editions. These are the Dīvān Būṭā Singh edition which, to distinguish it from the Hāfaz Qutub Dīn edition, will be referred to as 'the expanded 1871 edition', and, as a representative of the modern group, an edition published by Munshī Gulāb Singh and Sons of Lahore in A.D. 1942.

One reason which does much to explain the popularity of the *Bālā* version is its claim that the original *Bālā Janam-sākhī* was dictated in the presence of Gurū Aṅgad by Bhāī Bālā, a companion of Gurū Nānak, and that accordingly it represents an eye-witness account of the life of the first Gurū. This claim can be dismissed without hesitation, but the question then arises of a satisfactory substitute explanation to account for the origin of the *Bālā* janam-sākhīs. Two theories have been advanced. One is that the original janam-sākhī was composed by the heretical sect of Hindālīs during the first half of the seventeenth century; and the other is that a janam-sākhī of unknown but early origin was interpolated by the Hindālīs.[2]

There can be no doubt that the *Bālā Janam-sākhī* as it has survived in manuscript form is a Hindālī version of the life of Gurū Nānak.[3] This is not evident from the printed editions, for the publishers have purged almost all the references which expressed or seemed to imply Hindālī enmity towards Gurū Nānak, but the manuscript versions have whole *sākhīs* and a number of briefer references which were clearly intended to exalt Bābā Hindāl (and consequently the sect bearing his name) and to denigrate Gurū Nānak at the expense of Kabīr and Hindāl. Were these derogatory references an integral part of a Hindālī janam-sākhī deliberately composed as a contribution to the sect's campaign against the orthodox Sikhs, or should they be regarded as interpolations? Of the alternatives the former appears to be the more likely, but the issue is debatable. It is an issue of interest rather than of real importance and the same judgement can be applied to the question of whether or not a person called Bhāī Bālā actually existed. The actual existence of Bhāī Bālā is certainly a possibility, in spite of the failure of Bhāī Gurdās or of any other janam-sākhī tradition to mention

[1] The abbreviation *Bālā JS* refers to this edition.

[2] The heretical sect of Hindālīs, or Nirañjanīs, developed out of the enmity of a certain Bidhī Chand, the son of Bābā Hindāl of Jaṇḍiālā and a contemporary of Gurū Hargobind (1595–1644). Hindāl himself is said to have been converted by Gurū Amar Dās and to have displayed such loyalty, particularly through his service in the Gurū's kitchen (*laṅgar*), that he was appointed to a position of authority in the community. His son Bidhī Chand, however, married a Muslim woman and evidently responded to the reproaches of the Sikhs by turning apostate. Jaṇḍiālā became a centre of malignant opposition to the Gurūs and the mutual enmity which developed persisted until the Hindālī sect eventually declined into insignificance. During the period of Mughal persecution in the eighteenth century the Hindālīs disclaimed the title of Sikh and when Aḥmad Shāh Abdālī descended upon the Pañjāb they gave him their active support against the Khālsā (*MK*, p. 535. *A Glossary of the Tribes and Castes of the Punjab etc*, vol. ii, pp. 325–6).

[3] Macauliffe implies the existence of two separate janam-sākhīs, a *Bālā Janam-sākhī* (i, p. lxxix) and a *Hindālī Janam-sākhī* (i, p. lxxxi). This is incorrect.

him, and it is remotely possible that there was an association between a person of this name and Gurū Nānak.[1] It is not, however, possible to connect the extant *Bālā* janam-sākhīs with any such association except in the most distant and conjectural sense. The dominance of the manifestly fabulous within the *Bālā* tradition demolishes any such possibility and this verdict must hold until a more primitive *Bālā* version is discovered.[2] In a few cases the *Bālā* tradition evidently carries us further back than the other janam-sākhīs,[3] but for the most part it represents a selection from the common pool after it had become well stocked with fabulous incidents. It is a fascinating collection, but it is of only limited help in the search for the historical Nānak.

An important work based upon the *Bālā* tradition is Santokh Singh's *Gur Nānak Prakāś*, commonly called the *Nānak Prakāś*. This is a much later account of the life of Gurū Nānak, having been completed in 1823, but like its principal source it has acquired considerable importance as a result of its great popularity and consequent influence.[4] Relying as it does upon an untrustworthy source the *Nānak Prakāś* is itself unreliable and warrants mention only because its influence has been so extensive.[5]

The Gyān-ratanāvalī, *or* Manī Singh Janam-sākhī

The fourth and evidently the latest of the more important collections of *sākhīs* is the *Gyān-ratanāvalī*, a janam-sākhī attributed to Bhāī Manī Singh which has suffered from a surprising measure of neglect. It has not been totally ignored in the manner of the *Miharbān Jaham-sākhī* and indeed it evidently gathered to itself a considerable measure of respect. It was, however, a reputation based on awe rather than upon usage and the practical attention it has received has been relatively slight. This is difficult to understand, for unlike the *Miharbān Janam-sākhī* it has had no taint of

[1] The possibility receives some support from a brief work entitled *Sūchak prasaṅg gurū kā* attributed to Bhāī Bahilo. Shamsher Singh Ashok, *Pañjābī hath-likhatān dī sūchī*, vol. i, p. 361.

[2] The oldest so far found is a Hindālī manuscript which is said to bear the date S. 1715 (A.D. 1658). Rattan Singh Jaggi, *Dasam Granth dā paurāṇik adhiain*, p. 59.

[3] Its account of 'the country ruled by women' is a clear example (IOL, MS. Panj. B41, folios 70b–71b). The 1871 printed edition departs from the manuscript at this point and reproduces instead the *Purātan* version of the story (*Bālā JS*, *sākhī* 25, pp. 102–8). The *Bālā* version of the story of Rājā Śivanābh appears to be another illustration (*Bālā JS*, pp. 120–3). See *infra*, p. 74, numbers 46 and 54.

[4] Santokh Singh did not accept the absolute authenticity of the *Bālā* account, but he did accept its claim to have been originally written at the behest of Gurū Aṅgad and accordingly followed it very closely in the *Nānak Prakāś*.

[5] Its lengthy sequel, the *Gur Pratāp Sūray*, commonly referred to as the *Sūraj Prākāś*, which carries the account up to the tenth Gurū, contains a somewhat higher proportion of historical fact, but is untrustworthy nonetheless. The *Surāj Prakāś* was completed in 1844. Both works are in metre and have been edited in thirteen volumes by Bhāī Vir Singh. For a note on Santokh Singh's life see Macauliffe, i, pp. lxxvi–lxxvii.

heresy attached to it. On the contrary, it has been accepted as the work of one who ranks high amongst loyal Sikhs and who wrote the janam-sākhī with the express intention of correcting heretical accounts of Gurū Nānak's life.

Perhaps the most likely explanation for the neglect is that the original collection of *sākhīs* was made during a period of political disturbance which would have inhibited its circulation. These circumstances would not necessarily have had the same effect upon the *Bālā* janam-sākhīs, for the first half of the eighteenth century was the period of Hindālī influence. By the time more settled conditions returned the *Bālā* version had evidently established itself as the apparently authentic account and the need for other versions was no longer recognized.

Bhāī Manī Singh was a famous Sikh of Gurū Gobind Singh's time[1] and the circumstances which are said to have led him to write his janam-sākhī are set out in a prologue. In this prologue it is recorded that some Sikhs once approached him with the request that he should prepare an authentic account of Gurū Nānak's life. This, they assured him, was essential as the Mīṇās[2] had maliciously interpolated objectionable things in the current account and that as a result the Sikhs' faith in the Gurū was declining. Manī Singh referred them to Bhāī Gurdās's first *vār*, but this, they maintained, was too brief. What was required was an 'expanded commentary' on the *vār*. Manī Singh protested that such a task was beyond his limited capacities, but finally agreed to make the attempt.

> Just as swimmers fix reeds in the river so that those who do not know the way may also cross, so I shall take Bhāī Gurdās's *vār* as my basis and in accordance with it, and with the accounts which I have heard at the court of the tenth Master, I shall relate to you whatever commentary issues from my humble mind.[3]

At the end of the janam-sākhī there is an epilogue in which it is stated that the completed work was taken to Gurū Gobind Singh for his *imprimatur*. The Gurū, it is said, duly signed it and commended it as a means of acquiring knowledge of Sikh belief.[4]

This is the *Gyān-ratanāvalī's* own account of its origin. The claim is that Manī Singh took *Vār* 1 as his basis, that he supplemented it with *sākhīs* he had heard related at the court of Gurū Gobind Singh, and that he presented the complete work to the Gurū for his approval. Gurū Gobind Singh was Gurū from 1675 until 1708. If the janam-sākhī's own claim is to be accepted its date of composition must lie within the intervening period.

The claim is difficult to test as the version of the *Gyān-ratanāvalī* which we now possess is certainly not the work of Manī Singh. It may perhaps

[1] *MK*, p. 712, and Macauliffe, i, pp. lxxiv–lxxvi give brief biographies.
[2] See *supra*, p. 18, n. 4. [3] *GR*, pp. 3–4. [4] Ibid., *sākhī* 225, p. 592.

incorporate portions of a collection prepared by him, but the available manuscripts record a composite product which has drawn on more than one source and which has obviously been put together much later than the time of Manī Singh.

Three reasons point to this conclusion. In the first place, there are several references to Manī Singh in the third person which clearly imply that the writer of the *Gyān-ratanāvalī* is another person. In the prologue and at various points in the narrative[1] the author makes references which suggest that he is intended to be understood as one who was present while Manī Singh was relating the account.

Secondly, there is the comparative modernity of the *Gyān-ratanāvalī's* language. This cannot be blamed on the printers who lithographed the work in 1891 and 1907 as the manuscript copies possess the same characteristic.[2]

Thirdly, there is manifest lack of homogeneity in the work. Parts of the janam-sākhī are consistent and follow a relatively logical sequence, but there are groups of *sākhīs* and a number of individual ones which disrupt the basic pattern and which have obviously been drawn from extraneous sources. Some of this later material appears to be the result of simple interpolation, but most of it has been properly integrated into the janam-sākhī.

Most of the extraneous material is easily recognizable and its incidence divides the complete work into two distinct parts. The first part covers the period of the Gurū's early life, and of his travels in eastern and southern India. Most of this first section represents an independent selection of *sākhīs* which may well be a revised version of material dating back to the early eighteenth century, perhaps even to Manī Singh himself. Several of the *sākhīs* are also included in both the *Purātan* and *Bālā* versions[3] and just as these two versions differ in their presentation, so the *Gyān-ratanāvalī* account differs from both. A number are also to be found in the *Miharbān Janam-sākhī* as well and in these instances all four versions offer varying accounts. These differences which distinguish individual *sākhīs* from corresponding accounts in other known collections indicate an independent selection from the common stock of oral *sākhīs*.

In addition to the independent material, however, there are in this first part several *sākhīs* which have been borrowed from the *Bālā* tradition,[4] and in the second part the *Gyān-ratanāvalī* becomes, in substance, a *Bālā*

[1] e.g. *GR*, pp. 340, 516.

[2] Writing in 1885 Gurmukh Singh observed: 'This janam-sākhī is popularly attributed to Bhāī Manī Singh, although someone else wrote it because its language is modern.' He adds the comment: 'If Bhāī Manī Singh himself wrote a janam-sākhī it is no longer extant.' Introduction to Macauliffe's edition of the *Hāfizābād Janam-sākhī*, pp. 2–3.

[3] See *infra*, pp. 73–76.

[4] *GR*, pp. 46–48, 135, 194–200, 213, 214, 220–1, 237–42.

janam-sākhī. The change occurs with the sudden appearance of Bhāī Bālā in the *sākhī* which describes Gurū Nānak's return to his home village of Talvaṇḍī after his travels to the east and south.[1] In the first part the person of Bhāī Bālā has been dropped from the *sākhīs* which have been taken from *Bālā* sources,[2] but following the arrival in Talvaṇḍī he is introduced into the narrative and continues in it for most of the remainder of the janam-sākhī. A logical sequence of events is maintained during the first few *sākhīs* which follow his irruption,[3] but the record soon loses its coherence and assumes the characteristic disarray of the *Bālā* tradition. At one point Bhāī Bālā disappears and for a time the record reverts to the pattern of the first half of the janam-sākhī. It retains, however, a strong *Bālā* flavour.[4]

The second half of the janam-sākhī is accordingly an amalgam. Some of it continues the earlier pattern of an independent selection from the current stock, presented in a logical sequence, and the remainder is evidently material subsequently introduced from *Bālā* sources. This means that we have in the extant version of the *Gyān-ratanāvalī* two contrasting elements. The first half (with the evident exception of the prologue and a number of other individual *sākhīs*) represents an independent selection from the common stock of *sākhīs*, and the second combines this first element with substantial borrowings from the *Bālā* tradition. With the exception of a few minor points both elements have been integrated into a single janam-sākhī by an editor who provided an introduction and a conclusion, and who refers to Manī Singh in the third person. The language of the janam-sākhī and its relationship to the *Bālā* tradition suggest that this was probably done in the late eighteenth or early nineteenth century, although some individual *sākhīs* may have been added later. The first element representing the independent selection would, however, be older and may possibly go back as far as the time of Gurū Gobind Singh.

The value of the *Gyān-ratanāvalī* lies chiefly in this first element and as far as this material is concerned the janam-sākhī is a rather more satisfactory collection than those of the *Bālā* group. It has an order which the *Bālā* janam-sākhīs lack, it avoids many of their errors, and it offers appreciably less that is plainly fantastic. In spite of this, however, its usefulness is not much greater as far as efforts to reconstruct Gurū Nānak's biography are concerned. It does at times have a negative value in that its variant

[1] *GR*, p. 264. In some copies, including the edition lithographed in 1891, Bhāī Bālā appears prior to this point in a group of *sākhīs* which describe Gurū Nānak's meeting with Sālas Rāi, a jeweller in a town called Biṣambarpur (*GR*, *sākhīs* 99–107, pp. 247–59). The same *sākhīs* appear, in almost exactly the same words, in the expanded 1871 version of the *Bālā* tradition (Dīvān Būṭā Singh, Lahore, *sākhīs* 74–75, pp. 183–93). See *infra*, pp. 84–85.

[2] In one case (the Gayā *sākhī*, *GR*, p. 214) the omission of Bhāī Bālā's name has left an obvious hiatus, but for the most part the *sākhīs* have been successfully woven into the narrative.

[3] *GR*, *sākhīs* 110–20, pp. 264–85.

[4] *GR*, pp. 401–516.

account will strengthen a case against the historicity of a particular incident recorded in the older janam-sākhīs, and at a very few points, such as the date of birth question, it makes a positive contribution of some significance. In so far as it adds to what Bhāī Gurdās's *Vār* 1 contains it represents a relatively late selection from the fund of oral *sākhīs*, interesting for this reason and sober by comparison with the *Bālā* presentation, but still a supplementary source of only occasional usefulness.

The two versions of the Mahimā Prakāś

Two works which deserve a brief mention are the *Mahimā Prakāś Vāratak* and the *Mahimā Prakāś Kavitā*. The earlier of the two, the *Mahimā Prakāś Vāratak*, was written in 1741 by Bāwā Kirpāl Singh Bhallā, and the later longer version, the *Mahimā Prakāś Kavitā*, in 1776 by Sarūp Dās Bhallā, a descendant of Gurū Amar Dās.[1] The two accounts are basically the same, but the prose version, the *Vāratak*, is appreciably shorter, having only twenty *sākhīs* devoted to Gurū Nānak as opposed to sixty-five in the metrical version.

Neither work deals exclusively with Gurū Nānak, the remainder in each case concerning the lives of the Gurūs who followed him. The two versions occupy positions of importance in the history of Sikh tradition, for they were composed during a period which, although generally obscure, was certainly significant in terms of the development of such tradition. Like the *Gyān-ratanāvalī*, however, both are too recent to be regarded as primary sources for the life of Gurū Nānak. The portion of the *Mahimā Prakāś Vāratak* dealing with Gurū Nānak was printed privately in 1959,[2] but neither version has yet been published in full.

The relative value of the different janam-sākhī traditions

An attempt must now be made to assess the relative value of the different janam-sākhī traditions as sources for a biography of Gurū Nānak. As we have already indicated, the janam-sākhīs of the *Bālā* tradition are particularly unreliable, and the relatively late *Gyān-ratanāvalī* offers little which is not available in earlier janam-sākhī sources. Accordingly, these two sources may be summarily excluded and the discussion confined to Bhāī Gurdās's *Vār* 1 and the janam-sākhīs of the *Miharbān* and *Purātan* traditions. The *Bālā* janam-sākhīs and the *Gyān-ratanāvalī* will not, of course, be totally excluded from the analysis of the events of Gurū Nānak's life,

[1] The date S. 1833 (A.D. 1776) given in the text of the *Mahimā Prakāś Kavitā* refers only to the portion dealing with Gurū Nānak (Khalsa College, Amritsar, MS. SHR: 2300A, folio 145a).

[2] *Jīvan kathā Srī Gurū Nānak Dev Jī Mahimā Prakāś (Vāratak) vichon*, ed. Kirpal Singh, Dehra Dun, 1959.

for notwithstanding their limitations they do have a contribution to make.

The account of Gurū Nānak's life given in Bhāī Gurdās's *Vār* 1, and supplemented in *Vār* 11, is a very brief one, but within the limited range which it covers this account has generally been accepted as the most reliable available. There are three reasons for this reputation. The first and basic one is the indisputable fact that the author was a Sikh of impeccable orthodoxy who had close associations with the more prominent of his Sikh contemporaries. These would have included not only Gurū Arjan and Gurū Hargobind, but also older disciples whose memories might have extended back to the time of Gurū Nānak himself. Secondly, there is the coherence of the travel itinerary which may be deduced from the first *vār*. Thirdly, there is the belief that there is less of the miraculous in this account, and accordingly less that warrants a measure of scepticism. Khushwant Singh is expressing a generally accepted conclusion when he says of the events of Gurū Nānak's life, 'whatever reference he makes in the *Vārs* must be considered authentic'.[1]

The importance of the first reason should not be minimized, but we are nevertheless unable to accept the conclusion without some qualification. The belief that the account given in *Vār* 1 contains less of the miraculous than the janam-sākhīs is an illusion created by its limited range. If the comparison is narrowed down to the three incidents which are common to the *vār* and to either or both of the two older janam-sākhī traditions[2] it is at once evident that Bhāī Gurdās's account contains almost as many miraculous or otherwise unacceptable details as the *Purātan* version and, in one instance, more than that of the *Miharbān Janam-sākhī*. In the encounter with the eighty-four Siddhs on Mount Sumeru there is the anachronistic reference to Gorakhnāth and also the story of the jewels by the lakeside which the *Miharbān* account lacks. In Mecca we have the moving mosque, and in Achal Baṭālā the yogīs turning into lions, wolves, birds, and snakes.[3]

These details must prompt a measure of caution and constrain us to qualify Khushwant Singh's conclusion. We may attach a greater degree of trust to Bhāī Gurdās's account than to those of the *Purātan* and *Miharbān* janam-sākhīs, but it cannot be an unqualified trust. We must, moreover, conclude that even if the two *vārs* are the most reliable they are also the least satisfactory. The chief reason for this is the brevity of the account which they provide. The author's primary purpose was obviously to extol the Gurū rather than to provide a comprehensive record of his life, and so the *vārs* must disappoint us if we seek in them anything more than a brief

[1] Khushwant Singh, *A History of the Sikhs*, vol. i, p. 301.

[2] The Mount Sumeru, Mecca, and Achal Baṭālā incidents. See *infra*, p. 75, numbers 72, 79, and 90.

[3] See *infra*, p. 35. In Bhāī Gurdās's version it is Mecca itself which moves.

sketch of a small part of his travels and the names of a number of his followers. They retain a value in these respects, but it is to the janam-sākhīs that we must look for most of our material.

This restricts the discussion to the *Miharbān* and *Purātan* traditions. One point which at once becomes clear in any comparison of these two traditions is that as far as their biographical content is concerned they share a common heritage and a common distinction from the janam-sākhīs of the *Bālā* tradition. It is remotely possible that this is a result of one having copied from the other, but much more likely that they share a common source, or sources, of *sākhīs*. The similarities between the two accounts establish the connexion beyond all doubt, and the differences indicate that there is unlikely to have been any direct copying of one by the other. The parallels are marked, but so too are the divergences and it is on the basis of these divergences that an effort must be made to assess their relative values.

The most apparent difference is the greater length of the *Miharbān Janam-sākhī*. We are here concerned with the biographical content of the two janam-sākhīs and this means that the disparity is not nearly as great as might appear at first sight. Most of the *Miharbān Janam-sākhī* covers discourse, scripture, and interpretation, and the strictly biographical content is comparatively small. It is, however, greater than that of the *Purātan* janam-sākhīs. In the account of Gurū Nānak's marriage, for example, we find in the *Miharbān* version a lengthy catalogue of details which almost certainly owes its origin to an understanding of how marriages are usually conducted rather than to an authentic knowledge of the manner in which this particular marriage took place.[1] In the *Purātan* janam-sākhīs, on the other hand, the account of Gurū Nānak's marriage is dealt with in a single, brief sentence: 'When Bābā (Nānak) turned twelve he was married.'[2]

This is an extreme case, but Miharbān's accounts are generally longer. There are two possible reasons for this. The first is that the *Miharbān Janam-sākhī* may have drawn from the common pool of *sākhīs* later than the original *Purātan* version and that the individual *sākhīs* had been expanded in the meantime. This would mean that the *Purātan* version was a more primitive one, nearer to the time when memory still played a significant part, and was consequently more reliable.

The second possibility is that the additions represent the embellishments of a more sophisticated mind. There can be no doubt that the *Miharbān Janam-sākhī* is the work of a person of appreciably more learning than the person or persons responsible for the *Purātan* compilation. The less sophisticated mind would be content with the tradition as he found it, whereas a person such as Miharbān might feel compelled to embroider a simple account with details which do not materially affect the basic

[1] *Mih JS, goṣṭ* 11, pp. 29–33. [2] *Pur JS, sākhī* 3, p. 6.

elements of the account. The nature of the differences lends support to this latter possibility, but it may well be that both are true and that the *Purātan* version does carry us a little further back in the evolutionary process.

The other differences tend, however, to support the claims of the *Miharbān Janam-sākhī*. In the first place there is the fact that Miharbān is more careful with his material than whoever was responsible for the *Purātan* collection. This applies not just to his quotations from scripture, but also to his use of place-names and the names of people with whom Gurū Nānak is purported to have conversed. We do not find in his account such places as 'the land of Āsā'[1] or 'the land of Dhanāsarī',[2] and Gurū Nānak is said to have conversed not with Pīr Bahāuddīn[3] but with a descendant.[4] In this respect, however, the difference between Miharbān's account and that of the *Purātan* janam-sākhīs is one of degree, not an absolute one. His mistakes with scripture may be understandable,[5] but they are there nevertheless. There may be no lands of Āsā and Dhanāsarī, but there are numerous unidentified towns, deserts, and jungles. A conversation with a descendant of Pīr Bahāuddīn[6] cannot be given the summary treatment required in the case of a conversation with Bahāuddīn himself,[7] but an interview with Islām Shāh shows that Miharbān is also liable to record anachronisms.[8]

Secondly, although both accounts contain substantial quantities of the miraculous, the miracle stories recorded in the *Miharbān-Janam-sākhī* are, on the whole, less grotesque than those of the *Purātan* tradition. There is no description of Mardānā being turned into a lamb,[9] no reference to the victory of an army of insects possessing human faculties over an army of men,[10] no conversation with a man who had been reincarnated as a wolf,[11] no mention of Bahāuddīn's magic prayer-mat,[12] and no account of Rājā Śivanābh killing and stewing his son at Gurū Nānak's command.[13] Miharbān's janam-sākhī is by no means devoid of this kind of fantasy, but in general his miracles are of a more subdued nature.

[1] *Pur JS*, p. 40. [2] Ibid., p. 78. [3] Ibid., pp. 82, 108.

[4] *Mih JS*, p. 434. The word used is *potā* which generally designates a son's son, but which may be used of a more remote descendant in the direct male line.

[5] All but one of the extracts which he erroneously ascribes to Gurū Nānak appear in the *Ādi Granth* as parts of *vārs*. The *vārs* of the *Ādi Granth* are almost all composite works including the compositions of different Gurūs, and although the components are all identified a mistake made with *vār* material is more excusable than one involving a verse which plainly bears its author's title. The one exception, Gurū Amar Dās's *ślok* 104, is also explicable. It occurs in the collection of Sheikh Farīd's *śloks* and the same collection also includes *śloks* by Gurū Nānak.

[6] *Mih JS*, p. 434.

[7] *Pur JS*, pp. 82–84, 108–10. Bahāuddīn is believed to have died in A.D. 1266 (T. W. Beale, *An Oriental Biographical Dictionary*, p. 97).

[8] *Mih JS*, p. 114. See *infra*, p. 80.

[9] *Pur JS*, p. 34. According to the janam-sākhīs Mardānā the Bard was Gurū Nānak's companion during his travels.

[10] Ibid., p. 39.

[11] Ibid., p. 71.

[12] Ibid., pp. 82–84.

[13] Ibid., p. 88.

Thirdly, Miharbān offers a more satisfactory chronology and a more likely travel itinerary than the *Purātan* janam-sākhīs. According to Miharbān's *Pothī Sach-khaṇḍ* Gurū Nānak made two major journeys, followed by a brief excursion. During the first journey he travelled eastwards as far as Jagannāth Purī, southwards to Rāmeśwaram and perhaps to Ceylon, and then back to the Pañjāb up the west coast, calling at Ujjain and Bīkāner on the way. The second took him northwards into the Himālayas, westwards to Mecca, and then back through Sindh. The brief excursion took him no further than Pāk Paṭṭan.

This is much more likely than the traditional pattern of the *Purātan* account which follows the four cardinal points of the compass. It is not at all likely that Gurū Nānak would have returned home after an eastern journey and then gone to the south, and nor does it seem possible that he would have had sufficient time for such extensive travels.[1] Miharbān's description of a single all-embracing visit to the holy places of India is inherently more probable and offers a more reasonable time schedule. Moreover, Miharbān is supported by the brief outline which Bhāī Gurdās gives.

Fourthly, it is worth noting that Miharbān, for all his schismatic connexions, was a grandson of Gurū Rām Dās and a great-grandson of Gurū Amar Dās. The relationship would probably have meant access to relatively reliable traditions which might well have been denied to whoever gathered the *Purātan* material. This is an assumption, not a proven fact, but it is a reasonable assumption. These points would seem to indicate that of the three oldest sources the *Miharbān Janam-sākhī* is the most important. Before any conclusions are drawn, however, two of the arguments must be qualified. The second is qualified by the fact that the India Office Library manuscript B40, to which we have granted a *Purātan* affiliation, omits all but one of the miracles which are listed above;[2] and the force of the third is greatly reduced by the existence of another possibility which is much more likely than either the itinerary offered by the *Purātan* tradition on the one hand or that of Miharbān on the other. This third possibility is that neither of the collections is based upon a knowledge of the actual routes followed by Gurū Nānak in his travels, but rather that both represent patterns which were evolved by grouping the available *sākhīs* in a reasonable

[1] The likelihood appears to be that the *Purātan* pattern represents a later expression of the ancient *digvijaya* tradition. The term was primarily applied to a monarch's military triumphs in all four directions, but it had also acquired a hagiographic usage. In this latter sense it described the spiritual triumphs of a great saint, again with reference to the four cardinal points of the compass. Śaṅkara's biographies provide the most important illustrations of this usage and it seems that the *Purātan* pattern of Gurū Nānak's travels provides another example. I owe this suggestion to Professor A. L. Basham.

[2] The exception is the changing of Mardānā into a sheep (IOL, MS. Panj. B40, folio 83). This manuscript agrees with the *Bālā* and *Gyān-ratanāvali* versions in having him turned into a ram, not a lamb.

sequence.[1] Miharbān's more rational grouping probably amounts to no more than another example of his greater sophistication.

Even with these qualifications the arguments in favour of the *Miharbān* version still seem to indicate that of the three oldest sources it is the most satisfactory. The margin dividing the *Purātan* manuscripts and the *Miharbān Janam-sākhī* is, however, slender, and with the India Office Library B40 manuscript added to the *Purātan* group it virtually disappears. The differences are important not so much as a yardstick for measuring relative superiority, as a means of testing the reliability of individual *sākhīs*. Agreement between all versions may strengthen the claims of a *sākhī* and disagreement will have the opposite effect. Occasionally this factor is of appreciable significance, although generally in the negative sense.

Two things may be said with assurance. The first is that the normal practice of relying on the *Purātan* janam-sākhīs cannot produce reliable biography. The second is that any effort to use the *Miharbān Janam-sākhī* in the same way will be equally unsatisfactory. The janam-sākhīs must be regarded as examples of hagiography and any inclination to treat them as biographies will distort both our understanding of Gurū Nānak and our appreciation of the true value of the janam-sākhīs themselves. It is a value which includes the provision of strictly limited source material for the life of Gurū Nānak, but which is by no means limited to this function. It consists rather in the testimony which the janam-sākhīs give to the impact and continuing influence of the Gurū's personality, and even more in the evidence they offer of Sikh belief and understanding at particular points in the community's history. Having made this acknowledgement we must turn back to them. We are compelled to use the janam-sākhīs as best we can, for there is nothing better, but we must do so in the full understanding that they are thoroughly inadequate sources.

[1] See *infra*, p. 145.

3

THE LIFE OF GURŪ NĀNAK ACCORDING TO THE JANAM-SĀKHIS

THE ideal method of relating the janam-sākhī testimony to the life of Gurū Nānak would be to provide a connected account which harmonized in a single narrative the accounts given in our three principal sources. This, however, is impossible. The selection of incidents offered by Bhāī Gurdās can, by reason of its brevity, be assimilated with either of the two janam-sākhī narratives, but apart from the period covering the Gurū's childhood and early manhood it is not possible to fuse the accounts recorded in the *Miharbān* and *Purātan* traditions. Up to the point where Gurū Nānak sets out from Sultānpur on his travels there is relatively close correspondence and a harmony of the two versions could, if necessary, be provided. Following his departure from Sultānpur, however, the two narratives diverge so radically that reconciliation is out of the question. For the period of the Gurū's eastern and southern travels there is no correspondence at all. In the case of his northern and western journeys there are a number of incidents in common, but there remain crucial differences in sequence. It is accordingly necessary to set out the testimonies of our three principal sources as three separate accounts. Having done this we shall seek to analyse the material which they provide.

The life of Gurū Nānak according to Bhāī Gurdās

Bhāī Gurdās's account of the life of Gurū Nānak is to be found in stanzas 23–45 of his first *vār*, and in stanzas 13–14 of his eleventh *vār* he gives a list of the Gurū's more important followers. Stanzas 23 and 24 of the first *vār* provide little more than eloquent panegyric, but stanza 25 begins with the line:

> Bābā (Nānak) visited the places of pilgrimage; he went round seeing them all on festival days.

None of these centres are named, but it is clear from the description which follows that the line is meant to indicate a journey of considerable length.[1]

The first reference to a particular event comes in stanza 28 where it is related that the Gurū ascended Mount Sumeru and there held discourse

[1] *BG*, 1. 25–27.

with Gorakhnāth and the other eighty-three Siddhs.[1] The Siddhs questioned Gurū Nānak concerning the condition of the world below and received in reply a report of darkness, sin, and corruption. They then sought to persuade him to enter their sect and sent him to a nearby lakeside in order that he might be tempted by the masses of jewels which he would find in the lake. Their efforts failed, however, and the Gurū emerged victorious from the debate.[2]

Next he proceeded to Mecca and there went to sleep with his feet pointing towards the *miharāb*.[3] Observing this evident blasphemy a Muslim named Jīvaṇ kicked him and dragged his feet away from the direction of the *miharāb*. When he did this, however, the whole of Mecca miraculously moved in the same direction as his feet. A discourse followed in which Gurū Nānak emphasized that Rām and Rahīm, Hindu and Muslim names for God, designate one and the same God.[4]

Having left his sandals in Mecca as a relic,[5] the Gurū proceeded on to Medina,[6] and from there to Baghdad where, with Mardānā the Bard, he camped outside the city. From there he uttered the call to prayer whereupon the city at once became silent. A *pīr* named Dastgīr went out to investigate the newcomer's credentials and entered into a debate with him. In response to Dastgīr's request for enlightenment the Gurū took the *pīr's* son, ascended with him into the air, and in the twinkling of an eye revealed to him the multitude of heavens and underworlds. The two then descended into the regions below the earth and from there brought a bowl of *kaṛāh prasād*, the sacramental food of the Sikhs.[7]

Having returned to the Pañjāb Gurū Nānak proceeded to Kartārpur and there began to lead a settled life, surrounded by his followers. His sons proved rebellious and the seal of succession was accordingly set upon Aṅgad.[8]

On one occasion Gurū Nānak travelled from Kartārpur to the village of Achal Baṭālā[9] where many yogīs had gathered for the annual Śivrātri fair. In the debate which ensued the yogīs sought to overwhelm him with an impressive display of miracles. Disdaining to use the same methods, the Gurū eventually overcame them with his insistence upon the Name of God as the true source of power.[10]

From Achal Baṭālā he travelled south to Multān, but before he could enter the city some *pīrs* came out to him bearing a cup filled with milk. Gurū Nānak responded by plucking a jasmine flower and laying it on the surface of the milk.[11]

[1] See *supra*, p. 11, n. 10.
[2] *BG*, 1. 28–31.
[3] The niche in a mosque which indicates the direction of the *Ka'bah*.
[4] *BG*, 1. 32–33.
[5] *BG*, 1. 34.
[6] The reference to Medina comes in 1. 37, but the visit should presumably be placed after the Mecca visit.
[7] *BG*, 1. 35–36.
[8] *BG*, 1. 38.
[9] Four miles east of Baṭālā in Gurdāspur District.
[10] *BG*, 1. 39–44.
[11] *BG*, 1. 44. For the meaning of this gesture see *infra*, p. 142.

Following the Multān visit the Gurū returned to Kartārpur and settled down once again. There his glory daily increased and his fame spread throughout the world. Before he died he appointed his disciple Lahinā to succeed him as Gurū Aṅgad and then, merging his spirit in the spirit of his successor, he passed away.[1]

The life of Gurū Nānak according to the Purātan *janam-sākhīs*[2]

1 Bābā Nānak was born in the month of Vaisākh, S. 1526 (A.D. 1469). The date is given as the third day of the light half of the month, and the birth is said to have taken place during the last watch before dawn. His father, Kālū, was a khatrī of the Bedī sub-caste who lived in the village of Rāi Bhoi dī Talvaṇḍī and it was there that Nānak was born. His mother's name is not given. During his infancy he played with other children, but unlike them he had a concern for spiritual things and from the age of five began to utter mysterious sayings. The local Hindus declared that a god had been incarnated in human form, and the Muslims that a true follower of God had been born.

2 When he turned seven Nānak was taken to a paṇḍit to learn how to read. After only one day he gave up reading and when the paṇḍit asked him why he had lapsed into silence Nānak instructed him at length in the vanity of worldly learning and the contrasting value of the divine Name of God. The paṇḍit was greatly impressed and permitted him to return home.

3 The child now began to manifest disturbing signs of withdrawal from the world. He was set to learning 'Turkī'[3] at the age of nine, but returned home and continued to sit in silence.[4] The local people suggested to Kālū that he should have Nānak married. Kālū took their advice, a betrothal was arranged at the house of Mūlā, a khatrī of the Choṇā sub-caste, and at the age of twelve Bābā Nānak was duly married. No reference is made to where Mūlā lived or to where the marriage took place, and nor is the bride's name given. Nānak now took up a worldly occupation, but his heart was not in it and he spent his time consorting with faqīrs.

4 Two miracles are related of this period. On one occasion he went to sleep while grazing the family buffaloes and the unattended animals ruined a field of standing wheat. The aggrieved owner of the field haled the negligent Nānak before Rāi Bulār, the landlord of the village. Gurū Nānak insisted, however, that no damage had been done, and a messenger

[1] *BG*, 1. 45.

[2] The figure in the margin indicates the number of each *sākhī* as given in Vir Singh's *Purātan Janam-sākhī*. For a translation of the *Colebrooke Janam-sākhī* see E. Trumpp, *The Ādi Granth*, pp. vii–xlv.

[3] Persian.

[4] The IOL manuscript Panj. B40 inserts before the reference to Kālū's effort to have him taught 'Turkī' a very brief reference to his having been invested with the sacred thread (*janeū*) at the age of nine. Loc. cit., folio 6a.

despatched by Rāi Bulār found that the ruined crop had been miraculously
restored. On another occasion Rāi Bulār happened upon Nānak sleeping in 5
the shadow of a tree and was greatly impressed to observe that the shadow
did not move with the declining sun.[1] The same *sākhī* also records the birth
of Gurū Nānak's two sons, Lakhmī Dās and Sirī Chand.

Nānak's habitual withdrawal from the world continued to cause grave 6
concern and both his parents remonstrated with him unsuccessfully. Some 7
of the Bedīs suggested consulting a physician, but this merely prompted
utterances concerning the nature of what the Gurū regarded as the real
illness afflicting mankind. The family problem was eventually solved by 8
Nānak's brother-in-law, Jai Rām,[2] who was the steward of Nawāb Daulat
Khān of Sultānpur. Jai Rām sent a letter inviting Nānak to Sultānpur. The
invitation was accepted and Gurū Nānak departed, comforting his forlorn
wife with a promise that he would call her as soon as his work in Sultānpur
prospered.

As soon as Nānak arrived in Sultānpur Jai Rām petitioned Daulat Khān 9
to grant his brother-in-law an audience. The request was granted and as
a result of the interview Daulat Khān formed a very favourable impression
of Nānak. He presented him with a robe of honour and issued instructions
that he should be given employment. The nature of the employment is not
specified beyond the fact that it was evidently understood to be clerical
work. The *sākhī* records that each morning the Gurū would first take his
orders from the court and then would 'sit down to write'.[3] In the following
sākhī Daulat Khān refers to him as 'a good vazīr' and uses the same word
to describe him in *sākhī* 11.

During this period Gurū Nānak lived a very simple life, keeping only enough of his food allowance to meet his own limited needs and devoting the remainder to God's work.[4] Mardānā the Ḍūm[5] came from Talvaṇḍī to join him and was followed by others. All were commended to Daulat Khān by Nānak and received employment as a result. The group regularly sang the praises of God until late into the night, and during the last watch of the night the Gurū would go to the river and bathe.

One day Nānak went to the river[6] and removing his clothes left them in 10
the care of a servant. While he was bathing messengers of God came and
he was transported by them to the divine court. There he was given a cup
of nectar (*amrit*) and with it came the command, 'Nānak, this is the cup of
My Name (*Nām*). Drink it.' This he did and was charged to go into the
world and preach the divine Name.

[1] Rāi Bulār's relationship to Rāi Bhoi is not specified.
[2] Gurū Nānak's sister is not named.
[3] *Pur JS*, p. 14.
[4] That is, giving it to sādhūs and faqīrs.
[5] A depressed sub-caste of Muslim genealogists and musicians, also called Mirāsīs.
[6] The name of the river is not given.

In the meantime the servant had become anxious at his master's failure to emerge from the water. He returned to the town and informed Daulat Khān of the apparent tragedy. Daulat Khān rode out at once and had the river dragged, but Nānak's body was not to be found. Three days later, however, the missing Nānak suddenly reappeared at the point where he had entered the river. Daulat Khān joined the crowd which gathered, but Gurū Nānak evidently remained silent, for the people explained to the Nawāb that he had sustained injury in the river. Hearing this Daulat Khān departed with a heavy heart and Nānak, wearing only a loin-cloth, went with Mardānā to live with some faqīrs.

11 For one day Gurū Nānak maintained his silence and then on the following day he spoke, saying: 'There is neither Hindu nor Mussulman.' This was reported to Daulat Khān, but dismissed as the sort of utterance one might expect to hear from a faqīr. His qāzī, however, took a more serious view of what appeared to be a clear rejection of Islam's claims to superiority. Daulat Khān agreed to question Nānak on the subject, but found nothing offensive in the reply which he received.

It so happened that the appointed time for the second daily prayer came while Gurū Nānak was being examined. Everyone present arose and went to the mosque, and Nānak went with them. There he caused even greater offence to the qāzī by laughing out loud during the reading of *namāz*. The qāzī protested angrily to Daulat Khān, but Nānak explained that he had done so because the qāzī had been thinking, not of the prayer he was uttering, but of a new-born filly he had left in the compound, dangerously near a well. The qāzī was now convinced of Nānak's powers and made his submission. The people all followed his example and Daulat Khān was so impressed that he offered to surrender his entire authority and all his property to the Gurū. When he returned home he found that his treasury had been miraculously filled.[1] Gurū Nānak then left Sultānpur, taking with him Mardānā the Bard.

12 After leaving the town the Gurū and Mardānā first proceeded to a wilderness and for some time deliberately avoided all inhabited places. On one occasion Mardānā became hungry and was sent ahead to a village of Uppal khatrīs to receive the generous offerings they would make. On another occasion Mardānā entered a town where reverence, clothing, and money were lavished upon him. He returned laden to the Gurū, but was told to throw the offerings away as they were unnecessary encumbrances.

13 Journeying on they came to the house of a certain Sheikh Sajjaṇ. The house was situated out in the country and its owner had built both a temple and a mosque. These were ostensibly for the convenience of Hindu and Muslim travellers, but Sajjaṇ was a *ṭhag*[2] and his real purpose was to lure

[1] The IOL manuscript Panj. B40 omits this point.

[2] In its strict sense the word *ṭhag*, or thug, designates a member of the cult of ritual

travellers into his house in order that he might murder them and so acquire their wealth. His method of despatching his guests was to throw them into a well. Bābā Nānak and Mardānā were welcomed in the usual way and when night came they were invited to take rest. Before doing so the Gurū sang a hymn. The words which he sang convicted Sajjaṇ of his sin and falling at the Gurū's feet he implored forgiveness. This was granted on condition that he made restitution for all he had stolen. The *Hāfizābād* manuscript adds that the first *dharmsālā* was built there.[1]

After leaving Sajjaṇ they travelled to Pāṇīpat where Gurū Nānak held 14
a successful discourse with Sheikh Sharaf, the *Pīr* of Pāṇīpat. The name of
the *Pīr*'s disciple is given as Sheikh Ṭaṭihar. From Pāṇīpat they proceeded 15
on to Delhi where they encountered some mahouts employed by Sultan Ibrāhīm Beg.[2] The mahouts were bewailing the death of the elephant which had provided their employment. At the Gurū's bidding they stroked the dead animal's face and uttered, 'Vāhigurū!'[3] The elephant was instantly restored to life and the sultan, hearing of the miracle, asked for a repetition of it. The elephant duly died again, but Gurū Nānak made no effort to revive it. His cryptic explanation was, however, understood by the sultan and accepted as a thoroughly laudable one.

These early incidents were evidently a part of the Gurū's first journey 16
(*udāsī*), but this is not explicitly declared to have begun until after the Delhi visit. *Sākhī* 16 records that the first journey was to the east and that on this occasion the Gurū's companion was Mardānā. It also details the bizarre dress which he adopted for this journey. It is given as an ochre garment and a white one, a slipper on one foot and a wooden sandal on the other, a faqīr's *kafnī*[4] and a necklace of bones around his neck, a *qalandar's* hat on his head, and a saffron mark (*tilak*) on his forehead. His food is said to have consisted of air. The same *sākhī* also refers to a certain Sheikh Bajīd whom they happened to observe being transported in a litter and then being massaged and fanned by servants. In response to Mardānā's inquiry concerning the inequalities of the human condition Bābā Nānak replied, 'Joy and pain come in accordance with the deeds of one's previous existence.'

Travelling on they reached Banāras where they sat down in a public 17
square. A paṇḍit named Chatur Dās, who happened to pass, observed with surprise that Gurū Nānak had neither *śālgrām*, *tulsī-mālā*, rosary, nor sectarian mark. A discourse ensued, ending with a complete recitation of the lengthy work entitled *Oaṅkāru*[5] and with the conversion of Chatur Dās.

murderers who strangled and robbed in the name of the goddess Kālī. In the janam-sākhīs, however, it means any highwayman or violent robber.

[1] i.e. the first Sikh *dharmsālā*, or first building dedicated to Sikh worship and service.

[2] This is the *Hāfizābād* reading. The *Colebrooke* manuscript gives his name as Brahaṁ Beg.

[3] 'Wonderful Lord.' A characteristic Sikh name of God which originated after the time of Gurū Nānak.

[4] A piece of cloth worn round the waist.

[5] *AG*, pp. 929–38.

18 The next incident is set in a place which the *Purātan* janam-sākhīs refer to simply as Nānakmatā.[1] It was evidently a Nāth centre and the Siddhs[2] who were there at the time observed that a banyan tree which had stood withered for many years suddenly became green when the Gurū sat beneath it. They sought to persuade him to join their order, but ended by hailing him as one exalted.

19 The next four *sākhīs* are given no explicit geographical location. The first concerns a community of traders who were busy celebrating the birth of a son to their leading merchant and who ignored Mardānā in spite of his obvious hunger. Gurū Nānak is said to have smiled when Mardānā reported their ungracious behaviour and to have informed him that the new arrival would depart next morning. The prophecy proved to be correct, for the next day the community was lamenting the death of the infant.

20 The second unlocated *sākhī* briefly describes a watchman who, because he sought to give the visitors the best food he had available, received an undefined 'royal authority'.

21 The third is the story of a disciple whom the Gurū won while staying in a village during a rainy season. One day the new disciple's neighbour accompanied him to meet the Gurū, but on the way stopped instead at a prostitute's house. Thereafter the two would go out together, one to the Gurū and the other to his mistress, until one day they decided to test the merits of the radically different habits they were following. That same day the neighbour discovered a pot filled with coal, but containing also a gold coin, whereas the disciple had the misfortune to pierce his foot with a thorn. Gurū Nānak explained to them that the neighbour's gift of a gold coin to a sādhū in his previous existence had earned him a pot of gold coins. The disciple, on the other hand, had performed deeds meriting an impaling stake. The neighbour's subsequent immorality had, however, converted all but the original gold coin to coal, and the disciple's piety had reduced the impaling stake to a thorn.

22 The fourth of the unlocated *sākhīs* describes an encounter with some *ṭhags*. Like Sajjaṇ the *Ṭhag* (in the *Purātan* version) these *ṭhags* decided that the evident brightness of the Gurū's face must surely mean the possession of much concealed wealth on his person. Before killing the travellers, however, the *ṭhags* were persuaded to send two of their number to a funeral pyre which could be seen burning in the distance. There they observed angels of Rām snatch a body from messengers of Yam.[3] One of the angels explained that the man had been a monstrous sinner, and that accordingly

[1] The later janam-sākhīs add that it was formerly called Gorakhmatā (e.g. *GR*, p. 203). It is identified with a location in Nainī Tāl District, fifteen miles north-west of Pīlībhīt. Gurū Hargobind is said to have visited it (*MK*, p. 519). Bhāī Gurdās and Miharbān make no reference to the place or the incident.

[2] In this context the term Siddh designates a Nāth or Kānphaṭ yogī. See *supra*, p. 11, n. 10.

[3] The god of the dead.

he should really have been the rightful property of Yam. 'The smoke of his funeral pyre has, however, been seen by that divine *gurū* whom you came to kill, and as a result he has gained access to Paradise.' The *ṭhags* were appalled to think that they had been about to kill one who imparted salvation simply by seeing smoke. They made their submission and were pardoned on condition that they took up honest agriculture and devoted any surplus they might have to renunciate *bhagats*.

Sākhī 23 is set in a land called Kaurū,[1] or Kāvarū,[2] a land ruled by female 23
magicians. The queen's name is given as Nūr Shāh. Mardānā went ahead to beg for food and was turned into a lamb by one of the enchantresses. Gurū Nānak, following him, caused a pot to adhere to the woman's head, and told Mardānā to restore himself by saying 'Vāhigurū' and bowing down. The female magicians all converged on Gurū Nānak when they heard what he had done, some riding on trees, some on deerskins, some on the moon, several on a wall, and some on a whole grove of trees. When their efforts to enchant him failed Nūr Shāh herself came and tried magic and various sensual temptations. All failed and the women finally submitted.

Next the Gurū and Mardānā came to a wilderness where they rested. 24
At God's command Kaliyug came to try and deceive the Gurū.[3] To Mardānā's inexpressible terror a great darkness fell and trees were swept away. Next there appeared fire, with smoke ascending on all sides from four abysses of fire. Black clouds then gathered and rain began to fall. Finally, Kaliyug appeared in the form of a demon giant so tall that the top of its head reached to the heavens. It advanced towards them, but the nearer it came the smaller it grew, until eventually it assumed the form of a man and Kaliyug stood before Gurū Nānak in a posture of respect. In the discourse which followed he sought to tempt him with offers of a beautiful palace, of jewels, of women, of the power to work miracles, and finally of temporal sovereignty. All were rejected by the Gurū, and Kaliyug finally made his submission and asked for salvation.

Having left Kaliyug, the travellers came next to a city of insects. Where- 25
ever they looked everything was black and Mardānā was once again in the extremities of terror. Gurū Nānak related to him a macabre story of how a rājā had once shown disrespect to the insects, and of how they had first destroyed his army with poison and then revivified it with nectar.

Sākhīs 26 and 27 obviously constitute a single story. The first concerns a 26
village which refused hospitality, and the second a village which gave it 27

[1] *Pur JS*, p. 33. [2] *Pur JS*, p. 34.

[3] *Kaliyug*, the fourth and last in the cycle of *yugs* or cosmic eras, is the period of ultimate degeneracy. In this janam-sākhī context the meaning appears to be a manifestation in material form of all the characteristic evils and vices of the fourth *yug*. The evident impossibility of such a being subsequently led to the tradition that Kaliyug was the name of an evil person who lived in Jagannāth Purī and was converted by the Gurū. *MK*, p. 232. Teja Singh, *Sikhism: Its Ideals and Institutions*, p. 37.

liberally. After leaving the second village Gurū Nānak uttered the pronouncement: 'May this town be uprooted and its inhabitants scattered.' When Mardānā observed that this was strange justice indeed, he explained that the inhabitants of the first village would, if dispersed, corrupt others, whereas those of the second would spread true beliefs.

28 After this they reached the land of Āsā and there found the famous Sūfī Sheikh Farīd sitting in a jungle. Three incidents are recorded of the period which they spent with Sheikh Farīd. In the first a devout person offered the two holy men a cup of milk, having surreptitiously dropped four gold coins into it. When he returned later he discovered a gold cup filled with gold coins and realized that by offering worldly things instead of an open heart he had received a worldly reward and so had missed a great opportunity. The second describes a problem which was bothering the people of Āsā. The Rājā of Āsā, Śyām Sundar,[1] had recently died, but in spite of persistent efforts his skull would not burn. The astrologers had been consulted and had declared that he was in affliction as a result of once having told a lie, and that his salvation could not be effected until a sādhū set foot in the kingdom. For this reason Farīd and the Gurū were welcomed when they arrived. Farīd declined the honour and insisted that Gurū Nānak should be the one to pass through the gate which had been erected at the point of entry into the kingdom. The Gurū did so, the rājā's skull duly burst, and his soul went free. The third incident describes how Sheikh Farīd threw away a wooden *chapātī* which he had previously kept in order to have an excuse for refusing food. The rājā's unfortunate experience had shown him what would happen if he were to persist with this falsehood. The *sākhī* concludes with the statement that there is a *mañjī*[2] in the land of Āsā.

29 Much of *sākhī* 29 is incoherent, and the *Colebrooke* and *Hāfizābād* versions differ considerably. It concerns a visit to a land called Bisīar where everyone refused hospitality except a carpenter named Jhaṇḍā. Sitting on 'an island in the ocean',[3] Gurū Nānak composed a work called the *Jugāvalī* which he delivered to Jhaṇḍā. There is an obscure reference to a city called Chhuṭhaghāṭakā, and there is said to be a *mañjī* in Bisīar.

30 During these travels hunger was never a problem for the Gurū, who could subsist on air alone, but for Mardānā it was different. After leaving Bisīar they entered a great desert and here Mardānā's hunger became so extreme that he could proceed no further. Gurū Nānak showed him a tree

[1] This is the name given by the *Hāfizābād* manuscript. The *Colebrooke* manuscript gives Samundar.

[2] Literally a small string bed. Gurū Amar Dās, the third Gurū, is said to have divided his Sikhs into twenty-two districts, each under a superintendent (*mahant*). These districts were called *mañjīs* (*MK*, pp. 634, 750). References to *mañjīs* in the janam-sākhīs are anachronisms. The *mañjīs* were later superseded by the *masand* system of the fourth Gurū, Rām Dās (Teja Singh and Ganda Singh, *A Short History of the Sikhs*, vol. i, p. 27, n. 1).

[3] Literally 'a sandbank in the ocean'. *Pur JS*, p. 46.

which would provide him with fruit, but strictly enjoined him to take none with him when they proceeded on. Mardānā disobeyed the command and later ate some of what he had brought with him. He at once collapsed and Gurū Nānak explained that it was poisonous fruit which had turned to nectar because of the word he had spoken. He then cured him by placing his foot on his forehead.[1]

After twelve years of wandering they eventually arrived back at Tal- 31
vaṇḍī and stopped in the jungle at a distance of two *kos* from the village. Mardānā was given permission to enter the village, and was instructed to go to Kālū's house as well as his own. He was, however, to refrain from mentioning Nānak's name. In the village he received a reverent yet warm welcome. When asked where Nānak was he replied, 'Brethren, when the Bābā was in Sultānpur I was with him, but since then I have had no news of him.' The Gurū's mother refused to believe this and when he left the village she followed him at a distance. A touching reunion with her son followed. Kālū galloped after her as soon as he received the news and did his best to persuade Nānak to remain in Talvaṇḍī. The Gurū insisted, however, that they had renounced the world and that the settled life was not their calling.

Leaving Talvaṇḍī, Gurū Nānak and Mardānā visited the Rāvī and 32
Chenāb rivers, and then proceeded south towards Pāk Paṭṭan.[2] In a jungle, three *kos* outside the town, they encountered Sheikh Kamāl, a disciple of Sheikh Braham who was the contemporary successor of the famous Sūfī Sheikh Farīd. Kamāl informed his master and Sheikh Braham went out to converse at length with the Gurū.

From Pāk Paṭṭan the two travellers moved north-east and passing 33
through Dīpālpur,[3] Kaṅganpur,[4] Kasūr,[5] and Paṭṭī,[6] entered Goindvāl.[7] There no one would give them shelter except a faqīr who was a leper and who, as a result of the meeting, was healed. They then travelled on through 34
Sultānpur,[8] Vairovāl,[9] and Jalālābād,[10] and entered a village called Kiṛīān Paṭhāṇān[11] where the Gurū made more disciples.

From there they moved north through Baṭālā to Saidpur, or Sayyidpur, 35
the modern Eminābād in Gujranwālā District. By this time they had been

[1] The IOL manuscript Panj. B40, folios 30–32, places this *sākhi* immediately after *sākhī* 12 of the principal *Purātan* manuscripts, combining the two in a single *sākhī*. This corresponds with Miharbān's arrangement (see *infra*, p. 55). It is not possible to say whether the compiler of the B40 manuscript intended the incident to be placed at the beginning or the end of the first journey as it is the only incident he records between the departure from Sultānpur and the return to Talvaṇḍī, twelve years later.

[2] Multan District [3] Montgomery District.

[4] A village in Chūṇiā tahsil, Lahore District. [5] Lahore District.

[6] A village in Kasūr tahsīl. [7] Taran Tāran tahsīl, Amritsar District.

[8] Kapūrthalā District. See *sākhī* 8. [9] Taran Tāran tahsīl.

[10] There is a town of this name in Ferozepore District, but it is a common name and the itinerary which is being followed suggests a village in Amritsar District.

[11] Amritsar District (Macauliffe i, 108).

joined by some faqīrs and all were hungry. Gurū Nānak himself asked the townsfolk for food, but the Paṭhāns who lived there were all busy celebrating marriages and paid no heed to his requests. This lack of response made him exceedingly angry and in his wrath he uttered the verse which begins, *jaisī mai āvai khasam kī bāṇī*.[1]

A brāhmaṇ who had evidently heard the verse, and who had recognized it as a summons to Bābur the Mughal to punish the town, brought an offering of fruit and asked the Gurū to retract his curse. Gurū Nānak replied that what had been uttered could not be recalled, but assured the brāhmaṇ that if he were to remove his family to a pool twelve *kos*[2] away they would all be saved. The following day Bābur arrived and fell upon Saidpur. Everyone in it, Muslim as well as Hindu, was slaughtered, houses were looted and then razed to the ground, and the surrounding countryside was devastated.

At some stage the Gurū and Mardānā were seized and committed to the Saidpur prison under the supervision of a certain Mīr Khān. Both were made to do forced labour, Gurū Nānak as a coolie and Mardānā as a horse attendant. Mīr Khān, when he came to watch the prisoners, was startled to observe that the Gurū's load remained suspended a full cubit above his head and that the horse followed Mardānā without a halter. This information was conveyed to Bābur who declared, 'Had I known there were such faqīrs here I should not have destroyed the town.' He accompanied Mīr Khān to where the prisoners were working and observed that a hand-mill which had been issued to Gurū Nānak turned without any assistance.

Bābur then approached the Gurū who uttered two verses. Hearing these the Mughal fell and kissed his feet, and offered him a favour. Gurū Nānak asked for all the prisoners to be released, and Bābur at once issued orders to free them and restore their property. The prisoners, however, refused to go unless Gurū Nānak accompanied them. Mardānā subsequently asked why so many had suffered for the sins of one[3] and was told that he would be given his reply after he had slept under a nearby tree. While he was sleeping ants were attracted by a drop of grease which had fallen on his chest. One of the ants bit him and, without awaking, Mardānā brushed them away, killing them all as he did so. This, Gurū Nānak subsequently informed him, was his answer.

To this the *Hāfizābād* manuscript adds a lengthy account of the manner in which Bābur, who was really a clandestine *qalandar*, was impressed by the Gurū. When asked to free the prisoners he agreed to do so on condition that his throne should endure for ever. Gurū Nāṇak would promise only

[1] *Tilang* 5, *AG*, p. 722.
[2] *Colebrooke* manuscript. The *Hāfizābād* manuscript gives two *kos* (*Pur JS*, p. 59).
[3] The identity of the culprit is not indicated.

that the kingdom would endure 'for a time'. This was accepted as sufficient and the prisoners were all released.

Leaving Saidpur, Gurū Nānak and Mardānā passed through Pasrūr[1] and 36
came to the small fortress of a local celebrity named Mīā Miṭhā. They stopped in a grove at a distance of one *kos* and when Mīā Miṭhā was informed of the Guru's arrival he boasted that he would skim him as cream is skimmed off milk. Gurū Nānak replied that he would squeeze Mīā Miṭhā as he squeezed juice from a lemon. A debate followed and Mīā Miṭhā finally made his submission.

Next Gurū Nānak proceeded to Lahore where his coming was brought 37
to the notice of a wealthy Dhuppaṛ khatrī named Dunī Chand who happened to be celebrating his father's *śrāddh*.[2] In response to Dunī Chand's invitation Gurū Nānak came and, upon arrival, asked him what point there was in feeding brāhmaṇs when his father, in whose memory the *śrāddh* was being held, had not eaten for three days. Dunī Chand at once asked where his father was to be found, and was informed that he had been born as a wolf and was lying under a certain bush five *kos* away. Taking some food he went in search of his reincarnated father and was told by the wolf that the unfortunate rebirth was the result of having coveted some boiling fish when at the point of death.

Dunī Chand subsequently took Gurū Nānak to his house. Over the door were seven flags, each representing a *lākh* of rupees. The Gurū made no comment, but gave his host a needle with the request that he return it in the hereafter. 'Good God!' exclaimed his wife when he told her what the Gurū had said. 'Will this needle accompany you to the hereafter?' Appreciating the force of her rhetorical question Dunī Chand took the needle back to Gurū Nānak, who asked him, 'If a needle cannot go there, how can these flags get there?'

Sākhī 38 provides the setting for a denunciation of unnecessary cere- 38
monial purity. An excessively scrupulous brāhmaṇ refused Gurū Nānak's food and tried to dig a cooking-square which would satisfy his own notions of purity. After digging all day and everywhere turning up bones he finally made his submission.

The next incident evidently belongs to a later period, for it describes 39
Gurū Nānak's practice of daily communal *kīrtan*.[3] The Gurū happened to observe that a boy aged seven had become a regular attender at *kīrtan* and one day asked him why he engaged in such serious practices at such an early age. In reply the boy related that the necessity of doing so had been impressed upon him as a result of his having observed how when he

[1] Siālkoṭ District.

[2] A ceremony in which food and other commodities are offered to brāhmaṇs on behalf of deceased forebears.

[3] The singing of songs in praise of God.

kindled a fire the small sticks were consumed first. The boy's name is not given.

The two *sākhīs* which conclude the *Purātan* account of the first journey
40 are recorded in the *Hāfizābād* manuscript, but not the *Colebrooke*. According
to the first of them, Gurū Nānak took up residence on the banks of a river near Talvaṇḍī where crowds of people flocked to see him. A local official (*karoṛīā*) who lived in a neighbouring village concluded that Nānak was taking advantage of this popularity to corrupt both Hindus and Muslims, and that accordingly he should be imprisoned. He set out to make the arrest, but on the way was struck blind. This convinced him that Nānak must indeed be a great *pīr* and, greatly chastened, he remounted his horse, only to fall off again. The people who had observed these misfortunes assured him that the only proper way to approach a great *pīr* was on foot. This he did and was so impressed by the Gurū that he decided to build for him a village which was to be called Kartārpur.

41 The second of the *Hāfizābād sākhīs* relates the story of Bhāgīrath and an unnamed shopkeeper. A poor Sikh once came to the Gurū asking for financial assistance in order that he might have his daughter married. Gurū Nānak acceded to the request and dispatched another Sikh, Bhāgīrath, to Lahore with instructions to purchase everything that would be required, and to return at all costs that same day. Failure to do so would mean forfeiting his opportunity of salvation.

The shopkeeper to whom he went for his purchases provided him with everything except a set of bangles, informing him that these could not possibly be ready until the next day. When Bhāgīrath insisted that delay was more than his salvation was worth the shopkeeper became curious and decided to visit this gurū who could evidently give or withold salvation as he pleased. He provided a set of bangles from his own house and set off with Bhāgīrath. While they were still on the way the Gurū's voice came to them. The shopkeeper was instantly convinced and spent three years with Gurū Nānak before returning to Lahore.

When he eventually did return it was to entrust his property to other shopkeepers. He then embarked on a ship, sailed to the city where Rājā Sivanābh lived, and there established a trading business. He lived a life of great piety there, but it was not one which accorded with the superstitious practices of the local people. These people were not Hindus and they made a point of defiling any Hindus who went there. The shopkeeper did not observe local practices, but nor did he follow Hindu customs and so eventually he was reported to the rājā. Śivanābh summoned him, demanded an explanation, and was given a description of Gurū Nānak. This aroused a great longing in him for an opportunity to meet the Gurū. The shopkeeper replied that the proper place to meet him was in his own heart, but before leaving he comforted the rājā with the assurance that the Gurū would one day come to him in person. He warned him, however, that there could be no knowing the guise in which he would come.

After the shopkeeper had sailed away Rājā Śivanābh devised a method of testing all visiting faqīrs. Summoning a number of alluring women he instructed them to exercise their charms on any faqīrs or sādhūs who might arrive, knowing full well that in this degenerate age only the perfect Gurū would be able to resist such advances.

Sākhī 42 opens with the announcement that Gurū Nānak's second journey 42
was to the south. The *Purātan* janam-sākhīs are confused concerning the number and names of his companions on this journey. The *Hāfizābād* manuscript usually gives their number as two and their names as Saido and Gheho, both Jaṭs, but in one place it refers to three companions named Saido, Gheho, and Sīho, again all Jaṭs,[1] in another simply to Saido and Sīho,[2] and in yet another it adds the name of Mardānā.[3] The *Colebrooke* manuscript usually names them Saido a Jaṭ and Sīho a Gheho,[4] but in one place refers to them as Saido and Gheho.[5]

The first visit was to a country called Dhanāsarī where the Gurū's companions encountered Khwājā Khizar.[6] They had previously come to the
conclusion that Gurū Nānak's frequent visits to the river were for the
purpose of worshipping this deity, and had themselves begun worshipping
him. One night, however, they met Khwājā Khizar himself taking an
offering to the Gurū whom he worshipped daily. While in Dhanāsarī Gurū 43
Nānak conducted a successful discourse with Anabhī, the superior of a very
influential Jain monastery. He then completed *Mājh kī Vār*[7] and proceeded on.

The next recorded incident is set on 'an island in the ocean, in foreign 44
parts, where a savage man exercised tyrannical rule'. The savage seized the Gurū and set about cooking him in a cauldron. Instead of becoming hot, however, the cauldron became cooler. Perceiving this the cannibal fell at the Gurū's feet and asked for salvation. Sīho administered baptism and so he became a Sikh. The savage's name is not given.

The *sākhī* which follows is both confused and fantastic. It concerns a 45
meeting with Makhdūm Bahāuddīn whom Gurū Nānak encountered
sporting in the sea on his prayer-mat. After this Gurū Nānak is said to have 46
travelled out into the ocean to converse with Machhendranāth and Gorakhnāth.

[1] *Pur JS*, p. 81, n. **. [2] Ibid., p. 86.
[3] Ibid., p. 81, n. ††.
[4] In this case Gheho evidently means Ghei, a khatrī sub-caste.
[5] *Pur JS*, p. 79.
[6] A mythical Muslim saint who in many parts of India has been identified with a river god or with a spirit of wells and streams. *Encyclopaedia of Islam*, vol. ii, p. 865. R. C. Temple, *The Legends of the Panjab*, vol. i, p. 221.
[7] *AG*, pp. 137–50.

47 *Sākhī* 47 records another crossing of the ocean, this time to the kingdom of Śivanābh in Siṅghalādīp.[1] When Gurū Nānak arrived there Śivanābh's garden, which had remained withered for years, suddenly blossomed. The gardener reported this to the rājā who at once sent his alluring women to test the new arrival. Later Śivanābh came himself and after questioning the Gurū invited him to his palace. Bābā Nānak replied that he did not travel on foot, but that he required as his mount one who was of royal blood and ruler of a city. Śivanābh at once offered himself and the Gurū proceeded to the palace on the rājā's back.

At the palace Śivanābh and his wife, Chandarakalā, asked him what he wished to eat. In reply the Gurū asked for human flesh and specified that it was to be that of 'a son who is of royal parentage and twelve years old'. Śivanābh consulted his own son's horoscope and discovered that he was, as required, twelve years of age. Both the boy and his wife agreed that the Gurū's wish should be met, and while the mother held his arms and the wife his feet Śivanābh proceeded to cut his son's throat. The boy's body was then stewed and placed before the Gurū who instructed them to shut their eyes, utter 'Vāhigurū', and begin to eat. This they did and when they opened their eyes again the Gurū had disappeared. As a result of this experience the rājā became insane, but twelve months later was vouchsafed a *darśan*[2] and became a Sikh.

The partly incoherent conclusion of this *sākhī* records that while in Siṅghalādīp Gurū Nānak composed a work entitled the *Prāṇ Saṅgalī*. A group of believers met regularly in the *dharmsālā* and there secret teachings were revealed. Rājā Śivanābh received a *mañjī*[3] and Gurū Nānak departed.

48 The final *sākhī* of the second journey describes how Gurū Nānak wrecked the hut of an hospitable carpenter. The reason for this seemingly ungrateful action was revealed when the carpenter discovered under the remains of his broken bed four pots of gold.

49 The third journey was to the north and Gurū Nānak's companions this time were Hassū, a blacksmith, and Sīhān, a calico-printer. On his head and feet he wore leather and round his whole body he bound rope. The small group first travelled to Kashmir where a paṇḍit named Braham Dās came to meet them wearing an idol round his neck and bringing with him two camels loaded with Purāṇas. The discourse which followed converted him and he threw away his idol.

His conversion was, however, incomplete and one day Bābā Nānak told him to take a *gurū*. For this purpose he directed Braham Dās to some faqīrs

[1] Ceylon.

[2] An audience and, in contexts such as this, specifically an audience with a person of spiritual stature. It is not clear whether the writer intends this to be understood as another meeting or as a vision.

[3] See *supra*, p. 42, n. 2.

out in a tract of waste land, and they in turn sent him on to a nearby temple. There a woman in crimson beat him severely with a shoe and the wailing paṇḍit returned to the faqīrs to be informed that he had just met *Māyā*, the *gurū* he had hitherto served. This completed Braham Dās's conversion. He threw away his books and became a humble servant of the pious.

After leaving Kashmir, Gurū Nānak traversed many mountains and 50
eventually ascended Mount Sumeru where he conversed with Śiva, Gorakhnāth, Bharatharī, Gopīchand, and Charapaṭ. The Siddhs sent him to fill a pot with water, but when it kept filling with jewels the Gurū broke it, repaired it, exorcised the spell with a *ślok*, and then filled it with water. A lengthy discourse followed, at the end of which the Siddhs suggested that Nānak should proceed to the village of Achal where many Siddhs would be gathered for a fair. The journey, they informed him, would take them three days as they travelled on the wind. They then departed, obviously expecting to arrive well before him. The Gurū, however, was transported there in an instant and at their arrival the Siddhs from Mount Sumeru were amazed to hear from others at the fair that Nānak had appeared three days previously. A brief discourse followed.

The fourth journey took Gurū Nānak westwards to Mecca, evidently 51
without a regular companion. For this journey he wore leather shoes, pajama, a blue garment, and a necklace of bones. Having reached his destination he went to sleep with his feet in the direction of Mecca[1] and a qāzī named Rukandīn, who happened to observe him in this position, rebuked him severely. The Gurū suggested that the qāzī should drag his feet round and leave them pointing in a direction away from God and the *Ka'bah*. Rukandīn complied and was amazed to discover that as he moved the Gurū's feet the *miharāb* moved with them. He summoned Pīr Pataliā and the three engaged in discourse. At its conclusion Gurū Nānak uttered 'Vāhigurū' and water appeared in the wells, thus fulfilling a prophecy contained in the Muslim scriptures that Nānak, a *darveś*, would come and cause water to spring in the wells of Mecca.

The fifth journey was a much shorter one than any of the previous four. 52
On this occasion the Gurū travelled to Gorakh-haṭaṛī where he met Siddhs and held the discourse which is recorded in the work entitled *Siddh Goṣṭ*.[2] The Siddhs sought to impress him with displays of their magical power, but without success.

Sākhī 53 describes the conversion of Lahiṇā who was subsequently to 53
become Gurū Aṅgad. Lahiṇā lived in Khaḍūr[3] where he was the priest

[1] This may indicate the *Ka'bah*, or it may mean that the original *sākhi* was not set in Mecca. See *infra*, pp. 123–4. The B40 manuscript records that it was with his feet towards the *miharāb* that Gurū Nānak went to sleep (loc. cit., folio 51).

[2] *AG*, pp. 938–46.

[3] Amritsar District.

of the Tehaṇā (Trehaṇ) khatrīs. In the same town there lived a Bhallā khatrī who was a Sikh, the only person there who did not worship the goddess Durgā. One day Lahiṇā happened to overhear him reciting the *Japjī*[1] and this so impressed him that, having learnt the identity of the author, he went at once and became a disciple. The service which he rendered to his master was particularly devoted. He regularly scoured the Gurū's pots and waved the fan, and on one occasion willingly ruined a new suit of clothes in order to obey a command to bring in some wet grass. The *sākhī* also refers to Durgā's practice of coming every eighth day to serve the Gurū, and terminates with an incoherent story concerning a maid-servant who once sought to waken the Gurū by licking his feet.

54 Gorakhnāth once visited Gurū Nānak and the Gurū devised a test to show how many true followers he had. The two set out walking, followed by the Sikhs. At the Gurū's command copper coins appeared on the ground, and many of his followers picked them up and departed. Next silver coins appeared and then gold coins. Each time he lost more Sikhs and after the appearance of the gold coins only two remained. Further on they came to a burning funeral pyre. Over the corpse there was a sheet and from it there issued a foul smell. The Gurū asked if there was anyone prepared to eat the corpse and at this one of the two remaining Sikhs fled, leaving only Lahiṇā to obey the command. Lahiṇā asked which end he should begin to eat and was instructed to start at the feet. Raising the sheet he found Gurū Nānak lying there. Gorakhnāth, impressed by this display of loyal obedience, declared, 'He who is born from a part (*aṅg*) of you will be your Gurū', and the name Aṅgad was accordingly bestowed upon Lahiṇā.

55 In *sākhī* 55 Makhdūm Bahāuddīn reappears, this time as the *Pīr* of Multān and as one near death. Realizing that his end was near he sent a *ślok* to Gurū Nānak in Talvaṇḍī, informing him of the fact, and received in reply another *ślok* with the comment, 'You go and I shall follow after forty days'. Loudly lamenting the prospect of forty days of darkness Makhdūm Bahāuddīn passed away.

56 Gurū Nānak was also aware of approaching death. Before it took place he appointed Aṅgad as his successor by laying five copper coins in front of him and prostrating himself before him. The news at once spread that he
57 was about to die, and Hindus and Muslims flocked for a last audience. He then went and sat under a withered acacia, which at once blossomed, and his family gathered around him weeping. His sons asked what would become of them and were assured that they would be cared for. A dispute then arose between the Muslims and the Hindus, the former claiming that they would bury the Gurū's body and the latter that they would cremate it. The Gurū himself settled the argument by instructing the Hindus to lay flowers on his right and the Muslims to place them at his left. Whichever

[1] *AG*, pp. 1–8.

side's flowers were still fresh on the following day should have his body to dispose of as they wished. The assembled followers then sang *Kīrtan Sohilā*[1] and *Āratī*,[2] and the concluding *ślok* of the *Japjī*.[3] Gurū Nānak covered himself with a sheet and went to sleep. When the sheet was raised the body had gone and the flowers on both sides were still fresh. The Hindus took their share away and the Muslims did likewise. The date was the tenth day of the light half of Asū, S. 1595, and it was at Kartārpur that Gurū Nānak passed away.

The life of Gurū Nānak according to the Miharbān Janam-sākhī (Pothī Sach-khaṇḍ)

The *Purātan Janam-sākhī* contains only fifty-seven *sākhīs* and accordingly it has been possible to include them all in the outline given above. In the case of Miharbān's *Pothī Sach-khaṇḍ* this is not possible, but the exclusion of some individual *goṣṭs* need not involve any significant omissions as far as the biography of Gurū Nānak is concerned. Several of the *goṣṭs* offer no biographical details and frequently a single episode is spread over more than one *goṣṭ*.[4]

The first three *goṣṭs* of the *Miharbān Janam-sākhī* recount the greatness 1–3
of the first Rājā Janak and describe an interview with God wherein Janak is informed that he is to return to the world once again. His name is to be Nānak and his task is to be the salvation of the world from the evils and degeneracy into which it has fallen.

The details of Gurū Nānak's birth are given in the fourth *goṣṭ*. His 4
father was Kālū, a Bedī khatrī, and his mother's name is given as Tiparā. The Damdamā Sāhib manuscript gives the village of Chāhalāvāle[5] as the place where the birth took place,[6] but the second Khalsa College manuscript omits this detail and in *goṣṭ* 17 the Damdamā Sāhib manuscript gives 'Talvaṇḍī Rāi Bhoe kī' as the birthplace.[7] The date given in the Damdamā Sāhib manuscript is a moonlit night in the month of Vaisākh, S. 1526, and the second manuscript adds that it was the third day.[8] The hour is said to have been the last watch of the night. There was great celebration both in heaven and in the village, and Hindus and Muslims of all tribes and ranks

[1] *AG*, p. 12. [2] Ibid., pp. 13, 663. [3] Ibid., p. 8.

[4] The *Miharbān Janam-sākhi* is divided, not into *sākhis*, but into *goṣṭs* (discourses). The figures in the margin indicate the number of each *goṣṭ* as given in the edition of *Pothī Sach-khaṇḍ* edited by Kirpal Singh and Shamsher Singh Ashok and published under the title *Janam Sākhi Sri Gurū Nānak Dev Ji* by the Sikh History Research Department of Khalsa College, Amritsar, in 1962.

[5] The village of Chāhal in the area of Thāṇā Barakī, Lahore District, is traditionally regarded as the home of Gurū Nānak's maternal grandparents. *MK*, p. 345.

[6] *Mih JS*, pp. 9, 10. [7] *Mih JS*, p. 52. Also *goṣṭ* 141, p. 470.

[8] *Mih JS*, p. 9, n. 5.

came to offer their congratulations. On the ninth day after his birth he was given his name. Various faculties are recorded as having developed with consecutive months during the first year, at eighteen months, and with each year up to the age of five when he began to give utterance to spiritual wisdom. Hindus declared that he was the image of God, and Muslims that truly he was a godly child.

5 At the age of seven Nānak was taken to a paṇḍit to learn how to read. The paṇḍit wrote out the alphabet for him, but the child kept silent and refused to repeat it. A discourse followed based, as in the *Purātan* account, on the verse *Sirī Rāgu* 6,[1] and at its conclusion the paṇḍit acknowledged that one so wise should certainly be permitted to decide what was best for himself.

6 When he was eight years old Nānak would play with groups of other children and give them instruction in the things of God. During this period Kālū decided that he should learn 'Turkī'[2] and summoned a mullah for this purpose. This time Nānak applied himself to his studies and startled both the mullah and the village with his incredible progress. Within a matter of days he had mastered not only Persian but also Hindvī, Arabic, and accounting. After this he became silent and refused to communicate with anyone. The mullah was called again and with some difficulty managed to persuade Nānak to speak. When he did eventually speak it was to utter a verse expounding the transient nature of man's worldly abode.[3] Hearing it the mullah saluted him as a blessed child.

7 When he reached the age of nine arrangements were made for him to be invested with the sacred thread (*janeū*). It appears that he did not actually refuse it, as *goṣṭ* 11 makes reference to his wearing it,[4] but the occasion provided him with an opportunity to criticize external ritual, and to affirm inward acceptance of the divine Name and praises offered to God as the only true *janeū*.

8 The next recorded incident is the restoration of the crop ruined by Nānak's buffaloes. This is said to have occurred at the age of about ten or twelve and is substantially the same as in the *Purātan* account.[5] One significant difference is that the landlord's name is given as Rāi Bhoā, not Rāi Bulār. Two minor differences are that the field is said to have contained paddy, not wheat, and that the reason given for Nānak's negligence is
9 meditation, not sleep. *Goṣṭ* 9 relates the story of the tree's stationary
10 shadow[6] and in *goṣṭ* 10 Rāi Bhoā discusses with Kālū the significance of this

[1] *AG*, p. 16. *Sirī Rāgu* is the first of the *rāgs* in the *Ādi Granth*.
[2] Persian. It is also referred to as *Musalamānī*.
[3] *Tilaṅg* 1, *AG*, p. 721. [4] *Mih JS*, p. 29. [5] See *supra*, pp. 36–37.
[6] See *supra*, p. 37. Neither the *Miharbān* nor the *Purātan* account contains the popular story of how a cobra was once observed to be protecting the sleeping child from the sun's rays with its distended hood. This miracle appears in later janam-sākhīs. See *infra*, pp. 73, 77.

incident and that of the restored field. The owner of the field is summoned to ascertain that he had told the truth and Rāi Bhoā assures Kālū that Nānak is obviously no ordinary son. Nānak's age at the time when Rāi Bhoā observed the stationary shadow is given as thirteen or fourteen.

About the time of his sixteenth birthday Gurū Nānak was betrothed to 11
the daughter of Mūlā, a Choṇā (khatrī) of Baṭālā. The betrothal ceremony is said to have been held on the first day of the dark half of Vaisākh, S. 1542. The wedding took place in Baṭālā soon afterwards and when it was over Nānak returned with his family to Talvandī. In *goṣṭ* 22 his wife's name is given as Ghumī.[1]

At the age of twenty Gurū Nānak lapsed into silence and inactivity, and 13
his mother's efforts to rouse him were unavailing. In the following *goṣṭ* he 14
explains that his silence is the result of having no godly people to converse
with.[2] *Goṣṭ* 15 records that he neither ate, drank, nor spoke for four or five 15–16
days[3] and that eventually the anxious townsfolk persuaded Kālū to summon a physician. The physician duly came and feeling the patient's pulse pronounced it a case of madness. Nānak's reply was essentially the same as that given in the *Purātan* version,[4] and the physician acknowledged him as Gurū.

Next family pressure was tried. Gurū Nānak was summoned before a 17
family conclave and the Bedīs remonstrated with him, seeking to persuade him to take up agriculture. The effort was unsuccessful and so too was
another which the family made when he was twenty-two. 18

When Gurū Nānak was twenty-seven or twenty-eight his two sons, 22
Lakhmī Dās and Sirī Chand were born. At the age of thirty his renunciate tendencies became even more pronounced and he abandoned all other
activity in favour of discussions with yogīs and sannyāsīs. Efforts made by 22–23
both his father and mother to persuade him to take up agriculture, shop-keeping, trade, or civil service employment met with the usual negative response.

Eventually Jai Rām, his brother-in-law, came to the rescue with his 24
suggestion that Nānak should join him in Sultānpur. The invitation was accepted and Gurū Nānak departed, leaving his wife in the meantime but taking Mardānā the Dūm with him. Jai Rām is described as an Uppal

[1] *Mih JS*, p. 67.

[2] This *goṣṭ* is evidently out of sequence as it gives his age as twenty-six. The second Khalsa College manuscript gives it as *goṣṭ* 21 and the two versions differ appreciably. *Mih JS*, p. 40, n. 4.

[3] This is the reading of the second Khalsa College manuscript. The Damdamā Sāhib manuscript gives four months. *Mih JS*, p. 45, n. 8.

[4] Both versions give as his reply *Malār* 7 and 8, *AG*, pp. 1256–7; *Vār Malār*, *śloks* 1 and 2 of *pauṛī* 3, *AG*, p. 1280 (the second of which is by Gurū Aṅgad); and a verse which is not in the *Ādi Granth*. The *Purātan* manuscripts add *Gauṛī* 17, *AG*, p. 156, and a *ślok* which is not in the *Ādi Granth*. The greater length of the Miharbān account is, as usual, chiefly the result of the interpretation which is added to the quotations.

khatrī and as Daulat Khān Lodī's steward. The Damdamā Sāhib manuscript gives his home as Khānpur and the second manuscript as Sultānpur. The name of his wife, Gurū Nānak's sister, is not recorded. Gurū Nānak's age at the time is given as thirty-five years, six and a half months.

His meeting with Jai Rām and his interview with Daulat Khān are described in some detail. At the interview he presented to the Nawāb a fine Iraqi horse and an offering of money, and in return received a robe of honour. Daulat Khān pronounced himself highly pleased with the new arrival and commanded that all authority over his province and property be entrusted to Nānak. This was evidently to be understood as complimentary hyperbole as the employment to which he was actually assigned was in Daulat Khān's commissariat. His daily life, combining pious exercises with proper fulfilment of his secular duties, is also described.

25–26 It was not long, however, before doubts began to arise in the Gurū's mind. He continued to fulfil his responsibilities in the commissariat, but his mind turned increasingly to spiritual things, even while he was engaged in his
27 quartermaster duties. In a discourse with his cook he expressed his concern at his involvement in worldly affairs. Eventually the climax of his developing spiritual crisis came with the summons to the court of God, received while he was taking his regular early-morning bathe in the river.

28–29 As in the *Purātan* account the river is not named, but the author indicates that it was in the direction of Goindvāl. One morning Nānak plunged in as usual, but did not reappear, having been transported to the divine court. Miharbān's version is characteristically diffuse, occupying four times the space of the *Purātan* account without making any significant additions to it. The river was dragged without success and on the third day Nānak emerged to the acclamation of the crowd, gave away his belongings, and joined a group of faqīrs. The people were perplexed and many concluded that he must be possessed. Some of the common folk, observing that he appeared to be conforming to neither Hindu or Muslim practice, asked him what path he was now following. He replied, 'There is neither Hindu nor Mussulman so whose path shall I follow? I shall follow God's path. God is neither Hindu nor Mussulman and the path which I follow is God's.'[1]

32 This comment was communicated to the local qāzī and at his request Nānak was summoned before Daulat Khān to answer for it. Once again Miharbān provides an account which is appreciably longer than that of the *Purātan* janam-sākhīs, but which adds nothing except extra quotations from Gurū Nānak's works, protracted expositions, and incidental details of no importance. The Gurū successfully answered the qāzī's charge, humbled him by reading his thoughts during *namāz*, and expounded to him and to Daulat Khān the meaning of true *namāz*. At the conclusion of the exposition Daulat Khān prostrated himself adoringiy and Gurū

[1] *Mih JS*, p. 92.

Nānak assured him that he had attained salvation. Taking the dust of the Gurū's feet Daulat Khān returned home. No reference is made to his treasury having been miraculously filled.

Bābā Nānak and Mardānā then set out on the first journey (*udāsī*), having 34 spent two years in Sultānpur.[1] As in the *Purātan* janam-sākhīs the account of this journey begins with a description of how Mardānā would enter a 35 village to ask for food whenever necessary, and of how the Gurū commanded him to throw away the money and clothing which a generous village had bestowed upon him as offerings.[2] Following this experience they entered a wilderness devoid of human habitation. Mardānā became apprehensive, but the Gurū calmed his fears by assuring him that no place where the divine Name was repeated could be uninhabited. Some days later there occurred the incident of the forbidden fruit.[3] 36

After a conversation with some herons Gurū Nānak and Mardānā 37 reached Delhi where they observed food being distributed to mendicants on 38 behalf of the king, whose name is given as Salem Shāh Pathān. The Gurū preached to the people on the necessity of the divine Name and the entire population became his Sikhs. There is no mention of a resurrected elephant.

Leaving Delhi they proceeded on to the Ganges where, as it happened 39–40 to be a festival day, they observed thousands of people bathing in the river. The festival which was being celebrated was that of Baisākhī and the pilgrims were throwing water in the direction of the rising sun. Gurū Nānak also entered the river and began splashing water in the opposite direction. This provoked offended demands for an explanation. The Gurū responded by asking his questioners to whom they thought they were conveying water and they replied that they were sending it to their ancestors in heaven. Gurū Nānak then informed them that he was, in the same manner, watering his fields near Lahore. When this brought a scornful rejoinder he answered that if their water could travel as far as heaven his could certainly reach Lahore. This silenced them for they now realized that they were conversing with a person of exalted spiritual insight. Continuing the discourse on the banks of the river he emphasized the futility of *mantras* and cooking-

---

[1] In other words, according to Miharbān Gurū Nānak began his travels at the age of thirty-seven and a half.

[2] The *Purātan* manuscripts explicitly state that the first *udāsī* began after they had left Delhi (see *supra*, p. 39). It seems clear, however, that the four preceding *sākhīs* must belong to the first *udāsī*.

[3] Both the assurance concerning the Name and Mardānā's disobedient consumption of extra fruit are related in the *Purātan* janam-sākhīs (see *supra*, pp. 42–43), but the *sākhī* which includes them is placed at the end of the *Purātan's* first journey. Miharbān's setting is more logical. In both cases Mardānā promises to follow the Gurū if he will be patient with one who, unlike the Gurū himself, is subject to human limitations, and the terms in which the discourses are conducted fit the early stages of a journey more appropriately than the concluding stages.

squares.[1] Two more discourses follow. The first of these, another discourse
41 on cooking-squares, provides a setting for the verse *Basant* 3,[2] which in
42 the *Purātan* janam-sākhīs is set in an entirely different incident.[3] The
second refers to Hardwār as the location of these discussions.

43 From Hardwār Gurū Nānak and Mardānā moved on to Prayāg (Allahābād) where the Gurū's fame had preceded him and a large crowd had
gathered to pay their respects. After a discourse with some devout people
44–50 they proceeded on to Banāras where the Gurū engaged in several discourses
with paṇḍits and groups of devout believers. The first of these was with a
49 single paṇḍit, but he is not named. On another occasion the entire population of Banāras, and specifically all of the paṇḍits in the city, are said to
have been present at a discourse held on the Bisarāti (Viśrānti) Ghāṭ, and
at the conclusion of the discourse all of the paṇḍits became Sikhs.

51 After leaving Banāras they came to the city of Rājā Harināth in 'the east
country' where, to begin with, Gurū Nānak observed silence and was consequently mistaken for a *monī*.[4] Hearing of his arrival the rājā himself went
on foot to meet him, listened to his instruction, and asked if he might
accompany him as a disciple. He was, however, told to practise piety while
yet remaining a rājā.

52 From Rājā Harināth's unnamed city they proceeded 'to where Gusāī
Kambīr's house was'. Kabīr went out to meet Bābā Nānak and in the discourse which followed acknowledged him as the supreme Gurū. In reply
Gurū Nānak uttered his *Gauṛī Aṣṭapadī* 8,[5] a composition which if it were
to be applied to Kabīr would imply very high praise of him.

54 Travelling eastwards from where Kabīr lived they came next to Hājīpur
Paṭṇā where the Gurū discoursed with and converted a group of Vaiṣṇavas.
55 Continuing to the east they entered an unnamed city where Gurū Nānak
observed his common practice of initial silence and subsequently instructed the members of the town council in the nature of 'the true food',
namely God Himself.

56 From that city they turned south and, entering a wilderness, met and
57 conversed with an unidentified rājā. Next they arrived at another unnamed
city where Gurū Nānak's presence exercised an attraction so compulsive
that eventually the whole city gathered to pay him homage and declared
58 him to be an incarnation of God. In the following *goṣṭ* they are back in 'the
east country'. There they visited Ayodhyā where, after the Gurū had con-
59 ducted two discourses, 'all the *bhagats* gathered at God's command and
came to meet him—Nāmdev, Jaidev, Kabīr, Trilochan, Ravidās, Saiṇ,

[1] The conclusion of *goṣṭ* 40, which describes the pilgrims who accepted his teaching as the first Sikhs, is evidently an interpolation by sādhūs of the Udāsī sect. Its language is more modern, it conflicts with the earlier reference to the conversion of Delhi, and it affirms the adoption of celibacy.

[2] *AG*, p. 1169.

[3] *Sākhi* 38. See *supra*, p. 45.

[4] A faqīr or sādhū who observes complete silence.

[5] *AG*, p. 224.

Sadhnā, Dhannā, Beṇī'. A lengthy discourse followed, based on *Sirī Rāgu* 10–12,[1] at the end of which the *bhagats* hailed him and departed for heaven.
There they reported their experience to God who, well pleased to hear their 60
praises, summoned Nānak to an interview.

Leaving Ayodhyā they travelled down to Jagannāth where they met 61
Rājā Bharatharī, the famous yogī.[2] *Goṣṭ* 62 records that they spent three 62
years in 'the east country' and that having seen it all they turned south. Jagannāth Purī is accordingly the eastern terminus in Miharbān's account and after this visit we find Gurū Nānak travelling south, presumably down the east coast of India.

From Jagannāth Purī the Gurū and Mardānā travelled a considerable distance and eventually came to a temple surrounded by a desert. There a piece of brick happened to fall on Gurū Nānak after he had been meditating and the consequent pain greatly distressed him as he had believed his meditation would free him from such suffering. While he was lamenting this the voice of God was heard assuring him that all who live in the world must experience pain of this kind.

Two strange incidents follow. The first relates how the thirsty travellers 63
were led to water by a jackal, and how Gurū Nānak, entering the water,
travelled thence to the court of God and returned with food. In the second 64
story Gurū Nānak cures a fit of depression in Mardānā by revealing to him that the stars are worlds in which dwell those *bhagats* who have served God faithfully.[3]

Their journey southwards finally brought them to Rāmeśwaram where 65
Gurū Nānak recited the hymn in the *Dhanāsarī* metre entitled *Āratī*[4] and 66
held discourse with the worshippers of the idol installed there. Proceeding 67
on from Rāmeśwaram beyond Setu-bandha ('Adam's Bridge') they entered a foreign country in which an unknown language was spoken. There they passed through a series of regions in all of which the one God was worshipped. The first two of these were human kingdoms, but the remainder were areas inhabited only by either spirits or animals. In all of them they found the one God worshipped and Gurū Nānak gave praise accordingly.

Next they met Kaliyug who appeared to them as a man carrying fire in 68
his hand and raw meat in his mouth. He is an altogether milder being than the *Purātan* version[5] and explains his coming as simply the result of his
desire to see a great *bhagat*. A more fearsome monster is encountered in the 69
next *goṣṭ* where a high mountain turns out to be a massive creature. Gurū

[1] *AG*, pp. 17–18.

[2] See *supra*, p. 11, n. 2.

[3] Both *goṣṭs* are obviously later additions. The occurrences which they describe are altogether out of harmony with Miharbān's comparative restraint and their style is uncharacteristic in that they contain neither quotation nor interpretation. *Goṣṭs* 69 and 72 are also examples of later additions.

[4] *AG*, pp. 13, 663. In later traditions this hymn is set in Jagannāth Purī.

[5] See *supra*, p. 41.

Nānak distended himself to the equivalent size, seized the creature, and was about to eat it when Mardānā intervened and begged him to free it. His request was granted, but he was greatly upset to learn that he had been instrumental in freeing *Kāl* (Death). Gurū Nānak assured him, however, that it was really God who had spoken through him.[1]

71 Their next experience was the encounter with the cannibals who were
unable to heat their cauldron.[2] In Miharbān's account it is Mardānā whom
72 the savages try to boil. Following this the Gurū turned a deceitful people
to righteousness by causing a harvest to grow without moisture after local
śakti practices had failed to produce the necessary rain. Gurū Nānak renamed the country Sādiq and the people, following their rājā's example, all
became Sikhs. A *dharmsālā* was built and the Sikh devotional discipline
was adopted.[3]

73 Next, still in 'the south country', they met Sajjaṇ the *ṭhag*.[4] After his
exposure and confession his *dharmsālā* of blood was destroyed and a new
one built in its place. This is followed by a series of unimportant discourses,
most of which are held in wildernesses or various unidentified cities of
74 the south and none of which add any significant details. *Goṣṭ* 74, a discourse with God, is said to have taken place 'in a city of *ṭhags* in the south
75 country'. *Goṣṭ* 75 purports to be a discourse held in a desert with a certain
78, 83 Rājā Mitr Sain, and *goṣṭ* 78 concerns a Rājā Jagannāth. In *goṣṭ* 83 a storm
which kills all the birds in a grove where Gurū Nānak happened to be
sitting prompts a soliloquy on death. The birds are revived in the following
goṣṭ.

87–95 This group of south country *goṣṭs* is followed by another group which are
said to have taken place in the city of Ujjain or the area to the south covered
by the modern Indore District. This is still regarded as 'the south country'.
In the second of these Mardānā's name reappears, having been absent since
87 *goṣṭ* 72. The first of the Ujjain *goṣṭs* records a meeting with Bharatharī,[5]
88 but the discourse is with God. Gurū Nānak and Mardānā then left the city
89 and came to 'Vijhṇī where there are elephants'.[6] From there they continued
on to the Narabad river where Gurū Nānak conversed with a converted and
earnest sanyāsī named Chiti Giri.

90 After leaving the Narabad they turned north again and on the way back
to Ujjain fell among *ṭhags* who surmised that the Gurū must be a person
of much wealth who had disguised himself as a faqīr in order to conceal the

[1] These two *goṣṭs* are missing from the Damdamā Sāhib manuscript. The latter is, like *goṣṭs* 63 and 64, a later addition to the janam-sākhī, and for the same reasons.

[2] See *supra*, p. 47.

[3] The pattern of *goṣṭ* 72 resembles that of *goṣṭs* 63, 64, and 69, and like them appears to be a later addition.

[4] See *supra*, pp. 38–39.

[5] Cf. *goṣṭ* 61.

[6] Evidently the Vindhyā Mountains, which means that Miharbān is taking the travellers south again.

fact. The *ṭhags* of the *Purātan's sākhī* 22 based a like conclusion upon their conviction that a bright face must indicate a full pocket.[1] This appears, however, to be an entirely different story. There is no struggle on a funeral pyre as in the *Purātan* incident and the customary quotations differ. In Miharbān's account all that is required to effect the *ṭhags*' conversion is the recitation of an appropriate hymn.[2]

Goṣṭ 91 contains in its alleged meeting with Bharatharī a common kind 91
of anachronism and it also provides some unusually specific details concerning the location of the meeting.[3] The discourse on this occasion is said to have been held with celibate sādhūs, but Bharatharī is referred to in the introductory portion and appears as a participant during the latter part of
the conversation. Two more discourses with Bharatharī follow, then one 92–93
with God, and finally one with a group of Sikhs. 94, 95

Leaving Ujjain, Gurū Nānak and Mardānā continued their travels in 96–99
'the south country' and eventually, after a number of discourses with sundry people in various unnamed places, reached 'the Bīkāner country in
Rājputān'. Here they moved around for some time, holding discourses with 100–6
people both in Bīkāner city and in the surrounding countryside. After 107
leaving Bīkāner they entered 'the land of Soraṭhi'. Mardānā asked the Gurū if this meant they were in the land of the Soraṭhi who was associated with Bījc[4] and received an affirmative reply. This indicates Saurashtra[5] and means that Miharbān has taken them in a southerly direction once again.

Eventually, after spending five years in 'the south country', the travellers 109
moved on to the north and came to Mathurā. There they visited the Keśo Rāi temple, bathed in the Yamunā, and then proceeded to the eastern part of the town where a large convocation of sādhūs had gathered. After the usual discourse the sādhūs all became Sikhs.

From Mathurā they moved on to Kurukshetra where a festival was in 112
progress and many people were bathing. Gurū Nānak's arrival there brought a large crowd, and a discourse on the ineffectiveness of their
bathing. Finally they arrived back in Sultānpur where they received an 113
affectionate welcome from Daulat Khān Lodī. Three discourses followed, 114
in the second of which Daulat Khān declared that although God was 'the Master of hearts' no one had ever seen Him and that here on earth the title
belonged to Gurū Nānak. The Gurū also conversed with some pious people 116
and was acclaimed a *pīr* by both Hindus and Muslims.

After this interlude in Sultānpur Gurū Nānak set out through 'the north 117
country' to Mount Sumeru, evidently travelling alone. The only place

[1] *Pur JS*, p. 32. See *supra*, p. 40.

[2] *Dhanāsarī Chhant* 3, *AG*, pp. 689–90. The genesis of the story is obviously connected with the word *mūṭhārie* (*mūṭhāṇā*: to cheat, plunder, rob) which occurs in the first line and which would evoke associations of *ṭhagī* (thuggee).

[3] See *infra*, p. 91.

[4] The reference is to one of the famous Rājpūt cycles.

[5] *MK*, p. 175.

named on his journey there is a temple of Durgā. Climbing Mount Sumeru, Gurū Nānak found all nine Siddhs seated there—Gorakhnāth, Machhendranāth, Īśarnāth, Charapaṭnāth, Baraṅgnāth, Ghoṛācholī, Bālgundāī, Bharatharī, and Gopīchand. When Gorakhnāth asked the identity of the visitor his disciples replied, 'This is Nānak Bedī, a *pīr* and a *bhagat* who is a householder. Nānak Bedī is a great *bhagat*.' Gorakhnāth then addressed Gurū Nānak, asking him from where he had come. The Gurū replied that he had come from *Āsā-andesā* ('Hope and Fear') and that he dwelt there as a water-fowl floats on water. Gorakhnāth commented that a water-fowl knows all that is taking place along the river and asked him to tell them what was happening in the present evil age (*Kaliyug*). Gurū Nānak responded with three *śloks*, all of them describing a condition of degeneracy.

> There is a famine of truth, falsehood prevails, and in the darkness of *Kaliyug* men have become ghouls. . . .[1]

> The *Kaliyug* is a knife, kings are butchers, *ḍharma* has taken wings and flown. . . .[2]

> Men give as charity the money they have acquired by sinful means. . . .[3]

The discourse then takes up *Vār Rāmakalī*, *śloks* 2–7 of *pauṛī* 12,[4] and in
118–24 the succession of *goṣṭs* which follows there are quoted other *śabads* and
śloks which imply an audience of Nāths.

125 The series concluded with a discourse in God's court, after which Gurū
126 Nānak descended to 'this world' again and journeyed to Gorakh-haṭaṛī. He arrived there during a fair, conversed with 'the yogīs' *gurū*', and continued on. No reference is made to any attempt by the yogīs to overawe him with magic.

127 Leaving 'the north country', where he had spent one year, Gurū Nānak entered 'the west country' and proceeded towards Multān. Mardānā reappears in the janam-sākhī at this point and a group of Multān *goṣṭs* follows.
131 One of these was with a descendant of Pīr Bahāuddīn, and in the next *goṣṭ*
132 it is recorded that the Gurū visited the Pīr's tomb where, according to the people's report, he paid homage.

135 From Multān Gurū Nānak set out on a pilgrimage to Mecca. On the way he came to a village which belonged to a mullah and entering the village mosque without removing his shoes he lay down with his feet in the direction of the *Ka'bah*. When the mullah and his congregation entered the mosque for the *pesī*, the second prayer, they discovered him lying in this sacrilegious position. The mullah demanded an explanation and the

[1] *Vār Āsā*, *ślok* 1 of *pauṛī* 11, *AG*, p. 468.
[2] *Vār Mājh*, *ślok* 1 of *pauṛī* 16, *AG*, p. 145.
[3] *Vār Rāmakalī*, *ślok* 1 of *pauṛī* 11, *AG*, p. 951.
[4] *AG*, pp. 952–3.

Gurū replied, 'Bābā Sāhib, turn my shoes in that direction where the house of God will not go. Place my shoes in that direction where the *Ka'bah* is not.' The mullah did not accept the challenge. He first performed the office and then gave orders for the Gurū to be thrown into prison. Gurū Nānak asked for permission to make a single comment and when it was granted declared that God alone and not his accuser was the true Mullah. He then recited *Sirī Rāgu* 28:

> He is the true Mullah who has caused the world to blossom and be verdant. . . .[1]

The mullah, evidently acknowledging defeat, retired to the graveyard and there expired.

Proceeding on from the mullah's village he met two faqīrs who were 136
going to Mecca and who suggested that they should all travel together.[2] Further on, when they reached a village, the Gurū asked them their names. They informed him that they were called Rahīm and Karīm, and inquired what his name was. When he told them it was Nānak they commented with evident surprise that it sounded like a Hindu name. The Gurū replied that he was indeed a Hindu, and when he added that he was a khatrī and a Bedī they at last recognized him as the renowned faqīr of Sultānpur fame and became very respectful. When he refused food which the Muslim villagers brought, excusing himself on the grounds that he was fasting, word quickly spread that a great *darveś* had arrived and he was acclaimed by the village.

Next morning they all set out again and on the road the two faqīrs asked him how he, a Hindu, could hope to visit Mecca. He replied that if God so willed then it would come to pass. The faqīrs were carrying paper, pen, and ink, and at this point they wrote down the date. Gurū Nānak was then transported to Mecca in an instant. His two companions arrived on foot some months later and discovered the Gurū already there. When they asked the local people his date of arrival they were given the very date they had written down and as a result word soon spread in Mecca that a great *darveś* had arrived. Gurū Nānak remained there for twelve months.

After having visited Mecca and seen 'the west country' Gurū Nānak 138
travelled eastwards to Hiṅglāj.[3] There the pilgrims were unable to recognize his religion or his caste. They also observed that he seemed to neither sleep, walk, eat, nor drink.

Continuing on to the east he arrived back in the Pañjāb and passing 139
through Gorakh-haṭaṛī came to Saidpur. He had spent three years in 'the west country' and had seen all of it, including Rūm (Byzantium), Syria,

[1] *AG*, p. 24.

[2] Mardānā disappears following *goṣṭ* 135 and does not reappear in the record until *goṣṭ* 139.

[3] The *pīṭh-sthān* in the Makrān Coast Range about eighty miles west of the Indus Delta and some twelve miles inland.

Kābul, and Peshāwar.[1] When he reached Saidpur Mardānā suggested that they should enter the town to seek alms. This they did and discovered that weddings were being celebrated everywhere. No one, however, paid any attention to them. No food was offered to them, nor any place to rest, and wherever they asked they were ignored or refused. As punishment for its callousness the Gurū called down Bābur upon the town, invoking his coming by the utterance of the verse *Tilang* 5.[2]

As in the *Purātan* version the pronouncement of the curse came to the knowledge of a certain brāhmaṇ who was a friend of faqīrs. Knowing that God invariably heeds the request of a faqīr he hastened to the Gurū and, presenting him with a basket of fruit, begged him to be merciful. Gurū Nānak reminded him that the town had inflicted harm on faqīrs, thereby implying that the imminent punishment was merited. The brāhmaṇ, however, was told to take his family and go to a pool out in the waste land at a distance of fifteen *kos*. Bābur then fell upon the city and all save the brāhmaṇ and his family were massacred. 'And so Saidpur was devastated in accordance with the utterance given by the Gurū.'

140 Next day Gurū Nānak and Mardānā returned to Saidpur and the Gurū commented, 'Mardānā, see what has befallen Saidpur Saloī. Behold the will of God in what has taken place.' They looked upon Saidpur and there was nothing to be seen. From there they travelled to Ṭillā Bālgundāī. The following day Bābur also arrived there and, in accordance with an implied warning which Gurū Nānak had given the arrogant yogīs, assaulted the village.

141 After witnessing the sack of Saidpur and visiting Ṭillā, Gurū Nānak at last turned towards his home in Talvaṇḍī. They stopped at a distance of two *kos* from the village and Mardānā asked if he might continue on into the village. Permission was granted on condition that he was not to mention the name of Nānak and that if anyone should ask for news of him he was to give the following answer: 'Brother, since the time when Bābā Nānak left Sultānpur we, being separated from him, have continually held his name in remembrance. If anyone knows his whereabouts it is God.'

In the village the people showed great respect to him. He went to Kālū's house and prostrated himself before the Gurū's mother When she and others asked where Nānak was he replied that he did not know but was looking for him. After further conversation he departed and the Gurū's mother said to herself, 'There is meaning in his having come and then departed again. He has gone to Nānak.' Taking sweets, fruit, and clothing, she followed Mardānā out into the jungle called Sāndal Bār and there the
142–5 reunion took place. A series of discourses followed in which both his

[1] Rūm and Syria must be later additions to the janam-sākhī. The names are found in the later janam-sākhīs. Kābul and Peshāwar may also be later additions.

[2] *AG*, pp. 722–3.

parents unsuccessfully sought to persuade him to abandon his itinerant way of life and settle in Talvaṇḍī.

After leaving Talvaṇḍī Gurū Nānak moved south through the Mājhā[1] 147
to Pāk Paṭṭan, passing through a number of villages on the way and stopping two *kos* short of the town. The account of his meeting with Sheikh Kamāl, who was out gathering firewood, and of the first discourse with Sheikh Ibrāhīm is essentially the same as the *Purātan*'s *sākhī* 32,[2] except that Mardānā appears to be absent in the Miharbān version. Most of the scripture quotations are the same and both put Gurū Amar Dās's *ślok* 104[3] into Gurū Nānak's mouth on this occasion. Miharbān extends the meeting
with Sheikh Ibrāhīm over two more *goṣṭs*, but adds only scripture and 148–9
interpretation.

From Pāk Paṭṭan Gurū Nānak travelled north to Dīpālpur where a pious 151
merchant presented him with some dried fruit and some mangoes. The Gurū asked him why he was offering fruit from both Khurāsān and Hindustān together. The merchant explained that the mangoes were the first of a consignment which had just arrived from Delhi and in order that his business might prosper he wanted Gurū Nānak to be the first to taste them. The raisins had been left by Bābur's army, which had been in Dīpālpur, and some had been saved for any man of God who might come. Gurū Nānak tried a sample from each and then blessed both the donor and the town, reciting a *ślok* which is really by Gurū Aṅgad.[4] He then proceeded on through the areas of Shergaṛh, Mustafābād, Chuṇīān, Talvaṇḍī, Kaṅganpur, Harī, Kasūr, Rohevāl, Nanīer, Bahikiṛīā, and finally reached Khokhovāl.

The following *goṣṭ*, which is set in Khokhovāl, relates a series of bizarre 152
incidents, essentially disconnected but loosely linked by the presence of a brāhmaṇ boy. The language is later and the collection is evidently a subsequent addition.

Leaving Khokhovāl, Gurū Nānak moved through Kiṛīān Paṭhāṇān to 153
the village of Pokho.[5] The area so attracted him that he settled there on the banks of the Rāvī and soon crowds were coming to pay their respects. The local official,[6] however, was sceptical and, as in the *Purātan* version, set off to imprison the corrupter of Hindus and Muslims. The results were the same, except that the fall came first and blindness second, and that a third effort to proceed on horseback produced a pain in his stomach. When he continued on foot all was well. After his interview he donated some fertile

[1] The Bārī Doāb between the Rāvī and Beās rivers.

[2] See *supra*, p. 43.

[3] *AG*, p. 1383.

[4] *Vār Soraṭhi*, *ślok* 2 of *pauṛī* 28, *AG*, p. 653.

[5] Pokho dī Randhāvī, or Pakho, near the town of Dehrā Bābā Nānak. Gurū Nānak's father-in-law is said to have lived here before moving to Baṭālā.

[6] The *karoṛiā* of the *Purātan sākhī* 40. See *supra*, p. 46. The Miharbān account also describes him as a *karoṛiā*.

land for a village and built a *dharmsālā*. Gurū Nānak settled there, naming the new village Kartārpur.

At this point *Pothī Sach-khand* concludes.

Summaries

The three best available accounts of the life of Gurū Nānak have now been set out in some detail. In so far as they include references to specific dates, recognizable places, and people of some significance they may be summarized as follows:

Bhāī Gurdās's Vār 1

Gurū Nānak's visit to 'all the centres of pilgrimage'.
Mount Sumeru.
Mecca.
Medina.
Baghdad.
Kartārpur, on the right bank of the Rāvī, immediately opposite Dehrā Bābā Nānak.
Gurū Aṅgad appointed successor.
Achal Baṭālā, four miles east of Baṭālā.
Multān.
Kartārpur.

The Purātan *Janam-sākhīs*

Gurū Nānak was born in the light half of the month of Vaisākh, S. 1526 (A.D. 1469) in the village of Rāi Bhoi dī Talvaṇḍī where his father, Kālū, a Bedī khatrī, lived. The landlord of the village during his childhood was Rāi Bulār.

At the age of twelve he was married to the daughter of Mūlā, a Choṇā khatrī. Two sons, Lakhmī Dās and Sirī Chand, were subsequently born.

His brother-in-law Jai Rām, the steward of Daulat Khān, invited him to Sultānpur where he was given employment in Daulat Khān's service.

From Sultānpur he left on his first journey accompanied by Mardānā, a Ḍūm from Talvaṇḍī. This journey was to the eastern parts of India and included, in the following sequence:

Pāṇīpat (Sheikh Sharaf)
Delhi (Sultan Ibrāhīm Lodī)
Banāras
Nānakmatā
Kaurū or Kāvarū, evidently Kāmrūp in Assam (Nūr Shāh)
Talvaṇḍī, twelve years after leaving Sultānpur
Pāk Paṭṭan (Sheikh Ibrāhīm)
Goindvāl
Saidpur, or modern Eminābād (Bābur)
Lahore
Kartārpur

His second journey was to the south and his companions are variously given as Saido and Gheho; Saido and Sīho; Saido, Gheho, and Sīho; or Saido, Sīho, and Mardānā.

Ceylon (Rājā Śivanābh)

The third journey was to the north. His companions' names are given as Hassū Lohār and Sīhān Chhīmbā.

Kashmir
Mount Sumeru
Achal

The fourth journey was to the west. No regular companions are named.

Mecca (Qāzī Rukan-dīn)

The fifth journey was a brief one to Gorakh-haṭaṛī, perhaps the Nāth centre in modern Peshāwar. No companion is named.

Lahiṇā of Khaḍūr became a disciple, was subsequently renamed Aṅgad, and was eventually designated successor to the office of Gurū by Gurū Nānak himself.

Gurū Nānak died at Kartārpur on the tenth day of the light half of Asū, S. 1595 (A.D. 1538).

The *Purātan* janam-sākhīs also indicate that the Gurū was acquainted with Pīr Bahāuddīn of Multān.[1] Two prominent omissions from the places named are Baghdad[2] and Jagannāth Purī. The only dates of significance which are mentioned are those of his birth and death, and (by obvious implication) that of his marriage which would have been in A.D. 1481 or 1482. Two which may be added are those of the accession of Sultan Ibrāhīm Lodī in 1517[3] and Bābur's sack of Saidpur in 1520.[4] This at once involves a contradiction, as Gurū Nānak is said to have returned to Talvaṇḍī twelve years after the journey began,[5] and the journey is said to have begun after the occasion of Gurū Nānak's meeting with Ibrāhīm Lodī in Delhi.[6] One of the dates must be rejected forthwith and of the two incidents the one which has the greater claims to probability is obviously the Saidpur visit. The Delhi *sākhī* can have no claims whatsoever and accordingly the 1517 date may be summarily eliminated.

1 The IOL manuscript Panj. B40, folio 53, includes a discourse with Bahāuddīn's *potā* (grandson, or perhaps a remoter descendant in the male line), not with Bahāuddīn himself. The name of the *potā* is given as Rukandīn. Miharbān, who also has such a discourse, does not name the *potā*, referring to him simply as *Pīr Bahāvadī dā potā* or as *pirzādā* (*Mih JS*, p. 434. See *supra*, p. 60). In the *Colebrooke* and *Hāfizābād* manuscripts Rukandīn is the name of the Mecca qāzī who sought to drag Gurū Nānak's feet away from the direction of the *Ka'bah*. See *supra*, p. 49.

2 The IOL manuscript Panj. B40, folio 200, includes a *sākhī* describing a discourse held in Baghdad. The other participant's name is given as Sheikh Sharaf.

3 *Sākhī* 15. See *supra*, p. 39.

4 *Sākhī* 35. See *supra*, p. 44.

5 *Pur JS*, p. 48.

6 Ibid., p. 25.

The Miharbān Janam-sākhī

Gurū Nānak was born in the light half of the month of Vaisākh, S. 1526 (A.D. 1469), the son of Kālū, a Bedī khatrī, and Tiparā. The place where the birth took place is variously said to have been the village of Chāhalāvāle and Kālū's village, Rāi Bhoe kī Talvaṇḍī. The name of the contemporary landlord of the latter village is given as Rāi Bhoā.

At about the time of his sixteenth birthday Gurū Nānak was married in Baṭālā to Ghumī, the daughter of Mūlā, a Choṇā khatrī of Baṭālā. Two sons, Lakhmī Dās and Sirī Chand, were born when he was twenty-seven or twenty-eight years of age.

At the age of thirty-five years, six and a half months, he went to Sultānpur in response to an invitation from his brother-in-law Jai Rām, an Uppal khatrī and steward of Daulat Khān Lodī. There he was given employment in Daulat Khān's commissariat.

After two years in Sultānpur he left on his first journey, accompanied by Mardānā. This journey was to the east of India and then from there to the far south. It included the following places:

Delhi (Salīm Shāh Paṭhān)
Hardwār
Allahābād
Banāras
Hājīpur Paṭnā
Ayodhyā
Jagannāth Purī
Rāmeśwaram
A 'land of darkness' beyond Adam's Bridge (evidently Ceylon)
Ujjain (Rājā Bharatharī)
Vindhyā Mountains
Narabad River
Ujjain
Bīkāner
Saurāshtra
Mathurā
Kurukshetra
Sultānpur (Daulat Khān Lodī)

The second journey was to the north and then to the west.

Mount Sumeru
Gorakh-haṭaṛī
Multān (a descendant of Pīr Bahāuddīn)
Mecca
Hiṅglāj
Gorakh-haṭaṛī
Saidpur (Bābur)
Ṭillā Bālgundāī (Bābur)

Talvaṇḍī
Pāk Paṭṭan (Sheikh Ibrāhīm)
Dīpālpur
Khokhovāl
Pokho and Kartārpur

In Miharbān's account the notable omissions are Kāmrūp and Baghdad. Nānakmatā is also missing and Ceylon is not mentioned by name. The significant dates, stated or plainly implied, are the Gurū's birth in S. 1526 (A.D. 1469), his marriage (A.D. 1485), his move from Talvaṇḍī to Sultānpur (A.D. 1504), and his departure from there on his first journey (A.D. 1506). To these may be added the date of the attack on Saidpur (A.D. 1520) which means that according to Miharbān's account all of Gurū Nānak's travels outside the Pañjāb took place within the space of fourteen years and between the ages of thirty-seven and fifty-three. The period spent in 'the east country' was three years, in the south five years, in the north one year, and in the west three years, a total of twelve years. This leaves a balance of two years to be allocated to the initial journey from Sultānpur to 'the east country', and the gap between the departure from 'the south country' and the commencement of the second journey. The pattern would then be as follows:

From Sultānpur to 'the east country'	1506–7
Travels in 'the east country'	1507–10
Travels in 'the south country'	1510–15
The journey from 'the south country' to 'the north country' via Sultānpur	1515–16
Travels in 'the north country'	1516–17
Travels in 'the west country'	1517–20

4

THE LIFE OF GURŪ NĀNAK

THE three accounts set out in the previous section provide practically all of the material available for a reconstruction of the events of the life of Gurū Nānak. None of them can be accepted as it stands and our task must now be to seek and apply means of identifying what may be affirmed, what must be rejected, and what falls between the two. There is obviously much that must be rejected as impossible, and in contrast there is regrettably little which may be accepted without reserve. Some of the remaining material may be regarded as probable, but considerably more of it must be classified as unlikely. Finally there is a certain amount from which we must withhold judgement, material which records what is inherently possible, but for which there is no support other than that offered by the janam-sākhīs themselves.

We have here five categories which we may designate the established, the probable, the possible, the improbable, and the impossible. Into these five we must strive to fit the manifold traditions concerning the life of Gurū Nānak. In order to do so it is first necessary to determine the criteria which should be used.

The first criterion, and one which enables us to discard substantial portions of all the janam-sākhī accounts, is the incidence of the miraculous or plainly fantastic. It is, however, one which must be used with some caution. The inclusion of a miracle does not necessarily mean that the whole *sākhī* must be rejected. In most cases this is required, but in others the possibility of a substratum of truth must be borne in mind. The use of this approach should not, of course, suggest that legend possesses no significance and deserves to be wholly ignored. Legendary accretions frequently reflect the piety engendered by great religious figures and as such serve to communicate, in some measure, an impression of their power to attract and inspire.[1] In a study of this nature, however, legend must wherever possible be identified and set aside. The strict, at times ruthless, approach is as much required in a quest for the historical Nānak as it has been required in the quest of the historical Jesus.

A second criterion is the testimony of external sources. In most cases

[1] Tor Andrae, *Mohammed: The Man and His Faith*, Harper Torchbooks, New York, 1960, p. 31. H. D. Lewis and Robert Lawson Slater, *World Religions: Meeting Points and Major Issues*, p. 53.

where this criterion applies to the janam-sākhī accounts of Gurū Nānak's life it demands a negative judgement. The two important exceptions are the incidents involving Daulat Khān Lodī and the Emperor Bābur. There is also an inscription in Baghdad which requires careful consideration.

A third criterion which may be used is Gurū Nānak's own work as recorded in the *Ādi Granth*. This too offers us disappointingly little help for, as we have already observed, explicit references to the events of his life are entirely absent and implicit hints are few. The most important of these concern the connexion with Bābur and Gurū Nānak's relationships with Nāth yogīs. In other cases the help which his works offer us is generally negative. Occasionally it is possible to reject an incident because it is conspicuously out of accord with clearly stated doctrine or with the personality which emerges from his works as a whole.[1]

A fourth criterion is the measure of agreement or, conversely, disagreement which we find in the different janam-sakhis. This alone can rarely determine a particular issue, but in some cases it should certainly influence our judgement. One such instance is the story of Sajjaṇ the *ṭhag*.

In cases where there is disagreement between the different janam-sākhīs, or where only one janam-sākhī records a particular detail or incident, a fifth criterion is the relative reliability of the different janam-sākhīs. This criterion is of little use in issues which concern only the *Purātan* and *Miharbān* janam-sākhīs or *Vār* 1, but it certainly applies whenever the more recent janam-sākhīs enter the discussion. In general the testimony of the three older sources must be preferred to that of either the *Gyān-ratanāvalī* or the *Bālā* janam-sākhīs.

Sixthly, a measure of trust may be attached to genealogical references. Family relationships in the Pañjāb can normally be traced back accurately for several generations and it is reasonable to assume that at least the immediate family connexions of Gurū Nānak would still be known at the time when the older janam-sākhīs were committed to writing.

Finally there is a geographic criterion in the sense that a greater degree of confidence can be placed in details relating to Gurū Nānak's life within the Pañjāb than to those which concern his travels beyond the province.

[1] The so-called contextual argument is of use only in the case of the verses which refer to Bābur, and even here it must be qualified. According to this argument a *sākhī* is entitled to acceptance if the theme of the verse which it incorporates corresponds with the content of the *sākhī*. The argument is unacceptable for two reasons. In the first place it assumes a highly improbable degree of poetic spontaneity, particularly in the case of *sākhīs* relating to the Gurū's childhood. Secondly, such cases of correspondence are subject to a much more likely explanation. There seems to be little doubt that almost all *sākhīs* which are in significant accord with a particular verse should be regarded as examples of stories which have evolved out of a suggestive reference in a verse. The origin may be the theme of the complete verse, or it may be a single word. In some cases it may be the name or the nature of the person to whom the verse appears to be addressed. See *supra*, pp. 11–12 and *infra*, pp. 86–87, 119. It is possible that in a few instances a verse has been subsequently attached to a developed *sākhī* as a result of an evident affinity between the two.

This applies particularly to the period of his later years. The accounts of his childhood are all heavily charged with legend, but there is much that rings true in the brief accounts given of his Kartārpur period. This is to be expected, for the janam-sākhīs we are using must have emerged at a remove of only one or two generations from Gurū Nānak's death.

The relevance of this particular criterion is pointed up by the marked contrast between the geographical exactitude which characterizes the janam-sākhī accounts of his movements within the Pañjāb and the vagueness of those which describe his travels elsewhere. This certainly does not mean that we can accept a particular event as authentic simply because it is set in a recognizable and accurately described Pañjāb location, but it does enhance the possibility of acceptance. In the case of Gurū Nānak's travels beyond the Pañjāb the place-names are almost all either well-known capitals and centres of pilgrimage, or they are unidentifiable and evidently non-existent places such as 'Dhanāsarī'. Many of the *sākhīs* describing incidents which occurred during his journeys are unlocated or are said to have taken place in 'a certain city' or 'a certain country'. A high proportion are placed in deserts or jungles, and a number are said to have occurred on islands in the ocean. The incidence of the fantastic is particularly high in these latter cases. All *sākhīs* with indefinite oceanic settings must be regarded with marked scepticism.

The vagueness also emerges in such details as the names of Gurū Nānak's associates. In the case of the *Purātan's* southern journey the manuscripts disagree not just between themselves but also within their own individual accounts. There is the same evident uncertainty in the names of the people with whom Gurū Nānak is said to have conversed. Discourses with Sheikh Farīd, Sheikh Sharaf, and Pīr Bahāuddīn are anachronisms, but the names are at least those of real people, each of whom would have left a line of spiritual successors. This is more than can be said for such names as Nūr Shāh, Khwājā Khizar, and the eighty-four Siddhs. Such vagueness need not necessarily demand a definite rejection of a particular *sākhī*, but it must certainly weaken its claims to authenticity.

A synopsis of the janam-sākhī traditions concerning the life of Gurū Nānak

These are the seven principal criteria which will be used in this effort to reconstruct the events of the life of Gurū Nānak. Before proceeding to do so, however, it will be convenient to set out, in the form of a chart, a conspectus of the various *sākhīs* which have been used in Bhāī Gurdās's *Vār* 1 and the *Purātan* and *Miharbān* janam-sākhīs,[1] together with the correspond-

[1] In the case of the *Miharbān Janam-sākhī* numbers up to and including 153 represent *goṣṭs* from *Pothī Sach-khaṇḍ*, and numbers 172, 173 and 180 *goṣṭs* from *Pothī Harijī*.

ing *sākhīs* from the *Gyān-ratanāvalī* and *Bālā* versions. To these have been added a few *sākhīs* which do not appear in any of the three older sources, but which are included in most modern biographies of Gurū Nānak. A column has also been added to indicate which of the *sākhīs* have been used by Macauliffe in the first volume of his *The Sikh Religion*. Macauliffe's account is generally based upon the *Purātan* janam-sākhīs, but the author added several other incidents, mainly from the *Bālā* tradition, and in many cases he expanded the *Purātan* account with material drawn from *Bālā* sources. Occasionally he used the *Gyān-ratanāvalī* in the same way and added anything extra which was to be found in Bhāī Gurdās's *Vār* 1.

For this chart the *Miharbān Janam-sākhī* has been taken as the standard and the individual *sākhīs* are listed in the order in which they occur in that janam-sākhī. *Sākhīs* which do not appear in the *Miharbān* version but which include a specific chronological indication have been inserted in their appropriate places. Other *sākhīs* are listed as 'Miscellaneous *sākhīs*'. Each figure indicates the number of the relevant *sākhī*, *goṣṭ*, or *pauṛī* in the janam-sākhī under which it is listed, and the numbers given under 'Macauliffe' are those of the appropriate page numbers in volume i of *The Sikh Religion*.[1] The numbers which appear consecutively in the first column have been added by the writer for ease of reference in the discussion which follows.

The edition of the *Gyān-ratanāvalī* which has been used is the one which was lithographed in Lahore by Charāguddīn and Sarājuddīn in A.D. 1891. *Sākhīs* included in that edition which have obviously been borrowed from the *Bālā* tradition have been bracketed.

Three editions of the *Bālā* version have been included in the chart. These are: (*a*) the Hāfaz Qutub Dīn edition, lithographed in A.D. 1871, which generally follows the India Office Library manuscript Panj. B41 and the British Museum manuscript Or. 2754. I.; (*b*) the expanded 1871 edition lithographed by Dīvān Būṭā Singh, Lahore; and (*c*) a modern version published by Munshī Gulāb Singh and Sons of Lahore in A.D. 1942. *Sākhīs* have been listed under the third of these only if they do not appear in either of the 1871 editions. Numbers listed under (*a*) which are bracketed indicate *sākhīs* which have been taken direct from the *Purātan* tradition and do not appear in the India Office Library or British Museum manuscripts. An error has been made in the indexing of (*b*), the expanded 1871 edition, as a result of which the numbers 165–74 inclusive have been used twice in allocating consecutive numbers to *sākhīs*. In the chart such *sākhīs* are distinguished by the use of either (1) or (2).

It must be emphasized that although most *sākhīs* appear in the chart under more than one source, the different versions normally give differing

[1] One incident (number 93) is recorded in volume ii of *The Sikh Religion*.

accounts of the same incident. Occasionally the differences are such as to destroy practically all resemblances between two accounts. It should also be noted that the *sākhīs* listed in the chart do not cover the total range of all traditions concerning the life of Gurū Nānak. The selection is, however, an extensive one and includes all the important incidents from the older janam-sākhīs.

Sākhī	Mih JS	Pur JS	Vār 1	GR	Bālā janam-sākhīs a	b	c	Macauliffe
1. The birth of Gurū Nānak	4	1		27	2	2		1
2. Recitation of *Sapat Ślokī Gītā*				(31)		2		
3. Instruction by the paṇḍit	5	2		33–34	3	3		2
4. Instruction by the mullah	6	3		45		4		11
5. Investiture with the sacred thread	7			44		5		16
6. The restored field	8	4		46–47		6		15
7. The tree's stationary shadow	9	5		48	4	7		19
8. The cobra's shadow					4	8		19
9. Marriage of Jai Rām and Nānakī					7	13		18
10. Betrothal and marriage	11–12	3		50	11–12	17–18		18
11. The physician convinced	15–16	7		48		11		26
12. The true field	17							
13. The true merchandise	22	6		49		10		23
14. Birth of Lakhmī Dās and Sirī Chand	22	5		51	13	20, 25		29
15. The true harvest	23	6		49		10		21
16. *Kharā saudā*: the feeding of Sant Ren and the faqīrs					6	12		30
17. The *loṭā* and ring presented to a faqīr					8	14		32
18. Bhāgīrath and Mansukh		41		52		19		145
19. Mansukh and Rājā Śivanābh		41		82		27		146
20. To Sultānpur	24	8		53	9	15		32
21. Work in Daulat Khān's commissariat	25–27	9		54	10	16		33
22. Immersion in the river: his call	28–29	10		56	13	21–23		33
23. Nānak accused of embezzlement					10	25		42
24. The mullah seeks to exorcize his evil spirit					15	27		36
25. Discourse with the qāzī	30–32	11		57–58	15	28–29		37
26. Departure from Sultānpur	34	11		61	16	34		43
27. Mardānā commanded to throw offerings away	35	12				176		44
28. Mardānā eats the forbidden fruit	36	30			24	177		94
29. Nānak cooks meat at Kurukshetra				(62)	71	249		47
30. Discourse with Sheikh Sharaf of Pāṇīpat		14		65	(66)			52
31. Delhi: the real alms	38							
32. Delhi: the sultan's elephant resurrected		15		66–68		236		56
33. Sheikh Bajīd		16						58

Sākhi	Mih JS	Pur JS	Vār I	GR	Bālā janam-sākhis a	b	c	Macauliffe
34. Hardwār: the watering of his fields	39–40			71			81	50
35. Mount Govardhan, Mathurā, and Brindāban				(69–70)		251–2		57
36. Nānakmatā		18		72	(23)	90		59
37. Allahābād	43							
38. Banāras: discourses with paṇḍits	44–50			74		253		
39. Banāras: discourse with Chatur Dās		17				196		61
40. Rājā Harināth	51							
41. Meeting with Kabīr	52							
42. Hājīpur Paṭnā	54			77				
43. Ayodhyā: discourse with 'all the *bhagats*'	59–60							
44. Ayodhyā: discourse with paṇḍits				(75)		255		
45. Gayā				(76)		254		64
46. The country ruled by women		23		84	(25)	170(1)		73
47. Dacca					24			
48. Jagannāth Purī	61			78–79		254		81
49. The brick falls from the temple	62							
50. The jackal and the food from God's court	63							
51. The *bhagats* revealed in the stars	64							
52. Rāmeśwaram	65–66				60	{ 158 { 227		
53. The yogī of Jāpāpaṭan (Jaffna)				85–86				
54. Ceylon: Rājā Śivanābh and the *Prāṇ Saṅgalī*		47		87–91	29	169(1)		154
55. A girl turned into a boy				(92–94)		173–4(1)		
56. The meeting with Kaliyug	68	24		81	(26)	165(2)		78
57. The struggle with *Kāl*	69							
58. The cannibals' cauldron	71	44		83	30	72–73		152
59. A deceitful people turned to righteousness	72							
60. Sajjaṇ the *ṭhag*	73	13		73	63	239		45
61. Rājā Mitr Sain	75							
62. Rājā Jagannāṭh	78							
63. Ujjain	87, 91–95							
64. Vindhyā Mountains	88							
65. Narabad River	89							

66. Bīkāner district and city	100–6			108				
67. The land of Soraṭhi (Saurāshtra)	107							
68. Mathurā	109–11							
69. Kurukshetra: discourse on bathing	112							
70. Return to Sultānpur	113–16							
71. The Kashmīrī paṇḍit		49		(114)	(75)	217		163
72. Mount Sumeru	117–25	50	28–31	(139–42)	43–48	111–37		169
73. Gorakh-haṭaṛī	126	52						172
74. Multān: discourse with a descendant of Pīr Bahāuddīn	127–34							
75. The mullah's village	135							
76. Rahīm and Karīm	136							
77. The Mecca pilgrim and the following cloud		51		156				174
78. Mecca: Gurū Nānak's miraculous arrival	136			157				
79. Mecca: the moving mosque		51	32–34	157	39	104		175
80. Medina				(164)	40	106–8		179
81. Baghdad			35–36	161–3		228–31		179
82. Hinglāj	138							
83. The sack of Saidpur	139	35		(112)		470		109
84. Discourse with Bābur		35		(112)	73	470		113
85. Bābur attacks Ṭillā Bālgundāī	140							
86. Return to Talvaṇḍī and reunion with parents	141–5	31		110			101	95
87. Pāk Paṭṭan: discourse with Sheikh Ibrāhīm	147–9	32		36–37 (180)	83	258		101
88. The merchant of Dīpālpur	151							
89. The proud official humbled: the founding of Kartārpur	153	40		148–51		55		131
90. Achal Baṭālā: discourse with the Siddhs	173	50	39–44	170–7	61			157
91. Multān: the jasmine petal			44	178		233		180
92. First meeting with Lahiṇā	172	53		169	86	271		182
93. Lahiṇā's clothes ruined	172	53			86	271		ii. 4
94. Lahiṇā commanded to eat the corpse	180	54			86	279		183
95. Lahiṇā becomes Angad	172	54			86	271		185
96. Death of Makhdūm Bahāuddīn		55						186
97. Death of Mardānā				208				181
98. Death of Kālū and Tipārā				216–17		290		

Sākhi	Mih JS	Pur JS	Vār 1	GR	Bālā janam-sākhīs a	b	c	Macauliffe
99. The installation of Gurū Aṅgad		56	45	218	86	293		187
100. The death of Gurū Nānak		57		219	89–90	295–300		188
Miscellaneous Sākhīs								
101. The death of the trader's infant son		19				68		65
102. A watchman receives royal authority		20				160–1		68
103. The coal and the thorn		21						68
104. The *ṭhags* and the funeral pyre		22		120		198		71
105. *Kiṛ nagar*: the city of insects		25			(27)	376		
106. The inhospitable village unmolested		26						80
107. The hospitable village dispersed		27						81
108. The meeting with Sheikh Farīd in Āsā		28			(28)			84
109. Jhaṇḍā Bāḍhī and the *Jugāvalī*		29			34	170(2)		93
110. The leprous faqīr		33				202		107
111. The devotees of Kiṛīān Paṭhāṇān		34						108
112. Discourse with Mīā Miṭhā		36				171(2)		123
113. Dunī Chand and the wolf		37			(74)	62		129
114. Dunī Chand's flags		37			(74)	62		130
115. The brāhmaṇ's cooking-square		38						132
116. A pious boy		39				168(2)		133
117. The meeting with Khwājar Khizar		42				172(2)		147
118. Anabhī the Jain		43						150
119. The meeting with Makhdūm Bahāuddīn		45						153
120. The destruction of the hospitable carpenter's hut		48				167(2)		
121. Sālas Rāi				(99–107)	31	74–75		
122. *Pañjā Sāhib*: the rock stopped							147	171
123. Discourse with Abdul Rahmān				(119)	80	193 259–60		
124. Saidpur: Lālo and Bhāgo					19–20	47		43

Sākhīs which must be rejected

Of the *sākhīs* listed in the chart many may be treated in summary manner. A substantial proportion can be discarded at once, most of them in accordance with the first criterion, and many more must be relegated to the 'possible' category. The following may be rejected on the grounds that they are miracle stories without any features which suggest a substratum of truth.

2. Recitation of *Sapat Ślokī Gītā*
6. The restored field
7. The tree's stationary shadow
8. The cobra's shadow
23. Nānak accused of embezzlement
28. Mardānā eats the forbidden fruit
49. The brick falls from the temple
50. The jackal and the food from God's court
51. The *bhagats* revealed in the stars
53. The yogī of Jāpāpaṭan
55. A girl turned into a boy.
56. The meeting with Kaliyug
57. The struggle with *Kāl*
59. A deceitful people turned to righteousness
77. The Mecca pilgrim and the following cloud
78. Mecca: Gurū Nānak's miraculous arrival
94. Lahiṇā commanded to eat the corpse
104. The *ṭhags* and the funeral pyre
105. *Kīṛ nagar*: the city of insects
110. The leprous faqīr
113. Dunī Chand and the wolf.
115. The brāhmaṇ's cooking-square
117. The meeting with Khwājar Khizar
119. The meeting with Makhdūm Bahāuddīn
120. The destruction of the hospitable carpenter's hut
122. *Pañjā Sāhib*: the rock stopped

Several of these do not appear in the *Vār* or in either of the older janam-sākhī traditions, but have been included here either on account of their prominence in popular biographies of Gurū Nānak or because they provide illustrations of *Bālā* material incorporated in the extant version of the *Gyān-ratanāvalī*. In a number of cases these legends represent not an indigenous development within Sikh tradition, but a borrowing from another source. Number 8, the story of the cobra's shadow, is an obvious example, and another appears to be number 108, the city of insects.[1] In the latter case a legend from an external source, the Persian story of Hazrat Suleimān and a town of ants, may have come to be linked with a suggestive place-name. In Kāṅgṛā District of the Pañjāb there is a village which is now called Baijnāth, but which was formerly known as Kīṛgrām (literally 'insect-village') and which was, for a period, a centre of pilgrimage. It is at least possible that a tradition concerning a visit to the village by Gurū Nānak came to be associated with the Persian legend, and that the *sākhī* entitled *Kīṛ nagar* is the result.[2] The *ślok* which the *sākhī* incorporates must also have participated in the evolution of the story.[3]

A tradition which is accorded particular popularity in modern accounts is number 122, the story of how Gurū Nānak stopped a falling boulder. The story relates that the Gurū once visited Hasan Abdāl, a village in Attock District between Rawalpindi and Peshawar.[4] At the top of a nearby hill there lived a Muslim *darveś* called Bāwā Valī Qandhārī. Water issued from a spring at the summit, but none was available at its foot and Mardānā was accordingly sent up to draw some. Valī Qandhārī had, however, heard of the Gurū's reputation and, piqued by jealousy, he refused access to Mardānā, suggesting that if his master was such a great faqīr he should provide his own water-supply. A second request elicited a similar reply and so the Gurū proceeded to act in accordance with Valī Qandhārī's sarcastic advice. He caused a spring to open at the foot of the hill, whereupon the spring at the summit immediately ceased to flow. Seeing this, the enraged Valī Qandhārī rolled a huge rock down upon the Gurū. The mighty boulder failed, however, to reach its mark, for Gurū Nānak raised his hand and instantly terminated its headlong flight. An impression of his hand was left on the rock and it is for this reason that the place is known as *Pañjā Sāhib*, or the Holy Palm. Some accounts also claim that the flow of water in the spring greatly increased.[5]

The Sikh story concerning Hasan Abdāl is the latest in a line which has successively produced Buddhist, Hindu, and Muslim legends. General Cunningham identified the tank which is filled by the spring with that of the *Nāga* or Serpent King Elāpatra visited by Hsüan Tsang in A.D. 630.[6] The most interesting feature of the Sikh legend is the unusually late date at which it appears to have entered the janam-sākhī traditions. There is, of

[1] See *suprà*, p. 41.

[2] The writer owes this suggestion to Professor Pritam Singh of Government College, Ludhiana. For a brief discussion of Puranic elements in the janam-sākhīs see Rattan Singh Jaggi, *Dasam Granth dā Paurāṇik Adhiain*, pp. 58–63.

[3] *Vār Mājh, ślok* 1 of *pauṛī* 14, *AG*, p. 144. It includes the line: 'He confers kingship on an insect and reduces armies to ashes.'

[4] It is within the area of ancient remains which surround the site of Taxila. *Imperial Gazetteer of India*, vol. xiii, p. 70.

[5] Sewaram Singh, *The Divine Master*, p. 159.

[6] *Archaeological Survey of India, Report of 1863–4* vol. ii, pp. 135–6.

course, a hand-shaped depression in a rock at Hasan Abdāl and the gurdwara which has been built at the site is regarded as one of the most important of all Sikh temples.[1]

To the twenty-six *sākhīs* listed above the following three must, for all practical purposes, be added.

3. Instruction by the paṇḍit.
4. Instruction by the mullah.
5. Investiture with the sacred thread.

These three concern Gurū Nānak's childhood and the recitation of verses on these occasions obviously falls within the category of miracle stories. It is quite possible that Gurū Nānak was instructed by a paṇḍit and a mullah during his childhood, and that at the appropriate age he was invested with the sacred thread, but there seems to be little doubt that these incidents, like so many others, were introduced in order to provide settings for the verses. Moreover, the information they offer adds nothing to what we already know about Gurū Nānak. His works are not those of an illiterate or semi-literate person[2] and we may assume that his parents would have followed normal practices as far as the sacred thread was concerned.

58. The cannibals' cauldron

The story of the cannibals' efforts to boil Mardānā or, as in the *Purātan* version, Gurū Nānak himself[3] is one of the miracle stories which shows evident signs of having evolved out of references in particular verses, in this case a composition which is by Gurū Arjan and not by Gurū Nānak.[4] It may be argued that even if the story of the recalcitrant cauldron is to be rejected as legendary there still remains a possibility that Gurū Nānak, at some stage in his travels, encountered some savages. The possibility does indeed exist, but this *sākhī* cannot be accepted as evidence of such an encounter. The connexion between the *kaṛāhā*, or cauldron, used by the

[1] The *Gazetteer of the Rawalpindi District 1893–94*, p. 35, states that the 'hand-mark' is 'a rude representation of a hand in relief', and on the following pages stresses that it is *in relief*. G. B. Scott, who himself visited the site, refers to 'a small human hand carved in relief' (*Religion and Short History of the Sikhs 1469–1930*, p. 19). He records a conversation which, he claims, took place during his visit and which concludes as follows:

'That's where the Guru put his hand.'
'But,' I said, 'the mark of the hand would have been impressed into the rock, not carved outward.'
However, that was a detail not worth troubling about. Ibid.

The present 'hand-mark' is unmistakably recessed into the rock, not projecting in relief, and it is relatively large, not small (8-in. span and 7½ in. in length). It has been worn smooth by the touch of innumerable hands.

[2] The accusation has, however, been made. Cf. R. C. Śukl, *Hindī Sāhitya kā Itihās* (11th edition), p. 78.

[3] *Pur JS*, *sākhī* 44, p. 81.

[4] *Mārū Mahalā* 5, 14, *AG*, p. 1002.

cannibals, and the occurrence of the same word in Gurū Arjan's *Mārū* 14 offers a much more likely explanation for the whole *sākhī*. The fact that the incident is set outside the Pañjāb and, in the case of the *Purātan* and *Bālā* versions, on 'an island in the ocean'[1] further weakens any claims the *sākhī* may have had to an element of authenticity.

108. The meeting with Sheikh Farīd in Āsā

There is good reason to accept as at least probable the tradition that Gurū Nānak met the contemporary successor of Sheikh Farīd, but this *sākhī* which describes a meeting with Farīd himself is of an entirely different order. As recorded in the *Purātan* janam-sākhīs it recounts two impossible stories set in the non-existent land of Āsā. To these two legends has been added the story of how Sheikh Farīd used to carry a wooden *chapātī* as an excuse for refusing people who offered him food and so unwittingly threatened to upset his ascetic discipline. The story belongs to the traditions which have gathered around Sheikh Farīd.[2] but its inclusion in this *sākhī* does nothing to suggest that there can be any element of historicity in the janam-sākhī incident. On the contrary, it emphasizes its legendary nature, for it indicates that the person concerned is the original Farīd, who died in 1265, and not one of his successors.

The *sākhīs* considered so far have all been rejected on the basis of their almost exclusively miraculous or manifestly fictitious content. Others may be similarly discarded in accordance with our second criterion, the testimony of external sources. This group comprises the following six *sākhīs*:

31. Delhi: the real alms
32. Delhi: the sultan's elephant resurrected

Both of these are set in Delhi and both must be rejected on historical grounds. The first of them, which is to be found only in the *Miharbān Janam-sākhī*, is wide of the historical mark in that it names Salem Shāh Paṭhān as the contemporary sultan of Delhi. The reference is obviously to Jalāl Khān, the second son and successor of Sher Shāh, who adopted the regnal name of Islām Shāh but who is referred to by several of the contemporary chroniclers as Salīm Shāh.[3] Islām Shāh's reign did not begin until 1545, six years after the death of Gurū Nānak. The *sākhī* contains nothing else except the customary discourse and must accordingly be rejected.

The substance of the second Delhi *sākhī* consists of a miracle story which

[1] *Pur JS*, p. 81. *Bālā JS*, p. 123.
[2] Khaliq Ahmad Nizami, *The Life and Times of Shaikh Farid-u'd-din Ganj-i-Shakar*, p. 24, n. 4. Cf. Farīd *ślok* 28, *AG*, p. 1379.
[3] M. A. Rahim, *History of the Afghans in India*, p. 62, n. 1.

must be repudiated as such, but this still leaves open the possibility of a meeting with the sultan. In this case the sultan's name is given as Braham Beg in the *Colebrooke* manuscript and Ibrāhīm Beg in the *Hāfizābād* manuscript.[1] The name is clearly intended to be that of Sultan Ibrāhīm Lodī (1517–26) which means that in this particular instance the *Purātan* tradition comes nearer to historical possibility than Miharbān's account. It is not, however, near enough for, as we have already observed,[2] it is impossible to accept a visit to Delhi at a date later than Ibrāhīm Lodī's accession in 1517 without upsetting the complete pattern of the first journey. Were there any inherent probability in the substance of the *sākhī* it would constitute a sufficient reason for calling that pattern in question forthwith. The substance is, however, plainly impossible and accordingly the *sākhī* may be rejected.

43. Ayodhyā: discourse with 'all the *bhagats*'

Miharbān's description of a meeting with Nāmdev, Jaidev, Kabīr, Trilochan, Ravidās, Saiṇ, Sadhnā, Dhannā, and Beṇī must be rejected for the obvious reason that there can be no possibility of *bhagats* from different centuries and different parts of India ever having gathered in the same place at the same time. Nāmdev, Jaidev, and Trilochan all died well before the birth of Gurū Nānak and the same almost certainly applies to Saiṇ, Sadhnā, and Beṇī also. The *sākhī* has obviously been developed out of the *bhagat bāṇī*[3] of the *Ādi Granth*.

70. Return to Sultānpur

Miharbān records that after returning from the south Gurū Nānak passed through Sultānpur where he renewed his acquaintance with Daulat Khān Lodī. The incident is set in the context of the Gurū's travels and, regardless of which pattern is accepted for this period, it is clear that by this stage Daulat Khān Lodī would have been residing in Lahore, not in Sultānpur. The *sūbah* of Lahore was assigned to Daulat Khān in or shortly after 1500[4] which would certainly be before Gurū Nānak could have returned to the Pañjāb had he followed the itinerary laid down by either Miharbān or the *Purātan* janam-sākhīs. According to Miharbān's chronology this return visit would have taken place in 1516.[5] It is perhaps conceivable that Daulat Khān may have happened to be back in Sultānpur on a visit, but the possibility is remote. Moreover, the tradition is a weak one. It appears only in Miharbān's account.

[1] The *Gyān-ratanāvali* relates the incident without mentioning the sultan's name (*GR*, *sākhīs* 66–68, pp. 187–94).

[2] See *supra*, p. 65.

[3] The works of various *bhagats* which were incorporated in the *Ādi Granth* by Gurū Arjan.

[4] See *infra*, p. 109.

[5] See *supra*, p. 67.

30. Discourse with Sheikh Sharaf of Pānīpat
96. Death of Makhdūm Bahāuddīn

The first of these describes a discourse with Sheikh Sharaf, the Pīr of Pāṇīpat, and the second an exchange of messages between Gurū Nānak and Sheikh Bahāuddīn of Multān shortly before their deaths. Both of these famous Muslim *pīrs* died well before the time of Gurū Nānak.[1] It may be argued that the contacts must have been with successors of the two *pīrs*,[2] but this is not what the janam-sākhīs say. Had the names of the contemporary successors been known they would certainly have been given, for this has been done in the case of Farīd's successor, Sheikh Ibrāhīm.[3] A much more likely explanation is the natural tendency to introduce an association with the acknowledged great in order that the object of the writer's belief or affection may be shown to be even greater. This factor doubtless applies also in the case of number 84, the discourse with Bābur,[4] and in that of number 108, the discourse with Sheikh Farīd.[5] In the case of Farīd the janam-sākhīs present two irreconcilable traditions. Number 108, which names Farīd himself as the person with whom the Gurū conversed, is clearly spurious, whereas number 87, which specifies Sheikh Ibrāhīm, has good claims to at least a measure of authenticity.

This must lead us to reject these two *sākhīs*, for they evidently correspond to number 108 rather than to number 87. This is not to deny that Gurū Nānak must have had contact with some of his more prominent religious contemporaries, and nor does it necessarily mean that successors of these two *pīrs* could not have been amongst these contemporaries whom the Gurū would have met. The point is that these two *sākhīs* do not provide us with evidence of such contacts.

101. The death of the trader's infant son
103. The coal and the thorn

These two *sākhīs* may be discarded in accordance with our third criterion, for both are in evident conflict with what we know of Gurū Nānak's personality and beliefs from his works. The first of them records how the Gurū greeted the prospect of a baby's imminent death not merely with equanimity, but with apparent mirth, a description which is in sharp conflict with the character which emerges from his recorded works. The purpose in this case is clearly to show the fate of those who, like the infant's father, spurn the Gurū, but the illustration is an unfortunate one. The second of the *sākhīs* is based upon a naive understanding of the doctrine

[1] Sheikh Sharaf is said to have died in A.D. 1324 and Sheikh Bahāuddīn in A.D. 1170. T. W. Beale, *An Oriental Biographical Dictionary*, pp. 17, 97.

[2] This is Macauliffe's interpretation. *The Sikh Religion*, i. 52, 186. Cf. also i. 153.

[3] See *infra*, p. 140.

[4] See *infra*, pp. 134, 138.

[5] See *supra*, p. 80. Other examples are numbers 41 and 43.

of *karma* which would certainly not have accorded with Gurū Nānak's concept. The incident is clearly spurious.

Improbable sākhīs

From the impossible we move to the improbable and here too there are several *sākhīs* which can be relegated without lengthy analyses.

11. The physician convinced
12. The true field
13. The true merchandise
15. The true harvest

These four *sākhīs* are all set in the context of the Gurū's early life in Talvaṇḍī. None of them can be dismissed as absolutely impossible, but there can be little doubt that all four are examples of episodes which evolved as appropriate settings for certain *śabads* or *śloks*. The janam-sākhīs' own claim that the *śabads* and *śloks* were uttered in response to the situations which provide the settings assumes a quality of spontaneity which is difficult to accept, even in a poet as talented as Gurū Nānak.

16. *Kharā saudā*: the feeding of Sant Ren and the faqīrs
17. The *loṭā* and the ring presented to a faqīr

The two stories which concern gifts made by Gurū Nānak to faqīrs are also set in the period of his early life, but it is obvious that they have not developed out of suggestive verses in the manner of the previous four *sākhīs*. These two are narratives, not mere settings, and they are in no way dependent upon extracts from Gurū Nānak's works. Moreover, the stories which they relate, far from seeming intrinsically unlikely, sound like the kind of incident which might well have occurred in the life of a young man of pronounced religious inclinations. The first *sākhī* records how Gurū Nānak was once given a sum of money by his father and sent to use it in trading. The Gurū, however, spent the entire sum in purchasing food for a group of hungry faqīrs whom he happened to meet, and the incident has traditionally been referred to as *kharā saudā*, or the Good Bargain. In the second *sākhī* it is related that Gurū Nānak caused his parents further distress by donating his brass *lotā* and gold wedding ring to a faqīr whom he happened to encounter.

Neither story can be regarded as impossible, but there is nevertheless a serious objection which must be made against both of them. Both are to be found only in the *Bālā* janam-sākhīs. Had the stories been current at the time when the *Miharbān* and *Purātan* accounts took shape it is highly unlikely that either, much less both, would have omitted them, particularly such an interesting incident as the *kharā saudā* story. The conclusion indicated by their omission is that the two *sākhīs* represent a relatively late tradition. This cannot be established beyond all doubt, but it is certainly a strong likelihood and the fact that the *Gyān-ratanāvalī* also omits them strengthens it. The two *sākhīs* must accordingly be regarded as improbable.

The same argument applies to the following six *sākhīs*:

29. Nānak cooks meat at Kurukshetra
35. Mount Govardhan, Mathurā, and Brindāban
44. Ayodhyā: discourse with pandits
45. Gayā
121. Sālas Rāi
123. Discourse with Abdul Rahmān of Iran

All of these, unlike numbers 16 and 17, do appear in the 1891 edition of the *Gyān-ratanāvalī*, but all are clearly borrowings from the *Bālā* tradition. The first of them, number 29, appears to be a case of a situation evolving in order to give an answer to a later dispute concerning vegetarianism. To provide this answer an appropriate *sākhī* has been built around *Vār Malār*, *śloks* 1 and 2 of *pauṛī* 25.[1] Numbers 44 and 45 give precisely the kind of place one would expect the popular imagination to add to the story of Gurū Nānak's travels. Both Ayodhyā and Gayā are among the seven sacred cities of India and their inclusion within Gurū Nānak's itinerary is altogether natural.

The story of Sālas Rāi, the jeweller of Biṣambarpur who was converted by Gurū Nānak, is one which might well be classified with the categorically rejected. It includes elements of the miraculous[2] and it is set in a city which cannot be satisfactorily identified. Kahn Singh regarded Biṣambarpur as Bishnupur, the ancient city in Bankura District, Bengal,[3] whereas Vir Singh and Teja Singh, evidently following the *Nānak Prakāś*, both name Patna as the city of Sālas Rāi.[4] The compiler of the lithographed version of the *Gyān-ratanāvalī* was apparently unaware of either of these possibilities, for the *sākhīs* which concern Sālas Rāi have been inserted at a point which obviously implies a location in western India.[5] The combination of

[1] *AG*, pp. 1289–90. There are interesting divergences with regard to the meat which Gurū Nānak is said to have cooked. The three *Bālā* manuscripts in London all give goat. (IOL MS. Panj. B41, folio 206b; BM MS. Or. 2754. I, folio 198a; and SOAS MS. 104975, folio 218a.) The 1871 lithographed edition, which follows the IOL and BM manuscripts, reproduces exactly the same wording, but replaces *bakari* (goat) with *machhī* (fish) (*Bālā JS*, p. 314). The Dīvān Būṭā Singh expanded 1871 edition, p. 534, gives *mirag* (venison) and this is followed by the corresponding *sākhī* which has been interpolated in the 1891 edition of the *Gyān-ratanāvalī* (p. 135).

[2] An inscribed ruby which enabled Mardānā to find Sālas Rāi.

[3] *MK*, p. 140.

[4] Vir Singh, *Gurū Nānak Chamatakār*, vol. i, pp. 185–93. Teja Singh, *Sikhism: Its Ideals and Institutions*, p. 37. Also Khazan Singh, *History and Philosophy of Sikhism*, vol. i, pp. 82–83.

[5] *GR*, *sākhīs* 99–107, pp. 247–59. Gurū Nānak is at this stage travelling northwards from Ceylon to Bikaner.

legendary content, vague geography, and omission from the older collections renders the whole story most improbable. It is remotely possible that some fragment of truth may underlie the tradition, but if so it is unidentifiable.

36. Nānakmatā

In contrast with the story of Sālas Rāi the *sākhī* concerning Nānakmatā is both present in an early janam-sākhī collection and explicit in terms of location. Nānakmatā, which consists of little more than a temple in the jungle, is located in Satārgañj tahsil of Nainī Tāl District, fifteen miles north-west of Pīlībhīt and ten miles west of Khaṭīmā station on the Rohilkhaṇḍ–Kumāon railway.[1] The possibility that the area was visited by Gurū Nānak cannot be ruled out completely, but it seems much more likely that the tradition recorded by the *Purātan* janam-sākhīs can be traced to the existence of an important Udāsī centre at this spot. Udāsī sādhūs, led by a *mahant* named Almast, evidently evicted Nāth yogīs from this centre during the period of Gurū Hargobind (1606–44) and the name Nānakmatā was almost certainly bestowed by them upon the place.[2] The connexion with Nāth yogīs explains the claim made in later janam-sākhī traditions that the original name was Gorakhmatā.[3] This claim may well be true, but it is most unlikely that the original context was an incident involving Gurū Nānak.

40. Rājā Harināth
61. Rājā Mitr Sain
62. Rājā Jagannāth

These three *sākhīs* all name distinguished people with whom, according to Miharbān, Gurū Nānak held discourses in localities well beyond the Pañjāb. There are no details to support the existence of these three persons, none of the other janam-sākhīs mention them, and their sole function appears to be to provide suitable partners for three Miharbān discourses.

41. Meeting with Kabīr

Encounters with Kabīr are to be found in the *Miharbān Janam-sākhī*[4] and in the B40 manuscript.[5] The *Bālā* tradition also introduces Kabīr, but the *sākhīs* which include such references are evidently of Hindālī origin.[6] As they stand the *Miharbān* and B40 accounts can certainly be rejected. They are completely different, they are vague as far as location is concerned,

[1] *MK*, p. 519. *A Glossary of the Tribes and Castes of the Punjab &c*, vol. 1, p. 679.
[2] G. B. Singh, *Srī Gurū Granth Sāhib diān Prāchīn Birān*, pp. 280–1.
[3] *GR*, p. 207.
[4] *Mih JS*, pp. 154–6.
[5] IOL MS. Panj. B40, folios 136 ff.
[6] See *supra*, p. 23.

they offer no recognizably genuine information concerning Kabīr, and their obvious purpose is to exalt Gurū Nānak by having Kabīr acknowledge his superiority. Traditions which record such a meeting are to be found in Kabīr-panthī literature as well as in the Sikh janam-sākhīs,[1] but these must be similarly rejected. Kabīr-panthī traditions concerning the life of Kabīr are notoriously unreliable and can be accepted only when confirmed by other evidence. In this case there is no such evidence. This means that there is no authentic tradition concerning a meeting between Gurū Nānak and Kabīr.[2]

On the other hand, the chance of a meeting between the two cannot be completely ruled out. We may perhaps doubt whether Kabīr really lived to the year 1518, but we cannot reject the possibility of his having done so.[3] This means that if Gurū Nānak travelled through Banāras he may perhaps have met Kabīr. It is, however, pure conjecture, chronologically possible, but completely devoid of evidence. As such it must be classified as highly improbable.

124. Saidpur: Lālo and Bhāgo

The story of Lālo, the carpenter of Saidpur, is one of the most popular in the entire range of *sākhīs* concerning Gurū Nānak. The tradition relates that while Gurū Nānak was staying with this person of low caste a certain Malik Bhāgo gave a feast to which the Gurū was invited. The invitation was, however, refused and eventually Malik Bhāgo had to resort to constraint. When the Gurū was brought to him he demanded an explanation for the refusal. Gurū Nānak in reply took in one hand a quantity of Malik Bhāgo's rich food, and in the other a piece of Lālo's coarse bread. He then squeezed both. From Lālo's bread trickled milk, but from Malik Bhāgo's food there issued blood. The point of the miracle was obviously to demonstrate that Lālo's food had been earned by honest labour, whereas Bhāgo's was the product of extortion and oppression.

The story itself must be dismissed, in spite of modern efforts to rationalize it,[4] but there remains the question of whether there may in fact have been a carpenter in Saidpur around whom this and other lesser legends have gathered. The answer must be that it is extremely unlikely. In the first place Lālo does not appear in the older janam-sākhīs. Secondly, there is a likely explanation for his entry into the developing stock of traditions

[1] Puruṣottam-lāl Śrīvāstava, *Kabīr Sāhitya kā Adhyayan*, p. 311.

[2] Nor is there adequate evidence to establish that Gurū Nānak knew the works of Kabīr, although this has been commonly assumed. There exists a possibility that he did, but the likelihood is that he did not know them. See W. H. McLeod, 'Gurū Nānak and Kabīr' in *Proceedings of the Punjab History Conference*, 1965, pp. 87–92.

[3] See *infra*, p. 155.

[4] e.g. Kartar Singh, *Life of Guru Nanak Dev*, pp. 83–84. Narain Singh, *Guru Nanak Re-interpreted*, p. 151.

concerning Gurū Nānak. In the *Bālā* janam-sākhīs[1] Lālo is associated with the verse *Tilaṅg* 5 which begins:

jaisī mai āvai khasam kī bānī taisaṛā karī giānu ve lālo.[2]

All seven lines of the first stanza end in this same way with the words *ve lālo*. *Tilaṅg* 5 is one of the *śabads* which describe the suffering caused by Bābur.[3] The earliest traditions associate all of these *Bābar-vāṇī* verses with his attack on Saidpur and this would mean that the words *ve lālo* would be taken to refer to an audience addressed by Gurū Nānak in Saidpur. The words in this case would mean 'O beloved', a common form of poetic address. The next step must then have been to identify the word *lālo* as a proper noun and so in this manner there evidently developed a tradition concerning Lālo of Saidpur. This hypothesis does not completely destroy the tradition of a Saidpur carpenter called Lālo, but it does render it most improbable.

Possible sākhīs

The third category consists of *sākhīs* which cannot be rejected as inherently improbable or definitely impossible, but which must nevertheless be treated with a considerable degree of caution. They are *sākhīs* which offer only limited opportunities for the application of our criteria, and which accordingly cannot be either affirmed or denied, even in terms of probability or improbability. Many of them must be rejected in part, but in all there is at least some basic detail which requires us to withhold judgement.

The most we can say in these cases is that they generally tend towards the improbable rather than the probable. Many of them are the kind of story which inevitably gathers around a person of acknowledged spiritual stature, and there can be no doubt that several of these *sākhīs* will have entered the body of tradition in this manner. The difficulty is that when such accretions are both rationally and chronologically possible there is generally no means of separating them from incidents of a similar nature which may have a foundation in fact. We may well assume that a majority of such *sākhīs* are subsequent additions and that very few would have any factual connexion with Gurū Nānak, but we do not possess the means of determining which should belong to the majority group and which to the minority.

Many more of the *sākhīs* concern Gurū Nānak's travels, and here doubts must arise from the fact that most of the places named are the very locations which one would expect the popular imagination to associate with the

[1] *Bālā JS*, *sākhī* 21, pp. 88–89.

[2] *AG*, p. 722.

[3] See *infra*, p. 135.

wanderings of a person such as the Gurū. Places such as Hardwār, Allahābād, Banāras, Jagannāth Purī, Rāmeśwaram, and Ujjain are precisely the kind of pilgrimage centres one might anticipate. We cannot, however, assume that Gurū Nānak did not visit any of these places. On the contrary, it is safe to assume that he would have visited at least some of them and in a general sense we may accept the tradition, recorded by Bhāī Gurdās and implied by Miharbān, that Gurū Nānak's travels included visits to famous pilgrimage centres.[1]

What we have is the same problem of separating the likely from the unlikely without the means of identifying either. The fact that the incident or discourse which is set in a certain place is manifestly an invention does not prove that Gurū Nānak did not visit that particular place. We may with good reason decide that most of the *incidents* which are recorded of his travels beyond his own province are products of the imagination, but we must also conclude that Gurū Nānak obviously did make lengthy journeys outside the Pañjāb and that accordingly he must certainly have visited at least some of these places.

Most of the *sākhīs* which we shall classify as 'possible' fall into one or other of these two subdivisions. Either they are the kind of story which one inevitably finds associated with the person of a famous saint, or they concern visits to particular places during the Gurū's travels. The first subdivision includes the following:

27. Mardānā commanded to throw offerings away.
33. Sheikh Bajīd.
102. A watchman receives royal authority.
106. The inhospitable village unmolested.
107. The hospitable village dispersed.
111. The devotees of Kiṛīān Paṭhāṇān.
112. Discourse with Mīā Mithā.
114. Dunī Chand's flags.
116. A pious boy.
118. Anabhī the Jain.

Little can be said about any of these. Numbers 106 and 107, which really constitute a single *sākhī*, relate the kind of story which always finds a ready

[1] Gurū Nānak himself offers some support for this tradition.

taṭ tīrath ham nav khaṇḍ dekhe haṭ patan bājārā.

Gauṛī 17, *AG*, p. 156

I have seen places of pilgrimage on river banks, *tīraths*, the nine regions of the earth, shops, cities, markets.

The reference to 'the nine regions of the earth', i.e. the whole world, and the context in which the line occurs indicate that we have here an example of hyperbole, but it seems unlikely that Gurū Nānak would have expressed himself in this manner had he not visited places of pilgrimage. For the context see *infra*, p. 177.

welcome in hagiography and the convenient conjunction of an inhospitable village and a hospitable one strongly suggests legend.[1] The episode is one which indicates the narrowness of the distinction between our 'possible' and 'improbable' categories.

In the case of number 114 a comparison of the account given in the India Office Library manuscript B40[2] with that of the *Colebrooke* and *Hāfizābād* janam-sākhīs[3] shows that the incident has been expanded in the latter, but the kernel of the story remains the same in both versions. In both accounts the point of the story concerns the needle which Gurū Nānak delivered to the rich man, and the expansion of the two *Purātan* janam-sākhīs chiefly concerns the quantity of wealth which the rich man possessed. In the B40 version there are only four flags flying, signifying four treasure chests, whereas the *Purātan* account gives seven flags, each representing a *lākh* of rupees. It is also in this latter account that the name Dunī Chand appears. Once again we are confronted with a story which could possibly have roots in an authentic incident but which must prompt a considerable measure of scepticism.

The second sub-division, that of *sākhīs* which refer to specific places visited by Gurū Nānak, is a large one. The *sākhīs* listed here are those which we are obliged to classify without making detailed analyses. In other cases there are factors which make an examination possible and such *sākhīs* will be considered later.

34. Hardwār: the watering of his fields
37. Allahābād
38. Banāras: disc ourses with paṇḍits
39. Banāras: discourse with Chatur Dās
42. Hājīpur Paṭṇā
48. Jagannāth Purī
52. Rāmeśwaram
63. Ujjain
64. Vindhyā Mountains
65. Narabad River
66. Bīkāner district and city
67. The land of Soraṭhi (Saurāshtra)
68. Mathurā
69. Kurukshetra
71. The Kashmīrī paṇḍit
82. Hiṅglāj
88. The merchant of Dīpālpur
109. Jhaṇḍā Bāḍhī and the *Jugāvalī*

[1] Rattan Singh Jaggi, *Vichār-dhārā*, p. 16.
[2] IOL MS. Panj. B40, folios 189–90.
[3] *Pur JS*, *sākhi* 37, pp. 70–71.

In several cases it is necessary to reject the incident which a *sākhī* relates, but to retain the possibility that Gurū Nānak may have visited the location in which the incident is set. This necessity applies in the case of number 34, the story of how Gurū Nānak confounded the crowds who were devoutly throwing Ganges water towards their forbears.[1] The same story is to be found in earlier Buddhist traditions[2] and is obviously an example of the kind of legend which gains currency among the followers of different religious reformers.[3] The rejection of the actual incident does not, however, mean that the Gurū was never in Hardwār. On the contrary, it is a centre of pilgrimage which, by reason of its fame and proximity to the Pañjāb, he may well have visited.

Other *sākhīs* require, if not total rejection of an incident, at least the setting aside of substantial portions. This applies in the case of number 71, the Kashmīr *sākhī*.[4] It is obviously impossible to accept the story of how Braham Dās was sent in search of a *gurū*, but this certainly does not mean that Gurū Nānak never visited Kashmīr and nor need we conclude that the account of how Braham Dās initially became a convert is necessarily untrue. A considerable degree of doubt will persist as far as the latter aspect is concerned, but in the absence of acceptable evidence either for or against the tradition we must withhold judgement.

Number 109 may also be an example of legend superimposed upon an authentic tradition. The *Purātan Janam-sākhī* presents the story of Jhaṇḍā, the carpenter of Bisīar, as a single *sākhī* which has two distinct parts. Of these the second, which describes the composition of a work called the *Jugāvalī*, may be rejected without hesitation. The *Colebrooke* and *Hāfizābād* accounts differ, both are very corrupt, the poem is said to have been composed on 'an island in the ocean', Gurū Nānak's food at the time is said to have been air, reference is made to an unrecognizable city called Chhuṭhaghāṭakā,[5] and the work recorded in the janam-sākhīs under the title *Jugāvalī* is manifestly spurious.

The first part cannot, however, be dismissed in this manner, for it contains neither the inconsistencies nor the evident fantasy of the second part.

[1] See *supra*, p. 55. Khushwant Singh, *A History of the Sikhs*, vol. i, p. 35, gives a translation of the *sākhī* as it is to be found in the modern version of the *Bālā* tradition. The IOL manuscript Panj. B41 (*Bālā* tradition) and both of the 1871 lithographed editions omit the incident, although the expanded 1871 edition does include a discourse on the banks of the Ganges (Dīvān Būṭā Siṅgh 1871 edition, *sākhī* 250, p. 536).

[2] Thomas Watters, *On Yuan Chwang's Travels in India 629–645 A.D.*, London, Royal Asiatic Society, 1904, vol. i, pp. 320–1. I owe this reference to Dr. J. S. Grewal of Chandigarh.

[3] Another example, to which reference will be made later, is Bhāī Gurdās's account of a visit to Multān. See *infra*, p. 142.

[4] *Pur JS, sākhī* 49, pp. 90–94. See *supra*, pp. 48–49.

[5] This is the *Colebrooke* variant. The *Hāfizābād* manuscript has Chhuṭāghāṭakā. *Pur JS*, p. 46.

Bisīar may perhaps be a version of Bashahr in the Simla Hills[1] and it is possible that Gurū Nānak may once have met a person called Jhaṇḍā Bāḍhī. The fact that the *Miharbān Janam-sākhī* and the *Gyān-ratanāvalī* both omit the incident weakens the tradition, but there is at least a possibility that an actual encounter may underlie it. This first portion of the *sākhī* is very brief in the *Purātan* account. It merely records that in the inhospitable land of Bisīar only Jhaṇḍā gave shelter to Gurū Nānak and Mardānā, that Jhaṇḍā washed the Gurū's feet, that enlightenment dawned on him while he was drinking the water he had used for the washing, and that the experience led him to abandon wordly concerns in favour of a life of wandering.[2] It must, however, be emphasized that this remains mere possibility and that our acknowledgement of the possibility will be strongly tinged with scepticism. It is a scepticism which must be applied to all the incidents listed in this section.

In most of these travel *sākhīs* the geographical information given amounts to no more than the name of a city or locality. Occasionally, however, extra details are added and in rare instances they are supplied in abundance. Additional details of this kind do not necessarily indicate a sound tradition, even if they happen to be substantially accurate. One of the rare cases of abundant geographical detail is Miharbān's *goṣṭ* 91 which is set in Ujjain and which appears in the chart as a part of number 63. The details which it incorporates indicate a knowledge of the locality, but do nothing to strengthen the tradition. There can be no doubt that they represent the personal knowledge of a more recent visitor, not a report handed down from the Gurū himself.

Two *sākhīs* which do not fit either of our sub-divisions but which should be included in the category of 'possible' *sākhīs* are the following:

97. Death of Mardānā
98. Death of Kālū and Tiparā

Two dominant traditions exist concerning the death of Gurū Nānak's companion Mardānā. One is that he died in the year S. 1591 (A.D. 1534) on the banks of the river Kurram in Afghanistan, and that the last rites were performed there by Gurū Nānak himself.[3] The second is that he died in Kartārpur, before the death of Gurū Nānak but evidently towards the close of the Gurū's life. The first of these must be regarded as highly improbable. It is not recorded in any of the older janam-sākhīs and the evidence all suggests that Gurū Nānak's travelling days were well over

[1] This was Macauliffe's assumption (*The Sikh Religion*, i. 93). It is, however, unlikely. In the *Bālā* janam-sākhīs the location is given as 'on an island in the ocean' (*Bālā JS*, p. 193; IOL MS. Panj. B41, folio 88), a statement which accords with the second part of the *Purātan sākhī* and which strongly implies a legendary setting. Moreover, the resemblance of Bisīar, or Bisīhar as in the *Bālā* version, to Bashahr is not really close.

[2] The tradition is greatly expanded in the *Bālā* janam-sākhīs. See *Bala JS*, *sākhī* 34, pp. 142–57.

[3] *Bālā JS*, *sākhī* 59, pp. 280-81, *MK*, p. 714.

by 1534. The second tradition, which is to be found in the *Gyān-ratanāvalī*, cannot be regarded as proven, but it is certainly within the realm of possibility.

The *Gyān-ratanāvalī* tradition concerning the deaths of Kālū and Tiparā seems less likely. Gurū Nānak would have been sixty-nine or seventy at the time of his death and if his parents died only shortly before him they must both have attained advanced ages. The possibility exists, but it is one which tends strongly towards the improbable, particularly in view of the fact that the *Bālā* tradition refers in passing to their deaths at an unspecified but obviously much earlier time.[1]

Eighty-seven *sākhīs* out of the total of 124 listed in the chart have now been summarily classified as either possible, improbable, or impossible. The balance of thirty-seven *sākhīs* consists partly of incidents which can in like manner be assigned to the 'probable' category, and partly of *sākhīs* which can be discussed at some length before being classified. For convenience we may group them as follows:

Dates

1. The birth of Gurū Nānak
100. The death of Gurū Nānak

Family relationships

1. The birth of Gurū Nānak
9. The marriage of Jai Rām and Nānakī
10. Betrothal and marriage
14. Birth of Lakhmī Dās and Sirī Chand

Daulat Khān Lodī and Sultānpur

20. To Sultānpur
21. Work in Daulat Khān's commissariat
22. Immersion in the river: his call
24. The mullah seeks to exorcize his evil spirit
25. Discourse with the qāzī
26. Departure from Sultānpur

Visit to Assam

46. The country ruled by women

Visit to Dacca

47. Dacca

[1] *Bālā JS*, p. 288. The *Gyān-ratanāvalī* also records that Gurū Nānak's wife died fifteen days after her husband (*GR, sākhī* 219, p. 587). The older janam-sākhīs make no reference to her death.

Rājā Śivanābh and Ceylon

18. Bhāgīrath and Mansukh
19. Mansukh and Rājā Śivanābh
54. Rājā Śivanābh and the *Prāṇ Saṅgalī*

A ṭhag converted and the first dharmsālā built

60. Sajjaṇ the *ṭhag*

Discourse with the Siddhs on Mount Sumeru

72. Mount Sumeru

Mecca and Medina

75. The mullah's village
76. Rahīm and Karīm
79. Mecca: the moving mosque
80. Medina

Visit to Baghdad

81. Baghdad

The Emperor Bābur and the sack of Saidpur

83. The sack of Saidpur
84. Discourse with Bābur
85. Bābur attacks Ṭillā Bālgundāī

The conclusion of the travels

86. Return to Talvaṇḍī and reunion with parents

Visit to Pāk Paṭṭan

87. Pāk Paṭṭan: discourse with Sheikh Ibrāhīm

The founding of Kartārpur

89. The proud official humbled: the founding of Kartārpur

Discourses with Siddhs

73. Gorakh-haṭaṛī
90. Achal Baṭālā

Visits to Multān

74. Multān: discourse with a descendant of Pīr Bahāuddīn
91. Multān: the jasmine petal

Gurū Aṅgad

92. First meeting with Lahiṇā
93. Lahiṇā's clothes ruined
95. Lahiṇā becomes Aṅgad
99. The installation of Gurū Aṅgad

Gurū Nānak's date of birth

The janam-sākhīs agree with regard to the year of Gurū Nānak's birth, but there is a difference concerning the actual month and it is one which has resulted in a protracted controversy. The *Miharbān* and *Purātan* traditions, supported by the *Gyān-ratanāvalī*, record that Gurū Nānak was born on the third day of the light half of the lunar month of Vaisākh, S. 1526, a date which corresponds to 15 April A.D. 1469.[1] The *Bālā* janam-sākhīs, on the other hand, give the date as Kattak *Pūran-māsī*, S. 1526, the full-moon day of the month of Kattak, or Kārtik, more than six months later.[2]

The controversy concerns which of these two dates should be accepted as the birthday of the Gurū. A third is given in the *Mahimā Prakāś Kavitā*:

samat bikram nirap ko pandrah sahas pachīs,
vaisākh sudī thit tījā ko parau sant bāp īs.[3]

This gives the third day of the light half of Vaisākh, S. 1525, exactly one year earlier than the date given in the older janam-sākhīs. There seems to be little doubt that this third date must be an error. The suggestion that Sarūp Dās Bhallā, the author of the *Mahimā Prakāś Kavitā*, was using expired instead of current dating[4] cannot possibly be correct as he gives S. 1596 as the date of Gurū Nānak's death,[5] not S. 1595 as would be required by expired dating. Moreover, the older *Mahimā Prakāś Vāratak* gives the year as S. 1526.[6]

Bhāī Gurdās is silent on this particular issue, although it has been claimed that references in his works point unmistakably to a particular date. Proponents of both sides of the controversy have made this claim, each side

[1] *Mih JS*, p. 9. *Pur JS*, p. 1. IOL MS. Panj. B40, folio 1a. *GR*, p. 41. The word *sudī* (light half) is not used, but the word *chānaṇi* (moonlight) indicates the period of the waxing moon.

[2] *Bālā JS*, p. 7. Kattak and Kārtik both designate the eighth lunar month, Kattak being the form commonly used in Pañjābī and Kārtik the form generally used in Hindī. Kattak *Pūran-māsī*, S. 1526, corresponds to 20 Oct. A.D. 1469.

[3] Khalsa College, Amritsar, MS. SHR: 2300A, folio 5a.

[4] Karam Singh, *Kattak ki Visākh*, p. 224 n. *Gurapurb Niraṇay*, pp. 52–54.

[5] Op. cit., folio 143b.

[6] *Mahimā Prakāś Vāratak*, ed. Kirpal Singh, p. 1. Khalsa College, Amritsar, MS. SHR: 2308, folio 1a. It agrees with the *Mahimā Prakāś Kavitā* as far as the day and the month are concerned.

advancing a different reference in support of its case. A few supporters of the Vaisākh dating have argued that a line from stanza 27 of *Vār* 1 indicates the *first* day of Vaisākh as the correct date.

ghari ghari andari dharamasāl hovai kīratanu sadā visoā.

The claim is that the word *visoā* is a cryptic reference to the Gurū's birth having occurred on the day of the Baisākhī festival.[1] It is a claim which has received little support and there can be no doubt that it is incorrect. The translation should read:

In every house a *dharmsālā* was established and *kīrtan* was sung (as if it were) an unending Baisākhī festival.

From the other side of the controversy has come the claim that the first couplet of Bhāī Gurdās's *Kabitt Savayyā* 345 points to Kattak *Pūran-māsī*.

kārtik māsi rut sarad pūranamāsī
aṭh jām sāṭh gharī āj terī bārī hai.

It is the month of Kārtik, the season of coolness. Today, on this day of the full moon, this day of eight *jāms*,[2] of sixty *gharīs*,[3] it is thy turn.

This, it is argued, refers to Gurū Nānak's turn to enter the world, and on the basis of this interpretation it has been claimed that Bhāī Gurdās here testifies to Kattak *Pūran-māsī* as the date of the Gurū's birth.[4]

It is true that this couplet may be interpreted as a reference to a particular person's birth, but it is also true that it may be interpreted as a conventional reference to the month of Kārtik in the style of the *bārah-māhā*, the 'Twelve Month' or calendar poem. The balance of probability must be held to favour the latter. In the first place there is no reference to Gurū Nānak. Secondly, the form is a common one in Pañjābī literature and it would have been an entirely natural one for Bhāī Gurdās to have used. Thirdly, as one would expect in this particular poetic form, the reference is to the present, not to a past event. And fourthly, as we have already observed, the janam-sākhīs which belong to the Bhāī Gurdās period or soon after all specify Vaisākh. In the light of this fourth point the couplet could be admissible as contrary evidence only if it were to point unambiguously to the Kattak date, and this it certainly does not do. The fact that the poem stands in isolation and is not set in the context of a complete *bārah-māhā* does not affect this conclusion. Farīd's *Āsā* 2, which also makes a conventional reference to Kārtik, is not a part of a *bārah-māhā*.[5]

[1] The point is argued by Teja Singh Overseer in *Khālsā Rahit Prakāś*, pp. 73–75.
[2] *jām*, *yām*, or *pahar*: a period of three hours.
[3] A period of twenty-four minutes.
[4] For this argument see Trilochan Singh, article in the *Sikh Review*, vol. xii, no. 2, Feb. 1964, pp. 22–37.
[5] *AG*, p. 488.

Neither the third day in the light half of Vaisākh nor Kattak *Pūran-māsī* can be accepted as established beyond all doubt, but it is clear that of the two the former is much the more likely. The latter is evidently confined to the *Bālā* tradition and to subsequent works based upon it, notably Santokh Singh's *Nānak Prakāś*. It should be added, however, that the case against Kattak *Pūran-māsī* is, for all its strength, not quite as overwhelming as Macauliffe evidently believed. Macauliffe draws attention to what appears to be an interesting error in the *Nānak Prakāś*. Santokh Singh follows the *Bālā* tradition as usual and gives Kattak *Pūran-māsī* as the date of Gurū Nānak's birth,[1] but he also records that the Gurū lived seventy years, five months, and seven days. Counted back from the date which he gives for the Gurū's death[2] this gives a date close to Vaisākh *sudī* 3.[3] The printed editions of the *Nānak Prakāś* do indeed record that Gurū Nānak lived for seventy years, five months, and seven days,[4] but it is doubtful whether Santokh Singh actually wrote this. Vir Singh adds in a footnote that some manuscript copies of the *Nānak Prākāś* omit this reference.[5] The likelihood appears to be that it has been subsequently interpolated in the *Nānak Prakāś*. The inconsistency is patently obvious as it stands and it seems unlikely that Santokh Singh could have failed to perceive it.

Macauliffe describes the manner in which Kattak *Pūran-māsī* came to be generally adopted by the Sikh community,[6] but says nothing about how it ever came to be included in the *Bālā* tradition in the first place. This is not surprising as anything we may say in this respect must be pure conjecture. Karam Singh's theory was that the Hindālīs inserted it as a part of their effort to denigrate Gurū Nānak at the expense of Bābā Hindāl. His suggestion is that they must have had in mind 'the well-known Pañjāb superstition' that births which occur in the months of Bhādron and Kattak are inauspicious.[7] This is no more than a guess and it is unlikely to be correct. There is no evidence to support it, and it assumes a degree of subtlety which is by no means characteristic of the Hindālīs.

It is accordingly impossible to give any satisfactory explanation for the introduction of Kattak *Pūran-māsī*. There remains a possibility that it entered the tradition for the very good reason that it was the actual date

[1] *Nānak Prakāś*, canto 3 (70). In Vir Singh's edition vol. ii, p. 150.

[2] Asū *vadī* 10, S. 1596, the tenth day of the dark half of Asū, S. 1596.

[3] Macauliffe, *The Sikh Religion*, vol. i, p. lxxxiv. The formula is the exact difference between Vaisākh *sudī* 3, S. 1526, and Asū *sudī* 10, S. 1596 (Karam Singh, *Gurapurb Niraṇay*, p. 51).

[4] *Nānak Prakāś*, canto 57 (90). Vir Singh, vol. iv, p. 1255.

[5] Ibid., p. 1255, n.*.

[6] Macauliffe, i. lxxxiv–vi. He does not, however, give any adequate authority for his account of how Bhāī Sant Singh decided to declare Kattak *Pūran-māsī* the authentic date in order to draw Sikhs away from a Hindu fair which was held at Rām Tīrath on that date. He merely records that he owed his information to Bhāī Gurmukh Singh.

[7] Karam Siṅgh, *Kattak ki Visākh*, pp. 224–5.

of Gurū Nānak's birth, but it is a remote possibility. There can be no doubt that its claims to authenticity are much inferior to those of Vaisākh *sudī* 3. This latter dating has the support of all the better sources, whereas Kattak *Pūran-māsī* can be traced to nothing more reliable than the *Bālā* tradition. Most Sikh scholars now accept the Vaisākh date.[1] The only exceptions of any importance are Gyan Singh[2] and Khazan Singh,[3] writers who belong to generations now long past but whose works still exercise some influence. In Gyan Singh's case the adherence to Kattak *Pūran-māsī* is understandable as he produced his significant work before 1885, the year in which both the *Colebrooke* and the *Hāfizābād* manuscripts were published. Khazan Singh, whose *History and Philosophy of Sikhism* was published in 1914, uses Karam Singh's method in reverse. Just as Karam Singh sought in his *Kattak ki Visākh* to establish the Vaisākh date by attacking the whole of the *Bālā* janam-sākhī tradition as totally unreliable in all respects, so Khazan Singh denied it by affirming the reliability of the *Bālā* janam-sākhīs[4] and repudiating those of the *Purātan* tradition.[5]

The weight of evidence and scholarly opinion is thus strongly on the side of the light half of Vaisākh. If a choice is to be made between the two traditional dates the verdict should certainly go to the Vaisākh tradition. It cannot, however, be regarded as established beyond all doubt. There remains the possibility that *both* traditions are incorrect and that the actual date has been lost. The Vaisākh tradition may be regarded as probable, but not as definitively established.

As there is no dispute concerning the year of Gurū Nānak's birth this controversy would be of relatively slight importance were it not for the fact that a definite date must be acknowledged by the Sikh community in order that the anniversary may be celebrated. Kattak *Pūran-māsī* has been firmly entrenched for almost a century and there is little likelihood that the custom of holding the annual celebrations in November will be abandoned in favour of April.

[1] *MK*, p. 519. Teja Singh and Ganda Singh, *A Short History of the Sikhs*, vol. i, p. 2. Khushwant Singh, *A History of the Sikhs*, vol. i, p. 29. Kala Singh Bedi, *Gurū Nānak Darśan*, p. 45. Gopal Singh, *Sri Guru-Granth Sahib*, vol. i, p. xxxv. Sahib Singh, *Srī Gurū Granth Sāhib Darapaṇ*, vol. x, p. 756. Karam Singh's *Kattak ki Visākh* is devoted exclusively to repudiating the Kattak date.

[2] Gyan Singh, *Panth Prakāś* (6th edition), p. 28; *Tavarikh Gurū Khālsā* (3rd edition), vol. i, part i, p. 81. These works have been very influential.

[3] Khazan Singh, *History and Philosophy of Sikhism*, vol. i, pp. 30–35. Other writers who have accepted Kattak *Pūran-māsī* are Lajwanti Rama Krishna, *Les Sikhs*, p. 24, and Sewaram Singh, *The Divine Master*, pp. 18–19.

[4] loc. cit., vol. i, pp. 18–19.

[5] 'The whole work seems to be an incoherent collection of traditions, mostly wrong, and the date of birth recorded is apparently based on hearsay.' Ibid., p. 33. Khazan Singh is a very unreliable writer, but his work has been widely used.

Place of birth

If the testimony of the janam-sākhīs is to be accepted, Gurū Nānak's birth-place was his father's village, Rāi Bhoi dī Talvaṇḍī.[1] The name 'Nānak', however, raises doubts as it implies that the birth must have been in the home of the maternal grandparents.[2] Khushwant Singh accepts the implication as established fact:

> The janamsakhis and the *Mahimā Prakāś* state the place of birth to be "in the house of Mehta Kalu Bedi of Talwandi Rai Bhoe." This statement need not be taken literally. The custom of returning to the maternal home for confinement was well-established in Hindu families. The choice of the name confirms the fact of the birth taking place in the mother's parental home, which was in the village of Kahna Katcha. Cunningham supports this view and bases it on an old manuscript, but without giving its reference. Mehervan's janamsakhi mentions Chahleval near Lahore as Nanak's place of birth.[3]

It is true that the name 'Nānak' strongly implies that the birth took place at the home of the Gurū's maternal grandparents, but it is perhaps going too far to affirm this as proven. As Khushwant Singh indicates, all the janam-sākhīs except that of Miharbān specify Rāi Bhoi dī Talvaṇḍī as the place of birth. Miharbān's record is not clear at this point. The Damdamā Sāhib manuscript does indeed name the village of Chāhalāvāle[4] in the *goṣṭ* which describes the Gurū's birth,[5] but elsewhere it states with equal clarity that Rāi Bhoe kī Talvaṇḍī was the place where he was born.[6] Moreover, the second manuscript in the possession of Khalsa College omits the name Chāhalāvāle[7] and is consistent in specifying Rāi Bhoe kī Talvaṇḍī. It is impossible to say whether Chāhalāvāle is an interpolation in the account recorded by the Damdamā Sāhib manuscript or whether the subsequent references are the interpolations. It may even be that both names were in the original and that what we have here is simply a case of confusion.

We must, however, acknowledge that at some stage there was a tradition abroad that the birth-place was Chāhal and that this tradition may possibly have found expression in the original version of the *Miharbān Janam-sākhī*. This tradition, together with the implication borne by the Gurū's name, points to his mother's village as a strong possibility, but in view of the contrary testimonies of the other janam-sākhīs we cannot affirm it as definitely established. The village indicated in this manner would be

[1] The village is now named Nānakiāṇā Sāhib (sometimes spelt Nankana Sahib). It is situated in the Shekhupurā tahsīl of Lahore District, West Pakistan, approximately forty miles west-south-west of Lahore city.

[2] The word *nānā* means 'maternal grandfather' and *nānak* may be used as a common noun to mean 'a mother's family or lineage'.

[3] *A History of the Sikhs*, vol. i, p. 30, n. 11.

[4] The village of Chāhal, the traditional birthplace of Gurū Nānak's mother, is near Barakī in the district and tahsīl of Lahore. *MK*, p. 345.

[5] *Mih JS*, *goṣṭ* 4, p. 9.

[6] Ibid., pp. 52 and 470.

[7] Ibid., p. 9, n. 4.

Chāhal, not Kahnā Katchā as given by Khushwant Singh and also by Cunningham.[1]

Gurū Nānak's date of death

Just as there is disagreement between the janam-sākhīs concerning the date of Gurū Nānak's birth, so too there is disagreement regarding the date of his death. The divergence is more serious in this latter case, for it involves not simply a difference in the precise date given, but a disagreement concerning the actual year. Three dates are given. The *Purātan* janam-sākhīs give Asū *sudī* 10, S. 1595, the tenth day of the light half of the month of Asū, S. 1595, which would have fallen during September A.D. 1538.[2] The *Gyān-ratanāvalī* also gives Asū *sudī* 10 as the day of the month, but records that the year was S. 1596 (A.D. 1539).[3] The third date is that given in such of the *Bālā* janam-sākhīs as carry their accounts as far as his death. This tradition agrees with the *Gyān-ratanāvalī* as far as the year is concerned, but gives the actual date as Asū *vadī* 10, the tenth day of the *dark* half of Asū, fifteen days earlier than the *Gyān-ratanāvalī* date.[4]

These are the three dates and opinion has been divided concerning which of them has the stronger claims. Some writers have accepted the *Purātan* dating,[5] others follow the *Gyān-ratanāvalī*,[6] and a few the date which is to

[1] J. D. Cunningham, *A History of the Sikhs* (1st edition, 1849), p. 40, n. Khushwant Singh does not state whether he is here following Cunningham and the latter's unidentified manuscript, or whether he bases his statement on some other source. W. L. M'Gregor's *The History of the Sikhs*, which was published in 1846, gives 'the village of Maree, which is near Kot Kutchwa' as the place where the Gurū was born (loc. cit., vol. i, p. 32).

[2] *Pur JS*, p. 115. MS. no. 2310A of the Sikh History Research Department, Khalsa College, Amritsar, is a *Purātan* manuscript which gives S. 1596 as the year of Gurū Nānak's death (loc. cit., folio 185a). This manuscript was, however, written in S. 1829 (A.D. 1772) by which time the 1596 dating was well established in Sikh tradition. The *Colebrooke* and *Hāfizābād* manuscripts obviously represent the authentic *Purātan* tradition at this point and they are supported by the IOL manuscript Panj. B40 (folio 230). Moreover, the Khalsa College manuscript is evidently prone to error as far as recording dates is concerned, for it gives Gurū Nānak's year of birth as S. 1536 (A.D. 1479) instead of S. 1526 (folio 1a). MS. no. 2913 of the Central Public Library, Paṭiālā, is another *Purātan* manuscript which gives S. 1596 (folio 276a). In this case it is obvious that the figure 6 has been written over an original 5.

[3] *GR*, p. 587. Karam Singh, *Gurapurb Niraṇay*, pp. 47–49 and 57, gives 22 September A.D. 1539, as the exact equivalent of Asū *sudī* 10, S. 1596.

[4] SOAS, MS. no. 104975, folio 303. *Bālā JS*, p. 402. The expanded 1871 edition (Dīvān Būṭā Singh, Lahore), p. 587, gives the year as 1546 which may be either a simple error or an unsuccessful attempt made by the printer to convert the date given in the manuscripts to Christian reckoning.

[5] Macauliffe, op. cit., vol. i, p. 191. Indubhusan Banerjee, *Evolution of the Khalsa*, vol. i, p. 22. Volker Moeller, article 'Die Lebensdaten des Glaubensstifters Nanak' in the *Indo-Iranian Journal*, vol. vii, 1964, no. 4, p. 295. Mohan Singh, *A History of Panjabi Literature*, p. 23.

[6] *MK*, p. 519. Teja Singh and Ganda Singh, op. cit., vol. i, p. 17. Khushwant Singh, op. cit., vol. i, p. 37. Karam Singh, *Gurapurb Niraṇay*, p. 57. Sahib Singh, *Srī Gurū Granth Sāhib Darapaṇ*, vol. x, p. 759.

be found in some of the *Bālā* janam-sākhīs.[1] At this point the *Miharbān Janam-sākhī* offers no help as only the first three of its six sections have been found.[2] The last of the six presumably gave a date for the Gurū's death. The two versions of the *Mahimā Prakāś* are once again in conflict, the *Mahimā Prakāś Vāratak* supporting the *Bālā* tradition[3] and the *Mahimā Prakāś Ḳavitā* offering the same date as the *Gyān-ratanāvalī*.[4]

In an issue involving conflicting evidence from the *Purātan* tradition, the *Gyān-ratanāvalī*, and some *Bālā* janam-sākhīs, the usual procedure would be to accept the *Purātan* testimony as the most likely to be correct. In this particular case, however, the *Bālā* testimony is strengthened by other evidence. Indeed, this other evidence probably predates the references given in some *Bālā* janam-sākhīs, and should accordingly be regarded as the basis of the Asū *vadī* 10 claim. The absence of any account of Gurū Nānak's death in many *Bālā* manuscripts indicates that the date given in some versions has been introduced subsequently, and that the *Bālā* testimony should be regarded as supporting evidence, not as the actual foundation of the claim.

The primary evidence supporting Asū *vadī* 10, S. 1596, is to be found in manuscript copies of the *Ādi Granth*. Many of the extant manuscript copies of the *Ādi Granth* include lists of the dates on which each of the ten Gurūs died, and the testimony of these lists strongly favours the Asū *vadī* 10 dating.[5] It is true that practically all of these manuscripts are later than the period of the *Purātan* tradition, and that a large number must have been copied after the *Gyān-ratanāvalī* emerged, but this claim cannot be made in the case of the manuscript held by the Soḍhī family of Kartārpur,[6] the manuscript which is traditionally believed to be the original copy of the *Ādi Granth* dictated by Gurū Arjan to Bhāī Gurdās in 1603–4. This Kartārpur manuscript contains a list which gives the date of Gurū Nānak's death as Asū *vadī* 10, S. 1596,[7] and it is this entry which must be regarded as the primary evidence for the third of the conflicting dates.[8]

[1] Khazan Singh, op. cit., vol. i, p. 106. Kartar Singh, *Life of Guru Nanak Dev*, p. 263. J. C. Archer, *The Sikhs*, p. 65, unaccountably gives 1540 as the date of Gurū Nānak's death. There is no support for this date.

[2] See *supra*, p. 19.

[3] *Mahimā Prakāś Vāratak*. ed. Kirpal Singh, p. 38. Khalsa College, Amritsar, MS. SHR: 2308, folio 15b.

[4] Khalsa College, Amritsar, MS. SHR: 2300A, folios 143b–4a.

[5] All of the manuscript copies seen by the writer which include such a list give Asū *vadi* 10, S. 1596, as the date of Gurū Nānak's death. There are six such copies in London, five of them in the IOL (MSS. Panj. C3, C5, D2, D3, and F1) and one in the BM. (Or. 2159). If such a list is included it always follows immediately after the *tatkarā* (table of contents).

[6] This is not the Kartārpur in which Gurū Nānak spent his later years, but a town in Jullundur District founded by Gurū Arjan.

[7] *samatu 1596 aṃsū vadi 10 srī bābā nānak dev jī samāṇe*. Loc. cit., folio 25b.

[8] The Kartārpur manuscript is no longer available for public scrutiny, but access has been possible in the past. The author owes this reference to Dr. Bhāī Jodh Singh who himself made a copy from the manuscript.

It must, of course, be acknowledged that the entry in the Kartārpur manuscript may have been made appreciably later than the actual writing of the manuscript, and that accordingly we cannot accept the date it gives as definitely established. The nature of the entry does not, however, suggest a significantly later addition. Were this the case one would expect a uniformity of style in the complete list, whereas what the list actually contains is uniformity of calligraphy and pen in the case of the first four entries,[1] the same calligraphy but a finer pen in the case of Gurū Arjan's own date, and then an entirely different style for the two remaining names.[2] This suggests that the first four entries were made prior to the death of Gurū Arjan in S. 1663 (A.D. 1606). The point cannot be accepted as conclusively proven, but it does appear to be at least a likelihood.

This indicates Asū *vadī* 10, S. 1596, as the most likely of the three conflicting dates. The measure of uncertainty which must be attached to our interpretation of the entry in the Kartārpur manuscript requires a corresponding uncertainty in the case of the date which it gives and we must also acknowledge the possibility that all three dates are incorrect. The convergence upon the month of Asū suggests, however, that this latter possibility is a remote one. We may conclude that Gurū Nānak probably died on the tenth day of the dark half of Asū, S. 1596, a date which corresponds to 7 September, A.D. 1539. All accounts agree that he died in Kartārpur and this may accordingly be accepted as established. Needless to say, the miraculous disappearance of his body is legend. A similar story is recorded in the case of Kabīr.[3]

Family Relationships

The janam-sākhīs all give the names of at least a few of Gurū Nānak's relatives. As one might expect, the briefest list is that which may be compiled from the *Purātan* janam-sākhīs, and the longest that of the *Bālā* janam-sākhīs. The relatives mentioned in the various janam-sākhīs are as follows:

1. *Purātan janam-sākhīs*

Father:	Kālū, a Bedī khatrī of Rāi Bhoi dī Talvaṇḍī.[4]
Mother:	Referred to but not named.[5]

[1] Gurū Nānak, S. 1596 (A.D. 1539); Gurū Aṅgad, S. 1609 (A.D. 1552); Gurū Amar Dās, S. 1631 (A.D. 1574); Gurū Rām Dās, S. 1638 (A.D. 1581).

[2] Bābā Gurdittā, the elder son of Gurū Hargobind, S. 1695 (A.D. 1638); and Gurū Hargobind, S. 1701 (A.D. 1644). The differences in style and pen were noted by Dr. Jodh Singh when making his copy.

[3] Ahmad Shah, *The Bījak of Kabīr*, p. 28. G. W. Briggs records similar stories in connexion with Daryā Shāh of Uderolā, the founder of the Dayānāth Panth of Kānphaṭ yogīs, and of Ratannāth of Peshawar, a disciple of Bhartṛharī (*Gorakhnāth and the Kānphaṭa Yogīs*, pp. 65, 66).

[4] *Pur JS*, p. 1.

[5] Ibid., p. 8.

Sister: Referred to but not named.[1]

Sister's husband: Jai Rām.[2]

Wife: Referred to but not named.[3]

Wife's father: Mūlā, a Chonā khatrī.[4]

Sons: Lakhmī Dās and Sirī Chand.[5]

2. *Miharbān Janam-sākhī*

Father: Kālū, a Bedī khatrī of Rāi Bhoe kī Talvaṇḍī.[6]

Mother: Tiparā.[6]

Sister: Not mentioned but plainly indicated in a reference to Jai Rām as Gurū Nānak's *bahaṇoī*.[7]

Sister's husband: Jai Rām, an Uppal khatrī employed as steward by Daulat Khān Lodī of Sultānpur.[8]

Wife: Ghumī.[9]

Wife's father: Mūlā, a Choṇā khatrī of Baṭālā[10] and formerly of the village Pokho dī Randhāvī.[11]

Sons: Lakhmī Dās and Sirī Chand.[12]

3. *Gyān-ratanāvalī*

Father: Kālū, a Bedī khatrī of Rāi Bhoi kī Talvaṇḍī[13]

Mother: Tripatā.[13]

Sister: Nānakī.[14]

Sister's husband: Jai Rām.[14]

Wife: Referred to but not named.[14]

Wife's father: Mūlā, a Choṇā khatrī of Baṭālā.[14]

Sons: Sirī Chand and Lakhmī Dās.[15]

4. *Bālā janam-sākhīs*

Father: Kālū,[16] or Mahitā Kālū,[17] a Bedī khatrī and *paṭvārī*[18] of Rāi Bhoi dī Talvaṇḍī.

Mother: Tripatā.[19]

[1] *Pur JS*, p. 13. [2] Ibid., p. 12. [3] Ibid., p. 8. [4] Ibid., p. 6.
[5] Ibid., p.7. [6] *Mih JS*, p. 9. [7] Sister's husband. Ibid., p. 72.
[8] Ibid., p. 72. [9] Ibid., p. 67. [10] Ibid., p. 29. [11] Ibid., p. 516.
[12] Ibid., p. 73. [13] *GR*, p. 45. [14] Ibid., p. 112. [15] Ibid., p. 113.
[16] *Bālā JS*, p. 7. [17] Ibid., p. 8.
[18] The village land accountant. Ibid., p. 14.
[19] Expanded 1871 edition (Dīvān Būṭā Singh, Lahore), p. 5. The *Bālā JS* and the IOL MS. Panj B41 refer to her simply as *Bibī Kālū di isatri* (*Bālā JS*, p. 9) or as *Amā Bibī*, 'the Lady Mother' or 'the revered Mother' (ibid., p. 30).

Maternal grandfather:	Rām, a Jhaṅgaṛ khatrī.[1]
Maternal grandmother:	Bhirāī.[1]
Father's brother:	Lālū.[2]
Father's brother's son:	Nand Lāl.[3]
Mother's brother:	Kriṣṇa.[1]
Sister:	Nānakī.[4]
Sister's husband:	Jai Rām, a Paltā khatrī.[4]
Sister's husband's father:	Paramānand.[5]
Wife:	Sulakhaṇī.[6]
Wife's father:	Mūlā, a Choṇā khatrī and *paṭvārī* of Pokho di Randhāvī.[5]
Wife's mother:	Chando Raṇī.[7]
Sons:	Sirī Chand and Lakhmī Dās.[8]

Family memories are long in the Pañjāb and it is accordingly safe to assume that at least the two older janam-sākhīs are generally reliable in the information they give concerning the family of Gurū Nānak. All of the janam-sākhīs agree that his father was Kālū, a khatrī by caste and a Bedī by sub-caste, who lived in the village of Rāi Bhoi dī Talvaṇḍī. This may be accepted without reservation, and we may regard as at least possible the *Bālā* information that he was a *paṭvārī*, or village land accountant. The statement is confined to the *Bālā* janam-sākhīs, but it does receive some support from the *Miharbān Janam-sākhī* which records that Kālū was employed in *chākarī*[9] and which implies that the position was one which commanded at least a moderate measure of respect.[10] In the same manner we may also accept Tripatā as the name of his mother. The Tiparā form given by Miharbān is obviously a variant and a rather less likely one than the relatively common Tripatā, or Triptā.

His sister's name, which in the *Gyān-ratanāvalī* and the *Bālā* janam-sākhīs

[1] Ibid., p. 36.
[2] Ibid., p. 4.
[3] IOL MS. Panj. B41, folio 30a.
[4] *Bālā JS*, p. 22.
[5] Ibid., p. 30.
[6] The name is used only once in the IOL manuscript B41 and in the *Bālā JS* (*Bālā JS*, p. 48). Elsewhere in these two relatively early *Bālā* versions she is referred to as *Mātā Choṇī*, her family name.
[7] *Bālā JS*, p. 48.
[8] Ibid., p. 52.
[9] Employment in civil administration.
[10] *Mih JS*, p. 70.

is given as Nānakī, is perhaps a little more doubtful. It is clear that Gurū Nānak had a sister, but neither of the older janam-sākhīs name her, and in the *Gyān-ratanāvalī* the name appears in the context of a brief incident which is plainly legend and which may well be one of the later additions to the janam-sākhī.[1] On the other hand, no source offers an alternative name and it seems reasonable to accept the name Nānakī as at least probable.[2]

All of the janam-sākhīs agree that the sister's husband was called Jai Rām and that he was employed as a *modī*, or steward, by Daulat Khān Lodī of Sultānpur. There is, however, disagreement concerning his sub-caste. Miharbān refers to him as an Uppal khatrī and the *Bālā* janam-sākhīs as a Paltā khatrī. Of these the former appears to be the more likely. Miharbān is almost always more reliable than the *Bālā* record, and in this particular instance it is probable that as a descendant of the third and fourth Gurūs he would have had access to trustworthy information.

The name of Gurū Nānak's wife also seems, at first sight, to present a disagreement. Miharbān calls her Ghumī, whereas the *Bālā* tradition refers to her as Sulakhaṇī. The *Miharbān* form is, however, merely a corruption of Choṇī, the name of her sub-caste and the name which, in accordance with prevailing custom, would have been her usual designation. There is thus no conflict, and although the name Sulakhaṇī does not appear until relatively late in the janam-sākhī records there is no reason to dispute it. Family traditions can be safely trusted in this respect and there is no alternative name offered in the janam-sākhīs.

The janam-sākhīs are, however, in disagreement concerning the time of the Gurū's marriage to Sulakhaṇī, or Mātā Choṇī. The *Bālā* tradition dates it after he had gone to Sultānpur and secured employment there under Daulat Khān,[3] whereas the other three all record it prior to his departure from Talvaṇḍī. The *Purātan* janam-sākhīs give his age as twelve at the time of his marriage (A.D. 1481–2)[4] and the *Gyān-ratanāvalī* as fourteen (A.D. 1483–4).[5] Miharbān gives it as 'fifteen or sixteen' and states that the betrothal ceremony commenced on the first day of the dark half of Vaisākh, S. 1542.[6] The wedding evidently followed soon after, which would mean

[1] *GR*, *sākhī* 50, p. 113. It is recorded that Gurū Nānak caused Nānaki to conceive a son and a daughter by giving her a clove and a cardamom. He then caused his own wife to conceive two sons by giving her two cloves.

[2] This and other doubtful points relating to the family connexions of Gurū Nānak may one day be settled with the aid of the family records kept by the line of Bedī family *pāṇḍās*, or brāhmaṇ genealogists, in Hardwār. The common custom of regularly reporting genealogical details to a family *pāṇḍā* has been followed by the Bedīs and it is reasonable to assume that the details relating to Gurū Nānak's own generation must have once been recorded in Hardwār. Efforts to trace these records have so far failed. but they may yet be uncovered. The Bedī family *pāṇḍā* also serves the Soḍhīs, the family to which all the Gurūs from Gurū Rām Dās onwards belonged

[3] *Bālā JS*, *sākhī* 12, pp. 43–46.

[4] *Pur JS*, p. 6.

[5] *GR*, p. 112.

[6] *Mih JS*, p. 29.

that both betrothal and marriage took place, according to this account, in A.D. 1485. The *Miharbān Janam-sākhī* and the *Gyān-ratanāvalī* both give Baṭālā as the place where the wedding was held.

The unanimous testimony of the *Miharbān* and *Purātan* janam-sākhīs and the *Gyān-ratanāvalī* is certainly to be preferred to that of the *Bālā* tradition and we may accordingly conclude that the marriage probably took place before Gurū Nānak moved from Talvaṇḍī to Sultānpur. We may also accept Baṭālā as the place where it was held. The actual date must, however, be regarded with more caution. The period indicated by Miharbān and the *Gyān-ratanāvalī* (A.D. 1483–5) would be entirely possible, but both accounts show much evidence of the writers' imaginations and it may be that these were the sources of the dates which they give. Moreover, in their accounts of Gurū Nānak's early life both tend to attach consecutive ages to each successive *sākhī* and there can be no doubt that most, if not all, of these must be rejected.

All four versions are consistent in their descriptions of Gurū Nānak's father-in-law, and we may accordingly accept that he was Mūlā, a khatrī of the Choṇā sub-caste, originally from the village of Pokho di Randhāvī[1] but resident in Baṭālā at the time of the marriage. The *Bālā* account adds that he was a *paṭvārī* which may be correct but is more likely to be a transference from the tradition concerning Kālū.

The janam-sākhīs are also unanimous in naming two sons, Lakhmī Dās and Sirī Chand, as the Gurū's only children and there can be no doubt that this is also correct. The chief difference in the four accounts is that the two older versions imply that Lakhmī Dās was the elder,[2] whereas the two later versions explicitly state that Sirī Chand was born first.

This is as far as the *Miharbān* and *Purātan* janam-sākhīs and the *Gyān-ratanāvalī* take us. The *Bālā* janam-sākhīs add the names of several other relatives, but in the absence of support from any of the other accounts most of these must be regarded with some doubt. Lālū we may perhaps accept as at least probable. It is strange that Miharbān should have omitted all reference to a brother of Kālū had he in fact existed, but the name is firmly implanted in Bedī family tradition.

The traditions of the Bedī family may also be admitted as strong evidence in the case of Kālū's immediate forbears. These traditions record that the parents of Kālū were named Śiv Rām (or perhaps Śiv Narāyan) and Banārasī. Śiv Rām's father's name is given as Rām Narāyan of Dehrā Sāhib in the tahsīl of Taran Tāran, and he in turn is said to have been the son of Abhoj. Kālū's name is also given as Kaliyāṇ Rāi.[3]

[1] On the left bank of the Rāvī, near the town of Dehrā Bābā Nānak.

[2] They refer to both births in a single sentence, naming Lakhmī Dās first and Sirī Chand second.

[3] Kala Singh Bedi, *Gurū Nānak Daraśan*, pp. 268–71. *MK*, p. 830. See also the *Nānak Prakāś*, canto 3: 48, 50. Kala Singh Bedi, op. cit., pp. 271–2, also provides a family tree

Finally there are the names of two people who were not actually related to Gurū Nānak but who were, according to the janam-sākhī accounts, very closely associated with him. The first is Rāi Bulār, traditionally regarded as a son of the Rāi Bhoi, or Rāi Bhoā, whose name generally appears in references to Gurū Nānak's village. Most of the janam-sākhīs record that Rāi Bulār was the village landlord during Gurū Nānak's early years, and that he perceived in the young man signs of spiritual greatness which had evidently escaped Kālū.

The record of the janam-sākhīs concerning Rāi Bulār has been universally accepted, but there are reasons why it should be treated with some caution. In the first place, Miharbān states that the landlord during Gurū Nānak's early life was Rāi Bhoā, not Rāi Bulār.[1] Secondly, the *Purātan* references to Rāi Bulār are to be found in *sākhīs* which are manifestly unhistorical.[2] Thirdly, Bhāi Gurdās makes no mention of him in his list of Gurū Nānak's more important followers.[3]

These reasons do not mean that Rāi Bulār never existed, and nor do they necessarily mean that the role assigned to him in most of the janam-sākhīs must be rejected. What they do indicate is that we can no longer accept the janam-sākhī descriptions of him as beyond doubt. They may be basically correct, but there also exists the definite possibility that they are false.

This does not, however, apply to the second of the two close associates, Mardānā the Mirāsī.[4] Mardānā figures much more prominently in the janam-sākhīs than Rāi Bulār and Bhāī Gurdās refers to him explicitly as one of the Gurū's prominent followers.[5] His association with Gurū Nānak may be accepted without hesitation.

Daulat Khān Lodī and Sultānpur

The janam-sākhīs all record that while still a relatively young man Gurū Nānak spent a period in the town of Sultānpur,[6] working there for Daulat Khān Lodī.[7] The account is basically the same in all four janam-sākhī

showing the descendants of Lakhmī Dās. Sirī Chand, as the founder of the Udāsī sect of sādhūs, was celibate.

[1] *Mih JS*, p. 25.

[2] The restored field (*Pur JS*, *sākhī* 4, pp. 6–7); the tree's stationary shadow (ibid., *sākhī* 5, p. 7). He appears much more frequently in the *Bālā* janam-sākhīs.

[3] *Vār* 11, stanzas 13–14.

[4] Mirāsī or Ḍūm: a depressed Muslim caste of genealogists and musicians.

[5] *Vār*. 11, stanza 13.

[6] The town is situated in the Jullundur Doab, sixteen miles south of Kapūrthalā and near the confluence of the Satluj and Beās rivers. Its situation on the imperial high road between Delhi and Lahore made it a town of considerable importance during Mughal times. It was sacked by Nādir Shāh in 1739 and never recovered its former prosperity. *Punjab State Gazetteers* (*Kapurthala State*), vol. XIVA, p. 45.

[7] The *Purātan* janam-sākhīs do not append Lodī, referring to him simply as Nawāb Daulat Khān. There can, however, be no doubt that their reference is to Daulat Khān

traditions. All relate that Gurū Nānak moved to Sultānpur at the invitation of his brother-in-law Jai Rām, who was employed as a steward by Daulat Khān. Jai Rām commended Nānak to his employer and secured for him a position in Daulat Khān's commissariat. Some time later, while bathing in a nearby river,[1] Nānak was carried away to God's presence and there charged with the task of preaching the divine Name. Emerging from the river three days later he uttered the words, 'There is neither Hindu nor Muslim'. The local qāzī regarded this as an insult to the faith of Islam, and Nānak was brought to account before Daulat Khān. After successfully defending himself he left Sultānpur with Mardānā and began his travels.

All of the accounts include miraculous material which must be discarded,[2] but with the exception of the immersion in the river such material concerns only the details of the story and its rejection leaves the basis unaltered. The interview with God during a period of three days spent submerged in the river must also be rejected as it stands, but the incident is one which permits a rational interpretation. It would be entirely reasonable to regard the janam-sākhī accounts as the descendants of an authentic tradition concerning a personally decisive and perhaps ecstatic experience, a climactic culmination of years of searching issuing in illumination and in the conviction that he had been called to proclaim divine truth to the world. With this modification the story becomes wholly credible and we must now decide whether or not it can be accepted.

The evidence in this case leads us to regard the Sultānpur interlude as highly probable. In the first place it concerns events which took place in the Pañjāb. As we have already observed, traditions which relate to incidents or episodes within the province are generally more reliable than those which concern areas beyond its borders, for in such cases the corporate memory of the community can play a significant part. Although legend accumulates quickly it may be doubted whether such an important episode would be completely without foundation.

Secondly, the janam-sākhīs are unanimous as far as the basic details are concerned. Bhāī Gurdās does not refer to this period, but he does mention Daulat Khān as one of Gurū Nānak's followers.[3]

Lodī, and in the case of the *Miharbān Janam-sākhī* and Bhāī Gurdās it is explicit (*Mih JS*, p. 72, and *Vār* 11. 13).

[1] The janam-sākhīs do not name the river, but it would presumably be the Veīn, a small stream which flows past Sultānpur.

[2] Some elements are more accurately described as hagiographic anecdotes rather than as straight miracle stories. A particularly popular one is a late tradition which relates how Gurū Nānak, when distributing commodities in the commissariat, occasionally failed to get past the number thirteen. The word for thirteen (*terān*, or *terah*) is very similar to the word for 'thine' (*terā*) and having uttered the word *terān* the Gurū would sometimes fall into a trance and continue repeating the word *terā*.

[3] *Vār* 11. 13.

Thirdly there is the testimony of the *Dabistān-i-Mazāhib* to strengthen that of the janam-sākhīs.

Before the victory of the late Emperor (Babar) he (Nanak) was a *Modi* to Daulat Khan Lodhi, who was one of the high officials of Ibrahim Khan Emperor of Delhi. And, Modi is an official in charge of the granary.[1]

Fourthly, there is nothing in what we know of Daulat Khān Lodī which conflicts with the tradition. He occupied a position of considerable importance during the later years of Sultan Sikandar Lodī (1489–1517) and during the reign of Sikandar's successor, Ibrāhīm Lodī (1517–26), but nothing explicit appears to have been recorded of his early life up to his appointment as governor of Lahore at the very beginning of the sixteenth century. Bābur describes him in a brief, misleading paragraph.

This Tātār Khān, the father of Daulat Khān, was one of six or seven *sardārs* who, sallying out and becoming dominant in Hindūstān, made Buhlūl Pādshāh. He held the country north of the Satluj [*sic*] and Sarhind, the revenues of which exceeded 3 *krūrs*. On Tātār Khān's death, Sl. Sikandar (*Lūdī*), as overlord, took those countries from Tātār Khān's sons and gave Lāhūr only to Daulat Khān. That happened a year or two before I came into the country of Kābul (910 A.H.).[2]

This is incorrect in that it allows no gap between Tātār Khān and Daulat Khān in the government of Lahore, other than the indefinite reference to 'Tātār Khān's sons'. The *Tārīkh-i-Salātīn-i-Afghānā* and the *Tārīkh-i-Dāūdī* record that shortly before Bahlūl Lodī's death in 1489 Tātār Khān, who had risen in rebellion, was defeated and killed by Nizām Khān, the future Sultan Sikandar.[3] The omission of this incident from other chronicles, notably from the *Tabaqāt-i-Akbarī*, raises an element of doubt concerning its authenticity, but it seems clear that there was a break between the termination of Tātār Khān's governorship and the beginning of Daulat Khān's period, for Daulat Khān's appointment must have been made after the incumbent governor, Sa'īd Khān Sarwānī, was exiled in 1500 for his part in a conspiracy against Sultan Sikandar.[4] In other words, there must have been at least one other governor between Tātār Khān and Daulat Khān.

Bābur does, however, confirm that Daulat Khān was the son of Tātār Khān, and this would mean a connexion with Pañjāb administration prior to 1500. Apart from the janam-sākhīs there appears to be no hint of what

[1] Ganda Singh, *Nanak Panthis*, p. 4. The corresponding reference for Shea and Troyers' translation of the *Dabistān* is vol. ii, p. 247.

[2] A. S. Beveridge, *The Bābur-nāma in English*, vol. i, p. 383.

[3] *Tārīkh-i-Salātīn-i-Afghānā*, extract translated in N. Roy's *Niamatullah's History of the Afghāns*, part i, pp. 107–9. *Tārīkh-i-Dāūdī* in Elliot and Dowson, *The History of India as told by its own Historians*, vol. iv, pp. 440–4.

[4] *Tabaqāt-i-Akbarī*, trans. B. De, p. 369. *Tārīkh-i-Khān Jahānī*, in Elliot and Dowson, *The History of India as told by its own Historians*, vol. v, p. 96.

this connexion meant in terms of actual responsibility or achievement. Mrs. Beveridge twice states that he was the founder of Sultānpur,[1] but she does not name her source and neither the Persian chronicles nor the *Bābur-nāma* appear to offer this information. According to the *Kapurthala State Gazetteer* the town was founded in the eleventh century by Sultān Khān Lodī, a general of Sultan Mahmūd of Ghaznī.[2] It goes on to add that this information is 'according to tradition', but of these two possible origins it appears to be the more likely. The difficulty is that Mrs. Beveridge had access to the *Gazetteers* and she was certainly not inclined to make categorical statements without first ascertaining their basis. In one other case, however, she does err in her identification of a Pañjāb town[3] and it seems likely that her statements concerning the origin of Sultānpur represent another such error. It is possible that the janam-sākhīs are the ultimate source of her statements, although none of them records that Daulat Khān founded the town.

The most we can accept concerning Daulat Khān's life prior to his lengthy term as governor of Lahore is that his relationship to Tātār Khān must have meant a position of some standing in the Pañjāb, and that his appointment to Lahore would have been made within the first four years of the sixteenth century. The earliest possible date would be 1500, the year in which Sa'īd Khān Sarwānī was expelled. Bābur's reference to 'a year or two before I came into the country of Kābul' implies 1502 or 1503, as his arrival in Kābul in 910 A.H. corresponds to A.D. 1504. There is, however, an element of vagueness in his expression. An appointment soon after Sa'īd Khān Sarwānī's expulsion seems more likely.

These two conclusions certainly do not establish a connexion between Daulat Khān Lodī and Sultānpur prior to 1500, and if considered apart from the janam-sākhī tradition they do not even imply one. They do, however, render it at least possible. An appointment to Lahore in 1500 or shortly after would fit the chronology of Gurū Nānak's early life in the sense that the association, if it actually took place, must have been prior to this date.

The evidence available seems to indicate a two-fold conclusion. In the first place, we may accept as established the tradition that Gurū Nānak, as a young man, spent a period in Sultānpur, working in the employment of the nawāb of that town. The location of the incident within the Pañjāb and the basic unanimity of the janam-sākhīs appear to justify this conclusion. Secondly, we may accept as probable the claim that this nawāb was Daulat Khān Lodī. In this respect an element of doubt must remain, for it is possible that the connexion may have arisen through Daulat Khān's

[1] A. S. Beveridge, op. cit., vol. i, p. 442, and vol. ii, p. 461, n. 3.

[2] *Punjab State Gazetteers* (*Kapurthala State*), vol. XIVA, p. 45. Muhammad Nazim makes no reference to a general called Sultān Khān Lodī in his *The Life and Times of Sultān Mahmūd of Ghazna*.

[3] See *infra*, p. 133.

undoubted association with Sultānpur in 1524,[1] or through the common tendency to introduce associations with persons of acknowledged stature. The reference in Bhāī Gurdās and the *Dabistān* indicate, however, an unusually strong tradition and the external evidence raises no objections to its acceptance.

The visit to Assam

With the significant exception of Miharbān, all the janam-sākhīs include a *sākhī* which describes a visit to a country ruled by female magicians. The accounts vary in several respects, but the basis of the story is the same in all of them. All relate that Mardānā, who went ahead of the Gurū to beg for food, was put under a spell by one of these enchantresses and turned into a sheep. When the Gurū went in search of him efforts were made to work magic on him also, but to no effect. The women eventually acknowledged his superior power and made their submission to him.[2]

The substance of the *sākhī* must be rejected as a wonder story, but in this particular case we should examine the location ascribed to the incident in order to determine whether or not there may be an element of fact behind the legend. An examination is necessary in this case as such an element has been almost universally assumed. It is this *sākhī*, or more accurately two of the several versions of this *sākhī*, which provide the basis for the common statement that Gurū Nānak's travels extended as far as Assam, a statement which is to be found in practically every modern account of Gurū Nānak.

The two versions which have prompted this acceptance are those of the *Purātan* and *Bālā* janam-sākhīs, particularly the former. In the *Purātan* janam-sākhīs the story is set in a land which is called either Kaurū or Kāvarū,[3] both of which are evidently variants of Kāmrūp. This, at least, is the assumption which has been made by all who accept a visit to Assam and it is a reasonable one. The nature of the *sākhī* appears to confirm this. Assam is famed as a home of the Tantras, and the magic described in the *sākhī* has been taken as a description of tantric practices. All printed editions of the *Bālā* version give the name as Kārū, but in the manuscripts it appears, as in the *Purātan* janam-sākhīs, as Kaurū.[4] The *Bālā* manuscript version records a *sākhī* which differs radically from that of the *Purātan* janam-sākhīs, but it does concern women magicians who turn Mardānā into a sheep and make unsuccessful efforts to overcome the Gurū.[5] These

[1] A. S. Beveridge, op. cit., vol. i, p. 442, and vol. ii, p. 461.

[2] For the *Purātan* version see *supra*, p. 41.

[3] *Pur JS*, pp. 33–34.

[4] IOL MS. Panj. B41, folio 70b.

[5] The *Bālā sākhī* is, for once, much simpler and briefer than that of the *Purātan* janam-sākhīs and evidently represents a more primitive version. There is no reference to a queen called Nūr Shāh, and the miracles described differ from those of the *Purātan* account. According to the *Bālā* story, two women who seek to seduce the Gurū are changed, one

references to Kaurū have been accepted as satisfactory evidence of a visit to Assam and the point has not been challenged.

It must, however, be both challenged and rejected. In the first place, it is clear that Kāmrūp was not ruled by women during the period of Gurū Nānak's lifetime. The kings of western Kāmrūp[1] during the latter decades of the fifteenth century were Chakradhvaj (*c.* 1460–80) and his son Nilambar (*c.* 1480–98), and in eastern Kāmrūp authority was divided between a number of petty chieftains. In 1498 Nilambar was overthrown by Alāuddīn Husain, Sultan of Gaur, and a Muslim garrison was installed in the capital Kāmatapur under a general called Dānīyal. This garrison did not hold the city for long. Some time before 1505 it was attacked by a confederacy of Bhuyān chiefs and completely destroyed. The subsequent period is not entirely clear, but it seems that another king gained the throne, probably Nāgākṣa whom the *Kāmrūpar Buranjī* refers to as king in connexion with the building of the Bilveśvar temple in 1521. Nāgākṣa was evidently succeeded by his son Durlabhendra who was killed in 1540. There is certainly obscurity at this point, but there can be no doubt that the rulers of eastern Kāmrūp were men, not women.

The same applies also to western Kāmrūp where during the period following Nilambar's fall the various chieftains were brought under the authority of the Koche chieftain Hājo. This authority subsequently passed to Hājo's grandson Bisu (1515–40)[2] who greatly extended it and who in 1527 assumed the regnal name of Bisva Siṅgha.[3]

It is accordingly clear that no kingdom within Kāmrūp could have been ruled by women during the time of Gurū Nānak. Nor could it have been the Āhōm kingdom, for it was ruled during this period by King Suhungmung (1497–1539).[4] Indeed there is no likelihood whatsoever that such a kingdom would have been found amongst Kāmrūp's Assamese or tribal neighbours. Matrilineal descent was certainly a feature of Khāsi and Gāro society,[5] but it was not one which produced queens or chieftainesses. The result of this custom was not that women inherited power or property, but that such inheritances descended through them to their sons.[6]

into a ewe and the other into a bitch (ibid., folio 71a). In the earliest of the *Bālā* printed editions most of the manuscript version has been dropped and the *Purātan* version substituted in its place (*Bālā JS*, *sākhī* 25, pp. 102–8).

[1] It is usually referred to as Kāmata during this period.

[2] Hājo had two daughters, Hīra and Jīra, both of whom were married to a certain Haria Mandal. Bisu was the son of Hīra.

[3] E. A. Gait, *A History of Assam* (2nd edition), pp. 42–49. Rai K. L. Barua Bahadur, *Early History of Kāmrūpa*, pp. 283–4. See also N. N. Acharyya, *The History of Medieval Assam* (*A.D. 1228 to 1603*), a thesis submitted for the degree of Doctor of Philosophy in the University of London, 1957; and Francis Buchanan, 'General View of the History of Kamrupa' (Appendix C of S. K. Bhuyan's edition of the *Kāmrūpar Buranji*, pp. 139–43).

[4] E. A. Gait, op, cit., p. 86.

[5] *Jayantiā Buranji*, pp. x–xi.

[6] 'The chief of a Khāsi state is succeeded not by his own, but by his sister's son.' E. A. Gait, op. cit., p. 260.

The second reason for rejecting the *sākhī* is that it clearly reflects an earlier legend. Stories concerning *strī-deś*, 'the land of women', were already common currency long before the time of Gurū Nānak or the janam-sākhīs and in a number of traditions *strī-deś* had been identified with Kāmrūp.[1] The land of Kāmrūp was itself identified with an area in Assam or Bhutan, but its true location was in the realm of puranic and tantric mythology where it figured prominently as a symbol of erotic practice and dark magic.

There can be no doubt that it is this legendary land which is to be found in the janam-sākhīs. The *strī-deś*, or *triā-deś*, of the janam-sākhīs does not correspond to anything we know concerning the Assam of the early sixteenth century, but it does correspond closely to the *strī-deś* of puranic and tantric legend. Even the principal divergence separating the different accounts seems to reflect this correspondence, for it is a difference of location. The India Office Library manuscript B40 gives the land an unspecified location 'beside the ocean',[2] the *Gyān-ratanāvalī* places it in the south country immediately before the crossing to Ceylon,[3] and the *Purātan* and *Bālā* versions set it in Kaurū or Kāvarū. Miharbān and Bhāī Gurdās omit it altogether. The Kaurū or Kāvarū of the *Purātan* and *Bālā* janam-sākhīs must be regarded as the Kāmrūp of mythology, not the medieval kingdom of Kāmata or any part of it. Local traditions associated with particular gurdwārās in Assam will almost certainly have derived from the janam-sākhīs. Such traditions will have been planted in the area, as in other parts of India, by khatrī traders, Udāsī sādhūs, or soldiers, and then sustained by the foundation of a *saṅgat* and the erection of a gurdwārā.[4] It is not possible to state categorically that Gurū Nānak never visited Assam, but we must acknowledge that there is no acceptable evidence to support such a visit.

The visit to Dacca

The tradition concerning a visit to Dacca is weak in the janam-sākhīs, but it is one which nevertheless requires an examination as its authenticity has been defended on the basis of external evidence. In the janam-sākhīs such a visit is recorded only in the *Bālā* tradition, and within this tradition there are two conflicting versions of the circumstances. The older of the two sets the story of Mardānā and the forbidden fruit[5] in 'the region of

[1] Hazārī-prasād Dvivedī, *Nāth-sampradāy*, pp. 59–60. In this context the transcribed form is usually Kāmarūpa. Other traditions variously located it in the further regions of Gaṛhwāl-Kumāon, Kulū, near the source of the Satluj, and eastern Tibet. Ibid., p. 59.

[2] IOL MS. Panj. B40, folio 83.

[3] *GR*, pp. 227–30. This location may perhaps indicate a knowledge of Malabar matrilineal customs. Another possibility is that its source can be found in a reference to a *tiriā rāju* which occurs in the *Hakīkat Rāh Mukām Rāje Śivanābh kī*. See *infra*, p. 115.

[4] G. B. Singh, *Srī Gurū Granth Sāhib diān Prāchīn Biṛān*, *passim*.

[5] Number 28 in the chart.

Dacca, Bengal'.[1] There can be no doubt that this is a later addition to the *sākhī* for no such location is found in the versions given by the earlier janam-sākhīs. The second appearance of the name is an even more obvious case of interpolation, in this case a recent one made by a publisher or a printer. The modern versions which are available today set the story of Bhūmīā the Landlord in Dacca.[2] This same story is to be found in the expanded 1871 edition, but without a location.[3] The words 'in Dacca' are clearly a recent addition. The reason for the addition was probably the conviction, based upon the external evidence to be mentioned shortly, that Gurū Nānak must have visited the area. The Bhūmīā *sākhī* follows the 'Country ruled by Women' *sākhī* in the expanded 1871 edition; the latter is believed to have taken place in Kāmrūp; subsequent *sākhīs* indicate that Gurū Nānak moved south after visiting Kāmrūp; and therefore Bhūmīā must have lived in Dacca. This appears to have been the line of reasoning which led to the insertion of Dacca in most modern versions of the *Bālā* tradition.

The janam-sākhī references to such a visit can accordingly be rejected, but there remains the evidence which was put forward fifty years ago by Sardar G. B. Singh. In 1915 and 1916 a series of three articles on 'Sikh Relics in Eastern Bengal' were published in the *Dacca Review*.[4] The greater part of these articles relates to the period following the travels of the ninth Gurū, Tegh Bahādur (1621–75), but in the first of them G. B. Singh claimed to have discovered conclusive evidence of a visit to Dacca by Gurū Nānak. This evidence consisted of a well 'out in the waste near Jafarabad, half hidden in bramble growth'.[5] Local tradition held that the well had been dug by Gurū Nānak. In 1915 G. B. Singh evidently accepted this tradition as proof of a visit to the locality and later writers have concurred.[6]

The tradition must, however, be summarily dismissed. Uncorroborated traditions of this kind cannot possibly be accepted and in a subsequent work G. B. Singh explicitly renounced his earlier acceptance of this Dacca tradition.[7] Its origin is apparently to be found in the Sikh monastery which once stood on the site. During the seventeenth century khatrī traders and

[1] IOL MS. Panj. B41, folio 70a. *Bālā JS*, *sākhī* 24, p. 101.

[2] *Bālā* janam-sākhī, Munshi Gulab Singh and Sons, 1942 edition, *sākhī* 89, p. 311.

[3] *Bālā* janam-sākhī, expanded 1871 edition (Divan Buta Singh), *sākhī* 171, p. 358.

[4] *Dacca Review*, vol. v, nos. 7 and 8, Oct. and Nov. 1915, pp. 224–32; vol. v, no. 10, Jan. 1916, pp. 316–22; vol. v, nos. 11 and 12, Feb. and March 1916, pp. 375–8. An article by the same author also appeared in the now defunct *Sikh Review*, July 1915.

[5] Jafarabad, or Zafarabad, the area now occupied by the Dhanmandi Residential Area.

[6] Teja Singh and Ganda Singh, *A Short History of the Sikhs*, vol. i, p. 8, n. 2. Khushwant Singh, *A History of the Sikhs*, vol. i, p. 33. The latter writer refers to Chittagong as well as to Dacca and claims that tablets discovered there mention the stay of the first and ninth Gurūs (op. cit., p. 302). The authority he names is G. B. Singh's series of articles in the *Dacca Review*. The second and third articles do refer to Chittagong, but there is no reference to either Gurū Nānak or to any tablets mentioning him.

[7] G. B. Singh, *Srī Gurū Granth Sāhib diān Prāchin Biṛān*, p. 274.

sādhūs of the Udāsī sect travelled to Bengal from the Pañjāb and several Sikh communities (*saṅgat*) were founded in different parts of the province. The well discovered by G. B. Singh had evidently served one of these communities, for adjacent to it were the ruins of a small monastery. It seems safe to assume that the tradition developed within this community and subsequently lingered amongst the inhabitants of the locality after the monastery had been abandoned. The tradition is now completely extinct. The Hindu families which had preserved it left the area in 1947 and the well, although still in existence in 1951, has now disappeared.[1]

Rājā Śivanābh and Ceylon

The tradition that Gurū Nānak visited Ceylon and there met a ruler named Śivanābh is to be found in the *Purātan* and *Bālā* janam-sākhīs and in the *Gyān-ratanāvalī*. In all versions, except that of the earlier *Bālā* janam-sākhīs, it has two parts. The first is the story of how a Sikh trader, whom the *Gyān-ratanāvalī* and later *Bālā* accounts call Mansukh, sailed to the land of Rājā Śivanābh and there converted him to the religion of Gurū Nānak.[2] The second describes how the Gurū himself subsequently journeyed there in order to meet his royal disciple and while there composed a work entitled the *Prāṇ Saṅgalī*.[3] In the *Purātan* version the land is not named in the first part, but in the account of Gurū Nānak's own visit it is identified as Siṅghalādīp (Ceylon).

This tradition is one of the few which can be tested by reference to external evidence, for it specifies not just Ceylon but also the rājā whom, it claims, Gurū Nānak met there. The name Śivanābh indicates that the rājā, if he in fact existed, must have been a Śaivite and this must point to the kingdom of Jaffna. Elsewhere in Ceylon the contemporary dynasties were Buddhist, but in Jaffna the rulers of this period were Śaivites. None of them, however, was named Śivanābh. The two kings who occupied the throne of Jaffna during the time of Gurū Nānak's travels were Pararājasēkharaṇ VI (1478–1519) and Segarājasēkharaṇ VII (1519–61).[4]

Jaffna must accordingly be eliminated, but before concluding that Rājā Śivanābh did not live in Ceylon we must consider the testimony of the

[1] The writer owes this information to Dr. A. H. Dani.

[2] *Pur JS*, *sākhī* 41, pp. 76–78 (*Ḥāfizābād* MS. only). *GR*, *sākhī* 82, pp. 224–5. The IOL manuscript B41 and the *Bālā JS* do not contain this *sākhī*. In the expanded 1871 edition it is *sākhī* 27, p. 100. For the *Purātan* version see *supra*, pp. 46–47.

[3] *Pur JS*, *sākhī* 47, pp. 86–90. *GR*, *sākhīs* 87–94, pp. 232–43. *Bālā JS*, *sākhī* 29, pp. 120–3.

[4] The University of Ceylon, *History of Ceylon*, vol. i, p. 701. Segarājasēkharaṇ VII assassinated and succeeded his father. For a list of the Jaffna rulers for the period 1467–1620 see Mundaliyar C. Rajanayagam, *Ancient Jaffna*, pp. 373–4. See also V. Vriddhagirisan, *The Nayaks of Tanjore*, p. 78, C. S. Navaratnam, *Tamils and Ceylon*, p. 179, and S. Gnanaprakasar, *Kings of Jaffna in the Portuguese Period*.

Hakīkat Rāh Mukām Rāje Śivanābh kī,[1] a brief work attached to many old manuscript copies of the *Ādi Granth* which purports to be a description of how to get to Rājā Śivanābh's kingdom.[2] The *Hakīkat Rāh* claims that Rājā Śivanābh was the grandfather of Māyādunne. It errs in locating Māyādunne in Jaffna,[3] but he is at least an historical figure and his period is such that his grandfather could conceivably have been alive during the time of Gurū Nānak's travels. Māyādunne's grandfather was not, however, called Śivanābh. He was Parākramabāhu VIII who reigned in Kōṭṭē from 1484 until 1508.[4] Accordingly the *Hakīkat Rāh* must be rejected as evidence of a visit to Ceylon by Gurū Nānak.

What then are we to conclude concerning Rājā Śivanābh? G. B. Singh suggested that he may have been a khatrī landlord who had emigrated to Ceylon from the Pañjāb.[5] There is, however, no evidence whatsoever to support this theory. G. B. Singh makes his suggestion in the context of a reference to the *Hakīkat Rāh* which, as we have just noted, furnishes no confirmation of the tradition.

Our conclusion must be that if Rājā Śivanābh did exist he had no connexion with Ceylon. This seriously weakens the tradition of a visit to Ceylon, but it need not necessarily mean that it is wholly without foundation. We may still assume the possibility of such a visit and apply to it our fourth criterion, the measure of agreement or disagreement which we find in the different janam-sākhīs.

When this criterion is applied the possibility at once begins to crumble. In the first place, there is the failure of Bhāī Gurdās and Miharbān to offer any support to the tradition. Bhāī Gurdās makes no reference at all to any such visit, and although Miharbān's reference to 'a land of darkness' beyond Setu-bandha may be regarded as a clear pointer to Ceylon the description which he gives of the country plainly indicates that it is a product of the imagination.[6] Secondly, there is the fact that the India Office Library manuscript B40 records both the story of the Sikh trader and the subsequent meeting between Gurū Nānak and Rājā Śivanābh without any mention of Siṅghalādīp.[7]

[1] 'The truth (concerning) the way to Rājā Śivanābh's dwelling.'

[2] Almost all of the manuscript copies of the *Ādi Granth* in the British Museum and the India Office Library contain the apocrypha which includes the *Hakīkat Rāh*. In addition to the *Hakīkat Rāh* this apocrypha comprises several *śloks* and a *śabad*, all attributed to Gurū Nānak. This extra material is included at the end of each volume. It follows the *Mundāvaṇī* and Gurū Arjan's concluding *ślok*, but precedes the *Rāgamālā* with which all copies of the *Ādi Granth* end.

[3] Māyādunne was one of the conspirators in an uprising which took place in Kōṭṭē in 1521 and which led to the division of the kingdom of Kōṭṭē. The portion secured by Māyādunne was the territory of Sītāvaka in the south-west of Ceylon. *Çulāvaṃsa*, ii. 224, n. 1

[4] *Epigraphica Zeylanica*, vol. iii, pp. 41, 43. University of Ceylon, *History of Ceylon*, dynastic chart facing p. 851 of vol. i.

[5] *Dacca Review*, vol. v, nos. 11 and 12, Feb.–Mar. 1916.

[6] *Mih JS*, pp. 217–21. See *supra*, p. 57.

[7] IOL MS. Panj. B40, folios 138 ff.

This second point is a most significant one. Its significance lies in the contrast between the B40 and *Purātan* accounts, and in the fact that it is only the later of the two versions which gives the specific geographical location. The B40 account of the Sikh trader's conversion and of his journey to Śivanābh's kingdom corresponds almost exactly to that of the *Purātan*'s *sākhī* 41,[1] and although its treatment of Gurū Nānak's meeting with Śivanābh lacks the same measure of verbal identity and expands the portion which describes the efforts of the rājā's seductive women to tempt the Gurū, the basic details it gives are almost all the same as those of the *Purātan* account. The only exception is the omission of any reference to Siṅghalādīp in the B40 version.

As in the *Hāfizābād* manuscript, the B40 account records that following his conversion the merchant took ship and sailed 'to where Rājā Śivanābh lived'.[2] This nautical reference may be held to indicate Siṅghalādīp, but it is by no means a necessary assumption. On the contrary, it is a common feature of all the janam-sākhīs, except that of Miharbān, that Gurū Nānak is said to have crossed the sea to unspecified islands or lands. Such references are particularly frequent in the *Bālā* janam-sākhīs, but they are also to be found in the *Purātan* account.[3] Geographical inexactitude is generally associated with the historically dubious and this appears to be invariably the case when the inexactitude concerns a location somewhere over the sea. Indeed, references to the *samundar* (ocean) are almost always associated with incidents containing generous measures of the fantastic. The significance of these references is not that they must all point to Ceylon, but rather that their remote settings should prompt an even greater degree of caution.

The likelihood appears to be that the *sākhī* concerning Śivanābh had an early origin, but that it had no specific location in the early traditions, oral or written. This would mean that the whole of the B40 account and the first part of the *Purātan* version (*sākhī* 41) represent an earlier stage in the evolution of the story than the second part of the *Purātan* version (*sākhī* 47) or the later janam-sākhī accounts of the complete episode. It is impossible to identify with complete certainty the manner in which the name Siṅghalādīp came to be attached to the tradition. It may have been the result of visits to the south by Sikh traders, for it is conceivable that the reference to the converted shopkeeper sailing 'to where Rājā Śivanābh lived' may have come to be associated with these later trade contacts. This is one possible explanation and others could be the prominence of Siṅghalādīp in Pañjāb folklore,[4] or the simple fact that if an unspecified maritime location were to be given a name Siṅghalādīp would have been the obvious choice.

[1] *Pur JS*, pp. 74–78 (*Hāfizābād* manuscript only). [2] B40 MS., folio 140b.
[3] *Pur JS*, *sākhī* 29, p. 46; *sākhī* 45, p. 82; *sākhī* 46, p. 84.
[4] Cf. Mohan Singh, *An Introduction to Panjabi Literature*, p. 186.

The theory that the name Siṅghalādīp was introduced into an earlier tradition also receives support from *Pothī Harijī*, the second section of the *Miharbān Janam-sākhī*.[1] *Pothī Harijī* opens with a lengthy discourse between Gurū Nānak and the paṇḍit of Rājā Śivanābh, but gives no indication of who Śivanābh was or where he lived.[2] In a later *goṣṭ* Śivanābh reappears in a brief discourse which concerns him more directly, but which still makes no reference to his geographical location.[3] The only hint which it offers is the statement that after his conversation with Śivanābh Gurū Nānak returned to Kartārpur.[4] This does not suggest a location as far distant as Ceylon.

The conclusion which follows is irresistible. There was no contemporary ruler in Ceylon called Śivanābh and all the evidence points to a later introduction of the name Siṅghalādīp into *sākhīs* concerning him. The tradition that Gurū Nānak visited Ceylon must accordingly be rejected.

Sajjaṇ the Robber

According to the janam-sākhīs Sajjaṇ was a thief who posed as a pious philanthropist in order to lure unsuspecting travellers to their death.[5] It is an exceedingly popular story and appears in some form or other in all the janam-sākhīs,[6] but it is one which we must nevertheless regard with some considerable doubt.

In the first place, the janam-sākhīs disagree concerning the location of the incident. The *Purātan* version names no place at all, but implies that it must have been in or near the Pañjāb as the meeting is set between Gurū Nānak's departure from Sultānpur and his arrival in Pāṇīpat. This could conceivably be held to accord with the *Bālā* account which gives 'near Tulambā in the district of Multān' as the site.[7] The *Bālā* version differs radically from that of the *Purātan* janam-sākhīs in other respects, but almost all modern accounts, while rejecting the substance of the *Bālā sākhī* accept it as far as this single detail is concerned.[8]

No such compromise is possible, however, in the case of the *Miharbān* and *Gyān-ratanāvalī* versions. The latter names Hastināpur as the location

[1] See *supra*, p. 19.
[2] Khalsa College, Amritsar, MS. SHR: 427, folio 302a. In this *goṣṭ* he is called Śivanāth.
[3] Ibid., *goṣṭ* 171, folios 341b–2a. In this *goṣṭ* the name is Śivanābh.
[4] Ibid., folio 342b.
[5] *Mih JS*, *goṣṭ* 73, pp. 235–8. *Pur JS*, *sākhī* 13, pp. 21–22. *GR*, *sākhī* 73, pp. 207–10. *Bālā JS*, *sākhī* 63, pp. 290–4. See *supra*, pp. 38–39, 58.
[6] Bhāī Gurdās does not refer to it.
[7] *Bālā JS*, conclusion of *sākhī* 62, p. 290. The town is also called Ma<u>kh</u>dūmpur.
[8] The modern *Bālā* janam-sākhīs drop the earlier *Bālā* version and follow the *Purātan* account instead (*Bālā* janam-sākhī, Munshi Gulab Singh and Sons, 1942 edition, *sākhī* 67, pp. 269–70).

of the incident[1] and Miharbān sets it in 'the south country'.[2] The precise location is not named in Miharbān's account, but is evidently intended to be somewhere between Rāmeśwaram and Ujjain. It is clear that no definite geographical location can be assigned to the incident and that it should properly belong to the group of miscellaneous *sākhīs* which do not have a precise setting.

The janam-sākhīs also differ with regard to the actual content of the story, although in the case of Miharbān, the *Purātan* janam-sākhīs, and the *Gyān-ratanāvalī* these other differences are of little significance. The *Purātan* version calls Sajjaṇ a sheikh and records that he maintained a temple and a mosque in order to accommodate both Hindus and Muslims.[3] Miharbān's account, on the other hand, gives him no title and makes no reference to either a temple or a mosque, merely describing a handsome *dharmsālā* which had separate drinking facilities for Hindus and Muslims.[4] The *Gyān-ratanāvalī* adds that Gurū Nānak was aware of Sajjaṇ's intentions, having been surreptitiously informed by a bystander as he entered the city that Sajjaṇ was in reality a thug. The same informant added that Sajjaṇ was also in league with the local rājā who customarily received half of the booty.[5]

These are essentially differences of detail and there can be no doubt that all three accounts are relating a common tradition. The *Bālā* version, however, offers much more pronounced variations and indeed the *sākhī* it records is not really the same incident. Sajjaṇ's disguise is described as that of a Vaiṣṇava, not of a sheikh, and although he is obviously intended to be a scoundrel there is no reference to his being a thug. Nor is there any mention of his maintaining a temple and a mosque, of his throwing his victims into a well, or of subsequently building a *dharmsālā*.[6] His practice was evidently to do no more than steal his guests' clothes, for this is what he did to Mardānā's son.[7] The only real links with the story as recorded in the other three versions are his name and his sudden conversion as a result of hearing Gurū Nānak sing the hymn which appears in the *Ādi Granth* as *Sūhī* 3.[8]

Normally a variant of this kind would do no more than suggest that the *Bālā* version can be safely discarded in favour of the accounts given in the other three janam-sākhī traditions. In this particular case, however, the difference is more important, or rather the small area of agreement is

[1] *GR*, p. 207. This anachronistic appearance of the ancient Kuru capital will doubtless be a result of the influence of the *Mahābhārata*. The remains of the city are in Meerut District.

[2] *Mih JS*, p. 235.

[3] *Pur JS*, p. 21.

[4] *Mih JS*, p. 235.

[5] *GR*, p. 207.

[6] The *Bālā JS*, p. 290, refers to the temple and mosque, but the IOL manuscript B41 does not (loc. cit., folio 183b).

[7] Khazan Singh, *History and Philosophy of Sikhism*, vol. i, p. 95, follows this version.

[8] *AG*, p. 729.

important. The story given by Miharbān, the *Purātan* janam-sākhīs, and the *Gyān-ratanāvalī* on the one hand, and the different story given by the *Bālā* version on the other, both have as their key point Gurū Nānak's singing of *Sūhī* 3. This is significant for *Sūhī* 3 contains references which might well indicate the genesis of both stories. The hymn begins:

> Bronze shines brightly, but if I rub it blackness (like) ink (comes off it).
> Even if I clean it a hundred times (outer) cleaning will never remove its inner impurity.

The message which this and subsequent figures convey is that ultimate exposure must inevitably overtake all dissemblers who seek to conceal inner impurity behind an outward show of piety. The refrain then follows:

> They are my real friends who accompany me (now) and who will accompany me (into the hereafter);
> Who, in that place where accounts are called for, will stand up and give (a good) account (of their deeds).

The word used here for 'friends' is *sajaṇ*[1] and it seems likely that the message of the hymn, together with the word *sajaṇ*, produced two separate stories, both concerning an impostor called Sajaṇ, or Sajjaṇ. This cannot be affirmed categorically, but it is at least a strong possibility. Insofar as the two stories agree their agreement may be traced directly to the hymn, and it is when they move out into details which are independent of the hymn that they diverge.

There are accordingly good grounds for questioning the authenticity of the story and to these we may add the fact that Bhāī Gurdās makes no reference either to the incident or to a person called Sajjan. This is not surprising as far as the account of Gurū Nānak's travels given in *Vār* 1 is concerned, but had the tradition been a firm one a reference to Sajjaṇ might well have appeared in *Vār* 11.[2] The *sākhī* cannot be dismissed as totally impossible and nor can we rule out the possibility of a link with an earlier tradition concerning an encounter with a thief of some kind. As it stands, however, it must be classified with the improbable *sākhīs*.

The discourse on Mount Sumeru

The discourse with the Siddhs on Mount Sumeru is one of only three incidents which are to be found in Bhāī Gurdās and in all of the important

[1] *sajaṇ sei nāli mai chaldiā nāli chalanhi;*
jithai lekhā maṅgiai tithai khaṛe dasanhi.
AG, p. 729

[2] Bhāī Gurdās's list of Gurū Nānak's more prominent followers. (*Vār* 11, stanzas 13–14.)

janam-sākhīs.[1] This indicates a very strong tradition and one which cannot be lightly set aside. When Bhāī Gurdās and all of the janam-sākhīs unite in testifying to a particular claim we shall need compelling arguments in order to dismiss it.

In this case, however, the arguments which must be brought against the tradition do compel us to reject it. First, there is the mythical location which is given as the setting for the discourse. Mount Sumeru exists only in legend, not in fact.[2] It has been maintained that in this context Mount Sumeru represents Mount Kailāś,[3] but this is a claim which cannot possibly be sustained. The arguments which have been advanced in support of this identification are, first, a *Purātan* reference to Mahādeo (Śiva) as one of Gurū Nānak's interlocutors;[4] secondly, Bhāī Gurdās's account of how the Siddhs sent the Gurū to draw water from a lake;[5] and thirdly, the reported discovery of images of Gurū Nānak in the Kailāś area. The *Purātan* insertion of Mahādeo's name before that of Gorakhnāth can be traced to Gurū Nānak's use of the name Īśar in the series of *śloks* from *Vār Rāmakalī* which in large measure explain the origin of the Mount Sumeru tradition.[6] Bhāī Gurdās's description of a lake, which has been held to refer to Mānasa-sarovara,[7] must be rejected on rational grounds. Lake Mānasa is not filled with jewels in the manner related by the poet. The third justification concerns the report of an expedition which visited Lake Mānasa and claimed to have discovered images of Gurū Nānak in the four cave temples around the lake.[8] If in fact such images did exist they would certainly have been introduced by sādhūs at a later date.[9]

[1] The Mecca visit (nos. 78–79) and the Achal Baṭālā debate (no. 90) are the others. The association with Daulat Khān Lodī, though not treated as an incident in Bhāī Gurdās, is also referred to by all sources.

[2] Mount Sumeru or, more commonly, Mount Meru is the legendary mountain said to be situated in the centre of the earth. According to the geographical system of the *Purāṇas* the earth was flat and from its central point there arose this mountain. Seven continents (*dvīpas*) lay in concentric circles around it. The inmost of the seven, which was attached to Mount Meru and which included Bhāratavarṣa (India) was named Jambudvīpa. The summit of Mount Meru was believed to reach to the heavens, and the sun and planets revolved around it. The Himālayas were said to be its foothills. A. L. Basham, *The Wonder that was India*, pp. 320, 488–9. The influence of this Puranic mythology is to be found in all the accounts, but in varying degrees. In the *Miharbān Janam-sākhi* it is relatively weak and in the *Bālā* janam-sākhīs very strong.

[3] Vir Singh in his edition of Santokh Singh's *Nānak Prakāś*, vol. iii, p. 689, n.*. Kartar Singh, *Life of Guru Nanak Dev*, p. 190.

[4] *Pur JS*, p. 94. Vir Singh, op. cit., p. 690 n. Kailāś was believed to be the location of Śiva's paradise. Neither Bhāī Gurdās nor Miharbān include this reference.

[5] *Vār* 1. 31.

[6] See *supra*, p. 11, n. 2.

[7] Vir Singh, op. cit., p. 690 n. Kartar Singh, op. cit., pp. 190, 194. The *Pur JS* includes the same legend, but without specifying a lake as the source of water.

[8] Vir Singh, op. cit., pp. 691–2 n. Sewaram Singh, *The Divine Master*, pp. 139–41.

[9] Sewaram Singh also claims as evidence of Gurū Nānak's visit an oral report that the people who worship these images were aware that 'the Great Master . . . had appeared in Ten Forms and had founded the Great *Tirath* at Amritsar' (op. cit., p. 140). Such information could hardly have been derived from Gurū Nānak himself.

The second argument which must be brought against the tradition is the legendary nature not just of its location, but also of the story itself. Gurū Nānak and Gorakhnāth could not possibly have been contemporaries, and nor can it be claimed that the person referred to as Gorakhnāth must have been a Nāth yogī who bore the same name as the sect's founder. The names given to his companions plainly indicate that their origin is to be found in a confused amalgam of the popular traditions concerning the nine immortal Nāths and the eighty-four immortal Siddhs.[1] Bhāī Gurdās explicitly states that the meeting on Mount Sumeru was with the eighty-four Siddhs.[2]

The manner in which this legendary basis is developed varies in the different versions, but in all cases the development shares the nature of the basis. Miharbān relates discourses which surpass in length anything he offers elsewhere. Bhāī Gurdās sets out a denunciation of the degeneracy of life on the plains below and concludes with the miracle of the lake of jewels. The *Purātan* janam-sākhīs relate the story of the jewels and also a miraculous departure from the mountain. The *Bālā* version produces in this and other associated *sākhīs* its most sustained flight of Puranic fancy.

The third objection is the existence of an obvious explanation for the genesis of the whole tradition. There appears to be no doubt that the basic *sākhī* which has provided the foundation for all subsequent expansion of the tradition must have developed out of the *śloks* from *Vār Rāmakalī* which the janam-sākhīs set in the centre of the discourse.[3] This particular point has already been discussed as an illustration of the manner in which much of the janam-sākhī material must have evolved.[4] In the *śloks* from *Vār Rāmakalī* Gurū Nānak speaks successively as Īśar, Gorakh, Gopīchand, Charapaṭ, Bharatharī, and finally as himself. A discourse with yogīs was obviously implied, and the names used by Gurū Nānak seemed to indicate that these yogīs were none other than the famous Gorakhnāth and other celebrated Siddhs.[5] Around this nucleus there gathered details drawn from Puranic and Nāth mythology, and the result was the legend of the Mount Sumeru discourse as we find it in Bhāī Gurdās and the janam-sākhīs. All accounts have the same nucleus. They differ only in the nature and quantity of the detail which has been added.

The Mount Sumeru *sākhīs* provide us with a tradition which appears in all versions, but which must nevertheless be wholly rejected. This is not to say that Gurū Nānak never visited the Himālayas, nor indeed can we maintain with assurance that he did not penetrate as far as Mount Kailāś

[1] See Glossary for *Nāth*, p. 243, and *Siddh*, p. 245.
[2] *Vār* 1. 28.
[3] *Vār Rāmakalī*, *śloks* 2–7 of *pauṛī* 12, *AG*, pp. 952–3.
[4] See *supra*, pp. 11–12.
[5] Gorakhnāth was of course a Nāth, not a Siddh. This is an illustration of the common confusion of Nāths and Siddhs.

and Lake Mānasa.[1] The conclusion to which our analysis points is that Bhāī Gurdās and the janam-sākhīs do not provide us with acceptable evidence of such a visit, and that accordingly it cannot be a part of the biography which we are seeking to reconstruct.

Mecca and Medina

Although the tradition that Gurū Nānak visited Mecca was summarily dismissed by Trumpp as legend[2] almost all subsequent writers have accepted it and most have regarded it as the terminus of his western travels. Some popular accounts claim that he continued on to Egypt and adjacent African countries, and a few take him into Europe, but most follow the older janam-sākhīs in ending the westward journey at Mecca or Medina.

Once again it is convenient to draw a distinction between the content of the tradition and its geographical setting, and to reject most of the former as legendary. The portion which cannot be summarily set aside in this manner is the discourse recorded by Bhāī Gurdās.

> The qāzīs and mullāhs gathered and began questioning him on religious matters.
> God has unfolded an immense creation! None can comprehend His power!
> Opening their books they asked, 'Which is the greater—the Hindu or the Muslim?'
> Bābā (Nānak) answered the pilgrims, 'Without good deeds both lead only to suffering.
> Neither Hindu nor Muslim finds refuge in (God's) court.
> The safflower's pigment is not fast; it runs when washed in water.
> People are jealous of each other, but Rām and Rahīm[3] are one.
> The world has taken the devil's path.'[4]

This certainly accords with the convictions which we find expressed in the works of Gurū Nānak and it is possible that the tradition has descended from an authentic origin, though not one that took place in Mecca. It can

[1] The possibility of a visit to Tibet has been a recurrent topic for speculation, and support has occasionally been claimed for a particular theory on the basis of a local Tibetan tradition. For a recent example see the *Sikh Review*, vol. xii, no. 37, Jan. 1965, pp. 21–26. Our knowledge of these traditions is confined to reports of travellers who received them as oral traditions, and bearing in mind the linguistic problems normally involved in such communications we must treat these reports with considerable caution. Even when we can accept a report as a substantially accurate account of an existing tradition there will be a strong likelihood that the tradition communicated in this manner represents a later development resulting from the movement of sādhūs between India and Tibet. There remains, however, a small margin of doubt and even if no reports had been received we should still be unable to reject categorically the possibility that Gurū Nānak visited Tibet.

[2] E. Trumpp, *The Ādi Granth*, p. vi.

[3] Hindu and Muslim names for God.

[4] *BG*, 1. 33.

at least be accepted as an accurate representation of Gurū Nānak's teaching concerning the relationship between Hindu beliefs and Islam.

The portion which must be rejected consists of the miraculous events which the janam-sākhīs all associate, in varying forms, with the Mecca visit. These include an instantaneous journey to Mecca,[1] a cloud which followed the Gurū,[2] an issue of fresh water in the wells of the city,[3] and a moving *miharāb*.[4] Of these the last is the most important, for it constitutes in most versions the climax of the episode. Bhāī Gurdās, the *Purātan* janam-sākhīs, the B40 manuscript, and the *Gyān-ratanāvalī* all record that Gurū Nānak, after arriving in Mecca, went to sleep with his feet pointing towards a *miharāb* or, in the case of the *Purātan* version, towards 'Mecca'. A qāzī who happened to observe him in this posture kicked him and demanded an explanation for such blasphemy.[5] In reply the Gurū suggested that the qāzī should drag his feet round and leave them pointing in a direction where God and the *Ka'bah* were not. The qāzī proceeded to do so, but when he moved the Gurū's legs the *miharāb* moved with them. Confounded by this miracle the qāzī fell at his feet.[6]

This story has been rationalized by terminating it at the point where Gurū Nānak suggests that the qāzī should point his feet in a direction where God is not. Although this rationalized version is particularly common in modern accounts it is to be found as far back as Miharbān and evidently provides us with another illustration of the author's relative sophistication. In the *Miharbān Janam-sākhī* the incident is related without the concluding miracle, and the words attributed to Gurū Nānak indicate that the miracle has been deliberately excised.[7]

The second interesting feature of the story of the moving *miharāb* is that it apparently came to be located in Mecca after it had evolved as an explicit tradition. This is the conclusion indicated by a number of inconsistencies in the various versions. One is that the *Miharbān* and *Bālā* versions locate it elsewhere. In the *Miharbān Janam-sākhī* it is set in a village on the way to Mecca,[8] and in the earlier *Bālā* janam-sākhīs the location is given as Medina.[9] A second inconsistency is that the *Purātan* janam-sākhīs, while locating it in Mecca, state that Gurū Nānak went to sleep with his feet

[1] *Mih JS*, p. 453. See *supra*, p. 61. [2] *Pur JS*, p. 99.

[3] Ibid., pp. 99, 104. *Bālā JS*, p. 187.

[4] The niche in a mosque which indicates the direction of the *Ka'bah*.

[5] Bhāī Gurdās calls him Jīvan (*BG* 1. 32), the *Purātan* janam-sākhīs call him Rukan-dīn (*Pur JS*, p. 100), and the B40 manuscript refers to him as a descendant (*potā*) of Makhdūm Bahāuddīn of Multan (loc. cit., folio 53). The *GR*, p. 412, follows Bhāī Gurdās.

[6] *BG* 1. 32. *Pur JS*, pp. 99–102. IOL MS. Panj B40, folios 51–53. *GR*, pp. 408–20.

[7] *Mih JS*, p. 499. The rationalized version is also related in W. L. M'Gregor's *History of the Sikhs*, published in 1846 (loc. cit., vol. i, pp. 36, 159–60).

[8] *Mih JS*, p. 449.

[9] IOL MS. Panj. B41, folio 122a. According to this version Gurū Nānak and Bhāī Bālā both committed the alleged offence. Their feet are said to have been pointing towards the tomb of Muhammad.

pointing towards 'Mecca',[1] a reference which suggests an original setting away from the city. Thirdly, it can be assumed that had the original location been Mecca the Gurū's feet would have been pointing towards the *Ka'bah* rather than a *miharāb*.

All of this concerns, however, the superstructure of the Mecca and Medina traditions and it offers only limited help as far as the basic question is concerned. Did Gurū Nānak visit Mecca and Medina? Regardless of the actual content of the tradition, can its geographical basis be accepted?

In support of the tradition there is the fact that its more significant portion is referred to by all our sources. There is no reference to Medina in the *Miharbān* and *Purātan* versions, but the janam-sākhīs all record a visit to Mecca and Bhāī Gurdās supports them. This means that once again we have a strong tradition and one which cannot be lightly dismissed. The Mount Sumeru *sākhīs* show, however, that a unanimity of this kind is not in itself sufficient to place an incident beyond question and the Mecca *sākhīs* reinforce this conclusion.

The arguments which can be brought against the Mecca tradition are not compelling to the point of absolute certainty, but they are sufficiently strong to raise very grave doubts. In the first place there is the inherent improbability of a non-Muslim entering the city in the manner indicated by the janam-sākhīs. The janam-sākhīs do indeed inform us that Gurū Nānak dressed for the occasion as a Muslim pilgrim, but they also describe additional articles of apparel which implied Hindu affiliations and confused his fellow pilgrims.[2] If we accept the possibility of such a visit we must also accept a complete disguise. This Gurū Nānak may have worn, but it implies a measure of conscious deception which is altogether uncharacteristic of him.

A second reason for questioning the tradition is the fact that Mecca and Medina are precisely the kind of places which one would expect to find figuring in the popular versions of the Gurū's travels. We have already observed how prominently the chief centres of Hindu pilgrimage figure in the descriptions of his journeys beyond the Pañjāb. In the same manner it is to be expected that the principal Muslim centres would also appear in the itinerary. This in itself does not prove that Gurū Nānak did not visit Mecca, but it does provide an alternative theory to account for the genesis of the Mecca and Medina *sākhīs*.

Thirdly, we must note the dominant element of the miraculous in all versions of the story, including that of Bhāī Gurdās. The conclusion which we must draw from this feature is that, despite their unanimity concerning the actual visit, the janam-sākhī descriptions of what took place during the

[1] *Pur JS*, p. 100. See *supra*, p. 49, n. 1.

[2] *Pur JS*, p. 98. In Miharbān's account it is the Gurū's name which marks him as a non-Muslim (*Mih JS*, p. 451).

visit cannot possibly be trusted. Their accounts of the discourses which Gurū Nānak held in the city indicate the same conclusion. Such discourses would have divulged his identity at once and brought either instant expulsion or death.

The first of these three arguments is the significant one and it is an argument which must lead us very near to outright rejection of the tradition. Adventurers such as Burton and Keane have proved the possibility of non-Muslims entering Mecca, but they have also shown that success in such an attempt could be attained only by means of a thorough disguise, both in outward appearance and in behaviour.[1] Gurū Nānak would doubtless have been sufficiently conversant with Muslim belief and practice to have sustained the disguise, but it would have been a violation both of his manifest honesty and of his customary practice of plain speaking. The ban has, it is true, been applied with particular strictness during more recent times. It nevertheless existed during the period of Gurū Nānak's travels and would certainly have prohibited the kind of open entry which the janam-sākhīs describe. We may acknowledge a visit to Mecca as a possibility, but it must be regarded as an exceedingly remote one. The same reasons apply with only slightly less emphasis to the tradition of a Medina visit, and in this case the absence of such a visit in the *Miharbān* and *Purātan* accounts provides an additional argument for rejection. The Mecca and Medina *sākhīs* must accordingly be classified as highly improbable.

The visit to Baghdad

References to a Baghdad visit occur in two of the older janam-sākhīs. Of these the earlier is evidently the *sākhī* describing such a visit which is to be found in the India Office Library manuscript B40.[2] This *sākhī* records a discourse with Sheikh Sharaf who, according to this account, dressed in women's clothing, and applied black collyrium to his eyes and henna to his hands. The discourse which the *sākhī* records consists almost entirely of three hymns, two attributed to Sheikh Sharaf and one to Gurū Nānak. None of the three is to be found in the *Ādi Granth*.

The second reference occurs in Bhāī Gurdās's *Vār* 1 where two stanzas are devoted to a description of an incident in Baghdad.[3] Bhāī Gurdās's account bears no resemblance whatsoever to the B40 *sākhī*. Instead it records how Gurū Nānak, having arrived with Mardānā at the outskirts of the city, set up camp and then proceeded to utter the call to prayer.[4] Hearing this the astonished inhabitants of the city fell silent, and Gurū

[1] R. F. Burton, *A Pilgrimage to al-Madinah and Mecca*, vol. ii. J. F. Keane, *Six Months in the Hejaz*.

[2] IOL MS. Panj. B40, folios 200–2.

[3] *BG* 1. 35–36. The *Gyān-ratanāvalī* follows this account.

[4] The *bāṅg* normally uttered from a minaret by a *muezzin*.

Nānak was approached by a *pīr* who asked him to what order of faqīrs he belonged. A discussion ensued in the course of which Gurū Nānak assured the *pīr* that there exist many thousands of worlds both below and above the earth. To prove his claim he took the *pīr*'s son and, ascending with him into the air, revealed to him the multitude of heavens and underworlds. From above they descended into the nether regions and brought from there a bowl of *kaṛāh prasād*.[1] Gurū Nānak and Mardānā then left Baghdad and proceeded on their way to Medina and Mecca.

This is the testimony of the janam-sākhīs and it cannot be regarded as a strong one. In the first place there is the absence of any reference to such a visit in the *Miharbān* and *Purātan* janam-sākhīs. It is most unlikely that either would have omitted the tradition had it been known, and in this respect Miharbān's omission is of particular significance. Secondly, there is the fact that the B40 manuscript and Bhāī Gurdās record completely different traditions, the only point in common being the Baghdad location. Thirdly, neither of the traditions appears to offer an intrinsically convincing incident. Within the total range of janam-sākhī traditions Sheikh Sharaf is a ubiquitous figure who is to be found not only in Baghdad, but also in Pāṇīpat,[2] Bidar,[3] and Mecca.[4] In Bhāī Gurdās's account Dastgīr is the name given to the *pīr* with whom Gurū Nānak is said to have held discourse. Dastgīr is one of the more important of the numerous names given to the celebrated Sūfī 'Abd al-Qādir Jīlānī[5] and it seems clear that the name given by Bhāī Gurdās may be traced to this source. 'Abd al-Qādir Jīlānī spent most of his long life in Baghdad and subsequently came to be highly honoured in India as the *Pīr-i-pīrān*.[6] If this identification is correct the conclusion must be that we have in this Baghdad tradition another example of an association with a saint of acknowledged fame, introduced in order to magnify the fame of the Gurū. This is not to suggest that Bhāī Gurdās has related a deliberate falsehood. The likelihood appears to be that he has recorded a *sākhī* which had already evolved in oral tradition, gathering in the process a number of miraculous details. The silence of the *Miharbān* and *Purātan* janam-sākhīs indicates, however, that it could not have gained wide currency.

[1] The sacramental food of the Sikhs.

[2] *Pur JS*, p. 22. See *supra*, p. 39.

[3] IOL MS. Panj. B41, folio 187a.

[4] The (*Makke di goṣṭ*) which follows the *Bala* janam-sākhī in the IOL manuscript Panj. B41 names Sheikh Sharaf as one of the two Muslims with whom Gurū Nānak conversed in Mecca (MS. B41, folio 254).

[5] 'Abd al-Qādir of Jīlān, born 470 H. (A.D. 1077–78), died 561 H. (A.D. 1166), was the founder of the important Qādirī order of Sūfīs. *Encyclopaedia of Islam* (*New Edition*), vol. i, p. 71. See also J. A. Subhan, *Sufism: Its Saints and Shrines*, p. 178. The Qādirī order is particularly influential in India. A. J. Arberry, *Sufism*, p. 85.

[6] J. A. Subhan, op. cit., p. 264. The order was established in India in the fifteenth century by Sayyid Muḥammad Ghawth, tenth in the line of succession. He settled in Uch in A.D. 1428. Ibid.

By itself the testimony of the janam-sākhīs would permit us to classify the Baghdad visit as no more than possible, and the possibility would not be a strong one. In this particular case, however, the janam-sākhīs do not appear to stand alone. As in the case of the Dacca visit the authenticity of the Baghdad tradition has, it is generally believed, been established by the discovery of external evidence. Two inscriptions are said to have been found in Baghdad, both of them recording a visit to the city by Gurū Nānak.

For one of these two inscriptions we are bound to rely solely upon a poem published in 1919. It that year Swami Anand Acharya, who spent his later years living in Norway, published a book of English verse entitled *Snow-birds*,[1] and in this collection he included the following poem:

ON READING AN ARABIC INSCRIPTION IN A SHRINE OUTSIDE THE TOWN OF BAGHDAD, DATED 912 HEJIRA

Upon this simple slab of granite didst thou sit, discoursing of fraternal love and holy light, O Guru Nanak, Prince among India's holy sons!
What song from the source of the Seven Waters thou didst sing to charm the soul of Iran!
What peace from Himalaya's lonely caves and forests thou didst carry to the vine-groves and rose-gardens of Baghdad!
What light from Badrinath's snowy peak thou didst bear to illumine the heart of Balol, thy saintly Persian disciple!
Eight fortnights Balol hearkened to thy words on Life and the Path and Spring Eternal, while the moon waxed and waned in the pomegranate grove beside the grassy desert of the dead.
And after thou hadst left him to return to thy beloved Bharata's land, the fakir, it is said, would speak to none nor listen to the voice of man or angel;
His fame spread far and wide and the Shah came to pay him homage—but the holy man would take no earthly treasures nor hear the praise of kings and courtiers.
Thus lived he—lonely, devoted, thoughtful—for sixty winters, sitting before the stone whereon thy sacred feet had rested;
And ere he left this House of Ignorance he wrote these words upon the stone: 'Here spake the Hindu Guru Nanak to Fakir Balol, and for these sixty winters, since the Guru left Iran, the soul of Balol has rested on the Master's word—like a bee poised on a dawn-lit honey-rose.'[2]

This is the complete text. The author gives no further information concerning the location of the inscription or the circumstances under which it was discovered, and no one has subsequently found anything which corresponds to it.

In the case of the second inscription, however, the location is known and the inscription is accessible. To the south-west of modern Baghdad, in the

[1] London, Macmillan. [2] loc. cit., no. xc, pp. 182–4.

area occupied by the ruins of Old Baghdad, there is to be found the tomb of Bahlūl Dānā, believed to have been the court jester of Hārūn ar-Rashīd. Niebuhr described it as follows:

> Pas loin de là [the tomb of Zobeida] se trouve le tombeau, d'un nommé Bahlul Dâne qui étoit parent du Calife Harun Erraschid et son boufon. On a de lui un livre rempli de petites historiettes, que de pauvres savans racontent encore le soir dans les Caffés. Dans l'inscription inserée au bas de cette page[1] que l'on n'a mise sur son tombeau, que long temps après sa mort, en 501, on le nommoit le Sultan des pauvres en esprit; mais suivant quelques histoires que l'on rapporte de lui il paroit avoir aussi eu ses intervalles de bon sens.[2]

This tomb is now housed in a small two-roomed building. In 1916 some Sikh soldiers discovered in this building a brief inscription which, it is claimed, makes explicit mention of Gurū Nānak.[3] The inscription is set above a niche in the north-eastern corner of the building and below it there is a platform. The discovery was published in the January 1918 issue of the *Loyal Gazette*, Lahore,[4] and since that time has been accepted as conclusive proof of a visit to Baghdad by Gurū Nānak.

The language of the inscription is Ottoman Turkish and efforts to translate it have produced several different versions. Five of these translations are given below:

1. In memory of the Guru, that is the Divine Master Baba Nanak Fakir Aulia, this building has been raised anew, with the help of Seven Saints; and the chronogram reads: 'The blessed disciple has produced a spring of grace'—year 927 H.[5]
2. Guru Murad died. Baba Nanak Fakir helped in constructing this building which is an act of grace from a virtuous follower. 927 A.H.[6]
3. Murad saw the demolished building of Hazrat Rab-i-Majid, Baba Nanak, Fakir Aulia, and rebuilt it with his own hands, so that historic memorial may continue from generation to generation, and His *murid-i-s'eed* (the blessed disciple) may obtain heavenly bliss.—Year 917 H.[7]
4. When Murad saw the building of Baba Nanak, the Prophet of God, fallen in

[1] *hādha qabr sulṭān al-majdhūbin wa'l-nafs al-muṭmasa sanat khumsumāyah wa-wāḥid.*

[2] Carsten Niebuhr, *Voyage en Arabie et en d'autres pays circonvoisins* (French translation, 1776), tome ii, pp. 245–6. See also J. Oppert, *Expédition Scientifique en Mésopotamie*, tome i, p. 98; and C. Huart, *Histoire de Bagdad dans les Temps Modernes*, Introduction, p. xii. Niebuhr, op. cit., tab. xliv, provides a map of Baghdad which shows the tomb of Bahlūl Dānā as no. 13. The legend has been omitted in Niebuhr, but is supplied in Huart's reproduction of the same map.

[3] The actual words are read as 'Bābā Nānak'. A description of the building, together with a diagram of it, is given in Sewaram Singh, *The Divine Master*, pp. 155–6. Photographs taken in 1964 and 1965 indicate that the building is in considerable disrepair.

[4] Khushwant Singh, *A History of the Sikhs*, vol. i, p. 34, n. 20.

[5] Teja Singh and Ganda Singh, *A Short History of the Sikhs*, vol. i, p. 12.

[6] Indubhusan Banerjee, *Evolution of the Khalsa*, vol. i, p. 73.

[7] Sewaram Singh, *The Divine Master*, p. 157.

ruins, he built a new one instead, with the help of his own hands so that it may stand as a monument in history for generations to come, and that the meritorious act of his fortunate disciple may last for aye.[1]

5. Whoever saw this sacred place of Baba Nanak faqir was granted fulfilment of his heart's desire by the Great God and Seven Angels helped him. Its date lies in line [*sic*] He caused a spring of Grace to flow for His lucky disciple—year 927 H.[2]

The two different readings of the concluding date are the result of an obscure second figure. Normally it should be possible to determine the value of the indistinct figure by calculating the value of the chronogram, but here too there are evidently differences of opinion. Vir Singh sets out the value of the chronogram as follows:

$$27+59+205+215+13+254+144 = 917.$$ [3]

The writers who give 927 do not offer interpretations of the chronogram.

There are accordingly radical differences concerning the translation of the inscription and a fundamental disagreement concerning the reading of the date it gives, but no account of Gurū Nānak's travels written since 1918 has disputed the basic contention that the inscription refers to Gurū Nānak and proves that he visited Baghdad. Most writers have also accepted the authenticity of Anand Acharya's Arabic inscription and have inferred that the two inscriptions must describe a common event. The conclusion which follows is that Gurū Nānak conversed with 'Shah Bahlol, a local fakir'[4] or with 'a successor of Bahlol Dana'.[5] Vir Singh has offered a reconstruction based upon the two inscriptions and the account given by Bhāī Gurdās. His theory is that Gurū Nānak visited Baghdad twice. The first visit took place in A.D. 1506–7,[6] on the way to Mecca, and on this occasion the Gurū met Bahlol. The second visit was in A.D. 1511–12[7] and this time the discourse was with Dastgīr. Kahn Singh suggests a discourse with 'the descendants of Pīr Dastgīr, Bahlol, and other holy men'.[8] Several writers add that the discourse took place on the platform which is to be found beneath the inscription in the building which houses the tomb of Bahlūl Dānā. This assumption is evidently based upon the location of the inscription in relation to the platform, and upon Anand Acharya's 'slab of granite'.

Of these two inscriptions the Arabic one described by Anand Acharya must certainly be rejected as evidence of a visit to Baghdad. An inscription corresponding to the translation which he gives has never been discovered

[1] Kartar Singh, *Life of Guru Nanak Dev*, p. 214, n. 1. [2] Ibid.
[3] Vir Singh, *Gurū Nānak Chamatakār*, vol. ii, p. 664, n. *.
[4] Teja Singh and Ganda Singh, op. cit., p. 12.
[5] Kartar Singh, op. cit., p. 215. See also Sewaram Singh, op. cit., p. 155.
[6] 912 H., the date given by Anand Acharya.
[7] Vir Singh's reading of the date on the Turkish inscription. [8] *MK*, p. 622.

by anyone else, and without access to the original it is impossible to accept the Swami's poetic testimony as adequate evidence.

The most likely explanation of the missing original is that Anand Acharya's poem concerns not a separate inscription but the one which is to be found near the tomb of Bahlūl Dānā. The Swami might well have known of its existence and visited its location, for his book was published three years after its discovery. The experience which he records in the title of his poem could have taken place in or shortly after 1916.[1] Within the poem itself there are indications which point to an identification of his 'Arabic inscription' with the Turkish inscription. One such pointer is the name 'Balol' which he gives to the Gurū's disciple. The fact that this corresponds to the name of the court jester whose tomb lies near the Turkish inscription is much more likely to be a result of confusion than of coincidence. The reference to 'a shrine outside the town of Baghdad' also fits the Turkish inscription, and the 'simple slab of granite' may well be a poetic description of the platform beneath the inscription. Bahlūl Dānā's tomb is said to be adjacent to an old cemetery,[2] a location which would explain the Swami's reference to 'the grassy desert of the dead'; and the 'pomegranate grove' may perhaps correspond to the garden which is shown in diagrams of the tomb and its adjacent enclosure.[3]

In view of the translation difficulties which the Turkish inscription has presented the description of it as 'Arabic' need occasion no surprise, and the wording of the Swami's own translation probably arises from these same difficulties. If he did in fact see the Turkish inscription it would have been soon after its discovery and, consequently, prior to the more concerted efforts to produce a translation. The translation which he gives of the 'words upon the stone' is probably a poetic reconstruction, from memory, of an inscription only very imperfectly understood. The likelihood that he would have written from memory could also explain the date which he gives. It seems probable that Anand Acharya's poem represents an imaginative reconstruction of a Baghdad discourse, based upon the writer's recollection of a visit to the tomb of Bahlūl Dānā.

This leaves us with the Turkish inscription and in this connexion there are three basic questions which require answers. First, does the inscription actually refer to Gurū Nānak? Secondly, what date does it give? Thirdly, if it does refer to Gurū Nānak and if it does give a date which accords with the known events of his life, can it be accepted as authentic evidence of a visit to Baghdad? The writer owes the following comment to Dr. V. L. Ménage, Reader in Turkish at the School of Oriental and African Studies, London.

[1] It is also possible that he may have chanced upon the inscription before its reported discovery in 1916.

[2] Sewaram Singh, op. cit., p. 155.

[3] Ibid., p. 156. Vir Singh, op. cit., vol. ii, p. 663.

While in Baghdad in the summer of 1965 Miss D. Collon of the British Museum very kindly took a series of photographs of the inscription [in the tomb of Bahlūl Dānā], the clearest of which I enclose. She tells me that the inscription has been painted over several times with dark green paint, which has chipped in places and so made it difficult to read.

There is no doubt that the language is Ottoman Turkish and that the text is a quatrain, rhyming *aaba*, in the metre *mufta'ilun fā'ilun mufta'ilun fā'ilun*; this is a rather rare but standard metre of classical Persian and Turkish poetry.

Transliterating according to the system of the *Encyclopaedia of Islam*, I read the text as follows (lines 1 and 3 being certain, and line 4 practically certain):

1. Gör ne murād eyledi Ḥaḍret-i Rabb-i Medjīd
2. [five syllables] ola tā ki 'imāret djedīd
3. Yediler imdād edüb geldi ki tārīkhine
4. Yapdī thewāb edjr ede anī mürīd-i sa'īd

sene 917

1. See what the Glorious Lord proposed
2. [ ] that the building should be new.
3. The seven having given help, there came for the chronogram of it:
4. 'The blessed disciple performed a meritorious work; may He recompense it.'

year 917 [A.H. = A.D. 1511–12]

The five translations which you have shown me are all in varying degrees unsatisfactory.[1] Without going into detail, I mention three points which bear closely upon your problem:

(*a*) The word 'Guru' of versions 1 and 2 is a misreading of Turkish *gör* (line 1), 'see'.

(*b*) *murād* (line 1) is not a personal name, as versions 2, 3, and 4 interpret it, but bears its usual lexical meaning 'desire', 'wish'.

(*c*) The expression 'Glorious Lord' of line 1, correctly read in version 3 (i.e. 'Hazrat *Rab-i-Majid*'), and rendered 'Divine Master' in version 1, could not be applied to a human being, however saintly, but must refer to God.

The part of line 2 which I cannot understand is the passage where earlier translators have read *Bābā Nānak faḳīr* or, more grammatically, *Bābā Nānak-i faḳīr* (either six or seven syllables); and in the photograph the first letters certainly appear to be *bābānānk* and the next word, though not at all clear, might indeed be *faḳīr*. But the metre indicates clearly that this section contains only five syllables and that they scan – ◡ ◡ – –. The word *baba* being Turkish, both its vowels are by nature short, but since it is legitimate in poetry to lengthen a short vowel if necessary, the word could be scanned *bābă*. It would, however, be a grave fault of prosody to shorten the long vowel of *Nānak* in order to satisfy the demands of the metre for the third syllable of the line. Hence *Bābă Nānak faḳīr* does not fit the metre—and even if the reading is accepted the complete line does

[1] The same five translations are given above, pp. 128–9.

not make sense. I regret that I am unable to suggest the correct reading, but *Baba Nānak* seems to me to be excluded.

The last words of line 3 are an indication to the reader that line 4 constitutes a chronogram, i.e. that the total of the numerical values of the letters in it will reveal the date (by Muslim reckoning) of the event which the inscription commemorates. Vir Singh's calculation, giving 917, is based on two misreadings, the most serious of which arithmetically is *nwāb* = 59 for *thwāb* = 509. My reading of the line gives 27+509+204+20+61+254+144 = 1219. However, the poet's ingenuity has not stopped here. The phrase 'The seven having given help' in line 3 does not refer merely to the Ridjāl al-ghayb, the invisible Helpers who, in popular Muslim belief, come to the aid of the distressed. It is also a warning that 7 has to be added to the total given by line 4. (Examples of such enigmatic chronograms are given by Salâhaddin Elker, *Kitâbelerde (ebced) hesabinin rolü*, in *Vakiflar Dergisi* iii (Ankara, 1956), 17–25, esp. p. 22.) Thus the date indicated by the quatrain is 1219+7 = 1226 A.H., i.e. 26 January 1811–15 January 1812.

The date in the cartouche below certainly appears in the photograph as 917 (A.D. 1511–12). It is impossible to reconcile this figure with the chronogram. Bearing in mind the points (1) that it would be very surprising to find an Ottoman Turkish inscription of this date in Baghdad (first occupied by the Ottomans only in 1534), (2) that riddling chronograms of this type do not make their appearance, so far as I know, until the eighteenth century, (3) that the figures in the cartouche have evidently been touched up, and (4) that the width of the cartouche seems appropriate to the accommodation of four figures rather than three, I am forced to conclude that the original reading in the cartouche was '1226', and that this is an Ottoman inscription of the early nineteenth century.

To answer your three questions: (1) Does the inscription refer to Gurū Nānak? Almost certainly not. (2) What date does it give? Apparently 1226 A.H. = A.D. 1811–12. (3) Can it be accepted as evidence of a visit by Gurū Nānak to Baghdad? No.

The janam-sākhī traditions offer insufficient evidence and the support hitherto claimed on the basis of the inscription must be withdrawn. Although there remains a possibility that Gurū Nānak visited Baghdad we are now compelled to regard it as an unsubstantiated possibility. The tradition may be classified with the possible *sākhīs*, for Baghdad was certainly not beyond the range of a traveller from India and access to the city would not have been refused as in the case of Mecca. The weakness of the evidence indicates, however, a remote possibility, not a strong one.

Bābur and the sack of Saidpur

Bābur is the only contemporary figure of any significance who is referred to by name in the works of Gurū Nānak, and with the exception of Bhāī Gurdās's *Vār* 1 the principal janam-sākhīs all record that the Gurū was present as a witness when the Mughal army assaulted the town of Saidpur.[1] The *sākhīs* which offer a description of his experiences on this occasion are of very considerable importance as they provide the only reference in the janam-sākhīs to a recognizable and datable event in contemporary Indian history.

The attack upon Saidpur was made during the third of Bābur's preliminary expeditions into North India. Mrs. Beveridge has described it as follows:

The march out from Kābul may have been as soon as muster and equipment allowed after the return from Lamghān chronicled in the diary. It was made through Bajaur where refractory tribesmen were brought to order. The Indus will have been forded at the usual place where, until the last one of 932 A.H. (1525 AD.), all expeditions crossed on the outward march. Bhīra was traversed in which were Bābur's own Commanders, and advance was made, beyond lands yet occupied, to Siālkot, 72 miles north of Lāhor and in the Rechna *dū-āb*. It was occupied without resistance; and a further move was made to what the MSS. call Sayyidpūr; this attempted defence, was taken by assault and put to the sword. No place named Sayyidpūr is given in the Gazetteer of India,[2] but the *Ayīn-i-akbarī* mentions a Sidhpūr which from its neighbourhood to Siālkot may be what Bābur took.

Nothing indicates an intention in Bābur to join battle with Ibrahīm at this time; Lāhor may have been his objective, after he had made a demonstration in force to strengthen his footing in Bhīra. Whatever he may have planned to do beyond Sidhpūr (?) was frustrated by the news which took him back to Kābul and thence to Qandahār, that an incursion into his territory had been made by Shāh Beg.[3]

According to Mrs. Beveridge this expedition was made in 1520.[4] If the janam-sākhīs' claim that Gurū Nānak was present at the sack of Saidpur can be established it follows that he must have returned, at least temporarily, from his travels by that year. The question then arises of whether or not this date assists us in determining the end of his period of travelling.

The janam-sākhīs relate that Gurū Nānak and Mardānā happened to reach Saidpur at a time when its Paṭhān inhabitants were celebrating numerous marriages. The *Purātan* version adds that on this occasion the Gurū was also accompanied by some faqīrs who were weak with hunger.[5] The travellers asked for food, but were everywhere refused. This so enraged the Gurū that he uttered the verse which is recorded in the *Ādi Granth* as *Tilaṅg* 5.[6] A brāhmaṇ who, it seems, had heard the verse and

[1] It is also spelt Sayyidpur. The early janam-sākhīs refer to it as Saidpur, Saidpur Saṇḍeālī, Saidpur Siriālī, and Saidpur Saloī (*Pur JS*, p. 58, n. †; *Mih JS*, p. 463). It is the modern Eminābād, nine miles south-east of Gujranwālā. The *GR* uses the modern name (p. 112).

[2] Saidpur and Eminābād are identified in the *Imperial Gazetteer of India*, vol. 12, p. 24, and also in the *Gazetteer of the Gujranwala District 1893–4*, p. 173.

[3] A. S. Beveridge, *The Bābur-nāma in English*, vol. i, p. 429.

[4] Ibid., p. 428. See also Leyden and Erskine, *Memoirs of Zehir-ed-Din Muhammed Baber* (1st edition, 1826), p. 286.

[5] *Pur JS*, p. 58.

[6] *AG*, p. 722.

who recognized it as a summons to Bābur to punish the ungenerous town, begged him to retract his curse. This the Gurū was unable to do, but he promised the brāhmaṇ that he and his family would be spared if they took refuge at a certain pool some distance outside the town.[1] Bābur then descended upon Saidpur, sacked it, put all of its inhabitants to the sword, and ravaged the surrounding countryside. All this had happened because the churlish people of the town had failed to show proper consideration towards faqīrs.

Such was the destruction which Bābā (Nānak's) *śabad* brought upon the Paṭhāns. A Great Soul was filled with wrath and because faqīrs believe in God He hears their prayers. God hears the petitions of faqīrs and whatever is in a faqīr's heart He performs.[2]

Miharbān gives the same explanation for the town's misfortune. He concludes, as usual, with a *ślok* of his own.

Those who do not heed a faqīr's request are tormented in Hell. Behold their condition! The slave of Nānak says, 'The beliefs of faqīrs are true; all else is false.'[3]

After this the two principal accounts diverge. The *Purātan* janam-sākhīs relate an interview with Bābur,[4] whereas the *Miharbān Janam-sākhī* describes an assault by Bābur on Ṭillā Bālguṇḍāī.[5]

It is at once clear that much of what the janam-sākhīs relate must be rejected. The reason they give for the destruction of the town can be dismissed on rational grounds and also because it is completely out of character as far as Gurū Nānak is concerned. Nothing in his works, including the verse which is interpreted as a curse, offer the remotest sign that he could be capable of such vindictive behaviour. Most of the extra *Purātan* material,

[1] 'The Chaḍḍa (*sic* Chaḍḍhā, a khatri sub-caste) hold the *ak* sacred, because they say their forefathers once fought with Babar near Eminabad and all fell, save one who hid under an *ak* bush. He refounded the section and it still performs the *munnan* at Eminabad and worships the *ak*.' *A Glossary of the Tribes and Castes of the Punjab &c*, vol. ii, p. 518. This tradition and the janam-sākhī story evidently have a common origin.

[2] *Pur JS*, p. 59.

[3] *Mih JS*, p. 465.

[4] *Pur JS*, pp. 62–63. The *Hāfizābād* manuscript, which relates a longer interview with Bābur than the *Colebrooke* version, describes him as a clandestine *qalandar* (see *supra*, p. 44). The *Tārīkh-i-Dāūdī* also recounts a legend which depicts Bābur as a *qalandar*. This legend relates how a *qalandar* once visited Sultan Sikandar Lodī in Delhi. The Sultan accorded him due reverence and hospitality, and later learnt, to his great dismay, that he had missed an opportunity of capturing Bābur. The extract is translated in N. Roy's *Niamatullah's History of the Afghans*, part i, p. 123.

[5] A famous Kānphaṭ yogī centre thirteen miles west of Dīnā in Jhelum District. It is variously referred to as Ṭillā Bālguṇḍāī, Bālnāth kā Ṭillā, Ṭillā Ḍaṅgā, Jogīān dā Ṭillā, and Gorakh Ṭillā. See G. W. Briggs, *Gorakhnāth and the Kānphaṭa Yogīs*, pp. 101 ff. Bābur evidently camped below the village on his way into north India in 1525, but the reference in the *Bābur-nāma* makes no mention of any encounter with the inhabitants. A. S. Beveridge, op. cit., vol. ii, pp. 452–3. For the *Purātan* and *Miharbān* accounts of the complete episode see *supra*, pp. 43–45 and 62 respectively.

which describes the actual encounter with Bābur, must also be repudiated as a legendary wonder story, and so too must the *Miharbān Janam-sākhī*'s account of an attack upon Ṭillā Bālgundāī. This latter addition is a clear example of a story which has evolved out of a reference in one of Gurū Nānak's works, in this case the fourth stanza of *Āsā aṣṭapadī* 12.[1]

All of this may be rejected, but it still leaves open the two basic questions. Was Gurū Nānak present during the sack of Saidpur, and did he meet Bābur?

The principal argument which has been advanced in support of his presence at Saidpur, and one which has hitherto been accepted as conclusive, is the fact that Gurū Nānak himself refers directly to Bābur and describes the devastation wrought by his army. These references occur in the hymns *Āsā* 39,[2] *Āsā aṣṭapadī* 11,[3] *Āsā aṣṭapadī* 12,[4] and *Tilaṅg* 5,[5] four verses which are collectively known as the *Bābar-vāṇī*, or 'utterances concerning Bābur'. All four are set by the janam-sākhīs in the context of either the assault on Saidpur or Gurū Nānak's subsequent interview with Bābur soon afterwards.

There can be no doubt that in these verses Gurū Nānak is describing at least one of the Mughal expeditions for he does so explicitly.

> Now that Bābur's authority has been established the princes starve.[6]
>
> Thousands of *pīrs* tried to stop Mīr (Bābur by means of magic) when they heard of his invasion. Resting-places were burnt, rock-like temples (were destroyed), princes were hacked into pieces and trampled in the dust. (In spite of the *pīrs*' efforts) no Mughal was blinded. None of the spells had any effect.[7]
>
> Thou didst spare Khurāsān and spread fear in Hindustān. O Creator, (Thou didst this), but to avoid the blame Thou didst send the Mughal as (the messenger of) Death.[8]

But to which of Bābur's expeditions does he refer? The indications are that the two *aṣṭapadīs*, at least, concern the later invasions of 1524 and 1525–6. Saidpur is nowhere mentioned and the descriptions hardly accord with the limited nature of the 1520 incursion.

In the first place, there is one reference which indicates that the Lodī rule had come to an end prior to the composition of the *aṣṭapadī* in which it occurs.

> The wealth and sensual beauty which had intoxicated them became their enemies. To the messengers (of Death) the command was given to strip

[1] *AG*, pp. 417–18. See below. An *aṣṭapadi* is a poem or hymn of eight, or occasionally more, stanzas. *Rāg Āsā* is one of the principal metres of the *Ādi Granth*.

[2] *AG*, p. 360. [3] *AG*, p. 417. [4] *AG*, pp. 417–18.

[5] *AG*, pp. 722–3. [6] *Āsā Aṣṭ* 11 (5), *AG*, p. 417.

[7] *Āsā Aṣṭ* 12 (4), *AG* pp. 417–18. [8] *Āsā* 39, *AG*, p. 360.

them of their honour and carry them off. If it seems good to Thee Thou givest glory, and if it pleases Thee Thou givest punishment. Had they paused to think in time, then would they have received the punishment? But the rulers paid no heed, passing their time instead in revelry, and now that Bābur's authority has been established the princes starve.[1]

It seems clear that the reference here must be to the Lodīs, as there are no other 'rulers' or 'princes' to whom it could conceivably apply. These two stanzas bring out the point which Gurū Nānak makes in all four verses. The historical incident expresses for him a religious truth. It is for him an illustration of the truth that God's justice cannot be ignored, that the divine Order (*Hukam*) cannot be defied, that unrighteousness will be punished.[2] The Lodīs had acted in a manner contrary to the divine intention and they paid the inevitable penalty for having done so. This, however, must surely refer to the ultimate overthrow of the dynasty. The 1520 incursion was by no means a decisive defeat for the Lodīs and could scarcely be interpreted as the final penalty for their irresponsibility and unrighteousness.

Secondly, the description given of a battle fought by the Mughals and of the devastation caused by them does not tally with the evident nature of the 1520 expedition.[3]

The Mughals and Paṭhāns fought each other, wielding swords on the battlefield. One side took aim and fired guns, the other urged on (its) elephants. They whose letters were torn in (God's) court had to die.[4] Hindu, Muslim, Bhaṭṭ, and Ṭhākur women (suffered), some having their *burqās* torn from head to toe, others being slain.[5] They whose handsome husbands failed to return home, how did they pass the night, (what grief they must have endured)![6]

[1] *Āsā Aṣṭ* 11 (4–5), *AG*, p. 417.

[2] In the case of *Āsā* 39 this is only a subsidiary theme and is limited to the last stanza.

If anyone assumes an exalted name and indulges always in whatever his mind desires, he becomes as a worm in the sight of the Master, regardless of how much corn he pecks up. Die (to self) and you shall truly live. Remember the Name and you shall receive a portion.

The principal theme is the question of why the weak should suffer unmerited torment at the hands of the strong and in this respect the verse has obvious affinities with the Book of Job. God is called to account, just as Job summons Him, and the conclusion which Gurū Nānak reaches is expressed in the line:

Thou dost unite and Thou dost divide; thus is Thy glory manifested.

The only solution to the problem lies in the absolute nature of the divine will and authority —absolute and ultimately beyond human comprehension. This differs from the point made in the other *Bābar-vāṇī* verses, but both themes directly concern the nature of the divine *Hukam*.

[3] See *supra*, p. 133, the second paragraph of Mrs. Beveridge's note.

[4] The reference is to the custom of making a small tear in obituary notifications.

[5] Literally: becoming inhabitants of the cremation ground.

[6] *Āsā Aṣṭ* 12 (5–6), *AG*, p. 418.

This reads much more like a description of an important battle and the victors' subsequent devastation than simply the account of a siege. A battle-field is explicitly mentioned and the presence of elephants suggests that it was no mere skirmish. The reference to the bereaved wives whose husbands failed to return home also points to a battle rather than to an incident which involved no more than the fall of a small besieged town, and the same indications are evident both in the preceding stanza and in the extract quoted above from *Āsā aṣṭapadī* 11. The episode which appears to correspond most closely to this combination of fixed battle and subsequent devastation is the incursion of 1524. On this occasion Bābur defeated the army led by Bihār Khān Lodī which Ibrāhīm Lodī had sent to Lahore, and then sacked the city.[1] Neither Talvaṇḍī nor Kartārpur is far distant from Lahore and we may assume that if Gurū Nānak were in the Pañjāb at the time he would certainly have been well acquainted with the incident.[2]

The implied destruction of Lodī authority, together with the nature of the warfare described in the *aṣṭapadīs*, plainly suggests that these two works at least were written after 1526 and that they were prompted not by a single event, but rather by the series of events which culminated in the overthrow of the Lodī dynasty. The other two verses offer no clear indications. The fact that both express the same *Hukam* theme as the two *aṣṭapadīs* may imply a date subsequent to the Lodī downfall, but the point is not brought out with sufficient clarity to enable us to attach much significance to it.[3]

There are, accordingly, two principal conclusions which may be drawn from the four *Bābar-vāṇī* compositions. The first is that Gurū Nānak must have personally witnessed devastation caused by Bābur's troops. There is in his descriptions of agony and destruction a vividness and a depth of feeling which can be explained only as expressions of a direct, personal experience. The actual battle described in *Āsā aṣṭapadī* 12 may possibly

[1] A. S. Beveridge, op. cit., vol. i, p. 441.

[2] According to some traditions the cryptic *ślok* which runs:

lāhor saharu jaharu kaharu savā paharu

refers to the 1524 attack on Lahore. Literally translated the *ślok* reads:

Lahore city, poison, violence, a watch and a quarter.

It is number 27 in the collection 'Surplus *śloks* left over from the *Vārs*', *AG*, p. 1412.

[3] *Tilaṅg* 5, *AG*, p. 723, contains an enigmatic line:

He will come in seventy-eight and go in ninety-seven, and another disciple of a warrior will arise.

The usual explanation is that this refers to Bābur's entry into India in S. 1578 (A.D. 1521–22) and to Humāyūn's departure in S. 1597 (A.D. 1540). The *marad kā chelā*, 'disciple of a warrior', is said to refer to Sher Shāh Sūr. (*Śabadārath*, p. 723, n. 4.) The objections to this interpretation are that the third and fourth expeditions evidently took place in A.D. 1520 and 1523–4 respectively, and that although Humāyūn was certainly defeated by Sher Shāh in 1540 the reference would be to an event which followed Gurū Nānak's death.

be based upon hearsay, but even here one is left with an impression of close proximity to the event. The second conclusion is that the four verses were probably composed after 1526 in response to the complete series of invasions, rather than in response to any single event within the series. *Āsā aṣṭapadī* 12, with its battle scene, evidently refers to a specific event, but the nature of the reference points to the 1524 capture of Lahore, not to the 1520 sack of Saidpur.

This does not necessarily mean, however, that there can be no truth in the janam-sākhī traditions concerning Gurū Nānak's presence as a witness during the sack of Saidpur. The support claimed on the basis of his four *śabads* must go, but there remain others. In the first place, the janam-sākhīs all agree on this point. Secondly, the tradition concerns an incident which happened in the Pañjāb during the latter part of the Gurū's life. Thirdly, there appears to be a measure of accuracy in the janam-sākhī descriptions of the actual assault. And fourthly, it seems reasonable to assume that had there been no factual basis for the connexion with Bābur the narrators would surely have chosen the capture of Lahore or the Battle of Pāṇīpat as a setting rather than an obscure town besieged on one of the minor expeditions. These factors indicate a strong tradition and one which has good claims to acceptance. We may conclude from the janam-sākhīs that Gurū Nānak was probably in the Pañjāb during 1520, and from the *Bābar-vāṇī* verses that he was almost certainly there in 1526.

The same cannot, however, be said for the claim that Gurū Nānak actually met Bābur. The *Miharbān Janam-sākhī* omits it, the *Purātan* janam-sākhīs give divergent accounts,[1] and the familiar tendency to introduce interviews with the acknowledged great offers a much more likely explanation of its origin. It cannot be ruled out as completely impossible, but it certainly appears to be most unlikely.

The founding of Kartārpur

The *sākhīs* which describe the founding of Kartārpur raise two issues. First, there is the question of whether or not the account they give of the origin of the village can be accepted; and secondly, that of the incident's location within the total framework of the Gurū's travels.

In these *sākhīs* we have both a Pañjāb setting and general agreement amongst the janam-sākhīs as far as the content of the incident is concerned, but we also have a number of minor miracles. According to the janam-sākhī accounts a certain rich official[2] set out with the intention of apprehending the Gurū, but was persuaded to forsake enmity for reverence after

[1] *Pur JS*, p. 65.

[2] He is referred to by the janam-sākhīs as a *karoṛī*, a high-ranking revenue collector of the Mughal period. The term came into use in the time of Akbar and is accordingly an anachronism in the janam-sākhīs.

being smitten on the way with blindness and other afflictions.[1] This aspect of the story must be rejected, but its elimination leaves the essence of the *sākhī* unaffected. With the miraculous element excluded we are left with a brief account of a man of substance who in some manner developed a great reverence for the Gurū, and who gave this reverence practical expression either by building the small village of Kartārpur, or, more likely, by donating the land on which it was subsequently built, and by erecting a *dharmsālā*.

There can be no doubt that Kartārpur, if not positively founded by or for Gurū Nānak, was at least transformed from insignificance to importance by his arrival there. The tradition that he actually founded the village, or that it was founded for him, appears to be much the stronger of the alternatives, for the janam-sākhīs are here dealing with an issue which has a local setting and which should evidently be placed in the last two decades of the Gurū's life. The land for such a village would have had to be procured in some manner and there is nothing which leads us to doubt the story that it was donated by a wealthy Sikh. To this simple statement of the village's origin miraculous elements were subsequently added in its oral transmission. Stripped of them the story offers no difficulties and can be accepted.

This disposes of the first question. The second one arises because the janam-sākhīs, while generally agreeing as far as the actual content of the *sākhī* is concerned, disagree regarding the point at which they introduce the incident. For Miharbān the founding of the village marks the completion of the Gurū's major travels,[2] whereas the *Hāfizābād* janam-sākhī places it at the conclusion of the first of the *Purātan* tradition's five journeys.[3] The *Gyān-ratanāvalī* offers yet another alternative by setting it at the end of the Gurū's visit to the north.[4]

This seems to present us with three possibilities, but in all probability there are only two. The acknowledgement of three possibilities assumes that the different travel itineraries can be compared and a decision made in favour of one of them. As we shall see, however, the likelihood is that all three should be rejected and accordingly the question at this point is whether the founding of Kartārpur took place at some unknown point during the Gurū's two decades of travel, or whether it took place after their conclusion. The *Hāfizābād* janam-sakhi and the *Gyān-ratanāvalī* offer the first alternative, and the *Miharbān Janam-sākhī* the second.

There is no evidence which will either establish the one or disprove the other, but the second appears the more likely. Even if Miharbān's chronology is suspect it is at least a more likely pattern than that developed by the *Purātan* tradition. Moreover, this particular incident is, in a sense, outside

[1] See *supra*, pp. 46, 63–64. See also *BG* 24. 1.
[2] *Mih JS*, p. 516.
[3] *Pur JS*, p. 74. The *Colebrooke* manuscript lacks this *sākhī*.
[4] *GR*, p. 401.

the problem of travel chronology as far as the *Miharbān* version is concerned, as it comes at the conclusion of the travel period. The *Miharbān* alternative is also more satisfactory in that a sustained period of travel seems more likely than two such periods broken by an interlude of settled life at Kartārpur. We may accept that the land was donated by a wealthy follower of the Gurū, and we may add that the village was probably built after the conclusion of the Gurū's travels. This recognizes the stronger likelihood of the *Miharbān* alternative without according it an unqualified acceptance.

The return to Talvaṇḍī

The *sākhīs* which describe Gurū Nānak's return to his home village record nothing of importance apart from the fact that he did return and that he was there reunited with his parents. Their significance lies rather in the differing points at which the janam-sākhīs introduce the incident, a question which has already been considered in connexion with the founding of Kartārpur. The descriptions of Gurū Nānak's reunion with his mother are among the most beautiful passages in the janam-sākhīs.

The visit to Pāk Paṭṭan

There seems to be little doubt that Gurū Nānak must at some time have met Sheikh Ibrāhīm, the contemporary incumbent of the Sūfī line descending from Sheikh Farīd.[1] Pāk Paṭṭan was within easy reach and Sheikh Farīd's reputation would certainly have exercised a powerful attraction. Even without the testimony of the janam-sākhīs such a meeting might well be regarded as a likelihood. There are evident inconsistencies in the janam-sākhī descriptions of the encounter, but they are in substantial agreement as far as the principal details are concerned. We may assume that the discourse which they record owes more to imagination than to an actual knowledge of the event, but there is nothing which suggests that the event itself is open to doubt. Accordingly, we may accept as a strong probability the tradition concerning a meeting in Pāk Paṭṭan with Sheikh Ibrāhīm, the contemporary successor of Sheikh Farīd.

Discourses with Siddhs

The janam-sākhīs record two famous encounters with Siddhs within or near the Pañjāb. Of these one must be regarded with some scepticism, but the other may perhaps be authentic if for Siddhs we read Kānphaṭ or Nāth yogīs.

[1] For an account of the life and work of Sheikh Ibrāhīm see Lajwanti Rama Krishna, *Pañjābi Ṣūfi Poets*, pp. 1–11.

The story of Gurū Nānak's disputation with the Siddhs at Gorakh-haṭaṛī[1] must be regarded with considerable doubt as the *sākhīs* which describe it in the *Purātan* and *Miharbān* versions are both unsatisfactory. In the *Purātan* janam-sākhīs it amounts to no more than a wonder story of how the Siddhs sought to overwhelm him by assuming fearsome forms through the exercise of their occult powers.[2] It appears that the *sākhī* must originally have developed without having any specific location assigned to it, for Bhāī Gurdās sets the same story in the context of the Achal Baṭālā disputation.[3] The *Miharbān Janam-sākhī* gives an entirely different description and one which is equally unsatisfactory. All that it tells us is that a religious fair was being held there and that Gurū Nānak held a discourse with 'the *gurū* of the yogīs'. Gurū Nānak may have visited the locality, but neither of these *sākhīs* can be accepted as sufficient evidence for such a visit.

The Achal Baṭālā encounter, however, has a firmer basis. Bhāī Gurdās,[4] the *Purātan* janam-sākhīs,[5] the India Office Library manuscript B40,[6] the *Gyān-ratanāvalī*,[7] the *Bālā* version,[8] and *Pothī Harijī* of the *Miharbān Janam-sākhī*[9] all record such a dispute, and the fact that Achal Baṭālā is so near Kartārpur enhances the likelihood of the tradition. Bhāī Gurdās and the B40 manuscript both name the occasion as a Śivrātri fair. As usual there are details in the various accounts which must be rejected, but the basis of the tradition appears to be well founded. Gurū Nānak's own works also offer it some support. The location is not named in any of his compositions, but it is clear from many of them that his contacts with Nāth yogīs must have been frequent and it seems evident from such a work as the *Siddh Goṣṭ*[10] that he engaged them in formal debate.

Visits to Multān

Multān, like Pāk Paṭṭan, was a place which would almost certainly have drawn a person such as Gurū Nānak, for it too was a renowned centre of Muslim devotion within easy reach of Talvaṇḍī and Kartārpur. There is, however, nothing which may, with any assurance, be added to this assumption. In the *Purātan* janam-sākhīs the only reference to Multān occurs in the *sākhī* which describes the death of Bahāuddīn, 'the Pīr of Multān'.[11] This does not establish a connexion with the city for, as we have already noted, the reference to Sheikh Bahāuddīn must be regarded as an anachronism.[12] It appears that Miharbān's description of a discourse with the *potā*

[1] Generally identified with an elevated area in Peshāwar. *MK*, Addendum, p. 43, and *A Glossary of the Tribes and Castes of the Punjab*, vol. i, p. 679.
[2] *Pur JS*, pp. 104–6. This version concludes with a verse which is by Gurū Arjan.
[3] *BG* I. 41.
[4] *BG* I. 39–44.
[5] *Pur JS*, *sākhī* 50, p. 97.
[6] IOL MS. Panj. B40, folio 117. This janam-sākhī records a second visit to Achal on folio 181.
[7] *GR*, *sākhīs* 170–7, pp. 463–508.
[8] *Bālā JS*, *sākhī* 61, p. 287.
[9] Khalsa College, Amritsar, MS. SHR: 427, *sākhī* 173, folio 344a.
[10] *AG*, pp. 938–46.
[11] *Pur JS*, *sākhī* 55, p. 108.
[12] See *supra*, p. 82.

of Bahāuddīn must likewise be rejected as an anachronism.[1] The term *potā* generally designates a son's son and although it is occasionally used of a descendant further down the male line it is highly unlikely that it will be applied beyond the sixth generation. This brings Miharbān's reference within the bounds of remote possibility, but there is nothing in the discourse which strengthens its claims.

The tradition related by Bhāī Gurdās[2] must also be set aside. The incident which he briefly recounts concerns a symbolic gesture which the *pīrs* of Multān are said to have made when they heard of the Gurū's approach. A cup filled to the brim with milk was sent out to him, the intention being to indicate that the city already held all the holy men it could contain. Gurū Nānak laid a jasmine petal on the milk and returned it, thereby proclaiming that there was still room for one more. This is an example of the kind of anecdote which gains common currency in hagiography. An earlier version of this particular legend is related in connexion with 'Abd al-Qādir Jīlānī (A.D. 1077–1166), the founder of the Qādirī order of Sūfīs.[3] The details differ,[4] but the story is essentially the same.

There is accordingly nothing in the janam-sākhīs which may safely be added to the assumption that Gurū Nānak probably visited Multān. It is possible that he may have had contact with descendants of Sheikh Bāhāuddīn and that to this extent there is an element of truth in the *Purātan* and *Miharbān* accounts. As they stand, however, all of the accounts which describe Multān visits must be rejected. We are left with no more than our initial assumption that the fame and proximity of Multān would almost certainly have led Gurū Nānak to visit the city at least once during his lifetime.

Gurū Aṅgad

The *sākhī* describing the manner in which Gurū Aṅgad was tested and found worthy of the succession has already been rejected,[5] but there can be no doubt that the other basic details recorded by the janam-sākhīs are substantially correct. To say that Gurū Aṅgad succeeded Gurū Nānak is to state the obvious and unchallengeable, for the *Ādi Granth* includes works

[1] *Mih JS*, *goṣṭ* 131, p. 434. See *supra*, p. 60. The IOL MS. Panj. B40, folio 53, also describes a meeting with the *potā* of Bahāuddīn.

[2] *BG* 1. 44. The story is repeated in the *GR*, *sākhī* 178, p. 508.

[3] J. P. Brown, *The Darvishes or Oriental Spiritualism*, ed. H. A. Rose, pp. 100–11.

[4] According to this version the city was Baghdad, the cup was filled with water, and the flower which 'Abd al-Qādir Jīlānī laid on it was a rose. This legend is given as the origin of the Qādirī custom of wearing an embroidered rose in the cap (J. A. Subhan, *Sufism: Its Saints and Shrines*, pp. 181–2). Another version of the same story is to be found in Parsi tradition (H. Jai Singh, *My Neighbours*, p. 56, following A. R. Wadia, art. 'Dadabhai Naoroji' in *Bhavan's Journal* of 7 Aug. 1960).

[5] See *supra*, p. 77.

by him and Sikh tradition could not possibly be mistaken on such a point.[1] Nor need we doubt the family background which the janam-sākhīs give, for here too tradition would have been reliable. We may accordingly affirm that Gurū Nānak's successor was Lahiṇā, a resident of Khaḍūr[2] and a Trehaṇ khatrī by caste; that he met the Gurū and became a follower after the settlement of Kartārpur; that the Gurū bestowed on him the name of Aṅgad; and that he chose him as his successor in preference to either of his sons.

Gurū Nānak's decision to appoint a formal successor was one of critical importance, for there can be no doubt that it was the establishment of an effective succession of Gurūs which, above all other factors, ensured the transmission of the first Gurū's teachings and the cohesion of the religious community which he had gathered around him. The choosing and formal installation of Aṅgad was the first step in the process which issued in the founding of the Khālsā, and ultimately in the emergence of a Sikh nation. Other factors, such as the clarity of the teachings, the compiling and promulgation of a canon of scripture, the ethnic constitution of the community, and the incentive to greater cohesion provided by Mughal persecution, certainly played very important parts, but it is inconceivable that these elements could have had the same enduring effect without the original bond provided by Gurū Nānak.

The chronology of Gurū Nānak's travels

The analysis of individual *sākhīs* is now complete, but there remains the broader question of the total framework which each janam-sākhī compiler has constructed with the *sākhīs* at his disposal. In this respect none of the janam-sākhīs agree. There is general agreement for the period up to Gurū Nānak's departure from Sultānpur, but for the years which follow this event the *Miharbān*, *Purātan*, and *Gyān-ratanāvalī* accounts all give differing chronologies, and that of the *Bālā* version is fragmented to a degree which appears to render it meaningless. Many of the incidents which provide the substance of these differing chronologies have already been discarded and most of the remainder have been classified as no more than possible *sākhīs*, but there still remains the question of whether or not we can accept in a general sense any of the patterns which are given in the different janam-sākhīs.

In this examination it is possible to work from two fixed points. Neither of these points can be regarded as beyond doubt, but both have been accepted in this study as at least probable. The first may be located about

[1] *Vār Rāmakalī* by Rāi Balvaṇḍ and Sattā the Ḍūm refers to Gurū Nānak's appointment of Gurū Aṅgad in stanzas 1–4 (*AG*, pp. 966–7). See *supra*, p. 8.

[2] Tarn Tāran tahsīl, Amritsar District.

the year 1500. An association with Daulat Khān Lodī has been acknowledged as likely and from this it follows that Gurū Nānak probably began his travels in or about that year. The actual date may have been a few years earlier, but is unlikely to have been much later as it must have been in or soon after 1500 that Daulat Khān received his appointment to Lahore. The second point which we are probably entitled to regard as fixed is 1520, the year in which Bābur sacked Saidpur.

The pattern which has been generally accepted is the one set out in the *Purātan* version. This involves four major journeys (*udāsīs*) to the east, south, north, and west respectively, with a brief concluding excursion to Gorakh-haṭaṛī. The Saidpur *sākhī* is included in the first of these, and between each of the journeys Gurū Nānak returns to the Pañjāb.[1]

The *Miharbān Janam-sākhī*, on the other hand, gathers the various *sākhīs* into only two journeys. The first of these is a round trip to the east and then to the south of India. The second is to the north and west, and includes a visit to Gorakh-haṭaṛī. The Saidpur *sākhī* follows Gurū Nānak's return from the west.[2]

The third grouping, that of the *Gyān-ratanāvalī*, follows the *Miharbān* pattern in a general sense as far as the journey to the east and the south is concerned, but divides the Gurū's subsequent travels into separate northern and western tours. The Saidpur *sākhī* is placed at the beginning of the second, or northern, journey.[3]

Of these three, the *Purātan* pattern is the least likely. The Saidpur *sākhī* follows shortly after the *sākhi* which describes Gurū Nānak's return to Talvaṇḍī at the conclusion of his eastern journey, and this return is said to have taken place twelve years after the departure from Sultānpur.[4] The proximity to the Saidpur incident suggests that this *sākhī* should, according to the *Purātan* reckoning, be placed in 1519 or 1520. This does not accord with the Daulat Khān date. Moreover, it means that the remaining four journeys and the period of consolidation at Kartārpur must all be fitted into the last nineteen or twenty years of the Gurū's life. This seems to be most unlikely.[5]

The *Miharbān Janam-sākhī* is also in conflict with the Daulat Khān date as it indicates that the period of travels began in 1506.[6] It is, however, much nearer to reasonable possibility in placing the Saidpur *sākhī* at the end of the major travels, and in this respect it would appear to offer a more likely chronology than the *Gyān-ratanāvalī* pattern which records the northern and western journeys after the Saidpur incident.

[1] See *supra*, pp. 64–65. [2] See *supra*, p. 66. [3] *GR*, pp. 265–75.

[4] *Pur JS*, p. 48. In specifying twelve years as the length of the journey the *Purātan* janam-sākhīs are evidently following convention. Twelve years was the usual time taken by sādhūs for a *tīrath-yātrā*, or visit to the important pilgrimage centres.

[5] See also *supra*, p. 32.

[6] See *supra*, pp. 55, 67.

Comparisons of this nature imply, however, that we are bound to accept one or other of the three recorded patterns. This is certainly not the case. There is a fourth possibility and it is a much more likely one. In all probability the janam-sākhī chronologies represent not known fact, but rather the results of the compilers' reasoning. In other words, it seems likely that what the janam-sākhīs offer us are structures which have been devised in order to provide logical sequences for the stock of oral *sākhīs* at the compilers' disposal. This process need not have been a wholly conscious one. On the contrary, it is more likely to have been a gradual evolution rather than a deliberate ordering of isolated *sākhīs* at a particular point in time.

This is the conclusion indicated by the India Office Library manuscript B40. In this version the individual *sākhīs* are, for the most part, set down in isolation and only rudimentary efforts have been made to organize them into something resembling a sequence. The manuscript makes it plain that many of the incidents are set outside the Pañjāb, but it does not use them to construct an integrated itinerary. This manuscript offers a more primitive janam-sākhī than the *Miharbān* and *Purātan* janam-sākhīs or the *Gyān-ratanāvalī*, and the contrast between its lack of order and the developed continuity of the later versions strongly suggests that integrated itineraries should be regarded as a characteristic of the later stages of the janam-sākhī evolutionary process.

Such a conclusion should not, of course, imply that Gurū Nānak never travelled. All sources agree that he did and traditions which emerged within a century of his death could hardly have been mistaken in a general issue of such importance. This we can certainly accept, and we may also assume that the period of his travels probably covered the first two decades of the sixteenth century. The probable association with Daulat Khān Lodī provides a beginning for the period, and the likelihood that Gurū Nānak was present at Saidpur in 1520 indicates a probable terminus. Certainly he must have been back in the Pañjāb by 1526 at the latest. Within this period, however, it is possible to name neither destination nor sequence. The most we can do is accept as inherently probable Bhāī Gurdās's statement that Gurū Nānak travelled round visiting centres of pilgrimage.[1]

Gurū Nānak's life now falls into three clearly defined periods. The first three decades comprise his childhood and early manhood in Talvaṇḍī and Sultānpur. This first period evidently culminated in an experience of enlightenment and divine call. The fourth and fifth decades are the period of his travels in and possibly beyond India. The remaining two decades were then spent chiefly in Kartārpur, and we may assume that it was during this period that the real foundations of the Sikh community were laid.

[1] *BG* 1. 25.

The life of Gurū Nānak

We may now proceed to relate the life of Gurū Nānak.

Gurū Nānak was born in A.D. 1469, probably in the month of April. His father was Kālū, a Bedī khatrī living in the village of Rāi Bhoi dī Talvaṇḍī, and his mother was named Tripatā. Kālū and Tripatā had one other child, a daughter whose name was probably Nānakī and whose husband's name was Jai Rām. Gurū Nānak was married to the daughter of Mūlā, a Choṇā khatrī of Baṭālā who had formerly resided in the village of Pokho di Randhāvī. His wife's name was Sulakhaṇī and two sons, Lakhmī Dās and Sirī Chand, were born to them.

As a young man Gurū Nānak worked in the town of Sultānpur, probably in the employment of Daulat Khān Lodī. This must have been during the last decade of the fifteenth century. While in Sultānpur he experienced a sense of divine call and it was evidently in response to this that he began a period of travelling in and perhaps beyond India, accompanied for at least some of the time by a bard named Mardānā. Neither the pattern nor the extent of his travels can be determined, but it may be assumed that he visited a number of the more important centres of both Hindu and Muslim pilgrimage. The period of travelling probably ended in or shortly before 1520 as it seems likely that Gurū Nānak witnessed Bābur's attack upon the town of Saidpur in that year. It appears, however, that the references he makes to Bābur in his works point rather to the invasions of 1524 and 1525–6.

At some stage a wealthy follower evidently donated land on the right bank of the Rāvī and there the village of Kartārpur was built. This probably took place after the Gurū's travels had ended. For the remainder of his life he lived in Kartārpur, but made brief journeys from there to places within easy reach. These destinations probably included Pāk Paṭṭan and Multān. Contacts with Nāth yogis were frequent and on one occasion the Gurū evidently engaged a group of them in debate at the village of Achal Baṭālā.

During his years in Kartārpur Gurū Nānak must have attracted many disciples, one of whom was Lahiṇā, a Trehaṇ khatrī of Khaḍūr. Lahiṇā must have impressed the Gurū by his devotion and ability, for prior to his death Gurū Nānak renamed him Aṅgad and appointed him as his successor in preference to either of his sons. The Gurū died in Kartārpur towards the end of the fourth decade of the sixteenth century, probably in September 1539.

In this brief account we have everything of any importance which can be affirmed concerning the events of Gurū Nānak's life. It provides us with an outline, but it is a meagre one, leaving lengthy periods covered by no more than a general comment or a single detail. And yet in spite of this paucity of authentic biographical material there is much we can know about Gurū Nānak. In the numerous works by him which are recorded in the *Ādi Granth* we do not find biographical details but we do find a developed theology which points back to a person. It is to his teachings that our search for the historical Nānak must lead us for it is there only that we can hope to find him.

In the janam-sākhīs what we find is the Gurū Nānak of legend and of faith, the image of the Gurū seen through the eyes of popular piety seventy-five or a hundred years after his death. It is an important image, but it is not the primary object of this study. Here we seek the person who lived and taught in the Pañjāb almost five hundred years ago. Of this person the janam-sākhīs provide only glimpses and by their inadequacy force us back to the works preserved in the *Ādi Granth*. It is true, as we have several times observed, that the *śabads* and *śloks* attributed to Gurū Nānak are not sources of detail concerning the events of his life. As one might reasonably expect, however, it is also true that behind these works and the thought which they contain there can be discerned a personality. Our study of his teachings must be, in part at least, an exercise in discernment.

5

THE TEACHINGS OF GURŪ NĀNAK

Nānak, without the indwelling Name of God one endures suffering throughout the four ages.[1]

What terrible separation it is to be separated from God and what blissful union to be united with Him![2]

TERSE expression is common in the writings of Gurū Nānak and we find examples in these two extracts. Both concern the ultimate purpose of all life and all religion, and set it forth as union with God through the indwelling Name, an inward union which imparts eternal bliss. He who recognizes this, who accepts the proffered means and so attains such union, transcends the cycle of birth and death and passes instead into a condition of beatitude, infinite, eternal, and ultimately inexpressible.

Such a summary statement, however, can have meaning only in the light of a developed understanding of Gurū Nānak's beliefs. Who, or what, is this God with whom union is sought? Of what nature is He? Is He to be conceived in terms of personality? In what way is His being expressed to man? And what is man? Of what nature is his condition that he should seek to transcend it? What are the proffered means and how does he appropriate them? Having appropriated them how can he describe his regenerate condition, in so far as words are able to describe it? These and many other related questions must be answered if we are to reach an adequate understanding of Gurū Nānak's beliefs, of what may properly be called his theology.

Theology is the correct word to use in this connexion, for the whole of Gurū Nānak's thought revolves around his understanding of the nature of God. It was entirely appropriate that Gurū Arjan should place a declaration of the nature of God at the very beginning of the *Ādi Granth* and that it should be called the *Mūl Mantra*, the Basic Credal Statement.[3] Of all Sikh scripture none is more important than Gurū Nānak's *Japjī*, and in this work of surpassing beauty (which significantly follows immediately after the *Mūl Mantra* in the *Ādi Granth*)[4] the theme is God, the One whom men must praise and who yet far exceeds the most exalted conception which the mind of man can form. It is theology which we find in the *śabads* and *śloks* of Gurū Nānak and it is theology of a refined quality.

[1] *Tukhārī Chhant* 2 (4), *AG*, p. 1110.
[2] *Mārū* 1, *AG*, p. 989.
[3] *AG*, p. 1.
[4] *AG*, pp. 1–8.

This theology is not, of course, set out in any systematic form. Gurū Nānak's writings bear witness to his experience of God and the characteristic expression of that experience is the hymn of praise which it engenders. Neither Gurū Nānak nor Gurū Arjan, who compiled the *Ādi Granth*, sought to set out his beliefs in an integrated pattern and we should not expect them to have done so. Theirs was essentially a religion of experience, the 'real' rather than the 'notional'. The latter can, however, do much to impart an understanding of the former. 'Theology', as Professor Basil Willey reminds us, 'is the notional formulation of what the experience seems to mean'.[1] For the purpose of our own understanding an integrated pattern can do much to clarify the nature of Gurū Nānak's belief and accordingly the intention of this section is to seek such a pattern.

The fact that Gurū Nānak's thought is not set out systematically does not mean that it is necessarily inconsistent. On the contrary, one of the great merits of his thought is its very consistency. The accusation of inconsistency has been levelled against him,[2] but we believe that the system outlined in the present chapter will constitute a rebuttal of the charge. One can gauge the importance of this aspect of Gurū Nānak's works by comparing them with those of other *bhagats*. Kabīr's thought, for all its striking qualities, is by no means as consistent doctrinally as that of Gurū Nānak. In Nānak's case the consistency is there even if it is not at once apparent. There is certainly that doctrinal tension which is inevitable in a system upholding both the gracious activity of an absolute God and the necessary participation of man endowed with free will, but the person who seeks to extract the components of Gurū Nānak's thought and to fashion with them a systematic theology does not have to decide between statements which are mutually incompatible. Nor indeed does he have to grapple with the degree of obscurity which is found in so much of Kabīr's thought.

The comparison with Kabīr is an instructive one at this point. Gurū Nānak and Kabīr both offer syntheses and in each case the nature of the synthesis reflects the personality of its author. This is a point of critical importance as far as the subsequent effect of their thought is concerned. Kabīr was above all a mystic and the pattern of his thought is determined by this quality. The result is both profundity and obscurity. Kabīr's works have commanded an immense popularity ever since they were first circulated, but the popularity has been accorded to thoughts in isolation, not to an integrated pattern of belief. It has been the pithy saying, the striking aphorism, which has brought Kabīr his popularity. Those who claim direct allegiance to him, the Kabīr-panthīs, possess a system of belief, but it is one

[1] Basil Willey, *Nineteenth Century Studies*, Penguin edition, p. 104.

[2] J. E. Carpenter, *Theism in Medieval India*, pp. 477–8. J. N. Farquhar, *An Outline of the Religious Literature of India*, p. 337. Nicol Macnicol, *Indian Theism from the Vedic to the Muhammadan Period*, pp. 146, 153. E. Trumpp, *The Ādi Granth*, p. cv.

which only remotely resembles the original teaching of the sect's eponymous founder.

Gurū Nānak, on the other hand, produced a coherent pattern and one which, with some additions by later Gurūs, is followed to this day by orthodox Sikhism. In his own way Gurū Nānak was also a mystic and, as with Kabīr, the climax of his thought is to be found in an ineffable union with God, the Formless One. The climax itself was beyond analysis or expression, but not the path to it, and in this respect Gurū Nānak is much clearer than Kabīr. A person of pronounced mystical inclinations would doubtless find in Kabīr's works something of the depth of meaning which Kabīr himself had experienced, but most men would not. Many could, however, appreciate the pattern which Gurū Nānak sought to expound, for it is expressed in terms which are much more readily understandable. The fact that Gurū Nānak appointed a successor to continue his work is of primary importance as far as the perpetuation of his teachings is concerned, but it is not the only reason to account for the existence of modern Sikhism. The clarity and coherence of his thought have also been factors of fundamental significance.

For Gurū Nānak the meaning and purpose of human existence centres in the divine existence of the Eternal One, He who creates, sustains, and destroys, He who having created reveals Himself in His creation, He who by His grace communicates to man the way of salvation and calls forth the response which enables him to appropriate that salvation. Set over against this sovereign Master is man who, in his unregenerate condition, manifests a corrupt nature cutting him off from the divinely proffered way of salvation. Perverse and wayward, deluded by the transitory attractions of this world and the creature of evil impulses, he lives a life which binds him more firmly to the wheel of transmigration and condemns him to an endless cycle of death and rebirth.

To all men, however, is held out the means of escape from the misery of this self-centred life and continued transmigration. By His divine Order (*Hukam*) God has so created and regulated the world that the perceptive man can see in it an expression of the Creator's nature. The prerequisite perception is awakened in man by the *Gurū*, by the voice of God mystically uttered within. He who hears and responds to the *Gurū* will, through his response, begin to comprehend the Word (*Śabad*) of God made manifest in all that lies around him and in all that he experiences within himself. The necessary response is that of adoring love expressed through meditation on the Name (*Nām*) of God, on the nature of God communicated through His creation and through human experience within the creation. He who submits himself to this exacting discipline is cleansed from his impurities and grows progressively nearer to God. Ascending to higher and yet higher levels of spiritual perception he finally reaches the ultimate, a condition of ineffable union with the Eternal One in which all earthly bonds are dissolved and the cycle of death and rebirth finally brought to an end.

Many of these concepts Gurū Nānak shared with other earlier and contemporary religious figures, including Kabīr.[1] It is at once evident that his thought is closely related to that of the Sant tradition of Northern India and there can be no doubt that much of it was derived directly from this source. This is not, however, a sufficient answer to the question of his antecedents. Three issues require consideration in order to elicit this answer. First, there is the problem of how the Sant tradition itself evolved. Secondly, there is the question of other influences which may have operated upon the thought of Gurū Nānak, a question which chiefly concerns the extent of direct Islamic influence. Thirdly, there is the impact of Gurū Nānak's own originality upon the inheritance which he received. Of these three the second is comparatively unimportant. The system developed by Gurū Nānak is essentially a reworking of the Sant pattern, a reinterpretation which compounded experience and profound insight with a quality of coherence and a power of effective expression.

The Sant tradition of Northern India (the Nirguṇa Sampradāya)[2]

For the vast majority of Gurū Nānak's contemporaries, both Hindu and Muslim, the essence of religion was to be found in external authority and conventional ceremony. In the case of the Hindu community this authority was generally accorded to the brahmaṇs and through them to the Vedas and Purāṇas. The required response consisted in the performance of the customary rites appropriate to a man's station within the caste structure of society. For the Muslim also religion meant loyalty to an objective authority. In his case the authority was the Qur'ān and its exercise the acknowledged function of the qāzīs.

These conventional patterns did not, however, command universal acceptance. Customary religion had received numerous challenges and of the dissenting movements three were of particular importance. There was, first, the tradition of Vaiṣṇava bhakti which had spread to Northern India from the south, and which in the north was associated, above all other names, with that of Rāmānand. For bhakti the essential religious response was love, and in Vaiṣṇava bhakti this love was directed to one of the *avatārs* of Viṣṇu. Secondly, there was the ancient tradition of tantric yoga, expressed in Northern India during this period by the numerous adherents

[1] Cf. also F. R. Allchin, 'The Place of Tulsī Dās in North Indian Devotional Tradition', *JRAS*, parts 3 and 4 (1966), p. 140.

[2] For an explanation of the terms *Sant* and *Nirguṇa Sampradāya* see the Glossary, p. 245. The term *Nirguṇa Pantha* is also commonly used. The North India tradition should not be confused with the Vārkarī sect of Paṇḍharpur in Maharashtra, the exponents of which have commonly been referred to as *sants*. It seems highly probable, however, that Namdev provides a direct link between the two *Sant* traditions. See *infra*, p. 154.

of the Kānphaṭ or Nāth sect of yogīs. The sect was divided into various sub-sects, all claiming allegiance to the semi-legendary Gorakhnāth and all following essentially the same *haṭha-yoga* technique.[1] Thirdly, there were the members of the Sūfī orders, numerically far fewer than the adherents of orthodox Islam, but exercising a perceptible influence on the religious thought and practice of Hindus as well as Muslims.

Within each of these religious groupings there was a recognizable continuity, but none of them was completely insulated. All were to some extent influenced by one or more of the others and underwent corresponding modifications. In one significant case this reciprocal exchange issued not simply in the modification of an existing tradition, but in the emergence of a recognizable synthesis, a new pattern which in various respects strongly resembled other existing patterns but which in its wholeness corresponded to none of them. This was the Sant tradition of Northern India. The new movement was by no means the dominant religious tradition during this period, but it was certainly the most fertile and, as we have already observed, it is of fundamental importance as far as Gurū Nānak's religious antecedents are concerned.

The Sant tradition was essentially a synthesis of the three principal dissenting movements, a compound of elements drawn mainly from Vaiṣṇava bhakti and the *haṭha-yoga* of the Nāth yogīs, with a marginal contribution from Sūfism. For the Sants, as for the Vaiṣṇava *bhagats*, the necessary religious response was love, and for this reason the movement has frequently been regarded as an aspect of Vaiṣṇava bhakti.[2] In several respects, however, the Sants disagreed with traditional bhakti and some of these differences were fundamental. Their love was offered not to an *avatār*, but direct to the supreme God Himself, and their expression of this love was through strictly inward meditation and devotion. It was, moreover, a method which involved suffering, or at least some appreciable difficulties. It was not the easy path of traditional bhakti.

In spite of these differences bhakti elements provided the principal contribution to the Sant synthesis, particularly during the earlier stages of its development. Traces of Nāth influence are by no means absent during these earlier stages, but nor are they prominent and in some cases they may represent subsequent additions. It is not until the time of Kabīr that Nāth concepts assume a significant role. In the thought of Kabīr such concepts

[1] Gorakhnāth must be accepted as an historical figure, but practically all that is related concerning him must be regarded as legend. His period is uncertain, but appears to have been between the ninth and twelfth century A.D. See G. W. Briggs, *Gorakhnāth and the Kānphaṭa Yogīs*, pp. 228 ff., 250; M. Eliade, *Yoga: Immortality and Freedom*, p. 303; Rangey Raghava, *Gorakhnāth aur unkā yug*, pp. 29, 43. For a brief account of the Nāth sect see the Glossary, p. 243. The members of the sect are variously referred to as Nāth yogīs, Kānphaṭ ('split-ear') yogīs, and Gorakhnāthīs.

[2] The frequent use of Rām, as a name of God, and of other Vaiṣṇava names and epithets by the Sants has obviously encouraged this misunderstanding.

are both prominent and integral, and it is accordingly at this point that we encounter the developed synthesis. Nāth influence emerges in much of the basic terminology used by Kabīr (and later by Gurū Nānak), in a rejection of all exterior forms, ceremonies, caste distinctions, sacred languages, and scriptures, in a strong emphasis upon unity as opposed to 'duality', and in the concept of a mystical union which destroys this 'duality'. It is not without significance that the commonest of all terms used by both Kabīr and Gurū Nānak to express this experience of union is *sahaj*, a word which at once carries us back into Nāth theory and beyond the Nāth tradition into the earlier world of tantric Buddhism. The bhakti influence retains its primacy, but the Nāth content of Kabīr's thought is also of fundamental importance.

The Sants were monotheists, but the God whom they addressed and with whom they sought union was in no sense to be understood in anthropomorphic terms. His manifestation was through His immanence in His creation and, in particular, through His indwelling within the human soul. It was there that He, by grace, revealed Himself, and man's proper response was a love expressed through meditation on the divine Name. External authorities and ceremonies were useless for this purpose and religious texts, idol worship, formal religious exercises, pilgrimage, and ritual bathing were all accordingly rejected. The inward way to God was open to all who were prepared to accept the difficulties and the discipline which it would involve, and so caste was rejected also. Great importance was attached to the *gurū*, who might be a human teacher or who might be understood not as a person but as the inner voice of God. No value was accorded to celibacy or asceticism. Hindu and Muslim sectarian notions were spurned, not because the two systems were regarded as basically true, but because both were regarded as radically wrong and ultimately futile.[1]

These beliefs the Sants expressed not in the traditional Sanskrit, but in a language which was closely related to that of the common people to whom they addressed their teachings. Within the tradition and amongst other sādhūs there evolved a language which, with minor modifications, was used by Sants all over northern India. This language has been called *Sādhukkaṛī*. Its basis was Khaṛī Bolī, the dialect spoken around Delhi, and to this were added elements drawn from Old Rajasthānī, Apabhraṃśa, Pañjābī, and Persian.[2] Most of the Sants were from low caste groups and in such cases were generally poorly educated or completely illiterate. For this reason their compositions were usually oral utterances which came to be written down only after a period of circulation.

The first of the great Sants was Nāmdev (A.D. 1270–1350)[3] who lived in

[1] A particularly clear summary of the characteristics of the Sant movement is given by Dr. Charlotte Vaudeville in her *Au Cabaret de l'Amour: Paroles de Kabîr*, pp. 7–9.

[2] Ch. Vaudeville, *Kabīr Granthāvalī (Dohā)*, Introduction, pp. iv–v. Traces of Marāṭhī influence are evident in the works of Nāmdev and Trilochan.

[3] R. G. Bhandarkar, *Vaisnavism, Saivism, and Minor Religious Systems*, p. 92, disputed

Maharashtra and whose name is closely linked with the Vārkarī sect of Paṇḍharpur. The Vārkarī sect was well within the bhakti tradition and its worship centred on the famous idol of Viṭṭhal[1] which was located in Paṇḍharpur. Elements of traditional Vaiṣṇava bhakti are evident in Nāmdev's work, but his primary emphases are clearly in accord with Sant concepts. His influence extended into northern India as a result of his Hindi works and possibly as a result also of an extended visit to the Pañjāb. Doubts have been expressed concerning the assumption that the author of the Hindī works is the same Nāmdev as the famous Marāṭhī *bhagat* of Paṇḍharpur, but recent comparisons of the Hindī and Marāṭhī compositions have established it as at least a strong probability.[2]

The tradition of a Pañjāb visit must still be regarded as open to some doubt. According to this tradition Nāmdev spent twenty years in Ghuman, a village in the Baṭālā tahsīl of Gurdāspur District. In Ghuman itself the tradition is both strong and old, and there is certainly nothing improbable in a Sant wandering so far from home, but the complete absence of any reference in the older Marāṭhī accounts of Nāmdev's life raises an objection which cannot be overlooked. The tradition may still be regarded as possible, but certainly not as established.

The second of the important Sants was Raidās, an outcaste leather-worker (*chamār*) of Banāras.[3] Chronologically Raidās follows Kabīr, but his work corresponds more closely to that of Nāmdev. It belongs to the earlier stage of the Sant movement, to the stage in which the links with Vaiṣṇava bhakti are much more prominent and the evidence of influence from other sources much slighter. The Vaiṣṇava concept of the divine *avatār* is rejected, and likewise all external ceremonies or aids to worship,[4] but the nature of the devotion offered by these earlier Sants resembles the adoration of the *bhagats* rather than the deeply mystical experience of Kabīr.[5] There is also a stronger emphasis upon the immanence of God in external phenomena than in Kabīr's works.[6] In the latter the emphasis moves more to the inner revelation within the human soul.

these traditional dates, claiming that Nāmdev's works indicate a period one hundred years later. Recent work by Marāṭhī scholars favours the traditional dates. The question is fully discussed by Bhagirath Misra and Rajnarayan Maurya, *Sant Nāmdev ki Padāvalī*, pp. 9–31.

[1] A manifestation of Kriṣṇa.

[2] Bhagirath Misra and Rajnarayan Maurya, op. cit. There are sixty-one of Nāmdev's Hindī verses in the *Ādi Granth*. *Ślok* 241 of the Kabīr *śloks* (*AG*, p. 1377) may be by Nāmdev.

[3] In the *Ādi Granth* he is called Ravidās, and in it there are thirty-nine of his *śabads*. The number is generally given as forty, but *Soraṭhi* 4, *AG*, p. 658, and *Mārū* 2, *AG*, p. 1106, are the same composition. *Ślok* 242 of the Kabīr *śloks* (*AG*, p. 1377) may also be by Ravidās.

[4] Cf. Ravidās, *Dhanāsari* 3, *AG*, p. 694.

[5] Nāmdev: *Gond* 3, *AG*, p. 873; *Bhairau* 7, *AG*, p. 1164; *Sāraṅg* 3, *AG*, pp. 1252–3. Ravidās: *Soraṭhi* 3, *AG*, pp. 658–9; *Gūjari* 1, *AG*, p. 525.

[6] Nāmdev: *Tilaṅg* 2, *AG*, p. 727; *Goṇḍ* 2, *AG*, p. 873; *Malār* 1, *AG*, p. 1292. Ravidās: *Sirī Rāgu* 1, *AG*, p. 93; *Malār* 2, *AG*, p. 1293.

Little is known about Raidās's life and all that we can accept is contained in the occasional references which he makes in his works. In several verses he refers to his low caste status as a *chamār*,[1] and in one to his work as a cobbler.[2] Elsewhere he describes how the members of his caste carry away the cattle carcases from Banāras.[3] The tradition that he was a disciple of Rāmānand must be rejected. The traditional link between Rāmānand and Kabīr is barely plausible on chronological grounds, and it is evident that Raidās was younger than Kabīr. This is the conclusion which is indicated by the references which he makes to Kabīr[4] and it places him beyond the time of Rāmānand. Moreover, there is no hint of such a relationship in any of his works.

Raidās makes the characteristic Sant emphases, with an evident stress upon the irrelevancy of caste in all that concerns a man's salvation. An even stronger emphasis, and one which is peculiarly his own, is a recurring note of humility and confession. Raidās is a particularly attractive figure and one who has yet to receive the attention he deserves.

With Kabīr the Sant tradition moves into a more complicated phase. As in the case of Raidās little is known concerning his life, although a considerable quantity of legend has gathered around him.[5] The traditional date of his death, A.D. 1518, appears to be at least a definite likelihood, but his traditional date of birth, A.D. 1398, must be regarded as highly improbable. No definite year can be given to replace it, but a date in the vicinity of 1440 would appear to be reasonable.[6] Kabīr's life was spent in Banāras and his death probably took place in the village of Magahar, twenty-seven miles south-east of Bastī. His caste was that of *julāhā* and it seems clear from his works that he followed, in a somewhat erratic manner, his caste's hereditary occupation of weaving. Recent research has established a Nāth background as a strong probability. It now seems clear that

[1] Ravidās: *Gauṛi 2, AG*, p. 345; *Gauṛī Bairāgaṇi* 1, *AG*, p. 346; *Gauṛī Pūrabi* 1, *AG*, p. 346; *Āsā* 3, *AG*, p. 486.

[2] Ravidās: *Soraṭhi* 7, *AG*, p. 659.

[3] Ravidās: *Malār* 1, *AG*, p. 1293. A hymn attributed to the *bhagat* Dhannā and evidently revised by Gurū Arjan repeats this information concerning Raidās (Dhannā, *Āsā* 2, *AG*, p. 487).

[4] Ravidās: *Āsā* 5, *AG*, p. 487; *Mārū* 1, *AG*, p. 1106; *Malār* 2, *AG*, p. 1293.

[5] See Ahmad Shah, *The Bījak of Kabīr*, introductory chapter 'The Life of Kabīr in Legend', pp. 1–28.

[6] Ch. Vaudeville, *Au Cabaret de l'Amour: Paroles de Kabîr*, pp. 10–11. The question of Kabīr's dates is discussed at some length by Parasuram Chaturvedi, *Uttarī Bhārat kī Sant-paramaparā*, pp. 709–33. Chaturvedi decides in favour of A.D. 1448 as the date of Kabīr's death. The principal reason leading him to this conclusion appears to be a memorial in Magahar which is said to bear a date equivalent to A.D. 1450 (see *Archaeological Survey of India (New Series): the Monumental Antiquities and Inscriptions in the North Western Provinces and Oudh*, vol. ii, p. 224). Another reason may perhaps be a desire to maintain the traditional connexion with Rāmānand. The fact that 1518 has been consistently maintained in tradition in spite of its manifest conflict with the Rāmānand relationship is one of the principal arguments in favour of the later date. Another is the convergence of the Hindu and Muslim traditions at this point.

Kabīr belonged to a family of non-celibate yogīs converted only recently, and to a considerable degree superficially, to Islam.[1] The traditional association with Rāmānand cannot be rejected outright, but it is a most unlikely one. It involves chronological difficulties and the only references which Kabīr makes to Rāmānand are to be found in works of doubtful authenticity.[2] The numerous references which Kabīr does make to a *gurū* point unmistakably to the *Satgurū* within, the voice of God within the human soul.

The compositions attributed to Kabīr are seemingly numberless, but only two collections have adequate claims to be regarded as genuine. These are the *Kabīr-granthāvalī* and the selection included in the *Ādi Granth*.[3] To these the *Bījak* may be added, but with reservations. The *Bījak* is later than the other two collections and must be regarded as a Kabīr-panthī recasting rather than as the original work of Kabīr. There can be no doubt that the works included in the two older collections have also been altered in oral transmission, but to an appreciably lesser degree than those of the *Bījak*. The famous translation by Tagore from a collection made by Kshitimohan Sen cannot be accepted as authentic.[4]

The basis of Kabīr's belief was not, as has been commonly supposed, Vaiṣṇava bhakti or Sūfism but tantric yoga. Kabīr's name is certainly a Muslim one, but it has always been clear that his knowledge of Islam was relatively slight. In contrast to this there is a wealth of *haṭha-yoga* terminology and a thought-structure with obvious resemblances to that of the Nāths. In the light of this contrast the theory that Kabīr belonged to a caste which had recently been converted from tantric yoga to Islam is at once convincing.

Kabīr was, however, far from being a Nāth yogī. To this background he brought elements from Vaiṣṇava bhakti and perhaps from Sūfism also. His debt to the *bhagats* is evident in the primacy accorded to love, and his concept of such love as a way of suffering may possibly reflect, in some measure, a debt to the Sūfīs. These and other elements from the same sources he compounded with his own mystical nature and produced the synthesis which is the distinctive religion of Kabīr. It is a religion which in true Sant style renounces all that is mechanical or external, affirming as

[1] Ch. Vaudeville, *Kabīr Granthāvalī (Dohā)*, p. viii.

[2] *Bījak, śabad* 77. Tagore, *One Hundred Poems of Kabir*, no. xxix, p. 36.

[3] The *Ādi Granth* includes 226 *śabads* by Kabīr. Of these 225 are to be found in the *bhagat bāṇī* at the end of the various *rāgs*, and the remaining one is included amongst the works of Gurū Arjan (*Bhairo* 3, *AG*, p. 1136). The total number of Kabīr *śloks* included in the *Adi Granth* is either 237 or 239. The collection entitled *Ślok Bhagat Kabīr jīu ke* (*AG*, pp. 1364–77) has 243, but of these five are by Gurū Arjan (nos. 209, 210, 211, 214, 221), one by Gurū Amar Dās (no. 220), and two (nos. 241 and 242) may possibly be by Nāmdev and Ravidās respectively. Two extra *śloks* by Kabīr are included in the *bhagat bāṇī* of *Rāg Mārū*, *AG*, p. 1105. There are also three longer works: the *Bāvan Akharī* (*AG*, pp. 340–3), the *Thintī* (pp. 343–4), and the 'Seven Days' (pp. 344–5). A number of *śloks* are to be found in *vārs* (*AG*, pp. 509, 555, 947, 948), but all of these are duplicated in the collection at the end of the *Ādi Granth*.

[4] Rabindranath Tagore, *One Hundred Poems of Kabir*.

valid only that which may be experienced inwardly. Within a man's soul God may, by grace, reveal Himself. The revelation comes, however, only to him who has prepared himself to receive it. The way of preparation is the path of love, a love addressed directly to the supreme Lord who is both transcendent and immanent, and a love which will inevitably involve long periods in the anguish of separation. Few will have the courage to undertake it and fewer still the persistence to follow it to the point of revelation. The point at which the revelation occurs cannot be foreseen. It comes at the divine initiative and it comes with suddenness. God, the True Gurū (*Satgurū*), discharges the arrow of the Word (*Śabad*) and man is slain that in death he may find true life. This life is to be found in mystical union, an ineffable experience of dissolution in the divine.[1]

There is inevitably much that must remain obscure in Kabīr's attempts to describe his experiences, for they were of a fundamentally mystical quality and, as Kabīr himself repeats, ultimately inexpressible. There is also a measure of inconsistency in his utterances. In his efforts to impart some impression of his mystical experience he has frequent recourse to monistic terminology, but he uses it in senses which are his own. Monistic concepts certainly influenced him, but it seems clear from what he indicates concerning his own understanding of the nature of his relationship with God that his thought must be regarded as monotheistic, not monistic.[2] The works of Kabīr represent the highly personal record of an individual experience, but they nevertheless place him well within the framework of Sant beliefs.

It was this Sant tradition which provided the basis of Gurū Nānak's thought, an inheritance which, like Kabīr, he reinterpreted in the light of his own personality and experience. This is not to imply that he should be regarded as in any sense a disciple of Kabīr. There is no sound evidence to support the popular tradition that Gurū Nānak met Kabīr and little to suggest that he knew any of his works.[3] It is, however, clear that the Sant tradition was by far the most important element in all that he inherited from his past or absorbed from contemporary patterns.

This leads to the second question concerning the antecedents of the thought of Gurū Nānak, the question of direct influences which operated independently of his Sant inheritance. The dominant issue in this respect must be the extent of his debt to Islamic sources. Nāth beliefs certainly exercised an influence and we encounter many examples of Nāth terminology in his works,[4] but in so far as these influences and terms constitute integral expressions of his own beliefs they represent aspects of the Sant

[1] Ch. Vaudeville, *Au Cabaret de l'Amour: Paroles de Kabîr*, pp. 25–37.

[2] Ch. Vaudeville, art. 'Kabīr and Interior Religion' in *History of Religions*, vol. 3, no. 2, pp. 197–8, and *Au Cabaret de l'Amour: Paroles de Kabîr*, pp. 221–2.

[3] See *supra*, pp. 85–86.

[4] Cf. *Vār Malār*, *ślok* 1 of *pauṛī* 27, *AG*, pp. 1290–1.

inheritance. Gurū Nānak himself explicitly rejected Nāth beliefs[1] and his works bear clear witness to open controversy with Nāth yogīs. Nāth concepts were communicated to his thought through Sant channels which transformed their meaning, and in his usage such elements are, for the most part, naturalized. They are recognizably of Nāth derivation but they belong to the Sants, not to the Nāths.

Muslim influence

Sikhism has commonly been regarded as a blend of Hindu beliefs and Islam, and if for Islam we substitute Sūfism there appears, at first sight, to be much to support this view. It is at once evident that many elements in the thought of Gurū Nānak have affinities with Sūfī concepts and this would seem to suggest strong Sūfī influence. In his works we find an emphasis upon the unity of God, a revelation in creation, the paradox of God transcendent as well as immanent, an expression of God in terms of light, a perverse human organ[2] which requires purification, a doctrine of grace, an emphasis upon the suffering involved in separation from the Beloved, a concept of *nām simaran*[3] which appears to combine elements of both the *dhikr* and *murāqabat* of the Sūfīs, an ascent to union through a number of stages, a purging of self and an ultimate union which, although they are nowhere explicitly defined, do not appear to be inconsistent with the Sūfī notions of *fanā*' and *baqā*'. He also shares with many Sūfīs a belief in the needlessness of asceticism on the one hand, and upon the snare of worldly wealth on the other. In a few instances we encounter references which appear to be obvious echoes of the Qur'ān.

The appearance is, however, misleading. Affinities certainly exist, but we cannot assume that they are necessarily the result of Sūfī influence. Other factors suggest that Sūfism was at most a marginal influence, encouraging certain developments but in no case providing the actual source of a significant element.

In the first place, there is the fact that the Pañjābī Sūfism of Gurū Nānak's period had evidently departed radically from the classical pattern of Arab and Persian Sūfism. Gurū Nānak himself indicates this condition in references which place Sūfīs under the same condemnation as the conventional qāzīs and mullahs.[4] Classical Sūfism evidently had little opportunity to influence him, for there is no evidence to suggest that he came in contact with it during his formative years, nor even in subsequent years.

The evidence which can be derived from his works points not to a regular

[1] An arresting example is the verse *Sūhī* 8, *AG*, p. 730. See *infra*, p. 211.

[2] Gurū Nānak's *man* and the *dil-rūh-sirr* complex of the Sūfīs.

[3] 'Remembering the Name.' See *infra*, pp. 214–19.

[4] Cf. *Sirī Rāgu Aṣṭ* 17 (3), *AG*, p. 64; *Vār Mājh*, *ślok* 1 of *pauṛī* 13, *AG*, p. 143; *Gauṛī Aṣṭ* 14 (7), *AG*, p. 227.

direct contact with members of Sūfī orders, but rather to the kind of informal contact with ordinary Muslims which would have been inevitable in his circumstances. Amongst those Muslims there would certainly be some strict Sunnīs and we can assume that there would also be a number who might fitly be described as Sūfīs. The majority would, however, represent in varying degree the blend of modified orthodoxy and debased Sūfism which was dominant in the Muslim community of the Pañjāb during this period. Such contacts would explain the occasional references which seem to echo the language of the Qur'ān. It is, however, most unlikely that they could have had any significant positive influence upon the thought of Gurū Nānak, for they represented contacts with a version of Islam which he explicitly rejected.

Secondly, there is a conspicuous lack of Sūfī terminology in the works of Gurū Nānak. Even when a Sūfī term makes an appearance it is rarely used in a sense implying the precise meaning which it would possess in Sūfī usage, and in some cases such terms are introduced with the patent intention of providing a reinterpretation of their meaning.[1] This contrasts significantly with a wealth of Sant terminology and imagery derived from Hindu sources. Almost all of his basic terminology is of native Indian derivation. In choosing names of God his preference is strongly for Hindu names, and when dealing with a concept which has obvious affinities with Sūfī belief he will almost always use a non-Sūfī term.

Thirdly, we must observe that although there are certainly strong resemblances to Sūfī thought, almost all of the evident affinities can, with equal cogency, be traced back to native Indian sources. This is not to affirm that we must in all cases seek an Indian source; merely that an apparent affinity need not necessarily point to a Sūfī source.

Fourthly, there is the fact that in some fundamental respects Gurū Nānak's thought is in direct conflict with that of the Sūfīs. The obvious example of this is his acceptance of the doctrines of *karma* and transmigration.

Finally, and most significant of all, an examination of the more important points at which Muslim influence has been claimed can do little to support the claims made in this respect. The Islamic insistence upon the Divine Unity would presumably have strengthened the monotheistic basis of Gurū Nānak's thought, but his monotheism must be regarded primarily as an inheritance from the Bhakti Movement mediated through the Sant tradition. The word *hukam*, which possesses a particular significance in the thought of Gurū Nānak, is certainly an Arabic word, but the concept which it expresses is not a borrowing from Islam.[2] His doctrine of *nām simaran* does not correspond to the Sūfī technique of *dhikr*, and the five *khaṇḍs*, or 'realms', of *Japjī*[3] do not correspond, even remotely, to the *maqāmāt* of the Sūfīs.

[1] e.g. *faqīr* and *darveś*.

[2] See *infra*, pp. 199–203.

[3] *Japjī* 34–37, *AG*, pp. 7–8. See *infra*, pp. 221–24.

Muslim influence upon the thought of Gurū Nānak must accordingly be regarded as relatively slight. This conclusion should not, however, be pressed to the point of totally rejecting all such influence. The Sant tradition had already absorbed a limited measure of Islamic influence and this was obviously mediated to Gurū Nānak as a part of the Sant synthesis. Most of the elements in the thought of Gurū Nānak which suggest Muslim influence evidently descended to him in this indirect manner, for they are elements which he shared with his Sant predecessors. Instances of this are the encouragement which, we must assume, Islam provided in strengthening monotheistic tendencies, and the indeterminate pressure which the egalitarian emphasis of Islam exercised upon the Bhakti Movement. We may also assume that Sūfism, as opposed to orthodox Islam, must have subscribed to the characteristic Sant belief in the omnipresence of God, a feature of fundamental importance in the thought of Gurū Nānak.

To this we must add the likelihood that the Islam of Gurū Nānak's own environment must have exercised some direct influence, although here too stress must be laid upon the apparently limited nature of such influence. Very occasionally an evident borrowing can be detected, an example of which appears to be the 'veil' which conceals the Truth from man's perception.[1] Even here, however, we must observe that the debt is limited to the imagery and that Gurū Nānak imparts his own particular meaning to the Sūfī figure.

The conclusion to which we are led is that Islamic influence evidently operated upon the thought of Gurū Nānak, but that in no case can we accord this influence a fundamental significance. Sūfī and Qur'ānic imagery have certainly made their impress, and there must have been encouragement of tendencies which accorded with Sūfī teaching, but no fundamental components can be traced with assurance to an Islamic source. Gurū Nānak's principal inheritance from the religious background of his period was unquestionably that of the Sant tradition and evidence of other independent influences is relatively slight. We must indeed acknowledge that the antecedents of Sant belief are by no means wholly clear and that within the area of obscurity there may be important features which derived primarily from Sūfī sources. The complexity of the subject leaves some room for doubt and we are accordingly bound to own that at least some of our conclusions must be regarded as tentative, not as definitively established. It appears, however, that Sant belief owes none of its basic constituents to the Sūfīs. For Sant belief the major source is to be found in the Bhakti Movement, with Nāth theory entering as a significant secondary source.[2]

[1] *Japjī* 1, *AG*, p. 1.

[2] For a more detailed treatment of the question of Islamic influence see W. H. McLeod, 'The Influence of Islam upon the Thought of Gurū Nānak' in *History of Religions*, vol. 7, no. 4.

From this conclusion it follows that a common interpretation of the religion of Gurū Nānak must be rejected. It is not correct to interpret it as a conscious effort to reconcile Hindu belief and Islam by means of a synthesis of the two. The intention to reconcile was certainly there, but not by the path of syncretism. Conventional Hindu belief and Islam were not regarded as fundamentally right but as fundamentally wrong.

Neither the *Veda* nor the *Kateb* know the mystery.[1]

The two were to be rejected, not harmonized in a synthesis of their finer elements. True religion lay beyond these two systems, accessible to all men of spiritual perception whether Hindu or Muslim. It was the person who spurned all that was external and who followed instead the interior discipline of *nām simaran* who could be called a 'true' Hindu or a 'true' Muslim. Such a person had in fact transcended both.

It is accordingly incorrect to interpret the religion of Gurū Nānak as a synthesis of Hindu belief and Islam. It is indeed a synthesis, but one in which Islamic elements are relatively unimportant. The pattern evolved by Gurū Nānak is a reworking of the Sant synthesis, one which does not depart far from Sant sources as far as its fundamental components are concerned. The categories employed by Gurū Nānak are the categories of the Sants, the terminology he uses is their terminology, and the doctrines he affirms are their doctrines. This is not to suggest, however, that Gurū Nānak's thought was a precise copy of what earlier Sants had developed. He inherited the components of his thought from the Sants, but he did not transmit his inheritance unchanged. He received a synthesis and he passed it on, but he did so in a form which was in some measure amplified, and in considerable measure clarified and integrated. This applies in particular to his understanding of the manner of divine communication with man. Gurū Nānak's concepts of the *Śabad*, the *Nām*, the *Gurū*, and the *Hukam*[2] carry us beyond anything that the works of earlier Sants offer in any explicit form. It is Sant thought which we find in his works, but it is Sant thought expanded and reinterpreted. The result is a new synthesis, a synthesis which is cast within the pattern of Sant belief but which nevertheless possesses a significant originality and, in contrast with its Sant background, a unique clarity. It possesses, moreover, the quality of survival, for it remains today the substance of a living faith.

The verses which have been used in the following analysis are those which are recorded in the *Ādi Granth*. There have, as one would expect,

[1] *Mārū Solahā* 2 (6), *AG*, p. 1021. *Kateb* designates the Qur'ān. Sikh theology has traditionally interpreted *Kateb* as the four 'Semitic texts', namely the *Torah*, the *Zabūr* (Psalms), the *Iñjil* (Gospel), and the Qur'ān. Cf. also *Vār Āsā*, *ślok* 1 of *pauṛī* 6, *AG*, p. 465, and *BG* 1. 33.

[2] The Word, the Name of God, the divine Preceptor, and the divine Order.

been many other compositions attributed to Gurū Nānak,[1] but none of these have been used as there can be no guarantee, or even likelihood, of their authenticity. The restriction involves no appreciable loss, for the *Ādi Granth* contains a substantial number of works by Gurū Nānak.[2] These can all be accepted as authentic. It is clear that Gurū Arjan compiled the *Ādi Granth* with considerable care and the principal source which he used was a collection which had been recorded at the instance of the third Gurū, Amar Dās, who was only ten years younger than Gurū Nānak.

Two things remain to be added before beginning the analysis. The first must be a strong emphasis upon the primacy of religious concerns in the thought of Gurū Nānak. This has already been observed in the case of the celebrated verses which refer to Bābur where the purpose is not to provide a description of a Mughal invasion but to illustrate the fate of the unrighteous.[3] The message is religious, not political. The Lodīs had sinned and their misfortunes were the penalty for their sins. The same applies to a group of three *śloks* which are commonly quoted as evidence that insecurity and decadence were dominant features of the India of Gurū Nānak's time.[4] The three *śloks* refer to a far broader span of space and time than the period of the Gurū's own lifetime. Their primary application is to the whole of the present cosmic age, not to the contemporary conditions of the Lodī Sultanate or the early Mughal administration. The condition of degeneracy which they express is a characteristic of the *Kaliyug*, the era of ultimate degeneracy in the cosmic cycle, and although the specific conditions of the Gurū's own times would certainly be regarded as a reflection of this perversion they would, in this respect, be no different from those of other historical periods and other places. The issue is that of Truth, the quality which is so conspicuously absent in the *Kaliyug*. The absence of Truth means darkness and the unconquered self brings suffering.

This pursuit of Truth and so of salvation was, for Gurū Nānak, mankind's paramount concern, and as a result his comment on contemporary conditions relates almost exclusively to attitudes, customs, and institutions which obstructed this quest. Political, social, and economic issues find expression in his works only in so far as they relate to the pattern of religious salvation which he upheld, or to contemporary patterns which he rejected. This is not to deny that details relating to such issues can be gleaned from his works, and it is obvious that his teachings have had effects which

[1] The janam-sākhīs contain numerous apocryphal works attributed to Gurū Nānak, the most important of them being the *Prāṇ Saṅgalī* (*Pur JS*, pp. 89, 118).

[2] Kahn Singh, *MK*, p. 327, gives the figure 947 as the total of all Gurū Nānak's *śabads*, *śloks*, *chhants*, *pauṛis*, etc. in the *Ādi Granth*.

[3] See *supra*, p. 136. Cf. also *Vār Malār*, *ślok* 2 of *pauṛī* 22, *AG*, p. 1288.

[4] *Vār Mājh*, *ślok* 1 of *pauṛī* 16, *AG*, p. 145; *Vār Āsā*, *ślok* 1 of *pauṛī* 11, *AG*, p. 468; and *Vār Rāmakalī*, *ślok* 1 of *pauṛī* 11, *AG*, p. 951. The *Mih JS* sets these *śloks* in the context of the Mount Sumeru discourse. See *supra*, p. 60.

extend far beyond a recognizably religious context. Nor should it suggest that he was uninterested in human joy or human suffering. The *Bābar-vāṇī* verses make it abundantly clear that the wretchedness inflicted by Bābur's army had evoked a deep pity. There remained, however, the conviction of a condition transcending the misery and decay of this life. Gurū Nānak's concern was accordingly for salvation, for personal salvation and for the salvation of others.

Finally, it must be emphasized that this analysis concerns the theology of Gurū Nānak and not the theology of Sikhism. The two are largely but not completely coterminous and at one important point there is divergence. A theology of Gurū Nānak as opposed to Sikh theology must omit the contributions of Gurū Amar Dās, Gurū Rām Dās, Gurū Arjan, and Gurū Gobind Singh, and of concepts which evolved during the eighteenth century. In the case of the third, fourth, and fifth Gurūs the omission concerns amplifications which are certainly valuable, particularly in the case of Gurū Arjan, but which involve no significant modification of the pattern set out by the first Gurū. With Gurū Gobind Singh, however, comes the institution of the Khālsā, and finally the emergence of the belief that with his death in 1708, and the consequent termination of the line of personal Gurūs, the function of the Gurū had been vested in the scripture (the *Ādi Granth*) and in the corporate community (the Khālsā). This is of considerable importance. For modern Sikhism the scripture exists as a channel of communication between God and man, but obviously this could be no part of Gurū Nānak's theology. It must be understood, however, that this doctrine, its significance notwithstanding, is no more than a supplement to the teaching imparted by Gurū Nānak. The theology of Gurū Nānak remains the substance of Sikh belief.

I. THE NATURE OF GOD

I Oankas sati nāmu karatā purukhu nirabhau niravairu akāl mūrati ajūnī saibhan gur prasādi[1]

At no point is Gurū Nānak's quality of terseness better illustrated than in the *Mūl Mantra*, the basic theological statement with which the *Ādi Granth* opens. Principal Jodh Singh paraphrases it as follows:

This Being is One. He is eternal. He is immanent in all things and the Sustainer of all things. He is the Creator of all things. He is immanent in His creation. He is without fear and without enmity. This Being is not subject to time. He is

[1] The *Mūl Mantra*, *AG*, p. 1. The title *Mūl Mantra*, or 'Basic *Mantra*', was applied to an abbreviated form of this invocation by Bhāī Gurdās (*BG* 6.19). Gurū Nānāk himself declared that *Harinām*, the Name of God, was the *Mūl Mantra* (*Mārū Solihā* 20, *AG*, p. 1040). The two usages are not in conflict.

beyond birth and death. He is Himself responsible for His own manifestation. (He is known) by the *Gurū's* grace.[1]

Almost all accounts of Sikh belief refer to the *Mūl Mantra* and in Sikh commentaries considerable space is devoted to its exegesis.

In itself, however, the statement conveys relatively little. To a devout Sikh it imparts a wealth of meaning, but only because he has behind him an understanding of what the individual words mean. In themselves the words are not self-explanatory and in isolation may be interpreted in ways which would not accord with a comprehensive statement of Gurū Nānak's theology. The symbol *Om* is particularly open to misinterpretation if it be read without reference to Gurū Nānak's other works[2] and it is by no means self-evident why Dr. Jodh Singh should paraphrase *sati nāmu* as 'He is eternal'. It is in the light of the total range of Gurū Nānak's thought that the *Mūl Mantra* is to be interpreted, for it is the expression of his thought throughout his *śabads* and *śloks* which gives particular meaning and substance to each of the words. The *Mūl Mantra* may well serve both as a starting-point and as a final summary, but much remains to be filled in between the two.

1. *The unity of God*

At the very beginning of the *Mūl Mantra* stands the figure 1 and Sikh tradition is unanimous in accepting this as a declaration of the unity of God.[3] The conclusion is entirely reasonable, for the emphasis is strongly made in Gurū Nānak's works.

> The Lord is manifest in the three worlds. He is the eternal Giver and there is no other.[4]

'There is no other.' It is a characteristic expression of Gurū Nānak which recurs many times. God is for him simply *Ek*, the One.

> There are six systems of philosophy, six *gurūs*, and six patterns of instruction, but the *Gurū* of these *gurūs* is one though His manifestations be many.[5]

This affirmation of unity raises, however, an obvious question. Is this the one of monotheism, or is it the one of monism? Does it refer to the uniqueness of God, to His absolute difference in essence from all other beings; or does it denote the unity which denies ultimate reality to all phenomenal existence?

If we are compelled to choose between these two polar conceptions our

[1] Jodh Singh, *Guramati Niraṇay*, p. 1.

[2] The lengthy poem *Oaṅkāru* in the measure *Rāg Rāmakalī Dakhaṇī*, *AG*, pp. 929–38, provides an elucidation.

[3] Vir Singh, *Santhyā*, p. 3.

[4] *Oaṅkāru* 25, *AG*, p. 933.

[5] *Āsā Sohilā* 2 and *Āsā* 30, *AG*, pp. 12, 357.

choice must settle upon the former alternative. Gurū Nānak's thought cannot be made to conform to the categories of *advaita* doctrine without equating his concept of God with the ultimately unreal *Īśvara* of Śaṅkara's philosophy. The total range of Gurū Nānak's thought makes this equation manifestly impossible and accordingly requires us to reject the monistic alternative.

On the other hand, we must recognize that Gurū Nānak himself explicitly declares notions of 'duality' (*dubidhā*) to be the essence of man's problem, and the overcoming of such notions to be a vital aspect of man's quest for salvation. Moreover, we must also acknowledge the stress which he lays upon divine immanence and upon the fundamental importance of this immanent revelation in the quest for salvation. These aspects of his thought must prompt a measure of caution in our choice of terminology. If the thought of Gurū Nānak is to be designated monotheistic we must be clear that this is not to be construed in the Semitic sense.

The basis of Gurū Nānak's thought is best understood if approached as the thought of one who was essentially a mystic. 'Duality' is to be destroyed, but it is to be a swallowing up in mystical union. The creation does indeed provide a vital revelation of God, but the physical phenomena which impart this revelation are to be regarded as expressions of a God of grace who dwells not only in creation but also beyond it. The ultimate essence of God is beyond all human categories, far transcending all powers of human expression. Only in experience can He be truly known. Man must indeed seek to give human expression to this mystical experience, and Gurū Nānak's works are directed to this very end, but the human expression can communicate no more than a glimpse of the ultimate reality.

Gurū Nānak's own expressions of the experience and of the path to it plainly show that the One of whom he speaks is conceived as a personal God, a God of grace to whom man responds in love. His understanding of God as Creator and his repeated emphasis upon divine grace make this abundantly clear. As in the case of Kabīr monistic language does indeed occur, but the structure of monistic thought can provide no place for Gurū Nānak's concept of God. Strict pantheism is also excluded, for immanence is accompanied in the thought of Gurū Nānak by a notion of transcendence. If a label must be applied then monotheism is the label we must use, but it should be remembered that the vital expression of the One is through the many, through the infinite plurality of the creation.

This stress upon the many as the expression of the One must always be related to the concept of revelation through the created universe. It should not suggest any notion of implicit monotheism expressed through a plurality of deities, except in the sense that the deities of Hindu mythology are occasionally used as symbols to represent particular aspects of the divine activity. It has indeed been argued that Gurū Nānak accepted the *trimūrti*, the Hindu triad, and the justification for this claim is held to be the first couplet of the thirtieth stanza of *Japjī*.[1] Out of context these two lines could be translated:

> In the same manner a Mother conceived and bore three approved disciples—one the creator of the world, one the sustainer, and one who exercises the authority of death.[2]

Most Sikh commentators, however, begin their translations or paraphrases of this passage with some such words as, 'It is believed that . . .' and in the light of both the context and of Gurū Nānak's repeated references to the unity of God there can be no doubt that the addition is warranted. The same stanza continues with an emphatic assertion of the absolute authority of God:

> But Thou dost order (the three) as seems good to Thee and (they act) in accordance with Thy command.[3]

In the next stanza he declares that God Himself is both Creator and Sustainer.

> His abode is in every realm of the universe and every realm is His storehouse. That which He created He created once only and having created it He, the Creator, sustains it. This, Nānak, is the authentic work of the True One.[4]

Gurū Nānak does refer to Brahmā, Viṣṇu, and Śiva in ways which suggest that he accepted their existence as real, but they appear as the creatures of God, deprived of all functions and subject to *māyā* and to death. God did not merely create Brahmā. He created the world also and He it is who sustains it.[5] God is Himself Creator, Sustainer, and Destroyer, and His direct exercise of these functions reduces all demiurges and subordinate deities to meaningless shadows. Elsewhere they lose even this qualified acceptance.

> He, the One, is Himself Brahmā, Viṣṇu and Śiva, and He Himself performs all.[6]

They survive only as convenient illustrations, as conventional figures who will occasionally serve to exemplify a particular point.

As in the works of Kabīr this emphasis upon the unity of God emerges in the names which Gurū Nānak uses. Hari is the most common and there are other Vaiṣṇava names in his works, but there are also Muslim names.

[1] P. D. Barthwal, *The Nirguna School of Hindi Poetry*, p. 255. Indubhusan Banerjee, *The Evolution of the Khalsa*, vol. i, pp. 136–7.

[2] *Japji* 30, *AG*, p. 7.

[3] Ibid.

[4] Ibid. 31, *AG*, p. 7.

[5] *Mārū Solahā* 15 (14), *AG*, p. 1036.

[6] *Rāmakalī Aṣṭ* 9 (12), *AG*, p. 908.

God is Hari, Rām, and Gopāl, and He is also Allāh, Khudā, and Sāhib.[1] His manifestations may be many, but He alone is and there is no other.

My Master is the One. He is the One, brother, and He alone exists.[2]

2. *Nirguṇa and Saguṇa*

niragunu āpi saragunu bhī ohī.[3]

The words are Gurū Arjan's, but the doctrine which they so concisely express is also Gurū Nānak's. God, the One, is both *nirguṇa* and *saguṇa*, both absolute and conditioned, both unmanifest and manifest.

For Gurū Nānak, God in His primal aspect is *nirguṇa*—absolute, unconditioned, devoid of all attributes.

He who unfolded the three (*guṇa*[4]) has made His abode in the fourth.[5]

In other words, He is beyond the three *guṇa*. In this absolute aspect God is unknowable, completely beyond the range of human comprehension. God is not wholly beyond human perception, however, and for Gurū Nānak the explanation lies in His having endowed Himself with attributes which bring Him within the compass of man's understanding. He, the *nirguṇa*, of His own volition became *saguṇa* in order that man might know Him, and knowing Him enter into a unitive relationship with Him.

From His absolute condition He, the Pure One, became manifest; from *nirguṇa* He became *saguṇa*.[6]

There is at this point some danger of misunderstanding. The term *saguṇa* is generally used in connexion with Vaiṣṇava bhakti and in this customary sense it implies a belief in divine *avatārs*. This is certainly not the meaning which is to be attached to the word in Gurū Nānak's usage, nor in that of any of his successors. In Gurū Nānak's usage the term relates not to anything resembling anthropomorphism, but to his concept of divine immanence. One of the contributors to the commentary on the *Ādi Granth* entitled *Śabadārath Srī Gurū Granth Sāhib Jī* comments as follows on a relevant passage from Gurū Arjan's *Bilāvalu* 117:

In scripture God is said to have two aspects. One is that which He possessed when there was no creation and He existed solely in Himself. His qualities of power or of being unborn cannot thereby be diminished, but we can form no

[1] *Rāmakalī Aṣṭ* 1 (7), *AG*, p. 903. The characteristic Sikh term *Vāhigurū* is not found in Gurū Nānak's compositions. It first appears in the *savayye* of the *bhaṭṭs*. The *bhaṭṭs* whose works appear in the *Ādi Granth* were contemporaries of Gurū Arjan.

[2] *Āsā* 5, p. 350.

[3] Gurū Arjan, *Gauṛī Sukhamanī*, *Aṣṭ* 18 (8), *AG*, p. 287.

[4] The three vital 'qualities' or constituents of cosmic substance which by their varying proportions determine the nature of all that exists.

[5] *Mārū Solahā* 18 (4), *AG*, p. 1038.

[6] *Siddh Goṣṭi* 24, *AG*, p. 940.

impression of them in our mind. This is His *nirguṇa* aspect. Then He created and so revealed Himself in His creation. All the qualities or praiseworthy characteristics which can be attributed to Him are of this *saguṇa* aspect. Both are aspects of the one God.[1]

It is in this *saguṇa* aspect that man can know God and accordingly it is this aspect which is the object of Gurū Nānak's meditation and of his expository utterances. The *nirguṇa* nature of God, for all its fundamental quality, receives little attention for beyond the mere affirmation there is nothing man can say of it. In the ultimate condition of union man does indeed participate in this absolute quality and so in experience it can be ultimately known, but the way to God, the *sādhanā*, must be concerned with the *saguṇa* expression.

3. *Creator*

Gurū Nānak has set out his cosmology in the hymn *Mārū Solahā* 15. It begins:

> For countless aeons there was undivided darkness. There was neither earth nor heavens, but only the infinite Order of God (*Hukam*).[2]

He then details at length the things which did not exist, his point being that apart from God and His *Hukam* there was nothing. It is a striking picture with much that evokes the Genesis conception of primeval chaos. Finally:

> When it pleased Thee Thou didst create the world, establishing Thy creation without visible supports. Thou didst create Brahmā, Viṣṇu and Śiva, and Thou didst spread abroad the allurements of *māyā*.[3]

A number of references to the creative activity of God have already been quoted and there are many more available. The frequency with which they occur is significant in that it brings out a clear and explicit concept of the personality of God. Again the comparison with Kabīr is interesting. An affirmation of the personality of God does emerge from Kabīr's works, but it emerges rather by hint and implication than by explicit statement. References to God as Creator are comparatively scarce and lack the clarity of Gurū Nānak's declarations. The same also applies to other attributes which imply a notion of personality. In Kabīr's works we must often grope; in Nānak's we find clarity.

> Beings of various kinds, colours, and names—He wrote them all with a flowing pen. If anyone knew how to record the number what an immense account it

[1] *Śabadārath*, p. 827, n. ¶. The writer is almost certainly Principal Teja Singh. *Śabadārath* was issued as the work of a panel of commentators, but it is well known that practically the entire commentary was written by Principal Teja Singh.

[2] *AG*, p. 1035.

[3] *AG*, p. 1036.

would be! What power, what beauty of form, what gifts! Who can guess them! With a single command He unfurled creation and by that command there sprang forth thousands of rivers.[1]

The Fearless One, the Formless One, the True Name—the whole world is His creation![2]

4. *Sustainer*

God does not merely create. Having brought the world into being He watches over it and cares for it.

> He who created the world watches over it, appointing all to their various tasks.[3]

And in another passage which affirms both His creative and sustaining activity:

> True Creator, True Sustainer, and known as the True One! Self-existent, true, ineffable, immeasurable! Uniting both mill stones,[4] He separated them. Without the *Gurū* there is utter darkness. Having created the sun and moon He directs their paths day and night.[5]

Again the attribution of personality is evident. For Gurū Nānak God is a participant in the life of the universe which He has established, watching, directing, and upholding.

The latter passage also indicates the meaning of the term *saibhan* which is used in the *Mūl Mantra* and which is usually translated as 'self-existent'. God created Himself. In human terms this can have no meaning, but human understanding is bounded by strict limitations. The 'self-existence' of God is an affirmation of His absolute nature and beyond this human understanding cannot proceed. God in His fullness is, for Gurū Nānak, far beyond the human intellect and man can no more apprehend that fullness than he can encompass the infinite.

5. *Destroyer*

God, the One, is Brahmā and Viṣṇu, and so too is He Śiva. He who is the Creator and Sustainer is also declared to be God the Destroyer and Recreator.

> He who created also destroys; apart from Him there is no other. . . .
>
> Having destroyed He builds and having built He destroys. Casting down He raises up and raising up He casts down. Having filled the sea He causes it to dry up and then fills it again, for He, the One beyond care and anxiety, has the power (to do it).[6]

[1] *Japji* 16, *AG*, p. 3.
[2] *Vār Āsā*, *ślok* 2 of *pauṛī* 5, *AG*, p. 465.
[3] *Sūhī Chhant* 4 (1), *AG*, p. 765.
[4] i.e. creating heaven and earth.
[5] *Vaḍahaṃsu Dakhaṇī* 3 (1), p. 580.
[6] *Oaṅkāru* 31, 41, *AG*, pp. 934, 935.

Thou art absolute and whatever is in Thy will comes to pass. This world is a pretext.[1] The true Creator pervades the waters, the earth, and all between earth and sky. He, the true Creator, is ineffable, measureless, eternal. The coming (into the world) of a man is fruitful if he meditates single-mindedly (upon the Creator). Breaking down He reconstructs and by His Order He sustains all. Thou art absolute and whatever is in Thy will comes to pass. This world is a pretext.[2]

6. *Sovereign*

Thou art absolute and whatever is in Thy will comes to pass.

The refrain of the stanza from *Vaḍahaṃsu Alāhaṇī* 1 quoted above gathers the creative, sustaining, and destroying activities of God into that basic attribute from which all three flow. God is for Nānak the sovereign Lord, the wielder of absolute authority, the possessor of unqualified power.

Whatever pleases Thee, that Thou doest, and none can gainsay it.[3]

'Whatever pleases Thee.' We have here another of Gurū Nānak's characteristic expressions. Again and again one encounters a variety of forms which may be translated with these words, and repeatedly the same emphasis is made in other ways.

If it pleases Thee Thou dost exalt one to the throne and if it pleases Thee one renounces the world and goes begging. If it pleases Thee floods flow over the desert and the lotus blooms in the sky. If it pleases Thee one crosses the Ocean of Fear and if it pleases Thee (one's boat) fills (with water and sinks) in mid-ocean. If it pleases Thee Thou art a Lord of joy and I am rapt in Thy praises, Thou storehouse of excellences. If it pleases Thee Thou art a fearsome Lord and I go on dying in the cycle of transmigration.[4]

God is accordingly *anāth*, omnipotent, and as He is omnipotent so too is He omniscient.

The sovereign Lord created this visible world. He sees all, comprehends all, and knows all, permeating (all creation) both within and without.[5]

7. *Eternal*

The world, which is the work of God the Creator, is unstable and impermanent, but God Himself is not.

[1] The meaning of this phrase is not clear. Vir Singh's interpretation is probably correct: 'This world is a pretext (i.e. created to be an opportunity) for the liberation of souls.' *Santhyā*, vol. vii, pp. 3533–4.

[2] *Vaḍahaṃsu Alāhaṇī* 1, *AG*, p. 579.

[3] *Gūjarī Aṣṭ* 3 (5), *AG*, p. 504.

[4] *Sūhī Suchajjī*, p. 762. The Ocean of Fear, or the Ocean of Existence, is a conventional image representing the span of human existence with its multitude of attendant impediments which the soul must overcome in order to attain release from the cycle of transmigration.

[5] *Āsā Paṭṭī Likhī* 24, p. 433.

He, the true Lord, is eternally true. He is and will be, for unlike His creation He will not pass away.[1]

God is *abināsī*, eternal. He is *anādi*, without beginning, *akāl*, beyond time, the One who is ever firm and wholly constant. This is a logical corollary of the absolute nature of God, but it requires emphasis because of its importance to Gurū Nānak. To men his repeated appeal was that they should renounce their love of the world and all wordly attachments. These are *māyā*[2] and they are to be renounced, for in the experience of every individual they must inevitably betray the trust which is put in them. Nothing of the world can accompany man after his physical death[3] and so for every individual the world is a vain thing which must pass away. As opposed to this fickle destructible world, however, there stands the eternally constant *achal* God. He is *nirañjan*,[4] the One wholly detached (*atīt*, *alipt*, *niramal*, *niralep*), wholly apart from the *māyā* which He Himself created, wholly perfect.

The Alpha, the Holy One, without beginning and deathless, eternally immutable.[5]

This same concept lies behind the emphasis which Gurū Nānak lays upon God being *ajūnī*, unborn, non-incarnated.

Pervading all (as the heavens extend over all), infinite, absolute, not incarnated.[6]

To be incarnated means to be involved in death, which is the supreme enemy, the characteristic quality of the unstable world and the ultimate antithesis of God's own eternal being. God, however, is beyond death and transmigration.[7] This, by implication, means that there can be no place for a doctrine of *avatārs*,[8] but its primary purpose is to emphasize the total detachment of God from all that is unstable, mutable, or corruptible. The world, caught up in the cycle of birth and death, of endless coming and going, is real but it is *bināsī*, a corruptible reality subject to flux and decay and dissolution, whereas God, in contrast with it, is *abināsī*, *amar*, *achut*, the incorruptible, eternal Reality.

If an individual's affections are transferred from the world to God the result is a relationship which endures to eternity, and the person who is united with God in such a relationship himself participates in the divine immortality. This is Gurū Nānak's constant appeal, that men should

[1] *Japji* 27, p. 6. [2] See *infra*, pp. 185–7. [3] *Bilāvalu Aṣṭ* 2 (1R), *AG*, p. 832.
[4] See *infra*, p. 186. [5] *Japji* 28, *AG*, p. 6. Also stanzas 29–31.
[6] *Oaṅkāru* 20, *AG*, p. 932. [7] *Mārū Solahā* 18 (1–4), *AG*, p. 1038.
[8] Elsewhere the elimination is explicit.

Nānak, in comparison with the Fearless, Formless One, innumerable Rāms are as dust.

Vār Āsā, *ślok* 2 of *pauṛī* 4, *AG*, p. 464.

abandon worldly affections and attach themselves to the eternally tranquil and immutable God.

8. *Formless*

The absolute nature and the eternal being of God are metaphysical qualities and there now arises the question of whether for Gurū Nānak the human understanding of God can proceed from the strictly metaphysical to something more concrete. The answer is a firm negative and a negative which in its firmness rejects not merely idols and *avatārs*, but also anthropomorphic language. He is *arūp*, without form, *niraṅkār*, the Formless One. For Gurū Nānak and for all subsequent Sikh thought this word *Niraṅkār* has been one of the most important names of God. Stanzas 16–19 of *Japjī* all end with the salutation:

Thou the eternally unchanging Formless One (*niraṅkār*).[1]

In *Soraṭhi* 3 God is addressed in what is, for Gurū Nānak, a thoroughly typical manner.

Thou the Formless One, beyond fear and enmity, I blend in Thy pure light.[2]

Such significance has been attached to the name *Niraṅkār* that its derivative form *niraṅkārī* has since been used in conjunction with Gurū Nānak's own name to indicate the nature of the salvation which he himself achieved. Nānak Niraṅkārī he is called, Nānak who is one with the Formless One. Gurū Nānak himself used the word in just this sense.

Perceiving the nature of spiritual reality (lit. the self) he has become *niraṅkārī* (one with the Formless One).[3]

Niraṅkār is the characteristic epithet which Gurū Nānak uses to communicate this particular concept, but elsewhere the formless quality of God is expressed in other language.

He has neither form (*rūp*) nor material sign (*rekhiā*).[4]

Thou hast thousands of eyes and yet Thou hast no eye. Thou hast thousands of forms and yet no form, thousands of holy feet and yet no foot, and without a fragrance Thou hast thousands of fragrances.[5] I am dazed by such a wonder.[6]

9. *Ineffable*

God is the Formless One, uncreated, unborn, never incarnated. He cannot be present in an idol, He cannot be revealed by an *avatār*, and He

[1] *Japji*, *AG*, pp. 3–4.
[2] *Soraṭhi* 3, *AG*, p. 596.
[3] *Āsā Asṭ* 8 (7), *AG*, p. 415.
[4] *Sūhi Asṭ* 1 (3), *AG*, p. 750.
[5] Lit. nose, noses.
[6] *Dhanāsari Ārati*, *AG*, pp. 13, 663.

cannot be described in terms appropriate to the human condition. How then can He be apprehended? Is it in fact possible for human understanding to grasp the nature of God, or must man be content with defining Him in negatives, of describing Him in terms of what He is not?

The first answer to this question must be that God is ultimately incomprehensible, ultimately beyond human apprehension. For Gurū Nānak God in His fullness is far beyond the bounds of man's understanding. The intellect of man is strictly limited and any effort it may make to define the wholeness of God must be an effort to circumscribe the infinite, to bring within narrow bounds the One who is boundless. God is ineffable and man's proper and inevitable response to any authentic glimpse of the being of God can only be that of awe (*visamād*), of fear and wonder before Him who is beyond comprehending. He is *agam*, *agochar*, inscrutable, beyond the reach of the intellect; *agah*, unfathomable; *acharaj*, of surpassing wonder; *adriṣṭ*, beyond seeing or perception; *akāl*, beyond time; *alabh*, unsearchable; *anant*, infinite; *apār*, boundless; *abol*, *akah*, *akath*, *alekh*, beyond utterance or describing; *alakh*, ineffable.

> Beyond human grasp or understanding, boundless, infinite, the all-powerful supreme God! He who existed before time began, who has existed throughout all ages, and who shall eternally exist, (He alone is true). Spurn all else as false.[1]

> Beyond understanding, infinite, unreachable, beyond perception, free from death and *karma*, without caste, never incarnate, self-existent, subject to neither love (of worldly things) nor doubt. Thou, the ultimate Truth, to Thee I sacrifice myself. Thou hast neither form, colour, nor material sign, but Thou dost reveal Thyself in the true Word (*Śabad*).[2]

And as God and His dwelling place are beyond all telling so too is that expression of His will which is called the *Hukam*, the divine Order of creation.[3]

> No one has comprehended Thy *Hukam* and none can describe it. Were a hundred poets to gather together their singing could not even approach a description of it. No one has grasped its worth; all but repeat what they have heard.[4]

10. *Immanent*

All this, however, concerns God *in His fullness*. God is infinite and so ultimately beyond apprehension, but this does not necessarily mean that He is wholly unknowable, that He is *totally* beyond the range of human perception. For Gurū Nānak, as for Nāmdev, Kabīr, Raidās, and other

[1] *Āsā Chhant* 3 (1), *AG*, p. 437.
[2] *Soraṭhi* 6, *AG*, p. 597.
[3] See *infra*, pp. 199–203.
[4] *Siri Rāgu Aṣṭ* 1 (2), *AG*, p. 53.

Sants, there is certainly a revelation of God, partial no doubt but commensurate with the understanding and experience of man and accordingly sufficient for his salvation. The extract from *Sorațhi* 6 quoted above continues as follows:

> Thou hast neither mother nor father, son, relation, wife, nor sensual desire. Thou art without lineage, free from *māyā*, boundless. Thy light (shines) in all.[1]

And the passage from *Dhanāsarī Āratī* continues:

> Within all there is light and it is Thy light which is in all. Through the *Gurū's* leading the light is revealed. True worship is what pleases Thee.[2]

The figure is that of all-pervading light and its meaning is the all-pervading immanence of God.

> Wondrous, my Master, are Thy ways! Thou dost pervade the waters, the land, and all that is between the heavens and the earth, indwelling in all. Wherever I look there I see Thy light. Of what nature is Thy form? In a single form Thou dost move concealed (in all creation) and yet (in spite of Thy presence) no one person is the same as another.[3]

'Wherever I look. . . .' They are familiar words, both in the works of Gurū Nānak and in those of the Sants who preceded him. Wherever one looks there He is to be seen, for He manifests Himself in His own creation.

> Do not regard the Lord as far off for He is near, He, the One, pervading creation. He is the only One; there is no other. He, the One, pervades all.[4]

God the omnipotent and omniscient is also God the omnipresent.

> Thou art the ocean, the All-knower, the All-seer. How can I, a fish, perceive Thy limit? Wherever I look there Thou art. If I leave Thee I burst and die.[5]

This is accepted as a general truth and one of fundamental importance, but Gurū Nānak, in common with other Sants, goes further. The *Nirankār* who is immanent in all creation is specifically immanent in one particular part of creation.

> The Lord pervades every heart. He dwells concealed in the waters, the land, all that is between the heavens and the earth, but through the Word of the *Gurū* He is revealed. By His Grace the *Gurū*, the True *Gurū*, revealed Him to me in this world where all dies, in the nether world, and in the heavens. The non-incarnated Brahmā is and eternally will be. Behold the Lord within yourself![6]

[1] *Sorațhi* 6, *AG*, p. 597.
[2] *Dhanāsarī Āratī*, *AG*, pp. 13, 663.
[3] *Sorațhi* 4, *AG*, p. 596.
[4] *Oankāru* 5, *AG*, p. 930.
[5] *Sirī Rāgu* 31, *AG*, p. 25.
[6] *Sorațhi* 8, *AG*, pp. 597–8.

God who dwells in all creation has His particular abode within the human heart.

> The one *Omkār*, wholly apart, immortal, unborn, without caste, wholly free, ineffable, without form or visible sign, but searching I perceived Him in every heart.[1]

This is no mere aesthetic mystery, no mere source of numinous awe which, however impressive it may be, leaves man essentially where he was. Here we are at the crucial point, the point at which there can exist communication between God and man, and through which there can develop that relationship which means release and salvation. Failure to grasp this is regarded as fatal.

> Wearing ochre garments they wander around, but without the True *Gurū* none have found Thee. Roaming in all countries and in all directions they have grown weary (but their efforts are in vain for) Thou art concealed within.[2]

For Gurū Nānak the saving activity of God is expressed at this point. Here, in the divine Order (*Hukam*), is the inscription of His will for all who are able to read it. Here it is that the Word (*Śabad*) and the Name (*Nām*) acquire the substance which render them meaningful to the human understanding. And here it is that the *Gurū's* voice is to be heard.[3]

> Know Him who creates and destroys the world, know Him by His creation. Do not look far off for the True One, but recognize Him in the guise of the Word in every heart. He who established this creation, recognize Him as the true Word and do not imagine Him to be far distant. He who meditates on the Name finds peace. Without the Name the game (of life) is lost.[4]

> (Thou who art) inscrutable, beyond apprehending, ineffable, infinite, have mercy upon me! Thou who dost pervade the universe, Thy light shines in every heart.[5]

11. *The divine initiative*

In the pattern of salvation which is to be found throughout the works of Gurū Nānak effort on the part of the individual is essential, but it is not the only factor and nor would it appear to be the primary one.

> Nānak, the True King Himself unites (the believer) with Himself.[6]

It is God, says Gurū Nānak, who is responsible for that union which is the climax of the salvation process. Man must participate and unless he does

[1] *Bilāvalu Thitī*, *AG*, p. 838.
[2] *Vār Malār*, *pauṛī* 25, *AG*, p. 1290.
[3] This summary statement will be developed below under *Śabad*, *Nām*, *Gurū*, and *Hukam*, pp. 191 ff.
[4] *Vaḍahaṃsu Alāhaṇī* 4, *AG*, p. 581.
[5] *Bilāvalu* 2, *AG*, p. 795.
[6] *Sirī Rāgu* 10, *AG*, p. 18.

so there can be no release, no union.[1] His participation is, however, dependent upon the prior activity of God, and without this divine initiative the question of human participation does not arise as its need is not recognized.

Nānak, all we receive is by the grace of the Beneficient One.[2]

This aspect need not be developed here, for it will be dealt with in the section relating to the divine self-expression.[3] At this point it will be sufficient to draw attention to the stress which Gurū Nānak lays upon what is normally referred to as divine grace. It is an aspect which is integral to his total thought and it is one to which constant reference is made in his works. This divine grace is expressed in terms of divine activity made manifest in the created world and within man's inner being. It is not activity at a secondary level, but purposeful activity upon which the attainment of release depends. Nor is it an inflexible activity which could be interpreted as a mythologized version of natural laws. Natural laws are indeed acknowledged and, as we shall see, are regarded as a significant part of God's communication with mankind.[4] They are not, however, the ultimate basis, for behind them lies a will which is expressed in terms of decision, of giving and witholding. Without this divine grace a man is helpless.[5] If, however, God chooses to impart it the way of salvation lies open.

12. *The greatness of God*

The purpose of systematic theology is to construct a consistent framework, to develop a coherently integrated pattern out of what is dispersed throughout the record of an individual or corporate religious experience. In order to do this it is necessary to extract, analyse, and rearrange in a pattern which serves this particular purpose. By itself, however, such a pattern must be inadequate, for it will inevitably lose much of the spirit which prompted the original record. At the beginning of this section on the nature of God it was noted that the characteristic expression of Gurū Nānak's religious experience is the hymn of praise and it is appropriate that the section should close with extracts which convey something of this spirit. It is an impulse which Gurū Nānak shares with all *bhagats*. *Niraṅkār*, the Formless One, is the supreme Lord of the universe, eternal, absolute, ineffable, and yet purposing that man should know Him and find ultimate peace in union with Him. Before such majesty, infinite and yet condescending in mercy to stoop to man, the inevitable response for Gurū Nānak must be that of adoring praise.

Having heard of Thy greatness everyone speaks of it, but only by seeing Thee can one know the immensity of Thy greatness. No one can know or express

[1] *Vār Sāraṅg*, *ślok* 2 of *pauṛī* 2, *AG*, p. 1238. *Sirī Rāgu* 30 (3), *AG*, p. 25.
[2] *Japjī* 24, *AG*, p. 5.
[3] See *infra*, pp. 204–7.
[4] See *infra*, p. 201.
[5] *Japjī* 7, *AG*, p. 2.

Thy worth. Those who tell of Thee are gathered up into Thee. Great art Thou, my Lord, ineffable and of excellences beyond comprehending. None can encompass the measure of Thy greatness. The exegetes gathered together and expounded the scriptures; all extollers of Thy worth together determined that worth; men of understanding, men of contemplation, *gurūs* and *gurūs' gurūs*, (all proclaimed Thy greatness and yet) not a fragment of Thy greatness could they express. All truth, all (the merits of) austerities, all goodness, all the impressive works of *siddhs*, (all are from Thee). Without Thee none has reached the mystical consummation, but when Thy grace is received no obstacle remains. Thine is a storehouse filled with excellences beyond telling. He to whom Thou givest (support) what need has he of any other help? Nānak declares: Thou art the True One and all is in Thy hands.[1]

In describing only a tiny portion of the glory of the divine Name (men) have wearied themselves and yet failed to discover its worth. If all were to gather together and strive to describe it the glory would be neither heightened nor dimmed. He does not die and there is no occasion to mourn Him. He gives continually and His gifts do not cease. His particular quality is that He alone is, that there neither was nor will be another. His bounty is infinite as He is infinite, He who caused night to follow day. Low is he who forgets the Lord; wretched is he who is without the Name.[2]

II. THE NATURE OF UNREGENERATE MAN

O my Lord, who can comprehend Thy excellences! None can recount my sinfulness.

Many times was I born as a tree, many times as an animal, many times I came in the form of a snake, and many times I flew as a bird.

Many times did I break into city shops, strong buildings, and having burgled them return home. I looked ahead and behind, but how could it be concealed from Thee?

(I have visited) places of pilgrimage on river-banks, *tīraths*, shops, cities, markets; I have seen all regions of the world. Taking scales I have weighed (my merits against my demerits) in my heart.

As the oceans are filled with water, so immense is my sinfulness. Be merciful, show a measure of Thy grace that this sinking stone may cross over. An undying fire burns in my soul, within (my heart) a knife twists. Nānak prays: (Show me Thy grace for he who by it) understands Thy divine Order attains eternal peace.[3]

Man's nature is, for Gurū Nānak, dependent upon his affiliation, and that nature is transformed when his affiliation is transferred from the world to the divine Name. It is the nature of unregenerate man which concerns us at this point, the nature of man in the condition of attachment to the world. This is the condition of pride, of self-centredness, of sin, and so of

[1] *Āsā* 2, *AG*, p. 9. [2] *Āsā* 3, *AG*, p. 9. [3] *Gauṛī* 17, *AG*, p. 156.

death and transmigration. This is the condition which must be transcended if man is to attain release from transmigration.

For Gurū Nānak the key to an understanding of man's nature is an understanding of the human faculty which is called the *man*.[1] Cleanse the *man* and it becomes a fitting abode for the Name. Control it and you will no more wander from the One with whom you seek union. But let it retain its impurity, let it remain unbridled, and the penalty will be Death. Yam, the God of Death, will seize you, bind you, and march you off to his prison. There you will continue to suffer in the round of birth and death.

1. *The* man

mani jītai jagu jītu
To conquer the *man* is to conquer the world.[2]

The word *man* as used by Gurū Nānak has no satisfactory English translation. It is usually rendered 'mind', but the translation is unsatisfactory as the English word lacks the breadth of meaning and association which *man* possesses in Sant literature and Sikh scripture. It is true that the concept of mind is included within the range of *man* and that it is the dominant concept covered by the word. To translate it in this way alone is, however, inadequate in the context of Gurū Nānak's usage.

Man is a version of *manas*, a word with a lengthy history. In the *Ṛg Veda* it denotes 'soul' and is very close in meaning to *ātman*.[3] In the *Upaniṣads* the two terms tend to diverge, with *manas* moving towards *chitta* and assuming a quality best translated as 'mind',[4] whereas *ātman* becomes identified with the inmost essence in man.[5] In Vedānta *manas* emerges explicitly as an aspect or function of *antaḥkaraṇa*, the seat of collective thought and feeling.

> Vedanta does not regard manas (mind) as a sense (indriya). The same antahkarana, according to its diverse functions, is called manas, buddhi, ahamkara, and citta. In its function as doubt it is called manas, as originating definite cognitions it is called buddhi. As presenting the notion of an ego in consciousness ahamkara, and as producing memory citta.[6]

In these terms Gurū Nānak's understanding of the *man* could be described as synonymous with *antaḥkaraṇa* in that it embraces all of these functions,

[1] Attention is drawn to the italics. This is not the English word 'man', but a transliteration of the word used by Gurū Nānak and pronounced 'mun' as in 'mundane'. It is not translated as no accurate English translation exists.

[2] *Japji* 28, *AG*, p. 6.

[3] S. Dasgupta, *A History of Indian Philosophy*, vol. i, pp. 25–26. A Berriedale Keith, *The Religion and Philosophy of the Vedas and Upanishads*, vol. ii, pp. 403–4.

[4] Cf. *Chhāndogya Upaniṣad*, vii. 3. i.

[5] S. Dasgupta, op. cit., vol. i, pp. 45–46. Dr. Radhakrishnan identifies the *manas* of the *Upaniṣads* with the *antaḥkaraṇa* and uses 'mind' to translate it, but maintains a close relationship between the two terms (*The Principal Upanisads*, p. 471).

[6] S. Dasgupta, op. cit., vol. i, p. 472, n. 1.

in so far as they are distinguished in his thought, and is used interchangeably with *buddhi*, *chitta*, and *antaḥkaraṇa* itself. The comparison would, however, be misleading for Gurū Nānak was not a Vedāntist. His concept lacks the sophistication of developed Vedānta doctrine and extends to areas which are excluded from the *antaḥkaraṇa* of Vedānta. It comes much closer to the Yoga notion of the *manas* as 'the inner sense'.[1] Even here, however, the marked divergence from Yoga as a developed and integrated philosophy makes comparison risky, although there seems to be no doubt that in this, as in so much else, the Sant concept has roots in Nāth doctrine.

An impression of the range of meaning which the word covers in Gurū Nānak's works can be gathered from the actual contexts in which it is used, and from other terms which are used in similar contexts and which are obviously synonymous with aspects of *man*. It is with the *man* that one makes decisions and particular emphasis is laid upon its function as moral arbiter.

> The *man* acts as the *man* itself dictates. Sometimes it expresses virtue, sometimes sin.[2]

The *man* is the faculty by means of which Truth is apprehended.

> In his *man* is Truth and so Truth is in (the words of) his mouth also.
> With Truth as his banner he finds no obstacle remaining.[3]

And it is with the *man* that one meditates.

> Meditate in your *man*, cleave in union to the One, and the round of birth and death is at an end.[4]

In all of these the translation 'mind' would be appropriate and it is not surprising that such words as *surati*, *chitta*, *budhi*, and *mati* occur in similar contexts.

Other contexts, however, extend the meaning to express what in English is usually covered by 'heart'.

> If the strong smites the strong the *man* is not grieved.[5]

It is difficult to draw precise bounds between 'mind' and 'heart', but emotions of this kind are generally associated with the latter word. We also find the *man* specified as the seat both of such evil qualities as lust and anger, and of the *bhagat's* love for God.

> Within my *man* lurk the five (evil impulses) and so like a wanderer it has no resting place. My *man* has not found its resting place in the merciful Lord, for it is bound to *māyā*, (caught up in) greed, deceit, sin, and hypocrisy.[6]

[1] M. Eliade, *Yoga: Immortality and Freedom*, p. 20.
[2] *Bilāvalu Aṣṭ* 2 (1), *AG*, p. 832.
[3] *Bilāvalu Thitī* 9, *AG*, p. 839.
[4] *Gūjarī Aṣṭ* 1 (4), *AG*, p. 503.
[5] *Āsā* 39, *AG*, p. 360.
[6] *Āsā* 34, *AG*, p. 359.

Elsewhere *ghaṭ*, *hiradā*, *ridā*, *dil*, or *ur* are used interchangeably with *man*, for all are used to designate the specific abode of God within each individual.

Nor is this the limit, for *man* is also used to cover what in English is normally expressed with the word 'soul'. This applies to the usage which refers to the indestructible quality of the *man*. In such cases neither 'mind' nor 'heart' is adequate. The *man* is mind and it is heart, and it is also that human attribute which does not perish with physical death and which man must seek to unite with God, which he must strive to have carried across the Ocean of Existence.

> Be still, my *man*, and you shall not suffer hurt. Sing (His) praises, my *man*, and you shall enter into supreme tranquillity. Sing God's praises and you shall taste His sweetness. Apply the antimony of the *Gurū's* enlightenment (to your inward eyes) and by the light of that lamp which, fed by the Word, illuminates the whole universe you shall slay the five devils.[1] So shall you destroy your fears and in fearlessness you shall cross the dread Ocean of Existence. You shall meet the *Gurū* and find fulfilment. He upon whom God bestows grace finds a fullness of spiritual stature, spiritual joy, and love for God.[2]

Here we find *man* assuming the qualities of *jīv* and *ātmā*.

One solution to this translation problem is to translate *man* as 'mind' in some contexts, 'heart' in others, and 'soul' in yet others. In circumstances where an English word must be found if possible this is perhaps necessary, but such translations will normally fail to bring out the fullness of meaning which the term possesses. It is strictly untranslatable, for there is nothing in English which combines the functions of the mind, the emotions of the heart, and the qualities of the soul. Perhaps the closest we can get is the word 'psyche', but this too is inadequate and liable to mislead. *Man* is mind, heart, and soul. It is the faculty with which one thinks, decides, and feels, the source of all human good and evil, and that one indestructible attribute which must be released from the body and merged in the being of God.

In laying this stress upon the role of the *man* Gurū Nānak stands within a well-developed tradition. Dr. Vaudeville has described the importance which the *man* held for the Siddhs and the Nāths,[3] and to illustrate Kabīr's understanding of it she gives in her *Au Cabaret de l'Amour: Paroles de Kabîr* a translation of his *Gauṛī* 28, in which she renders *man* as 'âme'.

> Le caractère est inhérent à l'âme:
> Qui donc a jamais obtenu le salut en triomphant de son âme?
> Où donc est l'ascète qui a vaincu son âme?
> Dis-moi, qui donc a jamais obtenu la Délivrance par la défaite de l'âme?

[1] The five evil impulses. See *infra*, p. 184.

[2] *Tukhārī Chhant* 6 (3), *AG*, p. 1113.

[3] Ch. Vaudeville, *Kabīr Granthāvalī* (*Dohā*), p. xvi, and *Au Cabaret de l'Amour: Paroles de Kabîr*, p. 211, n. xxxv.

Pourtant, chacun éprouve cette certitude au fond de l'âme;
Le prix de l'amour divin, c'est la victoire sur son âme. . . .

Ceux qui ont pénétré ce mystère, dit Kabîr,
Contemplent en leur âme le Seigneur, le Maître de l'Univers.[1]

Gurū Nānak's understanding of the *man* is essentially that of Kabīr. The *man* of unregenerate man is erratic and leads him into worldly attachments which are the very antithesis of salvation.

The *man* is unsteady, it does not know the way. The man who puts his trust in his own *man* is as one befouled; he does not recognize the Word (*Śabad*).[2]

It is not, however, an inveterate enemy. It is to be restrained but not crushed, for this same *man* is something priceless, the treasury which contains all treasures, the abode of God Himself if man will but recognize it.

The *man* is a priceless pearl. (Dwelling on) the Name of God it has been accorded honour.[3]

In the *man* are the jewels of the Name, its pearls, its rubies, its diamonds. The Name is the true merchandise, the true wealth, deep down in every heart. If the grace of God, the precious One, is upon a man, then with the *Gurū*'s aid he obtains the divine Name.[4]

In unregenerate man, however, the *man* is impure, unrestrained. Its evil propensities are permitted to assert themselves, and in consequence man remains a slave to his passions and so to Death.

The heedless *man* is a wanderer, a vagrant.
Greedy beyond measure, it has indulged its desire by drinking the poison of *māyā*. Never does it find its peace in love of the One. It is like a fish, caught in the gullet by a hook. . . .
The heedless *man* flits hither and thither like a bumble-bee, seeking through its senses to indulge in many foolish evils. Like an elephant it is trapped because of its lust. It is bound and its head jabbed with a goad. . . .
The *man* is ever straying, never held in check. If it be not filled with love for God, He can give it neither honour nor trust. Thou art the omniscient One, the Protector of all. Thou dost uphold Thy creation, watching over all.[5]

2. Haumai

As iron is thrown into a furnace, melted, and recast, so is he who fastens his affections on *māyā* incarnated again and again. Without understanding (of the divine Word) all he gathers is suffering upon suffering. (Through the influence of) *haumai* he transmigrates and wanders in doubt.[6]

[1] loc. cit., p. 89.
[2] *Āsā Aṣṭ* 7 (8), *AG*, p. 415.
[3] *Sirī Rāgu* 22, *AG*, p. 22.
[4] *Sirī Rāgu* 21, *AG*, p. 22.
[5] *Basant Aṣṭ* 2 (1), (2), and (4), *AG*, pp. 1187–8.
[6] *Sūhī Aṣṭ* 4 (1–1R), *AG*, p. 752.

In unregenerate man the dominant impulse is that of *haumai*, a concept which is to be found in the works of Kabīr and those of other Sants, but which receives appreciably more emphasis in those of Gurū Nānak. For Gurū Nānak it is *haumai* which controls the *man* of unregenerate man and so determines the pattern of his life. The results are disastrous, for instead of leading a man to release and salvation his *haumai* will invariably stimulate affections which can only bind him more firmly to the wheel of transmigration.

The usual translation of *haumai*[1] is 'ego', another example of a rendering which is neither incorrect nor entirely satisfactory. The English word is certainly a literal translation,[2] but it is misleading for two reasons. The first is that it has already been appropriated in Indian philosophy to express a notion which has an equally literal original, but which offers a meaning different from that which *haumai* covers in Gurū Nānak's works. In Vedānta *ahaṃkāra* is an expression of *ajñāna*, a 'blending of the unreal associations held up in the mind (*antaḥkaraṇa*) with the real, the false with the true that is the root of illusion'.[3] This definition, in spite of the etymological connexion and the fact that the word has moved away from a neutral meaning, is not what Gurū Nānak meant, for it does not possess the moral content which is so strongly implied in *haumai*. Nor is 'ego' anywhere near *haumai* when used in a Yoga context, for in this case it is clearly neutral and precedes the emergence of *manas* in the evolutionary process.[4]

A second reason why there is a risk of misunderstanding is that the word 'ego' has at least three different usages in the West and that none of them can be said to accord with Gurū Nānak's usage. In its strictly philosophical application the term has a neutral meaning which is certainly not the case with *haumai*; in a psychological context it is too closely identified with Freudian theory; and in its loose popular usage it has become a mixture of 'pride', 'self-confidence', and 'morale'.

Macauliffe's translation was 'pride'.[5] It is true that *garab* and *haṅkār* are closely related to *haumai* and that in certain contexts they may be used in a sense which corresponds to it.

> Casting out pride (*garab*) we ascend to celestial heights. . . . Through His grace (the *Gurū*) reveals (God's) palace (within our own frame). Nānak, casting out our *haumai* (the *Gurū*) unites us with God.[6]

In general, however, *garab* and *haṅkār* must be regarded not as synonyms for *haumai*, but as a result of it.

[1] Or, in relevant contexts, of *hau* or *āp*.

[2] *hau-main*, 'I–I'.

[3] S. Dasgupta, *A History of Indian Philosophy*, vol. i, pp. 458–9.

[4] M. Eliade, *Yoga: Immortality and Freedom*, p. 20. There is, however, an obvious affinity between *haumai* and the *icchā* ('desire') of the *Yoga-vasiṣṭha* (S. Dasgupta, op. cit., vol. ii, p. 264).

[5] e.g. *The Sikh Religion*, vol. i, p. 227. Cf. also Jayaram Misra, *Sri Gurū Granth Daraśan*, p. 120.

[6] *Gauṛī* 9, *AG*, p. 153.

Another possible translation for *haumai* is 'sin'. It is not a literal translation in the way that 'ego' is, but its meaning corresponds closely. In its strict Christian theological usage 'sin' is always singular. It means self-willed disobedience to God, a condition naturally inherent in man and expressing itself in a multitude of ways. It would be difficult to distinguish this condition from *haumai*, for as applied to the individual the two correspond almost exactly. Just as such impulses as pride and greed are properly regarded as the results of sin, so too do we find that the five traditional evil impulses are the offspring of *haumai*. In both cases the evil impulses are regarded as the expressions in an individual's thoughts, feelings, and actions of a condition which determines the direction of those thoughts, feelings, and actions.

There are, however, two serious objections to the use of 'sin' as a translation. The first is that the word 'sin' extends in Christian usage beyond its application to the individual. In Christian theology it also possesses corporate and cosmic connotations. *Haumai*, however, is limited to the individual. The second objection is that 'sin', like 'ego', has its popular usage. It is a usage which is correct in its own right, but which differs from the strict theological definition. In general usage 'sin' refers to what is properly conceived as the result of sin and it is frequently used in the plural. This clearly does not correspond to *haumai*.[1] A discussion of the theological term 'sin' can certainly clarify the meaning of *haumai*, but the word itself does not provide us with a satisfactory translation.

'Self' and 'self-centredness' are also possible translations. In English 'self' can be used in a bad sense which comes close to *haumai* and its meaning in this sense has not been seriously distorted by popular usage. In this particular context, however, it is liable to be misunderstood because in Indian philosophy it has so commonly been used in its neutral sense as a translation of *ātman*. This leaves us with 'self-centredness' which is perhaps the best available, but which is nevertheless unsatisfactory in that it will frequently impart a weaker and more limited meaning than that which *haumai* was intended to give.

It is unfortunate that there is no really satisfactory English equivalent, for in the thought of Gurū Nānak this word *haumai* epitomizes the condition of unregenerate man.

In *haumai* he comes and in *haumai* he goes;
In *haumai* he is born and in *haumai* he dies;
In *haumai* he gives and in *haumai* he takes;
In *haumai* he acquires and in *haumai* he casts away;
In *haumai* he is truthful and in *haumai* he lies;
In *haumai* he pays regard sometimes to virtue and sometimes to evil. . . .[2]

[1] It is covered by such words as *pāp*, *gunāh*, and *āprādh*.
[2] *Vār Āsā*, *ślok* 1 of *pauṛī* 7, *AG*, p. 466.

Everything that a man does is done in the context of this condition which pervades the whole of his activity. Even that which men call right or good is done only if it accords with the individual's *haumai*, and if it is not in accord it is rejected in favour of that which is evil. The result is that the path of salvation is hidden. Attention is absorbed in *māyā* and so the round of birth and death continues. Only when one perceives the true nature of this condition does there come a recognition of the way of salvation.

> (In *haumai*) he fails to perceive the true nature of salvation. In *haumai* there is *māyā* and its shadow (which is doubt). By acting in accordance with *haumai* he causes himself to be born again and again. If he understands his *haumai* he perceives the door (of salvation), but without understanding he argues and disputes. In accordance with the divine Order (*Hukam*) our *karma* is inscribed. He who discerns the nature of the divine Order discerns his *haumai* also.[1]

The person who fails to discern the nature of the divine Order is a *manmukh*. His loyalty is to himself, to the wayward impulses of his own *man* instead of to the voice of the *Gurū*. In contrast to this pattern is that of the *gurmukh*. The *gurmukh* hears and obeys the *Gurū*'s Word; the *manmukh* ignores it. Offered truth, freedom and life, he chooses instead falsehood, bondage, and death, for such is the fate of the man who has not purged *haumai* from his *man*.

> The *manmukh's* mind is clogged with falsehood. He does not meditate on (the Name of) God and so suffers the penalties of sin.[2]

3. *Evil impulses*

The outward expressions of a *man* dominated by *haumai* are the evil passions and by this fruit the *manmukh* is to be known.

> Day and night are the two seasons when he crops his land; lust and anger are his two fields. He waters them with greed, sows in them the seed of untruth, and worldly impulse, his plough-man, cultivates them. His (evil) thoughts are his plough and evil is the crop he reaps, for in accordance with the divine Order he cuts and eats.[3]

Traditionally these evil passions are five in number—*kām* (lust), *krodh* (anger, wrath), *lobh* (covetousness), *moh* (attachment to worldly things), and *haṅkār* (pride). From these five basic impulses spring all the deeds of violence and falsehood which earn an adverse *karma* and so endlessly protract the cycle of transmigration.

[1] *Vār Āsā, ślok* 1 of *pauṛī* 7, *AG*, p. 466.
[2] *Āsā* 24, *AG*, p. 356.
[3] *Vār Rāmakali, ślok* 1 of *pauṛi* 17, *AG*, p. 955.

My adversaries are five and I am but one. How shall I defend my house, O *man*?

Daily they attack me and plunder me. To whom shall I cry?[1]

Violence, attachment to worldly things, covetousness, and wrath are four streams of fire, and they who fall therein are consumed. Nānak, clinging, through grace, (to the *Gurū*'s feet) one is saved.[2]

Such impulses and the actions which proceed from them are the marks of the *manmukh*, of the self-willed, unregenerate man. They are the outward evidence of an impure *man*, filled not with love for the divine Name, but with love of self. And these are the snares of Yam, of Death.[3] He who falls into them must assuredly suffer the endless misery of death and rebirth.

4. Māyā

My merchant friend, (you who deal in worldly things), in the third watch of the night[4] you fix your attention on wealth and the bloom of youthful beauty, and do not remember the Name of God which brings release. Forgetting the Name of God, the soul is led astray through keeping the company of *māyā*. Absorbed in wealth, intoxicated by bodily beauty, it fritters its opportunity away. You neither adhered to your duty nor performed good deeds. Nānak says: The third watch is the period of the soul's attachment to money and carnal beauty.[5]

A wayward *man* dominated by *haumai* inevitably means involvement in *māyā*.

She who is caught up in greed, covetousness and pride is sunk in *māyā*. Foolish woman! The Lord is not found by such means.[6]

Māyā in the thought of Gurū Nānak is not the cosmic illusion of classical Vedānta. The world is indeed *māyā*, but it is not unreal. It is an illusion only in the sense that it is accepted for what it is not. Delusion is a more appropriate word. The essence of the world is its impermanence. It is real, but it is impermanent, both in the sense that it is itself perishable and in the sense that its attributes cannot follow a man after his physical death. It offers qualities which are accepted as both good and desirable, but which constitute a fraud, a deception. He who accepts the world in this way and who accordingly seeks fulfilment in attachment to worldly things is a victim of *māyā*, of the pretence that these attachments, if not actually Truth itself, are at least not inimical to Truth.

[1] *Gauṛi* 14, *AG*, p. 155. [2] *Vār Mājh*, *ślok* 2 of *pauṛi* 20, *AG*, p. 147.

[3] See *infra*, p. 188.

[4] i.e. the third stage of human life. The four stages, corresponding in this *śabad* to the four watches of the night, are birth, childhood, adulthood, and death.

[5] *Siri Rāgu Pahare* 1 (3), *AG*, p. 75. [6] *Tilaṅg* 4, *AG*, p. 722.

Māyā is basically untruth as opposed to Truth and the expression of this untruth is the world. It is in worldly affections, in the desire to appropriate the things of this world, that man's great temptation lies and succumbing to this temptation means involvement in untruth. The result can only be separation from God and continued transmigration. *Māyā* is *añjan*, literally the black collyrium applied to eyes but traditionally the symbol of darkness and untruth. God, on the other hand, is *nir-añjan*, the One who is wholly apart from all that is false, the One who is Himself Truth. Man must choose one or the other, for Truth and its antithesis cannot coexist.

> The love of gold and silver, women and fragrant scents, horses, couches, and dwellings, sweets and meats—these are all lusts of the flesh. Where in the heart can there be room for the Name?[1]

The question is obviously a rhetorical one. If man accepts the world's attractions, if he accepts the pretences of *māyā*, he must inevitably choose to be separated from God. This is what unregenerate man does. Blinded by ignorance (*agiān*, *avidiā*), led astray by doubt (*bhram*) and forgetfulness (*bhulekhā*), he accepts the world at its own valuation. But it is *māyā*, it is a fraud (*kapaṭ*), a deceit (*chhal*), untruth (*kūṛ*, *jhūṭh*), a snare (*jāl*), and the penalty for accepting it is inexorable. By accepting it man involves himself in *dubidhā*, in 'duality', in all that stands in opposition to union, in that separation which must divide the self-willed *manmukh* from God. Rejecting Life he chooses instead Death.

> *Māyā's* disciple is false; he abhors the Truth. Bound up in duality he transmigrates.[2]

Some of the practical manifestations of *māyā* are set out in the extract quoted above from *Sirī Rāgu* 4. Wealth, women, sons, power, status, worldly honour, comfort, food—these are the attractions which the world extends and which call forth man's lust, greed, and pride.[3] These are the allurements which stimulate his evil impulses and so lead him into the trap.

> For the love of silver and women the fool is entangled in duality and forgets the divine Name.[4]

None of this, however, endures.

> Accumulating *māyā* (wealth, power, status) kings vaunt themselves, but the *māyā* to which they are so attached does not accompany them (after death).[5]

[1] *Sirī Rāgu* 4, *AG*, p. 15. [2] *Mājh Aṣṭ* 1 (5), *AG*, p. 109.

[3] Macauliffe uses 'Mammon' as a translation of *māyā* (e.g. *The Sikh Religion*, vol. i, p. 22). The word is useful in that it brings out the basic antagonism between *māyā* and God, but it is inadequate for it limits the application of *māyā* to worldly wealth. *Sampad* (riches) is certainly one of the primary manifestations of *māyā* in Gurū Nānak's works, but so too is *kāmaṇ* (woman). Other temptations receive less emphasis, but obviously they are not to be regarded as negligible.

[4] *Āsā Aṣṭ* 9 (2), *AG*, p. 416. [5] *Prabhāti Aṣṭ* 1 (2), *AG*, p. 1342.

Māyā is, of course, the work of God, for it consists in the creation and is inseparable from it.

> He who created the various colours, kinds and aspects of *māyā*, having brought His creation into being watches over it, the manifestation of His greatness.[1]

Māyā is an interpretation of the creation, or rather a misinterpretation of it, a misunderstanding of its nature and purpose. The creation is both a revelation of God and a snare. What matters is a man's response to it. If he perceives the revelation he is on the way to salvation. If, on the other hand, he regards it as a means of indulging his *haumai* he is on the road to ruin. It can be either his ally or his enemy, an opportunity or a trap, a firm path or a quicksand. Even evil is from God and is to be regarded as an aspect of man's opportunity.

> Many are endlessly afflicted by pain and hunger, but even these, O Beneficent One, are Thy gifts.[2]

Everything depends upon the response which a man makes, and unregenerate man makes the wrong response.

> *Bābā*, having come (into the world) one must depart again, and this world is but a fleeting show. The abode of Truth is found through serving the True One; attainment of Truth comes only by living in accordance with Truth, by following the path of Truth. Falsehood and covetousness disqualify a man and in the hereafter there is no place for him. No one invites him to enter and take his rest; he is like a crow in a deserted house. The cycle of birth and death is the great separation and in it all are destroyed. Involved through greed in the concerns of *māyā* people are led astray, and Death, standing over them, makes them to weep.[3]

5. *The fate of unregenerate man*

> They who have forgotten the Lord and indulged in sensual pleasures—they are the ones whose bodies are diseased.[4]

He who ignores God and follows instead the dictates of *haumai* is as one diseased. A remedy exists, but for the *manmukh* who refuses it the result can only be Death.

> Ineluctable Death smites the head of the false![5]

By Death in this sense Gurū Nānak does not, of course, mean the physical death which inevitably overtakes every person. Physical death, far from

[1] *Japji* 27, *AG*, p. 6.

[2] *Japji* 25, *AG*, p. 5. Dr. Vir Singh adds to this couplet the comment: 'Because as a result of this gift many people develop fear, abandon sin, and attain to the higher life.' *Santhyā*, vol. i, p. 120, n. § .

[3] *Vaḍahaṃsu Alāhaṇi* 5, *AG*, pp. 581–2.

[4] *Malār* 7, *AG*, p. 1256.

[5] *Gauṛī Aṣṭ* 14 (5), *AG*, p. 227.

being something to be feared, is for the *gurmukh* a joy to be welcomed when it comes, for it means a perfecting of his union with God. Gurū Nānak's *Gauṛī Dīpakī*[1] which is recited every night by devout Sikhs as a part of *Kīrtan Sohilā*, the Evening Prayer, is a sublime expression of the contentment with which a believer awaits his physical death and final release. The *manmukh*'s Death, however, is not the perfecting of union but the culmination of separation. To illustrate his meaning Gurū Nānak uses a variety of figures. The most common is the Vedic Yam who also figures prominently in the imagery of the Sants.

> Through Thy Name the *man* finds total bliss. Without the Name one goes bound to the city of Yam.[2]

Another is *narak*, the nether region, but demythologized as in Christian theological usage.

> He who forgets the Name must endure suffering. When the divine Order bids him depart how can he remain? He is submerged in the well of Hell (and yet dies as surely) as a fish without water.[3]

The various figures all point to the same thing. Submission to one's *haumai* and entanglement in *māyā* earn a *karma* which perpetuates the transmigratory process. In the constant coming and going there is separation from God and this is Death.

> No one can comprehend the Creator, He who is beyond human grasp, immeasurable. The soul is deluded by *māyā*, drugged by untruth. Ruined by the demands of greed (such a person) repents eternally, but he who serves the One knows Him, and his cycle of birth and death comes to an end. . . .
>
> Transmigration desolates us, the disease of duality has spread everywhere. A man who is without the Name collapses like a wall of sand. How can one be saved without the Name? (Such a person) must ultimately fall into Hell. . . .
>
> (The separated soul is like) the broken strings of a rebeck—severed and so giving no music. . . .
>
> (Man) is caught like a fish in Yam's net. Without the *Gurū*, the Giver, there is no salvation; one endlessly transmigrates. . . .
>
> (Innumerable people) have died begging *māyā* (to sustain them) but *māyā* accompanies no one (after death). The swan (-soul) mounts up and sadly flies away, leaving *māyā* here. The *man* which pursues untruth is tormented by Yam and with it go its evil qualities. . . .

[1] *AG*, pp. 12 and 157.

[2] *Prabhātī* 1, *AG*, p. 1327. The epithets used by Gurū Nānak are the common ones found in the works of the Sants. In addition to Yam we find Dharamrāj (with his assistants Chitr and Gupt) and Kāl.

[3] *Mārū Solahā* 8 (8), *AG*, p. 1028.

Those who focused their attention on themselves died. Devoid of the Name they received suffering. . . .

One may accumulate gold and silver, but such wealth is as poison, ashes. Gathering riches (a man) regards himself as an exalted person, (but his belief is vain). Caught up in duality he is destroyed.[1]

The fate of unregenerate man is the death of separation. How then can he escape this fate? In what manner is the way of salvation revealed to him and what must he do to appropriate it?

III. THE DIVINE SELF-EXPRESSION

I know that Thou art not afar. I believe that Thou art within. I have recognized the palace of God (within my heart).[2]

In the first section attention was drawn to Gurū Nānak's belief concerning the immanence of God in the human heart, and it was noted that this belief was for him of primary significance, for it is at this point that there may exist communication between God and man.[3] That the indwelling God should speak to man through his mind or what we call his heart is not in itself a remarkable doctrine and in a general sense it was universally accepted by the Sants. It is when we proceed from this point to inquire precisely *how* God communicates with man that we encounter the specific contribution of Gurū Nānak, a contribution which offers the most significant example of his positive originality. This is not to imply that his work is wholly original, for this can never be the case and much of what we find in Gurū Nānak, both in the total range of his thought and at this specific point, undoubtedly represents an inheritance from his contemporary religious environment. Nor does it necessarily mean that any single strand is without parallel elsewhere, for originality can lie as much in the pattern that is woven as in the threads which are used. There may have been earlier Sants who had arrived at similar conclusions concerning the medium of divine communication. In many there is silence at this point and it is possible that the notions which we find developed in the works of Gurū Nānak may have existed in an inchoate form in the minds of Sants who preceded him. It is true that even in Gurū Nānak's works there is not that manifest clarity which conveys an immediate understanding, but developed concepts of the divine self-expression are there nevertheless and exegesis will reveal them.

The obvious comparison is once again Kabīr and, as we have already noted, Kabīr and Gurū Nānak clearly share a common tradition. An outline of

[1] *Oaṅkāru* 6, 32, 39, 42, and 48. *AG*, pp. 930, 934, 935–6, 937.
[2] *Tukhāri Chhant Bārah-māhā* 6, *AG*, p. 1108.
[3] See *supra*, p. 175.

their respective patterns of belief (*sādhanā*) emphasizes the broad similarity of their thought and offers one reason to explain why the two figures have been so closely connected. The correspondence amounts, however, to no more than similarity. It is certainly not identity. Of Kabīr Dr. Vaudeville writes:

> La seule « révélation » valable, pour lui, est celle de la « Parole » (*çabda*) silencieuse que le Parfait Gourou (*Satguru*) prononce au « fond de l'âme » (*antari*) — et ce Gourou est Dieu.[1]

For Gurū Nānak, as for Kabīr, the Word of the *Satgurū* is the true revelation, and for him also this *Gurū* is God. Beyond this basic agreement, however, there is appreciable divergence. To speak of a 'Parole silencieuse' would not actually be incorrect in Gurū Nānak's case, but it would certainly be misleading. Moreover, we find in Gurū Nānak's doctrine of the divine Order (*Hukam*) and in his emphasis upon divine grace elements which carry him beyond Kabīr. The two are certainly within the same tradition, but their respective interpretations of it are by no means identical.

Our analysis at this point must concern six key words: Word (*Śabad*), Name (*Nām*), Divine Preceptor (*Gurū*), Divine Order (*Hukam*), Truth *Sach*), and Grace (*Nadar*).[2] Of these the first five bear a basic identity. In them we have five different words, but we do not have five radically different concepts. Instead we have five different aspects of a single all-embracing concept. This single concept is perhaps best expressed by the last of them, *Sach* or Truth, but in itself the word obviously has little substance and can only acquire it in the context of Gurū Nānak's usage. Frequently these words are used in ways which render them synonymous. All five are expressions of God; all are used to expound the nature, content, and method of the divine communication to men, of the divine truth which when appropriated brings salvation; all share a fundamental identity.

This does not appear to have received the emphasis which it deserves and the result has been an inability to give a satisfactory, coherent answer to the question of *how* in the thought of Gurū Nānak God communicates with man. The question has been allowed to remain a mystery. It is not sufficient to state that the *Gurū* is God, that the *Hukam* is His will, that the *Śabad* is the divine Word, and that the *Nām* represents the sum total of all God's qualities. Not all of these definitions can be accepted without qualification, and even if they could be so accepted the basic question would still remain unanswered. In what way is this divine Word so presented to the human understanding that it can be recognized, accepted, and

[1] Ch. Vaudeville, *Au Cabaret de l'Amour: Paroles de Kabîr*, p. 25.

[2] *Nadar*, or *nazar*, here represents a group of words which have the same or a closely related meaning: *kirpā, prasād, karam* (the Persian word), *bakhśiś, bhāṇā, daiā, mihar, taras*.

followed? This is the fundamental question and in order to answer it we must turn to the analysis of the six words.

Of the six the one which must receive the closest attention is *Hukam*. This it requires, partly because it has generally received much less attention than the other five, partly because it is in Gurū Nānak's use of this word that his development beyond the thought of Kabīr and other *bhagats* is most obvious, but above all because together with *Nadar* it carries us furthest in our efforts to set out Gurū Nānak's answer to the basic question. *Nadar* likewise demands careful scrutiny. It has not been overlooked in the way that *Hukam* is so often passed over, but neither has it normally received the degree of emphasis which it warrants. The translation of this and of the other words which bear the same meaning[1] is invariably the word 'grace', a translation which would appear to be the best available but which can be misleading in certain circumstances. The problem will be dealt with in the appropriate section.

1. Śabad: *the Word*

> None has encompassed Thy bounds so how can I describe Thee with a single tongue? He who meditates on Thy true *Śabad* is joined in union with Thee. . . . The *Gurū*'s *Śabad* is like a (sparkling) gem which reveals Thee by its light. One understands one's own self and through the *Gurū*'s instruction merges in the Truth.[2]

Śabad is one of the terms which evidently descended to Gurū Nānak through Sant channels from Nāth sources. The term has a significant history apart from its Nāth usage, but it appears to have been from this Nāth usage that it passed into Sant currency. In the context of Nāth theory the word is characteristically used in conjunction with *anahad*, or *anahat*, and refers to the mystical 'sound' which is 'heard' at the climax of the *haṭha-yoga* technique. The *anahad śabad* is, according to such theories, a 'soundless sound',[3] a mystical vibration audible only to the adept who has succeeded in awakening the *kuṇḍalinī* and caused it to ascend to the *suṣumṇā*.[4]

[1] *Kirpā*, *prasād*, *karam*, and *bakhśiś*. In some contexts *bhāṇā*, *daiā* and *mihar* may be translated as 'grace' and will always bear meanings closely related to it. *Taras* will normally be translated as 'pity'.

[2] *Vār Malār*, *pauṛī* 25, *AG*, p. 1290.

[3] 'Unstruck music'—Rabindranath Tagore, *One Hundred Poems of Kabir*, p. 20.

[4] According to the physiological theories of *haṭha-yoga* there are three principal channels (*nāḍī*) which ascend through the human body. These are the *iḍā* and *piṅgalā*, which terminate in the left and right nostrils respectively, and the *suṣumṇā*, or *sukhmanā*, which is held to run through the spinal column. Along the *suṣumṇā* are located six, or eight, *chakra* (discs, wheels, 'lotuses') and at its base, behind the genitals, is the *kuṇḍalinī*, a latent power symbolized by the figure of a sleeping serpent. By means of the *haṭha-yoga* discipline the *kuṇḍalinī* is awakened, and ascending the *suṣumṇā* it pierces each *chakra* in turn, thereby releasing progressively effectual stores of psychic energy. At the

Kabīr's usage distinguishes *Śabad* and *anahad śabad*. The *Śabad* is the *Gurū*'s 'Word', the revelation of God which is given in the depths of the human soul. *Anahad śabad*, however, he uses in a sense very close to that of the Nāths, although the experience which it expresses is, for him, in no way dependent upon the practice of *haṭha-yoga*.[1]

In the case of Gurū Nānak we find that, as with all such words which have Nāth antecedents, the term has travelled even further from its source. The expression *anahad śabad* has moved away to the periphery. It has become a useful figure of speech, a convenient means of conveying some impression of an experience which is strictly inexpressible.

> When one meets the *Gurū* then, casting aside doubt, one understands one's inner being. While yet alive prepare for the place where you must go when you die. (Prepare for it) by subduing the evil which is within you, and then die. Through meditation on the *Gurū* one hears the enchanting unstruck music (*anahad śabad*). When it is heard *haumai* is destroyed. I humble myself before him who serves the *Gurū*. He who repeats the Name of God receives a robe of honour in the (divine) court.[2]

The link with Nāth usage is very slender. Here there is no *kuṇḍalinī*, no *iḍā*, *piṅgalā*, and *suṣumṇā*, no *chakra*, no *prāṇāyām*. The expression, like other Nāth terms which are to be found in Gurū Nānak's works, has been naturalized. Its antecedents no longer cling to it as they do in the case of Kabīr's usage.[3] Moreover, such hints of the old Nāth association usually occur in verses which are obviously addressed to yogīs and which have a manifest dialectic or apologetic purpose. In such cases Gurū Nānak, like any effective apologist, has deliberately expressed himself in terms which would be related to a yogī's understanding.

Gurū Nānak's emphasis is wholly upon the concept of the Word (*Śabad*) as the vehicle of revelation. Inevitably, the Word is described by him more in terms of what it does than in terms of what it actually is. This is entirely natural as it is the function which concerns him and it is in experience that it is to be known rather than in any purely intellectual sense. The function of the Word is that it provides the means whereby man can know both God and the path which leads to Him, the means whereby the individual may secure release from his bonds and so attain union with God. Again and again the Word is declared to be the essential means of salvation.[4] It is for Gurū Nānak the revelation of God and so the only proper

climax of the ascent it pierces the *sahasradala*, 'the lotus of a thousand petals' said to be located at the top of the cranium. The *dasam duār* ('tenth door') then opens and the *jiv* passes into the ineffable condition of *sahaj*, the state of ultimate union with Brahman.

[1] Ch. Vaudeville, *Kabīr Granthāvali (Dohā)*, Introduction, pp. xxii–xxiii.

[2] *Sirī Rāgu* 18, *AG*, p. 21.

[3] Cf. Jodh Singh, *Guramati Niraṇay*, pp. 211 ff.

[4] Cf. *Sirī Rāgu* 19, *AG*, p. 21; *Gauṛī* 17, *AG*, p. 228; *Sūhī Aṣṭ* 2 (2), *AG*, p. 751; *Siddh Goṣṭi* 55 and 61, *AG*, pp. 944, 945.

object of man's contemplation. By contemplation of the Word and by the total conforming of one's life to its dictates the *man* is brought under control, self-centredness is cast out, the individual grows ever nearer to God until, ultimately perfected in His likeness, he passes into a condition of union which transcends death and the cycle of transmigration.

He has neither form, colour, nor material sign, but He is revealed through the true Word (*Śabad*).[1]

By the *Gurū*'s leading he obtains salvation and is no longer bound (to the wheel of transmigration).
Meditating on the Word (*Śabad*), (repeating) the Name of God, he is released.[2]

Without the Word (*Śabad*) one is condemned to wander. Worldly affections cause many to sink (in the Ocean of Existence). O *man*, apply your understanding to the Word (*Śabad*) and cross over. He who has not followed the *Gurū* and so has not understood the divine Name, (such a person) continues to transmigrate.[3]

Nānak, the Lord, the true Creator, is known by means of the Word (*Śabad*)![4]

Often the word *Śabad* stands by itself and often it is linked with the word *Gurū*. The latter may be regarded as the characteristic form, for the use of *Śabad* by itself normally assumes its connexion with the *Gurū*. The form may be *gurū kā śabad*, 'the *Gurū*'s Word', or it may be *gurū-śabad*, 'the *Guru*-Word'.[5] The latter carries us nearer the true meaning for it brings out the basic identity of the two terms. The development of this point must, however, await the section devoted to the *Gurū* and in the meantime we must continue to use the expression 'the *Gurū*'s Word', or 'the *Gurū*'s *Śabad*'.

For Gurū Nānak the Word is accordingly the *gurupadeś*, that expression of God's truth which is imparted to man by the *Gurū*. All that concerns God, all that relates to the path which leads to Him is the Word. It is this comprehensive quality which distinguishes his concept of the Word from that of Kabīr. Man's proper response to the divine revelation is, for Gurū Nānak, an inward one, but the revelation itself is by no means confined to a mystical inward experience. There is in his works a much stronger emphasis upon the significance of external circumstances and phenomena as aids to the necessary inward perception. The Word embraces all that is Truth, all that expresses the nature of God and the means of attaining Him, and this may be perceived in the divine laws governing the universe as well as in the ineffable mystical experience.

The difference between the thought of Gurū Nānak and that of Kabīr emerges not so much in their understanding of the ultimate experience of

[1] *Soraṭhi* 6, *AG*, p. 597. [2] *Gauṛi* 6, *AG*, p. 152.
[3] *Sirī Rāgu* 15, *AG*, p. 19. [4] *Dhanāsarī Chhant* 2 (3), *AG*, p. 688.
[5] Cf. *Dhanāsarī Aṣṭ* 1 (8), *AG*, p. 686, and *Rāmakalī* 10, *AG*, p. 879.

union, not so much in their conceptions of the condition of *sahaj*,[1] as in their differing notions of how that condition is to be attained. For neither is the path to God regarded as accessible to all, and both affirm that humanity suffers from a congenital blindness which is overcome in only a minority of cases. In Gurū Nānak's works, however, one can distinguish with much greater clarity the means whereby this spiritual sight is acquired and the path to God followed. There is in his thought relative clarity at a point where in the thought of Kabīr we are obliged to grapple with mystery.

In Kabīr's case, moreover, the experience of enlightenment comes with a suddenness which we do not find in Gurū Nānak's descriptions. Evidently there had come to Kabīr, at some particular point in time, a compelling and shattering illumination. The figure which he uses to describe it is that of the arrow which is discharged by the True Gurū (*Satgurū*) and which pierces the *man*.[2] The arrow represents the Word and the figure clearly illustrates the abruptness with which, according to Kabīr, it is apprehended. Gurū Nānak, by contrast, implies an ascent over a period of time as the normal pattern of an individual's salvation experience, of his apprehension of the Truth and the conforming of his life to it. This is clearly brought out in his doctrine of the five *khaṇḍs* ('realms' or stages in spiritual progress).[3] The *sākhī* which purports to describe the Gurū's divine call during his immersion in the Veīn stream near Sultānpur does not imply any denial of this.[4] The *sākhī* obviously owes much to a reverent imagination, but there is no need to doubt that Gurū Nānak as a young man did experience a definite sense of call. There is nothing, however, to suggest abruptness. On the contrary, the traditions all emphasize the piety of his youth and the call would accordingly come as the climax of a spiritual development.

The difference is not confined to their respective interpretations of the Word, but these interpretations are an illustration of it. Given the initial act of God's favour, the initiative which first arouses within a man the longing for union, the Word is for Gurū Nānak within the range of ordinary human understanding. It is by no means wholly within it, for the Word partakes of the infinity of God, but sufficiently within it to be readily accessible to all who desire it. God Himself is, in His fullness, a mystery far exceeding the comprehension of man, but in His Word He expresses Himself in terms which may be understood and followed. Here we are anticipating much that properly belongs to the section dealing with the divine Order (*Hukam*), but with terms which share a common basis a certain amount of anticipation is unavoidable.[5]

1 See *infra*, p. 225.

2 Cf. Kabīr *ślok* 183, *AG*, p. 1374 (= *KG sākhī* 14. 5); *KG sākhī* 1. 9.

3 *Japjī* 34–37, *AG*, pp. 7–8. See *infra*, pp. 221–4.

4 See *supra*, pp. 37, 54, 107.

5 In Sikh usage the term *śabad* is used as a synonym for an *Ādi Granth pad* (hymn or

2. Nām: *the Name of God*

For a diseased world the remedy is the Name. Without Truth the taint remains.[1]

This second category can be discussed with greater brevity than the first, not because it is any less important, but because for all practical purposes Name (*Nām*) is synonymous with Word (*Śabad*). The functions which are affirmed in the case of the Word may without exception be affirmed in the case of the Name also. It too is the revelation of God's being, the only proper object of contemplation, the standard to which the individual's life must conform, the essential means of purification and salvation.

Sacrifices, burnt offerings, charity given to acquire merit, austerities, and *pūjā*, (all are ineffective) and one's body continues to endure continual suffering. Without the Name of God there is no salvation. He who, by the *Gurū*'s aid, (meditates on) the Name (finds) salvation. Without the Name of God birth into this world is fruitless. Without the Name one eats poison, speaks evil, dies without merit, and so transmigrates.[2]

In this and in many other extracts 'Name' could be replaced by 'Word' without altering the sense at all. In other cases the close conjunction of the two terms renders their identity even more obvious.

Eating and drinking we die without knowing (the Truth). Recognizing the Word (*sabadu pachhāniā*) we die (to self) in an instant. The *man* has ceased to wander and it rejoices in this death. By the *Guru*'s grace we have recognized the Name (*nāmu pachhāniā*).[3]

It is obvious that in this context Word and Name are completely synonymous. The same applies to the following extract from *Bhairau* 2.

Without the Word how can one cross the Ocean of Fear? Without the Name the disease of duality has spread throughout the world. Men have sunk (in the Ocean) and so perished.[4]

In some cases, however, there is an implied distinction.

He who meditates on the true Name by means of the *Gurū*'s Word is accepted in the true court (of God) as a true follower of the *Gurū*.[5]

By means of the Word one enshrines the Name in one's heart.[6]

In such cases the Word appears as the medium of communication and the Name as the object of communication. Both remain, however, expressions

verse), the import being that all such *pads* are expressions of the divine *Śabad*. The word occasionally appears in this sense in *Ādi Granth* headings (e.g. *Rāg Mārū*, *AG*, p. 989).

1 *Dhanāsari Chhant* 1 (1), *AG*, p. 687.

2 *Bhairau* 8, *AG*, p. 1127.

3 *Oaṅkāru* 19, *AG*, p. 932.

4 *Bhairau* 2, *AG*, p. 1125.

5 *Āsā* 21, *AG*, p. 355.

6 *Prabhāti Aṣṭ* 1 (7), *AG*, p. 1242.

of God's Truth and the distinction is a very fine one, normally determined by the context. Almost invariably Truth as mediated by the *Gurū* is referred to as the Word, whereas Truth as received and meditated on by the believer tends to be expressed in terms of the Name. *Gurū ka śabad* and *nām japnā* are both thoroughly characteristic expressions. There is, however, no basic difference involved and occasionally one of the two is used where the other would be expected.

> Following the True *Gurū* one utters the Word which imparts immortality.[1]

Not only is it the Name which is normally used in the context of the believer's utterances but also it is *Nām* which is usually found in association with *amrit*, the nectar of immortality. The substitution is, however, entirely permissible, even if not common.

> Wherever the meaning of *Nām* is to be found in the *Gurū Granth Sāhib* there too is the meaning of *Śabad*.[2]

To all this we must add a couplet from *Japjī* which carries our understanding a stage further.

> Whatever he has made is an expression of His Name. There is no part of creation which is not such an expression.[3]

The creation is an expression of the Creator and so a manifestation of His Truth. We have here a preliminary answer to the question of how the individual is to perceive this Truth which is referred to as the Word or the Name. Look around you and within you, for in all that He has created you will see Him. Understand the nature of what you see and you will understand the nature of God and of the way to Him.

Once again we are verging on what can with greater clarity be treated under *Hukam*, the divine Order. In concluding this section we may note the radical difference between the Name of God and the names of God. Hari, Rām, Parameśvar, Jagadīś, Prabhu, Gopāl, Allāh, Khudā, Sāhib—these are all but names and none are essential. Some do indeed bear a special significance, as in the case of *Niraṅkār* and *Nirañjan*, but even these do not constitute the Name although they express aspects of it. The Name is the total expression of all that God is, and this is Truth. *Sati Nām*—His Name is Truth. Meditate on this and you shall be saved.

3. Gurū: *the Divine Preceptor*

Within Sikhism primary significance is accorded to the doctrine of the *Gurū* and considerable emphasis is laid upon his role as the communicator

[1] *Āsā* 13, *AG*, p. 352.
[2] *Srī Gurū Granth Koś*, pp. 210–11.
[3] *Japji* 19, *AG*, p. 4.

of divine Truth. But who is the *Gurū*? A contemporary answer is that the *Gurū* is a particular personality, a creative and perfect personality who stands as guide and exemplar.[1] This personality inhabited the ten personal Gurūs and with the death of Gurū Gobind Singh merged in the scripture and in the community.[2] Such an answer is certainly adequate as applied to a follower of Gurū Nānak, but it leaves unanswered the old question of who was the *Gurū* of Gurū Nānak. How was Truth imparted to Gurū Nānak himself?

The significance of the *gurū* in the bhakti tradition is well known and need not detain us here. Within this tradition the ancient respect for one's spiritual teacher had been magnified to the point where the *gurū* had become an object of devotion and his voice accepted as the veritable voice of God. In the case of the Sant tradition this inheritance from southern bhakti was reinforced by that tradition's link with the Nāth movement. In the Buddhist tantric tradition the master occupied a position of exalted authority as the mediator of esoteric knowledge and from this source the same emphasis descended to the Nāths.[3]

It is within the Sant tradition, however, that we encounter a major modification of the traditional doctrine. As we have already seen, there appears to be little doubt that Kabīr had no human *gurū*, but that for him the *Gurū* or *Satgurū* represented the inner voice, the mystical movement of God in the depths of the individual being, the light of God shed abroad in the inmost recesses of the human soul. The *Gurū* remains the vital link, the essential mediator of divine Truth, but no longer a human link.

In Gurū Nānak's case we must first note the characteristic emphasis upon the absolute necessity of the *Gurū*.

The *Gurū* is the ladder, the dinghy, the raft by means of which one reaches God;
The *Gurū* is the lake, the ocean, the boat, the sacred place of pilgrimage, the river.
If it please Thee I am cleansed by bathing in the Lake of Truth.[4]

Without the *Gurū* there can be no bhakti, no love;
Without the *Gurū* there is no access to the company of the *sants*;
Without the *Gurū* one blindly engages in futile endeavour;
But with the *Gurū* one's *man* is purified, for its filth is purged by the Word.[5]
When the True *Gurū* is merciful faith is perfected;
When the True *Gurū* is merciful there is no grief;
When the True *Gurū* is merciful no sorrow is known;

[1] Teja Singh, *Sikhism: Its Ideals and Institutions*, pp. 17–18.
[2] Ibid., pp. 23–25.
[3] M. Eliade, *Yoga: Immortality and Freedom*, pp. 206–7. P. D. Barthwal, *The Nirguna School of Hindi Poetry*, pp. 114–22.
[4] *Siri Rāgu* 9, *AG*, p. 17.
[5] *Basant* 6, *AG*, p. 1170.

When the True *Gurū* is merciful the love of God is enjoyed;
When the True *Gurū* is merciful there is no fear of death;
When the True *Gurū* is merciful there is eternal peace;
When the True *Gurū* is merciful the nine treasures are obtained;
When the True *Gurū* is merciful one blends in union with the True One.[1]

He knows fear who fears not (God). Without the *Gurū* there is darkness.[2]

Such passages recur constantly, but there is nothing remarkable in them apart from the quality of Gurū Nānak's expression. Others, however, carry us much further.

Renounce self-centredness and pride, O *man*! Serve Hari the *Gurū*, the Lake (of Immortality), for so you shall obtain honour in His court.[3]

The *Gurū* is God, ineffable, unsearchable. He who follows the *Gurū* comprehends the nature of the universe.[4]

Gurū Arjan makes the point explicitly.

The True *Gurū* is *Nirañjan* (God). Do not believe that He is in the form of a man.[5]

In the words of Dr. Jodh Singh:

All of the human *gurūs* who roam around nowadays have taken instruction from some person or other. Gurū Nānak's *Gurū*, however, was not a person. In the *sākhī* dealing with the Veīn River incident it is clearly stated that Gurū Nānak received the cup of the Name from the true court (of God). He himself has declared:

'*Nirañjan* is the essence of all and His light shines in all places. All is God and nothing is separate from Him. He who is the infinite, supreme God is the *Gurū* whom Nānak has met.'

Soraṭhi

The Tenth Gurū has also declared:

'Know that the eternal and incarnate One is my *Gurū*.'

Chaupaī[6]

This is the first stage in our effort to define Gurū Nānak's doctrine of the *Gurū*. We must, however, examine the nature of this identification of *Gurū* and God, for it requires some clarification. Many passages clearly imply a distinction between God and the *Gurū* and the question of their interpretation must now be considered.

[1] *Vār Mājh, pauṛī* 25, *AG*, p. 149.
[2] *Sirī Rāgu Aṣṭ* 3 (3), *AG*, p. 54.
[3] *Sirī Rāgu* 19, *AG*, p. 21.
[4] *Bhairau* 2, *AG*, p. 1125.
[5] *Rāmakalī* 39, *AG*, p. 895. Cf. also Gurū Arjan's *Goṇḍ* 9, *AG*, p. 864.
[6] Jodh Singh, *Guramati Niraṇay* (7th edition), p. 114. The passage quoted from Gurū Nānak is from his *Soraṭhi* 11, *AG*, p. 599.

He for whom we searched throughout the universe, Him we found by means of the *Gurū*. It is the True *Gurū* who brings us into union with the Lord.[1]

The Master is near at hand and yet, O my wretched soul, you do not perceive Him. It is the True *Gurū* who reveals Him.[2]

Here there is an evident contrast between the agent and the object of revelation. The conclusion which such extracts suggest is that our initial identification of the *Gurū* with God needs some qualification. A strict definition requires us to identify the *Gurū* not with God Himself, but with the voice of God, with the means whereby God imparts truth to man.

This brings us to what is essentially Kabīr's doctrine, but Gurū Nānak takes us one step further. In the case of Kabīr this step may be deduced; with Gurū Nānak it is categorically affirmed. The *Gurū* is in fact the *Śabad*, the Word. In the work entitled *Siddh Goṣṭ* the Siddhs put the following question to Gurū Nānak.

Who is your *gurū*, he of whom you are a disciple?[3]

Gurū Nānak replies:

The Word is the *Gurū* and the mind (which is focused on it) continually is the disciple. By dwelling on the Ineffable One, on Him the eternal *Gurū-Gopāl*, I remain detached. It is only through the Word that I dwell on Him and so through the *Gurū* the fire of *haumai* is extinguished.[4]

The *Gurū* accordingly is God; the *Gurū* is the voice of God; and the *Gurū* is the Word, the Truth of God.[5] Gurū Nānak uses the term in all three senses. One might perhaps raise logical objections to what may, at first sight, appear to be confused usage, but only if one forgets the basic identity which these three senses share in Gurū Nānak's thought. The passage quoted above from *Siddh Goṣṭ* brings out this identity not just with the pronouncement that the Word is the *Gurū*, but also with the reference to the *Gurū-Gopāl*. God Himself is Truth. In order to accommodate this fundamental belief to the limitations both of language and of the human understanding distinctions, if not absolutely essential, are at least very convenient.

4. Hukam: *the Divine Order*

Śabad, *Nām*, and *Gurū*—all three are to be defined as the Truth of God made manifest for the salvation of men, and all three share a fundamental identity. And yet the basic question remains unanswered. How is this Truth

[1] *Sirī Rāgu* 17, *AG*, p. 20.
[2] *Malār Aṣṭ* 3 (8), *AG*, p. 1274.
[3] *Siddh Goṣṭi* 43, *AG*, p. 942.
[4] *Siddh Goṣṭi* 44, *AG*, p. 943.
[5] And in *Bilāvalu* 3, *AG*, p. 795, God is identified with the Word.
Thou art the Word and Thou art its expression.

to be apprehended by man? The fourth key word brings us another stage nearer the answer.

The fundamental importance of the *Hukam* in the thought of Gurū Nānak is emphasized by its exposition at the very beginning of *Japjī*. The first stanza puts the basic question:

> How is Truth to be attained, how the veil of falsehood torn aside?[1]

And the concept of the *Hukam*, the divine Order, provides Gurū Nānak's answer. Truth is to be found through submission to the *Hukam*.

> Nānak, thus it is written: Submit to the *Hukam*, walk in its way.[2]

For Gurū Nānak this is an affirmation of the utmost consequence and one to which we must return. In the next stanza he proceeds to explain the nature of the *Hukam*.

> The *Hukam* is beyond describing, (but this much we can understand that) all forms were created by the *Hukam*, that life was created through the *Hukam*, and that greatness is imparted in accordance with the *Hukam*. Distinctions between what is exalted and what is lowly are the result of the *Hukam* and in accordance with it suffering comes to some and joy to others. Through the *Hukam* one receives blessing and another is condemned to everlasting transmigration. All are within the *Hukam*; none are beyond its authority. Nānak, if anyone comprehends the *Hukam* his *haumai* is purged.[3]

Several conclusions emerge from this description. The first is that just as God Himself is, in His fullness, beyond human comprehending, so too the *Hukam* is, in its total range, more than the understanding of man can grasp. Secondly, however, it can be understood to a sufficient degree and this much at least man can comprehend that it is the source of those differences and distinctions in man's condition which are seemingly beyond human control. It is the principle which determines the giving of differing forms, of greatness, of differences between high and low, misery and happiness, salvation and transmigration.[4] Thirdly, all are subject to the *Hukam*. And fourthly, understanding of this divine principle leads to destruction of self. Stanza 3 again sets it forth as the principle which regulates the universe in accordance with the intention of God.

> God's *Hukam*[5] directs the path—(God) the ever-joyous and carefree.[6]

[1] *Japjī* 1, *AG*, p. 1. [2] Ibid.

[3] *Japjī* 2, *AG*, p. 1. Vir Singh adds to this the note: 'This *haun* (*haumai*) is the veil of falsehood which prevents us from attaining to the Truth. When *haun* is destroyed Truth is attained.' *Santhyā*, vol. i, p. 48. For *haun*, or *haumai*, see *supra*, pp. 181 ff.

[4] Or more specifically the laws which determine who shall attain salvation and who shall continue to transmigrate.

[5] *hukami hukamu*. 'The *Hukam* of Him who exercises the *Hukam*.'

[6] *Japjī* 3, *AG*, p. 2.

Hukam has usually been translated as 'Will'. This is a literal translation, but it is unsuitable in the context of Gurū Nānak's usage for it fails to convey his precise meaning and is liable to be equated with the Islamic doctrine of the Will of God. In the thought of Gurū Nānak the *Hukam* signifies the divinely instituted and maintained principle governing the existence and movement of the universe. It is a constant principle, and to the extent to which it can be comprehended it functions according to a predictable pattern. This regularity and this consistency distinguish it from the Islamic concept. In Islam the divine Will, if not actually capricious is at least 'unpledged',[1] whereas the *Hukam* of Gurū Nānak's usage is definitely pledged and dependable. A better translation is 'divine Order'. This too is inadequate, but it comes nearer to Gurū Nānak's concept than 'Will' and it is not liable to be confused with the Will of Islam.

This divine Order is manifested in a variety of ways. It is represented as the agent of creation:

> By Thy *Hukam* Thou didst create all forms.[2]

It determines the regular cycle of human existence:

> My friend, (you who) trade (in the things of the world), in the first watch of the night, (the first stage of the human life), you are placed in the womb in accordance with the *Hukam*.[3]

All are under it:

> Speaking, seeing, moving, living, and dying—all are transitory. Thou, the True (Lord), having established the *Hukam* placed all under it (literally, in it).[4]

And it gathers into a single principle the sum total of all God's activity:

> (Of itself, i.e. apart from the *Hukam*) the soul does not die and it neither sinks nor crosses over. He who has been active (in creation) is still active. In accordance with the *Hukam* we are born and we die. Ahead and behind the *Hukam* pervades all.[5]

This principle is most immediately perceptible in the laws governing the structure and functioning of the physical universe, but it is by no means limited to this sphere. It is also expressed in moral terms in the law of *karma*.

> One receives in accordance with what one does. What you sow, that you must eat.[6]

> One reaps what one sows and one eats what one earns.[7]

[1] I owe this definition to Canon Kenneth Cragg.

[2] *Vār Mājh, ślok* 2 of *pauṛi* 27, *AG*, p. 150.

[3] *Siri Rāgu Pahare* 1, *AG*, p. 74.

[4] *Vār Mājh, ślok* 2 of *pauṛi* 15, *AG*, p. 145.

[5] *Gauṛi* 2, *AG*, p. 151.

[6] *Dhanāsari* 6, *AG*, p. 662.

[7] *Sūhi* 7, *AG*, p. 730.

This conviction is as much an aspect of the *Hukam* principle as the regular movement of the physical universe. Indeed it is a vital aspect.

> Hear me, O Lord. Each receives joy or sorrow in accordance with what his past deeds have earned him, and what Thou dost give is fair and just. Thine is the creation, but what is my condition! Without Thee I cannot live for a moment. Without my Beloved I suffer torment and there is none to give me aid. Grant that by the *Gurū*'s aid I may drink the nectar (of the Name). We remain entangled in the world which God has created; the supreme deed is to enshrine the Lord in the *man*. Nānak, the bride watches the way (for the Bridegroom's coming). Hear my cry, O God.[1]

The law of *karma* is here explicitly affirmed.[2] The conclusion which must be drawn from it is that each individual should perform those deeds which will, in accordance with the law of *karma*, bring the supreme reward. And 'the supreme deed is to enshrine the Lord in the *man*'.

> (In God's) presence Dharamrāj scrutinises our record of good and evil, and in accordance with our deeds we dwell near Him or far off. The labours of those who meditated on the Name are over. Their countenances are radiant and many others (through association) with them also find release.[3]

> Meditate on the One and harvest the fruit thereof.[4]

An exhortation of this nature assumes, of course, that man has the necessary measure of freedom to make such a decision. Such references clearly imply an area wherein man has the capacity to exercise free will, a capacity which permits him to live in discord with the divine Order instead of in harmony with it. This faculty is obviously of critical importance, for the manner in which it is exercised brings either salvation or continued transmigration. Disharmony is the normal condition, but it does not lead to Truth and its inevitable consequence is continued movement within the cycle of transmigration, with all the attendant sufferings of this condition. Submission, on the other hand, leads to union, the consequence whereof is freedom. He who recognizes the divine Order perceives the Truth; and he who, having recognized it, brings his life into conformity with it ascends to that eternal union with God which is the ultimate beatitude.

> Beloved, he who comprehends the divine Order of the Lord attains Truth and receives honour.[5]

[1] *Tukhāri Chhant Bārah-māhā* 1, *AG*, p. 1107.

[2] Cf. also *Vār Āsā*, *pauṛi* 10, *AG*, p. 468; *Vār Sūhi*, *ślok* 2 of *pauṛi* 17, *AG*, p. 791.

[3] *Japji*, *ślok*, *AG*, p. 8. In *Vār Mājh* (*ślok* 2 of *pauṛi* 18, *AG*, p. 146) this *ślok* is attributed to Gurū Aṅgad. The differences between the two versions are insignificant apart from the addition of the word *hor* in the last line of the *Vār Mājh* version.

[4] *Vaḍahaṃsu Alāhaṇi* 2, *AG*, p. 580.

[5] *Soraṭhi Aṣṭ* 3 (6), *AG*, p. 636.

He who meets the True *Gurū* knows Him. He recognises the divine Order and remains ever obedient to the will (of God). He who perceives the divine Order abides in the dwelling-place of Truth. Birth and death (the cycle of transmigration) are destroyed by the Word.[1]

He who recognises the divine Order of the Master needs no other wisdom.[2]

The divine Order, the *Hukam*, is accordingly an all-embracing principle, the sum total of all divinely instituted laws; and it is a revelation of the nature of God. In this latter sense it is identical in meaning with the Word (*Śabad*).

Thou didst create and Thou didst recognise (the true nature of Thy creation). Thou didst separate the heavens from the earth and Thou didst stretch out light in the heavens. Thou didst establish the sky without pillars and so revealed Thy Word.[3]

Again it is a case of basic identity with differing functions postulated only in order to bring out the fundamental truth with greater clarity. The creation is constituted and ordered by the *Hukam* and in this creation, physical and otherwise, the Word is made manifest. Understand this Principle, this divine Order, and you understand God. Look around you and within you and you shall perceive the Word, the Name, Truth. Herein is God revealed as single, as active, and as absolute; as *Nirankār*, as *Nirañjan*, as the eternal One beyond all that is transient and corruptible. Meditate on this, conform your life to it, acquire a nature which in accordance with the law of *karma* will carry you beyond the cycle of birth and death. Thus you shall find salvation.

When one meets the True *Gurū* and understands the *Hukam* one attains to Truth. Salvation is not wrought through one's own efforts. Nānak, such a claim would bring destruction, (not salvation).[4]

It is, as we have already noted, an extended process, an ascent, but in the end there is absolute harmony. With the ultimate attainment of Truth, with the *gurmukh* in the final stage of union (*sach khaṇḍ*) there is absolute fulfilment of the divine Order.

As the *Hukam*, so too the deed![5]

5. Sach: *Truth*

Sach, the fifth of Gurū Nānak's characteristic terms, does not require a detailed analysis for it too, as its normal meaning plainly indicates, is used

[1] *Bilāvalu Aṣṭ* 2 (7), *AG*, p. 832.
[2] *Mārū* 7, *AG*, p. 991.
[3] *Vār Malār, pauṛī* 1, *AG*, p. 1279.
[4] *Vār Malār, ślok* 1 of *pauṛī* 25, *AG*, p. 1289.
[5] *Japji* 37, *AG*, p. 8.

to express the Truth and an analysis would simply mean covering ground which has already been covered.

> One does not reach heaven through mere talk. It is through acting in accordance with Truth (*sachu*) that one finds release.[1]

6. Nadar: *the Divine Grace*

How does God communicate with man? How does man perceive the nature of God and the means of attaining union with Him? An analysis of *Śabad*, *Nām*, *Gurū*, and *Hukam* can bring us well towards an answer, but there remains one significant gap. According to Gurū Nānak God has revealed His Truth in creation, and specifically in the *Hukam* which orders creation. He who perceives this Truth and submits to it will find salvation. But how are we to explain the manifest fact that only a minority of men perceive it? The Truth may be there for all to grasp, but few there be who do in fact lay hold of it.

> Many there be who long for a vision of Thee, but few who meet the *Gurū*, the Word, and so perceive (Thee).[2]

Why are there so few? One explanation is that *karma* determines the issue. Those who in their previous existences have lived lives of relative merit acquire thereby a faculty of perception which enables them to recognize the *Gurū*. This theory has a logical consistency and in one place it would appear to be explicitly affirmed.

> If it is inscribed in the record of one's former deeds then one meets the True *Gurū*.[3]

Karma is one theory and the other is divine grace. According to the latter, the necessary faculty of perception is a gift from God and one which is not ultimately dependent upon the merit of the individual in this or any prior existence.

The latter theory is the one which we must accept, but not at the cost either of maintaining that Gurū Nānak denied the relevance of *karma* as far as this initial perception was concerned, or of admitting that at this point he was inconsistent. Extracts which affirm a belief in divine grace have already been quoted[4] and such affirmations recur with considerable frequency in his writings. The quotation from *Āsā Aṣṭapadī* 19 given above implies an inconsistency, but when the paucity of such references, direct or implied, is compared with the very considerable weight of

1 *Vār Mājh*, *ślok* 2 of *pauṛī* 7, *AG*, p. 141.
2 *Basant Aṣṭ* 3 (1R), *AG*, p. 1188.
3 *Āsā Aṣṭ* 19 (5), *AG*, p. 421. Cf. also *Basant Hiṇḍol* 12 (2), *AG*, p. 1172.
4 See *supra*, pp. 174, 176, 177.

emphasis which he lays upon his concept of divine grace there can be no doubt that in the last analysis it is this grace which must decide the issue. The solution which he himself provides to the seeming inconsistency is a compromise which does accord a necessary place to *karma* as far as the initial apprehension of the Word is concerned, but which specifies grace as the ultimate determinant. In a significant line from *Japjī* he contrast the two, *karma* and grace. *Karma* is certainly important in that it will produce a favourable or unfavourable birth, but it is through grace that the initial *opportunity* to lay hold of salvation is attained.

> *Karma* determines the nature of our birth (lit. the cloth), but it is through grace that the door of salvation is found.[1]

Even within its own domain the operation of *karma* is not irresistible. The divine Order, of which *karma* is a part, also provides the means of cancelling its effects, and he who brings his life into accord with the divine Order will find the effects of an adverse *karma* obliterated.

Man's understanding of the divine Order will not, however, provide him with an explanation for the fact that the prerequisite perception is awakened in some, whereas others remain blind. There is a point beyond which the human understanding cannot proceed and the giving or evident withholding of perception is an issue which lies beyond that point. It is for Gurū Nānak an ultimate mystery. The characteristic term used to express this mystery is *nadar*, or *nazar*,[2] but as we have already noted[3] the same doctrine is expressed in the words *kirpā* (or *kripā*), *prasād*, *karam* (the Persian word), *bakhśīś*, *bhāṇā*, *daiā* (*dayā*), *mihar*, and *taras*.

> If Thou dost impart Thy grace then by that grace the True *Gurū* is revealed.[4]
>
> He, the One, dwells within all, but He is revealed to him who receives grace.[5]
>
> Within us are ignorance, suffering, and doubt, but through the *Gurū*'s wisdom all are cast out. He to whom Thou dost show Thy grace and whom Thou dost bring to Thyself, he it is who meditates on the Name. Thou the Creator art ineffable, immanent in all. He whom Thou dost bring to the Truth, he it is who attains it. Let Nānak sing Thy praises.[6]

In order that the *Gurū*'s voice may be heard there must be a prior gift of perception and this gift comes by God's grace. If He gives it then the Word may be perceived, and if He does not there is nothing a man can do. This in itself is not sufficient for salvation, for even if a man accepts the proffered gift he must engage in a sustained discipline before he can attain ultimate release. The gift is, however, a prerequisite. Why it is given to some and withheld from others no man can say. There is much that must

[1] *Japji* 4, *AG*, p. 2.
[2] Literally: 'sight', the gracious glance.
[3] See *supra*, p. 190.
[4] *Vār Āsā*, *pauṛī* 4, *AG*, p. 465.
[5] *Oaṅkāru* 14, *AG*, p. 931.
[6] *Vār Malār*, *pauṛī* 28, *AG*, p. 1291.

remain hidden from the limited understanding of man and the exercise of God's grace is of this nature. Man is not given a complete understanding. What he is given is a sufficient understanding.

The translation we have used is 'grace', but a note of caution is required for the English word is liable to be misinterpreted in this context. The possibility arises from the fact that its usage in Christian theology assumes the specific Pauline doctrine of grace with its stress upon the universal nature of grace and of its absolute sufficiency for salvation. For a person nurtured in Sikh thought there is no problem, for he will take from the word 'grace' the meaning which is imparted by such words as *nadar* and *kirpā* in the context of Sikh scripture. The possibility of misinterpretation may exist, however, for the person whose background is Christian or western, and who may unconsciously read into the word specifically Christian connotations. 'Election' actually comes closer to Gurū Nānak's concept, but it is hardly a satisfactory alternative for it is too closely associated with neo-Calvinist theology and would almost inevitably be accorded an interpretation which implied an eternal double predestination, leaving no scope for the determinative exercise of the individual's free will. 'Favour' and 'choice' are both appropriate, but yet fail to convey a sufficient depth of meaning, although the word *bhāṇā* which corresponds exactly to the first of these is one of the words which is used to express this particular doctrine.

'Grace' remains the best word to express this aspect of the divine nature whereby there is imparted an initial and prerequisite illumination.

> He whom Thou hast enlightened understands. He to whom Thou hast given insight perceives all.[1]

Without this gift of perception, without a divine initiative, the *Gurū* will not be recognized. The gift alone does not mean automatic or irresistible salvation, for as we have already noted the gift must be actually accepted and the individual's life must be lived in accordance with what it imparts. Many, indeed most, to whom it is given refuse to accept it. Instead of listening to the *Gurū*'s Word they fasten their affections on *māyā*, on the attractions of the world.

The various terms may also be used in a sense which refers to the individual's own effort to conform to the Truth rather than to the prior gift of perception.

> The grace of the Master is on those who have meditated on Him with single mind, and they have found favour in His heart.[2]

Normally, however, the various terms are used with reference to the divine initiative, the prior act of grace whereby God implants the perception which enables the individual to hear and to understand the Word. It is not

[1] *Vār Mājh, ślok* 2 of *pauṛi* 27, *AG*, p. 150. [2] *Sirī Rāgu* 27, *AG*, p. 24.

salvation which is given, for this must be attained through the individual's own efforts. It is the prerequisite appreciation of the need for salvation and of the means to be followed in order to attain it—not salvation itself but 'the door of salvation'.

> Just as He, the Lord, is glorious, so too are His gifts glorious, gifts which He gives in accordance with His will. He upon whom the (Lord's) gracious glance rests, he it is who acquires the glory of the True Name.[1]

God has expressed Himself in the Word which He Himself as *Gurū* communicates to man. If by His grace any man be blessed with the perception which enables him to understand the Word he will discern around and within himself the nature of God and the means of attaining union with Him. In this manner the way of salvation is revealed. What must man do to grasp this proffered salvation? What effort must one make, what discipline must one follow in order to appropriate the Truth?

IV. THE DISCIPLINE

It has already been observed how the first stanza of *Japjī* expresses within a single couplet both the problem of salvation and its answer.[2] Stanza 44 of *Oaṅkāru* offers another summary statement. First it poses the problem:

> No one remains, neither kings nor faqīrs, neither poor nor rich. No one can stay when his turn comes round. The way is difficult, frightening, over seas and impassable mountains. I waste away because of the evil within me. Without the necessary merit how can one enter the house (of God)? Those who possess this merit meet the Lord. How can I meet them in love.[3]

Then follows the answer:

> By meditating on God in my heart I shall become like Him. (My heart) is filled with evil, but in it there also dwell redeeming qualities. Without the True *Gurū* these are not perceived and until they are perceived one does not meditate on the Word.[4]

The answer is two-fold. Salvation depends both upon God's grace, which is expressed by the *Gurū* in the Word, and upon the individual's own effort to cleanse himself of all evil and so appropriate the salvation which is offered to him. It is to the second of these which we must now turn, to the *sādhanā* or discipline which Gurū Nānak propounded as the individual's necessary response to the imparted Word. In this section we shall consider first the paths which he rejected and then the one which he affirmed. The goal is union with God. The prerequisite is a recognition of Him in all

[1] *Vār Mājh*, *ślok* 1 of *pauṛī* 19, *AG*, p. 147.
[2] See *supra*, p. 200.
[3] *Oaṅkāru* 44, *AG*, p. 936.
[4] Ibid.

creation and in particular within the human *man*. The way itself is meditation with adoring love upon the divine qualities revealed through such an understanding. The concomitant result is the cleansing and disciplining of the *man*, and a life brought progressively into total accord with the divine Order. And the end result is release from transmigration through the blending of the *man* in a union with God, a union which transcends all human expression. It is a pattern which denies the efficacy of all that is external or mechanical. For Gurū Nānak inward devotion of a specific kind is the way of salvation.

1. *Interior religion*

There is much obscurity in Kabīr, but at one point he is immediately and strikingly clear. No reader can possibly misunderstand his emphasis upon religion as a wholly inward experience, and the imprecations which he bestows upon all who trust in pride of birth or in outward ceremony have lost nothing of their mordant effect. Gurū Nānak does not manifest the same pugnacity, but his attitude in this repect is no less firm and clear. He too lived in an environment which set great store by birth, scriptures, ceremonies, and ascetic practices, and like Kabīr and other Sants he inevitably denounced them as entirely alien to true religion.

> They who read (scriptures) continually and forget (their spiritual duty) suffer the punishment (of spiritual death). For all their wisdom they continue to transmigrate.
>
> They who remember the Name and make fear (of God) their (spiritual) food —such servants, with the *Gurū*'s aid, dwell in union (with their Master).
>
> If the *man* is unclean how can it be purified by worshipping stones, visiting places of pilgrimage, living in jungles, wandering around as an ascetic? He who is united with the True One, he it is who acquires (eternal) honour.[1]

The brāhmaṇs do not receive a measure of scorn comparable with that shown by Kabīr, but we are left in no doubt concerning Gurū Nānak's attitude towards brahmanical pretensions.

> Hear me, paṇḍit, you who put your trust in all your religious works. The work which brings peace is meditation upon spiritual reality. You stand up and recite the Śāstras and Vedas, but your actions are those of the world. Inner filth and evil are not cleansed by hypocrisy. You are like a spider caught upside down (in the web you have spun)![2]
>
> One may have a cooking-square of gold with utensils of gold, (marked off) with lines of silver immensely protracted, water from the Ganges, a fire kindled with flint, and light food soaked in milk. But all these things are of no account, O *man*, unless one be imbued with the true Name. One may

[1] *Dhanāsarī Aṣṭ* 2 (5–6), *AG*, p. 686.

[2] *Soraṭhi Aṣṭ* 2 (1R–2), *AG*, p. 635.

have a hand-written copy of the eighteen Purāṇas and be able to recite the four Vedas by heart, one may bathe on auspicious days, give to each according to the rules prescribed for each caste, fast and observe regulations day and night; one may be a qāzī, a mullah, or a sheikh, a yogī, a *jaṅgam*, or one wearing ochre robes; one may be a householder and live accordingly, but without the understanding (which comes from meditation upon the Name) all are bound and driven off (to the abode of Yam).[1]

According to the *Purātan* janam-sākhīs this latter verse was the one delivered to the extraordinarily scrupulous brāhmaṇ who had refused even the uncooked food offered to him by Gurū Nānak, preferring instead to dig a cooking-square of unimpeachable purity. Wherever he dug, however, he found bones and after digging all day he finally accepted the Gurū's food.[2] The incident has no evident historical basis, but the spirit of the story certainly accords with Gurū Nānak's attitude towards caste status and purity regulations. In him we find the characteristic Sant rejection of caste as a necessary qualification for religious understanding. Gurū Nānak emphatically condemned pride based upon caste status, notions of purity and contamination arising out of caste distinctions, and above all any suggestion that caste standing was either necessary or advantageous in the individual's approach to God.

Perceive (in all men) the light (of God). Do not ask (a man's) caste for in the hereafter there is no caste.[3]

Caste and status are futile, for the One (Lord) watches over all. If anyone exalts himself the true measure of his dignity will be revealed when his record is produced (in the Lord's court).[4]

We who have taken shelter in God are neither high, low, nor in between. We are God's servants.[5]

Impurity, he declared, lay not in differences of birth but in the condition of the individual's *man*.

Your evil mind is a *ḍomaṇī*, your cruelty a *kasaiṇī*, your malicious tongue a *chūhaṛī*, your anger a *chaṇḍālaṛī*,[6] and all have led you astray. Why mark off a cooking-square when the four (outcastes) already keep you company? Let Truth be your manner (of drawing a cooking-square) and righteous

[1] *Basant* 3, *AG*, p. 1169.

[2] *Pur JS*, *sākhī* 38, p. 72. See *supra*, p. 45.

[3] *Āsā* 3, *AG*, p. 349.

[4] *Vār Sirī Rāgu*, *ślok* 1 of *pauṛī* 3, *AG*, p. 83.

[5] *Gūjarī Aṣṭ* 4 (1), *AG*, p. 504.

[6] The female members of four outcaste groups: *Ḍom*, *Kasāī*, *Chūhaṛā*, and *Chaṇḍāl*. The *ḍomaṇī* evidently refers to the caste of sweepers and corpse-burners which has been regarded as the type of all uncleanness (D. Ibbetson, *Panjab Castes*, no. 654, pp. 333–4). The *Mirāsī* caste of Muslim genealogists and musicians, to which Mardānā belonged, are also called *Ḍoms*, but the reference will not be to this group for it possesses an appreciably higher status than that of the sweeper *Ḍoms* (Ibbetson, op. cit., pp. 234–5).

deeds your lines. Let repeating of the Name be your ritual ablution. Nānak, hereafter it is he who does not teach sinful ways who will be exalted.[1]

This rejection of such notions was common among the Sants and was particularly strong in the case of Kabīr.[2] In Gurū Nānak's case it may have received a practical expression. One of the most attractive aspects of Sikhism is the *laṅgar*, the intercommunal refectory which is always attached to a gurdwārā. There can be little doubt that the institution was developed as a deliberate attack on caste distinction, but it is not entirely clear whether it was first introduced into Sikhism by Gurū Nānak or by the third Gurū, Amar Dās. Although the balance of probability strongly favours the latter there can be no doubt that the *laṅgar* expresses an ideal which we find clearly articulated in Gurū Nānak's works. It was an ideal which his successors faithfully upheld and in 1699 it received sacramental expression in the baptismal ceremony instituted by Gurū Gobind Singh at the founding of the Khālsā.[3]

Other expressions of external religion suffered a similar fate at Gurū Nānak's hands. Trust in the sufficiency of traditional acts of merit is rejected:

The man who possesses knowledge but knows not the *Gurū*, of what use are his good works and ceremonies?[4]

Idolatry is ridiculed:

The Hindus, straying in abysmal forgetfulness, have followed the wrong path. As Nārada (the Sage) taught, so they worship (idols). Blind and dumb (they walk) in pitch darkness, worshipping this ridiculous stone which they have set up. It sinks so how can it carry you across (the Ocean of Existence)?[5]

Gods and goddesses are worshipped, but what can one ask of them and what can they give? The stones (the idols) are washed with water, but they sink in water (and so are useless as vessels to carry you across the Ocean of Existence).[6]

Bathing at places of pilgrimage (*tīrath*) is rejected as completely ineffective:

If anyone goes to bathe at a *tīrath* with an evil heart and the body of a thief, one part (the exterior) is cleansed by the bathing, but the other (the heart) becomes even filthier. Outwardly he is washed like a faqīr's gourd, but

[1] *Vār Sirī Rāgu*, *ślok* 1 of *pauṛī* 20, *AG*, p. 91.

[2] Kabīr, *Mārū* 9, *AG*, p. 1105; *Bhairau Aṣṭ* 1, *AG* p. 1162; *śloks* 56, 57, and 82, *AG*, pp. 1367, 1368. *KG sākhī* 33. 7.

[3] See also *BG* 1. 23. I owe to Dr. S. Maqbul Ahmad of the Indian Institute of Advanced Study, Simla, the suggestion that the *laṅgar* may be a borrowing from the Sufi *khānaqāh*.

[4] *Sirī Rāgu* 13, *AG*, p. 19. For a condemnation of faith in astrology see *Rāmakalī Aṣṭ* 4, *AG*, p. 904.

[5] *Vār Bihāgaṛā*, *ślok* 2 of *pauṛī* 20, *AG*, p. 556.

[6] *Soraṭhi Dutukī* 4 (6), *AG*, p. 637.

inside he is poison and impurity. A sādhū[1] possesses goodness even if he does not bathe and a thief, even if he bathes, remains a thief.[2]

Shall I go and bathe at a *tīrath*? The true *tīrath* is the divine Name; it is inner contemplation of the Word and it is true knowledge (*jñān*). The *Gurū*'s *jñān* is the true *tīrath* where every day is an auspicious day. O Lord, Sustainer of the earth, I crave Thy Name eternally. Grant it (I pray Thee).[3]

Nor is salvation to be found in ascetic practices, in abandoning the world to pursue a solitary or an itinerant life, particularly if the renunciation is a hypocritical one designed to provide a life of irresponsible ease.

He who sings songs about God without understanding them; who converts his house into a mosque in order to satisfy his hunger; who, being unemployed, has his ears pierced (so that he can beg as a yogī); who becomes a faqīr and abandons his caste; who is called a *gurū* or *pīr* but who goes around begging—never fall at the feet of such a person.

He who eats what he has earned by his own labour and gives some (to others)—Nānak, he it is who knows the true way.[4]

The last couplet indicates the positive aspect of this particular rejection. Asceticism is rejected; a disciplined worldliness is affirmed. The way of Truth consists, in this respect, of living in the world yet unaffected by the attractions of the world. It is a common emphasis among the Sants and Gurū Nānak uses the conventional figure of the lotus to illustrate it.[5] The refrain of *Sūhī* 8, a verse which was evidently addressed to Kānphaṭ yogīs, is a striking expression of this belief.

The path of true Yoga is found by dwelling in God while yet living in the midst of the world's temptations.[6]

In this context it is to be noted that family attachments are not upheld as good or permissible. On the contrary, they too are of the nature of worldly attachments and are accordingly to be avoided.

Domestic involvement is a whirlpool; the sin (which lies upon us) is a stone which cannot cross over (the Ocean of Existence).[7]

[1] The word is used in its original sense meaning one who has attained self-control. In this context *bhagat* or 'true believer' would serve as synonyms.

[2] *Vār Sūhī, ślok* 2 of *pauṛī* 12, *AG*, p. 789.

[3] *Dhanāsarī Chhant* 1 (1), *AG*, p. 687. This extract is also of interest in that it illustrates Gurū Nānak's usage of *giān* (*jñān*). The word does not normally possess any particular significance in his thought and neither does it appear with any great frequency. When it does appear it usually corresponds to *śabad* as in the extract quoted here. The only instance where it is given a particular significance is in *Japjī* 35 where it is used to designate the second of the five *khaṇḍs*. See *infra*, p. 221.

[4] *Vār Sāraṅg, ślok* 1 of *pauṛī* 22, *AG*, p. 1245.

[5] Cf. *Gauṛī* 5, *AG*, p. 152; *Rāmakalī* 4, *AG*, p. 877. The beauty of the lotus is in no way diminished by the filthy water which may surround it, nor by the mud in which it takes root.

[6] *Sūhī* 8, *AG*, p. 730.

[7] *Mārū* 2, *AG*, pp. 989–90.

It is, however, the attachment, not the family itself, which is to be spurned. Those who love the Name do not need to isolate themselves in order to avoid such attachments.

> Meditation on the True One brings illumination and so one lives detached in the midst of evil. Such is the greatness of the True *Gurū* that even surrounded by wife and sons one can attain salvation.[1]

This freedom from attachment while yet living in the midst of temptations to attachment is the proper pattern for the true believer.[2] Ascetics and yogis wander in vain.

> If I live in a cave in a mountain of gold or remain immersed in water; if I remain buried in the earth, or ascend into the sky, or remain suspended head down; if I clothe myself completely and wash (my clothes) endlessly; if I read the white, red, yellow, and black Vedas at the top of my voice, or remain unwashed[3] (it is all in vain for) all (such practices) are error and evil misconception. Only if one meditates on the Word does *haumai* go.[4]

Qāzīs, paṇḍits, and yogīs in their traditional pursuits are all astray.

> The qāzī utters lies and eats what is unclean;
> The brāhmaṇ takes life and then goes off to bathe ceremoniously;
> The blind yogī does not know the way;
> All three are desolated.[5]

True religion is to be found not in external practices, but in the inward disciplines of love, faith, mercy, and humility, expressed in righteous and compassionate deeds and in the upholding of all that is true.

> The true yogī is he who recognizes the Way, who by the *Gurū*'s grace knows the One.
> The true qāzī is he who turns away (from the world) and by the *Gurū*'s grace dies while yet remaining alive.
> The true brāhmaṇ is he who meditates on Brahman; he saves himself and all his kin.[6]

> Make mercy your mosque, faith your prayer-mat, and righteousness your Qur'ān.
> Make humility your circumcision, uprightness your fasting, and so you will be a (true) Muslim.

[1] *Dhanāsarī* 4, *AG*, p. 661.
[2] Nāmdev's *Rāmakalī* 1, *AG*, p. 972, is an answer to the charge that such a life must be inconsistent with true devotion. Cf. also Kabīr's *śloks* 212 and 213, *AG*, pp. 1375–6, and Raidās's *Bilāvalu* 2, *AG*, p. 858.
[3] This reference is evidently intended to apply to Jain monks. *Vār Mājh, ślok* 1 of *pauṛī* 26, *AG*, pp. 149–50, directs a vigorous attack against their beliefs and practices.
[4] *Vār Mājh, ślok* 1 of *pauṛī* 4, *AG*, p. 139.
[5] *Dhanāsarī* 7, *AG*, p. 662. Cf. also *Vār Rāmakalī, ślok* 1 of *pauṛī* 11, *AG*, p. 951.
[6] Ibid.

Make good works your *Ka'bah*, Truth your *pīr*, and compassion your creed and your prayer.
Make the performance of what pleases (God) your rosary and, Nānak, He will uphold your honour.[1]

(Make the Merciful Lord) your *śālgrām*, your object of worship, O paṇḍit, and good deeds your garland of *tulsī*.
Construct a boat by repeating the Name of God and pray that the Merciful One may show mercy towards you.
Why waste your life in irrigating sterile land? Why plaster a mud wall when it will surely fall?[2]

2. *Loving devotion*

If one gains anything from visiting places of pilgrimage (*tīrath*), from austerities, acts of mercy,[3] and charity, it is of negligible value. He who has heard, believed, and nurtured love in his heart has cleansed himself by bathing at the *tīrath* which is within.[4]

The *tīrath* is within.[5] Religion is inward and its basic expression is love or, more accurately, loving devotion. This loving devotion, a devotion directed to the formless Lord, is the vital response required of all who have perceived the presence of God suffused throughout creation, and in whom has been awakened a longing for union with Him. It is at this point that Gurū Nānak shares with the Sants a particular debt to Vaiṣṇava bhakti. There is in his works the characteristic Vaiṣṇava emphasis upon the absolute necessity of love in the bhakti sense, commonly expressed in the figure of the bride yearning for her Beloved, the divine Bridegroom.

He who worships the True One with adoring love, who thirsts for the supreme love, who beseeching cries out, he it is who finds peace for in his heart is love.[6]

In addition to the basic bhakti emphasis we find in Gurū Nānak's works the more important of its corollaries. There must be fear of God, a recognition of His infinite immensity and of His absolute authority.

Fear (of God) is of great weight and hard to bear; the wayward mind, with all its effusions, is slight. (And yet) he who carries on his head (fear of God) can bear (its) weight. By grace he meditates on the *Gurū*'s (teaching). Without such fear no one crosses (the Ocean of Existence), but if one dwell in fear to it is added love.[7]

[1] *Vār Mājh, ślok* 1 of *pauṛī* 7, *AG*, pp. 140–1.
[2] *Basant Hiṇḍol* 9, *AG*, p. 1171.
[3] The reference is clearly to acts performed with the intention of acquiring merit.
[4] *Japjī* 21, *AG*, p. 4.
[5] Cf. also *Āsā* 32, *AG*, p. 358; *Vār Āsā, ślok* 2 of *pauṛī* 10, *AG*, p. 468.
[6] *Gūjarī Aṣṭ* 5 (1), *AG*, p. 505.
[7] *Gauṛī* 1, *AG*, p. 151.

There must be complete surrender to Him, an unconditional submission in faith.

> The Lord is near at hand (within you), foolish bride. Why seek Him without? Let fear be the *salāī*[1] (with which you apply antimony to your) eyes and let your adornment be that of love. She who loves her Master is known to be the bride united with Him. . . .
>
> Go and ask (those who are already the Master's) brides by what means they found Him. (A bride replies:) 'Accept whatever He does as good, put no trust in your own cleverness and abandon the exercise of your own will. Fix your mind on His feet.[2] (Cleave to Him) through whose love the priceless treasure is obtained. Do whatever He says. Anoint yourself with the perfume of total surrender to Him.' Thus replies the bride, 'O sister, by this means the Lord is found.'[3]

And there must be singing of God's praises.

> He who serves Him wins honour (in His court), so sing His praises Nānak, (sing of Him) the Treasury of excellences. Sing His praises, hear them, love Him. . . .[4]
>
> This is the belief which Nānak proclaims: It is through the singing of (His) praises that we find a place in the Lord's court.[5]

All of these are aspects of traditional bhakti and they represent a significant area of agreement between the Vaiṣṇava *bhagats* on the one hand and Gurū Nānak on the other. There are, however, basic differences separating them. In the first place, as we have already observed,[6] there is in Gurū Nānak's works an explicit rejection of *avatārs*. Like the Sants he addressed his devotion direct to God Himself, supreme and non-incarnated, not to any manifestation or intermediary. Secondly, there is Gurū Nānak's understanding of the practical expression of love, enunciated in his interpretation of *nām simaran* or *nām japan*. This interpretation is of fundamental importance. It provides the heart of his discipline and in it we find his distinctive understanding of the believer's proper response.

3. Nām simaran

> This world is entangled in earthly affections and so in the immense suffering of death and rebirth. Flee to the True *Gurū*'s shelter. There repeat the Name of God in your heart and so obtain salvation.[7]
>
> Nānak, he who is steeped in the divine Name is freed from his *haumai*, is gathered up in the True One, meditates on the way of (true) Yoga, finds the

[1] A small metal instrument for applying antimony to eyes.

[2] A conventional figure signifying humble, submissive devotion.

[3] *Tilaṅg* 4, *AG*, p. 722.

[4] *Japjī* 5, *AG*, p. 2.

[5] *Vār Mājh, ślok* 2 of *pauṛī* 12, *AG*, p. 143.

[6] See *supra*, p. 171.

[7] *Gūjarī Aṣṭ* 5 (5), *AG*, p. 505.

door of salvation, acquires an understanding of the three worlds, and attains to eternal peace.[1]

If the mind be defiled by sin it is cleansed with love of the Name. Virtue and sin are not mere words; we carry with us the influence of what we have done. As you have sown so will you reap, and in accordance with the divine Order you will transmigrate.[2]

The divine Order (*Hukam*) expressed, as we have already observed, in the law of *karma* ensures that one must reap in accordance with what one sows. In order to banish the influence of committed sin the individual must sow that seed which bears not the baneful fruit of transmigration but the blessed fruit of union. This seed (or, as here, this cleansing agent) is love of the divine Name. Sahib Singh comments as follows on the *Japjī* stanza:

As a result of the influence of *māyā* man falls into evil and his mind is sullied. This impurity separates man from the wholly pure God and the soul undergoes suffering. *Nām simaran* alone is the means whereby the *man* can be instantly cleansed. And so the practice of *simaran* is the means of cleansing the *man* from evil and of uniting it with God.[3]

Vir Singh has a similar comment:

The True *Gurū* has here informed us that the means of restoring purity to the mind or intellect clogged with sin is love of the Name. . . . God is supremely holy. Remembrance of His Name brings the *man* into a condition of meditation on Him. In this way the *antaḥkaraṇa*, coming into contact by means of the Name with the Possessor of the Name, is purified through His holiness. Through *nām simaran* it is separated from other impure inclinations. Thus it is drawn progressively nearer to both the *Hukam* and its Giver, and thus *haumai* is gradually purged.[4]

But how does one 'love the Name'? What is meant in Gurū Nānak's usage by the expressions *nām simaran* or *nām japan*?

Nām has already been dealt with. The divine Name is the revelation of God's being, the sum total of all His attributes, the aggregate of all that may be affirmed concerning Him. The two verbs which are normally attached to *nām* are *japanā* and *simaranā*, neither of which can be satisfactorily translated into English in the context of Gurū Nānak's usage. *Japanā* means 'to repeat' and is used in connexion with the recital of a divine name or *mantra*. In many contexts this literal translation is entirely appropriate, for mechanical repetition of this kind, often with the help of a rosary, was a very common practice. Mere mechanical repetition was not,

[1] *Siddh Goṣṭi* 32, *AG*, p. 941. See also stanza 33.
[2] *Japjī* 20, *AG*, p. 4.
[3] Sahib Singh, *Srī Gurū Granth Sāhib Darapaṇ*, vol. i, p. 87.
[4] Vir Singh, *Santhyā*, vol. i, p. 101.

however, Gurū Nānak's practice. Some references might indeed suggest this, as, for example, the following passage from *Japjī*.

> Let every tongue become a *lākh* of tongues, and let every *lākh* become twenty *lākhs*. And then let every tongue utter the Name of God a *lākh* of times. This path is a stairway which leads to the Lord, and having ascended it one passes into union with Him.[1]

Such examples must, however, be read in the context of his general usage. Here it is a case of hyperbole, an effort to convey the immensity of the divine majesty and not a claim that the infinite repetition of a single name or syllable is an assured path to salvation. Gurū Nānak would without doubt have been in complete agreement with the pronouncement of Gurū Amar Dās:

> Everyone goes around saying 'Rām Rām', but Rām is not found in this way.[2]

Simple repetition of this kind is not enough, regardless of how devout the repetition may be or how sophisticated a system may be built around the practice. It is a pattern which can include the repetition of a chosen word or brief formula, but only if the emphasis is upon the interiorising of the utterance, upon the paramount need of understanding the word so uttered and of exposing one's total being to its deepest meanings.

Simaranā, 'to remember' or 'to hold in remembrance', is more helpful, for 'remembering the Name' is nearer to a description of Gurū Nānak's practice than 'repeating the Name'. It too, however, falls short of an adequate description. How then is the practice to be described? Gurū Nānak himself provides a definition.

> Repeating (the Name) of the True God means engrafting (Him) in the *man*.[3]

And the method whereby this engrafting is carried out is meditation—meditation on the nature of God, on His qualities and His attributes as revealed in the Word (*Śabad*).

> God is found through meditation on the *Gurū*'s Word, the sublime utterance.[4]

> By meditating on the Word one crosses the Ocean.[5]

> You who are drowning (in the Ocean of Existence), you have laid waste your own dwelling. Walk in the *Gurū*'s love. Meditating on the true Name you shall find bliss in the palace (of God). Meditate on the true Name and you shall find bliss. Your stay in your father's house[6] is brief. When you go to your real home you shall know the Truth and you shall dwell eternally with your Beloved.[7]

[1] *Japjī* 32, *AG*, p. 7.
[2] *Vār Bihāgaṛā, ślok* 1 of *pauṛī* 18, *AG*, p. 555.
[3] *Vaḍahaṃsu Chhant* 2 (5), *AG*, p. 567.
[4] *Oaṅkāru* 47, *AG*, pp. 936–7.
[5] *Prabhātī Aṣṭ* 1 (1R), *AG*, p. 1342.
[6] i.e. in this world. The person addressed is the conventional figure of the bride.
[7] *Dhanāsarī Chhant* 3 (2), *AG*, p. 689.

The worship (*pūjā*) which we offer is meditation on the Name, for without the Name there can be no (true) worship.[1]

This meditation on the nature and qualities of God is the core of Gurū Nānak's religious discipline. The Word reveals the absoluteness of God. Meditate on this and make your submission before Him. The Word reveals the eternally stable permanence of God, the eternity of God. Reflect on this and abandon the fickle, fleeting world. The Word reveals the absolute freedom of God from all that is *māyā*. Meditate on this and so separate yourself from its deceits. The Word reveals the ineffable greatness of God. Reflect on this and humble yourself before Him. It is a meditation which must overflow in words and deeds which accord with the nature of the Name. It is remembrance of God *mani, bach, karami karakai*[2]—in thought, word, and deed.

This is the practical response which a believer is required to make. Meditate in love and you shall grow towards and into Him who is the object of your devotion and your meditation. It is a discipline which has been developed, interpreted, and expounded again and again, both by Gurū Nānak's successors and by devout Sikhs ever since. This should be remembered, for much of the detailed analysis which may be found in Sikh writings is taken from the works of the later Gurūs or represents assumptions based upon what is found in the scriptures. This is not to say that the assumptions are inconsistent with the basis, but merely that the basis as set out in Gurū Nānak's works is a relatively simple version of what the doctrine was later to become. Moreover, in the case of the Gurūs' followers the source of the Word and so the primary means of meditation has of course been the collection of works recorded in the *Ādi Granth*.

This meditation must be individual and it must also have a corporate application. Gurū Nānak emphasized both.

At the ambrosial hour (of dawn) meditate on the greatness of the true Name.[3]

In the company of true believers the joy of God's (presence) is obtained and when one finds the *Gurū* fear of death departs. This is your destiny, that repeating the Name of God in accordance with the *Gurū*'s instructions you find God.[4]

[1] *Gūjarī* 1, *AG*, p. 489. In these four quotations the expression used is either *śabad vichāranā* or *nām dhiāunā*. Cf. also *Vaḍahaṃsu Dakhaṇī* 4 (1), *AG*, p. 581; *Tukhārī* 2 (3), *AG*, p. 1110. In contemporary Sikh usage one also encounters the term *nām abhiās*, 'the regular practice of the Name'.

[2] *Pur JS*, p. 4.

[3] *Japjī* 4, *AG*, p. 2. This injunction has been accepted as an explicit commandment by the Sikh community. See the Sikh Book of Discipline, *Sikh Rahit Marayādā* (Śromaṇī Gurduārā Prabandhak Committee, Amritsar, 1961), p. 10. The same regulation lists the sections from the scriptures which should be recited by the individual in the morning and in the evening (pp. 10–11). Another section deals with attendance at the gurdwārā (pp. 14–17). The *Sikh Rahit Marayādā* has been translated in part by C. H. Loehlin, *The Sikhs and their Scriptures* (1st edition), pp. 39–42.

[4] *Soraṭhi* 10, *AG*, p. 598.

The importance of the company of true believers (the *satsaṅg*) as a vehicle of enlightenment which is so strongly stressed by Kabīr receives a corresponding emphasis in Gurū Nānak's works.

> Even if one were to possess infinite wisdom and were to dwell in love and concord with an immense number of people, without the society of the holy there would be no satisfaction, and without the Name there would be misery.[1]
>
> He who having created (the universe) watches over it dwells in every heart, (yet not beyond perceiving for) by the *Gurū*'s guidance He is made manifest in (the company of) the people of God.[2]

The traditional figure of the sandal tree is also used.

> Such is the nature of the true believer that like the sandal he imparts his fragrance to all (around him).[3]

The activity of the true believer in the *satsaṅg* is the singing of praises rather than the function implied by the word meditation, but *nām simaran* covers both, for both are concerned with God and with the individual's approach to Him. Music has always been used. Mardānā the Bard was Gurū Nānak's companion in at least some of his travels and there can be no reason for rejecting the janam-sākhī references to Gurū Nānak's practice of *kīrtan*, the corporate singing of God's praises.[4] The discipline must also be practised daily.

> Pain is poison but God's Name is the antidote. Let patient contentment be the stone on which you pound it and let your hand be that of charity. Take it daily and your body shall not waste away, and at the end Death itself will be struck down. Take this medicine, for the consuming of it will purge the evil that is in you.[5]

Meditation on the divine Name and the singing of praises must have seemed easy to many, but Gurū Nānak declares them to be otherwise. They are difficult and few are prepared to make the sacrifices which they demand. Those who do accept the discipline, however, find that the reward far outweighs the sacrifice.

> If I repeat the Name I live; if I forget it I die. Repeating the Name of the True One is hard, but if one hungers for it and partakes of it all sadness goes.[6]

This then is the discipline. The human body is a field in which the seed of the divine Name is to be sown. Cultivate it with love, humility, fear of God, true living, purity, and patience, and thus you shall reap your reward.

> Regard your body as a field, your *man* the plough, your actions the ploughing, and effort the irrigation. (In the field) sow the Name as seed, level it with contentment, and fence it with humility.

[1] *Siri Rāgu* 17, *AG*, p. 20.
[2] *Basant Hiṇḍol* 12, *AG*, p. 1172.
[3] *Tilaṅg* 2, *AG*, p. 721.
[4] See also *BG* 1. 38.
[5] *Malār* 8, *AG*, pp. 1256–7.
[6] *Āsā* 3, and *Āsā* 2, *AG*, pp. 9, 349.

Let your actions be those of love. (The seed) will then sprout and you will see your home prosper.[1]

Love is the soil, holiness the water, and truth and contentment the two buffaloes.

Humility is the plough, the mind the ploughman, remembrance (of the Name) the watering, and union (with God) the seed-time.

The Name is the seed and grace the crop. (These constitute Truth whereas) the world is wholly false.

Nānak, if the Merciful One is gracious all separation (from Him) comes to an end.[2]

4. *The concomitant results*

The practice of *nām simaran* results in experiences which develop progressively as meditation draws the individual nearer and nearer to God, and which find their ultimate perfection in the final absorption of the *man* into Him. They are at the same time results of the discipline and necessary aids to it, for they reveal more and more of the true nature of the Name and render the individual capable of rising to progressively greater heights.

The experience of *visamād* is, in this way, both a result of *nām simaran* and a stimulus to more exalted meditation. *Visamād* (Skt. *vismaya*) may mean either an immense awe, a prodigious wonder engendered by the overwhelming, indescribable greatness of God; or it may connote the actual condition of ecstasy resulting from the awe-inspiring vision of the greatness of God. The most sustained expression of *visamād* in Gurū Nānak's works is the lengthy *ślok* from *Āsā dī Vār* which begins with the line *visamādu nād visamādu ved* and in which almost every second word is *visamād*.[3] Stanza 24 of *Japjī* is also an expression of this same awe.

> Infinite are the praises (of the Creator), infinite the ways of uttering them. Infinite are His works and infinite His gifts. Infinite is His sight, infinite His hearing, infinite the workings of the divine mind. His creation is boundless, its limits infinite. Many have striven to encompass its infinity; none have succeeded. None there be who know its extent; whatsoever one may say much more yet remains to be said. Great is God and high His station; higher than high His Name. Only he who is of equal height can comprehend its loftiness; therefore God alone comprehends His own greatness. Nānak, all that we receive is the gift of the Gracious One.[4]

This is *visamād*, for Gurū Nānak both the inevitable result of true meditation and the food for even more refined and intense meditation.

The purging of *haumai* and its related impulses is likewise both a result and an essential aid. The further a believer proceeds in meditation on

[1] *Soraṭhi* 2, *AG*, p. 595.

[2] *Vār Rāmakalī*, *ślok* 2 of *pauṛī* 17, *AG*, p. 955. The word 'contentment' refers in these contexts to a condition transcending both pain and pleasure.

[3] *Vār Āsā*, *ślok* 1 of *pauṛī* 3, *AG*, pp. 463–4.

[4] *Japjī* 24, *AG*, p. 5.

the Name the less inclined he is to submit to his own *haumai*; and the less he submits to his own *haumai* the further he progresses towards the goal of ultimate union. The process is described, as in Kabīr,[1] in terms of dying to Self. Two kinds of death have already been noted in the thought of Gurū Nānak[2] and this is a third.

> Because my eyes are turned towards evil I have neither fear of God nor love for Him. Only if the Self is slain can one possess the divine Name. If one dies by means of the Word one dies not again. Without such a death how can one be perfected?[3]

It is a death which is accomplished by the overthrow of the *man*, a death to Self which the true believer dies while yet remaining physically alive. The *man* must remain, but not the self-willed *man* which finds its expression in evil. It must be a redirected *man* and this overthrow, this redirection, is effected through the believer's love for the Name and his meditation on it.

> He who smites his *man* knows the death which takes place while life yet remains. Nānak, through grace he recognises the Gracious One.[4]

> By the *Gurū*'s grace one perceives (the true nature of) the Self and so dies even while remaining alive.[5]

> The *Gurū* is an ocean, a mine of jewels in which lie a multitude of precious stones. I bathe in the seven oceans (of the *Gurū*'s teaching) and my *man* is purified. I bathe in the pure waters when it is the Lord's will and thus by meditation I acquire the five blessings.[6] I abandon lust, anger, deceit, and evil, and enshrine the true Name in my heart. The wave of *haumai* and covetousness has spent itself; the Merciful One has been found. Nānak, there is no *tīrath* like the *Gurū*, (nothing to compare to) the true *Gurū-Gopāl*.[7]

The *man* is cleansed of *haumai* and purged of all evil passions. Purified and disciplined it ceases to be man's enemy and is transformed instead into his ally. No longer does it lead him into the entanglements of *māyā*; no longer does it earn him a disastrous *karma*. Instead it leads him further and further into conformity with the divine Order, further into that same Truth by which it was itself cleansed.

> He who is steeped in fear of the True One casts out pride. Meditating on the Word he comes to a knowledge of God, for if the Word dwells (within) the True One is also within. Body and soul are immersed in (His) love and

[1] Kabīr, *Soraṭhi* 6, *AG*, p. 655; *KG*, *sākhī*, *aṅg* 19.

[2] Physical death which comes to all, and Death (personified in Yam) which is the fate of the *manmukh*. See *supra*, pp. 187–8.

[3] *Gauṛī* 7, *AG*, p. 153.

[4] *Prabhātī Aṣṭ* 3 (8), *AG*, p. 1343.

[5] *Oaṅkāru* 41, *AG*, p. 935.

[6] Truth, contentment, compassion, *dharma*, and patience.

[7] *Āsā Chhant* 2 (3), *AG*, p. 437.

(their passions) are cooled. Nānak, the consuming fires of lust and anger are extinguished by the grace of the beloved Giver of grace.[1]

Increasingly the believer becomes *like* God until ultimately he attains to a perfect identity.

He who is immersed in His love day and night knows (Him who is immanent) in the three worlds and throughout all time. He becomes like Him whom he knows. He becomes wholly pure, his body is sanctified, and God dwells in his heart as his only love. Within him is the Word; he is blended in the True One.[2]

5. *The ascent*

With the ever-widening *visamād* and the progressive subjugation of the *man* go a developing sense of joy and peace. It is a path leading onward and upward. The accent is strongly upon ascent to higher and yet higher levels of understanding and experience, an accent which is particularly evident in Gurū Nānak's famous figure of the five *khaṇḍs*.[3]

The pattern which is set out in this figure is sometimes said to represent a Sūfī contribution to the thought of Gurū Nānak, the theory being that its origin is to be found in the *maqāmāt* of the Sūfīs. There is, however, no evidence to establish this conjecture, and the parallel is not really a close one. A much closer one is to be found in the pattern of salvation enunciated in the *Yoga-vasiṣṭha*.[4] Sikh commentators understandably attach considerable importance to the figure of the five *khaṇḍs*, for it is clearly intended to represent the ascent of the *man* to its ultimate goal. There is, however, much that is obscure in Gurū Nānak's exposition and considerable differences of opinion are to be found in the commentaries. In the case of the third and fourth the very names of the *khaṇḍs* are translated in different ways.

Dharam Khaṇḍ, the first, is the clearest of the five.[5] *Dharam* represents here the law of cause and effect. This obviously applies in the physical universe and the person who has reached this initial stage perceives that it applies in a religious and moral sense also. God is just and in His court the true and the false stand revealed.

Giān Khaṇḍ (or *Jñān Khaṇḍ*) is the second stage.[6] It evidently represents a marked widening of the individual's understanding, chiefly due to a developing appreciation of the manifold qualities of the creation and of the significance of great figures who have preceded him. The precise

[1] *Siddh Goṣṭi* 47, *AG*, p. 943. [2] *Oaṅkāru* 10, *AG*, p. 931.

[3] 'Realms', or stages in spiritual progress. *Japjī* 34–37, *AG*, pp. 7–8.

[4] S. Dasgupta, *A History of Indian Philosophy*, vol. ii, p. 264, provides a summary of the seven stages set out in the *Yoga-vasiṣṭha*, vi, 120.

[5] *Japjī* 34, *AG*, p. 7. *Dharam* is the Pañjābī form of the Sanskrit *dharma*.

[6] *Japjī* 35–36, *AG* p. 7.

significance is not stated, but to some commentators the point is that such an understanding promotes a weakening of the individual's self-centredness.[1] One characteristic which is explicitly stated is the resultant joy of such a state.

> Knowledge shines in the Realm of Knowledge. In it there is joy of sound, sight, and deed.[2]

Saram Khaṇḍ, the third stage,[3] is the least clear and provides the most marked differences in interpretation. There are three views concerning the meaning of the word *saram*. First there are those who claim that it derives from the Sanskrit *śarma* and who accordingly interpret it as the Realm of Effort.[4] Secondly, there are the commentators who would derive it from the Sanskrit *śarman* and who interpret it as the Realm of Bliss.[5] Thirdly, there are those who favour the Persian *śaram* ('shame') and who interpret it as either the Realm of Humility or the Realm of Surrender.[6] The actual description given in *Japjī* does not provide an answer, but indicates rather that by this stage the nature of the religious experience involved is passing beyond the describable.

> There (in that Realm) are fashioned creations of surpassing wonder. None can describe them. Were one to try he would rue the effort.[7]

The only hint comes in the couplet:

> There inner perception and reason are fashioned; there the understanding of a divine hero or a spiritual adept is developed.[8]

The third of the suggested derivations is an attractive one, but the first seems the most likely. It harmonizes better with the above couplet and where Gurū Nānak uses *saram* in another context the meaning clearly seems to be 'effort'.

> Regard your body as a field, your *man* the plough, your actions the ploughing, and effort (*saramu*) the irrigation.[9]

The figure of the ploughman makes much better sense if *saram* is translated

[1] Harnam Singh, *The Japji*, p. 141. [2] *Japjī* 36, *AG* p. 7. [3] Ibid.

[4] *Śabadārath*, p. 7, n. 29. Teja Singh, *The Japji* (English trans.), pp. 13 and 39 ('self-exertion'). Jodh Singh, *The Japji* (English trans.), p. 54. Sahib Singh, *Sri Gurū Granth Sāhib Darapaṇ*, vol. i, p. 124. S. S. Kohli, *A Critical Study of the Adi Granth*, p. 367. Mohan Singh, *Pañjābī Bhākhā te Chhandābandi*, p. 218. *The Sacred Writings of the Sikhs* (UNESCO), p. 49. *Sri Gurū Granth Koś*, p. 243.

[5] Vir Singh, *Santhyā*, vol. i, p. 167. Khushwant Singh, *Jupji: the Sikh Prayer*, p. 22. Macauliffe, *The Sikh Religion*, vol. i, p. 216 ('happiness'). E. Trumpp, *The Ādi Granth*, p. 12 ('happiness').

[6] Harnam Singh, *The Japji*, p. 143 ('humility'). Gopal Singh, *Sri Guru-Granth Sahib*, p. 11 ('surrender'), although not in his earlier *The Song of Nanak*, p. 11, where his translation is 'the domain of Practice'. This Persian interpretation is general in the older, less important commentaries such as those by Baba Mangal Singh, Gurmukh Singh, and Sant Gulab Singh.

[7] *Japjī* 36, *AG*, pp. 7–8.

[8] Ibid., *AG*, p. 8.

[9] *Soraṭhi* 2, *AG*, p. 595.

as 'effort' and the idea of modesty or humility is covered by the word *garībī* which comes in the following line.

Karam Khaṇḍ is the fourth stage[1] and here there are two principal interpretations. First there is the majority opinion which takes *karam* to be the Persian word meaning 'grace' and which accordingly interprets the fourth stage as the Realm of Grace.[2] Secondly, there is a strong minority opinion represented by Macauliffe,[3] Teja Singh,[4] and Khushwant Singh.[5] All three have regarded *karam* as the Sanskrit *karma* and have translated *Karam Khaṇḍ* as the realm or domain of Action. The Persian school certainly has the weight of numbers to support it, but there is one serious objection to this theory. Grace does indeed occupy a position of primary importance in the thought of Gurū Nānak, but there is no indication in his works that the receipt of grace comes so late in the believer's ascent to union. On the contrary, it extends over the whole process and if any stage is of particular significance with regard to grace it is the very beginning. The Sanskrit interpretation, however, faces an equally strong objection. If *Saram Khaṇḍ* is to be regarded as the Realm of Effort and *Karam Khaṇḍ* as the Realm of Action there is little difference between the two stages.

A third possibility is that *karam* is the Sanskrit word and that it retains the normal meaning of *karma*. In this context the sense could well be that it is in the fourth stage that the *bhagat* begins to reap the reward of a *karma* earned through the faithful practice of *nām simaran*. This would accord with what we are told of the fourth stage, for the emphasis is upon fulfilment and one aspect of this fulfilment is that the *bhagat* is said to pass beyond error and transmigration.[6] Accordingly, an appropriate translation would appear to be the Realm of Fulfilment.

Sach Khaṇḍ is the fifth and final stage. This is the Realm of Truth, the true dwelling-place of the Formless One. Here the believer passes into a unity which can be described only in terms of infinity.

> Realms, worlds, universes exist there.
> Were anyone to number them, of his numbering there could be no end![6]

This is the ultimate climax of the search for Truth, for it is here that there is perfect and absolute accord with the divine Order (*Hukam*).

> As the *Hukam*, so too the deed![6]

[1] *Japji* 37, *AG*, p. 8.

[2] Vir Singh, op. cit., vol. i, p. 167. Kahn Singh, *MK*, p. 227. Jodh Singh, op. cit., p. 55. Sahib Singh, op. cit., vol. i, p. 125. Sher Singh Gyani, *Guramati Daraśan*, p. 329. Harnam Singh, op. cit., p. 144. Gopal Singh, op. cit., p. 11. S. S. Kohli op. cit., p. 367. *The Sacred Writings of the Sikhs*, p. 50. *Sri Gurū Granth Koś*, p. 352.

[3] Macauliffe, op. cit., vol. i, p. 216. His translation is 'the realm of action'. Trumpp's translation was 'the region of works' (op. cit., p. 13).

[4] Teja Singh, *The Japji*, pp. 14, 40, and *Śabadārath*, p. 7, n. *

[5] Khushwant Singh, op. cit., p. 22. Also Jogendra Singh, *Sikh Ceremonies*, p. 40.

[6] *Japji* 37, *AG*, p. 8.

But it is a condition which can be known only in experience.

> To describe it, Nānak, is as hard as steel![1]

6. *The ultimate*

Sach Khaṇḍ is the goal, the ultimate end and purpose of human existence, the final consummation of man's ascent to God. Gurū Nānak's references to this ultimate condition bring out three things. First, it is to be conceived in terms of a union of the individual *man* with the being of God, the supra-soul.[2] Secondly, this union means an end for ever to the transmigratory process, with all its attendant suffering, and instead an eternal, changeless tranquillity.[3] And thirdly, the true nature of this condition must ever elude description. It can be represented by nothing better than inadequate symbols and the broadest of generalizations. Its essential quality can be known only in the actual experience of union.

The characteristic word which Gurū Nānak uses to convey the nature of the ultimate experience is the verb *samāṇā* or *samāuṇā*. It is also used in the sense of 'to fill' or 'to pervade' in the context of the divine immanence, but here its meaning is rather 'to merge' or 'to blend'. *Sachi samāuṇā, śabadi samāuṇā, sahaji samāuṇā*, and *avigati samāuṇā*[4] are examples of the manner in which Gurū Nānak seeks to express the experience of union. It is a blending of the individual light in the Light of God (*jotī joti samāuṇā*),[5] a mingling of the individual drop in the ocean,[6] a dissolution of the individual *ātmā* in the *Paramātmā*.

> If God shows favour one meditates on Him. The *ātmā* is dissolved and is absorbed (in God). (The individual's) *ātmā* becomes one with the *Param-ātmā* and inner duality dies within.[7]

It is the *chauthā pad*, the 'fourth state' or absolute condition transcending the three *guṇa*;[8] the *turiā pad* or *turiā avasthā*;[9] the *param pad*;[10] the *amarāpad*;[11] the condition of supreme bliss beyond all that is corruptible and beyond all powers of human expression.

At no point in the whole range of Gurū Nānak's works is the link with the Nāth tradition, and beyond the Nāth tradition with tantric Buddhism, so clearly evident. Of all the terms used by Gurū Nānak in his effort to communicate something of the meaning of the experience the most

[1] *Japjī* 37, *AG*. p. 8.
[2] See *supra*, p. 180.
[3] Cf. *Gauṛī* 10, *AG*, p. 154; *Āsā Aṣṭ* 7 (4), p. 414; *Āsā Paṭṭī Likhī* (29), p. 434; *Sūhī Aṣṭ* 2 (1), p. 751; *Sūhī Chhant* 5 (3), p. 766; *Bilāvalu Aṣṭ* 2 (8), p. 832; *Mārū Solahā* 20 (4), p. 1040; *Sāraṅg* 2, p. 1197.
[4] The suffix '*i*' designates the word 'in'.
[5] *Tukhārī Chhant* 5 (3), *AG*, p. 1112.
[6] *Sirī Rāgu* 22, *AG*, p. 22.
[7] *Dhanāsarī* 4, *AG*, p. 661.
[8] *Dhanāsarī Aṣṭ* 1 (7), *AG*, p. 686; *Bilāvalu Thitī* (18), p. 840.
[9] *Gauṛī* 12, *AG*, p. 154; *Āsā* 22, p. 356.
[10] *Siddh Goṣṭi* (24), *AG*, p. 940; *Prabhātī* 14, p. 1331.
[11] *Tilaṅg* 1, *AG*, p. 725.

common is *sahaj*, the ineffable radiance beyond the *dasam duār*.[1] It is difficult to distinguish his *sahaj* from that of the Nāth yogīs, for in both cases we have a word which must be beyond the understanding of all who have not experienced the condition which it represents.[2] Gurū Nānak was in emphatic disagreement with Nāth method,[3] but in both cases similar claims are made on behalf of the ultimate state called *sahaj*. For both it has a climactic content which unfolds in absolute equipoise and absolute tranquillity, and for both it is a condition existing beyond the cycle of transmigration. The Nāths did indeed seek, in their own terms, to express their experience with some precision, but the descriptions are negatives or logically insoluble paradoxes which can have no real meaning outside the mystical experience which generated them. Moreover, the most characteristic of all such expressions, the *anahad śabad*, is used by Gurū Nānak as one of the symbols expressing the condition as he experienced it.[4]

Comparisons with Nāth descriptions can provide little help without the actual experience, and the same must also apply to any assistance which we may seek from Sūfī sources. The question which arises from the latter comparison is whether Gurū Nānak offers any symbol which seems to correspond in any way to the Sūfī concept of *baqā'*, of a continuing existence within the condition of union with God. The question cannot be finally answered, although there is certainly no evidence of direct Sūfī influence at this point. The image of the soul as a fish swimming in the ocean which is God seems to suggest such a continuing existence,[5] but the commoner figures of water merging in water and light blending in light point to a notion of total absorption. Gurū Nānak's own response would doubtless be that the answer can be found only in personal experience.

We are faced with the ineffable and must be content with descriptions which impart only a fragment of understanding. The condition of union is, as we have already observed many times, one which transcends the cycle of birth and death.

> He who meditates on the divine Name finds peace, for protected by the *Gurū*'s instruction he cannot be consumed by Death.
> Without the Name the cycle of birth and death remains with us and suffering is our lot.[6]

> If one meets Him and does not part from Him transmigration ceases, for He is the True One.[7]

[1] *Gauṛī Aṣṭ* 15 (2), *AG*, p. 227; *Rāmakali Aṣṭ* 3, pp. 903–4. For Gurū Nānak's usage of *dasam duār*, 'the tenth door', see *Mārū Solahe* 13 (1), 16 (2), 19 (4), and 20 (2), *AG*, pp. 1033–40 *passim*.

[2] M. Eliade, *Yoga: Immortality and Freedom*, p. 268. Ch. Vaudeville, *Kabīr Granthāvalī* (*Dohā*), pp. xviii–xix.

[3] *Siddh Goṣṭi*, *AG*, pp. 938–46.

[4] *Sirī Rāgu* 18, *AG*, p. 21; *Āsā Chhant* 2 (1), p. 436.

[5] *Sirī Rāgu* 31, *AG*, p. 25.

[6] *Tukhārī Chhant* 2 (3), *AG*, p. 1110.

[7] *Sūhī* 4, *AG*, p. 729.

It is a condition of supreme wonder (*visamād*).

> None can know Thy limits, but understanding comes through the perfect *Gurū*.
>
> Nānak, immersed in the True One we are intoxicated with wonder, and struck with this wonder we sing His praises.[1]

And it is a condition of peace, of consummate joy and perfect tranquillity, a condition transcending all human telling.

> The body is the palace of God, His temple, His dwelling-place wherein He has shone light infinitely radiant. By the *Gurū*'s word one is summoned within the palace; there one meets with God.[2]

Beyond this is the unutterable.

[1] *Mārū Solahā* 15 (16), *AG*, p. 1036.

[2] *Malār* 5, *AG*, p. 1256.

6
THE PERSON

AN analysis of the janam-sākhīs will reveal a few details concerning the life of Gurū Nānak, and exegesis will produce from his works an integrated theology. Our final task must be to seek a synthesis which will unite the glimpses provided by the janam-sākhīs with the personality emerging from the works recorded in the *Ādi Granth.* The result must be to some extent a disappointment, for we do not have the material to provide an adequate impression extending over the complete range of the Gurū's lifetime. The Nānak of faith and legend can be described at great length, but the historical Nānak must remain in large measure hidden. We can, however, form a distinct impression of the Gurū Nānak of a particular period in his lifetime, and it is the period which in terms of his posthumous influence is by far the most important.

One respect in which the janam-sākhīs provide significant help concerns the threefold division of the Gurū's lifetime which may be safely deduced from them. There seems to be little doubt that his seven decades should be divided into, first, a period of approximately three decades covering his childhood and early manhood in Talvaṇḍī and Sultānpur; secondly, a period of two decades spent in travelling; and, finally, two concluding decades of relatively settled existence in the village of Kartārpur.[1] The division into decades is unlikely to correspond exactly with the actual pattern of his life, but can be accepted as a sufficiently accurate method of defining the limits of the three recognizable periods.

It is the third of these periods which evidently emerges through the pages of the *Ādi Granth.* Many of Gurū Nānak's recorded works will have originated during the time of his travels, and some may go back even further, but the Kartārpur years must have been the period of definitive utterance. These were the years when Gurū Nānak was surrounded by disciples who received instruction from him and who presumably recorded what they had received. His compositions, if not actually committed to writing during his lifetime, must certainly have been recorded within a few years of his death. It is, indeed, entirely possible that they may have been first recorded in writing by Gurū Nānak himself, for unlike many of the religious figures of this period he was obviously not illiterate. This,

[1] See *supra*, p. 145.

moreover, was the period in which he gave practical expression to his own ideals, the period in which he combined a life of disciplined devotion with worldly activities, set in the context of normal family life and a regular *satsang*.

Of the first period we know relatively little, for the janam-sākhīs are almost totally unreliable in their accounts of these early decades. This applies particularly, and inevitably, to his childhood years. We may, however, assume a certain amount on the basis of the limited help provided by the janam-sākhīs and our knowledge of contemporary conditions, and in the light of the mature expression recorded in the *Ādi Granth*. We know, for example, that he was a khatrī of the Bedī sub-caste and that accordingly he belonged to a respected family. To this we may add the indisputable fact that he was brought up in a Pañjāb village and that his growth to manhood took place during a relatively settled period. This would mean a life dictated by the agricultural nature of the village economy and consequently by the seasonal round still so characteristic of rural Pañjāb. It would have been a round of contrasting cold and heat, of labour in the fields and enforced rest during the months of summer barrenness, of the striking resurrection of the land and of men's spirits with the breaking of the monsoon rains, and of the regular festivals marking the high points in this annual cycle. All of this would inevitably have constituted the stuff of his childhood experiences and the beauty of his *Bārah-māhā*[1] bears testimony to the manner in which it influenced him. It was presumably a healthy childhood, for there is no evidence of any serious physical illness having ever afflicted him, and the natural diet of the Pañjāb, with its wheat, its milk, and its green vegetables, is one of the best the world can offer. During this period he must also have received a regular schooling, perhaps from a private tutor but more likely in one of the small charitable schools which were attached to some of the mosques and temples at this time. The compositions recorded in the *Ādi Granth* are certainly not the work of an illiterate or semi-literate author.

The later part of this first period is more obscure, for during adolescence and adulthood individual experience diversifies and we can no longer make assumptions on the basis of a regular pattern. At some stage, presumably during adolescence, he was married and two sons were subsequently born to him, but there seems to be every likelihood that the janam-sākhīs are basically correct in depicting this as a time of increasing restlessness and of resort to sādhūs, faqīrs, and other such holy men. This would explain the subsequent years of travel and also seems natural in view of his deep understanding of contemporary religious belief and practice.

We can, however, affirm nothing categorically concerning the stages of

[1] *Tukhāri Chhant Bārah-māhā*, *AG*, pp. 1107–13. The *bārah-māhā* (literally 'twelve-month') is a conventional poetic form based upon the seasonal cycle.

development through which he passed during his growth to maturity, and any assumptions we make must be strictly tentative. It is perhaps reasonable to postulate a growing dissatisfaction with traditional religious beliefs and practices, and a growing attraction towards Sant ideas acquired from sādhūs with whom he happened to come in contact. In doing so, however, we offer little more than conjecture. That dissatisfaction and attraction of this kind did occur is an obvious assumption, but we do not really know when or in what manner this development took place, neither can we trace the procedures whereby he evolved his own interpretation of the Sant tradition. These years are not altogether hidden years, for we can accept the janam-sākhī claim that part of this period was spent in Sultānpur. They are, however, years of general obscurity.

This conclusion applies with even greater force to the second period, the years of travel. Having rejected the janam-sākhī accounts we are once again reduced to assumption and conjecture, neither of which can take us far. It is, of course, evident that during these years he must have lived the life of a wanderer, subsisting as so many have done in India on the charitable offerings of the devout. We may also assume that he would have sought the company of others of similar outlook and that with them he would have engaged in discussion, in the sharing of experiences, and in the singing of God's praises. Much of his time would be devoted to imparting teaching to those who were prepared to hear it, and at other times he would engage in debate people with whose religious beliefs or practices he disagreed. Such debates would have been held with yogīs, with other exponents of pronounced ascetic ideals, and with the upholders of traditional Hindu and Muslim observances. The years of restlessness were presumably succeeded by assurance and tranquillity, and we may assume that it would be during this period that his beliefs took definitive shape.

It must be emphasized that our procedure for this period is based upon assumption and conjecture. Such assumptions do, however, receive a measure of support from Gurū Nānak's own works. In them we encounter a recurrent didactic note, a repeated emphasis upon the value of singing praises in the company of true believers, and expressions which unmistakably evoke the atmosphere of debate. These features must be related primarily to the Kartārpur period, but by no means exclusively. It seems entirely reasonable to suppose that the pattern which they suggest must also have applied to the years of wandering.

It is when we reach the third period of Gurū Nānak's life that we at last pass beyond this dependence upon assumption and conjecture. We move now into a period which was spent in or near the Pañjāb, and which brings us as near as we can approach to the time when the janam-sākhīs were actually compiled. The janam-sākhī records accordingly assume a somewhat greater degree of reliability. They do not in fact tell us much about the events of the period, but this is understandable and significant, for it suggests that authentic knowledge and memory may have acted in some measure as checks upon the proliferation of legend. We also reach in this concluding phase the period in which Gurū Nānak must have communicated to his followers the works which have been recorded in the *Ādi Granth*.

During this third and final period we find Gurū Nānak settled on the banks of the Rāvī in the village of Kartārpur. The Gurū is now more than fifty years old. Behind him lie many years of religious endeavour and the time has come for the application of the ideals which have matured during those preceding years. His fame has spread and in accordance with immemorial tradition prospective disciples have gathered to learn from one whom they can acknowledge as a preceptor and master.

Within the Kartārpur community of those years there was evidently applied a pattern of threefold activity. In the first place there must have been an insistence upon regular disciplined devotion, both individual and corporate. The disciple was required, in imitation of his master, to arise early and devote the 'ambrosial hour'[1] to meditation upon the divine Name. This Gurū Nānak clearly enjoined and accordingly this must have been the discipline which he himself observed. Other hours are not specified, but the emphasis laid upon such meditation and also upon the corporate singing of praises (*kīrtan*) makes it clear that devotional activity must have occupied much of Gurū Nānak's own time and that his disciples would have been expected to follow his example. *Kīrtan* was presumably held both in the early morning, following individual meditation, and also in the evening following the conclusion of the day's work.

A second feature of the Kartārpur pattern would have been the regular instruction imparted by the Gurū. Such instruction would frequently have been given to individual followers, but the form in which we find it recorded in the *Ādi Granth* will correspond more closely to the instruction delivered in the regular gatherings of his disciples. The content would, however, be the same. In both cases there would be the same emphasis upon the greatness of God, upon His gracious self-revelation, upon the perils of the human condition, and upon the paramount necessity of meditation on the divine Name. Trust in conventional external forms would be exposed as essentially futile, sometimes by means of gentle irony and at other times by direct denial of their efficacy. Those who placed their confidence in status conferred by caste or by wealth would be sternly admonished, and any who descended to religious hypocrisy would be roundly condemned.

All of this is plainly evident from his works and so too is the recurrent dialectic strain which suggests frequent debates. Many disputations must

[1] *amrit velā sachu nāu vaḍiāī vichāru*. *Japji* 4, *AG*, p. 2. See *supra*, p. 217.

have been held with Nāth yogīs for, as we have already observed, members of this sect are addressed directly in several polemical compositions. Nāth yogīs would have been natural opponents, both because of the manner in which their theories and practices conflicted with those of Gurū Nānak, and because of the considerable influence which they still exercised over the popular mind of the Pañjāb. On one occasion the Gurū evidently travelled to a neighbouring Nāth centre in order to meet and dispute with yogīs of the sect.[1] It seems clear that they must have absorbed much of his attention and the subsequent decline of their influence in the Pañjāb must be regarded as one of his most striking victories.

The third feature of the Kartārpur pattern would presumably have been regular daily labour. In the works of Gurū Nānak asceticism is explicitly rejected and in its place a disciplined worldliness is set forth as the proper path for the believer. A necessary part of this disciplined worldliness was the insistence that the believer should live on what he had himself laboured to receive.[2] At this point we return once again to assumption, but in the light of Gurū Nānak's pronouncements on this particular subject it seems entirely reasonable to suppose that regular labour must have been a part of the Kartārpur community discipline. Whether Gurū Nānak himself participated is impossible to say. His position as leader of the community would certainly have freed him from any obligation to do so, but a concern to practise in his own life what he exhorted others to do may well have led him to join his followers in their daily labours. His concept of a disciplined worldliness also enjoined a continuation of normal family relationships and we may accordingly accept the janam-sākhī indications that his wife and sons lived with him in Kartārpur during this period.

The impression which emerges is that of a deeply devout believer absorbed in meditation and rejoicing in the manifestations of the divine presence, but refusing to renounce his family or his worldly occupation. Discipline there certainly was, but not renunciation and total withdrawal. The impression is also that of a revered teacher giving expression to his experience in simple direct hymns of superb poetic quality. Around him would be gathered a group of regular disciples, and many more would come for occasional *darśan*, or audience, with the master. And the impression is that of a man, gentle and yet capable of sternness, a man of humour and mild irony who could nevertheless reprimand and if necessary denounce, a man who experienced the inexpressible and who yet maintained an essentially practical participation in the everyday affairs of his community and of the world beyond it.

The combination of piety and practical activity which Gurū Nānak manifested in his own life he bequeathed to his followers and it remains

[1] His visit to Achal.
[2] See *supra*, p. 211.

characteristic of many who own him as Gurū today. At its best it is a piety devoid of superstition and a practical activity compounded with determination and an immense generosity. It explains much that has happened in the Pañjāb during the last four centuries and it explains much that can be witnessed there today.

BIBLIOGRAPHY

English, French, and German (including translations from Persian, Panjabi, etc.)

'ABDUL HALIM, *History of the Lodi Sultans*, Dacca, 1961.

ABU'L FAZL, *Āīn-i-Akbarī*, vol. ii, Eng. trans. H. S. Jarrett, Calcutta, 1891.

—— *Akbarnāma*, vol. i, Eng. trans. H. Beveridge, Calcutta, 1897–1903.

AHMAD SHAH, *The Bījak of Kabīr*, Hamirpur, U.P., 1917.

—— and ORMEROD, E. W., *Hindi Religious Poetry*, Cawnpore, 1925.

ANANDA ACHARYA, *Snow-birds*, London, 1919.

ARBERRY, A. J., *Sufism*, London, 1950.

ARCHER, JOHN CLARK, 'The Bible of the Sikhs', *The Review of Religion*, January 1949.

—— *The Sikhs in relation to Hindus, Moslems, Christians, and Ahmadiyyas*, Princeton, 1946.

ASHRAF, K. M., 'Life and Conditions of the People of Hindustan (1200–1550 A.D.)', *JRASB*, 1935, vol. 1, part i, pp. 103–359; and Jiwan Prakashan, Delhi.

AZIZ AHMAD, *Studies in Islamic Culture in the Indian Environment*, Oxford, 1964.

BADĀUNĪ, *Muntakhab al-Tawārīkh*, vol. i, Eng. trans. G. A. S. Ranking, Calcutta, 1898.

BANERJEE, I. B., *Evolution of the Khalsa*, vol. i, Calcutta, 1936.

BARTH, A. *The Religions of India*, London, 1882.

BARTHWAL, P. D., *The Nirguna School of Hindi Poetry*, Benares, 1936. Also in Hindi translation: *Hindī kāvya men nirguṇa sampradāya*, trans. Paraśu-rām Chaturvedī, Lucknow, S. 2007 (A.D. 1950).

BASHAM, A. L., *The Wonder that was India*, London, 1954.

BEALE, T. W., *An Oriental Biographical Dictionary*, London, 1894.

BEVERIDGE, A. S., *The Bābur-nāma in English*, London, 1921.

BHANDARKAR, R. G., *Vaisnavism, Saivism and Minor Religious Systems*, Strasbourg, 1913.

BINGLEY, A. H., *Sikhs*, Simla, 1899.

BRIGGS, G. W., *The Chamārs*, Calcutta, 1920.

—— *Gorakhnāth and the Kānphaṭa Yogīs*, Calcutta, 1938.

BRIGGS, JOHN (trans.), *History of the Rise of the Mahomedan Power in India till the year A.D. 1612* (Firishta), London, 1829.

—— *The Siyar-ul-Mutakherin* (G͟hulām Husain K͟hān), London, 1832.

BROWN, JOHN P., *The Darvishes, or Oriental Spiritualism* (ed. H. A. Rose), London, 1927.

BROWNE, JAMES, *Indian Tracts, containing a description of the Jungle Terry Districts. . . . Also an History of the Origin and Progress of the Sicks*, London, 1788.

CANDLER, EDMUND, *The Mantle of the East*, Edinburgh and London, 1910.

CARPENTER, J. E., *Theism in Medieval India*, London, 1921.

CHHABRA, G. S., *The Advanced Study in the History of the Punjab*, vol. i, Jullundur, 1960.

CHHAJJU SINGH, *The Ten Gurus and their Teachings*, Lahore, 1903.

COURT, HENRY, *History of the Sikhs*, Lahore, 1888 (Eng. trans. of Sardhā Rām's *Sikhān de rāj dī vitthiā*).

CUNNINGHAM, J. D., *A History of the Sikhs*, London, 1849.
CUST, R. N., 'The Life of Bâbâ Nânak, the Founder of the Sikh Sect', in the *Indian Antiquary*, iii (1874), pp. 295–300.
DALJIT SINGH, *Guru Nanak*, Lahore, 1943.
DASGUPTA, SHASHIBHUSAN, *An Introduction to Tantric Buddhism*, Calcutta, 1958.
—— *Obscure Religious Cults as Background of Bengali Literature*, Calcutta, 1946.
DASGUPTA, SURENDRANATHA, *A History of Indian Philosophy*, Cambridge, 1922–55.
—— *Yoga as Philosophy and Religion*, London, 1924.
DE BARY, WM. T., *et al.* (compilers), *Sources of Indian Tradition*, New York, 1958.
DOWSON, JOHN, *A Classical Dictionary of Hindu Mythology &c*, London, 1961.
ELIADE, MIRCEA, *Yoga: Immortality and Freedom*, London, 1958.
ELLIOT, H. M., and DOWSON, J., *The History of India as told by its own Historians*, vols. iii, iv, and v, London, 1871–3.
FARQUHAR, J. N., *Modern Religious Movements in India*, New York, 1919.
—— *An Outline of the Religious Literature of India*, London, 1920.
FIELD, DOROTHY, *The Religion of the Sikhs*, London, 1914.
FORSTER, GEORGE, *A Journey from Bengal to England &c*, London, 1808.
GANDA SINGH, *Contemporary Sources of Sikh History (1469–1708)*, Amritsar, 1938.
—— (ed.) *Early European Accounts of the Sikhs*, Calcutta, 1962.
—— (trans.) *Nānak Panthīs, or the Sikhs and Sikhism of the 17th Century*, Eng. trans. with original Persian text of a chapter from Muhsin Fānī, *Dabistān-i-Mazāhib*, Madras, 1939.
—— *A Select Bibliography of the Sikhs and Sikhism*, Amritsar, 1965.
GOPAL SINGH, *The Song of Nanak*, Eng. trans. of the *Japjī*, London, 1955.
—— *Sri Guru-Granth Sahib*, Eng. trans. of the *Ādi Granth*, Delhi, 1962.
GORDON, J. J. H., *The Sikhs*, London, 1904.
GREENLEES, DUNCAN, *The Gospel of the Guru-Granth Sahib*, Adyar, Madras, 1952.
GRENARD, FERNAND, *Baber, Fondateur de l'Empire des Indes*, Paris, 1930.
GRIERSON, G. A., *The Modern Vernacular Literature of Hindustan*, Special Number of the *Journal of the Asiatic Society of Bengal*, vol. lvii for 1888, Calcutta, 1889.
GRIFFIN, LEPEL, 'Sikhism and the Sikhs' in *The Great Religions of the World*, New York, 1901.
GURSHARN SINGH BEDI, *The Psalm of Life*, Eng. trans. of the *Japjī*, Amritsar, 1952.
HARBANS SINGH, *The Heritage of the Sikhs*, Bombay, 1964.
HARNAM SINGH, *The Japji*, Delhi, 1957.
HODIVALA, S. H., *Studies in Indo-Muslim History*, Bombay, 1939 and 1957.
HOPKINS, E. W., *The Religions of India*, London, 1896.
IBBETSON, DENZIL, *Panjab Castes*, Lahore, 1916.
IKRAM, S. M. (ed. Ainslie T. Embree), *Muslim Civilization in India*, New York, 1964.
IRFAN HABIB, 'Evidence for Sixteenth-century Agrarian Conditions in the Guru Granth Sahib', *The Indian Economic and Social History Review*, vol. i, no. 3, Jan.–Mar. 1964, pp. 64–72.
JIWAN SINGH, *Japjee Sahib*, Calcutta, 1935.
JODH SINGH, *The Japji*, Amritsar, 1956.
—— 'Religion and religious life as conceived by Guru Nanak' (tract), Anandpur Sahib, 1925.
—— *Some Studies in Sikhism*, Ludhiana, 1953.
JOGENDRA SINGH, *Thus Spake Guru Nanak*, Madras, 1934.
KAPUR SINGH, *Parasharprasna, or the Baisakhi of Guru Gobind Singh*, Jullundur, 1959.

KARTAR SINGH, *Life of Guru Nanak Dev*, Ludhiana, 1958. Also in Panjabi translation: *Jīvan kathā Srī Gurū Nānak Dev Jī*, Lahore, 1947.
KEITH, A. BERRIEDALE, *The Religion and Philosophy of the Vedas and Upanishads*, Cambridge, Mass., 1925.
KHALIQ AHMAD NIZAMI, *The Life and Times of Shaikh Farid-u'd-din Ganj-i-Shakar*, Aligarh, 1955.
KHAZAN SINGH, *History and Philosophy of Sikhism*, Lahore, 1914.
KHUSHWANT SINGH, *A History of the Sikhs*, vol. i, Princeton and London, 1963.
—— *Jupji: the Sikh Prayer*, London, n.d.
—— *The Sikhs*, London, 1953.
KIRPAL SINGH, *A Catalogue of Punjabi and Urdu Manuscripts in the Sikh History Research Department*, Amritsar, 1963.
LAL, K. S., *Twilight of the Sultanate*, London, 1963.
LANE-POOLE, S., *Babar*, Oxford, 1899.
LATIF, MUHAMMAD, *History of the Punjab*, Calcutta, 1891.
LEYDEN, J., and ERSKINE, WM., (trans.), *Memoirs of Zehīr-ed-Dīn Muhammed Baber Emperor of Hindustān*, London, 1826.
LOEHLIN, C. H., *The Sikhs and their Book*, Lucknow, 1946.
—— *The Sikhs and their Scriptures*, Lucknow, 1958.
MACAULIFFE, M. A., *The Sikh Religion*, Oxford, 1909. Vol. i also in Panjabi translation: *Jīvan Srī Gurū Nānak Dev Jī*, trans. Sujān Singh, Amritsar, n.d.
MACDONELL, A. A., *Vedic Mythology*, Strasbourg, 1897.
M'GREGOR, W. L., *The History of the Sikhs*, London, 1846.
MACNICOL, NICOL, *Indian Theism from the Vedic to the Muhammadan Period*, London, 1915.
MAHĪPATI, *Nectar from Indian Saints*, Eng. trans. of Mahīpati's Marāṭhī *Bhaktalīlāmrit* by Justin E. Abbott, N. R. Godbole, and J. F. Edwards, Poona, 1935.
—— *Stories of Indian Saints*, Eng. trans. of Mahīpati's Marāṭhī *Bhaktavījaya* by Justin E. Abbott, and N. R. Godbole, Poona, 1933.
MALCOLM, JOHN, *Sketch of the Sikhs*, London, 1812.
MOELLER, VOLKER, 'Die Lebensdaten des Glaubensstifters Nanak', in *Indo-Iranian Journal*, vol. vii, 1964, no. 4, pp. 284–97.
MOHAMMAD NOOR NABI, *Development of Muslim Religious Thought in India from 1200 A.D. to 1450 A.D.*, Aligarh, 1962.
MOHAN SINGH UBEROI, *A History of Panjabi Literature*, Amritsar, 1956.
—— *An Introduction to Panjabi Literature*, Amritsar, 1951.
—— *Kabīr—His Biography*, Lahore, 1934.
MONIER-WILLIAMS, M., *Brahmanism and Hinduism*, London, 1891.
MUHAMMAD IQBAL, 'Sikhs', art. in *The Encyclopaedia of Islam*, Leyden and London, 1934.
MUHSIN FĀNĪ, *Dabistān-i-Mazāhib*, Eng. trans. *The Dabistan or School of Manners* by David Shea and Anthony Troyer, Paris, 1843.
—— *Nānak Pānthis or the Sikhs and Sikhism of the 17th Century*, Eng. trans. of a portion of the *Dabistān-i-Mazāhib* by Ganda Singh, Madras, 1939.
NARAIN SINGH, *Guru Nanak Re-interpreted*, Amritsar, 1965.
—— *Our Heritage*, Amritsar, n.d.
NARANG, GOKUL CHAND, *The Transformation of Sikhism*, Lahore, 1912.
NICHOLSON, R. A., *The Mystics of Islam*, London, 1963.
NI'MATULLAH, *Niamatullah's History of the Afghans*, Eng. trans. of Ni'matullah's *Makhāzan-i-Afghānī*, part i, by Nirodbhusan Roy, Śantiniketan, 1958.
NIZĀMUDDĪN AHMAD, *Tabaqāt-i-Akbarī*, Eng. trans. by B. De, Calcutta, 1927–40.
OMAN, J. C., *The Mystics, Ascetics, and Saints of India*, London, 1903.

PANDEY, A. B., *The First Afghan Empire in India*, Calcutta, 1956.
—— *Early Medieval India*, Allahabad, 1965.
PANIKKAR, K. M., 'The Ideals of Sikhism' (tract), Amritsar, 1924.
PARKASH SINGH, *The Sikh Gurus and the Temple of Bread*, Amritsar, 1964.
PARRY, R. E., *The Sikhs of the Punjab*, London, 1921.
PAYNE, C. H., *A Short History of the Sikhs*, London, 1915.
PINCOTT, F., 'Sikhism', art. in T. P. Hughes's *A Dictionary of Islam*, London, 1885.
POLLET, GILBERT, *Studies in the Bhakta Māla of Nābhā Dāsa*, thesis presented to the University of London for the degree of Ph.D., 1963.
PRASAD, ISHWARI, *The Life and Times of Humayun*, Calcutta, 1955.
PRINSEP, H. T., *Origin of the Sikh Power in the Punjab and the political life of Muharaja Runjeet Singh*, Calcutta, 1834.
PRITAM SINGH, *Saints and Sages of India*, New Delhi, 1948.
PURAN SINGH, *The Book of the Ten Masters*, London, 1926.
QURESHI, I. H., *The Administration of the Delhi Sultanate*, Lahore, 1944.
RADHAKRISHNAN, S., *Indian Philosophy*, London, 1929.
—— *The Principal Upanisads*, London, 1953.
RAHIM, M. A., *History of the Afghans in India*, Karachi, 1961.
RAMA KRISHNA, LAJWANTI, *Les Sikhs*, Paris, 1933.
—— *Pañjābī Ṣūfī Poets*, Calcutta, 1938.
RANBIR SINGH, *Glimpses of the Divine Masters*, New Delhi, 1965.
RICE, CYPRIAN, *The Persian Sufis*, London, 1964.
RIZVI, SAIYID ATHAR ABBAS, *Muslim Revivalist Movements in Northern India in the Sixteenth and Seventeenth Centuries*, Agra, 1965.
ROSE, H. A. (ed.), *A Glossary of Tribes and Castes of the Punjab and North-West Frontier Province*, Lahore, 1911–19.
ROSS, DAVID, *The Land of the Five Rivers and Sindh*, London, 1883.
SARDUL SINGH CAVEESHAR, *The Sikh Studies*, Lahore, 1937.
SCOTT, G. B., *Religion and Short History of the Sikhs 1469–1930*, London, 1930.
SEN, KSHITIMOHAN, *Medieval Mysticism of India*, London, 1935.
SEWARAM SINGH THAPAR, *Sri Guru Nanak Dev*, Rawalpindi, 1904.
—— *The Divine Master*, Lahore, 1930.
SHARMA, KRISHNA, *Early Indian Bhakti with special reference to Kabir, a Historical Analysis and Re-interpretation*, thesis presented to the University of London for the degree of Ph.D., 1964.
SHER SINGH GYANI, *Philosophy of Sikhism*, Lahore, 1944.
SINGH, G. B., 'Sikh Relics in Eastern Bengal', in the *Dacca Review*, vol. v, nos. 7 and 8, Oct. and Nov. 1915, pp. 224–32; no. 10, Jan. 1916, pp. 316–22; and nos. 11 and 12, Feb. and Mar. 1916, pp. 375–8.
SOHAN SINGH, *The Seeker's Path*, Bombay, 1959.
STEINBACH, H., *The Punjaub*, London, 1845.
STULPNAGEL, C. REBSCH, *The Sikhs*, Lahore, 1870.
SUBHAN, J. A., *Sufism: Its Saints and Shrines*, Lucknow, 1960.
SURINDAR SINGH KOHLI, *A Critical Study of the Adi Granth*, New Delhi, 1961.
—— *Outlines of Sikh Thought*, New Delhi, 1966.
TARA CHAND, *Influence of Islam on Indian Culture*, Allahabad, 1963.
TARAN SINGH, *Guru Nanak as a Poet*, thesis presented to the University of Panjab for the degree of Ph.D., 1959.
DE TASSY, GARCIN, *Histoire de la Littérature Hindoui et Hindoustani*, vol. i, Paris, 1839.
TEJA SINGH, *Essays in Sikhism*, Lahore, 1944.

TEJA SINGH, *Growth of Responsibility in Sikhism*, Bombay, 1948.
—— 'Guru Nanak and his Mission' (tract), Lahore, 1918.
—— *The Japji*, Lahore, 1930.
—— *The Sikh Religion*, Kuala Lumpur, 1937.
—— *Sikhism: Its Ideals and Institutions*, Bombay, 1951.
—— and GANDA SINGH, *A Short History of the Sikhs*, vol. i, Bombay, 1950.
TEMPLE, R. C., *The Legends of the Panjâb*, Bombay and London, 1884–6.
THORNTON, D. M., *Parsi, Jaina and Sikh*, London, 1898.
THORNTON, T. H., *History of the Punjab*, London, 1846.
TITUS, MURRAY T., *Islam in India and Pakistan*, Madras, 1959.
TRIPATHI, R. P., *Some Aspects of Muslim Administration*, Allahabad, 1936.
TRUMPP, ERNEST, *The Ādi Granth*, London, 1877.
VAUDEVILLE, CHARLOTTE, *Au Cabaret de l'Amour: Paroles de Kabîr*, Paris, 1959.
—— *Kaḇīr Granthāvalī (Dohā)*, Hindi text with French translation, Pondichéry, 1957.
—— 'Kabīr and Interior Religion', in *History of Religions*, vol. iii, no. 2, Winter 1964, pp. 191–201.
WARD, WM., *Account of the Writings, Religion, and Manners of the Hindoos*, vol. iv, 'Account of the Sikhs', pp. 383–406, Serampore, 1811.
—— *A View of the History, Literature, and Mythology of the Hindoos*, vol. iii, chap. ix, London, 1822.
WESTCOTT, G. H., *Kabir and the Kabir Panth*, Cawnpore, 1907.
WILKINS, CHARLES, 'Observations and Inquiries concerning the Seeks and their College at Patna, in the East-Indies', an article reprinted in *Dissertations and Miscellaneous Pieces relating to the History and Antiquities, the Arts, Sciences, and Literature of Asia* by sundry authors, Dublin, 1793.
WILLIAMS, L. RUSHBROOK, *An Empire Builder of the Sixteenth Century*, London, 1918.
WILSON, H. H., *Sketch of the Religious Sects of the Hindus*, Calcutta, 1846.
—— 'A Summary Account of the Civil and Religious Institutions of the Sikhs', *JRAS*, vol. ix (1848), pp. 43–59.
YAHYĀ IBN AHMAD SIRHINDĪ, *Tarīkh-i-Mubārak Shāhī*, Eng. trans. K. K. Basu, Baroda, 1932.
YUSUF HUSAIN, *Glimpses of Medieval Indian Culture*, London, 1959.

ANON., *The History of the Sikhs*, Calcutta, 1846.
Cambridge History of India, vols. 3 and 4.
The Cultural Heritage of India, vol. iv, *The Religions*, Calcutta, 1956.
Encyclopaedia of Islam, Leyden and London, 1913–38. New edition: 1960—in progress.
The History and Culture of the Indian People, vol. iv, *The Delhi Sultanate*, Bombay, 1960.
Imperial Gazetteer of India, Oxford, 1908.
Punjab State Gazetteers.
Selections from the Sacred Writings of the Sikhs, trans. by Trilochan Singh, Jodh Singh, Kapur Singh, Harkishen Singh, and Khushwant Singh, London, 1960.
The Sikh Religion, a Symposium by M. Macauliffe, H. H. Wilson, Frederic Pincott, John Malcolm, and Sardar Kahan Singh, Calcutta, 1958.
Sikhism and Christianity in the Punjab, special issue of *Religion and Society*, vol. xi, no. 1, Mar. 1964.

Pañjābī and other works in Gurmukhī

Ādi Srī Gurū Granth Sāhib Jī, Srī Damdamī Bīṛ, various printed editions. Standard pagination 1430 pp.

Ādi Granth, BM MS Or. 1125.

DĀN SIṄGH, *Khālsā Tavārīkh dā Pahilā Pattrā*, Amritsar, 1937.

GOPĀL SIṄGH, *Pañjābī Sāhit dā Itihās*, Chandigarh, 1962.

—— *Srī Gurū Granth Sāhib dī sāhitak viśeṣatā*, Delhi, 1958.

GURBAKHSH SIṄGH (G. B. Singh), *Srī Gurū Granth Sāhib diān Prāchīn Bīṛān*, Lahore, 1944.

GURDĀS BHALLĀ (Bhāī Gurdās), *Kabitt Savayye*, Amritsar, 1925.

—— *Vārān Bhāī Gurdās*, ed. Hazārā Siṅgh and Vīr Siṅgh, Amritsar, 1962.

GYĀN SIṄGH, *Panth Prakāś*, Amritsar, 1923.

—— *Tavārīkh Gurū Khālsā*, Amritsar, 1914.

HARBANS SIṄGH, *Japu-niraṇay*, Chandigarh, 1963.

HARINDAR SIṄGH RŪP, *Bhāī Gurdās*, Amritsar, 1952.

JANAM-SĀKHĪ, *Colebrooke Janam-sākhī* (*Valāitvālī Janam-sākhī*), IOL MS Panj. B6, S 1728.

—— Photozincograph Facsimile of the *Colebrooke Janam-sākhī*, Dehra Dun, 1885.

—— Lahore Siṅgh Sabhā lithographed edition of the *Colebrooke Janam-sākhī*, Lahore, 1884.

—— a janam-sākhī published by M. Macauliffe with introduction by Gurmukh Siṅgh, being the *Hāfizābād Janam-sākhī*, Rawalpindi, 1885.

—— *Purātan Janam-sākhī*, edited by Vīr Siṅgh, Amritsar, several editions.

—— a janam-sākhī related to the *Purātan* tradition, IOL MS Panj. B40.

—— *Miharbān Janam-sākhī*, MS no. SHR: 427 of the Sikh History Research Department, Khalsa College, Amritsar, being *Pothī Sach-khaṇḍ, Pothī Harijī*, and *Pothī Chatarbhuj* of the *Miharbān Janam-sākhī*.

—— Miharbān Jī Soḍhī, *Janam-sākhī Srī Gurū Nānak Dev Jī*, being *Pothī Sach-khaṇḍ* of the *Miharbān Janam-sākhī*, edited by Kirpāl Siṅgh and Shamsher Siṅgh Ashok, Amritsar, 1962.

—— A *Bālā* janam-sākhī, IOL MS Panj. B41, S. 2885.

—— A *Bālā* janam-sākhī, BM MS Or. 2754. I.

—— A *Bālā* janam-sākhī, SOAS MS. no. 104975.

—— A *Bālā* janam-sākhī, Hāfaz Qutub-dīn, Lahore, S. 1928 (A.D. 1871).

—— A *Bālā* janam-sākhī, Mālik Dīvān Būṭā Siṅgh, Lahore, S. 1928 (A.D. 1871).

—— A *Bālā* janam-sākhī, Maulvī Maibūb Ahmad, Lahore, A.D. 1890.

—— A *Bālā* janam-sakhi, Munshī Gulāb Siṅgh and Sons, Lahore, several editions.

—— *Gyān-ratanāvalī* (*Manī Siṅgh Janam-sākhī*), Manuscript in the possession of Professor Prītam Siṅgh, Patiala.

—— *Gyān-ratanāvalī* (*Manī Siṅgh Janam-sākhī*), Charāg Dīn and Sarāj Dīn, Lahore, A.D. 1891.

—— *Mahimā Prakāś Vāratak*, Khalsa College, Amritsar, MS SHR: 2308.

—— *Mahimā Prakāś Kavitā*, Khalsa College, Amritsar, MS SHR: 2300A.

—— *Jīvan kathā Srī Gurū Nānak Dev Jī Mahimā Prakāś* (*Vāratak*) *vichon*, ed. Kirpāl Siṅgh, Bedi Printing Press, Dehra Dun, 1959.

JODH SIṄGH, *Bhagat Bāṇī Saṭīk*, Ludhiana, 1957.

—— *Gurū Nānak Simaratī Viākhiān*, Patiala, 1967. (Punjabi University Gurū Nānak Memorial Lectures for 1966–7.)

JODH SIṄGH, *Guramati Niraṇay*, Ludhiana, n.d.
—— *Ṭikā Japujī Sāhib*, Amritsar, 1911.
KĀHN SIṄGH NĀBHĀ, *Guramat Prabhākar*, Lahore, 1898.
—— *Gurumat Mārtaṇḍ*, Amritsar, 1962.
—— *Guruśabad Ratanākar Mahān Koś*, 1st ed. in four vols., Patiala, 1931; 2nd ed. revised with Addendum, in one vol., Patiala, 1960.
KĀLĀ SIṄGH BEDĪ, *Gurū Nānak Bhāṣā*, New Delhi, 1962.
—— *Gurū Nānak Niraṅkārī*, New Delhi, 1966.
—— *Gurū Nānak Daraśan*, New Delhi, 1965.
KARAM SIṄGH, *Gurapurb Niraṇay*, Amritsar, 1913.
—— *Kattak ki Visākh?*, Amritsar, 1913.
MAHINDAR SIṄGH RANDHĀVĀ, (ed.) *Pañjāb*, Patiala, 1960.
MAHITĀB SIṄGH, *Śrī Gurū Granth Sāhib Jī vich dite nāvān te thāvān dā koś*, Lahore, 1933.
MOHAN SIṄGH UBERĀI, *Pañjābī Bhākhā te Chhandābandī*, Lahore, 1938.
NARAIṆ SIṄGH, *Sikh Dharam diān Buniādān*, Amritsar, 1966.
PRATĀP SIṄGH, *Bhagat Daraśan*, Amritsar, 1944.
RATTAN SIṄGH BHAṄGŪ, *Prachīn Panth Prakāś*, Amritsar, 1962.
RATTAN SIṄGH JAGGĪ, *Dasam Granth dā Paurāṇik Adhiāin*, Jullundur, 1965.
—— *Vichār-dhārā*, Patiala, 1966.
—— (ed.), *Vārān Bhāī Gurdās: Śabad Anukramaṇikā ate Koś*, Patiala, 1966.
SĀHIB SIṄGH, *Bhagat-bāṇī Saṭīk*, Amritsar, 1959–60.
—— *Śalok Bhagat Kabīr Jī*, Amritsar, 1949.
—— *Srī Gurū Granth Sāhib Darapaṇ*, 10 vols., Jullundur, 1962–4.
SANTOKH SIṄGH, *Nānak Prakāś* and *Sūraj Prakāś*, 13 vols. edited by Vīr Siṅgh and comprising: vol. 1, *Śrī Gur Pratāp Sūraj Granthāvali dī Prasāvanā*, being Vīr Siṅgh's Introduction; vols. 2–4, *Śrī Gur Nānāk Prakāś*; vols. 5–13, *Śrī Gur Pratāp Sūraj Granth*, Amritsar, 1927–35.
—— *Vāratak Srī Nānak Prakāś*, prose summary of the *Nānak Prakāś* by Naraiṇ Siṅgh, Taran Tāran, 1941.
SARDHĀ RĀM, *Sikhān de Rāj dī Vitthiā*, Lahore, 1892.
SHAMSHER SIṄGH ASHOK, *Pañjābī Hath-likhatān dī Sūchī*, 2 vols., Patiala, 1961 and 1963.
SHER SIṄGH GIĀNĪ, *Guramati Daraśan*, Amritsar, 1962.
—— *Vichār Dhārā*, Ludhiana, n.d.
—— *Vichār Mālā*, Ludhiana, 1951.
TĀRAN SIṄGH, *Gurū Nānak, chintan te kalā*, Amritsar, 1963.
TEJĀ SIṄGH, *Japujī (Saṭīk)*, Patiala, 1952.
——*Sikh Dharam*, Patiala, 1952.
TEJĀ SIṄGH OVERSEER, *Khālsā Rahit Prakāś*, Lahore, 1914.
VĪR SIṄGH, *Pañj Granthī Saṭīk*, Amritsar, 1950.
—— *Santhyā Srī Gurū Granth Sāhib*, 7 vols., Amritsar, 1958–62.
—— *Srī Gurū Nānak Chamatkār*, 2 vols., Amritsar, 1928 and 1933.

Guru Śabad Ratan Prakāś, Line Index of the *Ādi Granth*, Patiala, 1963 (original edition compiled by Kaur Siṅgh Nihaṅg entitled *Srī Gurū Śabad Ratan Prakāś*, Peshawar, 1923).
Mahānkavī Gurū Nānak, Patiala, 1956.
Śabadārath Srī Gurū Granth Sāhib Jī, text and commentary on the *Ādi Granth*, n.p., 1936–41.
Srī Gurū Granth Bāṇī Beurā, Amritsar, 1914.
Śrī Gurū Granth Koś, 3 vols., Amritsar, 1950.

Hindī

BHAGĪRATH MIŚRA and RĀJNĀRĀYAṆ MAURYA, *Sant Nāmdev kī Hindī Padāvalī*, Poona, 1964.

GOVIND TRIGUṆĀYAT, *Kabīr kī vichār-dhārā*, Kanpur, S. 2009, (A.D. 1952).

HAZĀRĪ-PRASĀD DVIVEDĪ, *Hindī sāhitya*, Delhi 1955.

—— *Hindī sāhitya kā ādikāl*, Patna, S. 2009 (A.D. 1952).

—— *Hindī sāhitya kī bhūmikā*, Bombay, 1950.

—— *Kabīr*, Bombay, 1950.

—— *Nāth-sampradāy*, Varanasi, 1966.

JAYARĀM MIŚRA, *Śrī Gurū Granth Darśan*, Allahabad, 1960.

KABĪR, *Kabīr-granthāvalī*, ed. Śyāmsundardās, Prayag, 1928.

—— *Kabīr-granthāvalī*, ed. with introduction by Pāras-nāth Tivāri, Prayag, 1961.

—— *Kabīr kā pūrā Bījak*, ed. Prem Chand, Calcutta, 1890.

—— See also English etc., bibliography under Ahmad Shah and Vaudeville, Ch.

PARAŚU-RĀM CHATURVEDĪ, *Kabīr-sāhitya kī parakh*, Prayag, S. 2011, (A.D. 1954).

—— *Uttarī Bhārat kī sant-paramparā*, Prayag, 1951.

PRABHĀKAR MĀCHAVE, *Hindī aur Marāṭhī kā nirguṇ sant-kāvya*, Varanasi, 1962.

PURUṢOTTAM-LĀL ŚRĪVĀSTAVA, *Kabīr sāhitya kā adhyayan*, Varanasi, S. 2007 (A.D. 1950).

RAIDĀS, *Raidās jī kī bānī aur jīvan-charitr*, Belvedere Press, Allahabad, 1908.

RĀJNĀRĀYAṆ MAURYA, '*Hindī sāhitya men santamat ke ādi pravartak: Sant Nāmdev*', in *Journal of the University of Poona* (Humanities Section), no. 17, 1963, pp. 127–40.

RĀM-CHANDRA ŚUKL, *Hindī-sāhitya kā itihās*, Kaśi, S. 2014, (A.D. 1957).

RĀM-KUMĀR VARMĀ, *Sant Kabīr*, Allahabad, 1947.

RĀṄGEY RĀGHAVA, *Gorakhnāth aur unkā yug*, Delhi, 1963.

VINAY-MOHAN ŚARMĀ, *Hindī ko Marāṭhī santon kī den*, Patna, S. 2014 (A.D. 1957).

—— *Sant Nāmdev*, Delhi, n.d.

GLOSSARY

Ādi: first.
agiān (*ajñāna*): ignorance, nescience.
amar: immortal.
amrit (*amṛta*): the nectar of immortality.
anahad śabad: the mystical 'sound' or 'unstruck music' which is 'heard' at the climax of the *haṭha-yoga* process (q.v.).
antaḥkaraṇa: the collective mind; the seat of collective thought and feeling.
aṣṭapadī: a poem or hymn of eight, or occasionally more, stanzas.
Asū (*Aśvin*): the seventh month of the lunar year.
avatār: a 'descent'; incarnation of a deity, usually Viṣṇu.

Bābā: 'Father', a term of respect applied to sants, faqīrs, etc.
bāṇī (*vāṇī*): speech; the utterances of the Gurūs and *bhagats* (q.v.). recorded in the *Ādi Granth*.
baqā': the Sūfī concept of a continuing existence within the condition of union with God.
bārah-māhā: 'twelve-month' or calendar poem.
Bedī: a khatrī sub-caste.
Bhādon, Bhādron: the sixth month of the lunar year.
bhagat (*bhakta*): an exponent of *bhakti* (q.v.); a devotee.
bhakti: belief in, and adoration of, a personal God.
Bhāī: 'Brother', a title applied to Sikhs of learning and piety.
Bhallā: a khatrī sub-caste.
bhaṭṭ: a caste of bards and genealogists.
buddhi: the mind as the source of wisdom, intelligence.

chamār: an outcaste leather-worker.
chapātī: unleavened wholemeal bread.
chhant (*chhandas*): metre, measure; in the *Ādi Granth* a poem or hymn of variable length.
chitta: mind, intellect, reasoning faculty.
Choṇā: a khatrī sub-caste.

darśan: view, vision; audience with a person of regal or spiritual stature, visit to a holy shrine or object; the six systems of brahmanical philosophy.
darveś: dervish, a Muslim mendicant (esp. Sūfī).
dasam duār (*dasama dvāra*): 'the tenth door' as opposed to the nine physiological orifices of the human body; according to *haṭha-yoga* theory the mystical orifice which gives access to the condition of *sahaj* (q.v.).
deś: country.
dharma, dharam: the appropriate moral and religious obligations attached to any particular status in Hindu society.
Dharamrāj: *Yam* (q.v), the god of the dead in his role as divine arbiter of the fate of each individual.
dharmsālā: a place of worship; an inn (generally a religious foundation) for pilgrims and travellers.

dhikr: the Sūfī discipline of 'remembrance' or thinking on God.
Dhuppaṛ: a khatrī sub-caste.
dil: heart.
dīp **(*dvīp*)**: continent, island.
doāb: area between two rivers.
dohā: couplet.
Ḍūm, Ḍom: a depressed sub-caste of Muslim genealogists and musicians, also called *Mirāsīs*.

fanā': dying to self, the Sūfī concept of the merging of the individual self in the Universal Being.
faqīr: 'poor man', Muslim ascetic; loosely used to designate Sūfīs and also non-Muslim renunciants.

ghaṭ: heart; body.
ghāṭ: landing-place, bathing-place, place where corpses are cremated.
giān **(*jñāna*)**: knowledge, wisdom.
Gopāl: in Vaiṣṇava usage an epithet of Kriṣṇa ('Cow-herd'); in Sant and Sikh usage a name of the non-incarnated God.
goṣṭ: discourse.
guṇa: the three vital 'qualities' or constituents of cosmic substance which by their varying proportions determine the nature of all that exists.
gurdwārā: Sikh temple.
gurmukh: a follower of the Gurū.
gurū: a spiritual preceptor, usually a person but sometimes understood as the divine inner voice.
gurupadeś: the teaching of the Gurū.

Hari: in Vaiṣṇava usage Viṣṇu; in Sant and Sikh usage the non-incarnated God.
haṭha-yoga: 'yoga of force', a variety of yoga requiring physical postures and processes of extreme difficulty. For an account of its physiological theories see p. 191, n. 4. See also *Nāth* (q.v.).
haumai: self, self-centredness.
hiradā **(*hṛdaya*)**: heart.
hukam: order.

janam-sākhī: a traditional biography, esp. of Gurū Nānak.
janeū **(*yajñopavīta*)**: sacred thread.
jaṅgam: a member of a Śaivite sect of itinerant yogīs.
jīv: soul, spirit, psyche.
jñān: see *giān*.
julāhā: weaver caste.

kabitt: a poetic metre.
Kaliyug: 'the era of strife', the fourth and last of the cosmic ages; the age of degeneracy.
Kānphaṭ: 'split ear'; sect of yogīs, followers of Gorakhnāth and practitioners of *haṭha-yoga* (q.v.), so called because of their pierced ears in which rings are worn. Cf. *Nāth*.
karma: the destiny, fate of an individual, generated in accordance with the deeds performed in his present and past existences.
karoṛī: a high-ranking revenue collector of the Mughal period.

Kattak **(*Kārtik*)**: the eighth month of the lunar year.
kavitā: poem.
Khālsā: the Sikh order, brotherhood, instituted by Gurū Gobind Siṅgh.
khaṇḍ: region, realm.
khatrī: a mercantile caste, particularly important in the Pañjāb.
kīrtan: the singing of songs in praise of God, generally by a group and generally to the accompaniment of music.
kos, koh **(*krośa*)**: a linear measure varying from one to two miles in different parts of India. In the Pañjāb it has generally been computed as the equivalent of one and a half miles.

lākh: one hundred thousand.
laṅgar: public kitchen or refectory.
loṭā: a small metal vessel.

mahant: chief; superior of a monastery or other religious institution.
man **(*manas*)**: mind, heart, soul, psyche.
mañjī: a small string bed; areas of jurisdiction designated by Gurū Amar Dās.
manmukh: one who follows his own self-centred impulses rather than the guidance of the Gurū. (Cf. *gurmukh* q.v.)
mantra: a verse, phrase or syllable of particular religious import, in some cases believed to possess magical qualities.
maqāmāt: (plural form of *maqām*) the stages of spiritual development in the Sūfī ascent to mystical union.
mātā: mother.
mati: intellect.
maulānā: a title accorded to Muslim judges or other Muslims respected for their learning.
māyā: (in Vedānt) cosmic illusion; (in Sant and Sikh thought) the corruptible and corrupting world, with all its snares, presented to man as permanent and incorruptible and so masquerading as ultimate truth. In Sant and Sikh usage the term has strong moral overtones and is frequently symbolized by lucre and women.
miharāb: the niche in a mosque which indicates the direction of the *Ka'bah* (*qiblah*).
Mirāsī: See *Ḍūm*.
mullah: a teacher of the law and doctrines of Islam.
murāqabat: the Sūfī discipline of meditation.

nadar, nazar: sight, glance; grace.
Nām: the divine Name, the expression of the nature and being of God in terms comprehensible to the human understanding.
namāz: Muslim prayer, esp. the prescribed daily prayers.
narak: hell.
***Nāth*, sect**: A yoga sect of considerable influence during the time of Gurū Nānak. The origins of the sect are not wholly clear, but there can be no doubt that its development owed much to Śaivite teachings and to tantric Buddhism (the Vajrayāna or Sahajayāna school). The term *nāth* means 'master' and the *Ādināth*, or 'Original Master' was generally held to have been Śiva. In addition to the *Ādināth* there were believed to have been nine other *Nāths*, master yogīs who had attained immortality through the practice of *haṭha-yoga* (q.v.) and who were

supposed to be living far back in the fastnesses of the Himālayas. According to some traditions Śiva was one of the nine, but the leadership was generally accorded to Gorakhnāth. The idea of the nine immortal *Nāths* probably evolved by analogy with the eighty-four immortal *Siddhs* (q.v.) of tantric Buddhism, also accepted by the Nāth sect. All external ceremonies were rejected as futile, the inward discipline of *haṭha-yoga* being affirmed as the only means of obtaining immortality. Caste distinctions, sacred languages, and scriptures were also rejected as worthless. The yogīs of the Nāth sect exercised little influence upon the educated, but amongst the mass of the population they commanded a certain respect for their extreme austerities and a considerable fear on account of their supposed magical powers. The members of the sect are also called Kānphaṭ yogīs (q.v.).

nawāb: governor, viceroy.

nirguṇa: without 'qualities' or attributes, unconditioned. (Cf. *saguṇa*.)

Paltā: a khatrī sub-caste.

pāṇḍā: brāhmaṇ genealogist.

paṇḍit: an erudite person; a mode of address used for brāhmaṇs.

panth: path; sect; community.

param: supreme, ultimate.

paṭvārī: village land accountant.

pauṛī: lit. staircase; stanza.

pīr: the head of a Sūfī order; a Sūfī saint.

pīṭh-sthān: the fifty-one places where, according to tantric mythology, pieces of Satī's body fell after her dismemberment by Śiva.

poṭā: son's son; descendant in the male line.

pothī: volume.

prāṇāyām: breath control, a yoga technique.

pūjā: worship, esp. idol worship.

Pūran-māsī: the full-moon day.

qalandar: itinerant Muslim ascetic.

qāzī, qāḍī: a Muslim judge, administrator of Islamic law.

rāg: a series of five or more notes upon which a melody is based; melody.

ridā: heart.

Śabad (***Śabda***): Word, the divine self-communication. (The capitalization does not correspond to the Gurmukhī or Devanāgarī forms, but is used in transcription to indicate the distinction expressed in written English by 'Word' as opposed to 'word'. Cf. also *Nām, Hukam.*)

śabad (***śabda***): word. In Sikh usage a hymn of the *Ādi Granth*.

sach (***satya***): truth; true.

sādhanā: method of attaining or 'realizing' an ultimate spiritual objective.

sādhū: medicant, renunciant, ascetic. See also *Sant*.

saguṇa: possessing 'qualities', attributes; manifested, usually as an *avatār* (q.v.). Cf. *nirguṇa*.

sahaj: the condition of ultimate, inexpressible beatitude; the ultimate state of mystical union.

sākhī: (1) testimony, witness, evidence; (2) section of a *janam-sākhī* (q.v.); (3) *dohā*, couplet.

śakti: the energy or potency of a god (usually Śiva) expressed in his feminine counterpart. *Śakti* worship, performed by tantric sects (Hindu and Buddhist), commonly included magical *mantras* (q.v.) and symbols, sexual practices, and the consumption of flesh and alcohol. See also *Tantra*.

śālgrām (*śālagrāma*): ammonite found in the bed of the river Gaṇḍakī, prized as sacred stone on account of the spiral patterns in it which are regarded as representations of Viṣṇu.

sampradāya: sect, school, tradition.

saṅgat: a gathering, assembly, congregation.

Sant: In general usage *sant* serves as a synonym for *sādhū* (q.v.). The word has, however, two specific connotations: (1) a member of the Vārakarī sect of Maharashtra; (2) a member of the *Sant* tradition of Northern India, a loose fellowship of believers in a supreme, non-incarnated God. The usage in this study is normally the second of these two specific meanings. Within the tradition itself the term *sant* is used as a synonym for *sādh* or *sādhū* in the original sense of one who controls his senses (*indriya*) as opposed to the common modern and somewhat debased usage which designates an itinerant religious mendicant. In Kabīr's usage it denominates 'a perfected one', or 'one who has triumphed over death' (Ch. Vaudeville, *Kabīr Granthāvalī* (*Dohā*), pp. xiv–xv). The term is not used as a group or sectarian appellation until much later. It is to some extent an unsuitable designation, for it involves the risk of confusion with the Vārakarī sect. The alternative appellation *Nirguṇa Sampradāya*, or *Nirguṇa* tradition, avoids the risk of confusion in this respect, but the term *nirguṇa* ('attributeless', q.v.) is not a wholly accurate description of the Sants' understanding of the nature of God, except insofar as they explicitly rejected its antithesis, the *saguṇa* (q.v.) concept of divine *avatārs* (q.v.).

Satgurū: the True Gurū.

Sati Nām: the True Name.

satsaṅg: the fellowship of true believers, congregation.

savayyā: panegyric.

Siddh: Eighty-four exalted personages believed to have attained immortality through the practice of yoga and to be dwelling deep in the Himālayas. In the janam-sākhīs the term is frequently confused with *Nāth* (q.v.).

ślok: couplet or stanza.

sūbah: province.

sudī: the light half of a lunar month, the period of the waxing moon. Cf. *vadī*.

tahsīl: subdivision of a district.

takht: throne; seat of royal or spiritual authority.

Tantra: texts enunciating the forms of *śakti* worship (q.v.).

ṭhag: thug; strictly, a member of the cult of ritual murderers who strangled and robbed in the name of Kālī, but loosely used for any highwayman or violent robber.

ṭhāṇedār: officer in charge of a police station.

tilak: a sectarian or ornamental mark made upon the forehead.

tīrath: a sacred place, a place of pilgrimage.

tīrath-yātrā: a tour of important places of pilgrimage.

Trehaṇ: a khatrī sub-caste.

trimūrti: 'triple form', the Hindu triad comprising Brahmā, Viṣṇu, and Śiva, representing the creative, sustaining, and destructive principles respectively.

tulsī-mālā: a garland of basil leaves carried by Vaiṣṇavas.

turīā (*turīya*): the condition of ultimate bliss, a term derived from tantric Buddhism.

Udāsī: an order of ascetics who claim as their founder Sirī Chand, one of Gurū Nānak's two sons.

udāsī: lengthy journey, tour.
Uppal: a khatrī sub-caste.
ur: heart.

vadī: the dark half of a lunar month, the period of the waning moon. Cf. ***sudī***.
Vāhigurū: 'Wonderful Lord', God.
Vaikunṭh, Baikunṭh: the paradise of Viṣṇu.
Vaisākh, Baisākh: the second month of the lunar year.
vār: an heroic ode of several stanzas; a song of praise; a dirge.
vāratak: prose.
visamād: immense awe; ecstasy engendered by awe.

Yam: the god of the dead.
yug: cosmic era.

BIOGRAPHICAL INDEX

Events and relationships recorded in the janam-sākhīs *and other sources*

DOCTRINAL INDEX

Concepts and Terminology

GENERAL INDEX

Early Sikh Tradition

ACKNOWLEDGEMENTS

Early Sikh Tradition is the result of a year at the University of Cambridge made possible by a Smuts Fellowship. It is in fact the second and more substantial result of the academical year 1969–70, the first being the small volume of essays entitled *The Evolution of the Sikh Community* (Delhi 1975 and Oxford 1976). In *The Evolution of the Sikh Community* I expressed my deep appreciation to Professor E. E. Rich and the Managers of the Smuts Memorial Fund for their notable generosity and for the helpful interest which they took in my projects. I repeat these thanks with a sense of renewed gratitude. With the same recollection of pleasure and gratitude I also record once again my warm appreciation to the Provost and Fellows of King's College, and to the Dean and members of the Faculty of Oriental Studies. The friendship and the facilities which I received in my two Cambridge homes contributed handsomely to an enjoyable and productive year.

The original writing of *Early Sikh Tradition* and its subsequent revision have also been assisted by grants from other institutions. I owe a considerable debt of gratitude to the University of Otago for providing a thoroughly congenial place to work, for assistance with typing, and for continuing support in the form of research grants. One such grant covered the greater part of the expense required by a return visit to the Pañjāb in 1972. This visit was also aided by a grant from the Spalding Fund, a most welcome supplement for which I thank the Fund's trustees. I am likewise grateful to the British Academy for a generous grant towards the preparation of the book and to the trustees of the Isobel Thornley Bequest Fund for assistance with its actual publication. I acknowledge with thanks the fact that the trustees conferred on the book a sum which exceeded their normal maximum.

Numerous individuals have supplied information and advice or have assisted in the provision of research facilities and materials. In particular I should like to express my sincere thanks to Dr Raymond Allchin, Dr Amrik Singh, Professor N. G. Barrier, Mr Owen Cole, Mr Simon Digby, Miss E. M. Dimes, Mr Ben Farmer, Professor Fauja Singh, Dr Ganda Singh, Professor Richard Gombrich, Professor J. S. Grewal, Professor Harbans Singh, Professor Kirpal Singh, Dr Stuart McGregor, Professor Victor Ménage, Dr Albert Moore, Professor Piar Singh, Professor Pritam Singh, Principal Ram Singh, Professor G. S. Talib, and Dr John Webster. In thanking all who have assisted me I must expressly free them from association with any of the opinions expressed in this book and from responsibility for its errors. These I acknowledge to be mine alone.

Mr P. N. Kapoor of Delhi kindly permitted me to inspect his priceless *Bālā* manuscript, a favour for which I am most grateful. Guru Nanak Dev University and Punjabi University have frequently provided me with hospitality and with access to materials in their libraries. To their respective Vice-Chancellors I express my cordial thanks. For prompt, friendly and efficient service I thank and commend Messrs Singh Brothers, booksellers of Bazar Mai Sewan in Amritsar. For the same qualities as a typist I thank Miss Irene Marshall.

Ever since the early days of *Gurū Nānak and the Sikh Religion* I have enjoyed happy relationships with the Academic Division of the Oxford University Press. In particular I should like to thank Mr Peter Sutcliffe for his tactful guidance and unfailing encouragement. I should also like to thank his New Delhi colleague Mr Ravi Dayal and his Wellington colleague Mr John Griffin.

Finally, I must thank Margaret, Rory, Michael, Shaun and Ruth. They have been the principal sufferers, a fact which they seem determined to deny.

The University of Otago
Dunedin.

HEW McLEOD

CONTENTS

CONTENTS

ABBREVIATIONS

AG	The Ādi Granth.
Ā'in	Abu al-Fazl, *Ā'in-i-Akbāri*, trans. H. Blochmann and H. S. Jarrett, 3 vols., Calcutta, 1873–94.
AS	Piār Singh (ed.), *Śambhū Nāth vālī Janam Patrī Bābe Nānak Ji kī prasidh nān Ādi Sākhiān*, Paṭiālā, 1969. (Printed edition of a text of the *Ādi Sākhīs*.)
ASI	Alexander Cunningham, *Archaeological Survey of India* annual reports.
Aṣṭ	*aṣṭapadi*.
B40	The India Office Library manuscript Panj. B40. The folio numbers given in *B40* citations are the manuscript's original Gurmukhī numerals. The Gurmukhī pagination is given in the margin of both Piār Singh (ed.), *Janam Sākhī Sri Gurū Nānak Dev Jī* (Amritsar, 1974), and W. H. McLeod, *The B40 Janam-sākhī* (Amritsar, 1979).
B40(Eng)	W. H. McLeod, *The B40 Janam-sākhī* (Amritsar, 1979). English translation, with introduction and annotations, of the *B40 Janam-sākhī*.
B41	The India Office Library manuscript Panj. B41 (a *Bālā* janam-sākhī).
Bālā JS	The *Bālā* janam-sākhī lithographed by Hāfaz Qutub Dīn of Lahore in A.D. 1871.
BG	The *vārs* of Bhāī Gurdās.
BL	British Library.
Cole JS	The *Colebrooke Janam-sākhī*.
CPL	Central Public Library, Paṭiālā.
CUL	Cambridge University Library.
Enc Isl	*Encyclopaedia of Islam*, London, 1913–38.
Enc Isl (NE)	*Encyclopaedia of Islam* (*New Edition*) London, 1960– .
GNM	Sarūp Dās Bhallā, *Gurū Nānak Mahimā*, ed. Shamsher Singh Ashok and Gobind Singh Lāmbā, Paṭiālā, 1970. (Volume 1 of a printed edition of the *Mahimā Prakāś Kavitā*.)
GNSR	W. H. McLeod, *Gurū Nānak and the Sikh Religion*, Oxford, 1968. Repr. Delhi, 1976.
GR	The edition of the *Gyān-ratanāvalī* lithographed by Charāg Dīn and Sarāj Dīn, Lahore, A.D. 1891.
GTC	H. A. Rose (ed.), *A Glossary of the Tribes and Castes of the Punjab and North-West Frontier Province*, 3 vols., Lahore, 1911–19.
Haf JS	The *Hāfizābād Janam-sākhī*.

IA	*Indian Antiquary.*
IG	*Imperial Gazetteer of India.*
IOL	India Office Library.
LDP	The Languages Department of the Pañjāb Government, Paṭiālā.
LDP 194	Manuscript no. 194 of the LDP.
Macauliffe	M. A. Macauliffe, *The Sikh Religion*, 6 vols., Oxford, 1909.
Mih JS	*Janam-sākhī Srī Gurū Nānak Dev Jī*, ed. Kirpāl Singh *et al.*, 2 vols., Amritsar, 1962–9. (Printed edition of the extant text of the *Miharbān Janam-sākhī*.)
MK	Kāhn Singh Nābhā, *Guruśabad Ratanākar Mahān Koś* (commonly known as the *Mahān Koś*), 2nd edition revised with Addendum, Paṭiālā, 1960.
NPr	Santokh Singh, *Gur Nānak Prakāś* (the *Nānak Prakāś*.)
PHLS	Shamsher Singh Ashok, *Pañjābī hath-likhatān dī sūchī*, 2 vols., Paṭiālā, 1961–3.
PNQ	*Panjab Notes and Queries.*
PPP	*Panjab Past and Present.*
Pur JS	Vīr Singh (ed.), *Purātan Janam-sākhī*, 5th edition, Amritsar, 1959.
S	Samvat, dating according to the Vikramī era.
SLTGN(Eng)	Gaṇḍā Singh (ed.), *Sources on the Life and Teachings of Gurū Nānak* (English section), Gurū Nānak Birth Quincentenary edition of *PPP*, Paṭiālā, 1969.
SLTGN(Pbi)	Ibid. (Pañjābī Section).
SRL	Sikh Reference Library, Amritsar.

In the case of multiple-volume works footnote citations normally give two figures, separated by a full stop. The first figure specifies the volume number(s). The same form is also used for citations from Santokh Singh's *Gur Nānak Prakāś* (abbrev. *NPr*). In these *NPr* citations the first number indicates the section of work. (I designates the *pūrabāradh* section, and II the *utarāradh* section.)

In Ādi Granth references a single figure designates the number of a shabad or (in the case of a citation from a *vār*) the number of a *pauṛī*. A figure added in parentheses indicates a particular stanza (*aṅk*) within the designated shabad. (1R) indicates a reference from the *rahāu*, or refrain, of a shabad. Most *vār* references incorporate two figures, separated by a colon. This form is used for citations which refer to shaloks (*ślok*). The second figure designates the number of the shalok; and the first that of the *pauṛī* to which it is attached. For example, *Vār Malār* 3:2 designates the second of the shaloks attached to the third *pauṛī* of the *vār* in *Malār* rāga.

SECTION I

1

THE HISTORICAL SETTING

The Pañjāb 1500–1800

HISTORICAL periods always present problems of definition and Indian history is no exception. Sharp divisions must inevitably be blurred by persistent continuities. Most historians would agree, however, that the Mughal invasions together constitute an event of unusual importance, and for many this importance has been sufficient to warrant a clear period division at the year 1526, the occasion of Bābur's victory over Ibrāhīm Lodī on the field of Pāṇīpat.

In the case of the Pañjāb there is an additional reason for regarding the early decades of the sixteenth century as the prelude to a new period. During the last four-and-a-half centuries the most important development in Pañjāb history has unquestionably been the evolution of the Sikh community and its rise to a position of enduring prominence within the Land of the Five Rivers. This community had its beginnings in a group of disciples who gathered around their chosen teacher during the first half of the sixteenth century. While Bābur was securing his hold upon Northern India, Gurū Nānak was instructing his followers in a village of Central Pañjāb. Under his guidance there developed in the village of Kartārpur the religious community which we know today as the Sikh Panth. It was a community which during the period extending from the death of Nānak to the late eighteenth century was to ascend from the obscurity of Kartārpur to a position of predominance within the Pañjāb. As Mughal power in the north disintegrated, Sikh strength increased until eventually during the early decades of the nineteenth century the province became an avowedly Sikh kingdom, ruled in the name of the Khālsā by the celebrated Mahārājā Rañjīt Siṅgh.

Today the prominence of the Sikh Panth remains undiminished. Although the political and military glories of Rañjīt Siṅgh did not survive his death, the Panth, after a brief period of decline, soon recovered its vigour. Today its representatives are to be found scattered throughout the world. The wave of Indian immigration which in recent years has reached the United Kingdom consists largely of Pañjābīs, most of them Sikhs. An earlier wave of Pañjābī migration travelled to the east coast of North America, and during the same period ripples reached as far as the flax swamps and scrub-covered hills of New Zealand. During the past hundred years they have shown themselves to be a remarkably mobile people. In addition to the substantial communities in England, California, and British Columbia there are many thousands of Sikhs to be found in

South-East Asia, Hong Kong, Fiji, East Africa, and the Middle East.

Needless to say, the community as it exists today is no mere replica of the religious following which gathered around Nānak during the first half of the sixteenth century. Other influences have shaped the Panth during its subsequent history and the result is certainly not to be defined in exclusively religious terms. This should not, however, suggest an absence of direct links connecting the earliest disciples with their modern descendants. The Sikh Panth which confronts us today is the product of a process of transformation incipient within the earliest group of disciples and essentially complete by the end of the eighteenth century.

Nānak, the first of the Sikh Gurūs, was followed by a series of nine successors, all of them Pañjābīs. There was thus established a line of ten masters, corresponding in terms of time to the period of the Great Mughals. Gobind Siṅgh, the tenth and last of the succession, died in 1708, the year following the death of Auraṅgzeb.[1] Inevitably Sikh tradition concentrates almost exclusively upon the activities of the Gurūs and deals only indirectly with less obvious influences affecting the development of the community during the first two centuries of its existence. Of the more important of these influences one commands a particular significance in terms of its impact upon the evolving Panth. This was the caste constituency of the community.

The first six Gurūs all belonged to the mercantile Khatrī caste and all resided in villages of Central Pañjāb.[2] Their caste origins and their rural domicile were of crucial significance in the development of their following. The villages of Central Pañjāb contained a dominant concentration of Jaṭs, and in accordance with established tradition Khatrīs were accorded a role as the teachers of Jaṭs. This traditional status, together with the inherent appeal of the Gurūs' teachings, attracted a substantial following from amongst the Jaṭs, and during the course of the sixteenth and seventeenth centuries the Jaṭ segment of the Sikh community acquired a preponderance which it has never lost. The Sikhs entered the eighteenth century as a community still lead by a Khatrī succession, but strongly Jaṭ in membership. It was inevitable that the community should have been influenced by its numerically dominant element. Without relinquishing its loyalty to the teachings of Nānak it had assumed features which derived from its Jaṭ antecedents.

This pattern of development received a considerable impetus during the eighteenth century. In 1708 Gurū Gobind Siṅgh died without an heir. Ever since the time of the fourth Gurū a hereditary principle of succession

[1] The nine successors of Nānak were Aṅgad (1539–52), Amar Dās (1552–74), Rām Dās (1574–81), Arjan (1581–1606), Hargobind (1606–44), Har Rāi (1644–61), Har Kriṣaṇ (1661–4), Tegh Bahādur (1664–75), and Gobind Siṅgh (1675–1708).

[2] The remaining four Gurūs were also Khatrīs. Nānak and Aṅgad both passed over the members of their own families in choosing successors. Gurū Amar Dās bestowed the succession upon Jeṭhā, husband of his daughter and a Khatrī of the Soḍhī sub-caste. Jeṭhā assumed the name Rām Dās and in turn chose his youngest son Arjan as successor. Thereafter the succession remained within the male line of Soḍhīs descended from Rām Dās. The last four Gurūs were compelled to spend most of their time beyond the borders of the Pañjāb.

had been accepted and Gurū Gobind Siṅgh's death without surviving heirs brought a crisis. At first the answer appeared to be a transfer of the legitimacy to a different line and for this distinction the obvious candidate was a Sikh named Bandā Bahādur, or Bandā the Brave.

During the time of Gurū Arjan the Panth had begun to attract the unfavourable notice of the Mughal emperors and in 1606 Arjan had died in a Mughal prison. Skirmishes between Sikhs and the Lahore administration broke out during the period of Arjan's son, Hargobind, but these petered out when Hargobind withdrew to the Śivālik Hills in 1634. The period of peace which followed was abruptly terminated when in 1675 the ninth Gurū, Tegh Bahādur, was executed at Aurangzeb's command. Although Gurū Gobind Siṅgh remained in the Śivālik Hills for most of his life, his principal enemy was to be a Mughal force from Sirhind which entered a hills war against him. Immediately after his death and that of Aurangzeb Mughal authority in the Pañjāb declined rapidly. Persistent rural unrest now developed into a widespread rebellion and threw up a new Sikh leader. This was Bandā Bahādur.

Bandā's early successes against the Mughal administration in the Pañjāb qualified him in the eyes of many as a suitable successor to Gurū Gobind Siṅgh. It was, however, a disputed status, and his execution in 1716 finally settled the issue. A more dispersed variety of leadership now developed, together with other features which increasingly distinguish the later Sikh community from the earlier following of the Gurūs.

The eighteenth century was a period of considerable confusion. Earlier patterns of belief and behaviour were either extinct or largely unsuited to new needs and it is scarcely surprising that fresh patterns should have emerged during this turbulent period. As one might expect, the customs and ideals which now ascended to prominence within the Sikh Panth related closely to the cultural inheritance of the Panth's dominant element and to the distinctive circumstances which forced the change. The patterns which emerged under these pressures derived in large measure from Jaṭ antecedents and from the nature of the warfare which occupied the middle years of the century. For the Panth this crucial century began in 1699 and may be said to have concluded in 1799. In 1699 Gurū Gobind Siṅgh promulgated the Order of the Khālsā, the Sikh brotherhood which in its developed form has dominated subsequent Sikh history; and in 1799 Rañjīt Siṅgh secured control of Lahore, the key to the Pañjāb. The Khālsā brotherhood served as a focus of Sikh ideals throughout the century, faithfully reflecting in its evolving discipline the development and consolidation of these ideals.

Bandā's unsuccessful rebellion was followed by a period of restored Mughal authority and persecution of the Sikhs. This campaign was rarely pursued with any vigour, for the restoration was never strong and Nādir Shāh's invasion in 1739 brought another collapse. The restoration which followed Nādir Shāh's withdrawal was the last. The next invader, Ahmad Shāh Abdālī of Afghānistān, finally destroyed all hope of a Mughal revival in the Pañjāb.

Ahmad Shāh Abdālī's nine invasions covered the years from 1747 to 1769. The Afghān failed to establish himself in Northern India, but having destroyed the Mughals and seriously weakened the Marāṭhās Ahmad Shāh did serve to prepare the way for the establishment of Sikh authority. This authority first passed into the hands of twelve warrior bands or associations known as misls. These were independent groups of Sikhs bound in a loose confederation by their rural origins, by the ties of a common religious affiliation, and in the earlier days by opposition to a common enemy. The third of these was the more important, for the final withdrawal of Ahmad Shāh brought a period of internecine warfare amongst the misls. Eventually one of the chieftains, Rañjīt Siṅgh of the Shukerchakīā misl, secured an ascendancy over the remainder. This brought him to sovereignty over the entire area of the Pañjāb, and with the establishment of that sovereignty the most significant period in Sikh history came to an end. Although the teachings of Nānak had never been abandoned, the community which, in the form of the evolved Khālsā, emerged at the end of the eighteenth century was something radically different from the group of disciples who first gathered at Kartārpur.

This account covers in outline the period from the time of Nānak to the emergence of the fully-fledged Khālsā.[1] It should be added that whereas an outline can be sketched with a certain distinctness much of the detail remains very obscure. Sources for the period are few and generally unsatisfactory, and conclusions concerning this earlier period must be in part dependent upon social patterns described in sources which relate to later periods. An obvious source for the early period is the Ādi Granth, the scripture compiled by Gurū Arjan during the years 1603 and 1604. The Ādi Granth provides an abundance of information concerning the religious beliefs of Nānak and his immediate successors, but the historian who pursues a wider social, economic, or political interest must labour hard in order to extract from it the material which he requires. Material of this sort, although certainly present, is not provided in a readily accessible form.

The help offered by Persian sources is also limited. Several Persian chronicles deal with this period, but almost all of them direct their courtly interest away from the Pañjāb. Only two significant exceptions exist. One is the *Ā'īn-i-Akbarī*, which several times refers to features of the Lahore Sūba;[2] and the other the *Khulāsāt-ut-Tavarikh* of Sujān Rāi Bhaṇḍārī. Sujān Rāi was a native of Baṭālā and his narrative, which was completed in 1696, largely concerns his native province.[3] The section on the Nānak-panthīs in the *Dabistān-i-Mazāhib*[4] and Nūr Muhammad's

[1] For a fuller outline of the same period see W. H. McLeod, *The Evolution of the Sikh Community* (Oxford, 1976), chaps. 1 and 3.

[2] *Ā'īn* II. 310–47.

[3] For an English translation of Sujān Rāi's treatment of the Pañjāb see Muhammad Akbar, *The Punjab Under the Mughals* (Lahore, 1948), pp. 285–311.

[4] David Shea and Anthony Troyer, *The Dabistan or School of Manners*, vol. ii (Paris, 1843), pp. 246–88. Most of the section dealing with the Nānak-panthīs has also been translated by Gaṇḍā Singh in *PPP* I. i (April 1967), pp. 47–71. The portion of the latter translation dealing specifically with Guru Nanak also appears in *SLTGN(Eng)*, pp. 45–53.

Jaṅg-nāma[1] might also be added, but beyond these four works there is little except the brief comments included in such works as the *Bābur-nāma* and the *Tuzuk-i-Jahāṅgirī*. Although European visitors subsequently had much to say about the Pañjāb, and although some of their material is of great value, the principal contributors all arrived too late to observe the critical period of Sikh development or to secure access to reliable sources.[2]

In view of this paucity of source material it is perhaps surprising that the devotional literature of the Sikhs has not received more attention. In such circumstances problems associated with the reading and analysis of the Ādi Granth do not constitute a sufficient reason for continuing to neglect it, nor do they provide adequate justification for our undisturbed ignorance of other early products of the Sikh community. Three varieties of devotional literature deserve particular attention. First there are the poetic works of Bhāī Gurdās, a nephew of the third Gurū and a contemporary of the three Gurūs who followed him. The *vārs* of Bhāī Gurdās constitute a source of considerable importance, one which has yet to receive the close scrutiny and analysis which it deserves. Secondly, there is the substantial Dasam Granth, a heterogeneous collection of writings attributed to the tenth Gurū. Although the attribution seems plainly erroneous for the bulk of its contents this in no way impairs their value, for all are products of the period of Gurū Gobind Siṅgh or of the years immediately following his death. With this collection should be bracketed the Persian compositions of Nand Lāl Goya, another Sikh of the same period. Thirdly there are the *janam-sākhīs*, hagiographic accounts of the life of Nānak. These had their first beginnings in the late sixteenth century, flourished during the seventeenth century, and then decreased as other concerns increasingly dominated the Panth's interest. The decline has, however, never been total. Janam-sākhīs are still extensively read today.[3]

This study concerns the third of these categories. In the case of the janam-sākhīs the problem has been one of misunderstanding rather than total neglect. The various janam-sākhīs purport to narrate the events of the life of Nānak and it is as generally trustworthy biographies that they have hitherto been used. This accords them a reliability which they do not possess, while ignoring the considerable interest and value which they do in fact offer. The janam-sākhīs are important as examples of hagiographic growth-processes, as sources of Pañjāb history for the post-Nānak period within which they developed, as a cohesive factor in subsequent Sikh history, and as the earliest works of Pañjābī prose. The purpose of this study will be to examine these four aspects of the janam-sākhī literature.

[1] An English translation by Gaṇḍā Singh was published by Khalsa College, Amritsar, in 1939.

[2] The more important of these early observers were: James Browne, *History of the Origin and Progress of the Sicks* (published with his *Indian Tracts*, London, 1788); George Forster, *A Journey from Bengal to England &c.* (London, 1808); John Malcolm, *Sketch of the Sikhs* (first published in *Asiatick Researches*, vol. xi, Calcutta, 1810, pp. 197–292, and reprinted separately, London, 1812); H. T. Prinsep, *Origin of the Sikh Power in the Punjab &c.* (Calcutta, 1834); W. L. M'Gregor, *The History of the Sikhs* (London, 1846); J. D. Cunningham, *A History of the Sikhs* (London, 1849). See also Gaṇḍā Singh (ed.), *Early European Accounts of the Sikhs* (Calcutta, 1962).

[3] For surveys of all three varieties see W. H. McLeod, op. cit., chaps. 2 and 4.

2

THE JANAM-SĀKHĪS

A Definition and Summary Description

THE janam-sākhīs are commonly defined as 'biographies of Gurū Nānak'. This standard description is mentioned here only in order to reject it. Whatever else the janam-sākhīs may be they are certainly not biographies. It is true that they do concern the person of Gurū Nānak, and it can also be claimed that certain elements within the janam-sākhīs must assuredly derive from authentic incidents associated with the actual life of Nānak. This does not, however, mean that they can be regarded as biographies, nor that they can be uncritically used as sources for the life of the Gurū. Much misunderstanding has resulted from the application of this mistaken interpretation of the janam-sākhīs.

The janam-sākhīs are properly defined not as biographies of Gurū Nānak, but as hagiographic accounts of his life. They are tradition in precisely the same sense as the *Hadith*, and although they lack some of the features associated with their Muslim counterpart they have nevertheless developed in response to the same impulses, and in a less formalized manner they have fulfilled much the same role within their parent community. Although the distinction between biography and hagiography may seem obvious, it has in practice been largely ignored and much misunderstanding has consequently persisted. Until the distinction is clearly understood there can be no appreciation of the true nature of the janam-sākhīs, nor of their manifold contents. It is not sufficient to interpret them as nuclei of authentic tradition overlaid and in some measure obscured by the legendary accretions of later periods. There are indeed a few isolated anecdotes which appear to fit this description, but it is not an accurate representation of the janam-sākhīs as a whole. Even when stripped of all their wonder stories the janam-sākhīs do not offer an account of the actual events of the Gurū's life. What they do provide is an *interpretation* of that life, an interpretation springing from the piety and commitment of later generations.

This fundamental distinction may be expressed in a slightly different way. The janam-sākhīs find their origin not in the actual life of Nānak but rather in a myth which derives from that life. The word 'myth' will recur during the course of this analysis and it is of vital importance to the analysis that its meaning in this context should be clearly understood. This clarification is all the more important because the term is a newcomer to Sikh studies. Although 'myth' has for long been used in a technical sense by scholars working in biblical and Near Eastern studies, and although the concept has proved so valuable to social anthropologists, there are still extensive areas largely untouched by it. Sikh tradition provides one such area, one which offers considerable scope for fruitful application of a particular understanding of the concept.

In this context it is most important that the term 'myth' should not be interpreted as a synonym for 'legend'. Although legendary material has been extensively used in the janam-sākhīs to give expression to the myth which constitutes their origin the two terms must be kept rigidly distinct. As far as the purpose and the function of the janam-sākhīs are concerned this distinction between legend and myth is of much greater importance than the difference between legend and the authenticated historical event. Whenever the janam-sākhīs are used as a source for the actual life of Gurū Nānak the latter distinction becomes primary, and the historian who seeks to reconstruct the events of the Gurū's life must endeavour to separate the authentic elements embedded in the janam-sākhīs from the vast quantity of strictly spurious material within which they are set. This, however, is not the principal role or value of the janam-sākhīs. Their principal role has concerned their function within the later community; and as historical sources their value lies chiefly in their testimony to the period and the society within which they evolved. For an analysis of either the role of the janam-sākhīs or of their primary historical value the distinction between legend and history is of little practical importance. It is the myth which matters, and the myth can be served with equal advantage by both legend and history, provided only that the legendary element does not do serious violence to accepted conventions. In this sense myth is a fundamental aspect of the janam-sākhīs. It therefore follows that a firm grasp of this particular usage is a pre-requisite for any sufficient understanding of their true nature.

According to this usage a myth is a construct of the human imagination, developing out of an actual situation and seeking to give meaning to that situation. It is, in other words, an interpretation based upon a particular understanding of a given array of circumstances. This interpretation must be expressed in concrete form. It evolves in response to particular needs and if it is to survive it must continue to fulfil its distinctive function for the society within which it took shape. As long as it retains the capacity to do so it will survive. If it is to retain an acceptable relevance it must evolve in accordance with the changing needs and understanding of the society which it serves, for when it loses its capacity to fulfil a relevant function it will wither. Eventually it will either die or, if it lingers on, will survive as a cultural curiosity. Although every myth should accord with accepted norms of truth and reality, neither its rise nor its survival will relate primarily to such issues. It is the function which must sustain it and when a myth ceases to fulfil its function it must either change or make way for a more effective substitute.

Myths may be expressed in a wide variety of forms. They may exist in oral or in written tradition, and in either case they may be poetry or narrative prose. They may be drama, sagas, anecdotes, or series of discourses. Their conscious emphasis may be religious, historical, philosophical, or a mixture of all and much more besides. Though commonly expressed in oral or recorded tradition myth is not necessarily limited to the spoken or written word. It may be expressed in the ritual of a sacrifice, in the structure of a liturgy, in the design of a building, or in the multitude of customs observed by a particular society. The range of possibilities is enormous. Every society must find means of expressing its myths and any form which will provide a concrete and immediately comprehensible expression qualifies thereby as an appropriate vehicle.

It is in precisely this sense that the janam-sākhīs have served as the vehicle of a powerful myth, one which still commands a wide acceptance within the society which developed it. The myth which they express may be briefly stated as follows. Bābā Nānak was the divinely commissioned giver of salvation. To all who would seek salvation the way lies open. The means of salvation consists in loyalty to the person of Bābā Nānak and acceptance of his teachings. This is the myth. The form which was developed to give it expression was the narrative anecdote which, in relating some incident concerning the life of Nānak, sought to authenticate the claims made on his behalf. These anecdotes, collected into anthologies or structured 'biographies', constitute the janam-sākhīs.

Let it be stressed once again that the issue does not involve questions of historical truth, at least not in a primary sense. The fundamental question to ask of a myth should concern not its historical truth but its functional utility. Inevitably the janam-sākhī narrators have employed both historical and legendary material in order to give concrete expression to the myth of Bābā Nānak. It is, for example, safe to accept as historically accurate their claim that Nānak was born in Talvaṇḍī village, in the year S.1526 (A.D. 1469), and that he was the son of Kālū Bedī.[1] This is a statement of actual fact and it is also a part of the myth. Having made this statement concerning place, date, and parentage, the narrators add that a mighty concourse of celestial beings hailed his birth—three hundred and thirty million gods, eighty-four Siddhs, nine Nāths, sixty-four Yoginīs, fifty-two Vīrs, and six Jatīs.[2] Legend has been joined to historical fact but the myth remains the same.

This example will at once suggest the Lucan account of the Nativity. Jesus, the son of Mary and Joseph, born in Palestine, is greeted at his birth by the heavenly host of angels.[3] The authentic statement is coupled with a legendary element in order to express one aspect of the myth of Jesus. For an analysis of this kind the question is not whether the myth of Nānak or the myth of Jesus is true. In either case the issue can be affirmed only by an act of faith.

The nature of the janam-sākhī myth is clearly indicated by the declarations of purpose which some of the narrators attach to their collections of

[1] *B40*, f. 1.

[2] Ibid. For Siddhs and Nāths see below, pp. 68–9, 296. Yoginīs, Vīrs, and Jatīs are legendary figures possessing superhuman powers.

[3] Luke 2:2–14.

anecdotes. In one of the more important janam-sākhīs it is expressed in the following terms:

He who reads or hears this sākhī shall attain to the supreme rapture. He who hears, sings or reads this sākhī shall find his highest desire fulfilled, for through it he shall meet Gurū Bābā Nānak. He who with love sings of the glory of Bābā Nānak or gives ear to it shall obtain joy ineffable in all that he does in this life, and in the life to come salvation.[1]

The word *sākhī* which is here used by the writer to designate his work means, literally, 'testimony'. This is precisely what the janam-sākhīs are intended to be. They are testimonies to the belief which, in its concrete form, becomes the myth of Nānak. In a more specific sense they are, or claim to be, witnesses to actual episodes from the life of Nānak. These episodes are believed to authenticate the soteriological status of Nānak which constitutes the fundamental myth. For this reason the earliest collections were styled simply *sākhīān*, or 'Testimonies'.

It was not long, however, before the title was expanded and the word *sākhī* underwent a slight shift in meaning. One of the earlier collections assumed the title *janam-patrī* ('horoscope' or, more precisely, the piece of paper on which a person's horoscope is recorded).[2] Although in a strict sense the expression *janam-patrī* related only to the opening anecdote describing the birth of Nānak it came to be applied to the collection as a whole. It was consistently used as a title for the collection which had first appropriated it, and eventually coalesced with the earlier term. The word *patrī* was dropped and *sākhī* substituted to form the new compound *janam-sākhī*.

This compound has been used ever since and continues to be used today. Although in a literal sense it can be translated as 'testimonies to the birth (of Nānak)' it no longer projects this meaning. The coalescence has produced a different sense. The translation which best accords with the popular understanding of the meaning of janam-sākhī today is 'biography' and, as we have already observed, this is the term which is most commonly used in English translation. The word *sākhī* has, meanwhile, assumed a somewhat different connotation when used in this context. Occasionally one encounters a usage which implies the earlier meaning of 'witness' or 'testimony'. The usual meaning in modern usage is, however, an 'episode' or 'chapter' from the 'biography' of Nānak. Individual incidents are recorded separately or in integrated series, and each incident or series is called a *sākhī*. The individual *sākhīs* have been gathered into collections, some random and some ordered. These collections constitute the janam-sākhīs.

Although janam-sākhīs of other religious figures have since been

[1] *AS*, p. 101. See also *Mih JS* I. 1.

[2] This was the title used by the janam-sākhīs of the *Bālā* tradition. *Bālā JS*, p. 2. The same term is also affixed to the collection known as the *Ādi Sākhīs*, but in this latter case may perhaps be a copyist's addition. *AS*, p. 1. Piār Singh, 'A Critical Survey of Panjabi Prose in the Seventeenth Century' (unpublished Ph.D. thesis, Panjab University, 1968), p. 68.

written,[1] the term is generally restricted to collections of tales concerning Gurū Nānak, and if used without any specific indication of its subject it will invariably refer to him. As a result *janam-sākhī* is commonly translated not simply as 'biography' but as 'biography of Gurū Nānak'. Whereas this is certainly an accurate representation of the meaning popularly attached to the term today, it must again be emphasized that it is in fact a misrepresentation. The emphasis is necessary because of the extensive misunderstanding which still results from a persistent use of the janam-sākhīs as historical accounts of the life of Nānak. This was the method followed at the turn of the century by M. A. Macauliffe and in this sense his ghost is still very much with us. The janam-sākhīs do indeed have a considerable importance as historical sources, but only a limited measure of that importance relates to their usefulness as sources for the life of Nānak. Their primary significance as historical source-material lies elsewhere. It consists, first, in the role which the janam-sākhīs have played in the subsequent history of the Sikh community. Secondly, it is to be found in those elements incorporated within the janam-sākhīs which relate to the period of their actual emergence rather than to the earlier period of Gurū Nānak. In both respects the importance chiefly concerns the period stretching from the sixteenth century to the early eighteenth century. The first of these will be more fully explained when dealing with the function of the janam-sākhīs.[2] The second will be treated in the section which discusses the contribution of the janam-sākhīs as historical sources.[3]

The customary interpretation of the janam-sākhīs must accordingly be rejected and an effort made to redefine them. A janam-sākhī is a collection of hagiographic anecdotes concerning the person of Gurū Nānak (A.D. 1469–1539). These anecdotes, both individually and in their collective form, all serve to express a single myth relating to the life and teachings of Nānak, namely that he was sent into the world by God to demonstrate the way of salvation to an erring and confused mankind. In order to express this myth the anonymous narrators responsible for the various anecdotes have drawn in some small measure from authentic memories concerning the actual life of Nānak, and in considerable measure from current legend.

Some of the individual anecdotes are the product of simple borrowing from earlier traditions, whereas others derive from complicated growth processes. Most of the borrowings and much of the growth process must be related to the period of oral transmission. This not only preceded the first recording of anecdotes, but continues to the present day. As a result the expansion of the janam-sākhī traditions, though particularly active during the seventeenth century, is still continuing. It was during the late sixteenth or early seventeenth century that material drawn from oral sources was first recorded in written form. The earlier written collections (and some of their later descendants) recorded individual anecdotes in a random manner, the only deference to chronology being a simple sequence of birth, childhood, manhood, and death. Later collections devised more

[1] There exist janam-sākhīs of Kabīr and Nāmdev.

[2] See below, pp. 244–7.

[3] Chap. 14, pp. 250–67.

detailed chronological structures and reordered the individual anecdotes to accord with these predetermined patterns. In some instances a later manuscript will represent a generally faithful copying of an earlier version, but in most cases there will be some significant departures. Earlier versions are commonly augmented by the addition of minor details, extra anecdotes, or clusters of anecdotes, and are sometimes distinguished by alterations in the chronological pattern. In some instances supplementary manuscripts have served as sources for such additions, and in others the later copyist has drawn from current oral tradition.

The language of most janam-sākhīs is Pañjābī and until the nineteenth century the script was almost invariably Gurmukhī. Versions copied in the Arabic script do eventually appear, but they are exceedingly rare. Although distinct variations of language are to be found within the janam-sākhīs only occasionally are they sufficient to justify any claim that a writer has actually abandoned Pañjābī. Three principal varieties of linguistic difference are to be found. There is, first, a range of dialects extending from the Mājhī of the central tract (the Bārī Doāb) to the Poṭhohārī of Rāwalpiṇḍī District. Secondly, there is within the narrative traditions a gradual change from the primitive Pañjābī prose of the earliest manuscripts to the more refined language of the latest letterpress editions. Thirdly, there is a pronounced difference between the same crude Pañjābī of the earliest manuscripts and the sophisticated language of that variety of later janam-sākhī which stresses exegesis rather than narrative.

Several of the copyists have recorded the date on which they completed their work, and if to their manuscripts we add the modern printed editions the period which they span runs from the middle of the seventeenth century to the present day. It must be stressed that these dates refer to the actual copying of extant manuscripts. They do not necessarily refer to the original compiling of particular collections and in most cases it is abundantly evident that the extant work has been directly copied from an earlier manuscript or manuscripts. In a few important instances manuscripts bearing eighteenth-century dates must be related to the seventeenth century rather than to the time when they were actually copied, for it is clear that their material derives mainly from the earlier period. The seventeenth century was the formative period in the development of the janam-sākhīs, and it is with this century, running over into the opening decades of its successor, that any discussion of the janam-sākhīs must be primarily concerned.

The outcome of this continuing process is an indeterminate but obviously substantial number of manuscript janam-sākhīs. Most of these are concentrated within the Pañjāb.[1] Others are to be found scattered throughout India and the libraries of the western world, two of the most important being held by the India Office Library in London.[2] In 1870 the first printed edition appeared and the trade has flourished ever since. Most of the manuscript copies can be distributed amongst four, or perhaps five,

[1] See Appendix 6.

[2] IOL MSS. Panj. B6 and B40.

recognizable traditions. The printed versions, although they have continued the process of growth and diversification, are later extensions of these same groups or traditions. In our attempt to analyse the janam-sākhīs frequent reference will have to be made to these various traditions and to their principal manuscript collections. For this reason a description of the more important extant janam-sākhīs will precede the attempt to analyse their actual development.

3

THE PRINCIPAL JANAM-SĀKHĪS

MOST of the janam-sākhīs fall into one of a small number of recognizable groups or traditions, the only significant exception being the unique *B40 Janam-sākhī* held by the India Office Library. Each of these traditions possesses distinctive characteristics and there is rarely any difficulty in allocating a manuscript to its appropriate category. For this reason the various manuscripts will be described under the headings of their various traditions.

One feature common to all the traditions which should be made clear at the outset is that they are all, in their extant forms, composite products. All have drawn upon a diversity of earlier sources. Their identity as distinctive groups or traditions has arisen only because particular selections were subsequently copied, completely or in substantial part, by later hands. For this reason it is important to distinguish three varieties of participant in the development process. These are the original *narrators* of oral tradition; the *compilers* who made selections from oral tradition and recorded their individual selections in manuscripts; and the *copyists* who with varying degrees of faithfulness reproduced these earliest compilations in later manuscript or, even later, printed form. During the later stages of the development process participants occasionally combined the roles of both compiler and copyist. They were copyists in that they reproduced earlier manuscripts but compilers in that they combined extracts from more than one source to produce new selections.

Such details are, however, aspects of the discussion which must follow the account of extant janam-sākhīs. This account will be largely descriptive, its purpose being to provide a frame of reference for the analysis which will follow.

THE BĀLĀ *JANAM-SĀKHĪS*

When during his visit to the Pañjāb in 1805 Colonel Malcolm made inquiries concerning Sikh history and religion he was informed that Bābā Nānak had been accompanied on his travels by 'a person named Bālā Sandhū'.[1] He adds that it is on this person's authority that 'most of the miracles and wonders of his journeys are related'.[2] Although Malcolm does make passing reference to two other sources,[3] it is evident from his

[1] John Malcolm, 'Sketch of the Sikhs', in *Asiatick Researches*, vol. xi (Calcutta, 1810), p. 205.

[2] Ibid.

[3] The first is the *Bhacta Malli*, an unidentifiable work evidently confused with the *Bhakta Māla* of Nābhā Dās and perhaps with the *Bhagat-ratanāvalī* of Manī Singh. The second is Bhāī Gurdās

account that the *Bālā* version of the life and travels of Bābā Nānak had been accepted as standard by the beginning of the nineteenth century.

It is this status which constitutes the principal importance of the *Bālā* janam-sākhīs. In spite of their claims to be the 'original janam-sākhī' there can be no doubt that they represent an intermediate stage in the evolution of the form, and that others are accordingly more significant in terms of age and simplicity of structure. Having first emerged during the middle decades of the seventeenth century the *Bālā* tradition flourished increasingly during the eighteenth century and eventually secured its position as the standard version of the life of Nānak. This position it retained unchallenged until the rediscovery of the *Purātan* tradition late in the nineteenth century. The publication of Macauliffe's *The Sikh Religion* in 1909 eventually transferred the primary reputation to the *Purātan* version, but the *Bālā* janam-sākhīs yielded nothing in popularity and to this day they dominate the Pañjābī market.

Although the reasons for this *Bālā* ascendancy are not altogether clear, one which certainly played a major role was its confident claim to represent an eye-witness account of the life and travels of Bābā Nānak. All *Bālā* janam-sākhīs begin with a prologue which purports to describe the manner in which Bālā Sandhū (commonly known as Bhāī Bālā) was summoned before Nānak's successor Aṅgad and how he then proceeded to narrate all that he had witnessed as the first Gurū's constant companion. The earliest of the extant *Bālā* versions begins as follows:

The *Janam-patri* of Bābā Nānakjī

In the year Sammat fifteen hundred and eighty two, S. 1582, on the fifth day of the bright half of the month of Vaisākh, Paiṛā Mokhā, a Khatrī of Sultānpur, wrote this book. Gurū Aṅgad commanded it to be written. Paiṛā recorded the dictation of Bālā, a Sandhū Jaṭ who had come from Talvaṇḍī, the village of Rāi Bhoi. He had come in search of Gurū Aṅgad. The recording of his account took two months and seventeen days to complete. All the facts and all the places visited by Gurū Nānakjī were faithfully and fluently described by Bhāī Bālā, with the result that Gurū Aṅgad was greatly pleased with him. Bhāī Bālā and Mardānā the Bard accompanied Bābā Nānak on his travels and Bhāī Bālā was with him during the period he spent at the commissariat [of Daulat Khān in Sultānpur].[1]

The narrative then proceeds to describe how Gurū Aṅgad was one day sitting in his village of Khaḍūr disconsolately reflecting upon the fact that he did not know Bābā Nānak's date of birth. It so happened that Bālā Sandhū, the first Gurū's companion, had only recently learnt the identity of his Master's successor, and having discovered the location of Gurū Aṅgad's residence he arrived at this convenient moment to pay his respects. In response to a request from Gurū Aṅgad he agreed to go back to Talvaṇḍī and search for the horoscope (*janam-patrī*) which had been recorded on Nānak's birth. When he returned triumphantly bearing the

---

(see below, pp. 43–45), whom Malcolm mistakenly declares to have been the author of the *Gyān-ratanāvalī*. Ibid., pp. 203, 204.

[1] *Bālā JS*, p. 1. For *janam-patrī* as the title of a janam-sākhī see above, p. 11.

document it was discovered that the horoscope had been written in *Śastrī* (Nāgarī) characters. Fortunately there lived in Sultānpur a Sikh named Paiṛā Mokhā who knew 'both characters' and who could accordingly write Gurmukhī as well as read Nāgarī. Paiṛā was duly summoned and having received the horoscope he sat down to transcribe it.[1]

This process mysteriously turns out to be a recording of Bālā's lengthy dictation instead of a transcription of the horoscope. The horoscope incident is clearly a contrived episode designed to create an impression of authenticity, and the clumsiness of the transition from horoscope to narrative has evidently done nothing to frustrate this intention. It has, on the contrary, been abundantly fulfilled, and to this day there still survives a conviction that the *Bālā* tradition must be at least based upon an eye-witness account delivered in the presence of Gurū Aṅgad. This reputation it has retained in spite of numerous inconsistencies, a high incidence of fantasy, and a generally incoherent travel narrative.

Two theories have been advanced to account for the origin of the *Bālā* tradition. The first assumes the authenticity of the tradition's own claims as outlined above. There are, however, inescapable problems involved in the acceptance of these claims, problems which must in some manner be answered before there can be any prospect of sustaining them. The early *Bālā* manuscripts all include denigratory references which could hardly have proceeded from a loyal disciple and would never have been tolerated by the Gurū's successor. These references are plainly the work of the Hindālīs, a schismatic group which evidently regarded itself as Sikh but which accepted the leadership of a rival claimant in opposition to the claims of Gurū Hargobind (1595–1644). This rival was Bidhī Chand, son of Bābā Hindāl of Jaṇḍiālā, and because his claim was advanced in the name of his father the group bore the name Hindālī.[2]

Within the earliest extant janam-sākhīs of the *Bālā* tradition there are several episodes which seek to exalt Bābā Hindāl at the expense of Nānak. These references vary in emphasis. At one point there is propounded a threefold apostolic succession which begins with Kabīr, continues through Nānak, and reaches its climax in Hindāl.[3] Elsewhere Nānak and Hindāl are both accorded earlier incarnations in the court of King Janak, with Nānak cast in the humble role of oil-bearer (*telī*).[4] Finally, there occurs in some of the manuscripts a story which seems to suggest that Nānak once requested Aṅgad to grant him seignorial rights over his daughter.[5]

[1] *Bālā JS*, pp. 1–7.

[2] *GNSR*, p. 23. The group is also known as the Nirañjanī panth. Jaṇḍiālā in Amritsar District was the group's centre. Hindāl was himself a Jaṭ from the pargana of Baṭālā. *B41*, f. 142b.

[3] This is expressed in the form of a brief verse.

age hūā ab bhī hoi ik kambīrā nānak doi
tījā hor handāl jaṭeṭā jānko āp nirañjan bheṭā
aisī kirapā karī kambīr to dujai nānak bandhī dhīr

B41, f. 166b.

[4] *B41*, f. 189a.

[5] *B41*, f. 251a–b. This third element, although certainly a part of the same polemic, may be a later addition to the *Bālā* narrative.

The first theory concerning the origins of the *Bālā* tradition interprets these references as interpolations introduced into an earlier 'original' janam-sākhī narrated before Gurū Aṅgad. This theory was popularized by the early nineteenth-century Sikh hagiographer Santokh Singh, who thereby managed to reconcile the tradition's occasional Hindālī declarations with its confident claims to originality.[1] It was a relatively simple matter to excise the offending material, and having done this Santokh Singh used the *Bālā* version as the basis for his *Nānak Prakāś*.[2] Numerous successors have followed the same method, some confidently and some with evident misgivings.

A second theory claims that the entire janam-sākhī is the work of the Hindālīs and that it was first composed to serve as a vehicle for their polemic against the supporters of the orthodox line. This interpretation was vigorously if erratically propagated by Karam Singh in his *Kattak ki Visākh*, a book which in spite of its manifold inconsistencies did serve to strengthen doubts which had been raised by Macauliffe.

The first of these two theories must certainly be rejected. The reasons for this rejection will be treated in greater detail when discussing the sources used by janam-sākhī compilers.[3] At this point they need be only briefly summarized. There are, first, the numerous and irreconcilable inconsistencies involved in the tradition's own account of its origins. Secondly, there is the unusually strong element of fantasy which characterizes the *Bālā* version of the Nānak narratives. Thirdly, there is a significant absence of any reference to Bhāī Bālā in the other janam-sākhīs predating the eighteenth century. Even in the eighteenth century he receives only passing mention in other traditions.[4] This would have been inconceivable if in fact Bālā had been a regular companion of the Gurū. Their omission of his name further strengthens a conclusion which is already apparent from the first two objections. In terms of content, structure, and language the earliest *Bālā* version bears all the marks of a middle period in the pattern of janam-sākhī evolution and theories based upon its claim to originality must assuredly be repudiated.

Whilst this disposes of the first theory it does not necessarily mean that the second thereby stands affirmed. It does not follow that Karam Singh's alternative theory is automatically established by a repudiation of the claims which he so vigorously contested. Karam Singh insisted that the earliest extant versions represent an original Hindālī composition, not an earlier janam-sākhī corrupted by them. The incidence of the Hindālī references does, however, offer some support for the suggestion that they must be interpolations and it is accordingly necessary to postulate a third theory. The earliest extant versions of the *Bālā* traditions may represent a

[1] *NPr* I. 37. [2] See below, pp. 45–6. [3] See below, pp. 174–6.

[4] The *Mahimā Prakāś Vāratak* makes a single mention of Bhāī Bālā in its account of the life of Nānak, one which accords him no special importance. *SLTGN(Eng)*, p. 79. *SLTGN(Pbi)*, p. 42. At one point the *B40* and *Ādi Sākhīs* versions, following a common source, refer to 'another man' who was with Nānak in addition to Mardānā, a reference which might perhaps be intended to indicate Bālā. *B40*, f. 83b. *AS*, p. 27. The failure of Bhāī Gurdās to mention him in his *Vār* XI catalogue of principal disciples is of particular significance.

mid-seventeenth-century janam-sākhī interpolated by the Hindālīs. This remains no more than a possibility, for there is no manuscript evidence to support it, and if it is in fact correct the Hindālīs must have made use of it very soon after its first emergence. Either this or the second theory could be correct and if the Hindālīs were not actually responsible for the first *Bālā* compilation they must certainly have appropriated it almost immediately after it appeared.[1]

It will be observed that in describing the products of the *Bālā* tradition reference is made to the *Bālā* janam-sākhīs, not to a single *Bālā Janam-sākhī*. Although there is an obvious relationship linking all versions of the tradition, with much common material, there are also marked differences. These are almost certainly linear in the sense that the various versions can be regarded as successive amplifications of an original *Bālā* janam-sākhī, first recorded in the middle decades of the seventeenth century. There are two principal manuscript recensions extant, followed by four main printed versions. Although the latest of the printed editions differs greatly from the first manuscript recension the lineal connection can be easily traced. The one link which may still be missing from the chain is the first. Whereas one of the extant manuscript recensions *may* represent the first *Bālā* version there is no conclusive means of establishing this status.

Manuscripts

1. *Bālā MS Recension A* *Recension A* can be easily distinguished from *Recension B* by its omission of sākhīs describing the death of Nānak. There seems to be little doubt that *A* must be earlier than *B*. The earliest of all extant *Bālā* manuscripts bearing a date follows the *A* text, and the inclusion of death sākhīs adds one further inconsistency to the narrative. The introduction attached to all versions relates that Bhāī Bālā was unaware of the identity of Bābā Nānak's successor, an ignorance which would have been altogether inexplicable had he been present at the time of Nānak's death. The editor responsible for *Recension B*, taking cognisance of this fact, has Qurū Aṅgad narrate the death sākhīs for Bhāī Bālā's benefit. In order to do so, however, he borrows a significant portion of his account from a janam-sākhī of the *Miharbān* tradition. This brands the passage as a later addition, and implies that the briefer *Recension A* version must be earlier.

The earliest of all dated *Bālā* janam-sākhīs is a manuscript in the possession of a Delhi family, an illustrated copy bearing the date S.1715 (A.D. 1658).[2] Two of the three *Bālā* manuscripts in London also follow the

[1] The case in favour of an original Hindālī composition has recently been restated in a more developed form by Gurbachan Kaur, 'Janam Sākhī of Bhāī Bālā: authentic text and its critical editing' (unpublished Ph.D. thesis, Gurū Nānak Dev University, 1978). Dr. Gurbachan Kaur identifies Bālā with the elder son of Bābā Hindāl.

[2] The actual manuscript is in the possession of Shrī P. N. Kapoor of Hauz Qazi, Delhi. A photocopy is held by the Department of Punjab Historical Studies, Punjabi University, Paṭiālā. An abbreviated text is given in Kirpāl Singh, *Janam Sākhī Paramparā* (Paṭiālā, 1969), Appendix, pp. 221–329. See also Rattan Singh Jaggī, *Dasam Granth dā paurāṇik adhiain* (Jalandhar, 1965), p. 59.

Recension A text. The better of the two is the India Office Library manuscript Panj. B41. This consists of two parts, the first being the janam-sākhī proper (folios 1–253a) and the second a version of the two discourses entitled *Makke dī goṣṭi* and *Madīne dī goṣṭi* (folios 254a–348a, 348b–95). Between the two sections a shabad in *Gauṛī* rāga has been inserted. The copyist is named Ṭhākur Dās Faqīr and both portions of the work are said to have been completed in S.1831–2 (A.D. 1775).[1] The second London representative of the tradition is the British Library's manuscript Or. 2754.1. This is undated and omits the story of how Gurū Nānak asked Gurū Aṅgad to send his daughter to him.[2] Although it has been copied by various hands on inferior paper it is generally clear.

2. *Bālā MS Recension B* This version, with its *Miharbān* death addendum, is represented by MS 104975 of the School of Oriental and African Studies in London, and also by MS Add. 921 of the Cambridge University Library. Both are recent works. The London manuscript is dated S.1912 (A.D. 1855) and the Cambridge manuscript S.1922 (A.D. 1865). An example noted in the Pañjāb by Professor Piār Singh is manuscript no. 342 of the Pañjāb Archives in Paṭiālā.[3]

These are the two principal recensions available in manuscript form. Needless to say, a comparison of any two manuscripts will reveal many variants, some of them substantial.[4] These variants do not, however, upset the pattern of a relatively mature janam-sākhī emerging with strong Hindālī associations in the middle of the seventeenth century and subsequently augmented by the addition of sākhīs narrating a version of Nānak's death. Of all janam-sākhīs this is the most common. In his catalogue of Pañjābī manuscripts Ashok has listed twenty-two *Bālā* manuscripts.[5] This catalogue relates exclusively to the Pañjāb. It does not include the Delhi and United Kingdom manuscripts noted above, nor a *Bālā* manuscript in the possession of Mr Jan Nielsen of Denmark.[6]

[1] The first is dated Māgh *sudī* 13, S. 1831; and the second portion Vaisākh *sudī* 4, S. 1832. Loc. cit., ff. 253b, 395b

[2] See above, p. 17.

[3] Piār Singh in *AS*, Introduction. p. xxxv.

[4] Other sākhīs added to the original *Recension A* collection by later copyists are noted by Gurbachan Kaur, op. cit, Appendix.

[5] *PHLS* i. 342–9 and ii. 224–9, 235–6. The distribution of the manuscripts is as follows: Library of the former Mahārājā of Paṭiālā (6 MSS). Languages Department, Paṭiālā (3). Central Public Library, Paṭiālā (3). Pañjāb Archives, Paṭiālā (2). Pañjāb University, Chaṇḍigaṛh (2). Dr. Gaṇḍā Singh, Paṭiālā (2). Pañjābī Sāhit Ākādemī, Ludhiānā (1). Central Sikh Museum, Amritsar (1). Professor Prītam Singh, Amritsar (1). Sardār Shamsher Singh Ashok, Amritsar (1). Two manuscripts not noticed by Ashok are held by Khalsa College, Amritsar. Kirpāl Singh (ed.), *A Catalogue of Punjabi and Urdu Manuscripts in the Sikh History Research Department* (Amritsar, 1963), pp. 16–17. Both are nineteenth-century manuscripts.

[6] A microfilm copy of this manuscript is held by Punjabi University, Paṭiālā. The original, which was copied in Multān in S. 1884 (A.D. 1827), bears the following note signed by Mr. Rich. Ash. Hannaford: 'The Ghrunt of the Seikhs. Taken from the altar in one of their temples by Lieut: G: Moxon. Given to me by Mrs. Moxon Dec: 22, 1851.'

Printed editions

The printing of janam-sākhīs appears to have begun in 1870. In October of that year the owners of the Ganesh Prakash Press in Lahore issued a composite volume comprising three Sikh works lithographed in the Arabic script. The second of these was a version of the *Bālā* narrative, a popular retelling which plainly derived from a Gurmukhī original.[1]

The Gurmukhī version was not far behind and within months the dominant *Bālā* text had followed the 1870 forerunner into print. In 1871 a generally faithful replica of the *Recension A* Gurmukhī text was issued by another Lahore publisher, establishing thereby a firm link between the earlier manuscripts and the progressively expanding versions delivered by printing presses. During this same year the process of expansion was given a substantial impetus by the appearance of an extensively augmented version. The process continued into the twentieth century, each successive product claiming to represent the authentic text delivered by Bālā Sandhū to Gurū Aṅgad. The four Gurmukhī versions which constitute this developing sequence are as follows:

1. *Bālā Lithographed Edition A* (A.D. 1871) This edition, published in Lahore by Hāfaz Qutub Dīn, establishes the firm link with earlier *Bālā* manuscripts. Most of its text follows that of *Bālā MS Recension A* closely and thus effects only a slight advance in the expansion process. For this reason, and because it is more accessible than manuscript copies, this Hāfiz Qutub Dīn edition (*Bālā Lithographed Edition A*) will be used for most *Bālā* citations in this study.[2] It should, however, be noted that some significant variants do occur. These are set out in Appendix 1, together with a list of all *Recension A* and *Lithographed Edition A* sākhīs.[3]

2. *Bālā Lithographed Edition B* (A.D. 1871) The second of the 1871 editions is a much larger product, both in actual dimensions and in content. As indicated above, this second 1871 edition marks the first significant stage in the rapid and substantial expansion which transformed the *Bālā* tradition during the last three decades of the nineteenth century and created the twentieth-century *Bālā Janam-sākhī* still so popular in Pañjāb villages. From this point of view it commands a considerable interest, although it is of no help as a source for the primary period of

[1] The three works which comprise the volume are *Japjī paramārath* (50 pp.), *Pothī janam-sākhī* (114 pp.), and *Gur-bilās* (44 pp.). Each appears to have been lithographed as a separate booklet and the three subsequently bound as a single volume. The October 1870 date is recorded on the cover and evidently refers to the issue of the complete volume. A copy is held by the IOL (call number: VT 1552).

[2] It is to this edition that the abbreviation *Bālā JS* applies. The copy in the India Office Library is catalogued as Panj. 1522. The India Office Library also holds two later editions of the same version, one published in A.D. 1874 (Panj. 30.E.3) and the other in A.D. 1886 (Panj. 1523). The book is relatively small, measuring 25 × 15 cm.

[3] See below, pp. 271–5.

janam-sākhī development during the seventeenth century. The edition was published by Mālik Dīvān Būṭā Singh of Lahore.[1]

3. *Bālā Lithographed Edition C* (A.D. 1890) The *Bālā* tradition was further expanded by an even weightier volume published in 1890 by Maulvī Maibūb Ahmad of Lahore.[2]

4. *Bālā Letterpress Edition* The climax was finally reached with the twentieth-century letterpress edition which still sells well in the bazaar bookshops of the Pañjāb.[3] The first of the lithographed editions described above contains 90 sākhīs, the second jumps to 311, and the third leaps still further to 495. In the standard modern letterpress version the number is reduced to 183 by amalgamating earlier sākhīs. Some portions have been omitted, extra material has been added, and there has been some rearrangement, but the pattern of linear descent is still clear.

THE PURĀTAN *JANAM-SĀKHĪS*

Having established its supremacy during the course of the eighteenth century the *Bālā* tradition remained the standard account of the life of Nānak for more than a hundred years. It was only in 1872 that a serious rival reappeared, and it was not until the early twentieth century that this rival tradition began to make any serious impression upon the *Bālā* reputation. Because it was alleged by some of its promoters to be the oldest of all versions this variant account of the life of Nānak was dubbed the *Purātan* or 'Ancient' tradition.

The term *Purātan Janam-sākhī*, which has ever since been used with reference to this second major tradition, is misleading in two respects. It is misleading because it implies (and the claim has sometimes been expressed in explicit terms) that this must be the original janam-sākhī. The claim that the *Purātan* version represents the oldest of all *extant* accounts may perhaps be accurate. It is certainly disputable, but the possibility must be acknowledged. What is not acceptable is the suggestion that the *Purātan* tradition represents an 'original' janam-sākhī. The *Purātan* tradition is, like all extant janam-sākhī collections, a composite version based upon more than one antecedent source.

The term is also misleading in that its use of the singular implies the existence of a single *Purātan* janam-sākhī. This too is incorrect. As in the case of the *Bālā* tradition there is more than one *Purātan* janam-sākhī, and it is because more than one exists that the heading given above for this section uses a plural form. The intimate relationship which connects the various *Purātan* janam-sākhīs cannot be doubted and for this reason they

[1] IOL Panj. 31.I.9. A reprint was issued in A.D. 1890 (IOL Panj. 31.I.7).

[2] IOL Panj. 31.I.10.

[3] IOL Panj. H.18 is an example. The best available copies are those published by Munshī Gulāb Singh and Sons of Lahore.

are here grouped within a single definable tradition. This grouping should not, however, suggest identity. The terms '*Purātan* janam-sākhis' and '*Purātan* tradition' serve as convenient collective labels, whereas the singular form, the *Purātan Janam-sākhi*, must be restricted to the published text which bears this misleading title.[1] In addition to this and an earlier published text three of the more important *Purātan* manuscripts will be noted. Two of these manuscripts (the *Colebrooke* and the *Hāfizābād*) have enjoyed a particular fame. This they owe not to their dates (which are unknown) nor to any uniqueness of text, but rather to the manner of their discovery and to the fact that the names bestowed upon them have also been used to designate the two principal recensions of the *Purātan* tradition. The third manuscript, likewise undated but obviously later than its more celebrated analogues, deserves notice because it illustrates so well the persistent tendency of copyists to expand earlier collections.

Manuscripts

1. *The Colebrooke Janam-sākhi* In 1869 the Pañjāb Government commissioned Ernst Trumpp to translate the sacred scripture of the Sikhs.[2] Although Trumpp's responsibility was limited to the Ādi Granth he was naturally interested in surviving traditions concerning the lives of the Gurūs, and specifically those relating to Nānak. Knowledge of the Nānak traditions was largely confined to the *Bālā* version and because this version seemed to him to be so unsatisfactory Trumpp endeavoured to procure older and more trustworthy traditions regarding the life of Nānak. In India his search was unsuccessful, but after his return to Europe he chanced upon a manuscript which seemed to answer his need.

> After my return to Europe in 1872, some manuscripts of the Granth were forwarded to me from the India Office Library, for the prosecution of my labours, and to these some other Gurmukhi manuscripts were added in the expectation that the one or the other might prove useful in my researches. In looking them over, I found an old manuscript, partly destroyed by white ants, the early characters of which, resembling those of the old copy of the Granth, preserved at Kartarpur, and signed by Guru Arjun himself, at once caught my eye. On the first leaf it contained in Sanskrit letters the short title, *Nanak ka Granth Janamasakhi ka, A book of Nanak, referring to his birth* (*or life*). The copy had been presented to the Library of the East India House, according to the entry on the first leaf, by the famous H. T. Colebrooke, without his being aware, as it appears, of the contents of the book. As soon as I commenced to read the book, I observed with great pleasure, that this was a description of the life of Nanak quite different from all the others I had hitherto seen. As the characters, so also was the idiom, in which it was composed, old and in many words and expressions agreeing with the diction of Guru Arjun.
>
> After a lengthened examination and comparison of this manuscript with the later Janam-sakhis, I am satisfied that this is the fountain, from which all the others have been drawn largely: for the stories, as far as they are common to both

[1] See below, pp. 28–9.

[2] E. Trumpp, *The Ādi Granth* (London, 1877), p. III.

relations, very frequently agree verbally, with the only difference, that the later Janam-sakhis have substituted more modern forms for old words, which with the progress of time had become unintelligible. This old Janam-sakhi, as hinted already, belongs, according to all external and internal marks, to the latter end of the time of Guru Arjun or to that of his immediate successor. The Granth, which Guru Arjun compiled of the writings of his four predecessors and the old famous Bhagats, as well as of his own numerous poetical effusions, is cited throughout, without any paraphrase, whereas the later Janam-sakhis have deemed it already necessary to add to every quotation from the Granth a paraphrase in the modern idiom.

We are enabled now, by the discovery of this old Janam-sakhi, which is now-a-days, as it appears, quite unknown to the Sikhs themselves, to distinguish the older tradition regarding Nanak from the later one, and to fix, with some degree of verisimility, the real facts of his life.[1]

Although Trumpp was astray in his estimate of the age and reliability of the manuscript there can be no doubt that he had discovered one of the most important of the janam-sākhīs. H. T. Colebrooke had presumably presented the manuscript to the Library of East India House in 1815 or 1816. In English works it is commonly referred to as the *Colebrooke Janam-sākhī*, and in Pañjābī references as the *Valāitvālī Janam-sākhī*, or 'the janam-sākhī from overseas'.[2] The manuscript is almost complete, the only missing folios being 2–6, 12–13, and 18–19.

Trumpp had, in the manner of late nineteenth-century religious polemic, made some exceedingly discourteous remarks about the Sikh sacred scriptures and for this reason his book was ill received by the community when it was published in 1877.[3] His description and translation of the rediscovered janam-sākhī did, however, arouse considerable interest and in 1883 a group of Amritsar Sikhs petitioned the Lieutenant-Governor of the Pañjāb to have the manuscript brought to India for inspection. Sir Charles Aitcheson accepted the request and in the autumn of the same year the manuscript was sent to the Pañjāb. There it was made available for scrutiny in Lahore and Amritsar, where interest was sufficiently marked to persuade Sir Charles to have it reproduced. This was done by means of a zincographic process in 1885 and copies bearing the title *Janam Sakhi or the Biography of Guru Nanak, Founder of the Sikh Religion* were presented to selected institutions as gifts.[4] In the meantime a transcribed copy had been prepared and lithographed by the Singh Sabhā of Lahore.[5]

Although the manuscript bears no date for either an original compilation or the actual copying, a cryptic reference in the sākhī 'Jhaṇḍā the Carpenter and the *Jugāvalī*' points to the year A.D. 1635.[6] It is possible

[1] Ibid., p. ii.

[2] The manuscript is IOL MS Panj. B6.

[3] For examples of his opinion see E. Trumpp, op. cit., pp. VI–VIII, i–ii; and N. Gerald Barrier, *The Sikhs and their Literature*, (Delhi, 1970), pp. xix–xx.

[4] Loc. cit., prefatory note, p. ii. Because the reproduction was carried out at the Survey of India offices in Dehrā Dūn the *Colebrooke* version is sometimes referred to as the *Dehrā Dūn Vālī Janam-sākhī*. The India Office Library copy is catalogued as Panj. 30.E.4.

[5] IOL Panj. 30.E.2.

[6] *Pur JS*, p. 116n.

that this reference is intended to indicate the year in which the *Purātan* version was first compiled, and there can be no doubt that a janam-sākhī of the *Purātan* variety might well have been recorded at that time. A reference of this kind is, however, slender evidence. It occurs in the apocryphal *Jugāvali* (a work borrowed by the *Colebrooke* compiler from one of his sources), and it does not appear in all other *Purātan* manuscripts. The reference may relate to an original compilation, or to a later recension, or to a particular part of the composite *Purātan* tradition. Another possibility is that it may be entirely spurious. It occurs as an obscure reference within an esoteric work, circumstances which are scarcely favourable to positive conclusions. The text bears all the marks of an early seventeenth-century janam-sākhī, but beyond this supposition it is impossible to proceed. The actual manuscript is evidently later than this period. This conclusion is suggested by the salutation with which the manuscript concludes: *bolahu vāhi gurū jī kī fatai hoī.*[1] There is no evidence to suggest that this formula was used prior to the time of Gurū Gobind Siṅgh, from which it follows that the manuscript was probably copied during the early eighteenth century.

2. *The Hāfizābād Janam-sākhī* In 1884 Gurmukh Singh of Oriental College, Lahore, acquired a second *Purātan* manuscript from the town of Hāfizābād in Gujranwālā District. This manuscript he loaned to M. A. Macauliffe, who, having separated the individual words of the unbroken text, had it published at his own expense in 1885.[2] This version is variously known as the *Hāfizābād Janam-sākhī* or as the *Macauliffe-vālī Janam-sākhī*.

The *Hāfizābād* text differs from the *Colebrooke* version in three significant respects. First, it includes in addition to all the *Colebrooke* material (which it reproduces with minor variants) a small cluster of two consecutive sākhīs, neither of which appears in the *Colebrooke* analogue. These are the anecdotes entitled 'The Proud Karoṛī Humbled' and 'The Merchant and Rājā Śivanābh'.[3] Secondly, it contains a discourse with Bābur which the *Colebrooke* text lacks.[4] Thirdly, it omits the three lengthy compositions entitled *Āsā Paṭṭī*, the *Jugāvalī*, and the *Prāṇ Saṅgalī*.[5] One other difference reported by Gurmukh Singh in his introduction to the lithographed edition is that there were some folios missing from the end of the manuscript. In order to complete the text Macauliffe used the *Colebrooke* manuscript.[6]

Macauliffe's decision to publish a lithographed edition of the *Hāfizābād Janam-sākhī* was particularly fortunate in that the original manuscript is now no longer extant. When Gurmukh Singh died in 1896 his collection of

[1] Ibid., p. 115.

[2] *Janam Sākhī Bābe Nānak Jī kī: the Most Ancient Biography of Baba Nanak, the Founder of the Sikh Religion*, edited by M. A. Macauliffe, lithographed by the Gulashan Press, Rāwalpiṇḍī, 15 November 1885, with introduction by Gurmukh Singh.

[3] Ibid., pp. 184–97. *Pur JS*, pp. 73–8.

[4] M. A. Macauliffe, op. cit., pp. 163–7. *Pur JS*, pp. 65–7.

[5] M. A. Macauliffe, op. cit., introduction, p. 9.

[6] Ibid.

manuscripts passed to his widow Parameshari Devī; and when she died in 1923 they came into the possession of his adoptive nephew. The nephew's possession was disputed (presumably by other relatives of Gurmukh Singh) and although a court decision was delivered in his favour he evidently decided to dispose of the property which threatened to involve him in further litigation. This he did by casting the manuscripts into the Rāvī river. No inventory of the manuscripts exists, but it is presumed that the *Hāfizābād Janam-sākhī* must have been amongst them.[1]

In addition to the Macauliffe text at least two other extant manuscripts follow the *Hāfizābād Janam-sākhī* version of the *Purātan* narrative. These are manuscript number 2913 of the Central Public Library, Paṭiālā, and manuscript number 2310A in the Sikh History Research Department of Khalsa College, Amritsar.[2] The Paṭiālā manuscript is dated S.1747 (A.D. 1690)[3] and the Khalsa College manuscript S.1829 (A.D. 1772).[4]

Other manuscripts are distinguished by their use of both *Colebrooke* and *Hāfizābād*. An example of this pattern is provided by a *Purātan* manuscript dated S.1814 (A.D. 1757), copied in Burdwan and now in the possession of Sardār Kuldīp Singh Bedī of Baṭālā. This manuscript is much closer to *Colebrooke* than to *Hāfizābād* and is best classified as an example of the former. It does, however, include occasional readings which have evidently been adapted from a *Hāfizābād* source.[5]

3. *The Prāchīn Janam-sākhī* The title *Prāchīn Janam-sākhī* designates a manuscript in the possession of a private collector, Sevā Singh Sevak of Tarn Tāran. This manuscript represents a relatively late and substantially expanded *Purātan* collection. Although no date is given it is evident from the language and structure of the collection that the seventeenth-century estimate suggested by its owner must be too early.[6]

The bulk of the manuscript consists of *Purātan* material, rearranged in places but plainly attesting its basic source. To this foundation have been added sākhīs drawn from several other sources. Only a few of these have been introduced into the *Purātan* sequence. Most have been added at its

[1] Information supplied by Sardār Shamsher Singh Ashok of Amritsar, who reports having learnt it while scrutinizing the Lahore Singh Sabhā records in 1945.

[2] Piār Singh, op. cit., pp. 83–4. Kirpāl Singh, op. cit., pp. 11–12. *PHLS* i.340.

[3] Loc. cit., f. 276b. The manuscript is said to have been copied at Galgalā. The copyist adds: 'Galgalā is twelve *kos* from Bījāpur on the Kistna river. . . . It was written in the south, in the camp of Nauraṅg Pātśāh [Aurangzeb].' Ibid.

[4] Loc. cit., f. 185. Kirpāl Singh, op. cit., p. 12.

[5] Two other complete *Purātan* manuscripts and two fragments are *PHLS* i.340 and ii.225, 230. Ashok reports two additional *Purātan* manuscripts located after the compilation of *PHLS*, one in Ferozepore District and the other in Hoshiārpur District. Shamsher Singh Ashok, *Purātan Janam-sākhī Srī Gurū Nānak Dev Jī kī* (Amritsar, 1969), introduction, p. 46. He also reports having seen 'several *Purātan* janam-sākhīs' in Lahore prior to Partition in 1947. Ibid., p. 45. Karam Singh, writing in 1913, claimed to have seen five *Purātan* manuscripts in addition to *Colebrooke* and *Hāfizābād*, and to have received a report concerning a sixth. Karam Singh, *Kattak ki Visākh* (Amritsar, 1913), p. 218. It seems certain that one of these must have been the *B40 Janam-sākhī* (see below, p. 43). and in view of the looseness with which the term *Purātan* is used it is likely that other manuscripts to which this title has been applied may have been misnamed.

[6] Sevā Singh Sevak (ed.), *Prāchīn Janam Sākhī* (Jalandhar, 1969), introduction, pp. 28, 35.

conclusion.[1] A variety of sources lie behind these supplementary sākhīs. Several obviously derive from two major traditions unknown to the *Purātan* compilers but extensively used in some other janam-sākhīs.[2] The *Miharbān* tradition (discussed below) is well represented by several lengthy discourses, grouped within four sākhīs.[3] A cluster which plainly derives from a *Bālā* source manages to avoid all reference to the person of Bhāī Bālā.[4] Another cluster appears to be unique to the *Prāchīn Janam-sākhī*.[5] The manuscript also includes a version of the apocryphal 'Mecca Discourse'.[6]

Authorship and dating of the Purātan *version*

In *The Sikh Religion* Macauliffe states that the *Purātan* version 'was written by a Sikh called Sewa Das'.[7] He claims to have obtained 'several copies', and adds: 'One of them in our possession bears the date Sambat 1645 = A.D. 1588.'[8] The first of these claims can be safely dismissed. Macauliffe himself acknowledges the information to be hearsay, no manuscript bearing this name exists, and it seems clear that Macauliffe's informant (Sir Attar Singh of Bhadauṛ) must have mistaken the identity of a writer of Gurū Gobind Siṅgh's period named Sevā Dās Udāsī.[9] The second is also open to considerable doubt. Apart from the *Hāfizābād* manuscript in its printed edition none of Macauliffe's 'several copies' seems to have survived, and it is highly unlikely that a janam-sākhī as maturely structured as the extant *Purātan* version could have evolved by 1588. It is possible that Macauliffe may have seen a manuscript bearing this date, but if so it will almost certainly have been a much more primitive collection than the extant version.

Other attempts to devise a date for the compiling of the *Purātan* tradition must be treated with the same scepticism, for no specifically dated

1 Sākhīs 19, 33–6, and 51 have been interpolated; also portions of sākhīs 10, 41, and 53. The *Purātan* material concludes immediately prior to the *Purātan* account of Nānak's death, and the remaining sākhīs (58–81) are almost all taken from other sources. The sole exception is sākhī 80, a brief return to *Purātan* material immediately prior to the death sākhī.

2 These are the so-called *Narrative II* and *Narrative III* traditions. (See below, pp. 197–226) The former had, on earlier occasions, been extensively used by the compilers of the *Ādi Sākhīs* and the *B40 Janam-sākhī*, both following a common source-manuscript. In its recorded form the latter can be traced to the *B40 Janam-sākhī*, and it is possible that the compiler of the *Prāchīn Janam-sākhī* actually copied his *Narrative III* sākhīs directly from the *B40* manuscript. His source was at least very close to the original *B40*. It is also possible that he may have had access to a late recension of the *Ādi Sākhīs*, for sources which are blended in the later *Ādi Sākhīs* appear in the same form in the *Prāchīn Janam-sākhī*. *Narrative II* sākhīs in the *Prāchīn Janam-sākhī* are 58, parts of 59, and 62–5. *Narrative III* sākhīs are 71 and 75–9. Other sākhīs which may have been derived from the *B40 Janam-sākhī* are parts of 10 and 41, 51, 66–70, and 81.

3 Sākhīs 19, parts of 59, 60–1.

4 Sākhīs 72–4.

5 Sākhīs 33–6.

6 Sevā Singn Sevak, op. cit., p. 174.

7 Loc. cit. i.lxxxvi.

8 Ibid.

9 Sevā Dās Udāsī was the author of a collection of anecdotes entitled *Parchīān*, completed in A.D. 1708. Only one of these anecdotes (a version of the discourse on Mount Sumeru) refers to Bābā Nānak. Jagjīt Singh, 'A Critical and Comparative Study of the Janam Sakhis of Guru Nanak up to the Middle of the Eighteenth Century' (unpublished Ph.D. thesis, Panjab University. 1967), pp. 33–4. For the Pañjābī text of this anecdote see *SLTGN(Pbi)*, pp. 30–1.

reference survives. Calculations based on indirect references are of little help, except perhaps for the sākhī or poetic composition within which they occur. The extant *Purātan* version is, like all extant janam-sākhīs, a composite product and different portions have been incorporated at different times. A date within the middle decades of the seventeenth century may be assumed as highly probable but further than this it is not yet possible to go.

Printed editions

1. M. A. Macauliffe (ed.), *Janam Sākhī Bābe Nānak Jī kī*. Rawalpindi, 1885. This printed edition has already been briefly described in the section dealing with the *Hāfizābād* manuscript. According to Gurmukh Singh's introduction the lithographed text represents a faithful reproduction of the *Hāfizābād* manuscript, the only significant difference being the editor's separation of individual words, the addition of punctuation, and the terminal section drawn from the *Colebrooke* manuscript. Copies of this printed edition are now rare. The British Library possesses one,[1] but not the India Office Library. A few copies are still held privately and in libraries in the Pañjāb.

2. Vīr Singh (ed.), *Purātan Janam-sākhī*. In 1926 the distinguished Sikh novelist and theologian Bhāī Vīr Singh of Amritsar published a conflation of the *Colebrooke* and *Hāfizābād* versions under the title *Purātan Janam-sākhī*.[2] For this printed edition Vīr Singh took as his primary text the *Colebrooke* manuscript (using the zincographic reproduction) and added to it material included in the *Hāfizābād* manuscript which the *Colebrooke* manuscript lacked. For the portions covered by both manuscripts the more important of the *Hāfizābād* variant readings were listed in footnotes. This still left some gaps in the text, notably at the conclusion of the death sākhī. These Vīr Singh filled in his second edition (1931), by adding readings drawn from the *Purātan* manuscript in the possession of the Khalsa College Sikh History Research Department.[3] The three manuscripts were, like all Pañjābī manuscripts of this kind, written without gaps be ween individual words and with only rudimentary punctuation.

[1] BL 14162.c.14.

[2] Amritsar: Khālsā Samāchār. The complete title is *Huṇ tak miliān vichon sab ton Purātan Janam-sākhī Srī Gurū Nānak Dev Jī* ('The Earliest Extant Janam-sākhī of Srī Gurū Nānak Dev Jī'). Several subsequent editions have been issued by the same publisher and the book is still in print. The abbreviation *Pur JS* used in this study refers to the fifth edition of this work (February 1959). An abridged version appears in Kirpāl Singh, *Janam Sākhī Paramparā* (Paṭiālā, 1969), Appendix, pp. 1–57.

[3] One gap which still remained, and which can only be filled by speculation, is the prologue which evidently preceded the birth narrative in the *Colebrooke* manuscript. Although the extant manuscript begins with the birth of Nānak, the folio numbering indicates that five folios have been detached from the beginning of the manuscript. *Janam Sākhī or the Biography of Gurū Nānak* (Photozincograph Facsimile, Dehrā Dūn, 1885), Introduction, p. iii. These presumably recorded a pre-natal commissioning of Nānak by God in the manner of the introductory portions of the *Ādi Sākhīs* and the *Miharbān Janam-sākhī*.

In the printed edition the individual words have been separated and additional punctuation provided.[1]

Three other features of this printed version should be noted. First, Vīr Singh has added headings to the individual sākhīs and also section headings to mark the commencement of each of the five journeys which according to the *Purātan* version Bābā Nānak is said to have made. Secondly, he has amended the narrator's numerous quotations from Nānak's own compositions in order to bring them into conformity with the Ādi Granth text. This frequently involves substantial changes in the *Purātan* text. Vīr Singh defends these amendments on the grounds that 'because the authentic text of the Gurū's utterances is that of the *Gurū Granth Sāhib* it would be offensive to print a corrupt text'.[2] Thirdly, he has omitted from his main text compositions attributed by the janam-sākhī to the Gurū which he regards as apocryphal. These he has relegated to a series of appendices.[3] The shorter compositions are there printed in full, but for the remainder (including the important *Prāṇ Saṅgalī*) only the opening stanzas are given.

3. Sevā Singh Sevak (ed.), *Prāchīn Janam-sākhī*. Jalandhar, 1969. This volume represents a printed edition of the third of the *Purātan* manuscripts noted above. The text follows a brief Pañjābī introduction by the owner-editor.

4. Shamsher Singh Ashok, *Purātan Janam-sākhī Srī Gurū Nanak Dev Jī kī*. Amritsar, 1969. In spite of its title this recent publication is not strictly a *Purātan* text and it is included here only because claims to this status have been made on its behalf. It is, like Vīr Singh's *Purātan Janam-sākhī*, a conflation. Unlike Vīr Singh's version, however, the component texts are not all *Purātan*. Although the primary text has been provided by a *Purātan* manuscript the finished product contains much material derived from two non-*Purātan* manuscripts. It differs from the *Prāchīn Janam-sākhī* in that its non-*Purātan* sākhīs have been dispersed through the complete collection, extensively supplementing the *Purātan* content without disrupting its distinctive pattern. In the *Prāchīn Janam-sākhī* most of the non-*Purātan* sākhīs have been appended at the conclusion of the *Purātan* material.

Ashok has constructed his text in two stages. The first step was to conflate two *Ādi Sākhīs* texts (representatives of a separate tradition which is described below). These texts were taken from a manuscript in his own possession and from another in the library of the Mahārājā of Paṭiālā. The second step was to conflate this conflated *Ādi Sākhīs* text with the text of the *Purātan* manuscript in the possession of Sardār Kuldīp Singh Bedī of Baṭālā.[4] This *Purātan* text is basic in the sense that it supplies not only a

[1] *Pur JS*, Introduction, pp. *s–k*. [2] Ibid., p. *h*. [3] Ibid., pp. 116–20.

[4] Shamsher Singh Ashok (ed.), *Purātan Janam Sākhī Srī Gurū Nānak Dev Jī kī*, Introduction, pp. 13, 47. The two *Ādi Sākhīs* manuscripts are dated respectively S. 1791 (A.D. 1734) and S. 1758 (A.D. 1701). See below, p. 32. The *Purātan* manuscript is dated S. 1814 (A.D. 1757).

majority of the sākhīs but also the structure of the conflated product. In all *Purātan* manuscripts the narrative is distinguished by an ordering of the travel sākhīs into four major journeys, one to each of the four cardinal points of the compass, together with a minor journey to a place called Gorakh-haṭaṛī. This chronology has been retained by the editor and the extra sākhīs provided by the *Ādi Sākhīs* version have been introduced into this *Purātan* narrative individually or in clusters, at points which seemed appropriate.

Because the *Ādi Sākhīs* chronology disagrees with the *Purātan* pattern these supplementary sākhīs could not be interpolated in the same order as they appear in their *Ādi Sākhīs* form. In the case of common sākhīs, however, the editor has preferred their readings to that of his *Purātan* text. Wherever the *Purātan* and *Ādi Sākhīs* versions have sākhīs in common the conflated *Ādi Sākhīs* text has normally been used.[1] No indication of this is given in the printed text, the only manuscript identifications being occasional footnote references to variant readings. In a few places a passage included in one or more of the manuscripts has been omitted from the published text. An example is the *Ādi Sākhīs* explanation for Nānak's decision to visit the pilgrimage-centres.[2] The *Ādi Sākhīs* compiler, following a source used by other janam-sākhī compilers, records a tradition that Nānak's visit was in quest of a gurū.[3] This passage, which should have been attached to the end of sākhī 17[4] or the beginning of sākhī 24,[5] was evidently omitted because the suggestion that Bābā Nānak should ever have sought a gurū is now held to be offensive.

English translations

An English translation of the *Colebrooke* text is given by Trumpp in his introduction to his *The Ādi Granth*.[6] This rendering is exceedingly stilted and contains numerous inaccuracies. Much of the first volume of Macauliffe's *The Sikh Religion* is a paraphrase of the *Purātan* narrative, but no indication is given of the points at which the author briefly moves away from his principal source.

A list of the sākhīs included in the *Purātan* janam-sākhīs is given in Appendix 2.[7]

THE ĀDI SĀKHĪS

At some unspecified date prior to the partition of India in 1947 Dr Mohan Singh Dewana of Punjab University, Lahore, discovered in the Uni-

[1] Both versions of the 'Death of Nanak' sākhī are given. Loc. cit., pp. 191–3 (*Ādi Sākhīs* version) and pp. 193–6 (*Purātan* version).

[2] *AS*, p. 23.

[3] *B40*, f. 76b. *Mih JS* I.111. For a note on the common source see below, pp. 198–205.

[4] Shamsher Singh Ashok (ed.), op. cit., p. 40.

[5] Ibid., p. 52.

[6] Loc. cit., pp. vii–xlv. For a summary paraphrase of the *Purātan* narrative (*Hāfizābād* as well as *Colebrooke*) see *GNSR*, pp. 36–51.

[7] See below, pp. 276–7.

versity's library a janam-sākhī manuscript which recorded a version different from any of the extant traditions. This collection he named the *Ādi Sākhīs*, or 'First Collection of Sākhīs'.[1] Mohan Singh did not make a complete copy of the manuscript and efforts to trace it made in early 1969 proved unsuccessful.[2] In the meantime, however, four manuscript copies of the same collection had been located on the Indian side of the border by Professor Piār Singh of Punjabi University, Paṭiālā, and in October 1969 Piār Singh published a printed edition of the text.[3]

The name chosen by Mohan Singh for this collection is misleading, for it implies a precedence which in fact the janam-sākhī does not possess. This is made clear by an analysis of its contents. At least three distinct sources can be recognized,[4] and from the material provided by these sources the compiler of the collection has fashioned a coherent travel itinerary. These are features of a relatively mature janam-sākhī and any theory that the *Ādi Sākhīs* represent a 'first' collection must be rejected.

The composite nature of the *Ādi Sākhīs* collection must also prompt a measure of caution in attempting to place the janam-sākhī within any reconstructed sequence of janam-sākhīs. It has, for example, been argued that a reference to Akbar which is repeated in the *Miharbān Janam-sākhī* indicates that the *Ādi Sākhīs* is earlier than the *Miharbān* collection.[5] The portion of the *Miharbān Janam-sākhī* in which this reference appears claims to be a product of the year S.1707 (A.D. 1650),[6] and because the Akbar reference in the extant *Miharbān Janam-sākhī* appears to be later than the *Ādi Sākhīs* version it would seem to follow that the *Ādi Sākhīs* must antedate the middle of the seventeenth century. In fact, however, both the *Ādi Sākhīs* and the *Miharbān Janam-sākhī* in their earliest extant forms are the products of a continuing process of expansion. Whereas on the one hand there can be no doubt that the extant *Miharbān Janam-sākhī* embodies borrowings from the *Ādi Sākhīs*, on the other there seems to be little question that the extant *Ādi Sākhīs* includes reciprocal borrowings from the *Miharbān* tradition. The Akbar reference appears to be one of the latter, taken not from the extant *Miharbān Janam-sākhī* but from an earlier recension.[7]

[1] Mohan Singh's information is dispersed over several publications, summarized by Piār Singh in *AS*, pp. ix–xi. The copyist's name is given as Sibhū (or Śambhū) Nāth Brāhmaṇ and the manuscript's number as PUL 4141.

[2] Failure to locate the manuscript does not necessarily mean that it has been lost. The Gurmukhī manuscripts held by Punjab University, Lahore, are said to be in a condition of total confusion at present.

[3] See below, p. 33.

[4] See below, pp. 219–20.

[5] Piār Singh, 'A Critical Survey of Panjabi Prose in the Seventeenth Century' (unpublished Ph.D. thesis, Panjab University, Chaṇḍīgaṛh, 1968), pp. 94–5. *AS*, Introduction, p. *xlviii*. The *AS* reference reads: *ihu sākhī akbar pātisāhu suṇī thī*. 'The Emperor Akbar heard this sākhī.' *AS*, p. 90. The longer *Miharbān* version reads: *eh sākhī akbar pātisāh kari sunāī thī. jab gurū arjun lahauri āi miliā thā pātisāh kau*. 'The Emperor Akbar heard this sākhī related. [This happened] when Gurū Arjan visited Lahore to meet the Emperor Akbar.' *Mih JS* II.137.

[6] *Mih JS* II.357.

[7] See below, pp. 212–14. Piār Singh actually carries the date of the *Ādi Sākhīs* compilation as far back as a period preceding the compilation of the Ādi Granth (A.D. 1603–4), adding to the argument set out above the claim that anything later than this period would have utilized Bhāī Gurdās's

This cannot be affirmed in categorical terms, but it does at least demonstrate the perils of seeking to date janam-sākhīs on the basis of isolated references. The only positive assertions which may be regarded as permissible are, first, that the original *Ādi Sākhīs* collection must have been compiled during the seventeenth century; and secondly, that it incorporates material from earlier sources. The first is a safe assumption because two of the extant manuscripts bear dates corresponding to A.D. 1701 and both are evidently copies of an earlier manuscript.

Manuscript copies

The four manuscripts known to exist in Indian Pañjāb are located in the following places:

(1) Sikh Reference Library, Amritsar. MS no. S462.
(2) The library of the Mahārājā of Paṭiālā in Motī Bāgh Palace, Paṭiālā.
(3) The personal library of Sardār Shamsher Singh Ashok of Amritsar.
(4) Central Public Library, Paṭiālā. MS no. 495.[1]

Of these only the first two correspond in arrangement and content to the Lahore collection reported by Mohan Singh. Sardār Ashok's manuscript is limited to twenty-five of the thirty sākhīs included in the older manuscripts,[2] and the remaining manuscript records the *Ādi Sākhīs* anecdotes as part of a much larger collection.[3] The undated manuscript held by the Sikh Reference Library lacks its first five folios, but is otherwise complete.[4] Only one folio is missing from the Motī Bāgh copy. This manuscript is dated S.1758 (A.D. 1701), six months earlier than the Lahore manuscript.[5] Both manuscripts number their sākhīs up to thirty, but both have at different places overlooked a sākhī in the process.[6] Several of the sākhīs are composite and contain two or more separate anecdotes.

---

work and so would have included the anecdote which Bhāī Gurdās sets in Multān. *AS*, Introduction, p. *xlviii*. For Bhāī Gurdās and the Multān anecdote see below, pp. 118–20. With the sole exception of the *Gyān-ratanāvalī* none of the later janam-sākhīs use Bhāī Gurdās in this manner. The *B40 Janam-sākhī*, compiled in A.D. 1733, also omits Bhāī Gurdās's Multān anecdote.

[1] *AS*, Introduction, pp. *x–xii*. Jagjīt Singh claims that there is also a copy in the possession of 'S. Kundan Singh, a close friend of S. Randhir Singh, Department of Historical Studies, Panjabi (*sic*) University, Patiala'. 'A Critical and Comparative Study of the Janam Sakhis of Guru Nanak' (unpublished Ph.D. thesis, Panjab University, 1967), p. 31.

[2] Shamsher Singh Ashok (ed.), *Purātan Janam Sākhī Srī Gurū Nānak Dev Jī kī* (Amritsar, 1969), pp. 11–12. Ashok's manuscript is dated S. 1791 (A.D. 1734). He reports having obtained it from Bhāī Kirpā Singh Darzī of Guārā Upoke village. The manuscript contains twenty-five of the thirty sākhīs recorded in the longer versions. Ibid., p. 45.

[3] *AS*, Introduction, pp. *xi–xii*.

[4] The pagination begins with the figure 6. This, however, is not the original numbering. The fourth folio of the extant text also bears, in an earlier hand, the number 167. From this it is evident that the manuscript must originally have been part of a larger manuscript and it can be assumed that the *Ādi Sākhīs* portion must have commenced on folio 159. The extant manuscript concludes with folio 155 of the later numbering.

[5] *sammat 1758 māh asāṛ badī 13*. Mohan Singh reported the date of the Lahore manuscript as *sammat 1758 poh sudī 1*. *AS*, Introduction, p. *xi*. Ashok's manuscript is dated S. 1791 (A.D. 1734) and the Central Public Library manuscript S. 1813 (A.D. 1756). Ibid., pp. *xi–xii*.

[6] Sikh Reference Library manuscript no. 5462, f. 35b. *AS*, p. 81.

Printed edition

Piār Singh's printed edition of the *Ādi Sākhīs* was issued in 1969 under the title *Śambhū Nāth Vālī Janam Patrī Bābe Nānak Jī kī prasidh nān Ādi Sākhiān.*[1] In preparing this edition the editor followed the Motī Bāgh text supplementing it where necessary with the Sikh Reference Library manuscript. Footnotes have been added to indicate variant readings in the texts of the Sikh Reference Library and Ashok manuscripts. A list of the janam-sākhī's contents as printed in this edition is given in Appendix 3.

THE MIHARBĀN *TRADITION*

Soḍhī Miharbān, putative author of the discourses recorded in the *Miharbān Janam-sākhī*, occupies an unenviable position in Sikh annals. His father Prithī Chand, although the eldest son of Gurū Rām Dās, had been passed over as successor to the office of Gurū in favour of his younger brother Arjan. The succession of Arjan did not, however, go unchallenged. Prithī Chand, claiming to be the only legitimate heir, evidently managed to retain the allegiance of a portion of the Sikh community and when he died in 1619 he was succeeded by his son Miharbān. The followers of Prithī Chand and his successors were stigmatized Mīṇās, or unscrupulous rogues, by the adherents of Gurū Arjan's line[2] and enmity between the two groups persisted until the Mīṇā strength eventually dwindled to insignificance during the latter part of the eighteenth century. Miharbān himself led the Mīṇā sect until his death in 1640, when he was succeeded by his son Harijī.[3]

Although there persisted in Sikh tradition a belief that Miharbān had written a janam-sākhī it was not until well into the twentieth century that a copy was actually known to exist. In the absence of any text, and on the basis of the prologue to the *Gyān-ratanāvalī*,[4] it was assumed that the work of one so notoriously inimical to the established line of Gurūs would certainly be dangerously heretical, and in this assurance the absence of a copy went unmourned. It was only in 1940 that a copy was discovered in the village of Damdamā Sāhib.[5]

Unfortunately the manuscript found in Damdamā Sāhib covers only the first three sections (*pothī*, 'volume') of the six which constituted the complete janam-sākhī. To this day the three remaining sections are still untraced, except for the portion of the *Miharbān* account of Nānak's death

[1] Published by the editor, Paṭiālā, and printed at the Phulkiān Press, Phulkiān Mārg, Paṭiālā. Pañjābī introduction, pp. *ix–lii*, and text, pp. 1–101. The abbreviation *AS* used in this study refers to this edition.

[2] *BG* XXVI: 33, XXXVI: 1 ff.

[3] *GNSR*, pp. 18–19. See also the *Dabistān* reference in *PPP* I.1 (April 1967), p. 61.

[4] See below, p. 37.

[5] *GNSR*, p. 19. Damdamā Sāhib, also known as Sābo kī Talvaṇḍī, is located eighteen miles south of Bhaṭiṇḍā. It acquired the name Damdamā, or 'resting-place', in memory of the occasion when in 1705 Gurū Gobind Siṅgh rested there following the Battle of Muktsar.

which appears in the later *Bālā* tradition.[1] The three sections included in the manuscript are entitled respectively *Pothī Sach-khaṇḍ*, *Pothī Harijī*, and *Pothī Chatarbhuj*. According to the colophon of the first of these the three remaining sections were entitled *Keśo Rāi Pothī*, *Abhai Pad Pothī*, and *Prem Pad Pothī*.[2]

An examination of the extant portion indicates three important conclusions. The first is that if the works of Gurū Nānak are to be accepted as the standard of orthodoxy the sect responsible for the *Miharbān* tradition cannot possibly be branded as heretical. Differences between the teachings Nānak and the theology of the *Miharbān* sect can certainly be detected, but they represent no more than the shifting of interpretation and emphasis one might expect after a period of one hundred years. The followers of Miharbān must be regarded as loyal perpetuators of the Divine Name theology propounded by Nānak rather than as heretics. Their sin plainly was schism, not heresy.

The second point to be noted is that if the collection of *Miharbān* discourses is to be classified as a janam-sākhī the definition of that term will require some extension. The so-called *Miharbān Janam-sākhī* is not simply a collection of hagiographic anecdotes. It does indeed incorporate many such anecdotes, and *Pothī Sach-khaṇḍ* uses a janam-sākhī variety of travel sequence as a framework for its discourses. The interest of the *Miharbān* commentators, however, is not primarily in this narrative material. Their chief interest is in exegesis of the works of Nānak and it is for precisely this reason that they must be called commentators rather than narrators. For the same reason the word used to designate its subdivisions is *goṣṭ* ('discourse'), not *sākhī*. Anecdotes rarely provide more than settings for the scriptural quotations and exposition which the *Miharbān* commentators were so concerned to propagate. In *Pothī Sach-khaṇḍ* this exegetical interest is dominant and in the two succeeding sections it is overwhelming.

The third point to emerge from an examination of the manuscript is that the extant *Miharbān* text is a late and highly evolved product. According to the *Miharbān* group's own claim the janam-sākhī represents discourses delivered orally by Miharbān and recorded shortly after his death in 1640.[3] There may well be truth in this claim, but if it is to be allowed it must follow that the extant text does not correspond to the original version. The colophon at the conclusion of the manuscript declares that the actual copying was concluded in S.1885 (A.D. 1828).[4] It is to this early nineteenth-century period rather than to the early seventeenth century that the extant text should be related, for it clearly represents a process of growth requiring much more than a hundred years. This is indicated by the number of discourses it contains,[5] by the enormous length and variety of its scriptural commentary, by interpolations which can only have come

[1] *MS Recension B* of the *Bālā* tradition. See above, pp. 19, 20.

[2] *Mih JS* I.519.

[3] *GNSR*, p. 21.

[4] *Mih JS* II.624.

[5] *Pothī Sach-khaṇḍ* contains 153 discourses, *Pothī Harijī* has 61, and *Pothī Chatarbhuj* has 74. The total recorded in all six *pothīs* is said to have been 575. *Mih JS* I.519.

from late eighteenth-century sources, by evidences of earlier *Miharbān* recensions in other extant janam-sākhīs, and by comparisons of highly developed *Miharbān* narratives with the more primitive analogues recorded in these other janam-sākhīs. The basic structure of the *Miharbān Janam-sākhī* and an indeterminate quantity of its material may derive from the first half of the seventeenth century, but the text as it now stands is the composite product of several generations of later commentators. This expansion applies particularly to the scriptural quotations and exegesis which set the *Miharbān* tradition apart from all other janam-sākhīs.

The distinctive religious concerns expressed throughout the extant *Miharbān* material suggest that the tradition must have been sustained throughout the eighteenth century by groups (*saṅgat*) of Sikhs who did not subscribe to the evolving beliefs and discipline of the Khālsā brotherhood. These non-Khālsā *saṅgats* stand in a direct line leading from the teachings of Nānak through to the so-called *sahaj-dhārī* section of the modern Sikh community.[1] The followers of Miharbān may be regarded as seventeenth-century representatives of this Nānak-panthī stream and it would be entirely natural for the *Miharbān* writings, with their strongly religious emphasis, to survive within the eighteenth-century and nineteenth-century continuation of the same stream. The *Miharbān* following did not, of course, constitute the entire membership of this portion of the wider Sikh community, merely that of its most articulate section. It was also representative of this continuing Nānak-panthī tradition in that it perpetuated Khatrī influence, as opposed to the rapidly increasing Jaṭ dominance in the Khālsā.

Within the Khālsā the influence of the *Miharbān* tradition was negligible except in a purely negative sense and it was ironic that the principal *Miharbān* manuscript should have been discovered at Damdamā Sāhib, a village redolent with Khālsā associations. It is, however, possible that the *Miharbān* works may have commanded a continuing interest amongst sādhūs of the Udāsī sect and that versions of the *Miharbān* tradition may have been preserved in their *akhāṛās*.[2]

[1] The term *sahaj-dhārī* is normally translated 'slow-adopter', i.e. one who is moving towards a full acceptance of the Khālsā discipline but who has not yet proceeded further than an acceptance of Nānak's teachings concerning salvation. It is much more likely that the compound should be traced to Nānak's own distinctive usage of the word *sahaj*. In the works of Nānak *sahaj* is the most popular of several expressions used to designate the condition of ineffable bliss induced by the disciplined practice of *nām simaran*. *GNSR*, pp. 224–5. The term *sahaj-dhārī* probably assumed this usage and should accordingly be understood to mean 'one who accepts the *nām simaran* teachings of Nānak', without any reference to the adoption of the Khālsā discipline.

[2] The Udāsīs constitute an order of ascetics within the Sikh community. Although they claim as their founder Sirī Chand, one of Gurū Nānak's two sons, they are more accurately understood as a continuation within the new community of an earlier ascetic tradition. Nāth influence is plainly evident in some of their customs and beliefs. Their connection with the wider Sikh community is sustained by the reverence which they show towards the Ādi Granth and by close family ties. In theory, and generally in practice, the Udāsīs have been celibate and have relied largely upon the Jaṭ community for recruits. The word *akhāṛā*, 'arena', is used to designate their temples and monasteries. See H. A. Rose (ed.) *GTC*, vol. iii, pp. 479–81; and J. C. Oman, *The Mystics, Ascetics, and Saints of India* (London, 1903), pp. 194–6.

Manuscript copies

The manuscript discovered at Damdamā Sāhib in 1940 was acquired early in the following year by Khalsa College, Amritsar, and lodged in the College's Sikh History Research Department where it bears the number SHR 427.[1] This manuscript, as already noted, is dated S.1885 (A.D. 1828) and covers only the first three of the janam-sākhī's six sections. It is also incomplete in that two small clusters of folios are missing.[2] In 1961, however, the College obtained a second *Miharbān* manuscript (SHR 2190). This was no more than a large fragment covering seventy-two discourses of *Pothī Sach khaṇḍ*, but it did at least supply the two portions missing from the first manuscript. Its text corresponds closely to that of SHR 427. No date is given, but the copyist identifies himself as a Brāhmaṇ Sikh of Gujar Mal Maṇḍī in Lahore City.[3]

Apart from these two Khalsa College manuscripts no copies of any substantial portion of the *Miharbān* tradition are known to exist. There are, however, other works which were produced by the Mīṇās and of these one deserves a brief mention. This is the Mīṇā account of Miharbān's own life, a work attributed to his son Harijī and entitled *Goṣṭān Miharbān jī diān* ('Discourses of Miharbān'). The work deserves attention because of the light which it casts upon the nature of the *Miharbān* following and their distinctive beliefs. Two manuscript copies are extant, one dated S.1836 (A.D. 1779) held by the Sikh Reference Library in Amritsar, and the other an undated copy in the Central Public Library, Paṭiālā.[4] The text has not been published.

Printed edition

The text of *Pothī Sach-khaṇḍ* was published by the Sikh History Research Department of Khalsa College, Amritsar, in 1962 under the title *Janam Sākhī Srī Gurū Nānak Dev Jī* (edited by Kirpāl Singh and Shamsher Singh Ashok). This edition follows the text of SHR 427, supplemented where necessary by SHR 2190. The remainder of SHR 427 (*Pothī Harijī* and *Pothī Chatarbhuj*) was edited by Parkash Singh and published in 1969 as a second volume under the same title. Both volumes include a series of introductory essays by various contributors.[5]

[1] *Mih JS* I, Introduction, p. *v*, and personal communication from Dr. Gaṇḍā Singh of Paṭiālā. See also Kirpāl Singh (ed.), *A Catalogue of Punjabi and Urdu Manuscripts in the Sikh History Research Department* (Amritsar, 1963), pp. 13–15. *PHLS* i. 231.

[2] Loc. cit., ff. 82–84 and 121–125. The first cluster covered the concluding lines of *goṣṭ* 51, all of *goṣṭ* 52, and the opening portion of *goṣṭ* 53. The second cluster covered *goṣṭs* 68 and 69. *Mih JS* I, Introduction, p. *x*, and ibid., Introductory Essays, p. 153n.

[3] *Mih JS* I, Introduction, p. *x*. Kirpāl Singh (ed.), op. cit., pp. 12–13. *PHLS* i. 232.

[4] SRL MS no. 3510 and CPL MS no. 2527. *PHLS* ii. 255–6 and i. 375–6. The contents of the work are summarized in Piār Singh, 'A Critical Survey of Panjabi Prose in the Seventeenth Century' (unpublished Ph.D. thesis, Panjab University, 1968), pp. 150–4. For other Mīṇā works see ibid., pp. 138–50, 154–62. LDP MS no. 359 is a particularly valuable collection of Mīṇā material. Piār Singh, op. cit., pp. 142–9. *PHLS* i. 232–3. The Khalsa College MS no. SHR 2306 also deserves notice.

[5] In this study the abbreviation *Mih JS* I signifies the 1962 edition of the *Pothī Sach-khaṇḍ* text;

THE GYĀN-RATANĀVALĪ

Tradition attributes the authorship of the *Gyān-ratanāvali* to Manī Siṅgh, a famous Sikh of the early eighteenth century, executed by Zakaryā Khān of Lahore in 1738.[1] A prologue attached to extant copies of the janam-sākhī relates the circumstances of its composition as follows:

The Sikhs once made a request to Bhāī Manī Singh, saying, 'The *Chhoṭe Mel Vāle*[2] have in several places introduced errors into the record of the first Master's discourses and life, and as a result of hearing these the Sikhs' faith in the Gurū is declining. Just as milk is adulterated with water and the swan separates the two, so you be our Great Swan and separate the Gurū's words from those of the Mīṇās.' Bhāī Manī Siṅgh replied, 'At the time when the fifth Master established the canon of *Srī Granth Sāhib* the Sikhs besought him, saying, "There is no authenticated version of the discourses. The *Pañj Mel Vāle*[3] have all interpolated objectionable things in the janam-sākhī and are leading the Sikhs astray." Bhāī Gurdās was instructed to write a janam-sākhī in the form of a *vār* so that by means of the *vār* the Gurū's Sikhs might hear and read the record [of the Gurū's life]. Bhāī Gurdās's *vār*, that treasury of wisdom,[4] is a janam-sākhī.' The Sikhs then said, 'He has written [simply] the record. Please give us an expanded commentary on it so that faith may grow in the Sikhs who hear it.' Bhāī Manī Singh replied, 'Just as an ant cannot lift an elephant's burden and a turtle cannot raise Mount Mandar, so I am unable to prepare a commentary on the discourses of Bābā [Nānak]. But just as swimmers fix reeds in the river so that those who do not know the way may also cross, so I shall take Bhāī Gurdās's *vār* as my basis and in accordance with it, and with the accounts which I have heard at the court of the tenth Master, I shall relate to you whatever commentary issues from my humble mind.'[5]

This passage is certainly important in so far as it testifies to the early eighteenth-century influence of the Mīnās (the *Chhote Mel Vāle*) and to Khālsā hostility towards them. It may even be essentially accurate as an explanation for an original eighteenth-century *Gyān-ratanāvali*.[6] The professed connection with Manī Singh is, however, open to serious doubt and so too is the alleged period of composition. No eighteenth-century text

and *Mih JS* II signifies the 1969 edition of the two remaining *pothīs*. Extensively abridged texts of all three *pothīs* appear in Kirpāl Singh, *Janam Sākhī Paramparā* (Paṭiālā, 1969), Appendix, pp. 58–220.

[1] *MK*, p. 712. Macauliffe, i. lxxiv–vi.

[2] Lit. 'the lower congregation', a term which could be applied to any heretics or dissenters but which came to be attached specifically to the Mīṇās. *MK*, p. 603. See above, p. 33.

[3] The five execrated groups whom Khālsā Sikhs, in accordance with their baptismal oath, must spurn. These include the Mīṇās. *MK*, pp. 593–4. The usage in this context is anachronistic as the term dates from the seventeenth or early eighteenth century.

[4] *gyān* (*jñān*): knowledge, wisdom. *ratanāvalī*: a string of pearls or necklace of gems.

[5] *GR*, pp. 3–4. For Bhāī Gurdās see below, pp. 43–5.

[6] Although the prologue refers to Bhāī Gurdās's *vār* as the *Gyān-ratanāvalī* the title is more commonly applied to the janam-sākhī attributed to Manī Siṅgh. The *vār* in question is Bhāī Gurdās's first. The *Bhagat-ratanāvalī*, or *Sikhān dī Bhagat-māl*, a work based on Bhāī Gurdās's eleventh *vār*, is also attributed to Manī Siṅgh.

appears to have survived. All we have are lengthy nineteenth-century products which incorporate substantial quantities of extraneous material, much of it plainly derived from *Bālā* sources. In addition to numerous anecdotes this supplementary material also includes commentaries on *Āsā dī Vār*, Gurū Nānak's *Japjī*, and his *Siddh Goṣṭ*.

The evidence provided by extant texts suggests the following pattern. At some indeterminate date an amplified version of Bhāī Gurdās's first *vār* was produced. This, in its original form, probably comprised no more than the actual stanzas of the *vār*, with a comparatively brief paraphrase in each instance. Most stanzas were quoted individually, each with its corresponding paraphrase. Whenever a particular anecdote extended over more than one stanza, however, the relevant stanzas would be cited together and followed by a single paraphrase. The result would have been a brief janam-sākhī incorporating Bhāī Gurdās's limited selection of anecdotes together with his preliminary description of the darkness preceding the light of Nānak and also his summary treatment of Gurū Nānak's immediate successors.

This nucleus must have been a brief work, its contents apparently limited to quotation of the successive stanzas of *Vār* 1 and simple paraphrases of these stanzas. To it have been added materials drawn from all available sources. The original stanzas and paraphrases are still easily identifiable in most instances, but inserted between them one now finds a vast fund of supplementary anecdotes and commentary. This interpolated material is so substantial that the late nineteenth-century version of the *Gyān-ratanāvalī* rivals its *Bālā* contemporary in length.

The additions which have so impressively enlarged the *Gyān-ratanāvalī* cannot have been the work of a single interpolator. This is made clear by a division within the nineteenth-century collection. While covering the Gurū's early life and a period of travels which takes him to eastern and southern India the modern *Gyān-ratanāvalī* is relatively coherent. Parts of it are, moreover, distinctively different from the analogues provided by the other major janam-sākhī traditions. Instances occur of borrowings from the *Bālā* tradition, but most nineteenth-century texts omit the person of Bhāī Bālā from this first section. It is the introduction of Bhāī Bālā which marks the line of division between the two sections.[1] Some clusters of anecdotes continue to ignore him and these retain the essential consistency of the first section. On the whole, however, this latter portion of the modern *Gyān-ratanāvalī* resembles the disordered *Bālā* pattern and lengthy passages represent direct borrowings from the *Bālā* tradition.

One other element remains to be noted. At some stage in this growth process an explanatory prologue (quoted above) and epilogue were added. Like the supplementary anecdotes these two passages refer to Manī Singh in the third person and thus cannot be attributed to him personally. It seems likely that they were appended at a comparatively early date, before the introduction of significant interpolation, and that they provide a correspondingly early stage in the evolution of the bulky product which

[1] *GR*, p. 264. For further details see *GNSR*, pp. 26–7.

we now possess.[1] The final stage was reached when the heterogeneous result was lithographed at the end of the nineteenth century.

Manuscript copies

The only important collection of *Gyān-ratanāvalī* manuscripts consists of three copies in the possession of Professor Prītam Singh of Amritsar, all of them complete and all dated. One bears the date S.1778 (A.D. 1721) which, if correct, would firmly place the *Gyān-ratanāvalī* in the first two decades of the eighteenth century. It is, however, evident both from the modernity of the manuscript's language and from its actual contents that the date must be incorrect.[2] The two remaining manuscripts are dated S.1883 (A.D. 1826) and S.1927 (A.D. 1870). In addition to these three copies Shamsher Singh Ashok lists four undated manuscripts, two of them substantially complete and two incomplete.[3] Two more are held by the Sikh History Research Department of Khalsa College, Amritsar, both of them complete and both dated.[4]

Printed editions

At least three editions of the amplified *Gyān-ratanāvalī* text have been lithographed. One was published in 1891 by Charāg Dīn and Sarāj Dīn of Lahore; a second was published by the Sanskrit Book Depot of Lahore in 1892;[5] and a third was issued by Gulāb Siṅgh and Sons, also of Lahore, in 1908.[6]

THE MAHIMĀ PRAKĀŚ *TRADITION*

Internal evidence suggests that most of the important janam-sākhī traditions evolved in areas to the north and north-west of Lahore. The *Bālā* tradition may perhaps be an exception to this rule, but this has not yet been established. The only proven exception is the *Mahimā Prakāś*. This version of the life of Nānak represents a tradition which developed in Khaḍūr, a village south-east of Amritsar on the right bank of the Beās river. It was here that Gurū Aṅgad lived during his years as leader of the Sikh community (1539–52). Two centuries later the same village produced

[1] Jagjīt Singh argues that the original work was written in A.D. 1739 by Sūrat Singh of Bāṭh, a follower of Manī Siṅgh. 'A Critical and Comparative Study of the Janam Sakhis of Guru Nanak' (unpublished Ph.D. thesis, Panjab University, 1967), pp. 445–9.

[2] For examples see *PHLS* ii. 243.

[3] *PHLS* ii. 240–5.

[4] MSS nos. SHR 2300C, dated S. 1891 (A.D. 1834); and SHR 1440, dated S. 1895 (A.D. 1838). Kirpāl Singh (ed.), *A Catalogue of Punjabi and Urdu Manuscripts &c* (Amritsar, 1963), pp. 5–6.

[5] An abridged text of this 1892 edition is reproduced in Kirpāl Singh, *Janam Sākhī Paramparā* (Paṭiālā, 1969), Appendix, pp. 330–401. This edition was lithographed in Bombay.

[6] The abbreviation *GR* used in this study refers to the first of these. The book is now very difficult to procure. The British Library and the India Office Library each possess a copy.

its own distinctive janam-sākhī tradition, the *Mahimā Prakāś* or 'Light of Glory'.

Although two janam-sākhīs bearing the title *Mahimā Prakāś* now exist only one of these strictly qualifies as a separate and distinct janam-sākhī tradition. This is the collection of sākhīs known as the *Mahimā Prakāś Vāratak*, or '*Mahimā Prakāś* in Prose'. Unlike its predecessors this tradition does not deal exclusively with Nānak anecdotes, traversing instead the lives of all ten Gurūs and treating each of them relatively briefly. The first Gurū naturally receives special attention and the portion covering his life can be detached to form a complete janam-sākhī. It is, however, an unusually brief one, omitting many of the well-established anecdotes one might otherwise expect in an eighteenth-century collection. In the actual selection of anecdotes a primary criterion has obviously been the reputation of Khaḍūr. No reference to the village from earlier tradition appears to have been overlooked and some extra anecdotes relating to it have been added.

The second of the janam-sākhīs bearing the *Mahimā Prakāś* title is the so-called *Mahimā Prakāś Kavitā*, or '*Mahimā Prakāś* in Verse'. Apart from the actual title and the fact that both were evidently compiled in Khaḍūr there is little to suggest any close connection between the two janam-sākhīs. The third of the *Kavitā* sākhīs corresponds to one which first appears in the *Mahimā Prakāś Vāratak*,[1] but thereafter the *Kavitā* version follows a pattern which indicates a variety of sources. Sākhīs found only in the *Vāratak* collection are ignored and at two critical points (the dates of Nānak's birth and death) the two versions directly contradict each other.[2]

The *Mahimā Prakāś Kavitā* in its extant form evidently represents the product of two distinct phases. The first was the composition of a metrical janam-sākhī, based upon earlier narrative janam-sākhīs and probably the oral tradition of Khaḍūr. This first stage, representing the authentic *Mahimā Prakāś Kavitā*, has subsequently been augmented by later borrowings from other janam-sākhīs and from apocryphal works attributed to Gurū Nānak. In some instances these prose borrowings have been interspersed within particular sākhīs between sections of the original verse. Elsewhere they have been incorporated as complete prose sākhīs. Particularly obvious are extensive borrowings from a *Miharbān* source, complete with the exegetical supplements so characteristic of the *Miharbān* tradition.

The metrical portion of the *Mahimā Prakāś Kavitā* presents no apparent problems of authorship or dating. The author gives his name as Sarūp Dās and specifies S.1833 (A.D. 1776) as the year in which he composed his poetic account in Khaḍūr. In the case of the *Mahimā Prakāś Vāratak*, however, the extant text provides no information. The author is variously known in modern works as Kirpāl Siṅgh Bhallā and Kirpāl Dās Bhallā; and the date of composition as either S.1798 (A.D. 1741) or S.1830

[1] *GNM*, pp. 7–8. *SLTGN(Pbī)*, p. 32.
[2] *GNM*, pp. 5, 347. *SLTGN(Pbī)*, pp. 32, 46.

(A.D. 1773). Either date is possible. An earlier date is unlikely and any date more than two years later would appear to be impossible.[1]

Manuscript copies

Manuscript copies of both *Mahimā Prakāś* versions are surprisingly scarce. Only four *Mahimā Prakāś Vāratak* manuscripts are said to exist, and it is possible that the actual number is even smaller. One manuscript is (or was) in the library of the Languages Department of the Pañjāb in Paṭiālā.[2] A second is in the personal library of the late Bhāī Vir Singh, now housed in Dehrā Dūn; and a third is held by the Sikh History Research Department of Khalsa College, Amritsar.[3] The fourth is reported to have been in the Punjab Public Library, Lahore. The third of these manuscripts is a copy of the second, made in 1932. The second is itself a recent product, having been copied only four years earlier.[4]

Manuscript copies of the *Mahimā Prakāś Kavitā* are more numerous. Eight such copies are known to be extant.[5] Those which are dated range in age from S.1857 (A.D. 1800) to S.1897 (A.D. 1840).

Printed editions

A text of the portion of the *Mahimā Prakāś Vāratak* which deals with Gurū Nānak has been printed in *Sources on the Life and Teachings of Guru Nanak*, together with an annotated English translation.[6] This text follows the Khalsa College manuscript SHR 2308 noted above. An earlier edition of the same text which was privately printed in Dehrā Dūn in 1959 is now out of print.[7] A list of the Nanak anecdotes included in the *Mahimā Prakāś Vāratak* is given in Appendix 5.

A complete text of the *Mahimā Prakāś Kavitā* was published in two volumes by the Languages Department of the Pañjāb in 1970–1.[8] The first of the volumes, issued under the title *Gurū Nānak Mahimā*, covers

[1] For a more detailed discussion of the authorship and dating of the two versions, together with citations, see W. H. McLeod, introduction to an English translation of the *Mahimā Prakāś Vāratak*, in *SLTGN(Eng)*, pp. 55–7.

[2] Efforts made to trace it in 1969 were unsuccessful.

[3] MS no. SHR 2308. Kirpāl Singh (ed.), *A Catalogue of Punjabi and Urdu Manuscripts &c* (Amritsar, 1963), pp. 17–18.

[4] MS no. SHR 2308, f. 129a. The copyist, Akālī Kaur Singh, evidently left no information concerning the location of the manuscript which he used.

[5] LDP MS no. 176; SRL MS no. 1151; Khalsa College MS no. SHR 2300A; Pañjābī Sāhit Akādemī, Ludhiānā, MS no. 792 (incomplete); Pañjāb Archives MS no. 792/M; a manuscript in the possession of Giānī Prakaran Singh of Saṅgrūr; and two manuscripts in the Punjab Public Library, Lahore. *PHLS* i. 368 and ii. 249–51. Kirpāl Singh (ed.), op. cit., pp. 18–19. Gaṇḍā Singh, *A Bibliography of the Punjab* (Paṭiālā, 1966), p. 208. Gobind Singh Lāmbā, introduction to *GNM*, pp. 9–14. *LDP* MS no. 176 bears the date S. 1857.

[6] *SLTGN(Pbī)*, pp. 32–46. *SLTGN(Eng)*, pp. 59–87.

[7] Kirpāl Singh (ed.), *Jīvan Kathā Srī Gurū Nānak Dev Jī Mahimā Prakāś* (*Vāratak*) *vichon* (Dehrā Dūn, 1959).

[8] Sarūp Dās Bhallā (ed. Shamsher Singh Ashok and Gobind Singh Lāmbā), *Gurū Nānak Mahimā* (Paṭiālā, 1970), and *Mahimā Prakāś* (Paṭiālā, 1971). The abbreviation *GNM* refers to the first of these.

the portion which concerns the life of Nānak. The second volume, misleadingly entitled simply *Mahimā Prakāś*, contains a brief introduction by one of the editors and the portion dealing with the nine remaining Gurūs. The manuscript held by the Languages Department has been followed in the preparation of this text, with supplements and amendments drawn from three other manuscripts.[1]

INDIVIDUAL JANAM-SĀKHĪS

Two important janam-sākhīs which have not produced distinctive traditions are the manuscripts which for convenience will be referred to as *LDP 194* and *B40*. (In both cases the titles are library catalogue numbers.) Both are closely related to other traditions, notably to the *Purātan* and *Ādi Sākhīs* collections, but not to the point of justifying inclusion within either of them.

LDP 194 The abbreviation *LDP 194* designates manuscript no. 194 in the library of the Languages Department of the Pañjāb, Paṭiālā. At first sight it may appear that the manuscript is an early recension of the *Colebrooke* and *Hāfizābād* janam-sākhīs, and that it should accordingly be in the *Purātan* group. This would be misleading. Although the manuscript certainly stands within a line of descent leading to the *Hāfizābād Janam-sākhī*, it is the line which accounts only for the extra material added by the *Hāfizābād* compiler to the *Colebrooke* nucleus. Later it will be shown how an early tradition (designated *Narrative I*) divided into two streams (*Narrative Ia* and *Narrative Ib*). The first of these leads directly to the *Colebrooke* version and accounts both for the distinctive structure of the *Purātan* narrative and also for almost all of its material. To this *Colebrooke* version the *Hāfizābād* compiler added two anecdotes and a discourse drawn from a *Narrative Ib* source.[2]

It is to this second stream that *LDP 194* belongs, and as this was no more than a supplementary source for the *Purātan* tradition it would be misleading to bracket the manuscript with the *Colebrooke* and *Hāfizābād* janam-sākhīs in a common tradition. The link connecting it with the *Purātan* tradition is plain, but so too is its distinction from the main line of *Purātan* development. This same *Narrative Ib* tradition also contributes directly to the *Ādi Sākhīs* and *B40* compilations, and less directly to the *Miharbān* collection.[3]

The *LDP 194* manuscript is in poor condition. Several leaves are missing, some of the folios have been bound out of order, and having reached the figure 100 the pagination reverts to 43 in the middle of a sākhī. It is, however, easily read. The script, although very immature, is unusually clear. The manuscript bears no date.

The actual text of the manuscript consists of two principal elements. The first portion is narrative, and although it is not regularly divided into

[1] *LDP* MS no. 176, supplemented by the SRL, Panjab Archives, and Khalsa College MSS.

[2] See above, p. 25.

[3] See below, p. 195.

sākhīs a total of twenty can be distinguished. These are listed in Appendix 4. The second portion comprises extended quotations from the works of Nānak, notably the *Siddh Goṣṭ* and *Vār Āsā*. The *Siddh Goṣṭ* begins on folio 56a of the second set of folio numbers. The text briefly reverts to narrative with the Achal discourse on folio 77b and then continues its scriptural quotation through to folio 117b. A few folios of scriptural quotation in a different hand conclude the manuscript.

The B40 Janam-sākhī The *B40* manuscript (so called because of the number which it bears in the India Office Library catalogue) is perhaps the most important of all extant janam-sākhīs. This reputation it deserves partly because of the quality of its illustrations; partly because of the unusually specific information which is provided concerning its origins; but chiefly because it is of all janam-sākhīs the most representative in terms of content. It is, like all janam-sākhīs, a composite product. The range of sources and styles, however, is superior to that of any other collection. Oral and written sources have both been used by its compiler and from these sources he has drawn examples of all the major forms to be found in the janam-sākhī literature.

Two notes appended to the text describe the genesis of the *B40 Janam-sākhī*.[1] It was commissioned, the scribe informs us, by a certain Bhāī Sangū Mal, 'servant of the congregation'. The copyist identifies himself as Dayā Rām Abrol and his artist colleague as Ālam Chand Rāj. The work was completed in S.1790 on a date corresponding to 31 August 1733. In 1907 the manuscript was acquired from Lahore for the India Office Library.

An edition of the Gurmukhī text of the *B40 Janam-sākhī* was published in 1974 by Professor Piār Singh under the title *Janam Sākhī Sri Gurū Nānak Dev Jī*. To this has since been added an English translation by W. H. McLeod entitled *The B40 Janam-sākhī*. Its contents are listed below on pp. 230–2.

MISCELLANEOUS WORKS CLOSELY RELATED TO THE JANAM-SĀKHĪS

In view of their enormous and sustained popularity it is scarcely surprising that the janam-sākhīs should have stimulated an affiliated literature, most of it appearing in the nineteenth and twentieth centuries. Four representatives of this literature will be briefly noted. Reference must also be made to a related work composed during the early seventeenth century. This latter is the first of a collection of thirty-nine *vārs* by the distinguished Sikh poet Bhāī Gurdās, a collection which possesses a considerable importance for any understanding of the early Sikh community.

Vār 1 *of Bhāī Gurdās* Bhāī Gurdās Bhallā has three major claims to fame in the history of the Sikh community. The first of these is that he

[1] *B40*, ff. 84b, 230a–231a.

was a nephew of the third Gurū, Amar Dās. Secondly, he was the amanuensis employed by Gurū Arjan to record the contents of the Ādi Granth during its compilation in 1603–4. Thirdly he was himself the author of thirty-nine poetic works written in the *vār* form, and of 556 others composed in the *kabitt* form. Although none of these works was included in the Ādi Granth the *vārs* came to be regarded as 'the key to the Gurū Granth Sāhib' and the compositions of Bhāī Gurdās are specifically approved for recitation in Sikh gurdwaras. His date of birth is unknown, but his death is said to have occurred in 1637.[1]

Although Bhāī Gurdās's first *vār* is not strictly speaking a janam-sākhī no survey of the janam-sākhīs would be complete without reference to it. The *vār* differs from the standard janam-sākhī form in two respects. First, it uses a poetic form instead of the narrative of the janam-sākhīs; and secondly its primary intention is to eulogize the unique status and power of the Gurū. These are, however, only marginal differences. In order to fulfil his intention, Bhāī Gurdās has used anecdotes of precisely the same kind as those of the janam-sākhīs, all of them to be found at various points in different janam-sākhīs. A loose definition of the janam-sākhī would certainly embrace the relevant portion of Bhāī Gurdās's first *vār* (stanzas 23–45). To this portion should be added stanzas 13–14 of the eleventh *vār*, a passage in which Bhāī Gurdās lists the more prominent of Bābā Nānak's followers. The standard printed edition is that of Hazārā Singh.[2] An English translation is given in *Sources on the Life and Teachings of Guru Nanak*.[3]

Because of its relatively early date Bhāī Gurdās's contribution is of notable importance, and its value is enhanced by the personal links which connected the author to the line of Gurūs descended from Amar Dās. Its importance must not, however, be exaggerated. Bhāī Gurdās's *Vār* 1 has commonly been read as a historical account of the Gurū's life and a strong insistence has been laid upon an obligation to accept all that he writes as literally true. This scarcely does justice to Bhāī Gurdās's method and understanding. His purpose was to magnify the Gurū's greatness, a task which he performs with notable success. In early seventeenth-century Pañjāb there was no reason why his panegyric should have been written with scrupulous concern for the canons of later historical scholarship. It was the myth that mattered and, as already indicated in the discussion of the purpose of the janam-sākhīs,[4] legend and history were alike legitimate ingredients.

The point deserves to be stressed in this context because the defence of the historical reliability of the janam-sākhīs generally takes its stand upon an assumed inerrancy of the works of Bhāī Gurdās. To deny this inerrancy as far as strictly historical information is concerned is not to suggest that

[1] For citations and further details concerning Bhāī Gurdās see *GNSR*, pp. 14–15. See also Khushwant Singh, *A History of the Sikhs*, vol. i (London, 1963), pp. 310–12.

[2] *Vārān Bhāī Gurdās*, ed. Hazārā Singh and revised by Vīr Singh. Amritsar: Khālsā Samāchār, several editions. Also *SLTGN(Pbī)*, pp. 13–19.

[3] *SLTGN(Eng)*, pp. 32–44.

[4] See above, pp. 8–10.

Bhāī Gurdās was dishonest or even credulous. Bhāī Gurdās relates various miraculous occurrences,[1] sets a discourse with the long-deceased Gorakhnāth on the legendary mountain of Sumeru,[2] and attaches to Bābā Nānak an anecdote which had already been extensively used in earlier Sūfī hagiography.[3] None of these elements destroys the value of what Bhāī Gurdās has written, provided only that the nature of that value is understood. His approach and his understanding were not those of a twentieth-century historian, nor were they inferior. It is merely that he pursued a different understanding of the nature of truth, the truth which myth seeks to express and for which it may utilize legend as well as history. For those who believe in the divine inspiration of Gurū Nānak Bhāī Gurdās's words are eternally true, regardless of what use he may make of legendary material. To read him as a chronicler of literal historical facts is to misunderstand him.

None of the *vārs* of Bhāī Gurdās are dated and the only statement which may be made with any assurance is that they must have been written before 1637. The fact that he obviously had before him a janam-sākhī model[4] suggests a date close to 1637 rather than earlier in the seventeenth century, but falls far short of proof. A list of the anecdotes utilized in the composition of his Nānak stanzas is given in Appendix 5.

The *Nānak Prakāś* of Santokh Singh Santokh Singh's *Nānak Prakāś* was completed in 1823 and since that date has exercised a considerable influence upon the popular understanding of the life of Gurū Nānak.[5] It is of interest for two reasons. First, it did much to strengthen a *Bālā* dominance which by the beginning of the nineteenth century was already well established. Confronted by the Hindālī content of the extant *Bālā* manuscripts Santokh Singh decided that these manuscripts must represent a corrupted version of an original janam-sākhī delivered before Gurū Aṅgad. The original version had, he believed, been corrupted simply by means of interpolation and he accordingly concluded that an authentic text could be restored by excising the recognizably Hindālī portions of the janam-sākhī. This he did and the first section of his *Nānak Prakāś* (the *pūrabāradh* section) was based upon the remainder.

The *Nānak Prakāś* is also of interest for the extensive additions which it makes to the *Bālā* tradition as Santokh Singh had received it. Three supplementary sources are of particular importance. First, there is the *Purātan* tradition. This appears in such distinctively *Colebrooke* anecdotes as 'Dūnī Chand and the Wolf' and 'The Kashmīrī Paṇḍit'.[6] Secondly, there was the *B40 Janam-sākhi* or a source very close to it. The *B40 Janam-sākhī* is itself an amalgam drawn from several sources, one of them an oral tradition (designated *Narrative III*) which is peculiar to *B40*.[7]

1 *BG* 1:31, 32, 36, 41.
2 *BG* 1:28.
3 *BG* 1:44. See below, pp. 118–20.
4 See below, p. 204.
5 The correct title of the work is *Gur Nānak Prakāś*. The shortened form is, however, almost invariably used. For a brief account of Santokh Singh's life see Macauliffe, i. lxxvi–vii.
6 *NPr* II.4, 14. See also II.15, 20, 21, 25.
7 See below, pp. 220–6, 229–32.

Most of the *Narrative III* anecdotes recorded in the *B40 Janam-sākhī* reappear in the *Nānak Prakāś*.[1] Thirdly, there are numerous details together with a few complete anecdotes which have no antecedents in extant janam-sākhīs. Much of this material was presumably derived by Santokh Singh from current oral tradition. These three supplementary sources together contribute the bulk of the anecdotes recorded in the second of the two sections in the *Nānak Prakāś* (the *uttarāradh* section).

Like the *vārs* of Bhāī Gurdās the *Nānak Prakāś* is in verse, but in both form and intention it comes much closer to the standard narrative janam-sākhī. Although the form is clearly intended to be poetic the product offers constant reminders of its prose origins. A charitable judgement might describe it as narrative poetry, with the qualification that its merits are essentially narrative rather than poetic. Today even its narrative qualities are difficult to appreciate, for Santokh Singh's crabbed mixture of Pañjābī and Sanskritized Hindī is far removed from the simple language of the janam-sākhīs.

Even more important in terms of its subsequent influence was the lengthy sequel to the *Nanāk Prakāś*, a work entitled *Gur Pratāp Sūray* and popularly referred to as the *Sūraj Prakāś*. This substantial composition, completed in 1844, covers the lives of Nānak's nine successors. Whereas the *Nānak Prakāś* stands as one of several janam-sākhīs the *Sūraj Prakāś* commonly stands alone, and references by modern authors to incidents in the lives of the Gurūs can often be traced no further than statements by Santokh Singh. This is particularly true of the eight Gurūs between Nānak and Gobind Singh. An edited text of both the *Nānak Prakāś* and *Sūraj Prakāś* was published in fourteen volumes by Vīr Singh between 1927 and 1935, and is still in print.[2]

The *Nānak Prakāś* is divided into two parts, the *pūrabāradh* and the *uttarāradh*. In footnote citations these will be designated by the roman figures I and II respectively. Sections of each part (*adhyāya*) will be indicated by arabic numerals without parentheses, and for individual stanzas within an *adhyāya* arabic numerals within parentheses will be used. The actual title of the work will be represented by the abbreviation *NPr*.

The *Nānak Vijay* of Sant Ren Sant Ren's *Nānak Vijay*, or *Srī Gurū Nānak Dig Vijay* is another nineteenth-century contribution to the hagiographic literature concerning Gurū Nānak. Its importance has been slight and it warrants mention here only because the author has sometimes been represented as a contemporary of Nānak. This misunderstanding has evidently arisen because the leader of a group of sādhūs figuring in the *Bālā* anecdote entitled 'The Good Bargain' is also named Sant Ren. The

[1] *NPr* II.12, 13, 14, 40, 44. Also II.11, 38.

[2] Amritsar: the Khālsā Samāchār. No single title is applied to the complete edition. The thirteen volumes comprise the following: vol. i, *Srī Gur Pratāp Sūraj Granthāvalī* (Vīr Singh's Introduction); vols. ii–iv, *Srī Gur Nānak Prakāś*; vols. v–xiii, *Srī Gur Pratāp Sūraj Granth* (the *Sūraj Prakāś*).

account of Bābā Nānak which it offers is, as one would expect, another amplified version of the *Bālā* tradition.[1]

The *Sūchak Prasaṅg Gurū kā* attributed to Bhāī Bahlo Bahlo is said to have been an early Sikh who died in the month of Chet, S. 1660 (A.D. 1603).[2] If the composition entitled *Sūchak Prasaṅg Gurū kā* were in fact the work of such a person it would rank as the earliest of all extant accounts of the life of Nānak. It is, however, another *Bālā*-based nineteenth-century product. This is evident both from the modernity of its language and from its contents.

The *Sūchak Prasaṅg Gurū kā* differs from its nineteenth-century contemporaries in that it offers an epitome of the *Bālā* tradition instead of an expanded version, compressing a remarkable amount into a very brief space. Although the section dealing with Gurū Nānak consists of only thirty-eight couplets the author manages to mention more than fifty janam-sākhī anecdotes. Occasionally an anecdote receives more than one couplet, but normally each is limited to a single line or half a line. The terseness of the style is well illustrated by couplet 24:

alī yār nūn balī banāyā bimal jot nūn sudhu karāyā
māṇak chand kābal bich tārā bāl gudāī ṭille bārā[3]

Alī Yār he made a saint; Bimal Jot he cleansed.
Māṇak Chand he redeemed in Kābul; and Bālgundāī in Ṭillā.

This may be compared with a *Bālā* version similar to the source which the author has obviously used. In the India Office Library manuscript Panj. B41 the portion so summarily expressed in this couplet covers eleven folios.[4]

The only extant copy of the work is a manuscript in the possession of Dr. Gaṇḍā Singh of Paṭiālā. This bears the date S. 1907 (A.D. 1850).[5] The text of the portion which concerns Gurū Nānak has been published in *Sources on the Life and Teachings of Guru Nanak*.[6]

Vīr Singh's *Srī Gurū Nānak Chamatkār*. Bhāī Vīr Singh's two-volume work *Srī Gurū Nānak Chamatkār* is of interest as a singularly attractive twentieth-century representative of the continuing janam-sākhī form.[7]

[1] Jagjit Singh, 'A Critical and Comparative Study of the Janam Sakhis of Guru Nanak', pp. 190–3. Jagjit Singh, following Shamsher Singh Ashok, lists four extant manuscripts. A microfilm copy of one of these is held by the Languages Department in Paṭiālā.

[2] *PHLS* i. 361. [3] *SLTGN(Pbī)*, p. 27. [4] *B41*, ff. 187a–198a.

[5] *PHLS* i. 361. The text is inscribed upon account books (*vahī*) of the kind used by shopkeepers.

[6] *SLTGN(Pbī)*, pp. 26–8.

[7] Vīr Singh, *Srī Gurū Nānak Chamatkār*. Amritsar: Khālsā Samāchār. First edition: vol. i, 1928, and vol. ii, 1933. The work is still in print. Vīr Singh used the same form to re-create versions of the traditions concerning the lives of Gurū Aṅgad, Gurū Amar Dās, Gurū Rām Dās, and Gurū Arjan (*Srī Aṣṭ Gur Chamatkār*, Amritsar, 2 vols., 1952 and 1968), and Gurū Gobind Siṅgh (*Srī Kalgīdhar Chamatkār*, Amritsar, 2 vols., 1925). For another twentieth-century janam-sākhī see Kirpāl Singh, *Janam Sākhī Paramparā* (Paṭiālā, 1969), pp. 1–166.

Just as Santokh Singh and others rewrote the received *Bālā* tradition so in like manner Vīr Singh produced in contemporary language an augmented version of the *Purātan* tradition. Vīr Singh was an unusually gifted Pañjābī writer and his *Sri Gurū Nānak Chamatkār* can be regarded, in terms of language and style, as the climax of janam-sākhī development.

4

THE LANGUAGE OF THE JANAM-SĀKHĪS

Grierson, when dealing with the language of the janam-sākhīs, is both brief and confusing. In the primary definition given in *The Linguistic Survey of India* he declares: 'The celebrated *Janam-Sakhi* (a life of Nanak) is in Lahnda, not in Panjabi.'[1] Elsewhere he contradicts this statement. In an earlier volume, having claimed that 'Lahnda . . . contains no prose literature', he adds the footnote: 'The Janam Sakhi, a well known Sikh book, is written in a dialect which is half Panjabi and half Lahnda.'[2]

The contradiction is of less importance than might appear. It would be of importance only if Grierson's rigorous distinction between Pañjābī and Lahndā as two separate languages could be sustained. The line which, with due caution, he drew at 74° E. to distinguish the 'Indo-Aryan' Pañjābī from the 'Dardic' Lahndā[3] is meaningful only as a convenient division between two groups of Pañjābī dialects. Although the language group which he labelled Lahndā provides a viable linguistic unit, it must be regarded as a segment of the larger Pañjābī group, not as a separate language. The line which he drew amounts to no more than a convenience. There is, as Grierson well understood, a substantial area within which the Lahndā dialects merge into Mājhī and others of the eastern group.[4]

Once the essential vagueness of this distinction is recognized it becomes possible to accept an adapted form of Grierson's second definition. Most of the janam-sākhīs are written in varying blends of Pañjābī dialects, to which some exotic elements have also been added. In most instances Lahndā is dominant. Two notable exceptions are the *Mahimā Prakāś Vāratak*, in which Mājhī strongly predominates, and the *Miharbān Janam-sākhī* which generally uses Sādhukkaṛī. Partial exceptions also occur in the case of the *B40* and *Ādi Sākhīs* collections. A variety of sources have been used in the preparation of both, and because at least one of these sources happened to be in Sādhukkaṛī a small number of sākhīs in that language appear in both janam-sākhīs. This feature is more prominent in the *Ādi Sākhīs* than in the *B40 Janam-sākhī*.

The Lahndā group of Pañjābī dialects has been variously subdivided. Grierson's classification was based upon a primary distinction between a large southern segment and a smaller northern group, the line being drawn

[1] G. A. Grierson, *Linguistic Survey of India*, vol. ix, part i (Calcutta, 1916), p. 618. Grierson's use of the singular indicates the *Bālā* tradition.

[2] Ibid., vol. viii, part i (Calcutta, 1919), p. 247.

[3] Ibid., vol. i, part i (Calcutta, 1927), p. 136.

[4] Ibid. ix.i.608.

a little to the south of Jhelum. The northern group was further divided into north-eastern and north-western groups, and all three sections were then subdivided according to Grierson's understanding of their dialects. Most of the area covered by the districts of Gujrāt, Gujranwālā, and Lahore he classified as 'Panjābī merging into Lahndā'.[1]

Provided that the extreme vagueness of such definitions is given due stress this classification can be generally accepted. It is, however, convenient to ignore Grierson's subdivision of Northern Lahndā and to lay greater stress upon his principal subdivision of Southern Lahndā. In the case of the latter he drew an east–west line a little to the north of 30°N. This line deserves rather more prominence, and if with the usual insistence upon a necessary vagueness of definition it is given this prominence a threefold division emerges. In the north there is Northern Lahndā, with the Poṭhohārī dialect occupying a position of particular prominence; and in the south the dialects of Multān, Muzzafargaṛh, Bahāwalpur, and Derā Ghāzī Khān. This leaves Central Lahndā covering the area of Miānwālī, Shāhpur, Lyallpur, Montgomery, Jhaṅg and Maṅkerā.

The eastern portion of this central area must be closely linked with the immediately adjacent areas of Gujrāt, Gujranwālā, and Lahore. This link enables us to circumscribe the geographical area and the distinctive dialect which dominates the janam-sākhī literature. To this linguistic area belong the *Purātan*, *LDP 194*, and *Bālā* janam-sākhīs, and the greater part of the *B40* and *Ādi Sākhīs* collections.[2] *LDP 194* and the *Bālā* janam-sakhis are generally more homogeneous in terms of language forms, and in the case of the latter the language is more modern. The other three collections, all of them using a variety of sources, display a greater diversity of dialect forms. Of the exotic elements the more prominent are Persian and Braj.

The principal exception to this general rule is the *Miharbān Janam-sākhī* which for most of its material uses the language variously called Sādhukkaṛī or Sant Bhāṣā, 'the language of the Sants'. This language consists of a Khaṛī Bolī base, supplemented by elements drawn from Braj and other North Indian vernaculars. It served as a *lingua franca* for devotional works of the Sant tradition, a religious movement which spread over much of Northern India during the late medieval and early modern period.[3] Representatives of this tradition commonly took the Khaṛī Bolī of the Delhi area as their foundation and added to it vocabulary and supplementary grammatical forms derived from their own geographical areas. In the case of its Ādi Granth and janam-sākhī examples the supplement is, predictably, provided by Pañjābī dialects. This supplement is frequently insignificant to the point that the resultant language might well be described simply as Khaṛī Bolī.

Passages written in Sādhukkaṛī occur in both the *Ādi Sākhīs* and the

[1] Ibid. viii.i.233 ff., and ix.i.607 ff.

[2] All five display the terminal forms which constitute the most distinctive feature of Lahndā. The most prominent are the verb-endings *usu* (Perfective) and *sī* (Future). Gurcharan Singh *et al.*, *Pañjābī sāhit dā itihās* (*madh kāl*), section 5 (*Pañjābī gadd*), pp. 20–8.

[3] *GNSR*, pp. 151–8.

B40 Janam-sākhī. Such passages are normally confined to particular sākhīs and are of considerable help in identifying changes of source within both janam-sākhīs. This may be illustrated by three consecutive sākhīs from the *Ādi Sākhīs* collection. The brief narrative portion of sākhī 25 runs as follows:

tā phiri gurū horu sāgu kītā. bāki diā sikhā de vāsate. sūriā age litiā. dui kute nāli lite. laki chhurā badhā. je koī sā so sabh bhaji gae. koī ṭhaharāi na sakiu. tā sabh lage ākhani nānak bhalā fakīr sā par devānā hūā. bhalā fakīr kāmal daraves sā. paru devānā hūā. dhānakau raliā. tā bābe sirī rāg vichi sabadu kītā . . .[1]

This is unmistakably Pañjābī, and so too is the even briefer narrative portion of sākhī 26. There is, however, a hint of difference. The passage is in fact an editorial link connecting sākhīs 25 and 27:

jab ehu goṣṭi kari chuke tab gorakh nāth bābe no kahiā nānak tū pūrā purakh hai paru jog de ghari āu. tab bābā nānak boliā . . .[2]

In sākhī 27 the compiler, having changed his source, abandons the Pañjābī of the earlier source.

bābe nānak kau udāsī jo upajī chak te chaliā jātā thā. dekhai tā eku bāgu hai udiān ke bikhai. . . .[3]

This is not unadulterated Khaṛī Bolī but certainly it is much closer to Khaṛī Bolī than to the Pañjābī of the preceding sākhīs. It is Sādhukkaṛī of the kind so commonly found in the Ādi Granth and in the non-Pañjābī portions of the janam-sākhīs. Even within a passage as brief as this one both the Khaṛī Bolī base and Pāñjābī supplement are evident.[4]

In the *Ādi Sākhīs* Sādhukkaṛī is subordinate to Pañjābī, and in the *B40 Janam-sākhī* this same relationship is even more pronounced. Within the extant *Miharbān Janam-sākhī*, however, the balance moves strongly in the opposite direction. Although Pañjābī passages do occur, and although the *Miharbān* Sādhukkaṛī betrays ample evidence of Pañjābī influence, the language of the *Miharbān Janam-sākhī* must nevertheless be distinguished from the Pañjābī which, with varying blends of dialect, dominates all other janam-sākhīs. It is a distinction which corresponds to the fundamental difference separating the *Miharbān* tradition from the remainder of the janam-sākhī literature. Whereas the other janam-sākhīs are primarily concerned with popular narrative the *Miharbān* tradition is much more interested in religious discourse. Pañjābī was the natural language for the former and Sādhukkaṛī the appropriate language for the latter. In addition to its Pañjābī contribution the *Miharbān* language also includes elements derived from Braj.

The linguistic difference which distinguishes the *Miharbān* tradition

[1] *AS*, p. 84. The remainder of the sākhī consists of a recitation of the shabad *Sirī Rāg* 29.

[2] *AS*, pp. 84–5. The remainder of the sākhī consists of a recitation of five stanzas of the *Japjī Sāhib*.

[3] *AS*, p. 86.

[4] For a more detailed examination of the *B40* language see the introduction to *B40(Eng)*.

from all other janam-sākhīs has been considerably obscured by a consistent use of the Gurmukhī script. Although the distinction between Pañjābī language and the Gurmukhī script is now clearly understood there still persists a tendency to assume that Gurmukhī is used only for Pañjābī. The *Miharbān Janam-sākhī* provides an important example of the fallacy of this assumption. The same regular use of the Gurmukhī script is shared by all janam-sākhī traditions, regardless of their linguistic content.

SECTION II

5

THE ORIGINS AND GROWTH OF THE JANAM-SĀKHĪ TRADITIONS

THE ultimate origin of all the janam-sākhī traditions is the person of Nānak or, to be more precise, an interpretation of that person. Nānak had recast a particular range of popular religious doctrine in a uniquely coherent form, expressing it in poetry of a compelling directness and beauty. It was natural that such qualities should attract disciples, and those who in this manner gathered around their chosen teacher during the early decades of the sixteenth century constituted the nucleus of the *Nānak-panth*, 'the community of those owing allegiance to Nānak'. These were the first Sikhs, a word which in its literal sense means simply 'learner' or 'disciple'. It was in this sense that it was first used to describe the early followers of Gurū Nānak and only gradually did it acquire the distinctive and more restricted meaning which it now possesses. Although the Gurmukhi script makes no provision for capitalization the conventions of written English permit us to express the process in terms of a gradual change from 'sikh' to 'Sikh', from 'disciples' to 'Disciples'.[1]

Inevitably there developed within this community an interpretation of the life and teachings of its first Master. A religious community can have neither purpose nor coherence without a distinctive pattern of belief, and when such a community owes a conscious allegiance to a particular person it must assuredly incorporate within that pattern a particular understanding of the Master's mission and message. In the case of the emergent *nānak-panthī* or *sikh* community this understanding constitutes what we have already called the myth of Nānak. It is this myth which provided, and continues to provide, the source and origin of the ever-evolving janam-sākhī traditions.

At this point a clarification of terms is needed. Although the myth of

[1] A *Miharbān* commentator claims that in the earlier period the word *sikh* was reserved for the Hindu disciples of Nānak. Muslim disciples were called *murīd*. *Mih JS* II. 414. The other term commonly used in the janam-sākhīs to designate a follower of Nānak is, predictably, *nānak-panthī*. Although the term *nānak-panthī* is rarely used nowadays, the word *panth* from which it derives provides another example of the process which can be represented in terms of a change from the lower case to the upper case. The word *panth*, in its normal usage, designates a 'sect' or definable area of Indian religious tradition distinguished by loyalty to a particular teacher or adherence to particular doctrines. In this sense it clearly implies distinctiveness *within* Hindu tradition and society, and in this sense the early community of Nānak's followers may be properly designated a *panth*. As the community began to develop a consciousness of sharp differentiation *panth* tended increasingly to become *Panth*. In other words, it came to represent a religious community *distinct from* Hindu society. This distinction, however, has never become absolute. Whereas some Sikhs will draw the line with all possible clarity, others seem to be unaware of its existence.

Nānak has just been described as the source of the janam-sākhīs the word 'source' will not hereafter be used in this sense. Instead it will be reserved for the section which discusses the compilation of extant manuscript collections.[1] In all instances it is evident that the copyists responsible for the manuscripts now extant must have had access to one or more earlier manuscripts. These earlier manuscripts served as sources for the composite products we now possess and it is in this sense that the word will normally be used. The only extension beyond this usage will be to cover borrowings made by these copyists from developed oral traditions. It will be shown, for example, that the *B40* compiler has copied material from at least two recognizable manuscripts, and that he has drawn another substantial cluster of anecdotes from the oral tradition of his own area.[2] Both the oral tradition and the manuscripts will be referred to as sources, and the term will normally be limited to this usage.

This means that another term will be required to designate the materials utilized by those responsible for the earliest traditions. A few anecdotes can presumably be traced to actual incidents in the life of Nānak; others were obviously borrowed direct from even earlier pre-Nānak sources; and many developed organically in accordance with processes of varying complexity. In all three cases 'sources' were required in order to provide either the complete anecdote or the elements which were drawn together to form one. Wherever possible these 'sources' will be covered by the term 'constituents'. The word will have a particular relevance to the earliest traditions, but because the janam-sākhīs have persisted in growing there has always been a continuing if irregular inflow of constituents. For this reason the term will also be applied to the materials which, to the present day, continue to supply extra details or additional anecdotes. Occasionally it will be convenient to use the word 'sources' when indicating the origin of these elements, but its usage will be restricted and will be accompanied by a reference to the constitutents which derive from any such origin.

It seems safe to assume that the earliest of all constituents must have been authentic memories concerning actual incidents from the life of Nānak. Anecdotes concerning the Master will have begun to circulate during the Master's own lifetime, and although his actual presence will not have prevented the addition of legendary details it will certainly have served to inhibit their entry into the earliest tradition. They will have been added more as embroidery. The fabric will have been the narrative of authentic incidents.

This period was, however, brief, and an examination of the janam-sākhī literature plainly demonstrates that the vast bulk of their material entered the tradition after the death of Nānak. For this subsequent period of expansion three constituents proved to be of particular importance. One was the body of received tradition current in the Pañjāb during the seventeenth century. Some of the material which entered the janam-sākhīs in this manner has obviously been taken from the Epics and the

[1] See below, pp. 174ff.

[2] See below, pp. 187–94, 197–210, 220–6. See also the introduction to *B40(Eng)*, pp. 11–15.

Purāṇas. Other features evidently derive from the distinctive legends of the Nāth yogīs, and yet others betray a Sūfī origin. All three varieties represent a natural process. The Pañjāb of this period was impregnated with Puranic lore, and both the Nāths and the Sūfīs combined a considerable reputation with a well-stocked treasury of legend. Living within such a context the janam-sākhī narrators were inevitably directed by its more powerful influences.

The second of the major constituents was provided by the poetic works composed by Nānak for the benefit of his followers. There are many examples to be found in the janam-sākhīs of anecdotes which have been developed out of particular hymns by the Gurū, or out of isolated references from various compositions. Whenever this occurs in a sākhī the hymn which prompts the anecdote will be quoted during the course of the narrative, normally as the answer given by Nānak to an interlocutor or as his comment on the episode which provides the substance of the sākhī.

Although this is an important constituent it should be noted that all such quotations from the works of Nānak are not to be explained as the seeds from which their associated anecdotes grew. Many of the hymns which appear in the janam-sākhīs represent later additions to evolved sākhīs. A hymn introduced in this manner was normally added because its theme seemed to accord well with the subject of a particular anecdote. In other cases a hymn has evidently been quoted because the narrator wished to add to the hymn his own commentary on it. When this occurs in one of the narrative janam-sākhīs it commonly reflects a doctrinal issue current within the later community, the hymn with its commentary serving to express a particular view concerning the issue. Yet other hymns have been added to sākhīs for reasons which now elude us. In some cases the reason may have been nothing more than a narrator's partiality.

Most of the hymns quoted in the janam-sākhīs are by Nānak and are to be found in the Ādi Granth. In such instances the janam-sākhīs invariably depart from the standard Ādi Granth text and in some quotations their variant readings diverge extensively. A few hymns which are attributed by the janam-sākhīs to Nānak are listed in the Ādi Granth as the works of later Gurūs, and a number do not appear in the Ādi Granth at all. In the analysis which follows compositions of the latter kind are described as apocryphal. This they probably are, and in some cases there can be no doubt whatsoever. There remains, however, the possibility that genuine works may have escaped the Ādi Granth and yet been retained in an oral tradition later used by a janam-sākhī compiler.

The third of the important constituents was more restricted in scope than either the influence of received tradition or the impulses derived from Nānak's own words. This third element was provided by the continuing influence within the Sikh community of an ascetic tradition. Although Nānak himself had spurned extreme asceticism the conviction was too deeply rooted in Indian tradition to be easily eradicated and its influence emerges at several points in the janam-sākhīs.

Four principal constituents may accordingly be discerned in the janam-sākhīs. The first of these is fundamental in that it provided the original impulse and a significant portion of the earliest traditions. This is the authentic material derived from actual episodes in the life of Nānak. Subsequently this element comes to be vastly overshadowed by materials derived from received tradition, the works of Nānak, and resurgent ascetic ideals. These constituents are discussed at greater length in chapter 6.

This is followed in chapter 7 by a description of the various literary forms which have been used in order to give expression to these traditions. A preliminary survey of the janam-sākhī forms indicates an obvious division into two categories. First there are the narrative anecdotes; and secondly the numerous discourses which Nānak is said to have conducted. There is, however, a more meaningful distinction which becomes evident when the various discourses are analysed. This would link with the anecdotes the type of discourse which contains a strong narrative element, separating these two forms from the remainder of the discourses.

The first two forms we shall designate the *narrative anecdote* and the *narrative discourse*. The *narrative anecdote* is the janam-sākhī form *par excellence*. Sākhīs which employ it are normally brief and succinct, although a more complicated pattern sometimes emerges. During the later stages of janam-sākhī evolution composite sākhīs are commonly formed by grouping anecdotes which concern a single person, place, or theme. Some of these clusters enjoy a particular popularity and continue to grow as extra sub-sākhīs are added. The various traditions concerning Bābā Nānak's visit to Mecca provide a good example of this combination and growth process.

Narrative discourses are closely allied to the anecdotal form in terms of purpose, but can be easily distinguished in terms of structure. The term *narrative discourse* has been reserved for conversation pieces which have been developed out of quotations from the works of Gurū Nānak. A shabad or a shalok by the Gurū is sometimes incorporated within a sākhī in a manner which plainly marks it as the actual origin of the story in which it is set. In such instances the Gurū's actual composition serves as his answer, or series of answers, to questions or comments which are fashioned to suit the given reply. Several simple stories, communicating the same message as the narrative anecdotes, have been constructed in this manner.

These two narrative forms provide the bulk of the material recorded by the *Purātan* and *Bālā* janam-sākhīs, *B40*, the *Ādi Sākhīs*, and the *Gyān-ratanāvalī*. There are, however, two other distinctive forms which make occasional appearances in all of them. Both are discourses and both can be distinguished in terms of structure, content, and intention. One of them dominates the *Miharbān* tradition, thereby providing a clear line of demarcation between the *Miharbān Janam-sākhī* and all other important janam-sākhīs. This line can be drawn with a sharpness which might suggest that the *Miharbān Janam-sākhī* is not really a janam-sākhī at all. Any such conclusion would, however, mean carrying the distinction too far, for although the demarcation is certainly clear it cannot be regarded as an absolute one. The *Miharbān Janam-sākhī* differs not because it has abandoned the characteristic features of the janam-sākhī but because it has incorporated them within something larger.

The primary difference between the distinctively *Miharbān* variety of discourse and those of the narrative janam-sākhīs is the consciously preceptive nature of the former. For this reason it will be referred to as *didactic discourse*. Once again there are individual instances which are not easy to classify, but these are very rare. The shift of interest from narrative to doctrine is usually obvious, and is plainly reflected in the discourse structure which has been developed to give expression to doctrinal concerns.

The didactic discourse is, in a sense, an extension of the narrative discourse, for it commonly uses the narrative variety as a basis. The narrative form is however little more than a point of departure, a convenient framework within which to set the distinctively doctrinal portion of the discourse. Narrative settings and the introduction of interlocutors provide a context for the basic pedagogical purpose. This purpose was to provide an explanation or interpretation of Gurū Nānak's own works, an intention which seems to have been directed primarily to members of the community (or particular groups within it) but which might also extend to others outside.

The hermeneutic purpose was served by first quoting a passage from the works of Nānak and then attaching to it an *exegetical supplement*. Discourses which had already developed within the narrative traditions were appropriated for this purpose and transformed by means of adding passages of exegesis to every individual quotation of a stanza, shabad, or shalok by Gurū Nānak. These were, however, soon exhausted, and a substantial majority of the didactic discourses have been constructed with the obvious intention of expounding particular passages from the works of Nānak.

This blend of discourse and commentary constitutes the distinctive *Miharbān* approach. Examples which are to be found in other janam-sākhīs normally represent borrowings from the *Miharbān* tradition. Each division of the *Miharbān Janam-sākhī* is called a *goṣṭ*, not a *sākhī*, and because these divisions embody something characteristically different the term *goṣṭ* has been retained as a convenient means of reference when dealing with the *Miharbān Janam-sākhī*. Although its literal meaning is 'discourse' this translation will not be used for the *goṣṭ* form of the *Miharbān* tradition, this particular form being distinctively different from all other varieties of discourse. For the same reason the persons responsible for the development and transmission of the *Miharbān Janam-sākhī* will normally be designated commentators rather than narrators.

The exegetical portion of the *goṣṭ* is sometimes referred to as the *paramārath*. This is because the commentary which follows each quotation almost always begins with the formula *tis kā paramārath*, literally 'its sublime meaning'. The words 'is as follows' are understood, and the formula thus serves to distinguish the exegesis from the quotation. Modern usage does this by means of indentation, together with a separate line in the text to correspond to each line of a hymn or poem. Lacking these conventions the *Miharbān* commentators had to devise a method of their own to mark off exegesis from quotation.[1]

The last major form to be noted makes only rare appearances in the janam-sākhīs. This is the *heterodox discourse*, an independent form which has occasionally provided janam-sākhī compilers with acceptable material. The origins of these discourses are to be found in heretical doctrines and gnostic interpretation of earlier esoteric traditions (principally Nāth and Sūfī) which have found expression in a small group of apocryphal works attributed to Gurū Nānak. Most of these compositions were of sufficient length to warrant independent circulation, and for this reason they were commonly recorded as separate works, distinct from the janam-sākhīs. Their claim to authenticity was evidently viewed with suspicion by some of the compilers, but others were sufficiently impressed to include selections in their janam-sākhīs. All are, without doubt, spurious. Neither their curious doctrines nor their banal expression could possibly be imputed to Gurū Nānak.

The principal forms employed by the janam-sākhī narrators and commentators may thus be divided into two groups:

Narrative

1. Narrative anecdotes
2. Narrative discourses

Non-narrative

1. Didactic discourses, comprising both
   (a) Narrative discourses, and
   (b) Exegetical supplements
2. Heterodox discourses

These four forms together account for practically all that the janam-sākhīs contain. Other forms are exceedingly rare.

The chapter describing the various janam-sākhī forms is followed by a brief examination of oral transmission procedures and of the manner in which selections drawn from oral tradition were gathered into the written collections to which the term janam-sākhī is properly applied. Four stages can be observed in the development of recorded janam-sākhīs. The first is the random collection, a phase which continued long after the emergence of the more intricate second and third stages. For some compilers it was, however, and inadequate method. Random collections of anecdotes were regarded as an unsatisfactory way of narrating the Gurū's life-story and there soon emerged an impulse to order disjointed traditions into a coherent chronological sequence. This constituted the second stage. The

[1] In the English translation of the *B40 Janam-sākhī* the formula *tis kā paramārath* has been rendered: 'The exegesis [of this stanza etc. is as follows].' See for example *B40*, ff. 118b, 119b. *B40(Eng)*, pp. 134, 136. In sākhī 2 of this janam-sākhī the formula is reduced to *tis kā arath* (perhaps an earlier form) and is translated: 'Its meaning [is as follows].' *B40*, ff. 4a–5b. *B40(Eng)*, pp. 8–9.

third followed when to the narrative anecdotes there were added exegetical passages; and the fourth when the introduction of the printing-press enabled particular recorded versions to be widely disseminated.

In chapter 9 the discussion proceeds to a more detailed examination of the manner in which the different kinds of sākhīs evolved. This examination consists largely of an analysis of representative types. In some instances an anecdotal sākhī turns out to be little more than a repetition of pre-Nānak tradition. Others are simple anecdotes which have been suggested by a particular reference in one of Nānak's compositions, or discourses of the kind already noted which have been constructed on the basis of a complete hymn or a series of quotations. In such cases the pattern is relatively uncomplicated and requires little elucidation. Elsewhere the origins and structure of particular sākhīs are found to be more complex. Most of the samples chosen for analysis have been taken from these more complicated sākhīs. This is partly because the need for explanation is obviously greater, but also because the complex sākhīs usually embody sub-sākhīs which serve to illustrate the simpler forms.

The period of evolution was, of course, an extended one and is in fact still continuing. New sākhīs, though now a mere trickle, are still appearing, and older sākhīs are commonly modified in accordance with contemporary needs and understanding. Perhaps the most striking example of the latter feature is provided by the story of the moving *miharāb*.[1] Most janam-sākhī versions set this anecdote in Mecca and relate how Bābā Nānak, when he reached the city, lay down to sleep in a mosque with his feet in the direction of the mosque's *miharāb*.[2] An outraged qāzī commanded him to point his feet away from the house of God. Nānak, in reply, invited him to lay his feet 'in whatever direction the house of God is not'.[3] Accepting the invitation the qāzī dragged Nānak's feet away from the direction of the *miharāb*, whereupon the *miharāb* itself moved. Wherever the qāzī laid Nānak's feet, there the *miharāb* also swung round. Confounded by this miracle the qāzī fell at his feet.

For modern readers a wonder story of this kind raises obvious problems. Some have suggested that the *miharāb* only *seemed* to move, but a much more popular solution has been to terminate the sākhī at the point where Nānak invites the qāzī to point the offending feet 'in whatever direction the house of God is not', omitting all that follows except for the qāzī's submission.[4] This produces a neat anecdote, one which is entirely acceptable to the modern reader. The dwelling-place of God is everywhere! It is not, however, what the earlier janam-sākhīs say. What it illustrates is the continuing process of change and development. Another example of the same process has recently been provided by a new tradition concerning a visit to Sikkim (an aetiological legend explaining the appearance of rice

[1] See below, pp. 137–44.

[2] The niche which is aligned with the Ka' bah, thereby indicating the *qibla*.

[3] *B40*, f. 51b.

[4] Tejā Singh and Gaṇḍā Singh, *A Short History of the Sikhs*, vol. i (Bombay, 1950), p. 11. This ·ationalized interpretation appears in John Malcolm's *Sketch of the Sikhs* (Calcutta, 1810), p. 274.

and banana cropping in North Sikkim).[1] In this instance the new development represents an expansion of the received tradition, not a rationalizing contraction.

The last chapter of this section deals with the various sources used by janam-sākhī compilers. All the extant janam-sākhīs, regardless of the stage or stages to which they belong, include anecdotes drawn from a multiplicity of sources. Oral tradition continued to provide much supplementary material, but in no instance does the compiler of an extant janam-sākhī appear to have relied solely upon oral sources. All had access to at least one earlier manuscript and sometimes more than one. Needless to say the compilers do not acknowledge their various sources and the task of distinguishing them can be highly complex. The analysis included in chapter 10 covers no more than a sample. Whereas the *B40 Janam-sākhī* and the *Ādi Sākhīs* are treated in some detail, references to other janam-sākhī traditions are generally limited to points of close contact with the two primary examples. Although this limitation is necessary within the scope of a single volume it is regrettable, for it must involve many omissions. Two janam-sākhīs which should produce interesting responses to the same variety of analysis are the *Colebrooke* and early *Bālā* versions.

[1] *SLTGN(Eng)*, pp. 329–33.

6

CONSTITUENTS OF THE JANAM-SĀKHĪS

1. *EPISODES FROM THE LIFE OF NĀNAK*

ALTHOUGH the mass of extant janam-sākhī material must be classified as legend there can be little doubt that the earliest constituent will have been actual observation and authentic memory. There can be no doubt whatsoever concerning the broad outline of Nānak's life, nor of the fact that a community of disciples gathered around him in the village of Kartārpur during the early decades of the sixteenth century. It is also clear that many of these disciples continued to live in their own villages and expressed their devotion to the Master through regular visits to Kartārpur rather than through permanent attendance upon his person. Under such circumstances it was inevitable that anecdotes concerning the Master should have begun to circulate amongst his dispersed followers. These early tales will have been subjected to processes of expansion and embellishment even during the lifetime of the Gurū, but the basis of many of them will have been episodes from his actual experience, or authentic utterances which he had in fact made.

The problem presented by the authentic elements in the extant janam-sākhīs is that of recognition. Although their presence may be undoubted so too is the extreme difficulty involved in separating them from the quantity of supplementary material which now envelops them. The historian who is concerned to identify these elements can hope to achieve a certain limited success, but the analysis is arduous and the product scant.

Fortunately the solution of this particular problem is not vital for an understanding of the janam-sākhīs, nor for an appreciation of their chief importance. The importance of the janam-sākhīs concerns the myth which they express, and for this expression authentic history and legend can be equally serviceable. It is the quest of the historical Nānak which imposes a rigorous obligation to separate the two. For an understanding of the myth of Nānak the separation is always of interest and can occasionally be helpful, but it is not absolutely essential. At this point it is sufficient to note that authentic incidents from the life of Nānak form one of the several constituents which have contributed to the growth of the janam-sākhīs. In terms of temporal priority these authentic elements are primary and must form the basis of some of the earliest sākhīs. In terms of quantity they are of relatively minor significance. For the major constituents in terms of quantity we must turn to three other elements. The first is received tradition; the second is the corpus of Nānak's own compositions; and the third is a miscellany of ascetic ideals current during the period of janam-sākhī growth.

2. *RECEIVED TRADITION*

Received tradition in the Pañjāb of the janam-sākhī period consisted chiefly of an amalgam of Puranic lore, tales from the *Rāmāyaṇa*, the *Mahābhārata*, and the *Yoga-vasiṣṭha*, Nāth legend, and Sūfī hagiography. Occasionally it is possible to trace a connection with the Buddhist *Jātaka*, as in the popular story of how a tree's shadow stood still in order to shelter the sleeping child Nānak from the rays of the sun.[1] This is one among several prominent *Wandersagen* elements appearing in the janam-sākhīs, mediated by a variety of received tradition. Others include triumph over carnal temptations, the miraculous opening of springs, homilies on the curse of wealth, flight on magic prayer-mats, and shelter afforded by a cobra's distended hood.

Although the various sources can often be distinguished, it is important to remember that for the rural Pañjāb of the seventeenth and eighteenth centuries they commonly constituted a single tangled tradition. This coalescence is particularly advanced in the relationship to Puranic and Nāth elements. Sūfī traditions, by reason of their connection with Muslim belief, maintain a somewhat clearer definition. The difference is, however, one of degree and it is not a marked one. It would be altogether misleading to suggest that the traditions associated with celebrated Sūfīs were immune from the influence of native Indian traditions, or that those native traditions were screened from Sūfī influence. There was, in fact, no real clarity of definition. Boundaries were always blurred and commonly crossed. Details, structures, and complete anecdotes might be associated with a Sūfī pīr, a Nāth Master, or a prominent *bhakta*. Villagers who worshipped with equal reverence at a Śaivite temple or a Muslim tomb would not always distinguish between elements drawn from the *Bhāgavata Purāṇa* and those which derived from the *Hadīth*.[2]

This amalgam is faithfully reflected in much of the janam-sākhī material, particularly in the anecdotes which narrate encounters with Nāths. Needless to say, the point should not be laboured to the extent of suggesting that *all* janam-sākhī traditions necessarily manifest this composite character. In most cases of material derived from a received tradition it is possible to identify a dominant element and to label it Puranic, Epic, Nāth, or Sūfī. The point which does deserve to be laboured is the possibility of incorporating these diverse elements within a single tradition. To this possibility the extant janam-sākhīs bear ample witness.

One other misunderstanding which can easily arise from the composite

[1] *B40*, f. 9a. E. B. Cowell (ed.), *The Jataka*, vol. vi, pp. 246–7.

[2] The extent to which the exchange of ideas could be carried is well illustrated in the case of Nāths and Sūfīs by the *Rushd-nāma* of Sheikh 'Abd al-Quddūs (1456–1537). S. A. A. Rizvi and S. Zaidi, *Alakh Bāṇī* (Alīgaṛh, 1971).

nature of the janam-sākhīs is the assumption that the teachings of Gurū Nānak (as opposed to the traditions concerning his life) must necessarily reflect the same variety of synthesis. This misunderstanding is expressed in terms of a claim that the works of Nānak represent a blend of 'Hinduism' and 'Islam'. Although a diversity of influences can certainly be detected in Nānak's thought the synthesis to which he gave expression is not to be identified with that of the janam-sākhīs. Sūfī influence is much more pronounced in the janam-sākhīs than in the works of Nānak himself. The antecedents of Nānak's own thought are to be found primarily in the earlier Sant synthesis, and beyond this in the distinctive belief of Vaiṣṇava bhakti and in the *haṭha-yoga* of the Nāth tradition and other related cults.[1] Muslim influence, Sūfī and otherwise, is of marginal importance as far as the basic components of his thought are concerned. The janam-sākhīs, in contrast, show abundant evidence of the influence of Sūfī traditions. Whereas Nānak had found little of importance in contemporary Sūfī belief which was not already present in his Sant inheritance, his disciples found much in contemporary Sūfī hagiography to enrich their own narratives. It is partly to the Sūfī borrowings in the janam-sākhīs that the persistent misunderstanding of Nānak's own antecedents can be traced.

(a) *The Epics and the Purāṇas*

Puranic and Epic elements appear in the janam-sākhīs both as illustrative material and as the substance of particular sākhīs. The former application, which corresponds to Gurū Nānak's own usage of details from the Epics and the Purāṇas, is well illustrated by a passage which the *B40* compiler appends to an earlier narrative. The anecdote relates how Rājā Śivanābh tested Bābā Nānak by sending beautiful women to tempt him. To emphasize their comeliness the *B40* compiler adds:

> Their alluring appearance was like that of the Kāṃkandalās, the seductive sirens of Raja Indra; or like the four temptresses of Vaikunṭh. Whoever looked upon them—[even such] supermen and sages [as] the sons of Brahmā, [the generations of saintly heroes from] Janak onwards [or] ascetics and master ascetics such as Ṛṣya Śṛṅga—would have lost their heads.[2]

In this instance the passage appears to be an interpolation introduced because the anecdote following it so strongly suggested the popular Epic theme of the holy man tempted. Elsewhere complete stories from the Epics or the Purāṇas are given a distinctively janam-sākhī expression. One example is provided by the sākhī entitled 'The Robbers and the Funeral-pyre',[3] an anecdote which can be traced to the story of Ajāmila in the *Bhāgavata Purāṇa*.[4] Another which can be connected with a narrative in

[1] *GNSR*, p. 160.

[2] *B40*, ff. 146b–147a. Particular points occurring in the quotation are explained in the footnotes to the *B40* translation. See *B40* (*Eng*) p. 163. The *Ādi Sākhīs* compiler, following the same source, refers only to the supermen. *AS*, p. 65.

[3] *B40*, ff. 190b–193a. *Pur JS*, pp. 32–3.

[4] *Bhāgavata Purāṇa*, VI. 2. E. Burnouf, *Le Bhâgavata Purâṇa*, vol. ii, pp. 532–41. Purnendu Narayana Sinha, *A Study of the Bhāgavata Purāna* (Adyar, 1950), pp. 204–6.

the *Bhāgavata Purāṇa* is 'The Encounter with Kaliyug'.[1] This evidently derives its basic feature (notably the personification of the *Kaliyuga* or 'Age of Strife') from the episode concerning the chastisement of Kali by King Parīkṣit.[2] Both of these traditions entered the janam-sākhīs at an early date and acquired a considerable popularity. A later example appears in the *Mahimā Prakāś* story of how Gurū Aṅgad, having misunderstood a command of Bābā Nānak, remained rooted to the same spot for several years while ants gradually covered him with earth.[3] This tale can be traced to the *Mahābhārata* story of Ṛṣi Chyavana.[4]

The most prominent of all Puranic features to appear in the janam-sākhīs is Mount Sumeru (Mount Meru), legendary centre and axis of the earth and the setting for one of the most popular of all janam-sākhī discourses.[5] In this connection the 'Discourse on Mount Sumeru' is of particular interest for two reasons. First, it illustrates not merely the influence of Puranic legend, but also the manner in which Nāth and Puranic tradition are inextricably linked in the janam-sākhīs. The interlocutors in the discourse are Siddhs, which in this context plainly means Nāth Masters.

The second point of interest concerns the *Bālā* version of the discourse. Puranic influence is much more pronounced in the *Bālā* janam-sākhīs than in any of the others and at no point does this distinctive *Bālā* characteristic appear with greater prominence than in the mountain-climbing episodes which reach a climax in Bābā Nānak's ascent of Mount Sumeru.[6] The later *Bālā* janam-sākhīs also introduce sākhīs set in Govardhan, Mathurā, and Vrindāban, and from the details which they incorporate it is at once clear that they have derived their extra material from the *Bhāgavata Purāṇa*.[7]

(b) *Nāth tradition*

The Nāth *sampradaya*, or sect of Nāth yogīs, is a feature of medieval Indian society which has received only a fragment of the attention which it deserves. This neglect derives partly from the condition of the sect when first it became an object of interest to European observers. Monserrate, who accompanied Akbar on a visit to the Nāth centre at Ṭillā, indicates the kind of impression which the sect made upon an observer during the late fifteenth century.

When they heard of the King's approaching visit, a huge number of the members of that sect gathered at this place, many of whom, in order to show off their sanctity, betook themselves stark naked to certain caves which either nature or

[1] *B40*, ff. 44a–47a. *Pur JS*, pp. 37–8. *AS*, pp. 28–31.

[2] *Bhāgavata Purāṇa*, I.17.28–41. Cf. also ibid. I.18.5–10. Kaliyug is also personified in the *Mahābhārata*, III.58–62, 72. For another example of a janam-sākhī borrowing from the *Mahābhārata* see below, p. 162.

[3] *SLTGN(Eng)*, p. 83. *SLTGN(Pbī)*, p. 44.

[4] *Mahābhārata*, III.122.

[5] *B40*, ff. 86a–93a. *AS*, pp. 36–42. *Pur JS*, pp. 94–7. *Mih JS* I.384–416.

[6] *Bālā JS*, pp. 200 ff.

[7] Expanded 1871 edition, sākhīs 251–2

the art of man has made there. Many people did reverence to these naked ascetics and proclaimed their sanctity abroad. They are however extremely greedy of money. All their trickery and pretended sanctity is aimed at the acquisition of gain.[1]

Monserrate does, however, indicate more than mere knavery. The description which he gives of the Ṭillā establishment is, by his standards, a lengthy one[2] and implies that during this period Ṭillā must have commanded a considerable interest. Indeed, his report that Akbar stayed four days and while there paid homage suggests that the sect commanded not just interest but positive respect. This need occasion no surprise. The ignorant and arrogant charlatans described by Monserrate and later European observers have never constituted the entire sect, and their reputation obscures the importance of their antecedents. The antecedents and the later reputation are both necessary aspects of any attempt to understand either the thought of Nānak or the content of the janam-sākhīs.

The word 'sect' is, as always, a misleading term to use as a translation of *panth* or *sampradaya*. There were in fact several sects of Nāth yogīs. They are regarded as a single panth because they share a common allegiance to Gorakhnāth, a common adherence to the *haṭha-yoga* technique, and the common observance of a particular custom. This is the practice of wearing large ear-rings (*mudrā*), a custom which has earned them the name of Kānphaṭ (or 'split-ear') yogīs.[3]

The antecedents of the Kānphaṭ yogīs can be traced to the ancient tradition of esoteric Tantrism. This much is clear, but it does not in fact tell us much about the actual origins of the cult for it merely leads us into one of the most obscure areas of early Indian tradition. Little is known of Tantrism apart from its later expressions and it is only by inference from these later expressions that its origins and its earlier development can be described. Many of these influences relate to the geographical location of the earliest developments. It was along the northern perimeter of Aryan culture, from the Afghan highlands along the Himālayas to Āssām, that tantric beliefs evolved and flourished. This indicates alien antecedents, and the incorporation of these exotic elements within a Hindu tradition has suggested that Tantrism must represent an assimilation of the kind which enabled Hindu culture to extend into regions on its periphery. A secondary centre of Tantrism in the Dravidian country supports this theory.[4]

Tantrism emerges in two streams, one Buddhist and the other Hindu. The former represents an obscure blend of tantric traditions and Mahāyāna Buddhism; and the latter an equally obscure blend of tantric and Śaivite

[1] *The Commentary of Father Monserrate, S.J.*, trans. J. S. Hoyland (London, 1922), p. 115. For a note on Ṭillā see *B40(Eng)*, p. 193.

[2] Ibid., pp. 113–16.

[3] For a description of Nāth custom and belief see G. W. Briggs, *Gorakhnāth and the Kānphaṭa Yogīs* (Calcutta, 1938), *passim*; and Shashibhusan Dasgupta, *Obscure Religious Cults* (Calcutta, 1962), pp. 191–255. For an account of a Nāth establishment still surviving in the Pañjāb see B. N. Goswamy and J. S. Grewal, *The Mughals and the Jogis of Jakhbar* (Simla, 1967).

[4] Mircea Eliade, *Yoga: Immortality and Freedom* (London, 1958), pp. 201–2.

beliefs. Neither stream can be easily distinguished from the other, and later developments flowing from these earlier antecedents share their lack of clear definition. One important line seems to descend from Vajrayāna Buddhism (the classic Buddhist form of Tantrism) through Sahajiyā Buddhism to a Vaiṣṇava version of the Sahajiyā cult and thence through the Sant tradition of Northern India to Nānak himself.[1] Although the lines are by no means plain there can be no doubt concerning the Sant debt to a refined Tantrism. This is clear from the common denunciation of external forms of religion, from a common insistence upon an interior discipline, and from certain key terms which the Sants can only have derived from Sahajiyā usage.

The Nāths of Nānak's day and of the period following belonged to a different lineage. Once again it is impossible to trace the line of development with any clarity, but both the tantric origins and the radical distinction from the Sants are clear. The Nāth Masters are commonly called Siddhs, a feature which indicates a connection with the legendary Siddhāchāryas of the Buddhist Sahajiyā cult[2]. From this source the yogic beliefs and practices of the Nāths have evidently descended without being affected by the devotional concepts of the Vaiṣṇavas. It was bhakti belief which transformed the Sahajiyā cult in its Vaiṣṇava expression. Unaffected by this deviant development the Nāths continued the distinctively *haṭha-yoga* version of the Sahajiyā *kāyā-sādhana* ('culture of the body'). A particular prominence was accorded to belief in the nine Nāths, the legendary Masters who had achieved immortality through perfection in *haṭha-yoga* and who dwelt eternally in the further recesses of the Himālayas. Various lists of names are given for the nine Nāth Masters, all of them including the celebrated Gorakhnāth. Some lists name Mahādeva (Śiva) as one of the nine distinct from Gorakhnāth, whereas others merge the two.[3]

By the sixteenth century the various Nāth sects had achieved a considerable diffusion over Northern India, with two major centres in the Pañjāb and Nepāl. They were by this time in decline, but still commanded awe and a certain grudging respect for their extreme asceticism and their reputation as wonder-workers. The extent of their influence in the Pañjāb is plainly indicated by the number of compositions which Nānak addresses to Nāth yogīs. The same compositions also demonstrate the vigorous nature of Nānak's opposition to their teachings and their practices.

The reputation of the Nāths continued into the janam-sākhī period and its influence upon the evolving janam-sākhī traditions is patently clear. The attitude of the janam-sākhī narrators is ambivalent. On the one hand they naturally accept the case made by Nānak, and in both discourse and magical contest the Nāths are always worsted. On the other hand they give expression to a genuine respect for the person of Gorakhnāth. Although long since dead at the time when the janam-sākhīs were developing Gorakhnāth is a prominent choice as interlocutor for Nānak's discourses, and the pattern

[1] Shashibhusan Dasgupta, op. cit., pp. 51–2, 164–5, 345–6. *GNSR*, pp. 151–8, 191–2, 224–5.
[2] Shashibhusan Dasgupta, op. cit., p. 202.
[3] Ibid., pp. 191–7, 202–9.

which these discourses follow is generally one of accord between the two participants rather than the customary defeat.[1] It is Gorakhnāth who indicates a choice of succession to Bābā Nānak[2] and in the *Mahimā Prakāś* tradition it is he who first recognizes Nānak's greatness.[3]

One of the most prominent of the Nāth discourses, 'The Discourse on Mount Sumeru', has already been noted as an example of the manner in which the janam-sākhīs combine Nāth and Puranic legend in a single tradition. In this respect they merely reflect the Nāths' own understanding and that of sixteenth-century Pañjāb. The actual origin of this particular discourse is a series of shaloks by Guru Nānak which refer to several of the Nāth Masters by name.[4] To the names given by Nānak and the questions implied by his verses the janam-sākhīs have added the Puranic setting and many of the details needed in order to sustain the narrative. The chosen setting indicates that the legend concerning the immortal Masters was implicitly accepted by the janam-sākhī narrators and their audiences. It also illustrates the common confusion of the nine immortal Nāths with the eighty-four immortal Siddhs. Whereas the names of the interlocutors are those of Nāth Masters, Bhāī Gurdās and all his successors refer to them as representatives of the eighty-four Siddhs.[5]

A sākhī which owes rather more to the current reputation of the Nāths is the Achal discourse.[6] Like the Mount Sumeru discourse this sākhī derives in part from Nāth-oriented compositions by Nānak, but it deals with yogīs rather than immortal Masters and accords a particular prominence to their reputed power as wonder-workers. In the *Purātan* janam-sākhīs the wonder-working material is incorporated in a sākhī set in Gor-khatrī, a Nāth centre in Peshāwar.[7] Other discourse settings are Ṭillā,[8] Gorakh-matā,[9] Setu-bandha,[10] and 'in the midst of the ocean'.[11]

Most of the discourses are, like the Mount Sumeru sākhī, only partially derived from Nāth legend. The basis is generally provided by a shabad or series of shaloks from the works of Gurū Nānak, almost always a composition which by terminology or actual name indicates a Nāth audience. Nāth legend serves to supplement this basis with appropriate settings, details, and occasionally a sub-sākhī. It is an important supplement, one which bears eloquent testimony to the continuing influence of Nāth yogīs upon rural Pañjāb. The same influence emerges even more prominently in the apocryphal *Prāṇ Saṅgalī*, a work attributed to Nānak but expressing Nāth concepts of precisely the kind rebutted by the Gurū in his authentic compositions. The *Prāṇ Saṅgalī*, having penetrated the Sikh community or evolved within it, was soon appropriated by janam-sākhī

[1] Cf. *B40* sākhīs 23, 27b, and 53, ff. 86a–93b, 106b–110a, 208a–209a.
[2] *B40*, f. 93a.
[3] *SLTGN(Eng)*, pp. 59–60. *GNM*, pp. 7–8.
[4] *Vār Rāmkalī*, 12:2–7, *AG*, pp. 952–3. *GNSR*, p. 11.
[5] *BG* 1:28. *B40*, f. 86a.
[6] *B40*, ff. 117a–122a. See below, pp. 146–58.
[7] *Pur JS*, pp. 104–6. *GNSR*, p. 49. The janam-sākhīs call the place Gorakh-haṭaṛī. See below, pp. 146–51.
[8] *B40*, f. 182a. *Mih JS* 1.469. *Bālā JS*, pp. 308–11.
[9] *GR*, p. 203. *Pur JS*, pp. 27–8.
[10] *Bālā JS*, pp. 282–7.
[11] *Pur JS*, p. 84.

compilers.[1] Other apocryphal works used as sources for the janam-sākhīs provide further evidence of Nāth influence in certain sections of the post-Nānak community. An example is the *B40* sākhī 'Discourse with Kabīr'.[2]

One anecdote which can be traced directly to a Nāth source appears in the sākhī entitled 'The Country ruled by Women'.[3] This anecdote has enjoyed a notable popularity amongst the compilers of janam-sākhīs and varying versions are to be found in all collections except the *Miharbān Janam-sākhī*. The source of the anecdote is plainly the Nāth legend which relates the seduction of Machhendranāth (Matsyendranāth, or Mīnanāth). According to this legend Machhendranāth, while in the womb of a fish, overheard Śiva expounding the secret of the universe to his consort Gauṛī. Machhendranāth subsequently made slighting remarks concerning Gauṛī and as a result of her curse was transformed into a sheep by the women of Kadalī. From this sorry fate he was rescued by Gorakhnāth.[4] In spite of its more grotesque elements the janam-sākhīs' version of the anecdote has enjoyed a continuing popularity because two of them set it in an area variously called Kaurū or Kārū. This obviously indicates Kāmrūp, long regarded as the home of Tantrism and the darker magical crafts. Modern biographers have assumed that the Kāmrūp setting indicates a visit by Gurū Nānak to Āssām.[5]

(c) *Sūfī tradition*

In the use which they make of Nāth contacts the janam-sākhī compilers were, in large measure, following a pattern which had earlier been developed in Sūfī hagiography. A recent study of this aspect of Sūfī tradition enumerates three varieties of anecdote concerning encounters between yogīs and Sūfī pīrs.

Three classes of anecdotes regarding Jogīs in the Sūfī literature of the Dehli Sultanate can be arranged in a series of progressive elaboracy viz:—
(1) Plain anecdotes of the voluntary conversion of Jogīs followed by their attainment of a high 'station' on the Sūfī 'path'.
(2) Anecdotes of magic contests leading to the subjugation and conversion of the Jogī, again usually followed by his attainment of a high Sūfī station.
(3) Anecdotes of magic contest and conversion which have a regional significance, in that the Jogī is displaced as the *locum tenens* of a sacred or otherwise desirable site by the Sūfī Shaykh. Professing Islam and attaining a Sūfī 'station', the Jogī is accommodated in a subordinate capacity on the same holy site, or as an esteemed member of the Shaykh's entourage.[6]

This list indicates a striking but altogether natural similarity of Sūfī and janam-sākhī styles. The only significant difference is the extensive use

[1] See below, pp. 103–4.
[2] *B40*, ff. 136a–138a.
[3] *B40*, ff. 83a–85b. *Pur JS*, pp. 33–7. *AS*, pp. 26–8.
[4] Shashibhusan Dasgupta, op. cit., pp. 201–2, 244, 368n.
[5] *GNSR*, pp. 110–12.
[6] S. Digby, unpublished paper, 'Encounters with Jogis in Indian Sufi Hagiography'. For a discussion of the influence of Nāth doctrine upon Indian Sūfīs see S. A. A. Rizvi, 'Sufis and Natha Yogis in Mediaeval Northern India (XII–XVI Centuries)', *Journal of the Oriental Society of Australia*, vol. vii, nos. 1 and 2, pp. 119–33.

made by the janam-sākhī narrators of passages from the works of Nānak.

The close resemblance at this particular point indicates one of the janam-sākhī affinities with Sūfī hagiography. Other debts of an even more obvious nature can be observed throughout the janam-sākhī collections. Just as the Nāth discourses bear witness to a continuing Nāth influence in the Pañjāb of the sixteenth and seventeenth centuries, so in like manner do the numerous encounters with Sūfī pīrs testify to the extent of Sūfī influence. It must, however, be stressed that the influence derived from the hagiography of the Sūfīs and the personal fame of some of the more prominent pīrs. It did not derive from any extensive understanding of Muslim doctrine. Knowledge of the doctrines of Islam and the contents of the Qur'ān is conspicuously absent from the janam-sākhīs. The insistent interest of the janam-sākhī narrators in folklore traditions and their general ignorance of Muslim doctrines are both well illustrated by the following extract from the *Bālā* account of Bābā Nānak's visit to Mecca.

It is written in the *qibla* that one day a dervish named Nānak will come and that water will spring in the well of Mecca.[1]

Once again there emerges a contrast between the understanding of the janam-sākhīs and that of Nānak himself. Gurū Nānak, though relatively little influenced by Muslim doctrine, certainly possessed an extensive knowledge of it and commonly made use of its terminology.

In some instances janam-sākhī narrators have incorporated distinctively Sūfī features in anecdotes concerning Bābā Nānak. Many of these are easily recognized, particularly those which use a demonstrably Muslim context for stories involving miraculous locomotion, levitation, or *ṭai-i-safar* (instantaneous transportation achieved by the mere closing of the eyes). The *B40* story of the moving mosque of Kābul illustrates this variety of miraculous locomotion,[2] and Bhāī Gurdās provides an example of levitation in his account of how Bābā Nānak ascended into the air during his visit to Bāghdād.[3] The *ṭai-i-safar* tradition has been of occasional use to janam-sākhī compilers who have not followed chronological patterns in their order of sākhīs. When confronted by an evident need to explain how Bābā Nānak could traverse hundreds of miles in an instant they commonly found their solution in recourse to the example of Sūfī hagiographers.[4]

One specific application by the Sūfīs of their belief in miraculous movement of objects as a proof of spiritual power is the tradition that the Ka'bah may revolve around a pīr of the most exalted status. Ordinarily the Muslim circumambulates the Ka'bah, but in cases of supreme spiritual achievement the roles are reversed. It seems clear that one of the key elements in the janam-sākhī story of the moving *miharāb* should be traced

1 *Bālā JS*, p. 184. The *Purātan* janam-sākhīs give *kitābān* instead of *qibla*. *Pur JS*, p. 99.

2 *B40*, f. 154b.

3 *BG* 1:36. *GNSR*, p. 35.

4 This is a common feature in the chronologically disorganized *Bālā* janam-sākhīs. Cf. also *B40*, ff. 123b, 133b, 157a, 178a.

to this tradition.[1] Although the earliest version of the sākhī appears to have been given a setting away from Mecca[2] the movement of a *miharāb* amounts to the same thing as movement of the Ka'bah. The *miharāb* marks the *qibla* (the direction of the Ka'bah), and a mobile *miharāb* can only mean a corresponding movement of the Ka'bah.

In all of these Sūfī instances the janam-sākhī anecdote has been constituted by a combining of recognizably Sūfī elements with other material. This is the characteristic form of janam-sākhī borrowing. Occasionally, however, two other forms of direct borrowing may be noted. The first is the narration of a Sūfī anecdote in a manner which retains its earlier connection with a Sūfī pīr, but which sets the entire episode in the context of an encounter with Bābā Nānak. An example of this form is the *Purātan* story of a meeting with Sheikh Farīd in the legendary land of Āsā. One of the three anecdotes included in this sākhī describes Farid's attempt to maintain a rigorous ascetic discipline by carrying a wooden loaf (*chapātī*). This he did in order to provide an excuse for refusing proffered food. The anecdote, which properly belongs to the traditions concerning Farīd, retains this connection in the *Purātan* janam-sākhīs. The difference is that the meeting with Bābā Nānak convinces Farīd of the dangerous hypocrisy involved in the stratagem, as a result of which he abandons the wooden *chapātī*.[3]

Elsewhere a complete, or substantially complete, anecdote borrowed from Sūfī hagiography has been deprived of its Sūfī context and attached directly to the person of Bābā Nānak. The most striking example is Bhāī Gurdās's story of Nānak's encounter with the pīrs of Multān.[4] This anecdote, which is discussed below as an example of a *Wandersage*,[5] has obviously been taken directly from Sūfī traditions centring on Multān. Another example, also derived from a Multān source, is the Sūfī tradition concerning the manner in which Sheikh Bahā' al-Dīn Zakariyyā died.[6]

In addition to the direct borrowings, Sūfī influence is also evident in the choice of interlocutors for several of the janam-sākhī discourses. Sūfī pīrs commanded a considerable respect in the Pañjāb of the janam-sākhī period and it was of vital importance to the purpose of the janam-sākhīs that their reputations should be eclipsed by that of Bābā Nānak. The fact that the more impressive of Sūfī reputations were attached to pīrs long since dead did not affect the need to involve such men in discourses with Nānak and to demonstrate the superiority of the latter. There is no suggestion of conscious deceit at this point. Neither the janam-sākhī narrators nor their audiences were historians. History and legend could both serve their purpose and, as we have already observed, a consciousness of sharp distinctions between the two should never be expected in the janam-sākhīs. The discourses held with Sūfī pīrs of earlier centuries must be regarded as illustrations of the Nānak myth of the janam-sākhīs rather than as examples of their narrators' credulity.

[1] *B40*, f. 51b.
[2] See below, p. 140.
[3] *Pur JS*, p. 45. *GNSR*, pp. 42, 80.
[4] *BG* 1:44. *GNSR*, pp. 35, 142.
[5] See below, pp. 118–20.
[6] See below, p. 119n.

As a result of this need to contest the hold of Sūfī tradition the janam-sākhī compilers have sprinkled a series of appropriate discourses through their collections. In the *B40 Janam-sākhī* Bābā Nānak is said to have encountered, at various times, Rukn al-Dīn, Rattan Hājī, Ibrāhīm Farīd Sānī, and Sharaf al-Dīn.[1] Of these only Sheikh Ibrāhīm could have been a contemporary of Gurū Nānak. With the exception of Rattan Hājī all appear in the *Purātan* janam-sākhīs, where they are joined by Farīd al-Dīn Mas'ūd Ganj-i-Shakar and Bahā' al-Dīn Zakariyyā,[2] both of whom had long predeceased the birth of Nānak. Other janam-sākhīs add more names. Bhāī Gurdās and the *Miharbān Janam-sākhī* both describe encounters with 'Abd al-Qādir Jīlānī;[3] the *Mahimā Prakāś Vāratak* introduces Sākhī Sarvār Sultān;[4] and eventually Santokh Singh finds a place for the celebrated Shams al-Dīn Tabrīzī, Pīr of Multān and preceptor of Rūmī.[5] The same figure does not always appear in the same setting. Sheikh Sharaf is variously located in Pāṇīpat, Bāghdād, Bidar, and Mecca; Rukn al-Dīn is to be found in Mecca and Multān; and Jīlānī in Bāghdād and Kartārpur. Inconsistencies of this kind are, however, of no more importance than the fact that all three pīrs were long since dead. It is the pīrs' function which is important.

3. *THE WORKS OF GURŪ NĀNAK*

A second major constituent in the formation of the janam-sākhī traditions was provided by references in Nānak's own works. One important example of this feature has already been noted. In *Vār Rāmkalī*, shaloks 2–7 of *pauṛī* 12, Gurū Nānak refers by name to Īśar, Gorakh, Gopīchand, Charapaṭ, and Bharatharī, all of whom figure prominently in lists of the seven legendary Nāth Masters.[6] Whereas Gurū Nānak's own intention was clearly the expression of an imaginary dialogue, the janam-sākhī narrators quickly assumed an actual encounter. Elements from Puranic and Nāth legend were added and the result was the ever-popular 'Discourse on Mount Sumeru'. Other compositions employing Nāth names and terminology prompted similar discourses, and in like manner works which made prominent use of Muslim tradition or imagery soon found their way into sākhīs describing encounters with Sūfī pīrs. Works of this kind rarely indicate a specifically Sūfī audience, but Sūfīs were, like Nāth yogīs, prominent in seventeenth-century Pañjāb and it is natural that the janam-sākhīs should reflect this prominence.

1 *B40*, ff. 53a, 56a, 57b, 200a. 2 *Pur JS*, pp. 22, 40, 52, 82, 100, 104, 108.

3 *BG* 1:35–6. *Mih JS* II.179. Bhāī Gurdās refers to him as Dastgīr, one of the many names applied to Jīlānī. *GNSR*, p. 126.

4 *SLTGN(Eng)*, p. 72. For notes on Sākhī Sarvār see W. Crooke, *The Popular Religion and Folklore of Northern India*, vol. ii (London, 1896), pp. 208–11; R. C. Temple, *The Legends of the Panjab*, vol. i (Bombay and London, 1884), p. 66; and *GTC* i, p. 566.

5 *NPr* II.37(4). See *B40 (Eng)*, p. 59n. See also R. C. Temple, op. cit., vol. iii, pp, 90–1. R. A. Nicholson, *Rumi: Poet and Mystic* (London, 1950), p. 19. *ASI 1872–73*, p. 135. Alexander Burnes, *Travels into Bokhara*, vol. iii (London, 1839), pp. 116–17.

6 *AG*, pp. 952–3. See above, p. 69 and below, p. 148.

In such cases a complete shabad would normally be responsible for the discourse or anecdote. Elsewhere a brief reference or even a single word might be sufficient to spark the imagination. The words *lālo* in *Tilaṅg* 5, *sajjaṇ* in *Sūhī* 3, and *mūlā* in *Surplus Shaloks 21* have all been interpreted as proper names and as such have served as starting-points for prominent anecdotes.[1]

Sākhīs which have been developed out of compositions by Gurū Nānak are a common feature of all janam-sākhīs. When, as in most instances, the resultant sākhī takes the form of a discourse the process is generally as follows. Gurū Nānak's own words, as expressed in a suggestive shabad or shalok, provide, as a nucleus for the discourse, answers to an interlocutor's questions. A suitable person is chosen to serve as interlocutor (one to whom Nānak's words might appropriately have been directed), and the questions or comments to be uttered by him are framed in accordance with the known answer. This provides the basic pattern. The interlocutor's question or comment is followed by a shalok or by the first stanza of a shabad. Another question or comment is followed by the second stanza or another shalok, and so the discourse proceeds until the shabad has been completed or the supply of suitable shaloks is exhausted. A setting is provided in order to introduce the discourse and in a brief conclusion the interlocutor submits to the Gurū.

This is the standard procedure. It is, however, by no means invariable. A narrator's imagination was not limited to the images suggested by the text of Gurū Nānak's actual compositions and commonly it would range much more widely. This was particularly the case when the starting-point for a sākhī was provided by a single word or reference. It was, for example, inevitable that Nānak's references to Bābur and, in a less explicit way, to the Mughal invasions should attract attention. The resultant sākhīs do not, however, follow the pattern indicated by any of the shabads which include these references, for in no case are they well suited to discourse purposes. Instead the narrators utilize traditions concerning Bābur (notably the belief that he was a clandestine qalandar) and authentic memories relating to the Mughal conquest of the Pañjāb. The shabads evidently prompt the anecdotes and in this sense constitute their origin, but make only a small contribution to the substance of the narrative.[2]

The imagination of the narrator finds further expression during the period of subsequent circulation. Simple discourses become progressively longer and more complex, with extra details and complete episodes being drawn in from other sources. Some sākhīs which have evolved out of shabads or shaloks retain their individuality throughout this period of expansion, whereas others are combined to form a complex of sub-sākhīs. The Bābur narratives provide examples of both. The earlier traditions retain their central position, but extra material is added. This supplementary material includes a discourse developed in accordance with the standard process out of the shabad *Tilaṅg* 2. The shabad begins:

[1] See below, pp. 86–7, 121, 122.

[2] *B40*, ff. 66b, 73a(2). *GNSR*, pp. 132–8.

Fear of Thee, O Lord, is my bhang, and my mind
  the pouch in which I carry it.
Intoxicated with this bhang I have abandoned all
  interest in worldly concerns.[1]

Here the suggestive prompt is provided by the word bhang (cannabis). The narrator's task is relatively simple. Bābur, having heard Bābā Nānak sing an earlier shabad, has him brought to his presence. The earlier shabad is repeated and Bābur is converted. At this point the bhang sub-sākhī is introduced.

[Bābur] then opened his bhang-pouch and offered it to Bābā Nānak, saying, 'Have some bhang, faqīr.'[2]

To this Bābā Nānak replies:

Mīrjī, I have already eaten bhang. I have taken a kind of bhang which induces a condition of permanent intoxication.[3]

He then recites *Tilaṅg* 2 and the sākhī moves on to another episode. A discourse developed out of a shabad and complete in itself has thus been introduced as a sub-sākhī into an earlier cluster of sākhīs concerning Bābur.

The part played by the imagination of the narrator becomes even clearer when this Bābur anecdote is compared with the *Purātan* version of Bābā Nānak's visit to Mecca.[4] In this composite sākhī the same shabad appears within a different discourse, this time with a Mecca pilgrim serving as interlocutor. Evidently the bhang-consuming interlocutor had to be a Muslim. The *Colebrooke* narrator (to whom the Mecca version can be traced) chose a *hājī* whereas the unknown narrator followed by the *B40* and *Ādi Sākhīs* compilers decided that Bābur would be an appropriate choice.[5] The *Hāfizābād* compiler, with access to both sources, includes both discourses.[6]

These procedures will be further analysed when discussing the evolution of individual sākhīs. Two further points should, however, be noted before proceeding to the fourth important constituent of the janam-sākhīs. The first is that the processes indicated above should not be interpreted as explicitly conscious procedures and certainly not as examples of deliberate fabrication. Such an assumption would imply a variety of understanding which the janam-sākhī narrators did not possess and criteria which they could never have used. The point has already been made with the works of Bhāī Gurdās, but it is of sufficient importance to warrant repetition. The approach of the janam-sākhī narrators was not that of historians. Their primary concern was with a single belief, namely belief in the divine mission of Bābā Nānak. This was for them the essential truth. The variety and nature of the material which they employed was of secondary importance. No question of deceit would normally be involved in the use

1 *AG*, p. 721. 2 *B40*, f. 71a. 3 Ibid. 4 *Pur JS*, p. 98.
5 Photozincograph Facsimile (Dehrā Dūn, 1885), pp. 388–9. *AS*, p. 55.
6 M. A. Macauliffe (ed.), *Janam Sākhī Bābe Nānak Jī kī*, (Rāwalpiṇḍī, 1885), pp. 165, 250.

of 'unhistorical' material. It was the basic myth which demanded their faithful allegiance and with rare exceptions their allegiance was unswerving.

The second point to be noted at this stage is that although there are many sākhīs and sub-sākhīs which have been developed out of the Gurū's compositions their number is not nearly as substantial as first appearances might suggest. A cursory reading of almost any janam-sākhī will reveal numerous quotations from the works of Nānak, most of them presented as integral parts of the sākhīs in which they occur. Only a small minority of the large total have actually participated in the development of their contextual sākhīs. The large majority are subsequent additions to evolved sākhīs. Although they may still be regarded as constituents of the janam-sākhīs they are constituents in a much more superficial sense than works which have actually served to generate sākhīs.

Most extracts from the works of Nānak have been added because their terminology, content, or some particular reference seems to accord with the theme of an available sākhī. A transparent example is provided at the conclusion of the *B40* version of the sākhī 'Bābā Nānak's Visit to the Pilgrimage-centres'. The *Ādi Sākhīs* analogue terminates the sākhī at the point where Bābā Nānak's 'first disciples' give away all their possessions in order to live as *bairāgīs*.

Having given them his blessing he went on his way.[1]

The *B40* compiler has at this point responded to the ever-insistent impulse to expand.

Having given them his blessing he went on his way singing an *aṣṭapadī* in the measure *Tilaṅg* rāga.

Wondrous is the Kingdom of Poverty;
The domain wherein there are no pretensions to greatness.[2]

Whereas in this example it is the theme of the shabad which has prompted the addition, elsewhere a single brief reference has been sufficient to suggest a scriptural supplement. An example is provided by the anecdote entitled 'The Monster's Cauldron'. Once again it is the *Ādi Sākhīs* analogue which provides the earlier text and it is a text which completely lacks scriptural quotation.[3] In the *B40* and other versions, however, a shabad by Gurū Arjan has been added in the mistaken belief that it is by Gurū Nānak.[4] The sākhī describes how when the monster sought to boil Bābā Nānak in a cauldron the oil refused to heat.[5] The shabad by Gurū Arjan includes the line:

The seething cauldron has lost its heat, for the Gurū has applied to it the cooling Name.

Although it is clear that Gurū Arjan was using the cauldron as an image for the troubled human heart, the similarity in terminology was evidently

[1] *AS*, p. 26. [2] *B40*, f. 81a. The shabad is apocryphal. [3] *AS*, p. 28.
[4] *Mārū Mahalā* 5, 14, *AG*, p. 1002. [5] *B40*, f 40a–b. *Pur JS*, pp. 81–2.

too strong to be resisted and the shabad was accordingly added to the sākhī.[1]

The introduction of compositions by later Gurūs is a common inconsistency. Another is the manner in which different narrators interpolate the same shabad or shalok at different places. Many of the suggestive themes and references which have prompted interpolation can find congenial locations in more than one sākhī. An example is *Mārū* 6 in which Gurū Nānak describes himself as a slave (*lālā*).[2] His meaning can only be 'a slave of God', but this is not explicitly stated and two narrators have independently interpreted it in a literal sense. In the *B40* janam-sākhī it has been appended without further comment to a sākhī concerning a child who was to be sold into slavery by his parents.[3] The *Purātan* janam-sākhīs, in contrast, have introduced it into the sākhī describing the sack of Saidpur at the point where Bābā Nānak is said to have been committed to the Saidpur jail. In this latter instance a brief sub-sākhī has been developed from the shabad.[4]

Another example is provided by the shabad *Basant Hiṇḍol* 1, where the prompting issues from the fifth and sixth stanzas.

> And now the Primal One is called Allāh and it is the writ of the sheikhs which runs in Hindustān.[5]

One narrator, whose version was subsequently followed by the *Ādi Sākhīs*, *B40*, and *Miharbān* janam-sākhīs, somewhat inappropriately chose the Mecca visit as a suitable point to insert the shabad.[6] For him the reference to Muslims was sufficient. It was a more alert *Bālā* narrator who appreciated the distinctively Indian context of Nānak's comments and who was thus able to select a more suitable setting. The sākhī which he chose was a discourse between Bābā Nānak and a Muslim named Sheikh Mālo Takhān.[7] In this latter instance it is possible that the shabad may have been responsible for the development of the discourse. The same question arises in the case of a shalok from *Vār Āsā* which is said to have been addressed to a wealthy misanthrope named Bhāgo. In one tradition this Bhāgo appears as a resident of Saidpur in the celebrated story of Lālo the Carpenter;[8] and in the other as a chaudharī of Lahore.[9] Whereas the latter appears to be a direct development from the shalok the former is more doubtful.

It is thus evident that a majority of the scriptural quotations included in the janam-sākhīs are interpolations. Amongst those which appear as later supplements rather than original components some have been

[1] The interpretation suggested in *GNSR*, p. 79, is incorrect. The sākhī cannot have evolved out of the shabad.

[2] *AG*, p. 991.

[3] *B40*, f. 50a.

[4] *Pur JS*, p. 60. For an example of two complete sākhīs developed in this manner see below, pp. 128–9.

[5] *AG*, pp. 1190–1.

[6] *B40*, f. 134a–b. *AS*, pp. 43–4. *Mih JS* I.453–7.

[7] *Bālā JS*, p. 339.

[8] *SLTGN(Eng)*, pp. 75–6. In this tradition Bhāgo is said to be a Khatrī and a karoṛī.

[9] *Mih JS* II.385–6. The Bhāgo of the *Miharbān* tradition is said to be a Khahirā Jaṭ and to have been accompanied by a Dilāvarī Khatrī named Gaṅgū. The shalok is *Vār Āsā* 17:1, *AG*, p. 472.

introduced for pedagogical reasons, and a few for motives which are no longer evident. Pedagogical intentions are a prominent feature of the *Miharbān* tradition, particularly in the second and third sections of the extant *Miharbān Janam-sākhī*. In a sense, of course, all additions drawn from the works of Gurū Nānak are intended to serve this function. All have been introduced to strengthen the soteriological thrust of the janam-sākhīs. Because they represent subsequent additions to earlier traditions they are also of interest as a means of distinguishing later versions from their earlier sources.

An anecdote which illustrates most of the features associated with the use of scriptural quotations in the janam-sākhīs is 'Bābā Nānak's Discourse with the Physician'.[1] The anecdote represents, in the first place, a sākhī which has been developed out of a composition by Gurū Nānak, aided by a shalok of Gurū Angad and two apocryphal shaloks. The composition by Gurū Nānak is also a shalok:

> They called a physician to practise his art, to seize my wrist and feel my pulse.
> The ignorant physician was unaware that the pain is in my heart![2]

The other three couplets all express a similar message and there can be no doubt that the genesis of the sākhī is to be found in one or more of the four. In its original form the sākhī must have consisted of a brief introduction, at least one of the four shaloks, and the physician's concluding declaration.

The second feature illustrated by this sākhī is the subsequent addition of scriptural quotations which seem to accord with its theme. Having emerged as a brief, coherent anecdote the sākhī was taken up by two separate traditions. During transmission within one of these traditions it was expanded by the addition of Gurū Nānak's *Malār* 7, a shabad which seemed eminently suited to its theme. *Malār* 7 begins:

> Bring no medicine, O ignorant physician.
> It is this heart of mine which suffers, not my body.
> Such medicine is worthless, foolish physician.[3]

Meanwhile a narrator within the other tradition had made a different choice. Instead of *Malār* 7 he had selected *Malār* 8 as a suitable addition. This he did for precisely the same reason. *Malār* 8 begins:

> Bring no medicine, O ignorant physician,
> For it is my heart which suffers torment.[4]

[1] *B40*, between ff. 14b and 19a. The *B40* text of this sākhī is missing, but has been reconstructed with the help of the manuscript *LDP 194*. See *B40(Eng)*, introduction, pp. 28–31.

[2] *Vār Malār* 3:1, *AG*, p. 1279. *B40(Eng)*, p. 17.

[3] Photozincograph Facsimile (Dehrā Dūn, 1885), p. 35. In the Ādi Granth version this refrain follows the first stanza, and its second line reads:

> Pain lingers, agony still racks my body.
>
> *AG*, p. 1256.

The janam-sākhī tradition into which this addition was introduced has been designated *Narrative Ia*. See below, pp. 185–7.

[4] *B40*, between ff. 14b and 19a. *AG*, pp. 1256–7. The janam-sākhī tradition which incorporates this supplement is *Narrative Ib*. One compiler utilizing *Narrative Ib* sources quotes *Malār* 7, not *Malār* 8. *AS*, p. 13. *Malār* 8 is, however, confined to *Narrative Ib* janam-sākhīs and clearly represents an addition made within that tradition.

Both of these shabads were added because of their evident affinities with the subject of the anecdote.

A third feature appears only in the first of the two traditions. A narrator within this tradition later appended the shabad *Gauṛī* 17.[1] This he did for reasons which are difficult to understand. The theme of the hymn bears no obvious resemblance to that of the sākhī. Moreover the addition has been made at the conclusion of the sākhī, following the physician's final pronouncement. Unlike *Malār* 7 it has not been integrated into the narrative.

A fourth feature, already implied by the second and third, emerges clearly from a comparison of the various versions of the Physician sākhī. This is the manner in which the sākhī has progressively expanded with successive versions. Although no text of the original form exists, its presence in the earliest oral tradition may be deduced from the differences distinguishing the two recorded traditions. The earliest of the recorded texts is represented by *LDP 194*[2] and the reconstructed *B40* sākhī. This corresponds to the second of the traditions noted above. The first tradition emerges, in a much later form, in the *Colebrooke Janam-sākhī*.[3] Both traditions united in the composite *Hāfizābād Janam-sākhī*.[4]

The Physician sākhī provides a preliminary illustration of the manner in which the scriptural constituent has been utilized by janam-sākhī narrators. Other examples of greater complexity will be discussed in the section dealing with the evolution of selected individual sākhīs.

4. *ASCETIC IDEALS*

The last of the major constituents is of a markedly different nature from the remainder. It derives not from earlier compositions, whether current anecdotes or works of the Gurū, but from a prevailing attitude or ideology. This is the ancient and tenacious belief in the supreme merit of asceticism. In one sense this constituent can be regarded as an aspect of received tradition, for it was as a part of tradition in the wider sense that the ascetic ideal exerted its powerful pressure upon the janam-sākhī narrators. It could not, however, be classified as an aspect of the other major constituent noted above. The ascetic ideals which find expression in the janam-sākhīs are diametrically opposed to Gurū Nānak's own emphatically stated beliefs. Nānak himself maintained a moderate position, a disciplined worldliness which was opposed to laxity on the one hand and total renunciation on the other.[5]

It is a measure of the power exercised by the ascetic tradition that it could so effectively reassert itself against Nānak's explicit opposition. This

[1] Photozincograph Facsimile, pp. 36–8. *AG*, p. 156.
[2] Loc. cit., ff. 19a–21a.
[3] IOL MS Panj. B6, ff. 26b–29a. Photozincograph Facsimile, pp. 33–8.
[4] M. A. Macauliffe (ed.), *Janam Sākhī Bābe Nānak Jī kī* (Rāwalpiṇḍī, 1885), pp. 22–4. *Pur JS*, pp. 11–12.
[5] *GNSR*, p. 211.

is not to suggest that its resurgence affected all sections of the new community, nor that Nānak's own teachings were buried in an avalanche of restored traditions. On the contrary, the emphasis upon the old ideals seems to have been the work of a particular group within the community.[1] It was, however, an influential group and it could appeal to deeply rooted sympathies. Its strength is abundantly evident from the extent to which the ascetic ideal has affected many of the janam-sākhī narratives.

As with all janam-sākhī constituents the ascetic tradition mingles with other elements. Sometimes it is the dominant element, sometimes it plays a subordinate though integrated role, and sometimes it emerges in the form of an interpolation. An example of the third of these appears in the *Purātan* version of the sākhī variously entitled 'Bābā Nānak's Visit to Gujrāt' and 'Dūnī Chand's Flags'. This relates an anecdote concerning a wealthy man who flaunted his riches by means of a display of symbolic pennants.[2] According to the *B40* version (a narrative which seems to have been taken directly from oral sources) Bābā Nānak's response to the rich man's conversion is simply one of joy.[3] The *Purātan* janam-sākhīs add to this a statement which can only be interpreted as a commendation of the renunciant life.

'Give in God's name,' answered the Gurū. 'Feed ascetics (*atīt*) and wandering holy men (*abhiāgat*) for it is in this manner that your wealth will be carried into the hereafter.'[4]

Whereas the first instruction accords with Gurū Nānak's own ideals the second does so only in a strictly qualified sense which would not be the meaning intended by the narrator. Normally the distinction would be completely overlooked by a janam-sākhī audience. In this manner traditional beliefs which had been modified or rejected by the Gurū were soon restored to the community of his followers.

An example of combination with other constituents is the 'Sack of Saidpur' sākhī. Two primary elements can be recognized in this instance. The first is an authentic incident, namely the Mughal invasions of the Pañjāb and specifically Bābur's attack on the town of Saidpur;[5] and the second is a group of four shabads by Gurū Nānak which refer in general terms to Bābur's invasions.[6] The ascetic ideal provides a third constituent, subordinate to the other two but nevertheless important and richly embroidered by later narrators. Bābur attacked Saidpur (so it is claimed) because the churlish inhabitants of the town had refused hospitality to Bābā Nānak and the group of faqīrs who were with him.[7] In the proto-anecdote the explanation was probably limited to disrespect for the Gurū. The later narrators, however, magnify the explanation into something much larger. It is not merely the Gurū who was insulted but faqīrs in

[1] Probably the Udāsī sādhūs. The ascetic ideal obviously commanded a considerable following within the group responsible for the *Miharbān* tradition. It continues to find expression today in the surviving Udāsī panth and amongst the sādhūs of the Nirmalā panth. Both groups maintain their links with the wider Sikh community. For the Udāsīs see above, p. 35 and *B40(Eng)*, p. 96.

[2] *B40*, ff. 189a–190a. [3] *B40*, f. 189b. [4] *Pur JS*, p. 71.

[5] *GNSR*, p. 138. [6] Ibid., p. 135. [7] *B40*, ff. 66b–68b.

general, and faqīrs are explicitly distinguished from householders.[1] Once again the departure from Nānak's own teachings becomes apparent.

In this instance the ascetic element is secondary. A sākhī in which it plays a primary role is the *Bālā* anecdote entitled *Kharā Saudā* or 'The Good Bargain'.[2] Bābā Nānak, having received twenty rupees from his father for a small commercial enterprise, gives the entire amount to a band of wandering sādhūs. Once again the pressure of the ascetic ideal, with its marked deference to total renunciation, is abundantly evident.

From a number of sākhīs included in the *Ādi Sākhīs* and the *B40 Janam-sākhī* (and descending from the former to the *Miharbān Janam-sākhī*) it appears that a section of the Sikh community which subscribed to the ascetic ideal may once have produced its own distinctive janam-sākhī. In the *B40 Janam-sākhī* these sākhīs occur in two clusters (numbers 20–1 and 25–7).[3] There can be no doubt that these anecdotes have been taken from a single common source by the *B40* and *Ādi Sākhīs* compilers.[4] In view of the consistent emphasis laid upon asceticism and renunciation in these clusters it seems reasonable to conclude that they must have originated (at least in their extant form) within an ascetically inclined segment of the community. These sākhīs represent Bābā Nānak as a performer of austerities[5] and as one who sought total withdrawal from the world.[6] It is no accident that Gorakhnāth, with his immense reputation for ascetic accomplishments, should be accorded a particular respect within this group of sākhīs.

Received tradition and the works of Gurū Nānak provide the two most important constituents of the janam-sākhīs. A continuing ascetic ideal accounts for a third, and a fourth is occasionally supplied by memories of authentic incidents. A single constituent is rarely found in complete isolation. Most sākhīs are products of a blending of constituents, and in many instances the mingling process has reached a considerable degree of complexity. Whereas in all cases the choice of elements has been largely determined by the primary purpose of the janam-sākhī narrators, the form and content of their actual expression has been moulded by the cultural context within which the janam-sākhīs evolved. The impact of Gurū Nānak upon certain areas of sixteenth-century Pañjāb society produced a conviction concerning the meaning of his life and teachings. To give this belief concrete and convincing expression there soon accumulated a body of tradition, most of it consisting of anecdote and discourse. Although this tradition inevitably drew much of its material from earlier traditions it nevertheless possessed a freshness and a novelty of its own. This it acquired by reason of the new focus for the tradition and also as a result of the function it served in giving expression to the distinctive needs of the new community.

[1] *B40*, f. 68b. [2] *Bālā JS*, pp. 16–22. *GNSR*, p. 83. See also *SLTGN(Eng)*, p. 65.

[3] *B40*, ff. 76a–82a, 100a–110a. See below, p. 203.

[4] The source is the *Q2* manuscript. It appears that the *Q2* compiler may have used a particular source for these sākhīs. See below, p. 206.

[5] *B40*, ff. 76a, 102b–103a, 103b. [6] *B40*, f. 106b.

7

JANAM-SĀKHĪ FORMS

THE intention of the janam-sākhī narrators was to give expression to their interpretations of the life and teachings of Gurū Nānak. For this purpose they required appropriate forms. If the purpose was to be fulfilled it was essential that the chosen forms should provide coherent statements of their interpretations in a manner agreeable to their intended audiences, and it was inevitable that this requirement should be answered by means of extensive borrowing from contemporary models. The janam-sākhī narrators were not conscious artists, much less deliberate innovators. It was the message which concerned them and it was entirely natural that they should unconsciously adapt existing forms in order to give it expression. Narrative patterns which well suited their purpose were already abundantly familiar to their audiences. These provided the narrators with their models.

The principal exemplar followed by the janam-sākhī narrators was the *tazkira* of Sūfī hagiography. The Sūfī *tazkiras* were collections of biographical anecdotes which related the wondrous deeds of celebrated pīrs. This was precisely the pattern which the janam-sākhī narrators required and they slipped into it with complete ease. In some cases their debt to Sūfī tradition extended to exact borrowings of complete anecdotes.[1] Even the distinctively Indian elements in the janam-sākhī style can, in some measure, be associated with the Sūfī example, for Sūfī hagiography within India had itself engaged in extensive borrowing of native forms.

It is, of course, possible to carry this self-evident theory of correspondence too far and to assume that *all* varieties of janam-sākhī forms should be attributed to Sūfī models. This is certainly not the case. The beginnings of the janam-sākhī traditions must be closely linked with Sūfī forms and the continuing anecdotal method retains that connection. There are, however, other forms to be found within the janam-sākhīs and here the relationship is that of similarity rather than correspondence. Janam-sākhī discourse and commentary are not the same as the Sūfī forms.

The impression which emerges from a comparison of janam-sākhī and Sūfī traditions is that of an early assumption of the standard narrative forms used by the Sūfīs, followed by an increasing divergence as the janam-sākhīs grow in age and quantity. The needs of the Sikh community were not identical with the interests of Sūfī hagiographers, and just as the initial correspondence was inevitable so too was the later divergence. Although this applied to actual content rather than form the latter was by

[1] The anecdote concerning Bābā Nānak's visit to Multān provides an example. See below, pp. 118–20

no means uninfluenced by the distinctive needs of the evolving community.

The principal forms used by janam-sākhī narrators and commentators have already been briefly summarized. They will now be analysed in greater detail.

1. *NARRATIVE ANECDOTES*

The narrative anecdote was the earliest of all janam-sākhī forms and has ever since remained dominant in all janam-sākhīs except that of the *Miharbān* tradition. This at once indicates a plain debt to the Sūfī models. It should, however, be added that even without the example of the *tazkira* the janam-sākhī narrators would still have employed an anecdotal style. The anecdote is unusually well suited to the needs of hagiography. It provides ample scope for an unending series of decisive actions, pointed epigrams, and evidences of divine approval. These are the obvious concerns of the janam-sākhī hagiographers and their extensive use of the anecdotal form is a predictable consequence.

Although most of the individual anecdotes are marked by a pithy brevity this feature has been somewhat obscured by the general tendency of narrators to group them into clusters. A particular person, place, or theme has commonly attracted more than one anecdote and clusters of this kind have frequently been recast as a single composite sākhī or as a brief series of consecutive sākhīs. The process is clearly illustrated by the later janam-sākhī treatments of several Mecca anecdotes, and by some of the sākhīs which describe encounters with Nāths.[1] Most of the longer narrative sākhīs are fashioned in this manner from a number of separate anecdotes, often with a considerable degree of skill. It is only occasionally that the specifically narrative portion of a single anecdote will run to several folios of a manuscript, and whenever this does occur it usually succeeds only in weakening the force of the anecdote's message. An unusually clumsy example is the *B40* sākhī entitled 'Bābā Nānak Enslaved in the Land of the Paṭhāns'.[2]

Cumbersome narrative structures are, however, rare. Single anecdotes which run to excessive length normally do so because scriptural quotations have been inserted. These interpolations also tend to weaken the impact of an anecdote, and although they have obviously been introduced to serve the primary purpose of the janam-sākhīs it may well be suspected that they frequently produced the opposite effect. Whereas a single shabad would be tolerable a series which interrupted an interesting narrative could defeat the narrator's purpose.

A clarification which is required at this point concerns the distinction which must be drawn between anecdote and sākhī. In its normal usage 'sākhī' designates no more than a chapter or section of a janam-sākhī. A sākhī may, and often does, contain only one anecdote, but this should not imply an identity of meaning. The limitation of each sākhī to a single

[1] See below, examples 7 and 8, pp. 135–57.

[2] *B40*, ff. 163b–170b.

anecdote must have been a general feature of the earliest traditions, becoming progressively less common as the narratives diversify and the grouping of anecdotes advances. Whereas single-anecdote sākhīs dominate material drawn direct from oral tradition,[1] composite sākhīs containing more than one anecdote (or sub-sākhī) rapidly evolved within the recorded traditions. Moreover, these composite sākhīs frequently embodied distinctly different forms of anecdote and discourse. The term sākhī, in its strict sense, thus designates a convenient division. It is not itself a janam-sākhī prose form.

The narrative anecdotes of the janam-sākhīs may be subdivided into four categories. There are *moralistic anecdotes*, *chimeric fairy-tales*, *devotional legends*, and *aetiological legends*. All serve to express the same myth, but do so in distinctively different ways.

(a) *Moralistic anecdotes*

The *moralistic anecdote* serves, as its name so plainly indicates, to point a particular moral. This it may do either in a brief concluding statement by Bābā Nānak or, less commonly, by means of a parabolic action attributed to him. Brevity is vital if success is to be achieved and for this reason the moralistic anecdote is normally distinguished by succinct expression. The form is particularly prominent in the *Purātan* janam-sākhīs, a feature which indicates a special interest on the part of the principal *Colebrooke* compiler.[2] It is to this anonymous person that we owe the following five examples of highly effective moralistic anecdote.

The Inhospitable Village Unmolested and the Hospitable Village Dispersed

They departed from there and proceeding on their way they came to a village. They stopped there, but no one would give them shelter. Instead the inhabitants jeered at them. They moved on to the next town where they were warmly welcomed. Spending the night there they departed the next day. As they were leaving the Gurū declared, 'May this town be uprooted and its inhabitants scattered.'

'This is strange justice,' observed Mardānā. 'The place where we received no hospitality you left alone, and the town which welcomed us so warmly you have uprooted.'

'Mardānā,' replied the Gurū, 'the inhabitants of the first town would go to another and corrupt it. When the inhabitants of this town go to another they will bring it truth and salvation.'[3]

Sheikh Bajīd

On the road Bābā Nānak and Mardānā met Sheikh Bajīd Sayyid riding in a litter

[1] An example of this variety of material is supplied by the *B40* sākhīs 35–49 and 51. Loc. cit., ff. 154b–199a, 204a–205a. Even here there are instances of dual-anecdote sākhīs (e.g. 35, 43, 44, 49), although the two portions are rarely blended in the manner of the later composite sākhīs.

[2] The compiler of the *Hāfizābād Janam-sākhī* (the other major *Purātan* janam-sākhī) has evidently copied all his moralistic anecdotes from his *Colebrooke* source.

[3] *Pur JS*, p. 40. *GNSR*, pp. 41–2.

carried by six bearers. The Sheikh alighted beneath a tree and his bearers began to massage and fan him.

'Is there not one God?' asked Mardānā.

'God is indeed one, Mardānā,' replied Bābā Nānak.

'Then who created him, my Lord?' asked Mardānā. 'Who created the one who rides in a palanquin whilst these others are barefoot and their bodies naked? They bear him on their backs, whereas he reclines and is massaged.'

Bābā Nānak answered him, 'All who enter the world come naked from the womb. Joy and pain come in accordance with the deeds of one's previous existence.'

Mardānā prostrated himself.[1]

Sheikh Farīd and the Gold Coins

Bābā Nānak and Sheikh Farīd spent the night together in the jungle. A devout person happened to pass that way and seeing them he returned to his home. There he filled a bowl with milk and having dropped four gold coins into it he brought it back during the early hours of the morning. Sheikh Farīd took his share and left the Gurū his portion.

'Sheikh Farīd, stir this milk with your hand and see what is in it,' said Bābā Nānak. When Sheikh Farīd did so he discovered the four gold coins. The devout donor put down the bowl and departed. . . . Bābā Nānak and Sheikh Farīd also departed and when the donor returned he found the bowl sitting there. Picking it up he discovered that it was now made of gold and filled with gold coins. Then he began to lament, saying, 'They were true faqīrs. He who comes with an open heart finds true faith, whereas he who brings worldly things receives a worldly reward.' He picked up the bowl and returned home.[2]

Bābā Nānak explains the Destruction of Saidpur

One day Mardānā asked, 'Why have so many been slain when only one did wrong?'

'Go and sleep under that tree, Mardānā,' answered the Gurū. 'When you get up I shall give you an answer.'

And so Mardānā went and slept there. Now a drop of grease had fallen on his chest while he was eating and while he was sleeping it attracted ants. One ant happened to disturb the sleeping Mardānā who responded by wiping them all away with his hand.

'What have you done, Mardānā?' asked Bābā Nānak.

'All have died because one disturbed me,' exclaimed Mardānā.

Bābā Nānak laughed and said, 'Mardānā, thus does death come to many because of one.'[3]

A Pious Boy

One day the Gurū decreed that there should be communal singing (*kīrtan*) during the last watch of the night. A boy seven years of age used to leave his house and come and stand behind the Gurū during the *kīrtan*. After the *Āratī* had been sung he would depart. One day Bābā Nānak said, 'Detain the boy today.' After the boy had prostrated himself and was on his way out the other members of the congregation stopped him and brought him to the Gurū.

[1] *Pur JS*, pp. 25–6. *GNSR*, p. 39.
[2] *Pur JS*, pp. 43–4. *GNSR*, p. 42.
[3] *Pur JS*, p. 65. *GNSR*, p. 44.

Bābā Nānak addressed him, 'Boy, you who arise and come at such an hour, why do you come? This is the time of life for eating, playing and sleeping.'

'Sir,' replied the boy, 'one day my mother said to me, "Light the fire, son." I lit the fire and as I placed the wood on it the little sticks kindled first then later the bigger ones. I became afraid, thinking that like the firewood we who are small may have to depart first. We may perhaps reach adulthood—but then perhaps we may not. And so I decided that I should repeat the Gurū's name.'

Hearing this the congregation was struck with wonder. The Gurū was delighted and the boy fell at his feet.[1]

Of these five anecdotes only the last constitutes a separate and complete sākhī. The first has unaccountably been divided into two sākhīs, and the remainder have all been incorporated in composite sākhīs. Scriptural quotations have been added to all except the fourth. In the case of 'Sheikh Bajīd' the quotation (an apocryphal shalok) may have provided the actual genesis of the brief narrative.

Two anecdotes of the moralistic variety which have enjoyed a notable popularity within the Sikh community are the *Bālā* stories entitled respectively 'The Good Bargain' and 'Lālo and Bhāgo'.[2] The second of these, a relatively late development, provides perhaps the most striking of all parables within the range of the janam-sākhīs. Abbreviated versions of both anecdotes have been included in the *Mahimā Prakāś Vāratak*, and it is from the text of this latter collection that the following translations have been made.

The Good Bargain

Even after his marriage, however, Bābājī's spirit was still restless and Kālū, when he perceived this, was greatly disheartened. 'Whatever can we do to calm Nānak's restless spirit?' he asked himself. He tried another idea. 'Do some trading, son,' he said, and gave him a capital of twenty rupees, together with a servant, in order to procure some fine yarn. Bābājī set out to purchase the yarn. On the way he observed a large number of sādhūs sitting in a jungle, and tarrying in their company he conversed with them about God. Following this discourse Bābājī laid the twenty rupees before the sādhūs and returned home.

When he arrived Kālū said to him, 'Show us the merchandise which you have brought, son.'

'Father,' replied Bābājī, 'I have returned after striking a most profitable bargain!'

'He has returned after giving the money to faqīrs!' said the servant.

When he heard this Kālū was greatly disheartened and lost his temper. Rāi Bulār, the landlord, hearing what had happened summoned Kālū and said, 'Do not trouble Nānak. He is the image of God.' And so Kālū pardoned him.[3]

Lālo and Bhāgo

Next he visited the house of Lālo where he remained for some days. Meanwhile news of his arrival spread throughout that area. It so happened that at that time a certain Khatrī was holding a *yagya*. To secure blessings for his deceased forbears

[1] *Pur JS*, pp. 72–3. *GNSR*, pp. 45–6.
[2] *Bālā JS*, pp. 16–22, 80–90.
[3] *SLTGN(Eng)*, pp. 65–6. *GNSR*, p. 83.

he had ordered one hundred thousand cows for presentation to Brāhmaṇs and had invited oné hundred thousand Brāhmaṇs to the feast. Formerly the name of the village in which Lālo lived had been Saidpur Sarohā. Because of a sin committed by some Paṭhāns Bābājī had invoked a curse upon it and the Emperor Bābur had massacred its inhabitants. Subsequently the name was changed to Emīnābād in accordance with Bābājī's command, and having bestowed this new name upon it he had caused the devastated village to be reoccupied.

This foolish Khatrī karoṛī was at that time holding a *yagya* and when he heard of Bābājī's arrival he sent a man to the house of Lālo the carpenter to say that Nānak should dine at his house. Bābājī, however, refused the invitation and so when the Brāhmaṇs had taken their seats for the feast the karoṛī came to Bābājī and with insistent requests managed to persuade him to come to his own house. Setting a tray of food before him he said, 'How can an exalted sādhū such as you dine at the house of a mere carpenter? Tell me please why you decline to eat with Brāhmaṇs and Khatrīs?'

'In Lālo's house,' replied Bābājī, 'there lies my vegetable cake. Bring it here.' The vegetable cake was brought and Bābājī took it in one hand. In the other hand he took one of the karoṛī's fried pastries (*pūri*) and with both hands he squeezed the two articles. From the karoṛī's rich food there oozed blood and from Lālo's humble vegetable cake there flowed milk! Bābājī then recited a shalok.

ślok mahalā 1

If a thief burgles a house, and having robbed it offers the proceeds as an oblation for his departed forbears,
The stolen property will be recognised in the other world and your forefathers will be accused of theft.
The broker's hand will be cut off, for thus is divine retribution administered.
Nānak, only that which is given from honest earnings can be received in the other world.

Then Bābājī said, 'Close your eyes, brother karoṛī, and witness a spectacle.' And what should he see but his own forefathers being beaten with shoes by the forefathers of those whose cows he had taken. Awestruck he fell at Bābājī's feet, saying 'O Master, let me become your disciple. You are the saviour of the fallen. Let the purpose of my *yagya* be fulfilled.' Bābājī took mercy upon him and said, 'Pay everyone whose cows you have taken and when you have satisfied them make your offering to the Brāhmaṇs.' The karoṛī did as he was instructed and Bābājī, having brought the karoṛī's *yagya* to fulfilment, went on his way.[1]

Another anecdote of this kind which appears in both collections attributes its moral to Gurū Aṅgad:

[1] *SLTGN(Eng)*, p. 75. In the *Mahimā Prakāś Kavitā* version of the anecdote the Khatrī's name is given as Gurasū. *GNM*, pp. 293–4. This anecdote is also of interest as an example of a sākhī which owes a primary element to a reference in one of Nānak's shabads. The name 'Lālo' evidently derives from *Tilaṅg* 5 (*AG*, p. 722). See *GNSR*, pp. 86–7. Popular piety still identifies a house in Emīnābād with the actual residence of Lālo. This must be a later building. The town which existed during the lifetime of Gurū Nānak (it was at that time called Saidpur) was razed either by Sher Shāh Sūrī or earlier by Bābur. The Emīnābād which eventually replaced it was not constructed until the reign of Akbar and was built at a distance of one-and-a-half miles from the former site. *Gazetteer of the Gujranwala District 1893–94* (Lahore, 1895), p. 173. For the question of who actually destroyed Saidpur see below, pp. 93–4. See also *B40(Eng)*, pp. 69–70.

Absolute Loyalty

One night Bābājī asked Bābā Buḍhā, 'How much of the night remains, Buḍhā?'

'A watch and a quarter, my Lord,' replied Buḍhā.

'How do you know?' asked Bābājī.

'We who are rural folk can tell by observing the stars,' answered Buḍhā.

Bābājī then asked Gurū Aṅgad. 'How much of the night remains, my man?'

'My Lord,' he replied, 'You know full well that whether it is night or whether it is day I am yours. Night or day, it makes no difference.'

Hearing this response Bābājī was greatly pleased.[1]

To these examples many more could be added, particularly from the *Purātan* janam-sākhīs. Others included by the *Colebrooke* compiler are 'The Death of the Trader's Infant Son', 'A Watchman receives Royal Authority', and 'The Coal and the Thorn'.[2] The *B40* compiler was evidently less attracted by the moralistic approach, but does find space for two classic anecdotes of this kind, 'The Watering of the Fields'[3] and 'The Rich Man's Pennants'.[4]

The stories narrated in these anecdotes and the morals which they point are in every case related directly to the purpose of the janam-sākhīs. Moralistic anecdotes serve to express the wisdom of their principal participant, and the credit implied in the janam-sākhī specimens of this form is, of course, attached specifically to Bābā Nānak. In this manner the form provides its own distinctive and attractive contribution to the message of the janam-sākhīs.

(b) *Chimeric fairy-tales*

The *chimeric fairy-tale* is distinguished from other fairy-stories and legends by the presence of such figures of fantasy as magicians, ogres, and beasts endowed with human faculties.[5] Characters of this kind are to be found in all the janam-sākhīs, with a particular fondness for them evident in those of the *Bālā* tradition. Although the earlier *Miharbān* commentators were evidently reluctant to include the more grotesque variety a late redactor of the *Miharbān Janam-sākhī* has interpolated a series of unusually bizarre figures.[6] Chimeric fairy-tales are accordingly a significant feature of all extant janam-sākhīs.

Amongst the more popular instances of this form two which have enjoyed a particular prominence are 'The Monster's Cauldron' and 'The Country Ruled by Women'. The first of these relates how Bābā Nānak, having lost his way in a wilderness, was seized by a *rākaś* (demon or

[1] *SLTGN(Eng)*, pp. 80–1. The anecdote appears in *Bālā* manuscripts, but not in the printed *Bālā JS*.

[2] *Pur JS*, pp. 28–32. *GNSR*, p. 19. All three now include shabads. The first appears to have developed out of the shabad which it incorporates.

[3] *B40*, ff. 76b–79a.

[4] *B40*, ff. 189a–190a. See below pp. 124–5. The Sajjaṇ/Bholā story is also a moralistic anecdote. See below pp. 122–4.

[5] Aage Bentzen, *Introduction to the Old Testament*, vol. i (Copenhagen, 1948), p. 240.

[6] *Mih JS* I.206–31. *GNSR*, pp. 57–8.

monster). The monster's intention was to boil Nānak in a cauldron of oil, a plan which was frustrated when the Gurū dipped his finger in the oil. It immediately became cool and the monster, confounded by this miracle, became a disciple. This is the substance of the narrative as it appears in the *B40* version.[1] The *Ādi Sākhīs* account omits the reference to the wilderness, but actually places Bābā Nānak in the cauldron and describes in rather more detail the unsuccessful attempt to heat it.[2] In the interpolated *Miharbān* version it is Mardānā who is put in the cauldron.[3] The *Purātan* narrator makes Bābā Nānak a voluntary candidate for stewing and adds that the incident took place 'on an island in the ocean, in foreign parts'.[4] In a considerably expanded version the standard *Bālā* account adds that the monster's name was Kauḍā.[5]

The figure variously described in this manner is plainly of the chimeric variety. Although in modern usage this word can be rendered 'cannibal' or 'savage', and although the *rākaś* encountered by Bābā Nānak certainly numbered cannibalism amongst his qualifications, it is evident that the janam-sākhī narrators envisaged a creature of more than mere human proportions. This is clearly brought out in the illustration which accompanies the *B40* version[6] and to this day Kauḍā the Rākaś provides bazaar lithographers with their choicest opportunity for the exercise of ingenious fantasy. The figure was not, of course, an invention of the janam-sākhī narrators. Earlier tradition offered an abundance of incidents involving *rākaś* (*rakṣasa*). Rāvaṇ of Laṅkā is the obvious example.

The anecdote entitled 'The Country Ruled by Women' has already been noted as an example of a direct borrowing from received tradition.[7] In this episode interest is focused upon a group of female magicians who turn Mardānā into a sheep by means of an enchanted thread.[8] These are the famous women of *strī deś*, a popular theme in earlier legend.[9]

Other examples of the chimeric fairy-tale may be found in all janam-sākhīs. Another popular one, included in all major versions, is the encounter with Kaliyug.[10] Elsewhere in the *B40* janam-sākhī Bābā Nānak is confronted by a demon arsonist 'as high as the heavens' who made a monthly habit of setting fire to the houses in a particular area.[11] The *Purātan* janam-sākhīs relate anecdotes concerning a city of ants, a talking wolf, and the legendary K͟hwājā K͟hizar.[12] Although most of these are missing from the *Bālā* narrative other representatives of the same form more than compensate for their absence. The *Bālā* contribution includes a talking fish, seventy miles long and ten miles wide, which carries Bābā

[1] *B40*, f. 40a–b. [2] *AS*, p. 28. [3] *Mih JS* I.231. [4] *Pur JS*, pp. 81–2.

[5] *kauḍā*, lit. a fire lit specifically for heating purposes. *Bālā JS*, p. 125. The name Kauḍā also appears in the heading attached to the printed *Purātan* version. *Pur JS*, p. 81. This heading, like all others in the *Pur JS*, is an addition made by the editor of the published text. Such headings do not appear in the manuscripts.

[6] *B40*, f. 39b. Cf. also *Bālā JS*, p. 125. [7] See above, p. 70.

[8] *B40*, ff. 83a–85b. *AS*, pp. 26–8. *Pur JS*, pp. 33–7. *Bālā JS*, pp. 102–8.

[9] *GNSR*, p. 112. [10] *B40*, ff. 44a–47a. *AS*, pp. 28–31. *Pur JS*, pp. 37–8.

[11] *B40*, ff. 175a–176b.

[12] *Pur JS*, pp. 78–9, 70–1, 38–40. *GNSR*, pp. 41, 45, 47. The 'City of Insects' anecdote may perhaps owe its origin to the Quranic story of Solomon and the Valley of Ants (*sūrah* 27).

Nānak across the sea;[1] an encounter with Kāl (Death); a visit to the city of Demon Devalūt, ruler over 1,700,000 gods, who like Kauḍā the Rākaś is fond of boiling people in oil; and a meeting with some ape-men.[2]

As in the case of the moralistic anecdotes all of these chimeric fairy-tales are used to supplement the janam-sākhī myth. It is true that figures such as Kauḍā the Rākaś and Demon Devalūt appeal enormously to the popular imagination and that this feature alone might justify their inclusion. This, however, is not their primary significance. They have been introduced into the janam-sākhī narratives not merely to entertain but more particularly to provide further illustrations of the authority of Bābā Nānak. Although the women of *strī deś* wield magical powers of terrifying potency these powers are ineffective against Bābā Nānak. Only one who has received a divine commission could possibly withstand such assaults. Kauḍā, Devalūt, Kaliyug, and all the rest recognize the presence of divinity and fall at his feet. If they who hear these stories make the same submission they too shall find salvation. Thus does the chimeric fairy-tale, like all other forms, serve the basic purpose of the janam-sākhī narrators.

(c) *Devotional legends*

The basic purpose of the janam-sākhīs is expressed with even greater directness in the third variety of anecdote. The *devotional legend* seeks to convince or confirm by means of explicit reference to the power possessed by the Gurū, to the quality of his devotion, or to intervention by God on his behalf. This category may be further subdivided as follows:

(i) *Wonder-stories* The primary feature of the *wonder-story* is, in this context, the signification of divine status by means of miraculous deeds or supernatural phenomena. The essential feature of the story is not the miracle itself but rather the conclusion towards which the miracle points. Miracles can be performed only by the person chosen and endowed by God. Bābā Nānak worked miracles and God worked them on his behalf. Here surely is the seal of his divinity. The fact that Gurū Nānak himself laid no such claims in his works is of no importance. For the later believer miraculous events were both a staple tradition and a necessary proof. Their introduction into the janam-sākhīs was inevitable.

As one might expect, wonder-stories associated with the Gurū's childhood enjoy a considerable popularity. No janam-sākhī which deals with this period lacks 'The Ruined Crop Restored' or 'The Tree's Stationary Shadow',[3] both of them tales of how divine approval was signified by the suspension of natural laws. The child Nānak's discourses with the paṇḍit and the mullah[4] provide an interesting parallel to the child Jesus in the Temple; and the later *Bālā* introduction of a protective cobra illustrates a direct borrowing from earlier tradition.[5] Tales of dangers

[1] Cf. the *Mahābhārata*, *Mārkandeya-samāsyā parva* (*vana parva* CLXXXVI).
[2] *Bālā JS*, pp. 138, 141, 162–8, 168–9.
[3] *B40*, ff. 7a–9b.
[4] *B40*, ff. 2b–5b. *Pur JS*, pp. 1–6. *Mih JS* I.11–20.
[5] *Bālā JS*, p. 14.

survived are curiously absent, but not the predictable emphasis upon the degeneracy of the period into which Bābā Nānak was born.[1] The deeper the darkness the brighter the rising sun will appear to shine. This feature still survives in modern accounts of the life of the Gurū.

(ii) *Apologetic anecdotes* Some janam-sākhī anecdotes have a patently apologetic purpose, one which at times assumes a distinctly polemical character. In its positive form the *apologetic anecdote* seeks to uphold the claims made on the Gurū's behalf by means of explicit declarations, usually issuing direct from the mouth of God. Most janam-sākhī compilers regarded at least one such declaration as essential and an interview with God is accordingly a standard feature of almost all collections.[2]

In its negative form the apologetic anecdote involves encounters with Muslims and Hindus, particularly with the variety who commanded influence during the janam-sākhī period. Those whose distinctive beliefs or customs were understood to be in radical conflict with the teachings of Gurū Nānak also received attention. Bigoted qāzīs[3] and punctilious Brāhmaṇs[4] provided obvious targets. They were not, however, the most suitable interlocutors. Because they were so very obvious the anecdotes which relate encounters with such figures are usually less effective than those which concern a more sympathetic kind of Hindu or Muslim. A pīr convinced served the janam-sākhī purpose better than a qāzī humiliated.

(iii) *Sectarian narratives* In some instances the apologetic expressed by a particular anecdote concerns not the wider Sikh community but rather the distinctive beliefs of some segment of it. The result is the *sectarian anecdote*. Sākhīs which in the *B40*, *Ādi Sākhīs*, and *Miharbān* collections give expression to an ascetic ideal may be classified in this manner,[5] and likewise the Hindālī material which is to be found in manuscript versions of the *Bālā* tradition.[6]

(d) *Aetiological legends*

Although the *aetiological legend* is rare in the janam-sākhīs the few examples which do appear are of sufficient interest to warrant separate notice. They include popular etymologies, local legends, and at least one explanation of a natural phenomenon.

The earliest example of an aetiological legend appears to be the explanation offered by the janam-sākhīs for the second Gurū's change of name from Lahaṇā to Aṅgad. This, it is claimed, took place in accordance with a declaration attributed to Gorakhnāth: 'Nānak, he who is born from your body (*aṅg*) will be your Gurū.'[7] The classification of this anecdote as an

[1] *BG* 1:17, 22.
[2] *B40* sākhī 30, ff. 123b–126b, is an example.
[3] *B40*, ff. 19b–24b.
[4] *Pur JS*, p. 72. *GNSR*, p. 45.
[5] See above, pp. 80–81.
[6] See above, p. 17.
[7] *Pur JS*, p. 108. *B40* accepts the same etymology. *B40*, ff. 93a, 95a.

aetiological legend does not, of course, mean that the janam-sākhīs are necessarily mistaken in claiming that Gurū Aṅgad was originally called Lahaṇā. It is the etymological connection with Gorakhnāth which constitutes the legend.

Another popular etymology attributes the name of the Chinese city of Nanking to a supposed visit by Nānak. This legend, which emerged only very recently and which is still in the process of gaining currency, demonstrates that even today the travel narratives can still be expanded. Whereas the extant janam-sākhīs take Nānak only as far as the Himālayas (and Mount Sumeru), some modern hagiographers are evidently prepared, on the basis of this fanciful etymology, to extend his northern itinerary as far as eastern China.[1]

Two local legends of the aetiological variety are to be found in eighteenth- and nineteenth-century traditions. The earlier of the two is an obscure story recorded in the *Mahimā Prakāś Vāratak* which attributes a well in Khaḍūr village to the divination of the Gurū.[2] The second example is both unusually late and tremendously popular. This is the story of *Pañjā Sāhib*, an anecdote set in the village of Hasan Abdāl (Attock District). The anecdote relates how Bābā Nānak once came to the village and feeling thirsty he dispatched his companion Mardānā to bring water. The only available spring happened to be situated on the crest of a nearby hill, in the keeping of a Muslim dervish named Bāwā Valī Qandhārī. Jealous of the Gurū's fame Valī Qandhārī refused to permit access to the water, suggesting that if the Gurū were equal to his reputation he would provide his own spring. Bābā Nānak accepted the challenge and opened a fresh spring at the foot of the hill, whereupon the spring on the crest dried up. The enraged Valī Qandhārī then sent an avenging boulder hurtling down towards the Gurū who stopped it merely by raising his hand. The imprint of his hand upon the rock can (so it is claimed) be seen to this day, and for this reason the place is known as *Pañjā Sāhib*, or the Holy Palm.

This 'hand-mark' has added a second feature to a site which had already inspired a series of aetiological legends. The earlier legends, developed within Buddhist, Hindu, and Muslim tradition, all concerned the springs, which, as Jahāṅgīr was later to note, were unusually limpid.[3] Although in the Sikh tradition the springs still play an important role, primary attention has been transferred to the 'hand-mark'.

The legend of *Pañjā Sāhib* is of particular interest not merely for its aetiological characteristics, but for its relative lateness. None of the seventeenth- or eighteenth-century janam-sākhīs refers to it, nor does

[1] Surindar Singh Kohlī, *Travels of Guru Nanak* (Chaṇḍīgaṛh, 1969), pp. 57, 127. The same writer suggests that Nānak must have travelled by sea. He claims that the Gurū visited the Malay Peninsula and Singapore, and surmises that he must also have extended his travels to include the archipelago, perhaps also the Philippines and Japan. Ibid., pp. 55–7.

[2] *SLTGN(Eng)*, pp. 83–4.

[3] *The Tūzuk-i-Jahāngīrī, or Memoirs of Jahāngīr*, trans. A. Rogers, ed. H. Beveridge (London, 1909), p. 100. *ASI* ii.135–9.

Jahāṅgīr indicate any awareness of its existence.[1] Moorcroft and Trebeck, who passed through Hasan Abdāl in 1823, describe the story as 'the probable invention of a very recent date' and imply that it can be traced to the occasion of Rañjīt Siṅgh's occupation of the town in 1818.[2] In 1866 J. G. Delmerick, while visiting the town, was given an explanation which supported their opinion. Having related the standard tradition concerning the boulder and the 'hand-mark', he continues:

But there are many people still living in the town who openly deny the truth of this story. They remember to have grazed their buffalos on the site of the tank and temple. They state that one Kaman, a mason, for his own amusement cut out on a stone the impression of a hand, and that on one occasion during the reign of Ranjit Singh, the Sikhs having resolved to punish the inhabitants of the place for some marauding act, they all ran away, except one Naju, a *faqir*, to the Gandgarh Mountain. Naju was caught, but he declared that he was one of Baba Nanak's *faqirs*. He was asked how he came to know Baba Nanak, whereupon he showed the handiwork of Kaman, and invented the tale. The Sikhs believed him and set up the stone. Nanda, a very old man, and a Hindu, who is, moreover, a highly respectable resident of the town, admits that before Ranjit Singh's time there was no shrine or place for Hindu worship at Hasan Abdal.[3]

The 'hand-mark' witnessed by these early travellers was not an incision cut into the rock, but a representation projecting in relief. Hugel described it as a bas-relief[4] and the 1893–4 edition of the *Gazetteer of the Rawalpindi District* as 'a rude representation of a hand in relief'.[5] The same feature was again noted by G. B. Scott in 1930.[6] It was evidently during the course of 1940 that the original representation in relief was eventually replaced by a crude intaglio cut *into* the rock. The edges which were at first sharp have now been worn smooth.[7]

Two more aetiological legends offer points of particular interest. The janam-sākhīs explain the destruction of Saidpur by Bābur as divine punishment wreaked upon the town for its callous disregard of the Gurū and his company of faqīrs. The point of interest raised by this aspect of the Saidpur story is that it may well supply a historical fact which would otherwise be unknown. What was already known was that Saidpur was

[1] Valī Qandhārī does appear in the early *Bālā* tradition, but not in the context of the Pañjā Sāhib anecdote. *Bālā JS*, pp. 300–3.

[2] Wm. Moorcroft and Geo. Trebeck, *Travels in the Himalayan Provinces and the Panjab*, vol. ii (London, 1841), p. 320.

[3] J. G. Delmerick quoting an extract from his diary dated 11 February 1866, in *PNQ*, vol. ii, no. 23 (August 1885), p. 185.

[4] Baron Charles von Hugel, *Travels in Kashmir and the Panjab* (London, 1845), p. 225. Von Hugel, who visited Hasan Abdāl in December 1835, adds that the stone was moved to its present site following the Sikh occupation. Ibid.

[5] Loc. cit., p. 35.

[6] G. B. Scott, *Religion and Short History of the Sikhs, 1469–1930* (London, 1930), p. 19.

[7] This information was supplied to the author by three informants who visited the shrine at Pañjā Sāhib. According to the first informant the carving in relief was still there in early 1940. The second, who visited the site later in the same year, stated that the 'hand-mark' had been incised but that the edges were sharp. The third, whose visit took place in 1964, reported that the edges were smooth.

indeed destroyed and then later rebuilt as Eminābād. *The Gazetteer of the Gujranwala District* attributes the destruction to Śher Shāh Sūri, but does not name a source.[1] The janam-sākhīs were sufficiently close to the event to be in contact with authentic memories, and there is every likelihood that their attributing of the event to Bābur is correct. Upon this episode the ascetic ideal has erected an aetiological legend.

The same ascetic ideal was also responsible for a later explanation of how Bābā Nānak happened to have sons. To those of this ascetic persuasion it was unthinkable that the Gurū could be other than completely celibate. It was, however, equally unthinkable that the existence of Sirī Chand and Lakhmī Dās could be doubted. The dilemma was eventually solved by resort to a method of conception which would not involve a renunciation of celibacy. Bābā Nānak, after first resisting his mother's pleas for grandchildren, finally consented for her sake. To fulfil her wish he gave his wife two cloves, thereby inducing parthenogenetic conception of the two boys.[2]

2. *NARRATIVE DISCOURSES*

The closeness of the narrative discourse form to that of the narrative anecdote has already been noted and for this reason it has been allied to the latter rather than to the more developed discourse form which appears in the *Miharbān Janam-sākhī*. This should not, however, imply a complete identity. Whereas there is certainly an identity of purpose, the actual form of the narrative discourse is distinctively different from that of the anecdote.

The term *narrative discourse* designates sākhīs or sub-sākhīs which have taken their origin from compositions by Gurū Nānak and which incorporate these compositions within a contrived conversation or discourse as the response given by Nānak to the questions or comments of an interlocutor. This form should be distinguished on the one hand from the kind of conversation which has not been developed out of a shabad or a shalok; and, on the other, from discourses which have been consciously turned to a didactic purpose by the addition of exegetical supplements.[3] An example of the former is provided by the central portion of the *B40* version of the sākhī 'Bābā Nānak's discourse with Daulat Khān's Qāzī'.[4] Although this portion of the sākhī records a conversation and also includes a series of scriptural quotations the conversation element is in no way dependent upon the quotations. These are mere appendages. The actual conversation relates an independent anecdote and for this reason it has been classified as a narrative anecdote rather than as a narrative discourse. The earlier

[1] Loc. cit. (Lahore, 1895), p. 173.

[2] This particular explanation is to be found in the *Mahimā Prakāś Vāratak*. *SLTGN(Eng)*, pp. 78–9. The *Gyān-ratanāvalī*, which also relates this story (*GR*, sākhī 50), adds that Nānak also caused his sister Nānakī to conceive in the same manner. To her he gave a clove and a cardamom, as a result of which she gave birth to a son and a daughter.

[3] See below, pp. 98–101.

[4] *B40*, ff. 21b–24a.

portion of the same sākhī can also be regarded primarily as a narrative anecdote relating a conversation, but it should be noted that one of the quotations added to this portion has generated a brief sub-sākhī of the narrative discourse variety.[1]

Narrative discourse should also be distinguished from anecdotes which have developed out of individual works of Gurū Nānak but which have not been cast in the form of discourses. Although the celebrated stories of Sajjaṇ the Robber and Mūlā the Khatrī plainly derive from compositions of the Gurū neither can be described as a narrative discourse. Both are narrative anecdotes.

The nature of the narrative discourse and its manner of development have already been indicated in the preceding chapter. At this point it will be sufficient to recapitulate the standard pattern appearing in all discourses of this kind. The basis is provided by a quotation from the works of Gurū Nānak. This hymn (or series of couplets) provides the answers which Nānak is said to have given during the course of the discussion. A convenient interlocutor is then introduced and appropriate questions or leading comments are devised to match the answers which Nānak will give. These questions and their answers constitute the substance of the discourse. A brief introductory narrative furnishes a setting, and following the terminal quotation the interlocutor either falls at the Gurū's feet or (less commonly) withdraws defeated but unrepentant. Most of the compositions which are used in this manner can be safely regarded as the works of Gurū Nānak. The balance consists of a number of apocryphal works, a few by other Gurūs which have been erroneously attached to Nānak, and in one notable instance a series of shaloks attributed to Sheikh Farīd. All follow the same structural pattern.

One of the least complicated of the narrative discourses is the brief tale entitled 'Lamenting Women Commended' which the *B40* compiler attaches to his version of 'The Encounter with Kaliyug'.

Bābā Nānak and Mardānā then proceeded on their way and came to a village where a death had occured. Women were lamenting, crying out, 'Alas! Alas for our Lord! O God! O God!' Bābā Nānak heard their cries and was greatly saddened. 'Blessed be this town,' he said, 'and blessed be these women who repeat the Name of God.' He then recited a shalok.

'Alas! Alas!' they cry, 'Woe! Woe!'
They scream and tear their hair.
Let them instead take the divine Name and repeat it.
To such Nānak offers himself a sacrifice.

Bābā Nānak and Mardānā then left that place.[2]

The basis of this narrative is the cryptic shalok, quoted above in the course of the anecdote, which appears in the Ādi Granth as *Surplus Shaloks* 6.[3] This provides both the setting for the discourse and the words which the lamenting women utter in order to provide an appropriate point of entry for the shalok.

[1] *B40*, f. 21a–b. [2] *B40*, f. 47a–b [3] *AG*, p. 1410.

Brief discourses of this kind are not as rare as a cursory reading of the janam-sākhīs might suggest. They are easily missed, for most of them have been incorporated within composite sākhīs in a manner which largely conceals their independent origins. Another example has been given above in the chapter dealing with the constituents of the janam-sākhīs.[1] These single-comment discourses are, however, less common than the longer variety embodying a series of questions. 'The Encounter with Kaliyug' offers a more typical illustration of the standard pattern.[2] In this instance the basis of the discourse is furnished by the shabad *Sirī Rāg* 1, a highly suggestive work which begins with the words:

If for me there were to be built a palace of pearl encrusted with jewels,
Anointed with musk, with saffron, with the fragrance of aloes and sandal,
Forbid it, O Lord, that beholding it I should forget Thee and fail to call to mind Thy Name.[3]

Such a stanza indicates an obvious lead for the interlocutor.

Gracious one, if you command I shall erect a palace studded with pearls and anointed with musk.[4]

The second stanza is equally helpful to the narrator.

If the world were to be encrusted with diamonds and rubies, my bed studded with rubies;
And if there were to be an alluring damsel, her face glistening with jewels, tempting me with seductive gesture;
Forbid it, O Lord, that beholding such temptation I should forget Thee and fail to call to mind Thy Name.

For this reply the following lead-in has been devised:

If you so command I shall encrust the whole world with diamonds, and stud a bed with pearls and rubies.[5]

In this manner the discourse continues until the shabad reaches its conclusion.

The words of the shabad also indicated a narrow range of possible interlocutors. Plainly it would have to be someone who possessed the capacity to make such stupendous promises. An earthly king, however powerful, would be unsuitable. The interlocutor had to be one who could offer to 'encrust the whole world with diamonds' and this promise no human could ever fulfil. This indicated a superhuman interlocutor. In cases of this kind God can sometimes be introduced, but hardly in a discourse which involves an evidently sincere proffering of carnal temptations. The solution adopted by the first narrator was evidently suggested by a Puranic precedent. Kaliyug, a personification of the present evil age, had already appeared in earlier tradition and none could be more appro-

1 Bābur offers bhaṅg to Bābā Nānak. See above, pp. 74–5.
2 *B40*, ff. 44a–47a.
3 *AG*, p. 14.
4 *B40*, ff. 44b–45a.
5 *B40*, f. 45a.

priate for the present need.[1] A suitably fearsome context was accordingly devised with details drawn from traditions of the chimeric variety.

Gradually the darkness and the rain lifted. When they had cleared there appeared the figure of a demon with huge fangs, the top of its head touching the heavens and its feet the ground. Enormous was its belly and terrifying its evil eyes! Fearsomely it advanced towards them . . .[2]

Kaliyug, have failed to intimidate Bābā Nānak in this manner, then advances his series of offers. The Gurū utters each of the *Sirī Rāg* 1 stanzas in succession, Kaliyug makes his submission, and the proto-sākhī is complete.

This analysis concerns the first stage in the development of the discourse. The *B40* version indicates a second stage. To the simple structure provided by the proto-sākhī a number of extra details have been added, notably an apologetic addendum which gives expression to the evolving self-consciousness of the Sikh community.[3]

The proto-sākhī already provided an unusually clear example of the myth of Nānak, and this addition drives the point home with even greater force. It is, however, no more than an addition. A more advanced stage still is reached when simple discourses are incorporated within composite sākhīs, normally in combination with narrative anecdotes. In some instances the discourse provides the nucleus around which other elements cluster, and in others it is added to an existing nucleus. The composite sākhī concerning Bābā Nānak's meeting with Rājā Śivanābh is an example of the former.[4] The discourse with Bābur illustrates the latter.[5]

An obvious parallel to the narrative discourse of the janam-sākhīs would appear to be the Persian *munāzara* form. The resemblance is, however, strictly superficial and concerns little more than the evident fact that both embody dialogue. The *munāzara* is properly understood as a battle of wits, a genuine disputation in which both parties genuinely participate.[6] This distinguishes it from the one-sided question-and-answer, or contrived comment-and-answer, pattern of the janam-sākhīs. Similarly the regular occurrence of questions in the janam-sākhī form should not suggest that the janam-sākhī discourse bears any significant resemblance to the Muslim *mas'ala*. The *mas'ala* is a question arising from a dispute which is put to a *mujtahid* and which he answers with a *fatwā*. The nearest approach which the janam-sākhīs make to this form is the manner in which the *Miharbān* commentators provide suitable contexts for their exegesis by bringing a Sikh or group of Sikhs to Bābā Nānak with questions suited to the passages which they wish to expound. This is, however, far removed from the *mas'ala*. Moreover, it is distinct from the narrative discourse form. Exegetical intentions are a feature of the third of the janam-sākhī forms.

[1] See above, pp. 65–6. Buddhist traditions concerning the temptations of the Buddha may also have aided the structuring of the discourse.

[2] *B40*, f. 44a. [3] *B40*, ff. 46a–47a. [4] *B40*, ff. 144b–154a. See below, pp. 157–65.

[5] *B40*, f. 71a–b. See above, pp. 74–5.

[6] Jan Rypka, *History of Iranian Literature* (Dordrecht, 1968), pp. 97–8, 717.

3. *DIDACTIC DISCOURSES*

It is a fundamental difference of intention which distinguishes the narrative discourse from the *didactic discourse*. Most didactic discourses actually use the narrative discourse as a basis, but transform it by the addition of a lengthy *exegetical supplement*. The conscious intention of the *Miharbān* commentators responsible for the development of the didactic variety of discourse was exposition of the works of Nānak. The narrative discourse provided them with a convenient vehicle, and in accordance with their primary purpose they attached to the scriptural quotations which recur in many of the narrative discourses passages which purported to explain the meaning of those quotations. In most cases there was no need to depart from the established pattern of the narrative discourse form. It was sufficient to add the words *tis kā paramārath* after each quotation, and then insert the exegesis. The formula *tis kā paramārath* means 'its sublime meaning', and because these words appear with such unfailing regularity the exegetical supplement which they introduce is sometimes designated the *paramārath* form.[1]

The difference between the narrative discourse and the didactic discourse is conveniently illustrated by the *B40* version of the sākhī entitled 'Bābā Nānak's Discourse with Sheikh Braham'.[2] The sākhī is primarily based upon the series of shaloks attributed to Sheikh Farīd, together with some similar works of Gurū Nānak. These compositions were developed into a narrative discourse of the standard question-and-answer pattern, and this must have been the full extent of the proto-sākhī. The *B40* compiler has, however, interpolated a section borrowed from a *Miharbān* version of the same sākhī.[3] In this particular instance he does not use the customary *tis kā paramārath* formula, but much of the extra material which he introduces is of precisely this *paramārath* kind. Another example is provided by a similar interpolation in the sākhī 'A Discourse with Siddhs at Achal', where the borrowing includes the introductory formula.[4]

These two examples are, however, strictly interpolations, with neither making any substantial difference to the structure of the discourse in which it occurs. Didactic discourses are untypical of the *B40* collection and of all other janam-sākhīs except those of the *Miharbān* tradition. Whereas discourses of this kind are the standard form for the *Miharbān Janam-sākhī* they appear in other janam-sākhīs only as borrowings taken from various recensions of the *Miharbān Janam-sākhī*.[5] Exegetical supplements grafted on to narrative discourses are the stock form used by the commentators responsible for the *Miharbān Janam-sākhī*, and the term which they have applied to the form (*goṣṭ*) can conveniently be

[1] Mohan Singh Uberoi, *A History of Panjabi Literature* (Amritsar, 1956), p. 50.

[2] *B40*, ff. 57b–65b. For a more detailed analysis of the sākhī see below, pp. 131–5.

[3] *B40*, ff. 60a–64b.

[4] *B40*, ff. 118b–120a. The *Ādi Sākhīs* also include a similar interpolation at this point. *AS*, pp. 73–5. See below, p. 206. Both compilers have used the same source.

[5] In addition to the two examples noted above the principal *Miharbān* borrowings included in the *B40 Janam-sākhī* are to be found on folios 2b–5b, 112a–b, and 210a–218a.

retained as an alternative label for their variety of discourse. Although the word *goṣṭ* means simply 'discourse' its usage in this study is limited to didactic discourses bearing the hallmarks of the *Miharbān* tradition.

In its more advanced stages the didactic discourse is distinguished by more than the mere addition of exegesis. A developed *goṣṭ* expresses a particular theme and it is to the enunciation of this theme that the commentator's efforts are directed. In most cases the theme is suggested by the shabad or shalok which provides the nucleus of the discourse. A few have, however, been constructed in defence of a preconceived view concerning particular doctrinal issues.

This latter variety is well illustrated by the only *Miharbān* borrowing to have been recorded as a complete and separate unit by the *B40* compiler. The borrowing appears in the *B40 Janam-sākhī* as two consecutive discourses with closely related themes. The first (*B40* sākhī 54) insists upon an obligation to meditate upon the divine Name (*nām simaran*) during the early hours of the morning; and the second (*B40* sākhī 55) extends the same insistence to include an early-morning bathe. Both have been constructed point by point and may be represented in the following summary form:

The Way of Salvation

Goṣṭ 1 (*B40* sākhī no. 54, ff.210a–214a)

Theme:	The necessity of *nām simaran*.	
Interlocutor:	Gurū Aṅgad.	
Setting:	Bābā Nānak goes to bathe in the Rāvī river during the last watch of the night. He then meditates and sings praises to God.	210a–b
Treatment:	*Nam simaran* must be performed early in the morning every day.	211a
	An exhortation to resist the temptation to abandon the discipline.	211a–212b
	The reward of following the discipline.	212b
	The importance of associating with the few perfected devotees who have already discovered the way.	213b–214b

Goṣṭ 2 (*B40* sākhī no. 55, ff.214b–218a)

Theme:	The daily discipline.	
Interlocutor:	Gurū Aṅgad.	
Setting:	Bābā Nānak sits in Kartārpur during the third watch of the night.	214b
Treatment:	The merit of early rising and bathing.	214b–215b
	An exhortation to follow truth and goodness throughout the remainder of the day.	216a–b
	The fate of those who practise falsehood and deceit.	216b
	The necessity of *nām simaran* reaffirmed; oral repetition specified as the proper method.	216b–217a
	The human body as the dwelling-place of God.	217b

Each point of the argument is supported by an appropriate quotation, with intervening dialogue constructed out of the material provided by the passages quoted and from the distinctive doctrines which the commentator wishes to communicate. In some instances this is skilfully done; in others it is patently naive.

Gurū Aṅgadjī then asked, 'Respected Bābājī, He who is called God—where does He live? In what village does He dwell? . . .'[1]

This enables the commentator to introduce a quotation referring to the dwelling-place of the divine Name, but his method is on this occasion scarcely felicitous. Such crudities are, however, very rare.

It seems clear that the *B40* compiler introduced these two *Miharbān* discourses because of a personal interest in the practice of *nām simaran.* This same concern is expressed with even greater emphasis in the *Miharbān* interpolation which appears in the Achal discourse. The didactic portion is of particular interest in this latter case because it illustrates the manner in which a commentator would carry his exegesis beyond the meaning intended by Nānak to a position which is actually contrary to the Gurū's teachings. The particular point which the *Miharbān* commentator was anxious to communicate is that salvation is to be secured through constant repetition of the name of God (*rām*). The second stanza of Gurū Nānak's *Sūhī* 1 seemed to afford a suitable text to quote in support of the theory and in his exegetical supplement the commentator emphasizes the point by including a twelvefold repetition of the word 'Rām'.[2]

Although the second stanza of *Sūhī* 1 could, in isolation, be interpreted in this manner it does not actually make the point, and the burden of Gurū Nānak's teachings in their totality is clearly opposed to the commentator's exclusive insistence upon mechanical repetition. The commentator has reverted to an earlier interpretation which Nānak had deliberately opposed. The Gurū's own insistence was upon the interiorization of the process termed *nām simaran* or *nām japan*, and although this could include mechanical repetition it was by no means limited to it. When, as in this particular instance, Nānak uses the words *nām japai* they must be interpreted in the wider context of his teachings, not in isolation.

The commentator was, however, one who retained a firm belief in the efficacy of the old method and his conviction was shared by the author of a narrative source used by the *B40* and *Ādi Sākhīs* compilers. The *B40* compiler's unquestioning acceptance of the theory presumably explains an interesting slip which occurs when he quotes the stanza a second time. In the first instance he correctly reproduces the term *nām japai*, but in requoting it he substitutes *rām* for *nām.*[3] There can be no doubt that the *Miharbān*, *B40*, and *Ādi Sākhīs* compilers were all expressing the dominant interpretation of their period. The *Ādi Sākhīs* compiler adds to the repetition of *rām* an instruction to use the ascription *vāh gurū* ('praise to the Gurū') in the same mechanical manner.[4]

[1] *B40*, f. 217a. [2] *B40*, f. 118b. [3] *B40*, f. 119a.
[4] *AS*, p. 75. Cf. *B40*, f. 196b.

Having dealt with this subject the commentary then proceeds to discuss another critical issue. How could an idol-worshipper such as Nāmdev have attained to salvation?[1] His attainment could not be doubted, for he had been included in the sacred scripture compiled by Gurū Arjan. But nor could his idol-worshipping propensities be denied. Once again the commentary departs radically from the actual quotation which it purports to expound. The issue must have been a genuine problem within the community during the late seventeenth or early eighteenth century.

In yet another instance the *B40* compiler, in common with other compilers of narrative janam-sākhīs, has introduced an exegetical supplement which reverses a meaning intended by Gurū Nānak. In most versions the sākhī 'The Child Nānak's Discourse with his Teacher' largely consists of a didactic discourse based on the shabad *Sirī Rāg* 6.[2] The message which the third stanza communicates is that all men, whether high or low, pass their lives in vain if they neglect the paramount duty of meditation on the divine Name. Some are compelled to beg whereas others are exalted to kingship, but upon all there lies the same responsibility and the same penalty for neglecting it. In this stanza Gurū Nānak is not commending begging, and elsewhere he deprecates it. The commentator, however, interprets the passage as an expression of approval for the practice of begging. Having described the nature of divine retribution he concludes:

> Such will be the condition of those who enjoy the comforts and pleasures of sovereignty but neglect to repeat the Name of God, whereas they who remember God and live by begging shall receive high honour in the court of God.[3]

Exegesis of this kind represents the continuing pressure of the ascetic ideal. Didactic discourses offered a particularly convenient vehicle for such ideals, a feature which does much to explain the strong *Miharbān* preference for this particular form.

4. *HETERODOX DISCOURSES*

It has already been observed how later traditions, within the Sikh community or closely allied to it, are sometimes distinguished by a marked divergence from the teachings and evident intention of Gurū Nānak. Some of these deviant traditions can be traced to the influence of contemporary Islam in the Pañjāb, others derive from Nāth sources, and yet others are curious amalgams drawn from a variety of sources. Many give expression to gnostic interpretations whereas others are more concerned with trite epigrams. In tone and content they range from mild heresy to virulent polemic.

There is thus a considerable variety covered by the works of deviant

[1] *B40*, ff. 119b–120a. *AS*, p. 74. The *B40* version also introduces the idol-worshipping Dhannā into the discussion.

[2] *B40*, ff. 2b–5b. *Mih JS* I.11–15. *AS*, pp. 4–6. *Pur JS*, pp. 3–5. *Bālā JS*, pp. 10–14.

[3] *B40*, f. 5a.

traditions. Three features provide a common bond. The first is their generally heretical nature; the second is the uniformly poor quality of the verse in which they are expressed; and the third their strong preference for a discourse form. These reasons justify a convenient grouping under the common heading *heterodox discourse*. Occasionally a basis is provided for a discourse of this kind by an authentic composition of Gurū Nānak, but apocryphal verse is the general rule. As with other varieties of discourse settings are contrived and then largely ignored. It is the actual discourse which commands attention.

Most of the works incorporating heterodox beliefs developed apart from the janam-sākhīs and circulated independently. The purpose of their authors and promoters differed in some measure from that of the janam-sākhī compilers, and in most cases their products were too lengthy to encourage borrowing by the janam-sākhī compilers. The differences were, however, by no means absolute, and works which could not be included *in toto* might well provide extracts of manageable length. Heretical doctrine was not automatically excluded. The prerequisite was that it should purport to represent the authentic teachings of Bābā Nānak. This claim the heterodox discourses made explicitly and as a result a few extracts found their way into the various janam-sākhīs.

Independent works of this nature which circulated within the Sikh community during the janam-sākhī period may be divided into three categories. First there were two lengthy discourses set in the context of Bābā Nānak's alleged visit to Arabia. These are 'The Mecca Discourse' (*makke dī goṣṭi*) and 'The Medīnā Discourse' (*madīne dī goṣṭi*). The first of these purports to record a debate which Nānak conducted during his visit to Mecca, and the second an encounter with the quranic King Qārūn. During the course of the latter the Gurū recites a homily entitled the *Nasīhat-nāmā*. Neither discourse has been actually incorporated within any of the principal janam-sākhīs, but they have occasionally been recorded in conjunction with a janam-sākhī or included within a single manuscript binding.[1] An abbreviated version of both is to be found at the conclusion of the *B40* manuscript, obviously the work of a later copyist.[2] Both are plainly spurious in so far as they are attributed to Gurū Nānak. It is to the 'Triumph over Islam' theme of the janam-sākhī period that the two discourses properly belong.

A second group, closely allied to the Mecca and Medīnā discourses, consists of compositions attributed to Gurū Nānak which embody beliefs derived from the popular Sūfism of the period. These works are invariably set in the context of a debate held with a famous Sūfī, normally one who had lived prior to the time of Nānak. They are important in that they provide statements of the variety of Sūfī doctrine which evidently com-

[1] An example is IOL MS Panj. B41. The janam-sākhī terminates on f. 253. Thereafter the manuscript records the Mecca and Medīnā discourses (ff. 254–395). Sardar Kuldip Singh Bedi's manuscript also includes both discourses in addition to its *Purātan* text.

[2] *B40*, ff. 229–38 (Arabic pagination). The Gurmukhī pagination does not extend to this point. For an English summary of the *B40* version see *B40(Eng)*, Introduction, pp. 10–11.

manded a widespread following in the rural Pañjāb of the seventeenth and eighteenth centuries; and also for the testimony which in common with some of the narrative discourses they bear to the enduring reputation of certain Sūfī pīrs. 'Abd al-Qādir Jīlānī, Shams al-Dīn Tabrīzī, Farīd al-Dīn Mas'ūd Ganj-i-Shakar, Bahā' al-Dīn Zakariyyā, Rukn al-Dīn of Multān, and Sharaf al-Dīn of Pāṇīpat all figure in heterodox discourses. Two of the more important compositions included in discourses of this kind are the *Tīh Sipāre* and the *Hāzar-nāmā*.[1]

In one instance a discourse is said to have been held not with a figure who had predeceased Nānak but with one who came after him. This was Bābā Lāl of Dhiānpur, near Baṭālā.[2] Although Bābā Lāl was a Hindu, his celebrated association with Dārā Shikoh indicates that the Sikh 'Discourse with Bābā Lāl' should be included in the second category of heterodox discourses. The Sikh tradition derives directly from the record of Dārā Shikoh's own discourses.[3]

A third category of heterodox discourses is provided by works which owe their origin to the *haṭha-yoga* doctrines of the Nāth tradition. The distinctively Nāth element incorporated within narrative sākhīs bears ample witness to the widespread influence of the Nāth tradition in seventeenth-century Pañjāb, and from this third category of heterodox discourses it is evident that in spite of Gurū Nānak's strictures upon Nāth beliefs, these beliefs had in fact penetrated the later Sikh community. Within the community the doctrines and practices of *haṭha-yoga* were accorded a particular loyalty by the so-called Udāsī sādhūs, but it is clear that respect for these doctrines extended beyond the limited Udāsī circle. This is apparent from the willingness of the *B40* compiler to include such material in his janam-sākhī. An even clearer instance is provided by the *Colebrooke Janam-sākhī*. Like the *B40* janam-sākhī it is not to be identified as an Udāsī document, but it nevertheless includes an early version of the lengthy *Prāṇ Saṅgalī*.[4]

The *Prāṇ Saṅgalī* is the most important of the heterodox discourses with a Nāth orientation. Although it is not quoted *in extenso* by the *B40* compiler it does receive a passing reference at the conclusion of the Śivanābh sākhī.[5] In its extant form the entire work extends to eighty cantos and is plainly a collection of several compositions in verse connected by briefer narrative passages.[6] The collection takes the form of a discourse which, as the *B40* reference indicates, is set in the context of a visit to Rājā Śivanābh's domain in Siṅghalādīp. Śivanābh begins the discourse with Bābā Nānak and is later joined by Gorakhnāth and other Siddhs. The discourse proceeds in the usual manner, an appropriate question by one of the interlocutors being followed by Bābā Nānak's reply. Piār Singh attributes the composition of the various parts, and also

[1] *B40*, ff. 53a–55b, 56a–57a.

[2] Sujān Rāi Bhaṇḍārī, *Khulāsat-ut-Tavārīkh*, English trans. in Muhammad Akbar, *The Punjab under the Mughals* (Lahore, 1948), pp. 291–2.

[3] Piār Singh, 'A Critical Survey of Panjabi Prose in the Seventeenth Century' (unpublished Ph.D. thesis, Panjab University, 1968), p. 133.

[4] *Pur JS*, pp. 89, 118. [5] *B40*, f. 153b. [6] Piār Singh, op. cit., p. 129.

their collection into a single work, to the latter half of the seventeenth century.[1] Portions of it may perhaps pre-date this period, but there seems to be little doubt that his opinion is substantially correct.

Although the *Prāṇ Saṅgalī* must have enjoyed a considerable popularity during the eighteenth century it subsequently came to be regarded as apocryphal. A tradition related by Santokh Singh towards the middle of the nineteenth century implies this conviction. Santokh Singh relates that Gurū Arjan, while preparing the compilation of the Ādi Granth at the beginning of the seventeenth century, received news of a work which (so it was claimed) had been composed by Bābā Nānak during his visit to Sri Lanka and left there. A Sikh named Paiṛā Mokhā was forthwith dispatched to Sri Lanka, from where he returned bearing a copy of the *Prāṇ Saṅgalī*. Gurū Arjan examined the work, but being unconvinced of its authenticity declined to include it in the Ādi Granth.[2]

This opinion was evidently not shared by the eighteenth-century community, for manuscript copies of portions of the work were circulating freely in the Pañjāb during this period. Amongst the more important works which came to be included in the *Prāṇ Saṅgalī* were the *Dhiāo Bihaṅgam kā* ('The Bird Canto'), also referred to as the *Goṣṭ Niraṅkār Nāl* ('Discourse with God'); the *Goṣṭ Ātme Paramātme kī*; the *Sākhī Ved Sadāe*; the *Gyān Surodaya*; and the *Jugāvalī*.[3] The last of these is to be found in the *Colebrooke* manuscript.[4]

Another popular work belonging to this same cycle of Nāth-oriented traditions is 'A Discourse with Ajitta Randhava' (*goṣṭi ajitte randhāve nāl*). Bhāī Gurdās relates that Jittā (or Ajittā), a Randhāvā Jaṭ, was one of the more prominent disciples of Gurū Nānak.[5] Apart from a reference to his upright behaviour Bhāī Gurdās tells us nothing about him, but later narrators have enlisted him in a number of narrative anecdotes. The discourse in which he is said to have participated is of particular interest as an example of later polemic concerning disputed authority within the Sikh community. A version has been included in the *B40 Janam-sākhī*.[6]

[1] Ibid., p. 130.

[2] Santokh Singh, *Gur Pratāp Sūray* (the *Sūraj Prakāś*), *rāsi* 3, *aṅk* 32. Vīr Singh edition, vol. vi, pp. 2038–43. Mohan Singh Uberoi claims that the *Prāṇ Saṅgalī* was included in the proscribed *Khārī Bīṛ* version of the Ādi Granth. Mohan Singh, *Kabir—His Biography* (Lahore, 1934), p. 57. If this is correct it will have been an appreciably shorter work than the extant text. It appears, however, that Mohan Singh must be confusing the *Prāṇ Saṅgalī* with the *Hakīkat Rāh Mukām Rāje Śivanābh kī*, a description of the way to Sri Lanka attributed to Paiṛā Mokhā. Descriptions of the Banno manuscript (the earliest *Khāṛī Bīṛ* manuscript) make no reference to the *Prāṇ Saṅgalī*, and the *Prāṇ Saṅgalī* itself includes no description of Paiṛā Mokhā's alleged journey to Sri Lanka. For further descriptive accounts of the *Prāṇ Saṅgalī* see Piār Singh, op. cit., pp. 128–34; Jagjīt Singh, 'A Critical and Comparative Study of the Janam Sakhis of Guru Nanak' (unpublished Ph.D. thesis, Panjab University, 1967), pp. 9–10, 219, 278–82, 303–4, 332–4, 371; Rattan Singh Jaggī, *Gurū Nānak Bāṇī* (Paṭiālā, 1968), pp. 33–52. The extant text was edited by Sant Sampūran Singh and published in the Deva-nāgrī script by Mohan Singh Vaid of Tarn Tāran in 1928.

[3] Piār Singh, op. cit.

[4] Photozincograph Facsimile (Dehrā Dūn, 1885), pp. 170–93. Sākhī 46 of the *Pur JS* is also taken from the *Prāṇ Saṅgalī*. Jagjīt Singh, op. cit., p. 332. *Pur JS*, pp. 84–6.

[5] *BG* XI:14. *SLTGN(Eng)*, p. 44.

[6] *B40*, ff. 111a–116b. The reference to disputed authority occurs on f. 115a: 'Son, they will set

5. CODES OF DISCIPLINE

One last form which deserves to be noted is the *rahit-nāmā* or 'code of discipline'. This warrants a brief notice, not because it is accorded any prominence in the janam-sākhīs but rather because the rudimentary examples which do make occasional appearances in the janam-sākhīs were later to develop into a literary form of fundamental importance for the eighteenth-century Sikh community. It was during the course of the eighteenth century that the Khālsā discipline crystallized into a coherent code of conduct (*rahit*), and it was to give formal expression to this evolving code that the *rahit-nāmā* was developed. As links in the chain which connects the seventeenth- and the nineteenth-century communities the succession of *rahit-nāmās* is of some importance, and to this day modern versions continue to serve as a means of maintaining the coherence of the community on the basis of an agreed code of Khālsā conduct.[1]

Although the janam-sākhīs incorporate no evolved *rahit-nāmās* they do include statements which can safely be regarded as the seeds from which the later codes were to grow. These range from the brief and oft-repeated slogan *nām dān isnān* to more detailed lists of instructions issued by God to Nānak as patterns of conduct for his followers. The *B40* and *Ādi Sākhīs*, following a common source, include one such rudimentary *rahit nāmā* in the sākhī 'An Interview with God',[2] and another appears at the conclusion of a *Miharbān* interview of the same kind.[3] In both instances the setting is important. It was evidently believed to be necessary that the words of the *rahit* should proceed directly from God. The later *rahit-nāmās* of the eighteenth and nineteenth centuries consist largely of instructions ascribed to Gurū Gobind Singh.

---

up *mañjīs* [seats of spiritual authority] in their houses and sit on them, but these people will be punished.' The nature of the dispute appears to be indicated in a question concerning the shaving of heads on f. 113a. This suggests a conflict between an ascetic tradition and the Khālsā. The cryptic reference to 'the ninth garb' (? the ninth Gurū) on f. 111b probably relates to the same issue.

[1] Authorized editions are issued by the Shiromaṇī Gurdwārā Parbandhak Committee in Amritsar under the title *Sikh Rahit Maryādā*. For an English translation of the current version see Kanwaljīt Kaur and Indarjīt Singh (trans.), *Rehat Maryada: A Guide to the Sikh Way of Life* (London, 1971). An important example of an early *rahit-nāmā* available in print is the *Prem Sumārg Granth* (ed. Randhīr Singh, Jalandhar, 1965). Two others were published in the nineteenth century in English translation by Sir Attar Singh of Bhadaur under the title *The Rayhit Nama of Pralad Rai, or the excellent conversation of the Duswan Padsha, and Nand Lal's Rayhit Nama or rules for the Guidance of the Sikhs in Religious Matters* (Lahore, 1876). See also E. Trumpp, *The Ādi Granth* (London, 1877), pp. cxii–cxvi; and W. H. McLeod, *The Evolution of the Sikh Community* (Oxford, 1976), pp. 51–2.

[2] *B40*, ff. 125b–126a. *AS*, pp. 2–3.

[3] *Mih JS* II.156. This *rahit-nāmā* is particularly specific in its reference to intoxicants.

8

THE ASSEMBLING AND TRANSMISSION OF THE JANAM-SĀKHĪ TRADITIONS

IN their earliest stages the growth processes and the transmission of the evolving janam-sākhīs were evidently confined to oral tradition, and for fully three centuries oral tradition remained the area of major expansion. Although the first written collections must have been recorded within a hundred years of the Gurū's death (and probably earlier) their contribution has inevitably been more in terms of recording various phases of development than of actually stimulating it. The written word, though by no means static, tends to stabilize a tradition and to inhibit further expansion or radical diversification. By contrast, oral tradition can be vigorously dynamic, particularly when it lacks the conventional restraints commonly applied to the repetition of sacred texts. The oral tradition of the janam-sākhīs has, on the whole, lacked these.

The study of oral tradition has interested philologists for many decades and has long since demonstrated its critical contribution to the understanding of Old Testament development and transmission.[1] More recently its methodology, refined and extended, has been widely applied in such areas as African and Pacific pre-history.[2] As a result of this research much has been discovered concerning techniques of oral transmission and methods of analysing its products. Amongst the conclusions which must now be regarded as firmly established is the insistence that oral tradition does not necessarily lack safeguards. Oral traditions can in fact be transmitted with relatively little change provided that certain conventions are observed. These include specific memory training, mnemonic devices, control over the recital by certain groups or members of the audience, and a normal preference for poetry rather than prose.[3]

Oral traditions of this controlled variety are, however, much different from those which lie behind the janam-sākhīs. None of the conventional safeguards have been applied to the transmission of the anecdotes which eventually came to be collected into janam-sākhīs. These were anecdotes which did not need to be learnt by heart. The one essential feature was that

[1] A notable contribution has, in more recent years, been made by a Scandinavian school of Old Testament scholars. For a brief summary of their work see Eduard Nielsen, *Oral Tradition: A Modern Problem in Old Testament Introduction* (London, 1954). The more prominent names are those of Mowinckel, H. S. Nyberg, I. Engnell, G. Widengren, and Nielsen himself.

[2] For a useful introduction covering both the techniques of analysis and their application to particular African traditions see Jan Vansina, *Oral Tradition: A Study in Historical Methodology* (London, 1965).

[3] Ibid., pp. 31–43.

they should be seen to fulfil the requirements of the myth which they were intended to express. This imposed a certain limited restraint in that it required a general faithfulness to the current understanding of the person and mission of Nānak, but it was a restraint which could have little effect on wide areas of the evolving tradition. It was only the *bāṇī* (the actual works of Nānak himself) which had to be memorized. The traditions which were built around and beyond the *bāṇī* needed no such limitation.

The freedom to expand which was thus provided for the oral tradition concerning Gurū Nānak was greatly encouraged by other features. If in fact there were any members of the early Sikh community specifically appointed to narrate the tradition there is no evidence that any of these narrators ever received any training in memory or transmission skills. In practice the procedure was almost certainly that within a local community (*saṅgat*) the role of narrator would by general consent be accorded to a particular person. Age, social status, piety, or eloquence could presumably have determined the choice. This person, without either the benefit of training or the compulsion to adhere strictly to a received version, would relate anecdotes concerning the Gurū in words meaningful to himself and to his audience. The reactions of his audience would inevitably operate not as a control but rather as an encouragement to mutate and expand. The resultant pattern of development manifests, as one might expect, a pronounced affection for the simple wonder-story and a predictable reliance upon other traditions current during the period of growth.

Finally, it must be remembered that the anecdotes which together constitute the janam-sākhīs are prose narratives, not verse. Prose is not an impossible medium for a generally static oral tradition (the Icelandic sagas demonstrate this), but certainly it is vastly inferior to verse as a means of consistent preservation. Given this and the other features mentioned above it is scarcely surprising that the janam-sākhī traditions should expand with such speed and in such diverse forms. For the same reasons it is understandable that traditions relating to the authentic life of Nānak should be few and, in most instances, difficult to recognize. Although such elements certainly exist within the janam-sākhī traditions, they are deeply embedded and when extracted provide little more than glimpses of the historical Nānak.[1]

It seems clear that the main focus of the transmission process was the cult centre. For the early Sikh community this centre was the dharamsālā, a building or portion of a building which is nowhere described with any precision but which could evidently be anything capable of holding a small group of people. In some villages a separate structure may have been provided, in others the purpose may have been served by using a room attached to a private house, and in yet others a room in everyday use may have been appropriated for the regular meetings of the group. This much is reasonable conjecture. What seems certain is that a single room normally served as a dharamsālā, and what is certain beyond all doubt is that this dharamsālā was the cult centre.

[1] For an attempt to identify these elements see *GNSR*, pp. 68–147.

Within its dharamsālā a *saṅgat*, or congregation, would meet for *kīrtan* (the singing of devotional songs). *Kīrtan* would be the principal corporate activity of any local group of Sikhs, and an important supplement would be the recitation of narrative traditions concerning the first Gurū (*kathā*). There were many local *saṅgats* scattered throughout rural Pañjāb, and within each there will have been this regular pattern of *kīrtan* and *kathā*. In a few favoured instances a manuscript collection of sākhīs was obtained and thereafter the stories of the Gurū could be read. (The *B40* patron specifically states that he commissioned the writing of his janam-sākhī for the benefit of the *saṅgat* to which he belonged.[1]) For most *saṅgats*, however, there will have been a continuing dependence on oral tradition until at least the late nineteenth and perhaps into the twentieth century.

The home was presumably a second focus of the transmission process. There are no positive indications within the recorded janam-sākhīs to indicate that the written collections were used domestically during the seventeenth and eighteenth centuries, but this testimony relates only to the recorded tradition. Within Sikh homes the transmission process will almost invariably have been concerned with the continuing oral tradition. In this respect the home will normally have reflected the dharamsālā. The tradition current within any particular village or district will have found its primary expression in the dharamsālā, and a repetition in the Sikh homes of that district.

Because of the scattered nature of the Sikh community different areas inevitably developed their own local traditions. This produced variant versions of sākhīs which had gained a wide currency, and local sākhīs confined to particular areas. Some of the variants together with instances of unique local traditions find expression in the recorded collections and help to determine the geographical areas in which the different collections were compiled. It should not, however, be supposed that *saṅgats* lived in complete isolation from each other or from the community's principal centres of activity. Pilgrimage has been a regular feature of Sikh custom since at least the time of Gurū Amar Dās (1552–74), and right from the time of Nānak himself visits to the Gurū will have been a joy for many and an obligation for all who could reasonably make them. The cross-fertilization which was continually provided by such pilgrimages ensured that the pattern of janam-sākhī development constituted a close-knit web rather than a splay of lines connected only at their point of origin.

It has already been suggested that the agent of transmission within the local *saṅgat* could have been any person who possessed acceptable qualifications as a narrator. In practice the role will commonly have been performed by Khatrīs. The Gurūs were all Khatrīs, Bhāī Gurdās and Miharbān were both Khatrīs, and Dayā Rām Abrol, compiler and copyist of the *B40* janam-sākhī, was also a Khatrī.[2] Leadership by Khatrīs would

[1] *B40*, f. 84b.

[2] Manī Singh's caste connections are, like his janam-sākhī role, disputed. According to the late nineteenth-century writer Gyān Singh he was a Jaṭ. The traditional consensus claims, however, that he was a Kamboh. *MK*, p. 712n.

be no more than a continuation of a well-established pattern of leadership in rural Pañjāb. Social status, education, and a traditional role as teachers of the Jaṭs would serve as strong qualifications. It was not, however, an invariable pattern. The author of the *Dabistān-i-Mazāhib* reports that in the early seventeenth century Jaṭs were already moving into positions of authority,[1] and during the succeeding century they assumed a dominant status within the community. The recorded janam-sākhī collections seem to reflect this change. Whereas the *Miharbān Janam-sākhī*, *B40*, and the *Gyān-ratanāvalī* accord a greater prominence to Khatrīs, the *Bālā* tradition shifts attention to the Jaṭs. The latter tradition may, in fact, represent an aspect of the Jaṭs' ascent to dominance, and the later popularity of the *Bālā* janam-sākhīs may in some measure derive from the establishment of their dominant status.

Oral circulation from the time of Nānak's own lifetime constitutes the first major phase in the evolution of the janam-sākhīs. The second begins with the initial recording of a selection of sākhīs. This second phase will have been initiated for a number of reasons. One which can be safely assumed is the measure of sanctity which India traditionally attaches to holy books. Everyone else had their sacred scriptures, and although the fifth Gurū Arjan had provided his followers with their own Sikh scripture in 1604 there was no reason why they should not have more if there existed material suitable for recording. The *Sākhī Pothī*, or 'Volume of Sākhīs' was soon accorded a respect second only to the *Granth Sāhib* compiled by Gurū Arjan.

A second reason was presumably a growing awareness on the part of some literate Sikhs of the unreliability of oral tradition as a means of accurate transmission. All would have claimed a concern for accuracy, and a few will have perceived that uncontrolled oral transmission must seriously endanger the objective. The answer for such men will have been an attempt to fix the tradition by setting it down in writing.

These appear to have been the two main reasons for the earliest decisions to record the tradition. Others may be added as conjectures. In some instances a particular Sikh, having heard a recitation of the tradition at a location away from his home (perhaps from someone of renowned piety, or at one of the pilgrimage centres) may have desired to have it repeated to his own family or *saṅgat*. Rather than trust to his own memory he may have arranged to have the tradition recorded in order that he might return home with the manuscript.

Four principal stages may be observed in the recording of janam-sākhīs. The first is the random collection. A small number of sākhīs were selected from the current oral tradition and recorded in an essentially haphazard order. This phase appears to have been initiated during the late sixteenth century, or perhaps at the beginning of the seventeenth century. The earliest available examples suggest that the only deference paid to the notion of chronology was a rough grouping according to birth, childhood, manhood, and death. Chronology was of only secondary importance. The

[1] *PPP* I.1 (April 1967), p. 57.

janam-sākhīs were more concerned with the myth of Nānak than with the actual pattern of his life, and a coherent sequence of anecdotes was not essential to their primary purpose.

Amongst the extant manuscripts the earliest example of this first phase is provided by *LPD 194*. It is not, however, a particularly good example, for the impulse to order and arrange is already at work. A better example would have been the collection which evidently lay behind *LDP 194*,[1] and an even better example is provided by the janam-sākhīs of the *Bālā* tradition. Although the *Bālā* janam-sākhīs emerge later than the tradition which leads through *LDP 194* into the *Purātan* janam-sākhīs, these later manuscripts are actually more primitive in terms of structure. A generally consistent pattern is sustained up to the point where Nānak ventures out on his travels, but thereafter the selection and recording of anecdotes is essentially random.

The same feature is also evident in much of the *B40 Janam-sākhī*, particularly in the portion which was drawn directly from oral tradition.[2] Although it was compiled towards the middle of the eighteenth century this portion is perhaps the best of all available examples of the first primitive phase of janam-sākhī recording. Other portions of the *B40 Janam-sākhī* manifest the same disarray, but none are as primitive in structure as the group of sākhīs derived from the compiler's oral source. No other group of sākhīs has quite the same simplicity of narrative pattern nor its complete absence of quotations from the works of Nānak. The *B40 Janam-sākhī* is plainly an anthology drawn from a variety of sources, and as such it manages to combine highly evolved sākhīs with the most primitive we possess.

The second stage in the recording of janam-sākhīs closely followed the first. This new development was marked by a concern for chronology and a consequent effort to order the assortment of sākhīs into a coherent sequence. The process which is already evident in *LDP 194* reaches its climax in the detailed structures of the later *Purātan* manuscripts (the *Colebrooke* and the *Hāfizābād* janam-sākhīs). In the case of the childhood and early manhood sākhīs this task presented few problems. For this period of Nānak's life the chief issues concerned the timing of his betrothal and marriage, and the order in which his two sons were born. It was the period of Nānak's travels which provided the *Purātan* tradition with its greatest challenge and it was with considerable ingenuity that the challenge was answered. The result is a pattern of four major journeys corresponding to the four cardinal points of the compass, a schema which was presumably suggested by the ancient *digvijaya* tradition. Into this pattern numerous travel anecdotes have been fitted. There are, it is true, several flaws. The order is not always consistent, there are some obvious gaps, the compiler was obviously much more interested in outward rather than homeward journeys, and one anecdote which was evidently overlooked has been appended in the form of a fifth journey.[3] It is, nevertheless, something of a

[1] See below, p. 188. [2] *B40*, ff. 154b–199a, 203a–205a. See below, pp. 220–6.

[3] Sākhī 52, 'Discourse with Siddhs at Gorakh-haṭaṛī'. *Pur JS*, pp. 104–6.

tour de force and it marks the high point of janam-sākhī restructuring. Macauliffe followed this *Purātan* pattern closely in his account of the life of Nānak, and few biographers have since departed from it.

The manner in which different compilers used the same material to construct differing chronologies is illustrated by the varying placement of the sākhī 'An Interview with God'. The anecdote related in this sākhī describes how Nānak was summoned to the Divine Court and there ordained by God to go forth into the world to preach the divine Name. The *B40* compiler has taken this anecdote from an earlier collection, and following his predecessor's evident indifference to chronological concerns he has recorded it at a point more than half-way through his own collection.[1] If the *B40* collection were to be regarded as a coherent sequence it could only mean that Nānak had been preaching his message long before God had actually commissioned him to do so. The *B40* compiler is not, however, committed to any rigorous preservation of chronological sequences and follows them only when using a source which has already devised one. Most of his material represents the first stage of janam-sākhī compilation where sequence means little or nothing.

The compiler responsible for the *Purātan* chronology could not share this indifference. A logical place had to be found for the anecdote. In the *Purātan* janam-sākhīs it is recorded immediately before Nānak's departure from Sultānpur.[2] Nānak's travels (interpreted by the *Purātan* tradition as missionary journeys) begin with his departure from Sultānpur and this suggested a Sultānpur context for the anecdote. In accordance with this conviction the compiler has introduced it into the narrative relating Nānak's disappearance in the stream near Sultānpur. Other versions of this same narrative make it clear that the introduction of the commissioning sākhī at this point is an interpolation.[3]

The *Purātan* and *B40* compilers, following different sources, have recorded variant versions of the same anecdote. The source used for the *B40* version was also available to the *Ādi Sākhīs* compiler, a person who shared in some measure the *Purātan* concern for chronological consistency. For the *Ādi Sākhīs* compiler the logical place for a commissioning sākhī was the very beginning of the janam-sākhī and accordingly the narrative which appears at such an advanced stage in the *B40* collection is recorded as the first of all anecdotes in the *Ādi Sākhīs*.[4] Nānak is first commissioned by God and only then is he given birth in order to carry out his commission. In addition to this version, however, the *Ādi Sākhīs* compiler also had access to the *Purātan* version in a manuscript which recorded it in its distinctively *Purātan* place. Illogically he repeats it in this later setting[5] with the result that Nānak is twice commissioned in the *Ādi Sākhīs*. The two versions of the anecdote had diverged radically in earlier transmission and the *Ādi Sākhīs* compiler evidently failed to recognize them as separate recensions derived from a common origin.

In the case of the commissioning sākhī the feature which has attracted the attention and the varying interpretations of the different compilers is

[1] *B40*, ff. 123b–126b. [2] *Pur JS*, pp. 14–16. *GNSR*, p. 37.
[3] See below, p. 199. [4] *AS*, pp. 1–3. [5] *AS*, p. 16.

the theme. Elsewhere their decisions concerning placement within a sequence are evidently determined by minor references within the narrative. For the *Purātan* compiler the determinative reference in the Achal sākhī appears to have been the presence of Siddhs. Because the Achal encounter involves Siddhs the *Purātan* compiler bracketed this discourse with the other prominent confrontation with Siddhs, the discourse on Mount Sumeru.[1] For another compiler, however, an appropriate context was evidently suggested by the presence of Gurū Aṅgad in the Achal narrative. As a result the *B40* and *Ādi Sākhīs* compilers, following their common source, include the discourse in the cluster of Aṅgad anecdotes.[2]

The contrast between random and ordered recording can be further illustrated by sākhīs 32–4 of the *B40* collection.[3] This cluster covers a visit to Mecca, a discourse with Kabīr, and Bābā Nānak's encounter with Rājā Śivanābh. For the *B40* compiler there is no problem in the consecutive recording of sākhīs which jump from Western Arabia to Northern India, from Northern India to an unspecified location over the sea, and from there (in sākhī 35) to Kābul. He has, moreover, already recorded a different sākhī set in Mecca.[4] Sequence did not matter. The message could be communicated without coherent chronological patterns.

For the *Purātan* compiler, however, such inconsistencies were intolerable. If Nānak was to visit Mecca then it would have to be during the course of the westwards journey, and if both Mecca sākhīs were to be included they would have to come together. The result is a conflation of the two anecdotes, recorded as a single sākhī in its appropriate place.[5] The story of Rājā Śivanābh has, in like manner, been assigned a suitable place within the total structure. Having decided that the unspecified location over the sea can only mean Sri Lanka,[6] the compiler has included the Śivanābh sākhī in his southwards journey.[7] Kabīr does not appear in the *Purātan* collection, but the *Miharbān* tradition duly puts him in his proper place.[8]

There remains the question of why some compilers should have developed an impulse to order their material into a coherent sequence. The answer is probably the simple one that whereas certain minds will readily sustain a single theme through a disarray of circumstances, others prefer to systematize. Any desire to impart a stronger impression of authenticity probably had little to do with the earlier expressions of the systematizing impulse. For seventeenth- and eighteenth-century readers and listeners the essential questions of authenticity related to the myth expounded by the janam-sākhīs rather than to the incidents which served as a means of exposition. It is only in more recent times, following the

[1] *Pur JS*, p. 97.

[2] *B40*, ff. 117a–122b. *AS*, pp. 73–6. The common source was the manuscript *Q2*. See below, p. 198.

[3] *B40*, ff. 133a–154a.

[4] *B40*, ff. 51b–52b.

[5] *Pur JS*, pp. 98–104. See below, pp. 137–9.

[6] *GNSR*, pp. 115–16.

[7] *Pur JS*, pp. 86–90.

[8] *Mih JS* I.154–6. The *Miharbān* discourse is not the same as the *B40* version.

spread of western historicism, that the truth of the myth has been so intimately linked to the authenticity of the incidents expressing it. This misunderstanding of the janam-sākhī method does much to explain the vehemence with which the *Purātan* chronology is defended today.

The third of the four stages in the growth of the janam-sākhī collections is distinguished by the addition of expository material to the narrative anecdotes and discourses. In a sense it is misleading to define this feature as a third stage, for it is not dependent upon a prior ordering of earlier random selections. Exegetical passages can be added to disordered collections as well as to ordered janam-sākhīs of the second stage. Indeed, it can be argued that this third stage should properly be classified as the initial stage of a distinctively exegetical form, parallel to the first stage of the narrative janam-sākhīs. It is in fact claimed that the *Miharbān Janam-sākhī* is the direct product of an early oral tradition. Another work from the group which produced the earliest versions of the *Miharbān* tradition claims that the *Miharbān Janam-sākhī* records homilies which Miharbān delivered to his followers during the early years of the sixteenth century. These homilies (so it is claimed) were taken down by a disciple named Keśo Dās and later recorded as the *Miharbān Janam-sākhī* towards the middle of the century.[1]

This claim, even if true, does not gainsay the mature character of the extant *Miharbān* collection. *Pothī Sach-khaṇḍ*, the first portion of the *Miharbān Janam-sākhī*, is constructed on the basis of a substantial collection of narrative sākhīs, ordered into a coherent sequence. The narrative element is generally subordinate to the exegetical purpose of the collection but it plainly precedes it in terms of development. If Keśo Dās was in fact responsible for the structure of the extant *Pothī Sach-khaṇḍ* it follows that the introduction of exegetical material must represent a third stage in the development of the janam-sākhīs. The exponents of the *Miharbān* tradition have appropriated the coherent narrative form of the second-stage janam-sākhī and used it to develop a new form. In the remaining sections of the complete *Miharbān Janam-sākhī* this chronological interest largely disappears, but only because the travel itinerary has been almost completely covered in *Pothī Sach-khaṇḍ*. In a sense it is still assumed, for the remaining discourses are all set within the context of the later Kartārpur period of the Gurū's life.

The first three phases in the formation of recorded janam-sākhīs developed rapidly. If the *Miharbān Janam-sākhī*'s own account of its origins is to be believed (and there is no evident reason for doubting it), random, structured, and exegetical collections were all in existence by the middle of the seventeenth century. More than two hundred years passed before the next significant phase began. They were not, of course, sterile years. During the two intervening centuries the earlier janam-sākhīs were considerably supplemented, other distinctive traditions emerged, and individual compilers occasionally gathered all three phases into a single janam-sākhī. The two major developments during this period were a

[1] *Goṣṭān Srī Miharvān jī dīān*, quoted in *Mih JS* I, Introductory Essays, pp. 36–8.

considerable expansion of the *Miharbān* tradition and the increasing popularity of the *Bālā* janam-sākhīs.

The expansion of the *Miharbān* tradition can be safely assumed from the evident fact that the portion of the *Miharbān Janam-sākhī* now extant is obviously the product of sustained development over a lengthy period. The extreme rarity of *Miharbān* manuscripts indicates, however, that this development must have taken place within strictly limited confines. The ascetic emphases which find obvious favour with the *Miharbān* commentators suggest that these limited confines probably corresponded to a few *maṭhs* ('monasteries', ascetic communities). These *maṭhs* may have consisted of Udāsī sādhūs or perhaps sādhūs of the Nirmalā order.[1] Restricted circulation also seems to have been the fate of the *Purātan* tradition and likewise of the later *Gyān-ratanāvalī* collection. Increasingly it was the *Bālā* tradition which found favour in the eighteenth-century Sikh community, and by the nineteenth century its dominance was almost complete.

A number of reasons may be held to account for this widespread popularity of the *Bālā* janam-sākhīs. One will presumably have been its explicit claim to represent the actual words of a disciple who had accompanied Bābā Nānak on his travels.[2] No other janam-sākhī makes this same claim, and as there was no apparent reason for questioning it the janam-sākhī which advanced the claim was the one which won acceptance.

Secondly, the *Bālā* janam-sākhīs contain much that would attract the eighteenth- and nineteenth-century believer. The strong Puranic atmosphere of much of the *Bālā* narrative will have been thoroughly congenial to the rural Pañjāb of this period, and in no other janam-sākhī is the power of Bābā Nānak the wonder-worker more magnificently displayed. The *Bālā* tradition is, in fact, a faithful reflection of many aspects of contemporary Pañjāb rural culture, with its marked fascination for Puranic legends and Sūfī hagiography. Given such qualifications it is scarcely surprising that the *Bālā* janam-sākhīs should acquire such extensive popularity.

Thirdly there is the theory, to which passing reference has already been made, that the rise of the *Bālā* tradition may reflect the rise of the Jaṭs within the Sikh community. Although this is much less certain, it must be regarded as at least a possibility. The other important janam-sākhīs reflect a stronger Khatrī influence, both in terms of authorship and of references to particular disciples of the Gurū. In contrast, the *Bālā* janam-sākhīs mark a shift towards Jaṭ participation (Bālā himself is a Sandhū Jaṭ), and it can be argued that the tradition's dominant emphases accord better with Jaṭ cultural patterns than with those of the Khatrīs.

Whatever the reasons there can be no doubt concerning the eighteenth- and nineteenth-century success of the *Bālā* tradition. This success placed it in a position of considerable advantage when the fourth phase became

[1] Tejā Singh, *Sikhism: Its Ideals and Institutions* (Calcutta, 1951), pp. 58–66, 71–3.

[2] *Bālā JS*, p. 3.

possible. The fourth phase began with the introduction of the printing-press to the Pañjāb. In 1871 the first lithographed Gurmukhī text appeared in Lahore, closely followed in the same year by a second. Both were *Bālā* janam-sākhīs, the second much longer than the first,[1] and since that year progressively larger *Bālā* versions have completely dominated the market. Although Vīr Singh's *Purātan Janam-sākhī* has run through several editions its sales have been greatly assisted by its regular inclusion in university syllabuses. An earlier challenge advanced by two editions of the *Gyān-ratanāvalī* was soon overwhelmed, with the result that lithographed copies of the *Gyān-ratanāvalī* are now very difficult to obtain. To this day the popular market is still controlled by modern versions of the *Bālā* tradition. The spread of education must eventually destroy the *Bālā* reputation, but its disappearance from Pañjāb bookshops is still many years distant.

One last point may be briefly noted before terminating this survey of the janam-sākhīs' linear development. This is the appearance of works which are not strictly janam-sākhīs, but which relate in a generally uncritical manner the accounts given in the janam-sākhīs. In some instances these accounts depend almost exclusively upon a single tradition; in others they blend a variety of traditions, normally without any acknowledgement of source.

Two works of this derived nature have been of particular importance, one of them based upon the *Bālā* tradition and the other upon *Purātan*. The first of these has already been briefly noticed. This is Santokh Singh's *Nānak Prakāś*, a work which today is little read but which for earlier generations served as a valued confirmation of the *Bālā* tradition and as a supplement to it.[2] As far as scholars and writers were concerned its decline in popularity reflected in large measure a corresponding decline in the reputation of its principal source. The *Bālā* tradition retained its popularity amongst writers until after the turn of the century and as late as 1914 could still find an ardent supporter in Khazān Singh, author of *History and Philosophy of Sikhism*. Its reputation as a primary source had, however, declined sharply during the closing years of the nineteenth century and it suffered a particularly serious blow with the publication in 1909 of the second major work deriving largely from a single janam-sākhī source. This was the first volume of Macauliffe's *The Sikh Religion*, an account of the life of Nānak which diverted the attention of scholars and writers away from the increasingly discredited *Bālā* tradition to the newly discovered *Purātan* janam-sākhīs. It needed only the publication of Karam Singh's *Kattak ki Visākh* in 1913 to seal the *Bālā* fate.

Macauliffe, aided by Bhāī Kāhn Singh, established a pattern which has been generally followed ever since. The *Purātan* tradition provides the framework and much of the actual content for most subsequent biographies. This means that the Gurū performs his four major journeys to the east, south, north, and west, concluding with the brief journey to Gorakh-haṭaṛī (Gor-khatrī). To this *Purātan* itinerary are added the

[1] See above, p. 21.

[2] See above, p. 45.

three extra incidents mentioned by Bhāī Gurdās (the visits to Medīnā, Bāghdād, and Multān) together with others which command a particular popularity. (The water-splashing anecdote set in Hardwār is a prominent example.) Bhāī Bālā, the putative narrator of the tradition bearing his name, has presented a major problem. Macauliffe, firmly loyal to his *Purātan* source, rigorously excluded him[1] but others have been unwilling to go as far.

The situation established at the turn of the century by writers such as Macauliffe and Kāhn Singh continues to this day. Those who attempt biographies of Gurū Nānak almost invariably take their stand upon *Purātan*, and sometimes produce accounts which amount to little more than simple paraphrases. It must, however, be emphasized that this fashion is still largely limited to the authors of the more sophisticated variety of biographical study. Bālā still lives on. His continuing authority is everywhere considerable and in the villages of the Pañjāb it remains unchallenged.

[1] Macauliffe, i. lxxix.

9

THE EVOLUTION OF SĀKHĪS

INCLUDED in the *Purātan* janam-sākhīs is the sad story of a merchant who lost his infant son because he failed to pay proper respect to Bābā Nānak. The child had only recently been born and the proud father was busy celebrating the event when Bābā Nānak and Mardānā arrived on the scene. Mardānā sought the usual contribution due to itinerant faqīrs, but was ignored. When he returned and reported this disrespectful negligence to his master Bābā Nānak recited the shabad *Sirī Rāg Pahare* 1.

In the first watch of the night, O my merchant friend,
the divine order sets you within the womb. . . .
In the second watch of the night, O my merchant friend,
you wander heedlessly astray . . .
In the third watch of the night, O my merchant friend,
you are seduced by wealth and carnal beauty . . .
And in the fourth watch of the night, O my merchant friend,
the Reaper comes to gather your harvest . . .[1]

Next morning the child died and the two travellers moved on, leaving the merchant to bewail his fate.[2]

Although the narrator's choice of subject is not the happiest, the sākhī does at least provide a simple example of the manner in which anecdotes have been appropriated or developed in order to give expression to the basic janam-sākhī message. Gurū Nānak's own concern when composing *Sirī Rāg Pahare* 1 was to stress the futility of life without the divine Name. This message he repeats in a wide variety of ways, and in this particular instance he has chosen to use mercantile imagery. The basic theme of the janam-sākhī narrators is distinctively different. The message which they repeat with the same insistence is that salvation is to be found in submission to Bābā Nānak, and the corollary which this necessarily involves is that failure to make this submission can be an invitation to disaster. To give expression to this conviction the *Colebrooke* narrator or one of his predecessors has here taken a particular constituent (a shabad by Gurū Nānak) and from it has fashioned a brief anecdote demonstrating the fate of those who spurn the Gurū.

This illustrates in the simplest possible terms the manner in which one of the major constituents described in chapter 6 can be incorporated in one of the forms outlined in chapter 7. The purpose of this chapter will be to analyse other examples of the same process, particularly those which have developed more complex patterns.

[1] *AG*, pp. 74–5.

[2] *Pur JS*, pp. 28–30. *GNSR*, p. 40.

The present chapter will be concerned with sākhīs or clusters of sākhīs rather than with individual anecdotes or discourses, and for this reason a distinction which has already been mentioned must be repeated at this point. The term 'sākhī' should not be confused with the term 'anecdote'. A sākhī in its later normative usage is simply a division of a janam-sākhī (a 'chapter'). As such it may contain only one anecdote, or it may contain several. Where a multiplicity of anecdotes or discourses occurs within a single sākhī they may be expressed in a recognizable sequence, or they may be blended to form a composite 'episode'. Occasionally a sākhī will be found to contain no anecdotes at all. This variety is well illustrated by the agglomeration of miscellaneous statements which together constitute sakhi 26a of the *B40 Janam-sākhī*.[1] This consists of the following elements:

1. A statement that Bābā Nānak commenced a course of austerities (f. 102b).
2. A description of Bābā Nānak's cell (f. 102b).
3. A reference to Bābā Nānak's custom of retaining a *rabābī* (minstrel) for regular *kīrtan* (f. 102b).
4. Bābā Nānak's custom of taking an early-morning bathe, followed by devout prostrations (f. 103a).
5. A brief, incomplete reference to an unspecified meritorious deed performed by Gurū Aṅgad (f. 103b).
6. A reference to the custom of communal dining by Bābā Nānak's disciples in his presence (f. 103b).
7. The tradition that Bābā Nānak once sustained himself during a lengthy period with nothing more than a daily handful of sand and a poisonous *ak* pod (f. 103b).
8. A declaration concerning the world-wide fame of Bābā Nānak (f. 104a).

Miscellanies of this kind are unusual, but the list does at least serve to emphasize that a sākhī is essentially a division of a janam-sākhī and not necessarily a single anecdote. This should not suggest, however, that sākhīs are mere conveniences, devoid of any meaning other than the whim of a compiler. Most sākhīs, whether the single-anecdote variety or composite amalgams, deserve to be regarded as distinct units, and it is to the emergence of these units that the present chapter will be devoted. The method to be followed will consist of individual analyses of a series of representative examples.

Example 1: Bābā Nānak's visit to Multān

Narrative anecdote: simple form, direct borrowing from current tradition

The story of Bābā Nānak's encounter with the pīrs of Multān provides a simple example of an anecdote appropriated from earlier hagiography. In this instance the source is Sūfī tradition. The Sikh version retains all of the

[1] *B40*, ff. 102b–104a.

details intact, altering only the identity of the central participant. Bhāī Gurdās briefly relates the story as follows:

melio bābā uṭhiā mulatāne dī jārati jāi
agon pīr mulatān de dudhi kaṭorā bhari lai āī
bābe kaḍhi kari bagal te chambelī dudh vichi milāī
jiu sāgar vichi gang samāī

Bābā [Nānak] arose and journeyed from the [Achal] fair to Multān.
As he approached [the city] the pīrs of Multān came bringing a cup filled with milk.
Bābā [Nānak] plucked a nearby jasmine flower and laid it on the milk;
Just as the Gangā flows into the ocean![1]

As the water of the Gangā makes no evident difference to the volume of water already in the ocean, so did the jasmine make no difference to the volume of milk in the cup. Although Multān was already brim-full of pīrs there was still room for the crown and glory of them all.[2]

This particular anecdote had earlier been related in connection with ʿAbd al-Qādir Jīlānī (A.D. 1077–1166), the founder of the Qādirī order of Sūfīs. In this early version the city was Bāghdād, the cup contained water, and the flower which Jīlānī laid on the water was a rose.[3] The Jīlānī anecdote, however, was not the actual source from which Bhāī Gurdās derived his version. Prior to its appearance in Sikh tradition the legend had travelled to India where it had come to be associated with the city of Multān. In this context it had been attached to two different people, both of them celebrated Sūfīs of the city. The earlier was Bahā' al-Dīn Zakariyyā, the great Suhrawardī pīr who, according to Abu al-Fazl, died in A.D. 1266.[4] This version related the anecdote to Baha' al-Dīn's arrival in Multān from Bāghdād.[5] The second appropriation was in the name of the equally famous Sūfī pīr Shams al-Dīn Tabrīzī of the same period, who, according to legend, must bear the responsibility for having rendered the climate of Multān so unpleasantly hot.[6] This second version relates that when Shams al-Dīn first approached the city the symbolic cup was sent out by the incumbent Bahā' al-Dīn.[7] In both instances the cup contained milk, not water as in the case of the Jīlānī version.

[1] *BG* 1:44.

[2] The *Mahimā Prakāś Vāratak* offers another version of the same anecdote. See *SLTGN(Eng)*, p. 72.

[3] J. P. Brown, *The Darvishes or Oriental Spiritualism*, ed. H. A. Rose (London, 1927), pp. 100–11.

[4] *Ā'īn* III. 363. The tradition concerning Bahā' al-Dīn's actual death also appears to have been appropriated by one of the janam-sākhī traditions. Immediately prior to his death Bahā' al-Dīn is said to have received a sealed letter from 'an aged person of grave aspect'. Ibid. One janam-sākhī tradition links the deaths of both Bahā' al-Dīn and Nānak with an anachronistic exchange of letters immediately prior to their deaths. *Pur JS*, pp. 108–10. The *Mahimā Prakāś Vāratak* repeats this story, adding that Bābā Nānak subsequently received a mysterious letter which proved to be a harbinger of his death. *SLTGN(Eng)*, pp. 84–6.

[5] 'Abd al-Haq Muḥaddith Dihlawī, *Akhbār-al-Akhyār*, quoted by S. A. A. Rizvi, *Muslim Revivalist Movements in Northern India in the Sixteenth and Seventeenth Centuries* (Agra, 1965), p. 25n. The anecdote appears on page 27 of the 1914 edition of the *Akhbār-al-Akhyār*.

[6] Alexander Burnes, *Travels into Bokhara*, vol. iii (London, 1839), pp. 116–17.

[7] Lepel H. Griffin, *The Panjab Chiefs*, vol. iii (Lahore, 1890), p. 84.

The legend is particularly well suited to the concerns of hagiography and its entry into the janam-sākhī tradition need occasion no surprise. If there is any reason for surprise it is that the legend achieved only a limited circulation within the early Sikh community. The *Purātan*, *Miharbān*, *Bālā*, *Ādi Sākhīs*, and *B40* compilers all ignore it. In the eighteenth century, however, it was retrieved first by the *Gyān-ratanāvalī* and then by the *Mahimā Prakāś*. Thereafter its popularity was assured.

The Multān anecdote is an excellent example of a *Wandersage*, in this case a story which has travelled eastwards in a Sūfī form. Another such example is the ever-popular story of how Bābā Nānak claimed to be watering his Lahore fields by splashing water from Hardwār.[1] In this instance the earlier version is to be found in Buddhist tradition.[2]

Example 2: Mūlā the Khatrī

Narrative anecdote: simple form, evolved from quotation

The story of Mūlā the parsimonious Khatrī offers an uncomplicated example of a narrative anecdote which has developed out of a quotation from the works of Nānak. One day Bābā Nānak summoned Aṅgad to accompany him on a visit to 'a worldly fellow' named Mūlā the Khatrī.

> 'When I myself followed a worldly way of life this person, Mūlā the Khatrī, was my friend. If possible I should like to see him again.' And so Bābā Nānak, wearing the dress of a faqīr and accompanied by celibate *langoṭ-bands*, went and stood at the threshold of Mūlā the Khatrī's house.[3]

Mūlā's wife happened to observe the Gurū standing outside and suspecting that he had come to beg she urged her husband to conceal himself. This he did while she went out to inform Bābā Nānak that he was not at home. The Gurū was not deceived. He recited an imprecatory shalok and departed. Mūlā then emerged from his hiding-place, collapsed, and shortly afterwards died. Fortunately his companions managed to bring him to Bābā Nānak before he actually expired, and having thus beheld the Gurū (*darśan*) he died in the assurance of salvation.[4]

This brief cautionary tale has a dual origin. Its ultimate origin lies in the ascetic ideal which characterized a section of the later Sikh community and which produced several sākhīs with a distinctively austere message. Celibacy, renunciation, ascetic discipline, and respect for faqīrs are all affirmed; worldliness is proscribed. Bābā Nānak is made to fit this ideal and in a number of appropriate sākhīs is cast in the role of a celibate renunciant. The story of Mūlā the Khatrī belongs to this tradition and its earliest version is recorded within a cluster of ascetically inclined sākhīs.[5]

The story of Mūlā the Khatrī evidently developed within this tradition

[1] *B40*, ff. 76b–79a. [2] *GNSR*, p. 90. [3] *B40*, f. 100b.

[4] *B40*, ff. 100b–101b. *AS*, pp. 77–8. *Mih JS* II. 163–4. In all three janam-sākhīs the Mūlā anecdote is the second part of a composite sākhī. The first part is a brief description of Bābā Nānak's apparel, with specific reference to his adoption of both Hindū and Muslim customs; and a brief statement of his preaching methods. *B40*, f. 100a–b.

[5] See above, pp. 79–81 and below, pp. 203–4.

in the following manner. The ideal provided the impulse, and a pungent epigram by Gurū Nānak served as a nucleus. Out of this nucleus ingenuity fashioned a moralistic tale concerning the fate awaiting those who spurn faqīrs in general and the Supreme Faqīr in particular. The epigram providing the second element of the anecdote's dual origin is a couplet by Gurū Nānak which in the Ādi Granth appears as *Surplus Shaloks* 21.

nāli kirāṛā dostī eve kare guāu
maraṇu na jāpi mūliā āvai kitai ṭhāi

They who fraternize with merchants squander their affection.
Foolish one! None knows whence Death shall come.[1]

The key features of the couplet are the vocative form *mūliā*, the noun *kirāṛā*, and the mention made in the second line of the unpredictable nature of death. Although the word *mūlā* can be used as a proper name[2] the context provided by the shalok as a whole indicates that in this instance the literal meaning, 'O sad one' or 'O foolish one', is intended. The reference to *kirāṛā(n)* has been similarly misconstrued. In its literal sense the word means 'shopkeepers' or 'traders' and has been specifically applied in a somewhat pejorative sense to Khatrīs and Aroṛās. Within the context of the shalok it refers to those who 'trade' in worldly ambitions rather than in the things of God, providing thereby another example of Nānak's fondness for mercantile imagery. It has, however, been construed in a literal sense, the somewhat strained interpretation being that all traders are condemned because of one particular *kirāṛ* named Mūlā.

An anecdote has then been evolved to explain the condemnation and the result is the story of Mūlā the deceitful trader who out of niggardliness concealed himself when warned of the Gurū's approach. The second line of the couplet suggests his punishment. Bābā Nānank departs and Mūlā, overcome with shame, collapses and dies.[3] In the course of the narrative Mūlā is sometimes referred to as a *kirāṛ* and sometimes as a Khatrī. The latter designation presumably derives from the assumption that a trader or shopkeeper disciple would have been a Khatrī by caste.[4]

In the case of the Mūlā anecdote there has been a general acceptance of the janam-sākhī narrator's misinterpretation of Gurū Nānak's shalok. This is not invariably the case with all anecdotes which relate to specific references in the works of Nānak. An example of divergence is provided

[1] *B40*, f. 101a. The Ādi Granth version reads:
nāli kirāṛā dosti kūṛai kūṛī pāi
maraṇu na jāpai mūliā āvai kithai thāi
AG, p. 1412.

[2] Bhāī Gurdās refers to a disciple of Gurū Nānak named Mūlā the Kīṛ. (*BG* XI:13.) Although Kīṛ is the name of a Khatrī sub-caste Bhāī Gurdās is not referring to Mūlā the Khatrī of janam-sākhī fame. Unlike Mūlā the Khatrī, the Mūlā of whom Bhāī Gurdās makes mention is said to have been a loyal disciple, and in the *Nānak Prakāś* the two Mūlās are treated separately. *NPr* II. 38, 42. Another Mūlā, also a Khatrī, was Mūlā Choṇā, the father-in-law of Gurū Nānak.

[3] A later version of the tradition attributes his death to snake-bite. *NPr* II. 38 (69).

[4] In the area around Pakho and Kartārpur (the locality in which the story probably evolved) *kirāṛ* was normally identified with Khatrīs rather than with Aroṛās. *Census of India 1891*, vol. XIX (Calcutta, 1892), p. 290.

by the vocative form *ve lālo*, 'O beloved', which recurs in the shabad *Tilaṅg* 5.[1] The earliest janam-sākhī treatment of this shabad ignores these words and instead directs all attention to its Mughal references. For the janam-sākhī narrators the major event of the Mughal invasions was the sack of Saidpur and so the shabad takes its place within the sākhī describing this event.[2] In the *Bālā* tradition, however, the two words have been picked up and attached to another anecdote, thereby transforming it into a tale concerning a poor carpenter of Saidpur called Lālo.[3] The *Miharbān* tradition also notes the reference, but claims that the word *lālo* is an affirmative particle used by Paṭhāns.[4]

Example 3: Sajjaṇ/Bholā the Robber

Variant narrative anecdotes: simple, evolved from a common quotation

The anecdotes which have been developed out of Gurū Nānak's shabad *Sūhī* 3 are of interest for two reasons. First, they illustrate, like the preceding example, how the theme of a shabad, aided by a striking reference in its text, can prompt a narrative anecdote. Secondly, they demonstrate the manner in which a single extract from the works of Nānak can generate more than one distinct story. *Sūhī* 3 begins:

> Bronze shines brightly, but if I rub bronze it sheds an inky black.
> Though I scour it a hundred times polishing will never remove its stain.[5]

The theme of this hymn is the fate which must ineluctably overtake hypocrites and dissemblers, those who are outwardly pious but inwardly evil. This message evidently proved irresistible to the early community, for there emerged from its treatment of the shabad three distinct anecdotes with several variant forms, all describing pious rogues and all employing a recitation of *Sūhī* 3 as the means of exposing their pretences. In the *Ādi Sākhīs* the story concerns a man called Sajjaṇ, the name being derived from the word *sajaṇ* or 'friend' which Gurū Nānak uses to introduce the refrain of the shabad. The pious Sajjaṇ sits dressed in white, rosary in hand, devoutly repeating 'Rām, Rām' and dispensing water to all who pass. Bābā Nānak's recitation of *Sūhī* 3 converts him and he confesses to having murdered unsuspecting guests.[6] The *Purātan* manuscripts offer one variant of this story, the *Miharbān Janam-sākhī* a second, and the *Gyān-ratanāvalī* a third. In the *Purātan* and *Gyān-ratanāvalī* versions Sajjaṇ is said to be a *ṭhag* and is located in North India.[7] The *Miharbān Janam-sākhī* adheres more closely to the *Ādi Sākhīs* version and though much expanded is evidently derived directly from it.[8]

[1] *AG*, pp. 722–3.
[2] *B40*, ff. 66b–67a. *AS*, p. 53. *Pur JS*, p. 59.
[3] *Bālā JS*, pp. 88–9. *SLTGN(Eng)*, pp. 75–6. *GNSR*, pp. 86–7. See above, p. 87, n. 3.
[4] *Mih JS* I. 463.
[5] *AG*, p. 729.
[6] *AS*, pp. 31–3.
[7] *Pur JS*, pp. 21–2. *GR*, p. 207. The latter names Hastināpur as the location. The former merely indicates a place visited by Bābā Nānak prior to his arrival in Delhi.
[8] *Mih JS* I. 235–8.

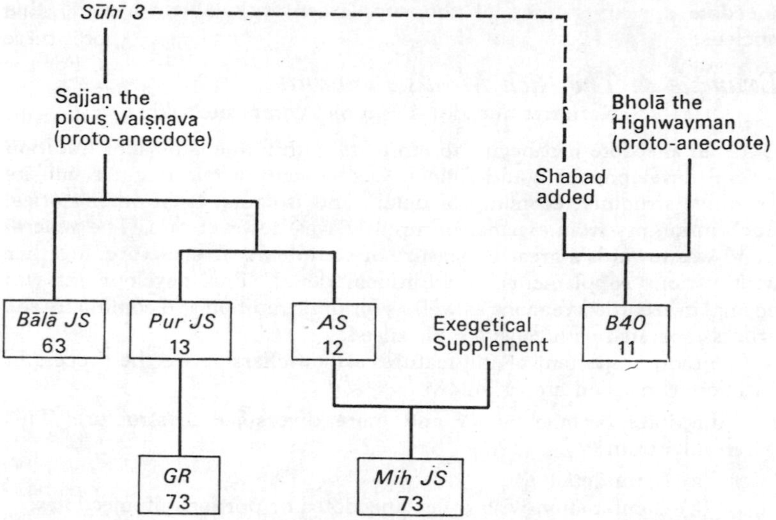

Figure 1

The *Bālā* version also concerns a hypocrite called Sajjaṇ, but portrays him as a rascally Vaiṣṇava who steals clothes.[1] This provides a second distinct tradition, and the *B40 Janam-sākhī* supplies a third. In the *B40* story yet another kind of thief appears. This time it is a highwayman named Bholā, and in the quotation of the shabad Gurū Nānak is said to have used the word *bholā*, or 'heedless one', instead of *sajaṇ*.[2]

The first two of these versions must have evolved out of the shabad, for there can be no other explanation to account for the key part which its recitation plays in the two stories. Only in the case of the *B40* version can we doubt the validity of this explanation. In this third case the story related by the janam-sākhī possesses a unity which is in no way dependent upon the shabad. A more likely explanation of the shabad's appearance in the *B40* version is that it was subsequently appended to an existing anecdote because its theme seemed to consort well with the theme of the anecdote.

The shabad *Sūhī* 3 has thus stimulated two separate stories and in addition has found a third place in the janam-sākhī traditions through incorporation within yet another tale. These anecdotes in their various versions may be diagrammatically represented as in figure 1.

One collection incorporates both the dominant Sajjaṇ version and also the Bholā anecdote. This is the so-called *Prāchīn Janam-sākhī*. The Sajjaṇ story is a part of the collection's *Purātan* foundation; and the Bholā

[1] *Bālā JS*, pp. 290–4. Although the Vaiṣṇava identity links the *Bālā* figure directly with the white-garmented rogue of the *Ādi Sākhīs* tradition, the two narratives diverge considerably.

[2] *B40*, f. 43a.

anecdote appears as one of the supplementary sākhīs added to this nucleus.[1]

Example 4: The Rich Man's Pennants

Narrative anecdotes: simple, composite sākhī

Once an anecdote had begun to circulate within a janam-sākhī tradition several developments could follow. Occasionally a tale might retain its primitive structure, economy of detail, and isolation from other stories. Such immunity from expansive impulses was however rare. The general trend was towards a greater measure of complexity in structure, together with various supplements of additional detail. This development was normal in recorded versions as well as for oral tradition and commonly the process operated with considerable speed.

The more important of the features which characterize the process of anecdote expansion are as follows:

1. Anecdotes become longer and more diversified in structure. This results from:
   (a) Extra detail
   (b) Combination with other anecdotes or portions of anecdotes.
2. Quotations from the works of Gurū Nānak are added.
3. Personal details are added
   (names of participants, their occupations, details of dress and appearance, etc.).
4. Specific locations are added.
5. Sākhīs are arranged in chronological order according to locations.
   (4 and 5 are commonly simultaneous processes.)
6. The more striking details (including miracles) tend to become exaggerated.
7. Anachronisms become more numerous.
8. Passages serving an apologetic or pedagogical purpose are added.

Although these eight features are rarely to be found within a single sākhī they are all common and the later janam-sākhīs provide an abundance of examples. All eight can be illustrated by comparing two extant versions of the anecdote 'The Rich Man's Pennants'. This tale has been recorded in a relatively primitive form by the *B40* compiler from a source which appears to have been the oral tradition of his area.[2] A much more developed version is to be found in the *Purātan* janam-sākhīs (both *Colebrooke* and *Hāfizābād*), and from a comparison of the *B40* and *Purātan* narratives it can at once be seen how the proto-anecdote has developed within a particular tradition.

The *B40* version is as follows:

The Rich Man's Pennants

Bābā Nānak left that place and appeared in another country. In the city to which he had come four pennants were fluttering aloft. Bābā Nānak asked what kind of

[1] Sevā Singh Sevak, *Prāchīn Janam-sākhī* (Jalandhar, 1969), pp. 27–33, 250–1.

[2] See *B40(Eng)*, Introduction, pp. 12–13, 22.

pennants they were and the people replied, 'There is a wealthy money-lender here. He has four coffers containing a large hoard of treasure and to signify this he flies four pennants over them.'

Bābā Nānak went to the money-lender and asked him, 'Shāh, what kind of pennants are these which have been hoisted up there?'

'Those pennants will accompany me after my death,' replied the money-lender.

Bābā Nānak then gave the money-lender a needle and said, 'Brother Shāh, keep this needle safe. I shall ask you to return it in heaven.' Having said this he arose and departed.

Later the money-lender began to worry. 'How can I take this needle with me when I die?' he asked himself. 'And how can I deliver it to that faqīr in heaven? I shall be put to shame.'

He arose and ran after Bābā Nānak, and after running more than two *kos* he caught up with him. Prostrating himself he said, 'Take back your needle. There is no point in my keeping it.'

'Shāh,' replied Bābā Nānak, 'if there is no point in keeping this needle of mine, then how can these four treasure-chests accompany you when you die?'.

Then the portals of the money-lender's understanding opened. Error was swept away! Joining his hands in supplication he stood before Bābā Nānak and begged for forgiveness. Bābā Nānak was overjoyed.

The money-lender then returned, gave away all his possessions, and applied himself to the threefold discipline of repeating the divine Name, giving charity, and regular bathing. He became a Sikh and found happiness. The transmigratory round of death and rebirth was broken, for the grace of the supreme Sādhū had come upon him. He had found happiness![1]

This simple version should be compared with the *Purātan* narrative, which here follows the *Hāfizābād* version. The *Colebrooke* version differs only slightly.

A. The Gurū then proceeded to Lahore on the River Rāvī. The karoṛī of the *pargana* of Lahore was Dūnī Chand, a Dhuppaṛ Khatrī. His father's *srāddh* was being held when he heard that Nānak the Ascetic had arrived. He went and reverently brought Bābā Nānak to his house. Bābā Nānak went in and sat down, and Dūnī Chand ordered milk, curd, and wood to be brought in from outside. When everything was ready he fed the Brāhmaṇs who had been invited for the *śrāddh* ceremony.

Bābā Nānak was also invited and when he arrived he asked, 'What are you celebrating?'.

'It is my father's *śrāddh*,' he replied. 'I have fed Brāhmaṇs in his name.'

'It is now the third day since your father had food,' said Bābā Nānak, 'and you say "I have fed a hundred Brāhmaṇs".'

'Where is he?' asked Dūnī Chand.

'He is lying under a *mal* tree, five *kos* away,' replied Bābā Nānak. 'He has been reborn as a wolf. But take food and go without fear. When he recognizes you his human intelligence will return. He will eat the food and speak with you.'

Dūnī Chand took food and went to the wolf. He prostrated himself, set down the food, and asked, 'Father, why have you been incarnated thus?'

The wolf replied, 'I was the disciple of a man who was scrupulous in the observance of his duties. It so happened that he had left a fish near me. When the

[1] *B40*, ff. 189a–190a.

hour of my death arrived I was suffering and the fish was stewing beside me. Its smell assailed me and I desired it. As a result I received this incarnation.'

The wolf arose and fled. Dūnī Chand returned and prostrated himself before the Gurū.

B. Dūnī Chand then took the Gurū to his home. Over his door were seven pennants, each representing a lakh of rupees. 'Whose are these pennants?' the Gurū inquired, to which Dūnī Chand replied, 'These pennants are mine.' Bābā Nānak then gave him a needle and said, 'Keep it safe for me. I shall ask for it in the hereafter.'

Dūnī Chand took the needle to his wife and said, 'Keep this needle. The Gurū gave it to me saying, "I shall ask for it in the hereafter." '

'Good God!' exclaimed his wife. 'Will this needle accompany you to the hereafter?'

'What can I do?' asked Dūnī Chand.

'Go and give it back,' answered his wife.

Dūnī Chand took the needle back to Bābā Nānak and said, 'This needle will not go with me into the hereafter. Please take it back.'

'If a needle cannot get there,' replied the Gurū, 'how will these pennants get there?'

Dūnī Chand bowed before him and said, 'Give me that which will go into the hereafter.'

'Give in God's Name,' answered the Gurū. 'Feed ascetics (*atīt*) and wandering holy men (*abhiāgat*), for it is in this manner that your wealth will be carried into the hereafter.'

Dūnī Chand distributed the seven lakhs of rupees symbolized by the pennants. He obeyed the command. The Gurū's command is such that whoever obeys it finds salvation. Dūnī Chand became a Name-believing disciple (*naudhariku sikh*) and began repeating 'Gurū, Gurū'. Bābā Nānak then said, 'Mardānā, play the rabāb" Mardānā played the rabāb.

[There follows a quotation from *Vār Āsā*]

The *vār* is to be completed later. Utter: 'Praise to the Gurū!'[1]

The eight features noted above are illustrated by the *Purātan* narrative in the following manner:

1. (a) The rich man's wife is introduced.
   (b) The anecdote B which in the *B40 Janam-sākhī* stands alone has been linked to an entirely separate anecdote A concerning a man who wasted money on futile ceremonies.
2. A quotation from *Vār Āsā* has been added.
3. The rich man has been named Dūnī Chand, his sub-caste is given as Dhuppaṛ Khatrī, and he is said to have been a government official of high rank (*karoṛī*)
4. The composite sākhī is set in 'Lahore on the river Rāvī'. (The *B40* compiler has also specified a location, namely the town of Gujrāt. This he does only in his table of contents.[2] The actual sākhī includes no such reference.)

[1] M. A. Macauliffe (ed.), *Janam Sākhī Bābe Nānak Jī kī* (Rāwalpiṇḍī, 1885), pp. 175–9. *Pur JS*, pp. 70–1. The quotation from *Vār Āsā* consists of *pauṛī* 10 with shaloks. *AG*, p. 468.

[2] *B40*, f. 228b (Arabic pagination).

5. The sākhī is set within the context of a tour of the Pañjāb which, according to the distinctive *Purātan* chronology, followed Bābā Nānak's return from his first major journey. The previous sākhī is set in a place near Pasrūr, approximately fifty miles from Lahore.[1] The narrator responsible for the *Purātan* sequence then brings the Gurū down to Lahore and the Rāvī river. Two unlocated sākhīs follow and the *Hāfizābād* compiler then introduces another incident on the banks of the Rāvī.[2]
6. The rich man has graduated from the status of a mere money-lender to that of a high government official; and the four pennants of the *B40* version have become seven. Each of these *Purātan* pennants represents a lakh of rupees instead of a coffer of treasure.
7. The rich man is anachronistically described as a karoṛī. The title was instituted by Akbar after the death of Nānak.
8. Two distinctive beliefs are given direct and emphatic expression in the *Purātan* version.
   (a) The authority of the Gurū: 'The Gurū's command is such that whoever obeys it finds salvation.' The *Colebrooke* version also adds as an explanation for the fate of Dūnī Chand's reincarnated father: 'I received this incarnation because I was without the perfected Gurū.'[3]
   (b) The ascetic ideal, and, specifically, deference to ascetics: 'Give in God's Name. Feed ascetics and wandering holy men, for it is in this manner that your wealth will be carried into the hereafter.'[4] At the beginning of the sākhī the Gurū is referred to as 'Nānak Tapā', Nanak the Ascetic.

Three concluding points may be noted. The first is that the relatively sophisticated commentators and redactors of the *Miharbān* tradition sometimes reverse the normal process in the case of miracles, excising rather than multiplying. In other respects, however, they follow the general pattern, commonly to a degree which far outstrips all other traditions.[5] Secondly, the *Purātan* version of the anecdote discussed above, although appreciably more developed than that of the *B40 Janam-sākhī*, is nevertheless still essentially primitive. It has not attained the measure of complexity which distinguishes a highly evolved version. Thirdly, it should be stressed that evolved products are not necessarily later in terms of time than more primitive analogues. The *B40* version of 'The Rich Man's Pennants' was drawn from an oral tradition and recorded approximately one hundred years after the *Purātan* version emerged in its present form.

[1] Sākhī 36. *Pur JS*, p. 66.
[2] Sākhī 40. Ibid., p. 73.
[3] Ibid., p. 71.
[4] Macauliffe's rendering of this sentence illustrates the arbitrary manner in which he altered his janam-sākhī material in order to bring it into accord with the known beliefs and teachings of Gurū Nānak. 'Give some of thy wealth in God's name, feed the poor, and thy wealth shall accompany thee.' Macauliffe, i. 130.
[5] The *Miharbān Janam-sākhī* does not include the anecdote discussed in this example.

Example 5: Bābā Nānak returns to Talvaṇḍī

Narrative discourse: simple, combined with narrative anecdote.

Most janam-sākhīs include in their accounts of how Bābā Nānak returned home after his travels a discourse based upon the shabad *Sirī Rāg* 7.[1] Having greeted him, his mother and later his father seek to divert him from his chosen path of itinerant sanctity. *Siri Rāg* 7 is unusually well suited to the construction of a discourse, and the result as it appears in the *B40*, *Ādi Sākhīs*, *Purātan*, and *Miharbān* collections is one of the most consistent examples of this form that the janam-sākhīs can offer.[2]

The theme of the shabad is self-denial and the choice is accordingly an appropriate one for the narrator's purpose. Gurū Nānak opens it with the following stanza and refrain:

> To believe in the divine Name is to taste all sweet flavours;
> to hear it all the salty.
> To utter the divine Name is to taste all tart flavours;
> to sing it all the spicy.
> In single-minded love of the Name lie the thirty-six delectable flavours, but only he can love like this upon whom falls the gracious glance of the Lord. 1.
> Bābā, to eat any other food would be to turn joy into suffering.
> He who eats it brings agony to his body and liberates evil within his *man*. *Refrain*

The narrator's task is an easy one. The vocative *bābā* is changed to *mātā* ('Mother, to eat . . .') and from the amended quotation has been fashioned the following introductory narrative:

> His mother laid the sweets and clothing before him and said, 'Eat, my son.'
> 'I am already filled,' replied Bābā Nānak.
> 'How can you have eaten your fill in this wasteland, my son?' asked his mother.
> 'Mardānā, play the measure *Sirī Rāg* on the rabāb,' commanded Bābā Nānak.
> Mardānā played *Sirī Rāg* and Bābā Nānak sang a shabad . . .[3]

This narrative is then followed by stanza 1 and the amended refrain.

The second stanza continues the same kind of imagery, so characteristic of Gurū Nānak's style.

> Let the crimson which you wear be a steeping of your *man* in God, and let your white be the giving of charity.
> Let your blue be the removal of the stain of falsehood and meditation the garment which you put on.
> I have bound around myself the sash of spiritual contentment. Thy Name, O Lord, is all my wealth and all my joy. 2.
> Bābā, to wear other garments would be to turn joy into suffering.
> He who arrays himself in any other brings agony to his body and liberates evil within his *man*. *Refrain*

Given this answer the narrator frames another suitable comment to precede it.

[1] *AG*, pp. 16–17.

[2] *B40*, ff. 34b–36a. *AS*, pp. 46–7. *Pur JS*, pp. 50–1. *Mih JS* 1.476–8.

[3] *B40*, f. 34b.

After he had concluded the first stanza his mother said,
'Remove that faqīr's robe and put on these new clothes.'
Bābā Nānak then sang the second stanza . . .[1]

The Gurū's mother then withdraws and his father offers him a mare. An offer of this kind might, under the circumstances, have seemed incongruous, but not when one observes that the third stanza refers to horses and riding equipment.[2] In this manner a narrative discourse of the standard comment-and-answer variety is constructed. The quotations from *Sirī Rāg* 7 provide ready-made answers for Bābā Nānak to utter, and on the basis of this given material the narrator devises suitable comments or questions for the interlocutors. Bābā Nānak's fourth stanza clinches the issue, and the discourse is brought to a rapid close.

The discourse which has thus been developed represents the dominant janam-sākhī usage of *Sirī Rāg* 7. It is not however the only one. *Sirī Rāg* 7 is of interest not merely because it has prompted a narrative discourse of unusual consistency, but also because within a different tradition it has been applied to an entirely different set of imaginary circumstances. The pattern outlined above belongs to the tradition which will later be designated *Narrative I*.[3] In contrast to this *Narrative I* product the *Bālā* tradition has developed from the same shabad a discourse set in the village of Pakho, with Mūlā Choṇā and Ajittā Randhāvā cast in the role of interlocutors. The actual questions inevitably correspond to a considerable degree, for both sets have been derived from the same given text. It is the setting devised for the discourse which differs and the difference is at once striking. In the *Bālā* version it is Mūlā Choṇā who offers the food and clothing, and Ajittā Randhāvā who offers the mare.[4]

The gap between the two traditions widens still further when later compilers link their *Sirī Rāg* 7 discourse with other anecdotes. In the dominant *Narrative I* tradition a partnership is formed with Bābā Nānak's homecoming sākhī, an anecdote which in the *Bālā* tradition is completely divorced from the *Sirī Rāg* 7 discourse. At an early stage the shabad *Vaḍahaṃsa* 1 has been added to the composite sākhī, and somewhat later a *Purātan* compiler has appended two more shabads, *Sūhī Chhant* 4 and *Mārū* 1.[5] Later still *Miharbān* commentators have added a shalok from *Vār Sāraṅg*, the shabads *Sirī Rāg* 4 and *Mārū* 5, extra details, and the usual quantity of *Miharbān* exegesis.[6] The *Bālā* compiler, on the other hand, has preserved the isolation of his *Sirī Rāg* 7 discourse. To the homecoming anecdote he has added an apocryphal shabad in the *Rāmkalī* measure and linked to it an episode concerning Rāi Bulār, the landlord of Talvaṇḍī.[7]

The various traditions have thus used a common shabad and a common anecdote in differing ways. The patterns of expansion and their relationship may be represented as in figure 2.

[1] *B40*, f. 35a.
[2] Because the interlocutor is now Nānak's father the vocative *bābā* can be retained.
[3] See below, pp. 181–5.
[4] *Bālā JS*, sākhī 70, pp. 312–14.
[5] *Pur JS*, pp. 49, 51. *AG*, pp. 557, 765, 989.
[6] *Mih JS* 1.475, 479–81, 482–4. *AG*, pp. 1243, 15, 990.
[7] *Bālā JS*, sākhī 22, pp. 93–9.

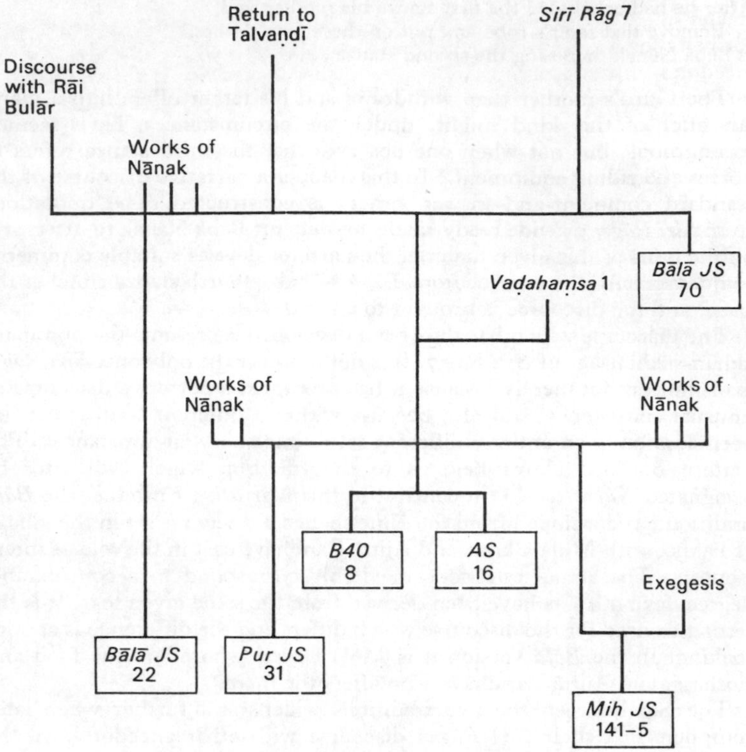

Figure 2

The five sākhīs so far discussed are all examples of relatively uncomplicated processes. Each includes either one or two anecdotes, and where two occur they are linked by means of simple juxtaposition. For various reasons they have proved resistant to incorporation within sākhīs of a more complex character. Although many anecdotes have preserved this measure of isolation, such simplicity of form and structure is by no means an invariable rule. Many other anecdotes obviously lost their independence very quickly. Instead of remaining isolated and subject in terms of sequence to the discretion of later compilers they were soon associated with other anecdotes and transmitted in an assimilated form. This process is particularly common in the case of anecdotes relating to the same person, place, incident, or theme.

In some instances various anecdotes associated in this manner have been blended to form a single composite sākhī. The earlier versions of these composite sākhīs normally betray clear indications of their diverse origins, but in the course of transmission the sharp divisions are blurred and a greater measure of unity is achieved. One or perhaps two anecdotes normally provide a focus for the composite sākhī, and these central anecdotes almost always survive any excising tendencies to which later narrators may occasionally be prone. Others of marginal significance to the central theme may drop away, although the general tendency favours expansion of a received tradition rather than contraction.

Three useful examples of this blending process are provided by the sākhīs set in Pāk Paṭṭan, Mecca, and Achal. In the first of these (example 6) the focus is a particular person, namely Sheikh Braham (Sheikh Ibrāhīm). This is a first step, and no more than a first step, in the movement away from simplicity. Although this sākhī in its various versions is more complex than any of the examples already discussed it was not a complexity which imposed serious demands upon the ingenuity of any janam-sākhī narrator. The measure of coherence sustained by the narrators in this lengthy sākhī was already implicit in the selection of quotations which provide a basis for the discourse.

A more subtle blend is demonstrated by the evolved Mecca sākhī (example 7). In this instance the factor primarily responsible for drawing together a number of separate anecdotes was their common setting, with a common theme aiding the process. In the case of the composite Achal sākhī (example 8 *inter alia*) the common theme provided the dominant impulse, with a common location serving a subsidiary role.

An even more impressive example of narrative skill and the blending of several anecdotes is to be found in the Rājā Śivanābh sākhī (example 9). This is the more impressive because it lacks the obvious focus provided by a common person, place, incident, or theme. The sākhī in its evolved form possesses a measure of unity which does much to obscure the multiplicity of its antecedents.

In all of these instances the end product in the more evolved janam-sākhīs has been a single sākhī. This is the general rule, but not an invariable one. In a few cases anecdotes with a common focus have retained their essential distinctions and instead of merging in a single, integrated sākhī have been transmitted as a cluster. This process is illustrated by the various anecdotes concerning Gurū Aṅgad which appear in the narrative janam-sākhis (example 10). In even fewer cases the result is neither a composite sākhī nor a cluster, but a recurrent reappearance within well-defined circumstances of a person who serves a distinctive function. This feature is illustrated in the last of the examples by the person of Mardānā the Bard (example 11).

Example 6: Bābā Nānak's discourse with Sheikh Braham

Narrative discourse and exegetical supplements: complex composite sākhī

A series of shaloks attributed to Sheikh Farīd have prompted a narrative discourse of unusual length and consistency. Although in this instance the germinal passages are not actually by Gurū Nānak the process which has operated upon them is the same. Quotations from the works of Gurū Nānak have subsequently been added in order to extend the discourse. Later versions contain more of these extra quotations, together with appropriate questions to introduce them, and the *Miharbān* treatment is distinguished by its customary fund of exegetical material.

The sākhī begins in all versions with an account of how Bābā Nānak once visited Pāk Paṭṭan,[1] the town in which was situated the Sūfī *khānqāh* established in the thirteenth century by the celebrated Sheikh Farīd-al-Dīn Mas'ūd Ganj-i-Shakar. There he held discourse with Sheikh Braham, a successor of Farīd. Sheikh Braham may be safely identified with Sheikh Ibrāhīm (born A.D. 1450), the twelfth successor of Farīd.[2] Because Nānak and Sheikh Ibrāhīm were contemporaries and because Pāk Paṭṭan lay within easy reach of the Pañjāb a meeting between the two must be regarded as at least a possibility. It should not, however, be inferred that any such meeting was directly responsible for the genesis of the sākhī entitled 'Bābā Nānak's Discourse with Sheikh Braham'. Its genesis is to be found not in this incident, if in fact it took place, but rather in a small group of shaloks bearing the name of Farīd.

Shaloks attributed to Sheikh Farīd had long been current in the Pañjāb and a selection had been included by Gurū Arjan in the Ādi Granth.[3] Several of these shaloks were cast in an interlocutory form and were for this reason admirably suited to inclusion within the pattern of a dialogue. The original Farīd had died in 1265, and although the janam-sākhīs of the *Purātan* tradition do include a sākhī relating an encounter with the first Farīd[4] the more sophisticated narrators would have recognized this as an impossibility. It so happened, however, that Sheikh Ibrāhīm, the contemporary of Gurū Nānak, was commonly known as Farīd Sānī, or 'Farīd the Second'. This may mean that the shaloks bearing the name of Farīd were in fact the work of Farīd Sānī, or it may merely have suggested to the janam-sākhī narrators that this was the case.[5] For reasons sound or mistaken the identification with Farīd Sānī, or Sheikh Ibrāhīm, was certainly assumed. The interlocutory tone of the shaloks implied discourse and from this there evidently followed the belief that the discourse which provided their original context was a conversation between Bābā Nānak and his contemporary Sheikh Ibrāhīm, erroneously called Sheikh Braham.

This process may have been encouraged by a tradition that Gurū Nānak had once visited Pāk Paṭṭan, and it is possible that such a tradition could

[1] Multān District, now in Pakistan.

[2] Lajwanti Rama Krishna, *Panjabi Sufi Poets* (Calcutta, 1938), p. 1.

[3] *AG*, pp. 1377–84.

[4] *Pur JS*, pp. 40–5. This sākhī illustrates the same process. It owes its origin partly to shaloks attributed to Farīd (only one of which is in the Ādi Granth), to two shabads attributed to Farīd in the Ādi Granth, and to shabads of Gurū Nānak. In this case, however, other processes have also operated. Some of the shabads have been added later, and earlier legends associated with Farīd have been worked into the discourse.

[5] W. H. McLeod, 'The Influence of Islam upon the Thought of Gurū Nānak', in ***Sikhism and Indian Society*** (Transactions of the Indian Institute of Advanced Study, vol. iv, Simla, 1967), pp. 296–7.

have derived from an actual incident. Even if no such tradition existed prior to the development of the discourse Pāk Paṭṭan would have been the obvious choice of location for the evolving discourse. In either case it is of secondary importance. For the actual origin and the substance of the discourse attention must be directed to the verses which were currently in circulation and which are now embedded in the sākhī. Both origin and substance are to be found in the Farīd shaloks, together with a few compositions by Gurū Nānak which seemed to accord with the occasion and with the tenor of the discourse. Four of the Farīd shaloks are included in the Ādi Granth collection. Two are extra-canonical.

With the solitary exception of Bhāī Gurdās all the important janam-sākhī traditions relate versions of this narrative discourse.[1] There are many minor variants in style and, as usual, the material progressively expands as the line of transmission grows longer. There can, however, be no doubt that all are based upon a common proto-discourse. This proto-discourse was formed by the addition of connecting passages of dialogue to the core provided by the verses. A visit to Pāk Paṭṭan provided an appropriate setting and the proto-discourse was then complete. Extra verses with related dialogue were later added, and later still we have the inevitable introduction of lengthy expository passages in the *Miharbān* version of the tradition.

If the analysis is confined to the *Colebrooke*, *Hāfizābād*, and *B40* janam-sākhīs the process may be diagrammatically illustrated as in figure 3. *Q1* represents a hypothetical manuscript which, for reasons to be discussed later, must have been used by the compilers of the *Hāfizābād* and *B40* janam-sākhīs.[2] Although in general the anecdotes recorded by this manuscript must have been briefer than their *Colebrooke* analogues, the Sheikh Braham discourse provides an instance of a *Q1* sākhī which is slightly more expanded than the corresponding *Colebrooke* version. An extra shalok (*Vār Malār* 23:1) which must have been added by the compiler of *Q1* appears in both *Hāfizābād* and *B40*, thereby distinguishing them from *Colebrooke*.

The pattern becomes a little more complicated when the *Ādi Sākhīs* version is introduced into the comparison. This version lacks the extra shalok and in consequence resembles the *Colebrooke* analogue rather than those of *Hāfizābād* or *B40*. The resemblance does not, however, amount to complete identity, and when other anecdotes common to all four collections are added to the comparison it becomes clear that the *Ādi Sākhīs* connection with *Hāfizābād* and *B40* is actually closer than its connection with *Colebrooke*. The introduction of the additional anecdotes also shows that the *Hāfizābād* compiler used not only *Q1* but also *Colebrooke*, or a manuscript very close to it. The pattern which now emerges is as shown in figure 4.

[1] *B40*, ff. 57b–65b. *Pur JS*, pp. 52–6. *AS*, pp. 47–52. *Mih JS* 1.488–510. *Bala JS*, pp. 360–77. *GR*, pp. 58–89, 509–10. *LDP 194*, ff. 45a–74a *passim*. (This portion of the manuscript includes some extraneous material.)

[2] See below, p. 191.

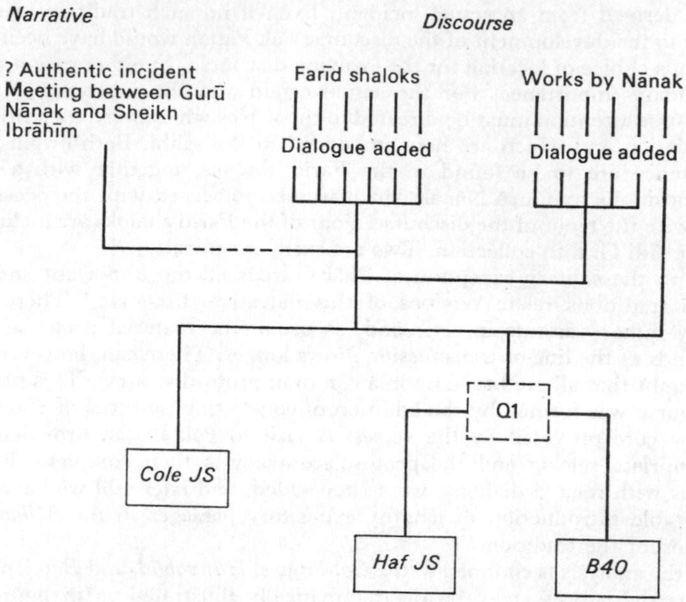

Figure 3

Further complications are introduced when the *Miharbān* version of the discourse is compared with the four represented above.[1] Although the *Miharbān* version includes all the quotations given by *Hāfizābād* and *B40* it cannot be assumed that any of the *Miharbān* redactors had access to *Q1*. The earliest *Miharbān* collection appears to predate *Q1*. To this original collection extra quotations were added, one of them the shalok which distinguishes *Hāfizābād* and *B40*. In addition to the extra quotations lengthy passages of exegesis were also introduced, thereby converting the original anecdote into three consecutive didactic discourses of the typical *Miharbān* variety.

This much is predictable for it merely illustrates the standard pattern of *Miharbān* growth. Less typical is the fact that some of the expanded *Miharbān* material has found its way into the *B40* version of the discourse. The *B40* version adds to the *Q1* text an extra quotation and five exegetical passages which can only have come from a *Miharbān* source.[2] A comparison with the extant *Miharbān Janam-sākhī* confirms this, and also indicates that the *Miharbān* version utilized by the *B40* compiler was a recension earlier than the extant text.

[1] *Mih JS* 1.488–508.

[2] The extra quotation is *Sirī Rāg* 33 (first stanza and refrain, part of second stanza and second refrain). *B40*, ff. 64a, 64b. The exegetical passages follow the quotations given on folios 60a–63a.

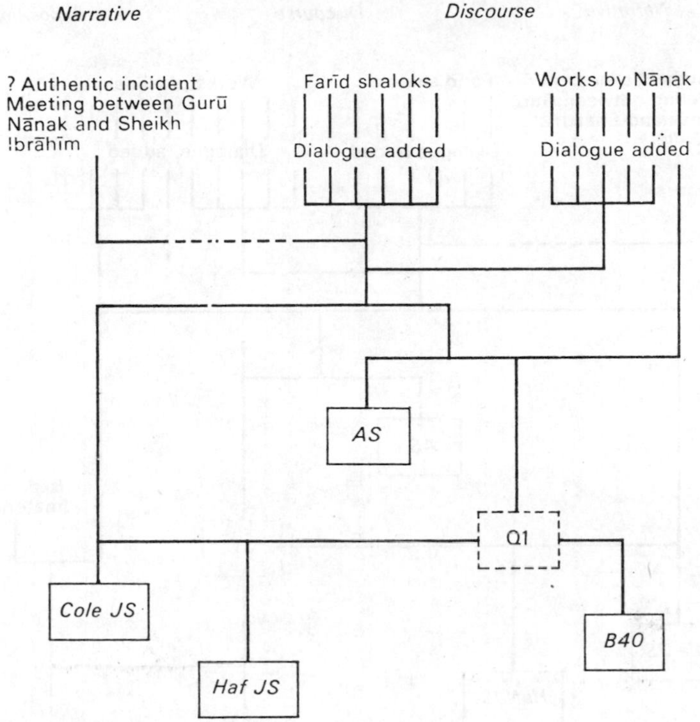

Figure 4

The addition of the *Miharbān* version of the discourse produces the extended pattern shown in figure 5.

Even this is not the full measure of the complexity, for the diagram omits the *Bālā*, *Gyān-ratanāvalī*, and *LDP 194* versions. It does, however, represent the principal components of the complete pattern, together with a sufficient indication of the growth process which has operated in all versions of the discourse.

Example 7: Bābā Nānak's visit to Mecca

Narrative anecdotes with subsidiary discourses and exegetical supplements: complex composite sākhī

Few janam-sākhī anecdotes can equal in popularity the tales concerning Bābā Nānak's visit to Mecca and Medīnā. The latter city is not mentioned in all versions, but in every janam-sākhī which is more than a mere fragment there is to be found an account of a journey to Mecca. The story is a particularly popular one, both because of its dramatic interest and for the function which it performs. There are, in fact, several distinct anecdotes

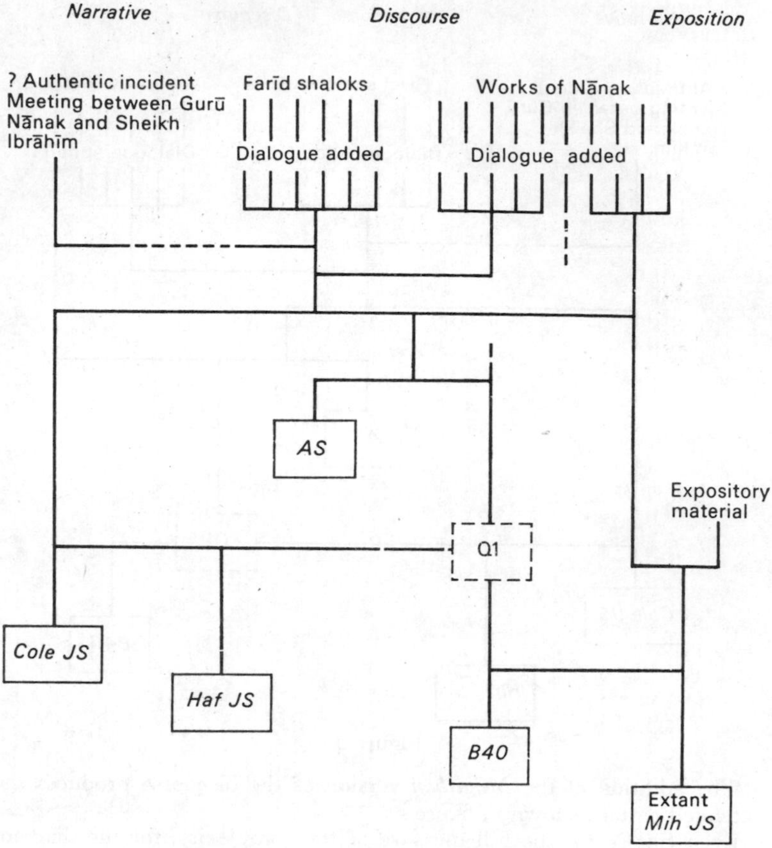

Figure 5

which the janam-sākhīs set in Mecca and which later compilers combine within single sākhīs. All have a common theme, through which they fulfil a common function. The common theme, the triumph of Bābā Nānak over Islam, is represented in three different ways corresponding to three original anecdotes.

There is, first, the entry of a Hindu into the forbidden city. The janam-sākhīs stress Nānak's identity as a Hindu, contrasting this with the insistence of various Muslims that no Hindu can ever enter the city. With divine assistance the impossible is achieved, thereby proclaiming the sanction of God upon the work of Nānak and the unique power which he possessed as a result of his divine commission.[1]

[1] Concerning the proscription of unbelievers from entering Mecca see the Qur'ān 9:28–9 and Reuben Levy, *The Social Structure of Islam* (Cambridge, 1962), p. 3. It has been suggested that

The same claim is expressed through the other two episodes which have descended from individual anecdotes to the composite Mecca sākhī of the later versions. The *miharāb* which moves as Nānak's feet are dragged round by an irate qāzī obviously moves in response to divine intervention, thereby confounding the representative of Islam and proclaiming once again the seal of divine authority upon Nānak. Even the *qibla* moves in response to the position occupied by Bābā Nānak. This claim, which evidently follows Sūfī precedents, is here applied to one who patently stood outside the bounds of Islam. Less spectacular but equally emphatic in making the same point is the religious discussion which, in its many different versions, Nānak is said to have held with qāzīs, mullahs, pīrs, and pilgrims in Mecca. The principal interlocutor in this discourse, and occasionally the only one, is said to have been the Sūfī Sheikh Rukn al-Dīn.

In these three anecdotes it may be seen how closely allied are the purpose and the function of the janam-sākhīs. All three attribute to Nānak an authority which is divine, unique, and invincible, an authority which is set in successful conflict with another claimant to the same titles in the same period and within the same geographical area. Such a claim demands a common loyalty from all who own Nānak as Master. At the same time it offers the assurance of divine approval upon the chosen Master and a corresponding assurance of salvation to those who follow him. In this manner it assists the efforts of the emergent Nānak-panthī community towards a distinctive identity, and at all subsequent stages of the community's development serves to strengthen its cohesion.

The common theme of these three episodes soon led to amalgamation in a single Mecca sākhī. The fact that the three anecdotes originally existed as separate expressions of the common theme is made clear by the testimony of the *B40 Janam-sākhī* and by an analysis of the single composite sākhīs which we find in the later versions. Amalgamation did not, however, follow a common pattern in all traditions, and in order to understand its various permutations the different traditions must be treated separately. In figure 6 an attempt is made to represent the distinctive *Purātan* pattern.[1]

As the diagram indicates, the three episodes which are combined in the

this proscription may not have been operative during the early sixteenth century. S. A. A. Rizvi in Harbans Singh (ed.), *Perspectives on Guru Nanak* (Paṭiālā, 1975), p. 216. The experience of the Italian traveller Ludovico di Varthema indicates that it must indeed have been operative during this period. When in 1503 Varthema decided to visit Mecca he clearly felt compelled to make the journey and the actual entry in disguise. The disguise which he chose for the purpose was that of a *mamlūk*. When challenged in the city he endeavoured to sustain his disguise. Only behind closed doors and when satisfied that his challenger would not betray him did he finally acknowledge that he was an Italian. Even then he continued to maintain the pretence that he was a Muslim. *The Itinerary of Ludovico di Varthema of Bologna*, trans. W. Jones, ed. Richard Carnac Temple (London, 1928), pp. 12–23. It is evident that Pêro da Covilhã, who visited Mecca between late 1491 and early 1493, also disguised himself as a Muslim. Conde de Ficalho, *Viagens de Pedro da Covilhan* (Lisbon, 1898), pp. 124–5.

[1] *Pur JS*, sākhī 51, pp. 98–104. For an English translation of the *Purātan* Mecca sākhī (*Colebrooke* version) see E. Trumpp, *The Ādi Granth* (London, 1877), pp. xl–xlii. See also *GNSR*, p. 49.

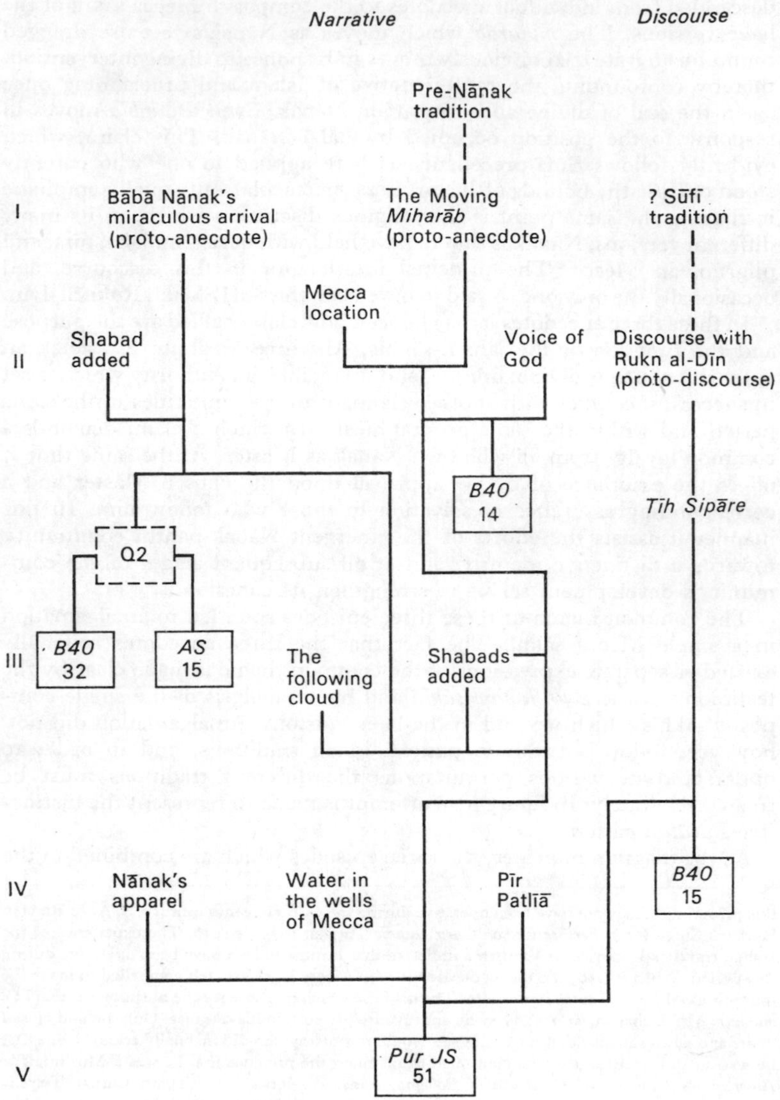
Narrative
Discourse
Pre-Nānak tradition
I
Bābā Nānak's miraculous arrival (proto-anecdote)
The Moving Miharāb (proto-anecdote)
? Sūfī tradition
Mecca location
II
Shabad added
Voice of God
Discourse with Rukn al-Dīn (proto-discourse)
B40 14
Tīh Sipāre
Q2
III
B40 32
AS 15
The following cloud
Shabads added
IV
Nānak's apparel
Water in the wells of Mecca
Pīr Patlīā
B40 15
V
Pur JS 51

Figure 6

single *Purātan* sākhī are still separate in the *B40 Janam-sākhī*.[1] This at once suggests that although the *B40* collection was actually compiled after the formation of the *Purātan* tradition its versions of the three anecdotes represent in each case an early stage in the evolution of the later sākhī. Such an assumption would indeed be correct, but it should not be carried to the point of concluding that any of the three represents an original version. An analysis of the *B40* analogues will show that they are themselves the product of a period of development and that none of them can be regarded as an accurate representation of a proto-anecdote. They are of interest merely as identifiable stages in the process which eventually produced the composite *Purātan* sākhī. In one instance it is evident that the *B40* compiler has used a source to which the *Ādi Sākhīs* compiler also had access (a hypothetical manuscript designated *Q2*).[2]

Although the *B40* analogues are thus to be regarded as more primitive than the *Purātan* sākhī it would be a mistake to assume that the three anecdotes as they appear in the *B40 Janam-sākhī* should all be placed at the same stage of development. The *B40* versions of 'The Miraculous Arrival' and 'The Moving *Miharāb*' are earlier products than the same manuscript's version of the Rukn al-Dīn discourse. The Rukn al-Dīn encounter, as it appears in the *B40* collection, embodies the kind of heterodox discourse (in this case the so-called *Tīh Sipāre*) which marks a later stage than the two wonder-stories. For this reason the *B40* sākhīs have been set at differing points in the diagram. The moving *miharāb* anecdote, lacking any scriptural supplements, has been represented as a second-stage product; the miraculous arrival anecdote, with its supplementary shabad, has been set at stage III; and the discourse has been aligned with stage IV. It should be emphasized that in this diagrammatic form these stages are intended to represent no more than highly simplified steps in what can commonly be a complex pattern of development.

From these three stages it is possible to work back to stage I archetypes. The story of 'The Journey to Mecca' is, in its *B40* form, very brief and simple, but to it has been added a shabad which will not have been a part of the earliest version of the tradition. There appears to be no reason to doubt that the proto-anecdote must have closely resembled the *B40* version without its attached shabad.

The *B40* account of 'The Moving *Miharāb*' is similarly primitive, and although it too has been supplemented the extra material is not a scriptural quotation. The voice from the cupola pronouncing a blessing upon Nānak is evidently a version of the highly popular 'Divine Voice' which in hagiographical traditions is a stock method of expressing divine sanction or approval.[3] Because this element appears in no other version it can be assumed that it was not a part of the proto-anecdote.

[1] *B40* sākhīs 14, 15, and 32, ff. 51b–55b, 133a–135a. Although the *B40* compiler has recorded two of the anecdotes consecutively, he has taken all three from different sources. See below, p. 230–1.

[2] See below, p. 198.

[3] A common variant is the 'Voice from the Tomb' communicating guidance from a deceased saint or from the Prophet Muhammad himself. Rukn al-Dīn is said to have indicated his final resting-place in this manner. *ASI* v. 133.

It seems likely that the location in Mecca represents another such addition. Had the proto-anecdote been set in Mecca it is most unlikely that the moving object would have been a *miharāb*. It is only outside Mecca that *miharābs* acquire their special significance as indicators of the *qibla* or direction of the Ka'bah. If the original anecdote had been set in Mecca the focus of the incident would almost certainly have been the Ka'bah itself, a conclusion which is strongly supported by the fact that the *Miharbān* version locates the incident in a village on the way to Mecca[1] and by the *Bālā* retelling of the same story in a Medīnā context.[2] A *Purātan* statement to the effect that Bābā Nānak's feet were pointing 'towards Mecca'[3] appears to be a remnant of the earlier location which the later narrator has failed to eliminate. The common theme linking 'The Moving *Miharāb*' and the 'Journey to Mecca' anecdotes, together with the heightened effect achieved by setting the incident at the geographical centre of Islam, presumably account for the change of setting. From this stage it is only a short step to a combining of the two tales within a single narrative.

The encounter with Rukn al-Dīn which constitutes the third of the contributory sub-sākhīs is of a different nature. The anecdote is not a simple wonder-story. It is a heterodox discourse of the kind which appears later in the janam-sākhī traditions. This particular example does not compare in length or complexity with most discourses of this kind, nor with the variety of didactic discourse which figures so prominently in the *Miharbān* tradition. Although it represents a form later than that of the two narrative anecdotes with which it has been linked it is less developed than most *Miharbān* discourses and for this reason has been treated as an example of fourth-stage development.

The remaining elements in the *Purātan* version of the Mecca sākhī have been added to one of these three primary elements, or perhaps to the single sākhī which has resulted from the blending of the three. It seems clear that some of the extra shabads must have been attached to the 'Journey to Mecca' anecdote in its earlier separated version and that others were added to the independent tale of the 'The Moving *Miharāb*'. There can be no doubt that the cloud magically following the pilgrims belongs to the former, and Pīr Patlīā is evidently a later contribution to the Rukn al-Dīn discourse. The point at which the two remaining elements were introduced is not altogether clear, although it seems likely that they represent the latest of all contributions to the final *Purātan* synthesis. One of them, the description of Bābā Nānak's apparel, is evidently a fragment which having developed in isolation came to be attached to the Mecca sākhī, perhaps as a result of a brief reference to dress which Bhāī Gurdās uses to introduce his version of the episode.[4]

[1] *Mih JS* I.449.

[2] *Bālā JS*, p. 188. The *Bālā* narrator evidently appreciated the incongruence of a *miharāb* in the Mecca setting. In its place he substitutes variously 'the gate of Mecca' or simply 'Mecca'. Ibid., pp. 184–5.

[3] *Pr JS*, p. 100.

[4] *BG* I:32.

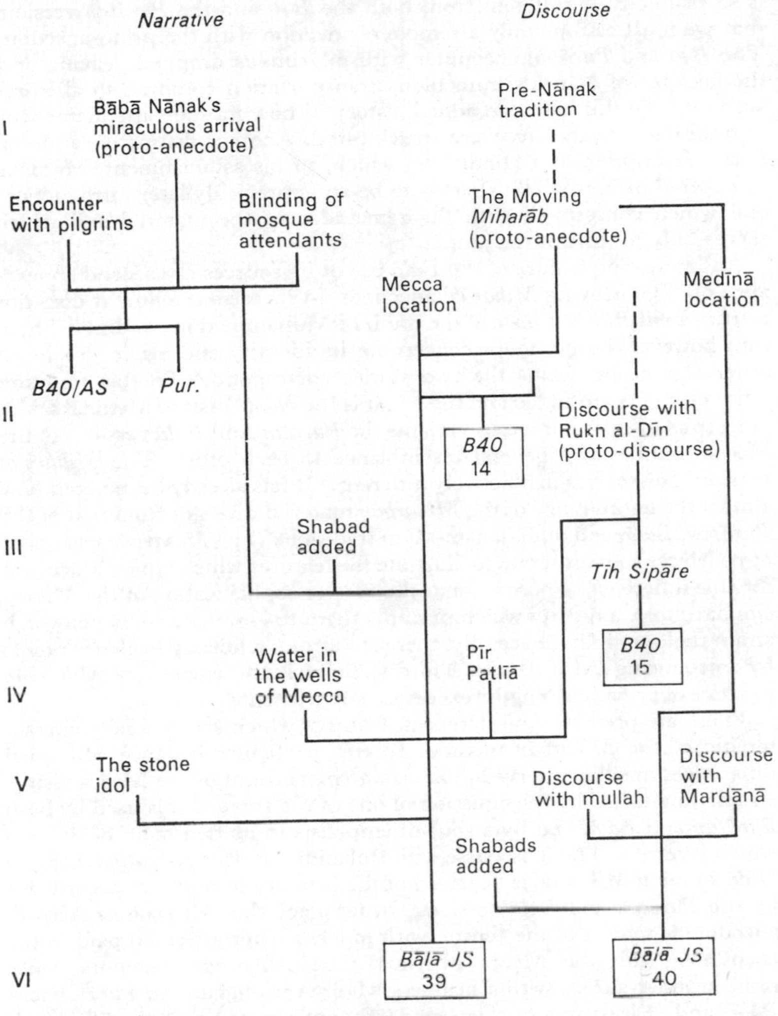

Figure 7

The mention of water springing in the wells of Mecca may possibly be a borrowing from the *Bālā* tradition.

The *Bālā* tradition provides a somewhat different pattern.[1] It embodies the same three constituents as the *Purātan* version, but the content of each betrays evident differences, particularly in the case of the 'Journey to Mecca' portion and the 'Discourse with Rukandīn'.[2] The first of these

[1] *Bālā JS*, pp. 182–94.

[2] The *Purātan* texts refer to Rukn al-Dīn as Rukandīn.

is so distinctively different from both the *B40* and the *Purātan* versions that we must assume only a remote connection with the proto-anecdote. The *B40* and *Purātan* encounter with pilgrims is dropped, leaving only the account of Nānak's miraculous transportation common to all three accounts. To this has been added a story of how mosque attendants who refused entry to the city were struck blind. Another distinctive addition is the description of a Hindu idol which, to his astonishment, Mardānā discovered in Mecca. This seems to be an appreciably later introduction, one which consorts ill with the remainder of the material and which serves only to disrupt the plot.

An interesting feature of the *Bālā* use of its sources is a second appearance of 'The Moving *Miharāb*' anecdote. In its second telling it does not feature a *miharāb* but instead the tomb of Muhammad in Medīnā.[1] There can, however, be no doubt concerning its identity and origin, for in all other significant details the two stories correspond.[2] To this tradition other elements are added and the result is the *Bālā* 'Visit to Medīnā' sākhī.

In spite of their numerous variants the *Purātan* and *Bālā* versions of the Mecca sākhī bear a general resemblance to each other. The *Miharbān* version, however, is distinctively different.[3] It has already been noted how almost the entire range of the *Miharbān* material diverges from that of the *Purātan*, *Bālā*, and other janam-sākhī traditions. The *Miharbān* treatment of its Mecca sources serves to illustrate the features which typically account for this difference. There is, first, the greater sophistication of the *Miharbān* narrators, a quality which prompts them to eliminate elements which strain their credulity. Secondly, there is a strong tendency to clarify points by introducing extra details. Thirdly, there is the customary *Miharbān* practice of providing lengthy exegetical supplements.

These are predictable differences, features which are generally characteristic of the *Miharbān* method. In this particular instance additional differences may be observed. The *Miharbān* account of the Mecca visit is also distinguished by the omission of one of the three sākhīs used by both *Purātan* and *Bālā*, and by a shift of emphasis in its treatment of the two which it retains. The 'Discourse with Rukandīn' is dropped altogether and 'The Moving *Miharāb*' is deprived of the primary importance accorded it by the *Purātan* and *Bālā* versions. In its place the 'Miraculous Arrival' anecdote is moved to the centre, with much greater attention paid to the encounter with the Mecca pilgrims. The *Miharbān* narrators could resist wonder-stories with a firmness wholly uncongenial to *Purātan* and *Bālā*, and at least one of them evidently appreciated that the 'Triumph over Islam' theme would be best served by the story of Bābā Nānak's encounter with the pilgrims.

In its *Miharbān* context 'The Moving *Miharāb*' anecdote contributes no more than a minor episode expressed in a much mutilated form. The

[1] *Bālā JS*, sākhī 40, pp. 188–94.

[2] A minor difference is that Bhāī Bālā joins Bābā Nānak in sleeping with his feet towards the tomb.

[3] *Mih JS* I.449–61. *GNSR*, pp. 60–1.

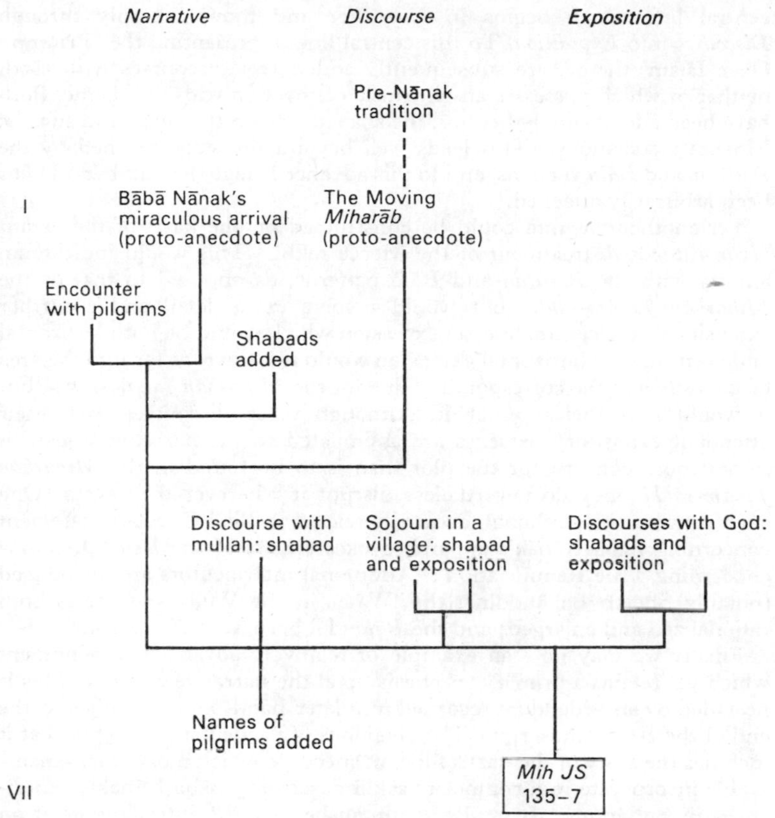

Figure 8

miharab is replaced by a reference to the Ka'bah, and its miraculous movement is, in characteristic *Miharbān* fashion, eliminated.[1] In one respect, however, this version seems to be nearer to the proto-anecdote. As we have already noted, the *Miharbān* narrator does not set the incident in Mecca.

An even more significant shift of emphasis is produced by the introduction of expository material. It is this feature which particularly distinguishes the *Miharbān* treatment in this as in almost all *Miharbān* material. The radical nature of the shift is illustrated in figure 8 by the

[1] It is, however, clear that the extant *Miharbān* version is based on a source which does relate the miraculous moving of the *miharāb*. This is made clear by the words, attributed to Bābā Nānak: 'Turn my shoes in that direction where the House of the Lord will not go. Place my shoes in that direction where the Ka'bah is not.' *Mih JS* I.449.

central line which begins in *Narrative* and moves sharply through *Discourse* into *Exposition*. To this central line, representing the 'Triumph Over Islam' theme, are subsequently added two discourses with God, neither of which possesses any intrinsic connection with the theme. Both have been added simply because the shabads which they expound suggest Muslim associations.[1] This leads well beyond the stage reached by the *Purātan* and *Bālā* versions, and to this advanced stage the number VII has been arbitrarily attached.

Yet another diagram could be constructed on the basis of the extant *Gyān-ratanāvalī* treatment of the Mecca sākhī.[2] This would indicate an affinity with the *Purātan* and *Bālā* patterns, as opposed to that of the *Miharbān Janam-sākhī*, but would involve extra detail and a further extension of the central line, an extension which would be both horizontal and vertical. The horizontal extension would not travel as far into the area of *Exposition* as the corresponding line for the *Miharbān Janam-sākhī*, but it would nevertheless enter it. Although these discourses with their attendant expository passages are assimilated to the narrative line with rather more concern for the plot than is to be found in the *Miharbān Janam-sākhī*, they do nevertheless disrupt it wherever they occur. One such conversation, although avowedly related to Bhāī Gurdās's statement concerning Bābā Nānak's apparel, evokes echoes of the *B40* 'Discourse concerning True Renunciation'.[3] Additional interlocutors are introduced (notably Sheikh Bahāuddīn); the 'Water in the Wells' episode is both rationalized and enlarged; and the *Bālā* idol becomes a *śiva-liṅga*.[4]

Finally we may note an example of relatively advanced development which yet retains a primary emphasis upon the narrative element. This is provided by an addendum recorded in a later hand on spare folios at the end of the *B40* manuscript.[5] The version is of particular interest in that it includes the story of the qāzī's filly, an anecdote which most other janam-sākhīs incorporate in a composite sākhī describing Bābā Nānak's experiences in Sultānpur.[6] It is also distinguished by the introduction of an associated Medīnā episode, one which differs from that of the *Bālā* janam-sākhīs.

Example 8: Discourses with Nāths

Narrative discourses with narrative anecdotes added: complex composite sākhīs with common theme

In the section dealing with the constituents of the janam-sākhīs particular stress was laid upon the influence of Puranic and Nāth traditions.[7] The cosmology of the Purāṇas, everywhere assumed, commonly appears in an explicit form. Echoes of Puranic legends can be distinguished in many

[1] A *Miharbān* commentator has also transferred the shabad *Basant Hiṇḍol aṣṭ.* 8 from its earlier Mecca setting (*B40*, ff. 134a–135a) to the context of the discourse with God (*Mih JS* I.453). This was evidently done because the shabad is so plainly addressed to God.

[2] *GR*, pp. 405–19.

[3] *B40*, ff. 205b–206b. *GR*, pp. 406–7.

[4] *GR*, pp. 405, 417.

[5] See *B40(Eng)*, Introduction, pp. 8–11

[6] *B40*, ff. 21b–22b.

[7] See above, pp. 65–70.

janam-sākhī anecdotes and a few of the more important Puranic figures make occasional appearances (particularly in the *Bālā* janam-sākhīs). References to Nāth Masters are even more common. Gorakhnāth figures in numerous discourses and in some of these anecdotes lesser Nāths also play key roles. The degree of prominence given to these legends plainly indicates that the Purāṇas and Nāth tradition must have exercised a considerable influence upon the rural Pañjāb of the sixteenth and seventeenth centuries.

In the case of the Purāṇas, as with the Epics, this was to be expected and to this day the folklore and beliefs of the Pañjāb are shot through with Puranic influence. The measure of the Nāths' hold on the imagination of rural Pañjāb is perhaps a little more surprising, for it no longer applies to nearly the same extent today. It is evident that the influence which still lingers must be a remnant of something much more powerful. The part played by Gorakhnāth in the janam-sākhī traditions reflects a substantial reputation, one which is surpassed only by a few distinguished disciples of Bābā Nānak. Anecdotes in which he or other Nāths appear also imply a considerable awe, and although Bābā Nānak invariably overcomes them he sometimes has to contend with an impressively fearsome display of magical powers. The Nāth yogīs who wandered through sixteenth- and seventeenth-century Pañjāb must have been held in some dread by the people for their alleged possession of such powers. They must have commanded both fear and a grudging respect, for asceticism of the Nāth order cannot go entirely unrecognized.

Strictly speaking Puranic and Nāth influences are two separate elements. In practice, however, the two were extensively confused by the common people who received and transmitted the legends. The Nāth yogīs themselves confused the two, grafting many of their distinctive traditions on to selected portions of the luxuriant Puranic growth. This confusion was further aggravated by a merging of the terms 'Nāth' and 'Siddh'. The latter properly relates to tantric Buddhism, and although the tradition of the nine immortal Nāths must have owed much to the earlier legends concerning the eighty-four immortal Siddhs the two should, in theory, be distinguished. The actual fact was, however, much more significant than the theory, and the fact was that the Nāth Masters and the Siddh Āchāryas were inextricably confused in the popular imagination.

This confusion is entirely characteristic of the janam-sākhī usage of legendary materials. It is on Mount Sumeru, the centre of the Puranic cosmological system, that Bābā Nānak is said to have held his longest discourse with Gorakhnāth and other Siddhs. In this, as in so many other respects, the janam-sākhīs plainly mirror the understanding of their own place and time. The amalgam of Puranic, Nāth, and earlier tantric legends must have exercised an enormous influence upon the rural understandings of sixteenth- and seventeenth-century Pañjāb.

This is not, however, the full extent of the janam-sākhī pattern. In the janam-sākhī treatment of these legendary materials a third element enters the amalgam. The influence of the Nāth yogīs is evident not only in the janam-sākhīs, but also in the works of Gurū Nānak himself. In his compositions he makes extensive use of Nāth concepts and terminology, and many of them are obviously addressed directly to a Nāth audience. This could not fail to impress the janam-sākhī narrators and inevitably these Nāth-directed compositions came to be linked with the traditions received from earlier sources. The characteristic janam-sākhī pattern is accordingly an amalgam of Puranic legend, Nāth legend, and evocative references from the works of Gurū Nānak.

Two locations command a particular popularity as settings for the janam-sākhī narratives which incorporate these influences, and others of lesser appeal are also used. Mount Sumeru and Achal are the two primary sites. Of these Mount Sumeru is certainly derived from the Purāṇas, and although Achal has been identified with a Nāth centre near the town of Baṭālā it is at least possible that its real origins are, like those of Sumeru, to be found in legend rather than in a factual location. The identification with a particular place in the Pañjāb may have come later, perhaps as a result of a tradition concerning an actual confrontation between Bābā Nānak and some Nāth yogīs at the site near Baṭālā.[1]

Other settings for discourses with Siddhs (or Nāths) are Ṭillā,[2] Gor-khatrī (which invariably appears in the janam-sākhīs as Gorakh-haṭaṛī),[3] Gorakh-matā,[4] Setu-bandha Rāmesvaram,[5] and a remote spot set 'in the midst of the sea'.[6] Occasionally Gorakhnāth comes to Kartārpur for a meeting with Nānak.[7] The first two of these locations deserve to be added to the list of primary janam-sākhī sites. Ṭillā, in Jhelum District, has for centuries ranked as the leading Nāth centre in the Pañjāb and one of the most important of all Nāth strongholds. In this sense there can be no doubt concerning its primacy. Gor-khatrī, near Peshāwar, did not possess the same status for the Nāths, but it was a place of some importance for Hindu pilgrimage and in the janam-sākhīs it receives as much attention as Ṭillā.[8]

[1] For a discussion of the identification of Achal with the site near Baṭālā see *B40(Eng)*, p. 132n

[2] *B40*, f. 182a. *Bālā JS*, p. 308. *Mih JS* 1.469.

[3] *Pur JS*, p. 104. *Mih JS* 1.416.

[4] *GR*, p. 407. The place is later referred to as Nānakmatā. *Pur JS*, p. 27. *GNSR*, p. 85.

[5] *Bālā JS*, p. 282.

[6] *Pur JS*, p. 84.

[7] *B40*, ff. 106b–107a. *Pur JS*, p. 107. Kartārpur is not always specified, but is indicated by the context.

[8] Gor-khatrī ('the tomb of the Khatrī', sometimes Kor-khatrī) is situated in the old city of Peshāwar. Bābur, having failed to locate the spot in 1505, returned to the area in 1519 and was able to pay the visit he had cherished for so long. He was, however, disappointed.

'Marching on next day, we reached Bīgrām and went to see Gūr-khattrī. This is a smallish abode, after the fashion of a hermitage (*ṣauma'at*), rather confined and dark. After entering at the door and going down a few steps, one must lie full length to get beyond. There is no getting in without a lamp. All round near the building there is let lie an enormous quantity of hair of the head and beard which men have shaved off there. There are a great many retreats (*ḥujra*) near Gūr-khattrī like those of a rest-house or a college. In the year we came into Kābul (910 A.H.) and over-ran Kohāt, Bannū and the plain we made an excursion to Bīgrām, saw its great tree and were consumed with regret at not seeing Gūr-khattrī, but it does not seem a place to regret not-seeing.' (A. S. Beveridge (trans.), *The Bābur-nāma in English*, vol. 1 (London, 1921), p. 394).

Each of these four locations has been used as a setting for at least one important discourse. There is general agreement amongst the various janam-sākhīs as far as the Mount Sumeru discourse is concerned, but marked divergences appear in the anecdotes set in Achal, Ṭillā, and Gor-khatrī. Although much of the material is common to the principal janam-sākhīs (including both narrative details and quotations from the works of Nānak) they disagree in the settings used for the different incidents and compositions. In general there is correspondence as far as Bhāī Gurdās, the *Miharbān Janam-sākhī*, the *Ādi Sākhīs*, and the *B40 Janam-sākhī* are concerned. This cluster must, however, be clearly distinguished from the *Purātan* janam-sākhīs and, with even greater sharpness, from the *Bālā* janam-sākhīs. The primary distinctions will later be seen to relate to recognizable traditions and, in some instances, to identifiable sources used by more than one janam-sākhī compiler.[1]

An effort will now be made to disentangle some of the strands which constitute this particular portion of the janam-sākhī web, and having done so to reintegrate them in a composite diagram representing all the major traditions. The principal emphasis will be upon the various versions of the Achal discourse, with only brief analyses provided for the Sumeru, Ṭillā, and Gor-khatrī traditions.

The Achal discourse has been selected for detailed analysis because it is one of the most illuminating episodes in the entire range of janam-sākhī traditions. Almost all the important issues arising from the evolution of the janam-sākhīs can be illustrated by reference to this particular sākhī. It combines narrative with discourse, and in some versions adds exegesis. Portions can be traced to earlier narrative traditions and others have obviously been developed out of references in the works of Nānak. Some quotations have been incorporated for this reason and others because they seemed to accord with the theme of the sākhī. The exegesis relates in part to the manifest intention of Nānak and in part to the doctrinal predilections of a narrator. Legendary details abound, but the actual location may perhaps be traceable to an authentic incident in the life of the Gurū. Earlier versions have been used by later compilers and the mode of expansion can be clearly traced in the latter. This is a substantial catalogue

---

See also ibid., p. 230. Abu al-Fazl reports a visit to Gor-khatrī by Akbar (H. Beveridge, trans., *The Akbarnāma*, III.528) and in the *Ā'īn-i-Akbarī* refers to it as 'a shrine greatly venerated . . . visited by people especially jogis from distant parts'. *Ā'īn* II.404. Jahāngīr also visited the spot, and like his great-grandfather was greatly disappointed by what he found. A. Rogers and H. Beveridge, *Tūzuk-i-Jahāngīrī*, I.102. A. H. Dani traces the history of Gor-khatrī back to a Buddhist foundation of the early Kushan period. *Idem*, *Peshawar the Historic City of the Frontier* (Peshawar, 1969), pp. 36–7, 171–3. See also A. Cunningham, *The Ancient Geography of India* (Calcutta, 1924), p. 93; S. M. Jaffar, *Peshawar Past and Present* (Peshawar, 1946), p. 74; and *GTC* i. 679. Gor-khatrī has been transformed into Gorakh-haṭaṛī by means of an interesting process of transmutation. The initial consonant of *khatrī* has been assimilated to *gor*, leaving a residual *h*; and the dental *t* and alveolar *r* have both been changed to retroflexes (*ṭ* and *ṛ*). 'The tomb of the Khatrī' has thus become 'the shop of Gorakhnāth'.

[1] This issue is discussed in chapter 10.

of qualifications for a single sākhī, one which attaches to it an unusual interest and importance.[1]

The analysis of this material concerns three principal elements, one of them basic and two of considerable subsidiary importance. The basic element is provided by the reputation of the Nāth yogīs and the influence of their legends. The two subsidiary elements are the influence of Puranic legend and the works of Nānak. Elsewhere either of these elements may be of primary importance. Within this particular area however both are subordinate to the dominant Nāth influence.

The simplest of the traditions to analyse and also the latest to evolve is that of the *Bālā* janam-sākhīs. This can be briefly outlined and then disregarded, for it had no evident influence upon the later evolution of the other traditions. The primary analysis must concern the other important janam-sākhīs. In the case of the *Bālā* version of the Sumeru discourse the most distinctive feature is the substantial quantity of Puranic material which has been added to the episode. No other janam-sākhī can match the range of Puranic borrowings utilized by the *Bālā* tradition to construct a mountaineering itinerary for Bābā Nānak. In order to reach Mount Sumeru Bābā Nānak climbs four legendary mountains many hundreds of miles high and having performed this feat he proceeds to ascend nine more (including Mount Kailāś, which in this context is strictly legendary as it provides a setting for a discourse with Dhrū Bhagat).[2] Indeed, it would be legitimate to regard the Puranic material as basic in this particular tradition, were it not for the fact that the core around which it all clusters remains the Sumeru discourse with Gorakhnāth and his colleagues. This discourse, as in all other traditions, blends a Puranic location (Mount Sumeru) with a Nāth audience (Gorakhnāth and others) and a content drawn from the works of Gurū Nānak (*Vār Rāmkalī*, shaloks 2–7 of stanza 12).[3]

The Ṭillā and Achal sākhīs offered by the *Bālā* tradition are both brief narratives, curiously remote from the other older traditions. The former relates a discourse with Bālgundāī, *mahant* of the Ṭillā *maṭh*;[4] and the latter another of the many discourses with Gorakhnāth, accompanied on this occasion by Bharatharī.[5] It is possible that the setting may derive from an actual visit to the Baṭālā area by Bābā Nānak, but the content of the *Bālā* sākhī, which includes an apocryphal composition, must be traced to other antecedents.

The *Bālā* pattern for these three sākhīs may now be represented as in figure 9. This is a relatively simple pattern. Simplicity of structure should not, of course, be confused with brevity. Apart from the *Miharbān Janam-sākhī*, with all its exegetical supplements, the *Bālā* versions are, in sum total, much the longest.

[1] The episode also provides another example of the manner in which Macauliffe conflated his material without indicating either his sources for various details or his reasons for setting the discourse at a particular point in his chronology. Macauliffe, i. 157–63.

[2] *Bālā JS*, sākhīs 43–59, pp. 200–79.

[3] *AG*, pp. 952–3. *GNSR*, pp. 11–12, 119–22.

[4] *Bālā JS*, sākhī 69, pp. 308–11.

[5] Ibid., sākhī 62, pp. 287–8.

A greater intricacy is encountered in the *Purātan* tradition. The *Purātan* version of the Sumeru sākhī is, in itself, simpler than the amplified *Bālā* version, but with it has been linked the *Purātan* Achal sākhī.[1]

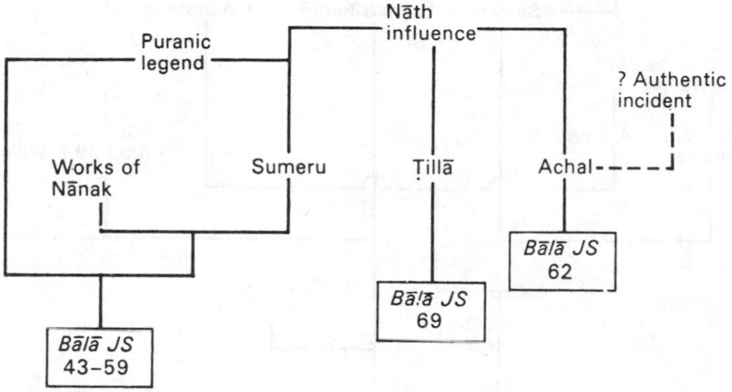

Figure 9

The two have been bracketed in a single sākhī for the apparent reason that they concern similar themes, the gap being bridged by one of Nānak's instantaneous journeys from one locality to another. In this *Purātan* version Achal produces only a minor anecdote. Bābā Nānak is offered an intoxicating drink by the assembled Nāths and in response recites his *Āsā* 38.[2] This shabad employs the intoxication produced by liquor as an image representing divine intoxication, and specifies raw sugar (*guṛ*) and the *dhāvā* or *mahūā* blossom as two of the constituents. In the *Purātan* narrative these are the constituents said to have been used by the Nāths and it is at once plain that the brief anecdote derives from the references in the shabad.

The Gorakh-haṭaṛī (Gor-khatrī) episode of the *Purātan* tradition is a more substantial anecdote.[3] Inevitably the composition by Gurū Nānak entitled *Siddh Goṣṭ*[4] found its way into the janam-sākhīs, and inevitably it was set in the context of a discourse with Siddhs (or Nāths). The actual context selected by the *Purātan* tradition is this Gorakh-haṭaṛī discourse. Following a recitation of Nānak's lengthy composition the Siddhs demonstrate their powers by making deerskins fly, stones move, and walls walk. Bābā Nānak replies by reciting *Vār Mājh*, shalok 1 of stanza 19, a brief work which proclaims the futility of both magic and extreme asceticism.[5] The Siddhs acknowledge defeat and the sākhī concludes with a recitation by Bābā Nānak of Gurū Arjan's *Gauṛī aṣṭapadī* 4.[6]

[1] *Pur JS*, sākhī 50, pp. 94–7.
[2] *AG*, p. 360. See *B40*, f. 91a–b.
[3] *Pur JS*, sākhī 52, pp. 104–5.
[4] *AG*, pp. 938–46. See *B40(Eng)*, p. 139n.
[5] *AG*, p. 147. See *B40*, f. 122a.
[6] *AG*, p. 237.

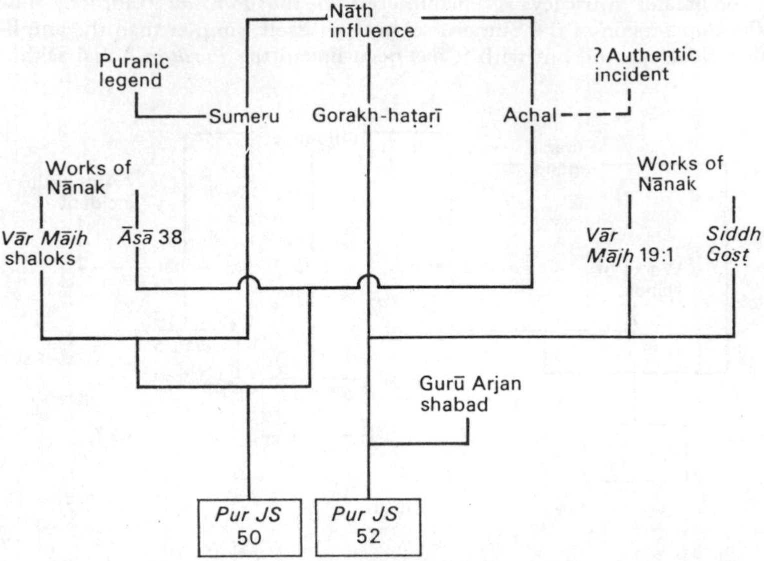

Figure 10

This *Purātan* pattern may be represented as in figure 10. The pattern, though more complex than that of the *Bālā* version, is still relatively simple. Another stage in the growing complexity results from an analysis of the material which, in various stages of growth, is found in Bhāī Gurdās's *Vār* 1, the *Ādi Sākhīs*, the *B40 Janam-sākhī*, and the *Miharbān Janam-sākhī*. This complexity does not derive from their several treatments of a single Sumeru tradition,[1] but rather from their versions of a single Achal tradition.[2]

Only two points relating to the former will be noted here. The first is the inclusion in the Sumeru discourse of the shabad *Āsā* 38.[3] This is the shabad which the *Purātan* tradition sets within its Achal discourse. The imagery of the hymn points unmistakably to a Nāth audience and with equal clarity suggests a liquor-drinking context. This leaves only the question of location for the compiler to decide. The *Purātan* tradition chooses Achal and the *Ādi Sākhīs/B40/Miharbān* tradition selects Mount Sumeru.

The second point to be noted is that the extant *Miharbān Janam-sākhī* appends to its version of the Sumeru discourse an account, both brief and vague, of a visit to Gorakh-haṭaṛī.[4] This *Miharbān* anecdote bears no

[1] *BG* 1:28–31. *AS*, pp. 36–42. *B40*, ff. 86a–93a. *Mih JS* I.384–416.
[2] *BG* 1:39–44. *AS*, pp. 73–6. *B40*, ff. 117a–122b. *Mih JS* II.70–137.
[3] *AS*, pp. 40–1. *B40*, ff. 91a–b. *Mih JS* I.407–9.
[4] *Mih JS* I 416–19. *GNSR*, p. 60

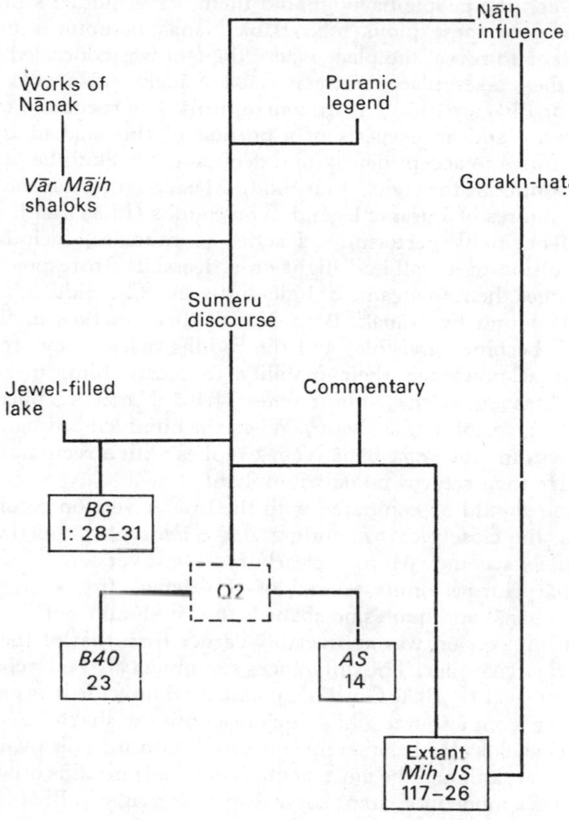

Figure 11

evident relationship to the Gorakh-haṭaṛī discourse of the *Purātan* tradition. It records a conversation with 'the yogīs' gurū' and incorporates an apocryphal shalok together with the shabad *Gauṛī* 15.[1]

The Sumeru discourse pattern which emerges from a comparison of these four versions is shown in figure 11. Once again the *B40* and *Ādi Sākhīs* compilers have the *Q2* manuscript as a common source.

This is still a relatively simple pattern and one which stands in marked contrast to the four corresponding versions of the Achal sākhī. The Achal sākhī as it appears in the *B40 Janam-sākhī* may be summarized as follows. Bābā Nānak proceeds to Achal on the occasion of the annual Śivrātri fair, taking with him his trusted disciple Lahaṇā (Gurū Aṅgad). There he observes pious folk performing various devout ceremonies. Meanwhile the sly 'Siddhs' (i.e. Nāth yogīs), evidently annoyed by the

[1] *AG*, pp. 155–6. The shabad clearly assumes a Nāth audience.

manner in which the people have ignored them, have hidden a brass pot (*loṭā*) belonging to these pious folk. Bābā Nānak confounds them by ordering Lahaṇā to reveal the place where the *loṭā* was concealed.

A debate then takes place between Bābā Nānak and a yogī named Bhagarnāth (or Bhāgarnāth). The discourse turns on a recitation of Gurū Nānak's *Sūhī* 1,[1] and an exegesis of a portion of this shabad is given. Bhagarnāth refuses to accept defeat, and declaring Nānak to be 'a worthless Bedī' he summons the eighty-four Siddh Masters, the nine Nāths, and sundry other figures of Puranic legend. The Siddhs (Bhāgarnāth and his fellow yogīs) begin by performing a series of miracles, including the magical propulsion of a wall and flight on a deerskin. In response Bābā Nānak challenges them to a game of hide-and-seek. The Siddhs hide first and are easily found by Nānak. Bābā Nānak then 'merges in the four elements' (i.e. becomes invisible) and the Siddhs, when they are finally compelled to acknowledge their inability to locate him, make their submission. As soon as they admit defeat Bābā Nānak reappears and utters *Vār Mājh,* shalok 1 of stanza 19. When the humbled Siddhs ask him to instruct them in true yoga Bābā Nānak replies with a recitation of the *Siddh Goṣṭ*. He then returns home triumphant.

This version should be compared with the briefer version recorded by Bhāī Gurdās, the closely corresponding *Ādi Sākhīs* text, and the much longer *Miharbān* account. All four clearly represent versions of the same tradition. Bhāī Gurdās omits several of the details (for example, the presence of Lahaṇā) and quotes no shabads, but it should not thereby be assumed that his version was appreciably earlier than that of the source used by the *B40* compiler. The differences can obviously be traced to the constraints imposed by Bhāī Gurdās's poetic medium, for it is clear that he was working from a source which includes both the shabad *Sūhī* 1 and the *Vār Mājh* shalok. He has merely converted both into his own briefer words. Moreover, although he omits some *B40* details he adds others. The Siddhs perform a much more impressive display of magic in Bhāī Gurdās's account.[2]

The *Ādi Sākhīs* version differs only slightly from *B40*. It omits the hide-and-seek story, and adds some extra exegesis which the *B40* sākhī lacks. The two are plainly from the same common *Q2* source and it appears that the *Q2* manuscript contained neither the hide-and-seek story nor the extra exegetical material. This is certainly a safe conclusion in the case of the former. The additional anecdote disturbs the unity of the story concerning the encounter with the Siddhs and can only be explained as an interpolation. The *B40* compiler presumably derived it from current oral tradition.

The extra exegesis included in the *Ādi Sākhīs* version raises issues which are a little more complex.[3] Although the absence of the extra material from the *B40* version seems to indicate another instance of inter-

[1] *AG*, p. 728.

[2] For an English translation see *SLTGN(Eng)*, pp. 40–3.

[3] The additional material consists of the exegetical passage which follows the fourth stanza of *Sūhī* 1, *AS*, p. 75.

polation it can hardly have been a simple addition of the kind made by the *B40* compiler when he introduced the hide-and-seek episode. This conclusion follows from a more extended comparison of the two versions. The *B40* text also includes two exegetical passages in precisely the same style as the additional *Ādi Sākhīs* material[1] and there appears to be little doubt that these *B40* passages (which the *Ādi Sākhīs* compiler uses in only a slightly different form) must have derived from the same source as the extra *Ādi Sākhīs* exegesis. The difference is merely one of quantity. The *B40* compiler has taken only a small amount from this supplementary source, whereas the *Ādi Sākhīs* compiler has incorporated rather more in his version of the discourse.[2]

It is clear that in both instances the exegetical material represents an interpolation within an earlier narrative tradition concerning the Achal discourse. Moreover, there can be no doubt concerning the source of the interpolation. The style is unmistakably that of the *Miharbān* tradition. A comparison with the extant *Miharbān* version confirms this and also indicates that the actual source must have been an earlier recension of this tradition.

This much is clear. The issue which remains obscure concerns the precise manner in which the *Miharbān* borrowings entered the two janam-sākhīs. Behind the *Ādi Sākhīs* and the *B40 Janam-sākhī* there lies the common *Q2* source for the Achal narrative. Did *Q2* include the *Miharbān* borrowing? If so did it include only the portion which appears in the *B40* text, or did it also incorporate the extra material recorded in the *Ādi Sākhīs*? If this manuscript did not include the *Miharbān* borowing, from where did the *Ādi Sākhīs* and *B40* compilers obtain it? Did they have access to another common manuscript (a *Miharbān* manuscript)? If so, does it mean that the *Ādi Sākhīs* and the *B40 Janam-sākhī* originated within the same geographical area? This is but the beginning of a series of related questions arising from this situation. There is, however, little value to be derived from posing them, for the available texts do not provide the means of reaching answers. We can merely affirm that the two janam-sākhīs incorporate borrowings of differing length, derived from an early recension of the *Miharbān* tradition and introduced into an even earlier Achal narrative.

The extant *Miharbān Janam-sākhī* carries the process of expansion much further. This it achieves partly by expanding the narrative element, partly by quoting the *Siddh Goṣṭ* in full, partly by introducing extra quotations from the works of Nānak, and above all by adding substantial quantities of exegesis in the characteristic *Miharbān* style. This, when compared with the *Ādi Sākhīs* and *B40* analogues, demonstrates the relative lateness of the extant *Miharbān* text. Although the origins of the *Miharbān* tradition may date from the early or mid-seventeenth century, the *Miharbān*

[1] Exegesis of the second and third stanzas of *Sūhī* 1. *B40*, ff. 118b–119a, 119b–120a.

[2] The *Ādi Sākhīs* compiler is rather more consistent, recording each stanza in turn with its appropriate exegesis attached. The *B40* compiler first records the second stanza with its exegesis and then the entire shabad followed by the exegesis of stanza 3 only.

Janam-sākhī as we know it today is obviously a product of the late eighteenth or early nineteenth century.

The evolved discourse may be represented in tabular form as follows:

Śivrātri fair at Achal	*BG*	*AS*	*B40*	*Mih JS*
Achal identified with Baṭālā site	*BG*			
Aṅgad as companion		*AS*	*B40*	*Mih JS*
The hidden *loṭā*	*BG*	*AS*	*B40*	*Mih JS*
Discourse with Bhagarnāth based on *Sūhī* 1	*BG*	*AS*	*B40*	*Mih JS*
Exegesis of stanza 1				*Mih JS*
Exegesis of stanza 2		*AS*	*B40*	*Mih JS*
Exegesis of stanza 3		*AS*	*B40*	*Mih JS*
Exegesis of stanza 4		*AS*		*Mih JS*
Contest of magical powers	*BG*	*AS*	*B40*	*Mih JS*
Hide-and-seek test			*B40*	
Recitation of *Sūhī* 6				*Mih JS*
Exegesis				*Mih JS*
Recitation of *Surplus Shaloks* 12–13				*Mih JS*
Exegesis				*Mih JS*
Recitation of *Vār Mājh* 19:1	*BG*	*AS*	*B40*	*Mih JS*
Exegesis				*Mih JS*
Recitation of the *Siddh Goṣṭ*				
Statement only	*BG*	*AS*	*B40*	
Recitation in full				*Mih JS*
Exegesis				*Mih JS*
Recitation of *Japjī* concluding stanzas				*Mih JS*
Exegesis				*Mih JS*

This evolved pattern combines three basic components and an extensive supplement. The basic components can be identified as three separate stories. One of these is a simple narrative anecdote. The remaining two are narrative discourses which derive from a blending of popular attitudes towards Nāth yogīs with evocative references in the works of Nānak.

The first identifiable component is the story of the hidden *loṭā*. It was presumably to this anecdote that the Achal location and Śivrātri occasion were first attached, and it is possible that an actual visit to the Nāth centre near Baṭālā may underlie it.

The second component is the discourse with Bhagarnāth (or Bhāgarnāth, or Bhaṅgarnāth) which has been developed out of Gurū Nānak's shabad *Sūhī* 1. In this instance the shabad is primary, and the Nāth references incidental. The brief narrative relates exclusively to the content of the shabad and although Bhāī Gurdās does not actually quote the shabad it is clear that he was working from a version which already incorporated it.

In the third story the Nānak composition is again primary but the Nāth reference is much more prominent. The nucleus of the discourse is provided by the shalok from *Vār Mājh* in which Gurū Nānak emphatically spurns the power to work wonders or the capacity to endure rigorous asceticism. The message which Nānak seeks to communicate through the shalok concerns the grace of God, and magical powers are mentioned merely in order to dismiss them as irrelevant. It was, however, the reference to magical and ascetic powers which attracted his later audience. The reference at once suggested the powers popularly attributed to Nāth yogīs and so the discourse began to evolve. The process ended with an anecdote which relates a contest of magical powers. These are demonstrated only by the Nāths, for Nānak's shalok provides a sufficient answer to their antics. For at least one disciple, however, this was unsatisfactory. If Nānak was greater than the Nāths, then plainly he could beat them at their own game. A story concerning Nānak's power to render himself invisible was developed and this erratic feature enters the *B40* version as the hide-and-seek test.

Before this *B40* interpolation had been introduced (and probably at the time when the discourse first evolved) another supplementary feature had been added. It was inevitable that Nānak's *Rāmkalī* composition entitled *Siddh Goṣṭ* should find its way into a janam-sākhī anecdote, and the 'Contest of Magical Powers' sākhī was chosen as an appropriate point to introduce it. At first it is merely mentioned. Later (in the *Miharbān* version) it is quoted in full.

This third discourse, 'The Contest of Magical Powers', is the anecdote which the *Purātan* tradition places in a Gorakh-haṭaṛī setting. In its *Purātan* context it remains an individual sākhī. In the *Bhāī Gurdās/Ādi Sākhīs/B40/Miharbān* tradition, however, it becomes a part of a composite Achal sākhī.[1]

The major supplement which is later added to this composite sākhī is the exegetical material introduced by the *Miharbān* compilers. Given the specific interests and purposes of the *Miharbān* compilers and redactors this was an inevitable development. In the late recension represented by the extant *Miharbān* manuscripts this feature has attained considerable dimensions and now provides a much greater proportion of the discourse's material than the three original anecdotes. The process of expansion has been achieved in this later recension not only by adding exegetical passages to *Sūhī* 1 and *Vār Mājh* 19:1, but also by quoting the *Siddh Goṣṭ* in full and by introducing additional extracts from the works of Nānak.[2] To these extra quotations exegesis had to be added, and the end product is a discourse of considerable length.

This proliferation of material must have been a continuing process within the *Miharbān* tradition, a process which eventually issued during the early nineteenth century in the extant *Miharbān* text. It was obviously an earlier and briefer recension which provided the exegetical interpolations appearing in the *Ādi Sākhīs* and *B40* accounts. These interpolations

[1] The introductory portion of the *B40* Ṭillā sākhī also relates a contest of miraculous powers with a Nāth yogī. *B40*, f. 182a. This is a much later tradition which may perhaps derive in part from the earlier tradition.

[2] The shabad *Sūhī* 6 (*AG*, pp. 729–30) has obviously been added because its key word, *bhāṇḍā* (pot, vessel), is also a key word of *Sūhī* 1 and of the discourse built around it. *Mih JS* II.70–4.

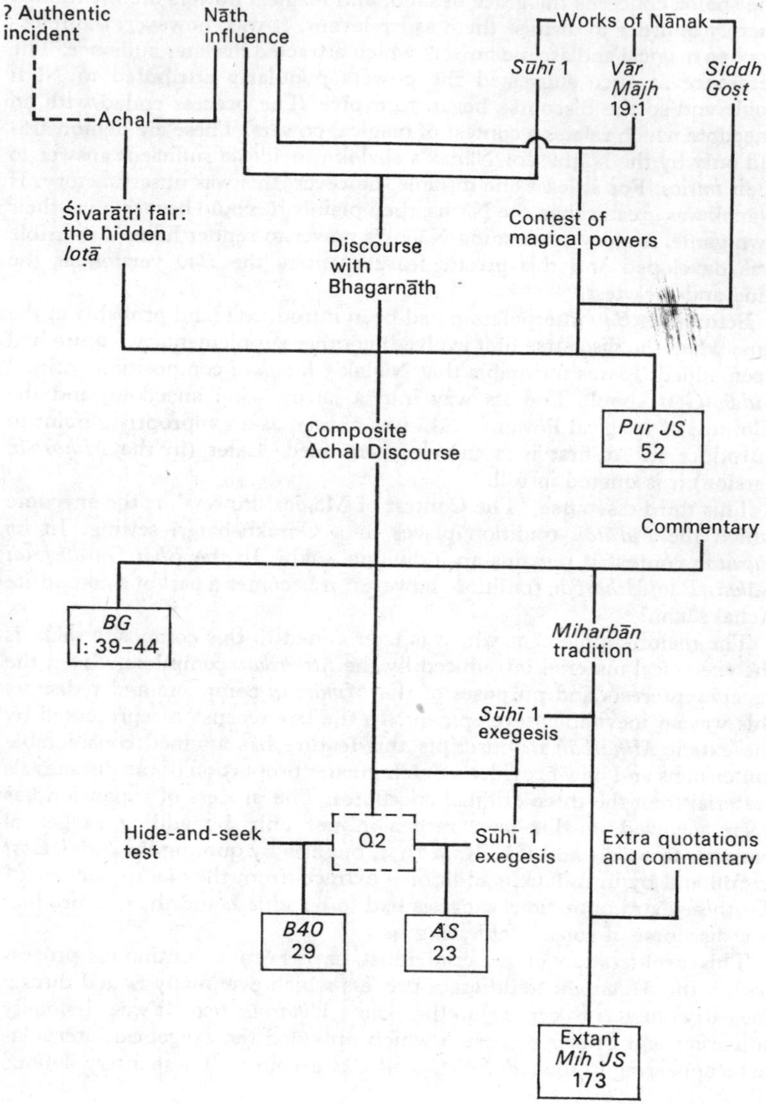
? Authentic incident
Nāth influence
Works of Nānak
Sūhī 1
Vār Mājh 19:1
Siddh Goṣṭ
Achal
Śivarātri fair: the hidden lotā
Contest of magical powers
Discourse with Bhagarnāth
Pur JS 52
Composite Achal Discourse
Commentary
BG I: 39–44
Miharbān tradition
Sūhī 1 exegesis
Hide-and-seek test
Q2
Sūhī 1 exegesis
Extra quotations and commentary
B40 29
AS 23
Extant Mih JS 173

Figure 12

were introduced into the second of the three original components (the discourse based on *Sūhī* 1).

The result of this process of blending and expansion is a single sākhī illustrating an unusual variety of janam-sākhī features. The pattern which accounts for its growth is illustrated in figure 12. A simplified version of this diagram and of the Sumeru diagram for the same group of janam-sākhīs can be compared with the corresponding discourses of the *Purātan* janam-sākhīs. This produces an interesting web of connecting strands, illustrated in figure 13.

This, it must be stressed, is a simplified pattern. Some of the minor strands have been omitted, the *Bālā* development is completely unrepresented, and the janam-sākhīs included in the diagram offer other instances of Nāth influence operating upon the janam-sākhī evolutionary processes. The diagram will, however, serve to illustrate a measure of that influence. At the same time it should provide a glimpse of the complex mechanics of sākhī and janam-sākhī development.

Example 9: Rājā Śivanābh

Narrative discourse with narrative anecdotes added: complex composite sākhī

The story of Bābā Nānak's meeting with Rājā Śivanābh consists, in its evolved form, of three distinct episodes. The first relates the story of how a merchant of Lahore visited Kartārpur and was there converted by Bābā Nānak. This is followed by the merchant's visit to the domain of Rājā Śivanābh and the conversion of the latter. Finally Bābā Nānak himself visits Śivanābh.[1] The *Purātan* janam-sākhīs add that the rājā's domain was in Siṅghalādīp (Sri Lanka).[2]

Although the reference to Sri Lanka must be dismissed as a later interpolation[3] it is possible that a Rājā Śivanābh did in fact exist and that Gurū Nānak actually met him. This possibility arises from the universal agreement amongst the janam-sākhī narrators concerning his existence and the apparent absence in pre-Sikh tradition of any figure to whom the janam-sākhī Śivanābh might be traced. It is, however, no more than a possibility. The well-known anecdote which the *Purātan* janam-sākhīs set in Siṅghalādīp is the product of a single tradition, not of all the janam-sākhīs. In the *Miharbān* tradition there appears an entirely different encounter with Śivanābh.[4] The area of agreement is thus confined to his mere existence and if in fact an authentic encounter did take place its details have been buried beyond recall.

The origin of the Śivanābh portion of the composite sākhī (the third of the three episodes noted above) lies not in any such encounter, real or imagined, but in Gurū Nānak's shabad *Mārū* 11.[5] The discourse which has been built around this composition follows the standard pattern of

[1] *B40*, ff. 138b–140b, 140b–144b, 144b–154a.
[2] *Pur JS*, p. 86. *GNSR*, p. 48.
[3] *GNSR*, pp. 114–17.
[4] *Mih JS* II.1–35, 65–6.
[5] *AG*, p. 992. *B40*, ff. 150b–151b.

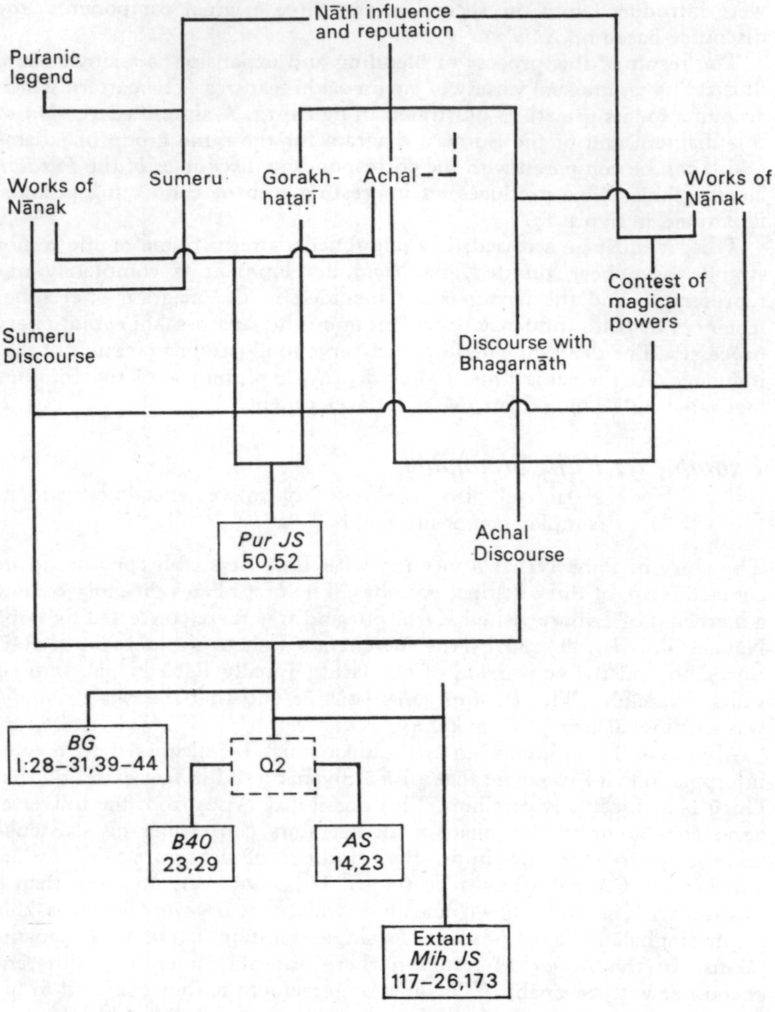

Figure 13

episodes developed out of works by Gurū Nānak. Each stanza serves as Bābā Nānak's reply, and Śivanābh's questions are framed in accordance with the given answers. Because of the manner in which it has been contrived the resultant discourse provides an unusually clear example of the standard pattern. Although the key words in Śivanābh's questions have obviously been taken from the stanzas which provide the replies the questions do not really correspond to the replies. This element of discord derives not from ineptness, but rather from the anecdotal concern of the narrator who first framed the questions. Whereas a close correspondence would not have produced a coherent discourse, a measure of freedom enables him to construct a neat little tale of how persistent cross-questioning finally enabled the rājā to identity his mysterious visitor.

The misinterpretations which are needed in order to make the shabad fit the narrative intention occur in a series corresponding to the stanzas of the shabad. The first quotation is the refrain, in which Gurū Nānak apostrophizes God in the following terms:

gusāī terā kahā nāmu kaise jāti
jā kau bhītari mahali bulāvahu pūchhau bāti niranti[1]

Master, where is Thy Name [to be discerned]? How art Thou to be known?
When Thou dost summon me within Thy palace let me inquire [of Thee the way of mystical] union.

The janam-sākhī narrator misconstrues this in three respects. First, he overlooks the word *kahā(n)*, 'where', which indicates that the question relates to locality; secondly, he takes *jātī*, 'known', to be *jāti*, 'caste'; and thirdly, he understands *mahal* to refer to an earthly palace. Were these three assumptions to be accepted a translation of the following kind would be required:

Master, what is your name and what your caste?
Let me invite you within [my] palace that I may inquire [of you the way of mystical] union [with God].

This is patently a mistranslation, but if the couplet is construed in this sense it can provide a narrator with a suitable query to put into his interlocutor's mouth. This initial query serves to introduce the discourse, and the actual stanzas can then be utilized as a series of responses by Bābā Nānak to a series of appropriate questions posed by the chosen interlocutor.

The same variety of misconstruction persists throughout the remainder of the discourse. The first stanza offers a brief description of the 'true yogī', a variety of reinterpretation which occurs commonly in the works of Gurū Nānak. It does indeed include the word *jogī*, but it does not (if properly construed) read like an answer to the interlocutor's question, 'Master, are you a yogī?' In all five instances the quotations from Gurū Nānak's shabad have been pressed into a use which they cannot really serve.

At two points the interpolations imposed by different narrators diverge. Stanza 4 begins with the words *dovai sire*, which may be variously translated as 'in both respects', 'both kinds', 'in both directions', etc. The *B40* narrator (or his source) evidently recognized the ambiguity, for in framing his introductory question he merely says, 'Master, tell me about

[1] *B40*, f. 150b. The Ādi Granth version corresponds almost exactly.

one *sirā* that I may understand',[1] thereby avoiding the awkward necessity of indicating what *sirā* means. The *Colebrooke* narrator evidently perceived the same difficulty and solved it by bracketing stanzas 3 and 4, without inserting a question to introduce stanza 4.[2] The *Hāfizābād* narrator is, however, prepared to offer an interpretation. The word *sirā*, he believes, must refer to the two dominant religious communities, and in accordance with this assumption he interposes the question: 'Are you a Hindu or a Muslim?'[3]

The second variant distinguishing the *B40* and *Purātan* discourses occurs in their treatment of the fifth stanza. For the *B40* narrator the suggestive word is *vāsi*, 'dweller' or 'resident', which occurs at the end of the first line. From this he has devised the question: 'Master, in what place is your home?'[4] The *Colebrooke* narrator (followed by *Hāfizābād*) has taken the key word to be *gorakh*, with the result that in the *Purātan* version we find the question: 'Are you Gorakhnāth?'[5]

The discourse which, in its variant versions, has been constructed in this manner constitutes the nucleus of the complete anecdote. Next an appropriate interlocutor and setting were required. The former had of necessity to be someone possessing a palace and for this role a rājā named Śivanābh was well fitted. A suitable setting is provided by the age-old story of the holy man tempted by women. Śivanābh, having previously determined to find a perfected sādhū, enlists a cadre of alluring damsels and charges them with the responsibility of tempting all visiting faqīrs. Only the most sublime will be able to resist their proffered charms and the rājā will in this manner find the teacher whom he seeks. This portion of the Śivanābh story bears a marked resemblance to the legend of Ṛṣya Śṛṅga, a resemblance which was noted by the *B40* compiler.[6] The theme is one which recurs in the Epic literature and there can be no doubt that the janam-sākhī tradition must derive either from one particular legend or from the cumulative effect of their recurrence in the *Mahābhārata* and the *Rāmāyaṇa*.[7]

A second introductory element is the brief episode which relates how Bābā Nānak's arrival caused a withered garden to blossom. The withered garden episode opens the narrative. Next comes the dispatch of the temptresses to test the mysterious wonder-working faqīr, followed by their failure and submission. The stage is then set and the discourse based on *Mārū* 11 duly follows.

[1] *B40*, f. 151a. In the English translation of the *B40* text this has been rendered: 'Master, tell me about one world . . .' See *B40(Eng)*, p. 169. This follows the interpretation of Tejā Singh in *Śabadārath*, p. 992, n. 28. Tejā Singh construes *dovai sirai* as a reference to this world and the next, to the present life and the hereafter. For yet another interpretation see Sāhib Singh, *Srī Gurū Granth Sāhib Darapaṇ*, where the term is understood to be a reference to *janam maran* (birth and death, the round of transmigration). Loc. cit., vol. vii, pp. 376, 377.

[2] *Pur JS*, p. 87. [3] *Pur JS*, p. 87, n. *. [4] *B40*, f. 151b. [5] *Pur JS*, p. 87

[6] *B40*, ff. 146b–147a. See above, p. 65. The legend of Ṛṣya Śṛṅga, the one-horned ascetic, is a much-travelled tale. See 'The youth who had never seen a woman' in Joseph Jacobs, *Barlaam and Josaphat* (London, 1896), pp. cxxx–cxxxi.

[7] Cf. *Mah.* I.71–2; III.110–13; V.9. Also *Rām.* I.9–11; III.11.

In its later recensions the narrative followed two different lines of development. One of these eventually produced the composite sākhī with its three distinct episodes, whereas the other presented the Śivanābh discourse as an isolated anecdote, considerably expanded but still separate. The first line leads to a common source utilized by both the *Ādi Sākhīs* and the *B40* compilers; and the second to the *Colebrooke Janam-sākhī* of the *Purātan* tradition. Both lines are eventually drawn together by the *Hāfizābād Janam-sākhī*.

The composite sākhī was formed by combining the Śivanābh discourse with the anecdote concerning the Lahore merchant. The simple tale of the merchant who was converted during a visit to Kartārpur is, in style and substance, completely independent of the Śivanābh discourse and presumably developed in isolation from it. The two anecdotes were subsequently linked by a third. The merchant, following his conversion, sails away to Śivanābh's domain, and having enrolled the rājā as a believer assures him that he will one day meet the Gurū himself. But, he adds, the Gurū may come in disguise. The rājā must watch alertly for his coming. This provides the link connecting the two sākhīs although it is unlikely that it was originally developed with this conscious intention. Had that been the case the beliefs and ceremonies attributed to Śivanābh and his subjects would probably have been Śaivite.[1] The distinctively Vaiṣṇava character of the accusations brought against the merchant by Śivanābh's outraged subjects suggests that an anecdote developed in association with a different person has been appropriated to provide the needed link.

The composite sākhī is now substantially complete and subsequent additions do not affect its structure. Of the later supplements the most obvious are two shabads which appear in the *B40* version of the tempting of the Gurū episode. Both illustrate the common practice of inserting quotations from the works of Nānak because their themes and terminology appear to accord well with the subjects of particular anecdotes. A simile commonly used by Gurū Nānak and his Sant predecessors is that of a woman representing the devotee. The imagery is often mildly erotic, the intention being to express in terms comprehensible to human understanding the nature of the devotee's mystical union with God. In several instances it is the faithless devotee who is portrayed, and in such cases the woman appears as one given to fleeting worldly pleasures.

> A woman desires elegance and carnal delights,
> Betel-leaf, flowers, the transient sweetness which turns to anguish.
> She revels and makes merry, but all must turn to lamentation.
> Let her cast herself upon the Lord's mercy and all her deeds will find fulfilment.[2]

Once again Gurū Nānak's meaning has been misunderstood by a janam-sākhī narrator. A real woman has been envisaged and the Śivanābh introduction has provided a convenient place to introduce Nānak's *Basant Aṣṭapadī* 1. This particular shabad was included in the version used

[1] *B40*, ff. 141b–142a.

[2] *Basant aṣṭ* 1, *AG*, p. 1187. *B40*, f. 147b.

by the *Ādi Sākhīs* and *B40* compilers.[1] The second shabad (Gurū Nānak's *Āsā* 35) has been interpolated by the *B40* compiler for the same reason as the *Basant* shabad and on the basis of the same misunderstanding.[2]

Meanwhile the original Śivanābh discourse had been receiving different treatment within the tradition which eventually issued in the *Colebrooke Janam-sākhī*.[3] This version lacks the two anecdotes concerning the Lahore merchant. It also relates the story of the temptresses in the briefest of terms and omits the extra shabads noted above. Instead two other episodes are introduced, both of them derived from pre-Sikh tradition. The first relates how Bābā Nānak insisted upon entering Śivanābh's city mounted on the rājā's back.[4] The second is a grotesque tale of how Bābā Nānak commanded Śivanābh to cut his son's throat and then eat the boy's flesh.[5] It is within this tradition that the reference to Siṅghalādīp appears. Other earlier versions lack it, indicating instead that the abode of Rājā Śivanābh was believed to be somewhere in North India and probably within the Pañjāb itself. A reference to Gorakh-haṭaṛī (Gor-khatrī) which has survived in the *Colebrooke* text suggests an original location within or near the Pañjāb.[6]

Pre-Sikh tradition has provided the extra *Colebrooke* material, and the manner in which it came to be added to the Śivanābh story is at once evident. In the *Mārkandeya-samāsyā parva* of the *Mahābhārata* there is to be found the tale of how a Brāhmaṇ once visited King Śivi, son of Uśīnara. He requested food and when Śivi asked him to be more specific he commanded that the king's son should be killed and cooked. In obedience to this command King Śivi duly slaughtered his son and took the cooked flesh to the visitor. The Brāhmaṇ then ordered the king to eat the flesh himself and only when Śivi began to do so did he stop him. King Śivi had passed the test. The Brāhmaṇ, who revealed himself to be Vidhātri (Viśvakarman) in disguise, commended the king's virtue, restored his son, and proceeded on his way.[7] The name Śivi was evidently confused by the *Colebrooke* narrator with Śivanābh and in this manner the *Mahābhārata* tradition came to be grafted on to the janam-sākhī anecdote.

One further stage in the evolution of the Śivanābh story is marked by the *Hāfizābād Janam-sākhī*. The person responsible for the *Hāfizābād Janam-sākhī* had access to a manuscript followed by the *B40* compiler (the hypothetical manuscript designated *Q1*) and also to either the *Colebrooke Janam-sākhī* or another manuscript very close to it. This meant that he was in a position to use either or both traditions. The rule invariably

[1] For the *Ādi Sākhīs* version see *AS*, pp. 60–9.
[2] *B40*, f. 148a–b.
[3] IOL MS Panj. B6, ff. 162a–176b. Photozincograph Facsimile, pp. 322–51.
[4] *Pur JS*, p. 87.
[5] *Pur JS*, pp. 88–9. *GNSR*, p. 48.
[6] In 1969 it was claimed that the authenticity of the Sri Lanka visit had been established by a newly discovered interlinear inscription incised on a slab now located in the Anurādhapura Museum. This claim must be rejected. For a discussion of the alleged inscription see W. H. McLeod, 'Inter-linear inscriptions in Sri Lanka', *South Asia*, no. 3 (August 1973), pp. 105–6.
[7] *Mah.* III.197. In the Buddhist version of this legend (the Śivi-jātaka) the Brāhmaṇ demands the king's eyes. E. B. Cowell (ed.), *The Jataka, or Stories of the Buddha's Former Births*, vol. iv (Cambridge, 1901), pp. 250–6.

observed by the *Hāfizābād* copyist was to use his *Colebrooke* manuscript as his principal source and to resort to the *Q1* source only where it contained important material which *Colebrooke* lacked.[1] Both manuscripts included versions of the Śivanābh discourse, and so the *Hāfizābād* copyist followed the *Colebrooke* alternative, in sequence as well as in its actual text. The *Colebrooke* manuscript did not, however, include the merchant anecdotes. For these the *Hāfizābād* compiler turned to his second manuscript, once again following its sequence as well as its text. The result is that the two portions of the composite sākhī have been separated in the *Hāfizābād Janam-sākhī*. The merchant anecdotes are recorded at the conclusion of Bābā Nānak's first journey, and the Śivanābh discourse towards the end of his second journey.[2]

The pattern which emerges from this analysis may be diagrammatically represented as in figure 14. This diagram illustrates only the basic structure of the composite sākhī. Within the sākhī a number of supplementary elements have been accommodated, most of them relatively late and all of them interesting. First, there is clear evidence of a distinctive Nānak theology. This is expressed in the doctrine, communicated by the merchant to Rājā Śivanābh, that Bābā Nānak is present wherever he is worshipped.[3] Secondly, the sākhī incorporates some apologetic passages, notably a clear definition of the nature of salvation.[4] These passages also include a polemic directed against Vaiṣṇava ceremonies and, in approving contrast, a description of the Nānak-panthī pattern of worship.[5] Thirdly, there is an interpolation which goes to unusual lengths in stressing the importance of ritual bathing.[6] This evidently reflects a controversy which must have troubled the Sikh community for many years. Other indications of the same controversy appear elsewhere in the janam-sākhīs.[7]

A final complication which deserves to be noted appears in the late *Purātan* manuscript owned by Sevā Singh Sevak of Tarn Tāran.[8] This manuscript, although clearly within the *Purātan* tradition, follows the *Q1* version in its entirety.[9] To this *Q1* version it adds two brief extracts drawn from the *Colebrooke* lineage. The first is the introduction appended to Bābā Nānak's discourse with Śivanābh, in which Nānak's crossing to Śivanābh's domain is incoherently described.[10] This sets the discourse explicitly in Siṅghalādīp. The second extract comprises the introductory portion of the anecdote in which Śivanābh is commanded to kill and consume his son.[11] Obviously the unknown copyist of this manuscript had access to a relatively late recension of the *Q1* version. Unlike his *Hāfizābād*

1 See below, pp. 188–91.

2 M. A. Macauliffe (ed.), *Janam Sākhī Bābe Nānak Jī kī* (Rāwalpiṇḍī, 1885), pp. 187–97, 216–25. In Vīr Singh's *Purātan Janam-sākhī* these appear as sakhis 41 and 47 respectively. *Pur JS*, pp. 74–8, 86–9.

3 *B40*, f. 144a. *Pur JS*, p. 77. *AS*, p. 63.

4 *B40*, f. 142b. *Pur JS*, p. 76. *AS*, p. 63.

5 *B40*, ff. 140b–143b *passim*. *Pur JS*, pp. 76–8. *AS*, pp. 61–4.

6 *B40*, f. 141a–b. *Pur JS*, p. 76. *AS*, pp. 61–2.

7 See below, pp. 227–8.

8 Sevā Singh Sevak, *Prāchīn Janam Sākhī* (Jalandhar, 1969). See above, pp. 26–7.

9 In common with the *B40* text it adds the shabad *Āsā* 35.

10 Sevā Singh Sevak, op. cit., p. 89.

11 Ibid., p. 94.

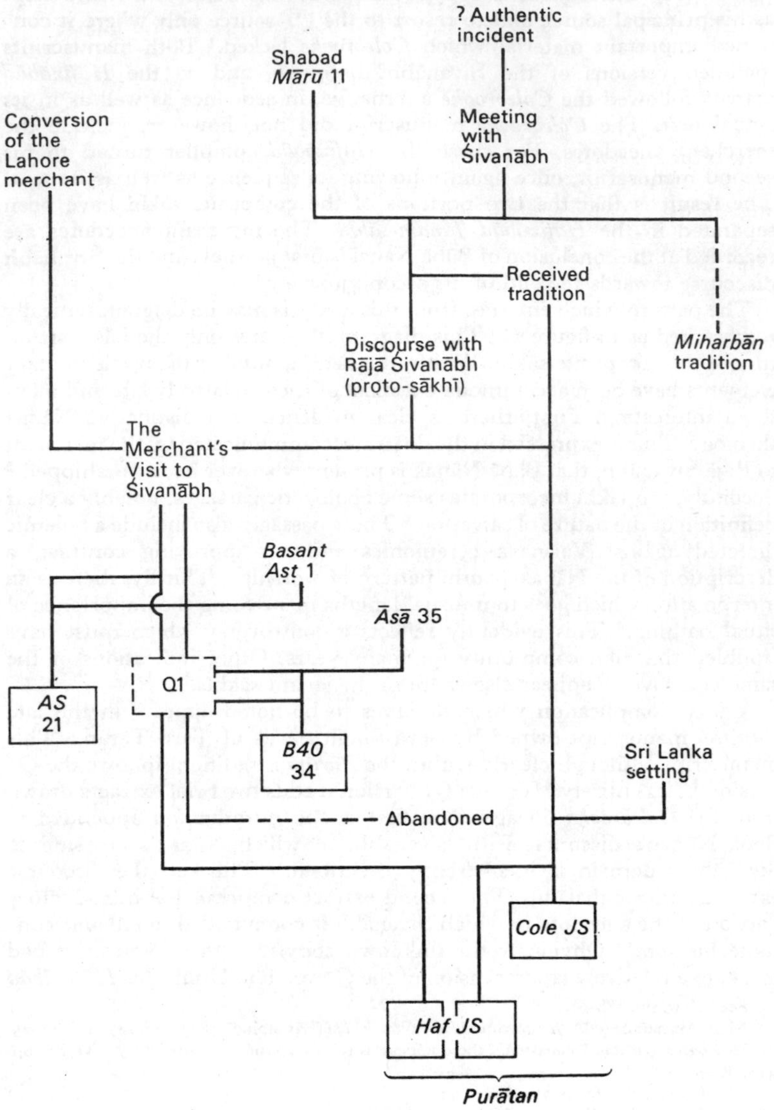
? Authentic incident
Shabad *Mārū* 11
Conversion of the Lahore merchant
Meeting with Śivanābh
Received tradition
Miharbān tradition
Discourse with Rājā Śivanābh (proto-sākhī)
The Merchant's Visit to Śivanābh
Basant Aṣṭ 1
Āsā 35
AS 21
Q1
B40 34
Sri Lanka setting
Abandoned
Cole JS
Haf JS
Purātan

Figure 14

predecessor he preferred to follow the more consistent and attractive *Q1* narrative throughout the entire sākhī, adding to it only the *Purātan* location and the inconsequential introduction to one of the *Purātan* anecdotes.

Example 10: Gurū Aṅgad

Narrative anecdotes: clusters

The ultimate origin of the Gurū Aṅgad cluster of anecdotes is to be found in a demonstrably authentic fact. Bhāī Gurdās briefly states it in the following words:

He shattered the old traditions and [before his death] appointed Aṅgad as Gurū,
For his sons did not obey him, becoming instead perfidious rebels and deserters.[1]

Before he died he installed Lahaṇā as his successor, setting the Gurū's canopy over his head.
Merging his light in [Aṅgad's] light the Satgurū changed his form.
None could comprehend this mystery; a wonder of wonders he revealed!
Changing his body he made Aṅgad's body his own![2]

There can be no doubt whatsoever that Aṅgad was the disciple chosen to succeed Nānak as Gurū. This is the starting-point and from this origin it is possible to trace an evolving pattern of supplementary anecdotes. These do not form a single cluster but rather three major clusters, each with its own distinctive sequence and selection of material. The analysis which follows will trace two of these three clusters. One emerges in the *Purātan* janam-sākhīs.[3] The other appears in both the *Ādi Sākhīs* and *B40 Janam-sākhī*,[4] and from the former descends to the *Miharbān Janam-sākhī*.[5] These two clusters were evidently the first to evolve, although some of their supplementary components are subsequent additions. The third cluster is a later development which came to be attached to the *Bālā* janam-sākhīs.

The pattern of development for both of the earlier clusters begins with the authentic tradition concerning Nānak's choice of Aṅgad as his successor. To this a second authentic element can be added, namely the fact that at least during his later life Gurū Aṅgad must have lived in the village of Khaḍūr.[6] The tradition now divides, one line of descent leading to the *Purātan* cluster and the other through the hypothetical *Q2* source to an *Ādi Sākhīs/B40* cluster.

According to the *Purātan* version Aṅgad resided in Khaḍūr prior to his first meeting with Nānak. There he served as the priest (*pujārī*) of the Trehaṇ Khatrīs who were worshippers of Durgā, and his conversion took place when he happened to overhear Khaḍūr's solitary Sikh singing the hymns of Bābā Nānak. His name during this pre-conversion period is said to have been Lahaṇā.[7]

1 *BG* 1:38. *SLTGN(Eng)*, p. 40.
2 *BG* 1:45. *SLTGN(Eng)*, p. 43.
3 *Pur JS*, pp. 106–8, 110–11.
4 *AS*, pp. 69–98. *B40*, ff. 94b–110a.
5 *Mih JS* II.66–156.
6 Amritsar District.
7 *Pur JS*, p. 106.

The other cluster agrees that Aṅgad was a Trehaṇ Khatrī named Lahaṇā who formerly worshipped Durgā, but in other respects it diverges markedly from the *Purātan* tradition. It relates that Lahaṇā dwelt in the village of Harike, near Matte dī Sarāi, and that he first heard of Bābā Nānak while passing by Kartārpur during an annual pilgrimage to a temple of Durgā. Only after his conversion and a period of three years spent in Kartārpur did he move from Harike to Khaḍūr in response to a command from his new Master.[1]

Two supplementary features are added to both of the evolving traditions before they finally diverge and go their separate ways. The first is the explanation which is given to account for the change of name from Lahaṇā to Aṅgad. The latter name was chosen because Lahaṇā was to be a replica of his Master. He was to be a 'limb' (*aṅg*) from Nānak's own body.[2] The other anecdote common to both clusters is the story of how Aṅgad ruined a new suit of clothes rather than disobey a command given by his Master. Nānak had instructed him to carry home a bundle of dripping grass (*Purātan*) or paddy (*Ādi Sākhīs/B40*). When Nānak's wife observed how the slime had ruined Aṅgad's clothes she rebuked her husband. In reply Nānak assured her that it was really an 'affusion of saffron', not a 'sprinkling of mud'. In other words, it was the seal of succession which she was observing.[3]

The two traditions now diverge completely, and it is only in a second recension of the *Ādi Sākhīs* that they come together again. To the common material the *Purātan* tradition adds the following supplementary anecdotes.

1. Aṅgad observes how every night the goddess Durgā comes to massage the Gurū[4]
2. The maidservant's vision[5]
3. Bābā Nānak tests his Sikhs by scattering coins before them. Only two pass the test (one of them Lahaṇā and the other unnamed)[6]
4. Bābā Nānak tests the two Sikhs by commanding them to eat a corpse[7]
5. Aṅgad is installed as Gurū[8]

Two shabads are added to the cluster, neither of them integral to the narrative.[9] The compiler's chronological concern has also prompted the insertion of an anecdote concerning Sheikh Bahā' al-Dīn Zakariyyā.[10]

All this appears to constitute a single tradition, developed by supplementing the original anecdotes with various sub-anecdotes. In contrast the *Ādi Sākhīs/B40* cluster is evidently a union of two such lines of development. One of these begins, like the *Puratan* tradition, with the original anecdotes and expands in the same manner. In addition to the supple-

[1] *B40*, ff. 94b, 96b, 97b.

[2] *Pur JS*, p. 108. *B40*, ff. 93a, 95a. See above, pp. 91–2.

[3] *Pur JS*, p. 107. *B40*, ff. 97b–98b. [4] *Pur JS*, p. 107. [5] Ibid.

[6] Ibid., p. 108. [7] Ibid. [8] Ibid., p. 110.

[9] *Sirī Rāg* 3 is appended to the corpse-eating test, and Gurū Arjan's *Mājh* 18 is said to have been recited at the installation ceremony.

[10] *Pur JS*, pp. 108–10. The anecdote has been interpolated by the *Purātan* compiler at this point because it relates to the imminent death of Bābā Nānak.

mentary anecdotes already mentioned it adds a variant account of Gurū Aṅgad's installation and also a version of the Achal discourse.

This tradition then unites with another issuing from different antecedents. The origin of this second contributory tradition is not an actual episode, but rather the ascetic ideal which, in accordance with the convictions of a particular group within the Sikh community, encouraged respect for faqīrs, celibacy, and withdrawal from worldly activity.[1] Elsewhere this ideal is expressed only as a gloss or as an interpretation laid upon an evolved anecdote. Here, however, it forms the basis of a small cluster incorporated within the larger Aṅgad cluster.

The smaller cluster has one principal component relating directly to the person of Gurū Aṅgad. This is the story of Aṅgad's loyal fortitude (an account of how he endured the torment of rain and cold in order to maintain a vigil while his Master was bathing).[2] The remainder relate to him less directly, but all involve his presence and emphasize his special status. Four anecdotes of this kind can be distinguished.

1. The story of Mūlā the Khatrī[3]
2. A course of austerities performed by Bābā Nānak[4]
3. Bābā Nānak's adoration[5]
4. Bābā Nānak seeks solitude[6]

The last of these narrates a series of stratagems adopted by Bābā Nānak at Gorakhnāth's suggestion to rid himself of the company of his disciples. First he imposes hard labour on them; next he reduces their food ration to vanishing point; thirdly he burns the harvest which they have so laboriously gathered; and finally, feigning madness, he threatens them with a dagger. (The last of these was evidently suggested by the theme of the shabad *Sirī Rāg* 29.) Although the origin of this series appears to be the ascetic emphasis upon the value of withdrawal it is implied at one point that the various stratagems are really tests designed to prove Aṅgad's worth.[7]

These two traditions were evidently recorded by the *Q2* compiler and then utilized by his *Ādi Sākhīs* and *B40* successors.[8] The only significant difference distinguishing the two successor versions of the common cluster is the omission from the extant *Ādi Sākhīs* of the 'Installation of Gurū Aṅgad' sākhī. This was probably present in an earlier recension of the *Ādi Sākhīs*, but omitted from the later recension because its redactor preferred another version of the same sākhī.

It was this preference which led to renewed contact between the *Ādi Sākhīs*/*B40* tradition and that of the *Purātan* janam-sākhīs. Although the precise source is not clear it appears that the *Ādi Sākhīs* redactor has used a version of the installation sākhī which finds expression in the *Purātan* tradition. This is the conclusion indicated by the same redactor's use of the corpse-eating sākhī, and even if some doubt must persist concerning

1 See above, pp. 79–81.
2 *B40*, ff. 104a–105a.
3 *B40*, ff. 100b–101b.
4 *B40*, ff. 102b–104a.
5 *B40*, f. 106a–b.
6 *B40*, ff. 106b–110a.
7 *B40*, f. 107b.
8 In the *Ādi Sākhīs* the two clusters appear as sākhīs 8b–d and 24–25e. *AS*, pp. 23–6, 76–84.

the installation sākhī the corpse-eating anecdote certainly provides a link between the two traditions. The two anecdotes are included in another supplementary cluster attached by the *Ādi Sākhīs* compiler to the ascetic cluster. This later supplement comprises the following anecdotes:

1. A recitation of *Japjī*
2. Dead birds revivified: Bābā Nānak's remorse
3. An interview with God: recitation of the shabad *Sodar*
4. Bābā Nānak summons the Gangā to thirsty Sikhs
5. Bābā Nānak continues testing his Sikhs
6. The story of Vasiṣṭ
7. Aṅgad commanded to eat a corpse
8. The installation of Gurū Aṅgad.[1]

The first four anecdotes should be separated from the remainder, for they evidently represent an interpolation drawn from a *Miharbān* source.[2] The remainder consists of additional anecdotes which further expand the Aṅgad cluster of the *Ādi Sākhīs* first recension.

This composite *Ādi Sākhīs* cluster underwent one further expansion. The entire cluster has been recorded, with some further additions, in *Pothī Harijī* of the *Miharbān Janam-sākhī*.[3] There can be no doubt that it appears there as a relatively late addition to the *Miharbān Janam-sākhī*, and little doubt that the source must have been the second recension of the *Ādi Sākhīs*. The precise point of inclusion within the *Miharbān Janam-sākhī* was probably determined by the earlier inclusion of a version of the Achal discourse. To the cluster was added an interview with God, and it is possible that one other anecdote included in this late *Miharbān* collection was also introduced at this time. This latter anecdote purports to describe a second marriage by Nānak.[4]

The extant *Miharbān* text represents the final stage in the evolution of the second tradition, just as the *Colebrooke* and *Hāfizābād* manuscripts provide a terminal point for the first. The two traditions diverge at an early stage and the only close link during the later stages of their respective developments is the small borrowing which appears in the second recension of the *Ādi Sākhīs*. There is, however, one other collection which combines elements drawn from both traditions. This is the account of Bābā Nānak's life given in the *Mahimā Prakāś Vāratak*. The *Mahimā Prakāś Vāratak* of Kirpāl Dās Bhallā (or Kirpāl Siṅgh Bhallā) is distinguished above all by the measure of attention which it devotes to Khaḍūr village and to the person of Gurū Aṅgad. In view of this special interest it is not

[1] *AS*, pp. 85–98. A concluding death sākhī follows this cluster.

[2] See below, pp. 212–14.

[3] *Mih JS* II.66–156.

[4] In the interview with God (*Mih JS* II.152–6) Nānak is said to have reproached the Almighty for the status bestowed upon him at birth. When God replies that he was given the respected status of a Khatrī he responds with the shabad *Sirī Rāg* 29 which the *Ādi Sākhīs*/*B40* version sets a little earlier in the narrative. The interview concludes with a ringing assurance from God that all who enter Nānak's panth will find salvation. It seems that this addition to the earlier version should be interpreted primarily as an attempt to sustain Khatrī authority within the community. The apocryphal account of a second marriage (*Mih JS* II.141–3) may have been included in an intermediate recension of the *Ādi Sākhīs* and then dropped by the redactor responsible for the extant text.

surprising that its author should have utilized so much of the available Aṅgad material. The following anecdotes appear in the *Mahimā Prakāś Vāratak*:[1]

1. The meeting with Lahaṇā (*Ādi Sākhīs/B40* tradition)
2. Lahaṇā's clothes ruined
3. The birth of Lakhmī Dās and Sirī Chand
   (Both conceived in response to Aṅgad's intercession)
4. The loyal fortitude of Aṅgad
5. Aṅgad shakes sweets from a tree
6. Absolute loyalty
   Bābā Nānak asks Buḍhā and Aṅgad to tell the time during the night.
7. The coins test
8. The corpse-eating test
   (Buḍhā named as the other disciple)
9. Lahaṇā becomes Aṅgad
10. Aṅgad instructed to move to Khaḍūr
11. The adoration of Māī Birāī
12. Aṅgad's lost children: the return of Dāsū and Dātā
13. Perfect obedience
    Aṅgad, misunderstanding a command of Bābā Nānak, remains rooted to the same spot for several years.
14. Bābā Nānak reveals a freshwater well in Khaḍūr.

Two concluding sākhīs follow this large cluster of Aṅgad anecdotes. The first is the Bahā' al-Dīn anecdote which has been added to the *Purātan* janam-sākhīs; and the second is a version of Bābā Nānak's death which obviously derives from the tradition used by the *Ādi Sākhīs* and *B40* compilers.[2]

Although this lengthy list includes anecdotes drawn from both the main traditions outlined above it does not necessarily follow that Kirpāl Dās Bhallā was using any of the manuscripts which today represent either of the two Aṅgad clusters. It seems much more likely that his sources were oral (probably the oral tradition current in Khaḍūr during the early eighteenth century), and if in fact they included any manuscripts these are unlikely to have been any of those mentioned above. Whereas the *Mahimā Prakāś Vāratak* appears to have come from Khaḍūr the other manuscripts all seem to have been located further to the north-west. The text of the *Mahimā Prakāś Vāratak* also supports this conclusion.

This pattern is represented diagrammatically in figure 15.

Example 11: Mardānā and Bālā

Dispersed references

The significant references to Gurū Aṅgad are almost all concentrated within three distinct clusters of sākhīs, and any attempt to understand his

[1] *SLTGN(Eng)*, pp. 77–84. *SLTGN(Pbi)*, pp. 41–4.
[2] *SLTGN(Eng)*, pp. 84–7. *SLTGN(Pbi)*, pp. 44–6.

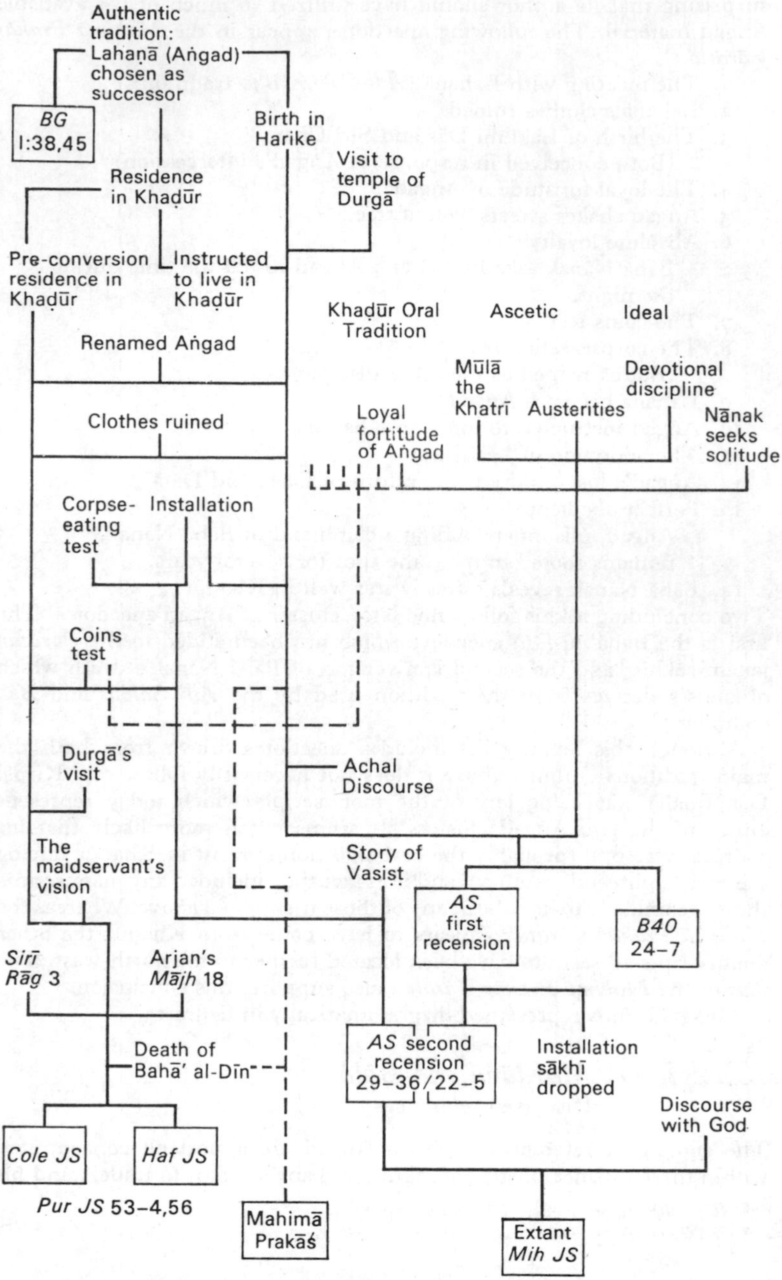
Authentic tradition: Lahaṇā (Aṅgad) chosen as successor
BG I:38,45
Birth in Harike
Visit to temple of Durgā
Residence in Khaḍūr
Pre-conversion residence in Khaḍūr
Instructed to live in Khaḍūr
Khaḍūr Oral Tradition
Ascetic
Ideal
Renamed Aṅgad
Mūlā the Khatrī
Devotional discipline
Austerities
Clothes ruined
Loyal fortitude of Aṅgad
Nānak seeks solitude
Corpse-eating test
Installation
Coins test
Durgā's visit
Achal Discourse
The maidservant's vision
Story of Vasist
AS first recension
B40 24–7
Sirī Rāg 3
Arjan's Mājh 18
AS second recension 29–36/22–5
Installation sākhī dropped
Death of Bahā' al-Dīn
Discourse with God
Cole JS
Haf JS
Pur JS 53–4,56
Mahimā Prakāś
Extant Mih JS

Figure 15

role within the janam-sākhīs need proceed little further than an analysis of this limited material. The *Miharbān Janam-sākhī* makes extensive use of him as an interlocutor, but for this purpose others could easily have been chosen. Gurū Aṅgad has, in most instances, been selected because for the later period of Bābā Nānak's life he could be regarded as a regular attendant upon his Master. The treatment of Mardānā and Bālā is, however, different and no single sākhī or cluster of sākhīs can adequately exemplify their roles.

Mardānā the Minstrel enjoys a particular prominence in modern accounts of the life of Gurū Nānak. This status he owes largely to the interest accorded him by the *Purātan* tradition. In other traditions his importance is considerably diminished, and in one significant source he is almost completely absent. The primitive tradition which will later be designated *Narrative III* mentions him only twice.[1] Within this tradition he is merely one of a number of companions to whom passing reference is made, with no special significance attached to his presence. He serves a purpose which could conceivably have been fulfilled by Ajittā Randhāvā or Gurū Aṅgad.

Mardānā acquires his distinctive function and corresponding prominence when the janam-sākhī narrators begin introducing into their anecdotes quotations from the works of Nānak. Almost all Nānak's numerous compositions are intended to be sung, and if the Gurū was to give utterance to them in the janam-sakhīs he would obviously require an accompanist as companion. Because Mardānā bore the title of Mirāsī (a low caste-grouping of Muslim minstrels) he was accordingly well suited to this role. This is not to suggest that Mardānā never existed. The united testimony of the janam-sākhī compilers suggests that his existence can safely be taken for granted and that he must have been intimately associated in some manner with Gurū Nānak. Moreover, it can be assumed that as a Mirāsī he must surely have participated as an accompanist in the hymn-singing (*kīrtan*) of the small community. It is the detailed description of his association with Gurū Nānak which cannot be taken for granted. These descriptions bear too close a correspondence to the function of Mardānā within the janam-sākhī narratives to permit any firm assumptions beyond the simple assurance that there must certainly have been an association of some sort.

For the janam-sākhī narrators Mardānā's distinctive function was that of minstrel to accompany the Gurū's singing. As the quotations from Nānak's works increase so too do Mardānā's appearances. This can be appreciated if the *Narrative III* sākhīs are compared with the source designated *Narrative I*.[2] The latter is a much more highly evolved tradition

[1] *B40*, ff. 158a–b, 164a. The number of references increases to four if *B40* sākhīs 56 and 57 (*B40*, ff. 219a–220a) are ascribed to the *Narrative III* tradition. For the *Narrative III* tradition see below, pp. 220–6. There is a passing reference to Mardānā at the beginning of sākhī 31, another of the *Narrative III* anecdotes. *B40*, f. 127b. This, however, occurs in a brief introduction which has been appended to the *Narrative III* sākhī, evidently by the *B40* compiler. The *Miharbān* version of the anecdote lacks the introduction. *Mih JS* I.231–2.

[2] See below, pp. 181 ff.

and as such it regularly includes suitable quotations in its sākhīs. Because *Narrative I* material has been extensively used by the *Purātan* compilers, and because their supplementary material is similarly evolved, scriptural quotation is a particularly common feature of the *Purātan* janam-sākhīs. Within this tradition Mardānā enjoys, in consequence, a particular prominence, a prominence which has been carried over into modern accounts as a result of the fondness for the *Purātan* source shown by Macauliffe and almost all his successors.

The process is well illustrated by example 4, 'The Rich Man's Pennants', where the *Purātan* narrator, having added a quotation from *Vār Āsā* also introduces Mardānā to accompany it.[1] This same feature may also be observed in the various versions of the anecdote entitled 'The Monster's Cauldron'. The *Ādi Sākhīs* text, which provides a version very close to the original proto-anecdote, includes no quotation from the works of Nānak and so makes no mention of Mardānā.[2] It is only when Gurū Arjan's shabad *Mārū* 14 is anachronistically introduced that Mardānā appears in the narrative.[3] If the examination is extended to other sākhīs it will be observed that Mardānā rarely participates in any active sense.[4] When he does it is in a manner which might well have indicated someone else.[5] In other words, he serves as one of a small panel of regular participants. It is only when the singing of shabads becomes a prominent feature that his importance escalates.

As time passed and interpretations shifted Mardānā gradually acquired a new role without abandoning his earlier function as minstrel. The earlier role continued to increase in importance as more quotations were introduced, and having acquired prominence in this manner he was increasingly used as a participant in preference to other regular candidates. His new role was, however, something distinctively different, one which he alone of the regular participants was fitted to play. As the janam-sākhīs developed their theme of recognition by both Hindus and Muslims of Nānak's divine status Mardānā was enlisted as a symbol of Muslim acceptance. This role has ever since gathered an increasing importance, strengthening the earlier emphasis of the *Purātan* tradition. As a result Mardānā now commands an eminence which stands in conspicuous contrast to his relative obscurity in the more primitive traditions. The fact

[1] See above, p. 126.

[2] *AS*, p. 28.

[3] *B40*, f. 40a. See above, pp. 76–7. The *Miharbān* version includes Mardānā without the shabad. *Mih JS* I.231. This version is, however, a relatively late addition to the *Miharbān* tradition, drawn from the *Ādi Sākhīs* or a source very close to it (i.e. from a source lacking both the shabad and Mardānā). See below, p. 202. It was interpolated at a point where Mardānā figures in the continuing narrative and where his absence would have seemed incongruous. *Miharbān* redactors normally noted this kind of inconsistency and it was presumably for this reason that they introduced Mardānā. In this late *Miharbān* version Mardānā's role undergoes a further extension. In order to avoid the necessity of putting Bābā Nānak in the cauldron later narrators make Mardānā suffer the indignity instead.

[4] *B40*, sākhīs 7, 8, 12a, 18a, 22, 37, and 57.

[5] The only exception amongst the *B40* sākhīs of this kind is number 57. This concerns Bābā Nānak's hymns and so indicates Mardānā as an obvious choice.

that as a Mirāsī he could also serve as a symbol of the lower castes has in recent times provided him with yet another role.

It must be repeated that this analysis does not question the actual existence of Mardānā, nor should it imply that he was never a companion of Gurū Nānak. On the contrary, there is sufficient evidence to conclude that he certainly did exist and that he must have been an intimate associate of the Gurū. Bhāī Gurdās's references to him put this beyond doubt.[1] The conclusion which follows from the analysis is that this historical person must be distinguished from the functions which Mardānā performs in the janam-sākhī traditions. The activities narrated in the traditions should be related almost exclusively to these roles. Only occasionally can they reasonably and safely be connected with actual incidents in the life of the historical Mardānā.

The same conclusion should also be applied to the figure of Bālā, putative narrator of the janam-sākhīs which bear his name. Little significance attaches to the doubtful historicity of the actual person. It is his function which matters. Bālā's original function was to set a seal of authenticity upon the janam-sākhīs of a particular tradition. The janam-sākhīs of this tradition begin by claiming that Bālā was the constant companion of the Gurū on all his travels, and if this claim were to be accepted it would follow that the narrative which he delivers must be an authentic account. Later he too acquires a supplementary role, and in precisely the same manner as Mardānā. Just as Mardānā symbolizes Muslim acceptance, so too does Bālā serve as a symbol of Hindu acceptance. His presence is essential to complete the image, an image which retains its popularity to this day. When represented in visual form it depicts Bābā Nānak sitting in the centre, flanked by Mardānā and his *rabāb* on one side and Bālā with his peacock-feather whisk on the other.[2] It is a representation which epitomizes a fundamental aspect of the janam-sākhī message.

[1] *BG* I:35, XI:13.

[2] For an excellent example see Khushwant Singh, *A History of the Sikhs*, vol. i (Princeton and London, 1963), plate facing p. 210.

10
SOURCES USED BY THE JANAM-SĀKHĪ COMPILERS

In chapter 8 a brief description was given of the assembling and transmission of janam-sākhī traditions. The concluding chapter of this section on the origins and growth of the janam-sākhī traditions will examine transmission procedures in greater detail. It will begin by postulating an early grouping of sākhīs to form the first coherent traditions concerning the life of Nānak. On the basis of this postulate it will attempt a description of the manner in which this primitive tradition must have expanded and diversified. It will also indicate how certain versions of it came to be consciously regrouped in order to provide a chronological sequence. Finally, it will analyse at some length the process of selection from both written and oral sources which constituted the method of later compilers.

All extant janam-sākhīs belong to the later stages of this pattern of development. Although some of the earliest include substantial quantities of material which must have been first recorded in the late sixteenth century or early seventeenth century all are, in their extant form, products of an augmented selection drawn from even earlier sources. The janam-sākhī which retains the closest connection with the initial stages of the pattern is the version recorded in the manuscript designated *LDP 194*. Even this manuscript must, however, be classified with other early manuscripts. Like them it is patently an expanded version of an even earlier tradition.

The fact that the janam-sākhīs are so obviously evolved works has naturally suggested the existence of an 'original' janam-sākhī. Two claims have been advanced in this respect. The earlier is based upon the express declaration made at the beginning of all versions and recensions of the *Bālā* tradition. All claim to record the words of an eye-witness to the life and travels of Bābā Nānak.[1] The association of the *Bālā* tradition with the schismatic Hindālīs occasionally prompted a measure of doubt concerning the authenticity of the eye-witness claim, but until a century ago such misgivings were rare. Santokh Singh suggested a solution to the problem during the early nineteenth century by acting on the assumption that the Hindālīs must have interpolated an earlier and authentic version of the tradition.

A more recent claim dates from the discovery of the two principal *Purātan* manuscripts (the *Colebrooke* and *Hāfizābād* janam-sākhīs). The version which they record appeared to be an early one, lacking both the

[1] See above, pp. 16–18.

Hindālī taint and the more fanciful flights of Puranic fancy which characterize the *Bālā* janam-sākhīs. It was accordingly accepted by many Sikh scholars as the earliest of all extant versions. Vīr Singh and Macauliffe expressed this conviction in the titles which they chose for their editions of this version. For Vīr Singh it was the *Purātan Janam-sākhī*, or 'Ancient Janam-sākhī', and for Macauliffe *The Most Ancient Biography of Bābā Nānak*. It is, of course, evident that both the *Colebrooke* and *Hāfizābād* manuscripts must be later recensions, but Macauliffe had referred to another manuscript in his possession dated S. 1645 (A.D. 1588).[1] Others have subsequently assumed that this must have represented either the 'original' janam-sākhī or a version very close to it. This point of view had already been expressed by Trumpp following his discovery of the *Colebrooke* manuscript. The newly discovered janam-sākhī was, he declared, 'the fountain from which all others have drawn largely'.[2] Recently a modified version of the same claim has been advanced by Professor Piār Singh. This qualified version claims archetypal status not for the *Colebrooke* manuscript but for an earlier hypothetical recension of the same tradition to which Piār Singh has attached the name *proto-Purātan Janam sākhī*.[3]

The *Bālā* claim is specifically stated in the prologue appended to all janam-sākhīs of this tradition. Bhāī Bālā, the putative narrator of the tradition, is represented as a constant companion of Bābā Nānak.[4] If this claim can be sustained it follows that the account which he is said to have related in the presence of Gurū Aṅgad must be an eye-witness account and the original janam-sākhī. It is, however, impossible to sustain the claim. Several features of the *Bālā* tradition require positive rejection of its self-proclaimed origins and its implied precedence over all other traditions.

A major objection to the *Bālā* claim derives from the complete absence of any reference to Bhāī Bālā in the works of Bhāī Gurdās (including his *Vār* XI list of Gurū Nānak's more prominent disciples) or in any non-*Bālā* janam-sākhī which predates the eighteenth century. Even the support offered by eighteenth-century janam-sākhīs is of no consequence. The portions of the extant *Gyān-ratanāvalī* which refer to Bālā are plainly later additions;[5] and the sole reference in the earlier *Mahimā Prakāś* is far removed from any suggestion of regular companionship.[6] This situation could never have arisen if in fact Bhāī Bālā had occupied the position claimed on his behalf by the *Bālā* janam-sākhīs.

A second objection concerns the ineptly contrived nature of the explanatory prologue. It would be altogether inconceivable that Gurū Aṅgad had never heard of one who had been a constant companion of Bābā Nānak, or that the same companion should never have heard of his

[1] Macauliffe, i. lxxxvi. See above, p. 27.

[2] E. Trumpp, *The Ādi Granth* (London, 1877), p. ii.

[3] Piār Singh, 'A Critical Survey of Panjabi Prose in the Seventeenth Century' (unpublished Ph.D. thesis, Panjab University, 1968), p. 80.

[4] See above, p. 16.

[5] *GNSR*, pp. 26–7.

[6] *SLTGN(Eng)*, p. 79. *SLTGN(Pbi)*, p. 42.

Master's successor. The date of the alleged encounter between the two (A.D. 1525) must also arouse some suspicion. Nānak died in A.D. 1538 or 1539.

Thirdly, it is evident from the structure of the janam-sākhī that its origins belong to a period which followed the assembling of the more rudimentary collections. The length and substance of the earliest *Bālā* travel itineraries, as implied in the prologue and worked out in the manuscripts, indicate that the originator or originators of the tradition were able to build upon earlier models.

There can be no doubt that some very early traditions have been preserved in several of the individual *Bālā* sākhīs, but equally there can be no doubt that the collection as a whole must belong to the middle seventeenth century, not to the late sixteenth or early seventeenth century. Although Bālā himself may perhaps have been a real person, he could not have been a constant companion of the Gurū in the manner claimed by the tradition which bears his name. His function within this tradition is manifestly that of lending it the measure of authenticity which would be required in order to establish its pretensions over those of other traditions.

Although Macauliffe made some of the more obvious objections abundantly clear, the theory of an 'original' janam-sākhī delivered before Gurū Aṅgad did not die an immediate death. Vīr Singh was perhaps the most influential amongst those who suggested that the original version delivered in this manner must have been destroyed by the Hindālī authors of the *Bālā* tradition. Without making his interpretation entirely clear he seems to have reverted to the old theory, associated with the name of Santokh Singh, which explains the *Bālā* tradition as an interpolated version of this 'original' janam-sākhī.[1] If this were to be accepted it would mean that the identification and excision of all Hindālī references from the earliest extant *Bālā* manuscripts would leave something very close to the account narrated before Gurū Aṅgad. There is, however, no evidence whatsoever to support this nostalgic assumption. An analysis of the *Bālā* contents shows that it must be regarded as a middle-period product, a predecessor of the *Gyān-ratanāvalī* and the two *Mahimā Prakāś* versions but later than the earlier portions of all other major janam-sākhī traditions.

This leaves the claim to originality advanced on behalf of the *Purātan* version. The *Purātan* claim cannot be rejected in the same summary manner, although as it stands it must certainly be qualified. In its extant form the *Purātan* tradition is a highly evolved product, and if in fact there lies behind it an 'original' janam-sākhī the *Colebrooke* and *Hāfizābād* manuscripts are far removed from this prototype in terms of development.

[1] Vīr Singh, *Srī Gur Pratāp Sūraj Granthāvalī* (Amritsar, 1964), p. 54. Macauliffe fails to make his opinion clear, but seems to imply acceptance of the *Purātan* claims. The Hindālīs, he states, were able to destroy 'nearly all the older accounts of the life of Guru Nanak'. Macauliffe, i. lxxxiii. Later he declares the *Purātan* version to be 'beyond dispute the most trustworthy detailed record we possess of the life of Nanak'. Ibid., p. lxxxvii. The first statement implies the survival of at least one 'older' account and the second suggests that this is to be identified with the *Purātan* version. He does, however, add that the *Purātan* account is 'deformed by mythological matter' (ibid.), thereby implying a measure of corruption in the *Purātan* text.

An analysis of the sources used by this tradition and by a number of other janam-sākhīs does, however, suggest that the *Purātan* janam-sākhīs may be directly descended from a nucleus of sākhīs which constituted the earliest tradition concerning the life of Nānak. If this hypothetical nucleus is to be designated the 'original' janam-sākhī there must be a clear understanding that it did not constitute a janam-sākhī of the kind represented by extant collections. It must obviously have been something much more rudimentary than the surviving janam-sākhīs.

A comparison of the *Purātan* janam-sākhīs with *LDP 194*, the *B40 Janam-sākhī*, the *Ādi Sākhīs*, and the *Miharbān Janam-sākhī* indicates that at some early date a small selection of anecdotes must have been grouped in a simple connected sequence. This cluster of primitive sākhīs will have constituted an archetype. In the following analysis of sources this earliest of all coherent collections will be referred to as the *Narrative I* tradition. The cluster was certainly small and almost certainly oral in its earliest version. This latter conclusion is implied by the absence of any manuscript version, by the obvious importance of oral tradition in the later development of the janam-sākhīs, and by analogy with similar collections of popular hagiography.

An important feature of this early nucleus will have been its links with authentic incidents from the actual life of Gurū Nānak. It is no accident that almost all of the few janam-sākhī constituents which withstand the test of vigorous historical analysis can be traced to this cluster. These authentic constituents, however, account for only a small proportion of the material included within the cluster. It is clear that the impulse to augment operated from the very beginning. This process will have followed the lines indicated by the analysis of individual sākhīs set out in chapter 9, and as a result of its operation the nucleus must have included appreciable quantities of legendary material by the time it emerged as a recognizable tradition. This need occasion no surprise. It is the basic myth which must retain its consistency, not the material which is used to give it expression.

Following the emergence of this first coherent tradition the augmenting impulse assumed complete control. Surviving memories which related to actual events were soon utilized in the continuing development of the tradition and within a short space of time were largely transformed by the addition of extra features, many of them essentially interpretative. Although passages from the works of Nānak continued to provide an indirect link, the sākhīs which were developed on the basis of such passages almost always related legendary rather than authentic anecdotes. In their choice of material the narrators responsible for the expansion of the earliest tradition were directed by the influence of traditional concepts, by the nature of the emergent community's needs, by its understanding of its role, and above all by the myth which justified and sustained its existence.

The consolidation of the first nucleus was thus followed by a rapid multiplication of anecdotes. Like the original nucleus these supplementary anecdotes will have originally developed as oral tradition. Many must have remained unrecorded and, after circulating within a particular area, assimilated to associated traditions or gradually disappeared.

In this manner there developed a large and ever-increasing fund of oral anecdotes. Some will have had a restricted circulation within certain areas and amongst certain groups within the Sikh panth, whereas others obviously enjoyed a much wider circulation. At various points in time a particular congregation (*saṅgat*) or individual evidently perceived the benefits of possessing a recorded version of the current tradition. In response to this realization collections of anecdotes were compiled for the edification of the congregation. In the case of the *B40* manuscript this is specifically declared to have been the origin of the collection.[1]

Although recorded versions could not have kept pace with the proliferation of oral anecdotes, the expansion of oral tradition was inevitably followed by a corresponding expansion of the written tradition, later and more restricted in content. These documents presumably began to circulate during the latter half of the sixteenth century and certainly continued to grow in length and number during the centuries which followed. The process reached a climax during the last three decades of the nineteenth century in a period of rapid *Bālā* development. Since then it has weakened but never disappeared. Collections of anecdotes which are essentially janam-sākhīs still appear as 'biographies' of Nānak.

Whereas the earliest of these collections will necessarily have relied exclusively upon oral tradition for its source the extant manuscripts show a marked preference for existing manuscripts. Oral tradition continued, however, to provide a supplementary source of considerable importance. Once again the *B40* collection serves as an example. Although the original basis of the *B40 Janam-sākhī* has obviously been provided by the *Narrative I* tradition, the largest single source was evidently the oral tradition of the locality in which the collection was compiled. In the analysis of sources which follows this major supplementary source is designated *Narrative III*.

The differences which so plainly distinguish *Narrative I* material from *Narrative III* anecdotes demonstrate the composite nature of the *B40* collection. In other instances a compiler's preference will incline him strongly towards a single major source and in many cases he will have had no choice other than a single available manuscript. As a result most extant manuscripts can be associated with well-defined traditions. The *Hāfizābād* compiler, for example, shows a marked preference for the *Narrative Ia* source which issues in the *Colebrooke* janam-sākhī. Other copyists reproduced the same material, with its distinctive content and sequence. The distinctive selection and arrangement constitutes the *Purātan* tradition, and manuscripts which follow this version can all be classified as *Purātan* janam-sākhīs. Others belong to the equally distinctive *Miharbān*, *Bālā*, *Ādi Sākhīs*, *Gyān-ratanāvalī*, or *Mahimā Prakāś* traditions.

One significant difference which distinguishes the *Bālā* janam-sākhīs and much of the *Miharbān* tradition from the others is their conspicuous

[1] *B40*, f. 84b.

lack of coherent chronological order.[1] In this respect the two traditions may reflect an earlier stage of development than the others. The earliest nucleus evidently possessed a recognizable order, but this was scarcely surprising as its content consisted largely of anecdotes concerning the childhood of Nānak. Only one sākhī related to the period in Sultānpur, one to his travels, one to his return, and perhaps one to his death. This imposed an obvious order upon the small cluster and all that remained was to add two miscellaneous anecdotes narrating incidents which had occurred in the Pañjāb.

If in fact the *Bālā* pattern represents a feature of early janam-sākhī compilation it means that at the earlier stage supplementary anecdotes drawn from oral tradition will have been added indiscriminately to the nucleus, the only deference to chronological sequence being a general grouping under the categories of childhood, manhood, and death. The obvious point at which the *Narrative I* cluster could be supplemented was its brief reference to Bābā Nānak's period of travels. The twelve years allocated to this period provided ample scope for expansion of the tradition and it is scarcely surprising that many anecdotes were introduced in order to fill the gap. Another such opportunity was provided by the period following Nānak's return from his travels, a period which he spent in the village of Kartārpur. Anecdotes relating to these periods must have been narrated with little regard for chronology, and only later could efforts have been made to order the generally incoherent collection into a chronological pattern.

This progression did not, of course, take place with a neat and orderly consistency. Whereas some janam-sākhī compilers have followed a developed chronological pattern others, contemporary or later, have paid heed to chronology only in the most general sense. There can be no doubt that the developed patterns have been devised by narrators who were adding to the nucleus, but it is not entirely clear at what stage this was done. All that can be affirmed is a tendency to develop increasingly intricate patterns, a process which reaches its most advanced phase in the chronology of the *Purātan* janam-sākhīs. The four major journeys (*udāsī*) of the *Purātan* tradition are evidently a later recording either of an earlier twofold pattern, or perhaps of a single travel narrative. The *Ādi Sākhīs* offer a travel narrative which groups a restricted number of anecdotes into a single journey; the *Pothī Sach-khaṇḍ* version of the *Miharbān* tradition (which evidently derives in part from the *Ādi Sākhīs* tradition) enlarges this to constitute two journeys; and the *Purātan* version, following the four points of the compass, devises four separate journeys. In all such instances the extra material required to fill out the itinerary has been added to the nucleus in the form of supplementary anecdotes.

Two distinct patterns have thus emerged as the collections of anecdotes have progressively expanded. One can be described as a pattern in only the loosest sense. Anecdotes are added singly or in small clusters with

[1] Chronological order is a feature of *Pothī Sach-khaṇḍ*, the first section of the *Miharbān Janam-sākhī*, but not of the succeeding sections.

regard being paid to nothing more than the most rudimentary of chronological sequences. These are the essentially unstructured janam-sākhīs which reach their climax in the twentieth-century collections of the *Bālā* tradition. To this same category belongs the *B40 Janam-sākhī* and the two versions of the *Mahimā Prakāś*. It should be added that their significant resemblance to the *Bālā* tradition is confined to this feature.

The other pattern is represented by the *Ādi Sākhīs*, *Pothī Sach-khaṇḍ* of the *Miharbān* tradition, the *Purātan* janam-sākhīs, and the *Gyān-ratanāvalī*. These versions are, in varying degrees, structured according to assumed chronologies. Sākhīs which occur indiscriminately in the *Bālā* or *B40* versions are here regrouped in order to constitute a logical sequence. None actually achieves the ultimate objective. The *Purātan* version, which comes closest to it, misplaces some individual anecdotes and records at the conclusion of its first journey a cluster of sākhīs which could more logically be assigned to the conclusion of the fourth journey. One important feature which derives from this impulse to arrange a coherent sequence is that anecdotes which in their earlier versions are unlocated are given definite geographical settings in order to accommodate them within a developed itinerary. This results in the same anecdote being set in different places by different compilers. Bābā Nānak's encounter with Sajjaṇ, for example, is located in South India by the *Miharbān* tradition (which is here following the *Ādi Sākhīs* pattern); in or near the Pañjāb by the *Purātan* janam-sākhīs; near Tulambā in Multān district by the *Bālā* janam-sākhīs; and in Hastināpur by the *Gyān-ratanāvalī*.[1]

It was in this manner that the janam-sākhīs evolved. All are collections of anecdotes, or of exegetical discourses strung on a loose sequence of anecdotes. Without exception the extant janam-sākhīs are either straight copies of earlier manuscripts, or composite collections based upon an earlier manuscript or manuscripts augmented with material drawn from current oral tradition. All are ultimately descended from oral tradition and all, whether directly or indirectly, represent the process of continuing expansion in accordance with the evolving understanding of the Sikh community and changes in its social patterns. In some instances a shift in understanding reflects the development of heretical notions within the community; in others the emergence of new social customs or a reversion to earlier practice. The introduction of new ideas into rural Pañjāb inevitably produced results which become particularly pronounced in the nineteenth and twentieth centuries, and the pressure of historical events, while reducing the functional importance of the janam-sākhīs, also left an impress upon their content. Finally (although this is much more difficult to document), it is apparent that the growing Jaṭ ascendancy within the Panth made its mark upon the development of the janam-sākhīs. This issue relates primarily to the emergence and later the overwhelming dominance of the *Bālā* tradition.

The process outlined above produced ever-expanding traditions with their abundance of anecdote and their wealth of exegesis. To this expansive

[1] *GNSR*, pp. 117–18.

impulse most narrators added a concern for chronology and with varying results reordered the received tradition and its supplements into a coherent sequence.

It must be stressed that the various stages of this growth have, since the late sixteenth century, been developing simultaneously, and although the printing-press and the spread of education have done much to arrest the process it continues to this day. A concern for sequence must have been evident in some of the earliest collections, and the oral tradition continues to develop new anecdotes while shedding others which have lost their relevance. As in the case of early accessions the more recent additions reflect new needs and new influences, many of which can be identified. One twentieth-century writer relates how Nānak, while travelling west, proceeded as far as the city of Rome. There he conversed with 'the Popes' and denounced their Indulgences as hypocrisy.[1] It is not difficult to identify the source of this particular supplement to the tradition.

The next task must be to examine the extant janam-sākhīs in order to determine their sources and, in a more precise sense, their manner of compilation. In the section which follows the term 'source' refers to actual manuscripts from which later narrators drew material in compiling their own manuscripts or to distinct oral traditions which were utilized in the same way. The analysis will be selective, for it would require an account of considerable length and complexity to unravel the multitude of tangled strands which connect the various janam-sākhīs to their sources and to each other. Attention will be directed primarily to the sources of the *B40 Janam-sākhī*, and secondarily to those janam-sākhīs which bear a close relationship to it. It can, however, be claimed that the same principles apply to the janam-sākhīs which receive only passing notice, and that in some instances these other janam-sākhīs are obviously drawing from sources close to those used by the *B40* compiler. The chief disadvantage of the selective approach is that there exists a distinct cleavage within the corpus of janam-sākhī traditions, the *Bālā* janam-sākhīs standing on one side and most of the remainder on the other. A concentration on the *B40* sources places us firmly on the latter side. Although it can be insisted that the same principles apply to any analysis of the *Bālā* development, it must at the same time be acknowledged that the *Bālā* tradition warrants a separate treatment which in this study it will receive only in the most cursory sense.

NARRATIVE I

One of the reasons why the *B40 Janam-sākhī* has received scant attention in the past has been the persistent belief that it is merely another *Purātan* manuscript. Karam Singh, author of the celebrated *Kattak ki Visākh*, included in his list of *Purātan* manuscripts a copy dated S. 1790 which he had noticed in a Lahore bookshop.[2] There can be little doubt that the

[1] Lāl Singh, *Tavarīkh Gurū Khālsā Panth*, vol. i (Lahore, 1945), p. 140.

[2] Karam Singh, *Kattak ki Visākh* (Amritsar, 1913), p. 218 (misnumbered 118). See *B40(Eng)*, introduction, p. 1.

janam-sākhī which he saw on this occasion was the *B40* manuscript now in the India Office Library, and likewise there can be little doubt that he did no more than scan its opening folios. Others following his example have declared the *B40* manuscript to be a version of the *Purātan* tradition.

This misunderstanding has arisen because the opening sākhīs of the *B40 Janam-sākhī* do indeed correspond closely to the analogue recorded in the *Hāfizābād* manuscript of the *Purātan* tradition. It is also true that this correspondence extends to a few sākhīs which are included at other points in the *B40* collection. A more thorough scanning of the manuscript soon reveals, however, that much of the *B40 Janam-sākhī* is totally distinct from the *Purātan* version. The correspondence is generally consistent up to the point where Bābā Nānak leaves Sultanpur, and the next two *B40* sākhīs do occur elsewhere in the *Purātan* narrative, but thereafter the two versions diverge and further correspondence is only occasional.

The common source which provides the area of correspondence is not to be described simply as one amongst several sources of equal importance utilized by the *B40* compiler. It seems clear that the sākhīs which have entered the *B40* manuscript from this common source constitute the primary basis of the janam-sākhī. Furthermore, it appears that this common cluster of sākhīs carries us close to the earliest nucleus or proto-janam-sākhī. This nucleus we have already designated *Narrative I*. It appears in the *Ādi Sākhīs*, in the *B40 Janam-sākhī*, and in the *Hāfizābād* and *Colebrooke* manuscripts. It also appears, vastly augmented, in the extant *Miharbān Janam-sākhī*, and in a transformed but recognizable form in the *Bālā* janam-sākhīs. Later still it is included in the *Gyān-ratanāvali*, and in every version of Nānak's life up to the most modern of accounts. The term *Narrative I* has been chosen because in its earliest version this nucleus must have consisted exclusively of simple narrative anecdotes. The figure *I* represents the assumption that it is upon the foundation provided by this cluster of anecdotes that all later janam-sākhīs have been erected.

Narrative I is, of course, a hypothesis. There exists no manuscript which corresponds exactly to our assumptions concerning its content and form. This is scarcely surprising, for it is clear that many manuscript records of janam-sākhī traditions have been lost, and a collection as crude as the early *Narrative I* version could hardly have appeared a strong candidate for preservation. Moreover, the *Narrative I* material must originally have circulated in oral tradition and even if the earliest recorded version had survived it would be unlikely to conform in all respects to the collection of simple anecdotes which constituted the initial form of the *Narrative I* cluster.

A hypothesis is, however, necessary in order to begin a reconstruction of the janam-sākhī sources, and apart from this *Narrative I* postulate there appears to be no satisfactory way of explaining both the relationship which links the various janam-sākhīs and also the differences distinguishing common anecdotes which are plainly amongst the earliest to have entered their narratives. This applies with particular force to the *Ādi Sākhīs*,

B40, *Colebrooke*, and *Hāfizābād* janam-sākhīs. It is also strongly supported by the form and content of *LDP 194*, and it may be possible to derive further support from the evident fact that almost all of the anecdotes with some claim to historical authenticity are to be found in this group.

The elements which, according to this hypothesis, constituted the earliest collection of the *Narrative I* tradition are the following:

1. Anecdotes concerning the birth and childhood of Nānak
2. Bābā Nānak's employment in Sultānpur
3. His travels and return to Talvaṇḍī
4. A visit to Pāk Paṭṭan to meet Sheikh Ibrāhīm, the successor of Sheikh Farīd
5. Bābā Nānak's presence at Bābur's sack of Saidpur
6. An encounter with a rājā named Śivanābh.

Certain features may be noted in this collection. First, there is a heavy concentration upon Nānak's childhood and early manhood. (Item 1, unlike the remainder, embodies several anecdotes.) Secondly, the few remaining anecdotes almost all relate explicitly to places within or very near the Pañjāb (Taḷvaṇḍī, Pāk Paṭṭan, and Saidpur). This observation may also apply to the encounter with Śivanābh. The belief that Śivanābh resided in Sri Lanka is certainly a much later addition to the tradition,[1] and the *Miharbān* references to this rājā suggest that an unspecified location 'over the sea' is also the product of later development.[2] Thirdly, there is only one travel sākhī.

This outline probably corresponds closely to the earliest tradition concerning the life of Nānak. It reflects, in the first place, a predictable interest in childhood anecdotes, with a strong emphasis upon the early manifestations of Nanak's greatness. Such episodes exercise a particular fascination in the development of legend and hagiography, and in this case the impulse will have been strengthened by an authentic knowledge of Nānak's family connections. It must, however, be remembered that these anecdotes will have been fewer in number and appreciably simpler in form than those contained in the versions recorded by our extant janam-sākhīs.

A second factor reflected by the hypothetical content of the earliest *Narrative I* tradition is an authentic knowledge concerning not merely the family connections of Bābā Nānak but also his adult life in the Pañjāb. An analysis of individual sākhīs has suggested that authentic episodes probably lie behind the accounts of the Gurū's experiences in Sultānpur, Pāk Paṭṭan, and Saidpur.[3] Although the conclusion cannot be set beyond all doubt, there exists in these instances a degree of probability which is conspicuously absent from almost all other janam-sākhī anecdotes.

These fragments of knowledge concerning the Gurū's life within or near the Pañjāb are set in contrast to a lack of information concerning his period of travels. It was obviously known to his later disciples that he had undertaken a lengthy journey beyond the Pañjāb, but apart from this

[1] *GNSR*, pp. 114–17. See above, p. 162.
[2] *Mih JS* II.1, 65–6.
[3] *GNSR*, pp. 106–10, 132–8, 140.

general statement there was evidently little that could be added from authentic knowledge. The small supplement must have included a tradition that Mardānā the Bard had accompanied him, for the single travel sākhī which can be included within the cluster centres upon the figure of Mardānā. It would, however, be rash to read too much into this emphasis or to assert on this basis that Mardānā did, in actual fact, accompany the Gurū wherever he went. Mardānā is absent from many of the later traditions relating to the period of travels and in most instances his entry into a particular anecdote can be explained by the function which he fulfils in the structure of the narrative. Although it would certainly be going too far to claim that Mardānā never existed, and although the tradition that he accompanied Nānak *may* be correct, it is nevertheless necessary to treat his appearances with some caution. His inclusion within the travel sākhī of *Narrative I* may possibly indicate that we have not pushed our hypothesis back far enough, that we have instead permitted an early development to appear as an element of the original tradition.

The same degree of caution is required in the case of the claim that Bābā Nānak travelled for twelve years. This appears in the earlier extant versions of the *Narrative I* tradition.[1] The fact that twelve years was a conventional figure for such pilgrimages suggests, however, that the earliest narrators did not actually know the extent of Nānak's travels in terms of years any more than they knew it in terms of his itinerary.

There is thus a distinct possibility that our hypothetical *Narrative I* nucleus, though primitive in form and brief in length, may nevertheless contain later elements. Later elements are certainly present in all extant versions of the *Narrative I* tradition, and for this reason it must be stressed that the earliest expression of this tradition would not have corresponded to any of the texts which are now available. In the *B40 Janam-sākhī* the *Narrative I* material is reproduced in the following sākhīs:

Narr. I	*B40*	
1.	1.	The Birth of Nānak
	2a.	Instruction by the Paṇḍit
	2b.	Bāba Nānak's Betrothal and Marriage
	3.	The Ruined Crop Restored
	4a.	The Tree's Stationary Shadow
	5.	Bābā Nānak's Discourse with the Physician
2.	6a.	Sultānpur
	6b.	Immersion in the River
	6c.	Bābā Nānak's Discourse with Daulat Khān's Qāzī
3.	7.	Bābā Nānak's Travels in the Uninhabited Wilderness
	8.	Bābā Nānak returns to Talvaṇḍī
4.	17.	Bābā Nānak's Discourse with Sheikh Braham
5.	18a.	The Sack of Saidpur
6.	34b.	Bābā Nānak and Rājā Śivanābh.

[1] *B40*, f. 221a. *AS*, p. 44. *Pur JS*, p. 48.

Certain elements contained within clusters as they appear in the *B40 Janam-sākhī* are certainly later additions to the earlier tradition. To sākhī 6, for example, there has been appended an account of Nānak's departure from Sultānpur which is obviously an expansion of the tradition.[1] Other versions of the same sākhī lack it and the fact that it consists largely of hymns attributed to Nānak indicates a later development. This amounts in practice to the addition of an extra sākhī, a feature which also appears in the *B40* version of the Saidpur visit. In this latter instance there has been introduced a discourse with Bābur based on current Sūfī tradition and upon references in Gurū Nānak's own works.[2] Elsewhere the expansion is evidently to be found in the addition of extra details to a primitive version of a sākhī. It has already been observed how most of the quotations from Gurū Nānak's shabads and shaloks have been interpolated at a later stage. All extant janam-sākhīs bear this impress. *LDP 194* illustrates a slighly less developed version than that of the *B40 Janam-sākhī*, whereas the *Colebrooke* and *Hāfizābād* manuscripts both represent a more advanced enlargement.

This differential development in the various janam-sākhī versions indicates that the elements responsible for the expansion of the original nucleus entered the tradition at different points in time. A comparison of the texts enables us to determine a sequence for these additions. It seems likely that the discourse 'The True Field and the True Merchandise', evolved out of the shabad *Soraṭh 2*, must have been added to the cycle of childhood anecdotes soon after the original nucleus first emerged in a coherent form.[3] 'A Discourse with Bābur' obviously entered the tradition later, and 'Bābā Nānak's Departure from Sultānpur' is evidently an even later addition made by the *B40* copyist himself.

Division of the Narrative I *tradition:* Narrative Ia

Another important development which becomes evident from a comparison of the *B40* and *Colebrooke* janam-sākhīs is a division of the *Narrative I* tradition. It is immediately clear from this comparison that although both versions contain *Narrative I* material they have received it through different lines of descent. The line which eventually issues in the *Colebrooke Janam-sākhī* we shall designate *Narrative Ia*. The other series of recensions, descending to the *B40 Janam-sākhi*, we shall designate *Narrative Ib*. This latter line also emerges in *LDP 194* and the *Ādi Sākhīs*. Both lines reunite in the *Hāfizābād Janam-sākhī*.

Narrative Ia evidently developed in the following manner. The primitive *Narrative I* nucleus, having already undergone a limited measure of expansion before the division, subsequently received a substantial accession of extra anecdotes and discourses. Most of the supplementary material related to the period of Nānak's travels, an area which inevitably commanded a particular interest. This interest it attracted partly because

[1] *B40*, sākhī 6d, ff. 24b–27b.

[2] *B40*, sākhī 18b, ff. 70a–73b (1).

[3] In the *B40* manuscript this discourse appears as the second part of sākhī 4. *B40*, ff. 9b–13b.

it had been left unfilled by the earlier tradition and partly because it provided unrivalled scope for the more fanciful variety of anecdote. The development or appropriation of anecdotes set within the Pañjāb was still inhibited by first-hand knowledge of the area and, to some extent, by authentic memories concerning the Gurū's life there amongst his disciples. The period of travels was, in contrast, largely devoid of such inhibitions. This feature will account for certain elements which figure prominently in the supplementary material, and others can be explained by the evident and altogether reasonable assumption that the Gurū, in the course of his travels, must certainly have visited some of the more important centres of Hindu pilgrimage. The same assumption also extended, with rather less justification, to the far-flung centres of Muslim pilgrimage.

First-hand experience and authentic memory did not, of course, constitute an insuperable barrier to the development of anecdotes and discourses set within the Pañjāb. Although such anecdotes are not as numerous as the travel sākhīs they are by no means absent. Expansion of the childhood narratives also takes place, and in all three areas (childhood, the period of travels, and adult life in the Pañjāb) there are to be found the characteristic constituents from which the janam-sākhīs draw their supplements. This supplementary material will have been entering oral tradition ever since the death of Nānak. From this fund of oral anecdotes a selection has been added to a recorded version of the *Narrative I* tradition. In this manner the *Narrative I* tradition acquired the distinctive form designated *Narrative Ia*.

There is no clear evidence of the order in which these supplementary sākhīs entered the recorded tradition and if it is suggested that there was a series of accessions in clusters it must at once be added that this is still in the nature of conjecture. It does, however, seem a likely conjecture, for several of the supplementary sākhīs are evolved products which have a history of development behind them. The *Colebrooke* version of the Mecca sākhī is an example. It has already been demonstrated, by means of a comparison with other versions, that the *Colebrooke* Mecca narrative represents a conflation of three separate anecdotes, one of which seems originally to have been set in a different context.[1] A comparison already drawn between two versions of the 'Rich Man's Pennants' sākhī similarly reveals that the *Colebrooke* version is a more highly evolved product than its *B40* analogue.[2] The fact that these sākhīs appear in conjunction with such primitive anecdotes as 'A Watchman Receives Royal Authority'[3] suggests that the latter variety represents a later borrowing from oral tradition.

Other distinctive points may be briefly noticed. The anecdote 'Bābā Nānak's Travels in the Uninhabited Wilderness', which constituted a single sākhī in the *Narrative I* nucleus, has, in the *Narrative Ia* tradition, been split into two parts.[4] Both portions have been expanded and between

[1] See above, pp. 137–41.
[2] See above, pp. 124–7.
[3] *Pur JS*, sākhī 20, p. 30. *GNSR*, p. 40.
[4] *Pur JS*, sākhīs 12 and 30, pp. 20–1, 46–8. *GNSR*, pp. 38, 42–3.

them seventeen travel sākhīs have been inserted in order to construct the 'Eastern Journey' of the *Colebrooke* version. The anecdote concerning Rājā Śivanābh has been expanded but still lacks the introductory portion which later enters the *Purātan* tradition through the *Hāfizābād Janam-sākhī*.[1] Quantities of scriptural quotation have been added at many

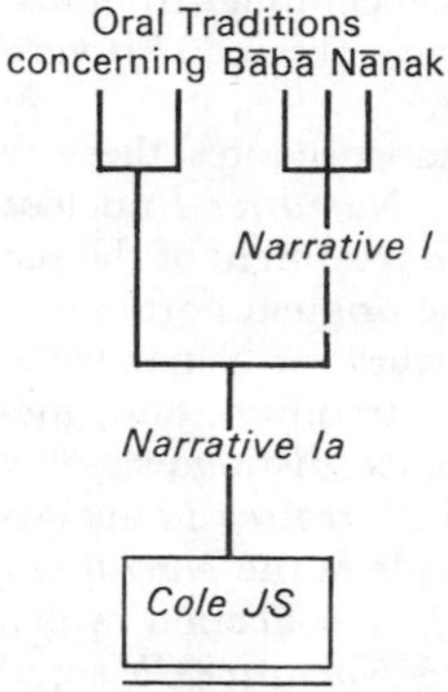

Figure 16

points,[2] and the entire collection has been arranged in the distinctively *Purātan* sequence with its travel itinerary based on the four points of the compass. This sequence obviously derives from the *Narrative Ia* line of development, not from the *Narrative Ib* line with which it is linked in the *Hāfizābād Janam-sākhī*.

It was in this manner that the *Narrative I* tradition, augmented with numerous additional sākhīs and ordered into a particular pattern, followed a line of development which ultimately produced the celebrated *Colebrooke Janam-sākhī*. This development may be diagrammatically illustrated as in figure 16. The precise location of this *Narrative Ia* development has not been determined, but the distinctly Poṭhohārī element in the language of the *Colebrooke Janam-sākhī* suggests that the tradition may have evolved in the area around Rāwalpiṇḍī.

Division of the Narrative I *tradition:* Narrative Ib

During the period of *Narrative Ia* growth the *Narrative I* nucleus had meanwhile been undergoing a variant development, probably in an area south-east of Rāwalpiṇḍī. To the original cluster a different selection of supplementary sākhīs had been added. In this case the supplement was evidently much smaller and the number of recensions appears to have been fewer. This was the line of development which we have designated *Narrative Ib*. To the original nucleus were added a discourse with Bābur;

[1] *Pur JS*, pp. 74–8.

[2] Several of the scriptural quotations included in the *Colebrooke Janam-sākhī* must have been added to the nucleus before the distinctive *Narrative Ia* tradition began to evolve.

an account of how a proud karoṛī, having been humbled by the Gurū, donated the land on which the village of Kartārpur was erected; and a story which related how contact with Rājā Śivanābh had first been established by a Khatrī disciple of Bābā Nānak.[1] It seems likely that the cluster of anecdotes which appear in the *B40* manuscript as sākhīs 10–14 were also derived by the *B40* compiler from his *Narrative Ib* source,[2] and it is possible that he may have obtained his version of the Achal discourse from the same manuscript.[3]

In addition to the extra anecdotes there was also expansion of the material inherited from the *Narrative I* nucleus in a manner distinguishing it from the *Narrative Ia* treatment of the same material. This certainly happened in the case of the original portion of the Śivanābh sākhī. Some extra quotations from the works of Nānak were added to those which had already entered the parent tradition, and, inevitably, numerous variant readings of lesser significance distinguished *Narrative Ib* renderings of common sākhīs from their *Narrative Ia* analogues.

The earliest extant example of the *Narrative Ib* tradition is provided by the manuscript *LDP 194*, a collection which consists of the original nucleus, together with the *Narrative Ib* supplement noted above. The supplement includes both the Achal and the Kaliyug sākhīs, but in a position which may indicate that they were additions to the manuscript by its copyist rather than integral parts of his *Narrative Ib* source. Both occur at the conclusion of the narrative portion of the manuscript, and the Achal sākhī is actually set within a lengthy section which otherwise comprises only scriptural quotation.[4] Because this section is so obviously a supplement to a basic *Narrative Ib* source it may follow that at least the Achal sākhī, and perhaps also the immediately preceding Kaliyug sākhī,[5] should be regarded as parts of the supplement rather than as elements of the basic source. On the other hand, the possibility that they may have belonged to the *Narrative Ib* tradition should not be obscured.

This same *Narrative Ib* tradition reappears in the *Hāfizābād Janam-sākhī*, where only a selective use has been made of it. The *Hāfizābād Janam-sākhī* is primarily based upon the *Narrative Ia* tradition. It is clear, however, that the *Hāfizābād* compiler also had access to a *Narrative Ib* manuscript. This he collated with his *Narrative Ia* text, a text which if not actually the *Colebrooke Janam-sākhī* must have been a manuscript very close to it. The *Hāfizābād* compiler obviously followed the longer *Narrative Ia* manuscript in preference to his *Narrative Ib* manuscript, and whenever a common sākhī appeared it was the *Narrative Ia* version which he copied. Only at points where the *Narrative Ib* manuscript recorded material missing from *Narrative Ia* did he turn to it. Having

[1] In the *B40* janam-sākhī these *Narrative Ib* sākhīs appear as numbers 18b, 19, and the first portion of 34. *B40*, ff. 70a–75a. 138b–145a.

[2] See below, pp. 192–4.

[3] Although a version of the Achal discourse may well have formed a part of the *Narrative Ib* tradition it seems much more likely that the *B40* compiler used a different source for this particular sākhī. See below, pp. 198 ff.

[4] *LDP 194*, ff. 56a–117b.

[5] Ibid., ff. 49a–54a.

copied the extra material he immediately reverted to his *Narrative Ia* source.

It is this feature which explains the *Hāfizābād Janam-sākhī*'s illogical placement of the introduction to the Śivanābh sākhī. In the briefer *Narrative Ib* manuscript the Śivanābh sākhī followed immediately after the story of the converted karoṛī. The Karoṛī anecdote was not to be found in the *Narrative Ia* recension and so had to be added to the new composite version. The *Narrative Ib* tradition had also attached an introduction to the Śivanābh sākhī (the story of the Khatrī disciple noted above). This introductory portion was retained in its *Narrative Ib* position by the *Hāfizābād* compiler and so follows immediately after the Karoṛī sākhī in the *Hāfizābād Janam-sākhī*.[1] The second portion of the *Narrative Ib* Śivanābh sākhī was, however, dropped in accordance with the compiler's preference for *Narrative Ia* versions wherever available. The *Narrative Ia* version comes later, having been allocated a position in the 'Southern Journey' narrative,[2] and the *Hāfizābād* compiler records it when he reaches it in his *Narrative Ia* source.

In this manner the *Narrative I* tradition reunited in the composite *Hāfizābād Janam-sākhī*, although in a fashion which involved a much greater dependence upon the longer and more evolved *Narrative Ia* line of development than upon the *Narrative Ib* line. The result was the so-called *Purātan* tradition, which in spite of obvious links must be distinguished from such distinctively *Narrative Ib* janam-sākhīs as *LDP 194*. The diagrammatic representation can now be extended as in figure 17.

This analysis is confirmed by a comparison of the two major *Purātan* manuscripts (i.e. the *Colebrooke* and *Hāfizābād* janam-sākhīs) with the *B40 Janam-sākhī*. Two conclusions follow from the comparison. First, it is clear that the *B40* compiler did not have access to the *Colebrooke* manuscript, nor to any other recension of the *Narrative Ia* tradition. Wherever the *B40* and *Colebrooke* janam-sākhīs contain analogues which cannot have existed in any *Narrative Ib* recension the *B40* version diverges widely from *Colebrooke*.[3] In such instances it is clear that the *B40* compiler derived his versions from sources other than the *Colebrooke Janam-sākhī* or its immediate antecedents.

Secondly, in contrast with this marked divergence from *Colebrooke* analogues, there is a remarkably close correspondence in the case of precisely those sākhīs which the *B40 Janam-sākhī* shares with the *Hāfizābād* manuscript but which are missing from the *Colebrooke* manuscript. In other words, the *B40* and *Hāfizābād* compilers agree when recording *Narrative Ib* sākhīs which were not included in the *Narrative Ia* tradition, but disagree when recording sākhīs which are common to both *Narrative Ia* and *Narrative Ib* (i.e. the sākhīs which must have been incorporated in the earlier *Narrative I* tradition before it branched into

[1] *Pur JS*, p. 74. *GNSR*, p. 46. [2] *Pur JS*, pp. 86–90. *GNSR*, p. 48.

[3] Cf. 'The Monster's Cauldron' (*B40*, f. 40a–b; *Pur JS*, pp. 81–2), the Mecca anecdotes (*B40*, ff. 51b–52b, 133a–135a; *Pur JS*, pp. 98–104), 'The Country Ruled by Women' (*B40*, ff. 83a–85b; *Pur JS*, pp. 33–7), 'The Meeting with Lahaṇā' (*B40*, ff. 94b–99a; *Pur JS*, pp. 106–8), etc.

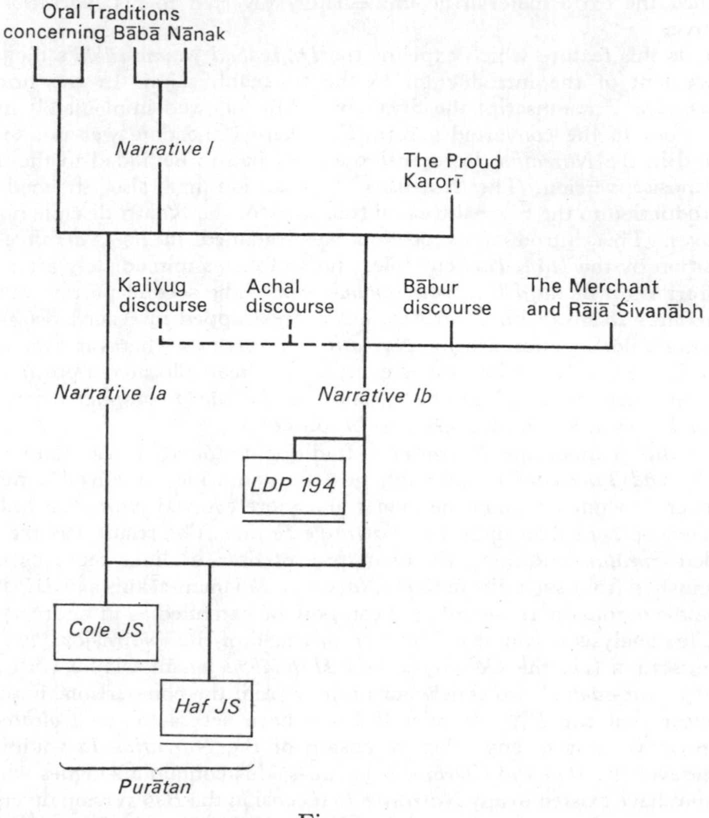

Figure 17

the two derived traditions). This can only mean that whereas the *Hāfizābād* compiler used a *Narrative Ib* manuscript as a mere supplement to his *Narrative Ia* source, the *B40* compiler regarded his *Narrative Ib* manuscript as a basic source, following it as far as it would take him and finding his supplements in non-*Narrative I* sources. Where the *Hāfizābād* compiler abandoned his *Narrative Ib* source in preference for *Narrative Ia*, the *B40* compiler adhered to it. This appears to be the obvious explanation for the pattern which emerges from a comparison of the *B40* and *Hāfizābād* janam-sākhīs, a pattern of close correspondence in some sākhīs and variant versions in others.

The degree of correspondence which distinguishes the *B40* and *Hāfizābād* readings of *Narrative Ib* sākhīs is so close that with only rare exceptions it amounts to a virtual identity. This suggests that the *B40* and *Hāfizābād* compilers must have had access to the same *Narrative Ib* manuscript. In the case of the Karoṛī sākhī only two differences of any significance emerge from a comparison of the *B40* and *Hāfizābād* texts, both of them evidently brief additions made to the source manuscript by the two later compilers. During the course of the narrative the *B40* compiler inserts a sentence which the *Hāfizābād* text lacks: *tā karoṛie kahiā ju nānaku vaḍā maradu hai* ('"Nānak is a great man," declared the karoṛī').[1] The second addition appears in the *Hāfizābād* text. Towards the end of the sākhī it repeats a sentence which the *B40* manuscript records only once: *bābā bahut khusī hoā* ('Bābā [Nanak] was filled with joy').[2] The former instance represents the kind of pious aside which so easily creeps into later recensions of any hagiographic tradition, and the latter is plainly a simple mistake by the *Hāfizābād* copyist.

Correspondence of such remarkable closeness suggests that the two compilers must have used a common source. This hypothetical manuscript we shall designate *Q1*. The existence of such a manuscript derives further support from hints concerning the original localities of the *Hāfizābād* and *B40* manuscripts. The *Hāfizābād* manuscript, as its name indicates, was discovered in Hāfizābād, a small town in Gujranwālā District. Although the *B40* manuscript first appears in a Lahore bookshop, internal evidence points to a location within Gujranwālā District, or perhaps the adjacent Gujrāt District, as a likely place of origin.[3] The convergence upon a limited geographical area renders the copying of a single manuscript by two different compilers entirely possible. Manuscript copies of janam-sākhīs would not be common, and if a *saṅgat* or individual within any particular area possessed such a manuscript neighbouring *saṅgats* would presumably be aware of its existence and, if proposing to acquire a janam-sākhī for their own use, would quite naturally turn to it as a source. *Q1* can accordingly be located in, or very near, Gujranwālā District.

After *LDP 194*, *B40*, and *Hāfizābād* the *Narrative Ib* tradition next appears in the *Ādi Sākhīs*. Although there can be no doubt that the *Ādi Sākhīs* compiler utilized a *Narrative Ib* source it is clear that his source was not *Q1*, at least not in an immediate sense. The *Ādi Sākhīs* analogue is longer and more developed than the version which derives directly from *Q1*. As the date given for its compilation (A.D. 1701) is earlier than that of the *B40 Janam-sākhī* (A.D. 1733) it seems more reasonable to postulate another *Narrative Ib* version which developed more rapidly during the late seventeenth century and emerged in a relatively mature form at the beginning of the eighteenth century. This suggests the pattern in figure 18. It will be observed that *LDP 194* has been affiliated with the *Q1* group rather than with the *Ādi Sākhīs*. This relationship is indicated by a comparison of the three texts.

To this extent the *Narrative Ib* tradition can be defined with reasonable assurance. There seems to be little doubt that the following anecdotes common to the *B40 Janam-sākhī* and the *Ādi Sākhīs* must have been taken from separate recensions of the tradition.

[1] *B40*, f. 74b.
[2] *Pur JS*, p. 74.
[3] See *B40(Eng)*, Introduction pp. 19–25.

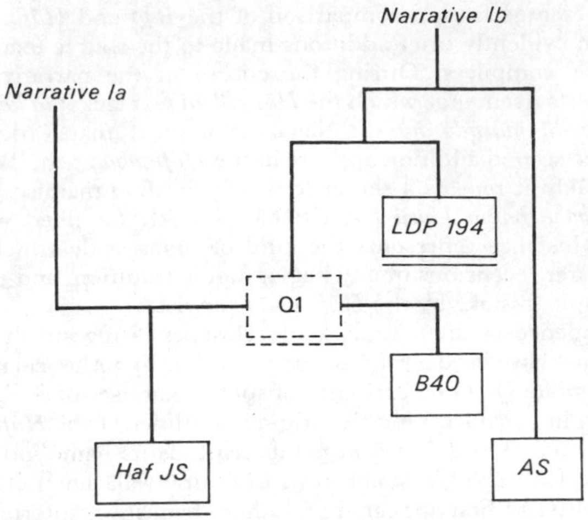

Figure 18

B40	*Ādi Sākhīs*	
1	2a.	The Birth of Nānak
2a.	2b.	Instruction by the Paṇḍit
2b.	3a.	Bābā Nānak's Betrothal and Marriage
3.	3b.	The Ruined Crop Restored
4a.	4.	The Tree's Stationary Shadow
4b.	5a.	The True Field and the True Merchandise
5.	5b.	Bābā Nānak's Discourse with the Physician
6a.	6.	Sultānpur
6b.	7a.	Immersion in the River
6c.	7b.	Bābā Nānak's Discourse with Daulat Khān's Qāzī
7.	8a.	Bābā Nānak's Travels in the Uninhabited Wilderness
8.	16.	Bābā Nānak returns to Talvaṇḍī
17.	17.	Bābā Nānak's Discourse with Sheikh Braham
18a.	18.	The Sack of Saidpur
18b.	19.	A Discourse with Bābur
19.	20.	The proud Karoṛī humbled
34a.	21a.	The Merchant and Rājā Śivanābh
34b.	21b.	Bābā Nānak and Rājā Śivanābh

Possible B40 *borrowings from the* Narrative Ib *tradition*

In the case of the *B40 Janam-sākhī* the anecdotes listed above were evidently copied from *Q1*. To this list the following should perhaps be added:

10. The Monster's Cauldron
11. Bholā the Robber

12a. The Encounter with Kaliyug
12b. Lamenting Women Commended
13. A Poor Sikh's Devotion
14. Mecca: the moving *miharāb.*

These six anecdotes obviously constitute a distinct cluster drawn by the *B40* compiler from a single source. This is indicated not only by the fact that they have been recorded as a group, but also by a general correspondence in terms of language, structure, and stage of development. The same distinctive verb-endings recur (notably *dā* followed by *thā* in the Imperfective past tense), Imperfective participles are commonly repeated, and some characteristic expressions are to be noted. These include *merā gunāhu bakhashie, charani lāuṇā, jāi baiṭhā,* and *pairī paiā* followed by *khaṛā hoiā.* The narrative style manifests a considerable degree of homogeneity and there appears to be no doubt that the *B40* compiler must have taken the six anecdotes from a single source.

Was this source the *Q1* manuscript? Arguments based upon language and style are inconclusive. Although the cluster does indeed correspond in general terms to *Narrative Ib* language and style, the distinctive features noted in the preceding paragraph are less prominent in other *Q1* material. A comparison of the cluster with recognizably *Q1* sākhīs leaves the question open.

A more serious objection is raised by the *Hāfizābād Janam-sākhī.* The *Hāfizābād* compiler, who also had access to *Q1*, fails to reproduce any of the six anecdotes in the same versions as the *B40 Janam-sākhī.* In the case of sākhīs 10, 11, 12a, and 14 this can be easily explained by a preference for the *Narrative Ia* analogues which he does in fact use, but this still leaves sākhīs 12b and 13.

Although these two *Hāfizābād* omissions cannot be altogether dismissed they are at least amenable to plausible explanations. Sākhī 12b, consisting of only a few sentences, may have been omitted by the *Hāfizābād* compiler because it was attached to the Kaliyug anecdote. The *Hāfizābād* compiler follows his *Narrative Ia* source both for the Kaliyug anecdote and for its successor. Under these circumstances it would scarcely be surprising if he were to follow through without interrupting the *Narrative Ia* text.

The omission of sākhī 13 can be explained in a different way. In order to purchase food for Bābā Nānak the poor Sikh of sākhī 13 voluntarily removes his hair and sells it in the market.[1] The objection to hair-cutting which receives such prominence during the eighteenth century was certainly upheld by many Sikhs during the seventeenth century, and if the *Hāfizābād* compiler shared this particular conviction he would have had a compelling reason for regarding the anecdote as mischievous.

These conjectures offer possible reasons for the omission of the two anecdotes by the *Hāfizābād* compiler. To them can be added the fact that the *B40* compiler records this cluster between two substantial blocks of *Q1* material. It is true that the cluster is immediately preceded by a single sākhī which is certainly not from the *Narrative Ib* tradition and that it is

[1] *B40*, f. 49a.

immediately followed by another two such sākhīs.[1] Elsewhere, however, the *B40* compiler interrupts one of his major sources in precisely this manner.[2] If we assume a separate source for this cluster we must also envisage a compiler with access to several manuscripts, abandoning one such manuscript for another and then reverting to the first for another run of sākhīs. This is by no means an impossibility, but it seems less likely than a continuation of the same basic manuscript. The cluster comprising sakhis 10–14 of the *B40 Janam-sākhī* will accordingly be assigned to the *Narrative Ib* tradition and specifically to the *Q1* manuscript. It must, however, be emphasized that this represents a cautiously tentative conclusion. The possibility of a separate, independent source should not be overlooked.

One further complication should be briefly noted before leaving the cluster. Three of its anecdotes have analogues in the *Ādi Sākhīs* and in all three instances the *Ādi Sākhis* compiler has used a source distinct from the *Narrative I* tradition.[3] This may perhaps mean that the cluster was added to the received *Narrative Ib* tradition by the *Q1* compiler or by a predecessor. Indeed, there may have been supplements added by both. The fact that *LDP 194* includes the Kaliyug sākhī may perhaps indicate that the six anecdotes were not added to the *Narrative Ib* tradition simultaneously.

Narrative I *material in the* Miharbān Janam-sākhī

Before leaving the *Narrative I* tradition reference should be made to its influence upon the *Miharbān Janam-sākhī*. It appears that an early recension of the *Narrative Ib* tradition must have been used by the first of the *Miharbān* compilers, or perhaps by a redactor who closely followed the original compiler. In its extant form the *Miharbān Janam-sākhī* is a late and highly evolved product, but a comparison of its contents with the *Narrative I* material indicates that *Narrative Ib* must have been used at a stage when the *Miharbān* tradition was assuming a coherent form. Whereas distinctively *Ia* sakhis are conspicuously absent from the *Miharbān* version, all the nucleus material and one of the unmistakably *Ib* anecdotes (the Karoṛī sākhī) have been included. This suggests that at some early stage in the evolution of the *Miharbān Janam-sākhī* use was made of a *Narrative Ib* recension, prior to the entry of the *Ib* Bābur discourse or the *Ib* development of the Śivanābh story. Although the *Miharbān Janam-sākhī* does include references to Śivanābh they indicate a much earlier source than the evolved *Narrative Ib* version.[4]

The *Miharbān* references to Śivanābh provide a rare instance of an early form preserved within the highly developed *Miharbān* tradition. A characteristic feature of the *Miharbān Janam-sākhī* is its considerable expansion of earlier tradition. This applies to most of the material which it derived from its early *Narrative Ib* source. Even the Śivanābh references

[1] *B40*, sākhīs 9 and 15–16. [2] *B40*, sākhī 28. [3] See below, p. 202.

[4] *Mih JS* II.1, 65–6.

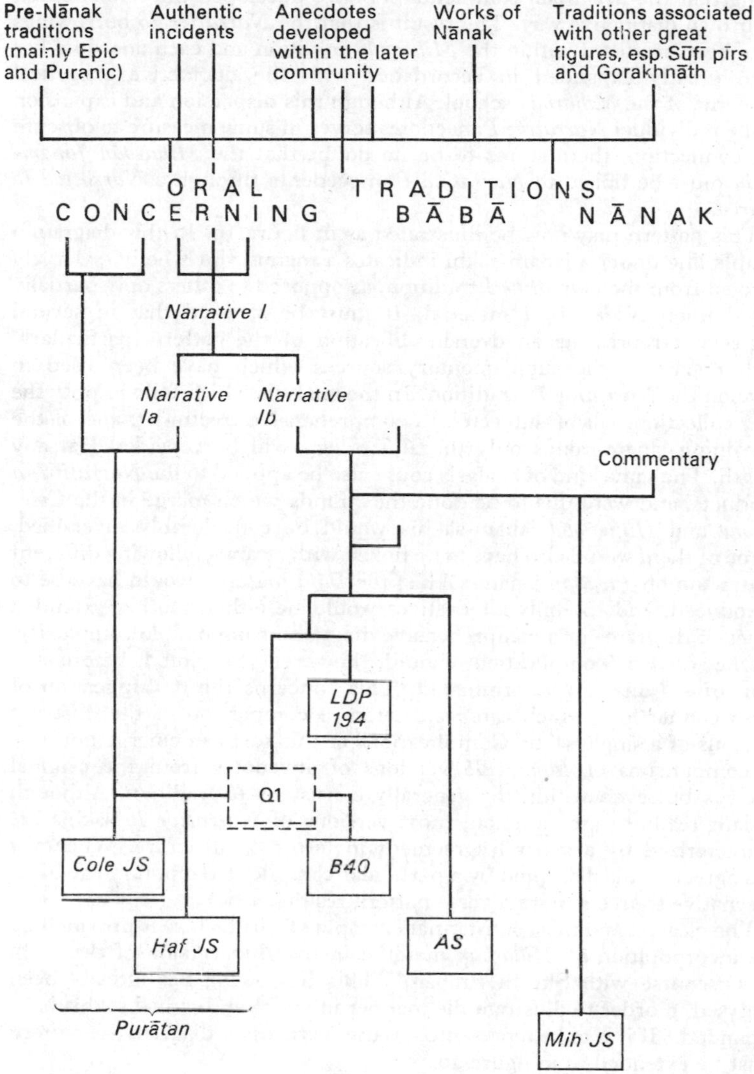
Pre-Nānak traditions (mainly Epic and Puranic)
Authentic incidents
Anecdotes developed within the later community
Works of Nānak
Traditions associated with other great figures, esp Sūfī pīrs and Gorakhnāth
ORAL TRADITIONS CONCERNING BĀBĀ NĀNAK
Narrative I
Narrative Ia
Narrative Ib
Commentary
LDP 194
Q1
Cole JS
B40
Haf JS
AS
Purātan
Mih JS

Figure 19

manifest the same feature, the essential difference from other versions being that the *Miharbān* commentators have developed the references in their own distinctive way. The result is that the *Narrative Ib* borrowings have been scattered within the *Miharbān* tradition and each anecdote has been greatly expanded in accordance with the distinctive exegetical concerns of the *Miharbān* school. Although this dispersion and expansion of the individual *Narrative I* anecdotes serves in some measure to obscure the connection, there seems to be no doubt that the *Miharbān Janam-sākhī* must be linked to *Narrative I* antecedents through a *Narrative Ib* source.

This pattern may now be illustrated as in figure 19. In this diagram a double line under a janam-sākhī indicates a manuscript wholly or largely derived from the *Narrative I* tradition, as opposed to others only partially based upon *Narrative I* material. It must be stressed that in several respects it represents an oversimplification of the pattern, particularly with regard to the supplementary sources which have been used to develop the *Narrative Ia* tradition. In the analysis which follows only the *B40* collection will be subjected to comprehensive treatment, and of the remaining janam-sākhīs only the *Ādi Sākhīs* will be considered at any length. The same kind of analysis could also be applied to the *Narrative Ia* products, and were this to be done the strands which merge in the *Colebrooke* and *Hāfizābād* janam-sākhīs would be considerably diversified. Some of them would also have to be linked with strands following different routes to non-*Purātan* janam-sākhīs, the *Bālā* material would have be to introduced, and the only alternatives would be either another extended series of diagrams or a comprehensive diagram of impossible complexity.

One further complication should, however, be noted before the *Narrative I* analysis is terminated. This concerns the multiplication of cross connections which can result from a comparison of the different versions of a single sākhī. Complications of this sort can emerge not only in comparisons of *Ia* and *Ib* versions of anecdotes from the original nucleus but even within the generally consistent *Ib* tradition. Although variant readings are common, most versions of *Narrative Ib* sākhīs are characterized by a general agreement in terms of structure. Whenever this agreement is disrupted by a particular compiler's temporary use of an alternative source a more diverse pattern results.

The clearest and most substantial example of this feature is provided by the incorporation of *Miharbān* material in the *B40* version of the sākhī 'A Discourse with Sheikh Braham'. This borrowing has already been analysed in order to illustrate the manner in which individual sākhīs have expanded.[1] If it is to be represented in the *Narrative I* diagram the pattern must be extended as in figure 20.

This concludes the analysis of *Narrative I*, the collection of anecdotes which was evidently the first to emerge in a coherent form and which,

[1] *B40*, sākhī 17, ff. 57b–65a. See above, pp. 131–5. The *B40* compiler later makes more extensive use of *Miharbān* material, presumably drawing it from the same source. See below, pp. 226–8.

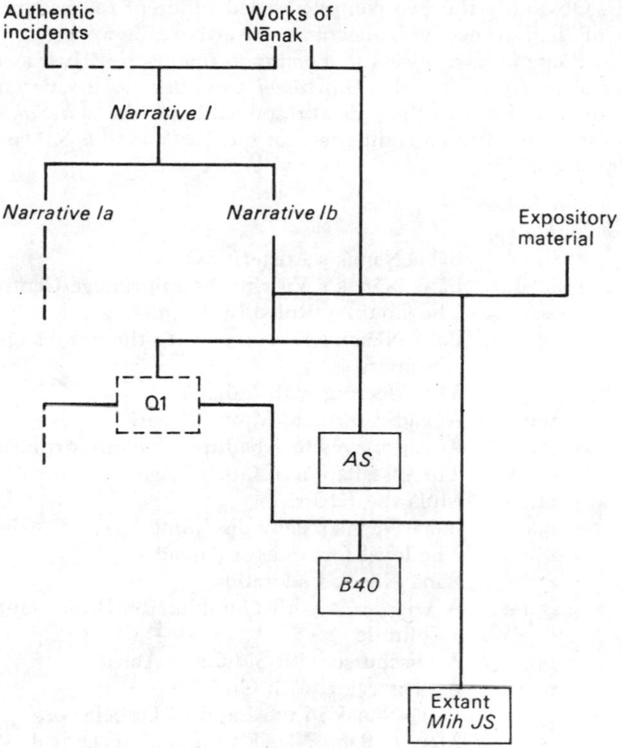

Figure 20

with varying supplements, has served as a basis for some of the most important of the extant janam-sākhīs.

NARRATIVE II

Although the *B40* compiler clearly began his work with a *Narrative Ib* manuscript before him, and although the anecdotes drawn from this tradition constitute the basis of his janam-sākhī, *Narrative Ib* material actually supplies only a small proportion of the complete *B40 Janam-sākhī*. In the case of the *Ādi Sākhīs* there is a higher proportion of *Narrative Ib* sākhīs, but only because the supplementary material is less than in *B40*. Almost half of the *Ādi Sākhīs* consists of *Narrative Ib* anecdotes. In the longer *B40 Janam-sākhī* the proportion is appreciably less.

A comparison of the supplementary sākhīs in the two collections reveals a second narrative source. It has already been observed that the *Narrative Ib* material in *B40* and the *Ādi Sākhīs*, although clearly descended from a common source, nevertheless shows marked divergences in the two versions. Obviously the two compilers used different recensions for this portion of their respective collections. Elsewhere, however, it becomes clear that they did have access to a common manuscript. Just as the *B40* compiler shared *Q1* with the *Hāfizābād* compiler, so too did he share another manuscript with the person responsible for the *Ādi Sākhīs*. This conclusion follows from a comparison of the *B40* and *Ādi Sākhīs* texts of the following sākhīs:

B40 *sākhī no.*	*Ādi Sākhīs* *sākhī no.*	
20.	8b.	Bābā Nānak's Austerities
21.	8c–d.	Bābā Nānak's Visit to the Pilgrimage Centres
22.	9.	The Country Ruled by Women
23.	14.	Bābā Nānak's Discourse with the Siddhs on Mount Sumeru
24a.	22a.	The Meeting with Lahaṇā
24b.	22b.	Aṅgad returns to Matte dī Sarāi
24c.	22c.	Aṅgad moves to Khaḍūr: his clothes ruined
24d.	—	The installation of Gurū Aṅgad
25.	24.	Mūlā the Khatrī
26a.	25a.	Bābā Nānak's daily discipline
26b.	25b.	The loyal fortitude of Aṅgad
27a.	25c.	Bābā Nānak's adoration
27b.	25d–e.	A Discourse with Gorakhnāth: Bābā Nānak seeks solitude
29.	23.	A Discourse with Siddhs at Achal
30.	1.	An Interview with God
31.	13.	Bābā Nānak in the Land of Unbelievers
32.	15.	Mecca: Bābā Nānak's miraculous arrival.

The degree of textual correspondence which can be demonstrated by a comparison of the two versions places the existence of a common manuscript source beyond all doubt. Most of the material constitutes in actual fact a single version, for variants within the main narrative of any of the sākhīs listed above are of little significance. A large majority can be explained by a tendency to assimilate to the compiler's own dialect, as where the *Ādi Sākhī* uses the verb-form *sī* in preference to a more common *B40* usage of *āhā*. More significant variants do appear outside the main narrative, but all such differences, whether of text, content, or arrangement are amenable to simple explanations.

This manuscript we shall designate *Q2* and the tradition which it records we shall distinguish with the title *Narrative II*. The latter term, when set in contrast with *Narrative I*, is intended to imply both similarities and differences. There is certainly a strong similarity in terms of style, for both consist almost exclusively of simple anecdotal narratives and of narrative discourses developed out of passages from the works of Nānak. The differences, though not absolute, relate chiefly to age and doctrine Whereas *Narrative I* offers an amalgam of the earliest traditions and later developments, *Narrative II* appears to lack the former. This should not, however, be understood to mean that *Narrative II* is late. Some of its material, though not a part of the original nucleus, is obviously very early.

In terms of doctrinal emphasis *Narrative II* is distinguished by the ascetic ideal which in *Narrative I* emerges only in an obvious interpolation.[1] A limited number of *Narrative II* anecdotes have found their way into the *Narrative I* tradition, both *Ia* and *Ib*,[2] but the measure of divergence in such instances is vast. This suggests that common anecdotes have been derived from oral tradition rather than from any recorded source, a feature which serves to emphasize the gap separating *Narrative I* and *Narrative II*.

The existence of *Q2* is indicated not only by the degree of textual correspondence linking *B40* and the *Ādi Sākhīs* but also by the differences which distinguish them. The two janam-sākhīs present edited versions of the common text and it seems clear from the nature of the editorial supplements that the later *B40* manuscript cannot have been copied from the earlier *Ādi Sākhīs*. The two compilers introduce sākhī divisions at different points, and it is actually the later *B40* version which follows a more primitive sequence in its arrangement of the common sākhīs. Although a particular manuscript must have been used by both compilers it is the *B40* collection of A.D. 1733 which brings us closer to it, not the *Ādi Sākhīs* of A.D. 1701.

Differences of arrangement are at once apparent from the list of *Narrative II* anecdotes given above. The two clusters recorded by the *B40* compiler (*B40* sākhīs 20–7 and 29–32) have been in some measure dispersed and rearranged by his *Ādi Sākhīs* counterpart. The *Ādi Sākhīs* order clearly derives from its compiler's concern for chronological order. Like the *Colebrooke* collection, but unlike *B40*, the *Ādi Sākhīs* offers a deliberate reordering of earlier sources designed to construct a coherent sequence. A discourse with God which comes relatively late in the *B40 Janam-sākhī* must have seemed out of place to the *Ādi Sākhīs* compiler. The sākhī which embodies this discourse relates the original commissioning of Nānak by God and the divine command to venture forth into the world for its salvation. The logical occasion for such a commissioning evidently appeared to be prior to the first appearance of Nānak in this world. This, it seems, was the line of reasoning which explains the placement of the sākhī at the very beginning of the *Ādi Sākhīs*, prior to the birth of Nānak. To a redactor of the *Narrative Ia* material a more suitable context appeared to be an experience of divine illumination in early manhood. In the *Purātan* janam-sākhīs the commissioning accordingly takes place during Nānak's submergence in the Sultānpur stream, and is immediately followed by the commencement of journeys which now assume the nature of missionary tours.

[1] *B40*, f. 68a–b. *AS*, pp. 53–4. *Pur JS*, p. 59.

[2] The Country Ruled by Women, the Sumeru discourse, the meeting with Lahaṇā and his appointment to succeed Nānak, the interview with God, the Achal discourse, and the miraculous arrival in Mecca.

The sequence which the *Ādi Sākhīs* develops by reordering its anecdotes is of considerable interest in that it represents the earliest extant example of a consciously coherent itinerary. In the *Ādi Sākhīs* the sequence assumes the form of a single journey lasting twelve years. Later *Ādi Sākhīs* manuscripts add to the geographical details,[1] but do not alter the structure. The *Miharbān* itinerary, which appears to be based in part on the *Ādi Sākhīs* pattern, divides the single journey into two, allowing for a temporary return to Sultānpur which is missing from the *Ādi Sākhīs*.[2] This pattern diversifies still further within the *Narrative Ia* tradition, perhaps by analogy with the *digvijaya* ideal.[3]

This chronological concern is conspicuously absent from the intention of the *B40* compiler, who apparently copied his material in the order he found it in *Q2*. It seems clear that he must have followed his model closely in terms of sequence, the only divergence being an interpolation which he introduced at one point. While copying from *Q2* the *B40* compiler turned briefly to another source in order to record an anecdote concerning Ajittā Randhāvā (sākhī 28). He then returned to *Q2*. In *Q2* the sākhīs which *B40* has recorded in two clusters presumably constituted a single cluster. This must have followed the order which results from a simple removal of the *B40* sākhī 28.

From the editorial supplements which have been added in both *B40* and the *Ādi Sākhīs* it appears that *Q2* must have been even less coherently structured than *B40*. Although *B40* lacks a consistent sequence it does indicate an awareness that one sākhī can often be linked with its predecessor. In the case of the *Narrative Ib* material this was normally unnecessary, for a comparison of the divergent *B40* and *Ādi Sākhīs* versions shows that this rudimentary editing had been performed by an earlier compiler. *Q2* did possess a certain measure of unity, but it was the common ascetic ideal which provided this unity rather than any emendation of earlier sources by the *Q2* compiler.

This was evidently as unsatisfactory to the *B40* compiler as to the person responsible for the *Ādi Sākhīs*. Both have added sentences and paragraphs with the obvious intention of improving the continuity of *Q2*'s disjointed narrative. The *B40* supplements are generally attached to the customary announcement that 'the sākhī is finished.' but occasionally an editorial clarification is worked into the actual narrative. The most prominent of the editorial additions occur, quite naturally, at the beginning or the conclusion of sākhīs. For example, *B40* concludes the Sumeru discourse by slightly extending a brief reference to the coming selection of a successor as Gurū.[4] The *Ādi Sākhīs* compiler has, however, decided to send Nānak to Mecca at this point. Accordingly he adds to the next sākhī a brief introduction which will serve to connect the Sumeru dis-

[1] An example is the addition of a reference to Setu-bandha Rāmeśvaram which is missing from one of the *Ādi Sākhīs* manuscripts. *AS*, p. 28.

[2] *GNSR*, p. 66.

[3] *GNSR*, p. 32n.

[4] *B40*, f. 93a.

course with the Mecca visit.[1] The variant conclusions with which the Achal discourse ends probably illustrate the same feature,[2] although in this instance it is possible that *B40* may have preserved a *Q2* reading which the *Ādi Sākhīs* compiler had dropped.

The same editorial concern has also produced two brief summaries of Bābā Nānak's travels. In the *Ādi Sākhīs* this summary is attached to the *Q2* Mecca sākhī and serves as a transitional passage leading back into *Narrative Ib* material.

And so all who were there prostrated themselves and became disciples (*sevak*). Having seen the entire territory of Mecca and Medīnā, and all the countries of that area, following the twelfth year [of his travels] Bābājī returned to Talvaṇḍī. Twelve years from the time when he had given away his property and left Sultānpur he returned to Talvaṇḍī. For two years he worked for Daulat Khān in Sultānpur. For twelve years he travelled. Then he returned home.[3]

The much briefer *B40* summary is attached to its concluding sākhī.[4]

Other additions to either *B40* or the *Ādi Sākhīs* can be explained by a variety of reasons. At one point the *B40* compiler has evidently been unable to resist interpolating a feature which he presumably derived from oral tradition. This seems to be the most likely explanation for the *B40* account of how Bābā Nānak eluded the Siddhs at Achal by means of a miraculous dissolution in the four elements.[5] It seems inconceivable that an episode of this kind would have been omitted by the *Ādi Sākhīs* compiler had it been present in *Q2*.

In other instances an addition can presumably be explained by reference to the doctrinal predilections of the compiler. An example appears to be a variant which occurs at the conclusion of the *B40* sākhī relating Bābā Nānak's visit to the pilgrimage centres, and at the beginning of the following sākhī in the *Ādi Sākhīs* version. The *B40* version, which probably adheres to the source at this point, declares that Bābā Nānak 'neither saw nor met a perfected gurū'.[6] The suggestion that Bābā Nānak, himself the divinely appointed messenger, should be in quest of a gurū was evidently more than the *Ādi Sākhīs* compiler could accept. This seems to be the explanation for his variant reading, which, by omitting several words, succeeds in making the 'perfected gurū' reference apply to Bābā Nānak.[7] At another point he indicates an interest in the meat-eating controversy by inserting a direct reference to flesh (*sugauti*) when specifying the diet which Bābā Nānak permitted his Sikhs to observe.[8]

One further reason for expanding *Q2* was the ever-present impulse to add quotations from the works attributed to Nānak at convenient (and sometimes inconvenient) points in the received narrative. This is obviously

[1] *AS*, p. 42. The *Ādi Sākhīs* version of the Sumeru discourse also provides an example of editorial clarification inserted during the course of the main narrative. To the extract *Vār Rāmkalī 12:2* there is added the note: 'Īśar Nāth said this.' *AS*, p. 39.

[2] *B40*, f. 122b. *AS*, p. 76.

[3] *AS*, p. 44.

[4] *B40*, f. 221a.

[5] See above, p. 152. The anecdote still figures prominently in the oral tradition of the Baṭālā area.

[6] *B40*, f. 82a.

[7] *AS*, p. 26.

[8] *AS*, p. 80. Cf. *B40*, f. 103b. The earlier portion of the *Ādi Sākhīs* version of this anecdote contains several sentences which are lacking in *B40*.

the source of the apocryphal *Tilaṅg Aṣṭapadī* 1 quotation at the conclusion of the *B40* sākhī 21.[1] The hymn is in no sense an integral part of the sākhī which purports to provide a context and it is absent from the *Ādi Sākhīs* version. Its introduction can be explained by its theme, which, in a limited sense, bears some resemblance to the theme of the sākhī's concluding anecdote.

All such variants do not, of course, prove an interpolation. In some instances a difference distinguishing the two versions arises from the obvious omission by one of the compilers of material which was evidently recorded in *Q2*. In the more significant instances (those which involve complete anecdotes) this feature can be explained by a compiler's preference for an alternative version to which he apparently had access. It seems likely that this must have been the reason for the *Ādi Sākhīs* compiler's omission of the account of Gurū Aṅgad's installation.[2] Elsewhere he introduces a different version, obviously a later, more evolved anecdote and for that reason a more attractive choice.[3] The *Narrative II* version was deliberately omitted and at the chronologically logical point (the period leading to Bābā Nānak's death) the alternative version was introduced.

The *B40* compiler also seems to have omitted anecdotes which were recorded in *Q2*, but for a slightly different reason. In the *Ādi Sākhīs*, between two clusters which are certainly from *Q2*, there occurs the following cluster:

10. The Monster's Cauldron
11. The Encounter with Kaliyug
12. Sajjaṇ the Robber.[4]

There is good reason for regarding these sākhīs as further borrowings from *Q2*. They accord with the other *Q2* clusters in terms of language and style, and they appear in the midst of *Q2* material where no evident reason for changing source exists. Moreover, they have analogues in the *Miharbān Janam-sākhī*. The significance of this parallel lies partly in the distinctive pattern followed by the *Ādi Sākhīs* versions, and partly in the material which the *Miharbān Janam-sākhī* associates with them.

The three anecdotes, as they appear in the *Ādi Sākhīs* version, are distinctively different from the better-known versions of the *Purātan* janam-sākhīs. The Monster's Cauldron sākhī omits Gurū Arjan's *Mārū* 14, which, because it contains a reference to a cauldron, has subsequently been attached to the anecdote; the encounter with Kaliyug is heralded by the approach of a hill which later turns out to be a man; and the Sajjaṇ of the *Ādi Sākhīs* is a different person from Sheikh Sajjaṇ of the *Purātan* tradition. All of these features appear in the *Miharbān Janam-sākhī*. As one would expect they have been amended and expanded, but they are plainly derived either from a source shared with the *Ādi Sākhīs*, or perhaps from a manuscript copy of the *Ādi Sākhīs* collection itself.

[1] *B40*, ff. 81a–82a.

[2] *B40*, sākhī 24d, ff. 98b–99a. The shabad *Sirī Rāg* 25 which *B40* appends may be an addition by ts compiler to his *Q2* source.

[3] *AS*, pp. 90–8.

[4] *AS*, pp. 28–33.

In the *Miharbān Janam-sākhī* these sākhīs constitute three of the anecdotes in a cluster of five.[1] The second in this group, a typical *Miharbān* discourse, is an expansion of a question concerning the existence of God which occurs in the fourth sākhī of the cluster. This fourth sākhī is the anecdote 'Bābā Nānak in the Land of Unbelievers'. It is a *Q2* sākhī, and there are several other examples of late *Miharbān* borrowings from the *Narrative II* tradition. The conclusion which this indicates is that the *Ādi Sākhīs* compiler must have taken the three sākhīs from *Q2*. The *B40* compiler's temporary abandonment of *Q2* can be explained by the fact that he had already recorded other versions of these same sākhīs.[2]

Although *Q2* must have been an early manuscript, it could not have represented a collection of anecdotes drawn from a single source. For the *B40* and *Ādi Sākhīs* compilers it constituted an important single source, but behind it lay several different sources. The *Narrative II* tradition was, in fact, a composite tradition. This diversity is evident from the varying content of the *Q2* material, and at least two of its sources can be positively identified. The major distinction can be observed in a comparison of the *B40* sākhīs 21 and 22. Sākhīs 20 and 21, the first of the *Narrative II* cluster, represent the ascetic ideal to which reference was made earlier in this section when distinguishing *Narrative II*. Here the emphasis is upon renunciation, upon separation from the world in order to obtain salvation, upon a philosophy which testifies to the reassertion of traditional ideals within the Sikh panth. When in *B40* sākhī 21 Bābā Nānak makes his first converts these 'first disciples' are said to have become renunciant *bairāgīs*,[3] and to this the *B40* compiler adds the apocryphal *Tilang* hymn in praise of renunciation.[4]

This was not a philosophy which commended itself to all within the community, but obviously it did retain a hold on some and their convictions emerge in these sākhīs. Other *Q2* borrowings which manifest the same concern are *B40* sākhīs 25, 26a, 26b, 27a, 27b, and, in a strictly qualified sense, 31. In the janam-sākhīs this element emerges later than the simple wonder-narrative and we shall accordingly designate it *Narrative IIb*. The origins of this tradition should probably be traced to the Udāsī panth, the sect within the Sikh community which was avowedly dedicated to the maintenance of ascetic belief and practice. The connection is indicated not only by the ascetic tone of the *Narrative IIb* material but also by a reference in the *B40* sākhī 31 which describes how Bābā Nānak, having arrived in the Land of Unbelievers, installed a *dhūān* (hearth).[5] The practice of constructing simple hearths was a Nāth custom which had been appropriated by the Udāsī sādhūs and subsequently the word *dhūān* was extended to designate any Udāsī establishment.[6]

1 *Mih JS* 1.226–38.

2 See above, pp. 192–4.

3 *B40*, f. 81a. *AS*, p. 26. *Mih JS* 1.120.

4 See above, p. 76.

5 *B40*, f. 128b. *AS*, p. 34. *Mih JS* 1.232.

6 For a description of the Nāth *dhūnī* see G. W. Briggs, *Gorakhnāth and the Kānphaṭa Yogīs* (Calcutta, 1938), p. 21. The words *dhūān* and *dhūnī* both mean, in their literal sense, 'smoke', but were used by the Nāths and Udāsīs to designate the ritual hearths which produced the smoke.

A change in tone within the *Q2* material becomes evident as we move from the *Narrative IIb* sākhī 21 into sākhī 22. Once again we are back in the realm of the wonder-narrative, the anecdote which expresses the basic janam-sākhī myth in its simplest terms. Bābā Nānak is the divinely commissioned giver of salvation. All who oppose him are humbled and converted. Even the most crafty of dark magic will fail to overcome him, for his strength lies in the infinite power of the divine Name. Needless to say, this theme is by no means absent from the *Narrative IIb* sākhīs. The primary distinction lies in the ascetic ideal which the *Narrative IIb* sākhīs attach to the common theme. The simpler sākhīs which lack this ideal we shall designate *Narrative IIa*. To this group belong the balance of the *B40* borrowings from *Q2*: sākhīs 22, 23, 24a–d, 29, 30, and 32. The three sākhīs recorded in their *Narrative II* form only by the *Ādi Sākhīs* (nos. 10, 11, and 12) also derive from this source.

Narrative IIa sākhīs are also distinguished from *Narrative IIb* material by an obvious link with the *Narrative I* tradition, probably in its *Ia* development. All of the sākhīs which omit the characteristic ascetic emphasis of the *Narrative IIb* anecdotes have analogues in the *Colebrooke Janam-sākhī*. In each case the *Narrative IIa* version (i.e. the version recorded in *Q2*) is obviously nearer to the common source than the *Narrative Ia* analogue as recorded in the *Colebrooke Janam-sākhī*. This is best illustrated by a comparison of the two variant treatments of the Mecca sākhī. In its *Narrative IIa* version this anecdote possesses a simplicity of form which must derive directly, or almost directly, from the earliest oral tradition. The *Narrative Ia* version, in contrast, has evolved its much more complicated narrative by conflating this anecdote with the story of the moving *miharāb* and with the separate Rukn al-Dīn discourse.[1]

This indicates a distinct but somewhat remote link with the *Narrative I* tradition. It appears that there may also be a link at this point with Bhāī Gurdās's *Vār* 1. Bhāī Gurdās's brief account of the life of Nānak is essentially an independent selection, including amongst its six anecdotes two which do not find a place in any of the major janam-sākhīs.[2] Of the remainder three do have analogues in both the *Narrative Ia* and *Narrative IIa* traditions,[3] and it is this feature which suggests a link with *Q2*, *B40*, and the *Ādi Sākhīs*.

An even closer connection may be observed in the case of the tradition which we shall be designating *Narrative III*.[4] This link is evident at two points. *Narrative III* is, of all traditions, the easiest to recognize, for it follows a distinctive structural pattern and includes several characteristic formulae. Some of these formulae appear in a brief prologue which is attached to sākhī 25 of the *B40 Janam-sākhī*.[5] The prologue does not

[1] See above, pp. 137–9.

[2] A version of Bābā Nānak's visit to Bāghdād, and the story of his encounter with the pīrs of Multān. *BG* 1:35–6, 44.

[3] The Mount Sumeru discourse, the Achal discourse, and the installation of Gurū Aṅgad. *BG* 1:28–31, 39–44, 45.

[4] See below, pp. 220–6.

[5] 'Mūlā the Khatrī.' *B40*, ff. 100a–100b (line 3). *AS*, pp. 76–7.

relate in any obvious way to the sākhī which follows it and there can be little doubt that it has been taken from the *Narrative III* tradition, probably by the *Q2* compiler himself.

The second appearance of *Narrative III* material occurs in *B40* sākhī 31, 'Bābā Nānak in the Land of Unbelievers' (*munāfik deś*).[1] This is another composite sākhī consisting, like *B40* sākhī 25, of a single anecdote prefaced by a brief eulogy of Bābā Nānak.[2] In this instance (unlike *B40* sākhī 25) it is the anecdote which derives from a *Narrative III* source. Whereas its prologue lacks the characteristic *Narrative III* formulae, the anecdote itself possesses both the typical *Narrative III* structure and its formulae. In its *B40* and *Ādi Sākhīs* form this sākhī accords reasonably well with the ascetic ideals of *Narrative IIb*, and this may explain its inclusion within the *Narrative II* tradition as recorded by *Q2*. Alternatively an earlier *Narrative III* anecdote may have been augmented with elements which conformed to the *Narrative IIb* ideal.

Another recognizable source which appears within the *Narrative II* material of *Q2* is the *Miharbān* tradition. This emerges in the form of another interpolation, this time within a *Narrative IIa* sākhī. The *B40* and *Ādi Sākhīs* versions of the Achal discourse both incorporate an exegetical passage wholly out of character for any of the *Narrative* sources.[3] The passage is however in complete conformity with the *Miharbān* style and there can be no doubt that an early recension of the *Miharbān Janam-sākhī* has provided its source. This particular feature has already been discussed in the section dealing with the evolution of individual sākhīs.[4] Once again the analogue in the extant *Miharbān Janam-sākhī* testifies to the lateness of this extant version.[5]

The *B40* and *Ādi Sākhīs* debt to the *Q2* manuscript (their *Narrative II* source) may be summarized as in the table on page 206.

The relationships linking *B40* and the *Ādi Sākhīs* to each other and to their common sources now form the pattern shown in figure 21. The twofold link with the *Miharbān* tradition represents first the interpolation from a *Miharbān* source in the Achal sākhī of *Narrative IIa*; and secondly the later appearance of *Narrative II* material in the *Miharbān Janam-sākhī*.[6] *Narrative II* sākhīs which appear in the *Miharbān Janam-sākhī* comprise all the *Narrative IIb* sākhīs, including the *Narrative III* borrowing;[7] the three *Narrative IIa* sākhīs which do not appear in the *B40* manuscript (*Ādi Sākhīs* numbers 10–12);[8] and the *Narrative IIa* cluster concerning Gurū Aṅgad which both *B40* and the *Ādi Sākhīs* record as a

[1] *B40*, ff. 127b–132a. *AS*, pp. 33–6.

[2] The preface occupies folio 127b of the *B40* manuscript and probably extends to line 12 of folio 128a. The portion which appears on folio 128a may, however, be the remnant of another anecdote. The *Ādi Sākhīs* and the *Miharbān Janam-sākhī* also record the sākhī in its composite form, including in it both the preface and the actual anecdote.

[3] *B40*, ff. 118a (line 3) to 120b (line 6). *AS*, pp. 73–5.

[4] See above, pp. 152–3. [5] *Mih JS* II.69–74. [6] See above, pp. 202–3.

[7] *Mih JS* I.111, 117–28. *Mih JS* II.143–7, 152–6, 163–4. *Narrative III* borrowing: *Mih JS* I.231–4.

[8] *Mih JS* I.226–31, 235–8.

B40	*Ādi Sākhīs*	*Colebrooke*			
22	9	23	The Country Ruled by Women	*Narrative IIa*	*Q2*
23	14	50a.	Discourse on Mount Sumeru		
24a–d.	22a–c.	53–4.	Anecdotes concerning Aṅgad		
29.	23.	50b	Discourse at Achal with *Miharbān* interpolation		
30.	1.	10.	Interview with God		
32.	15.	51.	Mecca: Bābā Nānak's miraculous arrival		
—	10.	44.	The Monster's Cauldron		
—	11.	24.	The Encounter with Kaliyug		
—	12.	13.	Sajjaṇ the Robber		
20.	8b.	—	Bābā Nānak's Austerities	*Narrative IIb*	
21.	8c–d.	—	Visit to the Pilgrimage Centres		
25.	24.	—	{Prologue from *Narrative III* / Mūlā the Khatrī}		
26a.	25a.	—	Bābā Nānak's Daily Discipline		
26b.	25b.	—	The Loyal Fortitude of Aṅgad		
27a.	25c.	—	Bābā Nānak's Adoration		
27b.	25d–e.	—	Discourse with Gorakhnāth: Bābā Nānak seeks solitude		
31.	13.	—	Bābā Nānak in the Land of Unbelievers	*Narrative III*	

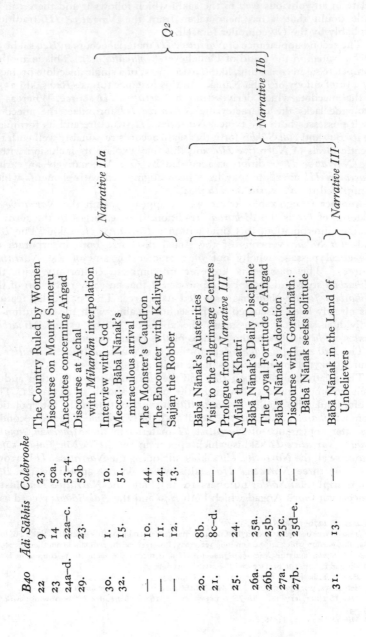

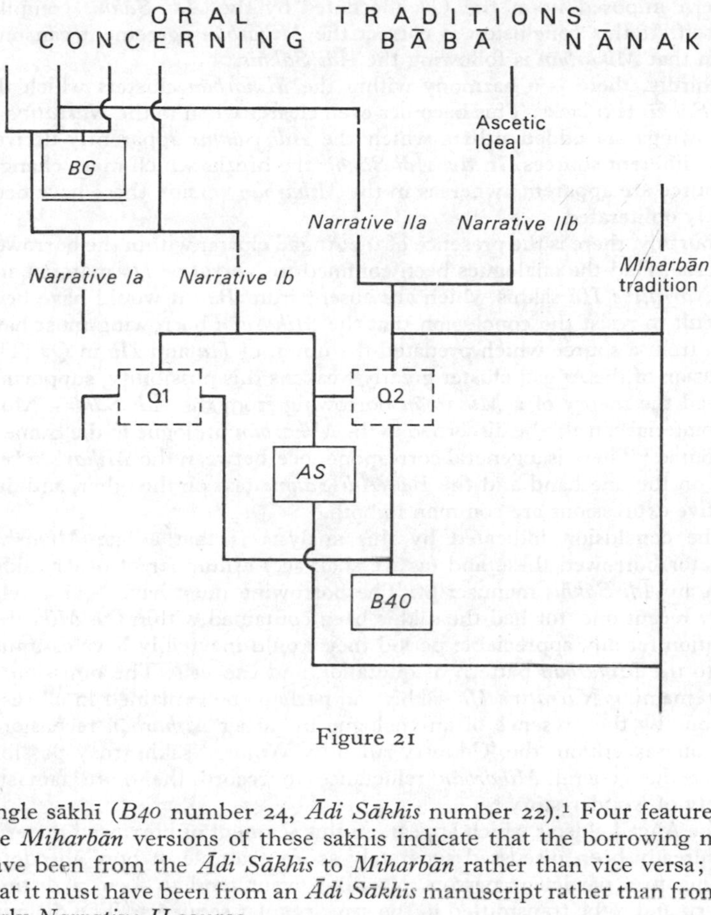

Figure 21

single sākhī (*B40* number 24, *Ādi Sākhīs* number 22).[1] Four features of the *Miharbān* versions of these sakhis indicate that the borrowing must have been from the *Ādi Sākhīs* to *Miharbān* rather than vice versa; and that it must have been from an *Ādi Sākhīs* manuscript rather than from an early *Narrative II* source.

First, it is immediately evident that the *Miharbān* analogues are conspicuously out of character for the *Miharbān* tradition. The typical *Miharbān* sākhī, or *goṣṭ*, consists of a brief narrative introduction followed by quotations from the works of Nānak and copious quantities of exegesis. Sustained narrative of the kind followed in these *Narrative II* sākhīs is alien to the *Miharbān* tradition and indicates a later borrowing.

Secondly, there is commonly an agreement in terms of sequence between *Miharbān* and the *Ādi Sākhīs*. A comparison of the *Ādi Sākhīs* and *B40* texts has already indicated that the *Ādi Sākhīs* sequence is a

[1] *Mih JS* II.66–8. Although most of the other *Narrative IIa* anecdotes also have analogues in the *Miharbān Janam-sākhī* all diverge widely from the *B40/Ādi Sākhīs* text. The *Miharbān* versions have clearly been taken from sources other than the *Narrative II* tradition.

pattern imposed upon the *Q2* anecdotes by the *Ādi Sākhīs* compiler himself. If this conclusion is correct the *Miharbān* agreement can only mean that *Miharbān* is following the *Ādi Sākhīs*.

Thirdly, there is a harmony within the *Miharbān* clusters which the *Ādi Sākhīs* text lacks. This becomes even clearer when to the *Narrative II* borrowings are added others which the *Ādi Sākhīs* apparently derived from different sources. In the *Ādi Sākhīs* the breaks which mark changes of source are apparent; whereas in the *Miharbān* version these have been largely obliterated.

Fourthly, there is the presence of the Aṅgad cluster within the borrowed material. Had the analogues been confined to *Narrative IIb* material and the *Narrative IIa* sākhīs which are absent from *B40* it would have been difficult to resist the conclusion that the *Miharbān* borrowing must have been from a source which predated the union of *IIa* and *IIb* in *Q2*. The inclusion of the Aṅgad cluster greatly weakens this possibility, supporting instead the theory of a *Miharbān* borrowing from the *Ādi Sākhīs*. More *IIa* material can also be discerned in the *Miharbān* prologue to the Sumeru discourse.[1] There is a general correspondence between the *Miharbān* version on the one hand and the *B40/Ādi Sākhīs* text on the other, and distinctive expressions are common to both.[2]

The conclusion indicated by this analysis is that a late *Miharbān* redactor borrowed these and (as we shall see) a number of other sākhīs from an *Ādi Sākhīs* manuscript. The borrowing must have been a relatively recent one, for had the sākhīs been contained within the *Miharbān* tradition for any appreciable period they would inevitably have assimilated to the *Miharbān* pattern of quotation and exegesis. The omission of the remaining *Narrative IIa* sākhīs can perhaps be explained in all cases but one by the presence of an analogue in earlier *Miharbān* recensions. The one exception, the 'Country ruled by Women' sākhī, may possibly reflect the general *Miharbān* reluctance to record the more fantastic variety of wonder-story.[3]

The Aṅgad cluster which appears in this segment of borrowed material has already been discussed separately as an example of how anecdotes relating to a particular person, place, or event tend to form a distinct pattern and to be transmitted in the same regular sequence. The diagram illustrating this process which appears on page 170 can now be reproduced with the various sources indicated.

The reason for including a second recension of the *Ādi Sākhīs* will be made clear in the next section.

[1] *Mih JS* I.384–5.

[2] For example, Bābā Nānak's claim that he had come from *āsā-andesā*, literally 'hope-anxiety'. *B40*, f. 86b. *AS*, p. 37. *Mih JS* I.385. Both texts also contain the word *viāh*. The *Miharbān* version clearly intends it to mean 'marriage', whereas the *B40/Ādi Sākhīs* text seems to be referring to the Beās river. See *B40(Eng)*, p. 92n.

[3] *GNSR*, p. 31. The fact that the *Miharbān* tradition already included a Kaliyug sākhī did not prevent the late redactor from borrowing the *Ādi Sākhīs* version, for it differed sufficiently to seem a different anecdote. The resemblance was nevertheless close enough to suggest a point at which one of the borrowed clusters could be interpolated. *Mih JS* I.226.

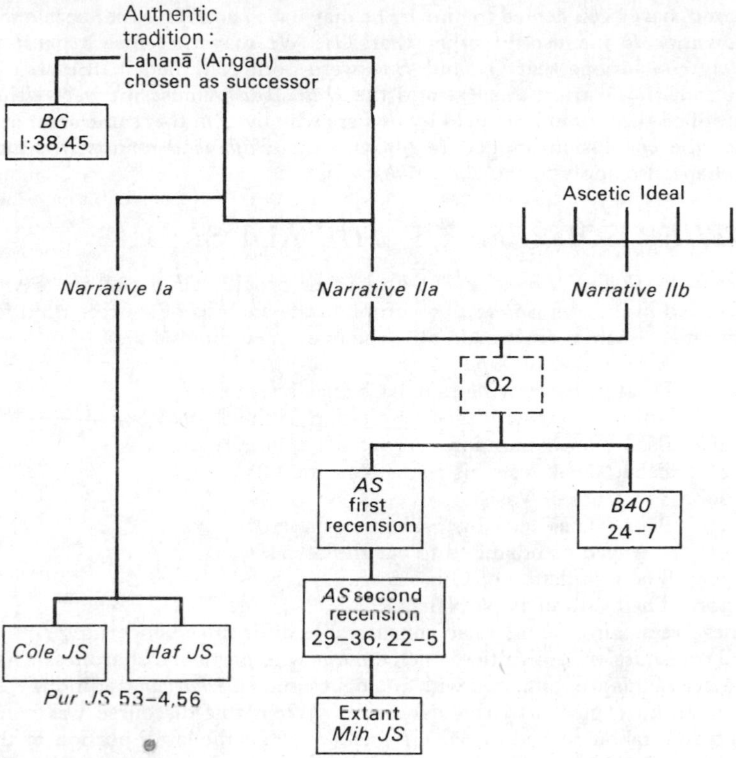

Figure 22

One final conclusion which may be drawn from this pattern is that *Q2* must certainly have been found within the same geographical area as *Q1*, *B40*, and the *Hāfizābād Janam-sākhī*.[1] This is indicated not only by the fact that the *B40* compiler had access to it, but also by the *Narrative III* borrowings which appear in *Q2*. *Narrative III* appears to have been the oral tradition current in the *B40* compiler's locality.[2] The fact that the *Ādi Sākhīs* compiler could also copy from *Q2* suggests that he too may have lived within this same area. This possibility must, however, be attended by some doubt. The connection of the *Hāfizābād Janam-sākhī* with the *Colebrooke* manuscript as well as with *Q1* indicates that a compiler could draw on sources which must have been widely separated in terms of geographical distance. If in fact *Q1* was located in the *B40* area, and if the *Ādi Sākhīs* compiler lived within easy reach of the same locality, it seems likely that he would have known of its existence and would have utilized it. On the other hand access to *Q1* may, for some

[1] See above, p. 191.

[2] See below, p. 223.

reason, have been denied to him, or he may have had even easier access to a *Narrative Ib* manuscript other than *Q1*. We may therefore suggest as likely conclusions that *Q2* and *B40* were both compiled in the area of Gujranwālā District; that *Q1* and the *Hāfizābād* manuscript were either compiled there or at least held by owners who lived in that same area; and that the conclusion applied to *Q1* and the *Hāfizābād* manuscript may perhaps also apply to the *Ādi Sākhīs*.

OTHER SOURCES OF THE ĀDI SĀKHĪS

Narrative Ib and *Narrative IIa–b* together provide almost all the sākhīs recorded in the *Ādi Sākhīs*. To complete the analysis of sources used for this janam-sākhī there remain only the five concluding sākhīs:

26. A recitation of *Japjī*
27. Dead birds revivified: Bābā Nānak's remorse
28a. An interview with God: recitation of the shabad *Sodar*
28b. Bābā Nānak summons the Gangā to thirsty Sikhs
29a. Bābā Nānak tests his Sikhs (continued)
29b. The story of Vasiṣṭ
29c. Bābā Nānak tests his Sikhs (continued): Aṅgad commanded to eat the corpse
30a. The installation of Gurū Aṅgad
30b. The death of Bābā Nānak.

These remaining sākhīs raise considerable difficulties concerning source and transmission, difficulties which emerge with particular sharpness when the five sākhīs are compared with analogues in the *Miharbān* tradition.

Sākhī 26 begins with the statement: 'When this discourse was completed Gorakhnāth said to Bābā [Nānak] . . .'[1] As the latter portion of the preceding sākhī is not in fact a discourse the sentence suggests that the *Ādi Sākhīs* compiler had at this point turned to a different source. This possibility is supported by the *B40* switch to a different source at the same point,[2] and the reference to Gorakhnāth (who had also appeared in sākhī 25) suggests a reason for the *Ādi Sākhīs* introduction of sākhī 26 at this particular juncture. These features indicate a break at the end of sākhī 25, without conclusively proving it. The fact that the brief narrative portion of sākhī 26 continues the Pañjābī of its predecessor means that some measure of doubt must persist, but it is scarcely a compelling doubt. The linguistic continuity could be the result of assimilation either to the language of the preceding *Q2* material or to the compiler's own usage. In view of the fact that this narrative portion comprises only two sentences such a process would be quite possible.

The question of language is, however, of subsequent importance, for the three anecdotes which immediately follow sākhī 26 are expressed in a Khaṛī Bolī (or a Sādhukkaṛī closely related to Khaṛī Bolī) which at once distinguishes them sharply from the *Narrative II* material of *Q2*. Whatever the origin of sākhī 26 there can be no doubt that for the next two sākhīs

[1] *AS*, pp. 84 5.
[2] *B40*, f. 111a.

the compiler is utilizing a source or sources other than *Q2*. In addition to the language difference three further features mark this distinction. First, there is the style, which, in sākhī 27, assumes the form of a soliloquy. This is not a feature to be associated with *Q2*. Secondly, a comparison of the *Ādi Sākhīs*' sākhī 28a with its sākhī 1 (sākhī 30 in *B40*) reveals that the two are analogues. Sākhī 1 comes from *Q2*, which suggests that sākhī 28a is unlikely to have derived from that particular source. Thirdly, there is the failure of *B40* to record this material. The conclusion which follows is that the *Ādi Sākhīs* compiler has almost certainly drawn sākhīs 27 and 28 (both 28a and 28b) from a source to which the *B40* compiler did not have access; and that sākhī 26 may have come from this same source.

A further conclusion which emerges from a study of these three sākhīs is that in all likelihood they entered the *Ādi Sākhīs* tradition as an addition made by a later copyist rather than as a part of the first recension. This conclusion is indicated by the failure of one of the extant *Ādi Sākhīs* manuscripts to include them.[1] The association of sākhī 26 with sākhīs 27 and 28, rather than with sākhī 25, derives further support from this omission.

The beginning of sākhī 29 marks a reversion not only to Pañjābī but also to the story of how Bābā Nānak tested his Sikhs. This was the theme of sākhī 25 and its reappearance at this point suggests a continuation of the same source following the irruption of sākhīs 26–8 in the later recensions of the *Ādi Sākhīs*. The story continues with an account of how Bābā Nānak tested Aṅgad by banishing him from his sight, but before reaching a conclusion it suffers another interruption. This consists of a lengthy anecdote concerning Ṛṣi Vasiṣṭ, Rām Chandar, and Lachhman (sākhī 29b).[2]

In a sense this anecdote, though distinctly alien to the janam-sākhī *Narrative* traditions, is not an interruption. It purports to be a speech of reassurance uttered by Aṅgad in order to comfort the Sikhs who had been puzzled and frightened by Nānak's sudden resort to threats of violence.[3] As such it seems to accord with the theme of the sākhī within which it occurs. It is, however, plainly an addition to earlier traditions concerning the tests which Bābā Nānak imposed on his followers in order to determine the measure of their loyalty to him. Moreover, it is at once clear that the source of the digression is the ever-popular cycle of *Rāmāyaṇa* legends. The issue which is not clear is whether the interpolation was limited to sākhī 29b, or whether it also included the setting provided by sākhī 29a and the beginning of sākhī 29c. In the *Ādi Sākhīs* version all three sections of sākhī 29 have been fused into a single coherent narrative with a link passage leading into the final anecdote of the series.[4] This suggests that the interpolation was not the compiler's own work, but that of his source.

The concluding anecdote of the series is the celebrated story of how Bābā Nānak tested Aṅgad's loyalty by commanding him to eat a corpse.[5]

[1] The manuscript in the possession of Shamsher Singh Ashok. *AS*, p. *xi*.

[2] *AS*, pp. 91–4. [3] *B40*, f. 109b. [4] *AS*, pp. 94–5.

[5] *AS*, pp. 95–7. *GNSR*, p. 50.

This reaches a climax with an ascription of praise to Bābā Nānak, the Giver of Salvation,[1] and leads naturally into sākhī 30a. The first part of this final sākhī narrates an account of the installation of Aṅgad as Gurū and introduces a brief reference to the objections raised by Nānak's own sons. At this point another obvious break occurs and it is evident that the compiler has once again changed his source.

The reason for the change evidently relates to the anecdote concerning Nānak's sons, for the new material takes up the account of their objections. The break is, however, patently obvious. The two sons who in the previous section are already arguing with their father are represented in the new material as absent from him, and for the first time hearing the news of his approaching death. They at once hasten to his bedside and begin lodging the objections already set forth in the earlier narrative. The two sentences which begin the new material do not in fact refer to the sons but to funeral preparations. This points back to a preceding narrative in the new source, a narrative which has been omitted by the *Ādi Sākhīs* compiler because the reference to the two sons seemed to provide a more appropriate point at which to introduce his new source material. The nature of the preceding narrative can be determined from the *B40* analogue,[2] for it is at this point that the *Ādi Sākhīs* and *B40* draw near to each other again. They do not, however, coincide. Somewhere behind the two versions there lies a common source for this 'Death of Nanak' sākhī. The two compilers have used widely divergent versions of this common material, and each has joined to it anecdotes drawn from mutually different sources.

Sākhī 30b concludes the *Ādi Sākhīs* narrative. Nānak's date of death is given as Asū *sudī* 10, S.1595,[3] and the janam-sākhī terminates with the customary offering of praise to the Gurū. An effort must now be made to identify the sources which have contributed to these five concluding sākhīs. Unfortunately the pattern which they present is unusually complicated and most conclusions concerning their origins must be regarded as strictly tentative.

The five sākhīs begin with a break, and two further breaks have been noted within the group. The initial break seems to mark the abandonment of *Q2* in favour of a Khaṛī Bolī source; the second marks a reversion to a Pañjābī narrative which appears to connect with sākhī 25; and the final break, while continuing the Pañjābī narrative, makes its presence clear by means of a clumsy repetition. This leaves us with three clearly defined sections. Within the second of these a lengthy sub-section (the *Rāmāyaṇa* borrowing) can be discerned. This indicates the pattern shown in figure 23. These four elements must be identified before the analysis of the *Ādi Sākhīs* sources is complete.

A possible source of the first cluster (26–8b) is the *Miharbān* tradition.

[1] *AS*, p. 97.

[2] *B40*, ff. 221a–227a.

[3] The appearance in some manuscripts of *vadī* (the dark half of the lunar month, or period of the waning moon) in place of *sudī* (the light half) is clearly a later amendment intended to bring the *Ādi Sākhīs* date closer to the generally accepted date. *AS*, pp. *xxxi–ii*, 100 n. 3. *GNSR*, pp. 100–1.

This identification is suggested by the sentence, quoted above,[1] with which sākhī 26 begins. Whereas the reference in this sentence to a discourse (*goṣṭ*) does not connect logically with the conclusion of sākhī 25, it could conceivably indicate a connection with the *Ādi Sākhīs* conclusion of sākhī 23 (the Achal discourse). At the end of this sākhī both the *Ādi*

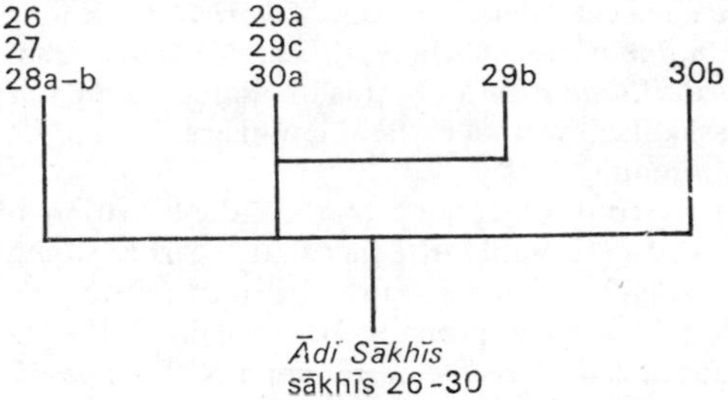

Figure 23

Sākhīs and *B40* state that Bābā Nānak, on this occasion, recited his *Siddh Goṣṭ*.[2] To this the *Ādi Sākhīs* adds a sentence which does not appear in the *B40* text: *tis kā nāle arath nāle paramārath*. 'With it (the text of the *Siddh Goṣṭ*) is the meaning and exegesis.'[3] This formula plainly indicates the *Miharbān* tradition and suggests that the *Ādi Sākhīs* compiler had before him a *Miharbān* source which at that point he was relinquishing. This source he may have been using earlier in the Achal sākhī, for his version of the *Miharbān* interpolation differs appreciably from the shorter *B40* version.[4] The nature of the difference consorts well with the possibility of a compiler having recognized a *Miharbān* borrowing within *Q2* and having thus been prompted to turn briefly to a *Miharbān* source which was in his possession.

It is possible that the introduction to sākhī 26 marks a return to this source. The reference to a *goṣṭ* seems to indicate this; the Khaṛī Bolī language of the cluster supports it; and the shift from narrative to soliloquy in sākhī 27 evidently adds to this support. Finally, there exist within the *Miharbān Janam-sākhī* analogues for all the sākhīs in the cluster.[5] The first sākhī of the cluster (the *Japjī* recitation) is set by the *Miharbān* version in the context of the Achal discourse, where it follows the *Siddh Goṣṭ* text and commentary. It includes more stanzas than the *Ādi Sākhīs* version, but agrees with it in beginning the recitation at the twenty-eighth stanza.

The existence of analogues, though seemingly the strongest argument of all, must be examined before it can be adduced in support of the

[1] See above, p. 210. [2] *B40*, f. 122a. [3] *AS*, p. 76.
[4] See above, p. 205, n. 3.
[5] *AS* sākhī 26 (*Mih JS* II.125–37). *AS* sākhī 27 (*Mih JS* I.269–71). *AS* sākhī 28a (*Mih JS* II.138–41). *AS* sākhī 28b (*Mih JS* II.137–8).

Miharbān identification. It has already been argued that the *Miharbān* tradition was itself indebted to the *Ādi Sākhīs* and it is possible that these analogues should be classified in the same manner. The case for an original *Miharbān* borrowing from the *Ādi Sākhīs* is, however, weaker in this instance. A much stronger case can be made when a *Miharbān* analogue follows a narrative pattern which can be recognized as untypical of the distinctive exegetical style of the *Miharbān* tradition. The passages in the *Miharbān Janam-sākhī* which appear to derive from *Narrative II* sources via the *Ādi Sākhīs* are all of this uncharacteristic narrative variety. In contrast the sākhīs now under examination are, with one exception, cast in the *Miharbān* mould.[1]

There are, it is true, objections to this identification of a *Miharbān* source for sākhīs 26–8, notably, the fact that the *Ādi Sākhīs* versions lack the exegetical passages which constitute the most prominent feature of the *Miharbān* style. This may perhaps be explained by the *Ādi Sākhīs* compiler's evident preference for narrative, a preference which may have prompted him to paraphrase his *Miharbān* source. It will be noted, however, that conjectures are accumulating with distressing speed. Our conclusion is that the *Miharbān* tradition provides the most likely source for the cluster, but that the identification can be no more than tentative.

The second cluster, sākhīs 29a–30a, connects with the narrative of sākhī 25 and suggests that the *Ādi Sākhīs* may at this point have reverted to *Q2*. Although this possibility receives further support from a general identity of language and idiom it cannot be accepted without question. A number of features point to a different source.

The first of these features is the structure and content of the sākhīs which constitute the cluster. In them we find a well-integrated narrative, developed by fusing different anecdotes with a skill unusual in *Q2* material. This implies a later stage than *Q2*, and some of the incidental details within the cluster indicate the same conclusion. When, for example, Aṅgad and Mardānā lift the shroud to eat the corpse they discover not putrid flesh but confectionery.[2] This is rather more sophisticated than the *Narrative Ia* analogue, which makes Nānak magically replace the corpse with his own body.[3] Sophistication of detail is not characteristic of *Narrative II* material.

A second distinctive element within the cluster is the stress which it lays upon a particular point of doctrine. 'The Gurū is God and not a man,'

[1] The exception is the brief anecdote which relates how Bābā Nānak once summoned the Gangā river to a group of thirsty Sikhs in a jungle. *AS*, p. 90. *Mih JS* II.175. See above, p. 31. Both versions claim that this story was related to Akbar. *AS*, p. 90. *Mih JS* II.137. The *Miharbān* version adds that the recitation took place on an occasion when Akbar met Gurū Arjan in Lahore. In the *Miharbān Janam-sākhī* the cluster which includes this anecdote and the interview with God (*goṣṭ* 176) also includes a narrative account of how Bābā Nānak contracted a second marriage, the second wife being a Muslim woman of the Raṅghaṛ caste (*goṣṭ* 177). This story, which has been omitted from the published text of the *Miharbān Janam-sākhī*, may possibly have been omitted by the *Ādi Sākhīs* compiler for similar reasons. There is no evidence to suggest that the story has a factual basis.

[2] *AS*, p. 96.

[3] *Pur JS*, p. 108. *GNSR*, p. 50.

it declares in sākhī 29a,[1] and repeats the claim in sākhī 29c.[2] This insistence, which provides the integrative principle linking the three parts of sākhī 29, is not to be found in *Q2*.

Thirdly, the lengthy digression which constitutes sākhī 29b has no parallel in *Q2* material; and finally it is difficult to understand why the *B40* compiler would have omitted these anecdotes had they been in *Q2*. The fact that he provides an alternative version of the installation of Gurū Aṅgad,[3] one which accords better with the general *Narrative II* style, suggests that *Q2* did not include these anecdotes.

Perhaps the most likely solution to the problem is a theory which envisages a later post-*Q2* extension of the *Narrative II* anecdote concerning Bābā Nānak's decision to test his Sikhs. This drew upon two sources. The first was the *Rāmāyaṇa* cycle, to which was added a narrative linking it to the *Narrative II* tradition and providing a context for the insistence upon Nānak's divinity. The second was a developed version of the corpse-eating anecdote, an anecdote which emerges in a cruder form in the *Colebrooke Janam-sākhī*. The distant connection with the *Narrative Ia* tradition indicated by the *Colebrooke* analogue continues up to the point where the compiler abandons his source during the course of his concluding sākhī. This source we shall designate *Narrative IIc*.

The last portion of the cluster is the most perplexing of all. Two obvious analogues exist, but neither enables us to make a positive identification. The first is *B40*, which records an appreciably longer and less coherent version of the death narrative.[4] Although there can be no doubt that *B40* and the *Ādi Sākhīs* have drawn from sources which must ultimately converge, it is equally obvious that the two versions are some distance apart. The greater length of the *B40* version can be explained only in part by the fact that the *Ādi Sākhīs* compiler chose to take up his source during the course of its narrative rather than at its beginning. During the later stages *B40* adds extra material which the *Ādi Sākhīs* lacks, and in the process jumbles the various elements to a degree which may perhaps reflect a haste to be finished with the janam-sākhī. The *Ādi Sākhīs*, though briefer and more coherent than *B40*, also has its inconsistencies. The disciple who seeks freedom for his *kuṛam* is variously named Sādhāran (as in *B40*[5]) and Bhagīrath.[6]

The second analogue is to be found in *Bālā* manuscripts which have obviously derived their 'Death of Nānak' sākhī from the *Miharbān* tradition. The earlier and more consistent *Bālā* tradition terminated its account prior to the death of Nānak. This was necessary as Bhāī Bālā had previously been represented as a companion of the Gurū who had left him prior to his death. Inevitably the deficiency proved to be unsatisfying to *Bālā* audiences and a supplement was later added, wherein Gurū Aṅgad narrated for Bhāī Bālā's benefit an account of the Gurū's death.[7]

[1] *AS*, p. 91.
[2] *AS*, pp. 95, 97.
[3] *B40*, f. 98b.
[4] *B40*, ff. 221a–230a.
[5] *B40*, ff. 225b–226a, 228a–b.
[6] *AS*, p. 99. Cf. *B40*, f. 138b.
[7] Cambridge University Library MS Add. 921, ff. 198b–205b.

This account, as we have already observed, was taken from a *Miharbān* source.[1]

Are any of these three analogues copies of either of the others? It seems probable that at least the *Bālā/Miharbān* version was a copy and that it was taken from the *Ādi Sākhīs*. This is indicated by two features.

First, there is the convincing hypothesis that much of the *Ādi Sākhīs* text, particularly the sākhīs which are recorded in its latter part, has been copied by a *Miharbān* redactor. *Narrative II* borrowings by the *Miharbān* tradition have already been noted, and the same procedure has also been followed in the case of sākhī 29a–c of the *Ādi Sākhīs*. These sākhīs, expressed in the same integrated form, constitute *goṣṭ* 180 of the extant *Miharbān Janam-sākhī*.[2] The fact that this *goṣṭ* immediately follows the analogue of sākhī 25 may possibly add further weight to the suggestion that sākhīs 26–8 represent an interpolated cluster within the later *Ādi Sākhīs* tradition. On the other hand it must be remembered that the constituents of this cluster also have their *Miharbān* analogues and that most of these immediately precede the *Miharbān* analogue of sākhī 25 in the *Ādi Sākhīs*.

The analogues of cluster 26–8 as they appear in the extant *Miharbān Janam-sākhī* may, indeed, represent a case of double borrowing. Some of this cluster, having originally entered the *Ādi Sākhīs* from an early *Miharbān* source, could have passed back into a later *Miharbān* recension in their *Ādi Sākhīs* form. The same process may also have applied in the case of the Achal sākhī. This theory is perhaps open to some doubt, but the doubt does not extend to *goṣṭ* 180. *Goṣṭ* 180 of the *Miharbān Janam-sākhī* must certainly be a late borrowing by the *Miharbān* tradition from the *Ādi Sākhīs* or a source very close to it. From this it follows that a borrowing of sākhī 30b would be entirely natural.

The second feature which supports this conclusion is a clear break within the *Bālā* text. It appears from the *Bālā* manuscripts that their *Miharbān* source provided them with an account beginning at precisely the same point as sākhī 30b of the *Ādi Sākhīs*. For the earlier portions of its death narrative the *Bālā* account relies on a source very close to *B40*, perhaps on *B40* itself.[3] It need occasion no surprise that the *Bālā* manuscripts do not follow a *Miharbān* version of the installation of Gurū Aṅgad, and that accordingly we possess no *Miharbān* analogue for sākhī 30a of the *Ādi Sākhīs*. The *Bālā* janam-sākhīs earlier record a different version of this episode, one which is important for the distinctive *Bālā* emphases which it expresses.[4] There was thus no need to copy the *Miharbān* version. This latter version, which like the death sākhī must have been included in the missing *Prem Pad Pothī* of the *Miharbān Janam-sākhī*, will presumably have followed the *Ādi Sākhīs* text.

This eliminates the *Miharbān* tradition as an original source, but leaves

[1] See above, p. 19; also *AS*, p. *xxxv*, note.
[2] *Mih JS* II.148–52.
[3] CUL MS Add. 921, ff. 197a–198b.
[4] Ibid., ff. 181a–184b.

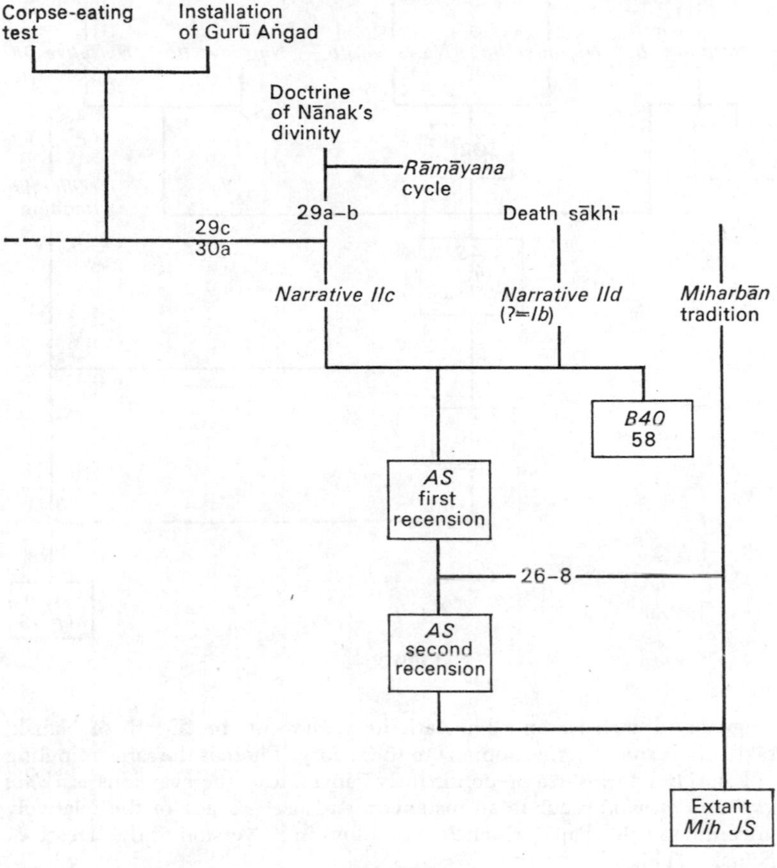

Figure 24

us unable to proceed further with any firm assurance. The hypothesis which seems to come closest to probability is that yet another *Narrative* source lay behind both accounts, and that for the area which it covers the *Ādi Sākhīs* version brings us nearer to this tradition than does the heterogeneous *B40* sākhī. With considerable hesitation we designate this source *Narrative IId*, adding that it may perhaps coincide with *Narrative Ib*.

This latter possibility is suggested by the nature of the relationship between the *Ādi Sākhīs* and *B40* versions. On the one hand they are clearly relating the same anecdote; on the other, the two texts are distinguished by a considerable measure of disagreement. This is the kind of relationship which links the two janam-sākhīs at points where they use common material from the *Narrative Ib* tradition, and a comparison of the *Narrative Ib*

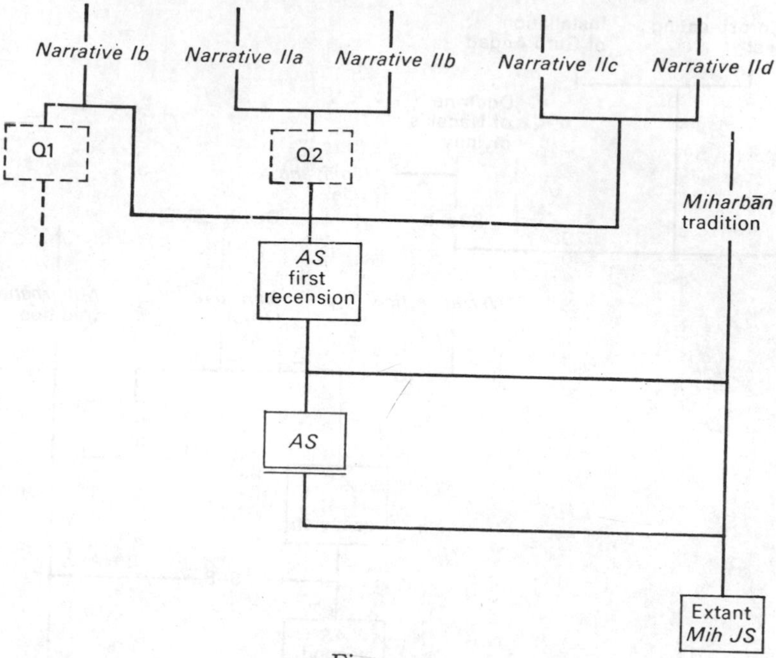

Figure 25

language in each janam-sākhī with its version of the 'Death of Nānak' sākhī offers some further support to the theory. There is the same mingling of Khaṛī Bolī forms in a predominantly Pañjābī text, such versions as *ākhan lagā* and *āi miliā* recur in all instances, and use is made of the relatively uncommon title 'Tapā' which *B40* employs in its version of the 'Death of Nānak' sākhī.[1]

It must, however, be acknowledged that this is a slender base upon which to erect a theory, for most of the similarities are to be found elsewhere in material which does not derive from the *Narrative Ib* tradition. The *Hāfizābād* manuscript does not help us at this point. Its failure to refer to the sākhī may merely mean that, as in other instances, its compiler preferred to use *Narrative Ia* material wherever possible. *Narrative Ib* remains a possible source, but not a proven one. An independent source could have equally strong claims. Finally, it should be noted that the *B40* compiler has evidently supplemented this principal source with material drawn from some other source or sources. The result is a composite sākhī at once the most muddled and the most sublime of all that the *B40* manuscript contains.

[1] For example *B40*, f. 224b. It has been translated as 'Master' in *B40(Eng)*.

The tentative pattern which now emerges for the five concluding sākhīs of the *Ādi Sākhīs* is shown in figure 24. Linked with the earlier paradigms this diagram produces the complete pattern for the sources of the *Ādi Sākhīs* shown in figure 25.

In this final diagram for the *Ādi Sākhīs* the upper link with the *Miharbān* tradition represents not only the cluster but also the later *Ādi Sākhīs* redactor's apparent reliance on his *Miharbān* source for his variant version of the sākhī 23 interpolation.[1]

Once again it is necessary to stress the tentative nature of portions of this *Ādi Sākhīs* pattern. It represents a combination of established sources and conjecture. The same qualification must be attached to the table, which indicates sources for individual sākhīs.

Sākhī no.	*Title of Anecdote*	*Source*
1.	An Interview with God	*Narrative II (Q2)*
2a.	The Birth of Nānak	
2b.	Instruction by the Paṇḍit	
3a.	Bābā Nānak's Betrothal and Marriage	
3b.	The Ruined Crop Restored	
4.	The Tree's Stationary Shadow	
5a.	The True Field and the True Merchandise	
5b.	Bābā Nānak's Discourse with the Physician	*Narrative Ib*
6.	Sultānpur	
7a.	Immersion in the River	
7b.	Bābā Nānak's Discourse with Daulat Khān's Qāzī	
8a.	Bābā Nānak's Travels in the Uninhabited Wilderness	
8b.	Bābā Nānak's Austerities	
8c.	Bābā Nānak's Visit to the Pilgrimage Centres	
9.	The Country Ruled by Women	
10.	The Monster's Cauldron	
11.	The Encounter with Kaliyug	
12.	Sajjaṇ the Robber	*Narrative II (Q2)*
13.	Bābā Nānak in the Land of Unbelievers	
14.	Discourse with Siddhs on Mount Sumeru	
15.	Mecca: Bābā Nānak's Miraculous Arrival	

[1] See above, p. 205.

Sākhī no.	*Title of Anecdote*	*Source*
16.	Bābā Nānak returns to Talvaṇḍī	*Narrative Ib*
17.	Discourse with Sheikh Braham	
18.	The Sack of Saidpur	
19.	Discourse with Bābur	
20.	The proud Karoṛī humbled: founding of Kartārpur	
21a.	The Merchant and Rājā Śivanābh	
21b.	Bābā Nānak and Rājā Śivanābh	
22a.	The Meeting with Lahaṇā	*Narrative II* (*Q2*)
22b.	Aṅgad returns to Matte dī Sarāi	
22c.	Aṅgad moves to Khaḍūr: his clothes ruined	
23.	Discourse with Siddhs at Achal.	
24.	Mūlā the Khatrī	
25a.	Bābā Nānak's Daily Discipline	
25b.	The Loyal Fortitude of Aṅgad.	
25c.	Bābā Nānak's Adoration	
25d.	Discourse with Gorakhnāth: Bābā Nānak seeks solitude	
25e.	Bābā Nānak tests his Sikhs	
26.	A Recitation of *Japjī*	*Miharbān*
27.	Dead Birds Revivified: Bābā Nānak's Remorse	
28a.	An Interview with God: Recitation of *Sodar*	
28b.	Bābā Nānak summons the Gaṅgā to Thirsty Sikhs	
29a.	Bābā Nānak tests his Sikhs (contd.)	*Narrative IIc*
29b.	The Story of Vasiṣṭ	
29c.	Bābā Nānak tests his Sikhs (contd.): Aṅgad commanded to eat the corpse	
30a.	The Installation of Gurū Aṅgad	
30b.	The Death of Bābā Nānak	*Narrative IId* (? = 1b)

OTHER SOURCES OF THE B40 JANAM-SĀKHĪ

1. Narrative III

It has already been shown that much of the *B40 Janam-sākhī* derives from *Narrative I* and *Narrative II* sources. The third and last of the *B40* compiler's major narrative sources is the easiest of all to recognize. He does not turn to it until he reaches sākhī 35 on folio 149b, but thereafter he uses it for most of the remainder of his janam-sākhī. Material drawn from this source runs without a break from sākhī 35 to sākhī 49, misses sākhī 50, and reappears with sākhī 51. The point at which the compiler finally abandons it is not clear. Another break certainly comes at the end of sākhī 51 and this may perhaps mark its terminus. There remain, however, two brief narrative sākhīs (56 and 57) which should perhaps be assigned to the same source. The nature of the narrative material which commences with sākhī 35 plainly indicates that this source cannot possibly be identified with any which have been included within either the *Narrative I* or *Narrative II* group. This source we shall designate *Narrative III*.

Most anecdotes drawn from the *Narrative III* tradition are readily distinguished by a number of characteristic features. In all cases their language is a simple, relatively modern Pañjābī, their sākhī structure is elementary yet generally consistent, and their narrative vigorous with little extraneous material. Within the entire cluster only one anecdote (sākhī 39) violates this rule of conciseness. Throughout the cluster there is a strong emphasis upon certain clearly defined ideals and in most sākhīs several formulae recur. In all sākhīs there is a complete absence of quotations from the works of Gurū Nānak.

The standard narrative pattern for these *Narrative III* anecdotes is as follows. Bābā Nānak arrives in a particular locality (commonly unspecified). Initially he is either neglected or positively rejected by the populace, but eventually one person is persuaded to associate with him and so to provide a means of contact with the local community. Having established this contact Bābā Nānak then performs a miracle, as a result of which the entire population is converted. To his new disciples he issues a set of stock instructions and then proceeds on his way.

It is in Bābā Nānak's concluding instructions and in the new disciples' response to them that the distinctive ideals and formulae of the *Narrative III* tradition are to be found. The most prominent feature of all is a brief threefold creed, *nām dān isnān*, which literally translated reads 'Name, Charity, and Bathing'. In the translation of the *B40 Janam-sākhī* it has been rendered: 'the discipline of repeating the divine Name, giving charity, and regular bathing'. Most sākhīs of the *Narrative III* tradition include this distinctive formula, sometimes in an expanded form,[1] but normally in its simple threefold expression.[2] It is at once a formula and an ideal, a brief credal statement which evidently enshrined all that was regarded as necessary for salvation. In almost all instances the verb which is attached to this formula is *diṛāiā*, 'inculcated' or 'instilled'.

A second basic formula occurring in most *Narrative III* sākhīs is the command to establish a *dharamsālā*, or place where the newly formed *saṅgat* (congregation) might meet for regular *kīrtan* (the singing of

[1] *B40*, ff. 157b, 162b, 170a.

[2] *B40*, ff. 155a, 157a, 165b, 167a, 169b, 173a, 174b, 176a, 176b, 186a, 190a, 193a, 205a. For a brief discussion of the formula see *B40(Eng)*, p. 110n. Gurū Arjan uses the formula in his shabad *Sirī Rāg* 21-2-29, *AG*, pp. 73-4.

devotional songs).[1] This image of the *saṅgat* gathered in the *dharamsālā* for *kīrtan* constitutes another of the central ideals of the *Narrative III* tradition, obviously reflecting a condition which actually existed in the contemporary Sikh community. It is also within this *Narrative III* tradition that we encounter the first signs of an emergent belief concerning the eternal presence of the Gurū within the gathered community of the faithful.[2] To this doctrine the *B40* compiler adds his own fervent assent.[3]

The invariable response of the newly converted Sikhs provides a third basic formula and corresponding ideal. Having accepted Nānak as Master, his new disciples at once adopt the practice of repeating the single word 'Gurū' (*gurū gurū lagā japan*).[4] Mechanical repetition of this word was evidently the understanding of *nām simaran* which the *Narrative III* tradition sought to inculcate. This is of considerable interest, for it diverges appreciably from the refined doctrine of *nām simaran* as taught by Nānak himself.[5] The *Narrative III* emphasis upon mechanical repetition, together with occasional references in other sources, indicates that the earlier pre-Nānak understanding of 'repeating the divine Name' very quickly reasserted itself within the community of his followers. Moreover, this particular formula is not confined to *Narrative III* sākhīs. Its appearance in other traditions, although less common than in *Narrative III*, indicates that the practice must have been extensively followed within the seventeenth-century community.[6]

These statements constitute the basic formulae of the *Narrative III* tradition. To them others of less significance may be added.

dhan eh deś jithai tusāḍe charan phirai, 'Blessed is this country wherein your feet have trodden.' Variant forms of the same formula use *bhāg* instead of *deś*, or *darśan hoiā* instead of *charan phirai*.[7]

tān sabhai sikh hoe, 'then all became Sikhs', or a variant of this form.[8]

maraṇ jīvaṇ kaṭiā, '[the transmigratory round of] death and rebirth was broken'.[9]

nihāl hoiā, 'he found happiness'.[10]

vāh gurū ākhi, 'Utter, "Praise to the Gurū" ', used not as salutation but as a magical formula.[11]

Narrative III sākhīs commonly apply the appellation *mahā purukh* ('Exalted One') to Bābā Nānak[12] and lay considerable emphasis upon the

[1] *B40*, ff. 155a, 157a, 158b, 162b, 165b, 167a, 170a–b, 173a, 174b, 176a, 185b, 193a. The formula occurs in two variant forms: *dharam-sālā hoiā* and *dharam-sālā badhiā*. These are sometimes expanded by the addition of the words *ghar ghar*, 'in every house', or *girāi girāi*, 'in every village'.

[2] *B40*, f. 197a. See below, p. 262.

[3] *B40*, f. 230b.

[4] *B40*, ff. 132a, 155a, 159a, 162b, 163a, 165b, 167a, 167b, 173a, 174b, 176a, 182a, 185b, 186b, 199a. In one place the formula is said to be *vāhi gurū, vāhi gurū*. *B40*, f. 196b.

[5] *GNSR*, pp. 214–19.

[6] For *Narrative Ia* examples see *Pur JS*, pp. 22, 27, 31, 33, 45, 71, 80, 89.

[7] *B40*, ff. 157a, 167b, 173a–b, 176a, 185b. Cf. also ff. 180a, 199a.

[8] *B40*, ff. 156b, 158b, 162b, 165b, 167a, 169b, 170a, 173a, 174b, 176a, 185b, 196b.

[9] *B40*, ff. 183a, 188b, 190a, 193a.

[10] *B40*, ff. 188b, 190a, 193a.

[11] *B40*, ff. 158a, 161a, 181b, 182b, 184b.

[12] *B40*, ff. 156a, 158b, 165a, 165b, 170a, 172b, 185a, 187b, 192b, 198b.

duty of *sevā*, or 'service', in the sense of ministering to the needs of visiting Sikhs.[1] In most instances these formulae occur towards the end of the sākhī and together constitute a standard conclusion for *Narrative III* stories. The closing sentences of sākhī 40 provide an illustration.

tā uhu mulaku sabho hī sikhu hoiā. lage gurū gurū japaṇi. ate gharighari dharamusālā hoiā. tā gurū bābe unā nū nāmu dānu isanānu diṛāiā. us mulaku de lage ākhaṇi jo dhanu asāḍe bhāgu ju tusāḍā darasanu hoiā. et mulaku tusāḍe charanu phire.[2]

The entire population of that land became Sikhs. They took up repeating 'Gurū. Gurū' and in every house a dharamsālā was established. Gurū Bābā Nānak inculcated in them the threefold discipline of repeating the divine Name, giving charity, and regular bathing. Everyone in that land declared, 'Blessed is our destiny that we have beheld your presence and that your feet have trodden in this land.'

The style is unmistakable, and likewise the structure of the sākhīs which follow this standard pattern.

From where did the *B40* compiler obtain his *Narrative III* anecdotes? The distinctive features of the *Narrative III* material suggest that the actual source was not a manuscript but oral tradition. The simple structure, the vigorous narrative, and the repetition of particular words, expressions, and formulae all point to this conclusion.[3] Further support is provided by the complete absence of scriptural quotation; by the conspicuous lack of features which indicate copying from another manuscript (haplography, dittography, metathesis, incorrect reading, etc.);[4] by the failure of any earlier janam-sākhī to reproduce this material in a form resembling the *B40* version;[5] and by the relative modernity of the language used in the narrative. Anecdotes drawn from oral tradition will be expressed in the language current during the period in which they were recorded. As expressed in the *B40* collection *Narrative III* anecdotes accord well with early eighteenth-century usage.

These *Narrative III* anecdotes constitute the most primitive element in the *B40 Janam-sākhī*. In them we have an excellent example of the first stage in the development of the recorded janam-sākhīs. A series of anecdotes has been drawn from the current oral tradition, grouped in a crude sequence, and recorded in much the same manner as a narrator would have uttered them orally. The oral tradition from which they have been drawn would presumably be that of the *B40* compiler's own area. This suggests that the *Narrative III* source used by the compiler was probably the oral tradition current during the early eighteenth century in a portion of Gujranwālā District or the immediately adjacent area of Gujrāt District.

1 *B40*, ff. 155a, 166a, 167a, 170b, 203a. Cf. also ff. 171b, 176b.
2 *B40*, f. 173a–b.
3 The material from this source provides examples not only of the Law of Repetition but also of the Law of the Number Three (viz. the formula *nām dān isnān*).
4 See *B40(Eng)*, introduction, pp. 7, 12–13.
5 Some *Narrative III* anecdotes are reproduced by a late manuscript, the so-called *Prāchīn Janam-sākhī*. See above, pp. 26–7. Some also appear in the *Nānak Prakāś*.

Narrative III sākhīs thus offer a generally consistent cluster of anecdotes, one which seems to have been recorded directly from an oral source. Having in this manner stressed both the general uniformity of the cluster and its immediacy to oral tradition we must now add three qualifications. The first arises from a comparison of the following two sākhīs with the *Narrative III* material surrounding them:

43 a. Ajittā Randhāvā rebuked for greed
   b. Abdul Rahmān humbled
44 a. Ajittā Randhāvā rebuked for revivifying dead birds at Achal
   b. A Visit to Ṭillā.

Sākhīs 43 and 44 do not present the distinctive *Narrative III* structure and they lack almost all the characteristic formulae. There can be no doubt concerning their close connection with the sākhīs which precede and follow, for the same language and idiom continues throughout the entire cluster. Moreover, the differences which distinguish the two sākhīs may perhaps be explained by the fact that they relate a different variety of anecdote. The likelihood still seems to be that the two sākhīs were recorded from the same oral source as the standard *Narrative III* material. The structural difference cannot, however, be overlooked and it raises the possibility that the *B40* compiler may have taken these two sākhīs from a different source.

The second qualification concerns the point at which the *Narrative III* material terminates. Specifically it concerns the question of whether or not the following brief sākhīs should be attributed to the *Narrative III* source:

56. An injunction to recite the *Ārati Sohilā*
57. The magnificence of Bābā Nānak's hymns.

This tiny cluster poses the same problems as sākhīs 43 and 44, enhanced by the fact that it has been recorded apart from the main *Narrative III* cluster instead of within it. On the one hand its two anecdotes lack the distinctive structure and formulae of the standard *Narrative III* pattern. On the other, they continue the same linguistic style and narrate a different variety of story. If they are not to be linked with the *Narrative III* cluster it will be necessary to postulate yet another narrative source, for there is little to support a connection with either *Narrative I* or *Narrative II*.

The third and final qualification merely repeats a point already made. It is, however, a point which deserves to be illustrated with reference to *Narrative III* material. Having stressed the distinctive qualities of the *Narrative III* tradition we must repeat that features indicating a distinctive tradition do not mean complete independence from other traditions. Even when the distinguishing features are as prominent as those of the *Narrative III* material this insistence must be maintained. Complete independence would mean no sharing of distinctive features and no analogues. In neither respect will the *Narrative III* tradition sustain a claim to complete independence.

Three examples of links connecting *Narrative III* with other traditions have already been noted. One of the distinctive formulae appears in the *B40* version of 'The Monster's Cauldron' sākhī (tentatively assigned to the

Narrative Ib tradition).[1] This may perhaps be a gloss by the *B40* compiler, for neither the *Narrative Ia* nor the *Narrative II* version of the anecdote contains it.[2] The same explanation cannot, however, be applied to the case of the two *Narrative III* portions which appear within the *Narrative II* material of *Q2*.[3] These represent a genuine penetration of *Narrative III* elements into a separate tradition. The process is scarcely surprising if, as we have already suggested, *Q2* is to be located in the same geographical area as *Narrative III*.

A more complex example of *Narrative III* influence is to be found in the *B40* version of the Śivanābh story (sākhīs 34a and 34b). In this version several of the distinctive *Narrative III* features appear and some of them occur more than once. Bābā Nānak does not inculcate the threefold *nām-dān-isnān* formula, but we do find that he inculcated the divine Word (*śabad diṛāiā*).[4] Stress is twice laid upon the building of a dharamsālā.[5] Śivanābh's slave-girls begin to chant 'Gurū, Gurū',[6] a reference is made to the *Narrative III* variety of *sevā*,[7] Bābā Nānak is frequently referred to as a *mahā-purukh*,[8] and Śivanābh declares in characteristically *Narrative III* style, '*dhan merā bhāg*.'[9] Other features strengthen this impression of *Narrative III* influence. 'The portals [of his understanding] opened' (*us de kapāṭ khuli gae*) is an unusual expression which occurs both in the Śivanābh story and in two sākhīs from the *Narrative III* cluster.[10] Finally, Śivanābh's collapse has an obvious parallel in the anecdote concerning Uttam Bhaṇḍārī and Sultānā Gujar.[11]

The two Śivanābh anecdotes are too highly developed to have been taken from the *Narrative III* source. There seems to be little doubt, however, that they have been strongly influenced by *Narrative III* style and ideals. This influence can be explained in the same manner as the elements which entered the *Narrative II* tradition. It has already been argued that the *B40* version of both parts of the Śivanābh story was derived from the *Narrative Ib* tradition. All the features mentioned above are to be found only in the *Narrative Ib* account of Śivanābh. They do not occur in the *Narrative Ia* tradition as represented by the *Colebrooke Janam-sākhī*.[12] This appears to support our earlier suggestion that *Q1* of the *Narrative Ib* tradition should also be located in the same geographical area as *B40*. Such a location would account for the appearance of so many *Narrative III* features in the *Narrative Ib* version of the Śivanābh story. It would also

[1] See above, p. 192.
[2] *Pur JS*, p. 82. *AS*, p. 28.
[3] See above, pp. 204–5.
[4] *B40*, f. 154a.
[5] *B40*, ff. 152b–153a, 154a.
[6] *B40*, f. 148b.
[7] *B40*, f. 146b.
[8] *B40*, ff. 140a, 140b, 142b, 143a, 143b, 149b, 150a.
[9] *B40*, f. 146a.
[10] *B40*, ff. 140a–b, 189b, 204b.
[11] *B40*, ff. 153a, 186a.
[12] The *Colebrooke Janam-sākhī* does, however, include three of the *Narrative III* formulae near the conclusion of its Śivanābh sākhī: *janam maraṇu . . . kaṭiā, sikhu hoā*, and *gurū gurū lagā japani*. Photozincograph Facsimile, p. 335. *Pur JS*, p. 89. The third of these is found elsewhere in the *Colebrooke Janam-sākhī*, but the other two are distinctively *Narrative III* expressions. In place of the second the *Colebrooke Janam-sākhī* normally uses the formula *nāu dharīk hoā*, 'he became a Name-believer'. *Pur JS*, pp. 22, 27, 31, 37, 45, 71, 79–80, 81, 82, 93. The appearance of the three formulae in this context suggests that the *Narrative Ia* tradition, though further removed from *Narrative III* oral tradition than *Narrative Ib*, was not altogether immune from it.

explain the appearance of the expression 'the portals [of his understanding] opened' in the *Narrative Ib* discourse with Bābur.[1]

Links with other traditions can also be found in a number of analogues. The two anecdotes which are common to *Narrative Ia* and *Narrative III* illustrate both the connection between the two traditions and also the distance which separates them. The anecdotes which, in the *B40* table of contents, bear the titles 'Bābājī visited Gujrāt' and 'A sākhī describing an encounter with robbers'[2] have analogues in the *Purātan* anecdotes entitled 'The Salvation of Dūnī Chand' (second part) and 'The Robbers' Salvation'.[3] In both cases the narrative differs considerably and in both the differences indicate the greater maturity of the *Purātan* version. The first has already been quoted in order to illustrate the manner in which an anecdote changes as it descends through different traditions.[4] The *B40* version of the second is actually longer than its *Purātan* counterpart, but lacks the shabad which has been attached to the latter and which distinguishes it as a more evolved product. Although the *Purātan* analogues were probably recorded at an earlier date than the *B40* versions they are actually later in terms of development.

Narrative III links with other traditions are certainly fewer and more tenuous than those which connect the *Narrative I* and *Narrative II* traditions or the sub-traditions within either. As these examples indicate, they do, however, exist. Their relative scarcity and the pronounced differences which distinguish them can evidently be explained by the oral quality of *Narrative III*. If this assumption is correct it means that the *B40* compiler was, at this point, carrying out the first stage in the development of the recorded janam-sākhīs. The fact that he was doing this in the year 1733 serves to illustrate the manner in which all stages could be operative at the same time. When set beside the blocks of material borrowed from other sources this large *Narrative III* cluster also illustrates the way in which several different forms and stages could be embodied within a single janam-sākhī. It is precisely because it incorporates so many different elements that the *B40* collection is of all janam-sākhīs the most interesting and useful.

2. *The* Miharbān *tradition*

All narrative sākhīs recorded in the *B40 Janam-sākhī* have now been assigned, confidently or tentatively, to their appropriate sources. The remaining *B40* sākhīs consist of two discourses borrowed from the *Miharbān* tradition and eight miscellaneous discourses inserted at various points throughout the janam-sākhī. Ideally any such reference to the *Miharbān*

[1] *B40*, f. 71a.

[2] *B40* sākhīs 47 and 48, ff. 189a–193a (Gurmukhī pagination), 228b (Arabic pagination). In the English translation of *B40* these sākhīs have been entitled respectively 'The Rich Man's Pennants' and 'The Robbers and the Funeral Pyre'.

[3] *Pur JS*, pp. 71, 32–3. *GNSR*, pp 45, 40–1. These two *Purātan* sākhīs are derived, through the *Colebrooke Janam-sākhī*, from the *Narrative Ia* tradition.

[4] See above, pp. 124–7.

tradition as a source should be preceded by a discussion of its own sources. This would, however, constitute a task of some considerable complexity, one which deserves a volume in its own right. Here we can do no more than note that the *Miharbān* tradition, having itself drawn on a number of sources, has regularly served as a source for other janam-sākhī collections.

One *Miharbān* borrowing within the *B40 Janam-sākhī* has already been noted.[1] This was merely a portion of a discourse interpolated in a *Q2* narrative sākhī. Later it was suggested that a small cluster of *Ādi Sākhīs* anecdotes might perhaps be another borrowing from the *Miharbān* tradition. This opinion, however, had to be qualified by a measure of doubt concerning the source and by an acknowledgement that the cluster, if in fact it had been derived from the *Miharbān* tradition, must represent a paraphrase rather than a copy.[2] It is only towards the end of the *B40 Janam-sākhī* that there appear complete discourses in the typical *Miharbān* style.

Although the *Miharbān* tradition in its various recensions owes some of its material to borrowings from narrative sources by far the greater portion of its content has been generated within the tradition itself in accordance with the obvious intention of its compilers and redactors. Narratives which describe the life and travels of Bābā Nānak express only a secondary purpose within the *Miharbān* tradition. Its primary purpose is, as we have already noted, exegesis of the works of Nānak. The distinctive form which it employs for this purpose is the *goṣṭ*, literally 'discourse' but more accurately described as discourse plus exegetical supplement.

A *goṣṭ* from the *Miharbān* tradition is easily recognized and for this reason there can be no doubt that sākhīs 54 and 55 of the *B40 Janam-sākhī* have been taken directly from this tradition.[3] Both are plainly discourses in the standard *Miharbān* style. In each instance the discourse begins with the characteristic *Miharbān* setting in Kartārpur, and following a brief introductory narrative the commentator turns to the quotation of passages from the works of Nānak and to the exegesis of these passages. The interlocutor who is introduced in order to pose necessary questions is one who commonly fulfils this role in the *Miharbān* tradition, namely Gurū Aṅgad.

The reason for introducing this small cluster from a *Miharbān* source evidently relates to the subject treated in the two discourses. The *Miharbān* commentators commonly chose their material in order to provide answers to questions of contemporary concern. One such issue was evidently the question of whether or not the early-morning bathe should be regarded as mandatory for all Sikhs, and within the *Miharbān* tradition an effort had been made to provide a divine sanction for the affirmative case by constructing a discourse from relevant works by Nānak. The effort was not entirely successful, and eventually the commentator, in order to clinch his argument, was compelled to put into Gurū Nānak's mouth words which were actually those of Gurū Aṅgad. The issue is treated at some length in the extant version of the *Miharbān Janam-sākhī*, and it seems clear from the commentator's efforts to provide a conclusive answer that an important

[1] See above, p. 205. [2] See above, pp. 212–14. [3] *B40*, ff. 210a–218a.

controversy within at least a section of the Sikh community must have lain behind the question.[1]

The importance of the controversy presumably accounts for this unique example of a direct *B40* borrowing of complete *goṣṭs* from a recension of the *Miharbān* tradition. This recension was obviously earlier than that of the extant *Miharbān Janam-sākhi*. A comparison of the two *B40* sākhīs with the analogue in the extant version of the *Miharbān Janam-sākhī* indicates that the latter has been considerably developed.

3. *Miscellaneous discourses*

The eight remaining *B40* sākhīs form a miscellaneous collection of heterodox discourses, drawn from a variety of sources and recorded at several different points in the janam-sākhī. This final group comprises the following:

9. A discourse with Abdul Rahmān
15. A discourse with Shāh Rukandī
16. A discourse with Rattan Hāji
28. A discourse with Ajittā Randhāvā
33. A discourse with Kabīr
50. A discourse with Sheikh Sharaf
52. A discourse concerning true renunciation
53. Discourses with Gorakhnāth and with Kāl.

Heterodox discourses are easily distinguished from the characteristic didactic form of the *Miharbān* tradition and there is little likelihood that any of them could have entered *B40* from a *Miharbān* source.[2] The *B40* compiler will almost certainly have taken them from independent manuscripts, some of which must have been limited to a single discourse. Manuscripts of this kind are still extant and their existence indicates that during the seventeenth and eighteenth centuries extra-canonical compositions of this kind enjoyed an extensive popularity within the Sikh community.[3] It was inevitable that some of these works, or selections from them, should be incorporated in the janam-sākhīs, and in this manner eight such discourses found their way into the *B40 Janam-sākhi*. The number suggests that they held a considerable fascination for its compiler, or perhaps for its patron.

The eight discourses which have been included in the *B40 Janam-sākhī* can be distributed between two of the three categories of heterodox discourse. Five of them belong to the popular Sūfism category. Rukn al-Dīn and Sharaf al-Dīn were both celebrated Sūfī pīrs;[4] and Rattan Hājī, though less famous internationally, must nevertheless have possessed a considerable local following within the Pañjāb.[5] The meeting with Rukn al-Dīn

[1] *Mih JS* II.395–401. W. H. McLeod, introductory essay in *Mih JS* II.xi–xii.

[2] For a definition of the heterodox discourse form see above, pp. 101–4.

[3] Piār Singh, 'A Critical Survey of Panjabi Prose in the Seventeenth Century' (unpublished Ph.D. thesis, Panjab University, 1968), pp. 122–37.

[4] *B40*, ff. 53a, 200a.

[5] *B40*, f. 56a.

provides the occasion for introducing a work entitled the *Tīh Sipāre*,[1] and to Rattan Hājī there is delivered a homily entitled the *Hāzar-nāma*.[2] Sheikh Sharaf, who is represented as a transvestite and located in Bāghdād, relates in verse the story of his failure to find union with God. Bābā Nānak replies with a brief poetic instruction in *Dhanāsarī* rāga.[3] Although Abdul Rahmān is remembered as a writer rather than as a pīr, the pattern followed in sākhī 9 indicates that this discourse should also be included in the popular Sūfism category.[4] Sākhī 52 names no interlocutor, adding instead the subtitle: 'A discourse took place with a learned faqīr'.[5] The content of the discourse certainly entitles it to be classified as a Sūfī-oriented work.

The three other discourses in this miscellaneous group can all be regarded as examples of esoteric Nāth-oriented compositions, although none of them gives particularly clear expression to *haṭha-yoga* doctrine. 'A Discourse with Ajittā Randhāvā' is perhaps more important as an expression of conflicts within the early eighteenth-century Sikh community.[6] The *haṭha-yoga* emphasis is similarly muted in the Kabīr discourse, although its presence can certainly be detected in the portions attributed to Gurū Nānak.[7] Finally there is sākhī 53, 'Discourses with Gorakhnāth and with Kāl'.[8] This brief composition is distinguished only by an abundance of cryptic allusions, producing a general impression of total obscurity. Once again *haṭha-yoga* concepts are nowhere expressed clearly and directly. The identity of the first interlocutor suggests, however, that this discourse should also belong to the third category. Its cryptic allusions may perhaps be a crude imitation of the 'intentional language' of the Nāths.

The fact that the eight miscellaneous discourses recorded by the *B40* compiler may be grouped in two categories should not imply that the compiler was using only two sources. Sākhīs 15 and 16 are almost certainly from a common source but there is no evidence of any such link connecting any of the remaining six discourses. The manner in which they are dispersed throughout the janam-sākhī suggests that several independent manuscripts (one of them incomplete[9]) were utilized by the compiler. In some instances he may perhaps have relied upon his own memory or upon an oral recitation.

A SUMMARY OF THE B40 *SOURCES*

The complete range of sources used by the *B40* compiler may now be summarized in tabular form.

[1] *B40*, ff. 53a–55b.
[2] *B40*, ff. 56a–57a. See *B40(Eng)*, p. 58n.
[3] *B40*, ff. 200a–202a. The *Colebrooke Janam-sākhī* correctly places Sheikh Sharaf in Pāṇīpat, but his dates render any such meeting completely impossible. *GNSR*, p. 82.
[4] *B40*, ff. 177b–180a.
[5] *B40*, ff. 205b–207b.
[6] *B40*, ff. 111a–116b. See above, p. 104.
[7] *B40*, ff. 136a–138a.
[8] *B40*, ff. 208a–209a.
[9] Sākhī 28, 'A Discourse with Ajittā Randhāvā', lacks a beginning. *B40*, f. 111a.

Sākhī no.	*Title of Anecdote*	*Source*
1.	The birth of Nānak	*Narrative Ib* (*Q1*)
2a.	Instruction by the Paṇḍit	
2b.	Bābā Nānak's Betrothal and Marriage	
3.	The Ruined Crop Restored	
4a.	The Tree's Stationary Shadow	
4b.	The True Field and the True Merchandise	
5.	Bābā Nānak's Discourse with the Physician	
6a.	Sultānpur	
6b.	Immersion in the River	
6c.	Bābā Nānak's Discourse with Daulat Khān's Qāzī	
[6d.	Bābā Nānak's Departure from Sultānpur]	
7.	Bābā Nānak's Travels in the Uninhabited Wilderness	
8.	Bābā Nānak returns to Talvaṇḍī	
9.	A Discourse with Abdul Rahmān	*Misc. Discourse*
10.	The Monster's Cauldron	*Narrative Ib* (*Q1*)
11.	Bholā the Robber	
12a.	The Encounter with Kaliyug	
12b.	Lamenting women commended	
13.	A poor Sikh's devotion to Bābā Nānak	
14.	Mecca: the moving *miharāb*	
15.	A Discourse with Shāh Rukandī	*Misc. Discourses*
16.	A Discourse with Rattan Hājī	
17.	Bābā Nānak's Discourse with Sheikh Braham	*Narrative Ib* (*Q1*)
18a.	The Sack of Saidpur	
18b.	A Discourse with Bābur	
19.	The proud Karoṛī humbled: founding of Kartārpur	
20.	Bābā Nānak's austerities	*Narrative II* (*Q2*)
21.	Bābā Nānak's Visit to the Pilgrimage Centres	
22.	The Country Ruled by Women	
23.	Discourse with Siddhs on Mount Sumeru	
24a.	The Meeting with Lahaṇā	

Sākhī no.	*Title of Anecdote*	*Source*
24b.	Aṅgad returns to Matte dī Sarāi	*Narrative II* (*Q2*)
24c.	Aṅgad moves to Khaḍūr: his clothes ruined	
24d.	The Installation of Gurū Aṅgad	
25.	Mūlā the Khatrī	
26a.	Bābā Nānak's Daily Discipline	
26b.	The Loyal Fortitude of Aṅgad	
27a.	Bābā Nānak's Adoration	
27b.	Discourse with Gorakhnāth: Bābā Nānak seeks solitude	
28.	Discourse with Ajitta Randhāvā	*Misc. Discourse*
29.	Discourse with Siddhs at Achal	*Narrative II* (*Q2*)
30.	An Interview with God	
31.	Bābā Nānak in the Land of Unbelievers	
32.	Mecca: Bābā Nānak's Miraculous Arrival	
33.	Discourse with Kabīr	*Misc. Discourse*
34a.	The Merchant and Rājā Śivanābh	*Narrative Ib* (*Q1*)
34b.	Bābā Nānak and Rājā Śivanābh	
35a.	Bābā Nānak's Visit to Kābul	*Narrative III* (*Oral Tradition*)
35b.	Water restored to a Land of Giants	
36.	A Visit to Bhūṭān	
37.	Cakes miraculously cooked	
38.	Bābā Nānak's Visit to Kashmīr	
39.	Bābā Nānak enslaved in the Land of the Paṭhāns	
40.	Bābā Nānak provides grain and fire	
41.	Floods banished from a land beside the sea	
42.	A Demon Arsonist converted	
43a.	Ajittā Randhāvā rebuked for greed	
43b.	Abdul Rahmān humbled	
44a.	Ajittā Randhāvā rebuked for revivifying dead birds at Achal	
44b.	A Visit to Ṭillā	
45.	Uttam Bhaṇḍārī and Sultānā Gujar: Springs from a mountain-side	
46.	A Visit to Hivanchal: Discourse with Datta	
47.	The Rich Man's Pennants	
48.	The Robbers and the Funeral Pyre	
49a.	A Robber Landowner Converted	
49b.	A Rājā's daughter turned into a boy	

no.	Title of Anecdote	Source
50.	A Discourse with Sheikh Sharaf in Bāghdād	*Misc. Discourse*
51.	The Reward of Meeting a Sādhū	*Narrative III (Oral Tradition)*
52.	A Discourse concerning True Renunciation	*Misc. Discourses*
53.	Discourses with Gorakhnāth and with Kāl	
54.	The Way of Salvation: A Discourse which Gurū Bābā Nānak held with Guru Aṅgad	*Miharbān Tradition*
55.	Another Discourse with Gurū Aṅgad concerning the Way of Salvation	
56.	An Injunction to Recite the *Ārati Sohilā*	*Narrative III* (?)
57.	The Magnificence of Bābā Nānak's hymns	
58.	The Death of Bābā Nānak	*Narrative IId*

Of these sources *Narrative III* was almost certainly an oral tradition. Some of the *Miscellaneous Discourses* may also derive from an oral tradition, but not from the same cycle as the *Narrative III* anecdotes. The remainder were all documentary sources. In diagrammatic form this pattern may be represented as in figure 26.

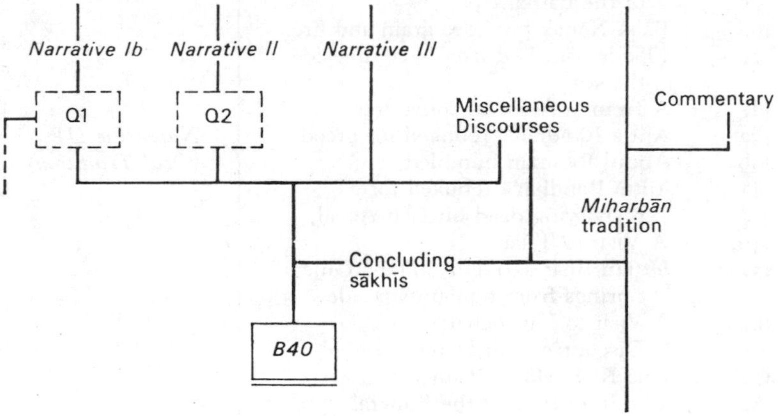

Figure 26

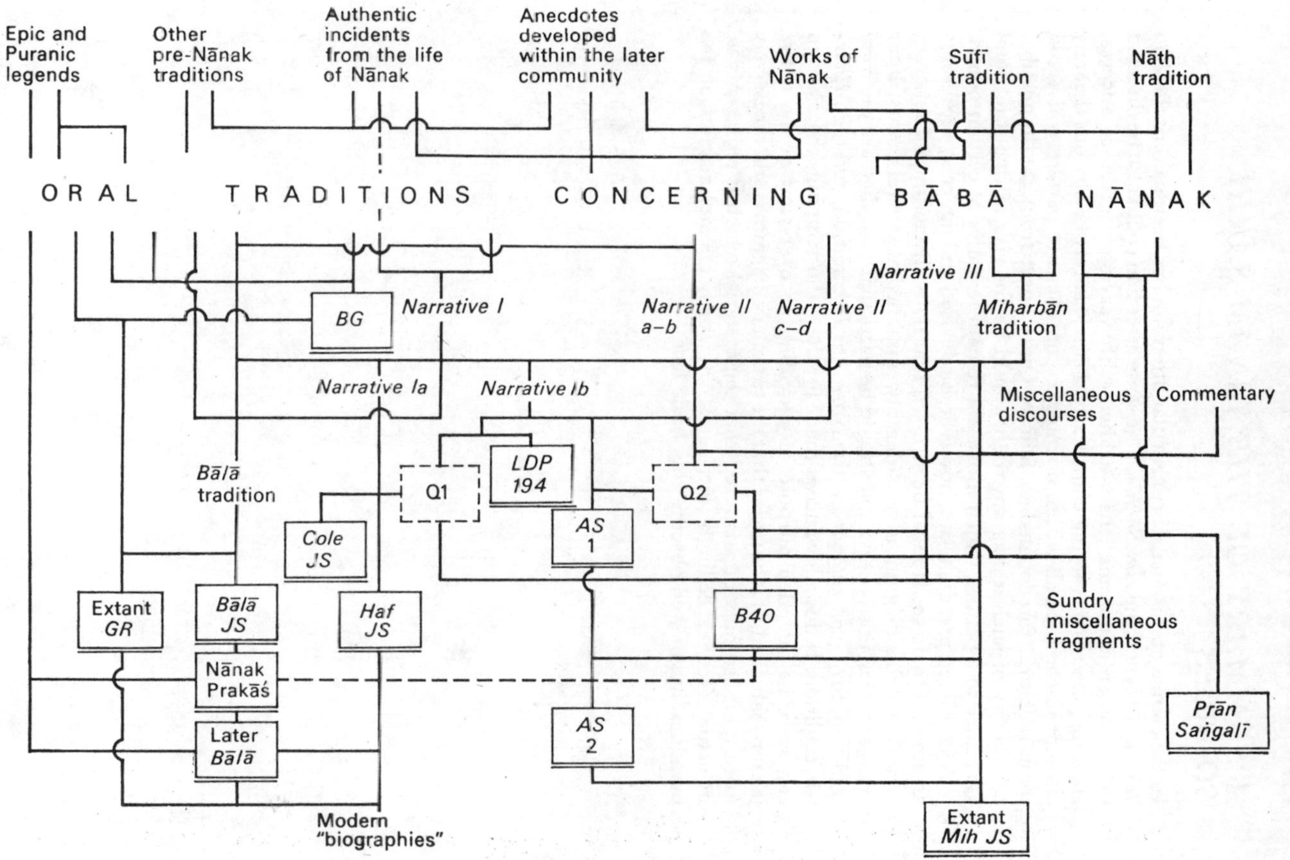
Epic and Puranic legends
Other pre-Nānak traditions
Authentic incidents from the life of Nānak
Anecdotes developed within the later community
Works of Nānak
Sūfī tradition
Nāth tradition
ORAL TRADITIONS CONCERNING BĀBĀ NĀNAK
BG
Narrative I
Narrative II a–b
Narrative II c–d
Narrative III
Miharbān tradition
Narrative Ia
Narrative Ib
Miscellaneous discourses
Commentary
Bālā tradition
Q1
LDP 194
Q2
Cole JS
AS 1
Extant GR
Bālā JS
Haf JS
B40
Sundry miscellaneous fragments
Nānak Prakāś
Later Bālā
AS 2
Prān Saṅgalī
Modern "biographies"
Extant Mih JS

Figure 27

A SUMMARY OF THE JANAM-SĀKHĪ SOURCES

In the course of this analysis particular attention has been paid to the *B40 Janam-sākhī* and the *Ādi Sākhīs*. The same attention could also be directed to the other important janam-sākhīs, with varying degrees of success, eliciting patterns of varying complexity. It must surely be obvious that any attempt to combine all within a single, comprehensive pattern will be, in some measure, foredoomed to failure. Quite apart from the impossible complexity of such a diagram there would be the risk of imputing total assurance to a pattern which must still remain tentative at certain points.

A simplified paradigm can, however, be devised and figure 27 represents an attempt to do so. It must be stressed that notwithstanding its apparent complexity this diagram is considerably simplified at several points. Four areas to which this observation should be particularly applied are the *Bālā* tradition, the *Gyān-ratanāvalī*, the *Narrative Ia* tradition, and the *Mihar-bān* tradition. If due allowance is made for these shortcomings the diagram can serve its intended purpose of providing an over-view of the entire janam-sākhī field. If it be urged that the summary diagram is still excessively intricate it can only be answered that the material which it represents is, in actual fact, exceedingly intricate. Any further simplification of the paradigm might well obscure this basic fact.

SECTION III

11
PURPOSE, FUNCTION, VALUE

ALTHOUGH the Sikh Gurūs are all regarded as manifestations of the same divine spirit two of the ten have in practice been accorded a particular affection, a loyalty of unusual intensity and duration. The two are the first and the last of the line, Gurū Nānak and Gurū Gobind Siṅgh. Both have been associated with particular phases in the development of the Sikh Panth and it is as symbols of these two major phases that their respective images have been of such substantial importance. Gurū Nānak stands as the image and ideal of the pre-Khālsā stage, the period in which the Panth's primary concern attached to a distinctively religious message. Gurū Gobind Siṅgh, in contrast, has symbolized the Khālsā era, the period in which primary allegiance moved away from the earlier soteriological concern to sociological patterns deriving from the dual impact on the Panth of Jaṭ custom and eighteenth-century disturbances.[1] Each period has given rise to a single dominant myth. The image of Gurū Nānak enshrines one of these; the image of Gurū Gobind Siṅgh expresses the other.

The janam-sākhīs belong to the period of religious ascendancy and for this reason they are exclusively concerned with the first of these images. It is an avowedly religious purpose which the janam-sākhī compilers pursue, and their products continue to serve a viable function for as long as religious interests retain a primacy within the Panth. Only when the religious concerns are largely submerged in the eighteenth-century flood do the janam-sākhīs become increasingly dysfunctional. New needs demand new ideals and new vehicles for those ideals. Functional substitutes are required for a role which the janam-sākhīs can no longer fulfil with a sufficient competence. The janam-sākhīs did not, however, suffer a total eclipse, for the community was not wholly transformed by its eighteenth-century experience. The teachings of Bābā Nānak have certainly not been lost, and wherever a concern for his message of salvation has survived there the janam-sākhīs have sustained their pre-Khālsā role. Even where they have lost much of their functional importance they have lost little of their audience appeal. To this day the janam-sākhīs are widely read in Sikh homes and gurdwaras, and evidences of a final recession have yet to appear in rural Pañjāb.

It will be noted that these comments concern the *function* of the janam-sākhīs within the Sikh community. The function of the janam-sākhīs must be clearly distinguished from their purpose, and it is because this distinction can be drawn so clearly that the two aspects of the janam-sākhī

[1] W. H. McLeod, *The Evolution of the Sikh Community* (Oxford, 1976), chaps. 1 and 3.

literature will be treated separately in the brief analysis which follows. Questions of purpose relate to the motives and intentions of narrators, compilers, and redactors; whereas the function of the janam-sākhīs concerns the role which they have played in the history of the Panth. This role accords only partially with the conscious intentions of the narrators and their later editors. It was a much more subtle need which provided the janam-sākhīs with their primary function and which earned them a significant status during the seventeenth and early eighteenth centuries. This is made clear by the manner in which the janam-sākhīs retreated from the centre of the community's life as the distinctively religious interest receded, and by the corresponding advance of functional substitutes fulfilling the same role in a strikingly different way. The primary function which they served from the late sixteenth century to the early eighteenth century must be construed in terms of panthic cohesion, a role which the narrators and compilers would never have suspected.

A functional analysis will reveal something of the importance of the janam-sākhīs for the Sikh Panth of three hundred years ago. This constitutes a major aspect of their importance as historical source material. Their chief value in this respect is closely related to their functional role. The janam-sākhīs' most notable fulfilment of their functional role took place during the seventeenth and eighteenth centuries, the period of their principal expansion. Because they were evolving during this period (and particularly during the seventeenth century) the janam-sākhīs record much that derives directly from its circumstances. As such they constitute a primary source for the two centuries extending from the late sixteenth century to the eighteenth century.

For this period the principal interest concerns the evidence provided by the janam-sākhīs of a religious community striving towards identity and self-understanding. Less obvious but nevertheless important are the recurrent glimpses of the wider life of the Pañjāb. For too long historians of Mughal Pañjāb have relied almost exclusively upon the standard Persian chronicles. The Persian chronicles do indeed retain a considerable value, particularly the relevant sections of Abu al-Fazl's *Ā'in-i-Akbari* and Sujān Rāi Bhaṇḍārī's *Khulāsāt-ut-Tavarīkh*. Alone, however, they are inadequate, for their range is strictly limited by their distinctive interests. The janam-sākhīs are also inadequate if compelled to stand alone, but at least their locus is the rural society so commonly ignored by the chronicler. For this reason the janam-sākhīs provide a valuable supplement to the Persian chronicles and the reports of early European visitors.

The value of the janam-sākhīs as historical source material is discussed in the fourth chapter of this section. In the fifth and concluding chapter there follows a brief note on the importance of the janam-sākhīs in the history of Pañjābī language and literature. This importance is twofold. The janam-sākhīs warrant attention as the first examples of sustained Pañjābī prose, and also as a continuing influence upon later creativity. The latter feature can be easily appreciated when one becomes aware of the extent to which the janam-sākhīs have been read in Sikh homes and gurdwaras. Together with the Ādi Granth, the works of Muslim Sūfīs from the Pañjāb, and eventually the example of western models, they rank as a major influence in the development of Pañjābī literature. When Pañjābī eventually receives the attention it deserves the janam-sākhīs will receive a significant share of this recognition.

12

THE PURPOSE OF THE JANAM-SĀKHĪS

He who from the depths of his being reads and hears this testimony will find salvation. Of this there is no doubt.[1]

IT is at once obvious that an important reason for the popularity of the janam-sākhīs has been an inveterate taste for anecdotes and wonder-stories. It is also evident that this affection was not confined to audiences, but that it extended also to the narrators who related the tales and to the compilers who gathered them into janam-sākhīs. The janam-sākhīs contain an abundance of these stories, many of which have lost nothing of their interest with the passing of several centuries.

It would, however, be entirely mistaken to interpret the purpose of the narrators and the compilers as the mere delectation of their audiences. The popularity of anecdote and legend was a means to a nobler end, to an objective which most compilers express in explicit terms at appropriate points in their collections. Salvation is the issue which concerns them and the promulgation of a particular way of salvation constitutes their conscious intention. This salvation is to be won through an acceptance of Bābā Nānak as Master. Nānak preached a particular method of attaining release from the cycle of death and rebirth. He who accepts Bābā Nānak as his guide and model will himself attain to the same salvation. In order to understand the method three things are essential. First, he must heed the actual words of the Master as enshrined in his sacred utterances; secondly, he must listen to the exemplary narratives of the Master's life; and thirdly he must join the community of the Master's followers. The janam-sākhīs served the second of these needs and increasingly they served the first also. The third must be the responsibility of the disciple, but at least the janam-sākhīs could be used to make his duty clear.

This is an explicitly soteriological concern and in giving expression to it the janam-sākhī narrators and compilers were following in the footsteps of their acknowledged Master. Nānak's own central and ever-present purpose had been salvation, and the janam-sākhīs remain faithful to this intention. There is, however, a radical shift of emphasis. Nānak insists repeatedly that salvation is to be obtained by hearkening to the divine Word (*śabad*) of the Gurū and, in accordance with the inward revelation imparted by the divine Word, by regular meditation upon the divine Name (*nām*). The janam-sākhīs do use the term *nām* in a sense akin to Nānak's meaning,[2] but

[1] *B40*, f. 116b.

[2] Cf. *B40*, f. 120a.

the words *śabad* and *gurū* have in their janam-sākhī usage acquired significantly different meanings. The *gurū* is no longer the inner voice of God, but the personal manifestation of that voice in Bābā Nānak. From this it follows that the divine Word must be identified with the actual utterances of Nānak, and so the term *śabad* (shabad) is almost exclusively used as a synonym for a *pada* or 'hymn' of Nānak. The same usage is also applied to the compositions of his successors, for all are but different manifestations of the same single Gurū.

The principal features of this janam-sākhī doctrine of salvation may be traced through a number of quotations. A basic element is the concept of *nām japan* or *nām simaran* as it was understood over a wide area of North Indian devotional life during this period. 'Remembrance of the divine Name' was practised in two ways, one individual and the other corporate. The individual discipline consisted of repeating a chosen word or *mantra* for protracted periods, the belief being that the qualities of the chosen word or *mantra* could thereby be acquired by the devotee. Mechanical repetition of this sort clearly had serious limitations as far as Nānak was concerned, but the janam-sākhīs plainly indicate that many of his later followers did not share his misgivings.[1]

The janam-sākhīs were, however, in complete accord with Nānak's interpretation of corporate 'remembrance'. Both for the Master and for his followers, as also for numberless other inheritors of the North Indian devotional tradition, the way of salvation required participation in the *satsaṅg*, the congregation of the faithful. Salvation depended not merely upon individual devotion (however it might be understood and practised) but also upon the singing of God's praises (*kīrtan*) at regular gatherings of the *satsaṅg*. It was for this purpose alone that the *satsaṅg* gathered, and in singing together each participant absorbed not merely the qualities of the divine words which he sang but also the qualities of the other pious participants. This activity was a prerequisite to salvation and it is clear that Nānak's own works were composed for use in this particular context.

The singing of *kīrtan* within the regular *satsaṅg* was accepted as normative by the janam-sākhī narrators and one of their purposes was to encourage the practice. It was, however, no more than a part of their wider concept of salvation. Devotional songs abounded, but all were by no means equal in value. Supreme value attached only to those of Bābā Nānak and, later, to those of his successors. The loyalty of the Sikh community was not to an idea nor to a particular doctrine of salvation but to the person who had propounded the doctrine with a unique clarity and beauty. Faith was due not to a theory but to a particular person.

This faith is explicitly affirmed at various points in the janam-sākhī literature, sometimes as a terminal declaration by a narrator or compiler, and sometimes as a statement attributed to one of the dramatis personae. A *Miharbān* discourse concludes with the following affirmation:

Gurū Bābā Nānak is the vessel which carries us across the Ocean of the World. Gurū Bābā Nānak has carried over the entire world. He who becomes a Nānak-

[1] Cf. *B40*, f. 118b.

panthī will be carried across. He who cleaves to the divine Word of Gurū Bābā Nānak shall be saved. Such was the grace of Gurū Bābā Nānak that he imparted the divine Name to the entire world. Glory be to Gurū Bābā Nānak! Praise be to Gurū Bābā Nānak, the True Gurū Bābā Nānak![1]

The status which is thus attributed to Bābā Nānak is explicitly declared to be the result of a divine commission received direct from God. This is made clear by the various versions of the sākhī entitled 'An Interview with God'.[2]

Datta the Sage carries the attribution of divinity one stage further. Bābā Nānak is not merely a supreme teacher. He is *joti sarūp*, the divine effulgence, God Himself incarnate in human form for the salvation of the world.

Blessed are you Bābā Nānak! Blessed are you Bābā Nānak! And blessed is this which you have done! You are yourself God, but for the salvation of the world you have come in this human guise. If anyone beholds your presence, sings and recites your sacred words, and instructs others in the recitation and singing of them he will be exalted. For him the round of birth and death will be brought to an end.[3]

It will be observed that three qualifications are specified as essential to salvation. The first is to behold the presence of Bābā Nānak (*darśan*); the second is to sing and recite his sacred utterances (*śabad*); and the third is to teach others the same way of salvation. The janam-sākhīs are concerned with all three but above all with the first. This need they alone can meet. While Bābā Nānak was present in the flesh *darśan* could be obtained by visiting him in Kartārpur or by meeting him during the course of one of his journeys. The same purpose might be achieved up to the beginning of the eighteenth century by appearing before one of the successor Gurūs, but as the community grew in numbers and in geographical distribution such personal visits became increasingly difficult. Moreover, an occasional encounter was no substitute for a permanent presence.

The primary purpose of the janam-sākhīs was to provide that permanent presence, or at least a satisfactory substitute. Death, disability, or distance need raise no insuperable obstacle to regular *darśan*, for *darśan* could be obtained through the true testimony (*sākhi*) of the Gurū's life and utterances. The understanding of *darśan* which this implied was the same as the understanding of a personal *darśan*. Whereas for some devotees a personal visit to the chosen Master would necessarily involve some direct teaching and also some observing of the Master's own example, others would be content merely to appear before him. The same variety of understanding could also be applied to the janam-sākhīs. For some there would necessarily be a conscious acceptance of the model set forth in the words of the testimony; for others it would be sufficient merely to hear the words.

Most of the narrators would, of course, belong to the former group. Their intention was not simply to tell a pious tale but also to point

[1] *Mih JS* II.178. Cf. also *Mih JS* I.461 (*goṣṭ* 137).

[2] *B40*, ff. 123b–126b. *AS*, pp. 1–3. *Pur JS*, pp. 14–16.

[3] *B40*, f. 188a–b.

deliberately to a particular pattern of pious behaviour. Faith alone was not enough. There must also be personal participation. For the narrator of the *Narrative III* tradition this is expressed in the insistent repetition of the formula *nām dān isnān*, the threefold discipline of repeating the divine Name, giving charity, and regular bathing. Occasionally the same narrator is even more specific, as in the prologue attached to the story of Mūlā the Khatrī.

Bābā Nānak revealed to the world a wise and enlightened belief concerning the remembrance of God. He established dharamsālās throughout the world and inculcated the virtues of remembrance of the divine Name, charity, bathing, mercy, and the performance of one's appointed duties (*dharma*). He would say, 'Son, if anyone is my Sikh let him remain firmly rooted in three things. In what three things? In the divine Name, charity, and bathing.'[1]

The disciple of Bābā Nānak is to follow a distinctive belief concerning the remembrance of God (*parameśar kā simaran*); he is to forgather regularly with the *satsaṅg* in the dharamsālā; and he is to observe a number of devout practices. All of these instructions proceed from Bābā Nānak himself. The *sākhiān* bear testimony to this authority and provide in their descriptions of the Gurū's life the perfect model of their fulfilment.

The purpose of the janam-sākhī narrators was thus to set forth a soteriological interpretation of the life of Nānak. This interpretation constitutes the myth of Nānak, a myth which is expressed in anecdote, in discourse, and in an occasional declaration of faith. A part of the intention was evidently the conversion of others to the same interpretation; an even greater part was obviously the confirming and strengthening of the faithful. For this reason the sākhīs were written down and then regularly read in the dharamsālās (which eventually became gurdwaras) and in the homes of devout Sikh families. No janam-sākhī contributor has expressed the basic purpose with greater force and clarity than the *Ādi Sākhīs* compiler, and his closing declaration is worth repeating.

He who reads or hears this sākhī shall attain to the supreme rapture. He who hears, sings, or reads this sākhī shall find his highest desire fulfilled, for through it he shall meet Gurū Bābā Nānak. He who with love sings of the glory of Bābā Nānak or gives ear to it shall obtain joy ineffable in all that he does in this life, and in the life to come salvation.[2]

[1] *B40*, f. 100a.

[2] *AS*, p. 101.

13

THE FUNCTION OF THE JANAM-SĀKHĪS

THE function of the janam-sākhīs must be clearly distinguished from their avowed purpose. Whereas their purpose concerns the conscious intention of their authors, their function concerns the role which they actually played within the later community.[1] There can be no doubt that the intention was in some considerable measure fulfilled and that to this extent the janam-sākhīs performed a function which corresponded to their purpose. This was not, however, their principal role. Their principal function was the maintenance of the community's cohesion during the pre-Khālsā period.[2] Although it was not the only cohesive agent during this period it was certainly a very important one, and it was largely because they fulfilled the cohesive role so well that the janam-sākhīs flourished during the seventeenth century. The seventeenth-century momentum continued into the following period and then weakened as eighteenth-century circumstances created new needs which they were ill suited to serve. During the Siṅgh Sabhā renewal movement of the late nineteenth century they recovered a considerable measure of their popularity, but never regained the stature which they had possessed during the seventeenth century.

For the first Sikhs identity and cohesion presented no problems. The first Sikhs were the disciples who gathered around Bābā Nānak during the first half of the sixteenth century, and for as long as their Master was present in the flesh there could be no serious difficulty as far as self-definition was concerned. Bābā Nānak provided in his person a focus for the loyalty of his disciples and no bond was needed other than their common allegiance to him. For this stage the word *sikh* is best represented with a lower-case initial letter. The word simply means 'disciple', and the principal difference distinguishing this particular group of disciples from innumerable others was their decision to accept Bābā Nānak of Kartārpur as their spiritual guide. A more appropriate designation for this stage (and one which the janam-sākhīs normally use in preference to *sikh*) is *nānak-panthī*. The early community constituted a panth, a loose congeries linked by a common ideal. Bābā Nānak provided in his person and in his teachings that ideal, and accordingly the panth of his followers bore his name.

[1] For a definition and discussion of the term 'function' as opposed to 'purpose' or 'motive' see Robert K. Merton's essay, 'Manifest and Latent Functions', in his *Social Theory and Social Structure* (Glencoe: the Free Press, 1957), pp. 19–84.

[2] In Merton's usage the fulfilment of the intended purpose constitutes a 'manifest function', and the more significant but unforeseen role a 'latent function'. Op. cit., p. 51.

For as long as Nānak lived in Kartārpur the question of identity required no attention, nor did it seriously concern the growing community during the period immediately following his death. Nānak had, in the usual manner, appointed a chosen disciple to succeed him as leader of the community, and the loyalty due to the first Gurū was automatically transferred to the second. This succession continued until the death of Gurū Gobind Siṅgh in 1708, not without challenge from various contenders but generally stable and always commanding a majority allegiance within the community. Its authority was considerably increased by attaching to it the ancient theory of spiritual transmission represented in the image of a succession of torches. Though the torches be many the flame is the same. Ten men were successively Gurū, but a single spirit inhabited them all and all bore the name Nānak.[1]

This projection of the first Gurū's personal authority through a line of successor Gurūs constituted the principal cohesive agent up to the death of the tenth Gurū in 1708. It was not, however, the only means devised by the community to determine its identity and maintain its cohesion. The personality of the first Gurū was projected not merely through the line of successors but also through the janam-sākhīs. Both the dynastic succession and the hagiographic tradition were fulfilling the same function in essentially the same way. Both were concerned with authority, identity, and cohesion; and both served these needs by sustaining a continuing loyalty to the person of the Gurū. The same answer could still be given to the ever-present question: What is a Sikh? A Sikh could still be defined as one who followed the Gurū.

This cohesive role the janam-sākhīs fulfilled by providing a single focus for a common loyalty. The single focus was not primarily any set of doctrines. The teachings of Nānak were certainly of vital importance, and the continuing reinterpretation of those teachings was a task necessarily imposed by a new experience and a new constituency. It was however the person of the community's first teacher which provided the actual focus, and in so far as any doctrines served to identify the community they did so only through a close connection with the acknowledged Master. Doctrine is in practice a treacherous maze within which a sect or community soon loses its compact unity. Loyalty to a person is a far more effective means of maintaining sectarian or communal cohesion, and although the janam-sākhī narrators could hardly have been aware of this fact their products certainly followed the more effective way. It is always the personality of the Gurū which receives their primary attention. Although later janam-sākhī narrators, and specifically the *Miharbān* commentators, developed a considerable interest in doctrinal issues, they were always careful to relate these issues directly to their image of Bābā Nānak.

The only point at which the janam-sākhīs do suggest an awareness of functional issues is in their occasional insistence that those who put their faith in Bābā Nānak must also identify themselves with the

[1] The Gurūs who composed shabads and shaloks all refer to themselves as 'Nānak' in these compositions.

community of his followers. To Aṅgad Bābā Nānak is said to have declared:

If anyone bears the title of *nānak-panthī* he will be saved.[1]

It is, however, no more than a vague awareness, and the precise meaning of such statements must always be obscured by the indistinctness of the word *panth*. Although such references do indicate a community struggling towards definable identity, they do not imply a clear consciousness of the issues involved in the endeavour. For the janam-sākhī narrators and compilers the maintenance of a single focus served a purpose which must be distinguished from its more important function.

It is, of course, an image of Nānak which provides this vital focus. The historical Nānak was soon replaced by the Nānak of myth and it was this latter figure to whom the common allegiance was so insistently directed. It was, moreover, a variable image. The community could never remain static, and any significant change in its needs and its self-understanding eventually produced a corresponding amendment of the image. The janam-sākhīs clearly reflect a community striving over a period of more than a century to attain an understanding of its own identity. The person and the teachings of the acknowledged founder provide the common loyalty and the common ideal. As new situations develop they raise new questions and demand different responses. The authentic person and teachings of Nānak provide a convenient core to which are added theories and conclusions emerging from subsequent experience.

These theories and conclusions are in some instances to be traced to a resurgence of earlier pre-Nānak ideals, and in others to social and economic pressures of the later Gurū period. Considerable changes inevitably resulted, but one thing remained constant. Loyalty to the person of the first Gurū remained a *sine qua non*. The person who owned this allegiance thereby qualified as a Nānak-panthī, and the common allegiance shared by all members of the Panth provided the essential cohesive factor. The theory was not a complete success, for schism did develop, and some contenders to the succession claiming to be the true heirs to the first Gurū's authority managed to detach segments of the community. It was, however, a generally successful ideal and a considerable measure of its success must be traced to the traditions concerning the first Gurū, both in their oral expression and in their recorded janam-sākhī form.

Throughout the seventeenth century and into the eighteenth, oral tradition and the janam-sākhīs continued to serve this function. Their decline came when the death of the last personal Gurū and the confused events of the eighteenth century forced a radically different situation upon the Panth. The inevitability of a later transformation had already been assured by the entry into the Panth of substantial numbers of Jaṭs. In 1708 the death of Gurū Gobind Siṅgh produced a leadership crisis, and the turmoil which persisted throughout the eighteenth century provided the occasion for a radical change in Sikh identity. Two elements within this situation

1 *B40*, f. 105a. Cf. also ff. 125a–126a.

dictated the actual form of the change. One was the dominant Jaṭ constituency and the other was the fact that the invasions of Ahmad Shāh Abdālī (1747–69) came to be understood as a war of Muslims against Sikhs. A third which also exercised some influence was the impact of Śakti ideals. The sixth Gurū, Hargobind, had moved to the Śivalik Hills in 1634 and all his successors spent substantial periods in this area. Śakti beliefs were strong in the Śivaliks and their influence can be detected in some of the later Sikh developments.

The principal elements were, however, the Jaṭ constituency and the conflict with Muslims imposed by the Afghān invasions. It was no longer possible to define a Sikh simply as one who followed the Gurū, and although the doctrines of *Gurū Panth* (the corporate community as Gurū) and *Gurū Granth* (the scripture as Gurū) successively emerged neither was sufficient to meet eighteenth-century needs. These needs were largely met by recourse to distinctively Jaṭ patterns and to institutions which explicitly distinguished the Sikh from the Muslim. Gradually there evolved and crystallized the distinctive Khālsā *rahit*, or Khālsā 'Code of Discipline', with its insistence upon such features as the obligatory symbols termed the *pañj kakke* or 'Five K's'.

This code provided a new and different answer to the old question of what is a Sikh. A Sikh is one who accepts baptism into the Khālsā and promises to abide by its discipline. Features of the discipline which commanded a particular importance were the Jaṭ custom of leaving hair uncut, and the anti-Muslim prohibition of tobacco and *halāl* meat. Other institutions which supplemented the code and served to strengthen the community's cohesion were regular assemblies in the cult centre (the *dharamsālā* which later became the *gurduārā*), a pronounced reverence for the sacred scriptures, and a new historiography which devoted primary attention to the perils and triumphs of the eighteenth century.

Meanwhile the janam-sākhīs gradually moved away from the position of central importance which they had previously held. Functional substitutes had become necessary and had been found. The janam-sākhīs were not stripped of their function entirely, but from the eighteenth century onwards they shared it with other elements, some of them far more efficient because they related with such greater intimacy to the transformed condition of the Sikh community. The retention of the janam-sākhīs actually involved some contradictions, for the janam-sākhī traditions are much different in tone and intention from the ideals and institutions erected by eighteenth-century experience. Their intention is, however, entirely understandable. A sanctity and an affection still adhere to them and their narrative power provides an anchor of considerable strength. If it be claimed that they will eventually decline to a status which interests only the occasional historian or student of literature, assuredly that day has not yet come.

14

THE JANAM-SĀKHĪS AS HISTORICAL SOURCES

> Lives of Baba Nanuk called 'Junum Sakhis' are very common, but they are so full of fable and invention, displaying such intense ignorance, that they are more calculated to deceive than instruct.
>
> R. N. Cust, *The Life of Baba Nanuk, the Founder of the Sikh Sect of the Hindu Religion in the Punjab*.

CUST'S brief account of Gurū Nānak was published in 1859.[1] Eighteen years later Ernst Trumpp repeated, in language of similar disdain and condescension, the same opinion of the janam-sākhīs.[2] Conventions have long since changed, and because their style now sounds highly insulting those who still accept their derogatory interpretation usually demonstrate a much greater degree of sensitivity in their choice of words. Against this extreme view can be set its more popular opposite, the attitude which persists in treating the janam-sākhis as generally trustworthy and accurate. Only minor changes are permitted by this popular interpretation. The more marvellous of the wonder-stories are commonly rationalized or removed, details which impose an undue strain upon the reader's credulity are similarly discarded, and the substantial balance is then accepted as historically reliable. Both extremes claim to be assessments of the janam-sākhīs as historical sources. Variously modified they represent every possible theory from total acceptance to total rejection.

Of the two interpretations the acceptance theory has, understandably, been much the more popular, and books relating the life and travels of Gurū Nānak are now legion. Ever since Macauliffe published the first volume of *The Sikh Religion* studies of the same kind have continued to appear, most of them in Pañjābī but several in English and other languages. Up to 1969 this succession of biographies could be more appropriately described as a trickle rather than as a stream. In that year, however, the trickle suddenly enlarged and briefly became a flood. The quincentenary of the Gurū's birth created an unprecedented demand and, as in the case of the Gurū Gobind Siṅgh tercentenary three years earlier, the demand produced a vigorous response.

Inevitably the authors who attempted biographies of Gurū Nānak were compelled to rely almost exclusively upon the janam-sākhīs for their material, and for those who purposed to write lengthy accounts of his life this reliance had to be generally uncritical. This has been the standard

[1] The essay was published in Lahore as 'a pamphlet for use in schools'.

[2] E. Trumpp, *The Ādi Granth* (London, 1877), p. *i*.

method from the time of Macauliffe onwards, and in so far as the janam-sākhīs have been used as historical source-material their usage has been almost exclusively limited to this biographical concern. Although this dependence upon the janam-sākhīs is inescapable two major qualifications are vital. The first is that the janam-sākhīs can tell us very little about the historical Nānak, of the man who lived in the Pañjāb during the late fifteenth and early sixteenth centuries. Although the investigation of his actual life must still rely largely upon the janam-sākhīs the source is for this purpose a very unreliable one and its yield necessarily scant.

The second qualification is that whereas the janam-sākhīs tell us relatively little of the historical Nānak they do communicate much concerning the later myth of Nānak and of its importance within the seventeenth- and eighteenth-century community of his followers. They also tell us much of the wider life of that community and of the Pañjāb in which it lived during that later period. It is most important that this potential contribution should be appreciated. For too long the use of the janam-sākhīs as historical sources has been confined to biographical endeavours, an approach which assumes that the janam-sākhī narratives relate primarily to the times of Nānak. It is to their own times, and particularly to the seventeenth century, that they primarily relate, and it is for this later period that they can make a major contribution to historical understanding.

1. *THE JANAM-SĀKHĪS AS SOURCES FOR THE LIFE OF GURŪ NĀNAK*

This issue may be treated very briefly, partly for the reason given above and partly because it is more extensively discussed elsewhere.[1] The procedure which must be followed in any attempt to use the janam-sākhīs as biographical sources should consist of a patient analysis of the anecdotes and discourses directed to the identification of elements which may safely be traced to the historical Nānak or his immediate environment. This amounts in practice to a lengthy series of tests, and for these tests a set of basic criteria must be devised.

One criterion to which constant appeal must be made is the evidence of external sources. This is an obvious procedure, but one which must be used with caution. References to Nānak which occur in other sources require careful checking, and if upon analysis they leave room for serious doubt this element of doubt should not be glossed over. There is, for example, a reference to the Gurū in the *Chaitanya Bhāgavat* which has been taken as conclusive proof of a meeting between Nānak and Chaitanya.[2] Such a meeting is certainly a possibility, but the reference does not provide sufficiently convincing evidence to permit any categorical affirmation. One must also take account of the age of the *Chaitanya Bhāgavat*, which, according to Bimanbehari Majumdar, 'could not have been written before the seventeenth century'.[3] Anecdotes concerning Nānak quickly became a

[1] *GNSR*, pp. 68–147. See esp. pp. 68–70.
[2] *SLTGN(Eng)*, p. 336.
[3] Ibid., p. 335.

feature of North Indian bhakti hagiography (as the works of Mahipati indicate) and traditions concerning Bābā Nānak had certainly reached Bengal by the seventeenth century. It could be argued that just as Nānak had to be represented as meeting Kabīr, so in like manner did Chaitanya have to encounter Nānak. Although it cannot be asserted that such a meeting did *not* take place, nor can it be affirmed that its historicity has been established.

The same caution must also be applied to the traditions concerning Nānak's visits to Sri Lanka and Bāghdād,[1] and likewise to the numerous conclusions based upon phonetic similarities or popular etymologies. The 'Land of Āsā' has in this manner been identified with Āssām; the 'Land of Dhanāsarī' is similarly identified with the valley of the Dhansirī river in the same province; *Munāfik Deś*, the 'Land of Unbelievers', is treated as a version of Kāfirstān in the Hindu Kush; and a visit to China has been declared proven on the grounds that the city of Nanking must have been named in memory of the Gurū.

In practice the appeal to external sources rarely sustains a janam-sākhī tradition. It is the reverse which is true, namely that such an appeal will commonly enable the historian to set particular claims aside. Whereas contemporary references to Nānak appear to be non-existent there is abundant evidence to indicate that many of the anecdotes or details attached to his person by janam-sākhī narrators were present in earlier traditions. External sources may not help much in confirming janam-sākhī claims, but they do render much assistance in distinguishing features which relate to the later image of Nānak rather than to the authentic historical person.

Most of the other criteria serve a similar purpose, their contribution being in terms of rejection rather than affirmation. The result, inevitably, is the conclusion that although much can be known concerning the teachings of Nānak very little can be positively affirmed concerning his life. Many incidents must remain unproven either way, but given the general unreliability of the janam-sākhīs as testimony to the historical Nānak the historian must usually incline strongly towards scepticism.

Three considerations will however mitigate any sense of disappointment which this conclusion may cause. The first is that the analysis does at least confirm the broad outline of his life in the Pañjāb. The second is that his works have been preserved and that from this source all aspects of his teachings may be known. The third is that for the historian the later image and its impact upon the later community will be of even greater interest than the historical figure. This image the janam-sākhīs describe in superabundant detail.

2. *THE JANAM-SĀKHĪ IMAGE OF BĀBĀ NĀNAK*

For the janam-sākhī narrators Bābā Nānak was above all else the Giver of Salvation. Although there is no single word to express this status explicitly,

[1] See above, p. 162. *GNSR*, pp. 125–32.

the promise of salvation (*mukti*) is repeatedly held out to those who will own Nānak as their Master and Guide. The single-word descriptions which do recur in the janam-sākhī narratives serve rather to express particular aspects of his saviour status. In all instances they are drawn from earlier usage, but there can be no gainsaying the uniqueness of the figure which emerges through the multitude of the janam-sākhī anecdotes. This figure, a blend of traditional symbols with surviving memories of the authentic personality, constitutes the janam-sākhī image of Nānak.

Although there is a generalized image common to all janam-sākhī traditions there are also a few features which are characteristic of particular sources. One of these, the image of Nānak the Ascetic, is of sufficient importance to warrant separate notice. The image depicts Nānak as one who consorted with celibate *langoṭ-band* sādhūs, lived by begging, practised *tapasya*, and sought withdrawal from the world in his quest for salvation. This particular representation is plainly the creation of the continuing ascetic tradition within the Sikh community and, as one would expect, its distinctive features find their fullest expression in the *Narrative IIb* source.[1] Their incidence is not, however, limited to this source. The ascetic ideal, though obviously stressed by a particular sect, exercised a wide appeal throughout the entire community, and occasional references to the Great Ascetic image are to be found amongst descriptions of a more conventional kind. One which begins in the *Narrative IIb* tradition but spreads much further is the belief that Nānak subsisted for many years on a daily *ak* pod and handful of sand, and that he made his bed upon stones.[2] In some references his diet is limited to either the *ak* pod[3] or the sand,[4] and elsewhere it is reduced to the consumption of air.[5]

Nānak the Ascetic is not, however, the dominant image of most janam-sākhī traditions. The *Miharbān* commentators do betray a certain fascination for an ascetic interpretation of the person and mission of Nānak, but their normal preference is for the image projected by almost all the narrative traditions. This generally consistent image also draws extensively upon traditional models, but not the same models as those of the dissenting *Narrative IIb* source. Various features may be identified and scrutinized separately.

Several of these features may be treated as aspects of piety, a quality which is represented throughout the janam-sākhīs by the regular title of Bābā. Whereas Nānak is now almost invariably called Gurū Nānak the janam-sākhīs with equal consistency refer to him as Bābā Nānak. 'Gurū' is certainly used and where it appears there is generally an evident stress upon Nānak's status as the Supreme Teacher.[6] It is, however, relatively

[1] See above, p. 203. For examples see esp. *B40*, ff. 76a, 102b.

[2] *B40*, ff. 76a, 103b. *AS*, p. 23. *Mih JS* I.111. *BG* 1:24.

[3] *B40*, f. 180a.

[4] *Pur JS*, p. 78. *AS*, p. 79.

[5] *Pur JS*, pp. 25, 89.

[6] Cf. *B40*, ff. 125a, 126b. The *Narrative IIb* tradition represents Nānak's travels as a quest for a gurū, implying thereby Nānak's willingness to accept the role of disciple. *B40*, f. 76b. It does, however, suggest that this was unnecessary, for later in the same sākhī a multitude of people at the Gangā acclaim him as their gurū. *B40*, f. 79b. Aṅgad, Rām Dās, and Arjan all refer to him as Gurū Nānak. *AG*, pp. 150, 710, 1297. The more exalted forms Satgurū and Gurūdev are occasionally used by janam-sākhī compilers.

uncommon in the earlier traditions and at no stage in the development of the janam-sākhīs does it overtake 'Bābā' in popularity. The fact that 'Gurū' was used so infrequently during the early period presumably reflects the standard convention of the period and the tradition. Modern usage can easily suggest that the title possesses an immemorial sanction. This was certainly not the case within the territory occupied by the early Sant tradition, nor by other movements with related beliefs and attitudes. If in fact Gorakhnāth was characteristically known as Gurū Gorakhnāth during the pre-Nānak period he must be regarded as something of an exception. The title was not commonly used in this sense and it should therefore come as no surprise to discover that the janam-sākhīs use it so sparingly.

The early use of 'Gurū' as a title applied to Nānak may also have been inhibited by an awareness of the meaning which Nānak himself had so explicitly attached to it. For Nānak the only *gurū* was the inner voice of God. Although the shift from actual voice to human mediator is a comparatively simple one, the stress laid by Nānak on his own understanding of the term is a clear one and may well have served to retard any such process. It is even possible that the ascription of praise, *vāh gurū* ('Praise to the Gurū'), and the practice of chanting *gurū gurū*, both of which were to become standard usages in the later seventeenth century, may have originally possessed the same meaning as Nānak intended. There is, of course, no doubt that in their later standard usage they refer to Nānak himself.[1]

Within the janam-sākhīs, however, 'Bābā' is strongly dominant. The honorific *bābā* (literally father, grandfather, old man) evidently goes back to the earliest disciples who attached themselves to Nānak during his lifetime. This assumption is based not merely upon the common usage of the term in the popular devotion of the period but also upon a reference which Nānak himself has left. In his shabad *Gauṛī Chetī* 13 he indicates that 'Bābā Nānak' is what others call him.[2] The meaning which it bears is that of respect based upon piety and religious wisdom. The later preference for 'Gurū' retains this sense, adding to it the dimension implied by the assimilation of the divine inner voice to the human communicator. It could also be urged that the increasingly specific application of *sikh* to the disciples of Nānak would encourage the same development. Although the janam-sākhīs sometimes use *sikh* in a general sense to designate the followers of other leaders or teachers, the term eventually acquires the exclusive Nānak-panthī meaning which it retains to this day. A *sikh* is necessarily the follower of a preceptor and although, as we have just noted, *gurū* had not conventionally been attached to a preceptor's name as an actual title of address it was nevertheless an appropriate one.

Increasingly, therefore, the preference shifted away from 'Bābā' to

[1] Cf. the final sentence of the *B40 Janam-sākhī* (loc. cit., f. 231a). Later still the two words *vāh* and *gurū* coalesced to form a name of God ('Vāhgurū', generally translated nowadays as 'Wonderful Lord'). See *B40(Eng)*, p. 45n.

[2] *AG*, p. 155. See Vīr Singh, art., 'Srī Gurū Nānak Dev Jī dī janam sākhī Srī Gurū Granth Sāhib Jī vichon saṅkalat', in the *Khālsā Samāchār*, vol. lxx, no. 1, p. 6.

'Gurū'. This, however, carries us beyond the janam-sākhīs. In so far as we can detect the beginnings of this gradual shift of preference operating within them there is little trace of any significant change in the image. Bābā Nānak, Gurū Nānak, and Srī Gurū Bābā Nānak are all expressions of essentially the same impulse and interpretation. The marked preference of the janam-sākhī narrators for the first of these affirms the piety and spiritual wisdom of the Master without denying those features subtly evoked by the later title. Although they opt so strongly for Bābā there can be no questioning their acceptance of Nānak as the mediator of a divine message, nor their own status as his disciples.

A conventional understanding of piety is also implied in the terms *bhagat*,[1] *sādh* (or *sādhū*),[2] and *faqīr*,[3] all of which are applied to Nānak by various janam-sākhī narrators. In referring to him as a *faqīr* they were not implying that he was to be regarded as a Sūfī. (On the rare occasions when they wish to attribute distinctively Muslim qualities they call him a *pīr*.) The word *faqīr* had been completely assimilated to popular Hindu usage as a synonym for *sādhū*, and both were commonly used as terms of respect due to those who had attained to spiritual wisdom and freedom from worldly desires. The same variety of assimilation is also evident in the *Purātan* affection for the Sūfī title *darveś* (dervish).[4] All four terms express the traditional form of piety which constitutes such a significant part of the janam-sākhī image.

Mere piety was not, however, the sum total of the janam-sākhī image. Bābā Nānak was a *baḍā bhagat* and a *bhallā faqīr*, and he was also much more. Others could be true sādhūs, but Nānak was unique. This uniqueness is represented by a number of characteristic terms which may be taken in ascending order of eminence.

He was, first, a *mahā-purukh* or 'Exalted One'. Rājā Śivanābh, in devising a method of recognizing Bābā Nānak, instructs his slave-girls to approach all sādhūs who visit his domain. Nānak when he first arrives is identified merely as another faqīr, but when he successfully resists the temptations proffered by Śivanābh's slave-girls he is declared to be a *mahā-purukh*.[5] Although uniqueness is implied it is not yet specifically stated. The term is particularly common in *Narrative III* material, but is by no means confined to it.

Secondly, Nānak is declared to be an *avatār*, a divine incarnation sent for the salvation of men. He is, in fact, said to be a reincarnation of Rājā Janak (presumably the first Janak, although this is not made absolutely clear).[6] For some obscure reason Rājā Janak held a curious fascination for the early Sikh community. A reference by Kīrat the Bard included in the Ādi Granth identifies Nānak with Janak;[7] the author of the *Dabistān-i-Mazāhib* was sufficiently impressed by the same popular belief to note it

[1] *B40*, ff. 86a, 94a. [2] *B40*, f. 192b. [3] *B40*, ff. 20b, 71a, 146a.
[4] *Pur JS*, pp. 22–3, 24, 40, 63. [5] *B40*, ff. 144b, 146a, 149b.
[6] This identification with the first Janak is implied in a reference to 'Janak Videha' which occurs in the *B40* sākhī entitled 'A Discourse with Kabīr'. *B40*, f. 137b.
[7] *Savāie mahale dūje ke* (3), *AG*, p. 1391.

in his account of the Sikhs;[1] and references to it appear at various places in the janam-sākhīs.[2]

The status of a divine *avatār* is high, but there is one higher still. The supreme status is that of God Himself and the climax of the janam-sākhī elevation of Nānak is the declaration that he is actually God. He is not merely one *avatār* amongst the small number of divine incarnations, nor even the most exalted of this tiny élite. The position which the janam-sākhīs finally reach is that Bābā Nānak must be identified with God, a unique and perfect manifestation of the Timeless One. 'Thou art the reader of inward thoughts,' confesses Rājā Śivanābh, and he continues, 'Thou art the supreme God!'[3] Many other references point to the same exalted status, and in a late addition to the *Ādi Sākhīs* the claim is stated in words which leave no room for doubt.

> The Gurū is God (*paramesar*). Whatever he does is true and whatever he says is true. The Gurū is God, not a man.[4]

The context makes it absolutely clear that the reference is to Gurū Nānak.[5] From his own works it is abundantly evident that Nānak himself could never have contemplated any such claim to divinity, but given the janam-sākhī doctrine of salvation his apotheosis is but a natural outcome.

All janam-sākhī narrators do not press their convictions to this logical conclusion, but with only one exception all unite in according Bābā Nānak a divine status far above that attained by any other incarnation of the divine. The one exception is the inimical Hindālī tradition appearing in the earliest *Bālā* janam-sākhīs. This claims a threefold succession from Kabīr, through Nānak, to a climax in Bābā Hindāl, seeking thereby to demonstrate the supremacy of Hindāl over both his predecessors.[6] Elsewhere the image is generally consistent and differs only in the degree of divinity attributed to Nānak. For the Sikh community of the seventeenth and eighteenth centuries Bābā Nānak was, in progressively ascending degrees of exaltation, a manifestation of God. Thus were the soteriological claims authenticated.

This image had to be set within a Pañjāb context. Inevitably this meant a confrontation with the conflicting claims of Hindu and Muslim doctrines of religious authority and salvation. For Nānak himself the conflict of claims was ultimately irrelevant for neither 'knew the mystery'.[7] Salvation could be obtained only by ignoring both and instead seeking direct access to God through the immanent Word.

The janam-sākhīs are by no means unfaithful to this vision, and the

[1] *PPP* I.1 (April 1967), pp. 55–6. *SLTGN(Eng)*, p. 50.

[2] *Mih JS* I.1–9. *AS*, p. 3. For *Purātan* references see *PHLS* i. 341 and ii. 230. For a *Gyān-ratanāvalī* reference see *PHLS* ii. 241.

[3] *pārabraham paramesar*. *B40*, f. 152a.

[4] *AS*, p. 91.

[5] *AS*, p. 97. For other examples in the *B40 Janam-sākhī* see ff. 79b, 85a, 140a, 140b, 162a, 188a–b, 205a, 217b, 229b.

[6] *B41*, f. 166b. BL MS Or. 2754. I, f. 162a–b.

[7] *Mārū Solahā* 2(6), *AG*, p. 1021. *GNSR*, p. 161.

most famous of all their pronouncements on the subject can be interpreted in a sense which would accord closely with Nānak's own intention.

> *nā koī hindū hai nā koī musalmān.*[1]
> There is neither Hindu nor Muslim.

There is, however, a distinctive difference to be noted between Nānak's own utterances and the janam-sākhī treatment of the issue. For Nānak the message alone was sufficient and his emphasis is strongly upon its positive aspects; criticisms of contemporary belief and practice are certainly present in his works, but they are strictly subordinate to his repeated insistence upon the divine Name as the vehicle of salvation. When he does pass strictures they are commonly aimed at Nāth yogīs. Muslims and Islamic doctrine receive much less attention.

The situation of the janam-sākhī narrators was, however, different. The growth of the Sikh Panth involved a growing measure of opposition, and this in turn involved the Panth in polemic. If the community was to sustain distinctive claims it could do so only by transgressing limits set by other communities. Increasingly this polemic came to mean rivalry between Nānak-panthīs and Muslims, and inevitably this later rivalry was reflected in the janam-sākhī reconstruction of the Gurū's own life and times.

As a result of this situation two allied themes run through the janam-sākhīs, both of them making substantial contributions to the janam-sākhī image of Nānak. The first is that of Nānak the Unifier, the one to whom both Hindu and Muslim must owe allegiance. This theme emerges in the opening sākhī with a united welcome accorded to the infant Nānak[2] and it receives a corresponding prominence at the very end when Hindus and Muslims quarrel over the disposal of Nānak's corpse.[3] Between these two events Bābā Nānak is pointedly called a Hindu,[4] but with equal emphasis he is described as one who mixed Hindu and Muslim garments and customs in such a manner that his precise affiliation was a puzzle to those for whom all men must belong to one religion or the other.[5] As a result crowds of both Hindus and Muslims flocked to him.[6] The theme also finds a later expression in the constant presence of two disciples, the Muslim Mardānā and the Hindu Bālā.

The second theme marked a stronger response to the contemporary situation. The principal challenge to the Panth came from Muslim claims and these claims had to be answered. The result was a 'Triumph over Islam' theme. This finds expression in Bābā Nānak's celebrated discourse with Daulat Khān's qāzī;[7] in missionary visits to Mecca, Medīnā, Bāghdād, and Multān; and in successful encounters with celebrated Sūfī pīrs.

The 'Triumph over Islam' theme is well illustrated by the *Bālā* sākhī

[1] *B40*, f. 19b.
[2] *B40*, f. 1b. *Pur JS*, p. 1. *GNSR*, pp. 36, 51–2.
[3] *Pur JS*, p. 114. *B40*, f. 228b. *GNSR*, pp. 50–1.
[4] *B40*, ff. 77a, 133a.
[5] *B40*, f. 74a, 100a. *Pur JS*, pp. 25, 98.
[6] *B40*, f. 104a.
[7] *B40*, ff. 22b–23b.

entitled 'How the Gurūjī met Mālo Takhān'.[1] This anecdote relates how Sheikh Mālo, a resident of Pakho or somewhere near it, heard that a Hindu called Nānak was showing respect to none of the traditional teachings of Islam. Filled with anger he came to Nānak but was promptly converted by the recitation of two shabads.

Sheikh Mālo prostrated himself before Gurū Nanākjī and laid his head upon his feet. 'Gurūjī,' he declared, 'you are my pīr and I am your murīd. Grant me even greater spiritual satisfaction. The Hindus make one claim and the Muslims another. Both are false. Whatever you say is true!'[2]

In such declarations the Hindu claims are commonly bracketed with Muslim so that both may suffer a common condemnation. It is, however, usually a Muslim who has to suffer the dialectical defeat and make the confession. Apart from the Nāths (who are treated separately) there are relatively few controversies involving representatives of Hindu society. When they do occur they normally involve obvious targets such as the overly scrupulous Brāhmaṇ or the miserly money-lender. The Nāth encounters should be noted as a third theme, one which plainly accorded rather more closely with Nānak's own attitudes.[3]

Of these three themes only the first commands a notable following today. Once again the pressure of contemporary circumstances is dictating the choice of material and the image which emerges in consequence. Whereas the Nāth conflict, so significant for Nānak himself, is now largely forgotten, the Muslim–Hindu unity theme answers a contemporary yearning and so receives a powerful emphasis in all modern representations of the Nānak image. This is well illustrated by the frequency with which a particular eighteenth-century couplet is quoted today.

bābā nānak shāh faqīr
hindū dā gurū musalmān dā pīr
Bābā Nānak, the supreme Faqīr!
The Hindu's Gurū and the Muslim's Pīr.[4]

The image is never static. There are, however, definable images for particular periods, and it is the image of the seventeenth-century Sikh community which the janam-sākhīs project.

3. *THE SIKH COMMUNITY IN THE SEVENTEENTH AND EARLY EIGHTEENTH CENTURIES*

It has frequently been observed how in terms of historical source-material the value of the *Jātaka* and *Hadīth* literature largely concerns periods later

[1] *Bālā JS*, pp. 338–41. Takhāṇ = Tarkhān, the carpenter caste.

[2] Ibid., p. 340. The same message is repeated in the three succeeding sākhīs, relating discourses with Ubārā Khān Paṭhān and Abdul Rahmān. Ibid., pp. 341–9.

[3] See above, pp. 144–57.

[4] Cf. Rattan Singh Bhaṅgū, *Prāchīn Panth Prakāś* (Amritsar, 1962), p. 30. The *Prāchīn Panth Prakāś* was written in A.D. 1841.

than those which the literature purports to describe. The *Hadīth* may be closer to Muhammad than the *Jātaka* stories are to Gautama, but the principle remains the same. As historical source-material they must be related primarily, and indeed almost exclusively, to the later periods which produced them. The same principle must be applied to the janam-sākhīs. The historical record which they provide is a record not of the early sixteenth-century period of Gurū Nānak but of the seventeenth- and early eighteenth-century situation of the Sikh community within which the janam-sākhī traditions evolved.

The image of Nānak projected by the janam-sākhīs is by no means the only feature to emerge with clarity from this record. Because the narrators were describing a person and not a set of doctrines it was essential that they should provide a setting within which the Gurū's activities might take place. Inevitably they drew the form and details of this setting from their own contemporary experience, and it is accordingly to the post-Nānak period that the janam-sākhī social patterns must be related. When for example the *Miharbān Janam-sākhī* provides a lengthy account of Nānak's wedding the description of this event must be applied not to the conventions of the late fifteenth century but to those of the early or middle seventeenth century.[1] The sole detail which can be related to the historical Nānak is the brief statement that at some indeterminate age he was married in Baṭālā to the daughter of Mūlā, a Choṇā Khatrī. The remainder concerns the later period. If it be protested that marriage customs in the Pañjāb change slowly and that a seventeenth-century description could still correspond closely to a fifteenth-century event the reply must be that this is no more than an assumption, and that it could be a very misleading one. It is to the seventeenth century that the detailed description applies, and it is accordingly as a source for seventeenth-century marriage procedures that the janam-sākhī must be used.

The same principle also applies to the janam-sākhī descriptions of Nānak's funeral,[2] and to other less formalized customs. In the case of the *B40* funeral rites it is interesting to observe the continuing authority of brāhmanical traditions.[3] These orthodox conventions may have been practised by the early followers who disposed of Nānak's body, but we cannot be sure. What we can assume with some assurance is that such customs must have been general within the Sikh community during the late seventeenth century.[4]

The general background against which the janam-sākhīs set their tales of Bābā Nānak is unmistakably that of rural Pañjāb, and it is clear from their descriptions that the Sikh Panth of this period must have been almost exclusively a rural community. This impression is in no way disturbed by the prominence given to Khatrīs in the janam-sākhī narratives. Although the Khatrīs constitute an urban-based caste grouping they are by no means

[1] *Mih JS* I.29–37.

[2] *B40*, ff. 222a–230a *passim*.

[3] *B40*, ff. 226a, 228a, 229b–230a.

[4] The source which in 1733 provided the *B40* compiler with material for his funeral sākhī was in existence more than thirty years earlier when the *Ādi Sākhīs* collection was compiled.

exclusively urban, and when the janam-sākhīs so commonly place their Khatrīs in rural contexts it must follow that most of the Sikh Khatrīs of the janam-sākhī period were in fact rural dwellers. Nānak himself had been a village Khatrī, and one popular anecdote has as its setting a village of Uppal Khatrīs.[1]

The rural base of the community is clearly implied by the absence of knowledgeable references to urban life, and by a corresponding abundance of authentic village descriptions. Lahore is occasionally mentioned, but there is no indication that any of the narrators have a distinct notion of its size or way of life. For the narrator who first related the story of the Lahore merchant converted on his way to Kartārpur the city was evidently envisaged in terms more appropriate to a large village.[2] The same applies to Sultānpur and other towns.

This rural consciousness is also to be detected in anecdotes which purport to have occurred outside the Pañjāb. When Nānak visits the Land of Unbelievers the locality is variously described as *vilāit* or *deś*, both of which imply areas at least as large as a modern district.[3] Elsewhere in the same sākhī, however, the reference is simply to a *nagarī* (small town or village),[4] a *piṇḍ girāu* (village),[5] or a *vasadī* (cluster of dwellings).[6] The narrator's description of the area plainly indicates that the diminutive terms correspond to his own understanding, and that this understanding is of a distinctively Pañjābī variety. From his narrative it soon becomes clear that *Munāfik Deś*, the Land of Unbelievers, consists of a single small town or village surrounded by its cultivated land. The situation which it reflects is that of the *bār* dweller, living in an interfluvial tract where streams are too far distant for irrigation and where well irrigation is exceedingly difficult or impossible.

To this instance many other rural references could be added. The anecdote entitled 'The Ruined Crop Restored' bears all the marks of an authentic village experience[7] and so too does the celebrated story of how Bābā Nānak directed the well-dressed Lahaṇā to carry dripping grass on his head.[8] The same sort of background is also evident in the account of how Nānak sent his servant Kamalā to cut grass for his horses and buffaloes from the village wasteland (*belā*).[9] These tales are products of rural Pañjāb, and the community which produced them was obviously reflecting its own situation. At certain points this is stated directly. When Bābā Nānak sets his Sikhs to work it is, inevitably, agriculture which he chooses.[10]

Within the general context of rural Pañjāb the janam-sākhīs indicate three social groups as primary constituents of the seventeenth-century Sikh community. The most prominent is the Khatrī caste grouping. From other sources it is well known that the ten Sikh Gurūs were all Khatrīs. The janam-sākhīs indicate that Khatrī influence in the Panth was not limited to the authority of the incumbent Gurū, but that it extended much

[1] *B40*, f. 28b. *Pur JS*, p. 20.
[2] *B40*, ff. 138b, 140b.
[3] *B40*, ff. 128a, 128b.
[4] *B40*, ff. 129b, 132b.
[5] *B40*, f. 131b.
[6] *B40*, ff. 128b, 131a.
[7] *B40*, ff. 7a–8a.
[8] *B40*, ff. 97b–98b.
[9] *B40*, ff. 221a–222a.
[10] *B40*, ff. 108a–109a.

further within the community. The three principal figures in the story of the Lahore merchant are all Khatrīs;[1] Dūnī Chand with his seven pennants is said to be a Khatrī;[2] in the *Purātan* account it is a Khatrī who converts Lahaṇā in Khaḍūr;[3] and the *B40* manuscript was actually written by a Khatrī.[4] In several instances their sub-castes are also given.[5] They are not always the heroes of janam-sākhī anecdotes (Mūlā and Malak Bhāgo are both said to be Khatrīs), but of their prominence in the janam-sākhīs there can be no doubt and this prominence must reflect substantial influence within the seventeenth-century community.

The Jaṭs, in contrast, receive much less attention than one might expect from their eighteenth-century and subsequent predominance in the community. Eighteenth-century developments indicate that their numbers must certainly have been substantial during the earlier period, and a direct reference by the author of the *Dabistān-i-Mazāhib*, recorded during the first half of the seventeenth century, confirms their importance within the community during that period.[6] The janam-sākhīs suggest nevertheless that their influence within the Panth must have been less than that of the Khatrīs, at least within those areas of Sikh life which interested their narrators and compilers. Perhaps the likeliest explanation is that whereas the Jaṭ Sikhs were prominent numerically, and also in communal administration and military activity, the Khatrīs retained their status as religious leaders. During the eighteenth century the Jaṭs rose to prominence through the *jathās* and the *misls* (both military organizations), whereas the Khatrīs retained their hold on the religious *saṅgats* where these were not transformed into military groups.

It should, moreover, be observed that although references are not as numerous as one might expect Jaṭs do nevertheless constitute a second prominent caste grouping within the janam-sākhīs, and with the advent of Bālā Sandhū their importance increases. A Randhāvā Jaṭ named Jittā, or Ajittā, is one of the most prominent of all disciples;[7] the *Hāfizābād Janam-sākhī* provides two Jaṭs as companions of the Gurū during his second *Purātan* journey;[8] and the *Bālā* tradition introduces another Randhāvā, this one bearing the name Buṛā or Buḍhā.[9] The *B40 Janam-sākhī* also refers to a single Gujar disciple.[10]

The third group consists of a number of artisan castes. Artisan Sikhs (the self-styled Rāmgaṛhiās) constitute an important segment of the community today and it is evident from the janam-sākhīs that their allegiance

[1] *B40*, ff. 138b ff. [2] *Pur JS*, p. 70. [3] *Pur JS*, p. 106.

[4] See below, p. 264. The *Bālā* janam-sākhīs also name a Khatrī as copyist. *Bālā JS*, p. 1. See above, p. 16.

[5] Bhagīrath is an Aṇad Khatrī, Dūnī Chand is a Dhuppaṛ, and the Khaḍūr Sikh a Bhallā. The *B40 Janam-sākhī* names a Bhaṇḍārī disciple (*B40*, f. 184a) and the *Colebrooke Janam-sākhī* mentions a Ghei (*Pur JS*, p. 79). Nānak, himself a Bedī, married the daughter of a Choṇā (*B40*, ff. 1a, 6a). Bhāī Gurdās, a Bhallā, refers to several more Khatrīs in a list of disciples notable for its strong predominance of Khatrī names (*BG* XI:13–14).

[6] *PPP* I.1 (April 1967), p. 57. [7] *BG* XI:14. *B40*, ff. 111a, 177a, 181a.

[8] *Pur JS*, p. 79. [9] *Bālā JS*, p. 335. *BG* XI:14. *MK*, p. 662.

[10] *B40*, f. 184a.

must date from at least the seventeenth century. Carpenters (*tarkhān*) are the most prominent.[1] Others named by the *Purātan* janam-sākhīs are a Kalāl (brewer), a Lohār (blacksmith), and a Chhīmbā (calico printer).[2] Ālam Chand, the illustrator of the *B40* manuscript, was a Rāj (mason) by caste.[3]

These three rural groups evidently constituted the bulk of the seventeenth-century community. Brāhmaṇs are almost completely absent except as convenient functionaries or as targets for some of the anecdotes. Outcaste groups are also conspicuously absent. The nearest approach to outcaste representation is Mardānā the Ḍūm. He, however, stands alone. There is no evidence to suggest that members of his caste entered the community in any numbers.

A constituency comprising three distinct caste groups inevitably raised the question of how the Sikh community should be defined. In theory a common allegiance to Nānak's message of salvation through the divine Name should have been sufficient, but in practice no community will tolerate such a slender base. The message of mystical union through *nām simaran* could sustain its appeal amongst a religious élite but it could not hold together the heterogeneous group which constituted the seventeenth-century Sikh community. Villagers who subscribed to the Panth because of simple piety, sub-caste solidarity, or a desire for social advancement needed objective conventions, and for their descendants born into the faith the need was even greater.

The janam-sākhīs reveal something of this struggle for identity, and of the tensions which it involved. There was, on the one hand, an evident awareness of links with the Hindu society from which the vast majority of Sikhs had come, and to which many still felt that they belonged. Without this continuing link it would have been impossible for the janam-sākhī narrators to have Nānak declare 'I am a Hindu'. On the other hand, there was a strong if ill-defined sense of difference and distinction from Hindu society. The nearest the janam-sākhīs come to defining this distinction is a pronouncement included in God's instructions to Nānak.

> Go, Nānak. Your panth will flourish. The salutation of your followers shall be: *pairī pavaṇā satigurū hoiā*. The salutation of the Vaiṣṇava panth is: *rām kriṣṇa*. The salutation of the Sanyāsī panth is: *namo narāyan*. The yogīs' salutation is: *ādeś ādi purukh kau*. The Muslims' cry is: *salām-'alaik*. You are Nānak and your panth will flourish. Your followers shall be called Nānak-panthīs and their salutation shall be: *pairī pavaṇā satigurū hoiā*.
>
> I shall bless your panth. Inculcate devotion towards Me and strengthen men's obedience to their *dharma*. As the Vaiṣṇavas have their place of worship, the yogīs their āsan, and the Muslims their mosque, so your followers shall have

[1] *B40*, f. 182b. *Pur JS*, pp. 45, 90. *Bālā JS*, p. 87. Tarkhān Sikhs are generally called Rāmgaṛhīā Sikhs. The name was assumed by the famous *misl* leader Jassā Singh of Ichogal following his capture of the Amritsar fort Rāmgaṛh in 1748. Jassā Singh was himself a Tarkhān and the name which he had adopted (or which had been bestowed on him) was subsequently assumed by all other Sikhs of the Tarkhān caste. The title is also applied, in a more general sense, to Sikhs of other artisan castes.

[2] *Pur JS*, pp. 65, 90.

[3] *B40*, f. 84b.

their dharamsālā. Three things you must inculcate in your panth: repeating the divine Name, giving charity, and regular bathing. Keep yourself unspotted while yet remaining in the condition of a householder.[1]

The stress which this passage lays upon a separate cult centre is confirmed by the numerous janam-sākhī references to Sikh dharamsālās. This term, which now designates a rest-house attached to a temple, clearly means in seventeenth-century Sikh parlance a room or building in which local groups would meet for communal singing (*kīrtan*). Repeated references are made to the dharamsālā, particularly in *Narrative III* material, and it is clear that these buildings provided a distinctively Sikh cult centre. Within these dharamsālās there would be regular conventicles, meetings of the *saṅgat* or *satsaṅg* at which the songs of the Gurūs would be sung. There was nothing either original or unique in this practice, for the *satsaṅg* had long been a feature of the bhakti tradition and during the janam-sākhī period it flourished in other parts of Northern India.[2] Its significance lay not in any feature peculiar to Sikh practice but rather in the existence of distinctively Sikh (or Nānak-panthī) *saṅgats* meeting in separate Sikh dharamsālās. These conventicles were concentrated in rural Pañjāb but already Khatrī enterprise was founding *saṅgats* in places far beyond its borders.[3]

The word *gurduārā* (gurdwara) does not appear during this period. For the seventeenth-century community the standard term was *dharamsālā*. No hint of size, pretentiousness, or furnishings is ever given and it seems safe to assume that these buildings were usually humble structures, perhaps rooms which served other purposes when not being used for *kīrtan*. This is suggested by a reference to a new disciple converting his house into a dharamsālā.[4] Other references indicate that a portion of a house might be used as a dharamsālā.[5]

A glimpse of a *saṅgat* meeting for *kīrtan* in a dharamsālā is given in the *B40* sākhī 49b, a *Narrative III* description which probably relates to early eighteenth-century conditions.

Beneath the rājā's palace was the dharamsālā where the Sikhs sang hymns and performed *kīrtan*. Sitting there the rājā would fix his attention on the music of whatever hymn the Sikhs were singing. One day the rānī said to the rājā, 'Rājā, how is it that no children have been born in our house? Let us go to the dharamsālā and lay our petition before the congregation, for the Gurū is present in the congregation.'...

Next day the rājā and the rānī both joined the congregation. It was an *Ekādasī* gathering. There was a congregational festival and a large gathering was present.

[1] *B40*, f. 125b. Malcolm reproduces a version of this declaration in his *Sketch of the Sikhs*, erroneously attributing it to Bhāī Gurdās. *Asiatick Researches*, vol. xi (Calcutta, 1810), pp. 275–6. For another statement of Sikh distinctiveness see *Mih JS* II.411–14.

[2] F. R. Allchin, *Kavitāvalī* (London, 1964), p. 52.

[3] G. B. Singh, *Srī Gurū Granth Sāhib dīān Prāchīn Bīṛān* (Lahore, 1944), p. 323. There is also evidence pointing to the early establishment of *saṅgats* in South India by Bhāṭṛā Sikhs. W. H. McLeod, 'Hakīkat Rāh Mukām Rāje Śivanābh kī', in F. S. Bajwa (ed.), *Papers on Guru Nanak* (Proceedings of the Punjab History Conference, Fourth Session, Paṭiālā, 1969), pp. 96–7, 101–2.

[4] *B40*, f. 162b.

[5] *B40*, ff. 167b, 173a. *BG* I:27.

A hymn was being sung and all were sitting enthralled. The rājā and the rānī then presented their petition, saying, 'You are the assembly of the Gurū and whatever is sought from you is granted. May it please you to hear our intercession so that the Gurū may grant a son.'

Those who were present in the congregation offered a prayer in order that the rājā's faith might remain unshaken. Then they assured him, 'The Gurū Bābā will grant you a son.'[1]

The passage is of interest for the picture of the *saṅgat* which it presents and also for the doctrine which it so explicitly declares. For the narrator of the janam-sākhī (and presumably for many others) the Gurū was believed to be present in the *saṅgat*, and decisions of the *saṅgat* were regarded as pronouncements of the Gurū himself. The doctrine to which this clearly points is that of the *Gurū Panth*, the Khālsā belief that decisions of the Khālsā brotherhood expressed the intention of the Gurū.[2] At the conclusion of the *B40 Janam-sākhī* the same conviction is expressed with even greater clarity.

The other members of the congregation (*saṅgat*) constitute the court of the perfect Gurū. And the abode of the perfect Gurū is in your midst.[3]

It was presumably this doctrine of the Gurū's presence which suggested the change from *dharamsālā* to *gurduārā* (gurdwara). No mention is made of the presence of the Granth Sahib, nor of any special authority accorded it as a book. The later doctrine of the *Gurū Granth* is still no more than implicit in the reverence attached to the hymns sung in the dharamsālā.

The theory of the Gurū's presence in the *saṅgat* is a relatively late development in the janam-sākhīs. A much earlier and less sophisticated doctrine of the Gurū's presence can be observed in declarations concerning the merit of *darśan*, or 'audience' with the Gurū. This belief, like the custom of gathering for *kīrtan*, is distinctively Sikh only in so far as it normally limits the benefits of *darśan* to the presence of Bābā Nānak. Even this limitation is not invariably applied. The *B40* sākhī 51 explicitly attaches the merit to a meeting with anyone who qualifies as a genuine sādhū.[4] This is, however, unusual. In other instances the benefit is reserved for those who appear before the Gurū. For these fortunate people the results can be dramatic. A leper is instantly cleansed of his disease as a result of *darśan*.[5] Lahaṇā is instantly converted and takes his place as the Gurū's successor.[6] A scurvy sinner is saved from perdition because the smoke from his funeral pyre is seen from afar by the Gurū.[7] Even the miserly Mūlā obtains salvation because at the point of death he was granted *darśan*.[8]

Another concept which obviously held much meaning for the seven-

[1] *B40*, ff. 196b–197a. For another description see *B40*, f. 102b.

[2] W. H. McLeod, *The Evolution of the Sikh Community* (Oxford, 1976), pp. 46–50.

[3] *B40*, f. 230b. Cf. also ff. 167b, 186a, 199a. All these examples come from the late *Narrative III* tradition.

[4] *B40*, ff. 203a–205a.

[5] *Pur JS*, p. 57.

[6] *B40*, f. 95a.

[7] *B40*, f. 192b. *Pur JS*, p. 32.

[8] *B40*, f. 101b.

teenth-century community was the merit of *sevā*, or 'service'. The content of this word has undergone some interesting changes within the community and its janam-sākhī meanings must be distinguished from later applications. In the janam-sākhīs it is sometimes used to designate worship or an act of devotion. Ignorant worshippers of the sun are said to have been performing *sevā*,[1] and the same word is used to describe Nānak's own devotional discipline.[2] The characteristic janam-sākhī usage is, however, a much more specific variety of 'service'. When the Sikhs are exhorted to provide *sevā* the duty to which they are directed is that of ministering to the needs of visiting sādhūs, particularly Nānak-panthī sādhūs. The supreme *sevā* is, of course, the welcome accorded to the Gurū himself. It is this which prompts the later development. After the janam-sākhī period *sevā* is increasingly directed to the abode of the Gurū, which means first the *saṅgat* and later still the gurdwara. Assistance in building a gurdwara, the maintenance or cleaning of an existing gurdwara, and donations in money, goods, or labour to a *laṅgar* (the gurdwara kitchen) are all common expressions of the modern concept of *sevā* within the Sikh community. Present indications suggest a further extension to cover humanitarian service to all mankind.

The janam-sākhī understanding of *sevā* marks a slight shift from Nānak's own meaning. A difference of a much more radical nature distinguishes the janam-sākhī understanding of *nām simaran* from the technique indicated by the Gurū. There is, it is true, more than one interpretation of 'remembering the divine Name' to be found in the janam-sākhīs, and a few narrators are evidently aware of Nānak's meaning. There is, however, a general insistence upon the sufficiency of mechanical repetition, the most common form being the chant 'gurū gurū'.[3] Nānak had sought to interiorize this devotional technique. The janam-sākhīs suggest a reversion to practices which he regarded as thoroughly inadequate as a means of salvation. Another evident deviation from the Gurū's teachings concerns the janam-sākhī concept of God. Whereas for Nānak God was strictly formless (*niraṅkār*, *nirguṇ*), the janam-sākhīs usually depict him in strongly anthropomorphic terms. Nānak's characteristic name for God, Niraṅkār, has passed into common usage, but its meaning has been so completely forgotten that a narrator can speak of Nānak actually seeing the Formless One with his eyes.[4]

Comments of this kind imply a general acceptance of such doctrines within the community. Elsewhere a narrator or commentator emphasizes an issue so deliberately that one must assume a background of contemporary controversy. The stress laid upon the importance of the daily ritual bathe suggests that the doctrine affirming it was either disputed or widely neglected during the seventeenth century.[5]

[1] *B40*, f. 171b.
[2] *B40*, f. 106a. Cf. also *AS*, p. 24.
[3] Other words or phrases recommended for repetition are *rām*, *vāh gurū*, *nānak*, and *vāh nānak*.
[4] *B40*, f. 123b.
[5] *B40*, f. 141a–b. *Pur JS*, p. 76. *AS*, pp. 61–2. *Mih JS* II.267, 383–98.

Although references to the ritual bathing obligation appear in several of the janam-sākhīs all do not treat the controversy with the same concern. In this, as with so many other issues, it is the *Miharbān* tradition which betrays the strongest interest.[1] This underlines the necessity of distinguishing the different janam-sākhī traditions and, wherever possible, of determining their particular interests, the date of their composition, and the dates of individual manuscripts. Conclusions are not always easy to reach, particularly in the case of the composite *Miharbān* tradition, but the effort should certainly be made. The historical value of a janam-sākhī is greatly enhanced when its distinctive point of view and period of compilation can be identified. For the same reason the geographical location of a janam-sākhī and information concerning its narrator or compiler can also be of considerable interest.

Whereas most janam-sākhīs raise serious problems of identification, one at least offers some explicit answers and where direct information is lacking it provides sufficient pointers in its text to suggest tentative answers. This is, once again, that most useful of all janam-sākhīs, the *B40* manuscript. The compiler of this janam-sākhī was a Khatrī, Dayā Rām Abrol by name, who completed his work in S. 1790 (A.D. 1733).[2] He does not name the geographical location of the *saṅgat* for which he prepared his janam-sākhī, but internal evidence points to the area of Gujranwālā or Gujrāt.[3] Several sources were used in compiling the collection, and most of these can be identified.[4] Two other members of the *saṅgat* are mentioned. These are the patron of the janam-sākhī, Saṅgū Mal, and its illustrator, Ālam Chand the Mason.[5]

The importance of this information and of the contents of the janam-sākhī becomes apparent when this 1733 janam-sākhī is set within its historical context, or, to be more accurate, within that historical context as generally understood today. Our twentieth-century understanding of the early and middle eighteenth-century Sikh community derives almost exclusively from Khālsā sources, most of them much later than the period which they purport to describe. These sources represent the history of the period as one of Mughal persecution and of Sikh triumph over the attempt to exterminate the community. Everything is related directly to the growing power of the Khālsā, which, with its distinctive doctrines and discipline, constitutes the orthodox Sikh Panth of today. This status it owed (according to later tradition) to the intention and explicit commandments of Gurū Gobind Siṅgh.

All this is completely absent from the *B40 Janam-sākhī*. It bears no evident mark of turbulent conditions, no mention of Bandā, no hint of persecution, no reference to the existence of the Khālsā or of either its

[1] See above, pp. 227–8.

[2] *B40*, ff. 84b, 230a–b.

[3] See *B40(Eng)* Introduction, pp. 19–25. The reference is to Gujrāt District in the Pañjāb, not to the Indian state of Gujarāt.

[4] See above, pp. 230–2.

[5] *B40*, ff. 84b, 231a. *B40(Eng)*, pp. 90–1.

military activities or its code of discipline. On the contrary, it suggests a *saṅgat* peaceably pursuing its devotional ideals with no evident awareness that the Khālsā brotherhood even exists. There is no evidence of a doctrine of the scriptural Gurū, the name Siṅgh is nowhere mentioned, there are none of the characteristic Khālsā prohibitions (the *kurahit*), and at one point there is an unconcerned acceptance of the greatest of all Khālsā sins. Sākhī 13 relates how a poor Sikh cut his hair in order that he might sell it to buy food for Bābā Nānak.[1] The complete indifference shown towards this detail suggests that for this particular compiler and his *saṅgat* the issue could have been of no importance.

The obvious explanation is that the *saṅgat* for which the *B40 Janam-sākhi* was written must have represented the continuing 'religious' tradition of the Nānak-panth as opposed to the growing martial and political traditions of the Khālsā. For this *saṅgat* it was the religious message of *nām simaran* that mattered and questions of Sikh identity could still be answered by reference to the old ideal of direct allegiance to the first Gurū. The Jaṭ depilatory prohibition was of no concern, and other features of the Khālsā discipline which derived from Jaṭ custom or the struggle against Muslim invaders are likewise absent. Either they had not developed by 1733 or else they had not yet affected this *saṅgat* of Nānak-panthī Sikhs living, it seems, in a rural area near Gujranwālā or Gujrāt. The only issue which suggests a significant link with Khālsā doctrine is the stress which the *B40* compiler lays upon belief in the Gurū's mystical presence within the *saṅgat*.

Eventually Khālsā doctrine was to emerge as the sole orthodoxy and the normative means of determining Sikh social identity. Circumstances favoured the Khālsā ideal, and its later eighteenth-century growth increasingly reduced the 'religious' tradition to insignificance. The tradition has survived as the so-called *sahaj-dhārī* segment of Sikh society and it has always continued to command a substantial Khatrī following.[2] Its influence upon the later development of the Sikh community has, however, been far less than that of the dominant Khālsā. As the Khālsā rose to predominance it reinterpreted both doctrine and history in the light of its own struggles and ideals. The *B40 Janam-sākhī* reveals the continuing existence of other ideals and of earlier patterns of Sikh life and conduct during a period when the martial tradition is supposed to have been sovereign in the Panth. There can be no doubt that the Khālsā tradition was strongly in the ascendant by 1733, but clearly its dominance did not emerge with the speed or the completeness of later interpretations.

The *B40 Janam-sākhī* speaks with an unusual clarity. Others, though less explicit, do make their own distinctive contributions, particularly for the seventeenth-century period. Although gaps, large and tantalizing, must inevitably remain there is much to be learnt from the janam-sākhīs concerning the pre-Khālsā Sikh community of the seventeenth and early eighteenth centuries. This, and not their testimony to the historical Nānak, is the primary value of the janam-sākhīs as historical sources.

[1] *B40*, f. 49a. Cf. also f. 113a.

[2] *GTC* ii. 507.

4. *THE JANAM-SĀKHĪS AS SOURCES FOR THE WIDER HISTORY OF THE PAÑJĀB*

Although the principal yield of the janam-sākhīs must be in terms of distinctively Sikh history their value is by no means limited to the community and its interests. The narrators never divorce themselves from their rural context and as a result there are recurrent references to the village community and its way of life. In some instances such features are directly described as settings for anecdotes or as essential elements in a narrative; elsewhere they appear as aspects of the imagery which rural narrators inevitably use. The fact that these features are recorded unconsciously adds considerably to their value. There could be no possible reason for misrepresentation on such points, for any failure to accord with the experience and understanding of the narrator's audience would merely defeat the purpose of his anecdotes. In the janam-sākhīs rural Pañjāb speaks with an authentic voice, and although they rarely tell us more than a small part of what we should like to know the janam-sākhīs do nevertheless provide a valuable supplement to the Persian chronicles and European reports of the same period.

The range of possibilities is wide, and different interests will extract different items from the janam-sākhī material. Only two brief examples will be offered here, examples which illustrate both the usefulness of the janam-sākhī contribution and its fragmentary nature. In the *Purātan* version of 'The Rich Man's Pennants' the central figure, Dūnī Chand, is described as a Khatrī of substantial wealth.[1] From a narrowly economic point of view the interesting feature of this anecdote is the use which Dūnī Chand makes of his wealth. It will be observed that he does two things. Much of it he spends on ostentatious ceremony (a large *śrāddh* feast) and the remainder he hoards as treasure. Such observations do not provide any final solution to the question of bullion disposal, but they do provide a glimpse of one seventeenth-century Pañjābī's views on the use of surplus wealth.[2]

The second example is to be found in the *B40* sākhī describing the death of Nānak, a portion of the janam-sākhī which consists of seventeenth-century material. Many years ago Moreland, while assuming the existence of landless labourers during the sixteenth century, acknowledged his inability to find any examples of such a class in the literature of the period.[3] Bābā Kamalā who served precisely this function[4] would not have provided a complete answer to Moreland's problem, but had this reference been known to him he could hardly have overlooked it.

It is generally in this circumstantial manner that the janam-sākhīs yield

[1] *Pur JS*, pp. 70–1. See above, p. 126.

[2] For a more detailed discussion of this and other mercantile issues arising from janam-sākhī references see W. H. McLeod, 'Trade and Investment in Sixteenth and Seventeenth-Century Panjab', in Harbans Singh and N. G. Barrier (ed.), *Essays in Honour of Dr Gaṇḍā Singh* (Paṭiālā, 1976), pp. 81–91.

[3] W. H. Moreland, *India at the Death of Akbar* (London, 1920), p. 112.

[4] *B40*, f. 221a.

their significant information concerning the wider life of seventeenth-century rural Pañjāb. When Nānak sets out on a minor trading enterprise it is the setting of the anecdote which refers the reader to issues beyond the essentially hagiographic interests of the narrator.[1] The story of the indigent Sikh who cut his hair briefly describes cooking procedures,[2] and a later discourse concerning true purity refers to the ritual purity of the Hindu cooking-square.[3] A declaration of Nānak's spiritual supremacy prompts a list of contemporary religious panths,[4] and an esoteric discourse on true renunciation provides an inventory of articles carried by a faqīr.[5] In some instances the value of a testimony lies in its failure to mention particular details, as for example the absence of references to irrigation. Elsewhere an absence noted by a narrator can be converted into a positive statement by the reader. When Chatur Dās, the paṇḍit of Banāras, comments on what Nānak is *not* wearing he thereby supplies a list of what a conventional Vaiṣṇava *bhagat* might be expected to wear.[6]

To many this variety of information may seem a poor return for the labour which is required in order to extract it. Much will depend on one's view of what is important in history. If the historian's interest is to be confined to dates, chronologies, and the mighty event then the janam-sākhīs have little to offer. The Persian courtly chronicles will be much better suited to his purposes. If, on the other hand, significance is to be found rather in the unspectacular life of the people of any particular place over any particular period of time, then there is much to be derived from the janam-sākhī testimony. Any significance of this kind will be considerably enhanced when a clear connection can be traced between an unspectacular past and living issues in the present. This certainly applies in the case of the janam-sākhīs. For any understanding of the modern Sikh community a knowledge of both Khālsā and pre-Khālsā Sikh history is vital.

1 *Bālā JS*, p. 16.
2 *B40*, f. 49a.
3 *B40*, f. 80a–b. See also *Pur JS*, p. 72.
4 *B40*, f. 106a. See also *Mih JS* II. 301.
5 *B40*, ff. 205b–207b.
6 *Pur JS*, p. 26.

15
THE JANAM-SĀKHĪS IN PAÑJĀBĪ LITERATURE

ALTHOUGH this examination of the janam-sākhīs is not intended to be a literary study it would be inappropriate to conclude it without some brief mention of their considerable importance in the history of Pañjābī literature. Their significance in this respect is twofold. The janam-sākhīs are important as the first examples of sustained Pañjābī prose, and in a more general sense they have continued to exercise a perceptible influence upon the style and imagery of all later generations of Pañjābī writers.

Pañjābī literature has, like most literature in South Asia, been predominantly poetic. It reached an early climax in the supremely beautiful compositions of Gurū Nānak and has since produced a steady stream of notable works. Prominent amongst these are the hymns of some of the later Gurūs (particularly the *Sukhmanī* of Gurū Arjan[1]) and the works of Pañjābī Sūfīs. The more celebrated amongst the latter include Shāh Husain (1539–93), Bulhe Shāh (1680–1758), and Hāsham Shah (1735–1823). The song cycles of *Hīr Rāñjhā*, *Sassī Punnū*, *Mirzā Sāhibān*, and *Sohṇī Mehivāl*, which have for centuries held a place of particular affection in the Pañjābī heart, are merely the most famous of a substantial corpus of poetic folk literature. This poetic impulse continues to the present day. Urdū is not the only language used at *mushā'aras* in the Pañjāb, and suggestions that Pañjābī is an uncouth language can only be made by those who have no knowledge of its literature.

Prose has been a less important part of this literature and with only one significant exception did not achieve widespread popularity as a literary form until the twentieth century. The single exception was the janam-sākhī. Pañjābī prose literature was inaugurated by the earliest janam-sākhīs and sustained by later representatives of the form for a period of almost three centuries. Today it has yielded this primacy, but it has done so to a literary form which is in some measure its descendant. The virile Pañjābī short story traces its antecedents to the janam-sākhī anecdote as well as to more obvious western models.[2]

It is not surprising that a hagiographic tradition should emerge as the first important contribution to Pañjābī prose. Early prose is commonly derived direct from a dominant oral tradition; and hagiography, which gives expression to an inevitable impulse, is better suited to prose anecdotes

[1] *AG*, pp. 262–96.

[2] Swinder Singh Uppal, *Panjabi Short Story: Its Origin and Development* (New Delhi, 1966), pp. 171, 186–7.

than to verse. Other Indian vernaculars have produced the same pattern, and the Pañjābī example shares most of the features observed in these other early representatives of regional prose traditions.[1] Although it is not true to claim that the janam-sākhī narrative style 'reads like poetry in bad prose rendering',[2] one will certainly find in the earlier janam-sākhīs a predictable absence of developed sentence structure and repeated recourse to a limited range of stylistic conventions. Conjunctions are rarely used, and punctuation is either restricted to pairs of vertical strokes (*do ḍaṇḍe*) or completely omitted. Sentences frequently begin with the adverbial *tā(n)* or *tab* ('then') or with such expressions as *bābāji ākhiā* ('Bābājī said . . .'). Tenses are restricted in range, compound forms are rare, and even the future tense is sparingly used.

Later janam-sākhīs gradually improve their prose style, but the process is a slow one. Although the printed *Bālā* versions of the late nineteenth century are not the primitive products of the early seventeenth century it can scarcely be claimed that they represent a mature prose style. This does not emerge in the janam-sākhī literature until the twentieth-century appearance of Vīr Singh's *Srī Gurū Nānak Chamatkār*.[3] In Vīr Singh's work it emerges in a highly distinguished form, a testimony to the author's considerable literary skills as well as to his deep personal piety. His was the last important contribution to the form. Vīr Singh himself marks the first significant beginnings of the Pañjābī novel, and the growth of the Pañjābī short story followed soon after.

The well-springs have thus run dry and the flow of sākhīs has at last ceased. We still live, however, in a period of continuing influence. There must be very few Sikh children who do not know at least some of the more popular janam-sākhī anecdotes, and Pañjābīs of all generations can readily call to mind stories of the first Gurū which have been firmly implanted in their earliest memories. Although this influence must certainly diminish, it is inconceivable that it could ever be completely extinguished. Memories of Nānak are too intimately tied to janam-sākhī images and impressions for this to occur. To suggest that the legacy of the janam-sākhīs may eventually disappear would be to imply that the Pañjāb may one day forget Gurū Nānak.

[1] Ian Raeside, 'Early Prose Fiction in Marathi, 1828–85', in *Journal of Asian Studies*, vol. xxvii, no. 4 (August 1968), pp. 791–2.

[2] I. Serebryakov, *Punjabi Literature* (Moscow, 1968), p. 43.

[3] Two volumes, Amritsar, 1928 and 1933.

APPENDIX 1

THE CONTENTS OF THE EARLIEST BĀLĀ *VERSIONS*

It was noted in the section dealing with the *Bālā* janam-sākhīs that the first of the Gurmukhī printed editions (*Lithographed Edition A*) generally corresponds closely to the earliest of the extant manuscript versions (*Recension A*). It was also observed that some significant differences do occur. Because *Lithographed Edition A* has been used for most *Bālā* citations in this study it is important that these differences should be distinguished. Three general differences are the omission of all Hindālī references in the lithographed edition; its occasional use of the *Purātan* tradition as a substitute for *Bālā* material; and inevitably the addition of a small cluster of death sākhīs. Although the latter feature suggests an association with *Recension B*, a textual comparison will at once demonstrate that the bulk of the printed material has been taken from a *Recension A* manuscript. Specific differences involving more than isolated words and sentences are as follows.

1. 'Bābā Nānak's Visit to Nānakmatā', sākhī 23 of the printed edition,[1] does not appear in the manuscripts. The editor of the printed edition has interpolated it from a *Purātan* source.
2. Sākhī 25 of the printed edition follows the manuscript text for only a few lines and then takes up a *Purātan* text. This *Purātan* text continues through to the end of sākhī 28 of the printed edition, covering in the process the following anecdotes:
   25. The Country Ruled by Women
   26. The Encounter with Kaliyug
   27. The City of Insects
   28. The Meeting with Sheikh Farīd in the Land of Āsā.

   The actual break takes place on page 103 of the printed edition at the beginning of line 13, and with the opening of sākhī 29 ('The Meeting with Rājā Śivanābh') the printed text reverts to that of the manuscripts. The manuscripts have a more primitive version of 'The Country Ruled by Women' sākhī. They do not have versions of the other three interpolated sākhīs.
3. The editor of the printed edition has introduced the *Purātan* version of the anecdote 'Mecca: the moving *miharāb*' into the *Bālā* Mecca sākhī. The interpolation begins in line 6 of page 184 and concludes with line 20 of page 185. In the manuscripts this anecdote appears in the Medīnā sākhī, and is there repeated in its distinctive *Bālā* form by the printed edition.[2]
4. In the course of an encounter with Kabīr the manuscripts introduce references to a mysterious Jaṭ who is obviously Hindāl.[3] This passage has been omitted from the printed text.
5. Both texts have a discourse with Sheikh Sharaf, but the printed edition abandons the *Bālā* manuscript version and uses instead a radically different *Purātan* version.[4]
6. Immediately after its Sharaf discourse the manuscript version records the

[1] *Bālā JS*, pp. 99–101.
[2] *B41*, f. 122a. *Bālā JS*, p. 188.
[3] *B41*, ff. 142a–143a.
[4] *B41*, f. 187a–b. *Bālā JS*, sākhī 66, pp. 296–300.

Hindālī narrative which describes previous incarnations in the court of Janak and contrasts Ḥindāl's exalted status with the lowly position occupied by Nānak.[1] This theme is continued in a briefer passage which occurs shortly after the principal narrative.[2] Both passages have been omitted from the printed edition.

7. The manuscript version includes a lengthy discourse with various persons (Lālo, Gopīnāth, Hayat Khān, Ajittā, etc.) which the printed edition has omitted.[3]
8. Sākhīs 74 and 75 of the printed edition do not correspond to the two sākhīs which appear at this point in the manuscripts. In the manuscript version both sākhīs relate discourses with Jittā (i.e. Ajittā Randhāvā) in Pakho village, and the second makes an insulting reference to an alleged liaison between Nānak and the daughter of a Muslim Raṅghaṛ.[4] The printed edition substitutes the *Purātan* sākhīs 'The Proud Karoṛī Humbled' and 'The Kashmīrī Paṇḍit'.
9. The manuscript version includes two further Pakho discourses which the printed edition omits.[5] One is said to have been held with Mātā Choṇī and Mañjot; and the other with a Sindhī.
10. The two texts diverge at their conclusions, with the printed edition recording the *Recension B* death sākhīs.[6] The manuscripts are not all consistent at this point. In the India Office Library *B41* manuscript the conclusion consists of three brief sākhīs, one of which narrates the mischievous tale of how Bābā Nānak asked Aṅgad for his daughter.[7]

These variants must be borne in mind when using the table of contents set out below or when consulting the printed edition published by Hāfaz Qutub Dīn in 1871.[8] The table of contents includes both the manuscript *Recension A* sākhīs and also those of the *Lithographed Edition A* (the Hāfaz Qutub Dīn edition). The serial numbers in the first column are the sākhī numbers used by the editor of the Hāfaz Qutub Dīn edition. Those of the second column are the numbers attached to successive sākhīs in the 1658 Delhi manuscript.[9] The third column lists the relevant folio numbers of the India Office Library *B41* manuscript. This latter manuscript, unlike the Delhi version, does not have a table of contents attached, and the numbering of sākhīs in the actual text is irregular.[10] For this reason each sākhī is identified by the folio on which it commences.

The titles used for individual sākhīs are not necessarily translations of Pañjābī titles appearing in either the manuscript or printed versions. Where a Pañjābī title conveys little or no impression of the actual content of a sākhī it has been replaced by a more helpful title.

Square brackets indicate sākhīs which appear only in the printed edition. They do not constitute a part of the authentic *Bālā* tradition and should not be regarded as such. The absence of a number in the first column indicates material which is present in the manuscripts but absent from the printed edition. This material

[1] *B41*, ff. 187b–190a. [2] *B41*, ff. 192b–193a. [3] *B41*, ff. 198a–205a.
[4] *B41*, ff. 214b–219b. Cf. above, p. 214n. [5] *B41*, ff. 228b–231b.
[6] *Bālā JS*, p. 384 (from line 12). [7] *B41*, ff. 250b–252b.
[8] The sākhī numbers are those used in the actual text, not those given in the book's table of contents. Numbers 60–6, as recorded in the table of contents, misdirect the reader.
[9] The table of contents appended to this manuscript was copied by Dr. Rattan Singh Jaggī of Paṭiālā and reproduced by Professor Piār Singh as an appendix to his doctoral thesis 'A Critical Survey of Panjabi Prose in the Seventeenth Century' (Panjab University, Chaṇḍīgaṛh, 1968), pp. 300–3.
[10] In so far as it retains consistency it agrees with the 1658 Delhi manuscript.

must be treated as a part of the authentic *Bālā* tradition. The absence of a figure from the second column does not, however, mean that the relevant sākhī is necessarily missing from the 1658 manuscript. This should be assumed only when the entry is bracketed. In some instances the 1658 manuscript has amalgamated sākhīs which appear separately in the printed edition, and at the very beginning of its table of contents the numbering is confused. It has also omitted number 43 by mistake.

Bālā *JS*	1658 MS	IOL MS B41	*Sākhī title*
1	1	1a	Prologue: the search for the *janam-patrī*
2	2a	4b	The Birth of Bābā Nānak
3	2b	6b	Instruction by the Paṇḍit
4		9a	Grazing the Buffaloes: the Tree's Stationary Shadow
4	3a	9a	The Cobra's Hood
5	3b	9b	Sowing the Field
6	4	10b	*Kharā Saudā*, the Good Bargain
7	5a	15a	The Marriage of Jai Rām and Nānakī
8	5b	17a	A Meeting with an Ascetic
9	6a	18a	Sultānpur
10	6b	19a	Employment in Daulat Khān's Commissariat
11	7	24a	Betrothal
12	8	29b	The Marriage of Nānak
13	9	35b	The Birth of Nānak's children
14	10	37a	An Encounter with Sāmā Paṇḍit
15	11–12	38a	Mūlā Choṇā appeals to Daulat Khān: discourse with the Qāzī
16	13	42b	Departure from Sultānpur
17	14	48a	Mardānā meets Firandā the Minstrel
18	15	49b	Bābā Nānak meets Firandā
19	16	55b	Bābā Nānak visits Lālo the Carpenter
20	17	59b	Malak Bhāgo's feast
21	18	61a	Discourse with Malak Bhāgo
22	19	69a	Return to Talvaṇḍī: Discourse with parents and Rāi Bulār
[23			Nānakmatā]
24	20	70a	Visit to Dacca in Bengal: Mardānā eats the forbidden fruit
[25	20	70b	The Country Ruled by Women] (MSS and printed edition differ)
[26			The Encounter with Kaliyug]
[27			The City of Insects]
[28			The Meeting with Sheikh Farīd in the Land of Āsā]
29	21	71b	Rājā Śivanābh
30	22	74a	The Monster's Cauldron
31	23	76b	Sālas Rāi the Jeweller
32	24	84a	A Monster Fish Redeemed
33	25	86a	Bābā Nānak's Meeting with Kāl and Nārad
34	26	88a	Discourse with Rājā Sudhar Saiṇ, Indar Saiṇ, and Jhaṇḍā the Carpenter in the Land of Biśahar
35	27	100b	Discourse with Rājā Madhar Bain on the Island of Silmilā

Bālā *JS*	1658 MS	IOL MS B41	*Sākhī title*
36	28	104a	Discourse with Rājā Devalūt and demons
37	29	108a	Discourse with Rājā Tīkhaṇ Vaiṇ and Jungle Men (*banmānus*)
38	30	109a	Discourse with Rājā Kaval Nain in Suvaranpur
39	31	119a	Mecca [The moving *miharāb*]
40	32	121b	Medīnā: the moving tomb
41	33	125b	Meeting with Nānakī in Sultānpur
42		127a	Mardānā drinks nectar (*ras*) in the Land of Mārūfar
43	34	128b	Mount Sirdhār in Himāchal: discourse with Gorakhnāth
44		131b	Mount Ūnā: discourse with Machhendranāth and Bharatharī
45		135a	Discourse with Bhaṅgarnāth
46		135b	Mount Kūnā: discourse with Kanīfā, Hanīfā, Gopīchand, etc.
47		143a	Mount Mīnā: discourse with Saṅgharnāth, Maṅgalnāth, etc.
48		148b	Mount Sumeru: discourse with Gorakhnāth
49	35	160a	Mount Byār: discourse with Datātre
50	36	162b	Mount Alalāchīn
51	37	163b	Discourse with Prahalād
52	38	166a	Mount Kailāś: discourse with Dhrū
53	39	166b	Discourse with Dhrū (contd.). Mount Akhand (the Topless Mountain): discourse with God and Kabīr
54	40	168a	Mount Kalkā: discourse with Mardānā
55	41	169a	Mount Sīlā: ambrosia
56	42	170b	Mount Uhār: discourse with Kalyān
57	44	173a	Mount Ikhan: discourse with Rājā Janak
58	45	174a	Discourse with Rakhīsar
59	46	175a	Mount Ulkā. Bābā Nānak proceeds to Khuramā City: death and cremation of Mardānā
60	47	177b	Rāmeśvaram: discourse with Gorakhnāth and Siddhs
61	48	181a	Achal Baṭālā: discourse with Gorakhnāth and Bharatharī
62	49	182a	Return to Talvaṇḍī: discourse with Mardānā's son Śahzādā at Chandar Bhān Sandhū's well
63	50	183a	Sajjaṇ the criminal Vaiṣṇava
64	51	186a	Śahzādā visits his father's *samādhi* in Khuramā
65	52	187a	Qandahār: discourse with Yār Alī
[66			Pāṇīpat: discourse with Sheikh Sharaf]
	53	187a	Discourse with Sheikh Sharaf Paṭhān of Bidar
	54	187b	Discourse with Dīnā Nāth Dayāl
67	55	190a	Discourse with Valī Qandhārī and Sharaf Paṭhān
68	56	192b	Kābul: discourse with Mān Chand Khatrī (MSS only include further references to Dīnā Nāth and Valī Qandhārī.)
69	57	196a	Ṭillā: discourse with Bālgundāī
	58–9	198a	Discourse with Lālo, Gopīnāth, etc.

Bālā JS	1658 MS	IOL MS B41	*Sākhī title*
70	60	205a	Pakho: discourse with Mūlā Choṇā and Ajittā Randhāvā
71		206b	Visit to Kurukshetra
72	61	208a	A Khatrī defames Nānak before Ibrāhīm Lodī: hand-mills turn miraculously. Bābur's invasion and capture of Bābā Nānak
73	62	211a	Discourse with Bābur
[74			The Proud Karoṛī Humbled]
[75			The Kashmīrī Paṇḍit]
	63	214b	Pakho; discourse with Ajittā, Mūlā Choṇā, Chando, and Mātā Choṇī
	64	217a	Discourse with Ajittā in Pakho
76	65	219b	Discourse with Būṛā Randhāvā in Pakho
77	66	221b	Discourse with Sheikh Mālo Takhān in Pakho
78	67	223a	Discourse with Ubārā Khān
79	68	224a	Discourse with Ubārā Khān and Shāh Adarmān (Abdul Rahmān)
80	69	226a	Discourse with Shāh Adarmān
	70	228b	Pakho: Mātā Choṇī and Mañjot
		229a	Discourse with a Sindhī
81	70–4	231b	Visit to Uch: meeting with Sayyid Jalāl
82		235b	Bābā Nānak decides to visit Pāk Paṭṭan
83	75–6	235b	Discourse with Sheikh Braham
84	77	247a	Talvaṇḍī: discourse with Lālū
85	78	247a	Pakho: Bālā leaves Bābā Nānak and returns to Talvaṇḍī
86	79	247b	Discourse: Gurū Aṅgad and Bālā
[87			The annunciation of Bābā Nānak's death: Kamalā and the yogīs. Sidhāran]
[88			Discourse with God]
[89			Final preparations: the Death of Nānak]
[90			The Disappearance of Bābā Nānak's Body]

APPENDIX 2

CONTENTS OF THE PURĀTAN *JANAM-SĀKHĪS*

The *Hāfizābād Janam-sākhī* contains the sākhīs listed below. The serial numbers correspond to the numbering used by Vīr Singh in his *Purātan Janam-sākhī*. Lower-case letters indicate the separate anecdotes included in composite sākhīs. The *Colebrooke Janam-sākhī* corresponds exactly in terms of contents, except that it lacks numbers 35b, 40, and 41, and includes number 29b which the *Hāfizābād* version lacks. Numbers 26 and 27, although recorded in the text as separate sākhīs, actually constitute a single anecdote. Most other janam-sākhīs which include both 8 and 9 incorporate them within a single Sultānpur sākhī.

1. The Birth of Nānak
2. Instruction by the Paṇḍit
3. Bābā Nānak's Betrothal and Marriage
4. The Ruined Crop Restored
5. The Tree's Stationary Shadow
6. The True Field and the True Merchandise
7. Bābā Nānak's Discourse with the Physician
8. The Departure for Sultānpur
9. Employment in Daulat Khān's Commissariat
10. Immersion in the River
11. Bābā Nānak's Discourse with Daulat Khān's Qāzī
12. Bābā Nānak's Travels in the Uninhabited Wilderness (I) (Mardānā commanded to throw offerings away)
13. Sajjaṇ the Robber
14. Discourse with Sheikh Sharaf of Pāṇīpat
15. Delhi: the Sultān's Elephant Resurrected
16. Sheikh Bajīd
17. Banāras: Discourse with Chatur Dās
18. Nānakmatā
19. The Death of the Trader's Infant Son
20. A Watchman receives Royal Authority
21. The Coal and the Thorn
22. The Robbers and the Funeral Pyre
23. The Country Ruled by Women
24. The Encounter with Kaliyug
25. The City of Insects
26. The Inhospitable Village Unmolested
27. The Hospitable Village Dispersed
28. A Discourse with Sheikh Farīd in the Land of Āsā (three anecdotes)
    a. Sheikh Farīd and the Gold Coins
    b. Sheikh Farīd and the Unbroken Skull
    c. Sheikh Farīd's Wooden Loaf

29a. Jhaṇḍā the Carpenter

29b. A Recitation of the *Jugāvalī* [*Colebrooke* only]

30. Bābā Nānak's Travels in the Uninhabited Wilderness (II) (Mardānā eats the forbidden fruit)
31. Bābā Nānak returns to Talvaṇḍī: Discourse with Mother and Father
32. Discourse with Sheikh Braham
33. The Leprous Faqīr
34. The Devotees of Kiṛīān Paṭhānān
35a. The Sack of Saidpur
35b. A Discourse with Bābur [*Hāfizābād* only]
36. A Discourse with Miān Miṭhā
37a. Dūnī Chand and the Wolf
37b. Dūnī Chand's Pennants
38. The Brāhmaṇ's Cooking-square
39. A Pious Boy
40. The Proud Karoṛī Humbled: the founding of Kartārpur [*Hāfizābād* only]
41. The Merchant and Rājā Śivanābh [*Hāfizābād* only]
42. The Meeting with Khwājā Khizar
43. Anabhī the Jain
44. The Monster's Cauldron
45. A Meeting with Makhdūm Bahāuddīn
46. A Discourse with Machhendranāth and Gorakhnāth
47. Bābā Nānak and Rājā Śivanābh
48. The Destruction of the Hospitable Carpenter's Hut
49. The Kashmīrī Paṇḍit
50a. A Discourse with Siddhs on Mount Sumeru
50b. A Discourse with Siddhs at Achal
51a. Mecca: Bābā Nānak's miraculous arrival
51b. Mecca: the moving *miharāb*
52. A Discourse with Siddhs at Gorakh-haṭaṛī
53a. The Meeting with Lahaṇā of Khaḍūr
53b. The Goddess Durgā serves Bābā Nānak
53c. Lahaṇā's clothes ruined
53d. Lahaṇā and the maidservant
54a. The testing of Aṅgad: the coins test
54b. Aṅgad commanded to eat a corpse
55. The Death of Bahāuddīn
56. The Installation of Gurū Aṅgad
57. The Death of Bābā Nānak

APPENDIX 3

CONTENTS OF THE ĀDI SĀKHĪS

This table of contents follows the text of the Motī Bāgh Palace manuscript of the *Ādi Sākhīs*, and Piār Singh's printed edition based on the Motī Bāgh text.

28b. Bābā Nānak summons the Gangā to thirsty Sikhs
29a. Bābā Nānak tests his Sikhs (contd.)
29b. The Story of Vasiṣṭ
29c. Bābā Nānak tests his Sikhs (contd.): Aṅgad commanded to eat a corpse
30a. The Installation of Gurū Aṅgad
30b. The Death of Bābā Nānak

APPENDIX 4

THE CONTENTS OF LDP 194

1. The Birth of Nānak
2. Instruction by the Paṇḍit
3. Bābā Nānak's Betrothal and Marriage
4. The Ruined Crop Restored
5. The Tree's Stationary Shadow
6. The True Field and the True Merchandise
7. Bābā Nānak's Discourse with the Physician
8. Sultānpur
9. Immersion in the River
10. Bābā Nānak's Discourse with Daulat Khān's Qāzī
11. Bābā Nānak's Travels in the Uninhabited Wilderness
12. Bābā Nānak Returns to Talvaṇḍī: Discourse with his Mother and Father
13. Discourse with Sheikh Braham
14. The Sack of Saidpur
15. A Discourse with Bābur
16. The Proud Karoṛī Humbled: the founding of Kartārpur
17. The Merchant and Rājā Śivanābh
18. Bābā Nānak and Rājā Śivanābh
19. The Encounter with Kaliyug
20. A Discourse with Siddhs at Achal

For a list of *B40* contents see above, pp. 230–2. The contents of the *Miharbān* and *Gyān-ratanāvalī* collections are much more extensive than those of the other major janam-sākhīs and for this reason are not listed in appendices. The more important anecdotes and discourses are included in the comparative table set out on pages 73–6 of *GNSR*. On pages 51–64 of the same work there appears a summary paraphrase of the contents of *Pothī Sach-Khaṇḍ* (the first and most important of the three sections of the extant *Miharbān Janam-sākhī*).

APPENDIX 5

ENGLISH TRANSLATIONS OF JANAM-SĀKHĪS

1. *The* Colebrooke Janam-sākhī

Trumpp included a translation of the *Colebrooke Janam-sākhī* in the introduction to his *The Ādi Granth* (pp. vii–xlv). Like his rendering of the opening rāgas of the Ādi Granth this translation contains numerous errors and is stilted to the point of being almost unreadable. Allowance must, however, be made for the pioneering nature of the work (Trumpp published it in 1877), and if one can look beyond the dullness of the work and its insulting references to the Sikh scriptures one must acknowledge that Trumpp was, for his period, an observer of considerable perception. The contents of the *Colebrooke Janam-sākhī* are listed in Appendix 2. For a note on the decision to commission the translation and also a brief biographical sketch of Trumpp see Robert Needham Cust, *Linguistic and Oriental Essays*, Third Series (London, 1891), pp. 262–5.

2. *Selections from the* Bālā *tradition*

(*a*) *E. Trumpp*, The Adi Granth, *pp. xlvi–lxxvi.*
Trumpp designated the *Colebrooke* manuscript *Janam-sakhi A*, and the *Bālā* manuscript catalogued as Panj. B41 in the India Office Library he labelled *Janam-sakhi B*. The latter he erroneously describes as an 'enlarged recompilation of A'.[1] His translation of the *Bālā* manuscript shares the characteristics noted above in the description of his *Colebrooke* translation. Of the sākhīs listed in Appendix 1 it covers only numbers 1–15, the opening sentences of 16, and 85–6. At its conclusion Trumpp adds a translation of the *Lithographed Edition A*[2] version of the death of Nānak.

(*b*) *Henry Court*, History of the Sikhs, *pp. 142–239.*
Court's *History of the Sikhs*, published in Lahore in 1888, is an English translation of Śardhā Rām's Pañjābī work *Sikhān de Rāj di Vikhiā* (*sic: Vithiā*), first published in Ludhiānā in 1884. Śardhā Rām had included a selection of twenty sākhīs from a late nineteenth-century *Bālā* version, and this selection Court reproduces in his translation. It comprises the following anecdotes. The titles are those used by Court, with explanatory comments added in parentheses where necessary to identify particular anecdotes.

1. Discourse with Gupāl the Teacher (Instruction by the Paṇḍit)
2. Discourse regarding the Brahmanical Thread
3. Discourse with the Physician
4. Discourse about the store (Talvaṇḍī, not Sultānpur)
5. Conversation regarding the betrothal of Nānak (Bābā Nānak's betrothal.

[1] Loc. cit., p. xlvi.

[2] See above, pp. 21, 271.

The departure for Sultānpur. Employment in Daulat Khān's commissariat. Nānak accused of embezzlement.)

6. The discourse regarding the marriage of Nānak
7. The discourse with Paṇḍat Sāmā
8. The discourse with Nawāb Daulat Khān (Bābā Nānak's discourse with Daulat Khān's qāzī)
9. The discourse with Rāi Bulhār
10. The discourse regarding the idol Sālig Rām
11. Conversation about the Ārtī Sohilā
12. The discourse in Sanglā with Rājā Siv Nāth
13. The discourse with Mīān Mitthā (Two parts, the first corresponding to *B40* sākhī 9, and the second to *Purātan* sākhī 36.)
14. The discourse with the Siddhs, or Hindū saints (The first part corresponds to *B40* sākhī 53. The second part set in an unnamed location over the sea.)
15. The discourse with the worshippers of Govind (in Ajudhiā)
16. The discourse with the Demon Kauṇḍā (the Monster's Cauldron)
17. The discourse with Sultān Hamīd Kārūn (Qārūn of Rūm)
18. The discourse with Paṇḍat Chattardās Banārsi
19. The discourse with Kālū (the Return to Talvaṇḍī: discourse with his mother and father)
20. The discourse with the Paṇḍats of Banāras (corresponding to a portion of *B40* sākhī 21)

3. *W. H. McLeod*, The B40 Janam-sākhī. An English translation with introduction and annotations of the India Office Library Gurmukhi manuscript Panj. B40, a janam-sākhī of Gurū Nānak compiled in A.D. 1733 by Dayā Rām Abrol. *Amritsar*, 1979.

4. *Bhāī Gurdās's* Vār I, *stanzas 23–45; and* Vār XI, *stanzas 13–14.*

An English translation of Bhāī Gurdās's account of Bābā Nānak has been published in *Sources on the Life and Teachings of Guru Nanak.*[1] Bhāī Gurdās's account includes, in full or in part, the following anecdotes. *Vār* I stanza numbers are given in parentheses.

1. Bābā Nānak's Austerities (24)
2. An Interview with God (24)
3. Bābā Nānak Visits the Places of Pilgrimage (25–6)
4. A Discourse with Siddhs on Mount Sumeru (28–31)
5. Mecca: the moving *miharāb* (32–4)
6. Bāghdād: Discourse with Dastgīr (35–6)
7. Visit to Medīnā (37. Brief reference only)
8. The Installation of Gurū Aṅgad (38, 44)
9. A Discourse with Siddhs at Achal (39–44)
10. Multān: the jasmine petal (44)

[1] *SLTGN(Eng)*, pp. 32–43. For the Pañjābī text see *SLTGN(Pbi)*, pp. 13–19.

5. *The* Mahimā Prakāś Vāratak

Sources on the Life and Teachings of Gurū Nānak also includes a translation of the portion of the *Mahimā Prakāś Vāratak* relating to Nānak.[1] The following anecdotes are to be found in it. Numbers in parentheses indicate the page-numbers of the English Section of *Sources on the Life and Teachings of Guru Nanak*.

1. The Birth of Nānak (59)
2. A Visit from Gorakhnāth (59–60)
3. The Naming of Nānak (60)
4a. Investiture with the Sacred Thread (60–1)
4b. Instruction by the Paṇḍit (61–2)
5. Instruction by the Mullah (62–3)
6. The Restored Field (63)
7. A field devastated by cattle and birds yields an abundant crop (63–4)
8. The Tree's Stationary Shadow (64)
9. Bābā Nāṇak's Discourse with the Physician (64–5)
10a. The True Field (65)
10b. Betrothal and Marriage (65)
11. *Kharā Saudā*: the Good Bargain (65–6)
12a. The Departure for Sultānpur (66)
12b. Employment in Daulat Khān's Commissariat (66–7)
12c. Nānak accused of embezzlement (67)
12d. Immersion in the River (67)
12e. Bābā Nāṇak's Discourse with Daulat Khān's Qāzī (67–8)
12f. Bābā Nāṇak's Travels: Mount Sumeru, Nānakmatā, and the return to Sultānpur. Discourse with Nānakī (68)
12g. Bābā Nāṇak Returns to Talvaṇḍī: Discourse with his Mother and Father (68–9)
12h. Discourse with Bābur in Kābul (69)
12i. Hasan Abdāl provides milk (69–70)
12j. Discourse with Sheikh Braham (70–2)
13a. Multān: the jasmine petal (72)
13b. Bābā Nānak opens a spring for Mardānā (72)
13c. Bābā Nānak's discourse with Sākhī Sarvār Sultān (72–3)
13d. Mecca: the moving *miharāb* (73–4)
13e. Khaḍūr: the devotion of Māī Birāī (74–5)
13f. Eminābād: Lālo and Malak Bhāgo (75–6)
13g. The Proud Karoṛī Humbled: the founding of Kartārpur (76–7)
13h. The Meeting with Lahaṇā (77–8)
13i. Lahaṇā's Clothes Ruined (78)
13j. The Birth of Lakhmī Dās and of Sirī Chand (78–9)
14a. The Loyal Fortitude of Aṅgad (79–80)
14b. Aṅgad shakes Sweets from a Tree (80)
15. Absolute loyalty: the hour of the night (80–1)
16a. The testing of Aṅgad: the coins test (81)
16b. Aṅgad commanded to eat a corpse (81–2)
17a. Aṅgad moves to Khaḍūr (82)
17b. The adoration of Māī Birāī (82)

[1] *SLTGN(Eng)*, pp. 59–87. For the Pañjābī text see *SLTGN(Pbi)*, pp. 32–46.

17c. Aṅgad's lost children: the return of Dāsū and Dātā (82–3)
17d. Perfect obedience: Aṅgad remains immobile for several years (83)
17e. Bābā Nānak reveals a well in Khaḍūr (83–4)
18. The Death of Bahāuddīn (84–5)
19. The Death of Bābā Nānak (85–7)

APPENDIX 6

HOLDINGS OF JANAM-SĀKHĪ MANUSCRIPTS

The principal library collections of manuscript janam-sākhīs within the Pañjāb are held by the following institutions:

1. The Sikh History Research Department of Khalsa College, Amritsar.
2. The Sikh Reference Library at the Golden Temple, Amritsar.
3. Bhāṣā Vibhāg, Paṭiālā (the Languages Department of the Pañjāb Government)
4. The Central Public Library, Paṭiālā.
5. Pañjab University, Chaṇḍīgaṛh.
6. The Pañjābī Sāhit Akādemī, Ludhiānā.

Important private collections are those of the former Mahārājā of Paṭiālā, Dr Gaṇḍā Singh of Paṭiālā, Professor Prītam Singh of Amritsar, and Sardār Shamsher Singh Ashok of Amritsar. Individual manuscripts are held by various families and institutions. For details of most manuscripts currently located in the Pañjāb see Shamsher Singh Ashok, *Pañjābī hath-likhatān dī sūchī* (Paṭiālā, 2 vols., 1961 and 1963, cited in footnotes as *PHLS*); Gaṇḍā Singh, *A Bibliography of the Punjab* (Paṭiālā, 1966); and Kirpāl Singh, *A Catalogue of Punjabi and Urdu Manuscripts in the Sikh History Research Department* (Amritsar, 1963).

The most significant of overseas collections is the India Office Library holding, a group of three manuscripts which owes its importance to the age and representative nature of its contents rather than to its size. For descriptions of its manuscripts Panj. B6, Panj. B40, and Panj. B41 see above, pp. 20, 23–5, 43. See also the introduction to *B40 (Eng)*; and C. Shackle, *Catalogue of the Panjabi and Sindhi Manuscripts in the India Office Library* (London, 1977), pp. 19–22. The smaller British Library holding merely duplicates a portion of the India Office Library collection. The libraries of the School of Oriental and African Studies in London and the University of Cambridge each possess one *Bālā* manuscript.

APPENDIX 7

THE ĀDI GRANTH

The structure of the Ādi Granth

One of the distinctive features of the Ādi Granth is the systematic order of its contents. A regular pattern is plainly evident throughout the volume and very few exceptions to this pattern can be found. In the case of the modern printed editions regularity is carried to the extent of maintaining a standard pagination. All editions have a total of 1,430 pages, and all correspond exactly in terms of the material printed on individual pages. The complete volume may be divided into the following primary categories:

A.	Introductory section	pp.	1–13
B.	The rāgas	pp.	14–1353
C.	Miscellaneous works	pp.	1353–1430

The first and third of these involve no further subdivisions, but within the second category individual works are recorded in accordance with a detailed system of classification.

Introductory section

The opening pages of the Ādi Granth record the following compositions:

1. The *Japjī* of Gurū Nānak, preceded by the *Mūl Mantra*[1] and ending with a stanza by Gurū Aṅgad. This work, which is regarded as an epitome of the teachings of Gurū Nānak, is customarily recited by devout Sikhs shortly after rising in the morning.[2]
2. *Sodar.* A collection of nine hymns, four of which are by Gurū Nānak, three by Gurū Rām Dās, and two by Gurū Arjan. The collection takes its name from the first word of the first hymn (a variant version of stanza 27 of *Japjī*). The nine hymns together constitute the greater portion of *Sodar Raharās*, a selection which is customarily sung at sunset.[3]
3. *Sohilā*, or *Kīrtan Sohilā*. A collection of five hymns, three of them by Gurū Nānak and one each by Gurū Rām Dās and Gurū Arjan. This selection is customarily sung immediately before retiring at night, and also at funerals.[4]

All the hymns which constitute *Sodar* and *Sohilā* are subsequently repeated under their appropriate rāgas (including the one which has already appeared as a stanza of *Japjī*). Their appearance at the beginning of the Ādi Granth suggests that they had already acquired a distinctive devotional or liturgical function by the time the original volume was compiled in A.D. 1603–4.

The rāgas

This section constitutes by far the greater portion of the Ādi Granth and it is within this section that we find the characteristic pattern of division and sub-division. The system of classification is as follows:

[1] See *B40(Eng)*, p. 3n.
[2] *Sikh Rahit Maryādā* (Amritsar, 1961), p. 10.
[3] Ibid., p. 11.
[4] Ibid., p. 11. *MK*, p. 173, App., p. 24.

1. The entire section is first classified according to rāga, or metre. The first of these, *Sirī Rāg*, begins on page 14 and continues to page 93. It is followed on page 94 by the rāga entitled *Mājh*, which in turn is followed by *Gauṛī* (pp. 151–346). Next comes *Āsa* (pp. 347–488), and in this manner the text continues through a total of thirty-one rāgas. The section finally terminates with the minor rāga *Jaijavantī* (pp. 1352–3).
2. Within each rāga there is a secondary classification, as follows:
   (a) *Chaupad*. Hymns by the Gurūs, each consisting of four short stanzas with refrain.
   (b) *Aṣṭapadī*. Hymns by the Gurūs, normally consisting of eight stanzas each (occasionally more), with refrain.
   (c) *Chhant* (*chhand*). Hymns by the Gurūs of variable length, commonly of four or six long stanzas.
   (d) Miscellaneous longer works by the Gurūs (e.g. Gurū Arjan's *Sukhmanī* in *Gauṛī* rāga; Gurū Nānak's *Siddh Goṣṭ* in *Rāmkalī* rāga).
   (e) *Vār*. The *vār* of the Ādi Granth is a distinctive form, to be distinguished from the ode-form to which the name is normally applied.[1] The framework of an Ādi Granth *vār* is constituted by a series of stanzas (*pauṛī*). Each *pauṛī* is preceded by a number of couplets or subsidiary stanzas called *ślok* (shalok). With one exception[2] the *vārs* are all composite structures embodying selections from the works of the Gurūs. The *pauṛīs* of any particular *vār* will all be by one Gurū, but the shaloks may be by any of the Gurūs. Of all the *vārs* the most famous is *Vār Āsā*, the *pauṛīs* of which are by Gurū Nānak.[3]
   (f) *Bhagat bāṇī*, 'the works of the bhagats', i.e. the compositions of religious poets whose doctrines accorded with those of the Gurūs. Particular prominence has been given to Kabīr, Nāmdev, and Ravidās (Raidās).
3. Yet another classification is made within the *chaupads*, *aṣṭapadīs*, and *chhants*. Each of these three groupings is itself divided according to author. First come the *chaupads* of Gurū Nānak, next those of Gurū Amar Dās, followed by those of Gurū Rām Dās, and finally those of Gurū Arjan.[4] These are followed by the *aṣṭapadīs* of Gurū Nānak, and in this manner the classification continues to the end of the *chhant* section. Each of the Gurūs is designated not by name but by the word *mahalā*, followed by the appropriate number. The formula *mahalā 1* denotes Gurū Nānak, *mahalā 3* denotes the third Gurū, Amar Dās, etc. The *śloks* of Gurū Aṅgad are distinguished in the same manner (i.e. with the formula *mahalā 2*).[5] The designation is often abbreviated to its initial letter (*M1* denoting Gurū

[1] I. Serebryakov, *Punjabi Literature* (Moscow, 1968), pp. 18–21.

[2] *Vār Rāmkalī* by Rāi Balvaṇḍ and Sattā the Ḍūm, *AG*, pp. 966–8. This *vār*, a panegyric of the Gurūs by two of their followers, is simply a series of stanzas with no shaloks. It represents the standard ode-form, not the composite form found elsewhere in the Ādi Granth.

[3] *Vār Āsā*, or *Āsā dī Vār*, *AG*, pp. 463–75, has acquired a liturgical function and is sung in gurdwaras during the early hours of the morning. It consists of twenty-four *pauṛīs*, each with attendant shaloks (normally two), and may be sung in full or in an abridged form. For the singing of the unabridged form a period of three hours is required.

[4] In the case of Gurū Aṅgad, the second Gurū, only shaloks have been recorded. A few compositions by the ninth Gurū, Tegh Bahādur, also appear, having been added later to the collection originally compiled by Gurū Arjan.

[5] See *B40(Eng)*, p. 3n.

Nānak, etc.) and is occasionally dropped altogether, leaving only the relevant number.

Miscellaneous works

The epilogue which follows the conclusion of the rāga section consists of a series of miscellaneous works. Prominent among these are a collection of *śloks* attributed to Sheikh Farīd, a similar collection attributed to Kabīr, and a collection of surplus *śloks* by the Gurūs for which no place could be found in the *vārs*.

In this unusually systematic manner the Ādi Granth was compiled. There are exceptions to the pattern, but they are few and unimportant.

Terminology relating to the Ādi Granth

The title *Ādi Granth* itself requires a brief note of explanation. *Granth* means simply 'book', and to this has been appended the adjective *ādi*, or 'first', to distinguish this *Granth* from the *Dasam Granth*, the 'Tenth Book'.[1] In Sikh usage the Ādi Granth is normally referred to as the *Gurū Granth Sāhib* (to which further honorifics may be added). This expresses the Sikh belief in the scripture as Gurū.[2] The contents of the scripture are commonly referred to as *bāṇī* ('utterance'), or as *gurbāṇī* ('the utterance of the Gurū').

Any individual hymn from the Ādi Granth (*chaupad*, *aṣṭapadī*, or *chhant*) is invariably called a *śabad*,[3] literally 'word'. The usage evidently derives from the weight of emphasis laid by Gurū Nānak and his successors upon the doctrine of the *Śabad*. According to the teachings of Nānak the *Śabad*, or divine Word, is the vehicle of communication between God and man.[4] The *bāṇī*, or 'utterance', of the enlightened *gurū* or *bhagat* embodies this divine Word, and the term used for the Word itself thus came to be applied to the composition which gave it expression.

The term is very extensively employed in the janam-sākhīs and in all later Sikh literature, and for this reason it has been given an anglicized form in this study of the janam-sākhīs. The word *śabad*, when used to denote a composition by Gurū Nānak, is rendered 'shabad'. For the same reason *ślok* has been rendered 'shalok'. The two forms 'shabad' and 'shalok' both approximate closely to Pañjābī pronunciation. (In speech, as in its written Gurmukhī form, Pañjābī normally separates conjuncts.) The third basic term, *pauṛī*, has been translated as 'stanza'.

[1] The appendage *dasam* is normally taken to refer to the belief that the contents of this later collection are all the works of the tenth Gurū, Gobind Siṅgh. It has, however, been suggested that it should properly be understood to mean 'one tenth', i.e. a tenth part of a much longer collection. Khushwant Singh, *A History of the Sikhs*, vol. i (London, 1963), p. 316.

[2] *GNSR*, p. 2.

[3] Hindī *śabda*. This particular usage corresponds to the Hindī term *pada*.

[4] *GNSR*, pp. 191–4.

APPENDIX 8

DATE CHART

INDIA (General)

1451 Accession of Bahlūl Lodī
1498 Arrival of Vasco da Gama

1526 Battle of Pāṇīpat Accession of Bābur
1556 Accession of Akbar

1605 Accession of Jahāngīr
1628 Accession of Shāhjahān
1659 Accession of Aurangzeb

1707 Death of Aurangzeb
1744–1749 First Anglo-French War
1757 Battle of Plassey
1784 Pitt's India Act

1828 Bentinck Governor-General

1848 Dalhousie Governor-General

1857 Sepoy Uprising

1885 Founding of Indian National Congress

1919 Government of India Act

THE PAÑJĀB

1469 Birth of Gurū Nānak

1520 Sack of Saidpur
1539 Death of Gurū Nānak

1603–1604	Compilation of the Ādi Granth
1606	Death of Gurū Arjan
1634	Gurū Hargobind's withdrawal to the Śivālik Hills
1675	Execution of Gurū Tegh Bahadur
1699	Founding of the Khālsā
1708	Death of Gurū Gobind Singh
1747–1769	Invasions of Ahmad Shāh Abdālī Rise of the Sikh *misls*
1799	Capture of Lahore by Rañjīt Singh
1839	Death of Rañjīt Singh
1845–1846	First Anglo-Sikh War
1848–1849	Second Anglo-Sikh War British annexation of the Pañjāb
1873	Singh Sabhā founded
	Gurdwara Reform Movement
1919	Jallianwālā Bāgh

JĀNAM-SĀKHĪS

	Development of *Narrative I* tradition
	Bhāī Gurdās's *Vārs*
	Period of *Purātan* and early *Miharbān* development
1658	Copying of earliest extant *Bālā* MS.
1701	Copying of earliest extant *Ādi Sākhīs* MSS.
	? *Gyān-ratanāvalī* development
1733	Copying of *B40 Janam-sākhī*
	Mahimā Prakāś Vāratak
1776	*Mahimā Prakāś Kavitā*
1823	Santokh Singh's *Nānak Prakāś*
1828	Copying of earliest extant *Miharbān* MS.
1870	First printed janam-sākhī (*Bālā*)
1877	Trumpp's *The Ādi Granth*

1885	Publication of *Colebrooke* and *Hāfizābād* texts
1909	Macauliffe's *The Sikh Religion*
1926	Vīr Singh's *Purātan Janam-sākhī*

SELECT BIBLIOGRAPHY

Janam-sākhīs: important manuscripts

Ādi Sākhīs manuscript in the Sikh Reference Library, Amritsar (MS no. S462), n.d.

Ādi Sākhīs manuscript in the library of Motī Bāgh Palace, Paṭiālā, dated S.1758 (A.D. 1701).

B40 Janam-sākhī. India Office Library MS Panj. B40, dated S. 1790 (A.D. 1733). Photocopies held by Languages Department of the Punjab, Paṭiālā (MS no. 474), Punjab Archives, Paṭiālā (microfilm), and Baring Union Christian College, Baṭālā (xerox).

Bālā Recension A. Manuscript dated S. 1715 (A.D. 1658) in the possession of Shri P. N. Kapoor of Delhi. Photocopies held by Department of Punjab Historical Studies, Punjabi University, Paṭiālā; and by the Library of Gurū Nānak Dev University, Amritsar.

Bālā Recension A. India Office Library MS. Panj. B41, dated A.D. 1775.

Bālā Recension A. British Library manuscript Or. 2754. 1, n.d.

Bālā Recension B. London School of Oriental and African Studies manuscript no. 104975, dated S. 1912 (A.D. 1855).

Bālā Recension B. Cambridge University Library manuscript no. Add. 921, dated S. 1922 (A.D. 1865).

Colebrooke Janam-sākhī (*Purātan* tradition). India Office Library manuscript Panj. B6, n.d. Also known as the *Valāit-vālī Janam-sākhī*.

Gyān-ratanāvalī. Three manuscripts in the possession of Professor Prītam Singh of Amritsar, dated S. 1778 (A.D. 1721), S. 1883 (A.D. 1826), and S. 1927 (A.D. 1870).

Gyān-ratanāvalī. MSS. nos. SHR 2300C and SHR 1440 in the Sikh History Research Department of Khālsā College, Amritsar, dated S. 1891 (A.D. 1834) and S. 1895 (A.D. 1838).

LDP 194. Manuscript no. 194 in the Library of the Languages Department of the Punjab, Paṭiālā, n.d.

Miharbān Janam-sākhī. MS. no. SHR 427 of the Sikh History Research Department of Khālsā College, Amritsar, dated S. 1885 (A.D. 1828). Contains first three of original total of six *pothīs*.

Miharbān Janam-sākhī. MS. no. SHR 2190 of the Sikh History Research Department of Khālsā College, Amritsar, n.d. Substantial fragment of first *pothī*.

Prāchīn Janam-sākhī (expanded *Purātan*). Manuscript in the possession of S. Sevā Singh Sevak of Tarn Tāran, n.d.

Purātan janam-sākhī (*Hāfizābād* text). MS. no. 2913 of the Central Public Library, Paṭiālā, dated S. 1747 (A.D. 1690).

Purātan janam-sākhī (*Hāfizābād* text). MS. no. SHR 2310A in the Sikh History Research Department of Khālsā College, Amritsar, dated S. 1829 (A.D. 1772).

Purātan janam-sākhī (*Colebrooke/Hāfizābād* text). Manuscript dated S. 1814 (A.D. 1757) in the possession of S. Kuldīp Singh Bedī of Baṭālā.

For additional janam-sākhī manuscripts see Shamsher Singh Ashok, *Pañjābī hath-likhatān dī sūchī*, 2 vols. (Paṭiālā, 1961 and 1963).

Janam-sākhīs: published texts

A *Bālā* janam-sākhī lithographed by Hāfaz Qutub Dīn, Lahore, S. 1928 (A.D. 1871).

A *Bālā* janam-sākhī lithographed by Mālik Dīvān Būṭā Singh, Lahore, S. 1928 (A.D. 1871).

A *Bālā* janam-sākhī lithographed by Maulvī Maibūb Ahmad, Lahore, A.D. 1890.

Gyān-ratanāvalī (*Manī Singh Janam-sākhī*), lithographed by Charāg Dīn and Sarāj Dīn, Lahore, A.D. 1891.

Gyān-ratanāvalī, lithographed by Lālā Mehar Chand, Bombay, A.D. 1892.

Gyān-ratanāvalī, lithographed by the Sanskrit Book Depot, Lahore, A.D. 1894.

Gyān-ratanāvalī, lithographed by Gulāb Singh and Sons, Lahore, A.D. 1908.

GURDĀS BHALLĀ (Bhāī Gurdās), *Vārān Bhāī Gurdās*, ed. Hazārā Singh and Vīr Singh, Amritsar, 1962.

KIRPĀL SINGH (ed.), *Janam sākhī paramparā*. Texts of the *Colebrooke Janam-sākhī*, the first three *pothīs* of the *Miharbān Janam-sākhī*, *Bālā* Recension A, and the 1892 Bombay edition of the *Gyān-ratanāvalī*. Paṭiālā, 1969.

LAHORE SINGH SABHĀ, lithographed edition of the *Colebrooke Janam-sākhī*, Lahore, 1884.

MACAULIFFE, M. A. (ed.), *Janam Sākhī Bābe Nānak Jī kī*, Rāwalpiṇḍī, 1885. (Macauliffe's edition of the *Hāfizābād Janam-sākhī*.)

Mahimā Prakāś Vāratak. Portion of text dealing with Gurū Nānak in Gaṇḍā Singh (ed.), *Sources on the Life and Teachings of Gurū Nānak* (Pañjābī section, pp. 32–46), Paṭiālā, 1969.

MIHARBĀN JĪ SOḌHĪ, *Janam-sākhī Srī Gurū Nānak Dev Jī*. Vol. 1, ed. Kirpāl Singh and Shamsher Singh Ashok, Amritsar, 1962, Vol. 2, ed. Prakāś Singh, Amritsar, 1969.

Photozincograph Facsimile of the *Colebrooke Janam-sākhī*, Dehrā Dūn, 1885.

PIĀR SINGH (ed.), *Janam Sākhī Srī Gurū Nānak Dev Jī*, Amritsar, 1974. (India Office Library manuscript Panj. B40).

PIĀR SINGH (ed.), *Śambhū Nāth vālī janam patrī Bābe Nānak jī kī prasidh nān Ādi Sākhīān*, Paṭiālā, 1969. (The *Ādi Sākhīs*.)

Pothī janam-sākhī, a version of the *Bālā* tradition lithographed in the Arabic script by Har Sukh Rai and Gobind Sahai, owners of the Ganesh Prakash Press, Lahore, 1870.

SARŪP DĀS BHALLĀ, *Gurū Nānak Mahimā* and *Mahimā Prakāś*, ed. Shamsher Singh Ashok and Gobind Singh Lāmbā, Paṭiālā, 1970 and 1971. (A text of the *Mahimā Prakāś Kavitā*.)

SEVĀ SINGH SEVAK (ed.), *Prāchīn Janam Sākhī*, Jalandhar, 1969. (A *Purātan* text.)

SHAMSHER SINGH ASHOK (ed.), *Purātan Janam-sākhī Srī Gurū Nānak Dev Jī kī*, Amritsar, 1969. (A conflation of one *Purātan* and two *Ādi Sākhīs* MSS.)

VĪR SINGH (ed.), *Purātan Janam-sākhī*, Amritsar, several editions.

English translations of janam-sākhīs

The *Colebrooke Janam-sākhī*

Trumpp, E., *The Ādi Granth*, London, 1877, pp. vii–xlv.

Much of the first volume of M. A. Macauliffe's *The Sikh Religion* (Oxford, 1909) consists of a free translation of the *Colebrooke* and *Hāfizābād* janam-sākhīs.

Selections from the *Bālā* tradition

Trumpp, E., op. cit., pp. xlvi–lxxvi.

Court, H., *History of the Sikhs*, Lahore, 1888, pp. 142–239.

W. H. McLeod, *The B40 Janam-sākhī*, Amritsar, 1979.

Gurdās Bhallā (Bhāī Gurdās)

Gaṇḍā Singh (ed.), *Sources on the Life and Teachings of Gurū Nānak*, Paṭiālā, 1969, English section, pp. 33–4. (A translation by W. H. McLeod of *Vār* I:23–45 and *Vār* XI:13–14.)

Mahimā Prakāś Vāratak

Gaṇḍā Singh (ed.), op. cit., English section, pp. 59–87. (A translation by W. H. McLeod of the portion of the *Mahimā Prakāś Vāratak* relating to Gurū Nānak.)

Other works

FAUJĀ SIṆGH and A. C. ARORĀ (ed.), *Papers on Guru Nanak*. Proceedings of the Punjab History Conference (Fourth Session, 1969), Paṭiālā, 1970. (Eng).

GURBACHAN KAUR, 'Janam Sākhī of Bhāī Bālā: authentic text and its critical editing'. Unpub. doctoral thesis, Gurū Nānak Dev University, Amritsar, 1978. (Pbī.)

HANS, S. S., 'The Mehrban *Janam-Sakhi*', in J. S. Grewal (ed.), *Studies in Local and Regional History*. Amritsar, 1974, pp. 86–108. (Eng.)

HARBANS SINGH, *Guru Nanak and the Origins of the Sikh Faith*. Bombay, 1969. (Eng.)

JAGJĪT SINGH, *Ādhunik Janam Sākhī*. Ludhiānā, 1970. (Pbī.)

JAGJĪT SINGH, *Ādi Sākhiān dā Ālochanātamak Adhiain*. Ludhiānā, 1973. (Pbī).

JAGJĪT SINGH, *Janam-sākhiān Srī Gurū Nānak Dev Jī dā Tārakik Adhiain*. Ludhiānā, 1970. (Pbī.)

KIRPĀL SINGH KOMAL (ed.), *Janam-sākhī Adhiain*. Farīdkoṭ, 1970. (Pbī.)

MACAULIFFE, M. A., *The Sikh Religion*, Vol. I. Oxford, 1909. (Eng.)

MCLEOD, W. H., *The Evolution of the Sikh Community*. Delhi, 1975; Oxford, 1976. (Eng.)

MCLEOD, W. H., *Gurū Nānak and the Sikh Religion*. Oxford, 1968; Delhi, 1976. (Eng.)

MCLEOD, W. H., 'Procedures in analysing the sources for the life of Gurū Nānak', in *Journal of Indian History*, Vol. XLV, Part I (April 1967), pp. 207–27. (Eng.)

MOHAN SINGH, *A History of Panjabi Literature*. Amritsar, 1956. (Eng.)

PIĀR SINGH, 'A Critical Survey of Panjabi Prose in the Seventeenth Century'. Unpub. doctoral thesis, Pañjāb University, Chaṇḍīgaṛh, 1968. (Eng.)

PIĀR SINGH *et al.*, *Gurū Nānak sambandhī tin khoj-pattar*. Paṭiālā, 1970. (Pbī.)

RATTAN SINGH JAGGĪ, *Dasam Granth dā Paurāṇik Adhiain*. Jalandhar, 1965. (Pbī.)

RATTAN SINGH JAGGĪ, *Janam Sākhī Bhāī Bālā*. 26 pp. Amritsar, 1974. (Pbī.)

GLOSSARY

Pañjābī forms are given in all instances. Corresponding Hindī forms are in some instances given in parentheses.

akhāṛā: 'arena', temple or monastery of the Udāsī panth.
āsaṇ: yogic posture; abode of yogīs.
aṣṭapadī: a hymn of eight (occasionally more) stanzas.
Bābā: 'Father', a term of respect applied to holy men.
baḍā: big, great.
bairāgī: Hindu renunciant.
bāṇī (*vāṇī*): speech; the utterances of the Gurūs and bhagats (q.v.) recorded in the Ādi Granth. The amplified form *gurbāṇī* is commonly used.
bhagat (*bhakta*): an exponent of *bhagti* (*bhakti*) (q.v.); a devotee.
bhagtī (*bhakti*): belief in, and adoration of, a personal God.
bhallā: good, noble.
chaudharī: head man of a village or caste grouping.
dān: gift, charity, alms.
darśan: view, vision; audience with a person of regal or spiritual stature, visit to a holy shrine or object; the six systems of brahmanical philosophy.
darveś: dervish, a Muslim mendicant (esp. Sūfī).
dharamsālā: in early Sikh usage a room or building used for devotional singing and prayer.
digvijaya: the conquest of territories in all four directions, an achievement imputed to particularly powerful kings or (as spiritual conquest) to a powerful preacher.
faqīr: 'poor man', Muslim renunciant; loosely used to designate Sūfīs and also non-Muslim renunciants.
goṣṭ, goṣṭi: discourse.
gurbāṇī: 'the utterance of the Gurū', cf. *bāṇī* (q.v.).
gurduārā: gurdwara, Sikh temple.
Gurmukhī: the script used for writing Pañjābī.
gurū: a spiritual preceptor, usually a person but sometimes understood as the divine inner voice.
halāl: 'lawful', in accordance with Muslim prescriptions.
haṭha-yoga: 'yoga of force', a variety of yoga requiring physical postures and processes of extreme difficulty.
iśnān: bathing.
jathā: military detachment.
kabitt: a poetic metre.
karoṛī: a high-ranking revenue collector of the Mughal period.
kathā: narrative; oral exposition.
Khālsā; the Sikh order, brotherhood, instituted in 1699 by Gurū Gobind Singh.
khānqāh: residence of a Sūfī pīr, with buildings for disciples, charitable purposes, etc.
kīrtan: corporate singing of hymns.
kos, koh (*krośa*): a linear measure varying from one to two miles in different parts of India. In the Pañjāb it has generally been computed as the equivalent of one-and-a-half miles.

kuṛam: the relationship subsisting between the fathers of a married couple. A husband's father is the *kuṛam* of the husband's father-in-law and vice versa.

langoṭ-band: celibate ascetic.

loṭā: small, round, metal pot.

Mahalā: a code-word used to distinguish works by different Gurūs in the Ādi Granth. Gurū Nānak, as first Gurū, is designated *Mahalā 1* or simply *M1*; the second Gurū, Aṅgad, is designated *Mahalā 2* or *M2*; etc.

mahant: chief; superior of a monastery or other religious institution.

mahā-purukh: a person of exalted spiritual status.

maṭh: religious establishment, monastery.

miharāb: the niche in a mosque which indicates the direction of the Ka'bah in Mecca.

misl: Sikh military bands of the eighteenth century.

mullah: a teacher of the law and doctrines of Islam.

murīd: disciple (Muslim).

mush'ara: an assembly gathered to recite and hear poetry.

Nāgarī, *Devanāgarī*: the script used for writing Sanskrit and Hindī.

nām: the divine Name, the expression of the nature and being of God in terms comprehensible to the human understanding.

nām japai: the same process as *nām simaran* (q.v.).

nām simaran: repeating the divine Name of God; meditating on God.

Nāth: lit. 'master'. A yogic sect of considerable influence prior to and during the time of the early Sikh Gurūs. Its members, who are also known as Kānphaṭ yogīs, practised haṭha-yoga (q.v.) in order to obtain immortality.

paṇḍit: an erudite person; a mode of address used for Brāhmaṇs.

panth: lit. path, road. System of religious belief and practice. The form 'Panth' designates the Sikh community.

pargaṅa: subdivision of a district.

pauṛī: stanza.

pīr: the head of a Sūfī order; a Sūfī saint.

pothī: volume, tome.

qalandar: itinerant Muslim ascetic.

qāzī, *qāḍī*: a Muslim judge, administrator of Islamic law.

qibla: the direction of the Ka'bah in Mecca.

rabāb: stringed instrument resembling a rebeck.

rāg: raga; a series of five or more notes on which a melody is based.

rahat, *rahit*: the code of discipline of the Khālsā (q.v.).

rahit-nāmā: a recorded version of the Khālsā code of discipline.

śabad: shabad; word; the divine self-communication; a hymn from the Ādi Granth.

sādh, *sādhū*: one who has attained spiritual excellence; holy man; renunciant.

Sahaj-dhārī: A Sikh who neither accepts baptism into the Khālsā (q.v.) nor observes its code of discipline.

sākhī (pl. *sākhiān*): (1) testimony, witness, evidence; (2) section of a janam-sākhī.

samādhi: tomb, cenotaph.

saṅgat: assembly, religious congregation.

satsaṅg: the fellowship of true believers, congregation.

sevā: deeds of piety; service rendered to a person or place of religious eminence.

Siddh: Eighty-four exalted personages believed to have attained immortality through the practice of yoga and to be dwelling deep in the Himalayas. In the janam-sākhīs the term is confused with *Nāth* (q.v.).

śiva-liṅga: phallic emblem of Śiva.

ślok: shalok; couplet or stanza.
śraddh: rite commemorating deceased forbear.
sudī: the light half of a lunar month, the period of the waxing moon. Cf. *vadī*.
tapā: ascetic, one skilled in the practice of *tapasya* (q.v.).
tapas, *tapasya*: religious austerities.
vadī: the dark half of a lunar month, the period of the waning moon. Cf. *sudī*.
vār: a heroic ode of several stanzas; a song of praise; a dirge.
yagya, *yajna*: sacrificial rite; ritual feast.

INDEX OF JANAM-SĀKHĪ ANECDOTES AND DISCOURSES

In some instances sākhīs listed below are referred to in the text by their sākhī numbers in particular janam-sākhī collections, not by their titles.

GENERAL INDEX

Indian personal names are listed below in accordance with the initial letter of the first name.

The Evolution of the Sikh Community

ACKNOWLEDGEMENTS

THE essays which together constitute this small book owe their origin to a series of four lectures delivered in the University of Cambridge during the Lent Term of 1970 under the auspices of the Faculty of Oriental Studies. The first four essays represent revised versions of these lectures. To the Dean of the Faculty, Professor John Emerton, and to all its members I offer my sincere thanks for the invitation which prompted the lectures and for the many kindnesses which I received during a pleasant year in their midst.

I must also record with deep appreciation the fact that the year in Cambridge was made possible by a generous grant from the Managers of the Smuts Memorial Fund. During the course of the year I discovered, to my great pleasure and advantage, the degree to which the Managers, individually as well as collectively, take a genuine and practical interest in their beneficiaries. With much gratitude I acknowledge the assistance which I received during the term of my fellowship from Professor E. E. Rich and his Committee. I also extend my grateful thanks to the Provost and Fellows of King's College for their generous hospitality during my year in Cambridge.

Several persons have aided either the original preparation of the lectures or their subsequent revision. One to whom I owe a special debt for this and much more besides is Dr. F. R. Allchin of Churchill College, Cambridge. Others who have rendered valuable assistance are Mr. Ben Farmer, Dr. Ganda Singh, Professor J. S. Grewal, Professor Harbans Singh, Dr. Stuart McGregor, Dr. Joyce Pettigrew, Mr. G. S. Rahi, Dr. Satish Saberwal, Professor E. Shils, Dr. Percival Spear, and Professor Peter Wilson. I thank them all, and in fairness to them hasten to add that for all opinions and conclusions expressed in these essays I alone am to be held responsible. This vicarious disclaimer must be stressed as the essays incorporate interpretations from which some of my friends and helpers would assuredly wish to dissociate themselves.

Thanks are also due to Professor Fauja Singh of the Department of Punjab Historical Studies at Punjabi University, Patiala, for permission to include in the second essay material previously used for a paper read at the 1969 session of the Punjab History Conference, and to Miss Irene Marshall for typing the entire work. And as always I owe to my wife gratitude beyond expressing for all her sympathy and help.

Finally I must thank my Sikh friends in the Pañjāb for the patience and tolerance which they have so graciously shown towards an interfering foreigner. I am acutely aware that some of the opinions expressed in this book will impose a measure of strain upon their tolerance. This is commonly the case when deeply held convictions are subjected to academic scrutiny and I am bound to recognize that my small volume will be no exception. In conversation with Sikh friends I have frequently referred to 'a concern for sympathetic understanding'. This concern continues undiminished and it is in this spirit that I offer these five essays to them.

The University of Otago, Hew McLeod
Dunedin

PREFACE TO THE SECOND EDITION

Although it is more than two decades since this work was first published there is very little that I would want to change in it. The first edition was a preliminary venture into the field of Sikh history, religion, and society, and much of it consisted of questions coupled with tentative answers. Those answers have yet to be significantly modified or overturned, and it therefore seems appropriate to reissue *The Evolution of the Sikh Community.*

It is true, of course, that there have been some major advances in knowledge since the book was first published. Our understanding of the Khalsa Rahit has certainly progressed, for example, and there has been useful work carried out concerning the Sikh diaspora. Most notable of all have been developments in our grasp of the Singh Sabha reform movement. The incisive analysis of Harjot Oberoi (*The Construction of Religious Boundaries : Culture, Identity and Diversity in the Sikh Religion* [Delhi, 1994/Chicago, 1994]) has greatly extended our understanding of this period, and were I to be rewriting the book I should certainly be demonstrating an awareness of the significance of the Tat Khalsa. The controversy between traditional Sanatan Sikhs and the radical Tat Khalsa, and the progressive growth of the latter's influence, are vitally important. Proven understanding of this kind must surely be accepted and we should be thankful for its increase.

None of this developing knowledge, however, has seriously undermined the information and the theories advanced in the first edition of this book. It has merely added to them, important though some of that new knowledge may be. The book seems therefore to warrant a reissue, with a firmer claim on the material which it communicates.

It comes, though, with the plea that whenever it is quoted as testimony of my views, all such quotations should take their complete context into account. It may be entirely accurate, for example, to quote me as having written of Guru Nanak that 'the term "founder" is misleading'. This I do indeed write, but it is not the complete sentence and it is not all that I say (first edition of this book [1975], p.5). I also say that 'in a certain sense he is legitimately described as a founder'. What I was endeavouring to demonstrate was that it all depends on one's perspective, and that if one is speaking about the person to whom the Panth's beginnings are traced, then of course Guru Nanak must be described as the founder. If, however, one is analysing the antecedents of his thought, the result must be different and one is required to choose other words in the interests of strict accuracy.

Another such quotation is provided by my treatment of the Banno version of the *Ādi Granth*. After describing the differences which distinguish the Banno version from the one held in Kartarpur I expressed the opinion that 'portions of the Kartarpur manuscript (the original manuscript written by Bhai Gurdas) were rather ineptly obliterated in order to bring the two versions into line' (ibid., p.78). Apparently some readers have stopped at this point, roundly condemning me for daring to say that the original was 'ineptly obliterated'. They should have read further. I had merely been describing some earlier thoughts, thoughts which I abandoned after reading Jodh Singh's *Sri Kartarpuri Bir de Darasan*. This is clearly stated further down the same page, and I conclude by stating: 'From this report it is clear that the issue should still be regarded as open' (ibid).

A third instance has been quoted in a paraphrased form: 'Though the Gurus denounced [the] caste system and preached against it, yet they did not seem sincere or serious in removing caste differences' (Gurdev Singh in Gurdev Singh [ed.], *Perspectives on the Sikh Tradition* [Patiala, 1986], p.9). I certainly wrote words which can be paraphrased in this manner (first edition of this book [1975], p.88) but I wrote them only in order to subsequently deny them. They represent a mistaken view, and this I was at pains to point out. The Gurūs were thoroughly consistent in that they renounced caste with regard to all notions of status and pollution, and practices introduced during their time make this perfectly clear. How else do we account for the custom in the laṅgar or for *amrit sanskar*? Caste renounced as a vertical distinction is, however, accepted in horizontal terms as a purely social convention designed to preserve the stability of Indian society. It is, in other words, accepted as a marriage convention, and this is the rule which the Gūrus followed in their own practice (ibid.).

These are the principal cases of misunderstanding arising from a reading of the first edition. There seems to be no reason for changing the text in this second edition as their treatment in the first edition is perfectly clear. It will, of course, make little difference to my more vigorous opponents. Those who regard my work as mischievous will, I fear, continue to take their own meaning from what I write.

This leads me to my final point. Conducting serious academic research concerning a living faith seems certain to generate antagonism. This is unhesitatingly conceded. At the same time, such hostility is not welcome and every effort will be made to overcome it. In the Acknowledgements to the first edition I wrote about 'a concern for sympathetic understanding'. That concern remains undiminished.

University of Otago
Dunedin 1995

Hew McLeod

CONTENTS

I

THE EVOLUTION OF THE SIKH COMMUNITY

TRAVELLING into New Delhi from Palam airport one is likely to find that the taxi is being driven by a Sikh. This will at once be evident from the driver's beard and distinctive turban. A prolonged stay in India will soon supplement this initial observation with a wider range of impressions concerning the Sikh people, impressions which in addition to the beards, turbans, and taxis will probably accommodate a reputation for physical prowess and a fund of mildly insulting jokes. This is the current stereotype. It suggests a community easily defined, one with well-marked bounds and an essentially homogeneous constituency. The available literature does much to encourage this impression and extends the same assurance to cover the period of historical development which produced the contemporary community. A superficial survey of this literature might well suggest that the pattern of Sikh history, like its contemporary expression, is simple and straightforward.

These impressions should be dispelled, for they misrepresent both the pattern of Sikh history and the nature of modern Sikh society. Historical antecedents and contemporary realities are both much more complex than the stereotype would suggest. This, surely, is to be expected. A community which in its contemporary form is constituted by a variety of cultural influences and by an eventful history of more than four hundred years is not to be summed up in terms of simple generalizations. These must be unravelled and examined. Only when we reach some understanding of those diverse cultural influences and obscure historical processes can we lay claim to any real understanding of the contemporary community.

A quest of this nature is well worth the labour which it involves. The Sikhs are an unusually interesting people, an extremely capable community which exercises upon the life of modern India an influence far greater than its numerical strength might otherwise warrant. To appreciate their importance one need look no further than Indian sport, political activity, and the armed services. Moreover, the community's impact is now to be felt in areas beyond the boundaries of India, a fact to which certain transport committees in the United Kingdom will bear testimony.[1] The record is an impressive one and it is matched by the considerable interest which attaches to the community's past. Sikh history presents us with a problem at once fascinating and perplexing. Those four and a half centuries of Sikh history offer an unusually coherent example of how a cultural group develops in direct response to the pressure of historical circumstances. The attempt to trace that history in detail must, however, encounter difficulties. The general outline may be clear but there are some blank patches, tantalizing gaps which in the condition of existing knowledge we can fill only by recourse to conjecture.

Before any attempt is made to trace this outline an important word must be introduced and defined. Up to this point the collective term used to designate the Sikh people has been the word 'community'. Conventional English usage sanctions the term and for this reason it appears in the title of this work. There are, however, disadvantages in continuing to use it. Within India the term has been sullied by association with the less admirable aspects of communalism, with the result that it no longer retains its neutral meaning when used in a specifically religious context. Moreover, by abandoning the word in this context we free it for a more convenient usage in a different context. For references to the religious community of the Sikhs the term normally used will hereafter be the word Panth (*panth*, literally 'path' or 'road' but customarily used with reference to particular systems of religious belief). The Sikhs themselves habitually refer to their own community as the Panth, and within the Pañjāb the word is so widely understood that it regularly appears in the English-language press without gloss or translation.[2] Deprived of this usage the word

[1] David Bentham, *Transport and Turbans: A Comparative Study in Local Politics* (London, 1970).

[2] The adjectival form 'panthic' is also commonly used, as in the expressions 'panthic welfare' or 'panthic unity'. For a discussion of Sikh usage of the term *panth* see J. S. Grewal, *From Guru Nanak to Maharaja Ranjit Singh* (Amritsar, 1972), chap. VI. The pronunciation of *panth* is very similar to the English word 'punt'

'community' can now be employed to designate specific social groups which have contributed to the membership of the Panth.[3]

There is nothing new in the idea that the Sikh Panth as we know it today is the evolved product of a period of many years. This merely states the obvious. In this particular context the concept of evolution, or of transformation, has been universally accepted, and major disagreements have concerned little more than the question of whether or not subsequent developments were in total accord with the teachings of Gurū Nānak. The orthodox Sikh interpretation insists upon the notion of complete accord, not merely with the teachings but also with the actual intention of the first Gurū; whereas some other commentators have suggested radical divergence from those teachings.

According to the generally accepted understanding of Sikh development there have been three major stages in the evolutionary process.[4] The first was the work of Gurū Nānak who is almost invariably referred to as 'the founder of Sikhism'. Gurū Nānak, it is maintained, propounded original teachings, established a new religion, and gathered round himself a following drawn from both Hindus and Muslims. This was the first and basic stage, and it took place during the first half of the sixteenth century.

The second came during the time of Gurū Hargobind, the sixth Gurū, whose period occupies most of the first half of the seventeenth century. Gurū Arjan, the fifth Gurū and father of Hargobind, had in some manner incurred the displeasure of the Mughal authorities and in 1606 had died while in custody. The incident is an obscure one, but later tradition tolerates no doubts. Gurū Arjan's death was, according to this later tradition, the death of a martyr at the hands of Muslims who feared his growing power as a religious leader.

This incident (so the tradition continues) indicated to the Sikhs a manifest intention to put down the developing panth

with the terminal consonant aspirated. The same pronunciation is used for the first syllable of 'panthic'.

[3] As such it will correspond to *zāt* or *jāti*, the endogamous caste grouping. See below, pp. 10, 89.

[4] For a summary statement of this interpretation see Harbans Singh, *The Heritage of the Sikhs* (Bombay, 1964), pp. 19–44. See also Gokul Chand Narang, *The Transformation of Sikhism* (Lahore, 1912 and numerous reprints), pp. 1–87: and Khushwant Singh, *A History of the Sikhs*, Vol. 1 (Princeton, N. J., 1963), pp. 96–8.

and persuaded the sixth Gurū that for the defence of his following he would have to resort to arms. He accordingly responded to the Mughal threat of violent repression by arming his followers and by inculcating martial instincts. Nothing basic had, however, been changed. The religious teachings of Nānak were retained intact, the only difference being that those who practised them would now be prepared to defend by military means their right to do so.

Tradition also attributes the third and final stage to the hostile intentions of the Mughals. This stage was marked by an event which took place on a particular day in the year 1699. The tenth Gurū, Gobind Siṅgh, having observed the growing hostility of both the hill rajas and the Mughal authorities, and having reflected upon the weakness of his own followers, reached a momentous decision. This decision he put into effect during the Baisākhī festival of 1699, and the result was the founding of the Khālsā.

The Khālsā is best described as an order, as a society possessing a religious foundation and a military discipline. The religious base was already in existence and a military tradition had been developed, but something much stronger was required. The military aspect had to be fused with the religious, and this Gurū Gobind Siṅgh achieved by promulgating the Order of the Khālsā on that fateful day in 1699. Thus were the sparrows transformed into hawks. Thus was there forged first in the mind of Gurū Gobind Siṅgh and then within the corporate body of his followers a community dedicated to the defence of righteousness by the use of the sword, an invincible army of saint-soldiers destined to withstand the most fearsome of persecutions, destined to overthrow the evil power of the Mughals, destined ultimately to usher in, under Mahārājā Rañjīt Siṅgh, the most glorious period in the history of the Pañjāb.

This, then, is the tradition—a theory of evolution in three stages which with greater or less sophistication still commands almost universal acceptance. It is, however, an interpretation which must be considerably modified. This insistence should not imply that the concept of development is to be discarded, nor is there any intention of disputing the importance of the three accepted stages. The purpose of this essay is to seek a more radical concept of development, one which will express a much more intricate synthesis of a much wider range of historical and sociological phenomena. Our basic disagreement with the traditional interpretation concerns its simplicity. It starts too late and ends too soon. It omits vital elements within the limited area which it claims to cover. It over-simplifies the events to which it does attribute importance and lays upon them a weight of emphasis which in all three cases is considerably in excess of their true significance.

Let us first consider the position of Gurū Nānak within this pattern. Gurū Nānak was born in the Pañjāb in 1469, travelled extensively in India as a religious pilgrim, and died in the Pañjāb in 1539. During the latter years of his lifetime he gathered a group of followers to whom the title 'Sikh' or 'disciple' came to be applied. This group constituted the original *Nānak-panth*, the religious following which was to develop into the Sikh Panth of today.

To Sikhs of all subsequent generations Gurū Nānak is the founder of the Sikh religion. Of his importance there can be no doubt whatsoever, and it must also be acknowledged that in a certain sense he is legitimately described as a founder. The following which gathered around this man was certainly the original nucleus of the Sikh Panth and if we are to follow organizational lines in our movement back through history we shall be able to proceed no further than this nucleus and this man.

In another sense, however, the term 'founder' is misleading, for it suggests that Gurū Nānak originated not merely a group of followers but also a school of thought, or set of teachings. This can be accepted as true only in a highly qualified sense. If we place Gurū Nānak within his own historical context, if we compare his teachings with those of other contemporary or earlier religious figures, we shall at once see that he stands firmly within a well-defined tradition. What Gurū Nānak offers us is the clearest and most highly articulated expression of the *nirguṇa sampradāya*, the so-called Sant tradition of Northern India.

Having recognized this affiliation we are also compelled to recognize that our search for the evolutionary pattern must take us back beyond the time and the teachings of Gurū Nānak. It must first take us to the earlier representatives of the Sant tradition, and then as we trace out the antecedents of their thought we soon find ourselves following those endless paths which eventually disappear in the mists of India's antiquity.

The school of thought which we call the Sant tradition of Northern India is commonly confused with that vast area of medieval devotion which is popularly referred to as the Bhakti Movement, or with the Vaiṣṇava expression of that movement.[5] Kabīr, the greatest of the Sants before Nānak, is normally regarded as one among many devotional poets of medieval India. It is true that Vaiṣṇava bhakti constituted a primary element of the Sant synthesis, but it was an element which had been largely transformed by its association with another important element. This second element was the doctrine of the Nāth tradition. The Nāth tradition was, in later medieval times, the most important expression of the ancient tantric tradition. Its exponents were yogīs who claimed to be followers of Gorakhnāth, and their distinctive discipline embodied the practice of haṭha-yoga. They are variously referred to as Nāths, as Gorakhnāthīs, and as Kānphaṭ or 'split-ear' yogīs, the latter designation arising from their custom of piercing the ears and inserting large ear-rings.

Haṭha-yoga affirms in an absolute sense a doctrine of interiority and finds its ultimate expression in an ineffable experience of mystical unity at the climax of a psycho-physical ascent within the human body. This absolute insistence upon the interior nature of their discipline inevitably involved the Nāths in a total rejection of all such external elements as idols, ritual, temples and mosques, pilgrimage and caste. They were also distinguished by their usage of vernacular languages.

It was the influence of Nāth doctrine and practice upon Vaiṣṇava bhakti which was primarily responsible for the emergence of the Sant synthesis. Muslim beliefs, both Sūfī and orthodox, had at most a marginal effect. The Vaiṣṇava insistence upon loving adoration remains central, but the understanding of the nature of this adoration has been transformed by Nāth concepts of unity, interiority, and the mystical ascent. In Kabīr we find a doctrine of unmediated interior devotion

[5] For the Sant tradition of Northern India see the introductions to Charlotte Vaudeville's *Kabīr*, Vol. 1 (Oxford, 1974), *Au cabaret de l'amour* (Paris, 1959), and *Kabīr Granthāvalī* (*Dohā*) (Pondichery, 1957). See also W. H. McLeod, *Gurū Nānak and the Sikh Religion* (Oxford, 1968), pp. 151–8.

directed to a formless, immanent, non-incarnated God. All external practices are spurned, and the sundering of the bond of transmigration is found in mystical union with God.

This is precisely the doctrine which we find in the works of Gurū Nānak. There is no strong evidence to suggest that Nānak knew of Kabīr, but there can be no doubt that both stand within the same tradition and that they share it with many lesser figures. Although the teachings of Gurū Nānak do indeed constitute a synthesis it is not that synthesis of 'Hinduism and Islam' which finds mention in most surveys of his thought. It is the Sant synthesis, a system which he inherited, reworked according to his own genius, and passed on in a form unequalled by any other representative of the tradition. The greatness of Gurū Nānak lay in his capacity to integrate a somewhat disparate set of doctrines, and to express them with clarity and a compelling beauty. Salvation for Gurū Nānak lay in interior meditation upon the divine Name, upon all that constitutes the divine Presence. Others accepted the teaching as valid and the teacher as inspired. In this manner the Sikh Panth was born.

Following the death of Gurū Nānak in 1539 the leadership of the Panth passed to a chosen disciple named Aṅgad.[6] Of Gurū Aṅgad's period we know very little that can be accepted with anything approaching assurance and we can only assume that the constituency and discipline of the Panth must have followed the pattern established under Nānak. With the third Gurū, however, we come to clear indications of one significant change, and to strong hints of another important development.

Gurū Amar Dās, who succeeded Gurū Aṅgad in 1552, lived in Goindvāl, at that time an important town on the imperial high road and on the right bank of the Beās river. If one visits Goindvāl today one will find there a *bāolī*, a large well with steps leading down to it. One may also observe that the steps

[6] The principal source used by most modern writers for the life of Gurū Aṅgad and for much of the subsequent Gurū period is Santokh Singh's *Gur Pratāp Sūray*, popularly known as the *Sūraj Prakāś*. This substantial work was completed in A.D. 1844, a date which at once indicates the risks involved in relying upon it (or upon the same author's earlier *Nānak Prakāś*) for authentic information concerning the period of the Gurūs. Santokh Singh was a hagiographer and as such produced works of considerable importance for an understanding of Sikh history during the early nineteenth century. His works cannot, however, be regarded as reliable sources for the period which they purport to cover and can be used for this purpose only with extreme caution.

number eighty-four. Tradition ascribes the original digging of this well to the command of Gurū Amar Dās and there is every reason to accept this particular tradition as accurate. The significance of the well lies in its relation to the teachings of Gurū Nānak on the one hand; and to other such watering-places on the other. The intention of Gurū Amar Dās, according to the tradition, was that this well should be the Sikhs' *tīrath*, or centre of pilgrimage, and certainly the eighty-four steps (corresponding to the traditional eighty-four lakhs of existences in the total transmigratory cycle) suggest that the purpose of the well was more than the mere provision of drinking-water.

If we set this new well against the teachings of Gurū Nānak we find an apparent contradiction. Gurū Nānak, with all the characteristic Sant emphasis upon interiority, had declared in very plain terms that there was only one *tīrath*, only one pilgrimage-centre for the true devotee, and that was within his own heart.[7] All others were useless. Here, however, we find his second successor apparently inaugurating the very thing he had spurned. Obviously we have in the establishment of this new pilgrimage-centre the response of a leader who is facing problems of definition and of organization. Such problems would have been slight in the early days, but now the Panth is growing. A second generation is coming up and the bond of immediate personal commitment is weakening. Bonds other than those based upon religious belief are becoming necessary and the third Gurū finds the solution in recourse to traditional Indian institutions. Not only did he provide this new pilgrimage-centre, but also distinctive festival-days, distinctive rituals, and a collection of sacred writings. Gurū Nānak had rejected all of these. Gurū Amar Dās, in different and more difficult circumstances, is compelled to return to them.

Change is accordingly taking place, but it should be stressed that the change is not yet radical. Two qualifications must be added. The first is that the developments which appeared during the period of Gurū Amar Dās should not be interpreted as a rejection of Gurū Nānak's primary emphasis upon interior devotion. The words of Gurū Amar Dās are in accord with those of the first Gurū, and the doctrinal lines laid down by Nānak are continued by his second successor. The innovations

[7] *Japjī* 21 (*Ādi Granth*, p. 4). W. H. McLeod, op. cit., pp. 210–11, 213.

introduced by Gurū Amar Dās must be seen as concessions to social needs, not as a conscious shift in doctrine.

Secondly, the innovations which Gurū Amar Dās evidently introduced were not really innovations at all, for he did little more than reintroduce traditional Hindu customs. There is, however, a strong element of distinction. The pilgrimage-centre is in Goindvāl. It is not at Hardwar, nor at Kurukshetra, nor at any of the other places which his followers might have visited. The Sikh Panth is developing a consciousness of its own separate nature. Links with Hindu tradition are very clear but so too is the intention to draw lines which will imply distinction. The point should not, however, be emphasized too strongly. Throughout Sikh history there has been constant movement into and out of the Panth along caste lines, and there have always existed many families whose allegiance to the community has been only partial. In such cases all members of the family do not own an explicit adherence to Sikh belief and practice. For a Pañjābī family of today this will mean that at least one member accepts the discipline in its entirety. Of the remainder some will claim doctrinal belief without formal observance of the discipline, and others will call themselves Hindus.

A second important development which appears to have been taking place during the period of Gurū Amar Dās concerns the constitution of the rising Panth. All ten Gurūs came from Khatrī families and there are other indications that the Khatrīs commanded a particular influence within the Panth during its early years. From the very beginning, however, many Jaṭs were attracted to the Gurū's following and it seems that by the time of the third Gurū their numbers within the Panth must have been increasing faster than those of any other caste group. It is true that the pattern is still in some measure unclear and that we may perhaps be pushing the significant growth of Jaṭ allegiance too far back in time. The dwelling-places of the first three Gurūs suggest, however, that the movement must have been under way by this time. All three lived within, or very close to, the Mājhā, an area in central Pañjāb which possessed and possesses a particularly high proportion of Jaṭs. Even if we allow a measure of doubt as far as this earliest period is concerned it is clear that the movement was certainly taking place by the time of the fifth Gurū, Arjan, whose period extended from 1581 to 1606. The founding of the villages of Tarn Tāran, Srī Hargobindpur, and Kartārpur (all of them in Jaṭ territory) puts this beyond doubt.[8]

To appreciate the meaning of this development it is obviously necessary to understand something of the contrasting features of Khatrī and Jaṭ society. In order to avoid using the misleading term 'caste' we shall here describe both the Khatrīs and the Jaṭs as communities, a word which was earlier deprived of its narrowly religious connotation that it might serve this purpose. The Khatrīs may be defined as an urban-based mercantile community, some of whose members are to be found living in villages. Trade has been their distinctive occupation, although many are to be found in administration, clerical employment, and industry. In contrast, the Jaṭs are a rural and agrarian community consisting largely of peasants and landlords. Although the two communities belong primarily to the Pañjāb representatives of both have migrated elsewhere in India and overseas.

The situation which now emerges is that within the Sikh Panth leadership drawn from a mercantile community secures a substantial and increasing following drawn from an agrarian community. This Jaṭ incursion was of considerable importance in the evolution of the Panth, particularly for the developments which took place during the seventeenth and eighteenth centuries. Even today a substantial majority of Sikhs are Jaṭs.[9] During the seventeenth and eighteenth centuries, prior to the admission of large numbers of Aroṛās and outcaste groups, their influence must have been even stronger. Although the respect accorded to Khatrīs obviously continued, the Jaṭ constituency was preponderant and the inevitable result was development along lines dictated by the influence of Jaṭ cultural patterns.

The origins of the Jaṭ community are still disputed, but fortunately we are not here concerned with those origins. The issue which concerns us here is neither the origin of the community, nor the label which we attach to it, but its nature.

[8] Note also the significant reference to Jaṭ influence made during the period of the sixth Gurū by the author of the *Dabistān-i-Mazāhib*. Ganda Singh, English translation in *The Panjab Past and Present*, Vol. 1, Part 1, no. 1, p. 57.

[9] See below, p. 93.

With their strong rural base, their martial traditions, their normally impressive physique, and their considerable energy the Jaṭs have for many centuries constituted the élite of the Pañjāb villages. They are also noted for their straightforward manner, for a tremendous generosity, for an insistence upon the right to take vengeance, and for their sturdy attachment to the land. They have long dominated rural Pañjāb and at certain times their influence has extended much further. Today, with agriculture expanding rapidly in the Pañjāb, they are experiencing another period of resurgence.

Why did the Jaṭs enter this new panth in such large numbers? Their evident willingness to do so was presumably facilitated by the fact that Khatrīs commonly served as teachers of the Jaṭs. Khatrīs could be expected to direct their teachings to Jaṭs, and Jaṭs could be expected to respond. Nānak, the first of the Khatrī line, was an unusually gifted teacher and the reputation earned by the emergent *Nānak-panth* was doubtless strengthened by the notable sanctity of his successors. For such men a sympathetic Jaṭ audience would be assured.

This traditional relationship can be regarded as one reason for Jaṭ accessions to the early Panth. By itself, however, it seems inadequate as a means of explaining the apparent volume of Jaṭ membership. An interesting solution to this problem has been offered by Professor Irfan Habib. The Jaṭs of the Pañjāb can, he suggests, be traced to a pastoral people of the same name who appear in reports dating from the period between the seventh and ninth centuries and who were distinguished by a notable absence of social or economic stratification. From Sind this Jaṭ people moved northwards via Multān into the Pañjāb and eastwards across the Jamnā River. In the course of their migration they changed from pastoralists to peasant cultivators. They thus advanced economically while retaining the social stigma attached to their earlier pastoral status. This widening disparity, fortified by their inherited egalitarian traditions, attracted them to a line of Gurūs who rejected the theory of caste and willingly raised Jaṭs to positions of high authority in the new Panth.[10]

The theory is an attractive one. Certainly there seems to be

[10] Irfan Habib, *Proceedings of the Punjab History Conference 1971* (Patiala, 1972), pp. 49–54 *passim.*

little doubt that in some sense the egalitarian emphasis of the Gurūs' teachings must be regarded as a primary reason for the extensive Jaṭ allegiance to the Panth. Whatever the reason, it is clear that many Jaṭs of the central Pañjāb did become Sikhs and that the Sikh Panth was deeply affected by its Jaṭ constituency. Inevitably it became in many respects a reflection of Jaṭ cultural patterns, adding to the interior devotion of Nānak features derived from their distinctive customs and values. It is in the light of this process that we must view the second stage of the traditional three-tier pattern of development.

This second stage concerns the conflict between the Sikhs and the Mughal authorities during the early seventeenth century. Tradition, as we have already seen, attributes the genesis of this conflict to Mughal fears concerning the growing power of the Sikh Gurū, and interprets the militant posture of Gurū Hargobind as a direct response to Mughal threats. There can be no doubt that Mughal hostility was developing during this period, but we must beware of attributing it solely to Jahāngīr's orthodoxy or to the promptings of his Naqshbandī courtiers. The increasing influence of the Jaṭs within the Sikh Panth suggests that Jahāngīr and his subordinates may well have had good reason for their fears, and that these fears would not have related exclusively, nor even primarily, to the *religious* influence of the Gurū.

It also suggests that the arming of the Panth would not have been the result of any decision by Gurū Hargobind. We may be sure that the Jaṭs did not enter the Panth empty-handed. They would have been bearing arms many years before Gurū Arjan died in Lahore. The death of Gurū Arjan may have persuaded Gurū Hargobind of the need for tighter organization, but we find it difficult to envisage a large group of unarmed Jaṭs suddenly being commanded to take up weapons. The Jaṭs will have remained Jaṭs. The development which tradition ascribes to a decision by Gurū Hargobind must have preceded, and in some measure prompted, the first Mughal efforts to curb the growing power of the community. The conflict with the Mughals certainly exercised a most important influence upon the subsequent development of the Panth, but not an influence of the kind attributed to it by Sikh tradition. The growth of militancy within the Panth must be traced primarily to the impact of Jaṭ cultural patterns and to economic problems which prompted a militant response.

There was, however, one important decision which Gurū Hargobind took in response to Mughal hostility. This was the decision to leave the plains and move to the Śivālik Hills, the low range which separates the plains of the Pañjāb from the Himālayas. This move took place in the year 1634 when the Gurū retired to the village of Kīratpur. From this time onwards Gurū Hargobind and all four of his successors spent most of their time in the Śivālik Hills. It was in these hills that the tenth Gurū was brought up, and for most of his period as Gurū he was exclusively occupied in Śivālik affairs. Only towards the end did a Mughal force from Sirhind enter what was essentially a Śivālik Hills war.

Why is this emphasis upon the Śivāliks so important? Its importance lies in the fact that the Śivālik Hills have long been a stronghold of the Devī or Śakti cult.[11] A journey from Ambālā up through the Śivāliks to Śimlā will, if one observes the place-names along the way, bear testimony to this fact. Ambālā itself is one such instance, Chaṇḍīgaṛh is the next, and Kalkā a third. The hills of the Pañjāb are culturally distinct from the plains and one of the most prominent instances of this difference is to be found in the Śakti aspects of the hills culture.

The result of prolonged residence within the Śivāliks was that elements of the hills culture eventually penetrated the Jaṭ Sikh culture of the plains and produced yet another stage in the evolution of the Panth. It is in the works of Gurū Gobind Siṅgh and in the developments which followed his death that we can observe this influence most plainly. God, for Gurū Gobind Siṅgh, was personified by steel and worshipped in the form of the sword. For him the characteristic name of God was *sarab-loh*, the 'All-Steel', and it is no accident that in the preparation for Sikh baptism the baptismal water is stirred with a two-edged sword. In his writings and in those which were produced at his court we find constant references to the mighty exploits of the Mother Goddess, one of the most notable being his own *Chaṇḍī kī Vār*.

[11] *śakti*, 'power', the active power of a male deity personified by his female consort. As a cultic term Śakti refers to the worship of Devī the Mother Goddess, consort of Śiva and variously manifested as Pārvatī, Kālī, and Durgā. I owe this hypothesis to Dr. Niharranjan Ray.

The source of these new emphases is quite clear. Obviously they are derived from the Śakti elements of the Śivālik Hills culture. The developments which took place within the Panth during this period cannot be explained without some reference to the *Mārkaṇḍeya Purāṇa* and to the beliefs which it so vividly expresses. This Śakti blended easily with the Jaṭ cultural patterns which had been brought from the plains. The result was a new and powerful synthesis, one which prepared the Panth for a determinative role in the chaotic circumstances of the eighteenth century.

We come now to that turbulent century, or rather to the year which stood at its very threshold. The year 1699 is, without doubt, the high point of Sikh tradition. According to this tradition all that had preceded 1699 was a preparation for the mighty climax which it produced; and all that follows has been the application and the product of that climax. The climax to which we refer was the founding of the Khālsā Brotherhood on the Baisākhī festival day of 1699.

What actually happened on that momentous day? Let us look first at the testimony of Sikh tradition, endeavouring as far as possible to preserve the spirit as well as the content of that tradition. It is believed that Gurū Gobind Siṅgh, having reflected upon the perils of his situation and the apparent weakness of his timid followers, had devised a plan whereby to infuse a spirit of strength and unity. This plan he put into effect on that Baisākhī day. Summoned from far and wide, his followers had gathered in their thousands at Anandpur Sāhib. The Gurū had, however, concealed himself in a tent which had been erected on the fair-ground. There he remained in seclusion until the fair was in full swing, when suddenly he emerged before his followers. With fearsome countenance and sword raised aloft he demanded the head of any one of his Sikhs.

A hush fell upon the mighty concourse and the Gurū repeated his demand. Eventually a loyal Sikh came forward and was conducted to the tent. Those who remained outside heard the thud of a descending sword and observed with horror that the Gurū, when he reappeared, bore a blood-stained weapon. Their horror increased when he demanded a second head, and when another Sikh came forward the same process was repeated. Eventually five such volunteers were escorted into the tent. When the Gurū reappeared after dispatching his fifth victim he proceeded to draw back the side of the tent. Horror changed to amazement when the gathering observed the five supposed victims alive and well. Beside them lay the corpses of five decapitated goats.

The Gurū then delivered a sermon. The five who had in loyalty to him volunteered their lives were, he declared, to constitute the nucleus of a new brotherhood, the Khālsā. Those who chose to enlist in this brotherhood were to abandon pride of caste; they were to abandon the old scriptures and places of pilgrimage; and they were to abandon the worship of minor gods, goddesses, and *avatārs*. Instead they were to follow only God and the Gurū.

Next the Gurū prepared *amrit*, or 'nectar', for a baptismal ceremony. Sweets were mingled with water in an iron bowl and stirred with a two-edged sword. The preparation was administered to the five foundation members who were then instructed to administer the same baptism to the Gurū himself. After this all who were willing to join the brotherhood and to accept its discipline were invited to take baptism, and it is said that many thousands of all castes came forward.

Finally the discipline was promulgated. Five groups of people were to be avoided, all of them either the followers of relatives who had at various times disputed the succession to the Gurū-ship, or else cutters of hair. Various prohibitions were enjoined, notably tobacco, meat from animals slaughtered in the Muslim fashion, and sexual intercourse with Muslim women. And five symbols were to be worn. These were the 'Five K's' (uncut hair, a comb, a steel bangle, a dagger, and a particular variety of breeches). All men who joined the brotherhood were to add the name Siṅgh, or 'Lion', to their given name, and all women were to add Kaur.

Thus was the Khālsā Brotherhood founded. An idea was born in the mind of the tenth Gurū and put into effect on that fateful Baisākhī day. A powerful brotherhood was established, one which in unity, loyalty, and courage was to struggle against overwhelming odds, survive the cruellest of persecution, and ultimately rise to supremacy on the ruins of Mughal power and Afghān pretensions. To this event we must add one more to complete the tradition concerning the birth of the Khālsā. It is believed that shortly before his death in 1708 Gurū Gobind Siṅgh declared the line of personal Gurūs to be at an end. Following his death the functions of the Gurū were to vest jointly in the body of believers (the *Khālsā Panth*) and the scripture (the *Granth Sāhib*).[12]

This is the traditional interpretation of the founding of the Khālsā. It leads us into the eighteenth century, for our understanding of these traditions must be evaluated in the light of what we find in the period extending from the institution of the Khālsā in 1699 to the capture of Lahore by Rañjīt Siṅgh in 1799. We must at once own that our knowledge of this century is still limited. Traditions abound but so too do compulsive reasons for scepticism. What we do know, however, indicates that the traditions relating to the period of Gurū Gobind Siṅgh must be, in some considerable measure, set aside. The slate must be wiped clean and must not be reinscribed until we have ascertained just what did take place during the eighteenth century, We may be sure that something certainly did happen on that Baisākhī day of 1699, and that some of the traditions will eventually turn out to be substantially accurate. Moreover, there can be no doubt that the Khālsā did eventually establish an effectual claim to represent the orthodox form of the Sikh Panth. Already, however, it is possible to demonstrate that many of the traditions are historiographical phenomena, features which developed subsequently but which came, in even later interpretations, to be related to the time and intention of Gurū Gobind Siṅgh.[13]

The eighteenth century was, even for the Pañjāb, an unusually disturbed period.[14] Immediately after the death of Gurū Gobind Siṅgh there followed a peasant revolt led by the Gurū's follower, Bandā. At one stage during this revolt Mughal authority was almost completely obliterated in the Pañjāb and

[12] Similar accounts of the founding of the Khālsā and of the termination of the line of personal Gurūs will be found in almost every modern work dealing with the period of Gurū Gobind Siṅgh. For examples see M. A. Macauliffe, *The Sikh Religion*, Vol. 5 (Oxford, 1909), pp. 84–97; Teja Singh and Ganda Singh, *A Short History of the Sikhs* (Bombay, 1950), pp. 68–72; Khushwant Singh, op. cit., Vol. 1, pp. 82–6.

[13] On the problem of what actually happened in 1699 see J. S. Grewal, *From Guru Nanak to Maharaja Ranjit Singh* (Amritsar, 1972), chap. IX.

[14] For a narrative account of Sikh history during the eighteenth century see Khushwant Singh, op. cit., Vol. 1, pp. 101–84.

it was not until the capture of Bandā in 1715 that the revolt was finally crushed. The execution of Bandā was succeeded by a period in which the restored Mughal authorities sought to strengthen their ascendancy over the scattered Sikhs, a period which in Sikh tradition is represented as an effort by the Mughals to exterminate the Panth completely. In 1738, however, Nādir Shāh invaded the area and dealt a severe blow to the Mughal restoration. After Nādir Shāh came the series of Afghān invasions led by Ahmad Shāh Abdālī, a catastrophe which by 1753 had brought the final collapse of Mughal power in the Pañjāb.

Ahmad Shāh Abdālī continued to invade the Pañjāb after 1753, but during the later invasions his chief opponents were the Marāṭhās and the Sikhs. During the Battle of Pānīpat in 1761 the Sikhs stood aside to watch the Afghāns and Marāṭhās destroy each other's hopes of dominance, and then taking advantage of this mutual destruction soon established their own supremacy. At first they were divided into a number of highly mobile bands called *misls*. These groups were loosely united by the ties of community, occupation, and religion in the Dal Khālsā, but in essence they were independent and following the final demolition of the Afghān threat they soon fell to fighting each other. Eventually, at the very end of the century, one of the misls secured a total ascendancy over all the others and the chaos of the misl period was followed by four decades of strong, centralized administration. The misl was the Śukerchakiā misl and its leader was Rañjīt Siṅgh.

The analysis of these eighteenth-century developments must be deferred until the third essay, for many of the more significant features represent efforts to define the nature of the Panth and to maintain its cohesion. There is, for example, the question of authority within the evolving Khālsā. As we have already seen, tradition attributes a definitive answer to Gurū Gobind Siṅgh, one which conferred his personal authority upon the sacred scripture and the corporate panth. This may perhaps be a retrospective interpretation, a tradition which owes its origin not to an actual pronouncement of the Gurū but to an insistent need for maintaining the Panth's cohesion during a later period. In the third essay an attempt will be made to explain the historical circumstances which stimulated this theory of dual authority within the Khālsā, and also to show how subsequent developments caused one part of the twofold authority to atrophy.

The highly interesting question of how the distinctive Khālsā discipline evolved also owes its development primarily to the need for panthic cohesion and must likewise be deferred until the third essay. The only point which requires emphasis at this stage is the fact that the Khālsā code of discipline is, like the Khālsā theory of authority, an evolved and evolving product. Although the actual institution of the code may be safely attached to a declaration made by the tenth Gurū in 1699 any analysis of its actual contents must extend over a much wider period. It must relate to cultural features which were already present within Sikh society at that time, and to events which came later, particularly to events which took place during the eighteenth century.

These two issues have been briefly noted both because they have been of fundamental importance in the evolution of the Panth and because they offer us the greatest scope for informed conjecture at the present stage. If we are to acquire an understanding of developments within the Panth during the course of the eighteenth century, then clearly we must devote considerable attention to these two basic questions. Other issues which must obviously have been of major importance are still too obscure to permit any but the most tentative of theories. There is, for example, the question of leadership patterns within the fragmented groups which constituted Sikh society throughout the greater part of the century. Although Khatrī Sikhs must have retained much of their authority within the religious congregations (*saṅgat*) these groups were no longer the sole representatives of the corporate Panth. The dynamic groups are the military jathās and the misls. In spite of their prominence in eighteenth-century Pañjāb history these military bands are still very imperfectly understood. It is obvious that their leadership was largely in Jaṭ hands and eventually it was a Jaṭ misldār, Rañjīt Siṅgh, who secured total ascendancy. Individual chieftains such as Jassā Siṅgh Kalāl (later known as Jassā Siṅgh Ahlūwālīā) and his namesake Jassā Siṅgh Rāmgaṛhiā represent leadership derived from lower-status groups, but do not disturb the dominant pattern. The Jaṭs are a pragmatic people, respecting good military leadership, and willing if necessary to co-operate with other rural communities. There are, however, many questions which remain unanswered. The framework of understanding which can be constructed in this manner is still little more than an outline.[15]

Another obscure topic concerns the impact of agrarian issues upon the course of eighteenth-century Pañjāb history in general and the Panth in particular. It seems clear that the rebellion associated with the name of Bandā was in some measure an agrarian uprising and we are also aware of the fact that the misl system was intimately related to rural society and its economy. But in precisely what manner? And what developments issued from such relations? The topic bristles with question-marks and other important issues offer a similar aspect.

It is indeed a tantalizing prospect which the eighteenth-century history of the Pañjāb offers us. At its conclusion we find a clearly defined Khālsā Panth with formulated religious doctrines, a coherent code of discipline, and the strong conviction that it has been born to rule. To explain the creation of this Panth we have an extensive, generally consistent, and almost universally accepted body of tradition. Confronting this the historian finds in the eighteenth century a period which provides in the midst of a considerable obscurity sufficient indications to call in question much of what has been passed down to us in the tradition. The impression which these glimpses communicate is that of a society in a critical period of evolution. Warfare, disaster, and eventually triumph all bring distinctive problems and distinctive solutions. In both tribulation and success the expanding Panth is ever seeking a self-understanding, a self-definition which in its essentials is maintained to this day. Plainly there can be no hope of comprehending the Sikh Panth of today without a prior understanding of its formative past.

[15] A promising sign of change has been the recent appearance of doctoral theses dealing with this period. Two which deserve special mention are Bhagat Singh, 'Sikh Polity in the Eighteenth and Nineteenth Centuries' (Punjabi University, Patiala, 1971) and Indu Banga, 'The Agrarian System of the Sikhs (1759-1849)' (Guru Nanak University, Amritsar, 1974).

2

THE JANAM-SĀKHĪS

MUCH misunderstanding in the field of Sikh history can be traced directly to the use of sources. The selection has been too narrow and the few which command a particular popularity have sometimes been misinterpreted. This second essay concerns one of the major misinterpretations.

For the period of Sikh history up to the beginning of the nineteenth century there are three main sources. There are the Persian chronicles of the period; the accounts which were written or commissioned by the British in the late eighteenth and early nineteenth centuries; and the corpus of Sikh devotional literature. The first of these tells us little about the Sikhs and not much more about the Pañjāb. With few exceptions the chroniclers were uninterested in the Pañjāb, except when an occasional crisis or royal visit drew their brief attention. The British accounts tell us much more (in most instances their very purpose was, after all, the communication of information concerning the Pañjāb and the Sikhs), but apart from their treatment of the late eighteenth century they are largely unreliable, for they are too far from the events which they purport to describe. This should not imply that these first two groups of sources are valueless. They can be very valuable indeed. Their contributions are, however, fragmentary. None of them contributes a narrative which is at once sustained and reliable.

This leaves us with the devotional literature of the Sikhs. Within this category the obvious work would appear to be the scripture compiled by Gurū Arjan, the *Ādi Granth*. It is, however, a source which is likely to prove something of a disappointment to the historian. For an understanding of later medieval religion it is priceless, but the historian who seeks to use it as a source for a wider knowledge of the culture of the period must work hard for a relatively limited return. A more useful source for this wider understanding is the devotional literature which constitutes the subject of this essay. In this introduction to the janam-sākhīs an attempt will be made to cover three aspects of the literature. First there will be an examination of the nature of the janam-sākhīs and in particular of their development, purpose, and function. This will be followed by a brief analysis of their usefulness as sources for the life of Gurū Nānak. Finally, the essay will conclude with a discussion of their value as sources for the later history of the Sikhs.[1]

A brief etymological excursus will explain the manner in which the term janam-sākhī acquired its present usage. The word *janam* means 'birth', and *sākhī* literally means 'testimony'. In its literal sense the composite term accordingly means a 'birth-testimony'. Originally only the latter term, *sākhī*, appears to have been used. Bābā Nānak was the giver of salvation and the duty of his disciples was to bear witness to this fact. In practice this meant the recitation of anecdotes which in various ways provided evidence in support of the claim. Collections of these anecdotes were soon made and were at first called simply *sākhīān*, or 'testimonies'. Two of these early collections are, however, entitled *janam-patrī*, or 'horoscope'. In a strict sense the title related only to the opening anecdote describing the birth of Nānak and it appears that the term was used in order to impart an impression of authenticity to the complete collection. The two terms both continued to be used and eventually coalesced. The word *patrī* dropped out and the compound *janam-sākhī* survived.

Although janam-sākhīs of other religious figures have since been written the term is generally restricted to collections of anecdotes concerning Gurū Nānak. The usual translation is, as one might expect, 'biography'. This translation is deliberately avoided here for the sufficient reason that the janam-sākhīs are not in fact biographical works. They are strictly hagiographic and only if this is borne in mind can they serve their proper use for the historian. Much misunderstanding has been caused, and continues to be caused, by a widespread acceptance of the janam-sākhīs as biographical, an acceptance which alone makes possible the lengthy accounts of the life and travels of Gurū Nānak which in the wake of his birth quincentenary are enjoying a new lease of life. This acceptance distorts our under-

[1] The janam-sākhīs are more fully discussed in W.H. McLeod, *Early Sikh Tradition* (Oxford, 1980).

standing of the historical Nānak and (what is equally serious) has led to a total neglect of the true value of the janam-sākhīs. This, as we shall see, consists in the expression which they give to the immensely important Nānak myth of early Sikh tradition,[2] and in their testimony to the period out of which they emerged in their present form, a period which begins almost a century after the death of Nānak.

This gap between the death of Gurū Nānak and the first known recording of janam-sākhī material does not, of course, mean that the literature is totally unrelated to the life of the person whom it purports to describe. The janam-sākhīs as we now possess them have been built upon oral traditions and there is every reason to suppose that these oral traditions must have begun to circulate during the lifetime of the Gurū. One can observe the same process happening today. Holy men flourish in the Pañjāb as much as in any other part of India and one does not have to venture very far into the Pañjāb villages of today to find anecdotes (complete with miracles) of men who are still living.

Oral traditions concerning Gurū Nānak obviously constitute the first stage in the development of the janam-sākhīs. These oral traditions will have sprung from a variety of sources. Some, which we also find related in connection with other celebrated figures, have clearly been borrowed from the common stock of hagiography, and this feature accounts for several of the most popular of all the janam-sākhī episodes. In other cases the source of a borrowing is the common stock of legend. Puranic elements are very prominent in the janam-sākhīs, and Nāth legends also occupy a position of some importance. Other episodes have their origin in some suggestive passage from the Gurū's works. The most obvious illustration of this (and one which at the same time provides an example of Puranic influence) is the discourse on Mount Sumeru with Gorakhnāth and other Masters of the Nāth sect, a story which owes its genesis to a composition in which Gurū Nānak refers to these Nāth Masters by name.[3] And a few must surely have derived from actual incidents in the life of Gurū Nānak, although the prob-

[2] It should be stressed that the word 'myth' is here used in a strictly technical sense and not as a synonym for 'legend'. The issue is more fully discussed in *Early Sikh Tradition*, chaps. 2 and 14.

[3] *Adi Granth*, pp. 952–3.

lem of how to recognize these authentic elements within the mass of legendary material is one of considerable complexity.

These oral traditions will have circulated for many years as isolated stories, or as small clusters. The period of oral circulation prior to the first recording of a selection was evidently lengthy (perhaps as much as a hundred years or more) and it requires little imagination to envisage the extent to which the traditions must have been transmuted as they passed from mouth to mouth. This does not mean, however, that they thereby lost their value for the historian. They lost much of their value as far as our knowledge of the historical Nānak is concerned, but they were always gaining in another sense. The nature of the transformation will have been, in considerable measure, dictated by the situation within which that trasformation took place, and if we can fix any particular janam-sākhī at a point in time we shall have in our possession a most useful means of furthering our understanding of the Sikh Panth at that particular point in time.

After many years of oral transmission the janam-sākhīs moved into a second stage, namely the first recording in written form of portions of the material. A few of the earliest manuscripts indicate that at this stage the various incidents must have been recorded as isolated episodes, the only deference to chronology being a rough grouping according to birth, childhood, manhood, and death. In some cases even this crude structure was evidently lacking.

Chronology characterizes the third stage. Episodes which had previously been related in a disjointed manner are now ordered into a reasonably consistent chronological pattern. Gurū Nānak was known to have travelled extensively. Itineraries are now devised and incidents which already had a particular location are set in appropriate places in the travel narrative. Other incidents which previously had no specific location are now given one. At first the Gurū's travels are relatively modest in extent, but as the years pass from the eighteenth into the nineteenth century we find him reaching Peking in the East and Europe in the West. One relatively recent contribution relates a meeting with the Pope in Rome, an opportunity which Gurū Nānak utilizes to denounce the sale of indulgences.[4]

[4] Lal Singh, *Tavārīkh Gurū Khālsā Panth* (Lahore, 2nd ed., 1945), Vol. 1, p. 140.

A fourth stage is reached when the janam-sākhī material is turned to a different use. Hitherto the emphasis has been upon narrative, and in particular upon the simple wonder-story. Now, in this fourth stage, it moves to exegesis. The various episodes are used as settings for quotations from the Gurū's works, and for lengthy expositions of the passages quoted in this manner. Within the context of a particular incident someone is made to ask a question. In reply the Gurū quotes a verse and the writer adds his own exegesis, normally at some length. This stage bears testimony both to the popularity of the janam-sākhī and to the intelligence of the religious teachers who used it to communicate their message. The people were obviously prepared to listen to janam-sākhīs; the teachers were resourceful enough to recognize this and to make the necessary adaptations.

Most of the janam-sākhīs which we now possess represent either the third or the fourth of these stages, or (more commonly) a combination of the two. They may be divided into a number of groups, or 'traditions', each of which represents the various products of a single source. The most important are the *Purātan* tradition, the *Miharbān* tradition, the *Bālā* tradition, and a version known as the *Ādi Sakhīs*. The janam-sākhīs of the *Purātan* tradition chiefly represent the third stage in the evolutionary pattern (the stage of chronological grouping), but also possess elements of both the second and fourth stages. The *Miharbān* tradition represents the fourth stage; and the *Bālā* a combination of the second and the third, with some elements of the fourth. It should be noted that the age of a tradition is not necessarily reflected in the stage which it represents. The *Bālā* tradition, although predominantly second stage, is actually later than either the *Purātan* janam-sākhīs or the nucleus of the *Miharbān* tradition. All four stages can be found from the early seventeenth century onwards, and all four are still given expression today.

A particular interest attaches, of course, to the seventeenth-century products and perhaps the most interesting of all is the India Office Library manuscript which bears the number *Panjabi B40*. This manuscript, although actually written in the eighteenth century, is essentially a seventeenth-century janam-sākhī in content. It is of particular interest because it best illustrates the second stage, while at the same time offering substantial portions of third-stage and fourth-stage material. Most of this janam-sākhī lacks structure, its individual sākhīs being recorded with little concern for chronology. The first twenty-seven folios are, however, a borrowing from a manuscript shared with the *Purātan* tradition and are related with the characteristic *Purātan* concern for chronological structure. This pattern occasionally recurs, and at other points there intrude exegetical passages which have been taken from a *Miharbān* source.[5]

Ever since the janam-sākhīs first emerged they have enjoyed a considerable popularity. They represent the first Pañjābī prose form, and the dominant prose form up to the emergence of the twentieth-century novel. To this day they retain much of their popularity. They are frequently read in devout Sikh homes and extensively used for instructional purposes in gurdwaras (Sikh temples). This popularity is not difficult to understand. The authors of the janam-sākhīs had developed a considerable narrative power, as a result of which their works make fascinating reading. Their popularity is matched only by their usefulness. To the student of Pañjābī language they are of unusual interest and help in tracing the development of modern Pañjābī prose; and to the historian they are of equal interest and assistance in the quest for an understanding of seventeenth- and eighteenth-century Sikh history.

As we have already observed, the chief use to which the janam-sākhīs have been put by historians of the Pañjāb relates to the life of Gurū Nānak. We have also briefly observed the risks involved in this emphasis, notably the almost universal practice of treating the janam-sākhīs as biographies of Nānak. Having stressed that they are not biographical let us hasten to add that this recognition does not warrant a total rejection of the janam-sākhīs as sources for the life of Nānak. If we reject them we are left with virtually no source for the Gurū's life. It is true, as we have already indicated, that the principal value of the janam-sākhīs relates to a later period, but if carefully scrutinized they can also serve a useful purpose with regard to our knowledge of the historical Nānak.

The basic point which needs to be made as far as the authentic

[5] W.H. McLeod, trans., *The B40 Janam-sākhi* (Amritsar, 1980), is a complete translation of the India Office Library manuscript, *Panjabi B40*. All janam-sākhi quotations used in this book have been taken from this translation.

Nānak material is concerned is that the janam-sākhī traditions can provide no more than pointers to possibilities. Each of these possibilities must be subjected to rigorous scrutiny and only when it is actually established can it be accepted. Unlike the prisoner in a court of law the janam-sākhī must be held guilty until proved innocent. A number of tests can be devised in order to test the various episodes in the janam-sākhīs. The incidence of legend is one such test, and a related procedure is the identification of material which has been appropriated from earlier hagiographic traditions. The application of these two obvious criteria will eliminate substantial portions of the janam-sākhī narratives from the authentic Nānak materials. On the other hand it is possible to sustain limited portions by the application of a genealogical criterion. Family memories are long and generally reliable in the Pañjāb, and it is reasonable to assume that when the janam-sākhīs relate details concerning close family relationships they are probably correct. If, of course, the various janam-sākhīs conflict in their testimony to such relationships we must withhold that acceptance, and herein we encounter yet another criterion, namely the measure of agreement or disagreement between the different janam-sākhīs.

The pursuit of this somewhat arduous analysis of the janam-sākhī material will show that most anecdotes are plainly legendary in their application to Gurū Nānak, and it will also establish a few points which withstand all tests. Much will be left between these two definitive extremes and this material we must set aside as unproved. Given the hagiographic nature of the janam-sākhīs and their general lack of reliability as far as the historical Nānak is concerned, material which cannot be positively established should only rarely be given the benefit of the doubt.

If a conviction regarding the unreliability of the janam-sākhīs as biographical records can be communicated it may be possible to develop an understanding of their primary value as historical sources. This primary value concerns the period and the situation out of which the janam-sākhīs emerged. Our earliest recorded janam-sākhīs developed during the early seventeenth century (at least seventy and perhaps as much as one hundred years after the death of Nānak). The seventeenth century was a period of particular popularity, but no generation since then has been without its janam-sākhīs and their importance as contemporary source materials continues to the present day. Once we are in a position to determine the approximate date of a janam-sākhī we shall have in our possession a document which can offer us many insights concerning the beliefs and the environment of the Sikh Panth during that particular period. These insights will chiefly concern the development of the powerful Nānak myth, but their range will extend much further. Inevitably the janam-sākhīs give expression to the wider expanse of Sikh belief and social practice, and at many points their interest passes beyond the confines of the Panth into the rural Pañjāb which was its home.

Let us, in this connection, stress once again the peculiar nature of the janam-sākhīs. The janam-sākhīs are hagiographic, a word which is commonly used in a pejorative sense as a synonym for 'legendary'. Hagiography (like myth) is not properly understood as a synonym for legend, notwithstanding the fact that hagiographic writing characteristically abounds in legendary accounts of mighty deeds. Hagiographic literature is properly understood not as a testimony to popular credulity but rather as a contemporary response to remembered greatness. Upon this memory are focused the needs and the aspirations of a particular group of people at a particular point in time. The treatment accorded to the object of a corporate remembrance will be constituted by a varying blend of authentic memory and subsequent accretion. The accretion must not, however, be dismissed as 'unhistorical'. It may certainly be unhistorical with regard to the person so described, but much of it will be truly historical with regard to the people responsible for the actual expression given to any tradition.

This result follows from the fact that the authors of hagiographic literature must inevitably develop their accounts upon the basis of their own circumscribed understanding. Much will be inherited, but much will derive directly from their own situation. Moreover, the particular expression which they give to their inheritance will draw heavily for its details upon their own experience. When, for example, they deal in any detail with a marriage ceremony they will describe the kind of ceremony which is known to them from their own experience. The janam-sākhī writer Miharbān, when he provides a lengthy account of the marriage of Gurū Nānak, describes not the marriage of Gurū Nānak but a marriage of the kind witnessed by Miharbān himself. The fact that Indian customs change very slowly does indeed mean that Miharbān's account may well be in its essential outline correct, but the principle remains unaltered. We must read this account as a description of a late sixteenth- or early seventeenth-century marriage, not as a late fifteenth-century marriage. As far as the life of Gurū Nānak is concerned it is only the bare statement of the actual event which retains an indisputable validity, namely the statement that he was married in the town of Baṭālā to the daughter of Mūlā Choṇā. This much we can relate to the authentic life of Nānak. The remainder, consisting of all the details which embellish the actual event, we must relate to the period in which the account was actually written.

An issue which serves to illustrate both the connection and the difference between the teachings of the historical Nānak on the one hand and the testimony of the janam-sākhīs on the other is the janam-sākhīs' deep involvement in the issue of reconciliation between Hindu and Muslim, a theme which runs right through the literature from the united welcome accorded the baby Nānak at his birth to the final dispute concerning the proper disposal of his body. It is strongly implied in the terminology used to designate the Gurū and it is explicitly stated at several points in all janam-sākhī traditions.

The janam-sākhī attitude towards this issue must be clearly distinguished from Gurū Nānak's own attitude. The latter can be easily ascertained from the Gurū's works recorded in the *Ādi Granth* where we find a conviction which interprets reconciliation in terms of an ultimate transcending of both Hindu and Muslim beliefs. The attitude to which the janam-sākhīs bear witness is the attitude of the Sikh Panth at a remove of some seventy or a hundred years from the Gurū's death. Although it cannot be said that the understanding which we find expressed therein is positively opposed to that of Gurū Nānak, it is not possible to affirm a total accord. The janam-sākhī understanding is pitched at a somewhat lower level, one which represents the Gurū as a Hindu to Hindus and a Muslim to Muslims, as one who 'dressed as a *bairāgī* and as a *faqīr*'. An indignant administrator regards him as a Hindu and Bābā Nānak is himself made to say, 'I am a Hindu.' This information he communicates to some faqīrs while journeying to Mecca and the faqīrs report it when they reach the city a year later. The people of Mecca have, however, formed a different opinion. 'This is no Hindu!' they declared. 'This is a great sage, one who recites the *namāz*. Everyone recites the *namāz* after him. He recites the *namāz* before anyone else.' 'He told us, "I am a Hindu",' explained the faqīrs, 'but in reality he is a Muslim and thus he has come near to God.'[6]

This narrative obviously represented a dominant conviction amongst Gurū Nānak's later followers and one which in the early seventeenth century must have commanded a considerable attention. It is an issue which illustrates the link between the historical Nānak and the testimony of the janam-sākhīs; and which at the same time plainly indicates how that testimony has moved away from the historical Nānak. The issue leads us from our second to our third point. We are now moving within the janam-sākhīs' own period, examining not the life and teachings of Gurū Nānak, but a later interpretation of that life and those teachings. It is essential that this distinction should be understood.

The early janam-sākhīs evolved during the period which extends from the late sixteenth century throughout the seventeenth century. This was unquestionably their season of major development and we must bear in mind that it precedes an unusually significant period in Pañjāb history. It precedes that tumultuous century which stretches from the founding of the Khālsā in A.D. 1699 through to the emergence of Mahārājā Rañjīt Singh. The early janam-sākhīs evolved during the pre-Khālsā period and this fact serves to underline their importance as sources of Pañjāb history. Our understanding of pre-Khālsā history has been moulded in large measure by post-Khālsā assumptions, and a source which lacks these assumptions acquires thereby an added significance.

The society within which the janam-sākhīs evolved was, of course, the emergent Panth and to this we can add that it was clearly a rural society. The imagery is rural, the various characters normally follow rural pursuits, and on the rare occasions when the Gurū is taken by the authors into a city there is little

[6] Ibid., p. 149.

awareness of the nature of urban life. The only exception to this, and that a very partial one, is the relatively sophisticated Miharbān who had evidently paid some visits to Lahore. This rural base will occasion no surprise and we do not need the janam-sākhīs to tell us that Pañjāb society was overwhelmingly rural during this period. In order to appreciate the janam-sākhīs we must, however, retain an awareness of this background. The locus of the janam-sākhīs is rural Pañjāb and it is a rural understanding which finds expression in them. We must also observe that it is an understanding conditioned and in large measure dominated by an amalgam of Puranic and Nāth legend. The janam-sākhīs bear overwhelming witness to this feature.

As one would expect, the fact that the janam-sākhīs evolved within a rising religious society has left a dominant impress upon the material which they offer. Religious issues are the primary concern of the authors and predictably we are treated to lengthy discourses on the way of salvation. Let it not be assumed, however, that these discourses offer nothing that will satisfy a wider historical interest. Religion was not, for the authors of the janam-sākhīs or their audiences, a set of doctrines. It extended far beyond this, ramifying throughout their society.

Inevitably the janam-sākhī narrators make repeated references to this society, few of them deliberate or contrived. We observe, in the first place, a developing self-consciousness, a growing awareness of the nature and function of the Panth as a distinctive religious group. It is by no means as coherent as it was to become in the eighteenth century, but the development is clearly taking place. In the janam-sākhīs it is possible to perceive a consciousness of distinction within the wider Pañjāb society.

Go, Nānak, [answered God]. Your Panth will flourish. The salutation of your followers shall be: 'In the name of the True Gurū I fall at your feet'. The salutation of the Vaiṣṇava Panth is: 'In the name of Rāma and Kriṣṇa'. The salutation of the Sanyāsī Panth is: 'In the name of Nārāyaṇ I bow before you'. The yogīs' salutation is: 'Hail to the Primal One'. The Muslims' cry is: 'In the name of the One God peace be with you'. You are Nānak and your Panth will flourish. Your followers shall be called Nānak-panthīs and their salutation shall be: 'In the name of the True Gurū I fall at your feet'. I shall bless your Panth. Inculcate devotion towards Me and strengthen men's obedience to their *dharma*. As the Vaiṣṇavas have their temple, the yogīs their *āsaṇ*, and the Muslims their mosque, so your followers shall have their dharamsālā. Three things you must inculcate in your Panth: repeating the divine Name, giving charity, and regular bathing. Keep yourself unspotted while yet remaining a householder.[7]

The awareness of difference is plainly evident, but it is not a difference which implies total separation. We must bear in mind the eirenic insistence of the janam-sākhīs upon the need for an understanding between Hindus and Muslims. The distinctiveness of the Panth is obviously assumed, but it is a distinctiveness set within a wider unity.

From the repeated references to the erection and use of dharamsālās it is clear that these buildings stood at the centre of the corporate life of the Panth and that much activity must have been conducted within them. When the hostile administrator is converted the first thing he does after donating land is to erect a dharamsālā and the *Miharbān Janam-sākhī* sets numerous discourses within the walls of this particular structure. The *B40* janam-sākhī concludes many of its individual stories with the statement that 'a dharamsālā was built' and the *Hāfizābād Janam-sākhī*, concluding its account of how a *ṭhag* named Sajjan was converted, makes pointed reference to the erection of 'the first dharamsālā'. These buildings obviously corresponded to the modern gurdwara, not to the hospice variety of dharamsālā which serves the needs of travellers and visitors. No indication is given of substantial size or ornamentation and we may accordingly assume that they were invariably simple structures, or single rooms set aside for this devotional purpose.

A particularly vivid picture of a saṅgat at worship in a dharamsālā is given in the *B40* janam-sākhī's account of how a childless rājā was granted a son by Bābā Nānak.

Beneath the rājā's palace was the dharamsālā where the Sikhs sang hymns and performed *kirtan*. Sitting there the rājā would fix his attention on the music of whatever hymn the Sikhs were singing. One day the rānī said to the rājā, 'Rājā, how is it that no children have been born in our house? Let us go to the dharamsālā and lay our petition before the congregation, for the Gurū is present in the congregation.' 'An excellent idea!' replied the rājā.

[7] Ibid., pp. 142–3.

Next day the rājā and the rānī both joined the congregation. It was an *Ekādasī* gathering. There was a congregational festival (*melā*) and a large congregation was present. A hymn was being sung and all were sitting enthralled. The rājā and the rānī then presented their petition, saying, 'You are the assembly of the Gurū and whatever is sought from you is granted. May it please you to hear our intercession so that the Gurū may grant a son.'

Those who were present in the congregation offered a prayer in order that the rājā's faith might remain unshaken. Then they assured him, 'The Gurū Bābā will grant you a son.'[8]

This not only provides a glimpse of a seventeenth-century Sikh congregation, but also indicates an early phase in the development of the doctrine of the *Gurū Panth.*[9]

Reference is made both in the passage just quoted and in many other places to the centrality of congregational singing (*kīrtan*) in the life of the Panth and from some references it is clear that certain selections of scripture had already acquired a liturgical function. For the compiler of the *B40* janam-sākhī the important liturgical office was evidently the selection of hymns called the *Ārati Sohilā* which is traditionally sung or recited before gong to bed. 'When Bābā Nānak was no longer listening the musician (*rabābī*) would sing the *Ārati Sohilā*. When he had sung the *Ārati Sohilā* there would come the command: "Go aside, my Sikhs, and sleep." The Sikhs would then go to sleep.'[10]

No reference is made in this janam-sākhī to the other traditional evening office, the *Sodar Rahirās*. A reference in another janam-sākhī indicates that it must have evolved by the early seventeenth century, but the silence of the *B40* janam-sākhī suggests that the practice was not followed universally during that century.

At certain points, particularly in the discourse material, a writer will introduce a question which must have been asked within the Sikh saṅgats, and then either give a direct answer or else narrate a symbolic response. ' "Nānak," asked Sheikh Ibrāhīm, "tell me, does grace follow service, does service follow grace?" '[11] To this question Bābā Nānak replies: 'First is his service, Sheikhjī, and if anyone perform it humbly God will

[8] Ibid., pp. 206–7.

[10] W.H. McLeod, *The B40 Janam-sākhi*, p.113.

[11] Ibid., p. 65.

bestow the virtue of piety upon him. If, however, a man performs service but is puffed up with pride, then even though his service be of a high order the Lord will not come near him. He will be rejected. The price [of grace], Sheikhjī, is service.'[12] For the Gurū Nānak of the *Ādi Granth* divine grace and human endeavour run parallel, both being vital to salvation. The only hint of priority comes in the indication that man's initial perception of the way of salvation is the result of grace. For the janam-sākhī writers, however, it is the other way round. Grace must be earned.

Many other doctrinal questions appear during the course of the narratives. A peasant in a place called 'the Land of Unbelievers' asks, 'Without having seen Him how can one know there is a God?' To this the janam-sākhī writers have no satisfactory direct answer and so resort to a miracle to make the point. Mardānā, a frequent companion of the Gurū, asks after having witnessed Bābur's destruction of the town of Saidpur, 'Why have so many been slain when only one did wrong?' In some cases brief answers are supplied to such questions; in others (as we have just noted) a convenient miracle resolves the difficulty; and in yet others we are given lengthy doctrinal statements which do much to illuminate beliefs which were evidently held within the Panth during the seventeenth century. No point receives greater emphasis than the repeated insistence upon the absolute efficacy of the divine Name. ' "Previously men performed austerities for a hundred thousand years," said Bābā Nānak to Kaliyug, "but in your age if anyone meditates upon the divine Name with undivided attention for a single *ghaṛī* he will be saved." '[13] This is a strikingly different emphasis from that which we find in the eighteenth-century Khālsā traditions.

Beyond the narrower bounds of doctrine and the practice of meditation we can observe certain social responses which flow from the religious convictions of the Panth. One which we would expect and which we do indeed find is a strong opposition to notions of caste or ritual purity. The scorn which is cast upon the ritually punctilious reflects not merely the teaching of Gurū Nānak but also the positive acceptance of this particular teaching by his later followers.

[12] Ibid. [13] Ibid., p. 49.

Another prominent feature, one which departs in some measure from the teachings of the Gurū, is a marked deference to the ascetic ideal. At certain points we encounter statements directed against the futility of austerities, statements which are in total accord with the words of Gurū Nānak. There is, for example, the answer which the Sikh trader Mansukh is said to have given to the King of Srī Laṅkā: 'I have already obtained the thing for which you perform fasts, religious observances, and discipline. Why then should I fast and perform these religious observances?'[14] The dominant emphasis is, however, opposed to this. Gurū Nānak himself is made to say: 'I have met so many people of this world. Let me leave them and dwell apart. Here there is the tumult of great numbers. What is there for me to obtain in the world? I shall go apart from the world, in seclusion and in hiding, and remaining there I shall meditate on God.'[15] Elsewhere the merit of austerities is vigorously affirmed and renunciants, both Hindu and Muslim, are treated with considerable respect.

We also find in the janam-sākhīs' choice of subject and treatment indications of some controversies which evidently troubled the Panth and which in certain cases extend beyond the area of doctrine to that of social behaviour. The most prominent of all relates to the question of whether or not the early-morning bathe should be obligatory, and from the amount of space devoted to the question we can only conclude that it must have been an issue of some concern. It is the *Miharbān* tradition which devotes the most attention to the question. The narrator's own mind is quite made up—the early-morning bathe is absolutely essential—but he has a problem. The *Miharbān* method is always to quote an extract from the works of Gurū Nānak in order to prove his point, but in this particular case no such extract can be found. First the narrator quotes a passage which has no possible bearing on the subject. Next he uses one which does indeed refer to bathing, but unfortunately contradicts his own point as it plainly says that the only essential bathing is a spiritual bathing in the divine Word. Finally he solves the problem by quoting an appropriate passage from the works of Gurū Aṅgad, putting it instead into the mouth of Gurū Nānak.[16]

[14] Ibid., p. 159. [15] Ibid., p. 118.

[16] *Janam-Sākhī Srī Gurū Nānak Dev Jī, likhat Srī Miharbān Jī Soḍhī*, Vol. 2 (Amritsar, 1969), p. xi.

Another issue has evidently been the question of whether or not the followers of Gurū Nānak might eat meat, although this one appears to have emerged somewhat later. Early janam-sākhīs indicate that it was definitely permitted, and it is only in later nineteenth-century versions that the question is seriously raised.[17] We may also note in passing that an incident recorded in the *B40* janam-sākhī indicates that at least some early Sikhs had no problems about cutting hair. A poor Sikh, unable to provide food for the Gurū, sells his hair and fulfils the requirements of hospitality with the proceeds. For this deed he is warmly commended by the Gurū.[18] Earlier we referred to the fact that the janam-sākhīs reflect pre-Khālsā Sikh society. To this we can add the claim that at certain points they reflect a condition prior to the firm establishment of Jaṭ patterns. No story illustrates the fact more dramatically than this hair-cutting episode.[19]

Comments of this kind concern the more obvious issues. They warrant a particular interest, but in bestowing this we must not overlook the host of passing references which together constitute a fascinating picture of the rural Pañjāb within which the janam-sākhī authors lived. Even when a narrative purports to represent some distant country its detailed descriptions will normally relate to the known Pañjāb of the writer's experience rather than to the unknown foreign place. These details are inconspicuous simply because they are so ordinary, and they should not for this reason be treated as insignificant. Needless to say, it is not possible to write a social or economic history of seventeenth-century Pañjāb from the janam-sākhīs alone, but they do nevertheless provide many useful glimpses of the period.

A catalogue of these passing references could run to great length. We are given glimpses of birth ceremonies, naming ceremonies, marriages, and funerals. A child sits with his teacher and is shown how to read. Labourers bring in the harvest for threshing or carry grass to the village for the buffaloes. Women attend to their cooking duties in their well-plastered kitchens. A Vaiṣṇava holy man appears, complete with tulsī-garland, sacred stone, rosary, and frontal mark. Sūfī pīrs pass in litters

[17] W.H. McLeod, *Gūru Nānak and the Sikh Religion*, p. 84n.1.

[18] W.H. McLeod, *The B40 Janam-sakhi*, p. 50.

[19] W. H. McLeod, *Early Sikh Tradition*, pp. 264–5.

and descend to greet their equals with the approved salutation. Nāth yogīs, squatting beside their hearths, pass round their intoxicating brew of molasses and *mahūā* petals. Many Muslims are to be seen in regular attendance at the mosque, but others less faithful neglect their prayers and instead devote their attention to the consumption of hashish and liquor. A scrupulous brāhmaṇ carefully prepares his ritually pure cooking-square. A band of pilgrims pass by on their way to a celebrated shrine.

Most prominent of all is the one who tramps the dusty roads or sits upon his string-bed under the shade of a pīpal tree, the man who with his ninth and last successor occupies a position of unrivalled affection and influence in the corporate memory of the Pañjāb. It may not be an entirely accurate representation of the actual man who was born five hundred years ago, but certainly it is a faithful representation of an image which exercised an immense influence on his seventeenth-century followers. This is the Gurū Nānak to whom the janam-sākhīs bear witness, and herein too lies a considerable measure of their value. It is an image which testifies to the fact that in history what is believed to have happened can commonly be more important than what actually did happen.

3

COHESIVE IDEALS AND INSTITUTIONS IN THE HISTORY OF THE SIKH PANTH

WHO is a Sikh and how is the Sikh Panth to be defined? At one level the answer is easily given. A Sikh is one who believes in the religion of the ten Gurūs and in no other. The primary criterion is strictly religious and it is accordingly on the basis of a distinctive religious belief and practice that the Panth's identity is to be established.

There are, however, serious problems to be encountered when this investigation is pressed further. The diverse constituency of the Panth has already been noted, with a particular emphasis laid upon the numerical dominance of Jaṭs. Although religious belief can provide a powerful bond it would nevertheless be naïve to assume that the conventional values of Jaṭs, Khatrīs, and others would involve no tensions within a religious grouping which included such distinctively different groups. There are, moreover, the conflicts which can arise from the characteristically powerful adherence of Jaṭs to narrower family and factional loyalties.[1] Inevitably these tensions are reflected in Sikh history and in the specifics developed for the maintenance of the evolving Panth's cohesion. Throughout Sikh history we observe a theory of religious unity contending with a diversity of social elements. This we find set within a context where lines of distinction are easily blurred. Periods of particular difficulty have been experienced during the waning of the original religious impulse, the persecution of the early eighteenth century, the anarchy of the mid- and later eighteenth century, the confused years which followed the death of Mahārājā Rañjīt Siṅgh in 1839, and the twentieth-century diaspora. All of these have raised acute problems of identity and cohesion, and have with varying success produced distinctive solutions.

[1] For an important analysis of contemporary factionalism within the Jaṭ community see Joyce Pettigrew, *Robber Noblemen: A Study of the Political System of the Sikh Jats* (London, 1975).

There is a sound practical reason why a functional analysis of this kind is so important in the area of Sikh studies. The analysis is necessary because the Panth is currently passing through another of its periodic identity crises and because the crisis now constitutes a significant aspect of a particular immigrant situation. Within the Pañjāb itself many of the younger Sikhs are disregarding their traditional symbols and discipline with increasing boldness. In some instances the rebellion amounts to no more than a covert trimming of the beard; in others it is an open rejection which extends to the use of that unlawful substance tobacco. Amongst the migrant Sikhs living in the United Kingdom this trend has been even more pronounced. The extent to which the old discipline has been abandoned can be appreciated only when we remind ourselves that at least three-quarters of the Indian immigrants in the United Kingdom are Sikhs.[2] This statement commonly evokes an incredulous response, for it is obvious that a majority of these immigrants no longer look like Sikhs. And this is precisely the problem as the orthodox Sikhs see it. More and more of their brethren are earning for themselves the title of *patit*, or 'apostate', by removing their turbans and cutting their hair.

It is generally assumed that Sikh history begins with Gurū Nānak. For present purposes this assumption can be accepted. Although many relevant developments predate this period,[3] such antecedents need not deflect the analysis at this point. The analysis concerns the Sikh Panth and there can be no doubt that the Panth originated in the loose following which gathered around Bābā Nānak during the first four decades of the sixteenth century.

In this earliest phase no specific agent was needed to maintain the cohesion of the Panth. All that was required was provided by the direct personal loyalty of the disciple who had voluntarily elected to place himself under this particular Master. The Master was present in the flesh and his word would certainly have been accepted as law by his more devout followers. Countless religious panths of this informal kind have risen in India and then slowly disappeared. This particular panth not

[2] E. J. B. Rose, *Colour and Citizenship* (London, 1969), p. 52. Roger T. Bell, writing in *New Backgrounds: the Immigrant Child at Home and at School*, ed. Robin Oakley (London, 1968), p. 52, gives the proportion as 80 per cent.
[3] See above, pp. 5–7.

only survived but also expanded, and inevitably it experienced in the process a need for something more than the personality of the first Master.

The personality of the first Master has, however, been of continuing importance as a cohesive factor, one which still survives to this day. Nānak's own personal influence in terms of Sikh cohesion was extended beyond his death in two distinct ways. The first protraction consisted of the line of successors who followed him as Gurūs of the community. The succession did not always take place without a dispute (Sikh history has also had its anti-popes), but in spite of these occasional difficulties the line continued unbroken up to the death of the tenth Gurū, Gobind Siṅgh, in 1708. Sikh tradition makes it abundantly clear that this line of Gurūs is not to be understood as a succession of one person following another. It is interpreted as one person following himself. There were ten Nānaks or, more precisely, ten manifestations in different bodies of the one original Nānak commissioned by God and sent into the world for the salvation of mankind.

The figure which is most commonly employed to express this doctrine is the conventional image of a torch lit from another torch. The actual torches may be different, but the flame is the same. The bodies may be different, but they are inhabited by the same spirit. Elsewhere the image is varied. Lahaṇā, the second Gurū, is renamed Aṅgad because he was an *aṅg*, or 'limb', from Nānak's own body. Nānak's formal investiture of Aṅgad as his successor is represented as light blending with light, and the divine origin of this light is stressed when the same idiom is used to describe Nānak's death. The *Ādi Granth* contains the works of six of the Gurūs, but these six own only one name. All are called Nānak.

There can be no doubt that the function of this doctrine was a simple extension of the first Gurū's authority and in this manner it continued to serve a cohesive role for more than a century and a half. It was not entirely successful, for some of the disappointed contenders to the succession did manage to attach followings of indeterminate size to their particular versions of the light. There was, however, no question about the majority allegiance and until the death of Gobind Siṅgh the office of Gurū served the cohesive role with a notable distinction. The crisis came at the death of the tenth Gurū because Gobind Siṅgh's sons had all predeceased him. During the late sixteenth century the office had become hereditary in the family of Soḍhī Khatrīs descended from the fourth Gurū, Rām Dās, himself the son-in-law of the third Gurū. Although this custom greatly restricted the number of possible claimants, it created serious dislocation when the tenth Gurū died without heirs. We shall see later how the dilemma was eventually resolved.

The second means of protracting the personal authority of the first Gurū was provided by the janam-sākhīs, the hagiographic accounts of Nānak which were described in the second essay. In the case of the janam-sākhīs function must be distinguished from purpose. The various compilers make their purpose clear by means of comments sprinkled throughout their collections of anecdotes, and commonly reinforce it with a concluding declaration. Their express purpose is soteriological.

> He who reads or hears this [janam-] sākhī shall attain to the supreme rapture. He who hears, sings, or reads this [janam-] sākhī shall find his highest desire fulfilled, for through it he shall meet Gurū Bābā [Nānak, the giver of salvation]. He who with love sings of the glory of Bābā [Nānak] or gives ear to it shall obtain joy ineffable in all that he does in this life, and in the life to come salvation.[4]

The intention, plainly, is to confirm and strengthen the believer, and to attract others to the same belief. In so far as they succeeded, the janam-sākhīs fulfilled (and continue to fulfil) the purpose for which they were recorded and circulated.

The latent function of the janam-sākhīs is, however, rather different. It is as a cohesive agent that the janam-sākhī literature has been of particular importance in the Panth, especially during its pre-Khālsā period. Whereas the purpose of the janam-sākhīs concerned the individual, their function has concerned the community as a whole. By persistently directing attention to the person of the first Gurū the janam-sākhīs provided a single focus, a common loyalty to which all members of the Panth could adhere. This personality received far more attention than any distinctive doctrine, and although the later janam-sākhī narrators are by no means uninterested in doctrinal issues

[4] Piar Singh (ed.), *Sambhū Nāth vālī Janam-patrī Bābe Nānak Jī kī prasidh nān Ādi Sākhīān* (Patiala, 1969), p. 101.

they invariably relate such issues directly to their image of Bābā Nānak. Anything which concerns belief or practice is incorporated in the narrative and is there represented as a statement uttered by Nānak or as an action performed by him. Janam-sākhīs of later Gurūs are conspicuous by their absence. Everything clusters around a single centre. If a person owes and owns allegiance to this single centre he is a *Nānak-panthī*, a Sikh of Gurū Nānak.

This cohesive role the janam-sākhīs performed with notable success for more than a century. It was as the constituency of the Panth became increasingly dominated by the growing Jaṭ membership that their effectiveness began to dwindle. There is evidence which suggests that one of the major traditions, the *Bālā* tradition, represents a distinctively Jaṭ venture into the field of janam-sākhī composition, and that here as in other respects the first response to their increasing dominance was a simple recasting of existing institutions. This particular institution related, however, to a pattern which was being superseded. The distinctively religious emphasis of the earlier Panth was losing its force. Its ideals were being replaced by concepts which derived from the culture of the Jaṭs. The more restricted religious interpretation survived, but increasingly it was pushed away to the periphery of Sikh life. Its recession was matched by a decline in the effectiveness of the janam-sākhī It would not, of course, be true to suggest that they had become positively dysfunctional. Only in these days of wider education and growing scepticism is this situation developing. They were, nevertheless, losing much of their efficacy and in the confusion which followed the death of Gurū Gobind Siṅgh the need for functional subtsitutes became acute.

Before reviewing the new pattern which emerged from this period of confusion it will be convenient to return to the earliest years of the Panth and briefly to trace the developments which finally issued in the eighteenth-century crisis. In the first essay it was suggested that although the pattern established by Gurū Nānak must have continued with little change under his first successor, supplementary features do become evident during the period of the third Gurū, Amar Dās.[5] By this time the bonds of personal commitment were apparently proving in-

[5] See above, pp. 7–10.

sufficient for the maintenance of the Panth's pristine cohesion. To this end Gurū Amar Dās encouraged his disciples to regard Goindvāl, where he resided, as a place of pilgrimage. Three of the traditional Hindu festivals became the occasions of large gatherings in Goindvāl, and tradition also accords to Gurū Amar Dās a decision to institute distinctively Sikh ceremonies for birth, marriage, and death.

All of these customs have served a cohesive function and even if tradition errs in ascribing them to the third Gurū there can be no doubt that they must have developed at a relatively early date. The same concern for the cohesion of the Panth must also have been responsible for the practice of appointing leaders of local congregations, commissioned by the Gurū to exercise certain aspects of his authority in areas away from Goindvāl. Although the actual details are exceedingly obscure it is evident that Gurū Amar Dās organized a system of *mañjīs* (literally 'string-bed' but meaning 'seat of authority') and that the individual appointed to a *mañjī* came to be called a *masand.* Under the fourth Gurū the actual centre of this growing network was moved a short distance away from Goindvāl to the new village of Rāmdāspur. This subsequently acquired the name Amritsar and although during the later seventeenth century its status was overshadowed by Śivālik sites it recovered during the early eighteenth century and has remained the unchallenged centre ever since.

These developments during the period of the third and fourth Gurūs supplemented the role of the personal Gurū and that of the janam-sākhīs. Had the Panth preserved its original pattern the combination would doubtless have been adequate for at least two hundred years and probably for even longer. The Panth would have lived in relative peace, it would probably have remained restricted in size, and it would certainly have lacked clarity of definition. The pattern did not, however, continue unchanged. It was transformed, as we have already seen, by the adherence of increasing numbers of Jaṭs. This produced not only new problems of cohesion, but also distinctive solutions. These solutions were in turn modified by the entry of Aroṛās, particularly during the early nineteenth century, and later still by the numerous outcastes who accepted the Khālsā discipline around the turn of the century.

At what point in time did these problems first become manifest? This is very difficult to answer. It is possible that one of the early succession disputes reflects the changing constitution of the Panth and that the truly radical changes were considerably delayed because victory went to the side which best accorded with Jaṭ expectations. This was the dispute which followed the death of the fourth Gurū, Rām Dās, in 1581. Gurū Rām Dās was succeeded not by his eldest son, Prithī Chand, but by his youngest son, Arjan. That at least is how the succession is represented in later tradition. In actual fact there was a division of the Panth between the followers of Prithī Chand and those of Arjan, with both leaders assuming the title of Gurū. It is now very difficult to envisage this situation, for our impressions have been deeply dyed in subsequent polemic. Although much invective must have issued from both sides we now possess little except that of the victors. This represents the followers of Prithī Chand as dissembling scoundrels and the name applied to them (Mīṇās) means precisely that. They are one of the five execrated groups which Khālsā Sikhs must, at the time of baptism, promise to spurn, and although the sect is now extinct its unhappy reputation lives on. The fact that the *Miharbān Janam-sākhī* was produced by this group means that a deep distrust still attaches to that janam-sākhī.[6]

It is accordingly assumed without any question that the segment of the Panth which elected to follow Prithī Chand represented a malignant heresy. A study of the *Miharbān Janam-sākhī* leads us to reject this traditional interpretation. Whatever else the Mīṇās may have been they certainly were not heretics, at least not if their surviving literature is any guide. Their literature suggests that this particular group may have been seeking to restrict the Panth's concerns to the more limited religious aspects of Nānak's teachings, that they were opposed to the wider social concern which increasingly occupied the Panth's interest and which increasingly was being used to define its nature.

Interesting though this speculation may be we must refrain from pressing it any further, for it is still little more than speculation. All we are entitled to affirm at this stage is that during the early years of the seventeenth century the pattern of Sikh

[6] See above, p. 24.

behaviour underwent a change which carried it some distance away from the religious concerns of Nānak and closer to the characteristic pattern of Jaṭ culture. It is, at this point in time, still only a tendency and although it was obviously a strong one it had not yet issued in a radical break with the past. Khatrī leadership continued and during the time of the seventh Gurū there was actually a movement back towards the earlier pattern. The personal Gurū was still the principal agent of cohesion and still a generally effective one. The truly radical break comes with the death of the tenth Gurū. This raised the question of authority (and so of the Panth's cohesion) in an exceedingly acute form. To whom should the Sikh's allegiance now be due? Who (or what) could now hold the Panth together?

Reference has already been made to the traditional version of how authority within the Panth was transferred at the time of Gurū Gobind Siṅgh's death. According to tradition, the question of authority was determined by a clear pronouncement uttered by Gurū Gobind Siṅgh at the point of death. The line of personal Gurūs was to come to an end and the functions of the Gurū were to vest jointly in the scripture and in the Panth. It seems clear that, as in so many other cases, the single event recorded in tradition must be replaced by an extended period of evolution. Well before the death of Gurū Gobind Siṅgh we can perceive in the literature of the earlier seventeenth century indications of a developing doctrine of the *Gurū Panth*, a doctrine which affirms that in the absence of the personal Gurū the local saṅgat, or congregation, within any area possesses the mystical power to make decisions on his behalf.[7]

The death of Gurū Gobind Siṅgh did indeed mark a crucial stage in this development, but not necessarily one which depended upon a personal pronouncement. We have already noted how, from the time of the fourth Gurū onwards, the office of Gurū remained hereditary within the Soḍhī family. Gurū Gobind Siṅgh had sons, but all had predeceased him and when he died in 1708 he was without an heir. This situation resulted in a leadership vacuum which was solved only in the course of time. The first answer appears to have been the personal leadership of Bandā. It was, however, a failure and even during his lifetime

[7] Another convention which had appeared prior to the time of Gurū Gobind Siṅgh was the use of the term *khālsā* to designate the Panth. J. S. Grewal and S. S. Bal, *Guru Gobind Singh* (Chandigarh, 1967), p. 115.

it was evidently a disputed answer. Following his death the Sikhs were scattered and a new theory of leadership was needed. The same problem persisted throughout the period of the misls. A pattern was required which would permit ample freedom to the small group while at the same time preserving a theory of unified authority, and it was essential that this theory should possess a powerful sanction. During the latter half of the eighteenth century latent enmities produced a series of shifting alliances and open conflicts between individual misls. The factional disputes which command such importance in Jaṭ society today evidently had their parallels in the misls of the eighteenth century.[8]

An answer to the need was provided by the doctrine of the corporate and scriptural Gurū. During the eighteenth century it was the corporate aspect of the doctrine which possessed the greater importance and which served to impart a measure of cohesion to the community. Later, as we shall see, the doctrine of the corporate Gurū effectively lapsed and an undisputed primacy was assumed by the scriptural Gurū theory, a primacy which continues to this day.

It would perhaps be wise to summarize at this point the eighteenth-century political and military developments which were covered in the first essay. Bandā's execution in 1716 was followed by a period of more than a decade during which the Mughal authorities attempted to bring the increasingly turbulent Jaṭ Sikhs under control. The Sikhs retaliated by organizing themselves into numerous small and highly mobile bands called *jathās*, each commanded by a *jathedār*. Recognizing the need for some sort of unified strategy the jathedārs evidently attempted to devise a confederation by meeting on the occasion of the Baisākhī and Dīvālī festivals. Although these meetings cannot have been held regularly they nevertheless expressed a continuing concern for solidarity and for some sort of common authority. At these gatherings the jathās were regarded as constituting the *Sarbat Khālsā*, or 'Entire Khālsā'. When during the fourth decade of the century efforts were made to extend the joint meetings to joint campaigning the resultant army (which generally existed in theory rather than in fact) was called the *Dal Khālsā*, the 'Khālsā Army'.

[8] Joyce Pettigrew, op. cit., esp. chap. 3, 'Significant Events in Jat History'.

Until the middle of the century these attempts to forge a permanent union of the jathās were conspicuously unsuccessful, particularly when the declining Mughal administration relaxed its efforts to control them. A closer unity did not develop until Ahmad Shāh Abdālī began his series of invasions from Afghanistan. The first of these was launched in 1747 and the last finally petered out in 1769. Ahmad Shāh Abdālī succeeded in defeating both the Mughals and the Marāṭhās, but he did not succeed in quelling the Sikhs. On the contrary, they grew and flourished, stimulated by the challenge of an external invasion. The invader in this particular instance added a religious dimension to the conflict, with the result that the distinctively Sikh character of the resistance was considerably strengthened. Ahmad Shāh Abdālī did much to restore unity to the Sikh ranks and at the same time to strengthen their self-awareness as Sikhs and their opposition to Muslims.

Even this, however, was not sufficient to develop a durable unity. Shortly after the beginning of the Afghān invasions the numerous small jathās had regrouped as twelve larger bands. These were the twelve misls, each commanding an ill-defined territory and each led by its own *sardār*, or chieftain. These misls were essentially independent, but the pressure of the Afghān invasions had been sufficient to compress them into a reasonably compact group, dominated by Jassā Siṅgh of the Āhlūwālīā misl. When the Afghān threat was removed the misls quickly drifted apart and soon fell to internecine warfare. Eventually the Śukerchakiā misl threw up in Rañjīt Siṅgh a leader of unusual ability and the ascendancy of this misl finally achieved by military means the unity which the Sikhs had sought for so long.[9]

A characteristic feature of the century which led up to this climax was, for the Sikhs, dispersion. The jathās were widely scattered and so too were the continuing congregations (*saṅgats*). Within both jathā and saṅgat the instrument of authority increasingly came to be identified with the group itself. The Gurū was present in the saṅgat and the corporate voice of the saṅgat was accordingly the voice of the Gurū. The saṅgat provided a

[9] For Ahmad Shāh Abdālī and the rise of the Sikh misls see Ganda Singh, *Ahmad Shah Durrani* (Bombay, 1959); Narendra Krishna Sinha, *Rise of the Sikh Power* (Calcutta, 2nd ed., 1946); H. R. Gupta, *History of the Sikhs*, Vol. 1 (Calcutta, 1939), Vols. 2 and 3 (Lahore, 1944).

religious context and the jathā a military extension of the same idea.

The termination of the line of personal Gurūs and the failure of Bandā to continue it had thus produced a new pattern. During the period of the personal Gurūs the problems encountered by the more distant saṅgats had already prompted the idea of the Gurū's presence within the local congregation. With the permanent removal of the Gurū's physical presence this doctrine was magnified in importance and during the middle years of the eighteenth century it assumed a position of primacy within the Panth. The Gurū, though absent in the body, is very much present in spirit wherever his words are devoutly sung. They who with genuine devotion participate in this *kīrtan* (communal singing) manifest in their assembly the Gurū's own presence, and when they speak as an assembly they speak as the Gurū. If for any particular purpose a limited number of participants was required, five representatives (the *pañj piāre* or 'five beloved') were chosen and temporarily invested with the authority of the saṅgat.

For its kīrtan sessions and other religious assemblies each saṅgat set aside a particular room or building. This was the *dharamsālā*, or prototype gurdwara, an institution which was briefly described earlier.[10] The frequency with which the dharamsālā is mentioned in the janam-sākhīs indicates that for the Sikhs of the seventeenth and early eighteenth centuries it occupied a central position in the life of the community. This role was substantially weakened later in the eighteenth century as the Khālsā rose to prominence. The energies of the Khālsā were largely absorbed in activities other than the devotional concerns of the dharamsālā and although some of the principal sites retained a considerable reverence many of the minor ones were allowed to remain the preserve of non-Khālsā Sikhs.

In this manner military needs and the extension of Khālsā influence shifted the Panth's primary interests away from the saṅgat towards the jathā and later the misl. This shift of interest carried with it the same belief in a mystical presence of the Gurū. As military and eventually political issues began to command an increasing attention, the doctrine was extended to cover the quasi-parliamentary sessions of the Sarbat Khālsā.

[10] See above, p. 31.

The need for cohesion did not end at the local saṅgat. The misl sardārs also had their problems to solve and the doctrine of the *Gurū Panth* proved to be well suited to their needs.

This doctrine eventually found an explicit practical expression in the institution of the gurmattā, in the theory that corporate decisions of the Sarbat Khālsā were to be regarded as the word of the Gurū with the full force of his authority to back it. The gurmattā is an unusually interesting feature of Sikh history, one which in any account of the period warrants more than a passing reference. During the invasions of Ahmad Shāh Abdālī it provided a useful means of deciding joint action, and it seems safe to assume that the disunity of the misl period would have been much more serious but for the respect accorded this institution.

The word *gurmattā* is a compound term meaning, literally, 'the mind, or intention, of the Gurū'. It was not, as some writers have assumed, a meeting of the Sarbat Khālsā, but rather a resolution passed at such a meeting. Sir John Malcolm was evidently responsible for this confusion. His description of the procedure is, however, worth quoting, for it is based upon inquiries made in 1805 and is accordingly one of the earliest accounts available.

When a Gúrú-matá, or great national council, is called, as it always is, or ought to be, when any imminent danger threatens the country, or any large expedition is to be undertaken, all the Sikh chiefs assemble at Amritsar. The assembly, which is called the Gúrú-matá, is convened by the Acális; and when the chiefs meet upon this solemn occasion, it is concluded that all private animosities cease and that every man sacrifices his personal feelings at the shrine of the general good; and, actuated by principles of pure patriotism, thinks of nothing but the interests of the religion and commonwealth to which he belongs.

When the chiefs and principal leaders are seated, the Adi-Grant'h and Daśama Pádsháh ka Grant'h are placed before them. They all bend their heads before these scriptures, and exclaim, *Wa! Gúrúji ka Khálsa! Wa! Gúrúji ki Fateh!* A great quantity of cakes made of wheat, butter, and sugar, are then placed before the volumes of the sacred writings, and covered with a cloth. These holy cakes, which are in commemoration of the injunction of Nánac, to eat and to give to others to eat, next receive the salutations of the assembly, who then rise and the Acális pray aloud, while the musicians play. The Acális, when the prayers are finished, desire the council to be seated. They sit down, and the cakes being uncovered, are eaten of by all classes of Sikhs: those distinctions of original tribes, which are, on other occasions kept up, being on this occasion laid aside, in token of their general and complete union in one cause. The Acális then exclaim: 'Sirdars! (chiefs) this is a Gúrú-matá!' on which prayers are again said aloud. The chiefs, after this, sit closer and say to each other: 'The sacred Grant'h is betwixt us, let us swear by our scripture to forget all internal disputes and to be united.' This moment of religious fervor and ardent patriotism is taken to reconcile all animosities. They then proceed to consider the danger with which they are threatened, to settle the best plans for averting it, and to choose the generals who are to lead their armies against the common enemy. The first Gúrú-matá was assembled by Gúrú Góvind; and the latest was called in 1805, when the British army pursued Holkar into the Penjáb.[11]

Malcolm was, of course, exaggerating. Disinterested patriotism of the kind indicated in this passage is not what we find throughout the history of the Sikh misls. It is, however, no more than an exaggeration. There undoubtedly did exist a sense of unity which survived the departure of Ahmad Shāh Abdālī and the inter-misl conflicts which followed. Evasions and direct violations there may have been, and it appears that the gurmattā was not, in fact, used very often. These factors notwithstanding, the gurmattā nevertheless expressed a continuing sense of unity and did much to sustain it during a disintegrative phase.

The potency of the gurmattā lay in the belief that ultimate authority within the Panth belonged neither to popular opinion nor to the assembly of sardārs. Authority within the Panth had been retained by the eternal Gurū whose presence at the meeting was symbolized by the sacred scriptures. Although the actual decision may have been the product of the sardārs' debate the sanction attached to the decision was commonly stronger than the military power of any misl or combination of misls. The sanction lay in the conviction that the Gurū's will had been elicited and that once the decision had been reached opposition amounted to blasphemy, or even apostasy. This can be an exceedingly uncomfortable situation and we need have no diffi-

[11] John Malcolm, *Sketch of the Sikhs* (London, 1812), pp. 120–3. Reprinted in M. A. Macauliffe, H. H. Wilson, *et al.*, *The Sikh Religion: A Symposium* (Calcutta, 1958), pp. 121–2.

culty in understanding the reluctance encountered by latter-day attempts to revive the doctrine.

During the eighteenth century, however, this doctrine served the Panth well. Although essentially a military instrument which had evolved in response to a military need, it expressed in an unusually coherent form the more general religious doctrine of the Gurū's continuing presence within any congregation of his disciples. As such it fulfilled a useful cohesive role. Ironically, its very effectiveness was largely responsible for the suddenness of its decline when the need which had produced it no longer existed. The need passed when Rañjīt Siṅgh extinguished the misl system, replacing it with a strong and relatively centralized monarchy. It was this monarchy which now assumed the cohesive role. A Jaṭ Sikh of remarkable ability had established the *Khālsā Sarkār*, the rule of the Khālsā. The disintegrative tendency had been replaced by a strong impulse towards reintegration of the Panth.

In this situation the gurmattā could only be regarded as a positive hindrance. Corporate decisions bearing a religious sanction could hardly be welcome to Rañjīt Siṅgh in his effort to bring all other leaders under his own control and he eventually imposed a ban upon all but strictly religious assemblies. The gurmattā had, in practice, rarely been applied to strictly religious issues, for the eighteenth century had not provided conditions congenial to careful religious disputation. As a result the theory of the *Gurū Panth* quickly lapsed into disuse, leaving the issue of religious authority to the doctrine of a scriptural Gurū, the *Gurū Granth.* All other questions previously determined by reference to the corporate Gurū were meanwhile appropriated by Rañjīt Siṅgh and later by his British successors.

This leads us into the nineteenth century, but before leaving the eighteenth century we must take notice of the other important agent of Sikh cohesion which emerged during this period. Unlike the doctrine of the *Gurū Panth* this second agent has suffered no permanent eclipse. Although it did for a brief period show signs of receding it soon recovered its strength and to this day it accounts for the most obvious features of Sikh custom and conduct.

The other important cohesive institution which crystallized during the eighteenth century was the *rahat*, or *rahit*, the Sikh 'code of discipline'. To be more explicit we should refer to it as the Khālsā code of discipline, and the development which we shall now examine reflects the eighteenth-century evolution of the Khālsā brotherhood. Our attention will, however, be focused on the actual discipline of the brotherhood, for it is the discipline which embodies the cohesive ideals of the Khālsā.

As in the case of the question of authority we have here an issue which, according to tradition, was definitively settled by a pronouncement of Gurū Gobind Siṅgh, but which we can now see to have been, in part at least, the result of gradual growth during the course of the eighteenth century. Tradition declares that the promulgation of a binding code of discipline was a part of the Baisākhī Day proceedings in 1699, and that this code continues essentially unchanged to the present day. It is, however, clear from the *rahat-nāmās* of the eighteenth century (the recorded 'Codes of Discipline') that the conventions of the Khālsā were in the process of evolution during this period. The evidence is not substantial in volume, but it suggests that the question of the 'Five K's', for example, was not finally settled until well into the eighteenth century.[12]

The term 'Five K's' refers to the five symbols which must be worn by the Sikh who is a baptized member of the Khālsā. All begin with the letter 'k' and hence the collective term *pañj kakke*, or 'Five K's'. The five symbols are the *keś* (uncut hair), *kaṅghā* (comb), *kirpān* (dagger), *kaṛā* (steel bangle), and *kachh* (a pair of breeches which must not reach below the knees). Although the origins of these symbols should probably concern the anthropologist rather than the historian the latter can nevertheless make some observations concerning their inclusion in the agreed 'Code of Discipline' which finally issued from the eighteenth century.

There can be no doubt that the Five K's reflect the complex of Jaṭ cultural patterns and contemporary historical events which produced so many of the features now associated exclu-

[12] For a note on the *rahat-nāmā* see E. Trumpp, *The Adi Granth* (London, 1877), pp. cxiii-cxvi. Attar Singh of Bhadaur provided an early translation of two of the more important *rahat-nāmās* under the title *The Rayhit Nama of Pralad Rai or the Excellent Conversation of the Duswan Padsha and Nand Lal's Rayhit Nama or Rules for the Guidance of the Sikhs in Religious Matters* (Lahore, 1876). See also J. D. Cunningham, *A History of the Sikhs* (London, 1849), Appx. iv, pp. 372-7; Kānh Singh Nābhā, *Gurumat Sudhākar* (Amritsar, 1901), pp. 453–507; J. S. Grewal, *From Guru Nanak to Maharaja Ranjit Singh* (Amritsar, 1972), chap. XII.

sively with the Khālsā brotherhood. Uncut hair was a Jaṭ custom which during and prior to this period was evidently observed by Hindu and Muslim Jaṭs as well as by Sikh Jaṭs.[13] The bearing of arms, represented by the dagger, was also a Jaṭ practice and one which received ample encouragement from the events of the eighteenth century. With these two symbols may be paired the comb and the bangle respectively. The breeches are rather harder to understand in this context, but it seems safe to assume that this symbol must also relate in some way to the same situation.[14]

The same complex of Jaṭ culture and contemporary circumstances also accounts for the explicit prohibitions which find a place in the Khālsā discipline. In this case it was the pressure of contemporary events which provided the dominant influence. Whereas the prohibitions directed against the consumption of *halāl* meat and intercourse with Muslim women do not reflect a 1699 situation, they do most certainly accord well with the eighteenth-century struggle against the Mughals and, more particularly, against the Afghāns. The same situation presumably accounts also for the ban on the use of tobacco.

With the Five K's and other features of the Khālsā code of discipline these prohibitions were recorded in the evolving *rahat-nāmās*. These *rahat-nāmās* purported to record the actual instructions of the tenth Gurū and because their claim was accepted they acquired the sanction which was needed to enforce the code. To flout the *rahat* would be tantamount to disobeying the Gurū himself.

An enumeration of the Five K's and the specific prohibitions provides merely two of the more prominent features of the Khālsā discipline. More could be cited in support of the claim that the discipline evolved gradually during the course of the eighteenth century in response to inherited cultural patterns and the impact of contemporary events. Such features are of con-

[13] *The Commentary of Father Monserrate, S. J.*, trans. J. S. Hoyland, ed. S. N. Banerjee (London, 1922), p. 110. Waris Shah, *The Adventures of Hir and Ranjha*, trans. C. F. Usborne, ed. Mumtaz Hasan (Karachi, 1966), p. 30. Cf also the Mirzā-Sāhibān cycle. See Eng. trans., line 273, in R. C. Temple, *Legends of the Panjab*, Vol. 3 (Bombay and London, 1886), p. 23. See also comments by John Griffiths and William Francklin in Ganda Singh (ed.), *Early European Accounts of the Sikhs* (Calcutta, 1962), pp. 88, 105; and Charles Masson, *Narrative of Various Journeys in Balochistan &c.*, Vol. 1 (London, 1842), p. 434.

[14] For a fuller discussion by a social anthropologist see J. P. Singh Uberoi, 'On Being Unshorn', in *Sikhism and Indian Society* (Simla, 1967), pp. 87–100.

siderable interest and could be pursued at much greater length. The temptation must, however, be resisted, for in the pursuit we should soon lose sight of the cohesive function with which this essay is primarily concerned. The Khālsā code of discipline which crystallized during the eighteenth century has fulfilled this role with conspicuous success. With the passage of time certain amendments have inevitably been imposed upon the discipline, but with one exception these have been surprisingly insignificant. The exception is the distinctive turban. The turban itself is, of course, as old as the Sikh Panth and much older. What interests us here is the manner in which the turban has assumed, like the other symbols, a particular status. This is a development which still lacks the formal sanction attached to the ban on hair-cutting, but which during the nineteenth and twentieth centuries has been accorded an increasing importance in the endless quest for self-identification.

This carries us forward into the nineteenth and twentieth centuries. Two final developments should be noted before leaving the eighteenth century behind. One which has already been briefly mentioned is the elevation of Amritsar to the rank of first amongst the community's religious centres. Amritsar had briefly occupied this status during the period of Gurū Arjan (1581–1606) and it was there that the *Gurū Granth Sāhib* was compiled. When, however, Gurū Hargobind moved to the Śivālik Hills in 1634 Amritsar lost its primacy and did not recover it until almost a century had passed. Its subordinate status during this period is highlighted by the fact that Gurū Gobind Siṅgh never visited the town. It was only when the dispersed jathās and misls began to use it as a convenient meeting-place that its primacy was restored. This restored status it retained even when Rañjīt Siṅgh established his political capital in Lahore. As chief of the Sikh pilgrimage centres Amritsar has ever since played an important cohesive role. Within the city a particular focus for piety and panthic activity has been provided by the most famous of all Sikh shrines, the celebrated Golden Temple.

Finally, there is the emergence of a distinctive Sikh historiography, an essentially eighteenth-century product which in an amplified form endures to this day. The events of the eighteenth century provided abundant material to develop and sustain a particular image of the Khālsā. Born in tribulation and nurtured in persecution, the Khālsā triumphed over all. To this day the cry of the eighteenth-century Panth can evoke a powerful response: *rāj karegā khālsā*, 'the Khālsā shall rule!' This too has been a most effective agent of cohesion in Sikh history.

The political ideal serves to link the eighteenth and nineteenth centuries, for it was believed that the ideal had found fulfilment in the person of Mahārājā Rañjīt Siṅgh. As we have already seen, Rañjīt Siṅgh terminated the disorders of eighteenth-century Pañjāb by establishing a strong if short-lived monarchy. This kingdom was regarded as a fulfilment of the Khālsā ideal and for four decades the Panth suffered no serious lack of cohesion. Beliefs which were in plain contradiction to the Gurūs' teachings penetrated the community, but did nothing to undermine its sense of strength and unity. Even the struggles which broke out within the Khālsā following the death of Rañjīt Siṅgh in 1839 did not immediately affect this sense of identity. The real threat did not emerge until power and patronage passed to the British.

The final annexation of the Pañjāb by the British took place in 1849 and was followed by a marked recession in Sikh fortunes, particularly those of the rural Jaṭ Sikhs. Several decades of relative peace under Rañjīt Siṅgh had brought increasing population pressure in the fertile plains tract, and the disbanding of the Khālsā army further aggravated this condition. British observers were soon commenting on the signs of dissolution which they saw all around them and confidently predicted the total absorption of the Sikhs into 'the great ocean of Hinduism'.[15] To these observers it seemed clear that the collapse of Sikh political power had cancelled the primary advantage of Khālsā observance and that accordingly a total relapse must soon overwhelm the Panth.

The signs of dissolution were certainly present, but they were soon to be belied. The credit for the reintegration which confounded the prophets is commonly ascribed to the British army authorities who insisted that their Sikh recruits should retain the traditional symbols intact. Although this insistence was not

[15] W. H. Sleeman, *Rambles and Recollections of an Indian Official*, ed. V. A. Smith (Westminster, 1893), p. 128. See also the quotations from Major R. Leech's *Notes on the Religion of the Sikhs and Other Sects Inhabiting the Panjab* in N. Gerald Barrier, *The Sikhs and their Literature* (Delhi, 1970), p. xviii.

without its importance the popular interpretation certainly involves a misplacement of emphasis. The primary significance of the army policy was the economic opportunity which it afforded. Military employment was congenial to the Jaṭs and for those of the central tract it provided a welcome means of alleviating the increasing land and population pressure. The measure of economic revival offered by the opportunity was further stimulated by the success of the canal colonies. This economic revival was the real basis for the restoration of a strong panthic consciousness and for the insistence upon a return to the orthodox Khālsā symbols which accompanied it.

During the last three decades of the nineteenth century this restoration found expression in the Siṅgh Sabhās, a group of closely related Sikh organizations dedicated to religious, social, and educational reform.[16] The Siṅgh Sabhā movement must be seen both as a response to the disintegration which threatened the Panth during the middle years of the century and as an expression of the revival which followed this period. The ideal which it so vigorously promoted was essentially the backward look to a golden age. Panthic revival, according to this ideal, depended upon a return to the earlier vision of the Khālsā, to the customs and beliefs which had brought glory during the eighteenth century and which had since been permitted to decay. Three points of emphasis were of particular importance. There was, first, the exhortation to resume in its full rigour the code of discipline. Secondly, there was an insistence upon the paramount authority of the Gurū. And thirdly, there developed a sustained campaign to secure Khālsā control of the Sikh temples (the erstwhile dharamsālās, now known as gurdwaras). The slide towards disintegration was halted. Once again the Panth had recovered its sense of identity and purpose. An influx of outcastes created problems which to this day remain unsolved, but even this must be seen primarily as an example of the new *élan*. Such an influx would never have taken place during a period of recession.

The authority of the scripture (the *Gurū Granth Sāhib*) is a subject which will be more fully treated in the fourth essay.

[16] For accounts of the rise of the Siṅgh Sabhā Movement and of the associated Chief Khālsā Diwān see N. Gerald Barrier, op. cit., pp. xxiii–xlv. Also Khushwant Singh, *A History of the Sikhs*, Vol. 2 (Princeton, N.J., 1966), pp. 136–47; and Harbans Singh, *The Heritage of the Sikhs* (Bombay, 1964), pp. 138–47.

Here it will be sufficient to note its place in the sequence of cohesive ideals and institutions. During the period when the doctrine of the *Gurū Panth* was accorded a particular authority the way was being prepared for the ascendancy of the *Gurū Granth* by the custom of deciding all gurmattās in the presence of the scripture. Following Rañjīt Siṅgh's suppression of the Khālsā assemblies the scripture assumed the role, at least in theory, of primary religious authority. This authority it has never relinquished and to this day it serves as the focus not merely of Sikh devotion but also of Sikh loyalty to the Panth. It still survives in situations which permit a growing neglect of the Khālsā discipline.

The campaign for control of the gurdwaras was undertaken because many of these temples were in the hands of superintendents (*mahants*) who made no pretence of observing the Khālsā discipline. If the Siṅgh Sabhā reformation was to have any meaning it must obviously extend to the Panth's shrines and to the mahants who still commanded a measure of influence as instructors in the faith. This was the purpose of the agitation. Its function (and this is what interests us here) was to reunite the Panth through the pursuit of a common objective.

The agitation achieved its declared objective when in 1925 the Pañjāb Government approved the Sikh Gurdwaras Act. This provided for a committee (the Shiromaṇī Gurdwara Parbandhak Committee, or SGPC), largely elected by the Sikh constituency and controlling a substantial proportion of the Pañjāb gurdwaras.[17] The purpose had been achieved and so the agitation ceased. With it went a significant measure of the Panth's cohesion. An expanded historiography sustained it in some degree, and both the code of discipline and the scripture still retained (at least in theory) an unchallenged authority. There were, however, evident signs of another disintegrative phase, for the very success of the so-called Gurdwara Reform Movement had introduced fresh problems. These problems derived from the pattern of political activity established by the successful agitation and from the prize which now lay within the grasp of a political victor.

[17] Baldev Raj Nayar, *Minority Politics in the Punjab* (Princeton, N.J., 1966), p. 177. The SGPC had been constituted by the Sikhs in 1920. The 1925 Act accorded it official recognition.

The prize was control of the substantial funds received by gurdwaras throughout the Pañjāb and now entrusted to the SGPC. Many gurdwaras drew large incomes from their endowments and when pooled these incomes provided an impressive source of financial supply. This wealth ensured that the SGPC should become the principal focus of Sikh politics and many gurdwaras (particularly the Golden Temple) have in consequence become primary centres of political activity. Control of the SGPC is fiercely contested, for it confers immense powers of patronage. These contests are by no means confined to the formal quinquennial elections required by the Sikh Gurdwaras Act.[18] The Akālī Party (the Akālī Dal) has always won these elections and in all recent instances it has dominated the polls, routing its Congress and Communist rivals and securing a superficially strong majority.[19] The more acrimonious disputes have taken place *within* the dominant Akālī Dal.[20] This situation is scarcely conducive to panthic cohesion, except when a particular objective serves to sustain a temporary unity. As a result the Panth has, during recent years, manifested a bewildering succession of struggles for political power, and an insistent quest for new causes. This phase is still with us and governments which resist claims for statehood or the possession of Chaṇḍīgaṛh help to stay the forces of disintegration.

In terms of formal religious observance and personal piety the gurdwaras have provided, and continue to provide, a strong bond of panthic unity. All who visit them join in a common service of worship, singing together and eating the same food in the *laṅgar* (the refectory attached to every gurdwara). At another level, however, they have had a reverse effect. As

[18] The total statutory membership of the SGPC is 160. Of these 140 are elected quinquennially and the remainder are either nominated or sit *ex officio*. The electorate consists exclusively of male and female Sikhs living in the states of Pañjāb and Haryānā who are over twenty-one years of age and are not apostate (i.e. have not renounced the formal external symbols of the Sikh faith). Those eligible for election must be Sikhs over twenty-five, literate in Gurmukhī, and not apostate. Baldev Raj Nayar, op. cit., p. 177. Elections are currently long overdue, the term of the last SGPC having expired in January 1969.

[19] The Akālī, Congress, and Communist parties all sponsor candidates for both the Pañjāb state legislature and the SGPC. At both levels the Akālī membership is almost exclusively Sikh although the party vigorously claims to be non-communal.

[20] In recent years the most celebrated of these disputes has been the struggle between Master Tara Singh and Sant Fateh Singh. The latter, originally a protégé of Tara Singh, organized his own Akālī Dal in 1962 and in the same year succeeded in wresting control of the SGPC from his former mentor. Baldev Raj Nayar, op. cit., pp. 194–5.

centres of political activity they divide rather than unite. In many respects the gurdwara can be regarded as an epitome of the Panth's current condition. It provides a focus for genuine personal devotion and for a continuing loyalty to traditional forms; and at the same time it serves as an arena for disruptive political strife.

A brief recapitulation concludes this survey of the ideals and institutions which have successively served a cohesive role in the history of the Sikh Panth. The survey began with the person of Nānak, the first Gurū. In this earliest phase the necessary and sufficient bond was provided by direct personal loyalty to the acknowledged Master. The loyalty owed to Nānak was extended for a period of more than 150 years after his death by the line of nine successor Gurūs and by the circulation of janam-sākhīs. At the beginning of the eighteenth century the personal line became extinct with the death of Gurū Gobind Siṅgh. An attempt to continue the personal line having failed the doctrine of the *Gurū Panth* was elevated to supreme authority. This doctrine found its clearest expression in the gurmattā, or resolution of the Sarbat Khālsā.

Meanwhile another powerful agent of cohesion was evolving from inherited Jaṭ patterns and in direct response to contemporary circumstances. This was the Khālsā, and specifically the Khālsā code of discipline. Following the rise of Rañjīt Siṅgh the code continued to be observed, but the doctrine of the *Gurū Panth* made way for the ascending doctrine of the *Gurū Granth*. Disintegration followed annexation and was in turn followed by reintegration under the impulse of the Siṅgh Sabhās. Siṅgh Sabhā objectives were at first pursued through education, preaching, and literature. As the Akālī movement overtook them, however, emphasis shifted increasingly to political methods, notably to political agitation. Although education survived this shift and continues to occupy an important place in panthic policy, it is primarily through political action that the Panth of today seeks to maintain its cohesion.

4

THE SIKH SCRIPTURES

BOOKS which refer to the Sikh scriptures can be very confusing. A variety of titles are used and it is not always clear which work is being described or cited. For this reason it may be helpful to begin this description with a brief explanation of some of the titles which one must inevitably encounter in an examination of the Sikh sacred scriptures. The scriptures of the Sikhs are not limited to a single volume, although it is true that one collection is accorded a particular degree of sanctity. Confusion can arise because this primary scripture has more than one standard title, and also because there are other scriptures which must be carefully distinguished from it.

The primary scripture is variously referred to as the *Granth Sāhib*, the *Gurū Granth Sāhib*, the *Ādi Granth*, or as an expanded combination of the latter two. *Granth* simply means 'book'. To this the honorific *Sāhib* is affixed to designate sanctity, and *Gurū* is normally prefixed as an indication of the status now attached to this particular scripture. In the third essay reference was made to the manner in which the gap left by the death of Gurū Gobind Siṅgh was filled first by the doctrine of the *Gurū Panth* and then later by the doctrine of the *Gurū Granth*. To both the body of believers (*panth*) and to the scripture (*granth*) there was accorded the authority previously exercised by the personal Gurū. Each thereby acquired the title which designated this status and it is as the *Gurū Granth Sāhib* that this primary scripture is most commonly known.[1]

The alternative title *Ādi Granth* tends to be confined to learned discussion. *Ādi* means 'first' or 'original', and is used to distinguish this first scripture of the Sikhs from their second scripture, the *Dasam Granth* or 'Book of the Tenth (Gurū)'. Although in its brief form this title is restricted in use it does appear frequently in conjunction with the more popular title. *Ādi Srī Gurū*

[1] The additional honorific *srī*, *sirī*, or *śrī* may also be prefixed to give *Srī Gurū Granth Sāhib*.

Granth Sāhib is the standard title for published editions of the scripture.

An examination of the *Ādi Granth* will occupy the greater portion of this essay. It will be followed by a brief description of the *Dasam Granth* and finally by an even briefer notice of the remaining works which can legitimately be regarded as sacred scripture. These are the poetic works of Bhāī Gurdās and Nand Lāl Goyā, and the narrative janam-sākhīs which provided the topic of the second essay.

According to tradition the *Ādi Granth*, or *Gurū Granth Sāhib*, was compiled by the fifth Gurū, Arjan, during the years A.D. 1603–4. To this extent the tradition appears to be well founded. A manuscript bearing the latter date is still extant and there is no sufficient reason to doubt its authenticity. Tradition also provides an explanation for Gurū Arjan's decision to compile this collection of hymns. It is said that his enemies (notably the Mīṇās led by Prithī Chand) were circulating spurious works bearing the name of Nānak in order to seduce the Sikhs from their loyalty to the legitimate succession. In order to combat this threat to his authority Gurū Arjan decided to prepare an authorized text bearing his own imprimatur.

Having reached this decision the Gurū established a camp in Amritsar during the year 1603 and there ordered a tank to be dug. Upon completion it was named Rāmsar and beside this tank he supervised the compilation of his authorized version. Hymns selected by the Gurū were dictated to his amanuensis Bhāī Gurdās and the bulky work was finally completed during the late summer of 1604. It was then installed in Harimandir, the principal Sikh shrine widely known in its present form as the Golden Temple.[2]

Gurū Arjan's principal source was a similar collection which tradition attributes to the third Gurū, Amar Dās. This collection consisted of two volumes, the so-called Goindvāl *pothīs*. These volumes included the works of the first three Gurūs together with those of the *bhagats*,[3] and so provided a substan-

[2] The temple is also commonly called Darbār Sāhib. This is the title generally used by Sikhs today. The term Golden Temple is largely confined to Europeans and to English-language sources.

[3] *bhagat*, or *bhakta*, literally 'follower of *bhagti* (*bhakti*)', 'devotee'. Both words are normally used as titles of respect and are applied to the more distinguished of the later medieval *bhakti* poets. Kabīr, who in Hindī tradition is referred to as Bhakta Kabīr (or Sant Kabīr), is in Sikh usage invariably known as Bhagat Kabīr.

tial nucleus. The actual copying of the volumes had been done by Sahansrām, a grandson of Gurū Amar Dās, and at the time when Gurū Arjan decided to prepare a second collection the two volumes were in the possession of Mohan, the elder son of Amar Dās and father of Sahansrām. Bābā Mohan (so the tradition continues) had not approved of his father's choice of Rām Dās as fourth Gurū, and so Arjan, the son of Rām Dās, had some difficulty in persuading him to part with the manuscript. His objections were overcome only when Arjan went in person to Goindvāl and sang a song in praise of him outside his window. Touched by the compliment, Mohan agreed to give the volumes on loan. They were carried with great reverence to Amritsar on a palanquin and subsequently returned in the same manner.

Although certain features of the tradition may arouse some suspicion,[4] there seems to be no doubt that the two volumes did in fact exist and that Gurū Arjan utilized them for his own collection. Two volumes purporting to be the original Goindvāl *pothīs* are still extant, or were extant until recently. If they do in fact still exist their precise location is uncertain, but descriptions left by the late Bābā Prem Siṅgh of Hoti support the claims which are made on their behalf.[5]

The Goindvāl volumes can thus be regarded as a first recension of the *Ādi Granth* and Gurū Arjan's collection as an enlarged second recension. To the nucleus which they provided he added the numerous works which he had himself composed, those of his father Gurū Rām Dās, and a small number by contemporary *bhagats*. Very few of the latter can have been included in this manner, for almost all of the *bhagat bāṇī* is said to be included in the Goindvāl volumes.

A considerable mystery surrounds the history of the actual manuscript which Bhāī Gurdās is said to have written at Gurū Arjan's dictation. The Soḍhī family of Kartārpur in Jullundur District possess the manuscript which is regarded as the original work of Bhāī Gurdās and, as we shall see later, there is sound reason for accepting this claim. But how did it find its way to Kartārpur? Once again we are compelled to fall back on the

[4] The story of Gurū Arjan's song under Mohan's window is plainly apocryphal. The hymn which he is supposed to have sung (*Gauṛī Chhant* 2, *Ādi Granth*, p. 248) does indeed use the word Mohan, but the context leaves no doubt that it is God who is being addressed by this name.

[5] Jodh Singh, *Srī Karatārpurī Bīṛ de Daraśan* (Patiala, 1968), pp. 123–5.

kind of tradition which, because it comes so much later than the actual events, must be treated with some caution. It is said that the sixth Gurū, Hargobind, kept the manuscript not in Harimandir but in his own house. From there it was stolen by his grandson Dhīr Mal who evidently intended that it should buttress his claims to the succession as Gurū. Some thirty years later followers of the ninth Gurū recovered it, but were instructed by their Master to return it. This was done by placing it in the Beas River, from where Dhir Mal recovered it miraculously unharmed. Gurū Gobind Siṅgh is said to have subsequently asked for it back and, when his request was refused, to have dictated another copy from memory.

From this point onwards even tradition fails to offer any coherent account of the manuscript's movements. The obvious conclusion is that throughout the eighteenth century it must have remained with Dhīr Mal's family, the Soḍhīs of Kartārpur. There are, however, fragments of tradition which indicate that this is not necessarily a safe conclusion. Not until 1849 does it emerge from obscurity. In that year, following the annexation of the Pañjāb, the volume together with its golden stand was discovered by the British in the custody of the Lahore court. An application was received from Soḍhi Sādhū Siṅgh of Kartārpur and in 1850 the volume was restored to him. Soḍhī Sādhū Siṅgh, 'out of respect and deference to the British Government', subsequently arranged for a copy to be made and presented to Queen Victoria.[6]

During the first two and a half centuries of its existence possession of the manuscript, though naturally something to be highly prized, was not an issue of prime importance. The doctrine of the scriptural Gurū had not yet been accorded the exclusive authority which it was later to acquire and current needs could be adequately served by the numerous copies (both complete and in part) which were in circulation. The significant change came with the rise of the Siṅgh Sabhā and, at almost the same time, the arrival of the printing press. The Siṅgh Sabhā reformers laid an insistent emphasis upon the absolute authority of the scripture, and the printing press pro-

[6] Nahar Singh (comp.), *Documents relating to Guru Gobind Singh's Swords and Sacred Books of the Sikhs in England* (Nangal Khurd, 1967), pp. 31, 36–7. The copy presented to Queen Victoria is now in the India Office Library (MSS. Panj. E2).

vided them with the means of disseminating it. Copies of the complete volume, with a standard text and pagination, have for many years been readily available and few Sikh families are without at least a *guṭkā* (a selection of the more important portions of the *Ādi Granth*, together with some extracts from the *Dasam Granth*).[7]

And yet, even today, the quest for a definitive authorized version is still not quite over. The final decision has been continually postponed by minor textual issues and by conflicting claims relating to the authenticity of the *Rāg-mālā* (the brief work which concludes the collection). In 1953 the Shiromaṇī Gurdwara Parbandhak Committee had blocks prepared for printing, but the completion of the work was indefinitely postponed by a dispute concerning the correct order of invocation and *rāg* title.[8] A decision was reached in 1962, but the actual printing of the approved version is evidently still pending.

To the outsider the points at issue may appear thoroughly insignificant and scarcely a sufficient reason for delaying the official version for so long. The orthodox Sikh, however, sees it differently. There may be some truth in the claim that a booksellers' lobby is hampering the work in the interests of unsold stock, but this is by no means the only obstructive element. To appreciate the problem it is necessary to understand something of the veneration in which a Sikh holds his scripture.

Perhaps the best method of acquiring this understanding is to visit the Golden Temple in Amritsar during the early hours of the morning. Numerous foreigners include Amritsar in their travel itineraries for the express purpose of seeing the Golden Temple, and then rob their visit of much of its potential value by going there during office hours. The truly interesting activity at the Golden Temple (or at any other gurdwara in India) is largely confined to the early morning and late evening. The best time to arrive is when the Temple opens at 3 a.m. If this can be managed the rewards are considerable, and amongst other things one can witness the daily installation of the *Gurū Granth Sahib*.

No one observing this event could possibly mistake the degree

[7] The *Ardās*, or 'Sikh Prayer', is also commonly included. See below, pp. 65–6.
[8] For the meaning and importance of *rāg* in the *Ādi Granth* context see below, p. 71.

of reverence which is bestowed upon the Book. It is, indeed, a little unnerving, for it demonstrates with abundant clarity that he who seeks a deeper understanding must assuredly find himself treading upon unusually sacred ground. The volume is greeted with affectionate reverence because for the Sikhs of today it is the Gurū. The same spirit which successively inhabited the bodies of ten men is now believed to dwell in this particular Book. This is no mere fundamentalism of the Western variety. The Book is endued with a personality in the literal sense of that word. Through it the Gurū speaks to his followers in the same manner that he spoke to them while present in the flesh. Let us hasten to add that this is not the same as bibliolatry and the Sikh quite rightly rejects the suggestion that his belief necessarily involves *worship* of the *Gurū Granth Sāhib*. The Gurū, while in human form, expressly disclaimed this right, insisting that worship was due to God alone. If the human Gurū was not to be worshipped, then neither is the scriptural Gurū.

It is of vital importance that the student of Sikh religion and society should appreciate the depth of this reverence, just as he should understand the offence which can be caused by the use of tobacco in the presence of orthodox Sikhs. The odium which in Sikh circles still attaches to the name of Ernst Trumpp derived in no small measure from his culpable insensitivity in this respect. During a visit to Amritsar he made the disastrous mistake of smoking a cigar while consulting a copy of the *Gurū Granth Sāhib*.[9] The *giānīs* who observed him doing so were, needless to say, outraged and the incident is remembered to this day. There may be signs of disintegration evident within the community today, but an obvious decline in reverence for the scripture is not one of them.

The place where most foreigners will observe a copy of the *Gurū Granth Sāhib* is in a gurdwara or, to be more precise, in a public gurdwara. Strictly speaking, any room which contains a copy is thereby constituted a gurdwara and Sikh families who can afford the extra room commonly set one aside as a family gurdwara. This will normally contain little except the

[9] The incident was described by M. A. Macauliffe in a published lecture entitled *The Sikh Religion and its Advantages to the State* (Simla, 1903), p. 2. Reprinted in M. A. Macauliffe, H. H. Wilson, *et al.*, *The Sikh Religion: A Symposium* (Calcutta, 1958), p. 1. This misleadingly titled book should not be confused with Macauliffe's six-volume work *The Sikh Religion* (Oxford, 1909).

sacred volume set in an elevated position. If the worshippers are to sit on the floor a low dais will serve the purpose. This is invariably the case in the Pañjāb itself, but in England chairs are sometimes used and in consequence the elevation of the volume has to be raised. The book will always be draped (normally in expensive cloth) and will commonly lie beneath a canopy. While it is undraped it is usually protected by the use of a fly-whisk. Whenever it has to be moved it should be carried on the head, and if being transported along a road some form of advance warning should be given in order to ensure that the people who witness its passing may show proper respect. On festival days a copy, mounted on a truck or bus and properly protected, will figure prominently in the customary procession.[10]

Within the structure of Sikh worship the *Gurū Granth Sāhib* is central in much more than a merely physical sense. All aspects of Sikh worship relate directly to it and practically the entire content of all worship is drawn from it. Many visit the gurdwara simply for *darśan*, or 'audience', with the *Gurū Granth Sāhib*. This consists of entering the gurdwara, prostrating oneself before the Book, making an offering, and accepting *praśād*[11] from the *granthī* ('reader') responsible for the care of the volume. Even when a formal service is in progress this is a common pattern. The formal service consists almost entirely of singing hymns from the scripture. Groups of three singers (*rāgīs*) lead the congregation and those present may, if they wish, join in hymns which they know. A garland may be offered and in return there may be given a garland, previously offered, which has meanwhile been in close proximity to the sacred volume. When the flowers wither the proper method of disposal is to cast the garland on flowing water.

The only important exceptions to the rule of drawing exclusively from the *Ādi Granth* are, first, the occasional use of selections from the other approved scriptures; and secondly, the regular recitation of *Ardās*, the so-called Sikh Prayer. The *Ardās*

[10] For a description of the modern gurdwara and its place in Sikh life, both in the Pañjāb and in England, see Alan G. James, *Sikh Children in Britain* (London, 1974), pp. 35ff, 64.

[11] The sacramental food distributed at temples, both Hindu and Sikh. The Sikh variety (consisting of equal parts of coarsely refined wheat flour, sugar, and *ghī*) is distinguished by the name *kaṛāh praśād*. See p. 87.

(literally 'Petition') is an unusually interesting text which, because it evolved during the eighteenth century, expresses with unusual clarity the ideals of that period. Earlier forms evidently concluded with an exhortation to accept the Panth as Gurū.[12] The version currently in use concludes with a similar exhortation to acknowledge the *Gurū Granth Sāhib*. The concluding passage is worth quoting, for no words are more familiar to a Sikh and none express with greater clarity the doctrine of the spiritual Gurū embodied in the scripture.

āgiān bhaī akāl kī
tabī chalāio panth
sab sikhān kau hukam hai
gurū mānio granth
gurū granth jī mānio
paragaṭ gurān kī deh
jā kā hiradā sudh hai
khoj śabad men leh

From the Timeless One there came the bidding,
In accordance with which was established the Panth.
To all Sikhs there comes this command:
Acknowledge as Gurū the *Granth*.
Acknowledge the *Granth* as Gurū,
For it is the manifest body of the Masters.
Ye whose hearts are pure,
Seek Him in the Word!

The prominence accorded the *Gurū Granth Sāhib* in regular gurdwara worship extends to all other Sikh ceremonies. The passages which the devout Sikh should recite in the morning and evening are taken from it. When he is married he circumambulates the sacred volume instead of the sacred fire, and when he is cremated the ceremony is performed in its presence. Before he proceeds to his daily labours he may 'take a command' from the scripture. This custom consists of opening the volume at random and reading the composition which appears at the top of the left-hand page. The passage which is turned up in this manner is believed to bestow a specific guidance for that particular day. A similar procedure is followed when choosing a name for a child. Once again the *Gurū Granth Sāhib* is opened

[12] E. Trumpp, op. cit., p. cxv, n. 2.

at random and the first letter at the top of the left-hand page must be the first letter of the chosen name.

The custom of taking daily guidance by means of a random opening may also be extended to provide a public oracle. Perhaps the most dramatic instance of using the scripture for this purpose was an event which took place in 1920. This was the period of the so-called mass movement when substantial numbers of Pañjābī outcastes, in quest of an enhanced social status, were joining either the Christian Church or the Khālsā. The Church, because it had previously been so tiny in the Pañjāb, suffered no serious dislocation, but for the much larger Khālsā the consequent problems were considerable. Inevitably the crisis assumed its most acute form over the issue of commensality, and specifically the question of whether or not converts from outcaste groups could offer and receive sacramental food (*kaṛāh praśād*) at the gurdwaras. A small group of Siṅgh Sabhā reformers advocated their right to do so and could point to passages in the scripture which supported their claim. The burden of tradition is, however, heavy and the prohibitions which obstructed a total acceptance of outcaste converts could not be so easily cast aside.

The issue came to a head in 1920 following a baptismal convention held in Amritsar. These conventions resembled the *śudhī* ceremonies of the Ārya Samāj in that they were held for the purpose of initiating outcastes, and on this occasion there had been the usual baptism of new converts into the Khālsā. But could these outcaste converts proceed to the Golden Temple in the expectation that they would there be permitted to offer and receive *kaṛāh praśād*? The administrators of the Golden Temple had already made it abundantly clear that they would be refused. The conference members nevertheless proceeded in procession to the Golden Temple and lodged their demand. This was again refused and it appeared that a serious disturbance might develop. Eventually it was agreed that the Gurū should be consulted and that his decision should be binding. With due ceremony the sacred volume was opened at random and revealed a passage which, it was maintained, put the issue beyond all doubt.

niguṇiā no āpe bakhasi lae bhāī satigur kī sevā lāi
satigur kī sevā utam hai bhāī rām nāmi chitu lāi

hari jīu āpe bakhasi milāi
guṇ hīṇ ham aparādhī bhāī pūrai satiguri lae ralāi

Upon the worthless He bestows His grace, brother, if
they will serve the True Gurū.
Exalted is the service of the True Gurū, brother, to
hold in remembrance the divine Name.
God Himself offers grace and mystic union.
Worthless sinners are we, brother, yet the True Gurū
has drawn us to that blissful union.[13]

Surely the words *niguṇiā* and *aparādhī* must embrace these lowly converts who had so recently declared their intention of seeking the Gurū's grace. The discomfited *sevādārs* withdrew in ignominy, leaving the triumphant reformers to dispense the *kaṛāh praśād*.[14]

One last ceremony to be noted is the *akhaṇḍ pāṭh*, or 'unbroken reading', a custom which tends to be restricted to the wealthier members of the Panth. An *akhaṇḍ pāṭh* is held in honour of a special occasion, as a special thanksgiving, as a supplication for some particular blessing, or as a means of averting a threatened disaster. A wedding will commonly be preceded by an *akhaṇḍ pāṭh* and likewise the opening of a new business. The return of a son from overseas may warrant one and for some it will be regarded as a wise precaution in the event of a serious illness. For the reading a team of readers is assembled and relieving each other in turn they intone the entire scripture without a break. This takes two days. Anyone may sit and listen at any time, and all who are involved in the occasion which prompted the ceremony will gather before the sacred volume as the reading approaches its conclusion (*bhog*). In the principal gurdwaras an endless chain of unbroken reading is maintained, and in smaller temples they may be performed as a prelude to important festivals. One finds throughout the Pañjāb that the invention of the loud-speaker has enabled the promoters of these readings to share their benefits with the wider community. The custom is a recent entrant into Sikh tradition (possibly derived from the Hindu *yajña*) and is by no means universally accepted within the Panth.

[13] Gurū Amar Dās, *Soraṭh Dutukī* 2, *Ādi Granth*, p. 638.
[14] Teja Singh, *Essays in Sikhism* (Lahore, 1944), pp. 168–9.

The centrality of the *Gurū Granth Sāhib* in Sikh custom, and the manifold uses to which it is put, leave no room for doubt concerning its enormous importance to the Panth. Before leaving this aspect of the subject let it again be stressed that the function of this customary usage is of fundamental importance. This function, as we have already seen, is the maintenance of the Panth's cohesion.

We turn now to the contents of the *Ādi Granth*—to its language, its script, its structure, and its dominant theme. Macauliffe must bear most of the responsibility for the misleading impression that the language of the *Ādi Granth* is unusually difficult. Having listed a number of other scriptures he continues:

> The languages in which the holy writings of these religions are enshrined, though all difficult, are for the most part homogeneous, and after preliminary study with tutors can generally be mastered by the aid of grammars and dictionaries; but not so the mediaeval Indian dialects in which the sacred writings of the Sikh Gurus and Saints were composed. Hymns are found in Persian, mediaeval Prakrit, Hindi, Marathi, old Panjabi, Multani, and several local dialects. In several hymns the Sanskrit and Arabic vocabularies are freely drawn upon.[15]

As a pioneer Macauliffe encountered difficulties which will account for this judgement. It is, however, far from accurate. Although there is diversity in the language of the *Ādi Granth* this feature is by no means as pronounced as Macauliffe claimed and in practice presents relatively few problems once the Gurmukhī script has been mastered. Most of the elements which seem to suggest a heterogeneous collection of linguistic forms are, in reality, closely related. There are certainly words from such diverse languages as Sindhī, Arabic, Persian, and Marāṭhī, but with very rare exceptions these provide no more than vocabulary problems. They do not affect the essentially homogeneous structure of the *Ādi Granth* language. A knowledge of Hindī and Pañjābī is the basic requirement. With this equipment one can proceed with relative ease to a study of Sādhukaṛī, or Sant Bhāṣā, a medium employed all over northern India by religious poets of the fifteenth and sixteenth centuries.

[15] M. A. Macauliffe, *The Sikh Religion*, Vol. 1, p. v.

Within this general pattern the different Gurūs and bhagats made different linguistic emphases. Gurū Nānak's language normally has a strong Pañjābī colouring, although in a few cases he drew heavily from the vocabulary of a different language. Gurū Aṅgad and Gurū Rām Dās are also predominantly Pañjābī. Gurū Amar Dās, however, shows more signs of Braj influence, and in the case of Gurū Arjan the Braj emphasis is pronounced.

One mistake which Macauliffe avoided, but which other foreigners have commonly made, is to apply the title Pañjābī to the script which is used in the *Ādi Granth.* The term Pañjābī applies to the actual language, whereas the script is Gurmukhī (literally 'from the mouth of the Gurū'). Tradition claims it to be an invention of the second Gurū. Although this cannot be strictly accurate, its name and its early association with the works of the Gurūs suggest that its development (as opposed to its actual origins) must be intimately connected with the rise of the Sikh Panth. As the vehicle of the sacred scriptures it has acquired a sanctity of its own. It is an exceedingly simple script—even simpler than the Deva-nāgrī script to which it is closely related.

Another distinctive feature of the *Ādi Granth* is the unusually systematic arrangement of its contents. Within it we find a complex and generally consistent pattern of division and subdivision. The first of these is a threefold division into an introductory section, main text, and epilogue. The introductory section consists of works which had evidently acquired a liturgical usage. It opens with the celebrated *Japjī* of Gurū Nānak, a work which must rank as one of the most difficult in the entire scripture but which is nevertheless regarded as its quintessence. It is this composition, running to thirty-eight lengthy stanzas, which devout Sikhs are expected to repeat from memory every morning. The remainder of this opening section comprises fourteen hymns which are used as set forms of devotion for other times of the day. All fourteen are repeated elsewhere in the scripture.

The epilogue consists exclusively of miscellaneous works which could not be accommodated in the main text. These include collections of shaloks (couplets) attributed to Kabīr and Sheikh Farīd, panegyrics in praise of the Gurūs, and at the very end the puzzling *Rāg-mālā* which is evidently intended to summarize the various *rāgs* used in the main text.[16]

The *rāgs* provide the primary subdivision of the main text. Immediately after the introductory section comes *Sirī Rāg*. Within this section have been recorded all the works composed in this particular *rāg* which find a place in the volume. Next comes *Mājh*, then *Gauṛī*, then *Āsā*, and so on through a total of thirty-one *rāgs*, concluding with *Jaijavantı*.

Each *rāg* is itself subdivided into several categories. First come the *chaupad* hymns (four brief stanzas with refrain), then the *aṣṭapadī* (eight stanzas with refrain), and then the *chhant*.[17] Next come works by the Gurūs which are in the appropriate metre, but which by reason of their greater length do not fit the earlier categories. These include Gurū Nānak's *Dakhaṇī Oaṅkār* and his *Sidh Goṣṭ*, both in the *Rāmakalī* measure; and Gurū Arjan's *Sukhmaṇī* in the *Gauṛī* measure. Still within the same *rāg* these longer works are followed by *vārs*, composite works consisting of a series of stanzas (*pauṛī*) each with attached shaloks. The stanzas of any particular *vār* are always the work of a single Gurū, but the shaloks (which are grouped in small clusters and prefixed to the stanzas) may be by different authors.

Finally, at the conclusion of each *rāg*, there is recorded the *bhagat bāṇī*, the compositions of various bhagats which, because they accorded with his own beliefs, had found a place in Gurū Amar Dās's earlier collection. Kabīr is the most prominent of the bhagats, followed by Nāmdev and Ravidās (Raidās). Two Ṣūfīs are included. Four hymns are attributed to Sheikh Farīd (in addition to the 117 shaloks recorded in the epilogue) and two to a lesser figure named Bhīkhaṇ. A single hymn is attributed to the celebrated Rāmānand.

The next subdivision takes place within the *chaupad*, *aṣṭapadī*, and *chhant*. These are arranged in a sequence which corresponds to the succession of Gurūs. The works of Gurū Nānak come first, and then those of Gurū Aṅgad, Gurū Amar Dās, Gurū Rām Dās, and Gurū Arjan respectively. All five Gurūs

[16] *rāg* (*rāga*): melodic organization. Any given *rāg* specifies particular notes to be used against the drone. Tradition and long usage have endowed each *rāg* with its own spiritual significance.

[17] *chhant* (Hindi *chhand*): lit. poem, song. In the *Ādi Granth* the term designates a hymn longer than a *chaupad* but shorter than an *aṣṭapadī*. Most examples consist of four stanzas, each comprising six lines.

styled themselves Nānak in their compositions,[18] but the differences of authorship are clearly distinguished by the use of the word *mahalā* with a figure corresponding to the Gurū's place in the succession. *Mahalā 1* precedes all of the compositions of Gurū Nānak, *Mahalā 2* those of Gurū Aṅgad, and so on through to *Mahalā 5* for the works of Gurū Arjan.[19]

Although this is not quite the end of the *Ādi Granth* system of classification, it must suffice for our present purpose. Not every *rāg* includes all of the categories just mentioned, but wherever they do occur they are almost always recorded in the sequence described above. Very few exceptions to this rule can be found and only one warrants a specific reference. There is a hymn by Kabīr which appears in the midst of a Gurū Arjan cluster, and which includes an unusually explicit rejection of both Hindu and Muslim authority.

nā ham hindū nā musalamān
alah rām ke piṇḍ parān.

I am neither Hindu nor Muslim.
(The One) Allah-Rām is the breath of my body.

The exception is worth noting because several writers, following Macauliffe, have accepted the hymn as the work of Gurū Arjan. This is probably incorrect, for an analogue appears in the *Kabīr-granthāvalī* tradition, and even in its *Ādi Granth* version it bears the name of Kabīr.[20]

The message of the *Ādi Granth* can be summarized very briefly. As in the case of its language we find beneath its superficial diversity a considerable degree of homogeneity. The Gurūs make one fundamental declaration. This they express in a wide variety of ways, building around it a coherent system of religious thought. The message is simply this: salvation is to be obtained through meditation on the divine Name. To recast this in terms which are perhaps more meaningful to a Western understand-

[18] In accordance with the standard procedure of Indian poetics the Gurūs incorporated their name in the last line or couplet of every composition. In every instance the name is Nānak. See above, p. 39.

[19] There are very few compositions attributed to *Mahalā 2* (Gurū Aṅgad). The standard text also includes some compositions attributed to Gurū Tegh Bahādur (*Mahalā 9*) and a couplet attributed to Gurū Gobind Siṅgh. See below, p. 75. The abbreviation *M* is frequently used in place of the word *mahalā* (*M1*, *M2*, etc.).

[20] *Bhairau* 5–3 (*Ādi Granth*, p. 1136) and *Kabīr-granthāvalī* 338 (Das version). Kabīr's *Bhairau* 12 (*Ādi Granth*, p. 1160) is also headed *Mahalā 5* (i.e. Gurū Arjan).

ing we can say that salvation is obtained by means of regular, persistent, disciplined meditation on the manifold expressions of the divine presence in the physical world and in human experience. It cannot be too strongly emphasized that the *Ādi Granth* is a collection of *religious* writings and that everything it contains relates directly to its soteriological concern.

The features which have been described above give an impression of order and clarity. In a general sense this impression is accurate and there can be few scriptures which possess a structure as consistent as that of the *Ādi Granth.* There are, however, certain aspects which are far from clear. The *Ādi Granth* is by no means without its problems (notably its textual problems) and some attention must now be directed to the more important of these issues.

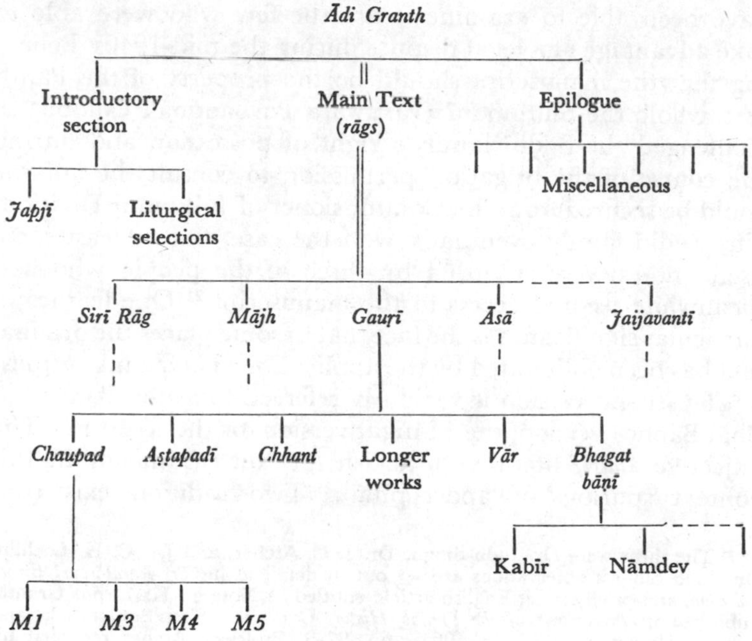

Structure of the *Ādi Granth*

The chief problem concerning the *Ādi Granth* arises from the fact that there is not one single version, but rather three different versions plus a number of variants. The variants can be disregarded in this discussion, but some attention must be directed to the three major versions. If the analysis succeeds only in muddying the water we must reply that a measure of obscurity is no more than an accurate representation of the present condition of our understanding.

Reference has already been made to the first of the three principal versions. This is the manuscript which, according to tradition, was written by Bhāī Gurdās at the dictation of Gurū Arjan, and which is now in the possession of the Soḍhīs of Kartārpur. It is variously known as the Kartārpur version, the Bhāī Gurdās version, or the *Ādi Bīṛ*. Unfortunately it is not possible to gain access to the manuscript. Although it is put on display once a month, no one is actually permitted to come close to the volume. The most one can do is to view it from afar and prostrate oneself before it. The only people who in recent years have been able to examine it are the few who were able to take advantage of a legal dispute during the mid-1940s. Believing that the manuscript should be the property of the Panth as a whole the Shiromaṇī Gurdwara Parbandhak Committee challenged the Soḍhī family's right of possession and during the course of the litigation permission to consult the volume could be secured from the Commissioner of Jullundur Division. The Soḍhī family eventually won the case, but at least some useful notes were recorded by three of the people who had meanwhile secured access to the manuscript.[21] One feature of particular significance is the fact that in some places the original text has been obliterated by the application of green ink (*haṛtāl*).

The second version is variously referred to as the Banno (or Bhāī Banno) version, the Māṅgaṭ version, or the *Khārī Bīṛ*. The adjective *khārī*, literally 'brackish' or 'bitter', means in this context 'spurious' or 'apocryphal'.[22] Two traditions exist con-

[21] The three were Dr. Jodh Singh, Dr. J. C. Archer, and Dr. C. H. Loehlin. Dr. Jodh Singh's observations are set out in detail in his *Srī Karatārpurī Bīṛ de Daraśan*, and briefly in an English article entitled 'A Note on Kartarpur Granth' published in *Proceedings of the Punjab History Conference*, First Session (Patiala: Punjabi University, 1966 for 1965), pp. 97–9. Professor Archer recorded his experience in an article entitled 'The Bible of the Sikhs', published in *The Review of Religion*, January 1949, pp. 115–25. Dr. Loehlin's account is to be found in his *The Sikhs and their Book* (Lucknow, 1946), pp. 44–5, and more recently in an article 'A Westerner looks at the Kartarpur Granth' published in *Proceedings of the Punjab History Conference*, First Session, pp. 93–6.

[22] It has been claimed that the name derives from Kharā, said to be an earlier name of Māṅgaṭ village. See Shamsher Singh Ashok, *Bhāī Banno jī te Khāre vālī bīṛ*,

cerning the origin of this version. According to one, Bhāī Banno, a resident of Māṅgaṭ village in District Gujrāt, visited Gurū Arjan and having developed a great interest in the new scripture asked permission to take it back to Māṅgaṭ on loan. Gurū Arjan was understandably loath to accede to the request, but eventually gave his permission on condition that Banno kept it at his village for one night only. Banno circumvented this condition by travelling very slowly to and from Māṅgaṭ. The lengthy journey afforded him time to make a copy of the volume without breaking his promise. The other tradition holds that he was entrusted with the responsibility of taking the original to Lahore for binding and he made his copy while on this mission.[23]

The third version has been briefly noticed in the account given above of the Kartārpur manuscript. Gurū Gobind Siṅgh, having been refused the latter, is said to have dictated his own copy from memory, adding to the original text fifty-nine hymns and fifty-six couplets of his father, Gurū Tegh Bahādur, and also one couplet of his own. Quite apart from the feat of memory the tradition is inaccurate, for the works of Gurū Tegh Bahādur had already been incorporated in at least one version which predates the period of Gurū Gobind Siṅgh.[24] This is, however, of small importance. The significant facts are, first, that a version incorporating this extra material did become current; and secondly, that apart from extra material it corresponds closely to the Kartārpur manuscript. This is the Damdamā version, so called because Gurū Gobind Siṅgh is said to have dictated it while staying at the village of Damdamā Sāhib.[25] Modern printed copies follow this third text in including the works of Gurū Tegh Bahādur and the couplet attributed to Gurū Gobind Siṅgh.

The problem which confronts us arises from a comparison of the Kartārpur and Banno versions. We note, in the first

in *Khoj Patrikā* (Patiala), no. 4, May 1970, pp. 36–7. Ashok's article gives a traditional account of the life of Banno.

[23] M. A. Macauliffe, op. cit., Vol. 3, p. 66.

[24] Khushwant Singh claims there are two such versions (op. cit., Vol. 1, p. 93, n. 35).

[25] Bhaṭinda District. The village is also known by its earlier name Talvaṇḍī. Sābo, or Sābo kī Talvaṇḍī. The name was changed in honour of the occasion when Gurū Gobind Siṅgh made the village his resting-place (*damdamā*), i.e. when he spent a period there following the Battle of Muktsar in 1705.

place, that the claim to originality made on behalf of the Kartārpur manuscript appears to be sound. Dr. Jodh Singh has argued this in a manner which seems to be entirely convincing.[26] At first sight, however, this manuscript appears to be an exception to the general run of early manuscripts which, until well into the eighteenth century, are almost always Banno texts or variants of it. And, as we have just observed, the Banno version is supposed to be spurious.

A solution is suggested by a comparison of the two texts. The significant differences consist exclusively of extra material included in the Banno version which is said to be absent from the Kartārpur manuscript. The three most important instances are a hymn by Mīrā Bāī, another by Sūr Dās, and a third by Gurū Arjan. Given this situation one is tempted to conclude that the extra material must originally have been included in the Kartārpur manuscript and then subsequently obliterated. Tact and persuasion having failed to secure access to the Kartārpur volume, I was compelled to fall back on the evidence which existed apart from the actual manuscript. An analysis of this evidence seemed to confirm a theory already tentatively formed.

Two of the basic points have already been noted. First, there is the universal agreement that the important differences distinguishing the Kartārpur manuscript from the Banno version consist exclusively of material included in the latter which is not to be found in the former. Secondly, there is the testimony of those who have inspected the Kartārpur manuscript concerning the obliteration of portions of its text.

A third factor is the presence in the standard printed editions of two fragments, corresponding to two of the three additional Banno hymns. In *Rāmakalī rāg* there occurs a single couplet where there should apparently be a complete hymn.[27] The remainder of the hymns in the same section indicate that the couplet must be either the first two lines of a *chhant*, or a shalok introducing a *chhant*. The second fragment corresponds to the Sūr Dās hymn in *Sāraṅg rāg*. In this instance the standard printed text contains only the first line.[28] There seemed to be only one possible reason for the appearance of these two fragments. The bulk of the hymn in each case must have been

[26] Jodh Singh, op. cit.
[27] *Ādi Granth*, p. 927.
[28] Ibid., p. 1253.

deleted, leaving a small remainder which was faithfully copied into the standard printed text.

A fourth point seemed to clinch the issue. The Banno text of the missing portions indicated good reasons for later deletion, particularly in the case of the *Rāmakalī* hymn by Gurū Arjan. This hymn describes the puberty rites conducted by Gurū Arjan at the initiation of his son Hargobind. The rites follow a standard Hindu pattern and in the third stanza there is a reference to the manner in which the boy's head was shaved.[29] This feature is in obvious contradiction to the later prohibition of hair-cutting. When the prohibition became mandatory, not merely for Jaṭ Sikhs but also those of other castes, the reference in the hymn could only be regarded as intolerable.

Finally, there was ample evidence that others had already formed the same suspicions concerning the Kartārpur manuscript and were seeking alternative explanations. One writer has declared that the present Kartārpur manuscript is a Banno version, adding that the original manuscript of the *Ādi Granth* must have been lost.[30] Another has suggested that the present manuscript must be a first draft, subsequently amended by the Gurū himself.[31] Their evident uneasiness strengthened a hypothesis which already seemed firmly founded.

By this time the hypothesis will have become obvious. The conclusion which seemed to be emerging with increasing assurance was that the widely disseminated Banno version must represent the original text; and that the Kartārpur manuscript must be a shortened version of the same text. A few portions must have been deleted because they could not be reconciled with beliefs subsequently accepted by the Panth. This much appeared to be well established and another point could be added as a possibility. It seemed likely that the amendments had originally been made by omitting the problem passages from later manuscripts rather than by deleting them from the Kartārpur manuscript. These later manuscripts reflected the distinctive pattern of Khālsā belief. The omission of the prob-

[29] India Office Library MS. Panj. F1, f. 462b. British Museum MS. Or. 2159, f. 582a/584a.

[30] Sant Indar Singh Chakarvarti, *Pañjābī Duniān* (Jan.-Feb. 1965), p. 196.

[31] This opinion was advanced orally during the discussion which followed the reading of Dr Loehlin's paper 'A Westerner looks at the Kartarpur Granth' at the first session of the Punjab History Conference. See above, p. 74, n. 21.

lem passages together with the addition of compositions by Gurū Tegh Bahādur constituted the Damdamā version of the *Ādi Granth*. Later still, portions of the Kartārpur manuscript (the original manuscript written by Bhāī Gurdās) were rather ineptly obliterated in order to bring the two versions into line.

That, however, was not to be the end of the problem. In 1968 Dr. Jodh Singh published his book *Srī Kartārpurī Bīṛ de Daraśan*. Dr. Jodh Singh was the person who had devoted the closest attention to the manuscript during the period when it was under litigation and had taken the opportunity to make copious notes. These notes form the substance of his book. They raise once again issues which previously had seemed to be satisfactorily settled, and although they do not altogether destroy the thesis based upon the comparison with the extant Banno text, they do deprive it of its earlier assurance.

From these notes it appears that the Mīrā Bāī hymn still fits the original thesis, for Dr. Jodh Singh confirms that it was in the original manuscript.[32] The hymns by Sūr Dās and Gurū Arjan are, however, in doubt. In the case of the former Dr. Jodh Singh reports that the opening line of the hymn (the line which appears in the standard printed text) is followed by four blank lines in the manuscript. This could accommodate the remainder of the hymn, but Dr. Jodh Singh assures us that there has been no obliteration at this point.[33] He reports a similar condition in the case of Gurū Arjan's *Rāmakalī* hymn. The solitary couplet is followed by a blank space which extends to more than two folios—and no obliteration. He also states that although the couplet is in the same hand as the text which precedes it the scribe has used a different pen.[34]

From this report it is clear that the issue should still be regarded as open. The importance of the questions which it raises deserves to be firmly stressed. Whereas the hymns by Mīrā Bāī and Sūr Dās involve interesting textual problems of no great significance, the same certainly cannot be said for the *Rāmakalī* hymn by Gurū Arjan. Did Gurū Arjan write this hymn? If it could be established that he did in fact compose it, the relationship of the later Khālsā discipline to the earlier teachings of the Gurūs could be made dramatically clearer. But

[32] Op. cit., p. 106. [33] Ibid., p. 113. [34] Ibid., p. 97.

did he compose it? Although the unity of the complete hymn as recorded in the Banno version implies the work of one man, the failure of the Kartārpur manuscript to record more than one couplet prevents us from drawing any firm conclusions.

This concludes the description of the *Ādi Granth*, or *Gurū Granth Sāhib*, except to add that there exist some excellent vernacular commentaries on the text of the standard printed edition.[35] The brief remainder of the essay will be devoted to a rapid survey of the other works which can be regarded as Sikh scriptures. It should be emphasized that the brevity of the treatment reflects no estimate of their importance. Although they are not to be compared to the *Ādi Granth* in terms of sanctity or actual use they are nevertheless works of very considerable significance, not least as historical source material.

The first of these supplementary scriptures to be noted is the *Dasam Granth*, or 'Book of the Tenth Gurū'.[36] This work must be distinguished from the Damdamā version of the *Ādi Granth* with which it is sometimes confused. The *Dasam Granth* is a large collection of miscellaneous writings attributed to Gurū Gobind Siṅgh which in no way overlap the contents of the *Ādi Granth*. In marked contrast to the consistent religious message of the earlier collection it embodies a considerable diversity of

[35] The first of the vernacular commentaries was the celebrated *Ādi Srī Gurū Granth Sāhibjī Saṭīk*, commonly known as the *Farīdkoṭ Ṭīkā* because it was commissioned by the Raja of Farīdkoṭ and published in four volumes under his patronage in 1905. A second edition appeared in 1924 and a third was published by the Languages Department, Patiala, in 1970. Its principal contributor was Bhai Badan Singh Giani. The best commentary is the four-volume *Śabadārath Srī Gurū Granth Sāhib Jī* (n.p., 1936–41), largely the work of the late Principal Teja Singh but published anonymously. The complete *Ādi Granth* text is given, with commentary on the facing page. Much fuller but still incomplete is Vir Singh's *Santhyā Srī Gurū Granth Sāhib* (Amritsar, 1958–62). Seven volumes have so far been published and the remainder, though long delayed, are said to be forthcoming. Another excellent work is Professor Sahib Singh's *Srī Gurū Granth Sāhib Darapaṇ*, published in ten volumes (Jullundur, 1962–4). Two supplementary works which are indispensable for a study of the *Ādi Granth* text are *Srī Gurū Granth Koś* (3 vols., Amritsar, 4th ed., 1950) and *Guru Śabad Ratan Prakāś* (Patiala, 1963). The first of these is a dictionary of difficult words occurring in the *Ādi Granth*, published anonymously but known to be largely the work of Vir Singh. The second is a line-index of the *Ādi Granth* compiled by Kaur Singh Nihang and originally published in 1923. To these should be added the noble *Guruśabad Ratanākar Mahān Koś* of Kahn Singh Nabha (Patiala, 2nd ed., 1960), commonly known simply as the *Mahān Koś* and justly claiming to be 'An Encyclopaedia of Sikh Literature'.

[36] A printed edition is available, published by Bhai Jawahar Singh Kirpal Singh, Bazar Mai Sewan, Amritsar. Two studies of the *Dasam Granth* are Dharam Pal Ashta, *Poetry of the Dasam Granth* (New Delhi, 1959), and C. H. Loehlin, *The Granth of Guru Gobind Singh and the Khalsa Brotherhood* (Lucknow, 1971). See also Khushwant Singh, *A History of the Sikhs*, Vol. 1, pp. 313–18.

material, owing a particular debt to the Purāṇas and to anecdotes from current oral tradition.

The contents of the *Dasam Granth* fall into four groups. First, there are two works which may be classified as autobiographical. The *Vichitar Nāṭak* is an account by the Gurū himself of his genealogy, of his previous incarnation as an ascetic in the Himālayas, and of his earlier battles. The *Zafar-nāmā* is a defiant epistle addressed to the Mughal emperor Aurangzeb.

Secondly, there are four compositions expressing the militant piety which characterizes the tenth Gurū. These are the *Jāp* (a work of great influence which must be distinguished from the *Japjī* of Nānak), the *Akāl Ustat*, the *Giān Prabodh*, and the *Śabad Hazāre.*

Thirdly, there are two miscellaneous works. These are the *Savaiyye* or 'Panegyrics'; and the *Śastar Nām-mālā*, or 'Inventory of Weapons'.

Fourthly, there are the lengthy portions relating legend and anecdote—the *Chaṇḍī Charitr*, *Chaṇḍī kī Vār*, the *Chaubīs Avatār*, and the *Trīā Charitr*. As these titles indicate the Mother Goddess Chaṇḍī figures prominently. Of the *avatārs* Kriṣṇa receives by far the greatest attention. The *Trīā Charitr* are tales of the wiles of women which have, with a certain aptness, been dubbed 'barrack-room ballads'.

These four groups differ considerably in terms of length as well as subject-matter and the differences are of significance in any attempt to define the true nature of the *Dasam Granth* collection. The two autobiographical works cover a total of 73 pages in the standard printed edition; the devotional compositions occupy 68 pages; and the miscellaneous works are contained within 96 pages. These three must be set in contrast with the legendary narratives which together account for 1,185 pages. Within this fourth group the *Kriṣaṇ Avatār* covers 316 pages and the *Trīā Charitr* 580 pages.

Were all these compositions the work of Gurū Gobind Siṅgh? The autobiographical and devotional compositions may well be the Gurū's own work, and perhaps also *Chaṇḍī kī Vār*. The remainder must be substantially, and probably entirely, the works of others who were present at his court. The various works were collected after his death (perhaps, as the tradition claims, by the celebrated disciple Manī Siṅgh) and because they had all come from the tenth Gurū's court the ordinal *dasam* was attached to the volume. The language is predominantly Braj, with some Persian, Pañjābī, and Khaṛī Bolī. As an expression of the Śivāliks' impact upon the Jaṭ culture of the Pañjāb plains the *Dasam Granth* is a historical source of critical importance for any analysis of the evolution of the Sikh Panth. It has yet to receive the close attention which it deserves.

Another anthology which may be regarded as a supplementary scripture is the collection of *Vārs* by Bhāī Gurdās,[37] a writer to whom we have already referred as the amanuensis of Gurū Arjan. A *vār* is, strictly, a heroic ode or ballad, but in Bhāī Gurdās's hands the form has been turned to a much more general use. In his thirty-nine Pañjābī *Vārs* he covers an extensive range of Sikh belief, history, and biography.[38] These compositions are renowned in Sikh tradition as 'the key to the *Gurū Granth Sāhib*' and as such are approved for recitation in gurdwaras. In spite of their extensive use they too have yet to receive from historians and philologists the attention which they warrant. The same can also be said of his 556 *Kabitts* which, because they are in a somewhat difficult Braj, have been largely ignored even within the Panth.[39]

A status similar to the *Vārs* of Bhāī Gurdās is accorded the Persian and Pañjābī works of Nand Lāl Goyā, and here too we must note not only their importance but also their neglect.[40] Although Nand Lāl was one of the poets at the court of Gurū Gobind Siṅgh, it is appropriate that his work should have been omitted from the *Dasam Granth*. Unlike most of the Gurū's other poets Nand Lāl betrays a dominant interest in philosophical issues.

Finally, there are the janam-sākhīs which, because they are so commonly read within the precincts of gurdwaras, may be regarded as semi-canonical. As a complete essay has already been devoted to this body of literature no further description will be offered at this point.

[37] The standard edition is *Vārān Bhāī Gurdās*, ed. Hazara Singh and Vir Singh (Amritsar: the Khalsa Samachar, 7th ed., 1962).

[38] The extant collection consists of forty *vārs*. There is, however, no doubt that the last of these is by a later hand.

[39] *Kabbit Bhāī Gurdās*, ed. Vir Singh (Amritsar: the Khalsa Samachar, 3rd ed., 1966).

[40] *Kulliyāt-i-Bhāī Nand Lāl Goyā*, ed. Ganda Singh (Malacca: Sikh Sangat, 1963).

The world is poorer for its ignorance of the Sikh scriptures. Although it is doubtless true that translations can rarely recapture the charm of a choice original, it is equally true that competence is always attainable and that a skilled translator who senses the power of the original Pañjābī will occasionally reproduce its spirit and beauty as well as its literal meaning. Already there are promising beginnings. We must hope that they prosper.[41]

[41] For three excellent articles on the *Ādi Granth* see those by C. Shackle in the *Bulletin on the School of Oriental and African Studies,* University of London XL. 1 (1977), pp. 36–50, XLI. 1 (1978), pp. 73–96 and XLI. 2 (1978), pp. 297–313. The third article concludes with a particularly helpful diagram on page 313.

5

CASTE IN THE SIKH PANTH

IT was during the last two decades of the eighteenth century that the Sikhs first became a subject of interest to British observers. Although the primary interest of the British was, predictably, in the military and political strength of the Sikh misls currently controlling the Pañjāb, the accounts which derive from this period also attempt to describe the rudiments of Sikh religion and society.[1]

Two comments relating to the caste constituency of the Panth recur in these accounts and in their early nineteenth-century successors. The first is that it consists 'mostly of the *Jaut* [Jaṭ] tribe'.[2] This 'tribe' is, however, generally recognized as the bulk and dominant nucleus of the Panth, not as its exclusive membership. Other castes were perceived within the Khālsā brotherhood and it was this mingling of castes which prompted the second recurring comment:

> The Article indeed of receiving Proselytes, in the Doctrine of the Seicks causes an essential deviation from the Hindoo system. It totally overthrows those wonderful Barriers which were constructed and affixed by Brimha [Brahma, *sic* Manu], for the arrangement of the different ranks and professions of his People.[3]

Caste distinctions were, in other words, obliterated within the eighteenth-century Panth.

Although the first of these observations can be accepted, the second must be substantially qualified. Another Englishman of the same period observed one major qualification clearly and dimly perceived another. Writing in 1803 William Francklin commented:

[1] These narratives have been edited by Ganda Singh and published in *Indian Studies: Past and Present*, Vol. 2, nos. 3 and 4; and Vol. 3, no. 2. *Indian Studies: Past and Present* subsequently published them collectively under the title *Early European Accounts of the Sikhs*, ed. Ganda Singh (Calcutta, 1962).

[2] James Browne, *History of the Origin and Progress of the Sicks* (1783). Ganda Singh, op. cit., p. 13. Also ibid., pp. 56, 105.

[3] Letter from George Forster to Mr. Gregory at Lucknow, dated in Kachmer 1783, Ganda Singh, p. 79. Also ibid., pp. 18, 56, 92.

The Seiks allow foreigners of every description to join their standard, to sit in their company, and to shave their beards, but excepting in the instance of the Jauts, they will not consent to intermarriages, nor will they eat or drink from the hands of an alien except he be a Bramin, and for this cast they always profess the highest veneration.[4]

The qualification which Francklin plainly marked was a restriction on commensality, overtly expressed in a continuing respect for Brāhmaṇ services. Pañjābī sources of the same period confirm the strength of this attitude.[5] Francklin also draws attention to a restriction on intermarriage. Although his reference concerns foreigners it seems clear that the comment should properly be applied to conventions observed within the Panth. This, at least, is the conclusion implied by nineteenth- and twentieth-century observations. These later observations reveal an insistent regard for marriage alliances along conventional lines, qualified only by a limited measure of freedom in the case of the Jaṭs. Entry to the Panth was open to all and within it caste was certainly discounted. It was, however, by no means obliterated. It survived in terms of commensality and marriage patterns, demonstrating in both respects that degree of tenacity which has proved so puzzling to successive generations of foreigners.

The comments by early British writers serve to introduce the important question of caste in the Sikh Panth. There are, in fact, two issues which warrant our attention. The first is the comparatively simple empirical question of the actual caste constituency of the Panth. This particular issue has already obtruded in the numerous references to Jaṭ dominance which appear in the earlier essays. The second question concerns the survival of caste observance within the Panth, a feature which for many Sikhs constitutes a continuing moral problem. On the one hand there are the egalitarian traditions inherited from the teachings of the Gurūs; and on the other one is confronted by the undeniable persistence of caste. There are thus separate issues of constituency and of attitude. They are, however, intimately related and it will accordingly be convenient to treat them concurrently.

[4] William Francklin, *Military Memoirs of Mr George Thomas*, Ganda Singh, p. 105.

[5] Chopā Singh, 'Rahit-nāmā', unpub. MS. no. 6124 of the Sikh Reference Library, Amritsar, f. 6a.

At first sight there seems to be no problem as far as the teachings of the Gurūs are concerned. Gurū Nānak declared his attitude in a famous and oft-repeated couplet:

phakar jātī phakar nāu
sabhanā jīā ikā chhāu

Worthless is caste and worthless an exalted name.
For all mankind there is but a single refuge.[6]

This is merely the most famous of his numerous pronouncements on this particular subject. Many more can be added.

Observe the divine light in a man and ask not his caste
For there is no caste in the hereafter[7]

Sacrifice, oblation, the reading of sacred texts—
all are futile.
Only that which pleases Thee is acceptable in
Thy sight.
Kingship, possessions, beauty, and riches—all
are but transient clouds,
And when the Sun's chariot ascends the true
landscape comes into view.
In the hereafter name and caste count for nothing.[8]

It was the quest for salvation which above all else concerned Nānak and in this quest caste status provided no assistance to the individual. It was, in fact, a positive hindrance for many in that it nurtured a detrimental pride. The way to God was through holy living, not through any accident of birth nor through the observance of any external ritual.

Nānak's successors repeat this same message both by precept and by the institution of distinctive customs.

When you die you do not carry your caste with you.
It is your deeds [and not your caste] which will
determine your fate.[9]

These are the words of Gurū Amar Dās and he, it seems, was

[6] *Vār Sirī Rāgu* 3:1, *Ādi Granth* (*AG*), p. 83.
[7] *Āsā* 3, *AG*, p. 349.
[8] *Malār* 8, *AG*, p. 1257: For other examples of Gurū Nānak's pronouncements on caste see *Vār Mājh* 10, *AG*, p. 142; *Vār Āsā* 11:3, *AG*, p. 469; *Sāraṅg* 3, *AG*, p. 198; *Prabhātī* 10, *AG*, p. 1330.
[9] *Āsā* 8, *AG*, p. 363.

the Gurū responsible for borrowing from the Sūfīs the practice of compulsory commensality.[10] To this day every Sikh gurdwara must have attached to it a dining-room (the *langar*) in which meals are served to any who may care to accept them. This strikes at the very heart of an important aspect of caste and there can be no doubt that the practice was instituted for this very reason.

The words of the fourth Gurū, Rām Dās, carry forward the same message.

> There are four castes and four traditional stages in
> the holy life.
> But he who meditates on God he it is who is supreme.[11]

The fifth Gurū, Arjan, repeats it yet again and significantly includes in the scripture which he prepared the works of two earlier poets who had made the same point with even greater force. Kabīr, a low-caste weaver (*julāhā*), and Ravidās, an outcaste leather-worker (*chamār*), had both insisted in their devotional poetry that the way of salvation was as open to them as to anyone else. Gurū Arjan indicated his agreement by retaining their hymns in the *Granth Sāhib*, the sacred scripture of the Sikhs. Also included were works attributed to Nāmdev, a low-caste calico printer (*chhīmbā*).

Finally, and most significant of all, there was the example set by Gurū Gobind Singh at the institution of the Khālsā brotherhood in 1699, specifically in the ceremony of initiation which he is said to have introduced on that occasion.[12] The climax of this ceremony was a form of baptism which required all candidates to drink from a common bowl, striking once again at the notion of ritual purity. In Sikh tradition the anti-caste quality of the Khālsā initiation is further strengthened by the belief that the first five to accept baptism included a representative range from high-caste Khatrī through middle-caste Jaṭ to low-caste barber and washerman.

The baptismal procedure of the Khālsā was strengthened and confirmed in the post-initiation experience of its members by the custom of presenting sacramental food (*kaṛāh praśād*)

[10] W. H. McLeod, *Gurū Nānak and the Sikh Religion* (Oxford, 1968), p. 210.
[11] *Goṇḍ* 4, *AG*, p. 861.
[12] See above, p. 15.

before copies of the scripture installed in gurdwaras. The significance of this rite lies not merely in the actual presentation, but also in the subsequent consumption of the food. Having been brought into a gurdwara by Sikhs of any caste the individual offerings of *kaṛāh praśād* are deposited in a single dish and a portion is distributed amongst all who are present in the congregation. All are expected to accept a share, regardless of their own caste or of the sources of the offering. This ensures that high castes consume food received in effect from the hands of lower castes or even outcastes and that they do so from a common dish. Although the actual period of introduction into Sikh usage is unknown a reference in the works of Bhāī Gurdās suggests that the custom (or something resembling it) was observed at least as early as the time of the fifth Gurū.[13] Those who wish to avoid receiving *kaṛāh praśād* from hands of inferior status can in practice do so, but the intention of the rite remains clear.[14]

And so it would appear that the Sikh Gurūs were, beyond all doubt, vigorous and practical denunciators of caste. From this it would seem to follow that continued evidence of caste distinction within the Sikh community must represent flagrant violations of the Gurūs' explicit commands. It is at this point that some critics of Sikh claims have introduced a suggestion which to Sikh ears must sound grossly impertinent. According to these critics the most prominent violators of the anti-caste commandments are the Gurūs themselves. Nothing rouses a Sikh to greater fury than a censure (direct or implied) of the Gurūs and it is presumably for this reason that the suggestion has rarely found its way into print. It is, however, uttered often enough in conversation and ought therefore to be brought into the open for examination.

The ten Gurūs were all Khatrīs by caste. In other words, they all belonged to a mercantile caste, claiming (as its name indicates) the elevated rank of Kshatriya and commanding a high status rating in Pañjābī society. This is widely regarded as

[13] *Vār* 1:36. Hazara Singh and Vir Singh (eds.), *Vārān Bhāī Gurdās* (Amritsar, 1962), p. 32.

[14] *Kaṛāh praśād* is prepared by boiling equal parts of coarsely refined wheat flour, clarified butter (*ghī*), and sugar in an iron pan (*kaṛāh*). For a more detailed description see Jogendra Singh, *Sikh Ceremonies* (Bombay, 1941), pp. 95–6; and Parkash Singh, *The Sikh Gurus and the Temple of Bread* (Amritsar, 1964), pp. 106–10.

a great pity, even within Sikh society where the numerically preponderant Jaṭs commonly bewail the fact that there was never a single Jaṭ Gurū. It is not, however, the point and substance of the impertinent suggestion. The suggestion concerns the marriage practices observed by the Gurūs. All, without exception, arranged marriages for their children in strict accordance with traditional caste prescription. There is no instance of a Gurū having contracted on behalf of his children marriages with boys or girls from lower castes (nor indeed from a higher rank, although in view of the elevated Khatrī status this is less significant). All the Gurūs, themselves Khatrīs, married Khatrī wives and this, declare their critics, is the true measure of their sincerity. How can one respect a commandment when its promulgators ignore it?

There are two answers which can be offered to this unpublished and unnecessarily embarrassing dilemma. The first is that the Gurūs were not concerned with the institution of caste as such, merely with the belief that it possesses soteriological significance. Caste can remain, but not the doctrine that one's access to salvation depends upon one's caste ranking. The way of salvation is open to all regardless of caste. Stripped of its religious content it can retain the status of a harmless social convention.

This deprives caste of some of its meaning, but by no means all. Was this what the Gurūs meant? Although their utterances (notably the stress upon there being no caste *in the hereafter*) might suggest this, their institutions (commensality in the *laṅgar*, distribution of *kaṛāh praśād* in the gurdwara, and baptism from a common bowl) indicate that they intended their denunciation of caste to be carried significantly further. A reasonable conclusion appears to be that whereas they were vigorously opposed to the *vertical* distinctions of caste they were content to accept it in terms of its *horizontal* linkages. This constitutes our second answer to the suggestion of inconsistency on the part of the Gurūs.

Whereas the first of these rebuttals is easily comprehended the second requires a brief explanation if the attitude of the Gurūs is to be fully understood. This is particularly necessary in the case of non-Indian readers who, having been nurtured on the concept of a traditional fourfold caste hierarchy, persistently apply this classical model to all areas of Indian society. Outside India caste is commonly understood as a single and generally uniform hierarchical 'system'. At the apex of the pyramid sits the Brāhmaṇ, or 'priest'. Below him we find the Kshatriya, or 'warrior'; then the Vaishya, or mercantile caste; and finally the Shudra, incorporating cultivators and such menials as possessed caste ranking. Below the pyramid we find the 'outcastes', notably the sweepers and leather-workers.

It is this classical hierarchy of four *varṇas* (literally 'colours') which is popularly supposed to constitute the 'caste system'. The classical *varṇa* theory certainly possesses a substantial importance as an ideal and in most parts of India the actual status of the two extremes (Brāhmaṇ and outcaste) generally corresponds to their theoretical status. In practice, however, there is no single pattern which can be applied to the realities of caste in India. The many and varied caste hierarchies one encounters in contemporary Indian society and for many centuries past have had only a weak reference to the traditional model.

The traditional pyramid provides a most misleading starting-point for any discussion of caste and for this reason we shall set it aside. Instead we shall begin with the two components of the 'system' most meaningful to those within it, namely the *zāt* (Hindī *jāti*) and the *got* (Hindī *gotra*).[15] The *zāt* is the larger grouping, distinguished above all else by the fact that it is endogamous. In the Pañjāb the important *zāts* include the Brāhmaṇs, Khatrīs, Rājpūts, Jaṭs, Aroṛās, Tarkhāns (carpenters), and many more. Each *zāt* is divided into several smaller groups. These are the *gots*, and the *got* (in contradistinction to the wider *zāt*) is exogamous.

As a convenient example we shall take the Khatrī *zāt*, the caste grouping to which all the Gurūs belonged. Gurū Nānak, a Khatrī by *zāt*, belonged to the Bedī *got*. This meant that his parents were required to arrange for him a marriage outside the Bedī *got* but within an approved range of other Khatrī *gots*. The *gots* into which Bedīs may marry include that of the Choṇās and it was to a Choṇā girl that his parents duly betrothed him. The second Gurū, Aṅgad, was a Khatrī of the Trehaṇ *got*, and his successor, Amar Dās, was a Bhallā. Since the Bhallā *got* may intermarry with the Soḍhī *got* it was to a young Soḍhī that

[15] These are North Indian terms. Other regions use different terms.

Amar Dās married his daughter. This young man, Rām Dās, became the fourth Gurū and thereafter the office was hereditary in the line of his male descendants. All married according to the correct *got* prescription.

This pattern still holds for the vast majority of Indian marriages, both in terms of parental arrangement and observance of the approved horizontal linkage. It is important to stress the horizontal nature of this, the most tenacious of all the many aspects of caste. It cuts across confessional boundaries, uniting Hindu and Sikh without hindrance, and imparting to Indian society a stability which Westerners find difficult to comprehend. Many will claim that Indian society would pay a high price for the abandonment of this relationship and the stability which is its consequence. Aliens may call it antiquated conservatism or unwarranted interference with the rights of the individual, but there are still comparatively few Indians who would agree with them and it seems clear that such critics would receive little sympathy from the Sikh Gurūs.

This emphasis upon the primacy of horizontal relationships is a necessary corrective to a popular misunderstanding. It should not suggest, however, that vertical relationships are unimportant. This would be far from the truth. Notwithstanding the importance of horizontal *got* and *zāt* relationships Indian society *is* strongly hierarchical and one can always expect to find the society of a particular area ordered within a distinct pattern of rank and status. While retaining an overriding loyalty to his *zāt* relationship each individual will also be well aware of who stands above and below him, even if his explicit declarations commonly lay claim to a status higher than that suggested by the general consensus.

Having thus sketched in the most general terms an outline of both the horizontal and vertical features of caste we can return to the question posed by the teachings and example of the Gurūs. We can affirm once again their apparent acceptance of the horizontal relationship, an acceptance unmistakably demonstrated by their willingness to observe customary marriage conventions. What they were apparently concerned to deny was the justice of privilege or deprivation based upon notions of status and hierarchy. They were, in other words, opposed to the discriminatory aspects of the vertical relationship while continuing to accept the socially beneficial pattern of horizontal connections.

Bhāī Gurdās, writing in the early seventeenth century, communicates the same impression. In his eighth *vār* he surveys the society which he knows, listing its principal categories and affirming a single way of salvation open to all men. The world, he declares, contains an abundance of different castes and the more important of these he enumerates in stanzas 9–12.[16] Their existence is evidently accepted without question, the point being that the differences of caste identity which they acknowledge are of no significance whatsoever in terms of salvation.

It is also to Bhāī Gurdās that we owe an important list of individual Sikhs, beginning with followers of Gurū Nānak and terminating (in Bhāī Gurdās's own period) with those of the sixth Gurū, Hargobind.[17] In most cases the caste name is given and we are thus provided with important evidence concerning the constituency of Panth during its first century. Three facts emerge clearly. The first is the point already indicated, namely that there is no evident attempt to conceal the caste origins of individual Sikhs. The second is that the early Panth incorporated a broad spectrum of castes, one which is much more diverse than the constituency observed from the late eighteenth century onwards. One particular caste does, however, emerge in notable prominence, and this feature provides the third significant fact. Of those who are identified in caste terms an absolute majority are Khatrīs, the *zāt* to which the Gurūs belonged. It seems clear from Bhāī Gurdās's evidence that Khatrī leadership within the early Panth must have extended well beyond the actual line of Gurūs.

The evidence provided by Bhāī Gurdās can, however, be supplemented by another source. It has already been claimed that the Jaṭ component must have been substantial by the early seventeenth century. This is no mere surmise. It is the testimony of the author of the *Dabistān-i-Mazāhib*, a contemporary of the sixth Gurū and an interested observer of his following.[18] From these two sources it seems reasonable to conclude that during the early seventeenth century Khatrīs enjoyed

[16] Hazara Singh and Vir Singh, op. cit., pp. 139–41.

[17] *Vār* 11. 13–31. Ibid., pp. 193–206.

[18] See above, p. 10. See also J. S. Grewal, *From Guru Nanak to Maharaja Ranjit Singh* (Amritsar, 1972), p. 43.

a particular prominence within the diverse following which constituted the Panth, but that a share of the leadership was also entrusted to individual Jaṭ members. This measure of authority presumably reflected the numerical importance of Jaṭs within the Panth.

During the course of the seventeenth and eighteenth centuries this numerical importance greatly increased, eventually producing the condition of strong Jaṭ predominance noted by the early European observers. An increase in Jaṭ authority matched their preponderance in members. Two processes evidently account for this late eighteenth-century situation. The obvious one is the accession of Jaṭs to the Khālsā. Less obvious was the failure of other castes (notably the Khatrīs) to join it in numbers corresponding to their position within the earlier Nānak-panth. Many non-Jaṭs appear to have preserved their connection with the Nānak-panth without accepting initiation into the Khālsā. This, at least, is the conclusion indicated by the emergence of non-Khālsā Sikhs in the early British censuses and supported by the content of the eighteenth-century *B40* janam-sākhī.[19]

Amongst these Nānak-panthī Sikhs Khatrīs are prominent and Jaṭs absent. The difference is presumably to be explained, in part at least, by the levelling implications of the Khālsā initiation rite, a feature which would offer a serious deterrent to Brāhmaṇs as well as Khatrīs. The Brāhmaṇ Sikh is hereafter a rare phenomenon. Khatrīs would at least retain a loyalty on the basis of their connection with the Gurūs. Together with a small number of other non-Khālsā Sikhs these unbaptized Khatrīs provide a direct link between the early pre-Khālsā Nānak-panth and the so-called Sahaj-dhārī Sikhs of the twentieth century.[20]

Throughout this intermediate period, extending through to the late nineteenth century, the general configuration of the Khālsā constituency seems clear. Jaṭs predominate, a few distinguished Khatrīs appear within its membership and service,

[19] W. H. McLeod, *Early Sikh Tradition* (in preparation).

[20] The *sahaj-dhārī* Sikhs are those who affirm an allegiance to the teachings of the Gurūs without becoming baptized members of the Khālsā (*amrit-dhārī*). The word *sahaj* is normally construed as 'slowly' and the compound as 'gradual-adopters', viz. those who are moving towards a full membership for which they are not yet worthy. A more likely etymology derives from Gurū Nānak's frequent usage of *sahaj* as a description of the spiritual ecstasy which climaxes the devotional practice of *nām simran*. W. H. McLeod, *Gurū Nānak and the Sikh Religion*, pp. 224–5.

and a sprinkling of other castes (all of them 'low-born')[21] can be discerned. The precise proportions are, however, far from clear. It is only with the 1881 Census that the curtain lifts and a degree of precision at last becomes possible.

The 1881 Census returns, while indicating a measure of exaggeration in earlier estimates of Jaṭ preponderance, nevertheless confirmed that this preponderance was indeed a fact. Of the 1,706,909 persons returned as Sikhs (viz. Khālsā Sikhs) 66 per cent proved to be Jaṭs. The second-largest constituent, however, came as a surprise to the British officials who conducted the census. From the Jaṭ total there was a spectacular drop to the next group who turned out to be the Tarkhāns (the carpenter caste) with 6·5 per cent. 'The [numerically] high place which the Tarkhans or carpenters occupy among the Sikhs . . . is very curious', commented Ibbetson in his report on the census.[22] Next came two outcaste groups, the Chamārs with 5·6 per cent and the Chūhṛās with 2·6 per cent. The Khatrīs proved to be sixth-largest with a mere 2·2 per cent. Slightly ahead of them with 2·3 per cent were the Aroṛās, a mercantile caste closely associated with the Khatrīs but ranking lower in terms of status. Twenty other castes produced Sikh returns, but of these only five managed to exceed 1 per cent of the Sikh total. These were the agrarian Kambohs with 1·7 per cent; the Lohārs (blacksmiths) with 1·4 per cent; the Jhīnwars (potters and water-carriers) and Nāīs (barbers) each with 1·2 per cent; and the Rājpūts with 1·1 per cent. The Chhīmbās (calico-printers) were returned as exactly 1 per cent.[23]

Although the 1881 Census certainly had its ragged edges subsequent returns have demonstrated that its analysis of the Panth's caste constituency was essentially correct. Two of the castes listed above (the Jhīnwars and the Rājpūts) can be ignored as their contribution to the Panth has been negligible. This leaves us with two agrarian castes (Jaṭ and Kamboh); two mercantile castes (Khatrī and Aroṛā); four artisan castes (Tarkhān, Lohār, Nāī, and Chhīmbā); and two outcaste groups (Chamār and Chūhṛā). To these we should add one smaller caste with a particularly interesting history within the modern

[21] Irfan Habib, *The Agrarian System of Mughal India* (London, 1963), p. 345.
[22] *Census of India 1881*, Vol. 1, Book 1 (Lahore, 1883), p. 108.
[23] Ibid., p. 107.

Panth. This is the Kalāl or distiller *zāt*, the Sikh members of which style themselves Āhlūwālīās. These eleven remain the principal constituents of the Panth.

A general comment which should precede the individual descriptions of the more important of these groups concerns the progressive increase in over-all Sikh numbers which has been evident ever since the 1881 Census. Whereas the 1881 total amounted to only 1,706,909 (including Delhi) the 1931 figure had risen to 4,071,624 (excluding Delhi).[24] The impact is slightly reduced by the inclusion from 1911 onwards of non-Khālsā Sikhs, but as these totalled only 281,903 in 1931[25] their numbers make comparatively little difference. Two separate processes must be distinguished here. The increment in excess of natural increase was clearly produced in almost all instances by a switch from Hindu to Sikh. This, as the 1931 enumerator pointed out, was to be observed chiefly amongst the agrarian and artisan castes (he should have added the outcastes) and was a response to a belief that enhanced status would result from the change.[26] The Panth still retained its egalitarian appeal and caste returns during the half-century 1881–1931 serve to document this process.[27] It was a process greatly stimulated by the reforming zeal of the Siṅgh Sabhā movement and later by the political concerns of the Akālī Dal. A fundamental aspect of Siṅgh Sabhā policy was recovery of the Gurūs' insistence on equality. In this respect their energies were enlivened by indications that Christian missionaries were managing to convert Sikh outcastes.

The Siṅgh Sabhā was also largely responsible for the second of the processes to be distinguished within the rising Sikh returns. In response to its insistence on Khālsā forms as the only proper observance for Sikhs many who had previously been content with Sahaj-dhārī status were persuaded to accept baptism into the Khālsā. Because the non-Khālsā pattern had been particularly common amongst Khatrīs and (to a lesser degree)

[24] *Census of India 1931*, Vol. 17, Part 1 (Lahore, 1933), p. 304.
[25] Ibid., p. 306.
[26] Ibid., pp. 293, 294.
[27] Caste returns do not appear after 1931. In 1961 Sikhs numbered 7,845,843 over the whole of India. Of these 6,695,099 were in the Pañjāb and Haryānā, 203,916 in Delhi, 557,935 in the adjacent states of Rājasthān and Uttar Pradesh, and the remaining 388,893 in other states. *India: A Reference Annual 1971–72* (New Delhi, 1971), p. 11.

Aroṛās, it was within these *zāts* that the appeal had a particular effect. It did not greatly increase over-all numbers, but it did bring firmly into the Khālsā Panth influential elements who were to affect its future policies significantly. The contribution of Khatrīs to the modern Panth has been far in excess of their numerical strength.

We turn now to individual descriptions, beginning with the Jaṭs.[28] Two vividly contrasting views of the Jaṭ emerge from the literature left by British administrators and from everyday conversation amongst urban Pañjābīs of today. An early expression of what was to become the characteristic British view was provided by Ibbetson in 1883. 'These men are the backbone of the Panjab by character and physique as well as by locality. They are stalwart, sturdy yeomen of great independence, industry, and agricultural skill, and collectively form perhaps the finest peasantry in India.'[29] The words of the civil administrator were endorsed and embellished by the recruiting officer,[30] contributing substantially to the developing British theory of 'martial races'. A contrary view emerges from the unpublished comments of many urban Pañjābīs. From these comments there emerges the impression of an uncouth rustic, hard-working perhaps but distinguished more for his attachment to liquor and feuding than for sophisticated pursuits such as commerce and higher education. It is this innuendo concerning Jaṭs which lies behind the many satirical stories featuring the alleged stupidity of Sikhs.

The second of these views is plainly gross caricature, based one suspects upon a mixture of fear and envy as well as on misunderstanding. The first is much fairer, but represents a somewhat naïve interpretation of Jaṭ attitudes and capacities. However 'sturdy' the Jaṭs may have been in the British experience their society offers much more than agrarian competence and military skills.

There is, nevertheless, truth in the observations of Ibbetson and his successors and its content should be acknowledged be-

[28] For a stimulating analysis of Jaṭ society see J. J. M. Chaudhri (now Pettigrew), 'The Emigration of Sikh Jats from the Punjab to England', *SSRC Report*, Project HR331–I, ed. A. C. Mayer, 1971. See also id., *Robber Noblemen* (London, 1975).

[29] *Census of India 1881*, Vol. 1, Book 1, p. 229.

[30] R. W. Falcon, *Handbook on Sikhs for the Use of Regimental Officers* (Allahabad, 1896), pp. 27–8, 65.

fore attempting to sketch other aspects of Jaṭ society. Agriculture is the traditional occupation of the Jaṭs and their success in this area has been impressive. Jaṭs are prepared to perform tasks which others would consider demeaning and their willingness to experiment with new methods of cultivation is producing handsome dividends at the present time. Their history has added military to agrarian traditions and many Jaṭs have distinguished themselves as soldiers. Military careers have served to relieve pressure on land, a purpose which in recent years has been further served by extensive participation in the transport industry. Distinction has also been won by Jaṭ Sikhs in such sports as hockey and athletics.

To these obvious features of Jaṭ society we must attach others which have attracted less attention. The first is the pronounced rise in status which marks the history of the Sikh Jaṭs over recent centuries. This achievement, already briefly noticed, deserves specific emphasis for the light which it sheds on the realities of caste. Although Jaṭs should, in theory, occupy a low-status ranking their experience as rulers and their dominance in rural Pañjāb have elevated them well above their humble origins. In terms of status no Jaṭ feels inferior or downtrodden.

The status which the Jaṭ Sikh now enjoys does not derive exclusively from economic success as an agriculturalist. It must also be traced, as one would expect, to political skills of a high order. Whatever truth there may be in the claim that Jaṭs show limited respect for formal education there can be none in the suggestion that they are unsophisticated people. Their political predominance in the Pañjāb of today demonstrates its absurdity. For the pursuit of political objectives the Panth serves as a firm base, one which has been skilfully exploited. Control and use of the gurdwaras as a platform and as a source of patronage provide the principal components of this considerable political strength. The chief minister of the Pañjāb does not necessarily have to be a Jaṭ, but it is difficult to imagine one surviving for any length of time without Jaṭ support. Although factional disputes persistently divide Jaṭ politics, effective leadership is never far from the Jaṭ grasp. In recent years this has been most strikingly demonstrated by Partāp Singh Kairon, chief minister from 1955 until 1964. The celebrated Master Tārā Singh was not a Jaṭ (he was a Khatrī), but he was supported by an effective Jaṭ lieutenant in Giānī Kartār Singh and was commonly honoured by the declaration that he possessed 'the heart of a Jaṭ'. When eventually he fell from power in 1962 it was a Jaṭ, Sant Fateh Singh, who overthrew him.

Two other features of Jaṭ society deserve to be noted. The first is the absence of formalized social stratification within the endogamous *zāt*. As with other *zāts* the Jaṭs are divided into numerous *gots* but within the *zāt* there is no recognized order which elevates some above others. Such claims have been made, as for example by the numerically large Gil *got* or more recently by the politically successful Ḍhillons. They are, however, claims which others would dispute.

As far as marriage is concerned Jaṭs follow the customary rules of propinquity which forbid alliances between those of the same *got* (i.e. the father's *got* in each case). Until comparatively recently the mother's *got* would also be excluded and in a few cases barriers survive between *gots* which are traditionally believed to be closely related. A large *got* may possess sub-*gots*, the most notable example being the Brāṛ sub-*got* of the large Sidhū *got*. Brāṛs are accordingly required to marry outside the Sidhū *got*.[31] There exist also prohibitions of varying duration which arise from inter-*got* feuds, an example being the long-standing refusal of Ḍhillons and Bals to intermarry. Jaṭs who migrated from Pakistan in 1947 are commonly regarded as unsuitable by those who have always resided in eastern Pañjāb; and in a few instances a *got* is regarded with suspicion on the grounds that it may not be genuinely Jaṭ.

These prohibitions are all informal and some of them are obviously impermanent. It is also evident that old distinctions based on geographical location are now breaking down. The Sikh Jaṭs have traditionally been divided into three categories corresponding to the geographical areas of Mājhā, Mālwā, and Doābā.[32] Mālwāī Jaṭs have tended to look down on Mājhāils, and both have looked down on Doābīs. This is a tradition well advanced in disintegration, amounting nowadays to little more

[31] The ruling families of Paṭiālā, Nābhā, and Jīnd states were all Sidhū. The ruling family of Farīdkoṭ was Brāṛ.

[32] Respectively (1) the lower plains tract between the Beās and Rāvī rivers, extending westwards beyond the latter for an indeterminate distance; (2) the area south and east of the Satluj river; and (3) the plains tract between the Beās and Satluj rivers.

than a traditional preference. Provided the *got* prescription is observed most will now marry across the old territorial lines.

Finally, we must note the distinctively Jaṭ attitude towards the Panth. Since the migrations of 1947 the Jaṭs of Mājhā, Mālwā, and Doābā have virtually all been Sikhs. Not all, however, are visibly Sikh as the Jaṭ Sikh commonly assumes a considerable freedom with regard to observance of the Khālsā discipline (*rahat*). In his own eyes and those of other Jaṭs he remains a Sikh even if he cuts his beard or smokes tobacco. For other castes it is very different. If a Khatrī shaves he is regarded as a Hindu by others and soon comes to regard himself as one.

It is to the Khatrīs that we now turn. Although Khatrīs claim Kshatriya status (the two terms are cognate) they are in fact a mercantile caste and a distinctively Pañjābī one. Their achievements in recent centuries have been impressive, notwithstanding the comparative smallness of the *zāt*.[33] Commerce has led them to distant parts of India and beyond, and many Khatrīs have distinguished themselves in positions of administrative responsibility.[34] They retain this prominence today. In industry and commerce, government service, higher education, and the professions the Khatrī community continues to demonstrate an enviable skill and many of its members reap substantial rewards. In spite of their mercantile traditions, the claim to Kshatriya status has generally been accepted. Even those who question it must perforce acknowledge that in terms of status the Khatrī occupies an elevated position in Pañjābī society.[35]

Traditional status provides one of the numerous contrasts between Jaṭs and Khatrīs. It is, however, a difference which has shrunk as the Jaṭs have moved upwards. Other differences have proved more stable. Whereas the Jaṭs remain a rural community heavily committed to agriculture, the Khatrīs are essentially urban-based. Many Khatrīs do live in villages, but of these a large proportion have pursued traditional Khatrī occupations (notably money-lending).

Prior to 1947 an important difference could also be observed

[33] The 1931 Census (Vol. 17, Part 2, p. 292) produced a total of 516,207 Khatrīs. Of these 460,851 were Hindus and 55,112, were Sikhs. The small balance were returned as Christians, Muslims, and Jains.

[34] Akbar's minister Ṭodar Mal and Rañjīt Siṅgh's general Harī Singh Nālwā were both Khatrīs.

[35] For an interesting description of Khatrī conventions see Prakash Tandon, *Punjabi Century* (London, 1963), esp. chap. 5.

in terms of geographical distribution. Since comparatively early times Jaṭ Sikhs have been largely concentrated within the plains area of the Mājhā, Mālwā, and Doābā. In this same area the pre-1947 incidence of Sikh Khatrīs was generally light except in the western Mājhā (notably in the cities of Amritsar and Lahore). West and north-west of this area their numbers increased, with a significant concentration appearing in the Poṭhohār territory around Rawalpindi.[36]

Khatrī society also differs from that of the Jaṭs in terms of its internal *got* organization. The Jaṭ *zāt* is, as we have already noted, truly endogamous and generally unstratified, apart from some comparatively minor exceptions. This is not the case with the Khatrī *zāt* which is internally divided into several endogamous units. The principal division is the traditional *chār bārah bavañjah* or *4:12:52* convention. Four *gots* claiming a particularly elevated status observe endogamy;[37] twelve more of intermediate status similarly constitute a separate endogamous grouping; and the remainder (conventionally fifty-two in number) together form a third. Other endogamies have emerged within the latter category, an example being the *gots* of the Sikh Gurūs (Bedī, Trehaṇ, Bhallā, and Soḍhī). The stratification thus generated within traditional Khatrī society is today showing signs of dissolving as increasingly its members form marriage alliances across the *4:12:52* lines. There remains, however, a distinct preference for the old order. Confessional differences are comparatively unimportant with the result that marriages between Hindu and Sikh Khatrī families have always been very common.

Differences between Khatrī and Jaṭ are also plainly evident in terms of their characteristic attitudes towards the Panth and their role within it. Unlike the Jaṭs the Khatrīs have never shown any interest in Sikh identity as a means of enhancing social or ritual status and for this reason a significant degree of Khatrī adherence has been *sahaj-dhārī* (or Nānak-panthī) rather than *amrit-dhārī* (baptized Khālsā). This feature also explains why in contrast to steady increases in Jaṭ membership over the period 1881–1931 Khatrī adherence actually declined during the period 1911–31.[38]

[36] *Census of India 1931*, Vol. 17, Part 2, p. 292.
[37] The four *gots* are Mehrā (or Malhotrā), Kapūr, Khannā, and Seṭh.
[38] *Census of India 1931*, Vol. 17, Part 1, p. 345.

This should not suggest, however, that Khatrī Sikhs characteristically regard their panthic membership with indifference. The reverse is true. Khālsā Khatrī Sikhs are generally punctilious in their observance of the *rahat* and many of them, both baptized and unbaptized, are conscientious in their practice of the *nām simran* devotional discipline. Their services to Sikh theology are unique and reform movements of a congenial nature have received notable support from many individual Khatrīs. Conservative reform stressing education and moral uplift is particularly congenial and Khatrīs have in consequence played major roles in the Niraṅkārī movement,[39] in the Siṅgh Sabhā, and in the surviving offspring of the latter, the Chief Khālsā Diwān. The hurly-burly of Akālī politics has been less to their taste and in this area their contribution has been less prominent.

Other contrasts distinguishing Jaṭs and Khatrīs reflect their basic differences of domicile, vocation, and tradition. Literature provides an example of derivative difference. Amongst Sikh writers, poets, critics, and theologians Khatrīs have been prominent in terms of activity and distinctive in terms of style. It would, however, be altogether false to suggest that visible contrast must necessarily mean deep cleavage or mutual hostility. Cleavages do indeed exist between some Jaṭs and some Khatrīs and there can be no doubt that the term 'Bhāpā' which Jaṭs commonly apply to Khatrīs and Aroṛās from the Poṭhohār area carries with it a perceptible degree of opprobrium. In general, however, the intention of the Gurūs is honoured. Sikhs of all backgrounds still regard the unity of the Panth as a meaningful concept.

One final and minor contrast will serve to link the Khatrīs with the Aroṛās. Whereas Jaṭ Sikhs almost invariably impart a vertical or slightly receding appearance to the apex of their turban, fashionable Khatrīs and Aroṛās commonly tie it in the form of a projecting 'beak'. Many Jaṭ Sikhs (almost certainly a substantial majority) fail to distinguish Khatrīs from Aroṛās, bracketing them in the same *zāt* and sometimes in the same condemnation. The confusion is understandable as their tradi-

[39] Bābā Dayāl (b. 1783), the *sahaj-dhārī* founder of the Niraṅkārī movement for Sikh reform, was a Malhotrā Khatrī. The movement's following has always been largely Khatrī and Aroṛā.

tional occupations are similar and intermarriage between the two is not uncommon nowadays. In terms of both status and occupation, however, the difference should be clear. Aroṛās rank lower than Khatrīs and concentrate on small-scale shopkeeping rather than on the more ambitious forms of industry, trade, or commerce. Most of the Sikhs one sees operating shops in Amritsar or any other Pañjābī city are Aroṛās.

It is not entirely clear when Aroṛās entered the Panth in substantial numbers. Bhāī Gurdās refers to at least two Aroṛā Sikhs in his eleventh *vār*[40] and another, Buhd Siṅgh Aroṛā, emerges as author of the *Risālah-i-Nānakshāh* in the late eighteenth century. Up to this point in time their numbers within the Panth appear sparse, a natural consequence of the Aroṛā concentration in areas beyond the direct influence of the early Panth. It is only with Rañjīt Siṅgh's invasions of Multan and the north-west that their area of major concentration is brought firmly within the Sikh domain, and it accordingly seems likely that the earliest Aroṛā accessions of any numerical significance date from the early nineteenth century. The first evidence they offer of corporate importance within Sikh society is the participation of many Aroṛās in the Niraṅkārī and Nāmdhārī reform movements of the mid-nineteenth century.[41]

British commentators (particularly the recruitment officers) were inexcusably unjust in their treatment of the Aroṛās, branding them as artful and cowardly people quite unsuited to military service. It is ironical that the surrender of the Pakistani forces in Bangladesh at the conclusion of the 1971 war should have been received on behalf of India by Lieutenant-General Jagjīt Singh Aurora. As with the Khatrīs military careers are still unusual for Aroṛās (and acceptable only in the case of direct commissioning). Individuals such as General Aurora do, however, point up the danger of uncritically accepting traditional stereotypes. The Aroṛās have been ill used in this respect.

In the case of artisan and outcaste Sikhs particular interest attaches to the methods used by depressed groups in attempts to raise their status. For all such groups membership of the Khālsā has obviously been regarded as a means of improving

[40] Bisnū Bībṛā (11:19) and Ugavandhā (11:23). The latter reference names another Sikh who may also be an Aroṛā.

[41] Balak Singh (d. 1862), founder of the Nāmdhārī movement, was an Aroṛā.

status. In the case of the Tarkhāns (carpenters) the pursuit of this ambition has taken an unusually interesting form. It can be assumed that many Tarkhāns must have entered the Panth in imitation of the Jaṭ landowners whom they traditionally served in a client relationship. The most famous of all Tarkhān Sikhs had been the misl leader Jassā Siṅgh Rāmgaṛhīā (so called because he had once been responsible for governing the Amritsar fort named Rāmgaṛh). The name Rāmgaṛhīā was taken up by an increasing number of Sikh Tarkhāns from the end of the nineteenth century onwards with the obvious intention of replacing a lowly title with one of acknowledged repute.

Sikh Tarkhāns (as opposed to Hindu Tarkhāns) are now generally known as Rāmgaṛhīās and have attracted to their name Sikhs from a few other artisan castes (Lohār, Rāj, and Nāī).[42] The result has been a new, composite, and distinctively Sikh *zāt*. Rāmgaṛhīā Sikhs have been particularly prominent in East Africa where many went to work in railway construction and funds repatriated to the Pañjāb have helped develop an important complex of Rāmgaṛhīā educational institutions in the town of Phagwāṛā. Many individual Rāmgaṛhīās have secured impressive economic successes by applying their traditional skills to modern needs. The small town of Kartārpur has become a centre of furniture manufacture while small-scale light-engineering industries have been developed in Phagwāṛā and Baṭālā.[43] Other concentrations of Rāmgaṛhīās are to be found in Gorāyā (Jullundur District) and in Ludhiānā.

Outcaste (or Harijan) Sikhs fall into two groups corresponding to their origins. Those who come from a Chūhṛā (sweeper) background are known as Mazhabī Sikhs, whereas those whose forbears were Chamārs (leather-workers) are called Rāmdāsiā Sikhs. One other title occasionally encountered is Raṅghṛetā. This designates Mazhabī families who trace their Sikh connection back to the time of the tenth Gurū. Following the execution of Gurū Tegh Bahādur by command of Aurangzeb a group of Chūhṛās managed to secure his severed head and deliver it for

[42] The Rāj *zāt* is that of the masons and bricklayers. Not all Sikh Nāīs have assumed the Rāmgaṛhīā style and it appears that few if any Chhīmbās have done so. The latter have instead adopted a new name of their own. Sikh Chhīmbās commonly call themselves Ṭaṅk Kshatriyas.

[43] For a fuller description of the Rāmgaṛhīās and also of the Āhlūwālīās see W. H. McLeod, 'Ahluwalias and Ramgarhias: Two Sikh Castes', *South Asia*, no. 4 (Aug. 1974)

honourable cremation to his son, Gurū Gobind Siṅgh. Their descendants subsequently came to be known as Raṅghṛetās, a title now generally superseded by Mazhabī.

A substantial proportion of both Mazhabīs and Rāmdāsiās represent the result of an influx into the Panth during the early decades of the present century, a movement paralleled by similar conversions to Christianity or to a new grouping designated Ād Dharmī.[44] There can be no doubt that the impulse behind this movement was a desire to purge the traditional taint of the outcaste status and that a majority of the converts regarded the egalitarian traditions of the Khālsā as the best hope of achieving this end. It would be false to claim that the hope has been fulfilled. Equally false, however, would be the claim that there has been no gain in status whatsoever.

Three summary points deserve mention before concluding this survey. The first concerns the present caste constituency of the Sikh Panth. Reference has already been made to the multiplicity of local hierarchies which one encounters in any investigation of caste patterns. Two general hierarchies can be discerned in Pañjābī society, one urban and the other rural. Within Sikh society the two intersect without losing their essential clarity. The Sikh component of the urban hierarchy is very small and very distinct, with Khatrīs plainly occupying a superior ranking and Aroṛās close behind. In contrast the rural hierarchy is much larger numerically and rather less clear in terms of order. Three levels are, however, evident. The massive Jaṭ constituency commands the heights. Beneath them and spilling into the urban hierarchy are ranged the Rāmgaṛhīās. At the base, and likewise extending across to the urban section, are the Mazhabīs and Rāmdāsiās.

The second point concerns attitudes and specifically those of foreign observers. Most foreigners regard the Sikh Panth as a generally uniform religious grouping manifesting such characteristics as agrarian skill and martial vigour. As we have seen, the Panth contains within itself a heterogeneous constituency, and many of the features so commonly regarded as

[44] Between the 1901 and 1931 censuses Sikh Chūhṛā returns rose from 21,673 to 169,247; and Sikh Chamār returns from 75,753 to 222,797. *Census of India 1931*, Vol. 17, Part 1, pp. 333, 334. The latter figure is incomplete in each case as many from both groups evidently returned themselves simply as Sikhs in the 1931 Census. Ibid.

typically Sikh should properly be regarded as characteristically Jaṭ.

The final point also concerns attitudes, in this case those of Sikhs themselves. Inevitably the stress in this essay has been placed upon the caste diversity of the Panth and on the fact that notions of status based on caste are by no means extinct within it. This should not conceal the significant degree to which the Panth has succeeded in eliminating many of the discriminatory aspects of caste. The Sikh insistence on equality is far from being a pious myth. Freedom within the Panth may not be a total freedom but it represents an impressive achievement nevertheless and an endeavour which is still proceeding. Sikhs are above all else loyal to the Gurū. The question of equality within the Panth offers no exception to this inflexible rule.

GLOSSARY

Pañjābī forms are given in all instances. Corresponding Hindī or Sanskrit forms are in some instances given in brackets.

Ādi Granth: the *Gurū Granth Sāhib* (q.v.), sacred scripture of the Sikhs.

Āhlūwālīā (*Āhlūvālīā*): the Sikh section of the Kalāl caste (q.v.).

Akālī: 'a devotee of Akāl (the Timeless One, God)'. During the eighteenth and early nineteenth centuries the title designated Sikh warriors noted for their bravery and (during the time of Mahārājā Rañjit Singh) their lack of discipline. In this sense their contemporary modern descendants are the so-called Nihang Sikhs. Early in the twentieth century the title was assumed by Sikhs agitating for freedom of the gurdwaras from private, hereditary control. Today it signifies a member of the Akālī Dal, the dominant political party of the Sikhs.

akhaṇḍ pāṭh: 'unbroken reading'; an uninterrupted reading of the entire contents of the *Ādi Granth* performed by a team of readers.

amrit: lit. 'nectar'; the water used for baptism in the initiation ceremony of the Khālsā (q.v.).

Āratī Sohilā: a selection of hymns from the *Ādi Granth* sung by devout Sikhs immediately before retiring at night, and also at funerals.

Ardās: the Sikh Prayer. See pp. 65–6.

Aroṛā: A mercantile caste of the Pañjāb.

Āsā: a *rāg* (q.v.); one of the sections of the *Ādi Granth.*

āsaṇ: yogic posture; abode of yogīs.

aṣṭapadī: a hymn of eight (occasionally more) stanzas.

avatār: a 'descent'; incarnation of a deity, usually Viṣṇu.

Bābā: 'Father', a term of respect applied to holy men.

bairāgī: Hindu renunciant.

Baisākh (*Vaisākh*): the first month of the Indian year (April/May).

bāṇī (*vāṇī*): speech; the utterances of the Gurūs and *bhagats* (q.v.) recorded in the *Ādi Granth.* The amplified form *gurbāṇī* is commonly used.

bāolī: a large masonry or brick well with steps leading down to the water.

bhagat (*bhakta*): an exponent of *bhagti* (*bhakti*) (q.v.); a devotee.

bhagti (*bhakti*): belief in, and adoration of, a personal God.

Bhāī: 'Brother', a title applied to Sikhs of acknowledged learning and piety. In a somewhat debased sense the term is often used as a synonym for *granthī* (q.v.), *rāgī* (q.v.), or other gurdwara employees.

Bhairau: a *rāg* (q.v.); one of the sections of the *Ādi Granth.*

Chamār: the leather-worker caste.

chaupad: a hymn comprising four short stanzas with refrain.

chhant (*chhand*): lit. poem, song. In the *Ādi Granth* the term designates a hymn of medium length. See p. 71, n. 17.

Chhīmbā: the calico-printer caste. Sikh members of this caste commonly call themselves Ṭank Kshatriyas.

Chūhṛā: the sweeper caste.

Dal Khālsā: the unified army of the Khālsā (q.v.).

Dasam Granth: 'the Book of the Tenth [Gurū]', a collection of writings attributed to Gurū Gobind Siṅgh. See pp. 79–81.

Devī: the goddess Durgā.

dharam (*dharma*): the appropriate moral and religious obligations attached to any particular status in Hindu society.

dharamsālā: in early Sikh usage a room or building used for devotional singing and prayer.

Dīvālī: Festival of Lights, celebrated by Hindus and Sikhs in the lunar month of Kattak (Kārtik, October/November).

Doābā: the plains tract of central Pañjāb bounded by the Beās and Satluj rivers.

Doābī: one who traces his ancestral origins to the Doābā area (q.v.).

Ekādasī: the eleventh day of each half of the lunar month.

faqīr: 'poor man', Muslim renunciant; loosely used to designate Sūfīs and also non-Muslim renunciants.

Gauṛī: a *rāg* (q.v.); one of the sections of the *Ādi Granth.*

ghaṛī: a period of twenty-four minutes.

giānī: one possessing *giān* (*jñāna*, knowledge or wisdom); a reputed Sikh scholar; a Sikh theologian.

got (*gotra*): exogamous caste grouping within the *zāt* (q.v.).

granth: book, volume.

granthī: a 'reader' of the *Gurū Granth Sāhib* (q.v.), the functionary in charge of a gurdwara (q.v.).

Granth Sāhib: the *Gurū Granth Sāhib* (q.v.), the Sikh sacred scripture.

gurdwara (*gurdvārā*, *gurduārā*): Sikh temple.

gurmattā: 'the mind, or intention, of the Gurū'; the will of the eternal Gurū (q.v.) expressed in a formal decision made by a representative assembly of Sikhs; a resolution of the Sarbat Khālsā (q.v.).

Gurmukhī: the script used for writing Pañjābī.

gurū: religious teacher; preceptor. Usually a person but sometimes understood as the divine inner voice. In later Sikh theology the continuing spiritual presence of the eternal Gurū in the *Granth Sāhib* (q.v.) and the *Panth* (q.v.)

Gurū Granth Sāhib: the *Ādi Granth*, sacred scripture of the Sikhs compiled by Gurū Arjan in 1603–4.
Gurū Panth: the presence of the eternal Gurū (q.v.) in an assembly of his followers.
halāl: 'lawful', in accordance with Muslim prescriptions.
Harimandir: 'the Temple of God', the central Sikh shrine in Amritsar commonly known as the Golden Temple.
haṭha-yoga: 'yoga of force', a variety of yoga requiring physical postures and processes of extreme difficulty.
janam-sākhī: traditional narrative, esp. of Gurū Nānak.
Jaṭ (*Jāṭ*): an agrarian caste with strong military traditions, dominant in rural Pañjāb.
jathā: military detachment.
jathedār: commander of a jathā (q.v.). Today the title designates a leader-organizer of the Akālī Dal, the Sikh political party.
kabitt: a poetic metre.
Kalāl: the brewer and distiller caste.
Kamboh: an agrarian caste.
kaṛah praśād: sacramental food dispensed in gurdwaras.
Kaur: lit. 'maiden', 'princess'; the name assumed by all female members of the Khālsā (q.v.). Cf. Siṅgh (q.v.).
Khālsā: the Sikh order, brotherhood, instituted in 1699 by Gurū Gobind Siṅgh.
Khatrī: a mercantile caste, particularly important in the Pañjāb.
kīrtan: the singing of hymns from the *Gurū Granth Sāhib*.
Kshatriya (*ksatriya*): the second *varṇa* (q.v.); the warrior caste.
lakh (*lākh*): one hundred thousand.
laṅgar: the kitchen attached to every gurdwara from which food is served to all regardless of caste or creed.
Lohār: the blacksmith caste.
Mahalā: a code-word used to distinguish works by different Gurūs in the *Ādi Granth*. Gurū Nānak, as first Gurū, is designated *Mahalā 1* or simply *M1*; the second Gurū, Aṅgad, is designated *Mahalā 2* or *M2*; etc.
mahūā: the tree *Bassia latifolia*. An intoxicating drink can be brewed from its flower.
Mājh: a *rāg* (q.v.); one of the sections of the *Ādi Granth*.
Mājhā, *Māñjhā*: lit. 'middle'. The area of central Pañjāb lying between the Beās and Rāvī rivers.
Mājhāil: one who traces his ancestral origins to the Mājhā area (q.v.).
Mālwā (*Mālvā*): the plains tract extending south and south-east of the Satluj river, particularly the area occupied by Ferozepore, Ludhiānā, and Paṭiālā districts.

Mālwāī (Mālvāī): one who traces his ancestral origins to the Malwa area (q.v.).

mañjī: lit. a small string-bed; areas of jurisdiction designated by Gurū Amar Dās.

masand: holder of a *mañjī* (q.v.); Sikhs appointed from the the time of Gurū Amar Dās onwards to exercise spiritual jurisdiction on behalf of the Gurū in designated geographical areas. During the course of the seventeenth century the masands became increasingly independent and were eventually disowned by Gurū Gobind Siṅgh.

Mazhabī: the Sikh section of the Chūhṛā or sweeper caste.

Mīṇās: the followers of Prithī Chand, eldest son of Gurū Rām Dās and unsuccessful claimant to the succession conferred on his younger brother Arjan.

misl: Sikh military bands of the eighteenth century.

misldār: chieftain of a misl (q.v.).

Nāī: the barber caste.

nām simran: repeating the divine Name of God; meditating on God.

namāz: Muslim prayer, esp. the prescribed daily prayers.

Nānak-panth: followers of Gurū Nānak.

Naqshbandī movement: Muslim revivalist movement introduced into India during the late sixteenth century, vigorously promulgated by Shaikh Ahmad of Sirhind (1564–1624).

Nāth: lit. 'master'. A yogic sect of considerable influence prior to and during the time of the early Sikh Gurūs. Its members, who are also known as Kānphaṭ yogīs, practised haṭha-yoga (q.v.) in order to obtain immortality.

nirguṇa sampradāya: the tradition or sect of those who believe God to be without form or incarnation; the Sant tradition of northern India.

pañj kakke: the 'Five K's', the five external symbols which must be worn by all members of the Khālsā (q.v.), both men and women, so called because all five begin with the initial letter 'k' (*kakkā*). The five symbols are: *keś* (uncut hair), *kaṅghā* (comb), *kirpān* (dagger), *kaṛā* (steel bangle), and *kachh* (a pair of breeches which must not reach below the knees).

panth: lit. path, road. System of religious belief and practice. The form 'Panth' designates the Sikh community. See p. 2.

panthic: (adj.) concerning the Sikh Panth.

patit: 'fallen'; an apostate Sikh, one who having accepted baptism into the Khālsā (q.v.) subsequently violates its code of conduct in some important respect (esp. the ban on cutting hair).

pīr: the head of a Sūfī order; a Sūfī saint.

pothī: volume, tome.

Poṭhohār: the area around Rawalpindi.
Purāṇa: lit. 'Ancient Story', though the *Purāṇas* are in fact comparatively recent and in their present form date from the sixth century A.D. There are eighteen *Purāṇas*. Together they offer a substantial quantity of legend and popular Hindu belief.
Puranic: of, derived from the *Purāṇas* (q.v.).
rāg (*rāga*): melodic organization, a series of five or more notes on which a melody is based. See p. 71, n. 16.
rāgī: a musician employed to sing in a gurdwara.
rahat, *rahit*: the code of discipline of the Khālsā (q.v.).
rahat-nāmā: a recorded version of the Khālsā code of discipline.
Rāj: the mason and bricklayer caste.
Rāmakalī: a *rāg* (q.v.); a section of the *Ādi Granth*.
Rāmdāsiā: the Sikh section of the Chamār or leather-worker caste.
Rāmgaṛhīā: a Sikh artisan caste, predominantly drawn from the Tarkhān or carpenter caste, but also including Sikhs from the blacksmith, mason, and barber castes.
Sahaj-dhārī: A Sikh who neither accepts baptism into the Khālsā (q.v.) nor observes its code of discipline.
śakti: lit. power. The active power of a male deity personified by his female consort. Cult worshipping the Mother Goddess, consort of Śiva. See p. 13, n. 11.
saṅgat: assembly, religious congregation.
sanyāsī: Hindu renunciant.
Sarbat Khālsā: the 'entire Khālsā'; assemblies of jathedārs (q.v.) and misldārs (q.v.).
sardār: chieftain; leader of a misl (q.v.). 'Sardār' is nowadays used as title of address for all Sikh men. The corresponding title for a Sikh woman is 'Sardāranī'.
sevādār: one who performs *sevā* (service); gurdwara attendant.
shalok (*ślok*): couplet or stanza.
Siṅgh: lit. 'lion'; the name assumed by all male members of the Khālsā (q.v.). Cf. Kaur (q.v.).
Siṅgh Sabhā: the 'Siṅgh Society', a movement comprising several local societies dedicated to religious and educational reform amongst Sikhs. The first Siṅgh Sabhā was founded in Amritsar in 1873.
Sirī Rāg: a *rāg* (q.v.); one of the sections of the *Ādi Granth*.
Sodar Rahirās: a selection of hymns from the *Ādi Granth* sung during the early evening.
Soraṭh: a *rāg* (q.v.); one of the sections of the *Ādi Granth*.
śudhī: 'purification'; a ceremony conducted by the Ārya Samāj to induct or restore to Hindu society those outside its bounds.
Tarkhān: the carpenter caste.
ṭhag: thug; strictly, a member of the cult of ritual murderers who

strangled and robbed in the name of the goddess Kālī, but loosely used for any highwayman or violent robber.
tīrath: a sacred place; a place of pilgrimage.
Vaiṣṇava: of, concerning the god Viṣṇu or the sect comprising his worshippers.
vār: a heroic ode of several stanzas; a sŏng of praise; a dirge.
varṇa: a section of the classical caste hierarchy. Four sections enumerated: *brāhmaṇ*, *kṣatriya*, *vaiśya*, and *śudra*.
zāt (*jāti*): endogamous caste grouping.

BIBLIOGRAPHY

AHLUWALIA, JASBIR SINGH, *Metaphysical Problems of Sikhism.* Chandigarh: Godwin, 1976.

———, *Sovereignty of the Sikh Doctrine.* New Delhi: Bahri Publications, 1983.

———, *Sikhism Today: The Crisis Within and Without.* Chandigarh: Guru Gobind Singh Foundation, 1987.

ALAM, MUZAFFAR, *The Crisis of Empire in Mughal North India: Awadh and the Punjab 1707–1748.* Delhi: Oxford University Press, 1986.

ALI, IMRAN, *The Punjab under Imperialism, 1885–1947.* Delhi: Oxford University Press, 1989.

AMRIK SINGH (ed.), *Punjab in Indian Politics: Issues and Trends.* Delhi: Ajanta, 1985.

ANAND, BALWANT SINGH, *Guru Nanak: Religion and Ethics.* Patiala: Punjabi University, 1968.

———, *Guru Tegh Bahadur: A Biography.* New Delhi: Sterling, 1979.

———, *Guru Nanak: His Life Was His Message.* New Delhi: Guru Nanak Foundation, 1983.

ANAND, G. S., *Guru Tegh Bahadur.* Agra: Agra University, 1970.

ASHTA, DHARAM PAL, *The Poetry of the Dasam Granth.* New Delhi: Arun, 1959.

ATTAR SINGH (trans.), *Sakhee Book or the Description of Gooroo Gobind Singh's Religion and Doctrines.* (Translated from Gooroo Mukhi into Hindi, and afterwards into English.). Banaras: Medical Hall Press, 1873.

——— (trans.), *The Rayhit Nama of Pralad Rai or the Excellent Conversation of the Duswan Padsha and Nand Lal's Rayhit Nama or Rules for the Guidance of the Sikhs in Religious Matters.* (Translated from the original Gurmukhi). Lahore: Albert Press, 1876.

AVTAR SINGH, *Ethics of the Sikhs.* Patiala: Punjabi University, 1970.

AZAD, MOHAMMAD AKRAM LARI, *Religion and Politics in India during the Seventeenth Century.* New Delhi: Criterion, 1990.

BAL, S. S., *Life of Guru Nanak.* Chandigarh: Panjab University, 1969.

———, *A Brief History of the Modern Punjab.* Ludhiana: Lyall, 1974.

BANERJEE, ANIL CHANDRA, *Guru Nanak and His Times.* Patiala: Punjabi University, 1971.

———, *Guru Nanak to Guru Gobind Singh.* Allahabad: Rajesh, 1978.

———, *The Sikh Gurus and the Sikh Religion.* New Delhi: Munshiram Manoharlal, 1983.

———, *The Khalsa Raj.* New Delhi: Abhinav, 1985.

BANERJEE, INDUBHUSHAN, *The Evolution of the Khalsa.* 2 Vols. Calcutta: University of Calcutta, 1936. Reprint, Calcutta: A. Mukherjee, 1979 and 1970.

BANGA, INDU, *Agrarian System of the Sikhs.* New Delhi: Manohar, 1978.

BARRIER, N. GERALD and VERNE A. DUSENBERY (eds.), *The Sikh Diaspora: Migration and Experience beyond Punjab.* Columbia, Missouri: South Asia Books, 1989; New Delhi: Chanakya, 1989.

BARSTOW, A. E., *Sikhs: A Handbook for the Indian Army.* Calcutta: Government of India Publications Branch, 1928. Reprint, Delhi: B. R. Publishing Corporation, 1985.

BHAGAT SINGH, *Sikh Polity in the Eighteenth and Nineteenth Centuries.* New Delhi: Oriental, 1978.

———, *Maharaja Ranjit Singh.* Patiala: Punjabi University, 1983.

———, *Maharaja Ranjit Singh and His Times.* New Delhi: Sehgal, 1990.

———, *History of the Sikh Misals.* Patiala: Punjabi University, 1993.

BINGLEY, A. H., *Sikhs.* Calcutta: Government Printing, 1918. Reprint, Patiala: Languages Department, Punjab, 1970.

CHETAN SINGH, *Region and Empire: Panjab in the Seventeenth Century.* Delhi: Oxford University Press, 1991.

COLE, W. OWEN, *Thinking about Sikhism.* London: Lutterworth, 1980.

———, *The Guru in Sikhism.* London: Darton, Longman and Todd, 1982.

———, *Sikhism and Its Indian Context 1469–1708: The Attitude of Guru Nanak and Early Sikhism to Indian Religious Beliefs and Practices.* London: Darton, Longman & Todd, 1984.

COLE, W. OWEN and PIARA SINGH SAMBHI, *The Sikhs: Their Religious Beliefs and Practices.* London: Routledge and Kegan Paul, 1978.

CUNNINGHAM, J.D., *A History of the Sikhs from the Origin of the Nation to the Battles of the Sutlej.* London: John Murray, 1849. Reprint, New Delhi: S. Chand and Co., 1985.

DALIP SINGH, *Dynamics of Punjab Politics.* New Delhi: Macmillan, 1981.

DALJEET SINGH, *Essays on the Authenticity of Kartarpuri Bir and the Integrated Logic and Unity of Sikhism.* Patiala: Punjabi University, 1987.

DARSHAN SINGH, *Western Perspective on the Sikh Religion.* New Delhi: Sehgal, 1991.

DHILLON, GURDARSHAN SINGH, *Character and Impact of the Singh Sabha Movement on the History of the Punjab*. Patiala: Punjabi University, 1973.

DUGGAL, KARTAR SINGH, *The Sikh Gurus: Their Lives and Teachings*. New Delhi: Vikas, 1980.

———, *The Sikh People Yesterday and Today*. New Delhi: UBSPD, 1994.

FALCON, R. W., *Handbook on Sikhs for the Use of Regimental Officers*. Allahabad: Pioneer Press, 1896.

FAUJA SINGH, *Guru Amar Das: Life and Teachings*. New Delhi: Sterling. 1979.

———, *After Ranjit Singh*. New Delhi: Master, 1982.

——— [Bajwa], *Military System of the Sikhs during the Period 1799–1849*. Delhi: Motilal Banarsidass, 1964.

——— [Bajwa], *Kuka Movement : An Important Phase in Punjab's Role in India's Struggle for Freedom*. Delhi: Motilal Banarsidass, 1965.

———, *Some Aspects of State and Society under Ranjit Singh*. New Delhi: Master, 1982.

FAUJA SINGH and A. C. ARORA (eds.), *Papers on Guru Nanak*, Patiala: Punjabi University, 1970.

——— (eds.), *Maharaja Ranjit Singh: Politics, Society and Economy*. Patiala: Punjabi University, 1984.

FAUJA SINGH, et al., *Sikhism*. Patiala: Punjabi University, 1969.

FAUJA SINGH and GURBACHAN SINGH TALIB, *Guru Tegh Bahadur : Martyr and Teacher*. Patiala: Punjabi University, 1975.

FAUJA SINGH and RATTAN SINGH JAGGI (eds.), *Perspectives on Guru Amar Das*. Patiala: Punjabi University, 1982.

FOX, RICHARD G., *Lions of the Punjab: Culture in the Making*. Berkeley, California: University of California Press, 1985.

GANDA SINGH, *Life of Banda Singh Bahadur*. Amritsar: Khalsa College, 1935. Reprint, Patiala: Punjabi University, 1990.

———, *A Brief Account of the Sikh People*. Patiala: Sikh History Society, 1956.

——— (ed.), *Early European Accounts of the Sikhs*. Calcutta: Indian Studies Past and Present, 1962.

———, *Guru Arjan's Martyrdom Re-interpreted*. Patiala: Guru Nanak Mission, 1969.

——— (ed.), *Sources on the Life and Teachings of Guru Nanak*. Guru Nanak's Birth Quincentenary Volume of *The Panjab Past and Present*, III (1969). Patiala: Punjabi University, 1969.

———, *Guru Gobind Singh's Death at Nanded: An Examination of Succession Theories*. Faridkot: Guru Nanak Foundation, 1972.

———, *The Sikhs and Their Religion*. Redwood City, California: Sikh Foundation, 1974.

———, *Martyrdom of Guru Tegh Bahadur*. Amritsar: Guru Nanak Dev University, 1976.

——— (ed.), *The Singh Sabha and other Socio-Religious Movements in the Punjab 1850–1925*. Vol. VII, Part I (April, 1973) of *The Panjab Past and Present*. Patiala: Punjabi University, 1984.

———, *Sardar Jassa Singh Ahluwalia*. Patiala: Punjabi University, 1990.

GANDHI, SURJIT SINGH, *History of the Sikh Gurus: A Comprehensive Study*. Delhi: Gur Das Kapur, 1978.

———, *Struggle of the Sikhs for Sovereignty*. Delhi: Gur Das Kapur, 1980.

GOBINDER SINGH, *Religion and Politics in the Punjab*. New Delhi: Deep and Deep, 1986.

SINGH, GOPAL, *The Sikhs: Their History, Religion, Culture, Ceremonies and Literature*. Madras: Seshachalam 1970; Bombay: Popular Prakashan, 1970.

———, *The Religion of the Sikhs*. Bombay: Asia Publishing House, 1971.

———, *History of the Sikh People (1469–1978)*. New Delhi: World Sikh University Press, 1979.

GORDON, JOHN H., *The Sikhs*. Edinburgh: William Blackwood, 1904. Reprint, Patiala: Languages Department, Punjab, 1970.

GOUGH, CHARLES and ARTHUR D. INNES, *The Sikhs and the Sikh Wars: The Rise, Conquest, and Annexation of the Punjab State*. London: Innes, 1897. Reprint, Patiala: Languages Department, Punjab, 1970.

GREWAL, J. S., *Guru Nanak in History*. Chandigarh: Panjab University, 1969.

———, *From Guru Nanak to Maharaja Ranjit Singh: Essays in Sikh History*. Amritsar: Guru Nanak Dev University, 1972. Revised edition, 1982.

———, *Miscellaneous Articles*. Amritsar: Guru Nanak Dev University, 1974.

———, *The Sikhs of the Punjab*. Vol. II. 3 of *The New Cambridge History of India*. Cambridge: Cambridge University Press, 1990.

———, *Guru Nanak in Western Scholarship*. Shimla: Indian Institute of Advanced Study, 1992. Reprint, New Delhi: Manohar, 1993.

———, *Guru Nanak and Patriarchy*. Shimla: Indian Institute of Advanced Study, 1993. 47pp.

GREWAL, J. S. and INDU BANGA (eds.), *Maharaja Ranjit Singh and His Times*. Amritsar: Guru Nanak Dev University, 1980.

GREWAL, J. S. and S. S. BAL, *Guru Gobind Singh: A Biographical Study.* Chandigarh: Panjab University, 1967. 2nd edition, 1987.

GULATI, KAILASH CHANDER, *The Akalis Past and Present.* New Delhi: Ashajanak, 1974.

GUPTA, HARI RAM, *A History of the Sikhs from Nadir Shah's Invasions to the Rise of Ranjit Singh (1739–1799).* 3 vols. Simla: Minerva, 1939–44.

———, *Short History of the Sikhs.* Ludhiana: Sahitya Sangam 1970.

———, *History of the Sikh Gurus.* New Delhi: Uttam Chand Kapur, 1973.

———, *History of the Sikhs.* 6 Vols. New Delhi: Munshiram Manoharlal, 1978–91.

GURDEV SINGH (ed.), *Perspectives on the Sikh Tradition.* Chandigarh: Siddharth Publications, 1986.

HANS, SURJIT, *Reconstruction of Sikh History from Sikh Literature.* Jullundur: ABS Publications, 1988.

HARBANS SINGH, *Heritage of the Sikhs.* Bombay: Asia Publishing House, 1964. 2nd edition, New Delhi: Manohar, 1983.

———, *Guru Gobind Singh.* Chandigarh: Guru Gobind Singh Foundation, 1966.

———, *Guru Nanak and the Origins of the Sikh Faith.* Bombay: APH, 1969.

———, *Bhai Vir Singh.* New Delhi: Sahitya Akademi, 1972.

——— (ed.), *Perspectives on Guru Nanak.* Patiala: Punjabi University, 1975.

———, *Maharaja Ranjit Singh.* New Delhi: Sterling, 1980.

———, *Guru Tegh Bahadur.* New Delhi: Sterling, 1982.

———, *Berkeley Lectures on Sikhism.* New Delhi: GNF, 1983.

HARBANS SINGH and N. GERALD BARRIER (eds.), *Essays in Honour of Dr Ganda Singh.* Patiala: Punjabi University, 1976.

HARJINDER SINGH, *Authority and Influence in Two Sikh Villages.* New Delhi: Sterling, 1976.

HASRAT, BIKRAMA JIT, *Life and Times of Ranjit Singh: A Saga of Benevolent Despotism.* Nabha: author, 1977.

HAWLEY, JOHN STRATTON and GURINDER SINGH MANN (eds.), *Studying the Sikhs: Issues for North America.* Albany: SUNY, 1993.

IBBETSON, DENZIL, *Punjab Castes.* Lahore: Government Printing, 1916.

IZMIRLIAN, HARRY (JR), *The Politics of Passion: Structure and Strategy in Sikh Society.* New Delhi: Manohar, 1979.

JAFAR, GHANI, *The Sikh Volcano.* New Delhi: Atlantic, 1988.

JAGIT SINGH, *The Sikh Revolution : A Perspective View.* New Delhi: Bahri, 1981.

Perspectives on Sikh Studies. New Delhi: Guru Nanak Foundation, 1985.

JODH SINGH, *Life of Guru Amar Dass Ji*. Ludhiana: Lahore Book Shop, 1953.

———, *Caste and Untouchability in Sikhism*. Amritsar: SGPC, 1976.

JOGENDRA SINGH, *Sikh Ceremonies*. Bombay: International Book House, 1941. Reprint, Chandigarh: Religious Book Society, 1968. Reprint, Ludhiana: Lahore Book Shop, 1989.

JOLLY, SURJIT KAUR, *Sikh Revivalist Movements: The Nirankari and Namdhari Movements in Punjab in the Nineteenth Century*. New Delhi: Gitanjali, 1988.

JUERGENSMEYER, MARK and N. GERALD BARRIER (eds.), *Sikh Studies: Comparative Perspectives on a Changing Tradition*. Berkeley, California: Berkeley Religious Studies Series, 1979.

KANWALJIT KAUR and INDERJIT SINGH (trans.), *Rehat Maryada: A Guide to the Sikh Way of Life*. London: Sikh Cultural Society, 1969.

KAPUR, RAJIV A., *Sikh Separatism: The Politics of Faith*. London: Allen and Unwin, 1986.

KAPUR SINGH, *Parasharprasna or the Baisakhi of Guru Gobind Singh*. Jullundur: Hind Publishers, 1959. Revised edition, edited by Madanjit Kaur and Piar Singh, Amritsar: Guru Nanak Dev University, 1989.

———, *Guru Nanak's Life and Thought*. Edited by Madanjit Kaur and Piar Singh. Amritsar: Guru Nanak Dev University, 1991.

———, *Guru Arjun and his Sukhmani*. Edited by Madanjit Kaur and Piar Singh. Amritsar: Guru Nanak Dev University, 1992.

KASHMIR SINGH, *Law of Religious Institutions: Sikh Gurdwaras*. Amritsar: Guru Nanak Dev University, 1989.

KHARAK SINGH, *et al.* (eds.), *Fundamental Issues in Sikh Studies*. Chandigarh: Institute of Sikh Studies, 1992.

KHILNANI, N. M., *Rise of the Sikh Power in Punjab*. Delhi: Independent, 1990.

KHUSHWANT SINGH, *The Sikhs*. London: George Allen and Unwin, 1953.

———, *The Fall of the Kingdom of the Punjab*. Bombay: Orient Longmans, 1962.

———, *Ranjit Singh: Maharajah of the Punjab 1780–1839*. London: George Allen and Unwin, 1962.

———, *A History of the Sikhs*. 2 Vols. Princeton, New Jersey: Princeton University Press, 1963, 1966. Revised edition, Delhi: Oxford University Press, 1991.

KHUSHWANT SINGH and RAGHU RAI, *The Sikhs*. Varanasi: Lutra, 1984.

KOHLI, SURINDAR SINGH, *A Critical Study of the Adi Granth*. New Delhi: PWCIS, 1961. Reissued as *Guru Granth Sahib: An Analytical Study*. Amritsar: Singh Brothers, 1992.

———, *Outlines of Sikh Thought*. New Delhi: Punjabi Prakashak, 1966.

———, *Sikh Ethics*. Delhi: Munshiram Manoharlal, 1973.

———, *Life and Ideals of Guru Gobind Singh*. New Delhi: Munshiram Manoharlal, 1986.

———, *The Sikh Philosophy*. Amritsar: Singh Brothers, 1992.

———, *The Sikh and Sikhism*. New Delhi: Atlantic, 1993.

———, *Real Sikhism*. New Delhi: Harman, 1994.

LAKSHMAN SINGH, *Bhagat Lakshman Singh: Autobiography*. Edited by Ganda Singh. Calcutta: Sikh Cultural Centre, 1965.

LOEHLIN, C. H., *The Sikhs and Their Book*. Lucknow: Lucknow Publishing House, 1946.

———, *The Sikhs and Their Scriptures*. Lucknow: Lucknow Publishing House, 1958.

———, *The Granth of Guru Gobind Singh and the Khalsa Brotherhood*. Lucknow: Lucknow Publishing House, 1971.

MACAULIFFE, MAX ARTHUR, *The Sikh Religion: Its Gurus, Sacred Writings and Authors*. 6 Vols in 3. Oxford: Clarendon, 1909. Reprint, Delhi: S. Chand, 1985.

MACAULIFFE, M., et al., *The Sikh Religion: A Symposium*. (Contains contributions by M. Macauliffe, H. H. Wilson, F. Pincott, J. Malcolm, and Kahan Singh.). Calcutta: Susil Gupta, 1958.

McLEOD, W. H., *Gurū Nānak and the Sikh Religion*. Oxford: Clarendon, 1968. 2nd Edition, Delhi: Oxford University Press, 1976.

———, *Early Sikh Tradition: A Study of the Janam-sākhīs*. Oxford: Clarendon, 1980.

——— (trans.), *The B40 Janam-sākhī*. Amritsar: Guru Nanak Dev University, 1980.

——— (trans.), *The Chaupā Singh Rahit-nāmā*. Dunedin: University of Otago, 1987.

———, *The Sikhs: History, Religion, and Society*. New York: Columbia University Press, 1989.

———, *Who is a Sikh? The Problem of Sikh Identity*. Oxford: Clarendon, 1989; New Delhi: Oxford University Press, 1989.

——— (trans.), *Textual Sources for the Study of Sikhism*. Manchester: Manchester University Press, 1984. Reprint, Chicago, Illinois: University of Chicago Press, 1990.

McMullen, Clarence O., *Religious Beliefs and Practices of the Sikhs in Rural Punjab.* New Delhi: Manohar, 1989.

Madanjit Kaur, *Golden Temple: Past and Present.* Amritsar: Guru Nanak Dev University, 1983.

Malcolm, John, *Sketch of the Sikhs.* London: John Murray, 1812.

Mann, Jasbir Singh and Harbans Singh Saraon (eds.), *Advanced Studies in Sikhism.* Irvine, California: Sikh Community of North America, 1989.

Mann, Jasbir Singh and Kharak Singh (eds.), *Recent Researches in Sikhism.* Patiala: Punjabi University, 1992.

Mansukhani, Gobind Singh, *Introduction to Sikhism.* New Delhi: India Book House, 1967.

———, *Guru Nanak: World Teacher.* New Delhi: India Book House, 1968.

———, *Life of Guru Nanak.* New Delhi: Guru Nanak Foundation, 1974.

———, *Guru Gobind Singh.* Delhi: Hemkunt, 1976.

———, *Guru Ramdas : His Life, Work and Philosophy.* New Delhi: Oxford and IBH, 1979.

———, *Aspects of Sikhism.* New Delhi: PWCIS, 1982.

———, *A Book of Sikh Studies.* Delhi: NBS, 1989.

Mansukhani, Gobind Singh and Surindar Singh Kohli, *Guru Gobind Singh: His Personality and Achievement.* New Delhi: Hemkunt, 1976.

Marenco, Ethne K., *Transformation of Sikh Society.* New Delhi: Heritage, 1976.

Mohinder Singh, *The Akali Struggle: A Retrospect.* New Delhi: Atlantic, 1988.

——— (ed.), *History and Culture of Panjab.* New Delhi : Atlantic, 1988.

Nabha, Kahan Singh, *Sikhs: We Are Not Hindus.* Translated by Jarnail Singh. Willowdale, Ontario: translator, 1984.

Narain Singh, *Guru Gobind Singh Re-told.* Amritsar: author, 1966.

———, *Guru Nanak Re-interpreted.* Amritsar: author, 1965.

———, *Guru Nanak and His Images.* 2 Vols. Amritsar: author, 1970.

Narang, Gokul Chand, *Transformation of Sikhism.* Lahore: Tribune Press, 1914. Revised and enlarged edition, 1945. Republished as *Glorious History of Sikhism.* New Delhi: New Book Society of India, 1972.

Nayar, Baldev Raj, *Minority Politics in the Punjab.* Princeton, New Jersey: Princeton University Press, 1966.

NAYAR, KULDIP and KHUSHWANT SINGH, *Tragedy of Punjab: Operation Bluestar and After.* New Delhi: Vision Books, 1984.

NAYYAR, GURBACHAN SINGH, *Sikh Polity and Political Institutions.* New Delhi: Oriental, 1979.

NRIPINDER SINGH, *The Sikh Moral Tradition: Ethical Perceptions of the Sikhs in the Late Nineteenth/Early Twentieth Century.* New Delhi: Manohar, 1990; Columbia, Missouri: South Asia Publications, 1990.

OBEROI, HARJOT, *The Construction of Religious Boundaries: Culture, Identity, and Diversity in the Sikh Tradition.* Delhi: Oxford University Press, 1994; Chicago: University of Chicago Press, 1994.

O'CONNELL, JOSEPH T. *et al.* (eds.), *Sikh History and Religion in the Twentieth Century.* Toronto: Centre for South Asian Studies, University of Toronto, 1988. Reprint, New Delhi: Manohar, 1990.

PATWANT SINGH and HARJI MALIK (eds.), *Punjab: The Fatal Miscalculation.* New Delhi: Patwant Singh, 1985.

PETTIGREW, JOYCE, *Robber Noblemen: A Study of the Political System of the Sikh Jats.* London: Routledge and Kegan Paul, 1975.

PETRIE, D., *Developments in Sikh Politics 1900–1911: A Report.* Amritsar: Chief Khalsa Diwan, n.d.

PRINSEP, HENRY T., *Origin of the Sikh Power in the Punjab and Political Life of Maharaja Ranjit Singh.* Includes appendix 'On the manner, rules, and customs of the Sikhs' by Captain W. Murray. Calcutta: Military Orphan Press, 1834. Reprint, Patiala: Languages Department, Punjab, 1970.

PURI, HARISH K., *Ghadar Movement: Ideology, Organisation and Strategy.* Amritsar: Guru Nanak Dev University, 1983.

PURI, NINA, *Political Elite and Society in the Punjab.* New Delhi: Vikas, 1985.

RANBIR SINGH, *The Sikh way of Life.* New Delhi: Indian Publishers, 1969.

RANDHIR SINGH, *Ethics of Sikhs.* Amritsar: SGPC, 1953.

———, *Autobiography of Bhai Sahib Randhir Singh.* Translated by Trilochan Singh. Ludhiana: Bhai Sahib Randhir Singh Publishing House, 1971.

RAY, NIHARRANJAN, *The Sikh Gurus and the Sikh Society: A Study in Social Analysis.* Patiala: Punjabi University, 1970.

SACHDEVA, VEENA, *Policy and Economy of the Punjab during the Late Eighteenth Century.* Delhi: Manohar, 1993.

SAGAR, SABINDERJIT SINGH, *Historical Analysis of Nanak Prakash: Bhai Santokh Singh.* Amritsar : Guru Nanak Dev University, 1993.

Sahib Singh, *Guru Gobind Singh*. Jullundur: Raj, 1967.

Sahni, Ruchi Ram, *Struggle for Reform in Sikh Shrines*. Amritsar: Sikh Itihas Research Board, 1964.

Samiuddin, Abida (ed.), *The Punjab Crisis: Challenge and Response*. Delhi: Mittal, 1985.

Santokh Singh, *Philosophical Foundations of the Sikh Value System*. New Delhi: Munshiram Manoharlal, 1982.

Sarhadi, Ajit Singh, *Punjabi Suba: The Story of the Struggle*. Delhi: U. C. Kapur, 1970.

Schomer, Karine and W. H. McLeod (eds.), *The Sants: Studies in a Devotional Tradition of India*. Berkeley, California: Berkeley Religious Studies Series, 1987; Delhi: Motilal Banarsidass, 1987.

Shackle, C., *An Introduction to the Sacred Language of the Sikhs*. London: SOAS, University of London, 1983.

———, *The Sikhs*. London : Minority Rights Group, 1984. Revised edition, 1986.

Sher Singh, *Philosophy of Sikhism*. Lahore: Sikh University Press. 1944. Reprint, Delhi: Sterling, 1966.

———, *Social and Political Philosophy of Guru Gobind Singh*. Delhi: Sterling, 1967.

———, *Sikhism and Indian Society*. Transactions of the Indian Institute of Advanced Study. Simla: Indian Institute of Advanced Study, 1967.

Singh, I. J., *Sikhs and Sikhism: A View with a Bias*. Columbia, Missouri: South Asia Books, 1994; New Delhi : Manohar, 1994.

Singh, Nikki-Guninder Kaur, *Sikhism*. New York: Facts on File, 1993.

Sinha, Narendra Krishna, *Rise of the Sikh Power*. Calcutta: University of Calcutta, 1936.

Talbot, Ian, *Punjab and the Raj 1849–1947*. New Delhi: Manohar, 1988.

Talib, Gurbachan Singh, *The Impact of Guru Gobind Singh on Indian Society*. Chandigarh: Guru Gobind Singh Foundation, 1966.

———, *Guru Nanak: His Personality and Vision*. Delhi : Gur Das Kapur, 1969.

——— (ed.), *Guru Tegh Bahadur: Background and the Supreme Sacrifice*. Patiala: Punjabi University, 1976.

Taran Singh (ed.), *Guru Nanak and Indian Religious Thought*. Patiala: Punjabi University, 1970.

———, *Teachings of Guru Nanak Dev*. Patiala: Punjabi University, 1977.

———, *Guru Nanak: His Mind and Art*. New Delhi: Bahri, 1992.

TEJA SINGH, *Essays in Sikhism.* Lahore: Sikh University Press, 1944.

———, *Sikhism: Its Ideals and Institutions.* Calcutta: Orient Longmans, 1951.

———, *The Gurdwara Reform Movement and the Sikh Awakening.* Jullundur: Desh Sewak, 1922. Reprint, Amritsar: SGPC, 1984.

TEJA SINGH and GANDA SINGH, *A Short History of the Sikhs (1469–1765).* Bombay: Orient Longmans, 1950. Reprint, Patiala: Punjabi University, 1989.

[THORNTON, THOMAS HENRY], *History of the Punjab and of the Rise, Progress & Present Condition of the Sect and Nation of the Sikhs.* 2 Vols. London: W. H. Allen, 1846. Reprint, Patiala: Languages Department, Punjab, 1970.

TRILOCHAN SINGH, *Guru Tegh Bahadur: Prophet and Martyr.* Delhi : Gurdwara Prabandhak Committee, 1967.

———, *Guru Nanak: Founder of Sikhism: A Biography.* Delhi: Gurdwara Prabandhak Committee, 1969.

———, *The Turban and the Sword of the Sikhs.* Gravesend: Sikh Missionary Society, 1977.

———, *Life of Guru Hari Krishan. A Biography and History.* Delhi: Delhi Sikh Gurdwara Management Committee, 1981.

THURSBY, GENE R., *The Sikhs.* New York: E. J. Brill, 1992.

TULLY, MARK and SATISH JACOB, *Amritsar: Mrs Gandhi's Last Battle.* Calcutta: Rupa, 1985.

TUTEJA, K. L., *Sikh Politics (1920–1940).* Kurukshetra: Vishal, 1984.

UPINDER JIT KAUR, *Sikh Religion and Economic Development.* New Delhi: National Book Organisation, 1990.

UPRETY, PREM RAMAN, *Religion and Politics in the Punjab in the 1920s.* New Delhi: Sterling, 1980.

WALLACE, PAUL and SURENDRA CHOPRA (eds.), *Political Dynamics of Punjab.* Amritsar: Guru Nanak Dev University, 1981. Revised edition, 1988.

WEBSTER, JOHN C. B., *The Nirankari Sikhs.* Delhi: Macmillan, 1979.

Translations of Sikh Scriptures

GOPAL SINGH (trans.), *Sri Guru-Granth Sahib.* 4 Vols. Delhi: Gurdas Kapur and Sons, 1960–2.

KHUSHWANT SINGH (trans.), *Hymns of Guru Nanak.* New Delhi: Orient Longmans, 1969.

MANMOHAN SINGH (trans.), *Sri Guru Granth Sahib.* 8 Vols. Amritsar: SGPC, 1969.

MANSUKHANI, GOBIND SINGH (trans.), *Hymns from the Holy Granth.* Delhi: Hemkunt Press, 1975.

——— (trans.), *Hymns from the Dasam Granth.* New Delhi: Hemkunt, 1980.

——— (trans.), *Hymns from Bhai Gurdas's Compositions.* Amritsar: Singh Brothers, 1989.

SEKHON, SANT SINGH (trans.), *Unique Drama: Translation of Benati Chaupai, Bachitra Natak and Akal Ustati.* Chandigarh: Guru Gobind Singh Foundation, 1968.

TALIB, GURBACHAN SINGH (trans.), *Sri Guru Granth Sahib.* 4 Vols. Patiala: Punjabi University, 1984–90.

TRILOCHAN SINGH, *et al.* (trans.), *Selections from the Sacred Writings of the Sikhs.* London: George Allen and Unwin, 1960.

Encyclopaedias, Dictionaries and Bibliographies

BARRIER, N. GERALD, *The Sikhs and Their Literature.* Delhi: Manohar, 1970.

COLE, W. OWEN and PIARA SINGH SAMBHI, *A Popular Dictionary of Sikhism.* London: Curzon, 1990.

GANDA SINGH (comp.), *A Select Bibliography of the Sikhs and Sikhism.* Amritsar: SGPC, 1965.

——— (comp.), *A Bibliography of the Punjab.* Patiala: Punjabi University, 1966.

HARBANS SINGH (ed.), *The Encyclopaedia of Sikhism,* 4 Vols. Patiala: Punjabi University, 1992–.

HAKAM SINGH (comp.), *Sikh Studies: A Classified Bibliography of Printed Books in English.* Patiala: Punjab Publishing House, 1982.

MCLEOD, W. H., *Historical Dictionary of Sikhism.* Metuchen, NJ: Scarecrow, 1995.

RAJWANT SINGH (comp.), *The Sikhs: Their Literature on Culture, History, Philosophy, Religion and Traditions.* Delhi: Indian Bibliographies Bureau, 1990.

ROSE, H. A. (comp.), *A Glossary of the Tribes and Castes of the Punjab and North-West Frontier Province.* 3 Vols. Lahore: Punjab Government Printing Press, 1919. Reprint, Patiala: Languages Department, Punjab, 1970.

INDEX

Who is a Sikh?

PREFACE

THIS book consists of lectures which could not be given. The Trustees of the Radhakrishnan Memorial Bequest had invited me to visit the University of Oxford and give the series for 1986–7. Dates had been arranged for March 1987, the six lectures had been duly written, and I was due to depart for Oxford in one month. It was then that the illness occurred which put an end to such plans. I had hoped that with rapid progress I would be ready to deliver them a year later than intended, but that also proved to be too optimistic. New Zealand was too far from England and eventually it was decided, with much reluctance, that the Radhakrishnan Memorial Lectures for 1986–7 would have to be cancelled.

The series had, however, been written and it was decided that even if they could not be heard it was at least possible that they could be read. It was unfortunate that they could not be presented before the members of an Oxford audience in order that due attention could be paid to their criticisms before publication. Such an advantage was not to be and it was felt that even in their uncriticized form they would be preferable to no lectures at all.

Punjabi words have presented the usual difficulty of when to italicize and when to leave as roman. Words indicating various kinds of people and organizations have been allowed to remain roman. Punjabi words which occur frequently in English usage (e.g. mañjī, saṅgat) have been italicized the first time and then printed in roman thereafter. Other Punjabi words have been italicized and marked with diacriticals throughout. All have been included in the Glossary, complete with diacriticals.

Three universities (or their various parts) deserve my gratitude. The University of Otago granted me the leave which was necessary if I was to be removed from distractions and diversions. To it I express my thanks and in particular to my fellow-members of the History Department for making my absence possible. The Centre for Religious Studies at the University of Toronto provided me with the facilities, without duties or interruption, to write the lectures. It too deserves my thanks. Finally there are the Trustees of the Radhakrishnan Memorial Bequest for their generous invitation to visit the University of Oxford and deliver the lectures. In this I failed, but I remain profoundly indebted to them for having prompted me to produce a text. To them, and to the memory of Sarvapalli Radhakrishnan, I offer in sincere gratitude these thoughts on who is a Sikh.

H. M.

The University of Otago
Dunedin

CONTENTS

1

What is Sikhism?

'WHAT is Sikhism?' I asked a Sikh gentleman many years ago. 'How would you define it?'

'Sikhism', he replied, 'can be defined as the fatherhood of God and the brotherhood of man.'

The answer is a popular one and it is an interesting response for several reasons. One reason is that it so clearly evokes the memory of Adolf Harnack and his famous Berlin lectures published as *What is Christianity*?[1] My informant was quoting the words which conventionally summarize Harnack's book and which were so commonly used to describe the essence of Liberal Protestant belief. Sikhism is scarcely the same as Liberal Protestantism, but one can easily understand why the vague formula should exercise such an appeal. Dogma is discarded and friendly benevolence retained.

Although the Liberal Protestant creed must be rejected as an adequate definition for Sikhism, we should pause before we dismiss all such summary statements. Concise or mnemonic summaries have been extensively used in the Sikh tradition and one early example retains its popularity to the present day. The earliest of all goes back to Guru Nanak himself, a saying consisting of nothing more than the three nouns *nām*, *dān*, and *iśnān*.[2] The *nām dān iśnān* formula evidently served as a kind of motto for the early community, neatly expressing the essence of Nanak's message and easily remembered by those who acknowledged him as their Guru.

Nām, or the 'divine Name', is a convenient shorthand for the total being and nature of Akal Purakh or God, a single word which effectively captures a broad range of direct meaning and indirect association.[3] One

[1] Adolf Harnack, *What is Christianity?* (1st Eng. edn., Williams & Norgate, London, 1901). The lectures were delivered in the University of Berlin during 1899–1900.

[2] Guru Nanak, *Siddh Goṣṭ* 36, Adi Granth, p. 942. The formula is extensively used in sakhis of the Narrative III janam-sakhi tradition. W. H. McLeod, *The B40 Janam-sākhī* (Amritsar, 1980), 110n. It also appears in the *Tanakhāh-nāmā* attributed to Bhai Nand Lal. Piara Singh Padam (samp.), *Rahit-nāme* (Patiala, 1974), 44. See chap. 3, n. 31.

[3] W. H. McLeod, *Gurū Nānak and the Sikh Religion* (Oxford, 1968; 2nd edn., Delhi, 1976), 195–6.

might well argue that the expounding of this single word should tell us all that we need to know about the fundamental doctrine which Nanak preached. The two remaining words merely amplify its meaning. If one is to secure deliverance from the cycle of transmigration, one must accept the reality of the *nām* and strive to bring one's own being into complete conformity with it. This purpose one achieves primarily through the practice of *nām simaraṇ* or meditation on the divine Name, though it is also assisted by alms-giving (*dān*) and necessarily involves pure living (*iśnān*).

The strength of this earliest of formulas obviously resides in its first word and it soon becomes clear that an extended explanation is required before it can be clearly understood. It is, moreover, evident that much of the developed Sikh tradition is missing. The same verdict must be applied to another formula popularly (but mistakenly) attributed to Guru Nanak. *Nām japo, kirat karo, vaṇḍ chhako*, he is believed to have declared. 'Repeat the divine Name, work [hard], and give to others a portion of what you earn.'[4] The ideal is an admirable one. As with *nām dān iśnān*, however, it must leave us with the distinct impression that much of the Sikh tradition has somehow been missed. Where, for example, is the mandatory reference to the Khalsa or to the Rahit which all its members should observe?[5]

A standard rule to follow when seeking summary answers to questions concerning the Sikh tradition is to consult Kahn Singh Nabha's encyclopaedia *Guruśabad ratanākar mahān koś*. How does Kahn Singh define what he calls *sikh dharam*? Having briefly summarized Nanak's doctrine of God and stressed the paramount need for the Guru's guidance, he lists the following as essential articles of faith:

I. Individual

1. To achieve mystical union with God (*Vāhigurū*) through meditation on the divine Name.
2. To read the sacred scripture (*gurbāṇī*) daily and to reflect on the doctrines which it imparts.
3. To view all men as brothers without concern for caste or race, bestowing love on all and performing service without expectation of reward.

[4] The origin is obscure, though apparently relatively recent. Dr Ganda Singh suggests it may owe its beginnings to the phrase *jinān nām japiā, vaṇḍ chhakiā . . . dī kamāī dā dhiān dhar ke*, which occurs in Ardas (the 'Sikh Prayer'). See chap. 7, n. 11. Personal letter 19 Nov. 1971.

[5] The Khalsa is the order instituted by Guru Gobind Singh in 1699, and its Rahit is the code of conduct which all who join it are expected to obey. See chap. 3.

4. To secure the benefits of religion (*dharam*) while continuing to live the life of an ordinary layman.
5. To spurn ignorant notions of untouchability, magic, idol worship, and superstition; and to accept only the teachings of the Guru.

II. Corporate

1. To observe the Sikh code of conduct (*rahit*) in the bonds of unity.
2. To accept the corporate community (*panth*) as Guru and to serve it with loyal devotion.
3. To proclaim the Guru's teachings to the world.
4. To accept with affection all Nanak-panthis as adherents of the Sikh religion, regardless of their outward appearance; and to treat people with respect and sympathy.
5. To observe in gurdwaras and other shrines the rituals enjoined by the Gurus.[6]

Kahn Singh was a master of the succinct statement and his skill is well represented by these Ten Commandments. In spite of their brevity they carry us a considerable distance, and, were we to examine each item in turn, we could reasonably expect to acquire a wide understanding of Sikh doctrine. The essential problem, however, remains. The Sikh tradition refuses to be thus encapsulated and a closer examination would certainly lead us into some major controversies. What, for example, is Kahn Singh telling us about the role and status of the Khalsa? The word does not appear in his catalogue although its presence is implied by his reference to the Rahit. A significant part of the answer is indicated by his reference to Nanak-panthis in item II. 4 and it is a view which some would certainly want to qualify.

The issue raised by this item concerns the difference between those who regard the Khalsa as the essential and definitive form of the Sikh tradition and those who affirm a broader identity. It is a fundamental issue which clearly signals the kind of problem which we expect to encounter as we endeavour to answer the question 'What is Sikhism?' Indeed some will maintain that no answer is possible until we abandon the term 'Sikhism' altogether. Amongst those who wish to retain the word there are some who hesitate to use it with reference to the early period of Sikh development, preferring to restrict its usage to the last three centuries. According to this latter view, the term 'Sikhism' should be reserved for that area of Sikh tradition which is amenable to clear definition, namely the Khalsa. Further complexity emerges when we discover that this restrictive view further subdivides, distinguishing those

[6] Kahn Singh Nabha, *Guruśabad ratanākar mahān koś* (2nd rev. edn., Patiala, 1960), 145.

who would accept non-Khalsa Sikhs as affiliates from those who would exclude them altogether.

Plainly we are running into difficulties and the time has come to indicate how we propose to deal with them. The only satisfactory method seems to be to treat the tradition historically. Observing how it emerges and grows, we should be able to comprehend something of the variety of doctrine and practice which develops within the tradition as its numbers increase and as changing pressures work upon it. In so doing we shall be led from the question 'What is Sikhism?' to the question 'Who is a Sikh?' The two issues differ, yet fundamentally they are the same. Most Sikhs (like most who identify with any of the major religious groupings) would have difficulty in recognizing much that is offered as an answer to the first question. They are nevertheless products of the tradition and of the history which has made it. Without the tradition they would be different people, identifying with a different tradition or with several.

We shall begin, predictably, with Guru Nanak and with the group of followers whom he attracted (the group which comes to be known as the Nanak-panth), exploring their beginnings and the pattern of development which was followed under the early Gurus. We shall proceed to examine the founding of the Khalsa by Guru Gobind Singh; and we shall then seek to follow the evolution of the Khalsa code of conduct (the Rahit) during the course of the eighteenth century. Another key period in the development of the Sikh identity, the decades occupied by the Singh Sabha and Akali movements, will then be considered. Answers to some crucial questions were given during the half-century from 1873 to 1925 and their effect has been to mould much that has taken place since then. Finally, we shall pose the question 'Who is a Sikh?', setting it in its modern context. In attempting to answer it we shall simultaneously endeavour to define the nature of Sikhism as it is generally understood today.

Although this procedure should help us to understand the Sikh tradition, let us not imagine that it will produce answers which are clear, definitive, and universally accepted. If that were our objective, we should assuredly fail, for Sikh identity cannot be described with the ease or clarity which so commonly we assume. Paradoxically it is the increasingly clear definition of Sikh identity which produces an increasingly acute problem of identity. When dealing with the Nanak-panth we may perhaps obtain some general definitions which apply to the tradition as a whole, but having reached the Khalsa we shall be confronted by a diversity of interpretations. As we have already noted, many Sikhs believe that the Khalsa definition and the distinctive Khalsa identity of today supply clear and immediate answers to all such questions. Others are less certain that the boundaries of the tradition can be drawn in a manner which effectively excludes those who claim to be Sikhs yet decline to observe the traditional code of the Khalsa.

This is one of the primary issues which awaits us and we mislead ourselves if we imagine that the debate covers only two distinct identities (the Khalsa and the non-Khalsa). The different between the punctilious Gursikh of the Khalsa and the so-called Sahaj-dhari Sikh may be clear enough, but what are we to make of those who observe much of the Khalsa discipline (particularly the uncut hair) without formally taking initiation?[7] Even more difficult are the questions implicitly raised by those who observe multiple identities, definable as neither clearly Hindu nor clearly Sikh. And how are we to classify those who belong to families which traditionally observe the Khalsa tradition yet cut their hair?

Amongst Sikhs living overseas the cutting of hair has long been a common practice, and, although recent events have slowed the process, there seems to be little doubt that the clearly established trend towards hair-cutting will continue. Such people still claim to be Sikhs. Are they mistaken, or should the boundaries of the Sikh tradition somehow be drawn in a manner which includes them? If they are to be included, what are we to make of the orthodox insistence on upholding the traditions of the Khalsa, and how should this latter variety of hair-cutting Sikh be compared with the Sahaj-dhari who has never kept his or her hair uncut?

It must be clearly recognized that a significant part of the problem derives from our typically Western insistence on clearly defined categories, on neatly labelled normative boxes into which all men and women should somehow be fitted. In this respect the problem is nevertheless the inevitable by-product of an essential process. We need the categories if analysis is to proceed; and we deceive ourselves only if we imagine that they can be arranged in a simple pattern.

A different kind of problem is raised by those who insist that the Sikh tradition can only be understood if we begin by acknowledging it to be an inalienable part of the larger Hindu tradition. It is futile to assert that this particular question need not be raised. Everyone knows (so it is claimed) that Nanak was a Hindu, and, although the Sikh tradition subsequently developed its own distinctive features, it remains firmly set within the

[7] A Gursikh of the Khalsa is a loyal Sikh of the Guru who, in obedience to the Khalsa rule, retains his or her hair uncut. A Sahaj-dhari is a Sikh who has never been a member of the Khalsa and has always cut his or her hair.

larger matrix of Hindu belief and social convention. This claim can be neither summarily accepted nor summarily dismissed, and the vehement assertions which it elicits are no substitute for patient analysis. For many Sikhs it is a very serious issue indeed, and if it is an important issue for them it must necessarily be an important issue for us also.

The problems are many and few of them will produce an agreed answer. The task is, however, worth undertaking, for in the process we can hope to draw nearer to that elusive consent. We begin at the beginning. What did it mean to be a Sikh of Guru Nanak in the early days of the community?

2

The Nanak-panth

NANAK was the first Guru of the Sikhs and his name requires no introduction. Everyone knows Guru Nanak, at least those who have the vaguest interest in Sikh history or religion. 'Panth', however, requires a preliminary definition. In its literal sense the word means 'path' or 'way' and it has traditionally been used to designate the followers of a particular teacher or of a distinctive range of doctrine. The early followers of Nanak thus constituted the Nanak-panth and came to be known as Nanak-panthis as well as Sikhs or 'Learners'. Eventually, as the line of Gurus lengthened and new ideals were introduced, Nanak's name was dropped and Sikhs increasingly referred to themselves simply as the Panth.

Panth is a word which yields no satisfactory English translation. 'Community' has been tainted in the Indian context by its association with communalism, and 'sect' (as we shall later see) is also inappropriate. The word has rich associations in Sikh usage and as such it is one which deserves to be a part of standard English usage. In all that lies ahead in this examination we shall respect that claim, referring only to the Panth and never to the Sikh community.[1]

The person who attracted the original Nanak-panth was born in the Punjab in 1469 and died there seventy years later. Nanak was a religious teacher who gave uniquely clear and attractive expression to doctrines and ideals which had developed within the Sant tradition of northern India. The Sant tradition must be distinguished from the larger and more diffuse Bhakti tradition with which it has generally been identified. The reason for the confusion is easily recognized, for the Sants shared with the Bhaktas a firm belief in the efficacy of personal devotion as the means to securing deliverance from the cycle of transmigration. In other respects, however, they diverge. The Sants would have nothing to do with incarnations, idol worship, sacred scriptures, temples, or pilgrimages, at least not

[1] For an extended discussion, see W. H. McLeod, 'On the Word *panth*: A Problem of Terminology and Definition', *Contributions to Indian Sociology*, 12/2 (1979), 287–95. See also id., *The Evolution of the Sikh Community* (Oxford, 1976), 2–3.

in the external sense conventionally associated with such beliefs and practices. Because these were typically performed as exterior acts of piety, they were regarded by the Sants as worthless.

Devotion for the Sants was strictly an interior discipline, one which spurned all exterior custom and practice as a means to liberation. The emphasis was one which they shared with the yogic tradition of the Naths and the frequency of Nath terminology in basic Sant usage clearly points to Nath antecedents. This is not to suggest that the Sants should be closely associated with the Naths in terms of general sympathy or actual practice. On the contrary, as Nanak so insistently reminds us, the Sant could have no truck with the hatha-yoga of the Naths nor with their stress on harsh austerities. The Sants were ordinary people, propounding in their hymns an interior discipline which other ordinary people could practise without regard for inherited status or ascetic withdrawal from the world.[2]

The Sant message was a simple one and to many it must have seemed naïve. Such a judgement could never have been applied to the teachings which Nanak delivered. In his many hymns we find a highly sophisticated doctrine, yet one expressed in an eminently accessible form. Religious songs are not well suited to the promulgating of a systematic theology, but an analysis of his works can demonstrate that behind them lies an integrated pattern of belief and a clear conception of how that belief should be applied in practice.[3] Although they may create difficulties in terms of intellectual analysis, religious songs can be very effective as a means of communicating the elements of a faith and in regularly reinforcing it. These objectives were certainly achieved by Nanak's hymns (*bāṇī*) and those who followed him as his early successors built upon the foundation which he had so securely laid.

The teachings of Nanak and his early successors focused on the *nām* or divine Name, a term which we have already noted as the dominant feature of the popular *nām dān iśnān* formula. For all mankind the fundamental problem is the suffering imposed by the cycle of transmigration. *Nām* is the sure remedy offered by Akal Purakh, the 'Timeless One' who created the universe and lovingly watches over it. Akal Purakh, the Creator and Sustainer, dwells immanent in all creation and, because all that exists is an expression of the divine being, his creation represents the

[2] Charlotte Vaudeville, '*Sant Mat*: Santism as the Universal Path to Sanctity', in Karine Schomer and W. H. McLeod (eds.), *The Sants: Studies in a Devotional Tradition of India* (Berkeley and Delhi, 1987), 21–40.

[3] W. H. McLeod, *Gurū Nānak and the Sikh Religion* (Oxford, 1968; 2nd edn., Delhi, 1976), 148–50.

supreme manifestation of the *nām*. The *nām* is the ever-present and all-pervading presence of Akal Purakh, and whoever perceives this presence gains access to the means of mystical unity with Akal Purakh. In that condition of supreme peace lies salvation, for the person who attains it thereby achieves release from the baleful cycle of transmigration.

Although the *nām* is thus revealed for all to see and accept, men and women are congenitally blind, unable to perceive the truth which lies around and within each of them. Deceived by the mischievous prompting of their weak and wayward spirits, they are held in permanent subjection to evil passions and false beliefs. Vainly they seek the elusive means of deliverance, foolishly trusting in such external conventions as the temple, the mosque, devout ceremony, or a pious pilgrimage. None of these practices can achieve the end which they seek and those who preach them are agents of doom. Release can be found only by opening one's eyes to the *nām* and by appropriating its wonders within the mind and the heart.[4]

How then is each misguided person to perceive the *nām*, and how is it to be appropriated? Akal Purakh is gracious and to those who are willing to listen he speaks the word which reveals his truth. The 'voice' of Akal Purakh is the eternal *gurū* and the 'word' which the Guru utters is the *śabad*. It can be effectively 'heard' only by engaging in the practice of *nām simaraṇ* or 'remembrance of the Name'. This involves regular meditation, the focus of the meditation being the *nām*, which reveals around and within us the immanent presence of Akal Purakh. The essence of the *nām* is order and harmony. The objective of *nām simaraṇ* must be to achieve that same harmony and thus to merge one's spirit in the being of Akal Purakh.

For those who achieve this objective, two results will follow. One is the experience of ever-growing wonder (*visamād*), leading eventually to the rapturous peace of total blending in the divine (the condition which Nanak calls *sahaj*). The other is the final ending of the cycle of transmigration with its painful sequence of death and rebirth. Instead of earning the vile *karma* which follows from passion and evil deeds, one achieves instead that harmony which separates the spirit from all that keeps the cycle in motion. The end is peace, and with passions finally

[4] The term used to designate the inner faculty which determines a person's thought and actions, and which provides the arena for the discipline leading to release, is the *man*. In this explanation it is variously translated as 'spirit' and as 'heart'. There is in fact no adequate translation available in English, for *man* draws together the range of thought, emotion, and spiritual being which English variously distinguishes as 'mind', 'heart', and 'soul'. For a discussion of *man*, see ibid. 178–81, 220.

stilled one attains release. It is a condition which can be achieved during the present life, preceding the physical death which is its final seal. It is also a condition which can be achieved only within one's own inner being. External props and practices merely delude. In spiritual terms their effect must be fatal.[5]

This is the pattern of belief and practice which emerges from an exegesis of Nanak's works (his *bāṇī*). The same pattern informs the works of his first four successors and it thus constitutes the message of the Adi Granth (the scripture compiled by Guru Arjan in 1603–4). In a certain sense it can be regarded as the foundation and enduring core of the Sikh tradition and of the Panth which embodies that tradition. Although some of the later Gurus left no *bāṇī*, it is clearly evident from the works of the last two in the succession that the message of the divine Name was loyally sustained.[6] It is also evident that the message commands the same continuing loyalty within the modern Panth as we know it today.

This, however, is not the appropriate perspective from which to view the actual birth and subsequent development of the Panth. The Panth does indeed preserve and transmit a particular pattern of doctrine and devotional practice. It also consists of people, and those who constituted the early Nanak-panth need not have been fully aware of the specific theology which lay behind the songs of Nanak. This could never have been the case. The primary basis of the Nanak-panth will have been veneration for the particular teacher who revealed beauty in his compositions and piety in his way of life.

Veneration is the key to understanding the original formation of the Nanak-panth. The phenomenon is actually a common one, as a cursory survey of the modern scene in north India will so quickly show. Teachers appear and in attracting disciples they create minor panths. Most of them soon wane, surviving as small remnants or returning to the larger tradition from which they originally emerged. What we still need to explain is why this particular panth achieved such notable permanence. We must also endeavour to determine how much of the original Nanak inheritance was carried forward by the Nanak-panth and what features it developed during its subsequent period of growth.

The answer to the second of these questions must obviously lie ahead of us. To some extent the same also applies to the first question, for

[5] Ibid., chap. 5. Id. (trans.), *Textual Sources for the Study of Sikhism* (Manchester, 1984), section 3.1.1.

[6] McLeod (trans.), *Textual Sources for the Study of Sikhism*, pp. 46–53, 54–63.

permanence is not something which can be initially achieved and thereafter taken for granted. There are, however, some important aspects of the answer which belong to the lifetime of Nanak himself and amongst these we must certainly include both the Guru's own reputation and the attractive quality of the hymns which he composed. To these we may also add a decision which he made, one which was plainly intended to ensure that the growing band of disciples and reverent admirers should not be permitted to dissolve after his death.

Before he died Nanak chose a successor, one who was to follow him as leader and guide of the Nanak-panth. The disciple chosen for this responsibility was Lahina, renamed Angad at the time of his selection.[7] A lineage was thus established and, although contending claimants were later to appear, a succession recognized as legitimate was maintained intact from the appointment of Guru Angad to the death of Guru Gobind Singh. It was a natural step to take, but not an inevitable one. Without a recognized succession the fledgling Nanak-panth could scarcely have survived, for there would have been no sufficient means of sustaining the loyalty of its adherents or their cohesion as an emergent tradition.

The Nanak-panth thus acquired a rudimentary organization, one which ensured a continuing existence beyond the lifetime of the first Guru. It was, however, too rudimentary for the strains which developed as the Panth grew older and its adherents increased in number. The appearance of later generations owing their adherence to birth rather than to personal choice imposes one variety of strain on a movement of this kind. Growing numbers impose another, particularly when there is a simultaneous expansion in geographical terms. To deal with these pressures a more developed form of panthic organization became increasingly necessary. There is considerable uncertainty with regard to the timing of the measures which were taken by Nanak's early successors, and indeed the actual measures themselves are not always clear. It seems that significant steps were taken during the time of Guru Amar Das (1552–74) and that the developments encouraged by these steps established the pattern of panthic organization which was to persist until the founding of the Khalsa at the end of the seventeenth century.[8]

The uncertainty associated with these developments should be stressed if we are to appreciate the shadowy nature of much that passes for historical fact during the period of the early Gurus. Measures which are traditionally associated with the period of Guru Amar Das and which

[7] J. S. Grewal, *Guru Nanak in History* (Chandigarh, 1969), 285–6.
[8] McLeod, *The Evolution of the Sikh Community*, pp. 7–10.

are viewed as the product of formal decisions may actually have longer pedigrees and less specific origins. Tradition is, however, reasonably firm on most of these points and, although our detailed understanding may be faulty, the eventual results seem beyond doubt. In these guarded terms we may attach to Guru Amar Das three distinct varieties of innovation. All three represent the kind of response which might well be expected of a second-generation panth passing through a predictable process of self-definition and crystallization.

One innovation attributed to Guru Amar Das can be regarded as strictly administrative. As the Panth expanded, new *saṅgats* or congregations came into existence. Immediate contact with the Guru became increasingly difficult to maintain and it thus became necessary to appoint deputies authorized to act on his behalf. Guru Amar Das is traditionally credited with having established the *mañji* system of supervision, and the later *masand* system is believed to have developed from this prototype.[9]

Manji jurisdictions certainly existed at an early stage of the Panth's history, and, although their precise nature is exceedingly vague, there can be little doubt concerning the role and authority of the masands. These were men who supervised individual sangats or clusters of sangats on behalf of the Guru, probably acting as spiritual guides and certainly empowered to collect the tithes or other contributions which a loyal Sikh might be expected to give to his Master. The masand system lasted until its formal abolition by Guru Gobind Singh in 1699.

A second innovation which is usually attributed to the third Guru concerns the institutionalizing of a key doctrine. Guru Nanak had made it abundantly clear that caste status (like all exterior conventions) could have no bearing on access to the divine Name and thus to the means of liberation. It was probably Guru Amar Das who borrowed from the Sufis the practice of compulsory commensality, thereby giving practical expression to the first Guru's ideal. In the Sikh tradition this inter-dining convention emerged as the *laṅgar*. This convention requires men and women of all castes to sit in status-free lines (*paṅgat*) and eat together

[9] Ibid. 42. A *mañjī*, literally a string-bed, designated authority over a sangat or group of sangats. *Masand*, derived from *masnad* or 'throne', came to be applied to the person who sat upon the manji. Traditionally the appointment to manjis is believed to date from the time of third Guru, and the masand system from the time of the fourth. Kahn Singh Nabha, *Guruśabad ratanākar mahān koś* (2nd rev. edn., Patiala, 1960), 750, 698. Fauja Singh argues persuasively that the manjis were actually preachers and they did not possess any territorial jurisdiction. *Guru Amar Das: Life and Teachings* (New Delhi, 1979), 116–29.

when they assemble on the sacred ground of the *dharam-sālā* or *gurduārā* (gurdwara).[10]

The langar is a particularly obscure institution as far as its period of introduction is concerned, but there can be no doubt concerning the central importance which it acquired nor the reason for actually introducing it. Caste is a contentious issue to which we must return. Here we note the early introduction of a convention which struck at a major aspect of caste, thereby advancing the process of defining a distinctive Sikh identity.

The third variety of innovation comprises a cluster of decisions (conscious or implicit) which concerned the developing ritual of the Panth. Whereas the langar plainly matched the intention of Guru Nanak, the new practices which together supply a distinctive panthic ritual might well seem to be in conflict with it. The first Guru had stressed the interior nature of devotion, dismissing as false and dangerous the kind of external ritual associated with conventional Hindu tradition or the orthodox Islam of the mullah. Decisions attributed to the third Guru may look suspiciously like the kind of thing which Nanak execrated. They include the digging of a sacred well (*bāolī*) in the Guru's village of Goindval to serve as a place of pilgrimage for Sikhs. They also include the introduction of particular festival days and the compiling of a collection which was later to become a sacred scripture.[11] Guru Amar Das is also credited with the decision to excavate the sacred pool which marked the founding of Amritsar.[12]

There are two answers which can be given to the problem thus presented. The theological answer is that the Guru is one and that decisions made by the third Guru proceed from precisely the same source as attitudes expressed by the first. This answer implies the second response, which is that changed circumstances require fresh decisions. No one is likely to be surprised by this development. A growing and maturing Panth could never have sustained the informality of the first Guru's practice. The formalizing of the tradition occurs at precisely the period when one would expect it and in much the manner that we might anticipate.

One last development deserves to be noted before we conclude this survey of the early Nanak-panth and turn to an examination of its actual

[10] McLeod, *Gurū Nānak and the Sikh Religion*, p. 210.

[11] McLeod, *The Evolution of the Sikh Community*, pp. 7–8.

[12] Kahn Singh, *Guruśabad ratanākar mahān koś*, p. 57. The actual excavation was conducted by Guru Ram Das. Ibid. McLeod (trans.), *Textual Sources for the Study of Sikhism*, pp. 28–9.

beliefs and practices. This is the critically important compiling of a sacred scripture by Guru Arjan in 1603–4. Guru Amar Das had evidently commissioned a preliminary compilation (the so-called Goindval *pothīs*) and the fifth Guru is believed to have used this prototype when producing the larger definitive version. The result was the Adi Granth.[13] There are unsolved textual problems associated with the Adi Granth, but none of these affect the powerfully cohesive role which the scripture was to assume during the later history of the Panth.

The death of Guru Arjan in 1606 marks a significant turning-point in the development of the Panth. Difficulties had emerged in the Panth's relationship with the local Mughal authorities and the hostility which fitfully developed during the course of the succeeding century has traditionally been held to account for the significant changes which eventually transformed the Panth. The analysis is rather more complex than this traditional summary might suggest and to that analysis we shall return in the next chapter. There can be no doubt, however, that the deteriorating relationship with Mughal authority supplies a large part of the explanation and that Guru Arjan's death in Mughal custody provides an appropriate symbol for the change which was taking place. Needless to say it is not a sudden change, instantly transforming the Nanak-panth of the sixteenth century into a prototype of the eighteenth-century Khalsa. The continuities remain evident and much that we may affirm concerning the early Panth applies with equal force to its seventeenth-century successor.

The permanence of the Nanak-panth was thus ensured by ritual and administrative measures introduced by the early Gurus. To what extent did the growing and crystallizing Panth present the authentic doctrines and ideals of the first Guru? There are two answers to be given to this question, the first of which has already been indicated. The early successors who followed Nanak as Guru continued to present the same teachings, cast in the same format and expressed in a very similar idiom. There is a developing richness in the poetry of the tradition, a trend which was significantly advanced during the period of Guru Arjan (1581–1606).[14] In terms of doctrinal content, however, the tradition remained essentially the same as that which Nanak had delivered to the first Sikhs.

[13] McLeod, *The Evolution of the Sikh Community*, pp. 60–1.

[14] Guru Arjan is the most prolific of all the contributors to the Adi Granth. Amongst his many compositions, his lengthy *Sukhmanī* in *Gauṛī* raga stands out (Adi Granth, pp. 262–96).

This response obviously describes a fundamental aspect of the early Nanak-panth, one which should certainly not be neglected. If, however, we are to achieve a balanced perspective, it must be accompanied by the second of the required answers. The second answer distinguishes the leaders of the Panth from the bulk of its adherents. By consulting the Adi Granth or the works of Bhai Gurdas, we encounter a normative response, an interpretation of the divine Name message as understood by the guides and leaders of the Panth. The full measure of Nanak's teachings demands a portion of our attention because it continues to inform the understanding of the Panth's acknowledged leadership during the pre-Khalsa period. There is, however, another range of understanding and to this more popular concept of Gurmat we must now turn.

The principal source for the popular variety of understanding is supplied by the janam-sakhis. The janam-sakhis are traditional narratives of the life of Baba Nanak, collections of anecdotes which relate in fond detail a wealth of stories concerning the first Guru. As records of accurate history or biography they must normally be discarded, but in so doing we must avoid any suggestion that the janam-sakhis provide source material of limited value. Properly understood, the janam-sakhis are very valuable indeed, quite apart from the endless fascination which their many anecdotes can supply. The janam-sakhis are properly understood as hagiography; and their appropriate context is not the lifetime of the first Guru but the later period within which they actually developed. Trustworthy information concerning the life of Guru Nanak is not what they supply. What they do provide is useful testimony to the life and understanding of the early Panth.[15]

This should not imply that the janam-sakhis will always yield their information easily. There are two general problems which must confront any attempt to use them as sources for the life of the early Panth. The first derives from the fact that the earliest of the surviving janam-sakhis belongs to the mid-seventeenth century and that prior to the eighteenth century it stands alone.[16] Although there can be no doubt that oral growth dates from the sixteenth century, the actual evidence belongs to a later period. It thus requires a process of careful deduction if we are to utilize the janam-sakhis as sources for the life and beliefs of the early Panth.

The second problem also demands careful analysis. Because the

[15] For a study of the janam-sakhis, see W. H. McLeod, *Early Sikh Tradition: A Study of the Janam-sākhīs* (Oxford, 1980).

[16] Ibid. 13, 19.

narrators and compilers of the janam-sakhis had their attention consciously focused on an earlier period, the contemporary information which they deliver is implicit rather than direct, nested within the story cycles which they generated. This may enhance its claims to authenticity. It also presents us with problems of exegesis and interpretation.[17]

This certainly does not mean, however, that the janam-sakhi contribution is invariably an obscure one. On the contrary, it delivers a distinct impression of the popular image of Nanak and also of the manner in which many devout Sikhs evidently applied his teachings. The image which they present is indicated by their strong preference for the title 'Baba' rather than for 'Guru'. The latter title does appear, particularly when Nanak's role as the Great Teacher is brought into focus, but typically he is Baba Nanak. As such he represents piety and spiritual wisdom, the supreme exemplar of the only sure path to deliverance.[18] All who acknowledge him as Master and practise the simple discipline which he enjoined will find peace in this present world and liberation in the hereafter.

The discipline which Baba Nanak is believed to have taught is indeed a simple one and it is here that we find ourselves drawn dramatically away from his actual teachings and from the faithful replicas which his successors produced. The janam-sakhis project a much less subtle understanding of the key doctrine of the *nām* and of its practical expression in the discipline of *nām simaraṇ*. This is plainly evident from a standard formula incorporated in the conclusion to many individual anecdotes. A common variety of anecdote (*sākhī*) records how Baba Nanak visited a particular place during his travels, converted the people by means of a miracle or wise pronouncement, and then proceeded on his way. One such anecdote relates how he conferred grain and fire on a people who possessed neither. It concludes:

> And so Baba Nanak gave them grain and fire. The entire population of that land became Sikhs. They took up repeating 'Guru, Guru' and in every house a dharamsala was established. Guru Baba Nanak taught them the three-fold discipline of repeating the divine Name, giving charity, and regular bathing [*nām dān iśnān*]. Everyone in that land declared, 'Blessed is our destiny that we have beheld your presence and that your feet have trodden in this land.'[19]

[17] Ibid. 248–67.

[18] Ibid. 250–2.

[19] W. H. McLeod (trans.), *The B40 Janam-sākhī* (Amritsar, 1980), 187. Brackets have been removed from this translation and the words *nām dān iśnān* have been indicated. Although the third word of the *nām dān iśnān* formula is now conceived as an injunction to live a pure life, the janam-sakhi understanding was plainly the literal sense of regular bathing. McLeod, *Early Sikh Tradition*, pp. 263–4.

From this and many other examples it is evident that *nām simaraṇ* was understood as a mechanical repetition of the single word 'Guru'. This, it may be argued, is a part of the total range covered by the concept of *nām simaraṇ*, but plainly it lacks the sophistication of Nanak's own understanding.

One other feature of this standard conclusion deserves to be noted. In every house, we are told, a dharamsala was established.[20] In other words, each house became a place where devout Sikhs would gather to sing the Gurus' hymns. The twin concepts of sangat and *kirtan* or hymn-singing are thus emphasized in the janam-sakhis as a regular feature of the corporate life of the Nanak-panth. Elsewhere in the janam-sakhis we encounter a reference which indicates that the dharamsala was one of the features which conferred a distinctive identity on the Nanak-panth. Sikhs of Guru Nanak can be distinguished from adherents of other panths because they possess their own special place of worship. Vaishnavas have their temple, Yogis have their *āsaṇ*, Muslims have their mosque, and Nanak-panthis have their dharamsala.[21]

This same passage from the *B40 Janam-sākhī* also claims that Nanak-panthis are distinguished by a unique salutation (*pairī pavaṇā satigurū hoiā*) and by the customary *nām dān iśnān* ideal.[22] A comment of this kind should be treated with caution, and we should not read too much into a single reference from an eighteenth-century janam-sakhi. There are, however, other indications which strengthen the impression of an emergent panth, one which is still in the process of drawing its own boundaries and defining its own distinctive identity. One such indicator is the clear janam-sakhi recognition of Guru Angad as the chosen successor, a feature which offers firm proof of an established lineage. Another is the prominence which they give to Baba Nanak's disputations with representatives of other recognized panths.[23]

In contrast to these positive indications we must also note features which imply hesitation. Nanak's janam-sakhi contestants conspicuously include Hindu pandits, Muslim qazis, and Nath yogis (the latter including the great Guru Gorakhnath himself.[24] Were such encounters

[20] McLeod (trans.), *The B40 Janam-sākhī*, p. 206. Id., *Early Sikh Tradition*, p. 261. *Vārān Bhāī Gurdās* 1: 27. The term *gurduārā* was later adopted as the name of the place where the Gurus' hymns were sung. W. H. McLeod, *The Sikhs* (New York, 1989), p. 57.

[21] McLeod (trans.), *The B40 Janam-sākhī*, p. 143. Id., *Early Sikh Tradition*, pp. 260–1.

[22] McLeod (trans), *The B40 Janam-sākhī*, pp. 142–3.

[23] The *Purātan Janam-sākhī* (5th edn. Amritsar, 1959) provides examples of the first feature on pp. 107–8, 110; and of the second on pp. 16–20, 22–4, 26–8, 40–5, 52–6, 66–70, 72, 80–1, 82–6, 96–106, and 108–10.

[24] A famous occasion occurs in the *Purātan* janam-sakhis, sakhi 54.

restricted to these three varieties of contestant, the sense of separateness would be very strong indeed. The effect is, however, diminished by implied comparisons with Vaishnavas, by the suggestion that Nanak might adopt various panthic identities,[25] and by the occasional claim that he regarded himself as a Hindu.[26]

These conflicting indicators point to a single definite conclusion. The Nanak-panth as refracted through the janam-sakhis can be recognized as a panth which is in the process of self-definition but which has not yet achieved a clear awareness of separate identity. This, it seems, was the status of the pre-Khalsa Nanak-panth and also of those adherents who retained a Nanak-panthi identity during the eighteenth century and beyond. It is, in other words, strictly an emergent panth. It is in the process of becoming without any certain awareness of having arrived.

This, we must stress, is a popular view of the Panth. References which can be cited from the works of both Guru Arjan and Bhai Gurdas offer some support for the claim that the leaders of the Nanak-panth had developed a strong sense of panthic identity by the end of the sixteenth century.[27] Such references match the reasonable expectation that the intellectual élite within the Panth moved more rapidly towards a sense of distinct identity than did the body of believers. Those who constituted the bulk of the Panth were much more exposed to inclusive ideals and blurred identities. There is nothing surprising about this. The same difference persists throughout the entire history of the Panth and, although it has receded during the last hundred years (particularly since 1947), there remains clear evidence of its presence today.[28]

This difference must be kept in mind whenever any attempt is made to define Gurmat or the distinctive Sikh identity. In the case of the early Nanak-panth the conclusion which follows is that no clear line of demarcation can be drawn in order to separate it from contiguous Hindu tradition. This does not mean, however, that the Nanak-panth lacked definition or the kind of distinctive ideals which signalled a conscious Nanak-panthi identity. In general terms this identity was defined by a

[25] McLeod (trans.), *The B40 Janam-sākhī*, p. 161.

[26] Ibid. 84, 148. Piar Singh (samp.), *Śambhū Nāth vālī janam patrī Bābe Nānak Jī kī prasidh nān Ādi Sākhiān* (Patiala, 1969), 24, 42.

[27] Guru Arjan, *Bhairau* 3, Adi Granth, p. 1136. *Vārān Bhāī Gurdās* 1: 21, 33: 2, 33: 4. Although the hymn attributed to Guru Arjan in Bhairau raga bears the signature of Kabir in the closing couplet and has a parallel in the *Kabīr-granthāvalī*, it is safe to assume that Guru Arjan would have accepted what it says: 'We are neither Hindu nor Musalaman'. The hymn is prefaced with his symbol and he after all compiled the Adi Granth.

[28] Paul Hershman, *Punjabi Kinship and Marriage* (Delhi, 1981), 24.

common loyalty, by common association, and by common practice.[29] Any man or woman who acknowledged the loyalty and joined with others to observe a particular pattern of worship would be plainly identified as a Sikh of Guru Nanak. The boundaries might be indistinct, but not the centre.

In specific terms the common loyalty was, of course, veneration for Nanak and for the legitimate succession of Gurus who followed him in the lineage which he had established. The stress is powerfully on the first of the Gurus, a feature which is indicated by the janam-sakhi focus on Nanak and through the conventional use of his name by the successors whose works appear in the Adi Granth.[30] The nature of the loyalty undergoes a progressive change as the Baba image of Nanak is displaced by the Guru image, and as the Guru status is supplemented by the attributes of royalty. The lineage which commences with the humble Sant ideal is thereby transformed into a succession of 'True Kings' (*sachā pādaśāh*). None of this, however, affects the basic assumption that all who regard themselves as Sikhs will acknowledge fealty to this spiritual lineage.

The custom of gathering as a *satsaṅg* for regular kirtan sessions was also a specific and essential feature of the Nanak-panthi identity.[31] The convention derived from the traditional Sant emphasis on the value of associating with the truly devout, an experience which enabled the humble participant to acquire a portion of the merit which emanated from the true *sādh*. It was greatly strengthened by the practice of singing the Gurus' own compositions at such gatherings and it was this latter feature which gave the Nanak-panthi gathering its own distinctive identity.

The singing of kirtan in the context of the satsang was not a ritual unique to the Nanak-panth. It was rather the nature of the kirtan which imparted distinction. The practice encouraged a particular concept of the *śabad* or divine Word, and, together with the actual recording of the Gurus' compositions as a scripture, it prepared the way for a fundamental doctrine. The doctrine which it foreshadowed affirms the eternal presence of the mystical Guru within the sacred scripture and wherever his followers gather as an assembly of the Panth.

29 *Vārān Bhāī Gurdās* 28: 15.

30 The Adi Granth uses the term *mahalā* to identify the works of the various Gurus (*mahalā 1* designating Guru Nanak, *mahalā* 2 Guru Angad, etc.). All five of the Gurus who follow Guru Nanak, however, employ the name Nanak as a signature in the final couplet.

31 *Vārān Bhāī Gurdās* 40: 11.

True to the teachings of the Gurus, these assemblies were obviously intended to be open to men and women of all castes. As we have already noted, this seems plainly to have been the essential purpose of requiring all who attended a ritual gathering of Sikhs to eat together in the langar. Although its primary purpose may well have been evaded by many Sikhs, it continued to be honoured as a Nanak-panthi ideal. This is not to suggest that the early Panth was casteless. What it does indicate is a continuing loyalty to the first Guru's insistence that caste had nothing to do with access to liberation.

Caste was, in fact, present and acknowledged within the Nanak-panth. The eleventh *vār* of Bhai Gurdas lists the names of prominent followers of the early Gurus,[32] thus enabling us to reconstruct a general profile of the Panth's leadership during the sixteenth and early seventeenth centuries. In his list Bhai Gurdas commonly identifies individual caste identities, and in so doing he indicates that one caste was particularly prominent in terms of leadership within the Panth. This was the Khatri caste, the caste to which all the Gurus belonged. The janam-sakhis support this feature and supply names which enable us to identify the other castes which were also conspicuously represented within the Panth. After the Khatris the principal contributors to janam-sakhi anecdotes are Jats, and they in turn are followed by members of artisan castes (notably Tarkhans or carpenters).[33]

None of this comes as any surprise. The janam-sakhis are strongly rural in tone and all three castes are to be found in rural Punjab.[34] When eventually the British began to enumerate Punjabi society, these three caste groups all emerged as prominent constituents of the Panth. The notable addition is the outcaste or untouchable Sikhs. The conspicuous attachment of the Mirasi minstrel Mardana to Baba Nanak implies access for the lowly, but Mardana was not strictly an outcaste and, even as a follower of marginal status, he remains an exception. Others can be noted in the early evidence,[35] but it seems likely that a significant outcaste membership did not develop until a later period of the Panth's history.

Actual numbers and proportions are impossible to determine. Bhai Gurdas deals only with the more notable members of the Panth and, in view of the Khatri status in rural Punjab, their prominence in this regard

32 Ibid. 11: 13–31.
33 McLeod, *Early Sikh Tradition*, pp. 258–60.
34 Ibid. 257–8.
35 For example, there is Paira Chandali noted by Bhai Gurdas. *Vārān Bhāī Gurdās* 11: 24. Outcastes were certainly not excluded from the Sikh Panth.

is entirely predictable. The janam-sakhis, with their broader coverage, offer no obvious clues concerning the numerical strengths of the three discernible groups. British figures reveal a substantial Jat majority in the late nineteenth century[36] and it is possible that this numerical preponderance extends back to the Panth's earliest days. Here, however, we must acknowledge uncertainty. What is clear is that three caste groups are conspicuously present within the Panth and that no effort seems to have been made to conceal their identities.

This acknowledgement of caste identities was presumably acceptable to the Gurus, for it receives unselfconscious treatment from the impeccably orthodox Bhai Gurdas, and the Gurus themselves married their own children according to traditional caste prescriptions. The anti-caste thrust of the Gurus' teachings must thus be seen as a doctrine which referred to spiritual deliverance and to the assemblies which helped individuals to achieve that objective. It is also legitimate to deduce a firm rejection of injustice or hurtful discrimination based on caste status. What is not implied is a total obliteration of caste identity.[37]

In this and other respects the Nanak-panth seems to have been generally loyal to the intention and example of the Gurus. Their stress on interiority was evidently understood, and, although the practice of *nām simaraṇ* may have been greatly simplified, the Panth kept some appropriate targets in view. This, at least, is the clear message communicated by the persistent janam-sakhi attacks on the punctilious pandit, the bigoted qazi, and the ascetic yogi. These assaults also implied what elsewhere the janam-sakhis make perfectly plain, namely the obligation to live as ordinary men and women. Deliverance from the cycle of transmigration was to be achieved by remaining in the world, not by withdrawing into ritual or ascetic seclusion.

This, it seems, was the Nanak-panth which developed during the course of the sixteenth century, and it retained its characteristic features throughout the century which was to follow. Veneration for Nanak and his line of successors qualified a person as a Nanak-panthi or Sikh. To express this allegiance each Nanak-panthi gathered with others in sangats, there to sing the kirtan composed by their Gurus. Most sangats

36 *Census of India 1881*, vol. 1, book 1 (Lahore, 1883), 107–8.

37 When this point was made in *The Evolution of the Sikh Community*, it prompted the accusation that the Gurus were being labelled as insincere in their opposition to caste. This was not the case. The Gurus accepted the marital obligations of caste, but were totally opposed to the idea that caste involved any discrimination or that it had any bearing upon the individual's access to liberation. The latter, all-important to the Gurus, was provided by loyalty to the divine Name.

were under masands appointed by the Guru and to them Nanak-panthis made their offerings for transmitting to the Guru. Nanak-panthis recognized *nām simaraṇ* as a standard practice of the Panth, but for most of its members it was evidently understood as the repetition of a simple formula. A small group within the Panth, however, practised it as it had been taught by Guru Nanak and in the way it still continued to be taught by his successors.

Caste had no place within the sangat, at least amongst those that were loyal to the Gurus. Sikhs were free to observe it as a marriage convention, but it had no bearing on liberation from transmigration nor did it justify discrimination of any sort. As such it was not to be recognized in the gurdwaras and the langar was instituted to prevent it being so. Although certain days were set aside as particularly appropriate for visiting the Guru and paying him respects, the Nanak-panthi was not to withdraw from the responsibilities of the world. Liberation was to be found by singing kirtan and practising *nām simaraṇ* in the context of an ordinary life.

This pattern of Nanak-panthi devotion was practised throughout the sixteenth and seventeenth centuries. It was during the seventeenth century, however, that external influences began to impinge significantly, and eventually these influences led to a radical reshaping of the Panth. The sixth Guru signals the formal beginning of the process and the tenth Guru is traditionally believed to have carried it to a dramatic climax. As always the actual experience turns out to be more diverse and complex than the tradition would allow. It is an experience which we shall examine in the next chapter.

3

The Khalsa and its Rahit

TO BE a Sikh at the beginning of the seventeenth century meant adherence to the Nanak-panth. This involved a professed veneration for Guru Nanak, continuing obedience to his legitimate successors, and regular association with others who acknowledged the same loyalty. Those who shared the same Nanak-panthi allegiance constituted local groups or sangats which gathered regularly in satsangs to sing the Gurus' hymns. Such gatherings took place in dharamsalas. Amongst the devout no caste barriers obstructed membership of the Panth or participation in its developing rituals, although caste identities were still recognized by Sikhs within the larger Punjabi society to which they belonged. A substantial majority of Sikhs were rural folk, most of them belonging to trader, cultivator, or artisan castes.

Special festival days had been appointed for observance by the Panth and on such occasions Sikhs would reverently visit the Guru or gather at places which had acquired pious associations. One location was regarded with particular respect by the end of the sixteenth century. This was Ramdaspur or Amritsar, and it was there that the fifth Guru supervised the compiling of a sacred scripture for the Panth. The Guru remained the key figure within the Nanak-panth, the object of devout veneration and source of continuing guidance.

Early in the seventeenth century that guidance seemed to be undergoing a significant change. Hargobind had succeeded his father Arjan as Guru in 1606 and the ever-faithful Bhai Gurdas reflects the concern which soon developed within the Panth. In a famous stanza from his *Vār* 26 he gives expression to criticisms which the sixth Guru evidently attracted.

> The earlier Gurus sat peacefully in dharamsalas; this one roams the land.
> Emperors visited their homes with reverence; this one they cast into jail.
> No rest for his followers, ever active; their restless Master has fear of none.
> The earlier Gurus sat graciously blessing; this one goes hunting with dogs.

> They had servants who harboured no malice; this one encourages scoundrels.

These are the criticisms. They are immediately followed by an assertion of the author's own continuing loyalty.

> Yet none of these changes conceals the truth; the Sikhs are still drawn as bees to the lotus.
> The truth stands firm, eternal, changeless; and pride still lies subdued.[1]

Guru Hargobind had adopted a new policy, one which tradition dramatically expresses in the donning of two symbolic swords. One sword represented the continuing spiritual authority (*pīrī*) which he had inherited from his five predecessors. The other proclaimed a newly assumed temporal power (*mīrī*). The Panth was to become more than an assembly of the devout, and its Guru was thereafter to wield an authority more expansive than that of his predecessors.[2]

A new building is also believed to have symbolized the same change. No one can be sure precisely when Akal Takhat was first erected, but Sikh tradition insistently maintains that it first appeared during the time of Guru Hargobind and that it has ever since represented the same ideal as the doctrine of *mīrī–pīrī*.[3] Akal Takhat faces Harimandir (the Golden Temple), and, whereas Harimandir symbolizes the spiritual message of the Gurus, it is Akal Takhat which represents their temporal authority. Together with the appearance of weapons, horses, dogs, and hunting expeditions, Akal Takhat also serves to represent the growing militancy of the Panth. The dual concept, whatever its actual origin, is traditionally located in the period and in the intention of Guru Hargobind. In its developed form it was to reflect a transformed Panth.

The actual reason for this significant shift in the nature and policy of

[1] *Vārān Bhāī Gurdās* 26: 24.

[2] Kahn Singh Nabha, *Guruśabad ratanākar mahān koś* (2nd rev. edn., Patiala, 1960), 198.

[3] The traditional date is s. 1665 (AD 1608–9). (s is the abbreviation for Samvat, used for dating according to the Vikrami era which begins approximately 56¾ years before the Christian era.) Ibid. 27, 198. The modern Akal Takhat was destroyed by the Indian Army in its attack on the Golden Temple complex in June 1984, and Jarnail Singh Bhindranwale was killed while defending it. It was immediately rebuilt, ostensibly by a Nihang chieftain Santa Singh but in fact by covert government assistance. Sikhs opposed to the central government immediately tore down the new building and are now engaged in erecting a much bigger one. For accounts of Akal Takhat prior to 1984, see Bhagat Singh in Fauja Singh (ed.), *The City of Amritsar: A Study of Historical, Cultural, Social and Economic Aspects* (New Delhi, 1978), 42–58; and Madanjit Kaur, *The Golden Temple Past and Present* (Amritsar, 1983), 168–72. A popular account is Harjinder Singh Dilgeer, *The Akal Takhat* (Jullundur, 1980), reissued as *Glory of the Akal Takhat* (Jullundur, 1984).

the Panth remains a subject of debate. Tradition delivers one answer and there can be no doubt that the traditional answer is at least partly correct. The sixth Guru, witnessing the increasing tyranny of the Mughal rulers, assumed an enlarged authority and armed his followers in order to resist their evil deeds. A modified version of the tradition views it as an essentially defensive move. Both variants offer Mughal threats as the reason and both interpret the change as a deliberate decision by the Guru to arm a Panth which had hitherto been peaceable and weaponless.

There is no evident reason why this response theory should be denied. There is, however, good reason for introducing a supplementary cause and it is this additional element which has generated some controversy in recent years. The supplementary claim focuses on the undeniable presence of Jats in the early Panth and it suggests that in becoming Sikhs they will have remained Jats. In other words, they are most unlikely to have shed the militant traditions which they certainly inherited as a major feature of their Jat culture.[4]

It accordingly seems necessary to assume that militant traditions were already present within the Panth by the time Hargobind became Guru in 1606. If this is correct, it means that the standard explanation can be accepted only in the sense that a decision by Guru Hargobind represented a formal adoption of militant means and a corresponding change in the Guru's own life style. In an informal sense militant traditions were already well represented within the Panth and the Guru's change of policy served to harness these traditions to a developing need rather than introduce them for the first time. Contemporary circumstances thus encouraged a process whereby the traditions of a significant segment within the Panth increasingly became the acknowledged policy of the Panth as a whole. To this extent the traditional explanation seems eminently plausible. Alone it remains inadequate.

During the middle decades of the seventeenth century the threat receded and during this period the Panth continued to live a life resembling that of its early experience. Serious trouble returned during the later years of Guru Tegh Bahadur (1664–75). This involved renewed and increasingly serious hostility on the part of the Mughals, a condition which Sikh tradition attributes directly to the bigoted policy of the

[4] The significance of Jats and Jat culture on the developing Panth was raised in W. H. McLeod, *The Evolution of the Sikh Community* (Oxford, 1976), chaps. 1 and 3. Amongst the responses produced by this tentative enquiry the most notable was perhaps Jagjit Singh, *Perspectives on Sikh Studies* (New Delhi, 1985), section 2. This section was reprinted (with amendments designed to make the criticisms more specific) in Gurdev Singh (ed.), *Perspectives on the Sikh Tradition* (Patiala, 1986), 326–85.

Emperor Aurangzeb. According to the dominant tradition, Guru Tegh Bahadur decided to confront Mughal power in response to a plea from Kashmiri Brahmans threatened with forcible conversion to Islam. He allowed himself to be arrested and executed in order that Mughal tyranny might stand revealed and that brave men might rise against it.[5]

Three themes are implicit in this tradition. The first is that Mughal rule spelt oppression and injustice. Though initially restricted to the Mughals, this theme was later to involve hostility towards Muslims as such. The second theme is the need to protect time-honoured conventions, notably those associated with Hindu tradition. The third, which is denied by the Guru's action but which follows as a deduction, is the ultimate need for force as a means of combating extreme injustice.

The tradition thus legitimizes the developments which were soon to follow. The protection theme is modified in that the rampart becomes *dharma* rather than Hindu rights; and *dharma* is variously conceived as the pattern of belief embodied in the Panth or as the moral order generally. With this amendment the three themes together supply the traditional interpretation of the crucial century which lies ahead. The moral order has been assaulted by evil men and, because the attack is fierce, those who would defend *dharma* must do so by means of the sword.[6] The assailants are Muslims, first Mughals and then Afghans. The defenders are to be Sikhs of a very special kind.

Here (as always) we are involved in the counterpoint of history and tradition, in the reciprocal interchange between the actual course of events in all its complexity and the comparatively simple interpretations with which those events are glossed. This is not to suggest that we should dismiss the latter and concentrate our attention only on the former. For present purposes that would be altogether inappropriate. If we are seeking answers to the question 'What is Sikhism?' or 'Who is a Sikh?', the double focus must be maintained. Traditional interpretations can be just as important as the actual facts and typically they are the more important. This is an axiom which needs to be kept clearly in mind as we venture upon the founding of the Khalsa and its development during the eighteenth century.

Tradition offers three inter-connected reasons for the founding of the Khalsa. The first derives directly from the scene of Guru Tegh Bahadur's execution, where, it is maintained, the Sikhs who were present shrank

[5] Harbans Singh, *Guru Tegh Bahadur* (New Delhi, 1982), 94–6. Trilochan Singh, *Guru Tegh Bahadur: Prophet and Martyr* (Delhi, 1967), 293–300.

[6] *Zafar-nāmā* 22, Dasam Granth, p. 1390.

from recognition for fear that they might suffer a like fate. Guru Gobind Singh, having learnt of their cowardice, determined to impose on his followers an outward form which would make them instantly recognizable. This would ensure that never again would Sikhs be able to take refuge in anonymity.[7]

The second of the traditional reasons focuses on the general problem of tyranny and injustice rather than on the specific instance provided by the ninth Guru's execution. According to this variant tradition, Guru Gobind Singh had realized that his Sikhs were mere sparrows, weak and timorous creatures who could never be trusted to face armed injustice without taking instant flight. The problem could be traced to the docile beliefs and customs which they had inherited, to traditions which might be appropriate in times of peace and order but which could never withstand the assaults of violent tyranny. Steel was needed, steel in their hands and steel in the soul of the Panth. Ratan Singh Bhangu, raised during the heroic years of the eighteenth century, gives forthright expression to this view in his *Prāchīn Panth Prakāś*. He concludes:

> Thus the Guru reasoned and from thought he proceeded to action. His followers were to emerge as splendid warriors, their uncut hair bound in turbans; and as warriors all were to bear the name 'Singh' [lion]. This, the Guru knew, would be effective. He devised a form of baptism administered with the sword, one which would create a Khalsa staunch and unyielding. His followers would destroy the empire, each Sikh horseman believing himself to be a king. All weakness would be beaten out of them and each, having taken the baptism of the sword, would thereafter be firmly attached to the sword.[8]

The third reason concerns the internal administration of the Panth. As we noted earlier, the problem of increasing numbers and geographical dispersion had been met first by developing the manji system and then by delegating authority to deputies called masands.[9] A century later many of the masands had acquired corrupt ways and an overweening arrogance. The Guru accordingly decided to disestablish the masands and summon all Sikhs to place themeselves under his own direct supervision. As such they would become members of his k͟hālis or k͟hālsā, that portion of the royal domain which remained under the direct supervision of the central authority.[10]

[7] W. H. McLeod (trans.), *The Chaupā Siṅgh Rahit-nāmā* (Dunedin, 1987), section 166, p. 168.

[8] Ratan Singh Bhangu, *Prāchīn Panth Prakāś* 16: 32–6. Vir Singh edn. (Amritsar, 1962), 42.

[9] See chap. 2, n. 9.

[10] Ganda Singh (samp.), *Kavī Saināpati rachit Srī Gur Sobhā* (Patiala, 1967), 5: 6, 5: 25, 5: 30, pp. 20, 23–4 (Gurmukhi pagination).

Although there is nothing intrinsically implausible in any of these reasons, or in a selective combination of all three, we must nevertheless maintain our insistent distinction between history and tradition. We are here dealing with tradition, with *post facto* interpretations which express a later understanding and which recast earlier events in the light of subsequent developments. The distinction between history and tradition must be maintained notwithstanding the fact that onc feature of the composite explanation can be strongly argued on the basis of etymology and other objective evidence. This concerns the role of the masands as a possible reason for the founding of the Khalsa as a formal order.[11] With the possible exception of this item we must deal with obscure history on the one hand and clear if variant tradition on the other.

The contrast becomes even more marked when we move from the reasons for the event to the actual event itself. From the traditional narratives we receive singularly dramatic accounts of what took place on Baisakhi Day 1699. The Guru is said to have circulated instructions that the regular Baisakhi Day assembly should be regarded as a particularly important one on this occasion. In response to the message a vast concourse gathered at Anandpur, eagerly awaiting the appearance of the Guru. When he stood before them he shocked all present into stunned silence by demanding the heads of five loyal Sikhs. His insistent demand finally produced a volunteer who was led into a nearby tent. A thud was heard and the Guru, emerging with a blood-stained sword, called for a second head. Eventually he secured five volunteers, each of them taken into the tent and there apparently dispatched.

The Guru then drew back the side of the tent, dramatically revealing five living Sikhs and five decapitated goats. The Sikhs were the *pañj piāre*, the 'cherished five' who had so convincingly demonstrated their total trust and loyalty. There were then initiated as the first members of the Khalsa order, and having completed the ceremony Guru Gobind Singh himself received initiation from their hands. For the ceremony he had provided an iron pot containing water into which one of his wives cast soluble sweets. The sweetened water, stirred with a two-edged sword, was the *amrit* with which each entrant was initiated. Some of the *amrit* was applied to the face and hair, and some was drunk. All were thus required to drink from the same vessel regardless of caste and subsequently all were given *kaṛāh praśād* from a single iron pan. The rejection of caste distinctions, inherited from Nanak and transmitted by

[11] J. S. Grewal, *From Guru Nanak to Maharaja Ranjit Singh: Essays in Sikh History* (Amritsar, 1972), 60–1.

his successors, was thus given ritual expression in the *pāhul* or initiation ceremony of the Khalsa.[12]

Properly told in all its vivid detail, the story is an unusually dramatic one, and it will seem churlish to suggest that it cannot be entirely true. If we are writing one sort of history, the obligation to do so is inescapable and the task has been very effectively discharged in a masterly essay by Professor J. S. Grewal of Amritsar. Professor Grewal does not deny that an important event took place at Anandpur Sahib on Baisakhi Day 1699, nor does he reject all the details traditionally associated with the occasion. He does, however, criticize the manner in which the available source materials have been used by other historians. Having shown that some features must certainly be discarded, he concludes that judgement should be suspended on many other points pending careful research which has yet to be done.[13]

Another sort of history (and a perfectly legitimate one) frees us from this obligation. If we are seeking to understand the fashioning of a Sikh identity, we can remain uncommitted as far as most of the details are concerned. It matters little whether five volunteers were actually summoned or whether five goats were actually slain. The overriding fact is that in its essential outline the story is firmly believed and that this belief has unquestionably contributed to the subsequent shaping of conventional Sikh attitudes.

Having thus evaded a significant portion of the historian's usual responsibility, we must acknowledge that our quest for Sikh identity requires us to examine one particular feature of the Anandpur event in some detail. According to the traditional narratives, Guru Gobind Singh included in the inaugural ceremony a sermon, and in this sermon he is said to have enunciated the way of life which each initiant was thereafter to follow. The injunctions supplied in this sermon supplemented certain key items incorporated in the actual *pāhul* ceremony. Together they constitute the substance of the Rahit, the only significant additions being those which the Guru delivered immediately prior to his death in 1708.[14] Such at least is the traditional view, and, because the Rahit is so

[12] Gian Singh, *Tavarīkh Gurū Khālsā* (2nd edn., Patiala, 1970), 856–61. M. A. Macauliffe, *The Sikh Religion: Its Gurus, Sacred Writings and Authors* (Oxford, 1909), v. 91–7. The lengthy *Tavarīkh Gurū Khālsā* was published between 1891 and 1919.

[13] J. S. Grewal, 'The Khalsa of Guru Gobind Singh' in *From Guru Nanak to Maharaja Ranjit Singh*, chap. ix.

[14] Macauliffe, *The Sikh Religion*, v. 93–7, 243–5. Khushwant Singh, *A History of the Sikhs*, i (Princeton, 1963), 83–6, 95.

intimately related to the question of identity, it is an aspect of the traditional account which plainly we cannot avoid.

'Rahit' is one of those words which, because it expresses a fundamental concept, deserves to be much better known.[15] Indeed, it deserves (like 'Panth') to be a part of standard English usage, at least for anyone interested in the Sikhs and their tradition. Kahn Singh defines the word as follows: 'The systematic statement of Sikh principles; the way of life lived in accordance with the principles of the Sikh religion.'[16] This is an interestingly inaccurate definition. It is significant because it draws us back to the problem which so persistently frustrates all attempts to produce a simple comprehensive statement of Sikh identity. Kahn Singh was committed to the view that authentic Sikhism was represented by the Khalsa mode and he accordingly uses the terms 'Sikh' and 'Sikh religion' where correct usage requires 'Khalsa' and 'Khalsa tradition'. If, however, we make these substitutions, his brief definition can be accepted. It is the way of life enunciated by the Khalsa tradition which is summarized in the word 'Rahit', and non-Khalsa Sikhs sustain a separate identity precisely because they decline to observe some key features of the standard Rahit.

The Rahit is thus the Khalsa way of life, the system of belief and distinctive behaviour which all who accept Khalsa initiation are expected to observe. Since the eighteenth century various attempts have been made to express the Rahit in written form and the manuals thus produced are called rahit-namas.[17] Some of these manuals are very brief, concentrating on particular features of the Rahit as understood by their authors at the time of writing. The comprehensive rahit-nama en-

[15] The word derives from *rahaṇā*, 'to live'. The word is sometimes spelt 'Rahat' or 'Rehat'. The former transcribes a variant Punjabi version. The latter is incorrect.

[16] Kahn Singh, *Guruśabad ratanākar mahān koś*, p. 760.

[17] There are nine such works which date from before the middle of the nineteenth century. For the early rahit-namas, see below, pp. 36–9. Two extended prose rahit-namas which probably belong to the first half of the nineteenth century are *Prem Sumārg* and *Sau Sākhīān*. One which is available only in Punjabi is Randhir Singh (samp.), *Prem Sumārg Granth* (1953; 2nd edn., Jalandhar, 1965). The second one was issued in an English translation by Attar Singh of Bhadaur as *The Sakhee Book, or the Description of Gooroo Gobind Singh's Religion and Doctrines* (Banares, 1873). This was the version used by the Namdhari or Kuka Sikhs. See chap. 5, n. 6. A version has more recently been published in Punjabi by Gurbachan Singh Naiar (samp.), *Gur ratan māl arathāt sau sākhī* (Patiala, 1985). Since the founding of the Singh Sabha in 1873 the quest for an agreed rahit-nama has raised recurrent difficulty. Finally an acceptable version was published in 1950 under the title *Sikh Rahit Maryādā* and has sustained its position ever since. Most of *Sikh Rahit Maryādā* is in W. H. McLeod (trans.), *Textual Sources for the Study of Sikhism* (Manchester, 1984), 79–86. For further information see the introduction to McLeod (trans.), *The Chaupā Singh Rahit-nāmā*; and id., 'The Problem of the Panjabi *rahit-nāmā*s' in S. N. Mukherjee (ed.), *India: History and Thought* (Calcutta, 1982), 103–26.

deavours to cover all aspects of the Rahit and may venture into such areas as denunciation of the faithless or promises of a glory yet to come. In a comprehensive rahit-nama we can expect to find four recognizable elements, distinct in themselves yet closely related as aspects of the total Khalsa tradition.

The first element consists of the fundamental doctrines which an orthodox Sikh of the Khalsa is expected to affirm. These include such basic items as belief in Akal Purakh, veneration for the personal Gurus, and recognition of the mystical presence of the eternal Guru in the pages of the Adi Granth (the Guru Granth Sahib). This is normally the least conspicuous part of a rahit-nama. Such doctrines are obviously crucial features of the Khalsa faith and identity, and all that follows must necessarily be perceived as strictly compatible with these basic beliefs. As far as the rahit-namas are concerned, however, they can be largely taken for granted. For the purposes of enunciating the Rahit, a summary statement is usually accepted as adequate.

In passing we should note that this portion of a rahit-nama will typically incorporate much that the non-Khalsa Sikh can accept. Both Khalsa and non-Khalsa can affirm a certain range of common doctrine, a range which essentially corresponds to the earlier Nanak-panthi foundation. It is when we come to the three remaining components of a comprehensive rahit-nama that the critical differences emerge. These portions modify and extend the range of doctrine, building upon it an impressively detailed structure of personal behaviour and panthic ritual.

Rules for personal behaviour constitute the second component of a rahit-nama. These rules (which may be very detailed and specific) include instructions concerning the devotional obligations of a Khalsa Sikh, the outward forms by which Sikh men and women proclaim their identity, a variety of practices which are proscribed, and a list of particular groups with which a Khalsa should not associate. In a more developed rahit-nama the detail can be very considerable indeed, with injunctions covering a wide range of behaviour from personal devotion to elementary hygiene. Predictably there is a strong emphasis on features which express the militant aspect of the Khalsa identity, features which so obviously reflect the social constituency of the Panth and the experience of warfare which it encountered during the eighteenth century.

Some of the typical rahit-nama prescriptions derive from earlier Nanak-panthi practice and are thus congenial to all who claim to be Sikhs. They include an insistent emphasis on the personal performance of a specific daily liturgy (the *nit-nem*) and regular attendance at a gurdwara, there to pay one's respects and participate in corporate kirtan with other members of the gathered sangat. Other items define the distinctively Khalsa identity. All rahit-namas, regardless of their age or provenance, stress the paramount obligation of retaining the hair uncut, and as the tradition works its way through early uncertainties this provision eventually becomes one of the celebrated *pañj kakke* or Five Ks. These are five items of external appearance which all Khalsa Sikhs must wear, each beginning with the letter 'k'. In addition to the uncut hair (*kes*), the cluster comprises a wooden comb worn in the hair (*kaṅghā*), a steel bangle (*kaṛā*), a sword or dagger (*kirpān*), and a pair of breeches which must not reach below the knee (*kachh*).[18]

Conspicuous amongst the practices to be avoided is smoking tobacco, an injunction which was originally aimed at the hookah but which now includes the European pipe and cigarette.[19] The origin of this particular ban is not altogether clear. A possible reason could be the fact that a hookah would encumber a soldier and that the prohibition should accordingly be understood as one of the many military injunctions incorporated in the Rahit. Alternatively, the hookah may perhaps have been identified as a distinctively Muslim artefact. If this latter theory is correct, the item becomes one of the numerous anti-Muslim injunctions of the Rahit.

Muslims and their distinctive practices provide an explicit target for the early rahit-namas and some other surviving injunctions can be traced to this particular source. The most obvious is the ban on *halāl* meat. For the Khalsa, meat is permitted, provided that it is not beef and provided also that it comes from an animal killed with a single blow (*jhaṭkā*). This eliminates the possibility that it may have been polluted by Muslim ritual, for animals slain by the *halāl* process must bleed to death.[20]

In the modern rahit-namas this eighteenth-century attitude towards Muslims has been greatly softened, but a few remnants of its earlier prominence still survive. *Jhaṭkā* meat provides a rare example of one which still proclaims its origin. Usually the origin is concealed by a recasting produced in response to later circumstances. An early prohibition of sexual contact with Muslim women thus becomes a commandment directed against adultery in general.[21] It seems probable

[18] McLeod (trans.), *The Chaupā Siṅgh Rahit-nāmā*, pp. 32–44. *Sikh Rahit Maryādā* (Amritsar, 1983), 26.
[19] McLeod (trans.), *The Chaupā Siṅgh Rahit-nāmā*, sections 7a, 80, and 438, pp. 150, 156, and 182. *Sikh Rahit Maryādā*, p. 26.
[20] McLeod (trans.), *The Chaupā Siṅgh Rahit-nāmā*, section 372, p. 179.
[21] *Sikh Rahit Maryādā*, p. 26.

that, in like manner, an original ban on the Muslim hookah was subsequently converted into a rejection of tobacco smoking in general.

Most of the injunctions directed against other eighteenth-century rivals of the true Khalsa survive in the modern Rahit as interesting relics rather than as reconstituted components of essential behaviour. Who now cares about the minor panths listed as *pañj mel* or 'the five reprobate groups'?[22] In many other respects, however, the early tradition holds firm. The ban on both hair-cutting and smoking is certainly firm as far as orthodox opinion is concerned. These are two of the four gross sins which earn the title of *patit* or 'renegade' and which today require re-initiation if repentance is offered and accepted.[23]

The third element in a standard rahit-nama consists of orders for the conduct of Khalsa ceremonies. Once again the distinction between Khalsa and non-Khalsa Sikh emerges. Some of these rituals can, it is true, be practised by the latter as well as by the former. The tone and content of the modern orders is, however, strongly Khalsa and the principal rite is unambiguous in intention. The prime ritual of initiation is exclusively Khalsa, for thus does one accept its discipline and adopt its outward identity. In the standard modern version of the Rahit many of the personal injunctions are actually incorporated within this particular rite, recited as portions of a standard homily which must be delivered to all who take *pāhul*.[24]

The fourth element in a comprehensive rahit-nama presents the sanctions which are to be invoked in the case of offences against the Rahit. Procedures designed to enforce the Rahit have, in practice, been very difficult to define and even more difficult to apply consistently. This, at least, appears to be the modern experience and there is evidence which suggests that carlier generations suffered a similar problem.

Any Khalsa Sikh adjudged guilty of violating the Rahit is branded *tanakhāhīā* and the penance imposed on the offender is called a *tanakhāh*.[25] Both terms emerged during the eighteenth century, clearly

[22] There is agreement concerning three of the five reprobate groups. These are the Minas and Dhir-malias (the followers of relatives of the orthodox line who asserted claims to the title of Guru) and the Masands. The fourth and fifth are disputed. According to *Gur Sobhā* they were *naṛī-mār* (users of the hookah) and *kuṛī-mār* (killers of female daughters). In the *Chaupā Siṅgh Rahit-nāmā* it is the Ram-raias (the followers of a third schismatic claimant to the title of Guru) and the Masandias (those who follow the Masands). Kahn Singh identified the fifth as the Sir-gum, or those who cut their hair (*Guruśabad ratanākar mahān koś*, pp. 593–4). *Sikh Rahit Maryādā*, p. 27, generalizes it to cover 'other enemies of the Panth'.

[23] Ibid. 27–8.

[24] Ibid. 25–8.

[25] McLeod (trans.), *The Chaupā Siṅgh Rahit-nāmā*, pp. 25, 234 (n. 300).

demonstrating that effective enforcement of the Rahit has long been a major concern within the Khalsa. There are, however, few indications of precisely how enforcement procedures were applied during the eighteenth century. In recent times the process has necessarily been selective, concentrating on important individuals or on issues which happen to be conspicuously present in the public eye. Individual sangats certainly possess the authority to impose penances. This authority is delegated to five chosen representatives (*pañj piāre*) and a guilty verdict requires the performance of a penance if the offender is to remain an accepted member of the sangat.[26] In practice, however, this simple procedure is too often frustrated by indifference or circumvented by the internal dynamics of a sangat. It is one aspect of the problem of authority, a general problem to which we must return.

In thus defining and briefly describing the Rahit we have necessarily used expressions which indicate that the system is not a static one, that it has in fact continued to evolve during the three centuries which have elapsed since first it was formally promulgated. In theory this pattern of change and development need pose no problem. Although the line of personal Gurus ended with Guru Gobind Singh in 1708, the mystical Guru continues to dwell in the Granth and in the Panth, ever-available for the kind of situational guidance which changing circumstances require. It is, therefore, perfectly consistent for an authorized assembly of the Khalsa to speak as the Guru, provided only that its message does not conflict with anything contained in the Guru Granth Sahib. Given this doctrine of the continuing authority of the eternal Guru, there should be no problem as far as changes to the Rahit are concerned.

In practice, however, the issue is much more complex. This is partly because it can be exceedingly difficult to secure the kind of corporate agreement which will command general acceptance; and partly because serious problems are raised by the eighteenth-century history of the Panth. The first of these difficulties must await our discussion of authority in a later chapter. It is the second of them which demands our attention at this stage.

Inevitably it has been assumed that the essence and substance of the Rahit must have been determined by Guru Gobind Singh during his own lifetime, and that in communicating the Rahit to his Sikhs he was effectively promulgating a definitive version. A large portion would have been delivered on the occasion of the founding of the Khalsa in 1699 and the remainder would have been added shortly before his death. One of

[26] *Sikh Rahit Maryādā*, p. 28.

the extant rahit-namas reinforces this impression by purporting to record words spoken by the Guru during his stay in Abchalnagar immediately before he died.[27]

It is the rahit-namas themselves which prevent us from accepting this traditional schema. The tradition demands consistency, a pattern which demonstrably derives from the actual utterances of the tenth Guru and which is thereafter transmitted through succeeding generations in a regular and unambiguous form. This is not the pattern which the early rahit-namas deliver. They constitute a very considerable problem, one which must be solved with reasonable certainty if we are to achieve a satisfactory understanding of the eighteenth-century notion of Khalsa identity.

The best of our early sources is not a formal rahit-nama, but it deserves to be included in any such discussion because it incorporates a portion which briefly describes the requirements of the Rahit. This is Sainapati's *Gur Sobhā*, 'The Radiance of the Guru'. As its title indicates, this work proclaims the marvels of the Guru's glory. It is actually an early example of the gur-bilas or 'splendour of the Guru' style which acquired a dominant popularity during the eighteenth and nineteenth centuries, and, because it is relatively close to the tenth Guru himself, it is a very important source indeed. It is also important for the brief rahit-nama which it supplies and no adequate discussion of the early Rahit can avoid reference to it.[28]

Gur Sobhā nevertheless fails to satisfy the need for a comprehensive statement of the Rahit, one which can be unequivocally traced to the actual utterances of the Guru. This is partly because Sainapati had a larger purpose, setting his brief exposition of the Rahit within his denunciation of the arrogant and corrupt masands. More particularly it is because the actual date of the work has not yet been conclusively determined. The two contending dates are 1711 and 1745. If the first of these can be definitively established, there will be a significant strengthening of the rahit-nama sequence.[29] As far as specific identity injunctions are concerned, two come through with particular force in Sainapati's version of the Rahit. Predictably they are the ban on hair-cutting and condemnation of the hookah.[30]

27 Piara Singh Padam (samp.), *Rahit-nāme* (Patiala, 1974), 53.

28 Ganda Singh (samp.), *Kavī Saināpati rachit Sri Gur Sobhā*. For the gur-bilas literature, see McLeod (trans.), *Textual Sources for the Study of Sikhism*, pp. 11–13.

29 Ganda Singh (samp.), *Kavī Saināpati rachit Sri Gur Sobhā*, pp. 21–3 (roman pagination).

30 Ibid. 5: 19, 5: 21, 5: 24, 5: 30, pp. 22–4 (Gurmukhi pagination).

The examples of formal rahit-nama style which usually attract attention first are four brief poems. These relate, in simple Punjabi verse, conversations which their authors allegedly had with Guru Gobind Singh prior to his death. Two of them are attributed to Nand Lal (*Tanakhāh-nāmā* and *Praśan-uttar*). A third is attributed to a Sikh variously called Prahilad Singh or Prahilad Rai; and the fourth to Desa Singh, a resident of Amritsar who claims to have obtained his information from the Guru and from Nand Lal. The Nand Lal of the rahit-namas is obviously intended to be Bhai Nand Lal, a celebrated member of the tenth Guru's entourage and one renowned for his Persian poetry. There also exists a brief prose rahit-nama attributed to him. With the same cluster we can also associate the brief prose rahit-nama attributed to Daya Singh (one of the five Sikhs traditionally believed to have offered their heads at the inauguration of the Khalsa in 1699).[31]

There can be no doubt concerning the importance of these six brief works in the history of Sikh doctrine (especially doctrine relating to the Rahit and thus to the nature of the Khalsa). Their significance in this regard is well illustrated by the repeated use which Bhai Jodh Singh makes of them in the relevant chapter of his influential study of Sikh doctrine entitled *Guramati niraṇay*.[32] It is also indicated by some very familiar expressions. From where do the words *savā lakh* and *rāj karegā khālsā* come? They are to be found in the *Tanakhāh-nāmā*.[33] And where do we first encounter such expressions as *gurū khālsā mānīahi, paragaṭ gurū kī deh* ('Accept the Khalsa as Guru, for it is the manifest body of the Guru') or *sabh sikhan ko bachan hai, gurū mānīahu granth* ('Every Sikh is bidden to accept the Granth as Guru')? These lines we find in the rahit-nama attributed to Prahilad Singh.[34] They are accordingly works which should be treated with great respect.

Unfortunately they are also works which the historian has to treat with great reserve. This is because it is still impossible to identify them in terms of author, place, or time. The authorship of such figures as Nand Lal and Daya Singh must be rejected and so too must the claims which each rahit-nama makes to immediate contact with the Guru himself. The distinguished Bhai Nand Lal Goya could never have written the kind of

[31] For texts of these six brief rahit-namas, see Piara Singh Padam (samp.), *Rahit-nāme*, pp. 42–67, 134–45. For a text and translation of the prose rahit-nama attributed to Nand Lal, see McLeod (trans.), *The Chaupā Siṅgh Rahit-nāmā*, pp. 133–8, 202–4. It first appears attached to the much longer *Chaupā Siṅgh Rahit-nāmā*.

[32] Jodh Singh, *Guramati niraṇay* (Ludhiana, n.d.; 1st edn. 1932). chap. 14.

[33] Piara Singh Padam (samp.), *Rahit-nāme*, 34 and 36, p. 47.

[34] Ibid. 24 and 30, p. 55.

verse which these rahit-namas offer, and in all cases the language indicates a significant remove from the Guru's own time and environment. There are, moreover, some conspicuous errors, such as Prahilad Singh's claim that he received his instruction from the Guru in 1696.[35] Had he received it in Abchalnagar (as he specifically claims) he should have supplied a date corresponding to 1708.

Such features separate this cluster of rahit-namas from immediate contact with Guru Gobind Singh, but we must take care not to exaggerate the distance. Other features indicate a relatively early date. The most important of these is the impression which these rahit-namas give of a Rahit still in the process of formulation. Although we may have to detach them from the person and period of Guru Gobind Singh, this does not necessarily mean that we shall have to advance them well into the eighteenth century or the early nineteenth century.

We have here summarized a very intricate problem, one which still awaits a satisfactory determination. Part of our problem derives from the lack of early manuscript evidence. In its absence we shall have to depend upon analysis of language and content, an analysis which has yet to be adequately performed. A reasonable hypothesis seems to be an origin located somewhere in the middle decades of the eighteenth century. In the meantime, however, it remains a hypothesis.

Fortunately the same does not apply to the only lengthy rahit-nama which belongs to the eighteenth century. This is the prose rahit-nama attributed to Chaupa Singh Chhibbar, tutor to the infant Guru Gobind Singh and later one of his trusted advisers. An analysis of the *Chaupā Singh Rahit-nāmā* indicates that it was compiled in its present form during the middle decades of the eighteenth century (between 1740 and 1765) and that it is accordingly the earliest of the datable rahit-namas. In its extant form it is a composite product mixing sections of classic rahit-nama material with anecdotes concerning Guru Gobind Singh, denunciation of the current Khalsa leadership, prophecies of imminent disaster, and a promise of ultimate glory.[36]

The composite nature of the *Chaupā Singh Rahit-nāmā* points clearly to earlier sources and it is conceivable that portions of it may indeed go back to Chaupa Singh Chhibbar of the tenth Guru's entourage. These portions are impossible to identify with any certainty, although some parts can be safely detached from the rahit-nama's putative author and

35 Ibid. 38, p. 56.

36 McLeod (trans.), *The Chaupā Singh Rahit-nāmā*, explains these in greater detail, pp. 24–8.

firmly located in a later period. The rahit-nama must be read as a mid-century interpretation of the Khalsa and its duty, as perceived by a particular family of Chhibbar Brahmans, once influential in the Panth but now pushed aside by coarsely aggressive successors.[37]

This firm identification is the basis of the rahit-nama's value today. Portions of its prolific content can be offensive to a modern Khalsa taste and it is easy to identify features which have made it an object of deep suspicion in orthodox circles. Notable in this respect is its claim that Brahmans are entitled to a special consideration in the Panth, a view which is unlikely to commend the source to those who support an egalitarian interpretation of the Panth.[38] Such features are nevertheless very valuable, for they sustain the credibility of the rahit-nama as a Chhibbar product and enable us to set it within a clearly definable context. Its profusion of detailed Rahit injunctions can thus be tagged in terms of source and period, and once this has been done the injunctions can be interpreted accordingly.

Although the Chhibbar connection arouses orthodox suspicions, it should not be assumed that these suspicions are necessarily valid. It does not follow that the rahit-nama will be unrepresentative or untrustworthy simply because of its Brahman provenance. On the contrary, the connection should considerably strengthen its claims, for this particular family had been very close to the tenth Guru and it can be plausibly maintained that for this very reason the rahit-nama deserves sympathetic analysis. The claim is strengthened by features which one might not have expected from a Brahmanic source. Strong emphasis is laid on the prime significance of the sword, on the role of the Khalsa Sikh as a soldier, and on the menace posed by polluting Muslims.[39]

Because the Rahit portions of the *Chaupā Siṅgh Rahit-nāmā* are so lengthy and detailed, it is impossible to summarize them here.[40] There are two such sections, one specifying duties which the loyal Khalsa must perform and the other listing offences which require a penance (*tanakhāh*).[41] In addition to their many injunctions concerning warfare and the sword, the two lists include such predictable items as rules for harmonious relations within a sangat, appropriate rituals, reverence for the sacred scripture, various means of avoiding pollution, and an

[37] Ibid. 16–19.
[38] Ibid., section 24, p. 151.
[39] Ibid. 40, 42.
[40] The injunctions are summarized in ibid. 32–43.
[41] Ibid. 149–66, 174–90.

insistent stress on maintaining the hair uncut. Practices to be strictly avoided include smoking a hookah and eating *halāl* meat.

The *Chaupā Siṅgh Rahit-nāmā* thus incorporates the customary stress on the *kes* (the uncut hair), but it does not include the Five Ks (the *pañj kakke* or *pañj kakār*). The earliest extant version omits them altogether, and when a later version introduces a fivefold cluster, the actual items which it lists do not correspond to the *pañj kakke*. Three of the Five Ks are included (*kachh*, *kirpān*, and *kes*) but two are missing (*kaṅghā* and *kaṛā*). In their place we find *bāṇī* (the Gurus' utterances as recorded in sacred scripture) and *sādh saṅgat* (the fellowship of the devout).[42] Precisely the same situation is presented by the brief rahit-namas which we have tentatively assigned to the mid-eighteenth century. There too we find no reference to the *pañj kakke* in the early versions, though a reference subsequently appears in a later text of the *Prahilād Siṅgh Rahit-nāmā*.[43]

This particular instance can be generalized in the sense that other features of the orthodox Rahit as understood today are absent from the eighteenth-century evidence or are present as prototypes which have yet to attain firm definition. Others possess a clear definition, but their content or emphasis is subsequently amended in response to changing circumstances. From this evidence we must draw the following conclusion. A version of the Rahit was certainly current during the lifetime of Guru Gobind Singh but that version must be regarded as a nucleus, not as the full-fledged twentieth-century Rahit. In the meantime (and particularly during the early and middle decades of the eighteenth century) a process of growth and development took place, one which had produced the essential lineaments of the modern Rahit by the end of the eighteenth century.

This process of change and development continued through the nineteenth century into the twentieth and it still continues today. The Rahit

[42] Ibid., section 7a, p. 150.

[43] The twentieth-century version of the *Prahilād Siṅgh Rahit-nāmā* has an addendum attached which affirms the use of the *pañj kakke*. It appears in *Pothī rahit nāmā te tankhāh nāmā* (Amritsar, 1922), 16, and is quoted as authentic by Jodh Singh, *Guramati niraṇay*, p. 303.

kachh kes kaṅghā kirapān / kaṛā aur jo karau bakhān /
ih kakke pañj tum māno / gurū granth sabh tum jāno /

The portion is missing from Attar Singh's *The Rayhit Nama of Pralad Rai or the Excellent Conversation of Duswan Padsha and Nand Lal's Rayhit Nama or Rules for the Guidance of Sikhs in Religious Matters*, which was published from Lahore in 1876, and from earlier versions of the rahit-nama.

has never been static. It still responds to contemporary pressures, producing shifts in emphasis which gradually emerge as significant changes. Two interesting (and closely related) examples are provided by changing attitudes towards illicit sexual intercourse and towards Muslims.[44] If one compares modern injunctions with those from the eighteenth century, some interesting (yet unsurprising) differences become evident.

It thus appears that the developed Rahit must be ascribed to an extended period of evolution rather than limited to explicit pronouncements on the part of the tenth Guru. If this is indeed the case, it raises the question of how one identifies sources for the various elements included in the developed Rahit. Three general sources may be briefly postulated.

The first is the traditional source, namely the intention of the Gurus applied during the formative years of the Panth's growth and codified by Guru Gobind Singh as a nucleus of the later Rahit. This source delivered items relating to the importance of the sangat and to devotional practices designed to achieve *mukti* or spiritual liberation. Duties associated with the growing militancy of the Panth will also have developed during the course of the seventeenth century and we must also accept that an outward identity had been defined by the end of the century. Given the insistent stress on the *kes* in all rahit-namas, we can assume that the dominant feature of this external identity was its insistence on uncut hair.

Militant conventions and uncut hair point to a second source. This comprises the culture and traditions of the caste group which was progressively moving towards ascendancy within the Panth, particularly after the founding of the Khalsa. This ascendancy had presumably been reached in numerical terms before the ending of the line of personal Gurus, and during the eighteenth century it was to assume a much larger connotation. The Jats have long been distinguished by their militant traditions and by the custom of retaining their hair uncut. The influence of these traditions evidently operated prior to the formal inauguration of the Khalsa, fusing with the purpose of Guru Gobind Singh and thus emerging as significant features of the Khalsa nucleus. During the course of the eighteenth century the same influence accelerated as Jat leadership assumed an increasingly high profile within the Panth.

The third source also affected the development of the Rahit during the

[44] Compare injunctions 10 and 396 of McLeod (trans.), *The Chaupā Siṅgh Rahit-nāmā*, pp. 150 and 180, with [44](3) of *Textual Sources for the Study of Sikhism*, p. 85. Injunctions aimed at relations with Muslims, common in the eighteenth and first half of the nineteenth century, are absent today. *The Chaupā Siṅgh Rahit-nāmā*, p. 42.

seventeenth century, growing significantly in influence during the eighteenth. This was the pressure of contemporary circumstances, specifically the experience of warfare against enemies who increasingly were identified as Muslims. These circumstances served to strengthen the influence of the Jat source in that they encouraged militancy within the Panth. They stand alone as the source of some notable eighteenth-century injunctions aimed clearly and directly at Muslims.

The Rahit must thus be viewed as an evolving system, one which began to emerge during the earliest days of the Nanak-panth. It thereafter continued to develop formally (in accordance with deliberate decisions) and informally (in response to internal influences and external pressures). The precise distribution of these factors cannot be determined, particularly as all three were intertwined to a considerable extent. It is, however, possible to identify the appearance of certain key items and to reconstruct a loose sequence. This should enable us to describe in general terms the nature of the Khalsa identity at the beginning of the eighteenth century; the pattern of development which progressively enlarged and consolidated the Rahit during the course of the eighteenth century; and the developed identity which the Khalsa carried forward into the nineteenth century.

In so doing we must take care to set this Khalsa identity within the context of the larger Panth, ever aware that, however dominant the Khalsa mode may sometimes seem, its boundaries have never coincided with those of the Panth as a whole. It all depends, of course, on one's point of view. For some strict members of the Khalsa the two sets of boundaries are indeed coterminous and those who fail to meet Khalsa requirements are *ipso facto* deregistered as Sikhs. Although no one has ever managed to isolate the strict or 'fundamentalist' sector of the Panth, there can be little doubt that it always constitutes a comparatively small minority. The majority consists of the liberal, the lax, and the ambivalent, all of whom would presumably acknowledge a Panth larger than the orthodox Khalsa.

This means that our basic problem will persist, emerging in each period and generation to frustrate the promise of easy definition which the Khalsa so insistently proffers. We must also remind ourselves that the problem of definition will not be confined to a simple distinction between loyal Khalsa on the one hand and clean-shaven Sahaj-dhari on the other. Punjabi society will not permit such an easy solution, particularly in the villages which are home to a majority of those who call themselves Sikhs. A major aspect of the practical problem is the willingness of many

Punjabis to merge identities which the academic and the devout would prefer to keep separate. We shall delude ourselves if we imagine otherwise, just as we so easily misunderstand Sikh society if we insist on keeping our normative categories carefully intact.

Those categories are nevertheless essential if our analysis is to proceed and the most important of them is unquestionably the Khalsa. In the chapter which follows we shall accordingly focus our attention on the development of the Khalsa.

4

The Khalsa in the Eighteenth Century

WHEN Guru Gobind Singh stood before his assembled followers on Baisakhi Day 1699 what did he actually say and do? We have already indicated two appropriate responses to this question, one cautiously sceptical and the other more positive. The first is that tradition has obviously embellished the occasion and that an analysis of the early sources requires the historian to suspend judgement on much of the traditional detail. The second is that something very significant obviously did happen in 1699 and that it should be possible to describe, in very general terms, the distinctive identity which marked those Sikhs who elected to join the Guru's Khalsa.

In attempting to envisage this identity we must always remember that it involves both an inheritance from the past and a continuing development in the future. This point, previously stressed when discussing the Rahit, means that certain features of the Khalsa discipline derive from the earliest days of the Nanak-panth. Others subsequently emerged in response to cultural influences operating within the Panth's constituency or to the pressure of political circumstances during the course of the seventeenth-century. The incorporating of such features in the formalized Rahit of the early Khalsa should serve to remind us that the 1699 event is set within a pattern of growth and development, and that the antecedents of this pattern extend well into the past. We should also remember that major features of the pattern belong to the future, evolving in response to the complex of influences which affect the Panth after 1699.

This should never suggest, however, that the 1699 event was unimportant. There is no reason to doubt that a rite of baptism was introduced on that famous Baisakhi Day, and, if indeed such a decision was implemented by Guru Gobind Singh, it marks a very significant development indeed. It means that a formal discipline was enunciated, one which required an explicit act of allegiance from all who accepted Khalsa initiation as the proper expression of loyalty to the Guru and his Panth. The discipline itself might continue to develop and mutate, but this has done nothing to diminish the conviction that Khalsa membership requires the outward observance of certain objective standards. Because a non-Khalsa option remained available, it also means that the Panth has ever since been compelled to grapple with the problem of differing identities. There is no evidence which suggests that in 1699 a choice was offered between Khalsa initiation and expulsion from the Panth.

The features of the 1699 tradition which seem to survive critical scrutiny are listed by Professor J. S. Grewal as follows:

> That a considerable number of the Sikhs used to visit Anandpur at the time of Baisakhi and that on the Baisakhi of 1699 many of the Sikhs were specially asked to come, that *khaṇḍe kī pāhul* [sword-baptism] was administered to those who were willing to become the Guru's *Khālsā* (though no exact figures are mentioned anywhere), that a considerable number of people—the *brāhmans* and *khatrīs* in particular—rejected the *pāhul*, that the *Khālsā* were required to wear *keshas* [uncut hair] and arms, that they were required not to smoke, that the appellation of 'Singh' came to be adopted by a large number of the *Khālsā*—all this is there in the earliest evidence.[1]

The fact that these points are to be found in the earliest chronicles does not necessarily mean that they were all introduced in 1699, nor does it tell us which of them (if any) were informally observed prior to 1699. It does, however, indicate that a 1699 introduction must be regarded as very likely in all instances and it definitively establishes them as features of the Rahit as observed in the early eighteenth century. Five such features emerge. An initiation ceremony involving the use of a sword was instituted; initiants were to keep their hair uncut; weapons were to be worn as a matter of course; smoking the hookah was forbidden; and many (though not necessarily all) who thus entered the Khalsa adopted the name 'Singh'.

This defines the essential Rahit as it was evidently understood at the beginning of the eighteenth century. The fact that Brahman and Khatri Sikhs were conspicuous amongst those who declined to accept the new order presumably means that the predominant response came from Jats, accompanied by smaller numbers from artisan castes. This assumption is certainly supported by later evidence[2] and arguably it is also strengthened by the distinctly militant tenor of the new dispensation.

Beyond these features we move into conjecture, supporting any

[1] J. S. Grewal, *From Guru Nanak to Maharaja Ranjit Singh: Essays in Sikh History* (Amritsar, 1972), 59.

[2] See above, p. 21.

proposal which we may offer with whatever evidence may be available from later sources. One range of conjecture concerns the continuing Nanak-panthi tradition, those members of the Panth who declined *pāhul* (Khalsa initiation) and came to be known as Sahaj-dhari Sikhs. The term *sahaj-dhārī* was applied during the eighteenth century to Sikhs who cut their hair, and it is used in precisely this sense by the *Chaupā Siṅgh Rahit-nāmā*.[3] The word *sahaj* can mean 'slow' or 'natural', and *sahaj-dhārī* was subsequently construed to mean 'slow-adopter' or 'a Sikh who is still on the path to full Khalsa membership'. This, however, represents the strained interpretation of a later generation, one which is unlikely to be correct. A much more plausible etymology associates the term with Guru Nanak's use of *sahaj* to designate the condition of ultimate spiritual bliss which climaxes the *nām simaraṇ* technique. Those who emphasized Guru Nanak's interior practice of *nām simaraṇ* as opposed to the outward symbols of the new Khalsa identity would thus come to be known as 'those who affirm *sahaj*', or Sahaj-dhari Sikhs.[4]

The continuing presence of such Sikhs is plainly indicated by the testimony of the *B40 Janam-sākhī*. In this work, completed in 1733, we are offered clear evidence of a Nanak-panthi sangat living somewhere in the Gujranwala or Gujrat area. A prominent member of the sangat (the patron responsible for the recording of the janam-sakhi) is a Khatri called Daya Ram Abrol.[5] Nowhere in the entire work is there any hint of a Khalsa awareness, nor of the military struggles in which the Khalsa was so deeply involved. Indeed, there is an evident willingness to accept without demur that most heinous of Khalsa sins, the cutting of hair. In one anecdote an impoverished Sikh cuts and sells his hair in order to purchase food for the Guru.[6]

It is thus evident that those who declined to accept pahul continued to live as Nanak-panthi Sikhs, loyal to their original inheritance. As such they continued to regard themselves as Sikhs, sustaining an identity which was much less precise than that of the baptised Khalsa. The non-Khalsa constituency presumably included Kes-dhari Sikhs, those who retained their hair uncut without actually taking pahul. In terms of identity such Sikhs would be associated with the Amrit-dhari (the Sikh who had formally taken pahul) rather than with the archetypal Sahaj-dhari who outwardly is indistinguishable from his or her

[3] W. H. McLeod (trans.), *The Chaupā Siṅgh Rahit-nāmā* (Dunedin, 1987), section 53, p. 154. Note, however, that his facial hair must be left untouched. See section 287, p. 176.

[4] McLeod, *Early Sikh Tradition: A Study of the Janam-sākhīs* (Oxford, 1980), 35 n.

[5] McLeod (trans.), *The B40 Janam-sākhī* (Amritsar, 1980), intro. pp. 19–25.

[6] Ibid., text p. 50. Id., *Early Sikh Tradition*, pp. 264–5.

Hindu neighbour. For some the choice would have reflected genuine convictions, and we must accept that this would apply to many of the Khatris and Brahmans who declined to accept initiation. For others it would presumably depend on circumstances. Periods of persecution would favour a discreet shedding of Khalsa symbols (particularly the *kes*), thereby producing a Sahaj-dhari identity. Khalsa success, by contrast, would favour a resumption of the symbols and a resurgence of the Kes-dhari identity.[7]

The Sahaj-dhari presence must always be kept in mind as we proceed through the eighteenth century, and likewise the existence of other identities which might claim an affiliation with the larger Panth. One which raises particular difficulties is the Udasi sect, an ascetic tradition claiming descent from Guru Nanak's elder son Siri Chand. The Udasi sect is distinguished by practices which clearly relate it to the Nath tradition, and, given Nanak's firm rejection of Nath practices, the Udasis should probably be set outside the Panth. The reputed descent from Siri Chand, aided by later connections of a distinctly tenuous nature, has nevertheless sustained an uncertain affiliation.[8] This was subsequently strengthened to some extent by the fact that during the eighteenth and nineteenth centuries many gurdwaras were maintained by individuals and lineages identified as Udasis. Although they are said to have been recognized by the later Gurus, they remain an obscure group, yet another of the many instances where uncertain tradition does service for established fact.[9]

In terms of visibility and participation in the Panth's evolving traditions, groups such as the Udasis are at one extreme. Sahaj-dharis are scarcely more prominent. Throughout the eighteenth century it is the Khalsa which occupies the stage, conspicuously dominant in all that passes as Sikh history and easily communicating the impression that all such history is in fact Khalsa history. This is not surprising. It is a development which can be easily understood in the light of political circumstances in eighteenth-century Punjab and in terms of the vigorous manner in which members of the Khalsa respond to those circumstances.

[7] Khushwant Singh, *A History of the Sikhs*, i (Princeton, 1963), 120. Teja Singh and Ganda Singh, *A Short History of the Sikhs* (Bombay, 1950), 110.

[8] The most significant of the Udasi connections with the orthodox Panth was the adherence to Udasi ideals of Baba Gurditta, eldest son of Guru Hargobind. Later Sikh tradition represents this allegiance as the route whereby Siri Chand eventually acknowledged the legitimate line of Gurus. Teja Singh, *Sikhism: Its Ideals and Institutions* (1938; rev. edn., Calcutta, 1951), 63.

[9] The Udasi panth is dealt with by Sulakhan Singh, 'The Udasis under Sikh Rule' (unpub. Ph.D. thesis, Guru Nanak Dev University, Amritsar, 1985). See also Teja Singh, *Sikhism*, pp. 58–66.

Uncertainty was followed by persecution, and persecution by counter-attack. The counter-attack proved to be increasingly successful and eventually resulted in armed bands of Khalsa Sikhs dominating much of the Punjab. This in turn led to internecine warfare, but unity was finally imposed by the Sikh leader Ranjit Singh and the eighteenth century closed with the effective establishment of his rule over most of the Punjab.[10]

In sketching the history of the Panth during the eighteenth century a special kind of caution is needed. Inevitably and quite properly we focus much of our attention on the chronic warfare of the period, and in dealing with the various participants we necessarily give prominence to Mughals and Afghans on one side and the Khalsa Sikhs on the other. In so doing we can easily fall victim to the compelling strength of Khalsa historiography, presenting a view of the period which essentially depends on the themes and assumptions of that interpretation. Let no one under-estimate its seductive power. This is the heroic period of Sikh tradition and its vibrant appeal can be very difficult to resist if one is predisposed to favour the Sikh cause. For those who are hostile to their cause the result is liable to be a comprehensive rejection of the tradition or a condemnation of what can easily be represented as bloody and uncouth. The tradition delivers a historiography and a mythology which tend strongly to polarize opinion. Although historians should be well aware of such a possibility, they are not necessarily immune from its extrovert charms or its subtle fascination.[11]

The warning to historians and their readers is, of course, a comment on the strength of the Khalsa ideal, a tribute to the influence which it exercises on those who subscribe to it as a belief and as a way of life. The fact that the heroic ideal has achieved such an ascendancy tells us something very important about Sikh identity, a message which power-fully reinforces Khalsa claims to represent all that is right and true in the teachings of the Gurus. *Here*, it insists, are the authentic traditions of the Panth. Others may perceive and practise vital aspects of the Gurus' message, but only in the Khalsa ideal does one find the fullness and the fulfilment of what Guru Gobind Singh intended his followers to be.

In thus emphasizing the strength of this tradition we will normally be referring to the modern Panth and to beliefs which exercise a consider-able influence today. Their contemporary relevance is a basic fact which

[10] J. S. Grewal, *The Sikhs of the Punjab* (Cambridge, forthcoming), chap. 5.

[11] This tradition informs the interpretation of Khushwant Singh, *A History of the Sikhs*, i, chaps. 7–11. In Teja Singh and Ganda Singh, *A Short History of the Sikhs*, pt. III, it is considerably more pronounced.

should certainly be acknowledged and it is one to which we shall return when we deal with the Panth in the late twentieth century. Here, however, our primary concern must be with the generating of the tradition, with the events which supply its content, and with the early interpretations which produce its distinctive mould. We are still in the eighteenth century and at this point we are concerned with the developing consciousness which accompanied Khalsa involvement in the unfolding events of the century.

It was an involvement which began in defeat and uncertainty. Guru Gobind Singh himself fought wars which a detached observer would regard as defeats, although we must also heed the interpretation which transforms these events by stressing the heroism and inflexible determination of the Guru. Uncertainty followed with Banda Bahadur, leader of the uprising which created a disturbance in the Punjab between 1709, and his capture by Mughal troops at the end of 1715. Although Banda has long since been incorporated within Khalsa tradition as one who loyally upheld its finest ideals, the contemporary situation was probably rather more ambiguous. There were evidently disputes between Banda and his immediate followers on the one hand and the so-called Tat Khalsa (the 'True Khalsa') on the other.[12] These disputes, which concerned the proper form of Khalsa observances, should come as no surprise. The Khalsa had been in existence barely fifteen years when disagreement first developed between the Bandai Khalsa and the Tat Khalsa, a period much too brief for clear definition to have emerged on all significant points.

As we have already observed when discussing the Rahit, it was a definition which developed during the course of the decades which followed. In so doing it reflected the circumstances encountered by the Khalsa, specifically the experience of warfare. For several years after Banda's capture and execution this involved a desperate defence against intermittent campaigns to destroy their influence, campaigns which are represented in Sikh tradition as attempts by vicious Mughal authorities to exterminate the Khalsa completely.[13] Names such as Zakarya Khan, Lakhpat Rai, and Mir Mannu figure prominently in Khalsa demonology and are still invoked today as examples of the kind of fierce enemy whom Sikhs must resist whenever they appear.

[12] Khushwant Singh, *A History of the Sikhs*, i. 121–2. Teja Singh and Ganda Singh, *A Short History of the Sikhs*, pp. 111–16. G. S. Chhabra, *Advanced History of the Punjab*, i (rev. edn., Jullundur, 1968), 344.

[13] Gopal Singh, *A History of the Sikh People 1469–1978* (New Delhi, 1979), ch. xv.

After Ahmad Shah Abdali began his long series of invasions in 1747, Mughals were replaced by Afghans as the principal persecutor and foe, but the essential pattern remains unchanged. It includes calamities such as the Lesser Disaster (*Chhoṭā Ghalūgārā*) of 1746 and the Great Disaster (*Vāḍā Ghalūgārā*) of 1762. Another important feature is martyrdom, a prominent example being the cruel execution in 1738 of the deeply revered Mani Singh. Throughout the entire period the tradition carries tales of heroism, stories of dedicated Sikhs of the Khalsa who expressed their faith and loyalty in determined resistance to the forces of tyranny and destruction.[14]

The figure who pre-eminently draws these themes together in a single episode is that most famous of all Sikh martyrs, Baba Dip Singh Shahid. Dip Singh, a Jat from Lahore district and a trusted follower of Guru Gobind Singh, had fought with Banda and had subsequently become one of the principal leaders of the Khalsa resistance. In 1757, after Afghan invaders had desecrated Harimandir (now commonly known as the Golden Temple), Dip Singh took a solemn vow to enter Amritsar and there endeavour to repossess the ruined temple. Near Tarn Taran his force was confronted by a large Afghan army and Dip Singh met a fate variously described in popular Sikh tradition. According to the dominant version his head was cut off, but clutching it with one hand he continued to fight his way forward for another fifteen kilometres before succumbing to his injury within the bounds of Amritsar.[15] A distinctly gory picture of the decapitated Dip Singh is perhaps the most popular of the coloured prints available today in the bazaars of the Punjab and Delhi.[16]

A significant detail in the Dip Singh tradition concerns the desecration of Harimandir. This was, of course, perpetrated by Muslims and it is believed to have included the dumping of cows' entrails into the sacred pool. Hostility towards Muslims is another of the themes illustrated by the martyrdom of Dip Singh, a theme which finds clear expression in the early rahit-namas.[17] Muslims can never be trusted, their touch will pollute, and Sikhs are required to avoid their company at all times.[18] If necessary the sword must be used against Muslims, for it is they who threaten *dharma*.

This, it should be noted, is not a message communicated by the janam-

[14] Harbans Singh, *The Heritage of the Sikhs* (New Delhi, 1983), chaps. viii and ix.

[15] Gian Singh, *Tavarīkh Gurū Khālsā* (2nd edn., Patiala, 1970), ii. 198–9. Teja Singh and Ganda Singh, *A Short History of the Sikhs*, p. 155.

[16] The picture appears in W. H. McLeod, *Popular Sikh Art* (New Delhi, forthcoming).

[17] McLeod, *The Chaupā Siṅgh Rahit-nāmā*, intro. p. 42.

[18] Ibid., injunctions 10, 31, 120, and 442, pp. 150, 152, 160, 183.

sakhis. In the janam-sakhis we find Guru Nanak portrayed as the conciliator of Hindu and Muslim. It is true that they often portray him as one who rebukes bigoted qazis and if necessary humbles them; and it is also true that the janam-sakhis develop their own distinctive 'Triumph over Islam' theme.[19] Their criticisms of Muslims and Muslim doctrine are, however, comparatively muted and they are accompanied by a 'Nanak the Unifier' theme, so effectively portrayed in the regular presence of the Hindu Bala and the Muslim Mardana.[20]

In this regard the rahit-namas differ dramatically from the janam-sakhis, and they also run counter to the philosophy of Guru Gobind Singh himself. A celebrated passage from *Akāl Ustat* declares that 'mankind is one, that all men belong to a single humanity',[21] and in the lines which follow it specifically relates this belief to the relationship between Hindu and Muslim. The rahit-namas put their emphasis elsewhere. Faithfully reflecting attitudes developed during the eighteenth century and possibly earlier, the more outspoken of the rahit-namas identify the Muslim as the enemy and record injunctions which express this conviction. A later generation of Sikhs, reared in different circumstances, was to perceive the issue differently and so to return to the janam-sakhi interpretation. For the eighteenth-century Khalsa, however, the enemy was typically a Muslim or the servant of Muslims. As a result Muslims as such were to be treated with wary caution or open hostility.

The enemies of the Khalsa, dominant at first and a continuing threat for most of the century, were eventually overcome. During the period of struggle the Khalsa looked forward to this ultimate triumph and at some point its confident expectation found expression in the triumphant words *rāj karegā khālsā*, 'the Khalsa shall rule'.

> The Khalsa shall rule, no enemy shall remain.
> All who endure suffering and privation shall be brought to the safety of the Guru's protection.[22]

Here we have another example of an eighteenth-century attitude requiring reinterpretation for a later generation. The eighteenth-century understanding, however, needs no such gloss. The Khalsa was involved in a struggle, first for survival and then for control. Through early defeat and later victory it moved steadily towards military triumph and political power, eventually securing the objective which destiny decreed. For

[19] McLeod, *Early Sikh Tradition*, pp. 255–6.
[20] Ibid. 172–3, 255.
[21] Dasam Granth, p. 19.
[22] Piara Singh Padam (samp.), *Rahit-nāme* (Patiala, 1974), 47.

many the climax and authentic fulfilment of the promise was to be the kingdom of Maharaja Ranjit Singh, established at the turn of the century.

The heroic ideals which thus developed during the course of the eighteenth century found expression in a variety of literature distinct from the rahit-namas. Reference has already been made to Sainapati's *Gur Sobhā* as the earliest example of the gur-bilas or 'splendour of the Guru' style.[23] Works which follow this style concentrate on the lives of the Gurus rather than on the events of the eighteenth century, but their treatment clearly reflects the ideals of the later period within which the style was developed. An obvious antecedent is supplied by *Bachitar Nāṭak*, an account of Guru Gobind Singh's early life which is attributed to the Guru himself. In *Bachitar Nāṭak* we find the same sense of destiny that characterizes the gur-bilas literature, the same emphasis on the paramount need to uphold *dharma* and on the obligation to use the sword in its defence if evil men persist in attacking it.[24]

Another eighteenth-century example of the standard form is Sukha Singh's *Gur-bilās Dasvīn Pātśāhī*, followed in the first half of the nineteenth century by Ratan Singh Bhangu's *Prāchīn Panth Prakāś*. Most of the gur-bilas literature actually belongs to the nineteenth century, sustaining through to the twentieth century a style and an interpretation which took shape within the Khalsa during the struggles of its heroic period. Some of its products have been extensively mined as sources for Sikh history, commonly without due regard for the date of composition or for the interpretation which so graphically informs them.[25]

It is when due allowance is made for these features that they yield their principal contribution. Examples of gur-bilas literature, like the rahit-namas, should be read primarily as works which reflect an unfolding perception of the mission of Guru Gobind Singh and of the divinely appointed role of the Khalsa. It is certainly not safe to assume that a particular incident or doctrine can be attached to the historical Guru Gobind Singh simply because it is so recorded in any or all of these works. We can, however, use them in our attempt to trace the development of convictions and attitudes which find expression in such references.

23 See above, p. 35.

24 Surjit Singh Hans, 'Historical Analysis of Sikh Literature, AD 1500–1850' (unpub. Ph.D. thesis, Guru Nanak Dev University, Amritsar, 1980), fos. 371–82, 392. Id., 'Social Transformation and the Creative Imagination in Sikhism' in Sudhir Chandra (ed.), *Social Transformation and Creative Imagination* (New Delhi, 1984), 99–101.

25 W. H. McLeod, *The Sikhs: History, Religion and Society* (New York, 1989), chap. 6. Id. (trans.), *Textual Sources for the Study of Sikhism* (Manchester, 1984), 12.

A conspicuous example, one which concerns the fundamental belief structure of the Khalsa, is the doctrine of the eternal Guru. This doctrine, having emerged in the early Nanak-panth, is carried forward from the period of the personal Gurus into the eighteenth century and beyond. For Nanak the Guru was the 'voice' of Akal Purakh, mystically uttered within the inner being of the individual believer. Because Nanak comprehended the divine message and relayed it to his Sikhs, he became for them an actual embodiment of the eternal Guru. This same spirit passed onwards from each of the personal Gurus to his successor as a single flame passes from one torch to another. Guru Gobind Singh, however, died without a successor.[26] What happened thereafter to the eternal Guru?

The orthodox doctrine affirms that Guru Gobind Singh, immediately prior to his death in 1708, declared that after he had gone there would be no successor as personal Guru. The eternal Guru would remain with his followers, mystically present in the sacred scripture and in the gathered community. The scripture thus becomes the Guru Granth and the assembled community becomes the Guru Panth.

Two early sources are commonly cited in support of the traditional doctrine and its formal delivery by Guru Gobind Singh. The first is Sainapati's *Gur Sobhā*.

> On an earlier occasion the Guru had been approached by his Sikhs and had been asked what form the [eternal] Guru would assume [after he had departed this earthly life]. He had replied that it would be the Khalsa. 'The Khalsa is now the focus of all my hopes and desires,' he had declared. 'Upon the Khalsa which I have created I shall bestow the succession. The Khalsa is my physical form and I am one with the Khalsa. To all eternity I shall be manifest in the Khalsa. They whose hearts are purged of falsehood will be known as the true Khalsa; and the Khalsa, freed from error and illusion, will be my true Guru.
>
> 'And my true Guru, boundless and infinite, is the eternal Word, the Word of wisdom which the devout contemplate in their hearts, the Word which brings ineffable peace to all who utter it, the Word which is wisdom immeasurably unfolded, the Word which none may ever describe. This is the light which is given to you, the refuge of all who inhabit the world, and the abode of all who renounce it.'[27]

The second source is the *Praśan-uttar* attributed to Nand Lal.

[26] By the time of Gobind Singh the successor as Guru was always chosen from amongst the male lineage in the Guru's own family, normally the eldest son of the deceased Guru. All four of Guru Gobind Singh's sons had predeceased him.

[27] Sainapati, *Srī Gur Sobhā*, 8: 40–3. Ganda Singh edition, pp. 128–9.

The Guru speaks: 'Listen attentively, Nand Lal, and I shall explain. I am manifested in three ways: the formless or invisible (*nirguṇ*), the material or visible (*sarguṇ*), and the divine Word (*gur-śabad*) . . . The second is the sacred scripture, the Granth. This you must accept as an actual part of me, treating its letters as the hairs of my body. This truly is so.

'Sikhs who wish to see the Guru will do so when they come to the Granth. He who is wise will bathe at dawn and humbly approach the sacred scripture. Come with reverence and sit in my presence. Humbly bow and hear the words of the Guru Granth. Hear them with affection and alert attention. Hear the Guru's Word of wisdom and read it that others may also hear. He who wishes to converse with me should read or hear the Granth and reflect on what it says. He who wishes to hear any words should attentively read or hear the Granth. Acknowledge the Granth as my visible presence, rejecting the notion that it is other than me.

'The Sikh himself is the third form which I take, that Sikh who is forever heedful of the words of sacred scripture (*gurbāṇī*). He who loves and trusts the Word of the Guru is himself an ever-present manifestation of the Guru. Such a Sikh is the one who hears the Guru's words of wisdom and reads them so that others may hear. It is he who attentively recites both *Japjī* and *Jāp*, who regularly visits the gurdwara, and who strictly avoids adulterous liaisons. The Gursikh who is faithful in serving his Master will find himself cleansed from all sense of self-dependence. He who is scrupulous in performing these obligations is the Sikh in whom I am made manifest.'[28]

Both sources provide clear statements of the orthodox doctrine, or at least of versions which can be construed as consonant with the standard *Gurū Granth*/*Gurū Panth* interpretation. The doctrine is, moreover, one which is easily related to elements in the earlier Nanak-panth which plainly foreshadow it. Each personal Guru incarnated the eternal Guru, and, because the sacred volume contains the compositions (*bāṇī*) of the Gurus, it implicitly represents the spirit which each embodied. Guru Ram Das explicitly identifies *bāṇī* and *gurū*,[29] and from this declaration it is but a short step to the formulated doctrine of the scriptural Guru (the *Gurū Granth*). In like manner the *Gurū Panth* doctrine is foreshadowed in the early Gurus' emphasis on the divine quality of a satsang or an assembly of true believers. A couplet from Bhai Gurdas points forward to the developed doctrine:

> He who receives the Guru's teachings must live a life which reflects their truth.

[28] Piara Singh Padam (samp.), *Rahit-nāme*, pp. 42–3.
[29] Guru Ram Das, *Naṭ Aṣṭapadī* 4(5), Adi Granth, p. 982.

> Let him take his place in the company of the faithful, absorbing their virtue in the presence of the Word.[30]

The line of doctrinal development is logical and clear, easily accommodating the final version within the established tradition of the Nanak-panth.[31]

There remain important questions, however, and these questions require answers before the process can be fully understood or its place within the Khalsa tradition satisfactorily determined. The first question concerns the point in time at which the dual doctrine actually crystallized. Was it immediately prior to the tenth Guru's death or did it occur later? Secondly, is the *Gurū Granth* doctrine confined to the Adi Granth (a common assumption today) or does it also include the Dasam Granth? Thirdly, is the expression *Gurū Panth* synonymous with *Gurū Khālsā* or does it possess a wider application?

We can dispose of the second of these questions summarily, for there appears to be no doubt concerning either the answer or its practical effect. As far as the eighteenth-century Khalsa was concerned, the Dasam Granth was as much a part of the canon as the Adi Granth.[32] The Dasam Granth breathes a militant spirit which matches that of the eighteenth-century Khalsa. Its influence on Khalsa ideals is well illustrated by portions of the *Chaupā Singh Rahit-nāmā* and by the strong fascination exercised within the eighteenth-century Panth by the Devi cult.[33]

The answer to the first question is rather more complex. It depends to some extent on the dating of *Gur Sobhā*, which, as we noted earlier, may be either 1711 or 1745.[34] If the former is correct, and if the relevant passage is demonstrably a part of the original text, the traditional connection with Guru Gobind Singh will be very difficult to dispute. It remains, however, one of the points on which we are compelled to suspend judgement in the meantime. What we can affirm with certainty is that the *Gurū Panth* doctrine performed a significant service to the Khalsa during the middle decades of the eighteenth century. It is also evident that a significant phase in the crystallizing process belongs to this period, a phase which produced a practical expression of the doctrine well suited to the contemporary needs of the Khalsa.

During the period of persecution and guerrilla warfare which followed

[30] *Vārān Bhāī Gurdās* 3: 9. [31] McLeod, *Early Sikh Tradition*, p. 262.

[32] John Malcolm, 'Sketch of the Sikhs', *Asiatick Researches*, xi (Calcutta, 1810), 221, 255, 281. For the Dasam Granth, see McLeod, *The Sikhs*, chap. 6.

[33] McLeod (trans.), *The Chaupā Singh Rahit-nāmā*, pp. 47, 172–3.

[34] See above, p. 35.

the execution of Banda, the Khalsa faced serious problems of co-ordinated strategy and organization. These derived partly from the absence of a single leader and partly from the scattering of Khalsa forces by its stronger enemies. For more than a decade following 1733 Kapur Singh was recognized as leader of the Khalsa, but the problem of consolidating its forces persisted and other individuals continued to function as commanders of separate *jathā*s or warrior bands.[35]

Towards the middle of the century many of the jathas were consolidated into twelve groups of varying size, each known as a *miṣl*. Although this development marked a significant strengthening of Khalsa power, it also conferred a greater influence on individual misl commanders. Men such as Jassa Singh Ahluwalia and Jai Singh Kanaihya led independent armies. All acknowledged a common Khalsa loyalty and all confronted the same foe, but the possibilities of fraternal conflict were ever present and an effective understanding was needed if the various jathas and misls were to overcome its dangers.[36]

A significant part of the answer was supplied by the doctrine of the Guru Panth. It was one thing to agree that Khalsa spells brotherhood and that the scattered groups should accept membership in a single united army, the Dal Khalsa. It was quite another matter to sustain a degree of unity sufficient to convert a pious ideal into a practical reality. The doctrine of the Guru Panth contributed significantly to the solving of this problem in that the leaders of the various groups believed that their meetings were held in the presence of the Guru and that decisions reached under such circumstances represented the will of the Guru.[37]

This conviction was defined in precise terms as the doctrine of the gurumata, or 'the intention of the Guru'. During the period of the Afghan invasions there developed the practice of holding biannual assemblies of the Sarbat Khalsa (the 'Entire Khalsa') before Akal Takhat in Amritsar. These meetings were held in the presence of the Guru Granth Sahib and a formal decision reached after debate by the leaders of the misls was called a gurumata. As such it was held to represent the will of the eternal Guru and a refusal to accept any such resolution constituted rebellion against the Guru himself.[38]

The belief was particularly effective during the years covered by the Afghan invasions, a period marked by increasing Khalsa strength but not

[35] Surjit Singh Gandhi, *The Struggle of the Sikhs for Sovereignty* (Delhi, 1980), 66–8.

[36] Khushwant Singh, *A History of the Sikhs*, i. 131–3.

[37] Teja Singh and Ganda Singh, *A Short History of the Sikhs*, pp. 111–12.

[38] J. S. Grewal, 'The Rule of Law and Sikh Thought', *Journal of Sikh Studies*, 11/2 (Aug. 1984), 137.

by total security. As the Afghan threat receded and individual misls acquired a more secure power, the doctrine weakened and disagreement within the Khalsa became more acute. Its practical effect came to an end with the triumph of Ranjit Singh. Having progressively subdued the other sardars (the misl chieftains), Ranjit Singh was eventually proclaimed Maharaja of the Punjab in 1801 and a single administration was established over most of the area previously divided amongst the various chieftains. Ranjit Singh continued to rule in the name of the Khalsa, but gatherings of the Sarbat Khalsa were unlikely to meet with his approval.[39] The practice of holding such assemblies was allowed to lapse and the doctrine of the Guru Panth gradually atrophied. As it declined, the doctrine of the Guru Granth assumed a larger prominence, acquiring an influence which it retains to the present day.

One other eighteenth-century result of the dual doctrine concerns the development of the gurdwara as an institution. During the period of the Nanak-panth the Guru's followers assembled for kirtan in rooms or buildings called dharamsalas.[40] This practice continued throughout the eighteenth century and by the end of the century the place of assembly was still called a dharamsala.[41] Meanwhile, however, there had developed the custom of erecting shrines called gurdwaras. These evidently marked locations associated with particular events in the lives of individual Gurus, places to which a Sikh might make a pious pilgrimage.[42]

Eventually this latter usage was enlarged to include the dharamsala and it seems likely that it was the doctrine of the eternal Guru which produced the change.[43] It may have been because the sangat which gathered in a dharamsala represented the corporate Guru, or it may have resulted from the practice of installing copies of the sacred scripture (the Guru Granth) in the room which served as a dharamsala. The former is perhaps the more likely, for copies of the sacred scripture would have been too expensive for many sangats until the printing press eventually made them obtainable. If the latter is the dominant reason it presumably

[39] Narendra Krishna Sinha, *Ranjit Singh* (Calcutta, 1951), 137. See also J. S. Grewal, *The Reign of Maharaja Ranjit Singh* (Patiala, 1981), esp. pp. 4–5.

[40] McLeod, *Early Sikh Tradition*, pp. 261–2.

[41] Malcolm, 'Sketch of the Sikhs', p. 278.

[42] McLeod (trans.), *The Chaupā Siṅgh Rahit-nāmā*, injunctions 111 and 120, pp. 159, 160. The word *gurduārā* (anglicized as 'gurdwara') can be translated either as 'by means of the Guru['s grace]' or as 'the Guru's door'.

[43] The use of the term in the *Praśan-uttar* attributed to Nand Lal suggests a later period in that it implies a much wider range of buildings than would have been covered by the early use of *gurduārā*. Piara Singh Padam (samp.), *Rahit-nāme*, p. 43.

means that the shift from dharamsala to gurdwara is comparatively recent.

There still remains the question of whether *Gurū Panth* and *Gurū Khālsā* are synonymous. In other words, is the voice of the eternal Guru uttered only in assemblies of the Sarbat Khalsa, or was it also accessible to Nanak-panthi sangats which lacked a Khalsa affiliation? There appears to be no doubt that Nanak-panthi sangats affirmed the doctrine and assumed the mystical presence of the Guru. This was certainly the view of the person responsible for the *B40 Janam-sākhī*: 'The sangat is the Court of the Supreme Guru and speaks as His voice. In your midst abides the supreme Guru and if any favour be asked of you [the sangat], it can be granted.'[44]

This response from the year 1733 is explicit, but it was not necessarily matched by assumptions developing within the Khalsa. We are confronted yet again by the persistent problem of the relationship between the Khalsa on the one hand and the Sahaj-dhari or Nanak-panthi Sikh on the other. During the course of the eighteenth century the difference became increasingly marked as the Khalsa tradition consolidated and political power passed into Khalsa hands. By the end of the century the Khalsa ideal was clearly dominant and to some foreign observers it seemed that all Sikhs were in fact Sikhs of the Khalsa.

Foreign observers provide us with some interesting and helpful commentaries on Sikh identity late in the eighteenth century and during the early years of the nineteenth. For the most part they seem to have been dependent on what they actually saw, and most of them were evidently unaware of the existence of Sikhs other than those who conspicuously displayed the symbols of the Khalsa tradition. The Sikhs whom they recognized were pre-eminently the troops of the Khalsa armies, flamboyant soldiers whom they admired for their riding skills and endurance while despising (or fearing) them for their loud voices and uncouth behaviour. Several such accounts derive from the last quarter of the eighteenth century and the first decade of the nineteenth, and together they present a reasonably consistent view of the Khalsa, as foreigners were able to observe it during that period. Although it was a partial view, based on an imperfect perception, it remains a useful one.[45]

[44] McLeod (trans.), *The B40 Janam-sākhī*, p. 241. Cf. also pp. 183, 198, 208.

[45] For these observers and their reports see Ganda Singh (ed.), *Early European Accounts of the Sikhs* (Calcutta, 1962). Ganda Singh's collection includes reports by Polier (1776 and *c.*1780), Wilkins (1781), Forster (1783), Browne (1787), Griffiths (1794), and Franklin (1803).

The various observations reported by these early European visitors can be consolidated as follows. The Sikhs whom they encountered late in the eighteenth century were impressive soldiers, particularly as horsemen.[46] Although the Sikhs admitted converts from all castes,[47] most were Jats[48] and very few came from Muslim origins (unless converted by force).[49] Following an initiation ceremony they refrained from cutting their hair,[50] wore an iron bangle on the wrist,[51] and clad themselves in dark-blue clothing with a prominent turban.[52] Smoking the hookah was strictly avoided, but not the free use of spirits, opium, and bhang.[53] They ate meat (including pork), but never touched beef.[54] A common utterance, frequently repeated, was 'Vah-gourou' (*Vāhigurū*).[55] The Swiss observer Colonel Polier notes the traditional antipathy towards Muslims;[56] and John Griffiths mentions the Khalsa assemblies held biannually in Amritsar, with the Guru Granth Sahib present on such occasions.[57]

One other passing reference which deserves to be noted is Polier's inclusion of 'a pair of blue drawers' as one of the few garments typically worn by the Sikhs whom he observed.[58] This, together with the uncut hair (*kes*) and bangle (*kaṛā*), brings us very close to the Five Ks, for we can probably assume the sword (*kirpān*) as clearly implicit in their emphasis on weaponry and the comb (*kaṅghā*) would be concealed in the conspicuous turbans which they noted. It seems, however, that no one drew their attention to the actual convention as such. This, together with the absence of clear eighteenth-century rahit-nama testimony, may indicate that at the end of the century the convention was still emergent rather than clearly defined.

The impression thus communicated by late-eighteenth-century observers is considerably strengthened by the most important of all these

46 Ganda Singh (ed.), *Early European Accounts of the Sikhs*, pp. 17, 25, 60, 81, 99.
47 Ibid. 18, 56, 83, 92, 100.
48 Ibid. 13, 56, 66. Griffiths and Franklin both drew specific attention to the connection which this feature established between Jats and Sikhs. Ibid. 88, 105.
49 Ibid. 59, 83.
50 Ibid. 18, 63, 65, 79, 92, 103–4.
51 Ibid. 18, 63, 65, 66, 79, 105. Franklin notes that the bangles (like weapons) may be gold, silver, brass, or iron 'according to the circumstances of the wearers'. Ibid. 104–5.
52 Ibid. 17, 63, 92, 100.
53 Ibid. 18, 63, 65, 79, 104.
54 Ibid. 63, 65, 92, 104.
55 Ibid. 63, 65, 73.
56 Ibid. 58–9.
57 Ibid. 91. Griffiths's reference to 'their Ghiruntejee' does not indicate whether the Granth was the Adi Granth, the Dasam Granth, or both.
58 Ibid. 93.

early European reports. In 1810 John Malcolm published his 'Sketch of the Sikhs', an account based on documents and information collected during a period spent in the Punjab in 1805.[59] Malcolm begins by describing Sikhs of the Khalsa as follows. 'The disciples of Govind were required to devote themselves to arms, always to have *steel* about them in some shape or other, to wear a blue dress, to allow their hair to grow, to exclaim when they met each other, *Wa! Guruji ka khalsah! Wa! Guruji ki futteh!*'[60] In the extended description which follows he largely confirms the reports of his earlier contemporaries as far as the outward identity of the Khalsa Sikh was concerned.[61] There are, however, two issues noted by Malcolm which deserve particular attention. One returns us to continuing distinctions within the Panth. The other concerns an evident awareness that Sikhs of the Khalsa were perceived as separate and distinct from Hindus.

The first of these contributions develops a point which had been mentioned in passing by his predecessor George Forster. In a letter written soon after his journey through the Punjab in 1783, Forster had briefly noted that all Sikhs were not 'Sings' of the 'military order'. There were also others, known as 'Khualasah Sikhs', who did not observe the outward forms of the Khalsa.[62] Malcolm deals with the distinction in greater detail. There are, he observes, several varieties of Sikhs, two of which deserve particular notice. First, and most assuredly foremost, there are the Khalsa Sikhs, easily identified by any casual observer. 'The character of the *Sikhs*, or rather *Sinhs*, which is the name by which the followers of Guru Govind, who are all devoted to arms, are distinguished, is very marked.'[63] This identity, he makes clear, is shared by 'the *Sikh* merchant, or cultivator of the soil, if he is a *Sinh*', not merely by the

[59] John Malcolm published his lengthy 'Sketch of the Sikhs' in 1810 in *Asiatick Researches*, xi. 197–292 (*Asiatick Researches: or Transactions of the Society Instituted in Bengal for enquiring into the History and Antiquities, the Arts, Sciences, and Literature of Asia*, Calcutta). It was subsequently issued as Lieutenant-Colonel Malcolm, *Sketch of the Sikhs, a Singular Nation, who inhabit the Provinces of the Penjab, Situated between the Rivers Jumna and Indus* (John Murray, London, 1812). All subsequent references to 'Sketch of the Sikhs' are from the 1810 edition in *Asiatick Researches*.

[60] Malcolm, 'Sketch of the Sikhs', p. 220.

[61] Malcolm describes the manner in which the Khalsa initiation was carried out. The initiant is required to 'allow his hair to grow', but the Five Ks (*pañj kakke*) are not mentioned. Instead 'five weapons' are presented to him (a sword, a firelock, a bow and arrow, and a pike). He is enjoined to avoid the company of 'men of five sects', though Malcolm's naming of them cannot be correct. Ibid. 285–7.

[62] George D. Forster, *A Journey from Bengal to England* (London, 1798), i. 266n, 268–9. The text presented by Ganda Singh omits this distinction.

[63] Malcolm, 'Sketch of the Sikhs', p. 259.

soldiers who so conspicuously paraded it.[64] The 'followers of Guru Govind' or Khalsa Sikhs are clearly distinguished by Malcolm from those whom he variously calls 'followers of Nanac' or 'Khalasa Sikhs' ('free' Sikhs, as opposed to those who abide by the Khalsa discipline).[65] The Khalasa Sikhs (Forster's 'Khualasah Sikhs') are of course, the Sahajdharis. Malcolm's prejudices show when he proceeds to describe them.

> Their character differs widely from that of the *Sinhs*. Full of intrigue, pliant, versatile and insinuating, they have all the art of the lower classes of *Hindus*, who are usually employed in transacting business; from whom, indeed, as they have no distinction of dress, it is difficult to distinguish them.[66]

We may ignore the insult, but not the important reference to the lack of visible identity.

Malcolm's other important contribution follows from his observations on caste. Sikhs, he acknowledges, observe routine caste distinctions with regard to both marriage and dining (except at gatherings of the Sarbat Khalsa). In many instances, he notes, their caste-fellows regard them simply as 'Hindus that have joined a political association' and continue to have customary dealings with them.[67] This, he continues, was not in accordance with the intention of Guru Gobind Singh. The tenth Guru sought to demolish all distinctions of caste, thereby separating Sikhs from Hindus. The Guru's intention found expression in the initiation ceremony and (he claims) those who understand the meaning of that ceremony will appreciate that 'Guru Govind has separated his followers for ever from the Hindus'.[68]

This Khalsa sense of separation from Hindu society is confirmed by Ratan Singh Bhangu, author of *Prāchīn Panth Prakāś* and contemporary with Malcolm. Ratan Singh's argument runs as follows. Guru Gobind

[64] Ibid. 260.

[65] Ibid. 257, 260–1. In spite of the apparent similarity when written in the roman script, *khalāsā* and *khālsā* are two different words. The former had evidently dropped out of use by the middle of the nineteenth century. J. D. Cunningham, *A History of the Sikhs* (1st edn., London, 1849; rev. edn., Oxford, 1918), 90 n. Malcolm also notes the existence of Acalis, Shahids, Nirmalas, and Nanac Pautras ('Sketch of the Sikhs', pp. 261–2). The Acalis (Akalis) and Shahids are easily identified as particularly enthusiastic Khalsas; and the Nirmalas constituted an order of scholar Sikhs. The 'Nanac Pautra' are the 'descendants of Nanac' and thus presumably the same as the 'Nanac Putrah' (ibid. 201). Presumably they are thus to be identified as the Bedi descendants of Guru Nanak, a familial group which received veneration because of its distinguished origins (correctly descended from Lakhmi Das). Alternatively they are a variety of Khalasa Sikhs. Malcolm also refers to 'the sect of Udasi', founded by Nanak's son Dherm Chand (*recte* Siri Chand). Ibid. 200–1.

[66] Ibid. 261.

[67] Ibid. 262–3.

[68] Ibid. 288. See also pp. 269–70.

Singh, having vowed to destroy Muslim power, was confronted by the manifest weakness of his cowardly followers. The root of the problem, he decided, was the kind of meek initiation which they received as entrants to the Panth. In its place he would introduce the baptism of the sword, imbuing his followers with a spirit which would strike fear in the hearts of all whom they assailed. Each would take up his sword and each would adopt the martial name of Singh. The frontal mark, the sacred thread, and the despised dhoti would all be cast aside. Together the members of the recreated Panth would constitute a single caste, all eating from the same dish and all united in the same resolve.[69]

As we move into the nineteenth century we are left with the distinct impression of an ascendant Khalsa and of a Rahit approaching the form familiar to the twentieth century. It is true that the Five Ks are absent and indeed will still be absent in a formalized sense half a century later. The old enmity towards Muslims still survived, moreover, but for some at least another clear line of demarcation had been drawn. This new line was not one which distinguished Hindu from Sikh in terms which most would necessarily accept. It distinguished the Khalsa from all who adhered to Hindu forms, a distinction which set the Sahaj-dhari Sikh apart from the Khalsa and identified him with those whom everyone recognized as Hindu.

Others saw it differently. There were 'Sikhs of Nanac' and there were 'Sikhs of Govind', both members of the same Panth though differing in their understanding of what constituted true loyalty. One portion of the Panth had entered a powerful claim to orthodoxy and had evidently succeeded in convincing some observers of the justice of their claim. Others were less sure. Although the balance had swung strongly in one direction, the problem of defining the Panth still remained.

[69] Ratan Singh Bhangu, *Prāchīn Panth Prakāś* 16. Vir Singh edn. (Amritsar, 1962), 40–2.

5

The Singh Sabha Reformation

AT THE beginning of the nineteenth century stands the youthful Ranjit Singh, conqueror of Lahore and soon to be invested with the title of Maharaja. At its end we find the Singh Sabha movement approaching the peak of its influence. During the course of the century the Panth had experienced the triumphs of Ranjit Singh, the rapid decline of his successors, and defeat in two wars with the British. The conclusion of the second Anglo-Sikh War was followed by the final annexation of the Punjab in 1849 and by confident British forecasts of the imminent dissolution of the Panth.

The first Singh Sabha, or 'Singh Society', was established in 1873 and for several decades thereafter its reformist leaders preached reform and regeneration of the Khalsa. Acknowledging that the Panth was indeed under threat, they devised a programme of reform designed to restore the Khalsa traditions and loyalties which seemed so plainly to be eroding. Their success was impressive. By the time the movement began to fade early in the twentieth century a persuasive interpretation of Sikh tradition had been fashioned and the Khalsa identity had been defined with a precision never before achieved.[1]

When Ranjit Singh became Maharaja of the Punjab in 1801 it must have seemed to many a fulfilment of the *rāj karegā khālsā* prophecy, a final vindication of the eighteenth-century belief that the Khalsa would rule. That, certainly, has been the interpretation placed on those famous words by some twentieth-century Sikhs and most, it seems, look back on the four decades of Ranjit Singh's rule as something resembling a golden age. Ever since he achieved the conquest of the Punjab, Ranjit Singh has been regarded as a folk-hero, as one who embodied in his person and in his administration the ideals for which the Khalsa had fought during the preceding century.[2]

Inevitably there has developed a mythology associated with Ranjit Singh and, as with all such mythologies, its features reflect the

[1] Harbans Singh, *The Heritage of the Sikhs* (2nd rev. edn., New Delhi, 1983), 233, 259.
[2] Khushwant Singh, *A History of the Sikhs*, i (Princeton, 1963), 291–6.

aspirations of those for whom he had acquired symbolic significance. It is popularly believed, for example, that, although he ruled in the name of the Khalsa, he did so in a truly secular spirit. In this context 'secular' must be construed in its modern Indian sense as 'respecting all religions' and as such it is a prominent feature of the reputation which the late twentieth century attaches to Ranjit Singh.[3] If European observers are to be believed, the administration of Ranjit Singh was informed by the spirit and attitudes of the eighteenth century.[4] Individual Muslims were employed as state servants (some of them with considerable authority) but the eighteenth-century hostility towards Muslims had not been wholly exorcised from all areas of government nor from Sikh society in general.

It is upon the Khalsa identity of the administration that the emphasis must be laid, with the significant qualification that Ranjit Singh placed strict limitations on the earlier ideal of popular participation in decision-making. Loyal sardars were duly rewarded, but assemblies of the Sarbat Khalsa were no longer held and the institution of the gurumata was effectively suppressed. Substantial largesse was, however, bestowed on prominent Sikh shrines and at the Maharaja's court conspicuous respect was paid to the traditions of the Khalsa. Coinage bore the image of Guru Nanak, the administration was known as *Sarkār Khālsājī*, and the royal court itself was called *Darbār Khālsājī*.[5] There could be no doubting the importance attached to the reputation of the Khalsa or to the individual identity associated with it. In this sense the state administered by Ranjit Singh was an authentic extension of eighteenth-century Khalsa ideals.

This did not mean, however, that all Sikhs were satisfied with the attitudes and behaviour generated by military success or political patronage. From the period of Ranjit Singh date two reform movements which still command significant followings today. These are the original Nirankaris and the group variously known as Namdharis or as Kukas. Both are strictly sects, emerging within the larger Panth during the same period and in the same part of the Maharaja's domains. Both, moreover,

[3] Surinder Singh Johar, for example, has entitled his study of Maharaja Ranjit Singh *The Secular Maharaja* (Delhi, 1985).

[4] John Malcolm, 'Sketch of the Sikhs', *Asiatick Researches*, xi (Calcutta, 1810), 256–7. 'A Tour to Lahore (in 1808)' by an officer of the Bengal Army, *Asiatic Annual Register*, vol. xi for 1809, repr. in *The Panjab Past and Present*, 1/1 (Apr. 1967), 120. Alexander Burnes, *Travels into Bokhara* (London, 1834), iii. 118–19. G. T. Vigne, *Travels in Kashmir &c* (London, 1842), i. 184. Charles Masson, *Narratives of Various Journeys in Balochistan, Afghanistan, and the Panjab* (London, 1842), i. 409–10. Charles von Hugel, *Travels in Kashmir and Punjab* (London, 1845), 190–1, 238.

[5] Khushwant Singh, *A History of the Sikhs*, i. 201.

stand under much the same condemnation as far as strictly orthodox Sikhs are concerned, for each acknowledges a continuing line of Gurus. Because of these obvious similarities the two movements are commonly mentioned in the same breath, a convention which may suggest that their resemblances are more important than their differences. Any such impression is wholly misleading, particularly in the context of a discussion concerning the nineteenth-century development of Sikh identity.[6]

Nirankaris trace their origins as a distinctive group to Baba Dayal Das, a Khatri shopkeeper of Rawalpindi. Baba Dayal's following came to be known as Nirankaris because of the emphasis which he laid on the formless quality (*nirankār*) of Akal Purakh, the attribute which contrasted so strongly with the contemporary understanding of piety and religious duty. External observance, whether idol worship or visible symbols, could never achieve liberation. Only by returning to Nanak's exclusive stress on the interior discipline of *nām simaraṇ* could this be attained.

Baba Dayal was not a member of the Khalsa, nor were most of his early followers. The sect was strictly a Nanak-panthi movement, one which preached a return to the original teachings of Nanak without significant reference to the later traditions of the Khalsa. As a result of the Singh Sabha campaign later in the century, many Nirankaris did eventually adopt the Khalsa insignia. The Nirankari tradition nevertheless retained its Nanak-panthi philosophy and it continued to attract a substantial number of adherents who identified as Sahaj-dhari Sikhs, as Hindus, or as both.[7]

Although the Namdhari movement started in much the same way, it significantly changed its complexion under its second Guru. The founder was Balak Singh of Hazro and, like Baba Dayal, he lived his life in the

[6] The Nirankaris and Namdharis are covered in all the standard histories. See Harbans Singh, *The Heritage of the Sikhs*, chap. xvii; and W. H. McLeod (trans.), *Textual Sources for the Study of Sikhism* (Manchester, 1984), 13–14, 121–31. There are few studies concerning only the Nirankaris. See John C. B. Webster, *The Nirankari Sikhs* (Delhi, 1979). The Namdharis, or Kukas, have been rather better treated. See Fauja Singh Bajwa, *Kuka Movement* (Delhi, 1965). There are also five volumes of documents. Three of these have been edited by Nahar Singh under the title *Gooroo Ram Singh and the Kuka Sikhs* (New Delhi and Sri Jiwan Nagar, 1965–6); and two of them by Jaswinder Singh as *Kukas of Note in the Punjab* (Sri Bhaini Sahib, 1985) and *Kuka Movement* (New Delhi, 1985). See also the short study by Gurmit Singh, *Sant Khalsa* (Sirsa, 1978). For a brief account, see W. H. McLeod, 'The Kukas: A Millenarian Sect of the Punjab', in G. A. Wood and P. S. O'Connor, *W. P. Morrell: A Tribute* (Dunedin, 1973), 85–103; repr. in *The Panjab Past and Present*, 13/1 (Apr. 1979), 164–79.

[7] Webster, *The Nirankari Sikhs*, pp. 9–11, 31–2.

north-western portion of the Punjab. His successor, in contrast, was from the village of Bhaini Raian in Ludhiana District. Ram Singh, having succeeded Balak Singh, returned to his native village, and it was within Ludhiana District and adjacent areas that the new sect developed its principal following. Its adherents were from castes with a strong Khalsa affiliation (notably artisans and poorer Jats) and predictably the Namdhari sect assumed a self-conscious Khalsa identity termed *Sant Khālsā*. Like their Nirankari contemporaries, Balak Singh and Ram Singh believed that there had been a grievous corrupting of Sikh practice during the period of the Sikh kingdom. The two responses were, however, widely divergent. Whereas one sought a return to pristine Nanak-panthi principles, the other preached a restored and regenerated Khalsa.[8]

The stress which is characteristically laid on the emergence of these two movements can easily suggest that the authentic spirit of the Khalsa had indeed dwindled during the later years of political power. This, moreover, was to be a part of the message of the Singh Sabha movement, an interpretation of the Panth's history which endeavoured to explain the perceived decay of the mid-nineteenth century by blaming the insidious influence of political strength and material affluence.[9] Like so much of the Singh Sabha message, it is an interpretation which needs to be carefully scrutinized before it is accepted. For the Singh Sabha reformers it was an important interpretation, one which supplied a major link in the historiographical chain which they fashioned, and as such it contributed to the justification which they offered in defence of their proposed reforms. A critical scrutiny suggests that their emphasis on growing decadence was considerably exaggerated. Decadence may well have been a feature of the royal durbar after the death of Ranjit Singh. It was not necessarily a feature of Khalsa practice in general.[10]

A theory of mid-century decline and decadence was congenial to the Singh Sabha reformers because their insistence on reform was based on the belief that their own version of Khalsa doctrine derived from Guru Gobind Singh himself. Their view assumed that there had been a clear and detailed statement of the Khalsa duty during the lifetime of the tenth

[8] Gurmit Singh, *Sant Khalsa*, pp. 27–33.

[9] Harbans Singh, *The Heritage of the Sikhs*, p. 228.

[10] On the Singh Sabha in general (which, amongst much else, disputes the claim to decadence as grossly exaggerated), see Harjot Singh Oberoi, 'A World Reconstructed: Religion, Ritual and Community among the Sikhs, 1850–1909' (unpub. Ph.D. thesis, Australian National University, Canberra, 1987). For the discussion of alleged 'decadence', see esp. fos. 146–7.

Guru, and later practice which deviated from that statement represented ignorance or perversity.[11] The task of the reformer must thus be to purge excrescence and recover what had been lost.

As we have already seen, however, the Khalsa Rahit was in the process of evolution during the course of the eighteenth century and by modern standards it was still only partially formulated by the end of that century. The outward forms of the Khalsa tradition which emerged during the course of the eighteenth century seem to have undergone comparatively little change during the first half of the nineteenth. Gurdwaras evidently assumed a larger importance during the more settled conditions imposed by Sikh rule, but the kind of Khalsa Sikh whom Joseph Cunningham observed during the period 1838–46 seems very similar to those whom Malcolm and his predecessors had described at the turn of the century.

In describing the customs and 'distinctive usages of the Sikhs', Cunningham refers to the merging of castes, the Khalsa rite of initiation, 'devotion to steel' (swords in all cases and also bracelets in the case of those zealous soldiers, the Akalis), uncut hair, blue clothing, use of the name 'Singh', and a strict ban on smoking.[12] The *kachh* (which he describes as 'a kind of breeches' or, in the more modern style 'a sort of pantaloons') is, he observes, a garment of particular importance, clearly distinguishing Sikhs from Hindus.[13] The presence of the Guru was recognized in 'the *Granth* of Nanak' (that is, the Adi Granth) and in any gathering of five Sikhs.[14] Frequently one heard the exclamation 'Wah Guru', or perhaps the lengthened versions 'Wah! Guru ki Fat[e]h' and 'Wah! Guru ka Khalsa'.[15]

Cunningham also agrees with Malcolm in affirming that Sikhs should be regarded as 'different from other Indians', and that, in spite of obvious resemblances in language and everyday customs, this involves a clear distinction between Sikhs and Hindus.[16] He is, however, more emphatic than Malcolm in emphasizing the predominance of the Khalsa identity amongst Sikhs. Nanak-panthis are to be found scattered through the cities of India and there exist several Sikh sects, but 'the great development of the tenets of Guru Gobind has thrown other denominations into the shade'. Within the Punjab at least the Khalsa identity prevails amongst those who regard themselves as Sikhs.[17]

[11] Kanh Singh Nabha, *Gurmat sudhākar* (1st edn., Amritsar, 1901; rev. edn., Patiala, 1970), intro.

[12] J. D. Cunningham, *A History of the Sikhs* (1st edn., London, 1849; rev. edn., Oxford, 1918), 70–4, 110, 346–9.

[13] Ibid. 349.

[14] Ibid. 82.

[15] Ibid. 347.

[16] Ibid. 84–5.

[17] Ibid. 90n.

This perception is strongly supported by the Sikhs' own literature. The gur-bilas tradition extends well into the nineteenth century and at least two of its prominent contributors produced their major work during the final decade of the Sikh kingdom. The celebrated works of Santokh Singh were composed during the first half of the nineteenth century and *Sūraj Prakāś* (the work which includes his Khalsa coverage) appeared in 1844. Three years earlier that most notable of all Khalsa dissertations had been completed. This was Ratan Singh Bhangu's *Prāchīn Panth Prakāś*, a work which vigorously affirms the distinctive nature of the Khalsa identity and the claim that this was the identity which Guru Gobind Singh intended his followers to adopt.[18]

The tradition is one which extends across the years of 'decadence' and into the period of Singh Sabha reform. Gian Singh's *Panth Prakāś* was issued in 1880, and the final instalment of his *Tavarīkh Gurū Khālsā* did not appear until 1919. By the time *Tavarīkh Gurū Khālsā* was completed, the Rahit had acquired its modern form and the works of Gian Singh can appropriately be regarded as examples of the unfolding pattern of Rahit observance. They can also be regarded as examples of the sustained predominance of the Khalsa identity, extending through from the early eighteenth century to the early twentieth century and onwards to the present day.[19]

The nineteenth-century rahit-nama tradition evidently communicates the same message, though in terms which are rather more difficult to decode. A serious problem persists because the rahit-namas which were current during the middle decades of the nineteenth century cannot yet be firmly located with regard to either time or place of composition. Until their contexts are identified and understood, all such texts must be used with great caution.

[18] In 1809 (s. 1866) Ratan Singh Bhangu, at Sir David Ochterlony's request, had provided Captain Murray in Ludhiana with information concerning the Khalsa. This he published in verse in 1841 (s. 1898) as *Panth Prakāś*, later known as *Prāchīn Panth Prakāś* to distinguish it from Gian Singh's work of the same name. Ratan Singh came from a distinguished Khalsa lineage, being the grandson of Matab Singh Bhangu who killed Massa Ranghar for desecrating Harimandir Sahib in 1740. Kahn Singh Nabha, *Guruśabad ratanākar mahān koś* (2nd rev. edn., Patiala, 1960), 594–5. Koer Singh's *Gur-bilās Pātaśāhī 10* and Sohan's *Gur-bilās Chhevīn Pātaśāhī* both claim to be eighteenth-century works. It has, however, been shown that both belong to the early nineteenth century. S. S. Hans, 'Gurbilas Patshahi 10 and Gurbilas Chhevin Patshahi as Sources for Early Nineteenth Century Punjab History', in Fauja Singh and A. C. Arora (ed.), *Maharaja Ranjit Singh: Politics, Society and Economy* (Patiala, 1984), 50–5. Id., 'Social Transformation and the Creative Imagination in Sikhism', in Sudhir Chandra (ed.), *Social Transformation and Creative Imagination* (New Delhi, 1984), pp. 104–6.

[19] McLeod (trans.), *Textual Sources for the Study of Sikhism*, pp. 12–13.

The fact that certain rahit-namas were in use during those middle decades can nevertheless be accepted as significant, and it seems likely that two of the major rahit-namas were actually composed during this period. These are the *Prem Sumārg* and the *Sau Sākhīān*.[20] Meanwhile (as Cunningham notes) the brief works attributed to Nand Lal and Prahilad Singh were in current circulation and were evidently accepted as authentic statements of the Rahit.[21] The Khalsa which is portrayed in these texts is not yet the Khalsa envisaged by the Singh Sabha reformers, but the line of development is clear and likewise the dominant features of the Khalsa identity as described by these rahit-namas.

If this should suggest that all was well with the Khalsa during the middle decades of the nineteenth century, the view is one which, looking back, the adherents of the reformist Singh Sabha would vigorously deny. It must be clearly understood that we do not speak here of the Singh Sabha as such, for the Singh Sabha was soon to be divided.[22] Those who dominated the founding of the Amritsar branch in 1873 were predominantly conservative Sikhs (Sanatan Sikhs) and it is not these men who concern us at present. It is the reformers, more common in the Lahore society, who agreed in large measure with the British observers' comments on the manifold signs of Khalsa decay. They certainly did not accept the common British assumption that decay spelt imminent dissolution, but it did seem likely that such would eventually be the fate of the Panth if vigorous measures were not taken to resuscitate the Khalsa ideal and restore traditional loyalties.

To the Singh Sabha reformers (at least the more ardent of them) disloyalty and decay were evident at all levels of Sikh society. Even Maharaja Ranjit Singh had betrayed the pure faith in death, distributing the material treasures of the Khalsa to Brahmans in the evident hope that he would thereby earn eternal merit. The same Brahmans participated prominently in his funeral rites and at the actual cremation four of his wives, together with seven 'slave girls', committed suttee.[23] The Maharaja's death epitomized both the danger and its source. It marked a threatening reassertion of Hindu tradition, the very superstitions which

[20] See chap. 3, n. 17. McLeod, 'The Problem of the Panjabi *rahit-nāmā*s', in S. N. Mukherjee (ed.), *India: History and Thought* (Calcutta, 1982), pp. 116–17. Mohan Singh, *An Introduction to Punjabi Literature* (Amritsar, 1954), 121–30, effusively praises the contribution of the *Prem Sumārg*, though with reference to an earlier period.

[21] Cunningham, *A History of the Sikhs*, pp. 372–6.

[22] Harjot Singh Oberoi, 'A World Reconstructed: Religion, Ritual and Community among the Sikhs, 1850–1909' (unpub. Ph.D. thesis, Australian National University, Canberra, 1987), fos. 202ff. and esp. chap. 6.

[23] Khushwant Singh, *A History of the Sikhs*, i. 289–90.

the Gurus had so vigorously denounced. If further evidence of the danger should be required, one need do no more than visit a gurdwara and observe the 'Hinduized' ritual practised therein. Even the precincts of the Golden Temple itself were disfigured by the presence of Hindu idols.[24] How, in such circumstances, could one deny the urgent compelling need for drastic reform?

Another 'Hindu' practice which conspicuously disfigured the nineteenth-century Panth was the observance of caste, particularly in terms of the discrimination applied to outcastes. To the Singh Sabha reformers the intention of the Gurus with regard to caste was crystal clear. The Gurus had denounced it in word and deed, conferring on their followers a scripture which incorporated the message and customs which gave it practical expression. How else could one construe the custom of sangat and pangat, the mingling of all in the langar, or the common water (*amrit*) of the initiation ceremony? Now, however, Sikhs were marrying strictly according to caste, and, following caste prescriptions, they ate in the manner of Hindus. Outcastes were prohibited from entering many gurdwaras and the sacred karah prasad was preserved from their contamination.[25]

The beliefs and customs of the Panth's élite supplied numerous examples of decadence and dire decay. Village life provided many more. In the villages of the Punjab it was often impossible to distinguish a Sikh from a Hindu and this was not merely because the outward symbols of the Khalsa were so indifferently observed. Frequently it was because the villager was quite unaware of the essential difference between a Hindu and a Sikh, easily moving from one identity to another and promiscuously combining elements from both. Indeed, the villager who was meant to be a Sikh might well adopt beliefs and practices which manifestly derived from Muslim sources. Seeking favours at the tombs of Muslim pirs was merely one such example. How could people who worshipped Gugga Pir or Sakhi Sarwar be regarded as loyal Sikhs of the Khalsa?[26] How could men who so brazenly cut their hair or smoked the hookah be accepted as devout servants of the Guru.

The facts were plain for all to see. The solution was also obvious, at least for those who accepted Singh Sabha analysis of a reformist persuasion. The Panth must be purged of false beliefs and superstitions,

24 Harbans Singh, 'Origin of the Singh Sabha', in Harbans Singh and N. Gerald Barrier (eds.), *Punjab Past and Present: Essays in Honour of Dr Ganda Singh* (Patiala, 1976), 274.

25 Teja Singh, *Essays in Sikhism* (Lahore, 1944), 133.

26 Harjot Singh Oberoi, 'The Worship of Pir Sakhi Sarvar: Illness, Healing and Popular Culture in the Punjab', *Studies in History* NS 3/1 (1987), 50–3.

both Hindu or Muslim. Sikhs must be summoned to a genuine reaffirmation of their Khalsa loyalty.

One other element deserves to be noted before we survey the various interpretations of the Singh Sabha movement. This concerns the contribution of the Indian Army. The British had been impressed by the strength of the opposition which they encountered during the two Anglo-Sikh wars and, although they were initially suspicious of their defeated enemies, their attitude towards the Sikhs changed significantly as a result of the assistance which they received from Sikh princes during the Mutiny. Sikhs were easily accommodated within the British theory of the martial races of India and Sikh enlistment increased steeply. For the British, however, martial Sikhs meant Khalsa Sikhs, and all who were inducted into the Indian Army as Sikhs were required to maintain the external insignia of the Khalsa.[27] This policy and its effective enforcement provide a significant element in the debate concerning Sikh identity during the crucial half-century from 1875 to 1925. As we shall see, the intention of the British policy and more particularly its practical effect have been variously interpreted.

The first Singh Sabha, as we have already noted, was formed in 1873. Four Sikh students attending the Mission School in Amritsar had announced their intention of taking Christian baptism and this event was evidently the reason for a meeting convened in the city by a group of prominent Sikhs. The first meeting was followed by others and from these discussions there emerged the decision to found a society called the Singh Sabha. Titled gentry, affluent landowners, and noted scholars were conspicuous amongst its founders, and the objectives which they framed for their new association gave expression to their distinctive ideals. Particular emphasis was laid on the promotion of periodicals and other appropriate literature, the assumption being that those who needed to be influenced would be accessible through the printed word. British officers were invited to associate with the Sabha and matters relating to government were expressly excluded from its range of interests.[28] The first

[27] Khushwant Singh, *A History of the Sikhs*, ii (Princeton, 1966), 113. See also R. W. Falcon, *Handbook on the Sikhs for the Use of Regimental Officers* (Allahabad, 1896); and A. H. Bingley, *Sikhs* (Simla, 1899), esp. chap. v.

[28] Rajiv A. Kapur, *Sikh Separatism: The Politics of Faith* (London, 1986), 16–17. For excellent summaries of the Singh Sabha, see the recent works of N. Gerald Barrier: 'The Roots of Modern Sikhism', in *Aspects of Modern Sikhism* (Michigan Papers on Sikh Studies, No. 1; 1985), 1–12; 'Sikh Politics in British Punjab Prior to the Gurdwara Reform Movement', in J. D. O'Connell *et al.* (eds.), *Sikh History and Religion in the Twentieth Century* (Toronto, 1988), 159–90; 'The Singh Sabhas and the Evolution of Modern Sikhism, 1875–1925', in Robert Baird (ed.), *Religious Movements in Modern India* (New

Singh Sabha was an élite organization, very similar to the urban associations which were emerging in other parts of India but specifically concerned with issues affecting the Sikh Panth.

Although the Singh Sabha movement never lost its élite texture, the Amritsar originators soon found themselves challenged by more strident exponents of the newly fledged ideal. In 1879 a second Singh Sabha was founded in Lahore and, although the two societies devised similar charters, the Lahore group soon proved to be much the more aggressive. Whereas the Amritsar organization was dominated by princely and landed interests, the Singh Sabha in Lahore attracted intellectuals with a more radical approach to the Panth's problems. Prominent amongst them was Giani Dit Singh, an outcaste Sikh who vigorously promoted social reform and a return to the casteless ideal of the Khalsa. Most radical of all was the small but embarrassingly noisy Singh Sabha of Bhasaur, led by Teja Singh Overseer.[29]

Each of these Singh Sabhas (particularly Amritsar and Lahore) attracted satellites as new sabhas were formed in various towns and villages. One feature which, in a general sense, distinguished the principal constellations was the contrast in their respective attitudes towards Khalsa exclusiveness. Amritsar, influenced by the weighty presence of Baba Khem Singh Bedi, tended strongly to support the claims of Sahaj-dhari Sikhs to an honoured place within the Panth. Bhasaur, at the other extreme, was militantly fundamentalist. The Lahore group also adopted a strict line, but with a somewhat sweeter reason and a more restrained idiom. Eventually its view came to be accepted as orthodox. The Khalsa tradition was to be regarded as standard. Sahaj-dharis were to be accepted only as 'slow-adopters', aspiring to the full status of the baptized Amrit-dhari Sikh but not yet ready to take formal initiation.[30]

Those who represented the reformist sector of the Singh Sabha movement came to be known as the Tat Khalsa (the 'True Khalsa' or the 'Pure Khalsa'). Opposing them, and increasingly disadvantaged by the strength of Tat Khalsa ideals and determination, were the conservatives of the so-called Sanatan Khalsa. By the turn of the century the exponents of Tat Khalsa theory had asserted an effective claim to interpret the nature of tradition and to enunciate the approved pattern of Sikh

Delhi, forthcoming); 'The Sikhs and Punjab Politics, 1882–1922', in Paul Wallace and Surendra Chopra (ed.), *Political Dynamics of the Punjab* (Amritsar, 1981; 2nd edn., forthcoming); etc.

[29] N. Gerald Barrier, *The Sikhs and their Literature* (Delhi, 1970), pp. xxvi–xxvii.

[30] Teja Singh, *Essays in Sikhism*, p. 117. N. Gerald Barrier, 'The Singh Sabhas and the Evolution of Modern Sikhism, 1875–1925'.

behaviour. When we speak of the Singh Sabha movement, we normally refer to its Tat Khalsa sector. When we describe the historiography, doctrinal formulations, and social policy of the Singh Sabha, we invariably do so.[31]

Prominent amongst the Tat Khalsa reformers were scholars such as Bhai Kahn Singh of Nabha and the prolifically versatile writer Bhai Vir Singh. Closely associated with them was the Englishman M. A. Macauliffe.[32] Together with others who shared the same attitudes and concerns, these authors were responsible for moulding and recording a version of the Sikh tradition which remains dominant in intellectual circles to the present day. It is important to remember that, when we read literature dealing with the Sikh tradition, we are usually reading perceptions which have been refracted through a Tat Khalsa lens. The reminder is essential if we are to achieve genuine detachment in any analysis of Sikh history, doctrine, or behaviour. Repeatedly we must draw attention to the impressive success achieved by scholars and writers associated with the Singh Sabha movement, for only thus can we hope to disengage our own interpretations from their continuing influence.

These men were largely responsible for the first of the interpretations which we must note in connection with the Singh Sabha. Their understanding of the Sikh tradition in general and the role of the Singh Sabha in particular can be summarized as follows.

Although Guru Nanak was born a Hindu, he separated his followers from Hindu society by requiring them to renounce caste. This intention

[31] A detailed analysis of the origin, nature, and spread of Tat Khalsa beliefs is given by Harjot Singh Oberoi, 'A World Reconstructed', chaps. 6–7. The thesis brings out very clearly the critical differences between the two principal groups within the Singh Sabha. The conclusion on fo. 307 deserves to be noted. See also id., 'From Ritual to Counter-ritual: Rethinking the Hindu-Sikh Question, 1884–1915', in J. D. O'Connell *et al.* (eds.), *Sikh History and Religion in the Twentieth Century*, pp. 136–58. The distinction is also clearly noted by N. Gerald Barrier in 'The Singh Sabhas and the Evolution of Modern Sikhism, 1875–1925'. In his 'The Sikhs and Punjab Politics, 1882–1922' it is identified as the 'Lahore or Tat Khalsa . . . message'. The other works of Harjot Singh Oberoi also deserve to be noted, in particular his 'Bhais, Babas and Gyanis: Traditional Intellectuals in Nineteenth Century Punjab', *Studies in History*, 2/2 (1980), 33–62 (a study of the Amritsar Singh Sabha leadership); and 'A Historical and Bibliographical Reconstruction of the Singh Sabha in Nineteenth Century Punjab', *Journal of Sikh Studies*, 10/3 (Aug. 1983), 108–30. The second of these refers to the principal differences distinguishing Sanatan and Tat Khalsa Sikhs on pp. 116–17.

[32] Sukhjit Kaur, *Bhāī Kāhn Siṅgh Nābhā te unhān diān rachanāvān* (Patiala, n.d.). Harbans Singh, *Bhai Vir Singh* (New Delhi, 1972), Id., 'English Translation of the Sikh Scripture: An Arduous Mission of a Punjab Civilian', in K. S. Bedi and S. S. Bal (eds.), *Essays on History, Literature, Art and Culture Presented to Dr M. S. Randhawa* (New Delhi, 1970), 139–44.

was expressly stated by Guru Arjan in the words 'We are neither Hindu nor Muslim',[33] and definitively confirmed by Guru Gobind Singh with the founding of the Khalsa. By establishing the Khalsa the tenth Guru bestowed on his followers a particular insignia (the Five Ks) and required them to observe a distinctive way of life. Admission to the recreated Panth was by initiation (the baptismal ceremony of *amrit sanskār*). All loyal followers of the Guru were expected to accept initiation and in so doing they were required to acknowledge the obligations of the Rahit.

The decades which followed the inauguration of the Khalsa brought a time of trial. Some faced the cruelty and fierce persecution with courage and determined loyalty, embracing martyrdom rather than betray their faith. Others, weaker in commitment, fell by the wayside. Eventually victory went to the brave and with the nineteenth century there came the period of triumph under Maharaja Ranjit Singh. The Khalsa ruled and with Ranjit Singh as leader it advanced to even greater glories.

Yet power can corrupt even the Khalsa. Political success and material affluence proved to be compelling temptations and many of the Khalsa were seduced by them. Hindu customs progressively reasserted their hold within the Panth, and, following the British annexation of the Punjab, this alarming tendency reached dangerous proportions. The British policy of insisting on Khalsa observances within the Indian Army helped to sustain the traditional loyalty, but because it affected such a small segment of the total Sikh population it could not provide a sufficient answer to the rapidly growing threat of disintegration.

It was to meet this challenge that the Singh Sabha movement was initiated, or at least so the Tat Khalsa believed. The message which it proclaimed was a simple one, easily comprehended and easily applied. Recognize that the Guru created a separate Panth, free from superstition and true to the doctrine of the divine Name. Recognize that all who seek membership in the Guru's Panth must accept the Guru's Rahit and that each must accordingly become a Sikh of the Khalsa. Recognize that *ham hindū nahīn*, we are not Hindus.[34] A Sanatan Sikh might demur, but for the Tat Khalsa it was obvious.

This interpretation has been vigorously contested by many who chose to identify as Sahaj-dhari Sikhs and by many more Punjabi Hindus who

[33] Guru Arjan, *Bhairau* 3, Adi Granth p. 1136. See chap. 2, n. 27.

[34] Two short works by Teja Singh summarize this point of view. See *Sikhism: Its Ideals and Institutions* (rev. edn., Bombay, 1951) and *Essays in Sikhism*. The title of a booklet by Kahn Singh Nabha first issued in 1899, *Ham Hindū nahīn*, was perhaps the most famous of all Singh Sabha publications.

laid no claims to a formal affiliation with the Panth. According to this second interpretation, Guru Nanak was a Hindu who remained a Hindu and who intended that his followers should likewise retain their traditional identities. There have been innumerable panths within the larger Hindu tradition and the panth of Guru Nanak is no different from the others in terms of its relationship to Hindu society. One may choose to follow the *nām simaraṇ* discipline taught by Nanak, but one does not thereby cease to be a Hindu (nor indeed a Muslim if that should be the inherited identity).

In establishing the Khalsa the tenth Guru certainly introduced a new element of great significance, but the relationship of the Sikh Panth to Hindu society remained unchanged. The Khalsa is a voluntary society within the Sikh Panth, formed to protect Hindus from Mughal aggression. Those who call themselves Sikhs have ever since had the choice of joining this strictly regulated society or of maintaining the kind of Nanak-panthi allegiance which was appropriate for all Sikhs prior to 1699. All remain Hindus, whether baptized Amrit-dhari or shaven Sahaj-dhari. All revere the Gurus and all who are devout will regularly visit a gurdwara for *darśan* of Guru Granth Sahib. Sikhs continue to observe caste, and Sikh marries Hindu in precisely the same way that Hindus traditionally intermarry. Some families observe the custom of having the eldest son initiated as an Amrit-dhari Sikh while all other members retain the identity of conventional Hindus.[35]

Some add that the real villains were the British. It was the British (so this extended version maintains) who taught the Sikhs to see themselves as distinct from other Indians and eventually to perceive the Panth as a separate 'nation'. This they achieved partly through their army practice, requiring all Sikh recruits to observe the Khalsa symbols and encouraging the Sikhs to see themselves as a 'martial race'. In part it was also achieved by means of an education which taught its pupils to think in Western terms. These involve clear distinctions whereas Indian tradition encourages the eirenic blurring of division and resolutely refuses to erect unbreachable barriers. Sikhs were also taught to see themselves as monotheists and to spurn the 'idolatry' of Hindus. Macauliffe was a notorious offender, ably assisted by Sikhs who had been trained to think

[35] Dharam Pal Ashta, 'Sikhism as an Off-shoot of Traditional Hinduism and as a Response to the Challenge of Islam' in *Sikhism and Indian Society* (Transactions of the Indian Institute of Advanced Study, vol. 4; Simla, 1967), 230–46. Gokul Chand Narang, *Transformation of Sikhism* (1st edn., Lahore, 1914; rev. edn., Lahore, 1946), app. ii–iii, pp. 346–69. Kapur, *Sikh Separatism*, p. 5.

in a Western mode. Christian missionaries added their enthusiastic support to the campaign.[36]

These two interpretations (the 'Sikh' and the 'Hindu') represent extreme views. In theoretical terms it is possible to formulate intermediate versions of Sikh identity. It is, for example, possible to argue that the Sahaj-dhari or Nanak-panthi identity is exclusively Sikh and that those who adopt it are no more Hindu than Sikhs of the Khalsa. In practice, however, one seldom hears such claims. Punjabis who believe that identities should be precisely formulated normally adopt one or other of the two interpretations summarized above. The debate has followed these lines throughout the present century, the intensity rising or falling as circumstances create divisive issues within Punjabi society or encourage a general sense of social satisfaction. Needless to say, it has risen sharply since the assault on the Golden Temple complex in June 1984. One seldom hears mention of Sahaj-dharis in the late 1980s, although that does not necessarily mean that the species is endangered or extinct.

Although the two interpretations are diametrically opposed, both suffer from the same basic flaw. Both are strictly intellectual formulations and both manipulate the historical past in order to defend contemporary perceptions. There is nothing unusual about such a procedure. It is perfectly normal, as all students of history should surely know. Accepting it as normal does not mean, however, that we must accept the procedure as sound historical analysis. Against it must be set two major objections, each of them affirming that these traditional interpretations are much too simple to be acceptable.

The first objection is implicit in our earlier treatment of the development of the Khalsa over a period of two eventful centuries. Though the linkage be both fundamental and obvious, the Khalsa which confronts us in the twentieth century is not the Khalsa of the early eighteenth century. The Singh Sabha interpretation distorts this reality by claiming that they are indeed identical in terms of their essential features, differing only because certain features of the tradition have been corrupted. This ignores the never-ending sequence of responses which any religious group must necessarily make to changing circumstances. Only the moribund escape this obligation.

The same general criticism applies to those who affirm the 'Hindu' interpretation. Changing circumstances mean changing attitudes and

[36] Sita Ram Goel, intro. to Ram Swarup, *Hindu–Sikh Relationship* (New Delhi, 1985), 7–9. Ram Swarup, ibid. 12–15.

changing identities. Whatever the original intention of Guru Nanak may have been, there can be no doubt about either the transforming influence of later experience or the attitude which has long been dominant within the Panth. Any attempt to persuade Khalsa Sikhs that they are Hindus is futile. Those Sikhs who are concerned with the defining of identities know that they are not Hindus and the rest of us must accept that assertion as a fact.

The second objection to both interpretations is that most people (Sikhs included) are not much bothered with identity differences, except perhaps in times of crisis. We must ever be aware that intellectual formulations are typically the concern of those who, by virtue of education, occupation, or family tradition, are encouraged to pursue such objectives. Much of the 'Who is a Sikh?' debate is, in fact, conducted within that area of Punjabi society which is occupied by the Khatri, Arora, and Ahluwalia castes, and it should come as no surprise to discover that such conventions as the baptizing of elder sons should be largely restricted to families from these castes. Jat society has fewer problems of definition precisely because it provides much less encouragement to debate. A Jat Sikh knows that he is a Sikh and there, for most, the matter ends.

The true nature of the problem can be easily understood by attempting to locate both Amrit-dhari and Kes-dhari Sikhs within a single consistent theory of Khalsa identity. For most it is not a problem because in normal circumstances few would question a Kes-dhari's claim to be accepted as a Sikh. It is only when the intellectual formulation assumes major importance that the issue becomes even remotely significant, and such occasions are rare. Even the so-called 'fundamentalist', ardent in advocating *amrit sanskār*, will normally accept a non-smoking Kes-dhari as a Sikh. If, however, one insists upon strict intellectual consistency, two options quickly emerge. Either one deregisters all but the diligent Amrit-dhari, or alternatively one faces endless confusion.

Discussions of this kind involve endless debate with no prospect of agreement. If we are to understand the role of the Singh Sabha and the nature of Sikh identity at the turn of the century, history must be used much more critically and the analysis thus produced will have to be rather more intricate. Any such analysis must certainly recognize the continuity which extends from the earliest days of the Nanak-panth to the end of the nineteenth century and beyond. By itself, however, this is insufficient. The force of intervening circumstances must also be recognized and the history of the Panth, like all history, must be seen as an endlessly evolving pattern. This may be regarded as the most elementary of historical truisms. The point nevertheless needs to be grasped if our discussion of Sikh identity is to proceed on rational lines.

A recent contribution which recognizes this need is Richard Fox's *Lions of the Punjab*.[37] Fox actually concentrates his attention on the Akali movement and on what he calls the 'Third Sikh War' of 1920–5 (usually known as the Gurdwara Reform Movement).[38] Much of his basic analysis nevertheless concerns the Singh Sabha period and the identity which developed under its auspices. The relevant portion of his argument may be summarized as follows.

The British, having conquered the Punjab, set about integrating it into the capitalist world economy. In so doing they successively pursued two conflicting policies. Whereas the earlier policy favoured a continuation of traditional agrarian production, the later version involved large-scale state investment in canal irrigation. The former policy encouraged the development of a rural class of petty commodity producers in central Punjab and also provided an opportunity for trading castes to form a lower-middle class.[39] The latter were initially attracted to the Arya Samaj (the radical Hindu society which was particularly strong in the Punjab), but, when a militant section of the Samaj attacked Sikh traditions, those who subscribed to those traditions went their separate way.[40]

The path which they elected to follow was one which had already been demarcated and defined by the British. The British had inherited a Punjab in which the term 'Sikh' carried no precise or agreed meaning. It covered a varied range of differing identities, no one of them accepted as standard or orthodox.[41] The British selected one of the available identities (the Khalsa identity) and insisted that its army recruits should thereafter observe routine Khalsa standards.[42] This identity was also assumed by those members of the trading castes who sought economic and educational advantage on the basis of their claim to be Sikhs.[43] They in turn communicated it to the petty commodity producers of central Punjab, already well prepared for its adoption by instruction received in the Indian Army.[44]

[37] Richard G. Fox, *Lions of the Punjab: Culture in the Making* (Berkeley and Los Angeles, 1985).

[38] The term 'Third Sikh War' was introduced by the Akali activist Sardul Singh Caveeshar, *The Sikh Studies* (Lahore, 1937), 191 ff.

[39] Fox, *Lions of the Punjab*, chaps. 2–4 *passim*.

[40] Ibid. 166–8.

[41] Ibid. 108–16.

[42] Ibid., chap. 8 and p. 178.

[43] Ibid. 168–71.

[44] Ibid. 80, 171–9.

During the early years of the twentieth century both the urban lower-middle class and the petty commodity producers of the villages experienced increasing economic pressure as a result of the investment policies more recently introduced by the British.[45] In addition to this shift in economic policy the British were also endeavouring to assert a more effective dominance over the Sikhs by controlling their gurdwaras.[46] By the time serious economic crisis developed after the First World War those most affected by it had been taught to regard themselves as Khalsa Sikhs and to perceive the incumbent owners of the gurdwaras (the mahants) as traitors to the Khalsa cause. A struggle which developed for economic reasons thus assumed the guise of a religious campaign.

Fox insists that his analysis should not be construed as simply a materialist explanation. Cultural factors were also involved. He maintains, however, that the latter are quite inadequate as an explanation for the developments which occurred during the early decades of the twentieth century. A basic feature of his argument is that

> those who labeled themselves 'Sikh' in the nineteenth century embraced no single cultural meaning, religious identity, or social practice; rather, an amalgam of what later reformers made into separate Hindu and Sikh cultural principles prevailed. Therefore, long-standing, widely shared, and consistent Sikh cultural principles cannot explain why the Third Sikh War was fought on the basis of Singh identity and over Sikh institutions. *In fact, no such tradition existed*.[47]

In thus isolating the identity issue we do some violence to the total argument which Fox develops. It is, however, fundamental to his theory as a whole as to our own present concerns, and it deserves to be scrutinized in isolation. In so doing we should acknowledge the truth of his claim that the nineteenth-century Panth incorporated a variety of identities.[48] As he presents it, however, the claim amounts to a serious exaggeration. To imply that no dominant tradition existed is to ignore the clear evidence of earlier periods. Although the Khalsa was not the sole claimant to the title of Sikh, it was by far the strongest and it carried into the British period conventions which enable us to recognize a clear connection between the Khalsa of the eighteenth century and that of the twentieth. The suggestion that the 'Singh identity' was selected by the British and then appropriated by a particular caste group for its own class

[45] Ibid. 76–8.

[46] Ibid. 158–9.

[47] Ibid. 106 (my italics). For a similar claim, see ibid. 116. Fox summarizes his argument on pp. 11–13 and 207–11.

[48] See also Harjot Singh Oberoi, 'A World Reconstructed', fos. 147–60.

purposes is unacceptable. As a theory it is no more valid than the claim that the Khalsa identity was invented by radical members of the Singh Sabha.

Such theories are nevertheless useful in that they stress the existence of alternate identities and the extent to which the Khalsa version acquired coherence during the Singh Sabha period. Fox also carries us closer to an acceptable analysis by emphasizing the role of the British. Although the emphasis which he lays on their economic and military policies may be altogether excessive, both features should certainly be incorporated in any such analysis. With them must come several other elements. As in other parts of India, the British presence in the Punjab amounted to much more than economic exploitation and a recruiting agency. Their economic influence was indeed significant, but we distort its results if we neglect the total range of their influence. There is a much larger context to be considered, and it is only within that larger context that the consequences of their presence can be appreciated.

The contribution of the British to Punjabi society involved economic policies, patterns of administration, a new technology, a fresh approach to education, and entry for Christian missionaries. Needless to say these elements did not operate in isolation, each exerting a distinct and separate influence on different areas of Punjabi society. Instead they meshed together, producing a web of influences which variously affected all Punjabis. Inherited status combined with new-found affluence might provide access to an education which supplied ideas subsequently propagated by means of printing presses. Economy, administration, education, and technology could combine to exert new pressures on Punjabi society and thus induce fundamental changes in that society.[49]

The emergence of the Singh Sabha movement provides a particularly important example of precisely this pattern. Most of the men who met in Amritsar or Lahore to form the first Singh Sabhas in 1873 and 1879 were from Sikh élites, those which had buttressed traditional status with British preferment. They were reacting to a perceived attack on their inherited traditions, and these traditions were to be defended in whatever ways might seem appropriate. The traditions derived from their pre-British past, reflecting the earlier acceptance of a dominant Khalsa with a Nanak-panthi appendage. The chosen methods of defence expressed educational influences and the available technology, a pattern which became increasingly evident as the movement progressed.

[49] Ibid., fos. 186–201.

The pattern which developed clearly reflected modes of thinking and ideals which the more influential of the Tat Khalsa reformers had acquired from their education and from the Western literature to which they were increasingly exposed. Prompted by these influences, they began to produce definitions and to shape systems which were congenial to a Western understanding. In so doing, however, they remained loyal to the inherited tradition. It was a Sikh tradition, and specifically a Khalsa tradition, which they developed and glossed. To suggest that they developed a new tradition is false. Equally it is false to claim that their treatment of it can be described as a simple purging of alien excrescence or the restoration of a corrupted original. The Khalsa of the Singh Sabha reformers was both old and new.

The Khalsa ideal which thus emerged from the Singh Sabha period was distinguished by a new consistency and a new clarity of definition. Earlier features which no longer seemed acceptable were abandoned or drastically modified, one notable result being a conscious shift away from the Panth's traditional hostility towards Muslims. Various practices were vigorously debated, the quest for distinctive rituals was initiated, and attempts were made to produce acceptable statements of the Rahit. An appropriate version of the Panth's history was formulated, a powerful stress was laid on the doctrine of the Guru Granth, and Sikhs were exhorted to observe conventions which would proclaim their separate Khalsa identity. Prominent amongst these conventions was observance of the Five Ks. A fierce debate developed with Arya Samaj apologists and insistent stress was laid on the claim that Sikhs could never be regarded as Hindus.

Throughout this process of study and debate we can observe the pressure of contemporary attitudes operating on the desire to protect traditional loyalties. Many Sikhs still rejected the claim that they were distinct from Hindu society, but within the Singh Sabha this Sanatan view was strongly opposed by the increasingly dominant Tat Khalsa.[50] The campaign to place a specifically Sikh wedding ritual on the statute books illustrates the nature of the general controversy and the kind of result which the reformers were seeking.

The marriage order which they so vigorously proposed was Anand Karaj, a rite which featured four circuits of the Adi Granth by the groom and his bride. Sikhs had earlier conducted marriages with a fire ceremony. Whereas this looked suspiciously like Hindu ritual, the Anand

[50] Ibid., fos. 278 ff.

ceremony was plainly Sikh and it was claimed that the rite represented early Sikh practice. Although this latter claim must be questioned, there can be no doubting the Sikh content of the ritual nor the ordered dignity which it presents. It well expressed the Tat Khalsa ideal and a vigorous campaign preceded the passing of the Anand Marriage Act in 1909. Within a comparatively short time Anand Karaj had become the standard form for Sikh marriages, a testimony to the determination of the reformers and to the influence which they had acquired.[51]

The successes achieved by the Tat Khalsa intellectuals and their supporters did not mean that the battle for an approved identity had been won by the time the Singh Sabha movement began to wane in the early twentieth century. Neither the passion of Giani Dit Singh nor the immensely versatile pen of Bhai Vir Singh could instantly dispatch attitudes which had persisted through much of the Panth's history. In particular there remained the problem of the Sahaj-dharis. Were they also to be regarded as Sikhs or was the Khalsa identity to be the only acceptable one? If the Sahaj-dharis were to be acknowledged as Sikhs, should their characteristic sense of a dual identity be conceded? Was it possible to live with their claim that they were both Hindu and Sikh?

The Tat Khalsa reformers were not the only people interested in the problem. The British had been responsible for much of the creative ferment which produced the Singh Sabha movement. They were now being forced to look closely at the question of who could legally be regarded as a Sikh.

[51] Harjot S. Oberoi, 'From Ritual to Counter-ritual: Rethinking the Hindu–Sikh Question, 1884–1915', pp. 150–53. The Nirankari Sikhs maintain that the Tat Khalsa borrowed the Anand ceremony from them. Webster, *The Nirankari Sikhs*, pp. 16–18. See R. S. Talwar, 'Anand Marriage Act', *The Panjab Past and Present*, 2/2 (Oct. 1968), 400–10.

6

Definition by Legislation

DURING its early years the Singh Sabha spoke in uncertain tones. Some individuals were convinced that the essence of the Panth was the casteless Khalsa and that Sikhs must be persuaded to see themselves as distinct from Hindu society. Others were much less certain that loyalty to their inherited tradition demanded such radical consistency. For the more conservative supporter of the Singh Sabha movement, attacks on caste observance, shared rituals, and multiple Sikh identities could go too far. These were routine aspects of the life which he knew, and, although reforms were evidently needed, the demands of the enthusiasts were altogether excessive.

Thus did Sanatan Sikhs regard the ideology of the Tat Khalsa, and it was only gradually that Tat Khalsa views gained ascendancy amongst the intellectual leaders of the Panth. Many of those who could be regarded as radical were not initially impressed by claims that Sikhs were so very different from Hindus. This was clearly indicated by the strong support which the Arya Samaj received from many Sikhs in its early days. For some the principal reason may have been the strength of the Arya Samaj amongst members of the Khatri and Arora trading castes, a constituency which also supplied many prominent members of the Panth. For others it was evidently the Arya Samaj rejection of idol worship and its apparent willingness to accept outcastes.[1] Whatever the reason, a close association with the Arya Samaj was unlikely to strengthen notions of an absolute distinction between Sikhs and Hindus.

Eventually the Tat Khalsa radicals did secure dominance within the Singh Sabha, at least with regard to doctrinal formulations and literary output. The early alliance with the Arya Samaj was soon abandoned by all but a handful of Sikhs, partly because of attacks on Sikh traditions by a sector of its adherents and partly because the two movements found themselves competing for outcaste support.[2] The Singh Sabha of

[1] Kenneth W. Jones, *Arya Dharm: Hindu Consciousness in 19th-century Punjab* (New Delhi, 1976), 2–6, 135–6.

[2] Ibid. 137–9. N. Gerald Barrier, *The Sikhs and their Literature* (Delhi, 1970), pp. xxxiv–xxxvii.

Amritsar continued to reflect the Sanatan conservatism of many of its early supporters, but increasingly the philosophical initiative passed to the more radical men who dominated the Lahore group.[3]

Although such prominent activists as Dit Singh and Gurmukh Singh were associated with the Lahore Singh Sabha, this should not suggest a simple distinction between Amritsar conservatives and Lahore radicals.[4] Both Singh Sabhas (with their respective satellites) had memberships spanning a range of attitudes and in neither group could one expect to find extreme opinions. Those whom we regard as radicals were actually men of very moderate views. Their strength, moreover, was the strength of ideas and effective communication rather than that of direct political influence. When the various Singh Sabhas united to form the Chief Khalsa Diwan in 1902, the leadership of the joint body was largely dominated by relatively conservative landowners such as Sundar Singh Majithia.[5]

For their own reasons these conservative leaders also supported many of the projects which served to advance the progressive cause. Khalsa College in Amritsar, founded with government assistance in 1892,[6] may have expressed the educational hopes of the radicals but that was not its sole function. It also reflected the status concerns of the Singh Sabha's more conservative supporters and their influence over its fortunes remained considerable.

In terms of debate and publications, however, the more conspicuous and influential contribution came from those who were eventually to be styled the Tat Khalsa. Exponents of the Tat Khalsa ideal promoted reform through education, journalism, and preaching. Although Khalsa College was certainly the most notable of the new educational institutions, it was by no means the only one. Literacy amongst Sikhs increased significantly during the Singh Sabha period and by 1921 it was approaching 10 per cent of all Sikh males.[7] For the educated élite there were newspapers, pamphlets, and books in English, Punjabi, and Urdu. For others the approach was through itinerant preaching and popular assemblies.[8]

[3] Barrier, *The Sikhs and their Literature*, pp. xxxii–xxxiii.

[4] Harbans Singh, *The Heritage of the Sikhs* (rev. 2nd edn., New Delhi, 1983), 252.

[5] Rajiv A. Kapur, *Sikh Separatism: The Politics of Faith* (London, 1986), 18. Khushwant Singh, *A History of the Sikhs*, ii (Princeton, 1966), 145.

[6] Harbans Singh, *The Heritage of the Sikhs*, pp. 245–8.

[7] Kapur, *Sikh Separatism*, pp. 40–1.

[8] N. Gerald Barrier, 'The Sikhs and Punjab Politics, 1882–1922', in Paul Wallace and Surendra Chopra (eds.), *Political Dynamics of the Punjab* (Amritsar, 1981; 2nd edn., forthcoming).

The key issue in this campaign was the nature of Sikh identity and during its course some ardent controversies were generated. One which greatly intensified the debate occurred with the death of the wealthy Dyal Singh Majithia in 1898. In his will Dyal Singh Majithia left his substantial fortune to a trust bearing his name. This was contested by his widow on the grounds that the bequest had been made in accordance with the Hindu law of inheritance and that, because her husband was a Sikh, the bequest was void. This claim required the Punjab High Court to determine whether or not Sikhs should be regarded as Hindus, a proposition which it eventually affirmed. In the meantime many others had joined in the fray. Two pamphlets appeared bearing the title *Sikh Hindū hain* ('Sikhs are Hindus'), both of them by Sikh authors. The contrary view was expressed in Kahn Singh Nabha's celebrated *Ham Hindū nahīn* ('We are not Hindus').[9]

Kahn Singh was also responsible for one of the several attempts made during this period to produce a coherent statement of the Rahit. In 1901 he published in Punjabi his *Guramat Sudhākar*, a compendium of works relating to the life and mission of Guru Gobind Singh.[10] Such a collection would obviously be expected to include material relating to the Rahit, but here Kahn Singh encountered a problem. Although there was much in the extant rahit-nama texts which met with his approval, there were also items which an enlightened Khalsa Sikh of the Singh Sabha period could scarcely be expected to accept. The solution which he adopted faithfully reflects the Singh Sabha approach to tradition, an approach which still commands substantial popularity today.[11]

The collection of rahit-nama extracts which appears in *Guramat Sudhākar* is no mere abridgement, nor is it a strictly representative selection from their material. It is a selection which mirrors the conviction of men such as Kahn Singh that the extant rahit-namas presented modified or corrupt versions of the tenth Guru's original Rahit. Whether by reason of ignorance or malice, they had acquired spurious items and some of them had discarded injunctions which the Guru must surely have uttered. If the harmful or misleading supplements were to be purged and authentic injunctions retained, a purer statement of the Rahit would emerge.

9 Kapur, *Sikh Separatism*, p. 19.

10 Wazir-i-Hind Press, Amritsar. The book had already been issued in 1898 in Hindi. A revised edition of *Guramat Sudhākar* is available published by the Languages Department, Patiala, 1970.

11 Ibid., *Bhūmikā*, 1970 edn., pp. u–ch.

This procedure eliminated many of the problems raised by the earlier rahit-namas without delivering a statement which would fully and accurately match Tat Khalsa ideals. The quest for an agreed rahit-nama continued and it remained unresolved throughout the Singh Sabha period. Much of the characteristic Singh Sabha understanding was incorporated in a manual of appropriate rituals issued by the Chief Khalsa Diwan in 1915 under the title *Guramat Prakāś Bhāg Sanskār*.[12] Although this book of order failed to attract a significant following, the Singh Sabha and its theologians should certainly not be judged on this basis alone. The complexity of its rubrics testifies to the distance which separated most of them from the Panth in general, but the ideals which they developed nevertheless took firm root amongst the educated and from there they have spread to a much larger sector of Sikh society. The order promulgated for the Anand marriage ceremony remains their most impressive success in this regard.

The thrust of the Tat Khalsa attempt to define Sikh identity was strongly towards the exclusive claims of the Khalsa definition and this impulse is clearly represented in *Guramat Prakāś Bhāg Sanskār*. All who participated in its preparation and revision were Khalsa Sikhs[13] and the actual orders for the various rituals are at least implicitly Khalsa in content. Apart from the order for Khalsa initiation, however, it leaves the way open for Sahaj-dhari use of the rites which it prescribes and this was the ultimate legacy of the Singh Sabha period.[14] Kahn Singh explicitly accepts the Sahaj-dhari status, his one condition being that all who claim it should acknowledge only the Guru Granth Sahib as sacred scripture.[15] A place was found for Sahaj-dharis within the general pattern of Khalsa dominance by translating *sahaj* as 'slow'. 'Sahaj-dhari' could thus be construed to mean 'slow-adopter', one who is on his way to the full-fledged Khalsa identity.

By 1915 the Singh Sabha reformers had succeeded in shaping a firmer definition of Sikh identity and in persuading a substantial proportion of educated Sikhs to accept that definition. Two major claims had been

12 Published from Amritsar, with subsequent reprints.

13 *Guramat Prakāś Bhāg Sanskār* (1952 edn.), app. 1–3.

14 The order for the conduct of Sikh funerals distinguishes the Amrit-dhari from other Sikhs in terms which may indicate that the authors had Sahaj-dharis in mind. Ibid. 47.

15 Kahn Singh Nabha, *Guruśabad ratanākar mahān koś* (2nd rev. edn., Patiala, 1960), 103. In a subsequent revision (published after his death) Kahn Singh strengthened this acceptance of Sahaj-dhari status by adding that 'Singhs who treat Sahaj-dharis with contempt are ignorant of the Sikh religion'. Ibid. 103n. He also included in the plate entitled 'Pictures of Nanak-panthis' a bearded figure labelled 'Sahaj-dhari Sikh'. Ibid., facing p. 518.

lodged and vigorously defended. First, Sikhs are not Hindus. Secondly, a true Sikh will normally be a Sikh of the Khalsa. As a result of their efforts a restored and redefined Khalsa identity had been effectively promulgated, carrying with it the clear implication that only the Khalsa of Singh Sabha definition could be regarded as orthodox.

It was, however, an interpretation which stopped short of any claim to exclusive possession of the entire Panth. Although their role and numbers within the Panth had been significantly diminished, a place still had to be found for Sahaj-dhari Sikhs. The direction of Singh Sabha doctrine might be clearly set towards a complete merging of the terms 'Khalsa' and 'Panth', but that result had not yet been achieved. Moreover, the Singh Sabha reformers had failed to deal adequately with the relationship of the Kes-dhari Sikh to a Panth increasingly defined in Khalsa terms. The definition of a Sikh, clearer now than it had ever been during the past two centuries, was still open to uncertainty and continuing debate.

If the Singh Sabha reformers could afford to be fuzzy at the edges of their definition, no such luxury was available to British administrators charged with framing laws and regulations based on communal distinctions. Apart from occasional issues such as a disputed will, there was the recurrent question of how the decennial census was to be conducted. If religious affiliations were to be returned (an obvious question for any British administrator to include), the census enumerators would have to be supplied with clear definitions of each acceptable identity. Who, in other words, was to be entered as a Sikh when answering census questions?

The initial British definition had been that of the army authorities for whom Sikh did indeed mean Khalsa. In the preliminary Punjab census Sikhs were included as Hindus, but from 1868 onwards they were listed separately.[16] No clear definition was supplied until the 1891 census, when enumerators were instructed to return as Sikhs those who followed the Khalsa order. The practical tests were to be uncut hair and abstinence from smoking. The definition thus implied the Amrit-dhari identity but in practice opted for the more general Kes-dhari form. Sahaj-dharis who failed either of the tests could return their sect as Nanak-panthi or identify themselves as followers of other Sikh Gurus.[17]

Ten years later the same model was adopted except that sects were not

[16] Kenneth W. Jones, 'Religious Identity and the Indian Census', in N. Gerald Barrier (ed.), *The Census in British India* (New Delhi, 1981), 79.

[17] Kapur, *Sikh Separatism*, p. 26.

included in the returns.[18] By 1911, however, it was realized that the 1891 tests were being generally ignored and it was accordingly decided to enter as a Sikh every person who claimed to be one. A new category, that of 'Sikh–Hindu', was also permitted. The same procedure was repeated in 1921,[19] clearly implying that, although administrators are meant to be neat and precise, this particular tangle had proven to be too daunting to unravel.

If that was the conclusion reached by the census commissioners, circumstances were already beginning to force the British back to the task of drafting a legal definition of who should be regarded as a Sikh. By 1921 the so-called Gurdwara Reform Movement was already under way and it was to continue until the British authorities eventually conceded that the principal Sikh gurdwaras should be transferred from their hereditary incumbents (the mahants) to elected representatives of the Panth.[20] Elections require voters, and individuals qualify as voters in accordance with specific criteria. Having accepted that such a transfer should indeed take place, the British were again confronted by the need to define a Sikh in statutory terms, and this time they were unable to evade the responsibility.

The history of gurdwara development and administration during the eighteenth and early nineteenth centuries is an obscure one. As we have already noted, the eighteenth-century gurdwara was distinguished from the less impressive dharamsala.[21] Routine kirtan was conducted in the latter, the term 'gurdwara' being reserved for shrines associated with particular events in the lives of the Gurus. Harimandir in Amritsar had become the Panth's principal gurdwara during the course of the eighteenth century. This rank it achieved in intimate association with Akal Takhat, the immediately adjacent gurdwara which symbolized temporal authority within the Panth. During the eighteenth century three other gurdwaras had received the title of *takhat* or 'throne' in recognition of their special role as repositories of Sikh tradition. The actual process whereby these four came to be regarded as takhats is not at all clear, except in the case of Akal Takhat.[22] Akal Takhat may have already

18 Ibid. 26–7.

19 Ibid. 27.

20 The history of this episode is narrated in ibid., chaps. 4–6; and Mohinder Singh, *The Akali Movement* (Delhi, 1978).

21 See chap. 4, n. 42.

22 The other three are Harimandir in Patna Sahib (where Guru Gobind Singh was born), Kesgarh Sahib in Anandpur (where he instituted the Khalsa), and Hazur Sahib in Nander (where he died). The fifth takhat, Damdama Sahib, which was not definitively designated until 1963, nevertheless surfaced from time to time as a candidate in the early years of the twentieth century. As such it lends some support to the view that the status of the takhat was still a matter of some uncertainty in the Singh Sabha period.

acquired its strongly symbolic identity and it certainly served as venue for the biannual gatherings of the Sarbat Khalsa during the eighteenth-century period of loose confederation.

This same lack of clarity applies to virtually all gurdwaras during the course of the eighteenth century. They were obviously regarded as appropriate destinations for pilgrims and some attracted pious donations from affluent or influential Sikhs.[23] It is, however, a very misty image which they present. Only with the provision of land grants and other privileges do they begin to emerge from obscurity, and they emerge in a form which was later to attract severe disapproval from the Singh Sabha reformers.

Most gurdwaras were in the hands of hereditary mahants and many of these proprietors were able to direct gurdwara income to whatever purposes they might choose. These purposes were not necessarily those which devout convention would approve and one of the standard complaints of reformers during the Singh Sabha period concerned the misappropriation of gurdwara funds. In some instances the income of a gurdwara was evidently directed to personal enrichment, and a few mahants adopted life-styles which piety could only regard as grossly immoral. Under the British their position was further reinforced by the granting of actual titles. In the eyes of the law they had become the owners of their gurdwaras and as such they were entitled to whatever protection the law might provide.[24]

The sins of the mahants were greatly compounded in the eyes of the reformers by the fact that so many of them declined to accept the Khalsa identity. Many described themselves as Udasi Sikhs, a claim which may once have had some justification but which survived as a relic rather than as a genuine identity. The usual assumption is that during the turmoil of the early eighteenth century Sikhs of the Khalsa were too conspicuous to serve as gurdwara custodians, and that later in the century they were too busy establishing Khalsa dominance. They accordingly left the care and conduct of their shrines to Nanak-panthis, who, because they declined to observe Khalsa standards, could hope to escape the hostile attentions of Mughals or Afghans. The preferred candidates were Udasis, celibate followers of the ascetic tradition established (so its adherents claimed) by Guru Nanak's son Siri Chand.[25]

If these assumptions are correct, it follows that the Udasi custodians

[23] W. H. McLeod (trans.), *The Chaupā Singh Rahit-nāmā* (Dunedin, 1987), 222.
[24] Teja Singh, *Essays in Sikhism* (Lahore, 1944), 175 ff.
[25] Kapur, *Sikh Separatism*, pp. 43–4.

must soon have abandoned their ascetic obligations, taken wives, and lived as ordinary Hindus. This was the usual life-style of the mahants who so offended the Singh Sabha reformers. The manner in which the mahants conducted gurdwara ritual also caused great offence. No acknowledged standards seemed to exist and the actual practice appeared to be strongly influenced by Hindu example. Amongst other objectionable features, this typically included a refusal to admit outcastes. Drastic reform was obviously needed if the gurdwaras were to serve their intended purpose in the life of the Panth.

In the event, however, the Singh Sabha reformers directed very little of their effective attention to the costly business of seeking a major change in gurdwara control. The Chief Khalsa Diwan had much to be proud of in social and educational terms, and it played a considerable part in bringing educated Sikhs closer together by means of newspaper journalism.[26] With regard to places of worship, however, they concentrated their attention on rituals, seeking to eliminate features which could be regarded as 'Hindu' and particularly those which implied idolatry. In 1905 a famous Tat Khalsa victory was won when idols were removed from the precincts of the Golden Temple,[27] but, apart from a continuing demand for ritual reform, the administration of the mahants was only occasionally challenged.

In thus retaining effective control the mahants had the implicit backing of the British authorities in the Punjab. The alternative, it seemed, would be Tat Khalsa control and this would obviously be unwelcome. A request for representative control of the Golden Temple, received from the Chief Khalsa Diwan in 1906, was ignored.[28] The Golden Temple was to remain under effective government control and mahants were to serve the same purpose in other major gurdwaras.

This eventually proved to be a mistaken policy. Because it involved resistance by government to a popular demand, it attracted a range of protest much wider than the ostensible issue would otherwise have attracted. The ostensible issue was one which could be powerfully represented in traditional terms and as such it could attract dedicated support. The Tat Khalsa claim which had received comparatively little attention or practical support during the first two decades of the twentieth century came dramatically to life after the First World War. A variety of new problems had arisen and the gurdwara issue provided a natural focus for the discontent which they were generating.

26 N. Gerald Barrier, 'The Sikhs and Punjab Politics, 1882–1922'.
27 Ibid. 28 Kapur, *Sikh Separatism*, pp. 47–8.

A foretaste of the strife to come was supplied by the protests which followed the government decision to appropriate a portion of the land attached to Gurdwara Rakabganj in order to achieve a desired street alignment during the planning of New Delhi.[29] This occurred in 1912, and, although the restoration campaign was effectively suspended during the war, it eventually provided a preview of later strategies. Meanwhile a host of new issues had developed. These included the growing pressure on many Punjabi cultivators,[30] the grievances of many Sikh migrants to North America, and economic difficulties following the conclusion of the war. Elsewhere in India a new nationalist phase was developing with the agitation against the Rowlatt Bills and when General Dyer opened fire in Jallianwala Bagh the Punjab situation became a major feature of Gandhi's campaign.

Gandhi was able to attract Sikh support for the Non-co-operation Campaign launched in 1920, but for the most part this support was supplied under auspices which were visibly and self-consciously Sikh. The Lucknow Pact of 1916 had not included the Sikhs and in 1917 the Chief Khalsa Diwan, acting under Tat Khalsa pressure, demanded separate electorates for Sikhs. Once again the identity issue was being forced into the legislative arena. Hindu politicians (including those who dominated the Congress Party in the Punjab) objected vigorously, with the result that politics in the Punjab assumed a stronger communal colouring. Tat Khalsa leaders responded by re-emphasizing their Sikh identity and their objections to Hindu practices within the Panth. The gurdwaras were associated with such practices and were accordingly drawn into the developing struggle.[31]

In 1918 the Montagu–Chelmsford Report conceded the claim for separate Sikh electorates and it was subsequently decided that the pragmatic definition of a Sikh would have to serve the purpose of determining the voter roll. Anyone claiming to be a Sikh 'and being prima facie what he represents himself to be' would be entitled to register on the Sikh roll.[32] The continuing controversy relating to this issue persuaded a group of Sikh politicians to found the Sikh League in 1919. The Sikh League endorsed the Congress decision to initiate non-co-operation in 1920, but it was soon superseded by organizations which

[29] Khushwant Singh, *A History of the Sikhs*, ii. 196–7.

[30] This particular issue is isolated and extensively discussed by Richard G. Fox in *Lions of the Punjab: Culture in the Making* (Berkeley and Los Angeles, 1985), especially in chaps. 3 and 4.

[31] Kapur, *Sikh Separatism*, pp. 70–6.

[32] Report of the Southborough Committee cited by Kapur, p. 79.

better expressed Tat Khalsa objectives. These were the Shiromani Gurdwara Parbandhak Committee (the SGPC) and its political associate, the Shiromani Akali Dal. Both were founded in late 1920.[33]

The Tat Khalsa now confronted the British, its demand supported by a considerable number of Sikhs (particularly rural Jats) and its campaign waged in alliance with Gandhi and the Congress Party. The objective of the campaign was eviction of the mahants from the gurdwaras which they controlled, and this purpose was kept steadily in view until it was finally achieved in 1925. Although the aim was thus a demonstrably religious one, a varied range of grievances had contributed to the formation of the movement's support, and in accepting Gandhi's non-violent strategy its leaders acknowledged their connection with the larger political campaign. The movement represented a continuation of the old Tat Khalsa purpose, significantly changed in terms of the following which it attracted and of the methods which it used.[34] As such it was appropriate that the Tat Khalsa leaders should form new organizations and that thereafter they should be known as Akalis.[35]

In the midst of these changes the identity issue persisted. The British soon found that the problem had become even more acute, for, having decided that the Akali demand would need to be conceded, they were compelled to negotiate a definition of Sikh identity which could be written into the empowering legislation. Amongst the Sikhs themselves a process already well advanced was accelerating. The Singh Sabha reformers had achieved considerable success with their insistence that the Khalsa should be recognized as the orthodox form of the Panth. The Akali movement further strengthened this claim, infusing it with a new version of the old heroic tradition. Although the Akalis may have

[33] Kapur, *Sikh Separatism*, pp. 82–100. Mohnder Singh, *The Akali Movement*, pp. 87–92. For the SGPC, see Gobinder Singh, *Religion and Politics in the Punjab* (New Delhi, 1986). For the Akali Dal, see Kailash Chander Gulati, *The Akalis Past and Present* (New Delhi, 1974).

[34] For a useful analysis of the relationship with Gandhi and the adoption of non-violent methods, see Partha N. Mukherji, 'Akalis and Violence: An Inquiry into the Theory and Practice of Non-violence', in Amrik Singh (ed.), *Punjab in Indian Politics: Issues and Trends* (Delhi, 1985), 71–118. The article is also of interest for its description of Gandhi's dawning awareness of Sikh identity. 'Till today', he explained to a Gujarati audience in March 1921, 'I had thought of them as a sect of Hinduism. But their leaders think that theirs is a distinct religion.' *The Collected Works of Mahatma Gandhi*, xix. 421, cited by Mukherji, p. 83.

[35] Akali means 'Follower of Akal [Purakh]'. In the eighteenth and early nineteenth century it was a name applied to those who are today called Nihangs. As such it designated one who was particularly ardent in pursuit of religious duties and it was an appropriate choice for the members of the new organization.

adopted a non-violent strategy during this period, they had certainly not parted company with their traditions. Eighteenth-century stories of heroism were invoked and old ideals were proclaimed in an idiom familiar to all nurtured in the Khalsa tradition. The actual events of the Akali campaign need not concern us.[36] What assuredly must concern us is the notable strengthening of Khalsa consciousness which accompanied those events and the definition of a Sikh which was written into the resultant legislation.

As far as the Akalis were concerned, the problem of definition had already been settled by the time the campaign began. When the first elections for the newly established SGPC were held in 1921, voting was restricted to Khalsa Sikhs and all elected members were required to bear the Five Ks.[37] The British eventually accepted a definition which was essentially the same and this was incorporated in the statutory definition of a Sikh written into the Sikh Gurdwaras Act of 1925. Before that point was reached, however, a debate was conducted over the five-year period of the campaign, with the final definition slowly crystallizing as the Akali strategy gradually forced government acceptance of their claims.

There were actually two definitions to be settled during the course of the campaign. In addition to determining who should be regarded as a Sikh, the government was also obliged to define the meaning of 'gurdwara'. Even with the two words 'Sikh' and 'gurdwara' defined to the satisfaction of the Tat Khalsa, there would still remain the question of non-Sikh participation in gurdwara administration. Should gurdwaras be regarded as the exclusive possession of Sikhs, however the latter word might be defined? There were plenty of Punjabi Hindus who stoutly maintained that Hindus were to be numbered amongst the Gurus' ardent devotees and that they, as regular and devout participants in gurdwara worship, were entitled to a share in the administration of the gurdwaras.

The quest for acceptable legislation was begun in 1921 with the introduction into the Punjab Legislative Council of a Sikh Gurdwaras and Shrines Bill. This failed to define either a Sikh or a gurdwara, but during the committee stage a definition was produced for the latter term. A gurdwara was to be defined as 'a Sikh place of public worship erected by or in memory of or in commemoration of any incident in the life of any

[36] In addition to Mohinder Singh and Kapur the early events can be followed in part in the older work by Teja Singh, *The Gurdwara Reform Movement and the Sikh Awakening* (Jullundur, 1922; 2nd edn., Amritsar, 1984). Fox's *Lions of the Punjab* is also principally concerned with this period.

[37] Kapur, *Sikh Separatism*, p. 124.

of the ten Sikh Gurus'.[38] This, of course, left 'Sikh' undefined and so too did a second bill introduced in 1922. The 1922 draft did, however, indicate that official opinion was moving down the track laid by the Tat Khalsa, for changes which it incorporated signalled that Tat Khalsa representatives would dominate the board of commissioners which was to control the gurdwaras.

Meanwhile, those who supported the Tat Khalsa cause continued to strengthen their grip on Sikh political activity. The SGPC elections held in July 1923 were again confined to Khalsa Sikhs, and in September of the same year the newly elected members agreed that the SGPC should sponsor candidates for both central and provincial legislatures. All who accepted nomination were to be Amrit-dharis who wore the Five Ks.[39]

The Akali campaign was finally terminated by the drafting and passing of the Sikh Gurdwaras Act of 1925. Chapter 1 of the Act defined a Sikh as 'a person who professes the Sikh religion', adding that the following declaration should be required if any doubt should arise: 'I solemnly affirm that I am a Sikh, that I believe in the Guru Granth Sahib, that I believe in the Ten Gurus, and that I have no other religion.'[40] No attempt was made to define 'gurdwara'. Instead a list of shrines to be covered by the Act was included, together with provision for having others added on appeal.[41] Committees of management were to be variously elected for individual gurdwaras of specified clusters,[42] and a central board was to be constituted for the purpose of general supervision. Of its 151 members, 31 were to be ex officio, nominated, or co-opted. The remaining 120 were to be elected by Sikhs who had passed the age of 21.[43]

As Rajiv Kapur points out, the key phrase in the definition of a Sikh is the concluding portion of the statutory declaration. Those whose Sikh identity might be questioned were required by the declaration to affirm that they had 'no other religion',[44] a form of words which supported the Tat Khalsa claim that Sikhs are not Hindus. For Sahaj-dhari Sikhs this could undoubtedly pose a serious problem, for many of them did indeed

[38] Ibid. 121.

[39] Ibid. 178.

[40] The Sikh Gurdwaras Act 1925, 2(9).

[41] Ibid. 7–17. The wording of the appeals made it clear that the term would not be limited to shrines associated with the Gurus. It could include shrines associated with celebrated Sikhs or important incidents and also those which had been established for public worship without reference to any particular person or event. Ibid. 16(2).

[42] Ibid. 85.

[43] Ibid. 43, 49.

[44] Kapur, *Sikh Separatism*, p. 187.

regard themselves as both Sikh and Hindu. Yet it was not the end of the affair, and, although Kapur rightly emphasizes these three words, he attributes to the Act a clarity and a finality which it did not possess. Although a Tat Khalsa interpretation of the Act would doubtless maintain that its definition of a Sikh necessarily implies the Khalsa identity, the Act does not specify this. A significant loophole remained.

There is, moreover, no sufficient reason for the conclusion which Kapur draws from the Act's reference to Patit Sikhs. The Act debarred Patit Sikhs from membership of individual committees or the central board and this provision, he maintains, automatically disqualified all non-Kes-dhari Sikhs.[45] This is certainly not a legitimate inference. The term *patit* ('fallen', apostate) applies to Amrit-dhari Sikhs who have committed any of the four gross offences specified in the Rahit (notably the cutting of hair or the use of tobacco). It can never apply to a Sahaj-dhari, nor can it strictly apply to an uninitiated Kes-dhari. Its inclusion certainly strengthened the Khalsa colouring of the Act, but it did not finally close the Khalsa circle.

After the passing of the 1925 Act, interest in Sikh affairs quickly receded and throughout the remainder of the British period little notice was taken of the Panth or of its politicians. This did not mean that they were inactive.[46] During the negotiations leading to independence, Sikh claims were pressed by Akali leaders (notably by Master Tara Singh) in an idiom which sustained the close connection between political objectives and Khalsa identity. The central board constituted by the 1925 Act had meanwhile decided to retain the name Shiromani Gurdwara Parbandhak Committee and this new SGPC was soon involved in the task of redefining the Rahit. A sub-committee convened by Professor Teja Singh of Amritsar was appointed to review the beliefs and customary practices of the Panth and to prepare a statement for the SGPC to consider.[47] On 1 October 1932 a draft document was duly submitted and after it had been publicly issued for discussion numerous submissions were received. Following a round of further discussions in 1936 the project was evidently shelved until after the Second World War. In early 1945 it was again revived and after some minor amending the sub-committee's proposed text was adopted by the SGPC on 3 February 1945.[48]

[45] Ibid.

[46] K. L. Tuteja, *Sikh Politics (1920–40)* (Kurukshetra, 1984), 135–207.

[47] This sub-committee included amongst its twenty-five regular members Kahn Singh Nabha, Vir Singh, and Jodh Singh.

[48] *Sikh Rahit Maryādā* (16th edn., Amritsar, 1983), 1–4. Although a lengthy delay occurred before the approved version was finally issued, an English translation of the draft

The statement thus prepared and formally approved was eventually published by the SGPC in 1950 under the title *Sikh Rahit Maryādā*. In terms of organization it had not been well drafted, particularly with regard to its curious distinction between 'personal discipline' (*śakhasī rahinī*) and 'panthic discipline' (*panthak rahinī*). It is, however, eminently clear as far as most of its definitions and rubrics are concerned. Ambiguity does occur at certain key points, but, as we shall see, this was evidently deliberate.

Whatever faults may be found with *Sikh Rahit Maryādā*, the manual has certainly stood the test of time, assuming since 1950 the status of sole standard authority within the Panth. Apart from the addition of a fifth takhat (Damdama Sahib) to the four recognized in the earlier tradition, its text remains unchanged.[49] By 1983 a total of 178,000 copies of the Punjabi text had been printed and English translations are also available.[50] As a statement of orthodox Sikh belief and normative Sikh conduct, it now stands virtually unchallenged. Although one may certainly encounter a wide range of unsanctioned doctrine and behaviour, the manual itself has no effective rival.

Sikh Rahit Maryādā begins by defining a Sikh. This it does in the following terms: 'A Sikh is any person who believes in Akal Purakh; in the ten Gurus (Guru Nanak to Guru Gobind Singh); in Sri Guru Granth Sahib, other writings of the ten Gurus, and their teachings; in the Khalsa initiation ceremony instituted by the tenth Guru; and who does not believe in any other system of religious doctrine.'[51] The new element is at once obvious. Amongst the items established by earlier convention there now appears the requirement that to be a Sikh one must believe in the Khalsa initiation (*amrit*). Does this mean that the Khalsa circle has finally been closed, that to be a Sikh one must be a member of the Khalsa?

At first sight this would seem to be the obvious conclusion to draw. A closer scrutiny will suggest, however, that such an assumption is still premature. The wording has obviously been chosen with great care, and,

had been published by Teja Singh in his *Sikhism: Its Ideals and Institutions* in 1938. As in all of Teja Singh's works, it is important that the Singh Sabha character of this book should be clearly recognized.

[49] See chap. 6, n. 22.

[50] Two English translations have been published under the title *Rehat Maryada: A Guide to the Sikh Way of Life*, one by Kanwaljit Kaur and Indarjit Singh (London, 1971) and an anonymous version issued by the SGPC (Amritsar, 1978). Neither adheres strictly to the authoritative Punjabi text. An abbreviated version is given in W. H. McLeod (trans.), *Textual Sources for the Study of Sikhism* (Manchester, 1984), 79–86.

[51] *Sikh Rahit Maryādā*, p. 8.

although it is certainly saying that the Khalsa form should be the standard version of the Sikh identity, it does not yet disqualify those who are outside the Khalsa. One is required to 'believe in' (*jo . . . nisachā rakhdā*) the need to take *amrit*. This form of words, strictly interpreted, can be construed to mean that, whereas a devout Sikh will certainly be expected to take *amrit* and assume the full range of Khalsa obligations, it is not an essential step. The essential requirement is that one should affirm the value of so doing. This will imply an intention to seek initiation at some time in the future, but it will not automatically deregister all who refrain from taking that step.

The form of words thus used to express the Khalsa aspect of Sikh identity is one which should accommodate the Kes-dhari Sikh without serious difficulty. The Kes-dhari demonstrates his or her attachment to Khalsa norms by maintaining its most conspicuous feature and for this reason can presumably be regarded as someone who believes in the virtue of proceeding to full Khalsa membership. The wording may also be construed as approval of the Sahaj-dhari form, provided only that the 'slow-adopter' definition is upheld and that the Sahaj-dhari can accordingly be viewed as someone progressing towards full participation in the Khalsa. Some stricter members of the Khalsa do indeed interpret the *amrit* reference as a mandatory obligation, one which allows no evasion or fudging. It appears, however, that this was not the view of Professor Teja Singh while drafting *Sikh Rahit Maryādā*, and it was certainly not the interpretation accepted by Kahn Singh Nabha.[52]

Sikh Rahit Maryādā is also ambiguous with regard to the precise status of the Patit Sikh, the 'apostate' or 'renegade' Amrit-dhari who wilfully commits any of the four gross sins (the *chār kurahit*).[53] Is a Patit still a Sikh or do these offences produce automatic excommunication? The wording which is actually used in references to the Patit seems to imply that offenders are indeed still Sikhs. It is, however, debatable. They are certainly not members of the Khalsa (this is made clear by the requirement that repentance must be followed by re-initiation) and the clear indication that the mere presence of a Patit is polluting signifies a very strong condemnation.[54] But are they to be altogether stripped of their Sikh identity? This seems not to be the case, although doubtless there will be a fundamentalist interpretation of this point also.

[52] Teja Singh, *Sikhism: Its Ideals and Institutions* (rev. edn., 1951), 84. Kahn Singh Nabha, *Gurumat mārtaṇḍ* (Amritsar, 1962), 111–14.

[53] *Sikh Rahit Maryādā*, p. 26.

[54] Ibid. 26, 27.

This combination of Khalsa norms and ambiguously implied exceptions informs *Sikh Rahit Maryādā* as a whole. Its version of Ardas (the so-called 'Sikh Prayer') includes repeated references to the Khalsa, yet it concludes with an eirenic couplet which gathers all people into a single blessing.[55] The Khalsa flag (*niśān sāhib*) is to fly above all gurdwaras, but access is open to all apart from particularly sacred areas within the takhats.[56] A reference in the order for the Anand marriage service seems plainly to imply that all Sikhs are not Amrit-dharis.[57] The funeral order, however, assumes that the deceased will have observed the Five Ks.[58] Whereas the 'Panth' consists of Sikhs, the 'Guru Panth' is limited to 'full-fledged Singhs' (*tiār-bar-tiār singh*).[59]

Although the ambiguity persists, the question of orthodoxy is put beyond all doubt. As far as the SGPC is concerned, standard belief and practice are defined by the Khalsa Rahit, and if others are to be accepted as Sikhs they should aspire to full membership of the Khalsa. But is the SGPC the ultimate authority, and must its pronouncements be accepted as the final word on any issue concerning doctrine and practice? Authority is one of the problems which still remains to be considered before we finally attempt to define who is a Sikh.[60]

Before concluding this narrative of the attempt to define Sikh identity by legislation, we should note one further contribution. When India became independent in 1947, the Punjab inherited the Sikh Gurdwaras Act of 1925 as a part of the legislative bequest from the British period. The Act is still in force and the definition of 'Sikh' which it enunciated remains unamended. It is, however, an Act which applies only to the Punjab and immediately adjacent territories. Because the gurdwaras of Delhi and New Delhi were beyond its jurisdiction, fresh legislation was required in order to regularize their administration.

The need for an act of Parliament to cover the Delhi territory gurdwaras provided yet another opportunity for the debate to recommence in earnest. Although it is by no means clear who exercised the determining influence, or for what reasons, the outcome was certainly an interesting one. In the course of 1971 two such Acts were passed by the Lok Sabha. The first of these was the Delhi Gurdwara (Management) Act 24 of 1971 and, in this first attempt to settle the issue, the word 'Sikh'

55 Ibid. 10.
56 Ibid. 12, 13.
57 Ibid. 21.
58 Ibid.
59 Ibid. 23.
60 See chap. 7.

was defined in terms closely following those of the 1925 Act.[61] The later Act significantly amended this definition. In the Delhi Gurdwara Act 82 of 1971 a Sikh is defined as follows:

'Sikh' means a person who professes the Sikh religion, believes and follows the teachings of Sri Guru Granth Sahib and the ten Gurus only *and keeps unshorn hair*. For the purposes of this Act, if any question arises as to whether any living person is or is not a Sikh, he shall be deemed respectively to be or not to be a Sikh according as he makes or refuses to make in the manner prescribed by rules the following declaration:—

'I solemnly affirm that I am a *Keshadhari* Sikh, that I believe in and follow the teachings of Sri Guru Granth Sahib and, the ten Gurus only, and that I have no other religion.'[62]

Between the two Acts a successful attempt had evidently been made to narrow the definition in such a way that Sahaj-dharis would be explicitly deprived of any right to call themselves Sikhs. It is clear, however, that there was no intention of limiting the definition to Amrit-dhari Sikhs. The chosen wording specifically enfranchises the Kes-dhari.

There is no reason why this piece of legislation should be regarded as representative of Sikh opinion in general, nor that it would necessarily have secured SGPC approval had that been invited. Legislation may well reflect the temporary influence of a particular pressure group and there seems to be little doubt that the second of these Acts should be regarded as an example of this effect.[63] Although this should certainly be acknowledged, it does not entitle us to dismiss the episode or its result as an issue of little consequence. It confronts us yet again with the central problem and with the importance which the problem commands. Who is a Sikh? A final attempt must be made to answer the question.

[61] Attar Singh, 'The Management of Gurudwaras' in Amrik Singh (ed.), *Punjab in Indian Politics*, p. 199.

[62] Quoted in ibid. The text is contained in Jitinder Kaur, *The Politics of Sikhs: A Study of Delhi Sikh Gurdwara Management Committee* (New Delhi, 1986), 242. The emphasis to *and keeps unshorn hair* was added by Attar Singh.

[63] Jitinder Kaur, *The Politics of Sikhs*, pp. 34–5.

7

Who is a Sikh?

IT WOULD be most convenient if there were to be an acknowledged authority, some individual or assembly to whom we might appeal for a clear and certain answer to our question 'Who is a Sikh?' Definitions are readily available and willingly dispensed, yet basic disagreements persist and the indisputable answer still seems to elude us.

There is, of course, one authority which most Sikhs will instantly cite. The Adi Granth, visible embodiment of the eternal Guru, is the divine Word which all devout Sikhs must accept and none may challenge. Its status is indeed beyond dispute, yet even this response must fail to answer our question, at least in terms sufficiently detailed to settle the issue in its present form. The Guru Granth Sahib will supply us with some basic features of the definition which we seek, and at least one of those features must be incorporated in any definition which we may finally present. This we must acknowledge without accepting the claim that it can deliver anything resembling a complete answer to our question. The Adi Granth was compiled prior to the founding and subsequent development of the Khalsa and, as we have repeatedly observed, any attempt to define Sikh identity must certainly take account of the Khalsa contribution. In this regard the Adi Granth may indicate some appropriate lines of enquiry, but it cannot be expected to supply the kind of answer which we require.

The one essential feature which the Adi Granth does provide derives from its emphasis on the doctrine of the divine Name. Guru Nanak and his early successors leave us in no doubt that for them this is the one fundamental belief which all must accept. The divine Name is the substance of truth and the practice of *nām simaraṇ* is the one assured means of liberation from the cycle of transmigration. The doctrine of the divine Name must accordingly be built into any adequate definition of Gurmat (or what we call, when speaking English, Sikhism). From this it follows that a definition of the person who accepts Gurmat must likewise include some reference to the divine Name and to the duty of regular *nām simaraṇ*.[1]

[1] See chap. 2.

We shall indeed include both the doctrine and the duty in our final definition, but let us be aware of the difficulties which it adds to our basic problem of framing that definition. It would be idle to suggest that all who regard themselves as Sikhs have a clear understanding of the Adi Granth doctrine of the divine Name or that they regularly practise anything resembling the technique of *nām simaraṇ* as enunciated by Guru Nanak and his successors. For many it will be acknowledged as nothing more than an occasional utterance of the pious ejaculation *Sati-nām* ('True is the Name'), while for others it will exist as a word recollected from childhood or as someone's personal name. A close acquaintance with the actual contents of the Guru Granth Sahib is not a feature of Sikh life which we should expect to encounter with any frequency. To assume it would be as unrealistic as imagining that all who call themselves Christians have a reasonable understanding of the Bible and its contents.

The two situations are very similar, for in both cases we are dealing with traditions which seek a measure of doctrinal precision. In examining the extent to which the Adi Granth is actually comprehended by Sikhs we are inevitably confronted by the problem of nominal identity as opposed to devout observance. Our task would be considerably eased by a decision to confine ourselves to the latter, concentrating our attention on a quest for the normative version of the tradition. It is, however, a temptation which should be resisted. A close analysis of the normative version is essential, but alone it is insufficient. It would lead us to an ideal rather than to a reality, to a definition which excludes many who regard themselves as Sikhs or to one which implicitly brands them as 'bad' Sikhs.

This decision complicates our task without eliminating the need for normative statements or the problem of identifying an acceptable authority within the Panth. The problem recurs when we proceed to examine the second of the standard answers to the general question of authority. Within the Panth the only organization which can claim representative status is the Shiromani Gurdwara Parbandhak Committee (the SGPC), and on occasion the SGPC has acted as if it were indeed an ultimate authority. Should this assumption of doctrinal power be accepted?

Most members of the SGPC are elected by popular vote of all who can establish their Sikh credentials in terms of the 1925 Sikh Gurdwaras Act.[2] This restricts the electorate to the Punjab and adjacent territories,

[2] Gobinder Singh, *Religion and Politics in the Punjab* (New Delhi, 1986), 79–85.

but a verdict delivered from the acknowledged heartland of the Sikhs is surely one to be respected by those who happen to live elsewhere. The SGPC has assumed the right to act as an ultimate authority in matters of doctrine and religious practice as well as in issues which more narrowly concern the administration of gurdwaras. *Sikh Rahit Maryādā* was prepared under its auspices and issued with its imprimatur. If *Sikh Rahit Maryādā* is to be accepted as an authoritative manual of Sikh doctrine and behaviour, it must surely follow that the SGPC is to be acknowledged as a court of final appeal in all matters relating to Sikh belief.

In practice this claim was widely rejected even before the present crisis, particularly amongst the educated and professional élites within the Panth. If one had asked a well-educated Sikh what he or she thought of the SGPC, the response was likely to be a prompt rejection of its claims to virtue, intelligence, or authority. Money was commonly identified as the culprit and politics as the curse which it conferred. Because the SGPC had access to such enormous funds through its control of gurdwara incomes, it offered an irresistible temptation to those who seek power and status. These funds it used (so the claim continued) to support a retinue of dependants within the gurdwaras themselves and an unstable programme of political action in the wider world of the Punjab.[3]

Even before the troubles of the middle and late 1980s these views were widespread. What opinions are held now would be difficult to ascertain, but it is safe to assume that the intellectual leadership of the Panth rejects the SGPC's right to pronounce on questions of doctrine and practice. There also appears to be abundant evidence which suggests that many more Sikhs see the SGPC as an essentially political body. It is conceived as a political organization, currently one which is in the hands of a distinctly militant group. As such it is certainly not one which can claim to determine religious principles which will carry weight in the Panth as a whole. This is not to say that the SGPC is devoid of power, nor that the exercise of that power is contrary to the interests of the Panth. That may or may not be the case. The essential fact is that its primary role is political. If it has a religious role, it is to exalt a narrowly Khalsa identity and to frighten away virtually all who would otherwise be prepared to call themselves Sahaj-dhari.

The same rejection is also extended to the so-called 'High Priests' of the Panth, a group of seven men who have received much attention in the recent past because of the use which has been made of them in pursuing

[3] Ibid. 154.

political advantage or settlement during the continuing crisis in the Punjab. The group comprises the Chief Granthis of Darbar Sahib (the Golden Temple) and Akal Takhat, together with the Jathedars or 'Commanders' of all five takhats. In normal circumstances their authority is limited and to call them 'high' is a somewhat doubtful usage. To call them 'priests' is wholly erroneous, for the Sikh tradition acknowledges no such role or authority. During the current crisis their newly bestowed status has been useful to both sides as a means of buttressing their own political strategies or obstructing that of their opponents. As authorities on matters of doctrine or practice their influence is negligible except in so far as they reflect the views of their masters.[4]

Sants supply another source of authority within the Panth, and within the range of an individual Sant's personal following that authority may be considerable. It will be all the stronger if he belongs to an established lineage of venerable repute. The title 'Sant' is in this sense a comparatively modern usage, although the actual role has been recognized within the Panth since the eighteenth century at least. A Sikh Sant is an individual (almost always a male) who develops a reputation for piety or pedagogical skill and thereby attracts an informal following of disciples. Sants are typically the products of rural society (most are Jats) and until recently their influence was largely limited to the villages where they imparted instruction in traditional Sikh doctrine or kirtan.

Because the Khalsa ideal stresses participation in worldly affairs, some Sants have been active in the larger life of the community, and the current participation of Sants in Sikh politics is an extension of this convention. This has significantly enlarged their range of influence during recent years, and so too has the increasingly popular practice of travelling overseas to minister to Sikhs in the diaspora. Amongst the recognized lineages one stands pre-eminent. This is the Damdama Taksal, led by Sant Jarnail Singh Bhindranwale until his death in 1984 during the storming of the Golden Temple complex.[5]

[4] W. H. McLeod, 'A Sikh Theology for Modern Times', in J. D. O'Connell *et al.* (eds.), *Sikh History and Religion in the Twentieth Century*, (Toronto, 1988), 42.

[5] Jarnail Singh Bhindranwale died during the army assault on the Golden Temple complex in June 1984. Other Sants who have achieved political prominence in recent times include Sant Fateh Singh of Punjabi Suba fame and the moderate Akali leader Sant Harchand Singh Longowal. For a description of the Sikh Sant and an analysis of his role, see W. H. McLeod, 'The Meaning of *sant* in Punjabi Usage', in Karine Schomer and W. H. McLeod (eds.), *The Sants: Studies in a Devotional Tradition of India* (Berkeley and Delhi, 1987), 251–63; and id., 'The Role of Sikh Doctrine and Tradition in the Current Punjab

Several Sants have achieved substantial influence in recent times and for many generations they have acted as effective mediators of traditional Khalsa attitudes. There are, however, major limits to their influence. Most live and work in the Malwa region (the area south and east of the Satluj River) and few command a following beyond traditional village society. The response which they elicit from most educated Sikhs ranges from tolerant indifference to strong condemnation. It is an important influence which they exercise and it should certainly not be disregarded. There is, however, no prospect that any Sant will be accepted as a final authority, except by those who choose to join his following.

The only other authority recognized within the Panth is that of the corporate community. This may be expressed in two forms, the ambitious version deriving from the doctrine of the Guru Panth and the less prominent from a traditional pattern of delegation within individual sangats.

According to the doctrine of the Guru Panth the assembled community constitutes the Sarbat Khalsa (the 'Entire Khalsa'), and any corporate decision which the Sarbat Khalsa may make in the presence of the Guru Granth Sahib bears the full weight of the eternal Guru's personal authority.[6] The doctrine still stands, but it is extraordinarily difficult to apply in practice. Indeed, it is altogether impossible to implement it in such a way that all Sikhs will acknowledge the outcome. Although attempts have been made to revive the practice in recent years, the doctrine is strictly dysfunctional, a convention which served a useful purpose during the eighteenth century but which has since been immobilized by changed circumstances and the ever-widening diversity of the Panth.

The other version of corporate authority is much less cumbersome and has consequently retained a portion of its original strength. This is the *pañj piāre* convention, the practice of choosing five members of a sangat to act on its behalf.[7] It is, however, a convention which retains its effect only within a comparatively small group of Sikhs, and only when the group is reasonably united in terms of purpose and understanding. Where these conditions are lacking, divisions commonly occur and splinter sangats appear (particularly amongst the more mobile diaspora

Crisis', in Jayant K. Lele *et al.* (eds.), *Boeings and Bullock-Carts: Rethinking India's Restructuring* (Leiden, forthcoming).

[6] See above, p. 55.

[7] The practice commemorates Guru Gobind Singh's choosing of five loyal Sikhs to receive the first initiation as members of the Khalsa in 1699.

Sikhs). As a means of decision-making on a large scale it can be effective only when a substantial majority of the Panth is fired by a common concern or a common indignation.

As a single authority exercised on behalf of the entire Panth the convention can seldom, if ever, hope to win general acceptance. Applied within individual sangats it can serve a useful purpose, but only within that sangat or its immediate environment. Each group of *pañj piāre* will normally reflect the attitudes of those who chose them, and the range of opinion which these groups represent will be as diverse as the full spectrum allows. To propose the *pañj piāre* convention as a decision-making system for the Panth as a whole would be a recipe for independency of the Protestant kind.

If, therefore, we seek an authority which will deliver an accurate and sufficient definition of a Sikh, our search will produce several differing results and consequently no result. We note the Adi Granth stress on the divine Name as one part of the final definition and proceed to ask if a consensus view can be identified. Granted that no text, individual, or institution can supply the answer which we need, is it nevertheless possible to isolate particular items which all Sikhs (apart from mavericks and recognized eccentrics) accept as essential features of their own identity? The enterprise is scarcely a promising one, but it may carry us a little nearer to an agreed definition. It can be assumed, for example, that apart from the truly secular all Sikhs will affirm the sanctity of the Guru Granth Sahib. Even the most ardent of secularized Sikhs will recognize this feature by ritually prostrating before the sacred book on the rare occasions when he is compelled to enter its presence.[8]

Entering the presence of the Guru Granth Sahib normally means entering a gurdwara and here we encounter another feature which few Sikhs would dispute. The religious centre for Sikhs is the gurdwara, an institution which wins grudging approval from many of the lax and secularized as well as firm support from the pious. This approval may be hedged with protests concerning the frequency of factional disputes within gurdwaras or their misuse for political purposes, and it may be accompanied by a lofty disdain for the gurdwara's role as a place of worship. Normally, however, the point will be conceded. When Sikhs

[8] It should be noted that 'secular' and 'secularized' are here used in the Western sense and thus designate a person who lacks religious convictions. The word 'secular' or its derivatives can cause much confusion if one is unaware of the radical difference between the Western usage and the meaning which the terms have assumed in Indian usage. In the latter context 'secular' typically means 'equal respect for all religions'. A pious practising Sikh (or Hindu, Muslim, Christian, etc.) can accordingly claim to be secular in outlook.

travel to foreign places, they usually find themselves drawn to a gurdwara, and if none should exist the deficiency will soon be remedied.

It is, moreover, recognized that the gurdwara is the place where the egalitarian principles of the Panth are most effectively applied, a feature which appeals to many who reject its devotional role. The langar is a convention which commands universal respect within the Panth and even the secularized can find meaning in the impartial distribution of karah prasad.[9] The same people may also accept the traditional concept of service (*sevā*). The concept may be construed as a kind of social welfare activity rather than the traditional variety,[10] but even that will normally prove acceptable to many of the more pious.

We can thus add reverence for the Guru Granth Sahib and acknowledgement of the gurdwara to the agreed features which together constitute Sikh identity. The gurdwara also directs us to another possibility. Within every gurdwara and during most Sikh ceremonies Ardas (the 'Sikh Prayer') is recited.[11] The structure of Ardas evidently derives from the eighteenth century, although the content of the version used today includes much that belongs to more recent times. Because Ardas is routinely recited in Sikh rituals, we can perhaps assume that its fundamental features should also be added to our list of agreed items. An actual analysis of its contents will soon reveal, however, that our luck is running out again.

The invocation with which Ardas begins calls to mind each of the Gurus by name and this portion of the prayer is surely acceptable to all but the narrowest of Nanak-panthis. Veneration for the Gurus is thus another of the features which can be added to our consensus list. The concluding petition is also likely to find general acceptance, although it adds little that will supplement a distinctive identity.[12] It is when we

[9] The langar is the kitchen and refectory attached to every gurdwara from which food is served to all regardless of caste or creed. Karah prasad is the sacramental food dispensed in all gurdwaras, again without reference to the individual's caste or creed.

[10] In a strict sense *sevā* is *sevā* done for the Guru, which in practice means *sevā* performed in the precincts of a gurdwara. Such activities as cleaning the shoes of worshippers, sweeping the sacred premises, and helping in the langar are all typical forms of *sevā*.

[11] For a translation of the version incorporated in *Sikh Rahit Maryādā* and in use today, see W. H. McLeod (trans.), *Textual Sources for the Study of Sikhism* (Manchester, 1984), 104–5. The complete prayer consists of three distinct sections (invocation, recollection, and petition). Only the first eight lines (the invocation) and the concluding couplet are unalterable. There is, however, a standard version for the second section and for most of the third. See ibid. 103–4.

[12] The concluding portion is the portion which begins with the words 'May Sikhs be humble of heart . . .'.

scrutinize the intervening section (the 'remembrance of past mercies') that we recognize the return of old problems. The middle portion is patently a prayer of the Khalsa and, if its text be treated as a statement of essential doctrine, the result must be a reaffirmation of the standard Khalsa interpretation. This portion of Ardas is in fact a product of the Tat Khalsa understanding of Sikh tradition. The element of ambiguity is still retained and determined exegesis may yield an interpretation acceptable to Sahaj-dhari claims. The import is, however, strongly that of the militant Panth and of the Kes-dhari identity.

The consensus approach thus provides some additional items before it runs into the difficulties which emerged during the Singh Sabha and Akali periods. At this point we shall abandon doctrine and try a generic approach to the problem of definition. Claims concerning the nature of Sikh society have been vigorously debated within the Panth and widely proclaimed as vital aspects of Sikh identity. Our next task must be to estimate the results of the debate. It requires us to venture on to distinctly risky ground, but the attempt must nevertheless be made if all aspects of the problem are to be adequately explored.

There are two terms which must be examined in the process of testing popular generic claims and the first of these is 'race'. Can we accept the claim that Sikhs constitute a separate race? The wording of race relations legislation in the United Kingdom has provided a defence for this claim and one can easily understand why Sikhs who wish to combat perceived discrimination should have recourse to the appropriate laws. This does not mean, however, that we must accept the claim in any general or universal sense. It is manifestly impossible to defend the claim that Sikhs are a distinct and separate race, except in the terms imposed by the race relations context in the United Kingdom. The narrowest possible definition will classify them as Punjabis and no one can claim that all Punjabis are Sikhs.

It is likewise impossible to claim that all Sikhs are Punjabis. It is indeed true that an overwhelming majority of Sikhs are Punjabis, and an interesting question with some relevance to our main purpose concerns the failure of the tradition to attract significant numbers of non-Punjabis.[13] No one, however, will deny the possibility that non-Punjabis may join the Panth and actual examples can easily be found. The claim that Sikhs are a distinct race need detain us no longer.

[13] Two suggested reasons may be that in other parts of India Sant teachings required no allegiance to the Nanak-panth (there were other panths which could be joined); and Khalsa symbols and conventions would have been regarded as alien.

The second generic term which we must examine is 'nation' and here we encounter a much knottier problem, one which is liable to generate very strong reactions. Although the first application of the word 'nation' to the Sikhs goes back to the earliest days of British contact, it did not receive significant emphasis until recent times. After the collapse of Ranjit Singh's kingdom, the British themselves used the word very loosely, and throughout the nationalist phase of the British period there was little questioning of the Sikh place within an independent India. Only as the Muslim League claim to nationhood crystallized and produced the threat of partition did the concept of a Sikh 'nation' begin to attract serious attention. Since independence it has designated the extreme version of the popular Sikh claim that the Punjab should receive a larger measure of political autonomy. In times of communal crisis it waxes strongly and in recent years its radical exponents have dramatized the claim as a demand for Khalistan.

There is much to be said in defence of the claim that the Panth constitutes a separate nation. The *mīrī–pīrī* doctrine affirms a political role for the Panth,[14] and the claim can be more generally defended in terms of the distinctive culture which the Panth embodies. There are, however, problems. Those who dispute the notion insist that too much of the Panth's culture is in fact Punjabi culture and that too much of its tradition overlaps with the larger tradition of India as a whole. There is, moreover, the difficulty of demarcating a viable area to be occupied by the Sikh nation, an essential feature of any realistic claim.

This is an argument which will presumably continue for quite some time to come. For present purposes a more realistic approach is to ask whether 'nation' is really the appropriate translation for what many of its more moderate exponents have actually had in mind. There seems to be little doubt that for many Sikhs 'nation' has served as a translation for the word *qaum*. If so, it is a thoroughly misguided choice, one of the many examples of how meanings can be seriously distorted by endeavouring to find single-word translations for terms which have no equivalent in English.

In its original Arabic form *qaum* designates 'a people who stand together' and this meaning has survived its adoption into Punjabi usage. As such it does indeed denote a strong sense of corporate identity and this fact is significant as far as our quest for a definition is concerned. It is nevertheless a meaning which differs from the strict sense of the English

[14] The *mīrī* part of the combination designates worldly authority (the authority of the *mīr* or *amīr*, the master of a realm). See above, p. 24.

word 'nation'. Whereas it certainly connotes a strong sense of ethnic identity, it does not bear a precise correspondence to 'nation'. There can be no doubt that some of those who today proclaim the existence of a Sikh nation are using the word in its strictly accurate sense. If, however, the essential content derives from *qaum*, the term should be discarded.

The conclusion must be that our attempt to use the generic approach has largely failed. The sense of a distinct Sikh identity will certainly be strengthened by an analysis of *qaum* in its specifically Sikh usage, but that alone will not serve to supply the distinctive features which we need. In a very real sense our quest has all along been an attempt to discover why Sikhs perceive themselves to be a *qaum*.

We turn next to the pragmatic approach. Regardless of what doctrine may declare or theory may claim, what do we actually see when we scrutinize the Panth?

One issue which we have not yet examined is the place of women in the Panth. The issue is one which concerns doctrines as much as observable behaviour and it might well have been discussed at an earlier stage. In practice, however, actual behaviour is normally much more important than doctrine when dealing with the status of women and for this reason it is generally more helpful to deal with the issue in pragmatic terms.

In theory women are regarded as the equals of men in the Panth. As one might expect, their actual status falls short of the theoretical claim, but this is not to suggest that women possess neither rights nor influence. Their right to participate in panthic rituals is generally recognized, even to the extent of permitting women to sit in attendance on the Guru Granth Sahib and read from the sacred scripture in public worship. Sikhs commonly claim that their women possess a much greater freedom than those who belong to other areas of Indian society. Sweeping assertions of this kind are difficult to test and it might be countered that in Punjabi villages (where most Sikh women live) there is little to distinguish the roles of Hindu and Sikh women belonging to similar castes. It must nevertheless be accepted that prima facie the claim is at least plausible and that as such it deserves to be examined.

The reality, as one would expect from Western experience, is that the actual place of women in the Panth is conspicuously subordinate to that of males. There exists a small élite of educated urban women with access to substantial influence and opportunity, but they are exceptions to a generally consistent rule. Women may take Khalsa initiation and having done so they are expected to observe the same code of conduct as men (with the exception of the turban, which is optional for women and very seldom worn).[15] Whenever the Rahit is discussed, however, or whenever the special claims of the Sikhs are debated, the focus is normally fixed on the male identity with a strong reference to beards and turbans. Those who exercise effective authority within the Panth are almost always men and likewise the various functionaries who serve in gurdwaras. Sants, granthis, jathedarṣ, members of the SGPC—virtually all are men.

It is, of course, possible to exaggerate the difference between male and female influence within the Panth and we should take care not to do so. Against the conspicuous prominence of male participation should be set the strong emphasis which is laid on girls' education, the traditional role of the mother in an Indian household, and the growing number of Sikh women in professional occupations. In many ways the situation is similar to that which Western societies are finally and hesitantly acknowledging. In some respects Sikh women may be starting further back than their Western counterparts, but at least there is clear doctrinal support for equal rights within the Panth.

Caste also presents an apparent conflict between doctrine or theory on the one hand and actual practice on the other.[16] Can a rejection of caste be included in our definition of Sikh identity? The answer has to be both yes and no. In ritual terms and within a gurdwara the answer can certainly be an affirmative, at least since the days of the Singh Sabha and Akali movements. The Khalsa rite of initiation is manifestly anti-caste in intention and involves the drinking of the same *amrit* from a common vessel. Within any gurdwara karah prasad is freely distributed to all, and in its langar all must sit in symbolic lines to receive the same food. Outside the gurdwara the same willingness to eat together is generally observed. Strict Sikhs of the Khalsa may refuse to eat with non-Sikhs,[17] but these same people are often in the vanguard of those who insist on full commensality within the Panth. The first answer to our question must be yes, the Panth does indeed reject caste.

The second answer must be no because within the Panth caste is still generally observed in terms of familial relationships and marriage alliances. Jat marries Jat, Khatri marries Khatri (or at least an Arora or an Ahluwalia), Ramgarhia marries Ramgarhia, and Mazhabi marries Mazhabi. Exceptions can easily be found, but they remain exceptions.

[15] *Sikh Rahit Maryādā*, p. 18. The European women who belong to Yogi Bhajan's 3HO following all wear turbans.

[16] For a description and discussion of caste in the Panth, see W. H. McLeod, *The Evolution of the Sikh Community*, (Oxford, 1976), chap. 5.

[17] *Sikh Rahit Maryādā*, p. 27.

Many Sikhs use their caste name as a surname (Singh or Kaur thus becomes a middle name) and political parties can generally depend on caste alignments in Sikh society as much as in Hindu. Even the gurdwara may be affected. Major gurdwaras have generally been immune since the early decades of the present century, but local gurdwaras are commonly the preserve of a single caste (particularly those serving Sikhs overseas). In the case of Ramgarhia gurdwaras, this identity is frequently proclaimed in the actual name. Gurdwaras dominated by other castes are usually more discreet in this respect, but wherever such an identity exists it will be well known to all members of the local community.

Issues requiring both affirmative and negative answers present obvious problems when we are endeavouring to establish an objective and describable identity. If we repeat our question, the accurate answer will presumably have to be that, whereas caste has been largely destroyed in ritual terms, it continues to exercise a fundamental influence on the social and political life of the Panth. Whereas the doctrine of the Panth expressly condemns caste,[18] a substantial majority of Sikhs observe certain significant features of caste in practice.

Although we have travelled a certain distance towards a definition of Sikh identity, we have still managed to avoid the most conspicuous issue of all. None of the items which we have so far managed to elicit from our various questions and approaches concerns the specific Khalsa identity or its relationship to non-Khalsa identities within the Panth. What conclusions are we entitled to draw in this regard when we apply the pragmatic approach? In particular, what results emerge when we scrutinize the actual observance of Amrit-dhari, Kes-dhari, and Sahaj-dhari identities?

A first conclusion is that in actual practice little distinction is drawn between the Amrit-dhari and Kes-dhari modes. Times of crisis (such as the recent past and the present) will typically produce a stronger emphasis on the former and one may find baptismal jathas touring the villages of the Punjab for the express purpose of administering *amrit* to as many people as possible. In normal circumstances, however, it is the visible evidence which matters. Those who retain their hair uncut and refrain from smoking will be accepted as Sikhs if they claim the identity, and for all practical purposes they will be regarded as Sikhs of the Khalsa.

The wearing of the supplementary Khalsa symbols will strengthen any such impression, but few eyes will look for them when credentials are being informally established. The bangle (*kaṛā*) will normally be worn

[18] Ibid. 12, 16, 17, 23, 24.

and one may assume that a regulation comb (*kaṅghā*) is concealed beneath the turban. Attached to the comb there may well be a miniature *kirpān*, a tiny replica which serves as a substitute for the real article (except when times of crisis focus a very specific attention on it). The *kachh* likewise presents no problems. The shorts which are actually worn may differ considerably in size and cut from the traditional style, but the actual article is normally concealed from sight and the issue seldom generates any fervour. The beard and tobacco are the two standard tests. Even these two criteria may be disregarded in some circles, though once either line is crossed claims to a Sikh identity will be treated as arguable.

At this point a debate may indeed develop and one aspect of any such debate will bring us back to the question of caste. If a Jat cuts his hair, there is a strong likelihood that his claims to be regarded as a Sikh will continue to be recognized. If, however, any member of the Khatri/Arora/Ahluwalia group should do likewise, he will usually be treated thereafter as a Hindu. The same is also true of Harijan Sikhs except that in their case the alternate identity could conceivably be Christian. Ramgarhias occupy an ambivalent middle ground. If they retain a strong Ramgarhia identity, they will probably be regarded as Sikhs, particularly in overseas communities. For most Ramgarhias the original identity is that of Tarkhan (the carpenter caste) and if the principal Khalsa symbol were to be abandoned the obvious designation in a village situation would be Hindu. We are, however, perilously near guesswork at this point and for the sake of safety we must retreat to the clearer identities of the Jat on the one hand and the Khatri/Arora/Ahluwalia group on the other.

The differing responses of these two groups can be explained in terms of the dominant affiliation in each case. The Jats involved in this comparison are those who live in the Indian state of Punjab or who trace their origins to that area. Jats who live in Pakistan are Muslims and those who reside in Haryana or adjacent Uttar Pradesh are Hindus. Each can be clearly distinguished from those who occupy the intervening territory, and in the case of the Hindu community the caste name changes from *Jaṭ* to *Jāṭ*. Those who occupy Indian Punjab (together with adjacent strips of Haryana and Rajasthan) identify strongly as Sikhs and they retain this affiliation regardless of their level of adherence to the Rahit. The punctilious may reject their claims, but few Jats will accept such a judgement.

We have here entered the one area where a generic claim can actually be sustained. When we move into the society of Khatris, Aroras, and Ahluwalias, the situation changes. Most Khatris and Aroras are Hindus and it is the Hindu affiliation (commonly Arya Samaj) which dictates the dominant tradition. Ahluwalias derive from a different origin, but, because they have chosen to identify closely with Khatris and Aroras, their own traditions have changed accordingly.[19] The perceptions of others have undergone a corresponding change, with the result that Ahluwalias are generally associated with Khatris and Aroras. If a Sikh from any of these three castes should cut his hair, most other people will eventually regard him as a Hindu.

This is an exceedingly complicated situation and it becomes even more complex when we acknowledge (as we must) that Khatris and Aroras who cut their hair or smoke do not necessarily regard themselves as Hindus. They may identify as Sikhs, as Hindus, or as both. This brings us back to the problem of the Sahaj-dhari, a problem which largely concerns the Khatri/Arora sector of the Panth. Is the person who claims to be a Sahaj-dhari actually accepted as a Sikh or is the claim rejected in practice? Present circumstances suggest that three answers can now be given to this question and that one of the three is assuming a strong dominance within the Panth.

The first answer is the old claim that it is possible to be a Sikh without regarding membership of the Khalsa as a necessary or preferred option. Many Punjabi Hindus still affirm this view, but it now has negligible support amongst those who actually identify as Sikhs. The second answer is the Singh Sabha interpretation. This affirms the orthodoxy of the Khalsa mode, but leaves a window open for those who reverence the Guru Granth Sahib without accepting the Rahit. Although this response still commands some support, it seems to attract little enthusiasm today. It seems clear that a substantial majority of those who regard themselves as Sikhs either reject the Sahaj-dhari option completely or treat it as irrelevant.[20] In practice it is now very difficult to find people who explicitly affirm a Sahaj-dhari identity. Changing circumstances may revive the debate in the future, but for the time being it seems to have lapsed.

This does not mean, however, that the question of Rahit observance

[19] W. H. McLeod, 'Ahluwalias and Ramgarhias: Two Sikh Castes', *South Asia*, 4 (Oct. 1974), 78–90.

[20] 'The absorption of the *sahajdhārī* Sikhs into the Hindu fold adds weight to the argument that there is no such thing as a clean-shaven Sikh. At one time *sahajdhārī* Sikhism was—as the meaning of the word signified, "those-who-take-time"—the halfway house to the hirsute form of Khalsa Sikhism. Now the process is reversed, and it has become a halfway house to Hinduism.' Khushwant Singh, *A History of the Sikhs*, ii (Princeton, 1966), 303.

has lapsed, nor that hair-cutting has ceased to be an issue as far as Sikh identity is concerned. Within the Punjab, tradition may still maintain a strong hold, but this certainly is not the case overseas. Although no one can offer actual statistics, the usual impression is that in England and North America a substantial majority of Sikhs cut their hair. The crisis of the middle and late 1980s has done something to slow the trend, but it still continues and it will presumably gather speed again when peace returns to the Punjab.

The trend is a predictable one because pressures to conform to the Khalsa ideal (which are usually very strong in the Punjab) are actually reversed in Western societies. Theoretically neutral on such issues, Western societies actually offer firm encouragement to remove the alien turban. A beard can be retained, but a Western-style beard with trimmed hair certainly does not qualify as an acceptable version of the Kes-dhari mode. For second-generation diaspora Sikhs the pressures can be even stronger, particularly for boys wearing turbans at school.

Are these clean-shaven or trimmed Sikhs of Southall and Toronto still Sikhs? It seems that the pragmatic answer largely depends on the individual's antecedents or on continuing contact with the gurdwara. Those who belong to families with a Khalsa tradition will still be regarded as Sikhs, a status which is normally signalled by retention of the names Singh and Kaur. This, in practice, includes all Jats. For others more will depend on the second criterion and if they maintain an association with a gurdwara few will question their right to regard themselves as Sikhs.

For overseas Sikhs this condition may prove to be a temporary one. The pressure to which they expose themselves in Western countries can be very powerful and these pressures will certainly encourage a dissolution of the traditional identity over the course of two or three generations (perhaps less). If this were to occur, there would be a general abandoning of Khalsa symbols accompanied by a continued yet diminishing loyalty to the gurdwara. It is, however, far from certain that any such collapse will occur overseas and it is inconceivable that it could happen in the Punjab. What is certain is that many who claim to be Sikhs will continue to cut their hair, leaving us with the problem of how to frame a definition which accommodates both the strict Khalsa and those who in practice set aside the Rahit.

We should clearly understand that those who set aside the Rahit in such circumstances are not adopting a Sahaj-dhari identity. As we have already noted, the term Sahaj-dhari properly applies to a small and rapidly dwindling remnant comprising those who have never accepted the Khalsa tradition. We speak now of those who retain a Khalsa affiliation and if we must find a label to distinguish them from the Kes-dhari Sikh the only one available appears to be Mona. It is, however, insufficiently precise for our purposes and it may one day be necessary to find a narrower substitute. The word *monā* means 'shaven' and it has been commonly used in the past to designate any Sikh who cuts his hair. As such it serves as the antonym to Kes-dhari, a broad term which incorporates the specific Sahaj-dhari identity. Because the Sahaj-dhari identity still sustains a fragile existence, it must be retained within any schema which may be devised. This means that we still lack a term which designates a Sikh who cuts his hair yet retains a Khalsa affiliation.

The pattern which emerges from this unsatisfactory state of affairs is represented in fig. 1. There are actually two terms missing from this

Khalsa	Affiliated Khalsa	Non-Khalsa
K e s - d h a r i	M o n a	
Amrit-dhari		Sahaj-dhari

Fig. 1.

diagram, both of them within the 'Affiliated Khalsa' category and together occupying the whole of that category. Just as we lack a term to designate the hair-cutting Khalsa affiliate, so too do we lack one which will distinguish the Kes-dhari who has not become an Amrit-dhari (see fig. 2). All Amrit-dharis are Kes-dharis, but most Kes-dharis are not Amrit-dharis. Similarly, all Sahaj-dharis are Monas but most Monas are not Sahaj-dharis. All will claim to be Sikhs and if their claims are to be respected an all-inclusive definition will have to be devised.

Khalsa	Affiliated Khalsa		Non-Khalsa
K e s - d h a r i		M o n a	
Amrit-dhari	?	?	Sahaj-dhari

Fig. 2.

One other uncertainty indicated by the diagram concerns the Patit Sikh. We have already noted that the Patit Sikh is one who has violated the Khalsa vow and that strictly speaking the term can only be applied to lapsed Amrit-dharis. A part of the uncertainty arises from the fact that it is frequently attached to any Kes-dhari who smokes or cuts his hair, not merely to the formally initiated Amrit-dhari.[21] The other aspect concerns the actual status of the Patit following his lapse. He (or she) must certainly be removed from the Khalsa category, but is the perceived destination to be 'Non-Khalsa' or 'Affiliated Khalsa'? (see fig. 3)

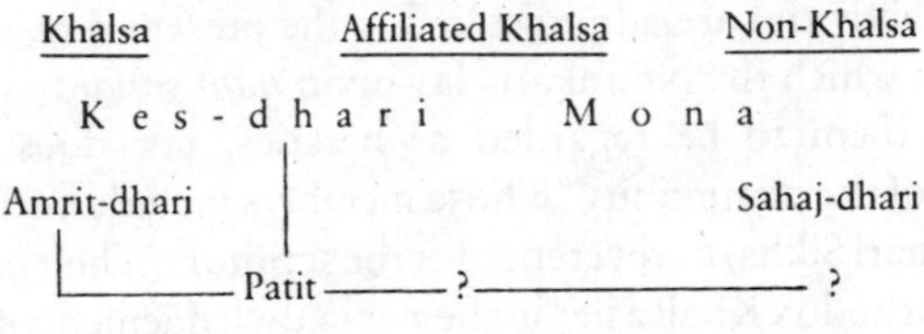

Fig. 3.

A strict answer would probably demand the former. A pragmatic answer would almost certainly indicate the latter.

One final question should be briefly considered before we attempt to draw these scattered items into a single definition. Certain sectarian groups (notably the Nirankaris and Namdharis) claim to be Sikh. Are these claims accepted?

It seems to be generally agreed within the Panth that acceptance should be withheld in the case of any group which draws a substantial body of support from Hindu society or adopts practices which orthodox Sikhs find offensive. Are the Nirankaris and Namdharis thereby excluded? What of the numerous other movements of which prominent examples are provided by the Radhasoami Satsang or the Sikh Dharma of the Western hemisphere? Should all sects be excluded or are there some which most Khalsa Sikhs will own as members of the Panth?

The Nirankaris, like the Namdharis, have been treated briefly above.[22] It is important to distinguish the Nirankaris (the so-called Asali Nirankaris or 'True Nirankaris') from the Sant Nirankaris, the sect whose bitter dispute with Sikhs of the Khalsa played such a prominent part in the events leading up to the storming of the Golden Temple complex in June 1984. The Asali Nirankaris, as we noted before, trace their beginnings to Baba Dayal (1783–1855), who endeavoured to reclaim the Sikhs of the Rawalpindi area from the temptations associated with military triumph under Maharaja Ranjit Singh. Sikhs were, he believed, increasingly

[21] The 1958 draft bill proposing improvements in the administration of gurdwaras included the following definition of a Patit Sikh: '"Patit" means a person who being a Keshadhari Sikh trims or shaves his beard or keshas or who after taking amrit commits any or more of the four kurahits.' *All India Sikh Gurdwaras Legislation* (Amritsar, 1958), 30.

[22] See above, pp. 63–65.

neglecting their duty to remember Akal Purakh through the practice of *nām simaraṇ*. His duty was therefore to preach the message of liberation through the *nām* and to insist upon *nām simaraṇ* as the one effective means. In 1947 the Nirankaris abandoned their centre in Rawalpindi and established themselves on the Indian side of the border in Chandigarh from where their activities are administered to the present day.

The stress which the Nirankaris lay upon *nām simaraṇ* certainly does not qualify them to be regarded as heretics, nor does the outward appearance of the community (whose members include both Amrit-dhari and Sahaj-dhari Sikhs) or reverence for the scripture. Their one fault in the eyes of the orthodox Khalsa lies in their acknowledgement of a continuing line of Gurus descending from Baba Dayal. In this respect the Nirankaris do not question the historic line of Gurus from Nanak to Gobind Singh, nor do they claim any connection with it beyond the beliefs which they share with all Sikhs. Baba Dayal preached renewal and it is for constant renewal in their Sikh faith that the adherents of the movement maintain their faith in the line of Gurus which descends from him.[23]

Confronted by this doctrine, an orthodox Sikh of the Khalsa would have to conclude that the Nirankaris were strictly heretical and some might well have difficulty in regarding them as fellow Sikhs. Such patent heresy is, however, accompanied by a conspicuous dedication to other features of the Sikh tradition and many more would give them the benefit of the doubt. Teja Singh was clearly speaking for the Singh Sabha when he declared that the differences were 'already obliterated almost completely'.[24]

Although the major emphasis of the Namdharis or Kuka Sikhs differs from that of the Nirankaris (a purified Khalsa as opposed to the Nanak-panthi professions of the Nirankaris), the same conclusion must also apply to them. Their origins were very similar to those of the Nirankaris apart from the caste membership of the predominant group.[25] From Hazro and the Peshawar region Baba Balak Singh (1797–1862) also preached the doctrine of *nām simaraṇ* as a remedy for the ills of Maharaja Ranjit Singh's time. He was succeeded by the most famous of all Namdhari Gurus, Baba Ram Singh (1816–85), who stressed the paramount need for a restored Khalsa and who moved the centre of the

[23] John C. B. Webster, *The Nirankari Sikhs* (Delhi, 1979), 9–11, 39–43. McLeod (trans.), *Textual Sources for the Study of Sikhism*, pp. 121–4.

[24] Teja Singh, *Sikhism: Its Ideals and Institutions* (rev. edn., Bombay, 1951), 71.

[25] The Nirankaris were principally Khatris and Aroras. The Namdharis, particularly under Ram Singh and his successors, were drawn mainly from the Ramgarhias and poorer Jats.

group's activities down the Punjab to Bhaini Raian in Ludhiana District. From there (with an important second centre at Sirsa in Haryana) the movement still continues to function.[26]

The Namdharis are more overtly heretical than the Nirankaris as they claim that their line of Gurus continues without break the sequence begun by Guru Nanak. (Guru Gobind Singh, they believe, lived his later life in secret as Baba Ajapal Singh until he 'departed for his heavenly abode' at the age of 146 in 1812.) Namdhari men also differ from ordinary Sikhs as they always wear white homespun clothing and tie their turbans horizontally across the forehead.[27] Their loyalty to the traditions of the Khalsa as they understand them is altogether too obvious to be ignored and only the strictly orthodox would be prepared to place them outside the circle of Sikhs. Faced by their devotion, the Singh Sabha in general and Teja Singh in particular concluded that, even if they were astray on one vital point, they were at least potentially aligned with the Panth.[28] Ganda Singh declares the story of Ajapal Singh to be 'pure fiction of recent creation',[29] but does little else to dispute the claims of the Namdharis to be regarded as Sikhs.

The battles over Nirankari and Namdhari membership were fought many years ago and the issue in their case has been reluctantly conceded. It is not so evidently conceded in the case of the Radhasoami Satsang of Beas, a movement which the Panth is finding much more difficult to digest. The comparatively recent origins of the Beas Satsang are only a part of the problem, for if this were the only objection it would be possible to treat it as the following of a Sant. A more serious objection (particularly in these days of heightened intercommunal tension) is the nature of their teachings and the substantial Hindu membership of the Satsang. If there is a place for Hindus in the Radhasoami Satsang of Beas, its doctrines will be regarded by a Khalsa Sikh at least with considerable suspicion and probably with outright condemnation.

The Radhasoami Satsang is a Sant movement which traces its origins to its foundation in Agra by Swami Shiv Dayal in 1861. During the movement's second generation the two principal disciples of Shiv Dayal organized separate branches, one of them on the banks of the Beas River

26 Fauja Singh Bajwa, *Kuka Movement* (Delhi, 1965). W. H. McLeod, 'The Kukas: A Millenarian Sect of the Punjab', in G. A. Wood and P. S. O'Connor (eds.), *W. P. Morrell: A tribute* (Dunedin, 1973), 85–103.

27 McLeod (trans.), *Textual Sources for the Study of Sikhism*, pp. 126–7.

28 Teja Singh, *Sikhism: Its Ideals and Institutions*, p. 71.

29 Ganda Singh, *Guru Gobind Singh's Death at Nanded: An Examination of Succession Theories* (Faridkot, 1972), 78.

in Amritsar District. This was the group led by Jaimal Singh, who in 1903 was succeeded by Sawan Singh or 'the Great Master'. A line of Gurus was thereby established, teaching the threefold message of *simaraṇ* (by which is meant repetition of the Lord's many Names until attention is focused on the Third Eye which lies within), *dhyān* (contemplation of the immortal form of the Master), and *bhajan* (listening to the celestial music within us).[30]

Not surprisingly the Satsang attracted many Hindus, adding to the offence which it caused by acknowledging a succession of Gurus. Equally unsurprising is the difficulty which most Khalsa Sikhs have in accommodating its teachings within the Panth, with the result that its Sikh members are viewed as marginal to say the least. What then do Khalsa Sikhs make of Sikh Dharma of the Western hemisphere, founded by its present leader Harbhajan Singh Khalsa Yogiji (or Yogi Bhajan)? This group, commonly known by the title of its educational branch as 3HO (Healthy Happy Holy Organization), was founded in the United States by Yogi Bhajan in 1971 and is thus a comparatively recent movement. Its members wear white apparel (including turbans for women as well as for men) and lead a rigorous life of yoga and meditation. The style of yoga practised by the group is called Kundalini Yoga and, although a successor to Yogi Bhajan has not yet been appointed, it is assumed that he will be followed by one of his disciples. An ordained ministry is also a distinctive feature of the movement.[31]

Sikhs who come in contact with Sikh Dharma are frequently perplexed by it, not knowing whether to embrace its followers as unusually devout or to avoid them as perversely unorthodox. To those nurtured on Guru Nanak's conflict with the Nath yogis, Kundalini Yoga seems distinctly suspicious and the enthusiasm of Yogi Bhajan's youthful followers makes them uneasy, particularly when it favours moral absolutes over

[30] Mark Juergensmeyer, 'The Radhasoami revival of the Sant Tradition', in Karine Schomer and W. H. McLeod (eds.), *The Sants: Studies in a Devotional Tradition of India* (Berkeley and Delhi, 1987), 331–5. The Beas Satsang has split several times. When Sawan Singh passed the succession on to Jagat Singh, a disappointed contender, Kirpal Singh, moved to Delhi and there founded the Ruhani Satsang. The family members of Maharajji, the boy guru at the centre of the Divine Light Mission, were also followers of the Beas Satsang. The American movement known as Eckankar was founded by Paul Twitchell, an initiate of Kirpal Singh. Ibid. 334–5.

[31] See the various articles by Verne A. Dusenbery, for example his 'Punjabi Sikhs and *Gorā* Sikhs: Conflicting Assertions of Sikh Identity in North America', in R. H. Brown *et al.* (eds.), *Tradition and Transformation: Essays on Migration and the Indian Diaspora* (New Delhi, forthcoming); and 'The Sikh Person, the Khalsa Panth and Western Sikh Converts', in Jayant K. Lele *et al.* (eds.), *Boeings and Bullock-carts: Rethinking India's Restructuring* (Leiden, forthcoming).

Punjabi notions of honour (*izzat*). But then the obedience of 3HO Sikhs to panthic ideals seems highly commendable and their loyalty to Khalsa observance appears to be beyond question. The answer appears to be to let them live their life of obedience, and Punjabis will live another, seldom the twain meeting in any meaningful way. They are accepted as Sikhs provided they maintain a separate existence.

The last of these groups to be noted produces an entirely different reaction. The Sant Nirankari Mandal elicits condemnation of the most violent kind, sufficient to ensure that no Sikh of the Khalsa will ever be a follower. Its foundation, although difficult to ascertain, probably occurred in the years immediately before Partition in 1947. Baba Buta Singh, often identified as the founder, was a member of the Nirankari Darbar who during the 1930s was asked to stay away from meetings of the Darbar until he had brought his drinking under control. In 1943 he died, still a Nirankari. He had, however, a group of followers and one of these, Baba Avtar Singh, seems to have been responsible for the breakaway in the years following Buta Singh's death.[32] Frequently, to the inexpressible dismay of the old Nirankari Darbar, the two groups are confused and the term Nirankari incorrectly used when the Sant Nirankaris are intended. By those who understand the difference, the Sant Nirankaris are commonly styled the Nakali Nirankaris (the 'Spurious Nirankaris') as opposed to the older Asali Nirankaris.

The principal differences are said to be the inclusion of other works together with the Adi Granth in the scriptures venerated by the Sant Nirankaris, together with the exalted homage which they pay to their leader as Guru. This, however, does not explain the depth of orthodox feeling towards them. For several years prior to 1978 relations between the Sant Nirankari Mandal and the Akali Dal, never cordial, had been deteriorating still further. On 13 April of that year there occurred a demonstration against a Sant Nirankari conference in Amritsar and the fatal police shooting. This was the event which thrust Jarnail Singh Bhindranwale to the forefront of public notice, for he was the leader of the protesters. His violent denunciations of the Sant Nirankaris were widely reported and in 1980 their leader, Baba Gurbachan Singh, was assassinated.[33] No Sikh of the Khalsa could possibly contemplate membership of the Sant Nirankari Mandal. Whoever a Sikh might be, he would not be Sant Nirankari.

32 Webster, *The Nirankari Sikhs*, pp. 34–5.

33 Khushwant Singh, 'The Genesis', in Abida Samiuddin (ed.), *The Punjab Crisis: Challenge and Response*, (Delhi, 1985), 96–7.

As one would expect, therefore, Khalsa attitudes towards sectarian movements are ambivalent. The Asali Nirankaris and the Namdharis are held by most to be Sikhs, a view which the strict might question but most would probably concede. Yogi Bhajan and his followers seem to attract a similar verdict, disputed by some yet grudgingly acknowledged by many more. The Radhasoamis, with all their offshoots, are distinctly marginal; and adherents of the Sant Nirankari Mandal are vehemently excluded.

We shall now attempt to draw these various items into a summary statement and we begin with what a Sikh is not. It seems clear that a very substantial majority of Sikhs now reject the claim that Sikhs are Hindus or that the Panth is a Hindu sect. The Panth's origins were Hindu and its partial retention of caste must be acknowledged, but the experiences and responses of the past five centuries have together generated a sense of separate identity. A few Sikhs may still regard themselves as Hindus. Most do not.

How then is their distinctive identity to be defined? By this time ample warning has been issued concerning the problems involved in this enterprise. The attempt must nevertheless be made, regardless of the certainty that its result will be subjected to a wide variety of criticisms. The following definition is offered on the basis of the foregoing interpretation.

> A Sikh is a person who reveres the ten Gurus (the lineage which begins with Guru Nanak and concludes with Guru Gobind Singh). The teachings of Guru Nanak and his successors concerning liberation through the divine Name are incorporated in the scripture known as the Adi Granth. Although some Sikhs may not be aware of the contents of this scripture, all will certainly venerate the scripture itself. They will also acknowledge the practice of *nām simaraṇ* to be mandatory, though for many the acknowledgement may be implicit and the actual practice rudimentary. The building or room which ritually houses the Adi Granth is called a gurdwara and all Sikhs acknowledge the sanctity which the scripture confers on it. They also recognize the role of the gurdwara in expressing the anti-caste ideals of the Gurus.
>
> Those who acknowledge allegiance to Guru Nanak and his successors constitute the community originally known as the Nanak-panth and now called simply the Panth. During the time of Guru Gobind Singh, members of the Panth were summoned to accept initiation into the Khalsa order and thereafter to observe its code of discipline (the Rahit). Prominent amongst the many features of the Rahit are a group of distinctive Sikh rituals and a series of personal

obligations which include the Five Ks. Two particularly conspicuous items are the prohibition of hair-cutting and a rigorous ban on smoking. It is believed that shortly before his death Guru Gobind Singh declared the line of personal Gurus to be at an end. Thereafter the authority of the Guru was to be vested in the Adi Granth (the Guru Granth) and the corporate community (the Guru Panth).

All orthodox Sikhs accept these statements as the authentic commandments of Guru Gobind Singh and, although they may not actually undergo initiation, they will at least observe the basic requirements of the Rahit. These may be defined in practical terms as a scrupulous observance of the bans on hair-cutting and smoking. Those who decline to accept the basic requirements of the Rahit can still be accepted as Sikhs, but only on the understanding that they are failing to discharge customary duties.

Sikhs are heirs to a history and a fund of tradition which they should regard as a continuing source of guidance and inspiration. Although the basic principles of the Panth include a denial of caste, the continuation of caste practices is nevertheless recognized as unavoidable, and those who observe such practices are not thereby deprived of their right to be regarded as Sikhs.

Within the Panth women enjoy a status which theoretically is equal to that of male Sikhs. Although most Sikhs are Punjabis, the Panth is open to any who accept its doctrines and practice.

It must surely be obvious that in the framing of this summary definition historical corners have been cut and that the word 'orthodox' has been used to cover what should properly be treated as an assumption rather than as a proven fact. The only possible defence is that complex communities can never be summarized in neat, concise, unqualified terms. In the end, however, the attempt must be made. Time and the response of others will decide its success.

SELECT BIBLIOGRAPHY

ENGLISH

ABIDA SAMIUDDIN (ed.), *The Punjab Crisis: Challenge and Response* (Delhi, 1985).

AMARJIT SINGH SETHI, *Universal Sikhism* (New Delhi, 1972).

AMRIK SINGH (ed.), *Punjab in Indian Politics: Issues and Trends* (Delhi, 1985).

ANUP CHAND KAPUR, *The Punjab Crisis: An Analytical Study* (New Delhi, 1985).

ATTAR SINGH, *Secularism and the Sikh Faith* (Amritsar, 1973).

ATTAR SINGH OF BHADAUR (trans.), *The Rayhit Nama of Pralad Rai or the Excellent Conversation of Duswan Padsha, and Nand Lal's Rayhit Nama or Rules for the Guidance of Sikhs in Religious Matters* (Lahore, 1876).

—— *The Sakhee Book, or the Description of Gooroo Gobind Singh's Religion and Doctrines* (Benares, 1873).

—— *Travels of Guru Tegh Bahadur and Gobind Singh* (Allahabad, 1876).

AVTAR SINGH, *Ethics of the Sikhs* (Patiala, 1970).

BALDEV RAJ NAYAR, *Minority Politics in the Punjab* (Princeton, 1966).

BALWANT SINGH ANAND, *Guru Nanak: His Life was his Message* (New Delhi, 1983).

—— *Guru Nanak: Religion and Ethics* (Patiala, 1968).

BANERJEE A. C., *Guru Nanak and his Times* (Patiala, 1971).

—— *Guru Nanak to Guru Gobind Singh* (New Delhi, 1978).

—— *The Khalsa Raj* (New Delhi, 1985).

BARRIER, N. GERALD, *The Sikhs and their Literature* (Delhi, 1970).

—— and DUSENBERY, VERNE A., *Aspects of Modern Sikhism* (Michigan Papers on Sikh Studies, No. 1; 1985).

—— and WALLACE PAUL, *The Punjab Press, 1880–1905* (East Lansing, 1970).

BEDI, K. S., and BAL, S. S. (eds.), *Essays on History, Literature, Art and Culture Presented to Dr M. S. Randhawa* (New Delhi, 1970).

BHAGAT SINGH, *Sikh Polity in the Eighteenth and Nineteenth Centuries* (New Delhi, 1978).

BHUSHAN CHANDER BHALLA, *The Punjab belongs to the Sikhs* (Lahore, 1947).

BIKRAMA JIT HASRAT, *Life and Times of Ranjit Singh* (Nabha, 1977).

BINGLEY, A. H., *History, Caste and Culture of Jats and Gujars* (1899; 2nd edn., New Delhi, 1978).

—— *Sikhs* (Simla, 1899).

BRASS, PAUL R., *Language, Religion, and Politics in North India* (Cambridge, 1974).

COLE, W. OWEN, *The Guru in Sikhism* (London, 1982).

—— *Sikhism and its Indian Context, 1469–1708* (London, 1984).

—— and PIARA SINGH SAMBHI, *The Sikhs: Their Religious Beliefs and Practices* (London, 1978).

COURT, H. (trans.), *History of the Sikhs* (Lahore, 1888).

CROOKE, W., *The Popular Religion and Folk-lore of Northern India* (Westminster, 1896).

CUNNINGHAM, J. D., *A History of the Sikhs* (1st edn., London, 1849; rev. edn. Oxford, 1918).

DALIP SINGH, *Dynamics of Punjab Politics* (New Delhi, 1981).

DALJEET SINGH, *The Sikh Ideology* (New Delhi, 1984).

—— *Sikhism: A Comparative Study of its Theology and Mysticism* (New Delhi, 1979).

DARSHAN SINGH, *Indian Bhakti Tradition and Sikh Gurus* (Chandigarh, 1968).

DATTA, V. N., *Amritsar Past and Present* (Amritsar, 1967).

DHARAM PAL ASHTA, *The Poetry of the Dasam Granth* (New Delhi, 1959).

ELLIOT, H. M., *Memoirs on the History, Folk-lore, and Distribution of the Races of the North Western Provinces of India* (2 vols.; London, 1869).

FALCON, R. W., *Handbook on Sikhs for the Use of Regimental Officers* (Allahabad, 1896).

FAUJA SINGH, *After Ranjit Singh* (New Delhi, 1982).

—— *Guru Amar Das: Life and Teachings* (New Delhi, 1979).

—— (ed.), *The City of Amritsar: A Study of Historical, Cultural, Social and Economic Aspects* (New Delhi, 1978).

—— (ed.), *Papers on Guru Nanak* (Patiala, 1969).

—— and ARORA, A. C. (eds.), *Maharaja Ranjit Singh: Politics, Society and Economy* (Patiala, 1984).

—— and GURBACHAN SINGH TALIB, *Guru Tegh Bahadur: Martyr and Teacher* (Patiala, 1975).

—— *et al.*, *Sikhism* (Patiala, 1979).

FAUJA SINGH BAJWA, *Kuka Movement* (Delhi, 1965).

FORSTER, GEORGE D., *A Journey from Bengal to England* (London, 1798).

FOX, RICHARD G., *Lions of the Punjab: Culture in the Making* (Berkeley and Los Angeles, 1985).

GANDA SINGH, *Ahmad Shah Durrani* (Bombay, 1959).

—— *Banda Singh Bahadur* (Amritsar, 1935).

—— (ed.), *Bhagat Lakshman Singh: Autobiography* (Calcutta, 1965).

—— (ed.), *Early European Accounts of the Sikhs* (Calcutta, 1962).

—— (trans.), *Nanak Panthis, or the Sikhs and Sikhism of the 17th century*, Eng. trans. of a chapter from Muhsin Fani, *Dabistān-i-Mazāhib* (Madras, 1939).

—— (ed.), *Sources of the Life and Teachings of Guru Nanak* (Patiala, 1969).

GOBIND SINGH MANSUKHANI, *Aspects of Sikhism* (New Delhi, 1982).

GOBINDER SINGH, *Religion and Politics in the Punjab* (New Delhi, 1986).

GOKUL CHAND NARANG, *Transformation of Sikhism* (1st edn., Lahore, 1914; rev. edn., Lahore, 1946).

GOPAL SINGH, *A History of the Sikh People, 1469–1978* (New Delhi, 1979).

GREWAL, J. S., *From Guru Nanak to Maharaja Ranjit Singh: Essays in Sikh History* (Amritsar, 1972).

—— *Guru Nanak in History* (Chandigarh, 1969).

—— *Miscellaneous Articles* (Amritsar, 1974).

—— *The Reign of Maharaja Ranjit Singh* (Patiala, 1981).

—— *The Sikhs of the Punjab* (Cambridge, forthcoming).

—— and BAL, S. S., *Guru Gobind Singh: A Biographical Study* (Chandigarh, 1978).

—— and INDU BANGA (eds.), *Maharaja Ranjit Singh and his Times* (Amritsar, 1980).

GURBACHAN SINGH TALIB, *Guru Nanak: His Personality and Vision* (Delhi, 1969).

GURDEV SINGH (ed.), *Perspectives on the Sikh Tradition* (Patiala, 1986).

GURMUKH NIHAL SINGH, *Guru Nanak: His Life, Time and Teaching* (Delhi, 1969).

HARBANS SINGH, *Bhai Vir Singh* (New Delhi, 1972).

—— *Guru Gobind Singh* (Chandigarh, 1966; 2nd rev. edn., New Delhi, 1979).

—— *Guru Nanak and the Origins of the Sikh Faith* (Bombay, 1969).

—— *Guru Tegh Bahadur* (New Delhi, 1982).

—— *The Heritage of the Sikhs* (Bombay, 1964; 2nd rev. edn., New Delhi, 1983).

—— and BARRIER, N. GERALD (eds.), *Punjab Past and Present: Essays in Honour of Dr Ganda Singh* (Patiala, 1976).

HARI RAM GUPTA, *History of the Sikhs* (3rd rev. edn.; 8 vols.; New Delhi, 1978–88).

HARJOT SINGH OBEROI, 'A World Reconstructed: Religion, Ritual and Community among the Sikhs, 1850–1909', unpub. Ph.D. thesis (Australian National University, Canberra, 1987).

HERSHMAN, PAUL, *Punjabi Kinship and Marriage* (Delhi, 1981).

IBBETSON, D., *Outlines of Panjab Ethnography* (Calcutta, 1883).

—— *Panjab Castes* (Lahore, 1916).

INDUBHUSAN BANERJEE, *Evolution of the Khalsa* (2 vols.; Calcutta, 1936).

JAGJIT SINGH, *Perspectives on Sikh Studies* (New Delhi, 1985).

—— *The Sikh Revolution* (New Delhi, 1981).

JAYANT K. LELE *et al.* (eds.), *Boeings and Bullock-carts: Rethinking India's restructuring* (Leiden, forthcoming).

JEFFRY, ROBIN, *What's Happening to India?* (London, 1986).

JITINDER KAUR, *The Politics of Sikhs: A Study of Delhi Sikh Gurdwara Management Committee* (New Delhi, 1986).

JODH SINGH, *Some Studies in Sikhism* (Ludhiana, 1953).

JOGENDRA SINGH (comp.), *Sikh Ceremonies* (Bombay, 1941).

JUERGENSMEYER, M., and BARRIER, N. GERALD (eds.), *Sikh Studies: Comparative Perspectives on a Changing Tradition* (Berkeley, 1979).

KAILASH CHANDER GULATI, *The Akalis Past and Present* (New Delhi, 1974).

KANWALJIT KAUR and INDARJIT SINGH (trans.), *Rehat Maryada: A Guide to the Sikh Way of Life* (London, 1971).

KAPUR SINGH, *Parasharprasna, or the Baisakhi of Guru Gobind Singh* (Jullundur, 1959).

KHAZAN SINGH, *History and Philosophy of the Sikh Religion* (2 vols.; Lahore, 1914).

KHUSHWANT SINGH, *A History of the Sikhs* (2 vols.; Princeton, 1963, 1966).

KULDIP NAYAR and KHUSHWANT SINGH, *Tragedy of Punjab: Operation Bluestar and after* (New Delhi, 1984).

LAKSHMAN SINGH, *Sikh Martyrs* (Madras, 1923).

LOEHLIN, C. H., *The Granth of Guru Gobind Singh and the Khalsa Brotherhood* (Lucknow, 1971).

—— *The Sikhs and their Scriptures* (Lucknow, 1958).

MACAULIFFE, M. A., *The Sikh Religion: Its Gurus, Sacred Writings and Authors* (6 vols. in 3; Oxford, 1909).

MCLEOD, W. H. (trans.), *The B40 Janam-sākhī* (Amritsar, 1980).

—— (trans.), *The Chaupā Siṅgh Rahit-nāmā* (Dunedin, 1987).

—— *Early Sikh Tradition: A Study of the Janam-sākhīs* (Oxford, 1980).

—— *The Evolution of the Sikh Community* (Oxford, 1976).

—— *Gurū Nānak and the Sikh Religion* (Oxford, 1968; 2nd edn., Delhi, 1976).

—— *The Sikhs: History, Religion and Society* (New York, 1989).

—— (trans.), *Textual Sources for the Study of Sikhism* (Manchester, 1984).

MADANJIT KAUR, *The Golden Temple Past and Present* (Amritsar, 1983).

MALCOLM, JOHN, 'Sketch of the Sikhs', *Asiatick Researches*, xi (Calcutta, 1810); republished as *Sketch of the Sikhs* (London, 1812).

MARENCO, ETHNE K., *The Transformation of Sikh Society* (Portland, 1974).

MEHAR SINGH CHADDAH, *Are Sikhs a Nation?* (Delhi, 1982).

MOHINDER SINGH, *The Akali Movement* (Delhi, 1978).

MUKHERJEE, S. N. (ed), *India: History and Thought* (Calcutta, 1982).

NARANG, A. S., *Storm over the Sutlej: The Akali Politics* (New Delhi, 1983).

NARENDRA KRISHNA SINHA, *Ranjit Singh* (Calcutta, 1951).

—— *Rise Of the Sikh Power* (Calcutta, 1946).

NIHARRANJAN RAY, *The Sikh Gurus and the Sikh Society* (Patiala, 1970).

O'CONNELL, JOSEPH D. *et al.* (eds.), *Sikh History and Religion in the Twentieth Century* (Toronto, 1988).

PARKASH SINGH, *The Sikh Gurus and the Temple of Bread* (Amritsar, 1964).

PETRIE, D., 'Secret C.I.D. Memorandum on Recent Developments in Sikh Politics', dated 11 August 1911, *The Panjab Past and Present*, 4/2 (Oct. 1970), 300–79.

PETTIGREW, JOYCE, *Robber Noblemen: A Study of the Political System of the Sikh Jats* (London, 1975).

PRINSEP, H. T., *Origin of the Sikh Power in the Punjab and the Political Life of Muharaja Runjeet Singh* (Calcutta, 1834).

PURAN SINGH, *The Book of the Ten Masters* (London, 1926).

RAJIV A. KAPUR, *Sikh Separatism: The Politics of Faith* (London, 1986).
RAVINDER G. B. SINGH, *Indian Philosophical Tradition and Guru Nanak* (Patiala, 1983).
Rehat Maryada: A Guide to the Sikh Way of Life (Amritsar, 1978).
ROSE, H. A. (ed.), *A Glossary of the Tribes and Castes of the Punjab and North-West Frontier Province* (3 vols.; Lahore, 1911–19).
RUCHI RAM SAHNI, *Struggle for Reform in Sikh Shrines* (Amritsar, 1964).
SAHIB SINGH, *Guru Nanak Dev and his Teachings* (Jullundur, 1969).
SANTOKH SINGH, *Philosophical Foundations of the Sikh Value System* (New Delhi, 1982).
SARDUL SINGH CAVEESHAR, *The Sikh Studies* (Lahore, 1937).
SCHOMER, KARINE, and MCLEOD, W. H. (eds.), *The Sants: Studies in a Devotional Tradition of India* (Berkeley and Delhi, 1987).
SHACKLE, C., *The Sikhs* (London, 1984; rev. edn., 1986).
SHER SINGH GYANI, *Philosophy of Sikhism* (Lahore, 1944).
Sikhism and Indian Society (Transactions of the Indian Institute of Advanced Study, 4; Simla, 1967).
SURINDAR SINGH KOHLI, *A Critical Study of Adi Granth* (New Delhi, 1961).
—— *Sikh Ethics* (New Delhi, 1975).
SURINDER SINGH JOHAR, *Handbook on Sikhism* (Delhi, 1977).
—— *The Heritage of Amritsar* (Delhi, 1978).
SURJIT SINGH GANDHI, *History of the Sikh Gurus* (Delhi, 1978).
—— *The Struggle of the Sikhs for Sovereignty* (Delhi, 1980).
SURJIT SINGH HANS, 'Historical analysis of Sikh literature, A.D. 1500–1850', unpub. Ph.D. thesis (Guru Nanak Dev University, Amritsar, 1980).
TARAN SINGH (ed.), *Sikh Gurus and the Indian Spiritual Thought* (Patiala, 1981).
TEJA SINGH, *Essays in Sikhism* (Lahore, 1944).
—— *The Gurdwara Reform Movement and the Sikh Awakening* (Jullundur, 1922; 2nd edn., Amritsar, 1984).
—— *Sikhism: Its Ideals and Institutions* (1938; rev. edn., Calcutta, 1951).
—— and GANDA SINGH, *A Short History of the Sikhs* (Bombay, 1950).
The Sikh Religion: A Symposium by M. Macauliffe, H. H. Wilson, F. Pincott, J. Malcolm, and Sardar Kahan Singh (Calcutta, 1958).
TRILOCHAN SINGH, *Guru Tegh Bahadur: Prophet and Martyr* (Delhi, 1967).
—— *The Turban and the Sword of the Sikhs* (Gravesend, 1977).
TUTEJA, K. L., *Sikh Politics (1920–40)* (Kurukshetra, 1984).
WALLACE, PAUL, and SURENDRA CHOPRA (eds.), *Political Dynamics of the Punjab* (Amritsar, 1981; 2nd edn., forthcoming).
WEBSTER, JOHN C. B., *The Nirankari Sikhs* (Delhi, 1979).

PUNJABI

Abnas Kaur, *Bhāī Mohan Siṅgh Vaid dī vārtak vanagī* (Patiala, 1976).
Amar Singh, *Siṅgh Sabhā lahir de ughe sānchālak Giānī Dit Siṅgh Jī* (Amritsar, 1962).
Avtar Singh, *Khālsā dharam śāstar* (Anandpur, 1914).
Bhagat Singh, *Giānī Giān Siṅgh* (Patiala, 1978).
Dalip Singh 'Dip', *Gurū Amar Dās* (Patiala, 1980).
Daljit Singh, *Siṅgh Sabhā de moḍhī Bhāī Dit Siṅgh Jī* (Amritsar, 1951).
Dit Singh, *Guramati ārtī prabodh* (Lahore, 1900).
—— *Gurū Nānak prabodh* (Lahore, 1890).
—— *Kalgīdhar upkār* (Lahore, 1899).
—— *Nakalī Sikh prabodh* (Lahore, 1895).
—— *Pammā prabodh* (Lahore, 1906).
Ganda Singh (samp.), *Pañjāb (1849–1960): Bhāī Jodh Siṅgh abhinandan granth* (Patiala, 1962).
Gian Singh, *Srī Gurū Panth Prakāś* (Delhi, 1870; rev. edn., Amritsar, 1923).
—— *Tavarīkh Gurū Khālsā* (2nd edn., Patiala, 1970).
Gobind Singh Mansukhani, *Gurasikh ki hai?* (Amritsar, 1979).
Gurbachan Singh Naiar (samp.), *Gur ratan māl arathāt sau sākhī* (Patiala, 1985).
Gurbakhsh Singh, *Merī jīvan kahānī* (2 vols.; Prit Nagar, 1969).
Gurdas Bhalla (Bhai Gurdas), *Vārān Bhāī Gurdās*, samp. Hazara Singh ate Vir Singh (Amritsar, 1962).
Gurmat Prakāś Bhāg Sanskār (Amritsar, 1915).
Gurmukh Singh, *Sudhārak* (Lahore, 1888).
Harbans Singh, *Bhāī Vīr Siṅgh te unhān dī rachanā* (Lahore, 1940).
Harjindar Singh Dilgir, *Śromaṇī Akālī Dal (ik itihās)* (Jalandhar, 1978).
Jagdis Singh, *Sāḍe rasam rivāj* (Patiala, 1976).
Jagir Singh, *Param Gurū Nānak* (Delhi, 1982).
Jagjit Singh, *Ādhunik janam sākhī (jīvan Srī Gurū Nānak Dev Jī)* (Ludhiana, 1970).
—— *Janam-sākhīān Srī Gurū Nānak Dev Jī dā tārkik adhiain* (Ludhiana, 1970).
Jit Singh Sital, *Amritsar: siftī dā ghar* (Patiala, 1978).
Jodh Singh, *Guramati niraṇay* (Ludhiana, n.d.).
—— (samp.), *Sikhī kī hai?* (Amritsar, 1911).
Kahn Singh Nabha (samp.), *Guramat sudhākar* (1st edn., Amritsar, 1901; rev. edn., Patiala, 1970).
—— *Gurumat mārtaṇḍ* (Amritsar, 1962).
—— *Guruśabad ratanākar mahān koś* (1st edn. 4 vols., Patiala, 1931; 2nd edn. 1 vol., Patiala, 1960).
—— *Ham Hindū nahīn* (Amritsar, 1899).

KARAM SINGH, *Itihāsak khoj*, samp. Hira Singh 'Darad' (2nd edn., Amritsar, 1975).

—— *Kattak ki Visākh?* (Amritsar, 1913).

KARTAR SINGH SARHADI, *Siṅgh Sabhā lahir dā sunaharī te mahān praupakarī itihās* (Yamunanagar, 1974).

MAN SINGH NIRANKARI, *Sikh dharam ate sikhī* (Amritsar, 1981).

MUNSHA SINGH DUKHI, *Jīvan Bhāī Sāhib Bhāī Mohan Siṅgh Jī Vaid* (Amritsar, n.d.).

NAND LAL, *Bhāī Nand Lāl granthāvalī*, samp. Ganda Singh (Malacca, 1968).

NARAIN SINGH, *Sikh dharam diān buniādān* (Amritsar, 1966).

PIAR SINGH, *Bhāī Jodh Siṅgh: jīvan te rachanā* (Patiala, 1983).

PIARA SINGH PADAM (samp.), *Rahit-nāme* (Patiala, 1974).

RANDHIR SINGH (samp.), *Prem Sumārg Granth* (1953; 2nd edn., Jalandhar, 1965).

—— *Sikh kaun hai?* (Ludhiana, 1973).

RATAN SINGH BHANGU, *Prāchīn Panth Prakāś*, samp. Vir Singh (Amritsar, 1914; 4th edn., 1962).

RATAN SINGH JAGGI, *Bhāī Gurdās: jīvanī te rachanā* (Patiala, 1974).

—— *Dasam Granth dā kartritav* (New Delhi, 1966).

—— *Dasam Granth dā paurānik adhiain* (Jalandhar, 1965).

—— *Vichār-dhārā* (Patiala, 1966).

S. S. AMOL, *Bhāī Mohan Siṅgh Vaid* (Patiala, 1969).

—— *Profaisar Tejā Siṅgh* (Patiala, 1977).

SAINAPATI, *Kavī Saināpati rachit Srī Gur Sobhā*, samp. Ganda Singh (Patiala, 1967).

SANTOKH SINGH, *Nānak prakāś* and *Sūraj prakāś*, samp. Vir Singh, 13 vols.; i. *Śrī Gur pratāp sūraj granthāvalī dī prasāvanā*; ii–iv. *Śrī Gur Nānak prakāś*; v–xiii. *Śrī Gur pratāp sūraj granth* (Amritsar, 1927–35).

SARDHA RAM, *Sikhān de rāj dī vitthiā* (Lahore, 1892).

SARDUL SINGH, *Sardhā pūran* (Amritsar, 1891).

SATIBIR SINGH, *Sāḍā itihās* (1957; 2nd edn., Jalandhar, 1970).

SEVA SINGH, *Bhāī Mohan Siṅgh Jī Vaid de jīvan de jhalak* (Tarn Taran, 1936).

SHAMSHER SINGH ASHOK, *Pañjāb diān lahirān* (Patiala, 1974).

—— *Prasidh vidvān Bhāī Kāhn Siṅgh Nābhā* (Guara, 1966).

Sikh rahit maryādā (1st edn., Amritsar, 1950).

SOHAN SINGH SITAL (samp.), *Sikh itihās de somen* (5 vols.; Ludhiana, 1981–4).

SUKHJIT KAUR, *Bhāī Kāhn Siṅgh Nābhā te unhān diān rachanāvān* (Patiala, n.d.).

SURAJ SINGH PRACHARAK, *Guramat kāj bivhār* (Lahore, 1913).

SURJIT HANS, *Sikh kī karan?* (Amritsar, 1986).

TEJA SINGH, *Sikh dharam* (Patiala, 1952).

TEJA SINGH OVARASIR, *Khālsā rahit prakāś* (Lahore, 1914).

VIR SINGH, *Śrī Aṣṭ Gur chamatakār* (2 vols.; Amritsar, 1952).

—— *Śrī Gurū Nānak chamatakār* (2 vols.; Amritsar, 1928–33).

—— *Śrī Kalgīdhar chamatakār* (2 vols.; Amritsar, 1925).

GLOSSARY

Ādi Granth: the Guru Granth Sahib, the sacred scripture of the Sikhs compiled by Guru Arjan in 1603–4.

Āhlūwāliā: a Sikh caste of the Punjab, by origin distillers but successful in acquiring a greatly elevated status.

Akālī: follower of Akal Purakh (q.v.); in the eighteenth and early nineteenth centuries a zealous Sikh soldier; in the twentieth century a member of the Akali Dal (Akali Party).

Akāl Purakh: the 'Timeless One', God.

Akāl Takhat: the principal centre of Sikh temporal authority, located immediately adjacent to Darbar Sahib (the Golden Temple).

amrit (amṛta): 'nectar of immortality'; baptismal water used in *amrit sanskār* (q.v.).

Amrit-dhārī: a Sikh who has 'taken *amrit*', viz. an initiated member of the Khalsa (q.v.).

amrit sanskār: the initiation ceremony of the Khalsa. (q.v.).

Anand Kāraj: Sikh marriage ritual.

Ardās: the 'Sikh Prayer', a formal prayer recited at the conclusion of most Sikh rituals.

Aroṛā: a mercantile caste of the Punjab.

Āryā Samāj: Hindu reform movement of the late nineteenth and twentieth centuries (particularly strong in the Punjab), at first sympathetic to the Singh Sabha (q.v.) but soon shifting to hostility.

asalī: true, real.

āsaṇ: mode of sitting adopted by yogis.

Bābā: 'Father', a term of respect applied to holy men.

Baisākhī Day: New Year's Day in India, the first day of the month of Baisakh or Visakh.

bāṇī: works of the Gurus and other poets included in the Sikh sacred scriptures.

bāolī: sacred well.

Bhāī: 'Brother', title of respect.

Bhakta: devotee, one who practises Bhakti (q.v.).

Bhakti: belief in, adoration of a personal god.

chār kurahit: the four gross sins against the Rahit (q.v.) (cutting one's hair, eating meat which has been slaughtered according to the Muslim rite, sexual intercourse with any person other than one's spouse, and using tobacco).

Chief Khalsa Diwan: united body formed in 1902 to conduct the affairs of the Amritsar and Lahore Singh Sabhas (q.v.).

darbār, durbar: court.

darśan: audience; appearance before eminent person, sacred object, etc.

Dasam Granth: the scripture attributed to the authorship or times of Guru Gobind Singh.

dharaṁ (dharma): in Sikh usage the pattern of belief embodied in the Panth; the moral order generally; panthic duty; (modern usage) religion.

dharamsālā: place of worship for early Sikh Panth (later gurdwara, q.v.).

Five Ks: five items (each beginning with the initial 'k') which Sikhs of the Khalsa must wear.

Granth: [the Sacred] Volume, the Adi Granth (q.v.) or Guru Granth Sahib.

granthī: custodian of a gurdwara.

gurbāṇī: works of the Gurus.

gur-bilās: 'splendour of the Guru'; hagiographic narratives of the lives of the Gurus (esp. the sixth and the tenth), stressing their role as warriors.

gurduārā: gurdwara, Sikh temple.

Gurmat: the teachings of the Gurus.

Gursikh: a Sikh of the Khalsa; a punctilious Sikh.

gurū: a spiritual preceptor, either a person or the divine inner voice.

Gurū Granth Sāhib: the Adi Granth (q.v.), specifically in its role as Guru.

Gurū Granth: the Granth in its role as Guru.

Gurū Khālsā: the Khalsa in the role of Guru.

Gurū Panth: the Panth (q.v.) in its role as Guru.

gurumata: 'the intention of the Guru', a resolution passed by the Sarbat Khalsa (q.v.) in the presence of the Guru Granth Sahib.

halāl: flesh of animal killed in accordance with the Muslim ritual whereby it is bled to death (cf. *jhaṭkā*).

Harijan: Outcaste or Scheduled Caste.

haṭha-yoga: the yogic discipline practised by adherents of the Nath tradition (q.v.).

janam-sākhī: traditional narrative of the life of Guru Nanak.

Jaṭ: Punjabi rural caste, numerically dominant in the Panth (q.v.).

jathā: military detachment; touring parties (commonly for singing kirtan or the administration of Khalsa initiation).

jathedār: commander (normally of a jatha).

jhaṭkā: flesh of an animal killed with a single blow, approved for consumption by members of the Khalsa (cf. *halāl*).

kachh: a pair of pants which must not extend below the knees, worn as one of the Five Ks (q.v.).

kaṅghā: wooden comb, worn as one of the Five Ks (q.v.).

Kānphaṭ yogi: 'split-ear' yogi; follower of Gorakhnath, adherent of the Nath tradition (q.v.)

kaṛā: steel bangle, worn as one of the Five Ks (q.v.).

kaṛāh praśād: sacramental food prepared in a large iron dish (*kaṛāhi*).
karma (karam): the destiny, fate of an individual, generated in accordance with the deeds performed in his/her present and past existences.
kathā: homily.
Khalāsā: a title used for Sahaj-dhari (q.v.) Sikhs in the late eighteenth and early nineteenth centuries.
Khālistān: 'Land of the Pure', the name adopted by proponents of an independent homeland for the Sikhs.
Khālsā: the religious order established by Guru Gobind Singh in 1699.
Khatrī: a mercantile caste of the Punjab.
kes: uncut hair, worn as one of the Five Ks (q.v.).
Kes-dhārī: a Sikh who retains the *kes* (q.v.).
kirpān: sword or dagger, worn as one of the Five Ks (q.v.).
kīrtan: singing of gurbani (q.v.) or other hymns.
Kūkā Sikh: a member of the Namdhari sect of Sikhs (q.v.).
laṅgar: the kitchen/refectory attached to every gurdwara from which food is served to all regardless of caste or creed; the meal served from such a kitchen.
mahant: the head of a religious establishment; incumbents of the gurdwaras until their disestablishment in 1925.
mañjī: administrative subdivision of the early Panth (q.v.).
masand: administrative deputy acting for the Guru.
Mazhabī: the Sikh section of the Chuhra or sweeper caste.
Mirāsī: a depressed sub-caste of Muslim genealogists and musicians, also called Dum or Dom.
mīrī–pīrī: doctrine that the Guru possesses temporal (*mīrī*) as well as spiritual authority (*pīrī*).
misl: a military cohort of the mid-eighteenth century Khalsa.
misldār: a lesser chieftain of a misl (under a sardar, q.v.).
Monā: a Sikh who cuts his/her hair.
mukti: liberation.
nakalī: spurious, false.
nām: the divine Name, a summary term expressing the total being of Akal Purakh (q.v.).
nām dān iśnān: the divine Name, charity, and either ablutions or pure living.
Nāmdhārī Sikh: member of the Namdhari Sikh sect (also known as Kuka Sikhs), followers of Balak Singh and Ram Singh.
nām japaṇ: devoutly repeating the divine Name.
nām simaraṇ: the devotional practice of meditating on the divine Name or *nām* (q.v.).
Nānak-panth: the community of Nanak's followers; the early Sikh community; (later) members of the Sikh community who do not observe the discipline of the Khalsa (q.v.).
Nāth tradition: yogic sect of considerable influence in the Punjab prior to and during the time of the early Sikh Gurus; practitioners of *haṭha-yoga* (q.v.).

Nirankār: 'Without Form', a name of Akal Purakh (q.v.) used by Nanak.

Nirankārī Sikh: member of the Nirankari Sikh sect, follower of Baba Dayal (1783–1855) and his successors.

nirguṇa: 'without qualities', formless, non-incarnated (cf. *saguṇa*).

nit-nem: the Sikh daily liturgy.

paṅgat: '[sitting in] line', the custom whereby equality is maintained in the langar (q.v.).

pāhul: the Khalsa initiation ceremony, baptism.

pañj kakke, pañj kakār: the 'Five Ks'; the five items, each beginning with 'k', which members of the Khalsa must wear.

pañj mel: the five reprobate groups.

pañj piāre: the 'cherished five'; the first five Sikhs to be initiated as members of the Khalsa in 1699; five Sikhs in good standing chosen to represent a sangat (q.v.)

panth: 'path' or 'way', system of religious belief or practice, community observing particular system of belief or practice.

Panth: the Sikh community (*panth* spelt with a capital 'P').

panthic: concerning the Panth.

patit: 'fallen', apostate, renegade.

Patit, Patit Sikh: a Kes-dhari (q.v.) Sikh who cuts his hair; an initiated Sikh who has committed one of the four gross sins (the *chār kurahit*) (q.v.).

pīr: the head of a Sufi (q.v.) order; a Sufi saint; (loosely) a holy man, whatever his religion.

pīrī: the authority of a *pīr* (q.v.); spiritual authority.

pothī: tome, volume.

Purātan: one of the extant collections of janam-sakhi anecdotes.

qaum: 'a people who stand together'.

qāzī: a Muslim judge, administrator of Islamic law.

rāga: metrical mode.

Rahit: the code of conduct of the Khalsa (q.v.).

rahit-nāmā: a recorded version of the Rahit (q.v.).

rāj karegā khālsā: 'the Khalsa shall rule'.

Rāmgaṛhīā: a Sikh artisan caste, predominantly drawn from the Tarkhan (q.v.) or carpenter caste but also including Sikhs from the blacksmith, mason, and barber castes.

śabad (śabda): word; a hymn of the Adi Granth (q.v.).

sādh: a virtuous person; practitioner of Sant teachings (q.v.).

sādh sangat: the fellowship of the devout; congregation of the pious.

saguna: 'with qualities', possessing form (cf. *nirguṇa*).

sahaj: slow, easy, natural; the condition of ultimate, inexpressible beatitude, the condition of ineffable bliss resulting from the practice of *nām simaraṇ* (q.v.).

Sahaj-dhārī: a non-Khalsa Sikh.

sākhī: a section of a janam-sakhi (q.v.), normally an anecdote.

Sanātan Sikhs: conservative members of the Singh Sabha (q.v.).

saṅgat: congregation, group of devotees.
Sant: one who knows the truth; a pious person; an adherent of the Sant tradition (q.v.); one renowned as a teacher of Gurmat (q.v.).
Sant Khālsā: 'the divine Khalsa', a title used by the Namdhari Sikhs (q.v.) for the Khalsa (q.v.).
Sant tradition: a devotional tradition of north India which stressed the need for interior religion as opposed to external observance.
Sarbat Khālsā: 'the Entire Khalsa'; representative assembly of the Khalsa (q.v.).
sardār: the chief of a misl (q.v.); in modern usage the standard mode of address for all Kes-dhari male Sikhs.
Sati-nām: 'True is the Name'; '[Thy] Name is Truth'.
satsaṅg: assembly of true believers.
savā lakh: 125,000, the number whom a single member of the Khalsa equals in battle.
sevā: service, commonly to a gurdwara.
Shiromanī Akālī Dal: the Akali Party.
Shiromanī Gurdwārā Parbandhak Committee: the committee which controls the historic gurdwaras of the Punjab (commonly referred to as the SGPC).
Siṅgh Sabhā: Sikh movement founded in 1873 for the reform and regeneration of the Panth.
Sūfī: a member of one of the mystical orders of Islam.
takhat: 'throne'; one of the five centres of temporal authority.
tanakhāh: a penance for a violation of the Rahit (q.v.).
tanakhāhīā: a person who is guilty of a transgression against the Rahit (q.v.).
Tarkhān: the carpenter caste.
Tat Khālsā: the 'True Khalsa' or the 'Pure Khalsa'. In the early eighteenth century the immediate followers of Banda Bahadur. In the late nineteenth and twentieth centuries radical members of the Singh Sabha (q.v.).
Udāsī: adherent of the Udasi panth (q.v.), an order of ascetics (normally celibate) who claim as their founder Siri Chand (one of Guru Nanak's sons).
Vāhigurū: 'Praise to the Guru'; the modern name for God.
Vaiśnava, Vaishnava: believer in, practitioner of bhakti (q.v.) directed to the God Visnu.
vār: ode; a poetic form.
visamād: wonder, awe.

THE TEN GURUS

1. Guru Nanak (1469–1539)
2. Guru Angad (1504–52)
3. Guru Amar Das (1479–1574)
4. Guru Ram Das (1534–81)
5. Guru Arjan (1563–1606)
6. Guru Hargobind (1595–1644)
7. Guru Hari Rai (1630–61)
8. Guru Hari Krishan (1656–64)
9. Guru Tegh Bahadur (1621–75)
10. Guru Gobind Singh (1666–1708)

INDEX